LEGACY OF SECRECY

LEGACY
OF
SECRECY

THE LONG SHADOW OF THE
JFK ASSASSINATION

Lamar Waldron
Thom Hartmann

COUNTERPOINT

BERKELEY

To my father, who showed me the way

To all those who have been inspired by John F. Kennedy,
Robert Kennedy, and Dr. Martin Luther King

Copyright © 2009 by Lamar Waldron.
All rights reserved under International
and Pan-American Copyright Conventions.

Library of Congress Cataloging-in-Publication Data
Waldron, Lamar, 1954-
Legacy of secrecy : the long shadow of the JFK assassination /
Lamar Waldron with Thom Hartmann.
p. cm.
Updated and expanded trade paperback edition.
Includes bibliographical references.
ISBN 978-1-58243-535-0
1. Kennedy, John F. (John Fitzgerald), 1917-1963—Assassination.
2. Official secrets—United States—History—20th century.
3. Conspiracies—United States—History—20th century.
4. Political corruption—United States—History—20th century.
I. Hartmann, Thom, 1951- II. Title.
E842.9.W275 2009   973.922092—dc22
2009033556

Cover design by Sarah Juckniess

Printed in the United States of America

COUNTERPOINT
www.counterpointpress.com
Distributed by Publishers Group West

10 9 8 7 6 5 4 3 2 1

Contents

___

Breaking News in This Updated
Trade Paperback Edition

This trade paperback edition has been expanded and updated with the latest information and breakthroughs about the assassinations of John F. Kennedy, Robert Kennedy, and Dr. Martin Luther King. The most significant developments concern Bernard Barker, the Cuban American best known as a Watergate burglar, who died on June 5, 2009.

For the first time, we can reveal Barker's longtime work for Mafia godfather Santo Trafficante, which includes Barker's involvement in the assassination of President John F. Kennedy on November 22, 1963. We document how Barker provided a critical link between the Mafia, the CIA, and secret White House operations during the most turbulent time in recent American history, from JFK's assassination to Watergate.

Robert Kennedy's closest Cuban exile aide, "Harry" Ruiz-Williams, first told us about Barker's connection to Trafficante and JFK's assassination in 1992. After seventeen years of research, this new edition finally details the full story of Barker's criminal life, starting with FBI files which say that Barker's involvement "in gangster activities" began in the late 1940s. Barker started working for the CIA in 1959, but CIA Director Richard Helms admitted in Congressional testimony that Barker was "fired" in 1966 because "we found out he was involved in certain gambling and criminal elements."

Barker's seven years with the CIA included working on President Kennedy's disastrous 1961 Bay of Pigs operation. However, this edition details Barker's work on a far more secret Kennedy operation: the plan to stage a coup against Fidel Castro on December 1, 1963, ten days after JFK's trip to Dallas. The leader of JFK's coup was to be Juan Almeida, Commander of Cuba's Army.

We reveal Bernard Barker's critical role in selling out the top-secret JFK-Almeida coup plan to Trafficante and Carlos Marcello, mob boss of Louisiana and Texas. Both godfathers later confessed their roles in JFK's murder, and Barker's inside role in the coup plan helped them kill JFK in a way that forced top officials—including the President's own brother, Attorney General Robert Kennedy—to withhold crucial information from the press, the public, and the Warren Commission. The secrecy protected Commander Almeida, who remained in Cuba and unexposed for decades, and prevented a nuclear confrontation with the Soviet Union, but it also prevented a full investigation of JFK's murder.

A Dallas deputy later placed Barker on the "grassy knoll" seconds after JFK was shot. Barker himself testified under oath that he saw JFK assassinated in the motorcade as it happened—but that was impossible unless he was in Dallas's Dealey Plaza, since JFK's motorcade wasn't televised live (or shown on tape delay) anywhere in the country. A new Special Addendum, written especially for this edition, examines these revelations and documents many more.

Before now, no book has revealed Barker's parallel careers in intelligence and crime, which extended all the way to Watergate. We show how Barker's work for Trafficante in 1961 and 1963 led to his central role in the Watergate break-ins that brought down Richard Nixon. This includes detailing for the first time the connections between Barker and Nixon that existed even before the Watergate operation.

The hardback edition of *Legacy of Secrecy* only hinted at Barker's role with Trafficante and in JFK's murder. This edition replaces those hints with definitive information about Barker, with more fresh information added throughout the book. However, most of the new revelations about Barker appear in the three-part Special Addendum, which follows the Epilogue.

Part I of the Special Addendum covers Barker's actions leading up to and during the time of JFK's assassination. Part II documents Barker's role in the operations that led to Watergate. Part III explains how readers can urge Congress and the administration to release what one official said were "over one million CIA records" related to JFK's assassination that remain secret, despite the 1992 law requiring their release. All three Parts are extensively documented with new endnotes. The new Barker material integrated into earlier chapters is not endnoted, to avoid disrupting *Legacy*'s nearly two thousand original endnotes, but all of the supporting documentation is included in the Special Addendum.

Even more new information about the assassinations of JFK, RFK, and Dr. King appears in this edition's greatly expanded Photo-Document section. It contains more revelations about Carlos Marcello's long-hidden confession to JFK's murder, which was obtained by a secret undercover FBI operation (CAMTEX). This section also includes new information about Marcello's possible role in the disappearance of his old ally, Jimmy Hoffa.

New photos and evidence reveal more about Georgia white supremacist Joseph Milteer, who played a small role for Marcello and Trafficante in JFK's death, but was a driving force in the assassination of Dr. Martin Luther King. Milteer was caught on police undercover tape two weeks before Dallas talking about JFK's murder and an earlier plot against Dr. King. Boxes of Milteer's personal records and effects, untouched for over thirty years, yielded new insights into his actions, painting a far different picture of the white supremacist than was previously known.

New disclosures about Robert Kennedy's assassination include the attempted murder of Sirhan's brother less than a month after Robert was shot. We also show for the first time FBI files about Jimmy Hoffa's hit contract on RFK and how the RFK contract involved Las Vegas.

This new, expanded edition of *Legacy of Secrecy* finally explains the mysteries surrounding some of the darkest episodes of America's past. It may disturb you, it may make you angry, but it will tell you things every American has a right to know.

Introduction and Overview

The assassination of President John F. Kennedy on November 22, 1963, triggered cover-ups by officials that continue to negatively impact American politics, life, and foreign policy. *Legacy of Secrecy* details those cover-ups and hidden investigations, many for the first time, including the reasons they were carried out under such intense secrecy. Most were spawned by John and Robert Kennedy's "top secret" 1963 plan to stage a coup against Fidel Castro—a plan so highly classified that it only started to be exposed in 2005 and is finally fully revealed in this book.[1]

Their own confessions now show that three Mafia bosses—Carlos Marcello, Santo Trafficante, and Johnny Rosselli—were behind JFK's assassination. They used parts of the secret coup plan to kill JFK in a way that forced Attorney General Robert Kennedy, President Lyndon B. Johnson, FBI Director J. Edgar Hoover, and high CIA official Richard Helms to withhold crucial information not only from the public and the press, but also from each other and sometimes their own investigators. It's important to keep in mind that JFK was murdered just a year after the tense nuclear standoff during the Cuban Missile Crisis. The main goals of US officials were to prevent a nuclear confrontation with the Soviets and to protect JFK's ally high in the Cuban government: Commander Juan Almeida, head of the Cuban Army in 1963—still listed as Cuba's No. 3 official today.

While US leaders managed to prevent a confrontation with Russia and preserve a critical ally high in the Cuban government, this limted the investigation into JFK's murder, allowing the three Mafia chiefs and their associates to remain free. As a result, the long shadow of secrecy surrounding both JFK's murder and the coup plan set the stage for the murder of Martin Luther King, ultimately driving two Presidents from office, and bringing about the murders of five Congressional witnesses in the mid-1970s.

Legacy of Secrecy breaks important new ground in key areas, detailing for the first time Louisiana godfather Carlos Marcello's clear confession to ordering JFK's assassination. Marcello's criminal empire ranged from Dallas to Memphis, and previously secret files at the National Archives have shown that he made this confession in 1985 to an FBI informant ruled credible by a federal judge, as part of a secret FBI undercover sting operation named CAMTEX. Exposed here for the first time, CAMTEX yielded Marcello's admission that he'd met Lee Harvey Oswald and set Jack Ruby up in business in Dallas. The operation also generated hundreds of hours of heretofore secret prison audiotapes of Marcello discussing his crimes, recorded using the FBI informant's bugged transistor radio. Yet the FBI and Justice Department withheld most of that information from the public and Congress for years, until its revelation in this book.

Carlos Marcello wasn't the only mob boss who confessed his involvement in JFK's murder to a trusted associate. *Legacy* also uncovers important new information about Marcello's partners in JFK's assassination, Tampa godfather Santo Trafficante and Johnny Rosselli, the Chicago Mafia's man in Las Vegas and Hollywood. Shortly before their deaths, both mobsters admitted their roles in JFK's murder to their attorneys. Two of their associates, with documented ties to the secret JFK-Almeida coup plan, likewise confessed.

Using exclusive new information, supported by FBI files apparently withheld from Congress, *Legacy* names two of the Georgia men who paid James Earl Ray to kill Dr. Martin Luther King: white supremacist Joseph Milteer and Hugh R. Spake. Milteer, who had been involved in Marcello's murder of JFK, was part of a small clique of racists in Atlanta who used Marcello to broker the contract to murder Dr. King. We document James Earl Ray's ties to Marcello's heroin smuggling operation and long overlooked evidence in FBI files linking Ray to Marcello's associate, Johnny Rosselli. Finally, *Legacy,* explains why Ray—while fleeing to Canada the day after killing Dr. King in Memphis—made a 400-plus mile detour south to Atlanta, where he contacted Spake to get help from Milteer.

In 1979, the last Congressional committee to investigate the murders of JFK and Dr. King—the House Select Committee on Assassinations (HSCA)—concluded "that Trafficante, like Marcello, had the motive, means, and opportunity to assassinate President Kennedy." The HSCA had been created in the wake of Rosselli's sensational murder, but the HSCA "was unable to establish direct evidence of Marcello's complicity," and the same was true for Trafficante and Rosselli—because the CIA,

FBI, and other federal agencies withheld so many relevant files. The HSCA, headed by civil rights figure Rep. Louis Stokes, also concluded "there was a likelihood of conspiracy in the assassination [of Dr. King]" and that "financial gain was [James Earl] Ray's primary motivation." But they were unable to determine who had paid Ray, or how the conspiracy had worked, because the FBI and other agencies hid critical files.

With the help of more than two dozen associates of John and Robert Kennedy—backed up by thousands of recently released documents at the National Archives, many of which are quoted here for the first time—*Legacy* tells the full story long denied to Congress and the American people.

Because top US officials covered up so much about JFK's assassination, of the dozen people knowingly involved in that murder, three were free to participate in Dr. King's slaying five years later. At the heart of the 1963 cover-ups lay the top-secret plans of John and Robert Kennedy to stage a coup against Cuba's Fidel Castro—set for December 1, 1963, ten days after JFK's Dallas trip. The Kennedys' goal was democracy for Cuba, after what they hoped would always appear to be a seemingly internal "palace coup." The Kennedys had banned the Mafia from the operation and from reopening their casinos if the coup succeeded.[2]

JFK's plans for a coup in Cuba—which included a "full-scale invasion" if necessary—were detailed in the authors' previous book, *Ultimate Sacrifice*. The 2006 expanded trade paperback edition first named Almeida as the coup leader after the National Archives released his identity after more than four decades of secrecy. *Ultimate Sacrifice* also exposed how Robert Kennedy had US officials secretly develop plans for dealing with "the assassination of American officials" if Fidel found out about the coup plans and retaliated.[3]

Legacy of Secrecy also adds important new information showing how Marcello, Trafficante, and Rosselli—desperate to end Robert Kennedy's unprecedented prosecutions of them and their associates—infiltrated the JFK-Almeida coup plan and used parts of it to murder JFK. Their first attempts to kill JFK, in Chicago (on November 2, 1963) and then during JFK's long motorcade in Tampa (November 18), failed—but because they had planted clues implicating Fidel, Robert Kennedy and other officials were forced to cover up those threats to protect the security of the JFK-Almeida coup plan. The Mafia chiefs made sure their murder of JFK in Dallas on November 22, 1963, involved ties to the coup plan and false clues pointing to Fidel. As a result, Robert Kennedy and other high officials had to withhold key information in order to prevent, in the words of President Johnson, a nuclear holocaust that could cost the lives of "forty million Americans."[4]

Legacy provides a well-documented and definitive account of the multi-faceted cover-up that followed JFK's murder, which lasted decades longer than anyone could have envisioned in 1963. The cover-up wasn't intended to shield JFK's killers, but to protect Commander Almeida and prevent a nuclear confrontation. However, high officials ranging from J. Edgar Hoover to the CIA's Richard Helms also used the opportunity to cover up their own misjudgments and misdeeds. Helms needed to hide his unauthorized Castro assassination plots with the Mafia, which he had withheld from both his own CIA Director and from Attorney General Robert Kennedy (tasked by JFK with overseeing covert anti-Castro operations).

Robert Kennedy had additional reasons for covering up as well, from protecting his brother's reputation to preserving his own political future. Shortly before JFK's murder, Robert Kennedy testified to Congress that it was almost impossible to prosecute top Mafia godfathers for any crimes, let alone ordering a hit.[5] Robert asked trusted associates to secretly investigate JFK's slaying, and he eventually concluded that Marcello was responsible. Prior to his own assassination, Robert confided to associates that only by becoming President could he conduct the truly thorough investigation needed to bring his brother's killers to justice.[6]

Robert's own murder ended any chance of that, and *Legacy* focuses on long-overlooked information about the criminal ties of compulsive racetrack gambler Sirhan Sirhan and some of his family. It analyzes the confessions of two associates of Johnny Rosselli regarding Robert Kennedy's murder, raising new questions about the official account.

It's important to point out that *Legacy* does not say that the same conspiracy that killed JFK also killed Martin Luther King and Robert Kennedy. Out of the dozen people knowingly involved in President Kennedy's assassination, *Legacy* documents that three of those who confessed or were caught on tape talking about JFK's murder were later involved to varying degrees in Dr. King's slaying. Because so much was covered up about JFK's murder, those three men—all career criminals— were able to get away with killing Dr. King. A like number may have been involved in Robert's assassination.

All three assassinations triggered cover-ups by US officials who had nothing to do with the assassinations themselves. Those efforts in turn caused still later cover-ups to protect the reputations of agencies and former superiors. Officials like Richard Helms, who initially covered up information about JFK's assassination to protect national security and his own career, essentially wound up protecting the criminal behavior of others in order to avoid exposing his earlier cover-ups and unauthorized operations. The career criminals behind the murders of JFK and Dr. King spent decades literally getting away with murder, and they knew from experience how to box in authorities by compromising law enforcement and intelligence operations.

Legacy of Secrecy was written because we discovered a tremendous amount of new and significant information in the National Archives, and from our sources, after the publication of *Ultimate Sacrifice*. While *Ultimate* covers the period from Oswald's death on November 24, 1963, to 2006 in only one chapter, the majority of *Legacy* focuses on the aftermath of JFK's murder. The deaths of several individuals involved in those events since the publication of *Ultimate Sacrifice* also allowed us to disclose more in *Legacy of Secrecy*. The most extensive example is E. Howard Hunt, whose work on the JFK-Almeida coup plan—while he was the CIA's liaison with US publishers and the press—is fully detailed here for the first time. In a posthumously released autobiography and tape recordings made for one of his sons, Hunt made seemingly contradictory claims about JFK's murder, sometimes saying they were only speculation. However, Hunt's self-serving accounts left out the most important information—not just his work on the JFK-Almeida coup plan, but also the ties of Hunt's associates, including his best friend Manuel Artime, to Santo Trafficante and the Mafia. As *Legacy* documents, seven associates of Hunt were among those who sold out the JFK-Almeida coup plan to the Mafia. The book also shows how Hunt's role in the JFK-Almeida coup plan led to his infamous work for Nixon during Watergate.[7]

Legacy of Secrecy tells the full story in five parts, plus a photo-document section that shows some of the most important files and people involved. The following are just some of the highlights from each part:

Part I (Chapters 1-10) reveals critical new information about the JFK-Almeida coup plan, an operation so secret that only a dozen US officials knew about it. Even JFK's Secretary of State, Dean Rusk, told us he wasn't informed about it until after JFK's murder. This part also identifies the twelve associates of Marcello, Trafficante, and Rosselli who learned about the coup plan, showing how that knowledge was used in the attempts to kill JFK in Chicago, Tampa, and Dallas. It describes Marcello's confession to ordering JFK's murder, his being introduced to Oswald by his pilot David Ferrie, and Marcello's meetings with Jack Ruby. Part I gives a new perspective on Oswald, pointing out his similarities to the ex-Marine patsy for the Chicago attempt and to the Tampa suspect linked to the Fair Play for Cuba Committee. Using witnesses overlooked or ignored by the Warren Report, Part I depicts the murder of JFK, followed by the killing of Dallas Police Officer J.D. Tippet.

Part II (Chapters 11-20) details the cover-ups that began within hours of JFK's murder. These include Robert Kennedy's initial suspicions that someone involved in the coup plan was tied to JFK's murder, and how two JFK aides' eyewitness accounts of shots from the "grassy knoll" impacted Robert's control of JFK's autopsy. It documents President Lyndon B. Johnson's efforts to avoid a nuclear showdown with the Soviet Union, while associates of Marcello, Trafficante, and Rosselli were spreading phony stories tying Oswald to Fidel Castro—even hinting to the press about JFK's top secret coup plan. Part II further shows how the CIA's Richard Helms and the FBI's J. Edgar Hoover withheld key information from investigators, President Johnson, and each other, as they sought to hide their own intelligence failures. Finally, Part II explains why Marcello had Ruby kill Oswald, how associates of Robert Kennedy spawned the Warren Commission, and why Robert tried to get LBJ to continue the coup plan with the still-unexposed Almeida.

Part III (Chapters 21-37, covering 1964 through mid-1967) shows why Richard Helms shut down his unauthorized Castro assassination operations after he was promoted to CIA Director, and how Johnny Rosselli's threats to reveal those operations stalled legal action against the Mafia don. It also shows how Marcello, Trafficante, and Rosselli compromised the JFK investigation of New Orleans District Attorney Jim Garrison, resulting in one suicide and one murder. Part III also describes Bobby's secret investigations of JFK's murder and briefly lays the groundwork for several of the men involved in the murder of Dr. King.

Part IV (Chapters 38-60, covering mid-1967 to mid-1969) extensively details explosive new information about the assassination of Martin Luther King, focusing on the previously unknown roles of Joseph Milteer, Hugh R. Spake, Carlos Marcello, and Johnny Rosselli in dealing with James Earl Ray. It reveals how Milteer and three Atlanta partners raised money for Dr. King's assassination, and—after several failed attempts—paid Carlos Marcello a huge sum to broker the contract on Dr. King. We show why Marcello agreed, and how James Earl Ray went from being a new member of Marcello's drug network to stalking Dr. King. Part IV also shows why J. Edgar Hoover and high FBI officials had to limit parts of their King inquiry, both to avoid compromising ongoing prosecutions of Marcello and Rosselli and because of their earlier failings in investigating the two mob bosses (and Milteer) for JFK's murder.

In addition, Part IV raises new questions about Robert Kennedy's assassination, including Johnny Rosselli's ties to Sirhan's main attorney and CIA officer David Morales. For the first time we expose David Morales's tie to an earlier plan to assassinate Fidel Castro by using a pistol-wielding assassin in a pantry. Part IV also reveals the little-known criminal ties of some of Sirhan's associates and family, including the attempted murder of Sirhan's brother shortly after Robert Kennedy's assassination.

Part V (Chapters 61-65, covering 1970 to the present) focuses significantly on Watergate, showing why a dozen participants in that scandal had ties to operations like the JFK-Almeida coup plan (and the Mafia's infiltration of it), and how three of those helped to expose Watergate. It quotes the document that the Watergate burglars were really after and explains why Johnny Rosselli and JFK's assassination became part of the Watergate investigation, which triggered five more government committees and commissions.

In Part V, we also document the murders of five witnesses slated for Congressional inquiries into JFK's assassination—including Rosselli, Sam Giancana, and Jimmy Hoffa—and four additional sudden deaths of witnesses. We show how the JFK-Almeida coup was withheld from all of those committees, including the HSCA, and the role played by a 1978 meeting between a US official and Commander Almeida. We also explain how Watergate spawned the BRILAB FBI sting that finally brought Marcello a long sentence in federal prison. There, the godfather became the target of the FBI's undercover CAMTEX sting, resulting in Marcello's JFK confession and his threat to kill the FBI informant who heard it.

Part V concludes with an Epilogue showing Commander Almeida's increasingly high profile in Cuba after the revelation (outside of Cuba) of his secret work for JFK. With Fidel having stepped aside, Almeida could be a key player in ending the forty-seven-year-old impasse and trade embargo between Cuba and the US. Ironically, several of JFK's Cuban exile allies from 1963 could still play important roles as well.

Legacy depicts the sometimes painful transformation of Robert Kennedy from aggressive Attorney General to a revered champion of civil rights and advocate for the poor, as he struggled to deal with his brother's murder. However, this book is not a biography of Robert Kennedy, JFK, or Martin Luther King, or a chronicle of the civil rights movement, even for the years we cover in depth (late 1963 to 1969). Unlike *Ultimate Sacrifice, Legacy* does not extensively document the development of the JFK-Almeida coup plan and the backgrounds of its participants. The same is true for the long Mafia careers of Marcello, Trafficante, and Rosselli prior to JFK's murder—including their work for the CIA in the Castro assassination plots that started in 1959— all of which are the subject of hundreds of pages in *Ultimate Sacrifice.*

For both the FBI and the CIA, where appropriate, we try to draw distinctions between the actions of top leaders like J. Edgar Hoover and Richard Helms and those of rank-and-file personnel, who were often at the mercy of superiors with agendas (and information) they didn't share with most in their organizations. The HSCA investigated and cleared the FBI of involvement in Martin Luther King's assassination, but because of the FBI's well-documented shameful track record in dealing with Dr. King, we tried to rely on government reports that were appropriately critical of the FBI.

Legacy is the result of twenty years of research—with help from some of the best investigators of today and from the past—that led to the continuing discovery of files at the National Archives that confirm (and add detail to) what Kennedy aides and associates told us years earlier. In 1990, former Secretary of State Dean Rusk first confirmed "active" plans for a "second invasion" of Cuba at the time of JFK's death and explained why JFK wasn't bound by any pledge not to invade Cuba. JFK aide Dave Powers told us in 1991 that he and another aide saw shots from the grassy knoll, but were pressured to change their story for the Warren Commission "for the good of the country." In 1992, Robert Kennedy's top Cuban exile aide Enrique "Harry" Ruiz-Williams first revealed Almeida's name and many details of the coup plan, while other former Kennedy aides pointed to Marcello, Trafficante, and Rosselli as being behind JFK's murder—something the mob bosses' confessions now confirm.[8]

All the secrecy that began in 1963 had tragic and lingering effects on America and the world, because intelligence and investigative agencies kept making the same mistakes. Several of those involved in the intelligence operations surrounding JFK's murder wound up being involved in US missions in Laos, Vietnam, Chile, Iran, and Central America—all with disastrous results. Because the reasons for the failure of JFK's coup plan were never exposed, later US coup attempts against dictators like Saddam Hussein failed for many of same reasons JFK's coup plan failed. The US intelligence failures noted in the 9/11 Report, which preceded that tragedy, are echoed in some cases almost word-for-word in documents depicting the intelligence failures prior to JFK's assassination.

The current impasse between the US and Cuba—essentially unchanged since the early days of JFK's administration—illustrates how the secrecy surrounding President Kennedy's assassination and the JFK-Almeida coup plan still affects America today. The economic stakes are higher now than ever before, especially with Cuba's vast oil reserves, but US economic sanctions make normal trade impossible. The continuation of those sanctions for decades is due, in part, to the mistaken belief of some former officials—like former Secretary of State Alexander Haig—that Fidel Castro killed JFK, a belief whispered among some US officials and Cuban exile leaders for decades. Those rumors persist because more than a million CIA records related to JFK's assassination and the JFK-Almeida coup plan are still withheld today, despite the 1992 JFK Act, passed unanimously by Congress requiring their release. *Legacy of Secrecy*'s Epilogue lists just a few of the most important document groups from 1963 that are still being withheld, and many more are detailed in almost every chapter.[9]

Legacy of Secrecy was written to reveal our hidden history, so that America does not have to keep repeating its tragic past. We believe it's better to know the truth, however painful, than to rely on the sometimes distorted or incomplete view of the history that has resulted from the withholding or destruction of so much vital information.

Author's note: Several key names have been simplified and standardized in this book. Dr. Martin Luther King Jr. will be referred to without "Jr.," while his father is identified with "Sr." Tampa godfather Santo Trafficante Jr. will be treated the same way, while his father will be referred to as Santos Trafficante Sr. The names of several important Cuban exiles will be standardized to their most common usage in government files and by associates: Manuel Artime, Manolo Ray, Eloy Menoyo, Tony Varona, and Harry Williams.

Also, to minimize disruption while reading, we sometimes put an endnote number at the end of a paragraph instead of putting it at the end of the particular sentence it refers to.

PART ONE

Chapter One

The rifle fire in Dallas that killed John F. Kennedy changed America forever, casting a long shadow on the history of the years that followed. JFK's murder didn't just start a frantic effort to find his assassins—it also triggered a series of covert actions to hide the fact that the United States was on the brink of invading Cuba. The exposure of this top-secret plan, part of a JFK-authorized coup to topple Fidel Castro, could have led to a nuclear confrontation with the Soviets only a year after the Cuban Missile Crisis. Revealing the coup, which was only ten days away, would have also cost the life of JFK's ally high in the Cuban government, Commander of the Army Juan Almeida, ending any chance the US had of toppling Fidel from the inside. The cover-ups by key US officials, including Attorney General Robert F. Kennedy, Lyndon Johnson, J. Edgar Hoover, and the CIA's Richard Helms, kept the JFK-Almeida coup plan secret from the public, not just at the time, but for decades to come. However, it also had the tragic effect of preventing a full investigation of JFK's assassination, spawning a legacy of secrecy that would lead to more deaths and impact presidents, Congress, and US foreign policy for the next forty-five years.

Important files that have been declassified in recent years, coupled with new disclosures from two dozen Kennedy associates, allow the story to be detailed for the first time. They allow us to chronicle the secret investigations into JFK's death undertaken by Robert Kennedy and others, which had to be conducted covertly to avoid exposing the JFK-Almeida coup plan and other intelligence operations. CIA officials, such as Richard Helms, had to protect not only legitimate covert operations, but also unauthorized schemes withheld from the Kennedys and Helms's own CIA Director, like the CIA-Mafia plots to kill Fidel Castro.

New revelations about John and Robert Kennedy, the CIA, the Mafia, and Cuba cast the aftermath of JFK's death in a whole new light. This new information shows who was actively involved in JFK's murder, who was covering up to protect their reputation, who was protecting national security, and who was really trying to solve the assassination. The information that Robert Kennedy and other officials decided to reveal, or not to reveal, would generate much of the controversy surrounding the JFK assassination that persists even today. The decisions they made on November 22, 1963, are why "well over a million CIA records" remain classified today, sixteen years after Congress unanimously passed a law requiring their release.[1]

To understand their actions, it's important to look first at what the key players had been doing in the weeks and months leading up to JFK's assassination. Much of the following is from the thousands of pages of formerly secret government files that were not available to the Warren Commission or the Congressional investigations of the 1970s, '80s, and '90s.

In 1963, the second most powerful man in America was the President's brother, Attorney General Robert F. Kennedy. Bobby, as he liked to be called by friends and associates, was far more than the nation's top law enforcement official. As the President's closest confidant and protector, Bobby advised JFK on most important official, political, and personal issues. Not yet the almost saintly idealist some would say he became before his own assassination, the Bobby of 1963 could be brash and cocky, a tough adversary. Acutely aware of the way government, the media, and big business really worked, he constantly tried—often with success—to get what he and JFK wanted. Yet he also inspired fierce loyalty from those who worked for him, who saw in him a determination to make America and the world a better place.

Bobby's path to becoming Attorney General was part of JFK's path to the presidency. In 1958, Senator John F. Kennedy started laying the groundwork for his presidential run by becoming the most publicized member of a Senate committee investigating the Teamsters and organized crime. Bobby, the committee's chief counsel, did much of the actual grilling of Mafia bosses and their associates, such as Jimmy Hoffa. Rumors about Mafia ties and Prohibition-era bootlegging had long dogged their father, Joseph Kennedy, one of America's wealthiest men, and going after mob bosses so aggressively was one way for JFK and Bobby to neutralize that issue. The crime hearings had become a matter of national urgency because the Mafia's power had grown tremendously during the administration of President Dwight Eisenhower and Vice President Richard Nixon. Nixon's early ties to the Mafia have been extensively documented, most recently by author Anthony Summers.

His best-selling book about FBI Director J. Edgar Hoover, *Official and Confidential*, makes a persuasive case that Hoover's soft treatment of the Mafia (Hoover denied the very existence of the Mafia for years) resulted from the Director's efforts to hide his own closeted life.

While Senator John F. Kennedy and Bobby couldn't prosecute Mafia bosses in 1958 and 1959, they could at least expose their criminal organizations to public scrutiny. This was true even when a mob boss repeatedly refused to answer questions by using his Fifth Amendment right against self-incrimination, as did Louisiana/Texas godfather Carlos Marcello. In a public session on March 24, 1959, Bobby posed dozens of incisive questions to Marcello, and when the crime boss declined to answer, Bobby's interrogation clearly outlined Marcello's criminal empire. This included Marcello's extensive involvement in the heroin trade, something he shared with his close associate Santo Trafficante, the godfather of Tampa, who controlled much of Florida.

The Kennedys had less success in getting Trafficante to appear, since he spent so much time visiting his Havana casinos. When Bobby Kennedy had the director of the Miami Crime Commission testify about Trafficante, Bobby noted in the hearing that there had been a mob hit in Tampa the previous day. Trafficante finally fled to Cuba in 1959, to avoid testifying about his role in the notorious barbershop murder of New York mob boss Albert Anastasia.

Much to Bobby's frustration, still another Mafia boss was able to evade testifying in 1959 because of his secret work for the CIA against new Cuban leader Fidel Castro.[2] Unknown to Bobby Kennedy, this plot to assassinate Castro had been brokered for the CIA by Jimmy Hoffa, who used his arms sales to Castro and Mafia ties to his own advantage, as later documented by Congressional investigators. This 1959 plot wasn't successful, and the following year the CIA took a fresh approach by avoiding Hoffa and working directly with a new set of mob bosses, including Trafficante and Johnny Rosselli (and eventually, Marcello). However, involved in both Hoffa's Cuban arms sales and the original 1959 Castro assassination plot was a small-time Dallas gangster and gunrunner named Jack Ruby.[3]

During the 1959 Senate crime hearings, Bobby was never able to find a man using the alias of "Jack La Rue," who was on the fringe of the first CIA-Mafia Castro assassination plots while smuggling armaments to Cuba. Much evidence and testimony shows that Dallas nightclub owner Jack Ruby was involved in the same operations as "Jack La Rue." Unbeknownst to Bobby in 1959 while he was fruitlessly looking for the mysterious "Jack La Rue," Jack Ruby was running guns to Cuba with La Rue's associates while also being used by Marcello as a messenger to Trafficante. Despite their setbacks in tracking down "La Rue" and Trafficante, JFK and Bobby were more successful in getting testimony from Chicago mob boss Sam Giancana and Teamster chief Jimmy Hoffa: Newsreel footage shows Bobby verbally sparring with each, with mutual contempt.

JFK officially launched his presidential campaign in that same Senate hearing room, before eventually winning the extremely close 1960 election. While the media often focuses on possible mob support in West Virginia arranged by Joseph Kennedy, and the Chicago Mafia's role in swinging that city to JFK (as if powerful Mayor Daley's help didn't matter), more Mafia support went to JFK's opponent, Vice President Richard Nixon. According to a trusted Justice Department informant, in September 1960, "Marcello had a suitcase filled with $500,000 cash which was going to Nixon" with the aid of Jimmy Hoffa. Marcello's half million was to be matched by other Mafia bosses, including "the mob boys in . . . Florida," like Trafficante, who were no doubt fearful of what a Kennedy presidency might mean for them.[4]

Once JFK took office in 1961, he appointed his brother Bobby as Attorney General of the United States, and, with a prosecutor's zeal, Bobby immediately made Carlos Marcello, Jimmy Hoffa, and Tampa's Santo Trafficante prime targets for investigation. Bobby eventually pressured J. Edgar Hoover, now officially Bobby's subordinate, into making some efforts against the Mafia, but in the meantime Bobby developed his own staff of special prosecutors in the Justice Department. In addition to his staff of Mafia prosecutors, Bobby organized a separate Justice Department group, informally called the "Get Hoffa Squad," to target the Teamster leader. Bobby Kennedy used compartmentalization for security and administrative reasons, keeping the Get Hoffa Squad and his Mafia prosecutors almost completely separate. This tactic would have grave repercussions around the time of JFK's assassination, when both groups were kept separate not only from each other, but also from Bobby's covert Cuban operations, and each group had crucial information the other needed.

In addition to Bobby's focus on the Mafia and Hoffa, the early 1960s were a turbulent and transitional time in the area of civil rights. This was the era of segregated schools in many parts of the country, though racial discrimination was worst in the South, where even public drinking fountains and movie theaters were often still segregated. Most state legislatures had no blacks or Hispanics, and all-white juries were the norm. Bobby and his Justice Department played a leading role in the growing civil rights movement, enforcing the law when local or state officials refused, or even broke the law themselves.

In June 1963, Governor George Wallace had stood in the doorway of the University of Alabama to block admittance to a black student, only weeks after Birmingham Police Chief Bull Connor had turned attack dogs and fire hoses on peacefully protesting children. A few days after that attack, the motel where Martin Luther King was staying was bombed, and JFK had to call out troops to maintain order in Birmingham. Though King was able to marshal two hundred thousand people to Washington in August 1963 to hear his "I Have a Dream" speech, civil rights crusaders faced a constant threat of violence. Mississippi civil rights leader Medgar Evers had been assassinated by a sniper in June 1963, and in September four little girls died when Birmingham's 16th Street Baptist Church was bombed.

Prosecutions for such crimes were largely local matters in 1963, since the comprehensive federal civil rights legislation sought by JFK and Bobby was proving problematic. Even with the help of Vice President Johnson, a consummate dealmaker when he had led the Senate in the late 1950s, passing such legislation would be difficult because of resistance from powerful conservatives in Congress, mostly from the South. Building Southern political support for JFK and his policies would be one reason for the President's open motorcades in Florida (on November 18, 1963) and Texas (on November 21 and 22).

Bobby would have had his hands full if he'd done nothing but focus on civil rights, the Mafia, and Hoffa, as well as his extensive advice to JFK about political and personal affairs, but there was still more on his plate. Bobby also had a hand in foreign policy, which included being one of several advisors to JFK about the growing problem of Vietnam. The country's dictator had been killed on November 2, 1963, following a coup by military officers. JFK had approved the coup to remove the corrupt dictator and his family from power, but hadn't expected them to be killed; a famous photo captured JFK's anguish when he first heard the news of their death. It's important to remember that in November 1963, there were officially no US combat troops in Vietnam (only several thousand "advisors"), and US casualties under JFK totaled less than a hundred. Even with that relatively low level of commitment, most scholars and former officials agree that JFK had decided to reduce US forces in Vietnam in 1964.

Of more immediate concern to Bobby Kennedy was Cuba, a problem in which he had taken a leading role that went far beyond just giving advice to JFK. In fact, Bobby's involvement surpassed anything that could remotely be considered the role of an Attorney General. JFK had delegated to Bobby the primary responsibility for defining and implementing Cuban operations, because the CIA had so badly bungled the Bay of Pigs operation in 1961 that JFK wanted someone he trusted to be in charge. JFK felt uncomfortable leaving Cuban operations entirely to the US military, since some of his Joint Chiefs had indicated an eagerness to attack Cuba during the Cuban Missile Crisis in 1962. Of the military brass, JFK fully trusted only his new Joint Chiefs Chairman, General Maxwell Taylor; Defense Intelligence Agency head General Joseph Carroll; and Secretary of the Army Cyrus Vance.

The complex, covert operations that made up the secret war against Cuba couldn't be delegated to cabinet officials like Defense Secretary Robert McNamara or Secretary of State Dean Rusk for several reasons. First, Defense and State had their own large bureaucracies, subject to Congressional oversight, a situation that wasn't conducive to their making quick decisions about complicated, top-secret operations where the hand of the US had to remain hidden. They also had their hands full with Vietnam, and the rest of the Cold War with Russia and China, whose fronts ranged from Eastern Europe to Asia to the Middle East. Finally, Rusk and McNamara were the administration's highest-profile officials to the press and public, which was hardly compatible with overseeing the Kennedys' highly secret operations against Cuba.

While the Joint Chiefs, Defense, State, and the CIA all had input into Cuba policy and operations, declassified files and former administration officials make it clear that JFK delegated control to his trusted brother, Bobby. Selected officials in those agencies participated in three subcommittees of the National Security Council (the Standing Group, the Special Group, and the Interdepartmental Coordinating Committee of Cuban Affairs), whose organization and responsibility were so confusing that detailed charts had to be prepared just to sort things out. Though Bobby Kennedy appeared on none of the charts, decades later Alexander Haig said that when it came to Cuban operations in 1963, "Bobby Kennedy was running it—hour by hour." Haig stated emphatically that as far as Cuba was concerned, "Bobby Kennedy was the President. He was the President! Let me repeat, as a reasonably close observer, HE WAS THE PRESIDENT!"[5] (Emphasis in original.) In 1963, Haig was the aide to Joseph Califano, the assistant to Army Secretary

Cyrus Vance. Haig's comments were confirmed in Califano's autobiography, as well as by a confidential source we interviewed who served on two of the three Cuba committees, and by other Kennedy associates.[6] CIA official Richard Helms told *Newsweek* editor Evan Thomas that "you haven't lived until you've had Bobby Kennedy rampant on your back [about Cuba]."[7]

For his secret Cuba operations, Bobby worked directly with officials like Helms and Vance, often bypassing their superiors, such as CIA Director John McCone and Defense Secretary McNamara. Bobby also dealt directly with several Cuban exile leaders he trusted, much to the resentment and frustration of CIA officials who had previously been in charge of controlling US-backed exile leaders.

Bobby sought out people he had confidence in, or felt he could control, because the Cold War was at its height and the stakes were high: It was just a year after the tense nuclear standoff of the Cuban Missile Crisis of October 1962, and thousands of Russian personnel were still in Cuba. A recently declassified "Top Secret . . . briefing for Mr. Robert Kennedy," makes it clear that one wrong move would result in "World War III."[8]

One reason for the Kennedys' secrecy and tight control was that America, and the world, were under two misimpressions at the time that remained in place for decades. As Secretary of State Dean Rusk revealed to us in an interview, JFK never made an ironclad pledge that the United States would not invade Cuba, in order to end the Cuban Missile Crisis. Rusk's revelation was later confirmed by hundreds of pages of formerly secret files published by the National Security Archive at George Washington University. As shown by these memos, and by JFK's own public statements to the press and on TV, his offer of a "no invasion" pledge depended entirely on Fidel Castro's allowing "UN inspections" for "weapons of mass destruction," to ensure that all the missiles had been removed.[9] Fidel never allowed UN inspectors into Cuba, so JFK's pledge never took effect. However, JFK was so anxious to avoid returning to the almost unbearable tension of the Missile Crisis that, during 1963, he and his top officials deliberately refrained from making Castro's failure to allow UN inspections an issue to the public or the media.

In stark contrast to the way Cuba had dominated the headlines and nightly newscasts in October and November 1962, by November 1963 Cuba was rarely front-page news. The relatively few stories that appeared focused mainly on the JFK administration's crackdown on most Cuban exile groups, dozens of which had formerly received lavish support from the CIA's huge Miami station. One could get the impression from media accounts in the fall of 1963 that Cuba was no longer much of an issue for JFK, despite growing attempts by his potential Republican opponents in the upcoming 1964 election to call attention to it. Republicans like Richard Nixon, Barry Goldwater, and Nelson Rockefeller tried to make the point that Soviet missiles might still remain in Cuba, or that they could be reintroduced as long as Fidel was in power. Though JFK refused to be drawn into public debate about hypothetical Cuban missiles, he knew such accusations would gain greater attention once the next presidential campaign officially began in January 1964.

JFK and Bobby were desperately trying to resolve the issue of Cuba by the end of 1963, so that it didn't become what two Kennedy aides called "a political football" during the 1964 campaign.[10] Because JFK and his officials had been vague to Soviet inquires about JFK's "no invasion" pledge and the lack of UN inspections, the Kennedys' actions had to be undertaken in utmost secrecy, even within their own administration. US involvement in the toppling of Fidel could never be revealed. The level of fear and mistrust between the United States and the Soviet Union in 1963 was extremely high. A direct "hotline" to the Soviet leader Nikita Khrushchev in Moscow had been installed in August 1963, but it was far more complex than the simple phone system depicted in popular movies. It involved encoded messages using wire and radio telegraph, with translators at each end.[11] If the Soviets felt betrayed over any obvious US intervention in Cuba, such a cumbersome system would be of limited use as JFK tried to explain the nuances of his justification for US action. The situation could quickly spiral out of control, and the earlier cited memo's prediction of "World War III" could well come to pass.

But one of the passages in that same memo provided the seeds of the plan JFK and Bobby started developing in May 1963:

> The [US] military could intervene overtly in Cuba without serious offense to national or world public opinion if we moved in response to a humanitarian requirement to restore order within Cuba [and announced we would] hold free elections; and that we would withdraw from Cuba as soon as the new government advised that they had the capability to maintain order without further assistance from OAS [Organization of American States] nations. [Also,] if the operation was conducted as quickly as possible and with sufficient force . . .[12]

What JFK and Bobby lacked when that memo was written was a logical reason for the United States to go into Cuba to "restore order." In mid-May 1963, the Kennedys finally got the opportunity they needed when one of the most powerful officials in Cuba—Commander Juan Almeida, the head of Cuba's army—contacted Bobby's top Cuban exile aide, Enrique "Harry" Ruiz-Williams. Commander Almeida told Ruiz-Williams that he would be willing to stage a coup to overthrow Fidel, if the Kennedys would back him. JFK and Bobby's acceptance of Commander Almeida's offer began a chain of events that would have a tremendous impact on the US presidency and American policy toward Cuba, one that still persists today.

Commander Almeida was a founding father of Castro's Cuba, one of the revered twelve who had gone into the Sierra Maestra mountains with Fidel to begin the Revolution. Almeida saved Che Guevara's life in the first battle of the Revolution and had gone on to found Cuba's Revolutionary Army. While Almeida's friend Che was a struggling economic bureaucrat by 1963, Almeida still commanded the loyalty of most Cuban troops, and was one of the most admired and respected officials in Cuba after Fidel and his brother, Raul. However, both Che and Almeida resented the increasing Soviet influence in Cuba, as well as Fidel's ongoing consolidation of his own personal power. In addition, Almeida was the highest-ranking black official in Cuba in 1963, an important consideration for a country in which, by some estimates, 70 percent of the population is of at least partial African descent.

Almeida's May 1963 offer to the Kennedys wasn't the first time he had rebelled against Fidel. Two recently declassified memos, first published in 2006, show that the CIA was aware more than two months prior to the 1961 Bay of Pigs disaster that Almeida "was disgusted with the communistic situation" in Cuba and wanted to defect. However, top CIA officials didn't pursue Almeida's offer then, apparently because they felt confident their plot with Mafia bosses Santo Trafficante and Johnny Rosselli would result in Fidel's assassination prior to the invasion at the Bay of Pigs. Not only did the CIA-Mafia plots fail to kill Fidel, but Almeida wound up being assigned the defense of the one-third of Cuba that included the landing site for the US-backed Cuban exiles at the Bay of Pigs. If the CIA had been working with Commander Almeida during the invasion, the resulting disaster might have been avoided.

The opportunity arose again in May 1963, because Almeida learned from an American newspaper article that the CIA was backing "a new all-out drive to . . . topple the Fidel Castro regime." The May 10, 1963,

Associated Press article went on to say that "the plan calls for a junta in exile [with a goal of] ultimate invasion [and] seeking to put together the junta was Enrique Ruiz-Williams, a Bay of Pigs veteran and friend of US Attorney Robert F. Kennedy."[13] Almeida had first met Ruiz-Williams, a successful mining engineer, in Cuba in the early 1950s. (Enrique Ruiz-Williams told us, and several Kennedy associates we interviewed, that he preferred to be called "Harry," so that is the name we will use for him.) Harry had provided supplies to Almeida when the revolutionaries were still in the mountains, but after the Revolution, Harry turned against Fidel and his increasingly repressive regime. He eventually fled Cuba with his family, and by 1960 was living in Miami, where he decided to join the Cuban exiles being recruited by the CIA to invade their homeland. Harry fought heroically at the Bay of Pigs until he was grievously wounded by an exploding shell, and Almeida had visited the recovering Harry in a field hospital. Harry was one of sixty injured prisoners released by Fidel in April 1962, to persuade JFK to free the remaining 1,113 Bay of Pigs prisoners from their deplorable prison conditions.

Harry grew close to the Kennedys, especially Bobby, while working to get the prisoners released by Christmas Eve 1962. After the prisoners' triumphant return and welcome at a huge ceremony at Miami's Orange Bowl, Bobby began to work with Harry on ways to deal with Castro. In Bobby's oral history at the Kennedy Presidential Library, Bobby says that Harry was "very brave" and "very bright," and had "very good judgment."[14] Their mutual friend, Pulitzer Prize–winning journalist Haynes Johnson, said that "Bobby trusted Harry. He loved it that Harry was full of shrapnel from the Bay of Pigs." Haynes, and no doubt Bobby as well, liked the fact that "Harry was bluff, candid, blunt." In addition, unlike many Cuban exile leaders in the US, who were content to sit safely in offices and collect support from the CIA and their fellow exiles, Haynes said that "Harry was willing to die at any moment."[15]

When Commander Almeida learned from the May 1963 newspaper article that his old friend was working for the Kennedys to topple Castro, he decided to contact Harry. Initially, Bobby and Harry had been angry the article had revealed so much information, but that changed when they learned of Almeida's interest. Thus began several months of secret negotiations and planning, with Harry acting as an intermediary between Bobby and Almeida, while Bobby kept JFK (and a handful of other officials) up to date. Bobby's official phone logs document some of these calls. For example, on May 13, 1963, at 5:50 PM, Bobby took a call from JFK. The next call Bobby took, at 6:05 PM, was from Harry. On

June 25, 1963, Bobby answered a call from CIA official Richard Helms at 10:15 AM, followed by a call from Harry at 10:25 AM.[16] Three days later, the CIA issued a memo establishing their largest operation to support the JFK-Almeida coup plan, code-named AMWORLD, a name so secret it had never appeared in any government report or book until we revealed it in 2005 in our previous book, *Ultimate Sacrifice*.

The JFK-Almeida coup plan was designed to avoid the main problems that befell the Bay of Pigs operation, which had been a relatively open secret known to dozens of officials, aides, agents, and military officers in the US government, as well as to numerous journalists and even partially to Fidel. This time, any knowledge of the coup plan would be tightly held and only about a dozen people—including JFK, Bobby, CIA Director John McCone, and CIA Deputy Director for Plans Richard Helms—would know the full plan. The United States' leading role in the coup plan was never supposed to be revealed, even after the coup succeeded—and not even years later, since US officials hoped Almeida and trusted exiles might play roles in Cuba's new government for many years to come. If things worked as JFK and Bobby hoped, it would simply appear as if JFK had responded well to the unexpected situation of Fidel's assassination (a term the Kennedys never used with their aides; they preferred "elimination").

Almeida would not take public responsibility for Fidel's death, and neither would Harry. The Cuban populace could hardly be expected to rally around new leaders who boasted of having killed Fidel, still admired by many on the island, so Harry made it clear that a patsy, someone to take the fall, would be used.[17] Evidence indicates that Fidel's death would have been blamed on a Russian or a Russian sympathizer, as a way to help neutralize the thousands of Soviet personnel still in Cuba.[18] Many newspaper accounts noted increasing tension between Fidel and the Soviets in the second half of 1963. As head of the army, Almeida knew the locations of all Soviet forces in Cuba, as well as Fidel's security plans. Almeida had enough personal prestige that if he went on Cuban TV and announced that their beloved Fidel had been killed by a Russian or Russian sympathizer, the people would accept his word, the same way most US citizens at that time would accept a pronouncement by a trusted figure like J. Edgar Hoover.

Remembering the debacle of the CIA-run Bay of Pigs, JFK and Bobby restricted the CIA to only a supporting role in the JFK-Almeida coup plan. This consisted primarily of providing secret support to a handful of trusted exile leaders, and getting additional US intelligence assets into Cuba prior to the coup. The largest part of the exile support operation, AMWORLD, was run largely out of Washington, with only a small component at the CIA's huge Miami station. Even within that facility, AMWORLD had its own separate communications operation, code-named LORK.[19] The exile leaders were supposed to all be based outside the United States so that the United States could publicly deny supporting them. Though AMWORLD itself was relatively secret within the CIA, as a program with a budget of over $7 million, more than a dozen CIA officials and their aides had to be told about it. However, most of those officials knew only that AMWORLD was a secret way for the CIA to provide JFK-approved funding and support to a select few exile leaders. Only a handful of CIA leaders, including Director McCone and Helms, knew about Almeida and the full plan to eliminate and overthrow Fidel.

The CIA was also responsible for helping Harry arrange an initial payment of $50,000 to Almeida (out of a promised $500,000, almost $3 million in today's dollars), and for helping to get Almeida's wife and children out of Cuba on a seemingly innocent pretext, prior to the coup. The US military would officially have the lead role in the coup operation and its aftermath, though in actuality Bobby would be calling the shots.

Historians have long known that the Kennedys initiated two separate back-channel attempts to negotiate with Fidel in the fall of 1963, one using pioneering TV journalist Lisa Howard and special UN envoy William Attwood, and the other through French journalist Jean Daniel. The JFK-Almeida coup plan finally explains the reason for the urgency of those efforts. As Dean Rusk explained to *Vanity Fair* magazine, when talking about the Kennedys' pursuit of peace negotiations with Fidel while they were also planning a violent coup to eliminate him: "There's no particular contradiction there. . . . It was just an either/or situation. That went on frequently." However, Rusk added that by doing so, JFK and Bobby "were playing with fire."

While the Kennedys wanted to avoid "a bloody coup" if possible, neither of their secret peace efforts had produced any breakthroughs by November 22, 1963. To maintain deniability in case the secret talks were exposed, JFK had to work through William Attwood, who in turn talked to Fidel's doctor, who dealt with Fidel. The parties were wary of each other, and the negotiations slow. Fidel also had to deal with factions within his own regime. A November 8, 1963, Attwood memo to JFK notes that Fidel didn't want Che Guevara to find out about the secret talks, because "there was a rift between Castro and the Guevara [and] Almeida group on the question of Cuba's future course."[20] JFK kept his own secrets from Attwood, not telling him that, barring some dramatic breakthrough in the secret talks, JFK and Bobby planned to allow Almeida to overthrow Fidel on December 1, 1963.

Frustrated by the slow pace of the Attwood negotiations, yet anxious to avoid a violent coup if possible, in late October 1963 JFK had asked French journalist Jean Daniel to talk to Fidel on his behalf. But Fidel had kept Daniel cooling his heels in Havana for weeks. Daniel had finally gotten to see Fidel on November 21, the day before JFK's trip to Dallas. No real progress was made, but Fidel was intrigued enough by Daniel's message from JFK that he invited the journalist to a follow-up lunch on November 22, at Castro's villa at Varadero Beach.[21] However, Daniel could not securely communicate directly with JFK or Bobby about his talks with Castro, so the Kennedys had no way to know that Daniel was finally speaking with the Cuban leader.

Even while JFK was making his final attempts to reach a peaceful solution with Castro, he continued his efforts to overthrow the Cuban leader. As the date for the coup approached, Almeida indicated to Harry that he wanted JFK's personal assurance that the President would fully support the coup once it began. On November 18, 1963, following JFK's long motorcade in Tampa, the President had gone to Miami to deliver a speech, several lines of which were written specifically to reassure Commander Almeida that he had JFK's personal backing. A CIA report from 1963, uncovered years later by Congressional investigators, confirms that in "Kennedy's speech of November 18, 1963 [in Miami], the CIA intended President Kennedy's speech to serve as a signal to dissident elements in Cuba that the US would support a coup." The CIA report states the wording was intended for "dissident elements in the Cuban Armed Forces [who] must have solemn assurances from high-level US spokesmen, especially the President, that the United States will exert its decisive influence during and immediately after the coup."[22]

Years later, according to Pulitzer Prize–winning journalist Sy Hersh, CIA officer Seymour Bolten told a Congressional investigator that he had personally delivered the key paragraph written for JFK's speech. Declassified files withheld from Congress and not seen by Hersh confirm that Bolten's supervisor was an important part of AMWORLD and the JFK-Almeida coup plan.[23] (Bolten's son, Joshua, became a cabinet official for President George W. Bush.)

———

According to a formerly top-secret memo sent by JFK's CIA Director John McCone on the morning of November 22, 1963, the date for the coup was "scheduled for" December 1, 1963, just ten days later.[24] Both that specific date and the general timing were important. First, as outlined by CIA memos and Bobby's top Cuban exile aide, Harry Williams, Fidel was launching a military draft around that date that would soon dilute Commander Almeida's loyal army units and allow for the introduction of army spies under Fidel's control. This was part of an ongoing trend noted in a cable to the CIA's Director, whereby top Cuban "officers such as . . . Almeida who [are] not completely reliable politically are slowly being isolated from troops [by the] current Regime."[25] Second, as a Kennedy aide who worked on parts of the JFK-Almeida coup plan told us, JFK and Bobby were determined to have the Cuban situation resolved by the end of 1963. They didn't want US troops fighting in Cuba over the holidays, so that part of the operation would have to be completed well before Christmas. Lastly, since the final versions of the "Plan for a Coup in Cuba" called for the use of US air power, the coup had to occur before the Pearl Harbor anniversary of December 7, so as not to raise the specter of that event and saddle the United States with accusations of a Japanese-style sneak attack.[26]

As noted earlier, Almeida's wife and children had already left Cuba on a pretext, and CIA operatives kept them under discreet surveillance in another country. Bobby had Harry Williams assure Almeida that he and the CIA would guarantee the family's safety and security if Almeida were killed or captured in the coup. At the time, Bobby, Harry, and CIA Director McCone never imagined that this part of the secret operation would go on for decades.

Bobby finished his final meetings with his key Cuban exile leaders in the week leading up to November 22, 1963. On that date, in the words of the *Washington Post*, Harry Williams was having "the most crucial of a series of secret meetings with top-level CIA and government people about . . . 'the problem of Cuba'" at a safe house in Washington, D.C.[27] Unless an unforeseen problem arose at that meeting, Harry had been instructed by Bobby to proceed to Miami, and then to the US base at Guantanamo. From there, he would slip into Cuba for a final meeting with Almeida before the coup and "elimination" of Fidel. Once Harry was inside Castro's Cuba, it would be difficult—perhaps impossible—to call off the coup. If all went according to plan, Harry would be inside hostile Cuban territory, beyond US protection and reliable communication, by November 24 (Sunday) or November 25 (Monday). That would leave only a few days between the time Harry met with Almeida inside Cuba and the day Fidel was eliminated, Sunday, December 1, 1963.

Setting the coup for December 1 was possible because almost every weekend Fidel traveled to—and from—his house at Varadero Beach in an open jeep. In those days, Fidel often rode in such a vehicle, instead of in a limousine, to evoke his triumphant jeep trip to Havana at the climax of the Revolution. As a Kennedy aide explained to us, and as numerous historians have confirmed, Fidel's security precautions were legendary: He often varied his schedule, used doubles, and had meetings at odd late-night hours to foil any potential plotting. Such safety measures meant that Castro's weekly jeep trip to Varadero was virtually the only reliable opportunity for an assassination attempt.

In 1962, and again in the fall of 1963, the CIA had reviewed a plan in which Fidel would be killed at a restaurant he frequented. Diagrams were drawn to show how a shooter could hide in the pantry, since Fidel always went into the kitchen to talk to the cooks and busboys.[28] But this plan was too risky and inflexible, compared with simply having snipers shoot Fidel in his open jeep as he traveled to or from Varadero Beach.

A later AMWORLD document talks about assassinating Fidel "when he goes to Varadero," and says one of Bobby's Cuban exile aides was given "the details and the exact locations where Fidel spends every Saturday and Sunday, and specifically every Sunday at Varadero."[29] Cuban exile Rafael "Chi Chi" Quintero, the assistant to one of Bobby's exile leaders, Manuel Artime, later said "the plot finally agreed on was a combined assassination-coup attempt at Varadero, the beach resort on Cuba's north coast, [where a CIA asset] was supposed to kill [Fidel] with a rifle."[30] Commander Almeida knew the local commander at Varadero, a man later said to have been one of the coup plotters. CIA propaganda expert David Atlee Phillips worked on AMWORLD and, years after his retirement, wrote a proposal for an autobiographical novel that lightly fictionalized his CIA work. In it, he said that Fidel would be shot "with a sniper's rifle from an upper floor window of a building on the route where Castro often drove in an open jeep."[31]

A later declassified memo that mentions Almeida says the assassination of Fidel "is to take place in public so that everyone can see that the leaders have been killed."[32] This was important, so that Fidel's death couldn't be hidden from the Cuban populace for days, weeks, or even months. Varadero is only seventy-five miles from Havana, so killing Fidel there in such a public way would ensure the news spread quickly. This would give Almeida and his associates a reason to immediately arrest the patsy, and to invite in US forces to prevent a civil war and a Soviet takeover. According to Harry Williams and several declassified memos about the coup, Raul Castro would be eliminated along with Fidel. CIA memos show that Almeida was involved with Raul's security, allowing him to ensure that Raul was taken care of at the same time Castro was killed.[33]

While December 1, 1963, was the coup date given in the CIA Director's memo (other CIA memos mention the same general time period), Harry Williams told us it was possible he might move the coup up by one day because he didn't trust one of the other Cuban exile leaders, Manuel Artime. In October and November 1963, growing friction had developed between Harry Williams and Artime, because the latter had starting going to Bobby about various matters, behind Harry's back. The extremely conservative Artime had agreed only reluctantly to work with more liberal exile leaders chosen by Harry and Bobby, and Artime would have preferred to become the sole leader of Cuba after Fidel's assassination. Artime was often called the CIA's "Golden Boy" because of all the money and attention lavished on him by the CIA and his best friend, CIA officer E. Howard Hunt, so Harry worried that Artime might try to get a jump on the other exile leaders. To prevent this possibility, Harry and Almeida could quietly move the coup date one day earlier, to Saturday, November 30, the day that Fidel would drive into Varadero. Once Harry was inside Cuba, meeting with Almeida, the final decision about the date for the coup and Fidel's "elimination" would be theirs.

According to two close associates of the Kennedy brothers, neither JFK nor Bobby considered the JFK-Almeida coup plan to be an assassination plot. They explained that the Kennedys saw Castro's "elimination" during a coup by Almeida as far different from the CIA's earlier (and, unknown to the Kennedys, ongoing) plan to simply have Mafia assassins shoot Fidel. As noted in declassified files and confirmed by our sources, the President and the Attorney General viewed the JFK-Almeida coup plan as providing aid to "Cubans helping other Cubans"—supporting Cubans outside Cuba (Harry and selected exile leaders) so they could help Cubans inside Cuba (Almeida and his allies).[34]

As described in the fourteen drafts of the "Plan for a Coup in Cuba"— most written in a flurry of activity after Almeida's May 1963 offer— extensive plans had been made for the coup, the US invasion, and the post-coup Cuban government. The Kennedys' goals were to bring about eventual free elections, and to produce a Cuba free of the Mafia influence that had been so pervasive during the Eisenhower-Nixon administration.

Though these drafts involved State, Defense, the Joint Chiefs, and the CIA, the Kennedys had devised a way for plans to be made without revealing Almeida's identity to so many officials and aides that it became an open secret, like the Bay of Pigs. As files released in recent years document, and former officials confirm, most of the planning involving those agencies occurred under the guise of a "what if" scenario: What if a very high official could be found to stage a coup against Castro?[35]

During the summer and fall of 1963, selected officials from those agencies knew about three ongoing attempts to find such an official. One was a plan code-named AMTRUNK by the CIA, though it was originally the brainchild of *New York Times* journalist Tad Szulc, a friend of JFK. The second was a joint CIA-DIA (Defense Intelligence Agency) Task Force designed to find a high Cuban official willing to stage a coup. The third centered on a disgruntled midlevel Cuban official named Rolando Cubela, with whom the CIA had been in contact since late 1960. Cubela was brought to the CIA's attention by a Trafficante associate, a businessman the CIA code-named AMWHIP-1, who remained in contact with Cubela in 1963 and later.[36] Inside the CIA, Cubela was referred to as AMLASH, but those in other agencies who knew about him simply referred to him by his real name.[37] Though Cubela, a physician, had no real power within the Cuban government, as the former leader of a prominent revolutionary student group (the DR[38]), he was allowed a large travel budget and frequently went to Europe and communist-bloc countries. One of Bobby's secret NSC subcommittees was told that the CIA was using Cubela to try to locate a high official willing to stage a coup.[39] Cubela himself wasn't powerful enough to lead a coup, since an October 18, 1963, CIA memo says "that Cubela has no official position in the government."[40] Because of his service during the Revolution, Cubela had been awarded a purely ceremonial military title, but according to an October 30, 1963, CIA memo, he lost that when he "resigned from the Army after difficulties with Raul Castro."[41]

Planning progressed on the coup, invasion, and post-coup Cuban government by Bobby's subcommittees "just in case" a high-ranking Cuban official could be found. This allowed JFK and Bobby to get representatives from those agencies to do extensive planning, without revealing prematurely that Cuban Army Commander Juan Almeida had already agreed in May 1963 to lead the coup. In one memo, Army Secretary Cyrus Vance lists several possible scenarios by which Fidel might be toppled, but states they will initially focus only on a "palace coup" by a powerful Cuban official; Vance says plans for the other scenarios will be prepared later. Of course, these plans were never made, because Vance knew they wouldn't be needed.

With the coup planning largely complete by November 22, 1963, the Kennedys thought they had no need to inform officials like Secretary of State Dean Rusk about Almeida until shortly before the December 1 coup. On November 22, Rusk and several other cabinet officials, as well as JFK's press secretary, Pierre Salinger, were flying to the Far East. A still partially classified series of memos between Bobby Kennedy and National Security advisor McGeorge Bundy reveals that as of November 20, "The Cuban problem is ready for discussion now . . . so we will call a meeting as soon as we can find a day when the right people are in town." With JFK going to Texas, while Bundy, Rusk, and other cabinet officials were in the Far East, that meant Monday, November 25, would be the soonest day all the parties would be available. But by that day, assuming there was no last-minute breakthrough in the secret peace talks with Fidel, Harry would be in Cuba to meet Almeida and the coup plan would be past its "fail-safe" point. That would be when Rusk and others could simply be told that all their efforts to find someone to stage a coup had yielded results, and that the action had been set for December 1, using the plans they had already developed and agreed to.

Bobby's method yielded an odd situation in which only some officials on the subcommittees knew about Almeida and realized all the planning was for real; officials in this group included Cyrus Vance, General Maxwell Taylor, CIA Director John McCone, Richard Helms, and only a few more. Others on the subcommittees didn't know about Almeida and thought the planning was just a "what if" exercise, contingent on finding a high-ranking Cuban official to lead the coup; those in this group included Robert McNamara and Dean Rusk.[42] This meant that in any particular meeting, some of those attending knew about Almeida and that the coup was fast approaching, and some did not. The declassified notes from those meetings show the torturous wording that was sometimes used to convey necessary information without revealing too much to those not yet fully in the loop.[43]

Bobby's method proved extremely effective in keeping secret both Almeida's identity and the imminence of the coup, while allowing him to maintain tight control of the overall plan. But it also contributed to disastrous intelligence failures, since some people in the meetings knew the urgency of the situation, while others viewed the planning as more of a routine bureaucratic exercise. Worse, important agencies such as the Secret Service, the FBI, and even Bobby's own Justice Department were excluded from domestic aspects of the planning, since membership on the secret subcommittees was kept so small. Some meetings of the Special Group included only three or four people. Even today, large portions of their meeting notes from the summer and fall of 1963 are still heavily censored, such as those from November 15, 1963. Other notes from that time period that aren't heavily censored, such as those from the November 6, 1963, meeting, often say to "see special minutes for additional items." Those "special minutes" have never been released, a sign of the secrecy that remains even after more than four decades.[44]

Chapter Two

By mid-November 1963, officials in Washington were putting the finishing touches on the final draft of the "Plan for a Coup in Cuba." While the plans were being approved by JFK's top military leaders, like Joint Chiefs of Staff Chairman Maxwell Taylor and Defense Intelligence Agency Chief General Joseph Carroll, much of the actual work was being done by Army Secretary Cyrus Vance. Helping Vance with some of the planning was his assistant, Joseph Califano, and Califano's aide, Lieutenant Colonel Alexander Haig. According to Harry Williams, Vance was fully aware of Almeida's role. Califano and Haig have gone to great lengths in their autobiographies and public comments to stress that Vance was privy to more information about the Cuban operations than they were, and have never acknowledged knowing about Almeida. However, Haig and Califano acknowledge freely that they worked extensively on covert Cuban operations in the summer and fall of 1963, and their names show up in several "Plan for a Coup in Cuba" documents.

Their public comments help to describe the situation at the time. On ABC's *Nightline,* Haig said that Bobby Kennedy was running the secret Cuban operations "hour by hour. I was part of it, as deputy to Joe Califano and military assistant to . . . Cy Vance, the Secretary of the Army, [who] was [presiding] over the State Department, the CIA, and the National Security Council [when it came to Cuba]. I was intimately involved."

Califano's autobiography wasn't published until 2004, and in it he says, "Presidential demands for a covert program to [eliminate] the Soviet military presence in Cuba . . . intensified. Helping develop this covert program and direct the Defense Department's role in it occupied much of my time in 1963."[1] Califano goes on to say, "I felt I was working directly for the Attorney General and through him, for the President, and with one exception I enthusiastically joined the administration's effort to topple Castro." Califano says that exception was a suggestion to assassinate Fidel, but he notes that at that meeting, "the CIA representatives sat silent." Califano later bemoans the fact that the Warren "Commission was not informed of any of the efforts of . . . the CIA and Robert Kennedy to eliminate Castro and stage a coup" in the fall of 1963.[2]

Those coup plans eventually grew to more than eighty pages by November 1963, and those didn't even include the US military's detailed invasion plans for Cuba. All of the quotes in the following brief summary are from the coup plans that Cyrus Vance sent to General Maxwell Taylor. CIA and State had also contributed to, and signed off on, the plans, which call for the leaders of the coup to "have some power base in the Cuban army," and to be in contact with the United States prior to the coup. The US would also "seek the cooperation of selected Cuban exile leaders." The whole point of the coup would be to stage a seemingly internal "palace coup in Cuba [that would] neutralize the top echelon of Cuban leadership." The term "neutralize" is simply a nice way of saying "kill." The plans stress that "from a political viewpoint, it is important . . . the revolt appear genuine and not open to the charge of being a facade for a forcible US overthrow of Castro [since] a well-planned and successful 'rescue' of a revolt could be made politically acceptable" to US allies and the Soviets.[3]

The coup plans say that after Castro's death, President Kennedy would "warn [the] Soviets not to intervene," an important consideration since "twelve to thirteen thousand Soviet military personnel of all kinds remain [in Cuba]."[4] The leaders of the coup "would have announced via radio and other means the . . . establishment of a Provisional Government. They would have appealed to the US for recognition and support, particularly for air cover and a naval blockade, ostensibly to make certain that the Soviets do not intervene but actually, by prearrangement, to immobilize the Cuban Air Force and Navy."[5]

After "completion of such initial air attacks as may be necessary, provision will be made for the rapid, incremental introduction of balanced forces, to include full-scale invasion if . . . necessary." The plans also say that "US military forces employed against Cuba should be accompanied by US military–trained free Cubans."[6] Several hundred such Cuban exiles had been trained at Fort Benning, Georgia, and Fort Jackson, South Carolina, and were ready to be deployed by mid-November 1963. If the coup went well, it was hoped those Cuban exile US troops might be the only US forces required.[7]

The United States wanted support from its allies, and the Kennedys' ultimate goal was a free and democratic Cuba. The plans say, "The OAS [Organization of American States] will send representatives to the island to assist the Provisional Government in preparing for and conduct of free elections."[8]

Among the Joint Chiefs, evidence indicates that only Maxwell Taylor and DIA Chief Joseph Carroll were fully informed about Almeida. Others, like Air Force Chief General Curtis LeMay, were too hawkish and close to JFK's conservative adversaries in Congress to be trusted to know everything, especially about a plan that might be canceled if there was a breakthrough with the secret peace feelers to Castro. As JFK biographer Richard Reeves discovered, JFK was worried about the possibility of a military coup by a US general if he was perceived to have suffered another disaster like the Bay of Pigs.[9]

Though military leaders like General Carroll had a greater role in the coup than the CIA, some of the CIA's activities caused him problems. A CIA memo describes General Carroll's frustration with the CIA regarding the coup, a dissatisfaction that the General expressed to a Cuban exile in a meeting held in a car in November 1963. Meeting about the upcoming coup in a car, instead of at the Pentagon, was apparently for security reasons, but that didn't prevent General Carroll's complaints about the CIA from being reported to that very agency.[10] Such domestic spying was all too common in those days, and General Carroll was part of that apparatus: His DIA was a newly created umbrella organization that was supposed to coordinate the activities of services like Army Intelligence and Naval Intelligence, which later Congressional investigations found had been involved in domestic surveillance for many years.[11] While the CIA had been tasked with getting more US assets into Cuba prior to the coup, some of those assets were current or former US military personnel who were also involved with the CIA. At least one of them was under "tight surveillance" in November 1963, as he had been since his return from the Soviet Union in 1962. As we first revealed in 2005, Naval Intelligence was maintaining phone, mail, and visual surveillance on Lee Harvey Oswald and his wife. Since Naval Intelligence lacked the resources to maintain such surveillance in many areas, they relied on assistance from the FBI and the CIA. Our source, who maintained reports about Oswald and other domestic surveillance targets, says that Oswald's folder contained a CIA phone number to call if he were ever involved in any problem.[12]

Today, the vast majority of Americans have no idea that in the days and weeks before JFK's trip to Dallas, Bobby Kennedy had a secret subcommittee developing plans for what to do if a US official were assassinated.

The development of "Contingency Plans" for dealing with the possible "assassination of American officials" grew out of planning for the coup, and involved many of the same officials. This planning had begun in September 1963, to deal with possible retaliation by Castro, if he learned that JFK and Bobby were plotting to overthrow him. However, since some of the officials working on these Contingency Plans didn't know about Almeida, they no doubt viewed the issue far differently, and with far less urgency, than the few who did. Only three of the many files this subcommittee generated have been declassified, though we also spoke with two members of the Kennedy administration who were familiar with the plans.[13]

One of the sources was an official who worked on the plans but had not been told about Commander Almeida. The other source was a Kennedy aide who saw the plans after they were drafted, but also knew about Almeida and the imminent coup. While declassified plans show that the subcommittee believed the "assassination of American officials" to be "likely" in the fall of 1963, they considered assassination attempts "unlikely in the US."[14] If Fidel found out about US plans and decided to retaliate, they felt he would risk assassinating an American official only outside the United States—for example, in a Latin American country.

Bobby and the officials working on the plans, especially those who knew about Almeida, were considering how the United States should react if, for example, the US ambassador to Panama was assassinated and his murder appeared to be linked somehow to Cuba and the upcoming coup. One of Vance's memos about the coup stresses the importance of having certain types of "information . . . to enable the President to make" viable decisions so they could avoid any situation where the President "would lack essential, evaluated information . . . but would at the same time be under heavy pressure to respond quickly."[15]

Bobby and the other officials didn't want JFK to be under pressure from the public, the press, or Congress to take hasty action against Cuba, if early reports pointed toward Cuban involvement in the death of a US official in Latin America. A hasty US military attack against Cuba could provoke devastating retaliation from Russia. Also, imagine the disaster if the United States started bombing Havana, only to have evidence emerge proving the US official had been killed not by Fidel, but in a routine robbery.

To avoid those problems, the Kennedy aide cautiously indicated some of the conditions necessary for JFK to make an informed, reasoned response to the apparent assassination of a US official in Latin

America: First, the US would need to control and limit initial publicity, to keep the news media from generating an outcry for an immediate military response against Cuba. To protect Almeida, any possible links between the assassination and the coup plan would have to be hidden from the press. US investigating agencies would need to take control of the investigation from local authorities as soon as possible, including gaining possession of important evidence. The autopsy would have to be conducted at a secure US military facility, to ensure that information couldn't be leaked to the press. All of this would give JFK the time and information needed to make an appropriate response.

In the third week of November 1963, the Cuba Contingency planning was still going on, even though most of those working on it hadn't been told crucial information: that officials had uncovered plots to assassinate JFK during his planned motorcades in Chicago on November 2 and in Tampa on November 18. In hindsight, it's hard to believe that most of those working on plans to deal with the assassination of a US official weren't told of the Chicago and Tampa attempts to assassinate JFK, especially since each appeared to have possible links to Cuba. However, as Chapter 5 documents, both attempts were kept out of the press because of all the secrecy surrounding the upcoming coup. Apparently, JFK and Bobby decided that sharing information about the attempts with the entire subcommittee—and potentially their supervisors, aides, and secretaries—could compromise the security of the entire coup plan.

In contrast to all the secret planning that JFK and Bobby hoped would never be revealed, the Kennedy brothers were also concerned with building positive publicity about the aftermath of the coup. If everything went according to plan, it would appear as if JFK had responded well to an unexpected crisis, removing Cuba as a liability to his 1964 presidential campaign. Part of their publicity plan included a Kennedy-backed book and television project about the Bay of Pigs, though the JFK-Almeida coup plan was unknown to the journalists involved.

While it may seem odd for JFK and Bobby to have wanted to remind voters of their biggest disaster, it makes sense given the individuals involved in the projects. Bobby was friends with Washington reporter Haynes Johnson, who was working on a book with the help of four Bay of Pigs veterans trusted by the Kennedys, including Harry Williams and Manuel Artime. Chet Huntley, another Kennedy friend and one of the top news anchors of the day, was handling the TV project. Along with David Brinkley, Huntley anchored America's most popular news broadcast each weekday evening on NBC. Bobby knew that Huntley's Bay of Pigs special was slated to run after the coup, allowing the program to end with the triumphant return to Havana of Bay of Pigs heroes like Harry and Artime.[16]

Harry Williams usually shied away from publicity, but at Bobby's request he was involved with both the book and TV projects. The personable Harry became close friends with journalist Haynes Johnson and friendly with Chet Huntley. Both men admired Harry for his bravery, as did JFK and Bobby. Harry had distinguished himself not only in fighting at the Bay of Pigs, but also even as he lay gravely injured in a field hospital after his capture. In a well-documented encounter, when Fidel showed up unexpectedly to visit the wounded captives, Harry weakly pulled a pistol out of his boot, pointed it at Fidel, and squeezed the trigger.

But Harry's pistol only clicked—his fellow prisoners had removed the bullets because they were worried Harry might use them on himself, due to his capture and grievous injuries. Coupled with Harry's agreement with Castro—to return to his Cuban prison if he were unable to get JFK and Bobby to make a deal to free the remaining prisoners—his actions cemented his heroic stature in the eyes of Cuban exiles, Bobby, and JFK. Journalists from Haynes Johnson to *Newsweek* editor Evan Thomas have written about the close personal relationship that developed between Harry and Bobby by 1963, which is why Bobby and JFK put Harry in charge of the exile side of the JFK-Almeida coup plan.[17]

It was up to Harry to recommend a handful of "selected Cuban exile leaders" who would become part of the coup plan, subject to approval from Bobby and JFK. Most of Harry's recommendations were accepted, and five groups were selected. The hundreds of other Cuban exile groups, many of whom had received lavish support from the CIA for years, had their financial aid cut back severely or cut off completely, creating much resentment.

The exile leaders and groups Harry, Bobby, and JFK chose were:
- Manual Artime, the extremely conservative former Bay of Pigs leader and best friend of CIA agent E. Howard Hunt.
- Tony Varona, a former Cuban senator who had recently headed the largest US-backed Cuban exile group, the CRC (Cuban Revolutionary Council).
- Manolo Ray, head of JURE (Junta Revolucionaria Cubana), considered one of the most liberal exile groups, and hence distrusted and disliked by Artime and Hunt.

- Eloy Menoyo of the SNFE (Second National Front of Escambray), also seen as very liberal; Harry called him "a man of action" because (unlike many office-bound exile leaders) he had been willing to personally lead raids into Cuba the previous year.
- The Cuban American US Army troops in officer training at Fort Benning, Georgia, considered the cream of the Bay of Pigs veterans from a military standpoint. This multiracial group of Cuban exiles would be the first US troops into Cuba after the coup.

Many of these men had worked with Fidel and Almeida during the Revolution and its immediate aftermath. One by one, they left Cuba or were forced to flee. Now, Harry was trying to meld them into an effective group that could help to rule Cuba after the coup, during the transition to democracy and eventual free elections. But this goal proved difficult, because their political differences were so great. Recently declassified memos show the scope of Harry's problem: As of June 26, 1963, an FBI informant reported that "Menoyo would not be welcome" to work with Ray's JURE group, and on September 26, 1963, Artime told one of his AMWORLD CIA case officers that "Menoyo . . . is indeed a traitor."

Artime also disliked Ray, and memos from the summer of 1963 show CIA officials lying to Artime, telling him "that [Ray] is not one of [the CIA's] chosen" leaders, when the CIA had actually being supporting Ray with an average of $25,000 a month since late June 1963.[18] If it had been up to CIA officials like Richard Helms and E. Howard Hunt, Artime would have been the sole exile leader receiving support, but that wasn't what the Kennedys wanted. After much work by Harry, by November 1963 Menoyo and Ray had met to reach a "working agreement," and exile informants began to report that Artime had reached an accommodation with each man. Also on board were Tony Varona and the leader of the Cuban exile troops at Fort Benning.[19]

The five were not a cohesive group, and their level of commitment to Harry and Bobby varied. This was partially because Harry felt he had to withhold some information about the coup plan from them (such as Almeida's identity), until the exile leader was fully committed to the operation. For example, newly released CIA files cited here for the first time confirm Harry's account of meeting with Manolo Ray in September 1963. Shortly after that, Almeida's name came up in a meeting between Ray and his CIA case officer, but they both talked so cautiously that it's hard to tell just how much Harry or Bobby had told Ray about Almeida. Menoyo was even more problematic, and as late as mid-November, after months of wooing, Harry Williams was still trying to get him fully on board.[20]

Tony Varona had been eager to join Harry's plan—perhaps too eager. Unknown to Harry and Bobby, Varona had ties to mob bosses Santo Trafficante and Johnny Rosselli. When the first round of CIA-Mafia plots to assassinate Castro in 1959 failed, the CIA began greatly ramping up their efforts in the summer of 1960, three months before the presidential election. Richard Nixon had been Eisenhower's point man for Cuba, and Fidel's death was apparently supposed to be the original October surprise that would propel the incumbent vice president to victory. The CIA admits they brought Varona into the plots at that time, along with Santo Trafficante, Johnny Rosselli, and his boss, Sam Giancana.[21] Carlos Marcello told an FBI informant that he joined the operation at a later date. Despite a series of failures, the CIA continued their work with the Mafia. Bobby Kennedy was told about some aspects of the CIA-Mafia plots in May 1962, after they threatened to interfere with the prosecution of Giancana. However, the CIA admits they told Bobby the plotting had stopped, when in actuality it continued. Without telling Bobby, JFK, or his own CIA Director, Richard Helms continued having Rosselli work with Varona on the project, through the rest of 1962 and into June 1963, under the supervision of William Harvey, Desmond FitzGerald's predecessor. The rotund, hard-drinking Harvey was sometimes called America's James Bond, though he was replaced after clashing with Bobby Kennedy during the Cuban Missile Crisis. Evidence indicates that the CIA-Mafia plots were still going on in the fall of 1963, and that Miami CIA Operations Chief David Morales grew close to Rosselli in the process.[22]

JFK, Bobby, and Harry were determined to exclude the Mafia from their coup plans and from any role in post-coup Cuba: The Mafia would not be allowed to reopen their casinos after Castro was eliminated. But Trafficante and Rosselli had other ideas. The Kennedys and Harry were never told that in August 1963, the CIA learned that Varona received $200,000 from associates of Rosselli. A few weeks later, CIA files show that Varona secretly aligned himself with Trafficante associate and former death-squad leader Rolando Masferrer, whom Harry had banned from the coup plan and who had once been arrested on orders from JFK. A CIA cable says Varona told Masferrer that he could become part of the coup plan once certain "obstacles" were removed.[23]

CIA files withheld from Warren Commission and Congressional investigators, and not published until 2005, confirm that Manuel Artime was also part of the CIA-Mafia plots in 1963. Neither Harry nor the Kennedys were aware of Artime's work with the Mafia. CIA memos show that Artime planned to use funds provided by the Kennedys to obtain an airplane in Dallas in the summer of 1963, with the assistance of Frank Fiorini, a bagman for Trafficante's organization. Also that summer, Artime briefly operated a minor-league exile training camp just outside of New Orleans, an operation that reportedly involved two associates of Carlos Marcello: Marcello's pilot, David Ferrie, and a low-level "runner" for Marcello's organization named Lee Oswald.[24]

Though Menoyo had been involved with Santo Trafficante in a 1962 arms deal that went awry, Menoyo was generally considered honest and was not actively involved with the Mafia by the fall of 1963. However, he was closely aligned with one of the most violent Cuban exile groups, Alpha 66, which JFK had denounced for mounting unauthorized attacks against Cuban ships earlier in 1963. Alpha 66 was not part of the JFK-Almeida coup plan, but it was so closely aligned with Menoyo's SNFE that the FBI considered them practically one group. The leader of Alpha 66, Antonio Veciana, told us that he was receiving aid from a CIA agent named "Maurice Bishop," who had introduced him to Lee Harvey Oswald in the summer of 1963 in Dallas; Veciana said he and Oswald discussed "killing Castro." Congressional investigator Gaeton Fonzi investigated the incident extensively and found it credible, identifying "Maurice Bishop" as CIA officer David Atlee Phillips. CIA files confirm that Phillips was assigned to support AMWORLD at that time, and used a variety of aliases and cover identities, at least one of which he withheld from Congressional investigators.[25]

Manolo Ray, of JURE, was considered by the Kennedys and Harry to be of very high integrity, and a natural leader. A CIA cable describes Ray as having the "highest intellect, sincerity, and conviction," though some CIA officials, like E. Howard Hunt, didn't like Ray's liberal politics.[26] In addition to the Kennedys' insistence on including Ray in the coup plan, Richard Helms knew that Ray was also in touch with Rolando Cubela and Cuba's top journalist, Carlos Franqui, connections that could also prove useful. While Ray had no known Mafia connections, two months before JFK's murder, three associates of Santo Trafficante (including Rolando Masferrer) were involved in a deliberate effort to link Ray's JURE to Oswald and the assassination. In that September 1963 effort, a JURE supporter in Dallas named Silvia Odio received a visit from two exiles, accompanied by a man said to be Lee Harvey Oswald. This incident, detailed in Chapter 13, would take on a huge significance for investigators after JFK's murder.

While that effort was a deliberate attempt to stage an encounter that would taint Ray and JURE after JFK's murder, another incident is not so clear cut. A CIA report from October 29, 1963, says that Ray's second-in-command boasted that "JURE had obtained military equipment through robbing unidentified [US] installation," a military base of some sort.[27] This didn't seem to alarm Ray's CIA case officer, because it was one way to equip US-backed Cuban exiles with "deniable" weapons. In a Texas incident involving arms stolen from a US military base, an exile had apparently hinted at the JFK-Almeida coup plan, according to FBI and Treasury Department reports from October 1963. The exile told a Dallas gun dealer that in "the last week of November 1963 . . . a large-scale amphibious operation would take place against the Cuba mainland [and] United States military forces or Government agencies would possibly be involved [as well as] rebel Cuban forces." (Jack Ruby's auto mechanic was involved in this gun-theft ring, and another Ruby associate had similar dealings.) FBI reports say that the Dallas gun dealer was probably the source of the bullet found in Oswald's rifle after JFK's assassination.[28] Thus, even Oswald's bullets were linked to pre-assassination reports of the JFK-Almeida coup plan.

It's important to point out the gun dealer was not knowingly part of JFK's assassination, and Ray's JURE might not have been the source of the talk about the coup plan; FBI files indicate it was a man linked to Eloy Menoyo. Still, it shows how the shadowy milieu in which the Kennedys' exiles operated gave the Mafia opportunities to learn about or compromise each of the chosen exile groups.

The Cuban exile officers at Fort Benning were largely beyond reproach, and many would go on to have distinguished careers. However, the base was a stop on Marcello and Trafficante's portion of the French Connection heroin network, which smuggled drugs into the US by hiding them in automobiles and appliances of servicemen returning from Europe. The Fort Benning part of the heroin network would not be exposed until two years after JFK's murder, though it was active in 1963.[29] The mob bosses had developed their ties to the area because Fort Benning was just across the river from Phenix City, Alabama, which until 1954 had a decades-long reputation as the most corrupt town in America (when it was largely run by Trafficante).

Before looking more closely at the CIA's role in the JFK-Almeida coup plan, we should point out two high officials who were not involved, and why: FBI Director J. Edgar Hoover and Vice President Lyndon B. Johnson. Both had been excluded from both the coup planning and the Cuba Contingency Plans due to the animosity between them and Bobby

Kennedy. Bobby had long been frustrated by Hoover's reluctance to go after the Mafia, and by the FBI director's racism. As for LBJ, Bobby had never gotten over their clashes when LBJ ran against JFK for the 1960 presidential nomination.

However, LBJ and Hoover were good friends, and by mid-November 1963, both probably knew something big was brewing about Cuba, because of reports from FBI agents about the Kennedys' exile leaders, and incidents like the one involving the Dallas gun dealer. Also, Hoover would have known about the FBI's involvement in maintaining the secrecy surrounding the November 1963 Chicago and Tampa assassination attempts against JFK.

Recently documented information about the state of Hoover's and LBJ's relationships with JFK by mid-November 1963 is important, because some researchers have claimed that Hoover and LBJ were behind JFK's assassination, even though no credible evidence has ever surfaced. Their most suspicious activity occurred during the cover-ups following JFK's murder, but extensive evidence now shows that Bobby Kennedy was equally involved, and that all three men had the same goal: to suppress information that could have triggered a dangerous confrontation with the Soviets.

By November 1963, Hoover was secure in his job even if JFK were reelected, thanks to a deal arranged the previous month. Hoover had first almost exposed—but had then agreed to cover up—JFK's liaison with an East German beauty. Anthony Summers first documented the meetings that resulted in Bobby and JFK's agreement to keep Hoover on as FBI director, even past normal retirement age and into JFK's possible next term, if information about the liaison was suppressed.[30]

JFK had been introduced to the East German woman by Bobby Baker, Lyndon Johnson's former aide. The press was starting to devote attention to Baker's and Johnson's activities in November 1963. But because what would become known as the Bobby Baker scandal touched JFK and involved members of both parties, it would soon be shut down. Some writers have said that JFK was going to drop LBJ from the ticket in 1964 because of the scandal, thus giving LBJ a theoretical motive to risk killing JFK. But JFK could hardly dump LBJ because of a scandal in which the President was also involved. Also, it would have made little sense for JFK to publicly tie himself to LBJ in numerous public events in Texas in November 1963 if he planned to dump LBJ a few months later.[31]

Rumors have long swirled that Hoover and Richard Nixon were in Dallas, meeting with powerful Texas oilmen, the night before JFK's assassination; by some accounts, LBJ was also at the meeting, which somehow involved JFK's murder. However, LBJ's busy schedule that evening is well documented, and no credible evidence exists that places the FBI director in Dallas on that date.[32] Although Nixon was in Dallas for a Pepsi convention, press reports verify that he was seen in public with Pepsi board member Joan Crawford at a Dallas nightclub during the time when he was supposedly meeting secretly with Hoover.

However, in November 1963, Hoover was keeping a crucial secret from the Kennedys and the Secret Service. The FBI had tracked to Texas, and then lost, a man using the name of Jean Souetre. Souetre was a former French officer who had been part of an attempt the previous year to assassinate French president Charles de Gaulle by spraying his car with gunfire.[33]

The story of the CIA's involvement in the JFK-Almeida coup plan, and in the intelligence failures that led to JFK's death, centers on AMWORLD and CIA official Richard Helms. Unlike the Agency's Director, John McCone, and the CIA's number-two man, General Marshall Carter, Helms was a career CIA man. As the Deputy Director for Plans, Helms was essentially the highest-ranking operations official in the CIA. In other words, Helms focused on covert operations instead of on the budgetary, personnel, publicity, and Congressional-oversight issues the CIA's top two officials had to deal with in addition to their main functions of gathering and evaluating intelligence.

Helms had not been involved with the Bay of Pigs, which is one reason he was promoted to Deputy Director for Plans after JFK had forced those who were responsible to leave the CIA. McCone was a wealthy industrialist and former head of the Atomic Energy Commission, with no intelligence experience. General Carter's background was in the military. The only other official technically above Helms was Lyman Kirkpatrick, formerly the CIA's Inspector General, who had delivered a scathing report about the CIA's performance during the Bay of Pigs. Kirkpatrick had been a rising star in the CIA until he was stricken with polio in the previous decade which left him confined to a wheelchair. By 1963, Kirkpatrick was in a newly created position called Executive Director, but he had little active role in covert operations. Essentially, that left Helms free to do whatever he wanted, with little or no effective oversight. With thousands of agents and operatives around the world, it usually fell to Helms to decide which operational reports addressed to the CIA's Director should actually be brought to McCone's attention.

Officially, the CIA's roles in the JFK-Almeida coup plan were limited to getting US intelligence assets into Cuba and assisting the officially sanctioned exile leaders: Harry, Artime, Ray, Menoyo, and Varona. As part of helping Harry Williams, the CIA also carried out several operations approved by Bobby and JFK. As described shortly, these included handling the initial payment of $50,000 to Almeida through a foreign account, and maintaining surveillance on Almeida's family after they had left Cuba on a pretext for another country. The CIA's role in assisting Artime was much bigger, and included helping him set up and supply exile camps in Central America, since any exile operations by Bobby's leaders were supposed to be based outside the US. The CIA's support for Artime eventually topped $7 million, and was handled under the code name AMWORLD. While JFK was President, support for Artime's small hit-and-run raids, as well as the lesser backing for those of Ray, Menoyo, and Varona, was not intended to have any serious effect on Castro. For JFK and Bobby, it was intended mainly as a way to deniably support seemingly "autonomous" exile groups that were really under their control. The exile leaders' role was really to have their own way to get into Cuba for the coup, so they could be part of the new provisional government with Almeida.

Even within the CIA, AMWORLD was an unusually secret operation, and many of those who knew about it saw it only as a way for the United States to offer Artime clandestine support; they didn't know about Almeida and the upcoming coup. For example, Desmond FitzGerald, the patrician blue blood who reported directly to Helms as his Chief of Cuban Operations, was fully aware of the JFK-Almeida coup plan, and Bobby had introduced FitzGerald to Harry at Bobby's Hickory Hill estate. However, FitzGerald's assistants apparently didn't know about Almeida, and were thus confused about why the US was secretly funneling so much money and support to Artime. With so much secrecy surrounding the JFK-Almeida coup plan and AMWORLD, officials like Helms and FitzGerald found ways to keep other secrets even from their own superiors.[34]

The secrets Hoover was keeping from the Kennedys pale beside those being kept by Richard Helms. Not only was Helms deceiving JFK and Bobby, he was also withholding crucial information from CIA Director John McCone. In addition to running authorized operations in support of the JFK-Almeida coup plan, Helms had inherited two earlier operations that he had decided to continue without telling the Kennedys. One was the CIA-Mafia plots to assassinate Castro, mentioned earlier.

In addition to Varona, these involved Trafficante, Rosselli, and, by his own admission, Carlos Marcello. Others later linked to the fall 1963 plots by news accounts included Dallas mobster Jack Ruby and Chicago hit man Charles Nicoletti. Coordinating with Rosselli for the CIA was Miami's David Morales.

The other operation Helms inherited involved a European assassin recruiter named QJWIN. Years later, the CIA would refuse to identify QJWIN to Congressional investigators, and even today, released documents and experts don't agree on his identity. His job was basically to spot potential assassins for the CIA, as part of the ZRRIFLE operation.

Finally, Helms had reactivated a former CIA asset named Rolando Cubela, code-named AMLASH within the CIA. As mentioned earlier, Cubela was a Cuban official with no real power, but who offered three main advantages to Helms. First, Cubela could travel freely and extensively throughout the world, making it possible for him to meet with his CIA contacts far from Cuba. Second, he was still on friendly terms with Fidel and several of his associates. Finally, Cubela owned a house at Varadero Beach, next to Fidel's.

As part of their work on the coup plans, several officials outside the CIA knew about Cubela. But, they viewed Cubela simply as someone who was helping to find higher officials to lead the coup, and who could provide intelligence if a coup developed. However, Helms and his Chief of Cuban Operations, Desmond FitzGerald, had other ideas. According to Cubela, his CIA contacts constantly pressured him to assassinate Fidel.

In October 1963, FitzGerald had even traveled to Paris to meet with Cubela in person, claiming to be the personal emissary of Bobby Kennedy, but Helms later admitted that Bobby and JFK were never told about the trip, or about Cubela's role as a possible assassin. By November 22, 1963, one of FitzGerald's men was in Paris meeting with Cubela again, this time offering him a poison pen to use to kill Fidel, as well as offering to arrange "rifles with telescopic sights" to use in assassinating Castro.[35]

A CIA report sent to McCone about Cubela's November 22 meeting with his CIA case officer in Paris makes it clear that Cubela didn't know about the real JFK-Almeida coup plan. Cubela didn't mention Almeida as one of the four officials who could "be trusted for a move against AMTHUG" (the CIA's code name for Fidel). Almeida wasn't even in the next group—officers who could "be counted on to support the coup" after Fidel had been "removed." Instead, Cubela listed Almeida at the top of the list of the *next* level of officers, those who would probably "fall in line" after "the coup appears successful."[36]

The cable, which would be sent to McCone by FitzGerald two weeks after JFK's death, doesn't explicitly mention Cubela as the person who would assassinate Fidel, something Helms acknowledged he never admitted to McCone or Bobby. However, the cable does show the intelligence value of using Cubela as someone to ostensibly seek out officers willing to stage a coup. It provides a list of potentially sympathetic plotters to supplement the allies Almeida had already developed himself. Moreover, the fact that Cubela clearly didn't realize that Almeida was already set to lead the coup, and had gotten his family out of Cuba for just that reason, shows that Almeida's work for JFK hadn't leaked, at least to officials on Cubela's level. So it's not hard to see why Helms felt he could get away with pushing Cubela to assassinate Fidel himself, since it was, in some ways, only a half step more than Cubela was officially doing anyway.

Desmond FitzGerald had suggested earlier schemes to kill Castro, which were never authorized by the Kennedys. In fact, the Kennedys were not told about them at all, because they involved having JFK's personal emissary, James Donovan, give Fidel a poisoned diving suit during their negotiations about a small prisoner release in the spring of 1963. Fidel and Donovan shared an interest in scuba diving, so Fitz-Gerald even suggested rigging an exploding seashell to kill Fidel.

Helms and FitzGerald were the highest CIA officials who knew about the unauthorized attempts to kill Fidel. From Helms's perspective, the CIA-Mafia plots, QJWIN, and Cubela-as-assassin might have been viewed simply as backup plans in case some problem developed with Almeida. Others might see them as an attempt by Helms to have Fidel eliminated by a CIA-originated plan, instead of one in which the CIA was only a supporting player. It's also possible that Cubela was being groomed as a patsy to take the fall when Fidel was killed by other means. Also, if at the last minute Almeida proved unwilling or unable to place assassins to kill Fidel at Varadero, it's possible that Helms wanted to make sure people were available to do the job.

On November 19, 1963, Helms had shown JFK an arms cache, supposedly from Cuba, that had been found in Venezuela, indicating that Fidel was exporting his Revolution to the rest of Latin America.[37] JFK and Bobby seemed impressed, and it may have been Helms's way to ensure that, just in case their secret peace feelers appeared to be meeting with success, they didn't get cold feet about the coup plan. (In subcommittee meetings, Helms had been opposed to any attempt at negotiation with Fidel.)

Of the CIA officers that declassified files linked to the AMWORLD portion of the JFK-Almeida coup plan, three were of particular importance in 1963 and the decades that followed: David Atlee Phillips, David Morales, and Henry Heckscher. They continued working together into the 1970s, even using aspects of AMWORLD for coup attempts in Chile.

David Atlee Phillips was officially the Chief of Cuban Operations at the CIA's Mexico City station, but he had a separate role for AMWORLD, in which he reported directly to Desmond FitzGerald in Washington. He used different cover identities (among them Lawrence F. Barker and Michael C. Choaden) for various operations, and dozens of aliases (including Maurice Bishop, according to Congressional investigator Gaeton Fonzi).[38]

Phillips was a writer and propaganda specialist; according to E. Howard Hunt, Phillips also "ran" the DRE, a small Cuban exile group that was not part of the coup plan. This raises suspicion about the unusual amount of TV, radio, and newspaper publicity Lee Oswald generated in August 1963, when he had a brief street altercation with the only member of the New Orleans DRE branch. At the time, Oswald was the only member of a phony Fair Play for Cuba (FPCC) chapter in New Orleans, though he avoided associating with real leftists or pro-Castro people in the city.[39] Shortly after Oswald's radio and TV appearances, Phillips supposedly met with Oswald and Menoyo's exile partner in Dallas. A short time after that, Oswald took his unusual trip to Mexico City, Phillips's main base. There, Oswald was one of three individuals linked to Artime associates who visited the Cuban embassy within days of each other (sometimes on the same day) in an attempt to get into Cuba.

Phillips's former boss in Cuba during the time of the Revolution was David Morales, a gruff Hispanic Indian from New Mexico. Though Phillips would eventually surpass Morales in CIA rank, in 1963 Morales was still the more senior of the two. Morales was seen within the CIA as someone willing to deal with the Mafia and assassinations, and he was close to Mafia don Johnny Rosselli in the fall of 1963. At that time, Morales was the Chief of Operations at the huge Miami CIA station, code-named JMWAVE. It was the largest CIA station in the world, even though it was based in the United States, where the CIA is not supposed to conduct covert operations. The CIA memo from June 1963 that created AMWORLD established a special communication center for it at JMWAVE that allowed Morales, FitzGerald, and Helms to bypass the normal bureaucratic structure and most employees at the Miami station. It's unclear how much the Miami Station Chief, Ted Shackley, knew about AMWORLD and Almeida at that time.

Morales's position in the AMWORLD part of the JFK-Almeida coup plan also gave him a way to use it for his own ends, or those of his close friend Johnny Rosselli. Morales had several code names and cover identities we know of so far, like "Stanley R. Zamka" and "Dr. Gonzales."[40] But if his close associate David Atlee Phillips is any indication, Morales had many more, and even one of those could have allowed him to funnel his time to aid Rosselli in a way that wouldn't be obvious to his superiors. Morales frequently traveled from his home base of Miami to Mexico City and to Washington, meaning that no one superior had a full view of his activities.

A fellow CIA agent said that Morales "was a roughneck. He was a bully, a hard drinker, and big enough to get away with a lot of stuff other people couldn't get away with." Yet Morales had polish when he needed it. By his own admission in a CIA file, he worked with "senior officials [in] Latin American countries," and ten years after JFK's murder, Morales would become "counterinsurgency advisor for Latin American matters to the Joint Chiefs of Staff in Washington."[41] Just prior to that, Morales had been one of four regional directors for the CIA in Vietnam for the Operation Phoenix assassination program, which resulted in the deaths of 20,857 people, according to the testimony of later CIA Director William Colby.[42]

Morales was capable of more than being a manager, and didn't mind killing people himself. His best friend says, "Morales claimed credit for having killed dozens of Tupamaro guerrillas in Uruguay in a door-to-door search of the apartment building where many of them lived."[43] According to the number-two man at the Miami CIA station in 1963, "if the U.S. government as a matter of policy needed someone or something neutralized, Dave would do it, including things that were repugnant to a lot of people."[44]

David Morales also reportedly met with Rolando Cubela, in September 1963, as one of the CIA men pressuring Cubela to assassinate Fidel.[45] As Chief of Operations in Miami, Morales would also have been responsible for providing rifles with scopes to Rolando Cubela in Cuba. It's important to point out that Cubela himself was not the one who asked for the meeting in Paris on November 22, 1963; the time was set by someone in the CIA, though it's unclear by whom. Also, Morales's Cuban exile informants (in the group code-named AMOT) were responsible for the hazy reports of a Cuban agent near Chicago, and in Florida, that helped to trigger national security secrecy after the Chicago and Tampa attempts.

Henry Heckscher's role in AMWORLD is documented by recently released CIA files, showing that he was Manuel Artime's CIA case officer in the summer and fall of 1963. However, Heckscher didn't work with any of our four sources who worked with the Kennedys on the coup plan, so it's not clear how much he knew about Almeida. Heckscher was a higher-level CIA official than either Morales or Phillips, and had first worked with them in 1954, on the successful CIA coup that overthrew the democratically elected president of Guatemala. Joining Heckscher, Phillips, and Morales in the 1954 coup operation was E. Howard Hunt, which makes it logical that Helms would have them working together again in 1963 on another coup.[46]

E. Howard Hunt, later infamous as a Watergate figure, was one of the CIA officers working most actively on the Almeida side of the coup plan. In his later years, Hunt was litigious, so we avoided mentioning certain things about him in our earlier book. But we can now reveal that Harry Williams confirmed in taped interviews that Hunt was part of the CIA effort that helped with the most sensitive parts of the JFK-Almeida coup plan. (A top Kennedy aide indicated that Harry's statements about Hunt were correct.) The activities involving Hunt included paying the first installment of $50,000 (out of $200,000) to Almeida in a transaction that Bobby Kennedy authorized and the CIA arranged. Hunt was also part of the secret operation in which Almeida's wife and children left Cuba under a pretext prior to November 22, 1963. The plan was for them to wait out the coup in another country, while under secret CIA surveillance. This may have been designed to ensure that Almeida didn't double-cross the CIA and the Kennedys. Bobby had also authorized Harry and the CIA to assure Almeida that his family would be taken care of financially if anything happened to Almeida and they couldn't return to Cuba.[47]

Harry told us that Hunt was one of two CIA officials assigned to assist him. According to former FBI agent William Turner, the other was Hunt's future Watergate partner, James McCord. However, McCord declined to speak with us about this, and *Vanity Fair* had a similar lack of success when it tried to contact McCord about the matter in 1994.[48] According to Harry, Hunt seemed to resent having to help him, since Hunt was used to giving orders to Cuban exiles, instead of taking them.

Prior to working on the JFK-Almeida coup plan, Hunt's career in the CIA had been erratic, but his friendship with Richard Helms had allowed him some measure of success. Before getting to know Helms, Hunt had worked with David Atlee Phillips, David Morales, and Henry Heckscher on the CIA's successful 1954 coup in Guatemala. According to Helms's biographer, Thomas Powers, Hunt first met Helms in 1956. Powers says that "Hunt conceived of Helms as a friend, admired him openly, and more than once called on him for help." David Atlee Phillips wrote that Hunt "idolized" Helms—perhaps because Helms helped him after Hunt's botched stint as the CIA chief in Uruguay.

It's often overlooked that while Hunt was in Uruguay in early 1960, "he was secretly organizing a plot to overthrow the Uruguayan government," according to noted journalist Tad Szulc. According to Szulc, it's not clear who ordered Hunt "to start organizing a coup," since "neither the White House nor the State Department ever entertained such ideas" about Uruguay. In any event, Hunt was transferred from Uruguay to work on the CIA's attempt to overthrow another government—that of Fidel Castro in the operation that eventually grew into the Bay of Pigs.[49]

E. Howard Hunt played an important role in the Bay of Pigs operation, until he dropped out at the last minute in April 1961, to protest including the liberal Manolo Ray in the post-Fidel government. If it had been up to Hunt, after Fidel's elimination Cuba would have been ruled by his good friend, the ultra-conservative Manuel Artime. But the Kennedys insisted on Ray's inclusion, so Hunt left the operation. Shortly after he did, the CIA-Mafia plots failed, as did the rest of the Bay of Pigs. More than a year earlier, Hunt had written a memo suggesting the assassination of Fidel in conjunction with a small invasion, so it's intriguing to speculate that Hunt may have had some role in, or knowledge of, the CIA-mafia plots. Buttressing that is that when Dominican dictator Rafael Trujillo was assassinated with CIA assistance just a month after the Bay of Pigs, Trujillo's Security Chief claimed that Hunt and Johnny Rosselli had been involved.[50]

In 1961, Richard Helms helped Hunt find new opportunities in the CIA. Hunt had been given permission to write spy novels under a pseudonym, and Thomas Powers notes that Helms "liked Hunt's books . . . he kept copies of them in his office which he sometimes gave to visitors."[51] Apparently, Helms's personal relationship with Hunt was enough for him to assign Hunt to work with Harry on the JFK-Almeida coup plan, despite Hunt's antipathy for some of its leaders, like Ray. From Helms's perspective, Hunt's experience in planning coups in Guatemala, Uruguay,

Cuba, and possibly the Dominican Republic must have made Hunt seem like a logical choice. Still, Hunt's friendship with Artime and dislike of Ray were well-known within the CIA, so Hunt couldn't have an official role with either of those exiles.

Harry told us about one occasion when Hunt sent one of his associates, a CIA officer, to see him. Harry thinks Hunt sent the associate because of the friction that existed between Hunt and Harry. Even though the CIA officer was driving an old car, as Harry said they often did to avoid attracting attention, the Agency man started telling Harry, "There is a lot of money to be made." Harry looked at him and said, "How?" The CIA officer said, "There is a lot of money in the budget for this thing, and some people have . . . "

Harry didn't realize it at the time, but the total budget for just the AMWORLD part of the JFK-Almeida coup plan would total at least $7 million, and some agents estimated it was much higher. But Harry felt the CIA man "was trying to buy me." So Harry told him, "Look, when I want to make money I [will] go back to my profession [as a mining engineer]. I am not here to make money. I am not interested." It's important to note that the CIA officer may have simply been testing Harry, to see if he could be bought. The same Hunt associate later took Harry to a Miami restaurant, where Trafficante himself tried to bribe Harry.[52]

By his own admission, Hunt's assistant in the early 1960s was Bernard Barker, who was also later involved in Watergate. Barker's official CIA position was as a Miami-based agent who frequently passed along information from Frank Fiorini, a Trafficante bagman. (Fiorini had changed his name to Frank Sturgis by the time he was apprehended at the Watergate with Barker, McCord, and others). While Barker has never acknowledged being officially privy to the JFK-Almeida coup plan, one of his CIA reports from November 14, 1963, mentions "rumors" of an "operation including Juan Almeida [to] overthrow" Fidel.[53] In a television interview, Barker told Bill Moyers, "I would have followed Howard Hunt to hell and back," and in another TV program, Barker said that "at the time [of] the Kennedy assassination . . . President Kennedy's government had reached its 'peak' in its efforts to overthrow Castro."[54]

However, as this edition's Special Addendum documents for the first time, by 1963 Barker was working for Santo Trafficante. The Kennedys didn't know that, so Hunt and Barker worked closely with Harry Williams on sensitive parts of the coup plan. Thus, whatever Barker knew, his real boss Trafficante could know as well—giving the godfather a direct pipeline into America's most secret operation.

Chapter Three

Almost twenty years ago, the House Select Committee on Assassinations concluded that mob bosses Carlos Marcello and Santo Trafficante had the "motive and means" to kill JFK, but the committee was unable to figure out how they did it, since crucial evidence was withheld from them, especially regarding the JFK-Almeida coup plan.[1] Based on conclusive evidence and testimonies that have come to light in recent years, it's now clear that Marcello and Trafficante worked together with Mafia don Johnny Rosselli to assassinate President John F. Kennedy. All three confessed their involvement to trusted associates shortly before their deaths, including stunning admissions in FBI files detailed here for the first time. It was the JFK-Almeida coup plan that gave the Mafia chiefs the opportunity they needed: to kill JFK in such a way that any true investigation would compromise the coup plan, exposing Commander Almeida and triggering a confrontation with the Soviets and Cuba. The committee was also denied important evidence about Johnny Rosselli, one of the small group of US intelligence assets who helped the Mafia infiltrate the coup plan, and use parts of it to kill JFK.

Marcello, Trafficante, and Rosselli had all faced an unprecedented and escalating onslaught throughout JFK's administration. Bobby's intense pressure on the Mafia in general, and those three mob bosses in particular, was at its peak by November 1963. The Mafia had been exposed on television in millions of homes in September 1963 by sensational Senate crime hearings in which the star witness, Joe Valachi, became the first "made" member of the Mafia to publicly reveal its secrets. Carlos Marcello controlled Louisiana and much of Texas, but November 1963 found him on trial in federal court in New Orleans by Bobby's own prosecutors and facing permanent deportation.

In Texas, Marcello and Trafficante's portion of the French Connection heroin network had recently faced a major bust for the second time in a year. All of Santo Trafficante's operations in Florida, from drugs to gambling, were under attack, and even his own brothers had been arrested and indicted. Trafficante himself had been the subject of Congressional hearings in October 1963, exposing him and his operations to public scrutiny for the first time. Mafia don Johnny Rosselli, the Chicago Mafia's dealmaker in Las Vegas and Hollywood, was under attack on several fronts. Bobby was getting ready to run the Mafia out of Las Vegas and had gotten the FBI to put Rosselli under surveillance, which it was able to do part of the time. Rosselli's power flowed from Chicago mob boss Sam Giancana, and Bobby had finally persuaded the FBI to go all out after Giancana. Marcello, Trafficante, and Rosselli had no options for survival as long as JFK was President and Bobby Kennedy was his crusading Attorney General.

The leading roles of Marcello, Trafficante, and Rosselli in JFK's murder were first revealed to us in 1992 by a top Kennedy aide, one whose personal integrity, honesty, and work for the Kennedys are confirmed by declassified files and a Pulitzer Prize–winning journalist. Unlike FBI and Congressional investigators, this Kennedy aide knew all about the JFK-Almeida coup plan and the Cuba Contingency Plans to protect it.[2] Since his revelation, more than four million pages of assassination files have been released, confirming what this aide and two dozen other Kennedy associates told us about these events. Even though more than a thousand pages about the coup plan and the Mafia's infiltration of it have been declassified, they are just a tiny fraction of the more than one million CIA records related to JFK's murder that will remain secret until 2017. However, information from Kennedy associates, the most important of the four million pages, and the findings of government investigators and journalists allow us to show why the three Mafia chiefs killed JFK, how they did it, and some of the most important people they used.

While all three Mafia bosses worked together to kill JFK, Marcello was the driving force, since he had the most to lose in the shortest time. After serving several years in prison in the early 1930s, Marcello had risen through the ranks to become the Louisiana Mafia's unchallenged ruler by the 1950s. Marcello was sometimes referred to as "the little man," though never to his face. His height was reportedly 5' 2", upped to 5' 4" by elevator shoes. But what he lacked in size, he made up for in ruthlessness and raw power. Traditional Mafia terminology can't convey the true measure of Marcello's power by 1963.

Two of Bobby's Mafia prosecutors used the term "godfather" to describe Marcello. John Diuguid, who prosecuted Marcello in New Orleans during much of November 1963, later read the transcript of the only instance in which Marcello's conversation was ever bugged during the 1960s. Since the FBI in New Orleans left Marcello alone, this single instance involved one visit to Marcello's headquarters by a very scared wired informant for the Bureau of Narcotics. Diuguid described the scene to fellow Mafia prosecutor, Ronald Goldfarb, who wrote that "the overheard conversation between Marcello and other supplicants who came to see him and seek his favors sounded like a scene from *The Godfather.*" Diuguid confirmed that to us, describing Marcello as a "godfather" who was "holding court."

However, Marcello was more powerful than any traditional god-father, or even a fictional one such as Don Vito Corleone, the character in *The Godfather*. Even he had to share New York City with the heads of other Mafia families, and the real Mafia families of New York sometimes feuded as they vied for power. In contrast, Marcello reigned supreme in Louisiana and large portions of the surrounding states, including Texas, where he controlled rackets in cities like Dallas and Houston. Instead of feuding with Mafia bosses in adjacent territories, Marcello became business partners with them, as he did with Florida's Trafficante.

There was another very important difference between Marcello and almost every other Mafia chief in America: As the head of America's oldest Mafia family, Marcello didn't need permission from the informal National Mafia Commission to stage major hits. This made Marcello more powerful in 1963 than far more famous mob bosses who had held sway over only a particular city, such as his friend Mickey Cohen (of Los Angeles) and New York's Vito Genovese, both of whom had still been subject to the commission. Unlike most other Mafia families in America, the Louisiana Mafia had a long tradition of murdering government officials, beginning with the assassination of a New Orleans Police Chief in 1890. Marcello himself had attempted to have New Orleans Sheriff Frank Clancy assassinated in 1955, and was linked to two successful hits on much higher-ranking government officials.

The Mafia assassinations of an attorney general in 1954 and a president in 1957 had a major impact on how Marcello, Trafficante, and Rosselli assassinated JFK. Marcello had learned in the 1950s that by working with other Mafia bosses like Trafficante and Rosselli, he could extend his considerable power even further. While Trafficante had primary control of corrupt Phenix City, Alabama, in the 1950s, Marcello also had vice interests in the town. Across the river from sprawling Fort Benning, Georgia, Phenix City was so lawless that even General George S. Patton had been unable to tame it. However, in 1954, an anti-corruption attorney general for the state of Alabama, Albert Patterson, was elected from the town, after he pledged to run the mobsters out of Phenix City once and for all. The mobsters faced a huge loss of revenue, so the state's new attorney general–elect was assassinated in Phenix City on June 18, 1954.

However, the vice lords had been so used to the lax attitudes toward organized crime by the state of Alabama, J. Edgar Hoover, and the Eisenhower-Nixon administration that they didn't bother to use a patsy to quickly take the heat and divert attention from the real culprits. This was a serious mistake, and suspicion quickly focused on Trafficante's lieutenants and a corrupt official, one of whom fled to Marcello's territory to hide, while two others went to Trafficante's Florida. The brazen assassination became a national scandal, causing a barrage of media coverage. After nationwide calls for action, President Eisenhower finally declared Martial Rule and sent in National Guard troops to clean up the city once and for all. Though their names stayed out of the investigation, Trafficante and Marcello had suffered a rare setback and would not repeat the same mistake.

The error was corrected when the president of Guatemala, Castillo Armas, was assassinated in 1957, at a time when Johnny Rosselli was very active in the country and Marcello was developing his extensive ties to Guatemala and to Rosselli. Guatemala's president was assassinated just four days after trying to close a casino owned by one of Rosselli's criminal associates. A seemingly lone, apparently communist patsy was quickly blamed and soon killed. Like Oswald, the patsy was ex-military, and supposedly an ardent communist who had never bothered to join the Communist Party. The investigation essentially ended with the death of the patsy, who was accepted as the sole assassin by the world press and much of the public.[3] Both Marcello and Rosselli would remember the importance of having a patsy to quickly take the blame and divert investigators.

Marcello's fellow mobsters continued to target government officials into 1963. Chicago Alderman Benjamin F. Lewis was assassinated on February 28, 1963, "the back of his head . . . shot off by three bullets," according to Hoffa expert Dan Moldea. He wrote that the hit man was "a close friend of [Jack] Ruby," in addition to being an associate of Johnny Rosselli.[4] The 1961 Mafia assassination of UAW-AFL President John Kilpatrick in Chicago was an important turning point, even though he wasn't a government official: It was the first Mafia murder solved in the city since 1934, and the first Chicago mob hit the FBI investigated, all because of new Attorney General Robert Kennedy. Guy Banister, the FBI's Chicago chief before his drinking and erratic behavior sent him on a downward spiral that eventually found him working for Marcello, once noted in a speech that more than one thousand gangland slayings in Chicago remained unsolved. Banister was exaggerating only slightly, since Moldea asserted that the assassination of Alderman Lewis was "the 977th unsolved underworld hit in Chicago since the early 1900s."[5]

Marcello's associates were even willing to target Bobby Kennedy. As mentioned earlier, Marcello's relationship with Hoffa went back to at least September 1960, when Marcello personally gave Hoffa $500,000 for Richard Nixon's presidential campaign against John F. Kennedy. That meeting was witnessed by Louisiana Teamster official Ed Partin, and shortly after receiving the money, the Eisenhower-Nixon administration dropped criminal charges against Hoffa.[6] By late 1962, Partin had begun helping the government and had agreed to testify against Hoffa for Bobby Kennedy's Get Hoffa Squad, headed by Walter Sheridan. Partin told Bobby's men that in the summer of 1962, Hoffa had talked about having Bobby assassinated by using "a gunman equipped with a rifle with a telescopic sight [while Bobby was] in the South . . . riding in a convertible." Hoffa had talked to the informant because "Hoffa believed him to be close to various figures in Carlos Marcello's syndicate organization."[7]

However, nothing happened to Bobby at that time, and Marcello may have had something to do with it. About a month after Hoffa talked about his plans to kill Bobby, two of Marcello's trusted associates introduced him to Ed Becker, an FBI informant. While at the immense Churchill Farms property, Marcello told Becker that if Bobby were assassinated, JFK would simply send in "the Army" to get whoever was responsible. Marcello later told another companion the same thing, saying that if Bobby were shot, then JFK "calls out the National Guard." Clearly, Marcello wanted to avoid another disaster like the National Guard's takeover of Phenix City. Marcello explained that the best way to effectively end Bobby's war against the Mafia and Hoffa was to kill JFK instead. Marcello said that since LBJ disliked Bobby so much, once the President was dead, Bobby's power would be over.[8]

New information, published here for the first time, shows how Marcello came to his decision to kill JFK, and offers the first information from FBI files tying Marcello directly to Lee Harvey Oswald and Jack Ruby.

These revelations provide unique insight into Marcello and his actions, because they are in the words of someone who heard them directly from Marcello himself, in many long talks with the Mafia chief. Marcello's confidant was a trusted FBI informant, for an undercover operation targeting Marcello (CAMTEX, for Carlos Marcello, Texas) that has never been revealed until now.

The Marcello informant's credibility was confirmed to us by two former FBI agents who worked on the case, including the supervisor of the operation, Thomas A. Kimmel. The files themselves also confirm the informant's reliability. FBI memos note that a federal judge found the informant's reporting so solid that he authorized extraordinary surveillance on Marcello while he was in prison. This included not just phone taps, but even an FBI bug in a special transistor radio the informant kept in the small prison cell he eventually shared with Marcello. These devices yielded "hundreds of hours" of tapes of Marcello, according to the files, a trove of information previously unknown to historians and journalists.

Most of the following information about Marcello comes from recently declassified FBI files, discovered at the National Archives in September 2006. They cover the time when Marcello was finally serving a long prison sentence, but years before debilitating illness overtook him. These files show the informant also helped FBI offices in San Francisco and Tampa target other criminals. For example, the FBI files praise the informant for helping them target a "Colombian drug fugitive" described by the DEA as "the head of the Medellín drug cartel," who was convicted in 1991.[9]

One of the FBI's CAMTEX memos says the "Informant's name is not to be disclosed in report or otherwise unless it has been decided definitely that he is to be a witness in trial or hearing."[10] While some of the internal FBI memos don't use the informant's actual name, others use his real name extensively. We did not disclose his name in the first edition of Legacy of Secrecy. However, in August 2009 the CAMTEX informant agreed to reveal his name to the public, after being told about this book and the files the FBI had released.

Jack Ronald Van Laningham, now 80 years old, was surprised that any of the FBI files about his work on the CAMTEX undercover operation against Marcello were available at the National Archives. But since they were, he decided to speak to one of the authors as part of a Discovery Channel documentary being produced by NBC. His mind is still sharp and he verified what he had written for the files more than twenty years earlier. All of the quotes that follow are from Van Laningham's FBI file, in which he wrote down in the 1980s what Marcello had told him. We have made only minor corrections for grammar and spelling.

Carlos Marcello and Van Laningham were incarcerated together at Texarkana Federal Prison in 1985. They eventually became roommates in the two-man cell that afforded the Mafia boss far more privacy than the large dormitory rooms that housed most inmates; even in prison, Marcello received extraordinary privileges and special treatment. Van Laningham writes that he became "pretty good friends" with Marcello, and that they "would talk for hours about his early life in New Orleans. He told me about all the gambling clubs that he had owned in New Orleans and all over. He told me how he had got started running the Mafia in Louisiana. This man had done everything at one time or another. He told me the way to make and keep money was to buy ground," meaning real estate. Marcello told Van Laningham "he owned hundreds of acres of ground that he had bought for peanuts and now it was worth millions." Marcello's real estate holdings in Louisiana and cities like Dallas were extensive, including his 6,400-acre Churchill Farms estate outside New Orleans, once mostly swampland. After extensive parts had been drained, Marcello used its remote farmhouse for some of his most private meetings—including some prior to JFK's assassination.

As a result of Van Laningham's long talks with Marcello, he began "to understand Marcello better and better. He was an uneducated slob that had taken everything that he had by force. Anyone that got in the way of what he wanted was eliminated one way or another. He told me about the bars and liquor business in New Orleans. He never bought bars; he took them. Marcello would send men to see the owner that he wanted to do business with. The owner was told that from now on, you will be selling our liquor. If the bar owner made trouble or refused, fights were staged, furniture broken up, and the guests harassed. Whores were sent in to cause trouble. The owner of the bar either went out of business or went into partnership with Marcello. Marcello had his own still in New Orleans and also shipped liquor in from Texas, in five-gallon cans. Since all of the police were on the payroll, it did no good to call them; he had them all in his pocket, along with the Judges."

In addition to Marcello's seemingly legitimate businesses, the Mafia chief told Van Laningham that if someone wanted to operate vice in New Orleans, they had to go through Marcello, who "made millions over the years, and all tax-free." Marcello also said that "in the early days, he had gambling casinos, but this was stopped." Marcello had indeed controlled several lavish but illegal gambling clubs around New Orleans, until Congressional hearings in the 1950s focused too much attention on them. But Marcello wasn't really out of the gambling business—as he told Van Laningham, his Louisiana gambling operations simply "went underground." The investigations of Robert Kennedy and the New Orleans Crime Commission bear this out, revealing that Marcello's gambling interests continued to gross hundreds of millions of dollars in 1963.

In addition, Marcello told Van Laningham "that he was partners with a man that ran the Mafia in Florida, [named] Trafficante. They were partners in a casino in Cuba, and made millions before Castro took over and shut them down." While Santo Trafficante's role in Cuban casinos was well known to law enforcement and historians, Marcello's involvement there has always been more difficult to pin down. Since Marcello wasn't a citizen and was in the US illegally, frequent travel to Cuba would have been risky for him when reentering the United States. But by working through Trafficante—who also utilized their mutual friend Johnny Rosselli to help manage casinos in Cuba, along with Jack Ruby's good friend Lewis McWillie—Marcello could reap the benefits of pre-Castro Havana without taking undue risk.

Marcello also told Van Laningham about his first Las Vegas casino business. The godfather said that he "tried to get into gambling in Vegas" by using a front man, and "all was going good until the Nevada Gaming Commission learned that Carlos Marcello was involved. They were shut down and lost a great deal of money in the venture." This statement refers to Marcello's initial role in the Tropicana hotel and casino in 1957, a deal brokered by Johnny Rosselli. Marcello told Van Laningham "that he stayed clear of Vegas after that."

According to a report by Van Laningham in his FBI file, "By far the most important thing that I reported to the FBI was Marcello's hatred for the Kennedys. In the early 1960s, Robert Kennedy was after anyone involved in organized crime. He was after Marcello and wanted him deported in the worst way. Marcello was born in Tunisia, North Africa. Kennedy knew that he was not a citizen, and played on this angle to have him deported. Marcello had to report to INS each month in New Orleans. One time when he reported [in April 1961], he was loaded on a plane and flown to Guatemala in [Central] America." (With the help of Rosselli and pilot David Ferrie, Marcello had arranged for a fake Guatemalan birth certificate.)

Marcello told Van Laningham that "the governments of these countries did not want Marcello, and he was forced to move on to another country. He . . . spent thousands as payola [to officials], but when the money ran out he would have to move on." Finally, Marcello was able to buy "new papers in Guatemala and returned to the [United States] through Florida. He said he hid out for a long time and moved around so he would not get caught. He finally turned himself in and was placed in a camp in Brownsville. His attorneys fought the case in court and he was allowed to stay. Marcello was furious and vowed to get even with the Kennedys."[11] However, the Kennedys weren't going to let Marcello stay in the United States without a fight; their determination resulted in the court case that Marcello faced in November 1963.

Before talking to Van Laningham about JFK's assassination, Marcello first mentioned his contacts with Lee Harvey Oswald and Jack Ruby, in a casual way, while talking about his criminal operations in New Orleans. There was only one other inmate whom Marcello felt comfortable talking to about his activities there. Van Laningham "had another friend at Texarkana [Prison] that had worked for Marcello's brother, as a bartender. The 'little man' would let him come to our room and they would talk about New Orleans for hours. One night, Marcello was talking about the Kennedys. He told me and my friend about a meeting with Oswald. He had been introduced to Oswald by a man named Ferris [Ferrie] who was Marcello's pilot. He said that the [meeting] had taken place in his brother's restaurant. He said that he thought that Oswald [was] crazy. They had several meetings with Oswald before he left town."[12]

Van Laningham said that Marcello "also told us about Jack Ruby. Marcello had met him in Dallas, Texas. He set him up in the bar business there. He said that Ruby was a homo son-of-a-bitch, but good to have around to report to him what was happening in town. Marcello told us that all the police were on the take, and as long as he kept the money flowing they let him operate anything in Dallas that he wanted to. Ruby would come to Churchill Farms to report to Marcello, so the little man knew what was happening all the time."[13]

Eventually, Marcello made a clear confession about JFK's assassination to Van Laningham, in front of a named witness. According to FBI files at the National Archives, Van Laningham wrote that "Marcello was talking about his favorite subject: the Kennedys and being deported. He flew into a rage, cussing the Kennedys, calling them every name that he could think of. I thought that he was going to have a stroke." Suddenly, Marcello "stopped talking for a minute, and then continued. He said, 'Yeah, I had the little son of a bitch killed, and I would do it again; he was a thorn in my side. I wish I could have done it myself.'"[14]

Chapter 65 will have much more about Marcello's JFK confession, including his threat to kill Van Laningham if he ever told, and how the FBI kept Marcello's JFK confession secret for years. For now, it's important to note that supporting evidence from independent sources, mostly government investigators and noted historians, exists for each part of the account that Marcello related to Van Laningham. For example, Marcello's admission about meeting Oswald is given credence by what the Mafia boss had told another FBI informant, Joe Hauser, a few years earlier. (Hauser's testimony in a government sting called BRI-LAB finally yielded Marcello a long prison sentence.) Marcello told Joe Hauser that he and some of his men knew Oswald: "I used to know his fuckin' family. His uncle, he work for me. Dat kid work for me, too." Marcello indicated that in 1963, Oswald worked briefly as a "runner" for his gambling network, in which Oswald's uncle, Dutz Murret, was a longtime bookie.[15]

In the spring of 1963, Oswald had moved to New Orleans, where he lived for a time with his uncle Murret. According to *Vanity Fair*, Oswald's "youth had been spent in New Orleans. Oswald's mother's friends included a corrupt lawyer linked to Marcello's crime operation and a man who served Marcello as bodyguard and chauffeur." In August 1963, when Oswald was "arrested, after getting into a brawl with Cuban exiles while passing out pro-Castro leaflets," the man who arranged Oswald's bail was close to "one of Marcello's oldest friends, Nofio Pecora, [who was] called three weeks before the assassination by Jack Ruby."[16]

FBI memos first published in Marcello's 1989 biography, *Mafia King-fish*, by John H. Davis, describe Oswald's receiving money from one of Marcello's men at the Town and Country Motel's restaurant in late February or early March 1963. The nondescript motel on the Airline Highway—far from the tawdry glitz of the French Quarter—served as Marcello's headquarters. According to the FBI memos, Oswald was sitting in the mostly empty dining room when the FBI's source saw the restaurant's "owner remove [a] wad of bills from his pocket, which he passed under the table to the man sitting at the table," whom the source identified as Oswald.[17]

Yet another well-documented link between Marcello and Oswald is David Ferrie, whom Van Laningham said "introduced Oswald to Marcello." Congressional investigators, FBI reports, and even photographic evidence confirm that Ferrie had been a leader in the teenage Oswald's Civil Air Patrol unit in 1955, shortly before the underage Oswald's first attempt to join the US Marines. By 1963, former Eastern Airlines pilot Ferrie was working for Marcello and his lawyer. Ferrie was supposedly helping with Marcello's defense against the federal charges being pressed by Bobby Kennedy's Justice Department, relating to Marcello's 1961 INS deportation and subsequent reentry. Both Marcello and Ferrie admitted to investigators that they spent several weekends together at Marcello's Churchill Farms estate in the weeks prior to JFK's assassination. Ferrie also admitted he flew to Guatemala twice, shortly before November 22, 1963. Based on what Marcello told him, Van Laningham accurately wrote that Ferrie "was an ex–airline pilot. It seems that he flew to Guatemala to pick up some new papers that Marcello needed to fight the INS in a court case."[18]

Also doing work for Marcello in the summer and fall of 1963 was private detective Guy Banister, Ferrie's associate and the former head of the Chicago FBI office. According to historian Richard Mahoney, six witnesses saw Oswald with Ferrie or Banister in the summer of 1963, when Oswald garnered an unusual amount of TV, radio, and newspaper publicity for his one-man New Orleans chapter of the Fair Play for Cuba Committee. Two witnesses said Oswald was working for Banister at that time.[19]

Marcello's admission about Ruby goes beyond anything previously reported, but is consistent with other evidence. Dallas journalist Earl Golz was one of the first to clearly establish the connection between Ruby and Marcello's organization, a link confirmed by the 1979 House Select Committee on Assassinations report.

Marcello biographer John H. Davis didn't have access to Van Laningham's information, but he was still able to detail tantalizing connections between Ruby and several Marcello associates. These included Marcello's Dallas mob lieutenants Joe Civello and Joe Campisi, the latter described as one of Ruby's closest friends and who met with Ruby the night before JFK's assassination. Davis documented that in the months and weeks prior to November 22, 1963, Ruby visited or made calls to five people in Marcello's organization. In addition to those five, he writes that "it appears that Jack Ruby knew at least two of Carlos Marcello's brothers" via slot-machine and strip-club businesses.[20]

Jack Ruby had worked for Chicago mobsters for years before moving to Dallas, where his duties for Marcello included being a low-level member of Marcello's part of the French Connection heroin network. In October 1963 in Chicago, shortly before the November 2 attempt to kill JFK in that city (discussed in Chapter 5), two witnesses saw Ruby receive $7,000 from a man who worked with Marcello's associate Jimmy Hoffa. Several witnesses say Ruby was in Houston on November 21, 1963, apparently shadowing JFK during his visit to that city. After Ruby returned to Dallas later that night and met with Marcello lieutenant Campisi, he heard that JFK's Secret Service agents were blowing off steam at an after-hours joint in Fort Worth—so he sent several strippers from his Carousel Club to join them.[21]

As for Marcello's remark that Ruby was gay, most people are unaware that Jack Ruby was homosexual (or bisexual), even though such information crops up almost forty times in Warren Commission documents, and Ruby's roommate at the time of JFK's murder described Ruby as "my boyfriend."[22] FBI files also back up Marcello's remark that "all the police were on the take" allowing Marcello to "operate anything in Dallas that he wanted to." The FBI interviewed witnesses who said that Ruby "was well acquainted with virtually every officer of the Dallas Police force" and was "the pay-off man for the Dallas Police Department."[23]

Marcello's claim to Van Laningham that Ruby went to his huge Churchill Farms property might explain a gap that Congressional investigators discovered as they compiled detailed information about Ruby's many calls and visits to New Orleans in 1963, usually to people or places connected to Marcello. They were unable to find where Ruby stayed during his visit to New Orleans from June 5 to June 8, 1963, leading one journalist to suggest that Ruby had stayed at Churchill Farms during that time. Ruby had called a Marcello associate several times before that visit, and Ruby called a club run by one of Marcello's brothers two days after he returned to Dallas.[24]

By June 1963, Ruby owed a small fortune to the IRS and was facing financial ruin, which would have made him amenable to a lucrative offer from Marcello. As Congressional investigators documented, in June 1963, Ruby's monthly long-distance calls built to a minor peak of more than thirty, up from his usual handful. The big peak would come during the three weeks prior to JFK's murder, when Ruby made more than 110 long-distance calls, many to associates of Marcello, Trafficante, Rosselli, and Hoffa.[25]

FBI files show that "on June 22, 1963"—two weeks after Ruby's visit to New Orleans—a horse trainer for one of Carlos Marcello's brothers said he was in a bookie joint in New Orleans, where he worked part-time. The horse trainer told the FBI that another one of Marcello's brothers came in and spoke to the owner. The trainer overheard Marcello's brother say, "The word is out to get the Kennedy family."

Independent accounts support Marcello's confession that he had JFK murdered. Congressional investigators took seriously the fall 1962 incident we noted earlier, when Marcello told Ed Becker at Churchill Farms that JFK was going to be assassinated.[26] John H. Davis uncovered a conversation that Marcello had with a close companion six months before JFK's assassination, in which Marcello said that to eliminate Robert Kennedy's prosecutions of him, "you gotta hit de top man. . . . This is somethin' I gotta get some nut for, some crazy guy . . . But I tell you as sure as I stand here, somethin' awful is gonna happen to dat man." That conversation occurred at Marcello's lodge in Grande Isle, Louisiana, a popular fishing area a hundred miles southwest of New Orleans, on the Gulf of Mexico. We found another witness who said that in early summer 1963 at Grande Isle, a cook on a large boat that Marcello used told the witness he overheard the godfather and a mobster from Los Angeles planning an attack on JFK.[27]

What Van Laningham said regarding Marcello's control of the New Orleans police and judges was true, according to Congressional investigators and the New Orleans Crime Commission. Much evidence shows that Marcello's corrupt control even affected congressmen, senators, governors, and other political leaders.[28] Marcello told Van Laningham about his scams with a Louisiana governor, which are described in Chapter 65. Marcello's reach also extended to federal law enforcement and intelligence activities.

The JFK-Almeida coup plan gave Marcello the opportunity he needed to kill JFK in a way that would prevent even Robert Kennedy—as well as Lyndon Johnson and J. Edgar Hoover—from pursuing a full or public investigation of JFK's murder. Though the Kennedys had barred the Mafia from any participation in the coup plan—and from reopening their Havana casinos after the coup—the work of Marcello and his associates on the CIA-Mafia Castro plots allowed the mob bosses to infiltrate the coup plan. While the CIA admits only that Rosselli and Trafficante worked on the CIA-Mafia plots, Marcello told FBI informant Joe Hauser he had been part of the operation as well. A private investigator for Marcello, Sam Benton, was indeed working on Castro assassination plans in the fall of 1963. It's important to remember that David Morales was working on the CIA-Mafia plots with Rosselli at the same time Morales had a significant role in the AMWORLD part of the coup plan.[29]

Twelve associates of Marcello, Trafficante, or Rosselli knew about the coup plan, and seven actually worked on parts of it (including Barker and Morales). This was a remarkable achievement, since we noted earlier that the JFK-Almeida coup plan was fully known to only about a dozen government officials at the time, and the first files about it weren't declassified until the 1990s.

An FBI memo shows that a close associate of David Ferrie told the FBI about Ferrie's "dealings with the late Attorney General Robert Kennedy [and] plans for a Cuban second invasion."[30] Another FBI memo written after November 22, 1963, quotes Jack Ruby as talking about "an invasion of Cuba [that] was being sponsored by the United States Government."[31]

A long-overlooked *New York Times* article quotes a Cuban exile, who had been in contact with Oswald in New Orleans in August 1963 and who knew David Ferrie, as saying that "Lee H. Oswald had boasted [about what he would do] if the United States attempted an invasion of Cuba." Prior to JFK's assassination, a close friend of Guy Banister wrote a description of "Kennedy Administration planning" for Cuba, in which Castro "would be the fall guy in a complete reorganization for the [Cuban] regime, which will [then] be free of Soviet influence." After Castro's removal, Banister's friend accurately noted that "a new government [for Cuba would be] set up with such men as . . . Manolo Ray."[32]

These are just a few of the associates of Marcello, Trafficante, and Rosselli who knew about the JFK-Almeida coup plan. More are documented in the next chapter and other parts of the book. One Marcello associate named John Martino not only boasted to journalists about his knowledge of the coup plan, but even taunted FBI agents with his inside information. So many of Marcello's men knew about the JFK-Almeida plan that it's inconceivable Marcello didn't know about it, too.

By November 1963, Carlos Marcello was confident that he could get away with assassinating the President of the United States, because he'd made sure that JFK's murder couldn't be fully or publicly investigated without exposing the coup plan. As documented earlier, even the bullets in Oswald's rifle could have led investigators to the plan with Almeida. Knowledge of the coup plan enabled Marcello and his associates to compromise each of Bobby and Harry's exile groups in some way. The Mafia chiefs used money to essentially bribe Artime and Varona, while they compromised Ray's and Menoyo's groups by linking them to Oswald.

As for Harry Williams, Marcello left him to his friend Trafficante. On one occasion, former death-squad leader Rolando Masferrer confronted Harry at Bobby Kennedy's New York apartment. As we noted previously, a CIA associate of E. Howard Hunt took Harry to an impromptu meeting with Trafficante, who fruitlessly offered Harry a bribe. Still later, on a trip to Guatemala to meet with Artime, Harry was attacked by two gunmen in a restaurant, and he barely escaped after shooting one of them.

The CIA ties of Guy Banister and David Ferrie, documented in Chapter 6, using new information from the CIA's Deputy Chief in New Orleans, also enabled Marcello to take advantage of US intelligence operations for his own ends. Memos show that the CIA almost recruited Banister in the summer of 1960, when the CIA-Mafia Castro assassination plots with Trafficante and Rosselli began. Guy Banister's secretary says that Rosselli visited their office in the summer of 1963, while the CIA-Mafia plots continued. Banister also had ties to Naval Intelligence through his close friend Guy Johnson. In addition, Banister had also served in the FBI on a major case with General Joseph Carroll, JFK's trusted head of the Defense Intelligence Agency, which included Naval Intelligence. Several years before JFK's assassination, Banister had even been business partners with Carmine Bellino, a close advisor to JFK who was part of Bobby's Get Hoffa Squad in 1963. In short, Banister had numerous ways to feed disinformation into various agencies.[33]

As for David Ferrie, Anthony Summers writes that "the former Executive Assistant to the Deputy Director of the CIA [confirmed that] Ferrie had been a contract agent to the Agency [CIA] in the early sixties . . . in some of the Cuban activities, [and Richard] Helms stated that David Ferrie was a CIA agent [in the fall of 1963]."[34] In the summer of 1963, Manuel Artime briefly had a training camp near New Orleans, and Summers writes that Guy Banister's secretary said that "Ferrie not only met Oswald but took him on at least one visit to an anti-Castro guerrilla training camp outside New Orleans."[35] A CIA note card about Lee Harvey Oswald, declassified in the mid-1990s, said "there had been no secret, as far as anyone was concerned, in regard to the fact that Banister, David William Ferrie, and Subj[ect, Oswald] may have known or been acquainted with one another."[36] Given all those connections, when Oswald talked to Marcello in the meeting Van .Laningham described, the young man may have thought he was being brought into the CIA-Mafia plots by Marcello and his associates.

Marcello faced losing his empire, his freedom, and even the ability to stay in America—unless he ended Bobby Kennedy's extraordinary power by killing JFK. In November 1963, when Marcello was being tried on federal charges that Bobby had brought against him, even a minor conviction could have resulted in his deportation. Marcello had already found a way to evade justice, by bribing a key juror. However, he knew that a new investigation would begin as soon as that trial was over (and Bobby did later prosecute him for bribing the juror). Bobby was already focusing on tax charges against Marcello, the same technique used to send Al Capone to prison, and the Mafia chief knew he would have no respite while JFK was alive.

Doing nothing about JFK and Bobby simply was not an option for Marcello. He knew that the JFK-Almeida coup plan was perhaps the only thing so sensitive that it could trigger a cover-up by high-ranking US officials. Just as the Kennedys felt they had to stage their coup with Almeida soon, Marcello knew he had to act before the coup took place and removed his only opportunity to force a cover-up by officials like Bobby Kennedy.

Marcello had nothing to gain, and everything to lose, by allowing the JFK-Almeida coup plan to go forward. As long as JFK was President, Cuba would not be a safe haven for Marcello or any other Mafia boss. Hence, Marcello had to kill JFK before December 1, 1963, the scheduled date for the coup. That's why Marcello organized three attempts to kill JFK during November 1963, in Chicago, Tampa, and Dallas.

Marcello relied on his trusted associates to help him: the Chicago mob's Rosselli, and Trafficante in Tampa. The men sometimes met at a secluded resort outside Tampa, the Safety Harbor Spa, whose exclusive clientele and distinctive staff freed the mob bosses from any possibility of law enforcement surveillance.[37] Trafficante also met with Marcello in New Orleans once or twice a year, and we noted earlier Rosselli's trip to New Orleans in 1963. In the JFK hit, these Mafia chiefs were only doing on a larger scale what they had done successfully in the past, and using only associates they knew they could trust.

Chapter Four

———

Though Carlos Marcello was the driving force behind JFK's assassination, he was joined at the highest level by Tampa crime boss Santo Trafficante and the Chicago Mafia's Johnny Rosselli. As Chapter 5 explains, in November 1963 they first attempted to kill JFK in Chicago and then in Tampa, before finally succeeding in Dallas. Their careful year of planning meant that even their backup plan (Tampa) had a backup (Dallas), and each city's Mafia family shared the risk. As with Marcello, both Trafficante and Rosselli also confessed their roles in JFK's murder to trusted associates shortly before their deaths. The same was true of some of the operatives they had used in the JFK hit, some of whose roles are described in this chapter.

Santo Trafficante's exclusive territory was not as large as Marcello's, but because of the groundwork laid by his crime-boss father, Santos Trafficante Sr., the Tampa crime godfather's reach stretched far beyond Florida and US borders. In the 1920s, the senior Trafficante began importing heroin from France into Cuba, and then into Florida. By the 1940s, the Trafficante network had worked out partnerships with other Mafia families that allowed them to bring in heroin through New York City. The elder Trafficante started his son in the Havana casino business in 1946. After his father died in 1954, Santo Trafficante became boss of the Tampa Mafia and prospered during the golden age of Cuban mob casinos in the mid- to late 1950s.[1]

Trafficante's Havana casino empire slowly crumbled after Castro ascended to power. Castro initially closed all the casinos, but then allowed them to reopen for more than two years before finally closing the last one in 1961, several months after the Bay of Pigs. However, Trafficante was still able to prosper by expanding his gambling and other criminal activities, which included smuggling contraband through Cuba while bringing in black-market goods barred by the American embargo. Trafficante controlled the rackets in most of Florida, and though Miami was considered an "open city" like Las Vegas, Trafficante's heavy presence there made him first among equals. While Trafficante lived in Tampa, he maintained a base in Miami, where he shared an office with a Hoffa Teamster local.

Trafficante also greatly expanded the French Connection heroin network, in partnership with Marcello and other associates, including Jimmy Hoffa.[2] By 1963, this heroin-importation network stretched from France to entry points like New York City, Montreal, Mexico City, New Orleans, Houston, and Miami. One of Trafficante's most common techniques for smuggling heroin was to hide it in special compartments in cars, bringing them into the United States at border crossings in Texas or from Canada, or on ocean liners, as depicted in the *French Connection* movie. Investigations by the Bureau of Narcotics and a Pulitzer Prize–winning team from *Newsday* show that the French criminal who perfected the car technique, Michel Victor Mertz, was an important part of Trafficante's network.[3]

Trafficante's heroin network was his most secure and ruthless operation because of the tremendous amounts of money it involved. It was a high-stakes, deadly enterprise in which one mistake could mean death. Although importing heroin was one of the most profitable operations that Trafficante and Marcello shared, it was under increasing attack by the Kennedys. This helps to explain why the mob bosses used trusted members of this network in the JFK hit, from Mertz to Ruby—and why one of the lowliest members of the network was almost able to prevent JFK's assassination.

Santo Trafficante talked about his decision to kill JFK in the fall of 1962, around the same time Carlos Marcello told Ed Becker that JFK should be killed to end Bobby's power. In Miami, Trafficante told a different FBI informant, Jose Aleman, that "JFK was going to be hit" and would never survive until the 1964 election. After that, the two Mafia chiefs began working together to target JFK, meeting several times in 1963 with Frank Ragano, the lawyer Trafficante shared with Hoffa. Years later, Ragano told Robert Kennedy's biographer and associate Jack Newfield that Hoffa had him take messages about JFK's assassination to Marcello and Trafficante in 1963.[4] Hoffa himself was under too much scrutiny to actively participate in the JFK plot, but he made it clear to Marcello and Trafficante that they would be well rewarded for carrying out their plan.

As explained in later chapters, Trafficante confessed his part in JFK's assassination to Frank Ragano, though the lawyer's account of

Trafficante's confession minimized Ragano's own role in the hit. In addition, Harry Williams told us that one of Trafficante's men, who also worked for the CIA, was involved in JFK's murder.[5]

By November 1963, Trafficante had even more compelling reasons to kill JFK in order to end Bobby's war against him and his Mafia allies. These ranged from the major busts that had disrupted Trafficante's part of the French Connection drug network to Bobby's relentless pressure on his associates, including Marcello, Hoffa, and Giancana. Both of Trafficante's own brothers were under indictment for tax violations, and two of his cousins had been arrested.[6] Bureau of Narcotics agents had even monitored the wedding of Trafficante's daughter, something that would have been unheard of just a few years earlier.[7] Also, Trafficante's operations had been exposed in Congressional hearings just five weeks earlier. While the testimony regarding Trafficante's activities hadn't received the same national exposure and live TV coverage as the Valachi hearings, such Congressional scrutiny threatened to generate further unwanted attention for Trafficante's normally secretive operations.

The October 15, 1963, hearings not only provide a good overview of some of Trafficante's operations, but also include details that presage how JFK was killed. The hearings were conducted by JFK's former mentor, Senator John McClellan. Bobby Kennedy had provided information for the hearings, which targeted many of the same Mafiosi his prosecutors were going after.

We can now reveal that Trafficante managed to have at the hearings his main operative on the Tampa police force, Sergeant Jack de la Llana, who was far more than just a corrupt cop for Trafficante. In Washington, Sgt. de la Llana not only monitored what witnesses said for Trafficante, but even testified himself, as a seemingly upright member of the force. In Tampa, Sgt. de la Llana's work for Trafficante extended to the whole state of Florida and beyond. That's because de la Llana, no doubt on Trafficante's behalf, had formed the Tampa Police Department's first criminal intelligence unit, and became its director. Neil G. Brown, Tampa's Police Chief in October 1963, proudly testified that Sgt. de la Llana was also the "chairman of the Florida Intelligence Unit, a statewide agency which coordinates information . . . throughout the State of Florida."[8] This cooperation even extended to other states, such as when Sgt. de la Llana exchanged information with the New Orleans Police Department about the Fair Play for Cuba committee.

Sgt. de la Llana's position allowed him to monitor developments in the city, state, and region for Trafficante, and to feed information to law enforcement agencies that could help the Tampa godfather. In this way, de la Llana was like a Tampa version of the Chicago Mafia's Richard Cain: The number-two man in the Cook County/Chicago sheriff's office, Cain was actually a "made" member of the Mafia named Ricardo Scalzetti. While de la Llana was not an actual member of the Mafia, a high-ranking Florida law enforcement source who worked with him said that de la Llana didn't try to hide his affinity for the Mafia: He "talked like a classic Italian gangster," and when he was off duty he dressed like one, too. Our source said that de la Llana was originally a good cop, but he had been "caught [up] in some mob deal" and "turned bad." By 1963, de la Llana was "feeding information to Trafficante" on a regular basis, his position secure because of Trafficante's political influence, even when new Police Chiefs came into office.[9] With someone like de la Llana in place, it's clear why Trafficante felt confident enough to plan a JFK hit in Tampa, since he would know if his plot leaked, and he had someone on the inside to ensure the patsy blamed for JFK's death was quickly killed.

In Sgt. de la Llana's brief testimony at the October 15, 1963, Senate hearings, he didn't mention Trafficante, though the godfather's name appears in a (no doubt carefully) prepared statement that was submitted for the record. That statement was devoted primarily to a minor Mafia courier who had already been arrested and who had an extensive FBI record. The main testimony about Trafficante came from Tampa Police Chief Neil G. Brown, who would soon be replaced by Chief J. P. Mullins.

Chief Brown's testimony foreshadowed the events to come in Dallas and explain why Trafficante felt his role in JFK's murder could stay hidden. Brown began by showing a large chart of organized crime in Tampa, with Trafficante's name at the very top. Brown also talked about Trafficante's ties to Rosselli's boss, Giancana, and to a French Connection heroin partner of Michel Victor Mertz. Next came accounts of Trafficante's direct ties to several murders, in addition to many others he had ordered.

Chief Brown called Trafficante a suspect in the notorious barbershop slaying of New York mob boss Albert Anastasia. Brown also said that Trafficante had "been picked up by the police for questioning about the gangland slayings of three [other] men" over the years, but authorities were unable to prosecute Trafficante for those hits. Usually, Trafficante took care to insulate himself from mob executions, using intermediaries and professional hit men to carry out his dirty work.

One of the Trafficante hits Chief Brown discussed would have particular resonance on November 22. Brown said that Trafficante had targeted a victim whose "head was blown off [while he] was seated in his automobile." In a further eerie foreshadowing of what would happen two days after JFK's murder, Brown said that in the Tampa case, the main "suspect in this murder was himself murdered."

Chief Brown pointed out the "relative infrequency with which such professional murders are successfully prosecuted," and explained why. He said that only one of twenty-three Mafia murders in Tampa had been solved, and the lone exception was not a typical Mafia hit. In contrast, he explained that 97 percent of non-Mafia murders in Tampa had been solved.

Brown explained that it was very "difficult to obtain evidence sufficient for successful prosecution of Mafia members, because the witnesses who might offer such evidence have always been reluctant to do so [due to] fear of Mafia reprisals, since it is common knowledge in Tampa that the Mafia does not hesitate to murder for such reprisals." Brown agreed with Senator McClellan's blunt assessment that the witnesses "know that the penalty for them talking would be death." In fact, Chief Brown was able to point out three reprisal hits in Tampa that were motivated by "the Mafia's knowledge . . . that the victims had given to legal authorities evidence incriminating Mafia members."[10]

Brown's testimony about "reprisal hits" helps to explain Trafficante's confidence that he would be able to get away with helping Marcello and Rosselli murder JFK. Not only witnesses, but also those in—and even on the fringes of—the underworld would know the danger of helping authorities. That was also why Trafficante and the other mob bosses used experienced people they had worked with before, who were familiar with the penalty for talking, or even for failure. This explains the risks Trafficante's associates took, such as Jack Ruby's shooting a suspect inside police headquarters after his efforts to find a policeman to silence Oswald apparently failed.

Chief Brown left office soon after his Congressional testimony, but his replacement, J. P. Mullins, was even tougher on Trafficante and organized crime. However, Sgt. de la Llana was still on the force, able to feed inside information to Trafficante.[11] This connection was crucial for Trafficante if word of the Tampa attempt threatened to leak to the public after JFK's assassination, or if leads from Dallas ever pointed to Trafficante.

If either of those scenarios occurred, Trafficante's infiltration of the impending JFK-Almeida coup plan could be used to prevent too much digging in his direction. Of the five major exile leaders and groups in the coup plan, Trafficante had bought off his old associate Varona, had arms and drug ties to Artime, had potentially neutralized Ray by linking Oswald to Ray's group in Dallas, and had formerly dealt arms to Menoyo (whose partner, Veciana, had also been set up to meet Oswald in Dallas). Trafficante's drug network with Mertz and Marcello ran through Fort Benning, home to the coup's Cuban American troops. As noted later in this chapter, Trafficante even had John Martino ready to tell journalists, if necessary, about JFK's invasion plan for Cuba.

We mentioned earlier Trafficante's significant use of his drug network in the JFK hit, which included Martino, Mertz, Ruby, and Nicoletti. Other Trafficante drug-trafficking associates linked to the hit included former death-squad leader Rolando Masferrer, whom Varona brought secretly into the coup plan after the $200,000 bribe mentioned in Chapter 2. There was also Masferrer's partner, Eladio del Valle, who was close to Marcello's David Ferrie—Cuban officials place del Valle in Dallas on November 22, 1963, based on the testimony of captured Cuban exile Tony Cuesta.[12]

According to Cuesta, former Trafficante bodyguard and drug trafficker Herminio Diaz was also in Dallas on November 22. Cuban officials say that the Cuban Diaz was "a hit man from the forties" who had been part of "an assassination plot against Costa Rican President Jose Figureres in 1956."[13] CIA files say that Diaz worked at a mob-owned casino in Havana, first as a cashier and then, in 1959–1960, as chief of security.[14] An FBI memo links Diaz to two of Trafficante's men, who were running guns to Cuba at the time with Jack Ruby.[15] In July 1963, Diaz came to America, where Cuban officials say he worked with Trafficante and Varona. By September 1963, Diaz was of interest to the CIA's Special Affairs Staff (SAS), which Desmond FitzGerald ran for Richard Helms. In addition to AMWORLD, FitzGerald and Helms were running the unauthorized CIA-Mafia plots and assassin recruiter QJWIN at the time.

One reason Herminio Diaz would have been of interest to FitzGerald was that in Diaz's July 1963 interview by one of David Morales's AMOT assets, Diaz mentioned the names of Juan Almeida and Rolando Cubela, saying they were part of a group of disgruntled Cuban officials who wanted to act against Castro. Diaz had some of the details wrong, but even mentioning Almeida and Cubela was enough to get FitzGerald's attention. Even though another CIA asset said that Herminio was "fond of gambling and capable of committing any crime for money," the CIA considered using him as an "agent candidate or . . . asset."[16]

Diaz was apparently part of one of Helms and FitzGerald's unauthorized Castro-assassination operations by November 22, because shortly after the events in Dallas, a State Department memo to the White House national security advisor would link Diaz to "an [unsuccessful] attempt to assassinate Castro in December 1963."[17] But even though Diaz caught the CIA's eye, he was still working in Trafficante's lucrative drug network. A CIA file confirms that Diaz was "smuggling narcotics or acting as courier between narcotics traffickers in Mexico and US." Diaz even "had meetings with local Mexican Police Chief, who [was his] personal friend. Diaz traveled frequently between Miami and New York and always seemed to have large amounts [of] money."[18] Cuban officials described Diaz as a "mulatto" or "dark skinned," and claimed he was in the Texas School Book Depository as JFK's motorcade approached.[19]

Based on statements from Harry Williams, law enforcement, and Bernard Barker himself, Barker's work for Trafficante apparently included helping with JFK's assassination. A Dallas deputy later said that seconds after JFK was shot, he encountered Barker behind the fence on the "grassy knoll." Barker had longtime ties to the Mafia and to Trafficante. He was close to two Trafficante drug associates, and to Frank Fiorini. Barker even had a way to learn about the Cuba Contingency Plans, since the boss of his CIA superior Hunt—Desmond FitzGerald—was part of the planning.[20] (See Special Addendum for more.)

Because Trafficante spoke Spanish well and had spent so much time in Cuba, he became the Mafia's main liaison to Cuban exiles, a role he would maintain into the 1970s (with exiles like Artime) and 1980s (with Artime's second-in-command, Rafael "Chi Chi" Quintero, linked to drug trafficking). For the JFK hit, Trafficante knew how to exploit the exiles' personal weaknesses and desire to see Fidel eliminated. Along with the Mafia, certain Cuban exiles had been excluded from the coup plan, so they had no incentive to see it go forward. Also, by November 1963 a few CIA exiles like Barker had learned of JFK's secret peace feelers to Castro. They no doubt worried that JFK would call off the coup if there was a breakthrough in the peace talks. Given the sense of betrayal that men like Barker and Morales felt over the Bay of Pigs, it's easy to imagine CIA assets working with Trafficante or Rosselli wanting to ensure they wouldn't suffer betrayal by JFK again. This explains why a few Cuban exiles and CIA operatives were willing to help assassinate JFK, even with the JFK-Almeida coup fast approaching.

To Artime's aide Rafael "Chi Chi" Quintero, even the Cuban Missile Crisis had been a betrayal by the Kennedys. Quintero said, "Talk about the word 'treason' at the Bay of Pigs; this [the Cuban Missile Crisis] was even bigger for us, the people involved." As Miami journalist Don Bohning wrote, exiles like Quintero had been certain the Missile Crisis "would be the end of Fidel."[21] When it wasn't, perhaps Quintero and a few others became receptive to what Trafficante had in mind. In a letter to the JFK Assassination Records Review Board, one of Quintero's associates says Quintero admitted to some involvement in JFK's assassination.[22]

Trafficante knew that getting rid of Fidel was still a priority for the exiles, but if he told them JFK's assassination could be blamed on a Cuban or apparent Cuban sympathizer, then the US military invasion they knew was almost ready might well go forward in retaliation. In such a scenario, the US invasion wouldn't be the carefully staged and sequenced operation in which Almeida invited US forces into Cuba, but would instead be a full-scale attack on the Cuban leaders who had apparently assassinated JFK.

Johnny Rosselli, the Chicago Mafia's pointman in Hollywood and Las Vegas, would later confess his role in JFK's assassination, as did Trafficante and Marcello. Rosselli was crucial to their plot to kill JFK, due to his years of clandestine work for the CIA. Though all of those involved with Marcello and Trafficante in the JFK plot had been CIA informants, assets, or operatives, Rosselli was the Mafioso with the highest role with the CIA.[23] After taking on a key position in the CIA-Mafia plots in the summer of 1960, Rosselli had grown close to hard-drinking CIA official William Harvey in 1962. After Harvey left Cuban operations in 1963, replaced by the more office-bound Desmond FitzGerald, Rosselli remained friends with Harvey while growing close to Miami's David Morales, who was prone to bouts of heavy drinking. Rosselli's friendships with Harvey and Morales, which he would exploit to the fullest in 1963 and for years afterward, were consistent with the high-level dealmaking and calculated schmoozing Rosselli had been doing for decades.

Rosselli had been the Chicago Mafia's representative in Hollywood during its golden age, controlling a key union for stagehands—until an informant named Willie Bioff sent Rosselli to prison. After the Chicago Mafia rigged an early release for Rosselli in 1947, Rosselli wanted a more legitimate position in Hollywood, but his prison record barred him from any position with a major studio. Court records confirm he was an uncredited producer for three B films in the late 1940s, including a film noir called *He Walked by Night,* about a young ex-serviceman who shoots a cop by his patrol car on a lonely street, then flees. The murderous ex-serviceman also keeps a rifle wrapped in a blanket and hidden away.[24] While the public had largely forgotten the film by 1963 (it wasn't even issued on video until the 1990s), Rosselli apparently hadn't, and echoes of those events would unfold on November 22 in the real-life actions of ex-serviceman Lee Oswald.

Rosselli was still a force with the major studios in Hollywood in the 1950s and early 1960s, but he could operate only in the shadows, behind the scenes. Congressional investigators cite Rosselli as the inspiration for the famous scene in *The Godfather* where a director finds a severed horse's head in his bed, because of the pressure exerted by Rosselli to win Frank Sinatra his comeback role in *From Here to Eternity*. A grateful Sinatra made Rosselli an unofficial member of his Rat Pack, while Rosselli was becoming a major Mafia force in Las Vegas. According to Rosselli's biographers, in the 1950s Rosselli was linked to two notorious murders in the area: the car bombing of Willie Bioff, who had sent Rosselli to prison; and the slaying of Gus Greenbaum, first mayor of the Las Vegas strip (most of the major Vegas strip hotels are in the unincorporated town of Paradise, not in the actual city of Las Vegas). Both Bioff and Greenbaum were very close to Arizona Senator Barry Goldwater, but Rosselli had no regard for government officials, as was made evident in the earlier noted assassination of the president of Guatemala in 1957.

The Sinatra-Rosselli connection even reached JFK, via Judy Campbell, a Hollywood beauty who slept with all three men (as well as with Chicago mob boss Sam Giancana). But JFK's affair with her had ended in May 1962, and Rosselli's attempt at having Campbell rekindle it had been rejected by JFK in early November 1963. On November 20, Rosselli moved Campbell into the Beverly Crest Hotel in Los Angeles, perhaps so his men could make sure she didn't do anything foolish after JFK was killed.[25]

Rosselli had also been close to Marilyn Monroe, but by November 1963 she was dead, and Campbell and Sinatra were of no use in trying to persuade the Kennedys to back off from their aggressive prosecution of the Mafia and Rosselli's boss, Giancana. Like Marcello, Rosselli was not a US citizen, and could be deported if the government ever found out about his status. The FBI's lockstep surveillance of Giancana was crippling the power of Rosselli's boss, and thus of Rosselli. As noted earlier, Rosselli was no doubt worried by headlines about Bobby's plan to run the Mafia and the Teamsters out of Las Vegas. With all of his important associates—Giancana, Marcello, Trafficante, Hoffa—under assault by the Kennedys, Rosselli joined Marcello and Trafficante in plotting to kill JFK.

Even though JFK and Bobby had barred the Mafia both from the JFK-Almeida coup plan and from reopening their casinos in Cuba after the coup, Rosselli's work on the CIA-Mafia plots to assassinate Castro gave him the opening he needed. Rosselli's two meetings with Jack Ruby in Miami in the fall of 1963 were no doubt ostensibly about the anti-Castro plots, which is why the routine FBI surveillance reports of those meetings—like all of the FBI reports about Rosselli in Miami in the late summer and fall of 1963—are missing. In the same way, Rosselli's close work with David Morales in the summer and fall of 1963 would look to CIA superiors like they were plotting to kill Castro, but the two conspirators really had another target in mind.

An army ranger assigned to the CIA in the summer and fall of 1963, Captain Bradley Ayers, wrote an account of his time in South Florida training Cuban exiles. Ayers wrote about a "Col. Rosselli," who also worked with one of the exile groups, saying that Rosselli's team included "a sharpshooter" who "did daily marksmanship practice . . . rehearsing for the day when he could center the crosshairs of this telescopic sight on Fidel." This individual was not a poor shot like Oswald, who some-times missed the entire target, even when he practiced regularly in the Marines. (Most people don't realize, when news accounts say Oswald was a Marine "marksman," that "marksman" was the lowest ranking, and Oswald scored only one point above the minimum required to achieve even that.)[26]

In contrast, Rosselli's "sharpshooter" was able to kill "three cormorants at a range of nearly five hundred yards." For someone like that, shooting a head of state in an open vehicle from a safe distance would be easy. Apparently, the CIA was preparing to have shooters available to kill Fidel if Almeida had problems getting someone into place. Capt. Ayers also documented Rosselli's work with David Morales at the time.[27] Rosselli's contact with Morales—authorized only by Richard Helms and not known by CIA Director McCone, JFK, or Bobby—also gave Rosselli a way to learn about, infiltrate, and take advantage of the JFK-Almeida coup plot. Rosselli could similarly compromise Helms's other unauthorized operations involving CIA assassin recruiter QJWIN and the attempt to get Rolando Cubela to assassinate Fidel.

CIA files show that three of the five exile groups working on the JFK-Almeida coup plan had groups in Dallas, who described things like Manuel Artime's looking into buying a large cargo plane from Trafficante's operative Frank Fiorini in Dallas. In light of these activities, sending men or supplies to or through Dallas, or having Rosselli go to Dallas himself, would not necessarily arouse any undue suspicion on the part of CIA officials.

Veteran FBI agent William Turner was the first to write about a pilot, an associate of John Martino, who says that he flew Rosselli from Tampa to New Orleans on November 21, 1963, in a private plane. The pilot then claims to have flown Rosselli to Houston around the time of JFK's motorcade there, then on to Dallas on the morning of November 22.[28]

John Martino, who worked with Johnny Rosselli in 1963 and was a longtime casino electronics expert and wireman for Santo Trafficante, later confessed his role in JFK's murder, to two trusted associates, shortly before his death.[29] Martino also had meetings with Carlos Marcello and Guy Banister in the summer of 1963, according to new witnesses uncovered by Dr. Michael L. Kurtz. Kurtz cites the former superintendent of the New Orleans Police Department as saying that Martino "met with Marcello himself at the Town and Country Motel."[30]

In addition to Martino's confessed role in JFK's assassination, FBI files cite several accurate descriptions Martino gave of the JFK-Almeida coup plan. Martino taunted the FBI with his knowledge that "President Kennedy was engaged in a plot to overthrow the Castro regime by preparing another invasion attempt against Cuba."[31] As well as helping with the assassination plot, Martino would raise the specter of the coup plan to selected media in the days, weeks, and months after JFK's assassination, to help ensure the investigation didn't go beyond Oswald.

By November 1963, Martino needed little extra incentive to want to see JFK dead. After being arrested in Cuba in 1959, when he was working with Santo Trafficante and Rolando Masferrer, Martino had to remain in a Cuban prison until 1962. Bitter toward the US government after that experience, Martino was working with Trafficante and Rosselli on various schemes by the spring of 1963.[32] By the fall of 1963, he was speaking for the ultra-right-wing John Birch Society and touring the country, promoting his book, *I Was Castro's Prisoner*. Martino lived in Miami, but he was conveniently in New Orleans in time to see Oswald passing out pro-Castro leaflets, and in Dallas, talking to the sister of Silvia Odio, a member of Ray's JURE exile group, around the time Oswald visited Silvia. At the time, Silvia Odio was living in the same apartment complex as the brother of Rolando Masferrer, Martino's associate, which was probably how she came to be targeted.[33]

In addition to Trafficante and Rosselli, Martino had numerous ties to other people linked to JFK's murder. He had known David Morales since at least 1959, and had even mentioned Morales by name in his book. According to witnesses Dr. Michael Kurtz interviewed, Martino was also seen with Oswald's uncle (and Marcello bookie) Dutz Murret and another Marcello associate, Emile Bruneau, who bailed Oswald out of jail after his arrest for the pro-Castro-leafleting incident. According to Kurtz, Martino "appeared to serve almost as a courier between Trafficante and Marcello."[34]

Martino would later admit to award-winning *Newsday* reporter John Cummings that "he'd been part of the assassination of Kennedy. He wasn't in Dallas pulling a trigger, but he was involved. He implied that his role was delivering money, facilitating things."

According to a CIA memo detailed in Chapters 8 and 17, notorious French Connection heroin trafficker and assassin Michel Victor Mertz was in Dallas at the time of JFK's assassination, and was deported from Dallas approximately forty-eight hours later.[35] Unlike the Cuban exiles working for Trafficante, Mertz's motivation was mostly financial. The Kennedys' war on the Mafia had resulted in two heroin busts in the network he shared with Marcello and Trafficante, resulting in the loss of millions of dollars' worth of heroin and of potential profits. Mertz had to make up for that disaster and prevent future losses. Also, 1963 newspaper headlines blared the findings of JFK's special commission on drug abuse, which recommended treating heroin addition as a medical problem; if the recommendation were adopted, the losses to Mertz, Trafficante, and Marcello would be enormous. All this made Mertz amenable to helping his heroin partners in their plot to kill JFK. Conveniently, all three mob kingpins shared heroin routes through Texas and Florida, as well as one through Fort Benning, Georgia, where the Cuban American troops were trained and ready for the coup.[36]

In the summer and fall of 1963, Mertz had been using the name of "Jean Souetre," an old associate from 1959, when Mertz had undertaken a mission for French Intelligence (the SDECE). Mertz, who won the French Legion of Honor for killing twenty Nazis for the French resistance in World War II, sometimes did work for French Intelligence to avoid prosecution for his crimes. His most famous exploit for the French government was in 1961, when he saved French president Charles de Gaulle from an assassination attempt by rebellious French military officers.[37]

The alias Mertz used in Dallas on November 22, 1963, "Jean Souetre," was the name of a fugitive French officer who in 1962 had participated in the attempted assassination of de Gaulle that inspired Frederick Forsyth's novel *The Day of the Jackal*. This attempt was more serious than the one Mertz had foiled a year earlier, since Soutre's group was able to hit de Gaulle's car with numerous bullets, though the French president survived. Souetre was one of several men imprisoned for the attempt, though he later escaped. Souetre himself did not travel to America in the 1960s; on November 22, 1963, the real Souetre was in Barcelona, Spain, and has witnesses to prove it. On the other hand, INS records that INS provided to the French show that Mertz traveled frequently to America as part of his heroin-smuggling activities. Former Senate investigator Bud Fensterwald found that "the FBI had traced [the man they thought was] Souetre to Dallas a day before the assassination and then lost him."[38]

Souetre has been consistent for almost twenty-five years in his claim to Fensterwald's associates and to us (via French journalist Stephane Risset) that Mertz was impersonating him in Dallas at the time of JFK's assassination. Souetre not only has been willing to talk with journalists for years, but also has allowed himself to be photographed, confident that no photograph could ever show him in Dallas. In contrast, Mertz was extremely reclusive and never talked to reporters, even when there were news stories about him in France. (In the 1980s, there was a report that a journalist disappeared after trying to track down Mertz.) Unlike Souetre, Mertz avoided being photographed whenever possible. *Newsday* found only two fuzzy photos of Mertz for the Pulitzer Prize–winning report it published in the early 1970s, at the direction of publisher William Attwood, JFK's former special envoy. A few years later, *Newsday*'s lead reporter for the story told researcher Gary Shaw that their Mertz photos had vanished from the files.[39]

In a similar way, Mertz himself had been mysteriously absent from the fall 1963 Senate hearings that spawned Joe Valachi's sensational testimony. Though all of Mertz's associates were named, and their actions in Texas, Mexico City, and Montreal were detailed, Mertz himself was not mentioned. That's likely because of Mertz's work for French Intelligence (in France, Mertz was known as one of "the untouchables"), and possibly because of work Mertz or his associates were doing for some American agency. Mertz had three associates who still operated in Cuba, which could have made him valuable to the CIA.[40]

As Chapter 15 documents, the CIA's William Harvey and Counter-Intelligence Chief James Angleton had been interested in using French assets to assassinate Fidel Castro. James P. Kelly, a former Senate investigator for Bobby Kennedy, later talked about members of French Intelligence "who [had] approached US w/capacity to hit Castro." That was confirmed by the former head of French Intelligence in the US in 1963, who was working for Angleton at the time, and who later told a Senate investigator about "an offer by French Intelligence to the CIA to carry out the Castro assassination for them."[41] For the CIA to turn to the French Connection for such assistance would be consistent with their past behavior, since the BBC News Service points out that "in 1947, the CIA's supply of arms and money to Corsican gangs recruited to harass French trade unionists in Marseilles docks was the beginning of the 'French Connection,' which supplied heroin to North America until the early 1970s."[42]

If Mertz was used in, or learned of, the CIA's use of French operatives against Fidel, it could have been through his or his associates' contact with QJWIN, retained by the CIA to look for just such people. QJWIN was involved in narcotics (the CIA had to intervene to keep him out of prison in 1962), and by 1963 there were more than a dozen parallels between QJWIN and Mertz (listed at www.legacyofsecrecy.com[43]). Definitive analysis isn't possible, because many of the files about QJWIN, including notes on French criminals QJWIN had targeted for recruitment, have not been declassified or are heavily censored. Also, William Harvey's notes for the ZRRIFLE project that included QJWIN say that files should be "forged and backdated," meaning that even the files that have been released could be suspect.[44] Harvey later claimed that QJWIN had never been used for Cuban operations, but Harvey's own expense reports prove this statement is false. INS provided some information to French authorities, which shows that while Mertz usually traveled to America alone on his frequent trips, an "unnamed colleague of Mertz" began traveling in "parallel [to] Mertz" shortly after JFK's assassination.[45] Given the many similarities between them, Mertz's colleague could have been QJWIN or one of his recruits.

From other associates in his heroin network, Mertz could also have learned of Helms's other unauthorized plots to kill Castro. For example, also named in the fall 1963 Senate hearings on narcotics was Chicago hit man Charles Nicoletti. By October 1963, Nicoletti was part of the CIA-Mafia plots with Johnny Rosselli, and unconfirmed reports place Nicoletti in Dallas at the time of JFK's death. Also, Mertz, using the Souetre alias, had apparently visited a Cuban exile training camp outside of New Orleans that was linked to Guy Banister, who was working for Carlos Marcello at the time.[46]

Mertz had once infiltrated Souetre's anti–de Gaulle group by passing out leaflets on a Paris street, getting into a fight, and being arrested. That could have been the inspiration for Banister's having Oswald do almost the same thing in New Orleans three months before JFK's assassination. Oswald might even have tried a dry run for his New Orleans stunt in Montreal, where Mertz maintained a home: According to information the Secret Service would receive just five days after JFK's death, the "Senior Customs Representative, US Treasury Department Bureau of Customs, Montreal, Canada" reported that several witnesses there saw Oswald passing out the same type of Fair Play for Cuba Committee leaflets he used in New Orleans. One of the witnesses was Customs Investigator Jean Paul Tremblay, who was "positive that this person was Oswald." Investigator Tremblay said that Oswald had been accompanied by three people, and he felt "he could identify [them] because he was working on cases involving Cuba at the time."[47] For reasons that remain unclear, the Secret Service and the FBI never pursued this lead.

Mertz's choice of "Souetre" as an alias was especially appropriate, since the real Souetre had been the subject of a memo from Richard Helms in July 1963,[48] and had met with a CIA representative (E. Howard Hunt, according to one report) in May 1963. This would help to ensure that Helms and his associates would want to cover up any indication that Souetre was in Dallas at the time of JFK's murder.

Chapter Five

Dallas was the third attempt by Marcello, Trafficante, and Rosselli to kill JFK in November 1963. The first had been in Chicago, the territory of Johnny Rosselli's Mafia family, on November 2, 1963. The second was during the longest domestic motorcade of JFK's presidency, in Santo Trafficante's Tampa on November 18, 1963.

The four-man plot to assassinate JFK during his November 2, 1963, Chicago motorcade was kept out of the press at the time, and was reported only briefly in one small article in 1967. Although it received a bit more press coverage in the mid-1970s, the story is still largely unknown to the American public. Parts of it were mentioned in Warren Commission documents (but not in the Commission's widely available Final Report), and in the late 1970s, the House Select Committee on Assassinations (HSCA) investigated the attempt.

The plot to assassinate JFK during his November 18, 1963, motorcade in Tampa (just hours before his speech later that evening, containing the lines written for Almeida) was also completely withheld from the press when it occurred. Just one small article about it appeared after JFK's death, but the story was quickly suppressed the following day. The Warren Commission was never told about the Tampa attempt, nor was the HSCA. None of the six government committees that investigated aspects of JFK's assassination were told about the Tampa attempt until we privately informed the JFK Assassination Records Review Board about it in 1994. Approximately six weeks later, the Secret Service destroyed files covering the Tampa motorcade, as they later admitted to the Review Board, despite the 1992 JFK Act requiring the files' preservation and release. Though we confirmed the attempt with the Tampa Chief of Police and with other Secret Service and Florida law enforcement sources, the public didn't learn about the attempt to assassinate JFK in Tampa until 2005, when we first published the information.

Before we describe the attempts to kill JFK in Chicago and Tampa, it's important to look at them from JFK and Bobby's point of view, keeping in mind the impending coup with Almeida and the Cuba Contingency Plans to deal with any retaliation by Castro, even the "assassination of American officials." Even as Bobby's subcommittee continued its Cuba Contingency planning in November, the Kennedys would use some of the thinking behind those plans in dealing with the Chicago and Tampa attempts. JFK and Bobby both had to keep a lid on the plots while they were investigated, as they proceeded with the coup planning (in case the attempts turned out to have nothing to do with Castro or Cuba). The ability of the President, Bobby, and key officials to suppress the news about the Chicago and Tampa attempts set the tone for what would happen in Dallas a short time later.

Even as Chicago residents had started to line the announced motorcade route on November 2, 1963, JFK canceled his trip literally at the last minute because the Secret Service had learned of the assassination threat. As Pierre Salinger explained to us, just after he had assured the press that JFK wouldn't cancel the motorcade because of a crisis in Vietnam, he had to quickly issue two different phony excuses to the news media.

According to Chicago Secret Service Agent Abraham Bolden, whose account was confirmed by other law enforcement sources uncovered by journalist Edwin Black, the plot involved four men, two of whom were briefly detained and released, and two who were never apprehended. A fifth man, an ex-Marine whose job reportedly overlooked JFK's motorcade route, was arrested. In his car, he had an M1 rifle and three thousand rounds of ammunition. Knowing of at least two potential assassins at large, JFK and Bobby apparently decided to cancel JFK's entire trip. They also decided to keep any mention of the assassination threat out of the press—and the press complied, even though years later several newsmen admitted to having heard about the four-man threat at the time.[1] The Kennedys had done this kind of news management on a smaller scale in the past, involving incidents as diverse as leaks about the Bay of Pigs and JFK's indiscretions. The CIA had handled smaller incidents related to Cuban operations, such as the September 1963 affair in Florida, when the CIA made sure "two local newspapers . . . suppressed" and turned over photos of several covert Cuban exile operatives after their boat had problems.[2]

Suppressing a news story on the scale of the Chicago threat against JFK took a new level of coordination among Bobby and several agencies, but the Cuban aspects of the threat seemed to justify it. Not until years later would the public learn that the ex-Marine who was arrested,

Thomas Vallee, had recent ties to a Cuban exile group affiliated with one of Bobby's exile leaders for the coup, Eloy Menoyo. Vallee also had ties to the John Birch Society, widely known at the time for its extreme stands against civil rights, Martin Luther King, and JFK, especially his seemingly soft stance on Cuba. The CIA and INS had also received reports of a possible Cuban agent named Miguel Casas Saez in Chicago, but they were unable to track him down. In addition, two of the men sought in the Chicago incident had Hispanic names, and a later CIA memo says the plot allegedly involved "Cuban dissidents," which meant "exiles." Those Cuban connections are why Bobby and JFK kept any mention of the four-man Chicago plot, and the real reason for JFK's sudden cancellation, out of the press at the time.[3]

As far as the Mafia bosses were concerned, their man Richard Cain was in a perfect position to help influence and monitor law enforcement's reaction to the Chicago plot. As we noted earlier, Cain was a "made" member of Giancana's Chicago Mafia, even while he was the Chief Investigator for the Cook County / Chicago Sheriff, heading a staff of more than two dozen. Congressional investigators documented that Cain had worked on the CIA-Mafia plots with Trafficante and Rosselli, had bugged a communist embassy in Mexico City in 1962, and in August 1963 had begun working for the CIA as an asset. CIA files withheld from Congressional investigators show that Cain had learned about AMWORLD, and that his information was sent on a secure path straight to Desmond FitzGerald. Cain also had inside knowledge of the $200,000 Mafia bribe to Tony Varona.[4]

Three weeks after Chicago, the Kennedys faced a huge dilemma when officials discovered another plot to assassinate JFK, this time during his long Tampa motorcade on November 18. Officials uncovered the plot less than twenty-four hours before JFK's arrival and advised him to cancel his visit, since at least two potential assassins were on the loose. However, another sudden cancellation was not a viable option for JFK. While he and Bobby had been able to keep the real reason for the Chicago cancellation out of the press, another major motorcade canceled at the last minute would surely raise questions they couldn't answer. JFK was set to give his important speech that night in Miami, which would include the important lines of assurance for Commander Almeida. How could JFK ask Almeida to risk his life to stage a coup if word leaked that JFK had been too afraid to travel in his own motorcade?

JFK's recent activities had been orchestrated to send a show of strength to Almeida and his allies. The previous day, Florida newspapers featured major front-page coverage of JFK viewing the launch of a Polaris missile from a submarine. In Tampa, JFK was scheduled to have a widely publicized private meeting with the head of Strike Force Command (now Central Command) and other military brass, some brought in from Washington.[5] Coupled with the special lines in JFK's speech, all this was designed to reassure Almeida that JFK would back him and the coup all the way, even with US military force.

However, JFK's plan to reassure Almeida was at risk after the Secret Service found "that the threat on Nov. 18, 1963, was posed by a mobile, unidentified rifleman shooting from a window in a tall building with a high-power rifle fitted with scope."[6] Tampa's Chief of Police, J. P. Mullins, confirmed to us that at least one other individual was part of that plot. Secret Service Agent Sam Kinney said he learned later that "organized crime" was behind the threat, and a high Florida law enforcement official later confirmed that Tampa mob boss Santo Trafficante was involved. But on the day of the motorcade, that information had not yet surfaced. Tampa was home to a large Cuban exile community, some of whom were angry about JFK's apparent crackdown on all anti-Castro Cuban exile groups in the US. (His support for a handful of exile groups for the coup plan was covert, and rare news reports hinting at it were quickly squelched.) The anger Cuban exiles felt toward JFK was even more pronounced in Miami, where some Bay of Pigs veterans threatened to protest outside his speech. However, Tampa was different from Miami in that some exiles in Tampa still supported Fidel Castro; there was even a Tampa chapter of the pro-Castro Fair Play for Cuba Committee, the same organization Lee Harvey Oswald had joined earlier that year.

Before JFK's Tampa motorcade, officials issued a lookout regarding the assassination plot, and its description of a potential assassin matched Oswald much better than the first descriptions issued after JFK's murder in Dallas. (An unconfirmed report later placed Oswald in Tampa the day before JFK's motorcade.) Yet the Tampa description also fit another individual who was named as a suspect in JFK's assassination in secret FBI and CIA documents, though he was never mentioned in the Warren Report, and information about him was withheld from the HSCA.[7]

By November 1963, Gilberto Policarpo Lopez had eighteen parallels with Lee Harvey Oswald, according to declassified government files. For example, both were about the same age, and both had left their wives a few months earlier, around the time each man moved to a new city. Both were former defectors with a Russian connection in their background. Each had returned to the United States in 1962 from a communist country. Both men had an unusual involvement with the small pro-Castro Fair Play for Cuba Committee in 1963, after it became the subject of Congressional hearings and newspaper accounts. Both got into fistfights over seemingly pro-Castro statements, but neither joined the Communist Party or regularly associated with American communists. Both men were persons of interest to Naval Intelligence in 1963, and both were alleged by officials to be informants for a US agency. Both men attempted to get into Cuba in the fall of 1963 by going to Texas, crossing the border at Nuevo Laredo, and proceeding to Mexico City for the air connection to Cuba. (Since travel between the US and Cuba was restricted, travelers from the US often went to Havana via Mexico City, a route undercover US intelligence agents also used.)[8] Both Oswald and Lopez went at least part of the way by car, though neither man owned a car or had a driver's license. Each was under CIA surveillance for at least part of his Mexico trip. And by November 1963, each had a job in the vicinity of an upcoming JFK motorcade.[9]

FBI and government files confirm that Lopez left Tampa shortly after JFK's motorcade and went to Texas, where an unconfirmed newspaper account places him in Dallas on November 22, 1963. But his whereabouts weren't known at the time, at least not by Bobby Kennedy; his movements were discovered only later, by the FBI, CIA, and several journalists.

Prior to JFK's Tampa motorcade, Bobby and JFK had been told about a Florida threat made by white supremacist Joseph Milteer, which had been picked up by a wired Miami police informant. Milteer was from the small town of Quitman in South Georgia, but he traveled extensively and was in touch with the most violent racist groups active in 1963.[10] He had inherited $200,000 from his father (over a million in today's dollars), and his determination to kill JFK was motivated by his racist ideology, not by money. Because Milteer was not arrested at the time of JFK's Tampa motorcade, before Dallas, or even afterward—and because Hoover withheld crucial information from Georgia FBI agents investigating Milteer—the white supremacist would continue his deadly pursuits. This would allow Milteer to play a crucial role in the assassination of Martin Luther King in 1968, which is revealed for the first time later in the book.

Undercover Miami police tapes recorded Joseph Milteer talking about JFK's murder less than two weeks prior to JFK's assassination in Dallas. Milteer told Miami police informant William Somersett about a plan "to assassinate the President with a high-powered rifle from a tall building." On the police tape from November 9, 1963, Milteer accurately states that authorities "will pick up somebody within hours afterwards ... just to throw the public off." Milteer said the assassination had been arranged in such a way as to "drop the responsibility right into the laps of the Communists . . . or Castro."[11]

Somersett also told authorities that Milteer had indicated "this conspiracy originated in New Orleans, and probably some in Miami." Milteer said "there was a lot of money" involved in the plot, not only from far-right extremists, "but from men who could afford to contribute," though the only one he mentioned by name was a Louisiana political boss who was tied to both Carlos Marcello and Guy Banister. The Miami police told the Secret Service and FBI about the tapes and plot. The FBI assigned Atlanta agent Don Adams to the case on November 13, and he went to Quitman, where Milteer lived, to quietly investigate him. However, Adams stated to us that his FBI superiors never told him about the police tapes of Milteer or about the recent threat against JFK in Tampa.

While parts of the Milteer story and the audiotapes have been known to investigators for decades, it was only in 2006 that Dr. Michael L. Kurtz published the accounts of reliable witnesses who could tie Milteer directly to Guy Banister and other associates of Carlos Marcello. He writes that on one occasion, a noted architect saw Banister and "Milteer conversing with some of Marcello's people in the French Quarter." Aside from sharing racist views and hatred of the Kennedys, Banister, Milteer, and Marcello also shared a connection to the illegal arms trade, since in 1963 the major buyers of illegal weapons from organized crime included Cuban exile groups and white supremacists. Dr. Kurtz also noted that "Milteer had close connections to Santos Trafficante," since Milteer was also involved in "illegal arms and narcotics trafficking."[12]

JFK had much to worry about during his November 18 motorcade in Tampa, and Police Chief Mullins and other officials were especially concerned about Tampa's tallest building, the Floridan Hotel, which overlooked a hard left turn JFK's motorcade would have to take. The red-brick Floridan looks similar to the Texas School Book Depository, only much taller and with more windows; almost a hundred had a clear view of JFK's motorcade. The hotel was full that day, and impossible to secure. In 1963, one could easily register under a false name—at that time, many travelers paid with cash—and every guest-room window in the Floridan could be opened. The hotel was just one short block away from the intersection where JFK's limo would have to come to almost a full stop to make its turn. For a sniper perched in one of the hotel windows, sitting back in the shadows, assassinating the President would have been easy. Chief Mullins and the Secret Service didn't know if the two suspects at large were Cuban agents (the same shadowy Cuban, Miguel Cases Saez, who was reported near Chicago just before JFK's motorcade there, had also been reported in Florida), disgruntled Cuban exiles, white-supremacist allies of Milteer, or someone else—hence their advice to JFK to cancel his entire motorcade.

But JFK disregarded their warnings, and insisted on going ahead. Just as in Chicago, a press blackout about the threat was informally ordered. The "bubble top" for JFK's limo wasn't used—it wasn't bulletproof anyway, and using it would send the wrong message to Commander Almeida. The Lincoln in which JFK rode in Tampa was the same one he would later use in Dallas. Jackie wasn't with him on the Tampa trip, so only JFK's life was at risk. According to Chief Mullins and other officials, when JFK was backstage and away from the press, he looked stressed and tired, though before the public he appeared to be the smiling, confident JFK the public knew. The press blackout about the threat was still holding when JFK began his motorcade, but there was no way to know if a media outlet might break the story while he was in his limo or giving a speech. Photos show that during part of the motorcade, JFK actually stood up in the car; we may never know whether he did so because of his ongoing back problems, or because it was his way of showing he wasn't afraid, even if word of the threat did leak to the public.

JFK gave several speeches in Tampa, including one at the International Inn. (Four days later, Santo Trafficante would publicly toast JFK's death at the same hotel, just hours after the assassination.) On the evening of November 18, the President flew to Miami and gave his most important speech, with lines directed at Commander Almeida and his allies in Cuba. The following day, several newspapers trumpeted those lines almost too clearly: The *Dallas Times Herald* said, "Kennedy Virtually Invites Cuban Coup"; the *Miami Herald* said, "Kennedy Invites Coup"; and the *New York Times* proclaimed, "Kennedy says US will aid Cuba once Cuban sovereignty is restored under a non-communist government."[13]

After JFK returned to Washington, JFK expressed his relief at surviving the trip to his close aide, David Powers. According to Kennedy biographer Ralph Martin, JFK told Powers: "Thank God nobody wanted to kill me today!" JFK explained an assassination "would be tried by someone with a high-power rifle and a telescopic sight during a downtown parade when there would be so much noise and confetti that nobody would even be able to point and say, 'It came from that window.'"[14]

After JFK's Tampa motorcade and Miami speech, JFK and Bobby could breathe a sigh of relief as they looked ahead to JFK's upcoming trip to Texas. They knew of no active threat in Texas, as there had been in Chicago and Tampa. Moreover, Dallas didn't have a large Cuban exile population to worry about, as did Tampa and Chicago.

JFK and Bobby would have been even more concerned had they known that the day before JFK's Tampa speech, he had been stalked by two Cuban exiles who hated him. Bitter Bay of Pigs veterans Alberto Fowler and Felipe Rivero had rented a house next to JFK's compound in Palm Beach, where the President was staying before his Tampa motorcade. While Fowler later wrote that their only interest was in playing loud music to annoy JFK, the facts suggest otherwise. Rivero was a leader in a Cuban exile group getting major funding from Chicago Mafia allies of Trafficante and Marcello, and Fowler would make a provocative call to Bobby's exile aide Harry Williams just hours after JFK was shot.[15]

Why did Trafficante call off the attempt to kill JFK in Tampa? According to our source, who was high in Florida law enforcement, Trafficante's man in the Tampa Police Department, Sgt. Jack de la Llana, "was in the motorcade meetings and was feeding information to Trafficante at the time." Our source, who also helped with JFK's security, said it was "likely that de la Llana could have tipped off Trafficante about the [security] plans or [the] threat alerts."[16] Besides, the ever-cautious Trafficante would still have an opportunity to hit JFK in Dallas.

Following the events in Tampa, we noted earlier an account saying that Rosselli went from Tampa to Louisiana and then on to Texas, but others were heading in that direction as well. One was a member of the lowest rung of the Mertz/Marcello/Trafficante heroin network, Rose Cheramie (one of many aliases used by Melba Christine Marcades). Cheramie was a sometime B-girl, prostitute, and heroin courier for Ruby. It's ironic that a woman who was one of the lowest members of Marcello's crime empire came close to saving JFK's life, and on at least three occasions would risk her own life to help law enforcement.

On November 21, 1963, Rose Cheramie had been dumped on the side of the road by two men she was riding with from Florida. She was eventually taken into custody by Louisiana State Police Lieutenant Francis Fruge, who drove her to East Louisiana State Hospital to be treated for heroin withdrawal. Cheramie told Lt. Fruge that she and her two male companions had been on their way to Dallas, where the men were going to "kill Kennedy." Her remarks were also heard by physicians at the hospital, including Dr. Victor Weiss, head of the hospital's Psychiatry Department, who said that on Thursday, November 21, "Cheramie was absolutely sure Kennedy was gong to be assassinated in Dallas on Friday and kept insisting on it over and over again to the doctors and nurses who were attending her." Dr. Weiss stated Cheramie said that "word was out in the New Orleans underworld that the contract on Kennedy had been let," and Dr. Weiss assumed she was referring to Carlos Marcello's organization.[17] Cheramie would later be proven an accurate informant regarding Marcello's part in the French Connection ring, but at this time, no one was taking her seriously.

Chapter Six

Lee Harvey Oswald's documented life, when stripped of years of speculation and conjecture, bears little relation to that of the supposed teenage communist the Warren Commission would later depict. Actually,
when Oswald was a young teenager, his favorite TV show was *I Led
Three Lives*, about a seemingly average American man who joined the
Communist Party but was really an FBI informant. This was the era of
movies like *I Was a Communist for the FBI*, which dramatized the true
exploits of deep-cover government agents who spent years undercover,
only to finally reveal their true status and reap the rewards of fame
and money. That was surely an enticing possibility to a young teenager
who had never known his father, who had died shortly before Oswald's
birth. Lee looked up to his two older brothers, both of whom served in
the military, one of them in an intelligence branch that guarded against
communist subversion.[1]

When Oswald was fifteen, he joined the Civil Air Patrol, not exactly
a hotbed of communist activity during the McCarthy era. (Staunch anti-
communist David Ferrie was one of Oswald's instructors.) Oswald then
not only tried to join the US Marines, but first tried to enlist a year before
he was old enough. Once he was finally in the Marines, Oswald was
assigned to a U-2 spy-plane base in Japan. There are numerous indications he became involved in intelligence work: He studied Russian and
spouted love for Russia so often that his Marine buddies called him
"Oswaldovitch," but even in those Cold War times, no Marine sergeant
or officer ever noted that behavior or disciplined him for it. According to
journalist Dick Russell, Oswald was one of five young men to defect to
Russia around the same time in 1959, with two more defecting in 1960.
Of those seven, six returned to the US, some with Russian wives.[2]

Such men and their wives could have been "dangles," who after their
return to the US would have been kept under covert surveillance in order
to see how KGB agents and operatives in America might try to recruit
them. Shortly after Oswald's return from Russia with his wife, Marina,

he was allowed to get a job at a firm in Dallas, Jaggars-Chiles-Stovall, that helped to prepare maps from U-2 spy-plane photos—at the height of the Cuban Missile Crisis! According to official records and the Warren Commission, this aroused no special concern on the part of the FBI or US intelligence, even though, as we noted earlier, Oswald was under "tight surveillance" at that time. We suspect that US authorities allowed, or probably arranged for, a recent defector to get a job at such a sensitive facility in order to make Oswald an even more attractive target for KGB recruitment.

In October 1962, four days before Oswald secured his job at Jaggars-Chiles-Stovall, a most unlikely individual befriended him: a former White Russian Count named George DeMohrenschildt. According to Oswald's mother, DeMohrenschildt had arranged the job for Oswald, which makes sense in light of DeMohrenschildt's later admission that he was a US intelligence asset. DeMohrenschildt was sophisticated and urbane, and he usually traveled in far loftier circles than Oswald's. George DeMohrenschildt knew Jackie Kennedy's family; the *New York Post* reported that he had briefly been engaged to Jackie's aunt and "nearly married [Jackie's mother] Janet Auchincloss." As a child, Jackie called him "Uncle George."[3]

Rumors circulated for years that DeMohrenschildt had intelligence connections, which declassified files, historians, and former government investigators have now confirmed. According to historian Michael Kurtz, the associates of DeMohrenschildt and his fourth wife, Jeanne, included Richard Helms, New Orleans CIA Deputy Chief Hunter Leake, and two CIA officials later involved with AMWORLD, including David Atlee Phillips.[4] Congressional investigator Gaeton Fonzi discovered that "a CIA memo . . . written by Richard Helms credits DeMohrenschildt with providing valuable foreign intelligence."[5] DeMohrenschildt knew another George in Texas, George H. W. Bush, an oil executive who would later become president of the United States.

Shortly before his controversial death, described in Chapter 64, George DeMohrenschildt confirmed his work for the CIA to Edward J. Epstein, a writer for the *Wall Street Journal*. DeMohrenschildt said he had befriended Oswald only at the request of Dallas CIA officer J. Walton Moore, who also told DeMohrenschildt that even before Oswald's stay in the Soviet Union, the CIA had an "interest" in Oswald.[6] From information provided by former CIA officials and declassified files, journalist Anthony Summers and former FBI agent William Turner have also confirmed DeMohrenschildt's intelligence work.[7] Moreover, Kurtz recently documented DeMohrenschildt's occasional work on CIA anti-Castro matters in 1963.[8]

The DeMohrenschildts remained friends with Oswald and his wife through the end of 1962 and into early 1963, and were no doubt part of the "tight surveillance" Naval Intelligence maintained on Oswald. Around the spring of 1963, when the DeMohrenschildts left Dallas for new intrigues in Haiti, DeMohrenschildt attended meetings between a business associate and the assistant director of Army Intelligence (part of the DIA, as was Naval Intelligence).

As for Oswald and his job at Jaggars-Chiles-Stovall, the KGB hadn't taken the bait, so Lee Harvey Oswald was apparently ready for another assignment by the start of 1963. Even before Lee Oswald left Dallas to move to New Orleans in the spring of 1963, he had made at least one earlier trip to the Crescent City. That was shortly after Oswald had joined the Fair Play for Cuba Committee (via mail; he never attended any meetings or met any of its officials), and Oswald—or someone using his alias, "A. Hidell"—had ordered a rifle and a pistol though the mail. Because Senate committees were investigating mail-order gun dealers and the Fair Play for Cuba Committee (FPCC), both were in the news at the time. Senator Thomas J. Dodd (father of current senator Christopher Dodd) headed the gun committee and served on the FPCC committee.

Oswald's unusual activities in early 1963 (leaving a mail-order paper trail by ordering guns that were easily available in his neighborhood, and joining the FPCC while avoiding meetings of real socialists, communists, and Castro sympathizers) have long concerned Congressional investigators and journalists. However, Oswald's actions leading up to his move to New Orleans in the spring of 1963 can be explained by looking at his associates in New Orleans, Guy Banister and David Ferrie.

History professor Michael Kurtz, while dean of the graduate school at Southeastern Louisiana University and a Louisiana state historian, uncovered new confirmation of the intelligence activities of Banister, Ferrie, and Oswald. Kurtz interviewed Hunter Leake, whom CIA memos confirm was the Deputy Chief of the New Orleans CIA station in 1963.[9] Leake told Kurtz, "in a quite definitive manner, that Oswald indeed performed chores for the CIA during his five months in New Orleans during the spring and summer of 1963." In fact, "Leake personally paid Oswald various sums of cash for his services." When Kurtz interviewed Richard Helms about this and other assertions, "Helms neither confirmed nor denied Leake's story."[10]

Leake said that in 1963, Oswald was in New Orleans, working with

Ferrie and Banister, both of whom also had intelligence ties. According to Kurtz, "Leake stated that Ferrie performed a series of tasks for the CIA: supplying weapons and munitions to Anti-Castro guerrilla fighters in Cuba; training Cuban units for the 1961 Bay of Pigs invasion; conducting propaganda sessions among refugee units, thus reinforcing their hatred of the Castro regime; and serving as an intermediary between the CIA and organized crime."[11] Ferrie must have found the last function easy, since during 1963 he was also working for Carlos Marcello.

As for private detective Guy Banister, Kurtz writes that, according to Leake, Banister "served as a key CIA liaison with many anti-Castro Cuban refugees in southern Louisiana. Banister often handled details of the training and supplying of various anti-Castro organizations. Typically, Hunter Leake or another CIA agent from the New Orleans office would meet Banister in Mancuso's Restaurant, located in the infamous 544 Camp Street Building."[12] That was the corner building that housed the office of the rabidly anticommunist and anti-Castro Banister, the same address that showed up on the pro-Castro leaflets Oswald was seen passing out in the summer of 1963.

Another witness uncovered by Kurtz, Consuela Martin, provides a new perspective as to why Banister's office address appeared on the pro-Castro leaflets. Kurtz writes that Martin's office was next to Banister's, and "she saw Oswald in Banister's office at least half a dozen times in the late spring and summer of 1963. . . . On every one of these occasions, Oswald and Banister were together." Oswald sometimes asked her to do translating work for him by typing documents into Spanish. Martin believes that the 544 Camp Street address was used in hopes of luring unsuspecting pro-Castro leftists to Banister's office, thus yielding more information for Banister's voluminous files.[13]

The CIA likely knew of at least some of Banister's activities with Oswald, since Oswald received such extensive local media coverage in the summer of 1963. Kurtz writes that Leake "provided Banister with substantial sums of cash, and Banister would use the money to purchase needed supplies and to pay the salaries of the men working in certain anti-Castro operations."[14] However, Banister and Ferrie were also working for Marcello in 1963, and the previous fall the Mafia chief had made it clear that he was determined to kill JFK in order to end Bobby Kennedy's pursuit of him. Banister and Ferrie were in a perfect position to assist the CIA regarding Oswald, while at the same time making sure Oswald would make a convincing fall guy for Marcello's assassination of JFK. It's possible that Oswald's activities in early 1963, such as ordering his

rifle and joining the Fair Play for Cuba Committee, were influenced by
Banister and Ferrie.

Kurtz recently disclosed the identity of a new witness to Oswald's
interactions with Banister and Ferrie: "Hamilton Johnson, a geologist
who later served on the faculty at Tulane University, stated that on
numerous occasions, he observed Guy Banister, David Ferrie, various
anti-Castro Cubans, and agents of both the CIA and FBI" at the Schlumberger facility in Houma, Louisiana, sixty miles from New Orleans.
Schlumberger provided equipment for oil drilling, but according to
Johnson "it was an open secret among company employees that the
federal government was using the large facility for intelligence activities." Johnson told Kurtz that "on at least two occasions in the summer of
1963, Lee Harvey Oswald accompanied Banister and Ferrie to Houma."
The anti-Castro material that "Johnson saw [included] such supplies
as guns, ammunition, hand grenades, howitzers, bombs, landmines,
propellers . . . and much more. On several occasions, Cubans told him
that they were using the equipment for 'training exercises for another
invasion of Cuba.'"

Until it was closed in early August 1963, Manuel Artime operated what
was essentially a minor-league exile training camp for the AMWORLD
operation near New Orleans, which Ferrie and Banister both reportedly
visited. Kurtz writes that "Hunter Leake verified Hamilton Johnson's
story about Schlumberger. . . . He also confirmed that Banister, Ferrie,
and even Oswald visited the camp from time to time."[15]

Oswald's public activities in New Orleans in August 1963 are well
documented because of their extensive media coverage. Oswald first
tried to join the local chapter of the DRE, an anti-Castro group, claiming he wanted to overthrow Fidel. Shortly after that, he very publicly
passed out pro-Castro leaflets on the street in New Orleans, an act that
provoked an attack by the local DRE head and two of his associates.
Oswald's arrest led to newspaper coverage, as well as radio and TV
appearances in which he handled himself remarkably well. How could
Oswald generate so much publicity? That was a specialty of CIA propaganda specialist David Atlee Phillips. Court records indicate that a "Mr.
Phillips . . . from Washington," who was involved with US intelligence,
met with Banister in New Orleans, at Banister's office, regarding an
anti-Castro TV appeal.[16] Earlier, Phillips had run an operation against
the Fair Play for Cuba Committee, and according to E. Howard Hunt's
sworn testimony to Congressional investigators, David Phillips ran the
DRE for the CIA.[17]

CIA files confirm that Phillips was working on the AMWORLD part of the coup plan, so it shouldn't be surprising that shortly after Oswald's publicity blitz, Phillips met with Oswald in Dallas, along with anti-Castro exile activist Antonio Veciana. Veciana and his Alpha 66 were barred from the JFK-Almeida coup plan, though Veciana was partners with Eloy Menoyo, an exile leader whom the Kennedys and Harry did want. Veciana's story of meeting Oswald and Phillips in the lobby of the new Southland Building in Dallas has long been controversial, though Congressional investigator Gaeton Fonzi concluded that such a meeting did take place. Veciana hinted that Phillips used the name "Maurice Bishop," and CIA official Ross Crozier later confirmed that to Congressional investigators. Kurtz got new confirmation, saying that "Hunter Leake told me that David Atlee Phillips . . . used the alias [Maurice Bishop]."[18] Veciana revealed to us that he originally named his group Alpha 66 after the Phillips 66 gas stations that were common in the early 1960s.[19]

David Atlee Phillips was from nearby Fort Worth, and by meeting Oswald in public—in the lobby of Dallas's newest glittering office tower—Phillips must have realized he could have been seen with Oswald by a relative or a high school classmate, or even photographed by a tourist. Such behavior seems illogical, and inconsistent with Phillips's long intelligence experience, if Phillips knew that Oswald was going to be any type of assassin or patsy for JFK's assassination. Such a meeting is much more consistent with Oswald's being used as an intelligence asset for an operation far from Dallas. Phillips appears to have been focused on using Oswald in the CIA's anti-Castro operations, as one of the US assets they had to get into Cuba before the coup. Apparently, Phillips hoped Oswald's pro-Castro media blitz would help him get into Cuba via Mexico City. Phillips was based in Mexico City, where he headed anti-Castro operations.

Oswald's trip to Mexico City in late September and early October 1963 has also been the subject of much controversy and Congressional investigation. William Gaudet, a CIA asset long known to have received the Mexican tourist card in New Orleans with the number just before Oswald's, told Kurtz that he was with Oswald in Mexico for the CIA.[20] This helps to explain why a later report said that Oswald had traveled one way to Mexico by car, though Oswald neither had a license nor owned a car. As our Naval Intelligence source told us, Oswald was under surveillance the whole time he was in Mexico City—something later confirmed by Win Scott, who at the time was the Mexico City CIA station chief.[21]

Oswald was not able to get into Cuba via Mexico City, especially after someone called the Soviet embassy, impersonating him. CIA officials found out about the impersonation because they had bugged the phones at the Soviet and Cuban embassies. Just as Banister and Ferrie were in a position to manipulate Oswald for Marcello while ostensibly helping the CIA, Marcello's Mafia associates also had ways to compromise Oswald's actions in Mexico City. Richard Cain, the high-level Chicago law enforcement official who had worked with Trafficante and Rosselli on the CIA-Mafia Castro assassination plots, had bugged a communist embassy in Mexico City the previous year. Monitoring the bugs for the CIA was the DFS, a Mexican police agency so corrupt and tied to drugs that it eventually had to be disbanded. The DFS was linked to the Mexico City arm of Trafficante and Marcello's French Connection drug ring with Michel Victor Mertz.[22]

As for Oswald, he may have thought he was simply going to be a US intelligence asset in Cuba, or that he was going to play a part in the CIA-Mafia plot to assassinate Castro. Given Oswald's long ties to intelligence activities, his favorite uncle's career as a bookie for Marcello, and Oswald's own brief work for Marcello as a runner, he probably would have had little problem with an operation that combined intelligence and the Mafia. However, Oswald would have been told as little as possible about his mission by people like Guy Banister and David Ferrie, whose real goal was to manipulate Oswald for Marcello and the JFK plot.

After Oswald failed to get into Cuba, he apparently had—or thought he had—a role to play for US intelligence. After a brief stint living at the Dallas YMCA, by November 1963, Oswald was living in a rooming house in the Oak Cliff neighborhood of Dallas, seeing his wife only on the weekends. He tried to find work at several businesses in downtown Dallas, which would later turn out to be near JFK's motorcade route, before finally settling on the Texas School Book Depository. However, for years others had determined Oswald's actions, and there is no reason to think his choice of work location deviated from that pattern. Even before JFK's final motorcade route through Dallas was announced, it was almost certain that the President would take a downtown route through Dealey Plaza, just as JFK had during his visits to Dallas in 1960 and 1961. Oswald was in the Soviet Union at those times, but JFK's visits would have been well known to a downtown Dallas businessman like Jack Ruby.

Oswald's starting salary at the Depository was small, yet evidence shows he was thinking of buying an expensive car: He told a car salesman on November 9, 1963, that he would be getting "a lot of money in the next two or three weeks."[23] Among Oswald's notes preserved—but apparently overlooked—by the Warren Commission are remarks apparently intended for a speech he would make after he finally emerged from his years of undercover work. Its tone and content are totally at odds with the pro-Marxist remarks he made on radio and TV in New Orleans. Oswald maintains that he hates communism, writing that "there are possibly few other Americans born in the US who [have] as many personal reasons to know—and therefore hate and mistrust—Communism." He says the US and Russia "have too much to offer to each other to be tearing at each other's throats in an endless cold war. Both countries have major shortcomings and advantages, but only in ours is the voice of dissent allowed opportunity of expression."[24]

By 1963, America had become a far different country than it had been during the McCarthy era, when Oswald loved *I Led Three Lives*, based on the true story of Herbert Philbrick, who pretended to be a communist for years before emerging to acclaim, Congressional thanks, and a long career as an author and popular speaker. Oswald's notes mention Philbrick and make it clear that he intended to surpass him in some way, apparently because of his role in the upcoming US operation against Cuba.[25]

Oswald's intelligence status had to be very closely held to remain secret, meaning that few federal agents in the field could be told about it. Oswald had been worried that a local Dallas FBI agent was going to blow his cover, which he had worked so hard to maintain for so many years, hoping he could make it pay off. FBI agent James Hosty had visited Oswald's wife on November 1 and again on November 5, and after Oswald heard about it, he wrote a note to Hosty warning him away, and Oswald personally dropped it off at the Dallas FBI office.

It's hard to tell where Oswald's legitimate US intelligence activities end and his manipulation by Mafia associates begins, given the true loyalty of US assets like Banister and Ferrie to Marcello, and the hatred of the Kennedys they shared with CIA officers like Morales and his good friend Rosselli. Any of Oswald's unusual actions during 1963 can be explained by three possibilities: 1. It could have been for legitimate intelligence purposes; 2. It could have been a legitimate intelligence purpose that was also furthering Marcello's goals; or 3. Oswald only thought he was acting for a legitimate intelligence purpose, but in reality he was being manipulated by Marcello's men. Imagine how difficult it must have been for officials from various agencies to sort through Oswald's actions after JFK's death, as they tried to figure out (in secret, and often not talking to other agencies) what Oswald was really up to.

In the weeks and months before Dallas, Oswald, or someone pretending to be Oswald, was reportly near Chicago prior to JFK's planned motorcade there, and in Tampa the day before JFK's motorcade there.[26] Since officials had uncovered assassination plots in each city before JFK arrived, that meant Oswald could have taken the fall if JFK had been shot in either of those two cities.

On Thursday, November 21, Lee Oswald went home a day early to see Marina and his children, who were living with Ruth Paine. When he awoke, he left $175 and his wedding ring for his wife. As he rode into work with Wesley Frazier on the morning of November 22, 1963, Frazier and his sister saw Oswald hold a package cupped in his hand and tucked under his armpit. It could not have been a disassembled Mannlicher-Carcano rifle, as the Warren Commission later asserted, because a disassembled Mannlicher was too long to be carried that way. Oswald told Frazier it was curtain rods, but it could have been almost anything— including an item Oswald had been told to bring to work (or the parking lot) that day by whoever he thought was his intelligence handler. According to Warren Commission testimony, Oswald did not have the package when he entered the Depository that morning. (One unconfirmed source linked to the deaths of two Artime associates claimed it could have been a pro-Castro banner, passed to a confederate who supposedly planned to unfurl it from a Book Depository window during JFK's motorcade. If Oswald went to the Cuban embassy in Mexico City and took credit for such a stunt, he might have thought he would surely be allowed into Cuba.) A Warren Commission counsel later outlined evidence, omitted from their Final Report, that Oswald may well have been preparing to go to Mexico that day.[27]

John Martino indicated that Oswald was supposed to leave work on the afternoon of November 22 to meet what he thought was an intelligence contact at the Texas Theater. In David Atlee Phillips's autobiography, *The Night Watch* (a completely different book from Phillips's autobiographical novel outline cited earlier), Phillips wrote about his own experience meeting contacts at movie theaters, setting up the time by phone and using "recognition procedures" that included code phrases. In Oswald's pocket on November 22 was half of a torn box top, as if Oswald expected to meet someone who had the other half at the theater.[28] Veciana told us about meeting the CIA official who first recruited Phillips, who gave Veciana half of a torn dollar bill to use as a recognition procedure later. Oswald had a couple of torn dollar bills in his room, and the torn-bill technique was also used in the Texas arm of the French Connection heroin ring.[29]

John Martino, Rosselli and Trafficante's Cuban exile associate, said shortly before his death that "Oswald had been 'put together' by 'anti-Castro types.'" Martino knew what he was talking about; as we noted earlier, he was acquainted with David Morales and had met with Marcello, Banister, Trafficante, and Rosselli in 1963. Martino told his son he even saw Oswald passing out the pro-Castro leaflets when Oswald was arrested, and he explained that "Oswald didn't know who he was working for. . . . He was to meet his contact at the Texas Theater" in Dallas on the day of the assassination. "They were to meet Oswald in the theater and get him out of the country. . . . "[30] However, according to Martino, Oswald didn't know that if he made it out of the theater, the plan was to "eliminate him." If Oswald appeared to have fled, or be fleeing, to Cuba after JFK's murder, that would have made the pressure to invade Cuba tremendous, especially since (as Martino and his Mafia associates knew all too well) the United States had a Cuban invasion plan ready to go.

Echoing Martino's words that "Oswald didn't know who he was working for," Oswald's wife would say, long after the assassination, that her husband had been "caught between two powers—the government and organized crime." According to the *San Jose Mercury News*, Marina said that "in retrospect, Oswald seemed professionally schooled in secretiveness, and I believe he worked for the American government. He was taught the Russian language when he was in the military. Do you think that is usual, that an ordinary soldier is taught Russian? Also, he got in and out of Russia quite easily, and he got me out quite easily."[31]

At his job at the Texas School Book Depository, Oswald sometimes used the pay phone near the first-floor lunchroom. On November 22, 1963, a foreman "saw Oswald near the telephone on the first floor" at ten or fifteen minutes before noon (just thirty minutes before JFK was shot). It's not known what calls he may have made or received that day. At noon, Oswald was still on the first floor, eating lunch in the small first-floor lunchroom used by minority and disabled employees. Unlike many employees, who started to drift out of the building on their lunch break to await the arrival of JFK's motorcade, Oswald seemed to have other things on his mind.[32]

Chapter Seven

As JFK and Jackie were beginning their motorcade through Dallas on November 22, 1963, Bobby Kennedy was having lunch at his Hickory Hill estate in Virginia, not far from CIA headquarters. The visiting US Attorney from New York, Robert Morgenthau, and his assistant joined Bobby by the pool. Morgenthau had handled the prosecutions resulting from the arrest of Joe Valachi, the Mafia heroin operative whose sensational televised Congressional testimony two months earlier had electrified the nation, dragging mob secrets out of the shadows and into American living rooms.

That Friday was a balmy Indian-summer day at Bobby's, with weather much like that in Dallas, and Bobby took a break for a bracing midday swim. Doing so gave him time to reflect on the morning meeting he'd had with his Mafia prosecutors at the Justice Department. Bobby must have felt pleased, since tremendous progress was being made on all fronts. Their investigation of a French Connection heroin bust in Texas, the second in two years, was going well. A year earlier, drug enforcement officers in Marcello-controlled Houston had seized twenty-two pounds of heroin linked to Trafficante. The most recent bust centered on a carload of heroin at the Texas–Mexico border that involved a Cuban exile and the Montreal Mafia.[1] Bobby knew from experience that heroin traffickers could be ruthless, so he had arranged for the main witness and his family to be placed under US protection in the coming months. In 1963, no Federal Witness Protection Program existed yet, and even arrangements to shield star Mafia witness Joe Valachi had to be done on an ad-hoc basis.

Bobby's morning meeting had also covered his Mafia prosecutors' pressure on Santo Trafficante and members of the Chicago Mafia, led by Sam Giancana. Bobby was pleased with that week's release of *The Green Felt Jungle*, a book that finally exposed Johnny Rosselli's leading role in Las Vegas on behalf of the Chicago mob. Bobby was no doubt relieved that JFK had ended his relationship with Rosselli's girlfriend, Judith

Campbell, a year and a half earlier, and that Campbell's recent attempt to contact JFK again—just after the Chicago assassination attempt—had been rebuffed.

Most important for Bobby, he was awaiting a verdict in Carlos Marcello's federal trial in New Orleans. A conviction would be the culmination of a battle Bobby and JFK had been waging against Marcello since 1958, and would result in Marcello's being either imprisoned or permanently deported from the United States.

Though Bobby kept his Mafia prosecutors separate from his Get Hoffa Squad, he knew they must have enjoyed the headline in the November 22 *New York Times* that proclaimed "Las Vegas: Casinos Get Millions in Loans from Teamsters Fund."[2] The article was just one in a recent series featuring information that Bobby's men had supplied, highlighting the ties of the Teamster president to casinos and gangsters. Hoffa himself was being tried for jury tampering in Nashville, and had reportedly tried to bribe a juror in that trial. Hoffa didn't realize that Bobby had a Teamster informer in Louisiana, who had revealed Hoffa's threats in the summer of 1962 about having Bobby assassinated in a car. We can only imagine what Bobby must have felt each time he made the trip by car from his Virginia home to his Justice Department office in Washington.

One of the most pressing concerns on Bobby's mind during his November 22 lunch and swim was something that he couldn't share with Morgenthau, his Mafia prosecutors, or his Get Hoffa Squad: the impending coup plan against Fidel Castro, just ten days away. Earlier in the week, Bobby had completed his final meetings with his trusted exile leaders: DIA files confirm he had met with Harry Williams and Manuel Artime on November 17, the day before JFK's Tampa motorcade, and that the following day Bobby had met with the leader of the Fort Benning Cuban American troops. On November 21, Bobby had met again with Harry Williams, for the last time before the coup.[3]

While Bobby had been meeting with his Mafia prosecutors that Friday morning, Harry was at an important meeting that Bobby had arranged, with CIA officials like Executive Director Lyman Kirkpatrick and E. Howard Hunt.[4] If no problems arose at the afternoon portion of the meeting, Harry would proceed immediately to Miami, to the US base at Guantanamo the next day, and then slip into Castro's Cuba to meet with Almeida.[5] At that point, it would be too late for any breakthrough in the secret peace negotiations to prevent the coup. Harry's entry into Cuba around November 25 would also coincide with Bobby's revelation to Dean Rusk and other cabinet officials that all the planning they had been doing in recent months was about to bear fruit, since they had found someone powerful enough in the Cuban government to "eliminate" Fidel and stage a coup.[6]

While Bobby knew that Cuban exile leaders Manuel Artime and Tony Varona were now fully on board, he also realized that two others, Manolo Ray and Eloy Menoyo, had not yet completely committed to Harry. However, CIA files confirm that Harry had met with both men in recent weeks to discuss what was generally going to happen, and that money was being provided to each of them (in Ray's case, more than $100,000). Bobby and Harry were confident that both Ray and Menoyo would cooperate fully once the coup began.

Like Harry, Bobby was sure that Almeida was sincere and not a double agent, because of his willingness to put his own family under covert US protection in another country. Still, if anything happened and the coup turned into a disaster, one of Bobby's associates indicated that the Attorney General planned to do the same thing he had offered to do after the Bay of Pigs fiasco: take full responsibility and resign, to minimize the political damage to JFK. Bobby wouldn't be risking his life during the coup, like Harry and Almeida would, but he knew his own political life was on the line.

Fully aware of a higher level of official planning kept mostly secret from Harry and the other Cuban exile leaders, Bobby knew about the flurry of eight drafts of the "Plan for a Coup in Cuba" that had been completed in just the past five months. (Only three, much smaller drafts had been completed in the six months before Almeida's May 1963 contact with Harry.) Bobby also knew—from trusted advisors like General Maxwell Taylor, General Joseph Carroll, and Army Secretary Cyrus Vance—about the updated invasion plans for Cuba, CINCLANT OPLANS 312 and 316, that might well have to be used if the coup didn't go smoothly.

Bobby's exile leaders also had not been made aware of the Cuba Contingency Planning for possible retaliation from Fidel if the Cuban dictator found out about the coup plan. One of Bobby's secretive subcommittees of the National Security Council was still trying to finalize the plans, but the thinking behind them had no doubt affected how Bobby had dealt with the recent assassination attempts against JFK in Chicago and Tampa. So far, Bobby and JFK's media skills and political savvy had kept any mention of the plots out of the press, and away from leaking officials and Congress. After Friday's motorcades in Dallas and

Austin, JFK would not take part in any more dangerous motorcades until after the coup had taken place. Bobby could take comfort in the fact that no active plot had been reported in Dallas, as there had been in Chicago and Tampa, and that, compared with those cities, Dallas had only a small Cuban population.

At a safe house in Washington, D.C., Harry Williams was eating a solitary lunch of sandwiches as his CIA meeting took a break. Whether Harry ate alone because of the lingering racism of D.C. and some in the CIA—an attitude that forced Hispanic CIA assets to stay only at certain hotels (the Ebbitt, for Harry and his associates)—or simply because of the busy schedules of the CIA participants isn't known.[7] The morning meeting had gone well, and no serious problems had arisen. Several CIA officials had slipped in and out of the meeting, including Lyman Kirkpatrick, the CIA's Executive Director and technically its third-highest official. Kirkpatrick had written a harsh report criticizing the CIA's performance during the Bay of Pigs debacle, so it made sense to have him carefully review all aspects of the plan before Harry slipped into Cuba for the coup. None of the men at the meeting were identified to Harry by their real names, but a top Kennedy aide later confirmed Kirkpatrick's presence for part of the meeting.

Kirkpatrick had left the meeting to appear with McCone and Helms before the President's Foreign Intelligence Review Board at the White House. (General Carroll had met with the Board the previous day.) Other important officials at Harry's meeting at various times have been identified as Richard Helms and Desmond FitzGerald. Present for most, if not all, of the meeting was E. Howard Hunt, one of the two CIA officers assigned to assist Harry. According to former FBI agent William Turner, the other CIA officer assisting Harry was James McCord. (McCord declined to speak to the authors or *Vanity Fair* about whether he was at the meeting.)[8] To Turner, Harry characterized McCord as cordial, professional, and helpful. But Harry said that E. Howard Hunt clearly resented being in an essentially subordinate role to a Cuban exile.

In Harry's morning meeting with the CIA officials, they had reviewed the plan to have Harry meet with Commander Almeida inside Cuba, then remain in place to await the coup. After Fidel had been killed, and his death blamed on someone else (not Almeida or Harry), then Artime, Varona, Ray, and Menoyo would join Harry. Almeida would proclaim a state of emergency to prevent civil war, and the Cuban American troops at Fort Benning would be invited in to help prevent a Soviet takeover.

Raul Castro would be killed as well; his death was easy for Almeida to arrange, since he worked closely with Raul.

Because of worries that Harry might be captured inside Cuba and tortured by Fidel's men, he had not been told some parts of the coup plan. While Harry knew someone else would take the fall for Fidel's death, he didn't know who that would be. Harry indicated that Bobby and the CIA were handling that aspect of the plan. Likewise, Harry was not told exactly how Fidel would be killed or who would do it; that was something he would learn only after he arrived in Cuba. The information about Fidel's being shot in an open jeep at Varadero Beach comes from later declassified AMWORLD documents and David Atlee Phillips's autobiographical novel outline.

Harry had been told that he was only one of several US assets going into Cuba in the coming days, in preparation for the coup. While the press was full of reports that the US was restraining groups from staging raids into Cuba, the handful of exile groups selected by Bobby and Harry had been encouraged to continue their operations. The CIA mounted its own small missions into Cuba, with future Watergate burglar Eugenio Martinez as its premier "boatman." All of those small raids and infiltration missions into Cuba during September, October, and the first three weeks of November were necessary so that there wouldn't be an obvious increase in activity just before the coup. In addition, exile leaders Artime, Ray, Varona, and Menoyo would need to find their own way into Cuba after the coup, from ports outside the United States, to maintain the plausible deniability of the whole operation.

As Harry Williams finished his lunch on November 22, 1963, he must have faced his afternoon session with the CIA men with a sense of both anticipation and dread. Unless one of the CIA men turned up some unforeseen problem, Harry would be in Guantanamo and ready to slip into Cuba in just two days. Harry had already visited Guantanamo for a couple of days, on a trip Bobby had arranged, just to check it out. He was certain he would be able to make his way into his Cuban homeland from there to meet with Almeida. Harry had risked his life to free Cuba several times before, but that didn't make doing it yet again any easier. Still, he was willing to take the risk because he knew he had the backing of Bobby and JFK, and thus the full force of the US government.

At CIA headquarters, Richard Helms prepared to have lunch with Director McCone, Kirkpatrick, and three other CIA officials in a small room next to McCone's office. Perhaps it weighed on his mind that he was keeping sensitive information about his unauthorized Cuban operations from his superiors. On the other hand, Helms might have viewed his own efforts to assassinate Castro using Rosselli, QJWIN, and Cubela as just part of an overall effort to eliminate Fidel at any cost, one that included the JFK-Almeida coup plan. Helms appeared to feel that as long as Fidel was terminated, the means didn't matter. Still, Helms knew about Bobby's massive effort against the Mafia, and he must have realized the Attorney General would have never approved the CIA's use of people like Rosselli and QJWIN.

Helms knew that in Paris, Cubela's CIA case officer was meeting with him and trying to give him a poison pen filled with Blackleaf-40, a deadly toxin. However, Helms may not have known that, two days earlier, a CIA officer had telephoned Cubela to set up the November 22 meeting. This meant that scheduling the date opposite JFK's Dallas motorcade originated with someone in the CIA, not with Cubela.[9] At the Paris meeting, Cubela's CIA case officer also told Cubela about JFK's speech four days earlier in Miami, citing it "as an indication that the President supported a coup."[10]

Cubela said assassination was the CIA's idea, and that it was constantly pressuring him to kill Fidel, both on November 22 and at other times. (In later years, Helms and his associates always testified and said in interviews that Cubela, not the CIA, wanted to assassinate Fidel.) According to the CIA, at the November 22 meeting Cubela "asked for the following items to be included in a cache inside Cuba: 20 hand-grenades, two high-powered rifles with telescopic sights, and approximately 20 pounds of C-4 explosive."[11] In charge of arranging for those items to be delivered would be the CIA official whom Cubela says he met in September 1963: David Morales.

David Morales's activities on November 22, 1963, cannot be documented, since files concerning his whereabouts that day have never been released by the CIA. Without the files, it's impossible to know whether he was in Miami, Mexico City, or even Dallas. However, by looking at Morales's documented actions and statements, we can get a good idea of what he was up to. For example, we know that at least some of the things Morales was doing that day involved the assassination of JFK, since he later admitted his involvement in the murder.

Ten years after President Kennedy's murder, Morales confessed to both his attorney and his longtime friend that he had some role in JFK's assassination, declaring: "Well, we took care of that son of a bitch, didn't we?"[12] As first documented by Congressional investigator Gaeton Fonzi, Morales's admission came at the end of a drunken tirade set off by the mention of JFK's name. According to one of the witnesses, Morales "jumped up screaming, 'That no good son of a bitch motherfucker!' He started yelling about what a wimp Kennedy was and talking about how he had worked on the Bay of Pigs and how he had to watch all the men he had recruited and trained get wiped out because of Kennedy."[13]

There is some support for Morales's claim. His remarks about JFK bear a remarkable similarity to those Carlos Marcello made regarding Bobby—apparently when it came to eliminating JFK, they both had the same goal, though for different reasons. While Oswald was in New Orleans, several witnesses reported seeing him in the company of a "Mexican," though it can't be determined if this was Morales or someone else. Also, more than twenty years after JFK's murder, Gaeton Fonzi uncovered a link between Morales and the French Connection drug smuggler who also helped French Intelligence (SDECE) agents like Michel Victor Mertz.[14]

Morales is the only person who confessed to JFK's assassination that was in a position to have both manipulated the date of the CIA's meeting with Cubela in Paris and have suggested that David Atlee Phillips meet with Lee Oswald in Dallas, in a public place, in September 1963. Morales had been Phillips's supervisor in Havana, and they were working closely together in the fall of 1963. As for Cubela, Cuban authorities say that Morales met personally with him in September 1963. It's also interesting to note that Cubela had originally been recruited for the CIA by a business associate of Santo Trafficante.[15] Morales would have realized that after JFK's assassination, the timing of the CIA-Cubela meeting and Phillips's meeting with Oswald would force both Helms and Phillips to cover up or destroy much crucial information to protect their own careers.

David Morales knew two men—Johnny Rosselli and John Martino—who later confessed their roles in JFK's assassination to trusted associates:[16] Martino even mentioned the normally secretive Morales by name in his 1963 book *I Was Castro's Prisoner*. Cuban authorities also linked Morales to former death-squad leader Rolando Masferrer, the associate of Martino and Trafficante who was secretly brought into the JFK-Almeida coup plan after Tony Varona received a $200,000 bribe in August 1963.[17]

More information also backs up Morales's JFK confession. Morales's AMOT informants had fed suspicious assassination-related reports to the CIA even before JFK went to Dallas. These would soon include claims that the supposed Cuban agent who appeared to shadow JFK in Chicago and Florida was also in Dallas, before returning to Cuba. Even Morales's own government associates felt he was capable of murder. The number-two official at the huge Miami CIA station, Tom Clines, told author David Corn that Morales "would do anything, even work with the Mafia." According to Corn, Morales once bragged about sabotaging the parachutes of "men he suspected of being communists" and "had the pleasure of waving good-bye to them, as they plummeted to [their] death."[18]

Former US diplomat Wayne Smith, who worked with Morales at the US embassy in Havana, said that "if [Morales] were in the mob, he'd be called a hit man." According to Smith (later America's highest-ranking diplomat in Cuba as head of the US Interests Section in Havana from 1979 to 1982), Morales said three years before his death that "Kennedy got what was coming to him." Smith has stated, "I am convinced that [JFK's] assassination was carried out by . . . men like David Morales, who I knew well from my days in Cuba."[19]

Chapter Eight

Carlos Marcello's whereabouts on November 22, 1963, at the time of JFK's murder are easily documented. The godfather who controlled Louisiana and parts of the surrounding states was sitting in a New Orleans federal courtroom, watching his trial enter its final stages. Although a conviction could lead to prison and permanent deportation, Marcello knew he would be acquitted, since he'd used intermediaries to bribe a key juror. In a few hours, his friends and family would be throwing a celebration for him, but Marcello anticipated celebrating more than just his acquittal.

Marcello knew that his hated enemy, Bobby Kennedy, was sure to investigate the circumstances of the verdict, and that he and his associate Hoffa couldn't go on bribing jurors forever. The Kennedy administration's additional prosecutions and investigations of Marcello and Hoffa, coupled with its relentless pressure on Trafficante and Rosselli, couldn't be allowed to continue. But after November 22, Marcello would no longer have to worry about the Kennedys' war on organized crime, because the Attorney General's brother would no longer be President.

Marcello's plan that was unfolding on November 22 was consistent with his criminal behavior for the past two decades, which had been careful, cautious, and ruthless. In the case of the JFK hit, even his backup plan (Tampa) had a backup (Dallas). The situation in Dallas looked much better than it had in either Chicago or Tampa. No active alert had been issued to law enforcement; no threat had been detected. In addition, Marcello had already seen in Chicago and Tampa that Bobby and top federal officials would cover up assassination information in order to protect national security, and there was no reason to think Dallas would be any different.

Marcello, along with Trafficante and Rosselli, had thoroughly planned and considered every aspect of the assassination for the past year, using all the skills they brought to their multimillion-dollar criminal business deals. They realized that JFK needed to be assassinated in public in order to force a quick reaction from Bobby and the government. Since parts of the slaying had already been linked to the top-secret JFK-Almeida coup plan, Bobby and top government officials would be forced into hurried decisions about limiting the investigation to prevent a nuclear confrontation over Cuba. As with the concealment of the Chicago and Tampa attempts, once such cover-ups had been put in place, they could be almost impossible to later admit or undo. These cover-ups would have to continue as officials and agencies tried to figure out in secret which parts of the extensive coup plan had been compromised.

Marcello also knew that by killing JFK during his motorcade, he would guarantee that JFK's death and its cause couldn't be hidden for even a short period of time. This meant that Bobby's archrival, Lyndon Johnson, would quickly assume office, before Bobby and his Justice Department prosecutors had a chance to seize control of the investigation. Marcello had contributed money to LBJ for years, as he did to many politicians in the region. The Mafia boss had originally supported Johnson for the 1960 Democratic nomination over JFK, since LBJ had never gone after the Mafia.[1] Because of LBJ's lack of interest in pursuing the Mafia, and his enmity with Bobby, an LBJ presidency was far preferable to having JFK in office.

Marcello was far more politically savvy than most Mafia chiefs—he employed his own powerful Washington lobbyist and had a close relationship with the Mafia boss of the nation's capital, Joe Nesline. Looking ahead, Marcello knew that any of the presidential options in 1964 were preferable to another four years of JFK. In November 1963, LBJ's political stock was so low that no one would have predicted that he would win the 1964 election by a landslide. Newspapers and TV indicated Richard Nixon or Arizona senator Barry Goldwater as the likely Republican nominees for the 1964 race, and neither represented a threat to Marcello. Nixon had the Marcello and Mafia support noted earlier and though Goldwater had served with JFK on the Senate crime committee, the Arizona senator had shown no real interest in going after the Mafia that had killed two of his best friends, in 1955 and 1958. In short, JFK's murder would be good for Marcello both now and for years to come.

In New Orleans, Marcello had the police and the local FBI in his pocket, minimizing his risk if the investigation of JFK's murder ever focused in that direction. The crime lord also had ties to lawmen in Dallas, like Sheriff Bill Decker, who was riding in the lead car of JFK's motorcade along with Dallas Police Chief Bill Curry. On an undercover police tape, Decker's predecessor described him as "a payoff man" for a Dallas gambling kingpin. Decker freely admitted to having a long friendship with Joe Campisi, a Marcello lieutenant in Dallas and one of

Ruby's good friends.[2] When Marcello's Dallas Mafia boss, Joseph Civ-ello, wanted to be paroled for a narcotics conviction, Decker provided a character reference for the mobster.[3] Sheriff Decker's mob ties were not that unusual for law enforcement officials in some major American cit-ies at the time, and while Decker had no knowing involvement in JFK's assassination, the connection was there in case Marcello needed it.

Marcello had many ways to feed disinformation even to federal authorities, and to essentially force agencies to protect his associates and even himself. As documented throughout this book, most of the dozen or so people knowingly involved in assassinating JFK were gov-ernment assets, informants, or agents who were all capable of supplying false or misleading information into the system, before, during, or after JFK's murder. We've noted the number of Marcello associates who had infiltrated the JFK-Almeida coup plan, and Marcello's own claim that he was part of the CIA-Mafia plots to assassinate Fidel Castro. Files at the National Archives from the JFK Assassination Records Review Board contain the allegation that an AMWORLD case officer was the liaison between the CIA and Marcello. Therefore, even if some lead should point to Marcello or his men, certain US intelligence officials would have to hide that information in order to divert suspicion from them-selves and their agency. They would have to either keep their suspicions to themselves or accept assurances from their men that any seeming involvement in JFK's death was simply a matter of their having been part of the same operation as Oswald, who was either a bad apple or working for some foreign power.

Marcello and his partners in the assassination had so many connec-tions to US intelligence and law enforcement that they are often over-looked by historians and journalists. For example, one way information could have gone directly to (or from) Desmond FitzGerald and Richard Helms was through E. Howard Hunt. The following is just a partial list of Hunt's anti-Castro associates who worked with the Mafia:

- Hunt's assistant Bernard Barker, also working for Trafficante
- Hunt's best friend, Manuel Artime, who was working on the CIA-Mafia plots and was soon involved in drug trafficking
- Artime's assistant, Rafael "Chi Chi" Quintero, involved in drug running by Iran-Contra, and likely much earlier
- David Morales, the Miami CIA Operations Chief who headed the CIA-Mafia plots at that time and was close to Johnny Rosselli
- Frank Fiorini, the Trafficante bagman who was a major source of information for Barker
- Exile leader Tony Varona, who worked with Trafficante and

Rosselli on the CIA-Mafia Castro assassination plots, and who had accepted a $200,000 bribe from Rosselli's mob associates just three months earlier

- Carlos Prio, the corrupt former Cuban president who was linked to drugs and angry at being excluded from the coup plan by the Kennedys

At a deniable arm's length, the list even includes Hunt's much admired patron, Richard Helms, who at that time was the highest CIA official to know about the continued use of the Mafia and European criminals like QJWIN. We noted earlier Helms's comment about David Ferrie's work for the CIA, which appears to have been corroborated by the later statements of New Orleans CIA Deputy Chief Hunter Leake. Marcello would have known that CIA officials had their own interests to protect if Ferrie's name ever threatened to surface after JFK's assassination.

In New Orleans on November 22, Marcello had David Ferrie sitting with him in the courtroom, as the closing arguments wound to a close.[4] Ferrie's presence gave him the perfect alibi for the time of JFK's murder. Marcello had spent much time with Ferrie in recent weeks, including two full weekends at the huge Churchill Farms property. From all indications, Marcello viewed Ferrie as a brilliant man, and in some ways he was. Based on papers later found by police, Ferrie had even calculated the distance shells ejected from a rifle would travel, as if he wanted to make sure that the shells police found after a shooting would be in the proper place. While Marcello may have thought the highly intelligent Ferrie had planned his actions carefully enough, the crime boss didn't realize there was one very small thing Ferrie had apparently overlooked.

In Dallas on November 22, Jack Ruby was both tired and wired from his busy previous day and late night. At noon, Ruby had been at the *Dallas Morning News* building, four blocks from Dealey Plaza. However, as JFK's motorcade neared the area, Ruby disappeared, apparently leaving the building for almost half an hour, according to an FBI report.[5] Ruby's exact location and activities at the time of JFK's assassination can't be established, aside from a comment by a Dallas TV reporter that he saw Ruby near the Texas School Book Depository within moments of the assassination.[6] However, Ruby's actions leading up to November 22 provide insight into what he was probably up to.

Ruby had recently been talking about leaving his modest Oak Cliff neighborhood (the same area in which Oswald lived) and moving to a new apartment in the most expensive and exclusive part of Dallas,

Turtle Creek. Three days earlier, Ruby had talked to his tax attorney, claiming "he had a connection who would supply him money to settle his long-standing [IRS bill]" of more than $40,000.[7] Ruby had been in Chicago just days before JFK canceled his motorcade there, where he had received $7,000 in cash from a Hoffa associate in the coffee shop of the Bismarck Hotel.[8] But that amount wouldn't come close to paying his IRS bill, let alone his expensive new rent. Clearly, on November 22, 1963, Ruby was expecting a huge sum of money, since his checking account contained only $246.65.

Ruby's clubs, the seedy Carousel strip club and the lesser-known Vegas Club, which he owned with his sister, weren't doing especially well, in spite of the shady side ventures Ruby ran, which included gambling and prostitution. Ruby's gunrunning was a fraction of what it had been around the time of the Cuban Revolution, especially now that the Kennedys had directed the CIA to cut off support for all but a small handful of exile groups. Ruby's mechanic, Donnell D. Whitter, was also involved in gunrunning, and had been arrested by Dallas police on November 18, 1963, as part of the gun ring that generated the FBI and Treasury Department reports about the upcoming US invasion of Cuba.

Ruby was part of Marcello's and Trafficante's portion of the French Connection heroin network. An FBI document notes that since 1956, "Jack Ruby of Dallas [had been given] the okay to operate [for a] large narcotics setup operation between Mexico, Texas, and the East." Journalist Michael Valentine has documented Ruby's ties to the heroin network, using Federal Bureau of Narcotics reports and interviews with retired agents. They confirm that Civello, who ran Dallas for Marcello, controlled the heroin business in that city. Valentine also cites the Kennedy crime hearings in January 1958, in which a Bureau of Narcotics supervisor linked "the Civello family in Dallas and . . . Carlos Marcello in New Orleans [and] Santo Trafficante in Tampa" to the drug rackets. Several Ruby associates and Dallas heroin traffickers also had links to Michel Victor Mertz. As with Ruby's strip club, gambling, and prostitution rackets, the Dallas nightclub owner gained protection from law enforcement for his narcotics activities by being helpful to them, and sometimes acting as an informant.[9]

However, Ruby was a relatively low-level, and thus low-paid, part of the heroin network, so his huge financial windfall would have to come from other activities. As we discussed earlier, Congressional investigators found that Ruby's long-distance calls had skyrocketed as November 22 approached, an indication that something big was in the works, something that required the careful use of cover stories and intermediaries.

JFK had been in Houston the previous day for a motorcade, and former FBI agent William Turner found and summarized a Secret Service report that stated: "Numerous witnesses identify . . . Jack Ruby as being in Houston, Texas, on November 21, for several hours, one block from the President's entrance route and from the Rice Hotel where he stayed."[10] Ruby was apparently shadowing JFK, getting a firsthand look at his security precautions.

Ruby's extensive police connections in Dallas were useful to Marcello. One of Ruby's musicians later told the FBI that he had seen "between 150 to 200 [Dallas] police officers at the Carousel [Club] at one time or another," and another Ruby associate put the number even higher, saying Ruby "was well acquainted with virtually every member of the Dallas Police."[11] Officers didn't have to pay for drinks at Ruby's clubs, and were sometimes provided with women. FBI reports note that Ruby was "very good friends" with Captain Will Fritz, who ran Homicide for the Dallas police, and that Ruby "was allowed the complete run of the Homicide Bureau." Ruby had even vacationed with the Dallas "Chief of Police" a few years earlier, according to another FBI report.[12]

Ruby could be helpful to Marcello by finding out things like the fact that 365 Dallas policemen were slated to be at Love Field when JFK arrived, and 60 would be at the Trade Mart as security at JFK's Dallas speech, but only a scattered few would be at Dealey Plaza.[13] Ruby would also have known that Dallas Officer J. D. Tippit, who worked after hours for Ruby's best friend, had been having an affair and had gotten his girlfriend pregnant.[14] Tippit needed money to deal with the crisis, and his situation allowed Ruby or his associates to exert pressure on him. If Tippit were told to be in a certain place to make an important arrest, for which he would be well paid, he wouldn't be in a position to refuse or ask too many questions.

Journalist Seth Kantor documented that later on November 22, 1963, Ruby had $7,000 on him, as well as his loaded pistol, so he might have had both when JFK went through Dealey Plaza. That's plenty of money for payoffs, a gun for any trouble, and even a built-in alibi if Ruby needed to shoot someone near the Depository or in his neighborhood (he could claim he thought he was being robbed). But all indications are that Ruby preferred to simply arrange for a Dallas policeman to take care of anyone who needed to be silenced.

As we've noted, about two months earlier Ruby had met with Johnny Rosselli in Miami twice, though FBI reports about the meeting vanished during a Congressional investigation. In fact, FBI surveillance reports for Rosselli in Miami are completely missing for the months surrounding those visits. Around the same time that Ruby met with Rosselli, author Peter Dale Scott notes that David Atlee Phillips was at the Miami CIA station, no doubt meeting with his associate David Morales, who was very close to Rosselli. Phillips even had a good friend in common with Ruby: Gordon McClendon, a Dallas radio station owner who would later cofound the Association of Retired Intelligence Officers with Phillips. Rosselli described Ruby as "one of our boys" to investigative journalist Jack Anderson. It's likely that the Ruby-Rosselli meeting was ostensibly about the CIA-Mafia plots to assassinate Castro, but a later admission by Rosselli makes it clear that the meeting had an even more sinister purpose.[15]

Johnny Rosselli's exact location during JFK's Dallas motorcade cannot be definitively established, because the FBI was unable to locate Rosselli between November 19 and November 27, 1963. However, we know what Rosselli was up to, because he told his attorney, Tom Wadden, that he was involved in JFK's assassination. According to noted historian Richard D. Mahoney, the first John F. Kennedy scholar at the Kennedy Presidential Library, Wadden revealed Rosselli's confession to one of Bobby's former Mafia prosecutors, William Hundley.[16] Rosselli's admission finally confirms what the Mafia don had hinted at to Jack Anderson over the years, and what a top Kennedy aide told us in 1992.

We noted earlier the account of a pilot associate of John Martino, who says he flew Rosselli from Tampa to New Orleans on November 21, then to Houston, and finally to Dallas on the morning of November 22. Three other unconfirmed reports place Rosselli in Dallas on November 22, most with Chicago hit man Charles Nicoletti. Newspaper accounts confirm that Nicoletti, who was also involved in narcotics smuggling, had joined the CIA-Mafia plots to kill Castro in October 1963. Nicoletti was best known in law enforcement circles for having a "hit car," with hidden compartments to hold weapons.[17] (Rosselli's biographers cite "an unconfirmed account [that] a woman drove 'Johnny Roselli and a second man, a sharpshooter from Miami, to the grassy knoll at the far end of Dealey Plaza,'" but none of these reports achieve the level of documented reliability we strive for.)[18] Perhaps when the remaining one million CIA records related to JFK's assassination are released, and the FBI finds and releases its missing Rosselli-surveillance files, we will be able to determine with certainty Rosselli's whereabouts at the time of JFK's death.

By the morning of November 22, 1963, Tampa godfather Santo Trafficante had no doubt already planned a celebratory dinner for that evening, to toast JFK's murder with Frank Ragano, the lawyer whose services he shared with Jimmy Hoffa. Trafficante's triumph would be all the sweeter because the dinner would be held at the posh International Inn, the site of one of the speeches JFK made in Tampa on November 18, 1963. According to Ragano, it was "the ritziest hotel and restaurant in Tampa," a place for special occasions, and Trafficante would no doubt delight in walking through the same "hotel lobby [where JFK] had shaken hands and waved at admirers" just four days earlier.[19]

Based on testimony from FBI informant Jose Aleman, by November 22, Trafficante had been planning JFK's assassination for over a year, so it's only natural that he would have wanted to celebrate the culmination of his long months of planning.[20] Ragano says that Trafficante confirmed his role in JFK's death to him, though, as we document later, the lawyer's account of Trafficante's confession downplays Ragano's own participation.

Normally extremely reclusive, Trafficante tried to stay out of the limelight. An average-looking man, he cultivated a nondescript image, and since he was not widely recognized or a media figure in Tampa, he knew he could celebrate at the exclusive restaurant without attracting undue attention. Also, Trafficante's inside man on the Tampa police force, Sgt. Jack de la Llana, could let him know if any suspicion started to come Trafficante's way.

We've noted accounts from a captured Cuban exile that Trafficante drug associates, like Eladio del Valle and Herminio Diaz, were in Dallas on November 22 and were part of JFK's assassination. Cuban officials described Diaz as a "mulatto" or "dark-skinned," and claimed he was in the Texas School Book Depository as JFK's motorcade approached.[21] Another longtime Trafficante associate, CIA agent Bernard Barker, would reportedly be on the "grassy knoll"—just down the street from the Book Depository—as JFK's motorcade passed.

On November 22, 1963, John Martino, Trafficante's electronics whiz, was at home in Miami. He had earlier told his wife, "They're going to kill him [JFK]. They're going to kill him when he gets to Texas."[22] As *Vanity Fair* reported, Martino made it clear that in Dallas there were "two guns, two people involved," and that some of those involved in the plot were "anti-Castro Cubans." Martino told both *Newsday* reporter John Cummings and his business partner that "Oswald wasn't" one of the shooters.[23]

In fact, one of the Cuban exiles involved had visited the Martino household just two months earlier, accompanied by a "man from Washington, tall and large . . . in a dark suit, like from the State Department." However, the man with the exile wasn't from State, since they didn't deal with Martino—but the CIA did. Several weeks before JFK's trip to Dallas, Martino says he was introduced to Oswald in Miami; in August Martino had seen Oswald passing out leaflets in New Orleans but had not met him.[24]

According to *Vanity Fair*, on November 22 Martino had "asked his son, Edward, to stay home from school that Friday. No reason given and no explanation offered. During the morning, Martino asked Edward . . . to watch television and notify him immediately of any special news or bulletins."[25]

Trafficante's heroin partner, Michel Victor Mertz, was in Dallas at the time of JFK's visit, according to one of the only memos the CIA has released about Mertz. It says that "on the morning of 22 November," Mertz "was in Fort Worth" at the same time as JFK; then Mertz "was in Dallas in the afternoon" later that same day.[26] While recently in Louisiana and Texas, Mertz had been using the name of "Jean Souetre," his old associate who was now a fugitive because of the 1962 attempt to shoot French president Charles de Gaulle in his limousine. The real Souetre was in Europe at the time, but Mertz's deception was sure to create consternation at—and cover-ups by—the CIA and FBI after the JFK hit. But Mertz frequently used aliases and cover identities in his work, and he would switch to another one after JFK's assassination. Doing so would ensure not only that he would be able to leave Dallas after JFK's murder, but also that he would be escorted to safety by the U.S. government.

As Marcello sat in the New Orleans courtroom, his men were in position and all of them knew their roles. Each was doing the same type of thing he had done successfully before. Only a dozen people appear to have had knowing roles in JFK's assassination and as with Marcello's heroin network, portions of the operation were compartmentalized, with people being told only what they needed to know. Now, everything was finally ready.

Chapter Nine

The activities of Oswald and others at the Texas School Book Depository have been the subject of tremendous debate for decades. As we'll document, witnesses who tended to support the initial lone-assassin conclusion were encouraged, and their stories often evolved over time to bolster it even more. Witnesses whose observations didn't support a lone-assassin conclusion were sometimes ignored, pressed to change their testimony, or threatened, or their remarks were altered in official reports. Entire books have been written about the hours surrounding JFK's murder, so the following is not intended as a complete list of accounts. But we have tried to exclude information that has been discredited, and to include details from early witnesses that some official reports often downplayed or ignored. This information tends to form a coherent scenario that helps to explain why Bobby Kennedy, Richard Helms, Lyndon Johnson, and J. Edgar Hoover took the actions they did after JFK's death.

The official version of events adopted quickly after JFK's murder says that Oswald—having decided to kill JFK—went to visit his wife Thursday night, November 21. The next morning, Oswald carried a large, suspicious package that contained his mail order rifle as he rode to work with a neighbor, who was also a coworker. Then, at lunchtime, Oswald was supposedly alone on the sixth floor of the warehouselike building, where he carefully arranged a "sniper's nest" of book boxes and waited to kill JFK for still-unknown reasons. Then, after having a perfectly clear shot as JFK's motorcade approached, with JFK looming ever larger in his sights, Oswald didn't fire. Even as JFK's motorcade slowed to a crawl to make a hard left turn below his window—when it would have been like shooting fish in a barrel—Oswald still didn't fire. Only as JFK's motorcade picked up speed, traveling away from the building and becoming partially obscured by trees on the hill leading up to the "grassy knoll," did Oswald supposedly start to fire. In approximately six seconds, this man, who was a poor shot when he left the Marines and who had no recent practice, completed a shooting feat scarcely matched—or, as some experts say, never matched—by the world's top sharpshooters.[1]

This story, which became the official version within less than twenty-four hours after JFK's death, has been shown to be problematic for many years, because of overlooked or ignored information in the government's own reports. As noted earlier, the man who drove Oswald to work (and his sister) said Oswald's wrapped package was too long for a disassembled Mannlicher-Carcano rifle, based on the way Oswald held it cupped in his hand and under his armpit. Oswald had ordered the old, unreliable weapon through the mail months earlier, using an alias, even though more reliable weapons at the same price were easily available in Dallas (with no ID required), and would have left no paper trail linking him to the weapon. When FBI officials later tried to test-fire the rifle, they found the scope so misaligned that it had to be redrilled and remounted before it could be fired with any accuracy—a fact that made Oswald's supposed marksmanship all the more remarkable (some would say impossible). The rifle also tended to jam frequently; when later a Discovery Channel show had a marksman test-fire a Mannlicher that one of the country's top gunsmiths had reconditioned (a service Oswald's rifle was never accorded), it still jammed a quarter of the time.[2] These are just a few of the many problems with the official scenario that experts have uncovered over the years, which raise new questions about what really happened that day at 12:30 PM (Central) when shots rang out in Dealey Plaza.

Carolyn Arnold was the "secretary to the vice president of the Book Depository," and on November 22, at 12:15 PM, she clearly saw Lee Harvey Oswald in "the lunchroom on the second floor." Oswald sometimes went up to the second-floor lunchroom to use the soft-drink vending machine, since there were none on the first floor. Arnold told investigative journalist Anthony Summers that Oswald "was alone as usual and appeared to be having lunch."[3] Another Depository employee would tell the Dallas police that "during the lunch breaks, Oswald usually made several phone calls, which were usually short in length."[4] Whom did he call? Aside from Marina, the FBI–Warren Commission's version of Oswald says he had no friends he would have called in Dallas, or anywhere else, for that matter. It's clear from their later testimony that Oswald was not calling his mother or brothers. It's conceivable that Oswald's "several phone calls" were brief, perhaps coded, messages regarding his intelligence work.

Just twenty-five minutes before Carolyn Arnold saw Oswald in the second-floor lunchroom, his supervisor had seen Oswald "near the telephone on the first floor." It's possible that Oswald made or received calls that day that would have required him to be away from other employees as Kennedy's motorcade neared Dealey Plaza. Meanwhile, on the sixth floor, Book Depository employee Bonnie Rae Williams ate his lunch on the sixth floor "at least until 12:15 PM, perhaps till 12:20 PM." When he left, he didn't see anyone else on the sixth floor.[5]

Arnold Rowland stood in Dealey Plaza with his wife, awaiting the arrival of the President's motorcade. Within minutes of Bonnie Rae Williams' leaving the sixth floor, Rowland looked up at the Book Depository to see a "man back from the window—he was standing and holding a rifle," a high-powered weapon with a scope. Rowland pointed out the gunman to his wife, saying he must be a Secret Service agent. This gunman was at the far left end of the Book Depository, away from the far right end that would later be called the sniper's nest. In the sniper's nest window, Rowland saw a man with a dark complexion.[6]

Also in Dealey Plaza was Carolyn Walther. By the time she glanced up at the Book Depository, in the area of the sniper's nest she saw two men, one with a gun. "I saw this man in a window, and he had a gun in his hands, pointed downwards. The man evidently was in a kneeling position, because his forearms were resting on the windowsill. There was another man standing beside him, but I only saw a portion of his body because he was standing." She thought, "Well, they probably have guards possibly in all the buildings," so she "didn't say anything" to anyone at the time. She observed that "the man behind the partly opened window had a dark brown suit, and the other man had a whitish-looking shirt or jacket, dressed more like a workman that did manual labor. It was the man with the gun that wore white." She also noticed that one of the men had a "darker complexion, perhaps a Mexican."[7]

Ruby Henderson was also one of the spectators in Dealey Plaza, and just after 12:24 PM (Central), she looked up at the windows of the highest floor of the Book Depository, in which people were visible. As she later told the FBI, she saw two men, one wearing a white shirt and one a dark shirt. The man "in the white shirt had dark hair and was possibly a Mexican, but could have been a Negro as he appeared to be dark-complexioned." She couldn't see the other man very well, but said both "were standing back from the window and . . . working" on something, even as they were "looking out the window in anticipation of the motorcade."[8] In light of Walther's and Henderson's accounts, it should be noted that Oswald was wearing what was described as a "reddish" shirt that day at the Depository.[9]

Meanwhile, Anthony Summers writes that on "the sixth floor of the Dallas County Jail," an inmate named John Powell was "in custody on minor charges." However, he had "an ideal vantage point for observation of the [sniper's nest]." Powell "and his cellmates watched two men with a gun in the window . . . 'fooling with the scope' [on a rifle]." Powell said that "one of the men appeared to have darker skin."[10]

Just down the street from the Depository was the area known as the "grassy knoll," topped by a picket fence, behind which was a parking lot usually used by Dallas deputies (it usually required a key to enter and leave). Behind the parking lot were a rail yard and a small tower. Inside the tower, Lee Bowers had noticed unusual activity behind the picket fence. First, he had seen a dirty 1959 Oldsmobile station wagon driven by a middle-aged white male enter the parking lot just before noon. As the vehicle drove slowly around the lot, he noticed it had out-of-state plates and a GOLDWATER FOR '64 bumper sticker, but the car soon left. As Bowers stated later that day to police, "at about 12:15 another car came into the area with a white man about 25 to 35 years old driving. This car was a 1957 Ford, black, 2-door with Texas license. This man appeared to have a mike or telephone in the car. Just a few minutes after this car left at 12:20 PM, another car pulled in. This car was a 1961 Chevrolet Impala . . . white, and dirty up to the windows," as if it had driven a long way. "This car also had a GOLDWATER FOR '64 sticker [and] was driven by a white male about 25 to 35 years old with long blond hair. . . . He left the area about 12:25 PM."[11]

Two minutes later, a young soldier named Gordon Arnold was walking behind the picket fence, in the parking lot, when he was confronted by a man "who showed me a badge and said he was with the Secret Service, and that he didn't want anybody up there."[12] However, there were no Secret Service agents stationed there, or anywhere else in Dealey Plaza. They were all either in the motorcade or at the Trade Mart, site of JFK's upcoming speech.

Just before JFK's motorcade arrived, Bowers, in the railroad tower, saw two men behind the picket fence. Summers quotes his description: "One was 'middle-aged' and 'fairly heavy-set,' wearing a white shirt and dark trousers. The other was 'mid-twenties in either a plaid shirt or plaid coat. . . . These men were the only strangers in the area. The others were workers that I knew.'"[13] Bowers later told the Warren Commission that "they were standing within 10 or 15 feet of each other" and were looking at the approach of JFK's motorcade, "following the caravan as it came down" toward the grassy knoll.[14]

As JFK's motorcade entered Dealey Plaza, the huge throngs that had packed downtown Dallas became smaller. Riding in the back seat of the limo with Jackie, President Kennedy must have felt very pleased that a city with such a conservative reputation had turned out in such numbers. John Connally was riding in the limo with his wife, in the seat ahead of JFK and Jackie, and he later said there had been "a quarter of a million people on the parade route." JFK had stopped the motorcade twice—once to shake hands with a little girl holding a sign that said: PRESIDENT KENNEDY . . . WILL YOU SHAKE HANDS WITH ME? and another time to speak with a nun and her group of schoolchildren.[15]

William Greer, the driver of JFK's limo, later said that when they turned toward the book depository, "he felt relieved. He felt they were in the clear, the crowds were thinning, and while he didn't relax, he did begin to feel relieved." He then made the turn onto Elm, in front of the Depository.[16]

In the limo, Nellie Connally had been delighted by the crowds, and she told JFK, "Mr. Kennedy, you can't say Dallas doesn't love you." JFK replied with his last words: "That is very obvious."[17]

In, and on the running boards of, the limo directly behind JFK's were eight Secret Service agents and two of JFK's closest aides, Dave Powers and Kenneth O'Donnell. Powers and O'Donnell are certain the first shot came from the right front of their limo, from the grassy knoll. Powers felt they were "riding into an ambush," so it was quite logical that JFK's limo driver, Greer, slowed down. Secret Service Agent Lem Johns, two cars behind Powers, is also certain the first shot came from the grassy knoll.[18] As the famous Zapruder film shows, JFK emerges from behind a sign, clutching his throat. The wound, just below his Adam's apple, will be described as a small entrance wound by one of the first doctors to see it.[19]

John Connally, hearing the first shot, turns to look at JFK, as Connally clutches his Stetson hat in his right hand. Moments later, Connally himself is hit in the back by a bullet that smashes his fifth right rib, exits his chest, shatters his right wrist, and buries itself in his left thigh. Dave

Powers will later stress to us that "the same bullet that hit JFK did *NOT* hit John Connally," something Connally and his wife will always say as well.[20] According to Connally, "because of the 'rapidity' of the shots, 'the thought immediately passed through my mind that there were two or three people involved, or more, in this.'"[21]

Secret Service Agent Glenn Bennett, riding with Powers and O'Donnell, sees "a nick in the back of President Kennedy's coat, below the shoulder. He thought the President had been hit in the back."[22] Agent Bennett is correct, and JFK's coat and shirt will be found to have bullet holes in them almost six inches below the top of the collar.[23] A shot is also fired that completely misses JFK and his limo; it strikes a curb and kicks up a piece of concrete that hits bystander James Teague.[24]

Finally, Powers and O'Donnell see the horrible, fatal head shot that shatters JFK's skull. Both are certain it came from the grassy knoll, as is Secret Service Agent Paul Landis, who is in the limo with them. Landis says he "saw the President's head split open and pieces of flesh and blood flying through the air. My reaction at this time was that the shot came from somewhere toward the front . . . along the right-hand side of the road."[25]

Motorcycle patrolman Bobby Hargis, riding behind and slightly to the left of JFK's limo, was splattered with JFK's blood and brain tissue. A piece of JFK's skull, from the back of his head, was thrown onto the median lawn to the left of Patrolman Hargis. Both the blood splatter on Hargis and the skull fragment indicate JFK's fatal head shot came from JFK's right front, from the grassy knoll.[26] From his vantage point in the railroad tower, Bowers said that "when the shots were fired at the President, in the vicinity of where the two men I have described were, there was a flash of light . . . or smoke."[27] In the motorcade, Jackie tried to crawl back to retrieve a piece of JFK's brain or skull on the trunk of the limo, before being pushed back in by Secret Service Agent Clint Hill, who had sprinted from Powers's limo to aid her. JFK's driver finally picked up speed and began rushing toward Parkland Hospital.

Chapter Ten

The immediate aftermath of JFK's murder, from the time the shots rang out in Dealey Plaza until Oswald's arrest one hour and twenty minutes later, is one of the most intensely analyzed time spans in recent history. Hundreds of authors have written about it, government committees have examined and reenacted the sequence of events, and thousands of documents about it are among the four million–plus pages of declassified JFK files at the National Archives. The following is not intended to be a definitive account. Instead, it focuses on credible evidence, most obtained by government investigators, that was overlooked, ignored, or suppressed in the rush to solve JFK's murder in a way that would avoid a confrontation with the Soviets and not cost the lives of Commander Almeida, his allies, and family—or cost certain officials their jobs or political futures.

Even as the motorcade's lead car picked up speed to leave Dealey Plaza, heading under the railroad bridge of the triple underpass toward the Stemmons freeway and Parkland Hospital, several of its passengers focused on the grassy knoll and the rail yards behind its picket fence and concrete terraces. Secret Service Agent Forrest Sorrels, in charge of the Dallas office, said that he "looked towards the top of the terrace to my right, as the sound of the shots seemed to come from that direction."[1] Dallas Police Chief Curry, driving the lead car, radioed to "get a man on top of that triple underpass and see what happened up there." Sheriff Bill Decker, sitting beside Sorrels, sent the order to "move all available men out of my office [and] into the railroad yard to try to determine what happened in there."[2]

Patrolman Hargis, covered in JFK's blood, parked his motorcycle and headed up the grassy knoll.[3] Dallas Deputy Sheriff Harold Elkins said he "immediately ran to the area from which it sounded like the shots had been fired. This is an area between the railroads and the Texas School Book Depository," where the knoll is.[4] Dallas Deputy Harry Weatherford "heard a loud report, which . . . sounded as if it came from the railroad yard." After hearing two more shots, he began "running towards the railroad yards where the sound seemed to come from."[5]

Just after the shooting, off-duty Dallas policeman Tom Tilson was driving near the knoll. Anthony Summers writes that Officer Tilson "saw a man 'slipping and sliding' down the railway embankment from behind the knoll." The man was "38-40 years, 5' 8" . . . dark hair, dark clothing," and resembled Jack Ruby (whom Tilson knew). The man "had a car parked there, a black car. He threw something in the back seat and went around the front hurriedly and got in the car and took off." Tilson attempted to follow the car, but lost it. Shortly after, a car with a stolen Georgia license plate was reported speeding through downtown Dallas.[6] A witness on the roof of the Terminal Annex Building, J. C. Price, told the sheriff's office he saw a man running through the rail yard "after the volley of shots. This man had a white dress shirt, no tie, and khaki-colored trousers. His hair appeared to be long and dark and his agility running [meant he] could be about twenty-five years of age. He had something in his hand [that] may have been a head piece" or "a gun."[7] Deputy Seymour Weitzman ran to the knoll after hearing the shots. A railroad worker there told the Deputy he "thought he saw somebody throw something through a bush," and pointed out an area of the fence "where there was a bunch of shrubbery" as the place the shots had come from.[8]

Several law enforcement personnel saw someone behind the picket fence claiming to be a Secret Service man, even though no real Secret Service agents were stationed there. Dallas Police Officer Joe Smith ran to the knoll after hearing a woman scream, "They're shooting the President from the bushes!" Once Officer Smith was behind the fence, he noticed "the lingering smell of gunpowder." Smith noticed a man near one of the cars, and, as he later testified to the Warren Commission, Smith pulled his pistol on him. The man then "showed me that he was a Secret Service agent."[9] Smith later explained that the credentials "satisfied me and the deputy sheriff," who had joined him. The deputy was Seymour Weitzman, who confirmed in his Warren Commission testimony that he had met the fake Secret Service agent.[10] (As explained in the Special Addendum, Deputy Weitzman later identified Bernard Barker as the fake agent on the knoll.) Officer Smith later explained his regret at allowing the phony agent to leave, because—instead of looking like a typically clean-cut, suit-and-tie Secret Service agent—this man "had on a sports shirt and sports pants. But he had dirty fingernails . . .

and hands that looked like an auto mechanic's hands." Smith explains that "we were so pressed for time," looking into the cars, that "we just overlooked the thing. I should have checked the man closer."[11]

Three other witnesses—Jean Hill, Malcolm Summers, and soldier Gordon Arnold—also saw what they thought were Secret Service agents on the knoll.[12] Dallas Police Sergeant D. V. Harkness talked to two men behind the Book Depository who said they were Secret Service agents.[13] Yet the Secret Service has repeatedly confirmed there were no authentic Secret Service agents stationed in, or even near, Dealey Plaza.[14] As for the cars in the parking lot behind the knoll fence, their trunks were never searched. And railroad workers who ran to that area, where they thought the shots came from, noticed "footprints in the mud around the fence, and there were footprints on the wooden two-by-four railing on the fence." Two workers noticed muddy footprints "on a car bumper there, as if someone had stood up there, looking over the fence" at JFK's motorcade.[15]

Films and photos of that day confirm that most people ran toward the grassy knoll, not the Book Depository. NBC Radio reporter Robert MacNeil (later of PBS's *MacNeil/Lehrer Report*) was in Dealey Plaza, and wrote that "a crowd, including reporters, converged on the grassy knoll, believing it to be the direction from which the shots that struck the President were fired." MacNeil "saw several people running up the grassy hill beside the road. I thought they were chasing whoever had done the shooting and I ran after them."[16]

Anthony Summers noted that "a dozen people were actually on the grassy knoll when the President was shot, and almost all of them believed some of the gunfire came from behind them, high up on the knoll itself." Many were never called by the Warren Commission. These witnesses included four women who worked at the *Dallas Morning News;* one of them talked about "a horrible, ear-shattering noise coming from behind us and a little to the right," from behind the picket fence.[17]

Abraham Zapruder, filming the motorcade as he stood on a concrete step on the knoll, testified that the shots "came from back of me." On the knoll steps, not far from Zapruder, Emmett Hudson said, "The shots that I heard definitely came from behind and above me." Photos and films show a couple—the Newmans—and their two children on the knoll all on the ground because, as Mr. Newman said later, "I thought the [first] shot had come from the garden directly behind me," and "it seemed that we were in the direct path of fire."[18]

Others in Dealey Plaza heard shots from the knoll as well. Jean Hill was one of the closest witnesses to JFK when the shooting started. From where she stood, Hill was looking at the knoll from the other side of the street as her friend Mary Moorman took what would become a famous Polaroid photo of JFK. Hill said, "I frankly thought they were coming from the knoll . . . people shooting from the knoll."[19] Summers found that "sixteen people, in or outside the Book Depository, indicated some shooting came from the knoll. They included the Depository manager, the superintendent, and two company vice presidents."[20]

Six witnesses, including three in the motorcade, said they smelled gunpowder around the knoll. They include Senator Ralph Yarborough, Congressman Ray Roberts, the Dallas mayor's wife, and two police officers.[21] Seven witnesses on the railroad bridge of the triple underpass said they saw something that appeared to be smoke in the area of the grassy knoll.[22]

It appears that those on or near the knoll tended to hear at least some shots from there, while others farther away reported one or more shots from the vicinity of the Book Depository. But even the number of shots witnesses reported—two, three, four, even five or more shots—varied widely. Several witnesses near the knoll said they heard only two shots, perhaps indicating the number fired from there.[23] In an interesting parallel, investigator Josiah Thompson found that, "with no exceptions, all those witnesses who were deep inside the Depository (either at work or in hallways) report hearing fewer than three shots"—either just one shot or two.[24]

Over the years, different investigators have created many charts, trying to make the case for where most witnesses said the shots originated, but this tactic is problematic for several reasons: Witnesses sometimes changed or hedged their initial statements after "only three shots from the Book Depository" became (in less than twenty-four hours) the official story; others say authorities changed their statements to reflect that official version; and others, like JFK aides David Powers and Kenneth O'Donnell, say they were pressured to change their story about shots from the knoll "for the good of the country."

Our point is simply that there were many credible reports from the start, including from officials and law enforcement, that some shots came from the knoll. As events unfolded and suspicion finally fell on the Book Depository, this evidence became a problem for officials in Dallas and Washington. More than one shooter would mean a much more complicated case, with unknown suspects still at large, and no real leads.

Once a Book Depository suspect emerged who had seeming ties to both Russia and Cuba, there were dangerous Cold War implications as well, just a year after the tense standoff at the Missile Crisis. This accounts for the fact that, within hours of the shooting, authorities began to ignore or suppress evidence indicating a wider, more complicated case, even as troubling reports of just such complexities rose through channels to authorities in Washington. Such reports created concern at the highest levels, especially among those who knew, or were just finding out, about the JFK-Almeida coup and invasion plans. Because no official could know where leads pointing toward more than one shooter might go, both local and national law enforcement seemingly wanted to declare "case closed" before the investigation really begun.

Even as crowds swarmed the area of the grassy knoll, a few people were paying attention to the Book Depository. A man named Howard Brennan, whose statements to authorities would be very inconsistent, later became the star witness in making the case against Oswald. Though he initially appeared to have gone toward the knoll after the shots, he later claimed to have seen Oswald fire a shot from the Depository. As Anthony Summers notes, Brennan couldn't identify Oswald in a lineup on the night of November 22, even though a month later he said he could, and then, three weeks after that, said he wasn't sure. Finally, Brennan told the Warren Commission he was sure he had seen Oswald in the Depository window, even though Brennan's vision was questionable. Also, the initial lookout for a suspect, apparently based on Brennan's description of the man in the window, was for a man older and heavier than Oswald.[25] (As noted earlier, the lookout issued in Tampa on November 18 fit Oswald much more closely.)

Still, two other witnesses say they saw "a rifle being pulled back from a window" in the Book Depository. One was *Dallas Times Herald* photographer Bob Jackson, who would later win a Pulitzer Prize for his famous photo of Ruby shooting Oswald. The other was WFAA-TV cameraman Malcolm Couch, who was riding with Jackson in the press car, five cars behind JFK. Couch said he saw about a foot of rifle being pulled back into the window. (A shooter wouldn't need to extend the rifle out of the window at all in order to fire at JFK—unless he wanted to call attention to his position.) Neither Couch nor Jackson immediately contacted police about what they had seen, which even a Warren Commission counsel considered unusual, especially for a newsman. Also, when Couch tried to tell the Warren Commission that TV reporter Wes

Wise had seen Jack Ruby near the Book Depository "moments after the shooting," the Commission dismissed the statement as hearsay. (Wise, who later became mayor of Dallas, was never called to testify.)[26]

In contrast to the rush toward the grassy knoll, only one policeman, Marion Baker, headed into the Book Depository. His attention had been drawn to it because he saw a flock of pigeons fly from the roof, and he wanted to check it out for a possible sniper. As author Michael Benson summarized, based on testimony and documents, Baker first encountered Book Depository manager Roy Truly, who told the officer to follow him. (Truly initially thought the shooting had come from the area of the knoll.) However, both elevators were stuck on upper floors, so Baker took the stairs to the second floor, with Truly following. On the second floor, "between seventy-five and ninety seconds after the assassination," Officer Baker glimpsed Oswald "standing near a Coke machine in the building's lunchroom." Baker ordered Oswald to "come here." Baker then asked Truly if he knew the man; Truly said he did, and that Oswald worked for him. Baker and Truly then continued up the stairs. About thirty seconds later, "Oswald was seen drinking a Coke by Mrs. Elizabeth Reid," who worked on that floor. Officer Baker's initial report stated that Oswald had been "drinking a Coke," though those words were later scratched out. Both "Reid and [Officer] Baker reported that Oswald was not breathing hard." It's unlikely Oswald could have raced down all seventy-two steps of the eight flights of stairs from the far corner of the sixth floor, and gotten a Coke, in the seventy-five to ninety seconds since the last shot, especially since the "sniper's nest" was on the opposite corner of the building from the stairs.[27]

Meanwhile, at the back entrance to the Book Depository, James Worrell saw a man in a dark sports jacket and lighter-colored pants emerge and then run down Houston Street. Worrell later told police and the Warren Commission that the man was in his early thirties, 5' 8" to 5' 10," with dark hair and of average weight. Another witness saw a man he'd noticed earlier, in an upper floor of the Depository, "walking very fast" south on Houston Street. The man eventually got into a Rambler station wagon driven by a black man. Two other witnesses reported seeing someone enter a similar car from the front of the Depository, and one witness—a Dallas deputy—said it was driven by a black man.[28]

It's easy to document the time Oswald left the Depository, because he met newsman Robert MacNeil on his way out of the building. After checking out the area behind the grassy knoll, MacNeil tried to find a phone so he could file his report. He wrote that he "ran . . . into the first building I came to that looked as though it might have a phone . . . the Texas School Book Depository. As I ran up the steps and through the door, a young man in shirt sleeves was coming out. In great agitation I asked him where there was a phone. He pointed inside to an open space, where another man was talking on a phone. . . . "[29] Within about a minute, MacNeil found an open phone, and, as a recent article by Don Thomas noted, "MacNeil called NBC headquarters in New York, and the tape of the call has MacNeil saying that 'police chased an unknown gunman up a grassy hill." According to phone billing records, MacNeil made the call at 12:34, meaning Oswald left the building at 12:33 (the shooting occurred at 12:30, and the encounter with Officer Baker happened between 12:31 and 12:32, all Central time).[30]

That's the last definite timing for Oswald until his capture at the Texas Theater—every minute of every action in between has been the subject of intense debate for decades. But it's important to note one reason why Oswald might have left the first-floor lunchroom, where he had eaten with the minority employees, to go up to the second floor to get a Coke. Unlike the all-white, main lunchroom on the second floor, the minority lunchroom had no soft-drink machines. Oswald's association with minority employees is why suspicion fell so heavily and quickly on him, even though several other employees also left the building soon after the shooting. At the Book Depository, Oswald's eating lunch with minorities helped to typecast him as a brazen leftist. Hence, once a rifle was found on the sixth floor of the Depository, and it was noted that Oswald was one of the people who had left the Depository, he became a suspect even before the events with Officer Tippit.

After JFK's assassination, police detained at least twelve men but all would be released. No records were kept about some of them, like a young man wearing a black leather jacket and gloves who was arrested at the Dal-Tex building, across from the Depository (some witnesses said they thought shots came from the Dal-Tex, which did have a clear view of the motorcade). Another man taken into custody at the Dal-Tex was released, even though Congressional investigators later found he was a convicted criminal from Los Angeles who once had an associate who "knew Jack Ruby well"; the same associate "was an acquaintance of both Carlos Marcello and Santo Trafficante." The man arrested at the Dal-Tex even used an office in New Orleans that was on the same floor as an office used by David Ferrie.[31]

At 12:38 PM, Parkland Hospital admitted JFK and Governor Connally. As with so much in the assassination, thousands of pages have been written about the desperate, fruitless attempt to save JFK's life. In order to understand the later reactions of Bobby Kennedy and other officials, it's important to note the nature of the wounds observed by the doctors and nurses at Parkland. A general medical principle demonstrates the significance of what the medical personnel saw at Parkland and what was later seen at JFK's autopsy at Bethesda Naval Hospital. Usually, a bullet makes a small entrance wound and a larger exit wound. In the case of test bullets fired from rifles like the Mannlicher-Carcano found in the Book Depository, the exit wound was usually at least 50 percent larger, sometimes more.

Doctors at Parkland noticed two wounds, a small wound of entrance just below JFK's Adam's apple, and his massive head wound. If JFK had been shot from the front, the largest part of the head wound could have been expected to be located toward the rear of his head. According to Summers, "seventeen of the medical staff who observed the President in Dallas have described the massive defect as having been more at the back of the head than at the side." Dr. Robert McClellan, a surgeon who worked on JFK, approved a drawing of the wound in the 1960s that showed a huge wound just behind JFK's right ear.[32]

In a video oral history, Dr. Charles Carrico later described and demonstrated what he saw: "With the president laying on his back, I could see the whole wound in his head." He said that the head wound "was about right here, as I recall [placing hand on right side of head, toward the back], and it was about as big as I'm showing it with my hand [opening hand about grapefruit size]. You know, a big chunk of bone and scalp missing."[33]

As for the small throat wound, a neat tracheotomy incision was made over it, to insert a breathing tube. Michael Benson wrote that "every medical professional who saw JFK in Parkland described the throat wound as an entrance wound," including Dr. Perry, who made the tracheotomy incision.[34] The Dallas doctors were so busy trying to revive JFK that they apparently didn't notice the small bullet wound in his back.

Also present at Parkland was the President's personal physician, Admiral George Burkley, the only doctor present at both Parkland and the autopsy. However, Burkley's car had not headed to Parkland immediately, so he arrived fifteen minutes after JFK's body. He did not witness the throat wound before it was obscured by the small tracheotomy incision, though it's unclear if one of the other doctors told him about it.

As the Dallas doctors worked desperately on JFK, several other things happened at Parkland that would impact the case. As Hugh Sidey (later the editor of *Time* magazine) observed, Secret Service agents cleaned and wiped down JFK's limousine. While cleaning removed the gruesome remains of the shooting, it also eliminated crucial blood-spatter evidence that could have helped to determine the source of the shots.

Lyndon Johnson was in a frantic state when he arrived at Parkland; though he was uninjured, onlookers feared he was having a heart attack. His condition was not surprising, considering that one or more of the shots that hit JFK and Connally had traveled over LBJ's head as he sat just two cars behind JFK. Anyone who still thinks that LBJ was behind JFK's assassination should consider the foolishness of someone's planning an attack in which he himself could have been killed, if the gunmen had been jostled or attacked while firing.

Also at Parkland was Jack Ruby, who spoke with noted journalist Seth Kantor at the hospital at around 1:28 PM. Another witness saw Ruby at Parkland as well, though Ruby later denied being there. About fifteen minutes later, the so-called "magic bullet" was found on a hospital stretcher by Parkland senior engineer Darrell Tomlinson. The almost pristine bullet was found on a stretcher Tomlinson was sure had not been used for either JFK or Connally. However, the stretcher had fresh bloodstains on it (from a bleeding child, less than an hour earlier), and was next to another stretcher, so someone might have thought those stretchers had been used for JFK and Connally.

Experts have noted numerous problems with the "magic bullet," from differing accounts of its description to chain-of-evidence and identification problems. Just recently, for example, the FBI agent who supposedly took the bullet back to Parkland to show witnesses has denied that he ever had the bullet in his possession, according to Dr. Gary Aguilar and Josiah Thompson.[35]

After JFK was pronounced dead, a struggle ensued over his body. Around 2:00 PM, JFK aides Dave Powers and Kenneth O'Donnell, along with the Secret Service, tried to take JFK's body back to Air Force One. But the Dallas medical examiner, Dr. Earl Rose, and Justice of the Peace Theron Ward refused, saying the autopsy had to be done there, according to Texas state law. The impasse quickly escalated. As Anthony Summers concisely described, after Judge Ward said JFK's murder "was just another homicide as far as I'm concerned," an angry O'Donnell said, "Go screw yourself." Then "the Secret Service agents put the doctor and the judge up against the wall at gunpoint and swept out of the hospital with the President's body."[36]

About five minutes after JFK's assassination, Dallas Police Officer J. D. Tippit sped away from a Texaco service station toward the Oak Cliff neighborhood, where Oswald lived in a rooming house and Ruby lived in an apartment. Three witnesses interviewed by former FBI agent William Turner say that just before Tippit left the station, he had been looking at traffic in an area that was only a few blocks from the triple underpass and Dealey Plaza.[37] Twenty-five minutes later, at 1:00 PM, Dallas police headquarters tried to radio Officer Tippit, but he didn't answer.[38]

Also at 1:00 PM, just half an hour after JFK's shooting, Lee Oswald was seen running into his rooming house by its housekeeper, Earlene Roberts. Two minutes later, she saw a Dallas police car pull up slowly, park in front of the house, and sound its horn twice. Then it slowly pulled away. Roberts later said she saw two men in the car, but William Turner has pointed out that Tippit's uniform jacket was hanging in the car's window, so she might have thought that was a second officer. She later recalled the car's number as 107—Tippit's car number was 10.

About two minutes after the patrol car pulled away, Mrs. Roberts saw Oswald leave the house. She last saw him waiting at a bus stop. Around 1:06, Officer Tippit went into an Oak Cliff record store to use the phone, as he often did. However, this time, two witnesses found by veteran Dallas reporter Earl Golz say that Tippit was in a big hurry, telling customers to get out of the way so he could use the phone. Tippit dialed a number, let it ring for about a minute, and then hurried out of the store.[39] A 1:08 PM call from police headquarters to Tippit went unanswered—and that's the last thing most experts can agree on until Oswald's arrest at the Texas Theater, at 1:48 PM (Central).

As described by researcher Michael T. Griffith, the official Warren Commission story says that after Tippit saw a man who matched the description of JFK's assailant that had been broadcast over police radio, Tippit "drove up slowly behind the man, pulled up alongside him, and then asked him to come over to the driver's window for what was described as having the appearance of a 'friendly chat.'"[40] Oswald, the ex-serviceman turned killer, then pulled out his pistol, shot the officer, and fled.

For decades, numerous historians, experts, and government investigators have noted important evidence, witnesses, and timing that don't support the Warren Commission's version. The actions of Tippit and Oswald, the evidence, and the witnesses have been debated in books, articles, and websites, and have been the subjects of one entire book. We can't cover even a fraction of that here, but we can point out important problems with the official story and highlight some of the facts that weren't available to the Warren Commission.

Noted journalist Henry Hurt pointed out that "one of the oddest assumptions of the Warren Commission was that Officer Tippit stopped Oswald because he was able to identify him as the man described in the police broadcasts that started about 12:45 PM. . . . The description itself was of a 'white male, approximately thirty, slender build, height five feet, ten inches, weight 165 pounds,' believed to be armed with a .30-caliber rifle. This description missed Oswald by six years and about fifteen pounds." Michael Griffith points out that "the police description could have fit a good quarter to a third of the male population of Dallas." And yet "none of the witnesses who saw Tippit's assailant just before Tippit stopped him said the man was walking unusually fast or in any way acting strange or suspicious."[41]

We've noted that the married Officer Tippit had been having an affair, and that the woman had gotten pregnant. Complicating the situation, just over a month earlier, the woman had reconciled with her former husband. She was employed at the restaurant where Tippit worked part-time, which was owned by one of Jack Ruby's best friends. The bottom line is that Tippit could have been subject to blackmail or manipulation to keep his personal situation from being exposed, which in those times probably would have cost him his job.[42]

As *Vanity Fair* reported, one of Johnny Rosselli's associates, John Martino—who also confessed his role in JFK's murder—said that Oswald "was to meet his contact at the Texas Theater" in his Oak Cliff neighborhood.[43] As we soon document, Oswald's actions in the theater were more like those of a man trying to meet a contact than those of someone who was trying to hide after shooting a policeman. As noted earlier, it's odd that the official Oswald-Tippit story mirrored a scene in a then-forgotten B movie Johnny Rosselli had helped to produce in 1948, *He Walked by Night*. The murderous ex-serviceman in that film even kept one of his weapons hidden away, wrapped in a blanket, just like Oswald had.

Rosselli's associate Jack Ruby lived just a few blocks from the Tippit murder scene. America's foremost investigative journalist in the 1960s and '70s, Jack Anderson, later obtained information from Rosselli on several occasions. Anderson wrote that Oswald had to be killed because, according to "Johnny Rosselli, . . . underworld conspirators feared he would crack and disclose information that might lead to them . . . so Jack Ruby was ordered to eliminate Oswald."[44] Before Ruby had to do the job himself, he apparently tried to persuade one of his many police contacts to do it. In fact, the night of Tippit's death, Ruby met with one of Tippit's police-officer friends for more than an hour. According to Hurt, this officer had been "working privately as a guard at an Oak Cliff home when Tippit was murdered nearby."[45] Perhaps when Tippit was killed before he was able to silence Oswald, Ruby tried to get another officer to eliminate Oswald.

As for Tippit's slaying, the evidence and witnesses are so inconsistent that there are at least four possible explanations for his murder: 1. Oswald shot Tippit, just as the Warren Commission said he did, in the manner depicted in Rosselli's movie; 2. Someone with Oswald might have shot Tippit; 3. While Tippit was talking to Oswald, the officer might have been shot by someone nearby who was unconnected with Oswald; 4. Oswald might have already been in the Texas Theater at the time of Tippit's death, and Tippit might have been shot by an unknown person.

The physical evidence is troublesome, to say the least. As Griffith noted, "the offending firearm was initially—and firmly—identified as an automatic pistol, based on a shell that was found at the scene."[46] Oswald was carrying a revolver when he was arrested. Shells were found at the murder scene, and numerous experts have pointed out how odd it would have been for someone who had just killed a policeman to take the time to open his revolver and remove the shells, conveniently leaving incriminating evidence at the scene of the crime. Casting further doubt on the Warren Commission version, three of the shells were Winchester and one was a Remington. But the bullets removed from Tippit's body were two Winchesters and two Remingtons—clearly, something didn't match up.[47] The chain of evidence regarding the shells, and three of the bullets, has also been called into question.

As documented in numerous books over the past forty years (we've listed a few of the best in this endnote[48]), witnesses were inconsistent in their description of the shooter, the number of people involved, and how they fled. For example, witness Acquilla Clemmons said the killer was "kind of short" and "kind of heavy," and was with another man. (The day Oswald was shot, a Dallas policeman told Clemmons that she might get hurt if she told anyone what she saw.) Even the Dallas assistant district attorney at the time said later that "Oswald's movements did not add up then and they do not add up now. . . . Certainly, he may have had accomplices."[49] While most witnesses said the shooter fled on foot, another saw him speed away in a gray car.

Witnesses also said different things at different times, possibly because they were intimidated or threatened. Witness Warren Reynolds first told the FBI he couldn't identify Oswald as Tippit's killer. Two days later, Reynolds was shot in the head. (A suspect was arrested, but released after one of Ruby's former strippers gave him an alibi. According to the FBI, two days later she "hung herself.")[50] After Reynolds recovered, he decided that he could identify Oswald as the killer after all. The witness closest to the Tippit slaying, Domingo Benevides, said he couldn't identify Tippit's killer as Oswald, even after seeing pictures of Oswald on TV and in newspapers. That left as the Warren Commission's star witness a woman so inconsistent (she claimed to have talked to Tippit after he was dead) that she was later described by one of the Commission attorneys who dealt with her as "an utter screwball."[51]

The Texas Theater was not the first place police converged on in an attempt to apprehend Tippit's killer. Instead, police radio calls went out, saying, "A witness reports that he [Tippit's killer] was last seen in the Abundant Life Temple. . . . We are fixing to go in and shake it down." Another patrolman said, "Send me another squad [car] to check out this church basement." The Abundant Life Temple is a huge building, three stories tall (counting a large daylight basement), just one block from the Tippit slaying site. But even as several policemen were getting ready to enter the Temple, another call came in, erroneously reporting that Tippit's slayer was at a library several blocks away. All of the police left, and the Temple was never searched.[52] Later, it was alleged that the Temple had been the site of Cuban exile activity.

The Warren Commission's version of how and when Oswald got into the Texas Theater has been challenged by numerous authors and witnesses. But Oswald's documented actions inside the theater seem inconsistent with those of someone fleeing a murder scene. According to theater patron Jack Davis, Oswald sat next to him for a few minutes before Oswald got up and moved to sit next to another person for several minutes. Then Oswald stood up and walked to the lobby, as if looking for someone, before eventually returning to the auditorium. At the time, Oswald had half of a torn box top in his pocket, and was perhaps looking for someone with the other half. (Dollar bills torn in half were later found in his rooming house, indicating Oswald had used that technique before. The CIA file of Cuban exile leader Manuel Artime confirms that the CIA also used this technique for Artime during AMWORLD in 1963.)[53]

Oddly, once the police arrived, they mirrored Oswald's unusual behavior by going to two people before going to Oswald. It was almost as if one or more of the policemen wanted to give Oswald a chance to flee; if Oswald had been shot trying to run from the theater, things would have been much simpler for Jack Ruby and his Mafia bosses. Oswald was arrested after a scuffle, though Henry Hurt and other journalists have noted "conflicting testimony among arresting officers about just what happened during the arrest," and "most of the dozen or so patrons . . . were never canvassed and questioned in any inclusive fashion by the FBI or the Warren Commission."[54] Mob associate John Martino later told his wife that when police "went to the theater and got Oswald, they blew it . . . there was a Cuban in there. They let him come out . . . they let the guy go, the other trigger."[55]

Questions have also arisen about the fake ID card Oswald had in his wallet, with the name of "Alek Hidell," the same alias he had apparently used to obtain his mail-order weapons nine months earlier. The rifle had been found on the sixth floor of the Book Depository just thirty minutes before Oswald's arrest, and the alias on the fake ID would let the FBI quickly trace the guns to Oswald's post office box. As with many other details in the case, writers have debated whether the rifle the FBI found really was Oswald's, since each factory that produced the Mannlicher-Carcano used its own set of serial numbers, meaning several rifles could have the same serial number.[56]

Later, at the home where Marina was staying and where Oswald had spent the night, Marina told police that Oswald had kept his mail-order rifle wrapped in a blanket. She had last seen the wrapped rifle two weeks earlier, but at the time of her interview, the blanket was empty. When Oswald's rooming house was searched, police found a miniature Minox spy camera, three other cameras, and several rolls of exposed Minox film.[57] (A November 27, 1963, memo shows that David Morales's Miami CIA station used Minox cameras.)[58]

One theater patron placed Jack Ruby at the theater at the time of Oswald's arrest, though Ruby's known movements would have made the timing for that appearance very tight.[59] But shortly after that, Jack Ruby was seen at his bank with a large sum of money. According to journalist Seth Kantor, "Bill Cox, the loan officer at [Ruby's bank], vividly remembers Ruby standing in line at a teller's cage on the afternoon of November 22, after President Kennedy was slain. 'Jack was standing there crying, and he had about $7,000 in cash on him the day of the assassination. . . . I warned him that he'd be knocked in the head one day, carrying all that cash on him.'"[60]

Perhaps Ruby was crying because he knew the risk he was going to have to take himself, now that Tippit was dead. Bank records show that Ruby didn't deposit the money; he may have gotten it from, or put it into, a safety deposit box, or switched out the bills to make it harder to trace. Seven thousand dollars was the amount Ruby had received from a Hoffa associate in Chicago just before JFK's planned motorcade in that city, the one canceled because of an assassination threat. Two other Marcello associates involved in JFK's assassination, David Ferrie and Joseph Milteer, had received similar amounts. Perhaps $7,000 was either the down payment, or the expense money, for helping to kill the President.

PART TWO

Chapter Eleven

The initial reactions of Bobby Kennedy and Richard Helms to the unfolding events in Dallas would impact not just the immediate investigation, but also lives, political careers, and US foreign policy for years to come. The decisions they and other key officials made—including the information they decided to release or withhold—would both generate and impede government investigations for the next four decades. Bobby's goal, beginning that afternoon and continuing until his death, was to find out what had happened to his brother without revealing information that could trigger World War III or cost the lives of Almeida and his allies. Helms shared some of Bobby's concerns, but he also decided to protect his own reputation and that of the CIA, while maintaining a capability to assassinate Castro. The actions of Bobby and Helms on and after November 22, 1963, are why "well over a million CIA records" related to JFK's assassination remain classified today, more than sixteen years after Congress unanimously passed a law requiring their release.[1] Among these files are more than one thousand identified in a lawsuit seeking the release of documents about a CIA-backed Cuban exile group linked to Oswald, a lawsuit that the CIA has been fighting for years.

Fifteen minutes after the gunfire in Dealey Plaza, Bobby received a call from J. Edgar Hoover informing him that his brother had been shot in Dallas. Bobby was still eating lunch by the pool behind his Hickory Hill mansion with his wife, Ethel, New York's US Attorney Robert Morgenthau, and another guest when he got the news. Hoover, in a flat tone, told Bobby that he thought it was serious and that he'd call back when he found out more. According to William Manchester, after Bobby hung up he turned toward his guests: His "jaw sagged ... it seemed that every muscle was contorted with horror. 'Jack's been shot,' he said, gagging, and clapped his hand over his face."[2]

At that point, neither Hoover nor Bobby knew that the President was essentially dead, so Bobby's first thought was to fly to Dallas, an idea he soon abandoned. He made a flurry of calls to people like Secretary of Defense McNamara (who was getting his information from General Carroll's DIA), as well as to Parkland Hospital in Dallas and to CIA Director John McCone, who was only five minutes away at the Agency's headquarters in Langley, Virginia.[3]

McCone was dining in a small private room beside his office when his assistant came in with the news that JFK had been shot. Eating with McCone were CIA Executive Director Lyman Kirkpatrick, Richard Helms, and three other CIA officials. Helms's own account of that day in his autobiography is self-serving and incomplete at best, glossing over most of his activity. He perpetuates the myth that there was nationwide TV coverage of JFK's Dallas trip, writing that "one of McCone's aides who had been following the President's trip to Texas on live TV in a nearby office brought the news of the shooting in Dallas." It's important to stress that there was no live TV coverage of JFK's motorcade in Dallas, let alone in the rest of the country, which is why so many facts about the shooting are still in dispute. Presidential motorcades were simply too common in those days to be of national interest. Only one radio station in Dallas provided live coverage of the motorcade, but the reporter's commentary wasn't recorded; thus, a potential audio record of the event was lost. The clip of a Dallas radio announcer that's often used in documentaries, saying, "There has been a shooting in the motorcade," was a later re-creation by the original announcer. However, Helms's version avoids potentially troubling questions about how and when CIA headquarters was first informed of JFK's shooting.[4]

Though Helms's usually cool outward demeanor probably didn't show it, he must have been shocked upon hearing the news, and for reasons beyond those of the others present. The stunning news had additional resonance for Helms even aside from the JFK-Almeida coup plan, which was known to at least several in the room. Of all those present, only Helms knew about a host of unauthorized Castro assassination operations he was running, including at least one going on at that very time, in Paris. In that room, Helms alone knew that, in the words of a later CIA Inspector General's report, "at the very moment President Kennedy was shot, a CIA officer was meeting with a Cuban agent in Paris and giving him an assassination device for use against Castro."[5] As the news from Dallas continued to arrive, Helms decided to withhold information about the Paris meeting—and his other plots—from CIA Director McCone and the others in the room.

McCone's lunch meeting had included a discussion of Cuba, reviewing the morning briefing that he, Kirkpatrick, and Helms had given the President's Foreign Intelligence Advisory Board (PFIAB) at the White House. Those PFIAB notes have finally been declassified, and they include McCone's saying, "The CIA has had a very active operation against Cuba," and that the "CIA has vastly improved its agent net[work]s and internal agent sources among legal travelers." However, an entire paragraph apparently relating to Cuba is still censored. Though it's unlikely McCone would have revealed a closely held secret like the JFK-Almeida coup plan to an advisory board, the presence of Helms and Kirkpatrick at the meeting means it's possible they might have at least laid the groundwork for what could happen with Cuba in ten days.[6]

It's not known if McCone's CIA lunch meeting included discussion of the JFK-Almeida coup plan, though the secure setting and the high-level CIA attendees make that much more likely. Kirkpatrick had met that morning with Harry Williams and the other CIA personnel, such as E. Howard Hunt, for the final review of the plans before Harry went into Cuba. This was the last, most critical meeting, with the plan only a few days away from its fail-safe point. Kirkpatrick had raised no major objections in the meeting with Harry, and would no doubt want to give his assessment to McCone and Helms, who had overseen the CIA's role in the coup plan up to that point. After their discussion and McCone's final approval, Kirkpatrick was set to return to the meeting with Harry in Washington to give him the go-ahead to proceed.

However, events in Dallas disrupted those plans. McCone first checked with the Agency Crisis Watch Committee, whose files about that day have never been made public or shown to Congressional investigators.[7] McCone then called Bobby Kennedy, who asked that McCone come to his Hickory Hill estate, so McCone left the meeting and headed there. Kirkpatrick apparently returned to resume the meeting with Harry, Hunt, and the other CIA officials. Helms's actions the rest of the day remain sparsely documented, though in recent years enough information he first withheld from the public and Congress has emerged to make it possible to reconstruct the most important decisions he made, and the actions he did and didn't take.

Helms allowed McCone to leave without telling him about any of the unauthorized Cuba operations Helms was still running in 1963. When Helms made this decision, the die was cast regarding what he could reveal, or allow the CIA to reveal, not just for the coming weeks but for decades. Helms must have felt tremendous pressure—because of the events in Dallas and all that he was withholding—as he realized that his career would be finished if his unauthorized schemes came to light.

Many of Richard Helms's actions after JFK's murder make sense in light of Helms's position and psychological makeup, as outlined by his biographer, Thomas Powers, and other journalists. Helms was usually cool under pressure, able to manage a crisis, and not prone to be emotional under stress, as his subordinate Desmond FitzGerald was. On the other hand, Helms was also detached (some might say cold-blooded), at times sarcastic, and quick to divert blame or responsibility. Above all, Helms was able to keep secrets.[8]

Though Helms was from an affluent family, he was not independently wealthy to the degree that FitzGerald or his former boss Allen Dulles was. Helms had recently turned fifty; his whole career, personal life, and future depended on the CIA—and on avoiding any type of controversy like the Bay of Pigs disaster that had cost Dulles and other associates their careers.

It's helpful to think of all the unauthorized Cuban operations Helms was running not as separate programs, but as parts of one overall unauthorized operation, since they often crossed over and usually involved the same agents and supervisors. Helms and his immediate subordinate for Cuba, Desmond FitzGerald, apparently relied on a small, trusted clique of CIA men to deal with the unauthorized portions of the operation. They included David Morales, David Atlee Phillips, E. Howard Hunt, and and his assistant, Bernard Barker.

The unauthorized operations Helms was running on November 22, 1963, unknown to McCone or Bobby, included the ongoing CIA-Mafia plots to assassinate Fidel with Johnny Rosselli and David Morales, as well as the assassination part of the Rolando Cubela (AMLASH) operation. (McCone and Bobby knew of Cubela only as someone who could provide intelligence on more powerful Cuban officials.) Helms had also authorized continuing payments to European assassin recruiter QJWIN (CIA files show his regular monthly salary was paid on November 22, 1963), and there are indications that French assets were also part of the CIA's own assassination plot against Fidel.[9] In addition, Helms knew that David Atlee Phillips was using CIA officer George Joannides to support a small Cuban exile group called the DRE, which had interacted with Oswald during his flurry of publicity in New Orleans in August. The DRE wasn't part of the JFK-Almeida coup plan, and one CIA memo says it was "mob controlled."[10] Evidence shows that Phillips was also helping to support Alpha 66, the violent anti-Castro group the Kennedys had excluded from the JFK-Almeida coup plan. Finally, newly released CIA files show that after Trafficante enforcer Herminio Diaz expressed an interest in assassinating Fidel in September 1963, Helms's CIA chief in Miami, Ted Shackley, expressed an interest in Diaz. In the same memo, Shackley also showed an interest in Rolando Masferrer, Trafficante and Martino's notorious associate.

While all those details may seem complicated, they start to make sense when viewed simply as parts of one large, unauthorized Castro assassination plan. If Helms wanted his own plan as a backup—in case something happened to Almeida, or to supplement the President's plan, or if JFK got cold feet—he would need someone to assassinate Castro. Helms would also need someone to take the blame, a fall guy whom the American public and much of the world would logically accept. Rosselli's marksmen could handle the shooting. They could easily be assisted or supplemented by those who could freely travel in and out of Cuba, like Diaz, QJWIN, or any French assets helping the CIA. Cubela's beach house near Fidel's at Varadero Beach gave the assassins a place to operate when Fidel made his regular weekend visit in an open jeep. As for who could take the blame, some of the US assets going into Cuba had Russian connections that could be used to make it seem as if they had killed Fidel on behalf of the Soviets. Among those assets were Lee Oswald and Gilberto Policarpo Lopez.

Helms also knew information about Oswald that was being withheld, at least in part, from McCone and Bobby. Dr. John Newman, a noted historian and major with twenty years' experience in Army Intelligence, documented that when Oswald made his odd trip to Mexico City in late September 1963, two tracks of information about him had been sent to CIA headquarters. The most secret track clearly showed Oswald to be of operational interest to Desmond FitzGerald's anti-Castro activities. In the days, months, and years to come, Helms would maintain to the public and Congress that the CIA "had no real knowledge of [Oswald's] presence" in Mexico City until after JFK's assassination. Even today, this is still the CIA's official stance. However, Dr. Newman uncovered CIA files and statements proving that assertion false. The CIA's Mexico City chief at the time, Win Scott, later wrote that "Oswald 'was a person of great interest' to the CIA during his visit to Mexico City between Sept. 27 and Oct. 2, 1963." Clearly, Oswald was part of an extremely sensitive anti-Castro operation that FitzGerald and his supervisor, Helms, were running. In charge of surveillance of the Cuban and Soviet embassies that Oswald visited in Mexico City was David Atlee Phillips, who, in addition to his duties in Mexico, worked directly for FitzGerald and on AMWORLD with David Morales and Manuel Artime.[11]

The AMWORLD connections show why Helms thought he could get away with running his own plot to assassinate Fidel without telling McCone or Bobby. The watchword for AMWORLD and the other aspects of the JFK-Almeida coup plan was "deniability," a theme that would come up repeatedly in the Congressional investigations of the 1970s. Just as JFK and Bobby wanted their coup with Almeida to look like an internal "palace coup," with no apparent ties to the US government, Helms had worked to establish a cover for many aspects of his own, unauthorized Castro assassination plotting.

For example, Helms could always claim that Cubela decided on his own to assassinate Fidel, instead of just providing intelligence on other Cuban officials, as McCone and Bobby thought he was doing. It's ironic, but years later we learned that Helms had not needed to keep the assassination part of the Cubela operation secret from Bobby: As a close Kennedy aide told us, Bobby would not have minded Helms's assassination operation with Cubela as long as it had not interfered with the JFK-Almeida coup plan.[12] Still, Helms did withhold it, not only from Bobby, but also from JFK and McCone. On November 22, even as Helms pondered his options in the wake of JFK's shooting, Cubela was still meeting with his CIA case officer in Paris. In addition to trying to get Cubela to take the CIA's special poison pen, the case officer was also offering to place a cache of weapons and explosives in Cuba for Cubela's use. The Paris meeting only ended when they received word that JFK had been shot.[13]

In the hours after JFK's murder, Helms no doubt reviewed the rationalizations and justifications for his unauthorized programs, in case they surfaced or he needed to convince other CIA officials to keep them hidden from McCone. As for the CIA-Mafia plots, Helms knew that if the Mafia ever appeared to have murdered Castro, few tears would be shed in Washington. Then, too, Rosselli was operating within the structure of secret CIA exile training camps in Florida that JFK had approved, and Bobby had visited (without realizing Rosselli's involvement).[14]

Helms knew that even if Alpha 66 seemed to be involved in Castro's death, the group's role would be hard to link to Helms, since the CIA's contact with the group had been through very deep cover for more than a year. As a 1963 memo from CIA Miami Chief Ted Shackley to FitzGerald stated, regarding an Alpha 66 offshoot, "current efforts to support them are being made through other channels." By "other channels,"

Shackley could mean CIA support funneled through what appeared to be a private citizen, or via military-intelligence channels. As the memo said, for the CIA to keep supporting the group while maintaining "the desired degree of plausibility in our denial of support," it was important that even the exile group itself "be unable to track . . . [its] support to [the CIA]."[15] If even the group didn't know about or couldn't prove CIA backing, Helms could be fairly confident he could keep his unauthorized support of Alpha 66 from being exposed. Even if it were, Helms could rationalize that JFK and Bobby had pressed the CIA to include Eloy Menoyo, of the SNFE, in the JFK-Almeida coup plan, and it wasn't Helms's fault that Menoyo was partners with Alpha 66's Antonio Veciana. In the same way, if someone like former Russian defector Oswald were blamed for assassinating Fidel, Oswald had been a Marine, and was (as Helms would later testify to Congress) the responsibility of Defense Department agencies like Naval Intelligence and the DIA.

In retrospect, it's easy to see why Helms had thought he could get away with running his own unauthorized Castro assassination operation without telling JFK, McCone, or Bobby. With the impending date for the coup rapidly approaching, everything would come to a head in less than two weeks anyway, and if the Kennedys' coup plan failed, Helms could even be rewarded for already having a backup plan in place. However, after JFK's shooting, the backup plan for which Helms might have once been praised now suddenly looked incredibly suspicious. The unauthorized plans would have to remain hidden from McCone and Bobby if Helms were to have any future in the CIA.

After McCone had left for Bobby's estate, Helms received the news that JFK was dead. Along with learning that JFK had been shot in an open car, by one or more snipers, Helms's anxiety must have increased to new heights. The way in which JFK was shot mirrors later AMWORLD memos, and a passage in David Atlee Phillips's autobiographical novel outline about the CIA's plan to shoot Fidel at Varadero beach.[16] Phillips later wrote that JFK was shot using "precisely the plan we had devised against Castro [which involved using] a sniper's rifle from an upper floor window of a building on the route where Castro often drove in an open jeep."[17]

Now, just ten days before Almeida's coup, Helms had to wonder if some aspect of his plans had been turned on JFK. Clearly, a massive intelligence failure had occurred somewhere along the line, and Helms, as essentially the head of CIA operations, was responsible. But had Castro somehow retaliated against JFK, because of the coup plan or one of Helms's unauthorized operations? Or had someone involved in Helms's own plots turned their sights on JFK instead of Fidel?

When Oswald surfaced as the prime suspect in JFK's slaying, Helms must have been crushed. What had been a horrible situation just got even worse since JFK's murder was now tied to someone with CIA connections. The words of one of Helms's top subordinates can help us gauge Helms's reaction to hearing that Oswald was the prime suspect in JFK's murder. John Whitten was Helms's covert operations chief for all of Mexico and Central America. In a detailed report that he wrote soon after JFK's death and that was kept classified for thirty years, Whitten said that after "word of the shooting of President Kennedy reached the [CIA] offices . . . when the name of Lee Oswald was heard, the effect was electric." [18]

And that was just the effect for those who knew only that the CIA had been monitoring Oswald's activities, especially in Mexico City. There is no evidence that Whitten and the others had been fully informed about the JFK-Almeida coup plan, and (based on Whitten's later testimony) they knew nothing about Helms's unauthorized operations, which had crossed paths with Oswald in recent months. For Helms, who knew that Oswald was also linked to his unauthorized Castro assassination operations, the effect was surely more than just "electric"; it was probably devastating.

To Helms, it would have appeared that someone linked to, or even part of, his unauthorized operations had murdered the President. That meant those operations would have to remain unexposed to the public, the press, Congress, McCone, and even the new president, or else the CIA itself would come under suspicion. On a more personal level, the ambitious Helms, who would later become CIA Director under two presidents, not only would be washed up professionally, but could even become a target of suspicion himself. The same would apply to the people Helms had working on his unauthorized operations, like FitzGerald, Morales, Phillips, and Hunt—they would have to keep quiet as well if they wanted to continue their careers and avoid suspicion, or even prosecution.

However, there was one small potential silver lining for Helms, one that meant he would not have to bear all the responsibility for an Oswald cover-up. Oswald was a "former" Marine, and thus the responsibility of Marine and Naval Intelligence, and General Carroll's DIA. It wasn't unusual at that time for military men to be assigned to the CIA, or vice versa, and the evidence shows that Oswald's intelligence ties encompassed both groups. Naval Intelligence (along with Marine Intelligence, G-2) had been responsible for the "tight surveillance" on Oswald since his return from Russia, while Oswald's operational activities appear to have involved the CIA. That meant officials at Naval Intelligence would have to cover up as well, as we'll soon show. In addition, the FBI had aided with the "tight surveillance" in places where Naval Intelligence had few resources, meaning that top FBI officials like J. Edgar Hoover would also have to conceal information about Oswald.

John McCone returned from his long meeting with Bobby Kennedy at around 5:00 PM and met with Helms, Kirkpatrick, and two other CIA officials. But Helms still didn't tell McCone about the unauthorized operations, then or later. It's interesting to speculate how history might have been different if Helms had come clean to McCone about the Mafia, Cubela, Alpha 66, QJWIN, the DRE, and everything. The course of the investigation of JFK's assassination might have taken a dramatic turn toward dozens of other leads. On the other hand, relations between the CIA and the FBI were always strained, and it's possible that McCone and even LBJ were so overwhelmed by the scope of the possible leads and what they might expose—and so worried about the reaction of the press, the public, and the world—that they might still have withheld information from law enforcement.

Declassified files show two reasons in particular why Helms didn't tell McCone about the unauthorized operations. Just three months earlier, Helms had sparred with the CIA's new Inspector General (IG), John Earman, over telling McCone about the CIA's longtime behavior-control program known as MKULTRA, which was later exposed during Senate hearings in the 1970s. Like the CIA-Mafia plots to assassinate Castro, QJWIN, and Cubela, Richard Helms had inherited the MKULTRA program, but he had continued it. (In 1963 it focused on using LSD, then legal, to influence behavior, though it also tested more tried-and-true methods, like prostitutes.) After an IG staffer had stumbled across the program earlier in 1963, Helms had tried to avoid telling McCone about it. But IG Earman persisted, and he presented a detailed report to McCone that concluded the program was "unethical," likely illegal, and dangerous. IG Earman also said the program was shrouded in such secrecy that it was hard to make a complete report.[19] That also would have been true of Helms's unauthorized Castro assassination operations in 1963.

That Helms would have continued the dangerous MKULTRA program without telling McCone says a lot about Helms's arrogance and tendency to take dangerous risks (or rather, to have others do so) as if he were accountable to no one. If Helms had chosen to tell McCone on November 22 about his unauthorized Castro assassination operations, it would have looked like a pattern of deceit on Helms's part, something a hard-nosed businessman like McCone would not tolerate.

Even worse for Helms, he hadn't just withheld information about his unauthorized operations from McCone (as well as JFK and Bobby)—he had actually lied, three months earlier, to his Director about one of those operations. In August 1963, an article had appeared in the *Chicago Sun-Times* about Chicago mob boss Sam Giancana, then under "lockstep" surveillance by the FBI. (Unlike the tight surveillance on Oswald, which was entirely covert, the lockstep surveillance was designed to be very visible to both the subject and the general public in order to intimidate Giancana's criminal associates in restaurants, on golf courses, etc.) The article had mentioned Giancana's work for the CIA regarding Cuba. Though the article didn't mention the CIA-Mafia Castro assassination plots, and limited its focus to Giancana's help in getting intelligence on Cuba, the article got McCone's attention. After McCone demanded an explanation from Helms, Helms told him that the plots had stopped in May 1962, even though Helms had secretly continued them.[20] For Helms to tell McCone now that he'd been lying about that, and withholding even more, was simply not an option if Helms wanted to keep his job.

However, while Helms was withholding crucial information about the unauthorized operations from McCone on November 22, others were probably withholding important information from Helms about those same operations. After all, Cuba was not Helms's only focus; he essentially headed covert operations for the whole CIA. It was the height of the Cold War, which meant he had to focus not only on Russia but also on its communist bloc in Eastern Europe, including the often-tense divided city of Berlin. Helms also had to contend with China, Central and South America, and the Middle East (where a CIA-backed 1963 coup in Iraq had brought to power the party Saddam Hussein would later control). Moreover, Helms had the growing problem of Vietnam to deal with. Helms's point man for Cuban operations, Desmond FitzGerald, had been in charge of Cuba for less than a year, having formerly been responsible for Far East operations. Between Helms's divided attentions and FitzGerald's newness on the job (he didn't even speak Spanish, and had no previous experience in Cuban affairs), many details could have slipped by Helms.

To use business terminology, if we consider McCone a chairman of the board, then Helms would be the CEO for covert operations, with FitzGerald and Shackley as corporate vice presidents, and people like Morales, Phillips, and Hunt in middle management. Below them was another layer of more hands-on managers, like Joannides (who ran the DRE for Phillips) and Morales operative Tony Sforza. And below those managers were the people doing the real dirty work, from shooters being trained to kill Castro to agents like Barker, and others slipping in and out of Cuba (or going in overtly, with the right cover) to assets like Banister and Ferrie helping with CIA-backed Cuban exiles. As in many large corporations, those lower down the ladder can get away with things the CEO doesn't know about.

For example, the CIA had been targeting the Fair Play for Cuba Committee for years, and Phillips took part in those activities. It's probable that Phillips and even Helms were aware of the operation under which Oswald joined the Fair Play for Cuba Committee in early 1963. But they might not have known that Oswald had ordered a Mannlicher-Carcano rifle around the same time, using an alias—something he may have done on the orders of someone like Banister or Ferrie.

It's probably not a coincidence that the three mob bosses involved in the CIA-Mafia Castro assassination plots—Rosselli, Trafficante, and (by his own admission) Marcello—were the same three Mafia bosses who later confessed their roles in JFK's assassination. Their involvement, and that of the men who worked for them, gave them a way to appear to be working to kill Castro, while they actually planned to kill JFK. Manuel Artime is a good example: AMWORLD memos show that one way "to cover CIA support [for Artime]" was to use the "Mafia." Another CIA memo says that at the very same time, "Artime was also [being] used by the Mafia in the Castro operation." Hence, Morales's help to Artime for AMWORLD and the CIA-Mafia plots to eliminate Castro provided cover for Morales's work with Rosselli to assassinate JFK.[21]

Still another example was in Mexico City, where someone impersonating Oswald made phone calls to the Russian and Cuban embassies, calls that would come back to haunt Helms and the CIA just after JFK's death. Rosselli's associate Richard Cain was in the perfect position to have set up the phone calls, and he would have known the CIA would secretly record them. Cain had previously bugged a communist embassy in Mexico City for the CIA, and he had ties to the corrupt Mexican police force (the DFS) that helped monitor the calls for the CIA.

The bottom line is that the three Mafia bosses were in a perfect position to compromise not just the JFK-Almeida coup plan, but also Helms's unauthorized operations—and to use parts of them to murder JFK in a way that would force Helms and other officials to cover up important information.

The question of whether Richard Helms was knowingly involved in some aspect of JFK's assassination has dogged him since the time of Watergate and the subsequent public revelation of the CIA-Mafia plots to kill Fidel. After all, Helms was the highest-ranking CIA authority at the crossroads of the authorized and unauthorized Castro assassination operations, including those with mobsters like Santo Trafficante, who began to be linked to JFK's assassination in the press by the late 1970s. As the rest of the story unfolds, the significant weight of the evidence argues against Helms's knowing participation in JFK's murder. As a Washington insider, Helms would have known that JFK's murder would at least severely delay, and probably end, any chance for a coup with Almeida. Helms knew that LBJ hated Bobby, who had kept LBJ out of the loop about the coup plan, and that there would be little chance LBJ would continue Bobby's pet project. Also, as of November 22, Helms had everything he wanted from the Kennedys. They had bought his story of Cuban weapons being found in Venezuela, reducing any chance of a breakthrough with the secret peace initiatives of William Attwood and Jean Daniel.

Memos from Bobby's Cuban subcommittees show that Helms was not in favor of the peace feelers to Castro, but he didn't have to kill JFK to ensure that those efforts failed. These memos say that if there had been a next step in the Attwood peace process, it would have involved Attwood's going to Varadero Beach to meet with Fidel. That would have given Helms a prime opportunity to have Castro assassinated. In the spring of 1963, Helms had already shown a willingness to endanger JFK's emissaries in his quest to assassinate Fidel. These included not only the exploding seashell he considered, which would have also killed JFK's representative James Donovan, but also in his actual attempt to assassinate Fidel with guns while Donovan was in Cuba, negotiating the release of several prisoners (including four CIA men) with Castro.

It's difficult to envision a scenario in which it would have made sense for Helms to have JFK assassinated when the JFK-Almeida coup plan, and even his own unauthorized Castro operation, were so close to fruition.[22] The same is true for Desmond FitzGerald, who was closer to, and sometimes socialized with, Bobby Kennedy. Additionally, neither man had been involved with the Bay of Pigs, so they lacked bitterness over that failure as a motivating factor. The same can't be said, however, for David Morales and others like Bernard Barker. Additionally, one can ask whether Helms trusted his protégé Hunt too much, or if Hunt trusted his aide Barker too much. Did Helms come to suspect any of them in the JFK assassination? Helms cleaned house of only a few, like Tony Varona and Barker; others continued working with him until the time of Watergate and even beyond. Certain Cuban exiles, and others in positions to know about Helms's unauthorized operations, continued to receive CIA support for years, sometimes decades, despite their committing other crimes, and even spectacular terrorist acts, against innocent civilians. Was this part of the price Helms and others paid to keep their secrets from being exposed? (Many of Helms's secrets, from AMWORLD and the JFK-Almeida coup plan to Artime's involvement in the CIA-Mafia plots were not publicly exposed until after Helms's death in October 2002.) The rest of the book will help to answer those questions.

Even without being involved in JFK's assassination, Helms still had plenty of motivation for cover-ups afterward: to protect the viability of the coup plan with Almeida, to prevent a crisis with Russia over Cuba, and to block the exposure of his own unauthorized operations. These cover-ups would help him rise in power, which allowed him to cover up even further. As his biographer said, "when Helms said secret, he meant *secret*—in the words of Lyman Kirkpatrick, secret from inception to eternity."[23] Starting on the afternoon of November 22, Helms would spend the rest of his life making sure that was the case.

Helms's early background as a journalist helped him continue to expand his influence in media circles, which in turn allowed him to influence their coverage of him and the CIA. His biographer writes that "Helms's reputation for integrity extended to the Washington press corps. . . . He lunched frequently with reporters like the Alsop brothers, James Reston, and C. L. Sulzberger of the *New York Times,* Hugh Sidey of *Time,* [and] Chalmers Roberts of the *Washington Post.*" They saw him as "well wired in the Washington establishment and one who could be trusted not to mislead."[24] In light of the many CIA operations, authorized and unauthorized, that we now know Helms kept secret, as well as his later conviction for lying to Congress, the media's view of Helms as truthful seems incredible, to say the least. Yet it goes a long way toward explaining how he was able to keep so much about JFK's assassination so secret for so long.

The change in presidents also allowed Helms to keep his secrets from being exposed. LBJ would learn much about the anti-Castro operations in the coming days. But Helms wouldn't inform him of some aspects until 1967, and other parts Helms would never reveal to either LBJ or his successor in the White House, Richard Nixon.

Other CIA officials involved in the unauthorized operations heard the news in different ways. Desmond FitzGerald was said to be having lunch with an aide in Georgetown, a short drive from the site where Harry had been meeting with CIA officials until they took a lunch break. The aide said that after FitzGerald got a call about what had happened in Dallas, FitzGerald was "white as a ghost." After FitzGerald told the aide, "The President's been shot," the aide said, "I hope this has nothing to do with the Cubans." [25] Also in Washington, the CIA's Counter-Intelligence Chief, the spectral James Angleton, was also having lunch when he got the news. Angleton probably knew about some of Helms's unauthorized operations, since the safe houses where Artime and other exile leaders working for Bobby and Helms stayed were sometimes bugged, because Counter-Intelligence was supposed to make sure Castro's agents didn't infiltrate exile operations. [26] Angleton was meeting at a restaurant with a colonel in the French Secret Service (the SDECE, the same organization Michel Victor Mertz sometimes worked for). Ironically, the restaurant's owner was linked to the French Connection heroin bust that eventually sent Mertz to prison. [27]

Miami Station Chief Ted Shackley didn't deal with the day of JFK's assassination in his 2005 autobiography, which avoids many sensitive topics. Shackley did write that many months before JFK's death, his operations chief "Dave Morales and I spent many a Miami evening by my swimming pool, discussing the problem" of Bobby Kennedy's pressure to do more about Cuba. [28] Shackley surely knew about the actions of Rosselli with Morales in terms of the unauthorized Castro assassination plot. How much Shackley knew, suspected, or came to learn later regarding Morales's work with Rosselli on the JFK hit may never be uncovered.

A far more objective book about Shackley, by *Nation* writer David Corn, accurately notes that "in the fall of 1963, Shackley had a lot to track. His own officers were planning attacks. Artime's forces were building up, [as was] the CIA-backed JURE of Manolo Ray." [29] We have examined much of the raw cable traffic—at least, those cables that have been released—that went from or to the CIA's huge Miami station in the weeks before and after JFK's assassination. The number of ongoing operatives and operations was staggering at a time when the general public—and, even later, Congressional investigators—had been told that the CIA's Cuban operations had been practically eliminated. Some of the cables are completely coded, some partially, and others are still censored. While few operational cables have been released, CIA informants were often talking about Harry Williams, Bobby Kennedy, Manuel Artime, Manolo Ray, Eloy Menoyo, and Tony Varona, with hints of the impending coup.

Clearly, Shackley had a lot to keep under control on November 22, ranging from AMWORLD to whatever he had been told about the JFK-Almeida coup plan to Helms's unauthorized plots. It's important to keep in mind that even though cables might appear to have been sent from Shackley to CIA Director McCone, they usually went to Helms, who decided which cables to show or tell McCone about. As David Corn later wrote, for Shackley's actions in the immediate aftermath of JFK's murder, "in 1979, the House Select Committee [on Assassinations] judged Shackley harshly. . . . His station, its report declared, ought to have debriefed thoroughly all its sources to determine if there were any links between Oswald and Havana, and it should have swept fully its contacts to see if any anti-Castro partisans possessed knowledge pertaining to the murder of the President." [30] What the Committee didn't realize then was the extent to which Shackley had been at least aware of unauthorized operations, like the use of Rosselli, and operations that were still being withheld from the Committee in 1979, like Phillips's use of Joannides to run the DRE exile group that had contact with Oswald. As detailed in Chapter 64, in 1978 Shackley was still a high-ranking CIA official when Joannides was assigned to be the CIA's liaison with the Committee—and Joannides told the Committee he couldn't locate the CIA man who had run the DRE.

As CIA Director John McCone sped toward Bobby's Virginia estate, he later told author William Manchester he was thinking, "You wonder who could be responsible for a thing like this? Was this the result of bigotry and hatred that was expressed in certain areas of the country, of which Dallas was one? Was this an international plot?" In the CIA's copy of the original transcript of Manchester's interview with McCone, declassified in 1998, McCone admitted that "this was a question that plagued us day and night for a long time." In stark contrast to the lone-assassin story that Hoover presented in private within hours, and to the public by the following morning, McCone said, "I don't recall that I reached an immediate judgement." McCone said that after Oswald surfaced as the prime suspect, "we went to work in depth on this thing to determine whether Oswald had any association [with] or was receiving direction from any external [source]. And there were days there where we didn't know. There were of course conflicting reports."[31]

This situation worsened after Oswald (whom McCone called "the main source of information") was murdered, because "nothing could be proven, nothing could be checked, so people get so convinced themselves that something is a fact that they feel that they must convey them."[32] McCone appears to be addressing the situation in the days and weeks after Dallas, when he received many disturbing reports—which turned out not to be true—linking the Soviets or Fidel to JFK's murder, and McCone apparently didn't consider the possibility that the false information had been planted deliberately.

Of course, McCone didn't know that Helms was withholding a wealth of critical information from him. And when McCone met with Bobby Kennedy at Hickory Hill, he was talking to someone else who'd had much of the same important information withheld from him. Their lack of knowledge prevented both of them from realizing that the individuals originating or pushing some of those "conflicting reports" may have had ulterior motives, designed to deflect attention from themselves or their associates.

When McCone arrived at Bobby's mansion, the Attorney General and his wife "were alone . . . in the library of the second floor." Earlier, Bobby had placed calls to Parkland Hospital in Dallas. Not long after McCone's arrival, Bobby received a call from Secret Service Agent Clint Hill telling him his brother was dead. McCone described Bobby as "being just aghast, as though he had received unbelievable news." But McCone said that Bobby was initially stoic, and though "obviously shaken to an unbelievable degree [he] retained his composure in a most remarkable manner" as he called his brother Edward and family members to deliver the devastating news.[33]

McCone later told Manchester that "the Attorney General and I then went out into his yard and we walked for a long time and talked about a great many things." Manchester interviewed McCone for his book *Death of a President* just months after JFK's death, so it's not surprising that McCone would have been vague about some of the "great many things" he talked about with Bobby. To Manchester, McCone focused on things like whether Bobby should fly to Dallas. Bobby's initial impulse was to head to Dallas and "return with the body and Mrs. Kennedy." McCone says that he "urged that he not do that" because it would take so much time and Bobby "would be out of touch all the time that he was in the air." Bobby agreed, and stayed put while they continued their almost two hour–long talk.

Chapter Twelve

On November 22, 1963, Bobby Kennedy was running on the adrenaline that would sustain him, with only a few exceptions, through that day and much of the next. McCone said that during their talk, Bobby "never cracked—he was steely." McCone adds that their talk "was punctuated by these phone calls that would come in. . . . [Bobby] has a White House phone in the corner of the swimming pool." As more information came in about the events in Dallas, Bobby confronted McCone with a surprising question. As Bobby later told his top Hoffa prosecutor, Walter Sheridan, "At the time, I asked McCone . . . if they [the CIA] had killed my brother, and I asked him in a way that he couldn't lie to me, and [McCone said] they hadn't."[1]

McCone left Bobby's estate less than thirty minutes after Oswald arrived at police headquarters in Dallas, and well before any news flash or FBI report named Oswald as the prime suspect. (Hoover himself would first call Bobby about Oswald thirty-one minutes after McCone left.) That timing makes it almost impossible for Oswald's name to have triggered Bobby's question to McCone. More likely, Bobby asked McCone because both men knew they were only about ten days away from Almeida's coup, which could have involved Fidel Castro being assassinated by snipers as he traveled in an open car. On one hand, it could have been Fidel retaliating in one of the ways Bobby's subcommittee had been discussing for more than two months: with the "assassination of American officials." But the subcommittee had considered that unlikely to happen inside the United States. Bobby apparently agreed with that assessment, because his suspicions on the afternoon of November 22 were not directed at Castro, but instead at someone involved with the JFK-Almeida coup plan who had used part of that plan to kill JFK instead of Castro. It's important to note that at some point after JFK's murder, McCone told Bobby that he "thought there were two people involved in the shooting."[2]

McCone apparently gave Bobby an answer that afternoon that reassured the Attorney General that the CIA *hadn't* killed JFK. But, as we documented earlier, McCone (and Bobby) didn't know about Helms's unauthorized operations with mob bosses like Rosselli, dealings that had allowed several of Bobby's exile leaders to be compromised by the Mafia. While Bobby felt he could "ask McCone in a way that he couldn't lie to me," Bobby couldn't account for what McCone himself didn't know. In light of the impending JFK-Almeida coup operation that both men had been working on for months, Bobby's question was probably framed in a way that addressed the coup plan.

Certainly, Bobby and McCone would have discussed what to do about the coup, and what to tell incoming president Lyndon Johnson.[3] Starting the next day, McCone would meet with LBJ every day, sometimes several times a day, for several weeks.[4] LBJ had been completely excluded from the Cuba planning, as well as from many foreign-policy decisions. While Rusk and McNamara could bring LBJ up to speed on most of the world's hot spots, they didn't know all that McCone did about Cuba. Chairman of the Joint Chiefs of Staff General Maxwell Taylor and Defense Intelligence Head Joseph Carroll would be able to fill LBJ in about the big picture and military side of the coup and invasion, but only McCone knew details about key parts of the operation, such as how the CIA had gotten Almeida's family out, where they were, and the $50,000 payment to Almeida.

Bobby and McCone would undoubtedly have had the CIA check to see if anything unusual had happened to Almeida's family that might indicate the Kennedys had been double-crossed. One of the CIA agents who would have been involved in such activities was E. Howard Hunt, who had helped to provide the CIA assistance Harry had promised Almeida. Apparently, no problems were found because, as we'll soon describe, Bobby was ready to reactivate the coup plan within weeks of his brother's murder. There were others involved in the coup plan to consider as well, such as Cuba's leading journalist, Carlos Franqui. According to CIA files, including a report from Hunt's assistant, Bernard Barker, Harry had helped Franqui leave Cuba and go to Paris with a large sum of money ($200,000–$300,000), possibly with the aid of Manolo Ray. Like Almeida's family, Franqui hadn't overtly defected, and it appeared that he was just visiting Paris. There, Franqui would have been able to favorably write about the coup and influence the world media when it happened.[5]

Based on Bobby's question to McCone, it's clear that the Attorney General was determined to find out who had killed his brother, even as he struggled to deal with his own grief, family, and other government matters. Bobby made at least two phone calls that day that showed where his suspicions lay: Journalist David Talbot writes that one was to "Julius Draznin in Chicago, an expert on union corruption for the National Labor Relations Board. [Bobby] asked Draznin to look into whether there was any Mafia involvement in the killing of his brother. Draznin knew this meant Sam Giancana." Draznin would turn in his report five days later, three days after Ruby had shot Oswald in the basement of Dallas Police headquarters, on live television. Draznin's report" detailed Ruby's labor racketeering activities and his penchant for violence," as well as Ruby's "wide syndicate contacts." As Talbot notes, "later, Kennedy would remark that when he saw Ruby's phone records, 'The list was almost a duplicate of the people I called before the Rackets Committee.'"[6] However, Draznin found nothing definite because Bobby hadn't told him about the plots to kill JFK in Chicago and Tampa, the JFK-Almeida coup plan, or the earlier CIA-Mafia plots with Giancana and Rosselli. Those were simply too sensitive to divulge, even to Bobby's own investigators. This situation would be repeated in several secret investigations Bobby had associates undertake in the coming years: They couldn't investigate what they weren't told about.

From the afternoon of November 22 forward, Bobby would remain trapped by his desire to find out what had happened to his brother without revealing the coup plan and exposing Almeida or his family to harm. He also wanted to preserve Almeida as an asset in place, a willing ally who might be ready to stage a coup at some future time. Historian Thomas Borstelmann compared Commander Almeida to Colin Powell—a good analogy that shows why Bobby, McCone, and the few others who knew Almeida's identity were so careful not to expose it.[7] The odds were overwhelming against the United States ever finding another Cuban official with Almeida's power and prestige who was willing to risk his life to stage a coup, and even willing to put his own family under the watchful eye of the CIA. Almeida was also agreeable to sharing power with Bobby's trusted Cuban exile leaders on a path eventually leading to free elections, something any other dissident Cuban leader might not be willing to do.

Avoiding exposing Almeida also meant continuing to cover up other information, like the Chicago and Tampa assassination attempts. On the afternoon of November 22, that was pretty much Bobby's call to make, and something he may have discussed with McCone, who no doubt knew about the attempts because of their national security implications. One can only imagine how different history would have been if Bobby had been willing to make those attempts, and their similarities to Dallas, public on November 22. But that would have led to questions about why the attempts had been kept secret when they occurred, and to investigations about possible Cuban involvement, which could have exposed the coup plan. With JFK gone, and Bobby having such hostile relationships with both new president Johnson and J. Edgar Hoover, he was in no position to conduct or control any significant covert investigation himself. Other organizations—from the FBI to the Secret Service to local police and prosecutors—would control the handling of evidence, witnesses, and testimony. Killing, or attempting to kill, a president was not a federal crime in 1963, meaning Bobby had no real standing in the matter as Attorney General. Therefore, the Chicago and Tampa attempts were kept secret on November 22 for the same reasons they had been kept secret in the first place; that lid of secrecy would be slammed shut the following day, when word about Tampa started to leak in one small article. Basically, the pattern set by Bobby and McCone that afternoon would continue in the days to come, and would be adopted by other officials as well.

John McCone left Bobby's estate around 3:30 PM (Eastern), twenty minutes before the FBI in Washington would be officially notified of Oswald's arrest.[8] Either just before McCone left, or more likely soon after, Bobby made another phone call that revealed whom Bobby suspected in JFK's assassination. Bobby's instincts would prove quite accurate, and one of the people he spoke with would play a crucial role, almost thirty years later, in helping us vindicate Bobby's initial suspicion.

As we mentioned earlier, Harry Williams had met with several CIA officials—including CIA Executive Director Lyman Kirkpatrick and E. Howard Hunt—on the morning of November 22, 1963, and was supposed to resume their talks after lunch. Pulitzer Prize–winning journalist Haynes Johnson later wrote in the *Washington Post* that it was "the most crucial of a series of secret meetings with top level CIA and governmental people" that Harry had been having in recent months. Haynes wrote that Harry was the Cuban exile leader closest to JFK's administration, and that Harry's work with the Kennedys "had reached an important point."[9] Harry confirmed to us that his friend Haynes Johnson hadn't been told about the JFK-Almeida coup plan, but Haynes was close enough to Bobby and exile leaders like Artime to know that something big was brewing.[10] Haynes would have seen the Kennedys' backing being given to Harry, and the large financial support going to Artime and the Cuban exile troops at Fort Benning.

Harry explained to us that "Bobby told me to be at this meeting," planned as Harry's final high-level Washington meeting before he headed to Cuba for the coup. During the morning session, Harry said he felt that "we were really advancing." Harry was set to go to Miami that night and to Guantanamo the following day; from there he would slip into Castro's Cuba to meet with Almeida. Harry would remain in Cuba to await the coup, which at that point would be only a few days away. Either it would happen on December 1 (as one CIA memo noted) or, as Harry told us, he might move it up by a day, to keep Artime from jumping the gun.[11] There was some flexibility regarding the date, since Fidel could be shot either on the day he drove into Varadero Beach or on the day he left.[12]

According to Harry, one of the topics discussed at the November 22 meeting was looking at "all the ways of eliminating Castro." Seeds of a misunderstanding might have been planted that morning, when Harry told the CIA men that they should "get a professional" to kill Fidel. Harry told them, "I am sure that you guys know more people, a hell of a lot more people that could, you know, could do these things." He also told them that he had "a couple [of people] that could be used" to kill Fidel. But when Harry used the term "professional," he was not referring to a mob hit man, but to an experienced, professional soldier—in this case, Almeida and one of his allies in the Cuban government. In any event, unbeknownst to Harry, the CIA already had that aspect covered, whether Almeida or one of his men personally pulled the trigger or not. For months, the CIA had been training snipers in Florida, like the Cuban exile sharpshooter we described previously. Harry, and probably even Kirkpatrick, did not know that Johnny Rosselli was also part of that training.

How much E. Howard Hunt knew at that point about Rosselli, and Helms's other unauthorized operations, is a matter of some speculation. CIA memos confirm that Hunt's best friend, Artime, had ties to the CIA-Mafia plots with Rosselli, and that "rumors of Mafia support of Artime had long pervaded Artime's organization."[13] Hunt's assistant, CIA Agent Bernard Barker, worked for Trafficante, who had originally been part of the CIA-Mafia plots. Barker also provided a steady stream of reports from Trafficante operative Frank Fiorini, who had been involved in a potential aircraft deal with Artime in Dallas.[14] Hunt knew and sometimes worked with Rosselli's good friend David Morales. When added to the information about Hunt mentioned in Chapter 2, it appears likely that Hunt did know about Rosselli's work on the unauthorized Castro assassination plots.

Whether E. Howard Hunt knew Rosselli had also been conspiring with Carlos Marcello and Santo Trafficante to assassinate JFK is another matter. Harry told us that Bernard Barker was involved in JFK's assassination, while working for Trafficante. But Harry didn't say that Hunt participated—even though Harry considered Hunt "a son of a bitch" and a man of "dubious" character, whom Harry didn't trust. Hunt's varying stories about his whereabouts on November 22 could be due to the secrecy surrounding his meetings that day about the JFK-Almeida coup plan, since it had never been exposed or declassified while Hunt was testifying in court or to Congressional committees. Also, various photos that some researchers thought were of E. Howard Hunt in Dealey Plaza have so far all turned out to be of someone else. Weighing against Hunt's knowing involvement is the fact that he knew the coup was only ten days away: Killing JFK would delay, if not prevent, the assassination of Fidel, whom Hunt hated with a passion. Hunt was extremely ambitious, and it seems counterintuitive for him to have sabotaged a covert plan in which he had a pivotal role, one that would be rewarded if the coup succeeded.

It's possible Hunt was simply used by his associates with mob ties, men who were working for Trafficante and Rosselli. It's also conceivable that Hunt's culpability was at the level of having "guilty knowledge," a term an informant used to describe Hunt's longtime friend Artime to Congressional investigators. However, given the fact that so many of Hunt's associates were working with the Mafia—specifically people, like Trafficante, who had JFK killed—it can't be ruled out that Hunt was knowingly involved, that his hatred of JFK overshadowed any desire the ardently anticommunist Hunt had to see Fidel eliminated. The actions of Hunt and his associates described in future chapters provide additional insights that will help to make his role clearer.

While Harry was at lunch, he learned that JFK had been shot. This must have been a stunning blow for Harry, both on a personal level (since he had gotten to know JFK) and for Harry's crusade to free Cuba. As his meeting with the CIA men resumed, they learned that JFK was dead. Harry said that Hunt and the other agent present both acted cool when they heard the news, unlike the very high-ranking CIA official who was present. That was likely Lyman Kirkpatrick, who had probably just arrived from CIA headquarters. Harry said that the high official "really felt it" and was "upset"—so much so that he got mad at Harry because he felt Harry was acting too calm in response to the news. Harry explained to us that the word of JFK's death really shocked him, but "when things get tough, I get very cool" and he tried to keep calm, just as he had when he was under fire at the Bay of Pigs.

But Kirkpatrick said, "Don't you feel" anything? Don't "you care that President Kennedy was killed?"

Harry looked at him and said, "Look, let's talk about all this." But Kirkpatrick seemed suspicious of Harry after that, and the meeting soon broke up. Perhaps Kirkpatrick had misinterpreted Harry's remark in the morning session about getting professionals to eliminate Fidel, and wondered if Harry or his associates had something to do with JFK's death. In actuality, Kirkpatrick should have been much more suspicious of Hunt and some of his associates.[15] For that matter, when Kirkpatrick met with McCone and Helms at CIA headquarters at 5:00 PM, the former Inspector General would have been suspicious of Helms if he had known the secrets Helms was keeping from him and McCone.

Harry headed back to his room at the Ebbitt Hotel, where the CIA had its Cuban and other Hispanic visitors stay. He had arranged earlier to meet journalist Haynes Johnson there. Haynes didn't know it, but Harry had thought it would be their last meeting before he went to Cuba for the coup. Along with Artime and two other exiles, Harry had been working with Haynes on a book about the Bay of Pigs. It was part of the publicity blitz engineered by Bobby Kennedy mentioned earlier, that would include an NBC News special about the Bay of Pigs, hosted by the leading news anchors of the day, Chet Huntley and David Brinkley. Bobby hoped it would all be timed to show off the former Bay of Pigs leaders who would become part of the new leadership in Cuba after the coup.

Two months earlier, Artime had told one of his CIA case officers about the book, in a memo that has recently been declassified. Artime told CIA officer Henry Hecksher that he believed the book was "being published under the auspices of the Attorney General, who [had] introduced the author" to Artime. At that point, Artime had "received royalties in the total amount of $2,800," and Artime said, "The book is about ready for publication." (Its appearance was apparently delayed after JFK's death.) Artime had been concerned that the book might criticize the CIA, and Hecksher reported Artime's concerns to Desmond FitzGerald.[16]

Before Haynes arrived at the Ebbitt Hotel, Harry had already put in a call to Bobby's office at the Justice Department. Bobby called back shortly after Haynes arrived. Anthony Summers, who investigated the timing of the call for *Vanity Fair*, puts Bobby's call at approximately 4:00 PM (Eastern), fifteen minutes before the first network news reports of Oswald's arrest. It could not have happened even a minute later, because at 4:01 PM, Bobby received a phone call from J. Edgar Hoover alerting him to Oswald's arrest. Based on Hoover's declassified notes, that call must have lasted at least ten or twelve minutes; Bobby then left his estate at 4:15 PM, heading for the Pentagon, to meet with General Maxwell Taylor and Defense Secretary McNamara.[17] Our most recent analysis indicates that Bobby's call to Harry was probably made at least a few minutes prior to 4:00 PM, sometime after McCone left Bobby's at 3:30 PM.

After Bobby had spoken on the phone to Harry for a few moments, Harry mentioned that Haynes Johnson was with him. Bobby asked to speak to Haynes, who writes that "Robert Kennedy was utterly in control of his emotions when he came on the line, and sounded almost studiedly brisk as he said: 'One of your guys did it.'"[18]

It's important to stress that both Haynes Johnson and Harry agree that Bobby said, "One of your guys did it"—killed JFK—to Haynes, not to Harry. Haynes confirmed that to us in 1992, and again in May 2007. Harry said Bobby never voiced any suspicion like that to him on that day or any other; a close Kennedy associate—who knew Bobby, Haynes, and Harry—backed up Harry's statement.[19]

Haynes wrote that he assumed at the time that Bobby had received an early FBI or Secret Service report that "had identified Lee Harvey Oswald as being involved with the anti-Castro group." Haynes may have been correct, but in ways he didn't realize, since he was unaware of the JFK-Almeida coup plan. If Bobby received a report about Oswald prior to Hoover's 4:01 PM call, there is no record of it. Any such report would have had to come from the CIA or the DIA (particularly Naval Intelligence), since certain officials at both agencies knew that Oswald had been under "tight surveillance." Oswald's involvement with "the anti-Castro group" included a visit to one of Artime's small training camps outside of New Orleans, the work with Banister and Ferrie described by CIA agent Hunter Leake, and even Oswald's trip to Mexico City.

However, the tight timing makes it uncertain if Bobby had even heard Oswald's name by the time he spoke to Haynes. Even J. Edgar Hoover didn't find out about Oswald until 3:50 PM (Eastern time). That means it's possible, even probable, that Bobby's reaction and comment to Haynes was due to whatever feeling or clue had caused him to question McCone a short time earlier. That was likely the fact that JFK was shot by one or more snipers while riding in an open car, mirroring the plan for Castro that a later AMWORLD memo revealed. In any event, the evidence shows that the link Bobby had in mind was Artime or someone in his organization, and would also explain why Bobby would make the "your guys" comment to Haynes and not Harry, due to the friction that had developed between Harry and Artime.

Haynes would later write that within a year or so after JFK's death, he heard that Artime was involved in the drug trade. In addition, Haynes also wrote about one of Artime's protégés during Watergate, who became a major Miami drug lord at the same time Trafficante still wielded power there.[20]

Only after twenty years had passed would Haynes Johnson write a detailed account of his November 22, 1963, meeting with Harry Williams. Even then he would avoid naming Harry, whose name had not appeared in any of the Congressional reports on JFK's assassination issued a few years earlier (though it had surfaced in some staff memos). In 1981 Haynes mentioned Bobby's remark very briefly in a long article about a distinguished Bay of Pigs veteran. Otherwise, the only time Haynes talked about those activities was in 1973, when he was interviewed by a researcher about Harry, Bobby, and the exiles. However, only a few parts of the interview were summarized in a small newsletter, so it received no attention from newspaper or television journalists.

Why have so many mainstream journalists been reluctant to investigate or write about the evidence of a conspiracy in JFK's death? One reason involves just how many highly regarded journalists were friends with JFK or Bobby, or Helms, or Hoover, or others involved in various aspects of the story. For example, Ben Bradlee, the longtime *Washington Post* editor who became famous during the newspaper's Watergate investigation, was very close to JFK. Another example is *New York Times* reporter Tad Szulc, who actually worked with Bobby, Morales, and others on developing the AMTRUNK operation, trying to find a high-ranking Cuban leader to stage a coup before Almeida emerged. However, it's also worth noting that a few journalists, like Haynes and Szulc, did eventually attempt to make some of their information known.

Not long after Bobby spoke to Harry and made his provocative remark to Haynes Johnson, he left his estate and headed for the Pentagon. But sometime prior to that, earlier in the afternoon and probably while McCone was en route to Bobby's Hickory Hill estate, Bobby had made another intriguing call—to CIA headquarters, according to journalists George Bailey and Seymour Freidin. (Freidin was the *New York Herald-Tribune's* foreign-affairs editor, later revealed by Jack Anderson to have been a paid CIA informant in the 1960s; author David Talbot believes Freidin got his information about Bobby directly from one of his CIA contacts.) Freidin says that Bobby spoke to a high-level CIA official at headquarters about the shooting of JFK and demanded to know: "Did your outfit have anything to do with this horror?"[21]

Viewing this call in context with Bobby's similar question to McCone, his flat-out statement to Haynes, and his call to Julius Draznin, we can clearly see Bobby's suspicion, that someone connected with the anti-Castro operations and the Mafia had turned their sights on JFK. Also, it's possible that information Bobby received from McCone during their long talk, or as additional details about the shooting emerged, allowed Bobby to evolve from questioning the CIA to making a declaration to Haynes.

As cited earlier, the timing probably prevented Bobby from knowing Oswald's name when he made his statement to Haynes, but the possibility can't be excluded. A few years ago, a Cuban exile associate of Artime made an uncorroborated claim to several authors that Oswald's name had been reported to Bobby prior to JFK's death, but this man did so while apparently trying to justify a preassassination encounter he claimed to have had with Oswald. Also, this Artime associate never mentioned any of Artime's Mafia ties, thus seriously undermining his own credibility. However, even without those claims, we can't rule out that Bobby might have had some general awareness of Oswald (or Hidell, the alias first found by police on an ID card in his wallet) as one of the US intelligence assets being sent into Cuba before the coup.[22]

Back at the Ebbitt Hotel, Haynes Johnson said farewell to his friend Harry Williams without mentioning Bobby's statement that "One of your guys did it." Haynes writes that he "stumbled out of the Ebbitt lobby [still] shaken by . . . what Robert Kennedy had said to me."[23] Alone in his hotel room, Harry Williams soon received a provocative call, the first of what appear to have been several attempts by certain exiles to quickly spread word of Oswald's guilt and his apparent Castro ties to the news media.

The man who called Harry was Alberto Fowler, the bitter former Bay of Pigs prisoner who had shadowed JFK in Palm Beach the day before JFK's Tampa motorcade. To Harry, Fowler implied that Oswald had been acting on behalf of Castro, urging Harry to tell Bobby Kennedy that Oswald had been passing out pro-Castro leaflets on the streets of New Orleans and spouting pro-Castro remarks on New Orleans radio and television. Fowler indicated that Oswald's pro-Cuba activities had been well-covered by New Orleans news outlets. When Harry said getting through to Bobby would be very difficult, Fowler urged Harry to contact his friends in the news media, since word had traveled through exile circles that Harry was helping with the upcoming NBC News Bay of Pigs special.

Harry knew Fowler, but not well, and Fowler was not part of the JFK-Almeida coup plan. Cultured and sophisticated, Fowler had been left psychologically scarred by his grueling ordeal as a Bay of Pigs prisoner. But Fowler was a highly respected member of the exile community and the Director of International Relations at the New Orleans Trade Mart. He had formerly been a member of Tony Varona's exile group, which is probably how Fowler knew to reach Harry at the Ebbitt Hotel.

Harry thought Fowler's information was important, and tried without success to reach Bobby. (Harry would hear from Bobby the following day.) Next, Harry tried calling Chet Huntley at NBC News. At an informal meeting at RFK's Virginia estate, Bobby had introduced them in preparation for the Bay of Pigs special. Harry said that he and Chet Huntley had "hit it off. He had said, 'Call me whenever you want,' because Huntley wanted the news" about exile activities.

On November 22, Harry wasn't able to speak to Huntley directly because the newsman was anchoring much of NBC's by-then-continuous coverage of the events from Dallas. But Harry left a message with a detailed account of what Fowler had told him. At 7:00 PM (Eastern time), Huntley introduced the audio of Oswald's interview on New Orleans's WDSU-TV. At 7:43, NBC ran both the audio and video of Oswald's interview, allowing America to see and hear Oswald praising Castro, talking about the Fair Play for Cuba Committee, and declaring, "I am a Marxist."[24]

Fowler's call to Harry was the first of three efforts to quickly publicize Oswald's seemingly pro-Castro sentiments, but each attempt was by people or groups tied to the Mafia and close associates of David Morales. In addition to Fowler's admitted shadowing of JFK on the day before the Tampa assassination attempt, Fowler has made other interesting admissions. Fowler would later tell the New Orleans District Attorney that as far as JFK's assassination was concerned, "I didn't kill him . . . but I wish I had." Fowler cast the comment as a joke, the same way he later tried to explain away his shadowing of JFK from an adjacent house.[25]

However, Fowler admitted to the New Orleans Times-Picayune that he "had been resentful of Kennedy; in fact, I had even written a long article for *U.S. News & World Report,* showing my resentment for the lack of air cover that had been promised for [the Bay of Pigs invasion]." The article appeared less than two weeks after Fowler's release from a Cuban prison. Fowler, like other Bay of Pigs prisoners, had been freed as part of the deal worked out by Bobby and Harry.[26] Writing his slam of JFK must have been one of the first things the embittered Fowler did after he was released.

Fowler's associates were involved with Artime's exile training camp outside New Orleans, the one David Ferrie and Oswald allegedly visited. It was closed after several associates of Marcello, Rosselli, and Trafficante were arrested with an arms cache less than a mile away.[27] The arms cache had been the idea of Frank Fiorini, and Fowler had a close friend in common with the Trafficante bagman.

Fowler also had ties to Tony Varona, who worked with Rosselli and Trafficante, and to other CIA assets. Originally, the CIA had wanted Fowler to head the New Orleans chapter of Varona's exile group, but Fowler declined.[28] Two CIA assets worked at the Trade Mart with Fowler, including William Gaudet, who helped with the CIA's surveillance of Oswald. Fowler himself was on the International Advisory Committee for INCA, the group that helped to arrange and publicize Oswald's radio debate. Also on the Committee with Fowler was Oswald's childhood idol, Herbert Philbrick, whose television series *I Led Three Lives* detailed his years as a deep cover undercover US intelligence asset pretending to be a communist.

Was Fowler part of the plot to kill JFK—or was he being used or manipulated by someone else? While Fowler was extremely conservative, and very intolerant of minorities such as blacks and gays, he had no history of criminal behavior or violence (aside from his days as a fighter at the Bay of Pigs for the CIA). However, the same is not true for the man who assisted Fowler in shadowing JFK just before Tampa: Felipe Rivero.

At the time of JFK's assassination, Rivero was one of the highest-ranking members of an exile group—usually called by its initials, the JGCE, or "the Junta"—whose major funding came from the Chicago Mafia. Three months before JFK's assassination, in August 1963, Rivero and his group had tried to become involved in Harry's plans. Files confirm that he was rejected, and was instead referred by Bobby and Harry to the State Department, as sometimes happened to groups deemed unsuitable for inclusion in the coup plan.[29]

In April 1963, a month before Almeida contacted Harry about

staging a coup, declassified CIA files show that Rivero was working with Manuel Artime on a scheme to embarrass JFK. A cable from the Miami CIA station to CIA Director McCone said that Rivero "had the backing of Manuel Artime, who has been with him quite frequently" to publicize a request from a group of Bay of Pigs veterans that "President John F. Kennedy return the Brigade flag" that JFK had been given at the Orange Bowl on December 29, 1962, to celebrate the prisoners' release.

The CIA memo calls "Felipe Rivero the official front man for this plan," which would involve sending announcements to "all local radio and television outlets" about their demand. Rivero and Artime were acting in response to a perceived lack of action on JFK's part to topple Fidel; the information in the report came from Bernard Barker and one of David Morales's AMOT informants.[30] The plan apparently fell apart when the Kennedys increased their attention to and support of Artime. Just over a month later, the opportunity with Almeida presented itself, and a month after that, Artime was being set up in what would eventually become the $7 million AMWORLD operation. Harry Williams once indicated that Artime's support from the Kennedys always involved a touch of "blackmail"—perhaps Artime's threat to demand the flag's return was what Harry was referring to. Rivero, on the other hand, turned to a Mafia-backed organization for his own support.

In the years after JFK's assassination, Rivero would help plan a wave of terrorist bombings in the United States, Canada, and Latin America. Rivero's most infamous bomb attack occurred on September 21, 1976, when a car bomb exploded in the middle of Washington, D.C., taking the life of former Chilean diplomat Orlando Letelier. With Letelier were two Americans: Michael Moffit, who survived, and his wife, Ronni. As journalist Joseph Trento described, Ronni Moffit "drowned in her own blood" from a severed artery, while Letelier's body was "torn in two."[31] Files from the Dade County Manager's office state that "authorities believed that Rivero had planned Letelier's assassination."[32] However, Rivero was never prosecuted for this or other acts of violence he was connected to in the 1970s. In 1975, two close friends of Rivero blew up Trafficante associate Rolando Masferrer in Miami in another car bombing. The same Rivero associates were also linked to the bombing of a packed Cubana airliner less than two weeks after the Letelier bombing.[33]

Felipe Rivero wasn't just intolerant toward minorities, like his friend Alberto Fowler; Dade County files described Rivero as a "neo-Nazi." His beliefs became abundantly clear in 1992, when Rivero invited and hosted ex-Klan head David Duke to speak to his organization. Several other participants in JFK's assassination, including Joseph Milteer and Guy Banister, were also white supremacists. They were part of the nexus of illegal arms sales by the Mafia, whose two largest customer groups were Cuban exiles and white supremacists. The day before JFK was shot and Fowler called Harry Williams, a Cuban exile backed by Rivero's group had made a suspicious remark to an associate. According to *Vanity Fair*, on November 21, 1963, while a Cuban exile was "negotiating an arms purchase in Chicago," the exile stated that "the money for the guns would come through shortly . . . 'as soon as we take care of Kennedy.'"[34]

The Chicago Secret Service heard about the remark and began investigating. But author Vince Palamara writes that "Chicago Secret Service agent Joseph Noonan . . . and other agents were uneasy that the Cubans might have some ties to the CIA." The agents were correct, because the suspect had ties not only to Rivero's group, but also to the DRE, which David Atlee Phillips ran for the CIA with the help of George Joannides. Palamara writes that "a little later, they received a call from (Secret Service) Headquarters, to drop everything . . . and send all memos, files, and their notebooks to Washington, and not to discuss the case with anyone."[35] The case was taken over by the FBI, which let it die. This was just one of many examples in the aftermath of JFK's murder in which potential ties to Cuba, exiles, or the Chicago or Tampa threat weren't adequately explored, for fear of where they might lead or what they might expose.[36]

Rivero's partner, Alberto Fowler, would later take a more active role in diverting suspicion from himself, Rivero, other exiles, and the Mafia when Fowler became the main Cuban exile investigator for New Orleans District Attorney Jim Garrison in 1967. Shortly after Fowler started working for Garrison, Fowler's gay associate at the Trade Mart, former occasional CIA asset Clay Shaw, became the primary focus of Garrison's investigation.

Fowler's call to Harry late in the afternoon of November 22 was soon followed by two more attempts to quickly tie Oswald to Fidel Castro, thereby implicating Fidel in JFK's death. The reason was made clear in a CIA memo a few days later, which said that "rumors are now circulating among Exile groups [about Castro's] involvement in Kennedy's death. Authors [of] these rumors not identified but it['s] clear this [is] being done primarily in [an] attempt to provoke strong US action against Cuba."[37] The memo obscures the fact that some in the CIA knew, or should have known, the source of "these rumors," since the following two incidents involved groups being run by David Atlee Phillips and George Joannides for the CIA.

On the evening of November 22, a CIA memo confirms that members of Phillips's DRE had information about Oswald's time in the Soviet Union, stemming from Oswald's radio debate with a DRE member three months earlier. However, the author of the CIA memo (someone at the Miami station, where Morales ran operations) says that the "above info has not been passed to the Secret Service, State, or FBI as [the DRE] plans a news release" to publicize its information. It seems odd that the CIA would withhold information from other federal agencies just so a small exile group could issue its own news release.[38]

Later that night, another DRE member contacted Clare Booth Luce, wife of the publisher of *Time* and *Life* magazines. She and her husband were ardent anticommunists, and she had been funding several DRE members.[39] *Vanity Fair* reports that her caller made the most direct accusation tying Oswald to Fidel, telling Luce that Oswald was "the hired gun of a Cuban Communist assassination team." The caller also mentioned the trip Oswald had made to Mexico City in late September, a trip that would not be reported in the press until two days later.[40]

While several CIA-backed Cuban exiles were trying to leak incriminating information about Oswald to the press, some in the US military were desperately trying to conceal information about Oswald. Our confidential Naval Intelligence source—who had helped to compile the reports resulting from the "tight surveillance" of Oswald since his return to the US from Russia—said that "on the day of the assassination," he and a coworker "were called back to their office in Washington." After receiving orders from their commander, they "destroyed and sanitized lots of the Oswald file."[41] Confirmation for such document destruction comes from FBI memos, which describe their own interviews with Marines who had served with Oswald. However, the FBI agents discovered that some of the Marines had earlier been interviewed by Naval Intelligence—but those Naval Intelligence reports were all missing, leading an FBI agent to say in a memo, "Perhaps they have been destroyed."[42]

The Naval Intelligence file our source handled in the fall of 1963 concerned only the close surveillance of Oswald, not any operational duties Oswald might have had. Those were apparently being handled by, or coordinated with, the CIA. Our source said there was "a note on the top of the file jacket [that] said to contact the CIA if Oswald was arrested or got into any trouble. There was a name and some sort of code given for someone at the CIA."[43] The one person at the CIA who is alleged to have been in contact with Oswald is David Atlee Phillips. In his later autobiographical novel outline, Phillips wrote that Oswald was part of the effort to assassinate Castro and had "used [against JFK] precisely the plan we had devised against Castro."[44]

Naval Intelligence and its close counterpart, Marine Intelligence (G-2), were components of the Defense Intelligence Agency (DIA) headed by General Joseph Carroll. A journalist told former Senate investigator Bernard Fensterwald that "Oswald had connections to an 'intelligence service . . . called the Defense Intelligence Agency. . . . The General who . . . supposedly made the arrangements [was] General Joe Carroll, founder of the DIA. . . . The Army was going nuts over Oswald's part in the assassination.'"[45] Army Intelligence destroyed its entire Oswald file in 1973.[46]

However, General Carroll had problems with both the CIA and some of the agencies theoretically under his control. As noted earlier, a Cuban exile associate of Manuel Artime says that during a meeting in a car (apparently to avoid prying ears in the Pentagon), General Carroll expressed frustration with some "CIA activities because they [were] interfering with Plan Judas." "Plan Judas" was a name some exiles used for the JFK-Almeida coup plan, since Almeida had been one of the legendary twelve who founded the Revolution with Fidel. General Carroll's concerns were promptly reported to the CIA and preserved in a memo sent to CIA Director John McCone by the Miami CIA station. The same CIA memo also discussed Harry Williams, Bobby Kennedy, and Manolo Ray.[47]

Even on the day of JFK's death, a memo shows that Naval Intelligence considered withholding information from General Carroll. Carroll asked to see Oswald's Naval Intelligence file, but Naval Intelligence was "cautious about passing [the] file to DIA." Eventually, after Joint Chiefs Chairman General Maxwell Taylor had made a request, General Carroll was allowed to look at the file, but he was not permitted to keep a copy.

It's hard to say if Naval Intelligence was initially reluctant to share the file for bureaucratic reasons, or because by that time it was probably already incomplete. The DIA had been formed only two years earlier, as the brainchild of JFK and Defense Secretary McNamara. Several top generals were opposed to its creation, since it would dilute the power of the individual intelligence services. Branches like Naval Intelligence were already ostensibly accountable to the Navy Chief of Staff, the Secretary of the Navy, and the Secretary of Defense. Now, they were also beholden to General Carroll, who advised both the Joint Chiefs and McNamara.[48] That was a difficult position for General Carroll, since General Maxwell Taylor was probably the only other member of the Joint Chiefs who was fully informed about the JFK-Almeida coup plan; McNamara says that he wasn't told about it.[49]

Based on the few DIA files from the fall of 1963 that have been declassified, it appears unlikely that General Carroll knew about the destruction of parts of Oswald's Naval Intelligence file, at least initially. While the CIA is still withholding more than a million files related to JFK's assassination, the amount of DIA and Naval Intelligence files about the JFK-Almeida coup plan and anti-Castro operations—which could be related to JFK's assassination—should be equally vast, if the files still exist.

As for General Carroll's superior, General Taylor, his concerns on November 22 were more global. DEFCON indicates the degree of US defense readiness, and declassified files show that the level was raised to DEFCON 4, from 5, an hour and twenty minutes after JFK was shot. One command even raised it to DEFCON 3. FBI Agent James Hosty said that just after Oswald's arrest, "fully armed warplanes were sent screaming toward Cuba." Peter Dale Scott wrote that the "planes would have been launched from the US Strike Command at MacDill Air Force Base in [Tampa] Florida," the very base JFK had visited for a conference with its top brass just four days earlier.

Scott also noted that a "cable [had been issued] from US Army Intelligence in Texas, dated November 22, 1963, telling the Strike Command (falsely) that Oswald had defected to Cuba in 1959 and was 'a card-carrying member of the Communist Party.'" Clearly, someone had been feeding erroneous intelligence into the system—stories similar to the false tales that John Martino would soon spread. Luckily, cooler heads started to prevail, and "just before [the US planes] entered Cuban airspace, they were hastily called back." *U.S. News & World Report* says, "The Air Force and the CIA sent a 'Flash' worldwide alert for all [US surveillance flights] to return to their bases, lest the Soviet Union be provoked." But it would be almost two days before the DEFCON alert status finally returned to normal.[50] Even then, the specter of a nuclear crisis with the Soviets over Cuba would keep coming up in the days and weeks after JFK's assassination.

Chapter Thirteen

On the afternoon of November 22, 1963, in the packed federal courtroom in New Orleans, Carlos Marcello waited anxiously as the judge finished charging the jury. Marcello wasn't concerned about his case because he knew a bribe had ensured he wouldn't be convicted; he was eager to hear the news from Dallas. Finally, one hour after the shooting, the rest of the courtroom learned what Marcello already expected: After getting a note from the bailiff, the judge announced to the stunned courtroom that JFK had been shot and might be dead. The judge declared an immediate recess, and Carlos Marcello and David Ferrie left the courtroom.

Court resumed an hour and a half later, at 3:00 PM (Central), though Bobby's Justice Department prosecutor for the case, John Diuguid, told us he recalls that David Ferrie was no longer with Marcello. The jury then began its deliberations, reaching a verdict in less than fifteen minutes, thanks to the key juror Marcello had bribed. The juror later boasted that "he had also convinced several of his fellow jurors to vote not guilty." Marcello had also threatened the government's main witness during the trial, compromising his testimony and ensuring Marcello's acquittal on both charges: conspiracy and perjury. With no conviction, there would be no deportation for Marcello.[1] Marcello, his family, and his supporters all headed out for a big celebration, with Marcello surely savoring the moment of his greatest triumph.

In Miami, Marcello's associate John Martino got the news from his son that JFK had been shot. Martino's son later told *Vanity Fair* that his "father went white as a sheet. But it wasn't like 'Gee whiz,' it was more like confirmation." John Martino's wife said that her husband "got I don't know how many calls from Texas. I don't know who called him, but he was on the phone, on the phone, on the phone. . . . "[2]

Also in Miami was another Marcello associate, Teamster President Jimmy Hoffa. From the Miami Beach apartment he sometimes used during the cooler months, Hoffa called Frank Ragano, the attorney he shared with Santo Trafficante. According to Ragano, Hoffa could barely contain himself: "Did you hear the good news? They killed the son-of-a-bitch bastard." Ragano said, "I had never heard him sound happier or more elated."[3] Hoffa could be confident and happy because he knew that a month earlier, one of his associates had paid Jack Ruby approximately $7,000, as part of an arrangement to ensure that whoever took the fall for JFK's death didn't live to talk about it.[4] As for Ragano, he would soon be celebrating and toasting JFK's death with Trafficante.

In Washington, Secret Service officials had their Chicago office check on the ex-Marine who had been arrested on the day of JFK's canceled Chicago motorcade. The man, Thomas Vallee, had been quickly released in early November and had resumed his regular job. A later report says that on November 22, "Vallee was employed at his place of business during the entire day." Yet neither the Secret Service nor the FBI bothered to interview Vallee to see if he had any knowledge of Oswald or his associates, or to see if they had any links in common.[5] The Secret Service files on Vallee seem oddly incomplete, because some files treat him as a subject of intense interest for years to come. It's possible that the Secret Service, or some other agency, had been keeping Vallee under surveillance since the time of his release, which would account for the Secret Service's relative lack of official interest in Vallee in the days after JFK's murder. It's also possible the Secret Service or FBI did more to investigate possible links between ex-Marine Vallee and ex-Marine Oswald, but that those files were treated with the same degree of secrecy as other aspects of the Chicago assassination plot.

Only an hour after Oswald's arrival at Dallas police headquarters, and just ten minutes after J. Edgar Hoover learned Oswald's name, Hoover was able to tell Bobby Kennedy not only that he "thought we had the man who killed the President," but also that he even knew that Oswald was "not a communist." Several factors account for Hoover's ability to know so much so quickly.

First, the FBI had assisted Naval Intelligence with some of its tight surveillance on Oswald, especially in landlocked cities like Dallas, where Naval Intelligence had few assets. This information apparently almost slipped out right after the assassination, when James Hosty, the Dallas FBI agent assigned to Oswald, allegedly told Dallas police "officer Jack Revill on November 22 . . . that Oswald . . . had been under observation. When Revill protested that the information had not been shared with the

Dallas police, he was reminded of the FBI policy forbidding the sharing of information pertaining to espionage."[6]

If the public learned that the FBI had Oswald under surveillance before he shot JFK, it would destroy the sterling image of Hoover's FBI that the director had spent decades building. It addition, many FBI surveillance efforts in the early 1960s, such as "black bag" break-ins and phone taps, were illegal. If they became known in Oswald's case, public awareness of those methods could unravel the whole network of illegal domestic surveillance the FBI maintained, often in cooperation with the CIA and various branches of military intelligence. Therefore, the Dallas FBI agent's alleged comments about Oswald's being under observation were quickly disavowed.

Hoover could never reveal that the FBI had ever had more than a routine interest in Oswald, and had made a few run-of-the-mill, above-board efforts to contact him after Oswald returned to Dallas. Hoover didn't even want some of those efforts publicized, once it appeared that Oswald had killed JFK. Shortly after Oswald's death, Hoover would order the Dallas FBI office to destroy a note Oswald had left there just ten days before JFK's assassination. The contents of the note and the circumstances of Oswald's visit were the subject of three conflicting stories that Congress investigated in the mid-1970s, following Hoover's death in 1972. The essence of Oswald's note was that Agent Hosty should "stop bothering my wife [and] talk to me if you need to." The secretary in the Dallas office recalled a phrase about "blowing up" the FBI office.[7] However, surely a written threat to blow up the Dallas FBI office, delivered in person by a former defector to an enemy of the US like Russia, would have provoked a swift response in 1963, as it would today. We feel that Oswald was simply trying to keep the local FBI agent from "blowing" the deep cover Oswald had carefully maintained for so long.

We also noted that Hoover was able to tell Bobby Kennedy that Oswald was not a communist, just an hour after Oswald arrived at Dallas police headquarters. This was probably a function of both Hoover's access to some of the additional surveillance on Oswald, and the FBI's thorough infiltration of the Communist Party USA by the early 1960s. It has been claimed that one out of every four members of the Communist Party by that time was an FBI informant, asset, or agent. Still, the initial reports that Oswald was a self-proclaimed Marxist, a former defector, and a member of the Fair Play for Cuba Committee were more than enough for someone with Hoover's mindset to believe Oswald was guilty of JFK's murder.

Though America was nine years past the height of the McCarthy-era blacklist—which gave rise to popular entertainments like *I Led Three Lives* and *I Was a Communist for the FBI*, that had so enthralled a young Oswald—its effects still lingered throughout much of the United States. The first small crack in the Hollywood blacklist had occurred only three years earlier, and even in 1963 many former film and TV stars and directors were still unemployable in Hollywood or working in exile. Many of the film shorts produced ten years earlier, which claimed that freedoms needed to be sacrificed to fight the communist menace, were still shown in schools and on Sunday-afternoon local television. The John Birch Society was at the height of its influence, courted and joined by prominent politicians, judges, and other officials, even as it used anticommunism to mask what many saw as an undercurrent of racism. (Its newsletters denounced any attempt at civil rights as a communist plot and called Martin Luther King Jr. a communist who wanted to found a "Soviet Negro Republic . . . with Atlanta as its capital.")[8]

For Hoover, and many American newspapers and television stations, initial word of Oswald's apparent Soviet and Cuban connections was all they needed to convict him. By Friday night, and into Saturday and Sunday, many newspapers were in an odd state of duality. Their editorials, written in the immediate aftermath of JFK's murder, denounced the far-right paranoia and racism that many initially felt must have been behind the shooting. But even as those editorials appeared over the next two days, the newspaper's front pages were trumpeting that JFK had been murdered by a communist with ties to Russia and Cuba.

For someone like former FBI supervisor Guy Banister, it would not have been hard to guess Hoover's reaction, on two fronts. First, Oswald's seeming Soviet and Cuban ties would have made him a logical suspect. Banister had long been an ardent anticommunist, first for the FBI and then running checks for corporations to root out those with the taint of communism, so he knew the mindset of someone like Hoover. Second, Banister would know that because of the FBI's participation in the tight surveillance of Oswald (which probably involved Banister's friends in the New Orleans FBI office), Hoover would immediately have to begin covering up any information that could reflect badly on the FBI. That is exactly what happened in the coming days, weeks, months, and years. The smallest step out of line by a reporter would bring a response from Hoover, which might include having an FBI agent contact the reporter, his or her editor, or even the publisher. Several examples of attempted FBI suppression involved stories that emerged from Chicago, some

about the events in Dallas and others about the whispers among reporters regarding the attempt to assassinate JFK in Chicago.

What Hoover said publicly, or had his staff leak to reporters, could be
different from what Hoover said in private. Even as he told Bobby Kennedy and others that Oswald had killed JFK, only sixteen hours later, on
Saturday morning, Hoover would tell new president Lyndon Johnson
that "the evidence that they have at the present time is not very, very
strong" against Oswald.[9] We now know that saying one thing in public and almost the opposite in private was consistent with the contrast
between Hoover's own public and private lives. In public, he presented
himself as the personification of right-wing, conservative family values,
while in private he led a closeted gay life with his longtime companion,
Clyde Tolson. By 1963, Bobby Kennedy had finally dragged Hoover
into the war against the Mafia; in public, Hoover presented himself as
leading the FBI's fight against organized crime, even as his New Orleans
office gave carte blanche to Banister's patron Carlos Marcello.

Over the coming days, Hoover would no doubt learn more about
the JFK-Almeida coup plan and the other authorized, and unauthorized, CIA operations against Castro. Though the FBI had no official role
in any of those operations, Hoover already had some information. Six
weeks before JFK's death, Hoover had been sent a report from a Miami
FBI informant who said that Cubela was working for the CIA.[10] Also,
the FBI had sometimes been in touch with Harry Williams throughout
the summer and fall of 1963, specifically after Harry's encounter with
Trafficante in Miami (arranged by an associate of E. Howard Hunt) and
before Harry's almost fatal trip to Guatemala City, when an FBI agent
warned Harry the FBI had picked up information that he was in danger.
In addition, Miami FBI informants (such as those code-named "MM T-1"
and "MM T-6") provided information about Harry to the local office.[11]
Harry's FBI file, like his CIA file, has never been released.

President Lyndon Johnson, like Hoover, would learn much about
secret anti-Castro operations in the coming days. Because Hoover had
so many informants, prior to JFK's death Johnson probably knew even
less than Hoover about the JFK-Almeida coup plan and the CIA's other
operations. Yet Johnson's new position allowed him to start learning
about those operations directly from CIA Director McCone. Close
friends Johnson and Hoover no doubt shared much of this information
with each other. However, the huge amount of data each man learned in
such a short time undoubtedly made it hard to keep all the operations
straight. After a summary that lasted only a few minutes, distinguishing

the JFK-Almeida coup plan and AMWORLD from AMTRUNK and from AMLASH wouldn't have been easy. Hoover would eventually have to figure out where the assassination part of the Cubela operation fit in, and how the CIA-Mafia plots were involved. (Hoover knew about the earlier phase of the CIA-Mafia plots, and had informant reports about the actions of Rosselli and others still involved in the fall of 1963.) In addition, LBJ would learn about the detailed files for the "Plan for a Coup in Cuba," and the even more extensive US military invasion plans. This mass of information would have been confusing to digest in the best of times, let alone in the aftermath of JFK's murder.

At 7:25 PM (Eastern time) on the evening of the assassination, Lyndon Johnson called J. Edgar Hoover "at his home, and requested that the FBI take complete charge of the case involving the assassination." William Manchester observed that "this was one of the first calls that the President made upon returning to Washington that evening." Hoover had already begun investigating on his own authority, but now the new president had given him primary control of the entire case. Hoover "also told the President that he was concerned about the great amount of publicity coming out of Dallas."[12] We have only Hoover's account, to historian Manchester, of what was said that night, and the publicity-savvy Hoover was well aware that his words would be published in Manchester's upcoming book *Death of a President*. No doubt Hoover and LBJ discussed urgent national security matters that Hoover didn't share with Manchester. For example, some of the "publicity coming out of Dallas" was about the possible role of communist Russia and Cuba in JFK's murder. Just a year after the tense nuclear standoff of the Cuban Missile Crisis, this could have spelled disaster for the new president.

Journalist Jack Anderson knew both men well, and later said he was confident that LBJ would have said to Hoover something like "Help me save my country."[13] That would have meant keeping the investigation from spreading into areas that could trigger a call for an attack on Cuba or the Soviet Union. This concern helps to account for the actions of the FBI as the investigation unfolded. While critics of the FBI and Warren Commission have long complained about FBI witness intimidation, misrepresentation of statements, and missing or altered evidence, an increasing number of former FBI agents have gone on record about the pressure they were under.[14] As recounted in *Vanity Fair*, "former agent Harry Whidbee [said] the Kennedy investigation was 'a hurry-up job' ... we were effectively told, 'They're only going to prove (Oswald) was the guy who did it. There were no co-conspirators, and there was no international conspiracy.'" The retired agent says that he "had conducted a couple of interviews, and those records were sent back again and were rewritten according to Washington's requirements." Laurence Keenan, a retired FBI supervisor, confirmed his account. He told *Vanity Fair* that "within days we could say the investigation was over. 'Conspiracy' was a word which was verboten. . . . The idea that Oswald had a confederate or was part of a group or a conspiracy was definitely enough to place a man's career in jeopardy."[15]

As even more information emerged in the coming days and weeks that seemed to implicate Russia or Cuba, the pressure from Hoover to contain the investigation only increased. Hoover had his own reasons, aside from national security, to withhold information, and it's important to keep those motivations in mind as the various cover-ups unfold. Some have tried to blame JFK's assassination on Hoover because of these investigative shortcomings, but they overlook the fact that Bobby Kennedy also withheld similar information for some of the same reasons. Also, if Hoover wanted to get rid of JFK before the 1964 elections, he could have easily done so simply by leaking accounts of his affairs to conservative press outlets, something Hoover had done in a small way in October 1963 in order to secure his job throughout JFK's current (and any future) term as president.[16]

Several important phone calls to Hoover on November 22 show just how powerful and influential he was at that time. That morning, even before JFK was shot, former president Dwight Eisenhower called Hoover. At 4:18 PM, just minutes after Hoover finished his call to Bobby about Oswald, Hoover received a call from former vice president Richard Nixon, then seen as a probable contender for the 1964 Republican presidential nomination. Coupled with the fact that the first call LBJ made when he got back to Washington was to Hoover, this call from Nixon confirms that Hoover had assumed the mantle of the second-most powerful man in America after JFK's death (which was especially true since there was no vice president once LBJ ascended to the Oval Office). That's why it was important for the conspirators to have someone quickly blamed for the assassination who could force Hoover, as well as LBJ and Bobby, to cover up any information pointing at suspects besides Oswald. Once Hoover's considerable media and political connections were brought into play, the lone-assassin information Hoover and the FBI conveyed would quickly become gospel.

But in the first hours after JFK's death, Hoover (and LBJ's staff) had not yet begun to exert the more extensive spin control they soon would.

This allowed some early reports to appear that did not conform to the "lone assassin" scenario that would be prevalent by the following morning. News reports from Parkland talked about JFK's throat wound being an entrance wound, indicating a shooter from the front. This was repeated by CBS reporter Dan Rather on KRLD-TV in Dallas, who said that "we are told that the gunshot wound, the fatal wound, inflicted on the President of the United States entered at the base of the throat and came out the base of the neck, on the back side."[17] But by the following day, Rather had so accepted the FBI's official lone-assassin story that—as he later acknowledged in his autobiography—he did not clearly relate what the Zapruder film actually depicted.

It's important to note the media's reporting of the overwhelmingly sympathetic reaction of most Americans, and much of the world, to JFK's assassination. This is something a racist in the Deep South, like Marcello, might not have anticipated, given JFK's razor-thin margin of victory in 1960 and his loss of support since that time among conservative Democrats, due to JFK's increasing concern over civil rights. However, 1963 was a very different era from today, when President George W. Bush's approval rating has hovered near 30 percent for more than a year. In contrast, JFK's popularity never dipped below 56 percent, despite problems like the Bay of Pigs. His highest disapproval rating was only 30 percent, which is very good by historical standards. No other president in recent history has been as popular; even if people disagreed with JFK politically, many still liked and admired him personally. Hence, by Friday evening and over the weekend, newspapers throughout the country noted only a few officials or people who made it clear that they weren't sad to see JFK gone; the vast majority of those cited were shocked and saddened by the President's death.

The reaction was similar throughout much of what was then called the "free world": Countries like England, France, Ireland, and Germany in particular showed tremendous concern from both officials and the general populace. Perhaps more surprising in light of the low status of the US presidency among the people of Latin America in the 21st century, in 1963 those countries were mostly sympathetic toward the slain US president.

That's because JFK had courted, and managed to win over, many in Latin America, and that effort had an impact on his coup plan with Almeida. Because JFK had managed to reverse the mostly negative, heavy-handed image of the United States that grew under Vice President

Richard Nixon in the 1950s, JFK hadn't wanted to simply invade Cuba to remove Castro. That's why JFK had wanted US forces to be "invited in" after a coup, and for the Organization of American States to be involved in the immediate aftermath and transition to democracy. It's ironic that JFK was set to make remarks about his Latin American progress in Austin, Texas, on the evening of November 22. JFK had planned to say, "I can testify from my trips to Mexico, Colombia, Venezuela, and Costa Rica that American officials are no longer booed and spat upon south of the border"[18]—a reference to Nixon's treatment in Latin America.

As for Richard Nixon, the former vice president was one of the few people who had trouble remembering exactly what he was doing on November 22, 1963, when he heard that JFK had been assassinated—which is ironic, since that day's events eventually played a role in forcing him to step down as president. Nixon told three different stories over the years about where he was when he heard JFK had been killed. Once, he even lied to the FBI about it, claiming he had been in Dallas only "two days prior to the assassination of President John F. Kennedy." However, as noted earlier, it was no secret that Nixon had been in Dallas attending a soft-drink convention; it is well established that he flew out of Dallas about three hours prior to JFK's assassination; and there is no credible evidence to support the tales of Nixon, J. Edgar Hoover, and wealthy Texas oilmen plotting in secret the night before JFK's murder.[19] While Nixon had no role in JFK's death (it certainly would have been uncharacteristically foolish for him to be in Dallas if he had anything to do with it), his associates knew people who were on the fringes of the plot—including former Cuban president Carlos Prio, the Trafficante associate who was trying to infiltrate the JFK-Almeida coup plan.

In a CIA memo based on information obtained shortly before JFK's death, Prio is reported as talking about various aspects of the coup plan, then mentioning two exile associates who were part of Prio's operation "and have become associated [with] Richard Nixon in accordance with [the] Republican Party plan [to] bring up the Cuban case before elections."[20] Ties like these help to explain why Prio would have a little-known role in the plots surrounding Watergate, as would Artime, while other veterans of the 1963 anti-Castro operations—like E. Howard Hunt—would become infamous for their Watergate exploits.

In New Orleans, Carlos Marcello was suddenly consumed with two problems that threatened to tie David Ferrie, and thus Marcello, to JFK's assassination. By Friday evening, a third problem would surface, setting off a chain of events that would cause Ferrie to hastily flee New Orleans on Friday, have authorities looking for him by Saturday, and have him under arrest by Monday.

The first problem for Marcello was that Oswald, his former "runner" who had been introduced to him by Ferrie, was still alive. According to an FBI report, Marcello's second problem was word from his lawyer, G. Wray Gill, that "Lee Oswald, when he was picked up, had been carrying a library card with David Ferrie's name on it." Both of these problems had an immediate impact on Marcello, who realized they could unravel his entire carefully planned scheme. Marcello biographer John Davis wrote that Marcello had initially celebrated after his bribe-induced acquittal, "embracing his attorneys and receiving congratulations from his family, friends, and supporters." But Marcello decided to skip "a family celebration [and instead] went to his office in the Town and Country Motel." A source Davis interviewed said that Marcello looked "as if he had something urgent on his mind."[21]

Ferrie was apparently frantic about the news. Congressional investigators wrote that "Oswald's former landlady in New Orleans . . . told the Committee she recalled that Ferrie visited her home on the night of the assassination and asked about Oswald's library card." The investigators also found that a former New Orleans "neighbor of Oswald's [said] that Ferrie had come by her house after the assassination, inquiring if [her husband] had any information regarding Oswald's library card."[22] In a few days, the Secret Service would ask if Ferrie had loaned Oswald his library card. But before that, Ferrie took an unusual late-night weekend trip to Texas, apparently in response to the news from Dallas.

Ferrie must have been alarmed. The fact that Oswald was still alive, and hadn't been killed soon after the assassination by Ruby or one of his policemen, was bad enough, but the library card would tie him directly to Oswald. To have something that small slip by after all the months of careful planning, and the long weekends going over every detail with Marcello, must have been devastating. Something as simple as a library card could now unravel the whole plot. And Ferrie had worked with Marcello long enough to know that the godfather wouldn't hesitate to have him killed if Ferrie couldn't figure some way out of the problem.

Ferrie did not flee to Texas on Friday night to avoid Marcello, since he went to cities that were under Marcello's firm control; instead, Ferrie's trip was part of his attempt at damage control. Ferrie didn't panic, and tried to give the sudden trip at least the veneer of plausibility, though most investigators are skeptical. Ferrie seems to have suddenly decided to drive more than 350 miles to go ice skating, taking two teenage boys with him as companions.

The many unusual aspects of Ferrie's trip have been chronicled in many books and articles. Ferrie didn't leave until after nine o'clock on the night of November 22, and later admitted the trip was connected to his work with Marcello attorney Gill.[23] The first leg of Ferrie's trip must have taken at least five hours, probably more. Anthony Summers wrote that Ferrie drove to a Houston ice-skating rink, where in the late hours he would "spend a great deal of time at a pay telephone, making and receiving calls." Ferrie then checked into a Marcello-owned hotel, from which Congressional investigators found he called "the Town and Country Motel, Marcello's New Orleans headquarters." He then went to Galveston and checked into a motel there, while he was still registered at Marcello's motel in Houston.[24]

Jack Ruby made several calls to Galveston just before Ferrie's arrival. Also, associates of Ruby had left Dallas and traveled to Houston and Galveston just before Ferrie's arrival in each city. We think it's possible Ferrie went to Texas to retrieve his library card. Perhaps one of the corrupt members of the Dallas police, close to Marcello's Dallas boss, Joe Civello, or to Ruby, had taken possession of the card. The lawman could have simply been bribed or told by someone like the CIA's Morales or Banister that the card involved a sensitive national-security matter (which was technically true, given Ferrie's CIA-sanctioned anti-Castro activities). The bottom line is that by Monday, Ferrie would be able to produce his library card when FBI agents confronted him about it.[25]

In the meantime, Carlos Marcello had a third major problem, this one involving Guy Banister as well as David Ferrie. As detailed by Congressional investigators, one of Banister's employees, Jack Martin, had an altercation with Banister on the evening of JFK's death. Banister pistol-whipped Martin, causing Martin to call an assistant District Attorney and accuse Banister of being involved in JFK's assassination. Martin later said that Ferrie had gone to Texas "to serve as the getaway pilot for the men involved in the assassination."[26] One of Bobby Kennedy's Mafia prosecutors in New Orleans told us that he had heard that "Ferrie was supposed to have flown some conspirators out of Texas," though it wasn't anything he could confirm or had firsthand knowledge of.[27] In any event, authorities issued a lookout for Ferrie on Saturday, and by Monday would have him under arrest.

One of Banister's associates was unaware of those difficulties and thought the plan was still on track, even with Oswald alive for a while longer. White supremacist Joseph Milteer told Miami police informant William Somersett that "Oswald hasn't said anything and he will not say anything." Milteer also made it clear that, despite the initial reports of Oswald's stay in Russia and his seeming public support of Fidel Castro, "Oswald was not connected with Moscow, or any big communist leaders."[28]

Two vastly different women, each with connections to JFK's assassination, were in the hospital on the evening of November 22. At East Louisiana State Hospital, the self-described "dope runner" for Jack Ruby, Rose Cheramie, was still suffering the effects of withdrawal from her heroin addiction. After JFK's murder, Louisiana State Police Lieutenant Frances Fruge recalled the comments Cheramie had made to him about the impending assassination of JFK. He immediately called the hospital and ordered them to hold Cheramie so that he could question her further. But Cheramie was too ill to be questioned at that time, though Lt. Fruge was assured she would be held until he could interview her.[29]

In Dallas, the second hospitalized woman was the beautiful, sophisticated Cuban exile Silvia Odio. Earlier that day, she had been listening to the radio, as she returned to work from lunch, when she first heard of JFK's assassination. As mentioned previously, Odio was part of Manolo Ray's JURE exile group, though her father was in prison in Cuba because of a Castro assassination attempt by Alpha 66's Antonio Veciana. On November 22, it had been just two months since Silvia Odio had been visited by two Cuban exiles and an American introduced to her as Leon Oswald. The following day, one of the exiles had called her to say that Oswald was a former Marine, an expert marksman who had said the exiles "should have assassinated Kennedy after the Bay of Pigs."[30]

Odio later told Congressional investigator Gaeton Fonzi that upon hearing of JFK's death on the radio, "she immediately thought of the visit of the three men to her apartment. . . . It produced a tremendous amount of fear in her." When she reached work, everyone was being sent home because of the tragedy. Fonzi writes that, as Odio thought more about the assassination, "she began to feel terribly, uncontrollably frightened, and, while walking to her car, fainted. She remembers waking up in the hospital."[31]

Odio's younger sister Annie, who had also seen the three men back in September, joined her at the hospital. The notes from Fonzi's first interview with Silvia Odio say that later on November 22, Silvia was:

> . . . watching television with her sister and seeing Oswald . . . one of the men who came to the apartment. "We were just so scared because we both recognized him immediately." They both were extremely frightened and very anxious about the welfare of their many siblings and their mother and father in prison in Cuba and, since they didn't know what was going on or whether or not there had been a conspiracy of many involved in the assassination, they both decided not to bring their experience to the attention of the authorities. ("I never wanted to go to them, I was afraid. I was young at the time, I was recently divorced, I had young children, I was going through hell. Besides, it was such a responsibility to get involved because who is going to believe you, who is going to believe that I had Oswald in my house? I was scared and my sister Annie was very scared at the time, she was only 14.")

The only authority figure Silvia had told about Oswald's visit at the time it happened was Dr. Burton Einspruch, who had had been counseling Silvia about her family difficulties. Dr. Einspruch confirmed that to Fonzi, saying he recalled Silvia's telling him about the three men's visit prior to JFK's assassination.

The only other person Silvia confided in was her sister Sarita. However, Sarita told a mutual acquaintance, who told a friend, who told the FBI. This action started a chain of events that threatened to unravel the Warren Commission investigation just before its close, almost a year later. As documented in declassified files and in *Ultimate Sacrifice*, what has become known among historians as the "Odio incident" can be linked to four associates of Santo Trafficante, including two who had learned about parts of the JFK-Almeida coup plan: John Martino, who met with Sarita Odio around the time of the incident, and Rolando Masferrer, whose brother lived in the same Dallas apartment complex as Silvia Odio.[32]

In Tampa, Santo Trafficante greeted his lawyer, Frank Ragano, at the International Inn, the posh hotel where JFK had spoken just four days earlier. The hotel's fancy restaurant, usually full on a Friday night, had less than a dozen customers besides Trafficante, Ragano, and Ragano's girlfriend. With so few people around, the normally cautious Trafficante could be effusive without worrying.

Trafficante beamed as he told Ragano, "Isn't that something—they killed the son-of-a-bitch." Ragano says that Trafficante hugged and kissed him on the cheeks as the Tampa godfather gloated, "The son of a bitch is dead." According to Ragano, Trafficante's face was "wreathed in joy" as he boasted, "We'll make big money out of this and maybe go back to Cuba." Trafficante also said he was glad for their mutual associate Hoffa, since Bobby's power would end under LBJ. In his autobiography, Ragano claims he doesn't know what Trafficante meant about returning to Cuba, but it's clear Trafficante hoped that blaming the seemingly pro-Castro Oswald for JFK's murder would provoke the invasion that Trafficante's associates, like Martino, knew had been planned. Even if there weren't an invasion, with JFK out of the way and Bobby no longer controlling Cuban operations, Trafficante and his men would be free to return to Cuba if Castro were assassinated. (CIA and FBI files would later confirm that associates of Trafficante knew about Helms's unauthorized plots to use Cubela/AMLASH to assassinate Fidel.)[33]

Ragano writes that he and an ebullient Trafficante raised their glasses of scotch "as Santo said merrily, 'For a hundred years of health and to John Kennedy's death.' Santo and I both started laughing." Those words no doubt rang hollow in the somber, mostly empty restaurant. Ragano's girlfriend, a young college student, was horrified. After a few words with Ragano, "she rushed out of the restaurant." Ragano stayed to continue the celebration with Trafficante.[34]

Trafficante had much to celebrate that night, in the hotel where JFK had spoken so recently. His close associate Marcello had successfully bribed his way to an acquittal, and now that JFK was dead, Bobby's extraordinary power was coming to an end. Also, the JFK hit hadn't had to occur on Trafficante's turf. Moreover, Trafficante's man on the Tampa police force, Sgt. Jack de La Llana, could let him know if any word of the Tampa assassination attempt started to leak, or if the JFK investigation started to point toward Trafficante.[35] Finally, Trafficante knew Jack Ruby, and he apparently felt confident that Ruby would be able to take care of silencing Oswald.

Chapter Fourteen

As night fell in Washington, D.C., on November 22, 1963, Bobby Kennedy was on his way to Bethesda Naval Medical Center, along with Jackie and a caravan that included JFK's body. During the twenty-minute ride, Bobby heard Jackie's account of the shooting; once they arrived at Bethesda Naval Hospital, he would also hear what JFK aides Dave Powers and Kenneth O'Donnell had witnessed. According to historian Richard Mahoney, as they passed the Capitol building, Bobby later "recalled reflecting on his and Jack's dramatic days together on the McClellan Committee," when they first began investigating organized crime and Mafia bosses like Marcello and Trafficante.[1]

Entire books have been written about JFK's autopsy, which several government commissions studied over the course of thirty-five years, yet substantial controversies remain. The location and size of wounds on some autopsy x-rays and photos don't match what others show, or what some at Parkland or Bethesda observed. Even worse, crucial evidence is missing, ranging from photos and tissue samples to JFK's brain. At the root of these controversies is the fact that Bobby Kennedy controlled the autopsy.

A few basic facts about the autopsy are not in dispute. All agree that the Bethesda doctors didn't realize that JFK had been shot in the throat, since that wound was obscured by a tracheotomy incision. But the Bethesda doctors did find JFK's small back wound, which the Dallas physicians had missed in their rush to perform the tracheotomy and deal with JFK's massive head injuries. The Bethesda doctors initially assumed JFK had been shot once in the back and once in the head, and that Connally had been hit by a separate shot. It was only the next day, Saturday, that lead autopsy physician Dr. James Humes learned about the throat wound. Dr. Humes later admitted that he burned his first draft of the autopsy report on Sunday, November 24.[2]

Beyond those key points, much has been disputed over the years and remains controversial, ranging from what the autopsy doctors did or didn't do (and why) to what kind of casket JFK arrived in to whether he was in a body bag. By focusing only on the most glaring issues here, in layman's terms when possible, we can illustrate why some of the problems arose that night and why they persist today. (For detailed accounts, see *In the Eye of History,* by William Matson Law, and *Best Evidence,* by David Lifton.)

At Bethesda Naval Hospital, the man really calling the shots was Bobby Kennedy, from the family suite on the hospital's seventeenth floor. There, Bobby was part of a group that included Jackie, as well as JFK aides Dave Powers and Kenneth O'Donnell. Bobby was no doubt shocked when he heard what Powers and O'Donnell had seen from their vantage point in the motorcade, in the limo directly behind JFK's. As Powers told us, and as he and O'Donnell both confirmed to former House Speaker Tip O'Neill, they clearly saw shots from the grassy knoll.[3] Powers and O'Donnell had known and worked with Bobby for years; the Attorney General would have trusted their observations. In addition, Admiral George Burkley—the only doctor at Bethesda who had also seen JFK at Parkland—later stated that he believed JFK had been killed by more than one gunman.[4] All of this presented a dilemma for Bobby: If Oswald had been shooting from the rear, as Hoover and the news were now reporting, who had been shooting from the front?

Bobby's suspicions, expressed to Haynes Johnson just hours earlier, pointed to someone connected with a CIA-backed exile leader like Artime, who was involved in the JFK-Almeida coup plan. That belief tied into the suspicions Bobby expressed to CIA Director McCone about the CIA. Bobby's own subcommittee of the National Security Council had been making Cuba Contingency Plans for two months, to deal with the possibility that if Fidel learned about the coup plan, the Cuban leader might retaliate by assassinating an American official. The possibility of a shooter from Cuba, or even a double agent, couldn't be ruled out. Also, Oswald had spent more than two years in Russia—what if the other shooter had been sent by the Russians?

Any of those options could have led to a crisis with Cuba or Russia or both, especially if it were prematurely exposed. At the very least, the coup plan with Commander Almeida would have been compromised, resulting in the death or imprisonment of Almeida and his allies. The plan's exposure would have ended Bobby's political career and any chance he had to find out what had really happened to JFK. Bobby's concerns about Cuba, Russia, and Almeida would have been shared by other officials in the know, like Joint Chiefs Chairman General Maxwell Taylor, who had ultimate authority over a military facility like Bethesda. One of the main points of Bobby's subcommittee's planning had been to avoid a situation in which the premature release of information could back JFK into a corner and cause a crisis that could go nuclear. Now the thinking behind some of that planning would have to be implemented to deal with JFK's own death.

Some have tried to claim that shadowy generals, the CIA, or J. Edgar Hoover ran the autopsy without Bobby's knowledge, but much evidence shows that is simply not true. Several of the people in the autopsy made it clear that JFK's personal physician, Admiral Burkley, wielded a heavy hand at the autopsy on Bobby's behalf. Francis O'Neill, one of two FBI agents present at the autopsy, told Congressional investigators that there was "'no question' that Burkley was conveying the wishes of the Kennedy family."[5] Jerrol F. Custer, the radiology technician who took x-rays in the autopsy room using a portable x-ray machine, stated that Admiral Burkley said, "I am JFK's personal physician. You will listen to what I say. You will do what I say."[6]

A laboratory technician at the autopsy, Paul O'Connor, said that "Admiral Burkley controlled what happened in that room that night, through Bobby Kennedy and the rest of the Kennedy family." O'Connor says they only "did a perfunctory examination" of JFK's internal organs "because Admiral Burkley kept yelling that the Kennedy family wanted just so much done, and that's all and nothing else." O'Connor said that when Burkley came into the autopsy room, he "was very agitated— giving orders to everybody, including higher-ranking officers."[7]

But at least the appearance of observing military rank had to be maintained, and the Commandant of the Bethesda facility, Admiral Calvin Galloway, was present in the autopsy room, so Burkley sometimes conveyed Bobby's wishes using Galloway. James Jenkins, a navy man from Bethesda's clinical laboratory who helped at the autopsy, said that the main autopsy doctor "was probably being directed by Burkley through [Admiral] Galloway."[8] One of the assisting autopsy physicians, Dr. J. Thorton Boswell, said that "Dr. Burkley was basically supervising everything that went on in the autopsy room, and that the commanding officer was also responding to Burkley's wishes." Dr. Burkley himself stated in his oral history at the JFK Library that "during the autopsy I supervised everything that was done . . . and kept in constant contact with Mrs. Kennedy and the members of her party, who were on the seventeenth floor."[9]

Bobby was calling the shots to Dr. Burkley, and JFK military aide

General McHugh later testified that "Bobby Kennedy frequently phoned the autopsy suite." According to Gus Russo, the Commander of Bethesda's Naval Medical School, Captain John Stover, said that "Bobby went so far as to periodically visit the autopsy room during the procedure."[10]

However, Bobby also had someone—an individual whom we spoke with in 1992—assisting him in dealing with Burkley and the autopsy room. The presence of this very sensitive, confidential source at the autopsy has been confirmed by an official account, and his credibility is not only clear based on the public record, but has been vouched for by numerous associates of John and Robert Kennedy. These include Secretary of State Dean Rusk, Harry Williams, and Bobby's trusted FBI liaison Courtney Evans.

It's significant that our source who assisted Bobby at the autopsy was fully knowledgeable not only about the JFK-Almeida coup plan, but also about the Cuba Contingency Plans designed to protect it. The bottom line is that whatever went on at the autopsy most likely happened with the full knowledge, and probably at the ultimate direction, of Bobby Kennedy. Further proof of this concept is the fact that some of the most important missing evidence, such as JFK's brain, wound up under Bobby's control.

Even such a basic fact as when the autopsy started has caused much debate and uncertainty over the past four decades. There was a delay of at least forty minutes, and possibly as much as an hour, between the arrival of JFK's body at the facility and the start of the autopsy. While that might not be very unusual in itself, something else was: There were two ambulances—one was a decoy supposedly meant to throw off reporters and sightseers who might have made it onto the base. After JFK's body arrived at the front of the building, the *Washington Post* reported that Admiral Galloway himself "pushed into the front seat and drove to the rear of the hospital, where the body was taken inside."[11]

However, author David Lifton found that the men who were to guard the ambulance with JFK's body lost sight of the ambulance as it sped away. The guards chased after the ambulance, but couldn't find it. This was followed by much confusion on their part, before they finally arrived at the rear of the facility and found the ambulance at last.[12] Oddly, Secret Service Agent Kellerman says the autopsy started at 7:30, while the casket team's report says JFK's casket was not carried in until 8:00 PM. The two FBI agents say the first incision was made at 8:15 PM.

In addition to the unusual timing discrepancies, there were also easy-to-document differences between how JFK's body looked at Parkland

and how it looked (and was photographed) at the start of his autopsy in Bethesda. The most obvious example is JFK's throat wound, where the tracheotomy incision had been made. Dallas's Dr. Perry said that his small, neat incision was only 2–3 centimeters. However, photos of JFK's body at the start of the autopsy show a very ragged incision, spread open in the middle, that was at least two or three times larger. JFK's official autopsy report (now known to be at least the second completed, and possibly the third) says the incision was 6.5 centimeters when the autopsy began, while the lead autopsy physician, Dr. Humes, said under oath that it was 7–8 centimeters.[13] The throat incision was not enlarged during the official autopsy, because, as assisting autopsy physician Dr. Pierre Finck later testified, the doctors had been ordered not to.[14]

How did the small, neat incision in JFK's neck more than double in size to a wound so ragged that the autopsy physicians didn't even realize there had been a bullet hole there? Some experts have suggested a solution that would also account for the timing inconsistencies regarding the start of the autopsy, as well as the missing brain and other evidence. They say there could have been a brief, hurried, unofficial "national security autopsy" before the start of the official one. They point out that on the night of November 22, the official autopsy results and evidence were expected to be used in Oswald's trial, and would have to be turned over to his defense.

If Bobby Kennedy and other top officials were worried that evidence of another shooter from the front could have generated calls to invade Cuba and a conflict with the Soviets, this line of reasoning suggests they might have wanted to learn as much as possible before the "official" autopsy began. The greatly enlarged throat wound certainly appeared as if someone had hurriedly explored it to see if a bullet was still lodged inside.

While the official autopsy was jammed with officers and other personnel, such a national security autopsy might have been conducted with only a few people present. This scenario could also explain other discrepancies that have been documented. As the official account would evolve, JFK's back wound was supposedly caused by the complete "magic bullet" found at Parkland on a stretcher—no bullet (or substantial part of a bullet) was found at the autopsy. Yet Dr. Osborne—then a Captain and later an Admiral and the Deputy Surgeon General—told Congressional investigators he saw "an intact bullet roll . . . onto the autopsy table" when JFK was removed from his casket. Osborne reiterated to David Lifton that "I had that bullet in my hand and looked at it." He said it was "reasonably clean [and] unmarred," and "the Secret Service took it."[15]

Dr. Osborne's account is somewhat confirmed by the account of x-ray technician Custer, who said that "a pretty good-sized bullet" fell out of JFK's "upper back," where his back wound was located. He said that when "we lifted him up . . . that's when it came out."[16] Finally, the Commanding Officer of the Naval Medical School at the time, Captain John Stover, told author William Law, "Well, there was a bullet." To Lifton, "Stover confirmed there was a bullet in the Bethesda morgue" from JFK's body. However, Stover thought it was the bullet found on the stretcher at Parkland. But it wasn't, since that bullet was at the FBI laboratory, many miles away.[17]

A brief national security autopsy prior to the start of JFK's official autopsy, as well as national security concerns after the official autopsy, could also account for the many problems surrounding the autopsy photographs and x-rays. Douglas Horne was the Chief Analyst of military records for the congressionally created JFK Assassination Records Review Board (ARRB) for three years in the 1990s. In addition to the problem with JFK's throat wound, Horne recently wrote, "There is something seriously wrong with the autopsy photographs of the body of President Kennedy. . . . The images showing the damage to the President's head do not show the pattern of damage observed by either the medical professionals at Parkland Hospital in Dallas, or by numerous witnesses at the military autopsy at Bethesda Naval Hospital. These disparities are real and are significant."

To cite just two of several discrepancies he uncovered, Horne writes that "Navy photographer John Stringer, under oath before the ARRB, disowned the [JFK] brain photographs in the Archives, because (1) they were taken on a type of film he did not use; (2) they depict 'inferior' views of the underside of the brain which he was certain he did not shoot; and (3) the photographs of several individual sections of brain tissue that he did photograph were not present." Horne also cites FBI Agent Frank O'Neill, who "testified to the ARRB that the brain photos in the National Archives could not possibly be of President Kennedy's brain, because there was too much tissue present; O'Neill testified that more than half of President Kennedy's brain was missing when he saw it at the autopsy following its removal from the cranium, and his objections to the brain photographs in the Archives were that they depict what he called 'almost a complete brain.'"[18]

FBI Agent O'Neill, now retired, made other interesting observations.

Along with his colleague at the autopsy, Agent James Sibert, he doesn't believe in the "magic bullet" theory that was later proposed. Sibert says he looked at JFK's back wound from only two feet away. Measurements of the bullet holes in JFK's jacket and shirt show they were almost six inches below the tops of the collars, well below the neck. Agent Sibert says, "There's no way that bullet could go that low, then come up, raise up, and come out the front of the neck, zigzag and hit Connally, and then end up in a pristine condition over there in Dallas." Agent O'Neill concurs, saying, "Absolutely not, it did not happen."[19]

O'Neill also recently revealed something that Secret Service Agent Roy Kellerman said to him at the autopsy: "He told me he [had] cautioned Kennedy that morning not to be so open with the crowds for security reasons. Kennedy told him that if someone wanted to kill him, all they would have to do was use a scope rifle from a high building."[20] This statement was just one more indication of JFK's mindset following the Chicago and Tampa assassination attempts. When the events of the autopsy are considered in terms of the cloak of secrecy those attempts generated for national-security reasons, it starts to provide a rationale for many, if not all, of the autopsy discrepancies.

The fact that there were national-security concerns for what should have been a routine autopsy is confirmed by the fact that thirteen people—including the three main autopsy physicians, most of the lower-ranking people present at the autopsy, and even Admiral Galloway's secretary—were ordered to sign a secrecy order four days later. As O'Connor said, they were told they were "under the penalty of general court martial, and other dreadful things like going to prison."[21] The orders were finally rescinded at the request of the House Select Committee on Assassinations in March 1978. However, it's not known what orders covered the higher-ranking people present at the autopsy, or whether those orders were ever rescinded. As we document in Chapter 64, in 1978 Commander Almeida was still high in the Cuban government, and his secret work for JFK had not yet been exposed. In fact, on April 22, 1978, Almeida met at the UN with a representative of then–Secretary of State Cyrus Vance, and the JFK-Almeida coup plan was never revealed to the Committee.

At the time of JFK's assassination, Vance was Secretary of the Army and fully aware of the JFK-Almeida coup plan. After the autopsy, JFK's body and funeral arrangements were put in the hands of Vance's two trusted aides, Joseph Califano (who would serve in the Cabinet with Vance in the late 1970s) and Alexander Haig (later a Secretary of State

himself). Haig has written that he "was assigned the duty of helping
with the preparations for the President's funeral [and] handling details
concerning the burial site."[22] Califano has written that after JFK's murder, he went to the Pentagon and met Vance, who put him in charge of
arranging JFK's burial at Arlington National Cemetery and meeting
Bobby there the next day.[23]

Califano and Haig have always been careful to distance themselves
from the most sensitive parts of Vance's work on Bobby's plans to eliminate Castro, and neither has ever admitted to knowing about the JFK-
Almeida coup plan. But declassified files confirm that Califano and Haig
worked on the Cuba Contingency Plans for dealing with the possible
"assassination of American officials" when that planning started, in late
September 1963.[24] Vance's use of Califano and Haig makes sense, even
if both men had not yet been told about the JFK-Almeida coup plan.
Because of their admitted work on some of Bobby's anti-Castro activities, and their involvement in the Cuba Contingency planning, Vance
knew he could count on each man if any problems arose that might
involve national security.

In fact, when a problem did arise, Haig showed how information
could be destroyed for reasons of national security. In his autobiography, Haig wrote that "very soon after JFK's death, an intelligence
report crossed my desk. In circumstantial detail, it stated that Oswald
had been seen in Havana in the company of Cuban intelligence officers
several days before the events in Dallas . . . the detail—locale, precise
notations of time, and more—was very persuasive. I was aware that
it would not have reached so high a level if others had not judged it
plausible. . . . I walked it over to my superiors. . . . 'Al,' said one of them,
'you will forget, as from this moment, that you ever read this piece of
paper, or that it ever existed.' The report was destroyed."[25] Unfortunately, Haig didn't realize that there were many similar reports later
shown to be bogus, most connected to associates of David Morales,
Johnny Rosselli, Santo Trafficante, and Carlos Marcello.

While JFK's autopsy continued at Bethesda, the lines were buzzing
between the White House and Dallas in an effort to rein in public comments and legal action that could launch an outcry for action against
Cuba or the Soviet Union. Earlier that evening, the Dallas Assistant
District Attorney, Bill Alexander, had talked about filing charges against
Oswald for murdering JFK "as part of an international communist conspiracy."[26] Reports like that quickly reached Washington, alarming Pres-

ident Lyndon Johnson, now at the White House. Given the constant stream of TV news coverage on all three networks, much of it from Dallas, LBJ knew that one inflammatory statement on live TV by an official in Texas could generate demands for retaliation that could be hard for a new president to resist.

On the night of November 22, an LBJ aide placed urgent calls to Texas Attorney General Carr, US Attorney Sanders, Dallas District Attorney Wade, and Police Chief Curry. Author Larry Hancock says the message was the same in each case: "Avoid any official statements, charges, or discussion relating to conspiracy" that involved Russia, Cuba, or international communism.[27] DA Wade later said that "President Johnson's aide called me three times from the White House that Friday night. He said that President Johnson felt any word of a conspiracy—some plot by foreign nations to kill President Kennedy—would shake our nation to its foundation." Hancock notes that "the FBI also moved quickly to bring pressure on Chief Curry to retract statements . . . that Oswald was known to be a Communist and potentially dangerous."[28] Curry agreed, though it would be a constant struggle for Hoover to limit Curry's public statements about the case. Curry had easily grasped that the FBI wanted the public to know that Oswald was guilty, but he appeared to have trouble understanding why Hoover's usually rabidly anticommunist FBI didn't want him or anyone else to imply that Cuba, Russia, or communism was behind Oswald's actions.

Both Hoover and LBJ knew how carefully public statements and the media had to be managed as the national and international press converged on Dallas. Numerous reporters, who would later become famous, first received national notice in Dallas, sometimes becoming part of the story. We've already mentioned Dan Rather, but his successor as anchor of *CBS Evening News*, Bob Schieffer, also received his big break that day. As a reporter for the *Fort Worth Star-Telegram*, Shieffer not only gave Oswald's mother a ride to Dallas; he escorted her into police headquarters. Peter Jennings from Canada was there, and in addition to the earlier mentioned Robert MacNeil, his later partner on PBS, Jim Lehrer, was also covering JFK's murder, as a reporter for the *Dallas Times-Herald*. National anchors like Chet Huntley, David Brinkley, and Walter Cronkite held down the fort in New York and Washington; indeed, Cronkite's performance on November 22 and throughout the following days propelled him to the legendary status he soon attained.

Unfortunately, the fact that so many careers were launched that day helped to stifle serious journalistic investigation of JFK's assassination for many years. As Dan Rather implied in his autobiography, if there were a conspiracy behind JFK's death, why didn't the reporters there find it? The answer is also in his autobiography, and in the later comments of newsmen like Schieffer: The reporters' biggest concerns were scooping the competition and getting something sensational out quickly.[29] The whole atmosphere was not conducive to careful, methodical investigation, or questioning the information stated publicly or leaked by authorities (something that was rare in those pre-Watergate days). In later years, newsmen like Rather and Cronkite would find themselves defending the "lone assassin" theory almost as a matter of professional pride, as if anyone questioning it were somehow calling the newsmen's judgment into question.

A good example of the media feeding frenzy in Dallas that weekend was Oswald's press appearance, held after midnight on Friday, which Jack Ruby attended. As described to journalist Jack Anderson by Johnny Rosselli, after "Oswald was picked up . . . underworld conspirators feared he would crack and disclose information that might lead to them. This almost certainly would have brought a massive US crackdown on the Mafia, so Jack Ruby was ordered to eliminate Oswald."[30] That Friday evening, as Ruby tried to get close to Oswald, he found himself incredibly busy. Ruby had free access to police facilities because, as Tippit's attorney later said, Ruby was "very close friends" with Captain Fritz, who was running the homicide investigation, and "Ruby, in spite of his reputation of being a 'hood,' was allowed complete run of the Homicide Bureau."[31]

Ruby later admitted he was carrying his pistol that evening. He was seen on the third floor of police headquarters that night at 6:00 PM (Central) and again an hour later. Not long after that, Ruby attempted to open the door to Captain Fritz's office, where Oswald was being interrogated. If Ruby had succeeded, he probably would have done then what millions of people would see him do on live television less than forty-one hours later. But that night two policemen stopped Ruby, one cautioning him, "You can't go in there, Jack."

Jack left the police station, but not for long. At 10:30 PM, while Oswald was being interrogated, Ruby called one of the officers and offered to bring them sandwiches, but the officer declined. Ruby was seen at the police station again around 11:30 PM. Soon after, Ruby attended a press briefing by Chief Curry and DA Wade, where he learned that Oswald was going to be shown to newsmen in a press conference in the basement. Ruby made sure he was there, and he is clearly visible in film of

Oswald's brief press conference. However, the film also shows that Ruby was too far away to get a clear shot at Oswald (and in the packed room, swarming with police, one shot was all he could count on).

But Ruby was able to helpfully correct Wade when the DA mistakenly said that Oswald was a member of the "Free Cuba Committee." That was the name of an anti-Castro group run by Eladio del Valle, the criminal associate of Ferrie, Trafficante, and Masferrer (the last two also knew Ruby). Ruby shouted out a correction to Wade, saying it was actually the "Fair Play for Cuba Committee," which was a pro-Castro organization.[32]

During the rowdy press conference, Oswald said in response to a question that he "didn't shoot anybody, no sir" and correctly stated that he had not been charged with shooting the President. Oswald also asked for someone to "come forward to give me legal assistance," possibly an appeal to one of his contacts, like Banister or Phillips, to clear him with the authorities. (Two lawyers connected to Marcello received calls about representing Oswald, but Oswald never saw a lawyer while he was in custody.) Interestingly, Chief Curry later said that "one would think Oswald had been trained in interrogation techniques and resisting interrogation techniques," and that Curry believed Oswald could have been some type of agent. That was based on the way Oswald handled himself during the twelve hours of interrogation that weekend, none of which were recorded or stenographically transcribed. Assistant DA Alexander said that he "was amazed that a person so young would have had the self-control he had. It was almost as if he had been rehearsed, or programmed, to meet the situation that he found himself in."[33]

Alexander apparently didn't consider the possibility that Oswald had been trained to handle KGB interrogation before he went to Russia, or to deal with the possibility of interrogation by Cuba's secret police if Oswald successfully entered that country. DA Alexander also didn't entertain the prospect that Oswald might have been innocent of shooting JFK. (As many authors, such as Anthony Summers, have documented, "nobody has ever made the flimsiest allegation that the authentic Lee Oswald had anything but good to say about John Kennedy." This was true in Oswald's interrogations, his media appearances, and his private talks. Three months before JFK's murder, Oswald had been interviewed by a New Orleans police lieutenant who later said that Oswald "seemed to favor President Kennedy [and] in no way demonstrated any animosity or ill feeling toward President Kennedy . . . he liked the President.")[34]

After Oswald had been taken from the room after the press conference,

Ruby ran up to DA Wade, saying, "Hi, Henry!" Wade shook hands with Ruby and asked, "What are you doing here?" William Manchester wrote that "Ruby waved his hand about and said grandly, 'I know all these fellows,'" meaning the many policemen in the room.[35] Ruby realized he wouldn't have any more chances to get to Oswald that night, so he left and went to a radio station owned by Gordon McClendon, a close friend of David Atlee Phillips. McClendon was also friends with Ruby, who had tried to call McClendon's home earlier that evening.

Oswald was finally charged with killing JFK at 1:30 AM (Central); he had been charged with killing Tippit earlier, at 7:30 PM. Anthony Summers writes that Assistant DA Alexander later said Oswald was charged with killing JFK because of his departure from the Book Depository, his story about bringing curtain rods to work that morning, and the "'communist' literature found among Oswald's effects at the rooming house."[36] (Several years earlier, Guy Banister had found and displayed for New Orleans media a very similar stash of incriminating communist literature.)[37]

By 2:00 AM, Ruby had left the radio station for an suspicious meeting at Simpson's Parking Garage. There, Ruby met with a Dallas police officer and his girlfriend, a dancer for Ruby. Those involved gave varying accounts of the length of the meeting and who was present, but the policeman said it lasted between two and three hours. That seems like a long time for a meeting in the middle of the night at a parking garage. Some have speculated that Ruby was trying to talk the officer into shooting Oswald, helping Ruby find an officer who would, or helping Ruby get close enough to Oswald to do the job himself.

Chapter Fifteen

In the predawn hours of November 23, 1963, another piece of evidence surfaced that would seal the case against Oswald. Historian Richard Mahoney writes that at "4:00 AM (Central), executives at Klein's Sporting Goods in Chicago discovered the *American Rifleman* [magazine] coupon Oswald had allegedly used to order the Mannlicher-Carcano [found on the sixth floor of the Book Depository.] CIA files from the Assassination Archives reveal that the first lead as to the location of the rifle came from the chief investigator of the Cook County Sheriff's Office, Richard Cain, a Roselli-Giancana confederate."[1] Like most of those involved in the JFK assassination operation, Cain also knew Trafficante and had worked on the CIA-Mafia plots—and CIA files confirm that he knew about the AMWORLD part of the JFK-Almeida coup plan. Cain, a "made" member of the Chicago Mafia, was also an active CIA asset at the time.[2]

Cain had been feeding information to the CIA since August that would impact the course of the investigation, and he continued to plant phony stories in the press after JFK's death, saying that Oswald had received money in Chicago. However, when Chicago Secret Service Agent Abraham Bolden was asked by the Dallas office to get information about "Oswald's rifle and the possibility that Oswald received money from Chicago . . . neither Bolden, nor any other Secret Service agent, could get any information on either lead and they were preempted by the FBI, who had . . . warned all concerned to talk to no one, including the Secret Service."[3] Because of LBJ's close relationship with J. Edgar Hoover, the FBI would win the turf war with the Secret Service over the JFK investigation. However, both agencies continued to cooperate in squelching the release of problematic information, including any news about the Chicago and Tampa attempts.

As for mob lawman Richard Cain, a CIA memo says he was "heavily involved" in the JFK assassination investigation, but almost none of those files have been released.[4] Months later, when Abraham Bolden would try to bring the Chicago and Tampa attempts to the Warren Commission's attention, Cain would have the motive, means, and opportunity to help frame Bolden.

Thousands of pages have been written about the odd circumstances of the rifle's ordering, its abysmal condition, and whether or not the rifle that was found was the same one that Oswald apparently ordered.[5] However, even Warren Commission and military testimony confirm the rifle found on the sixth floor had a scope that "was installed as if for a left-handed man." All evidence shows that Oswald was right-handed, despite later questioning of Marina Oswald and grilling of Lee's brother in a vain attempt to show otherwise. Also, the scope was so badly misaligned that shots later fired by military experts all landed "high and to the right of the target." This was no accident caused by a fleeing assassin's dropping the rifle and knocking the scope out of alignment. Military experts at the Aberdeen Proving Ground would later tell the Warren Commission that "three shims [had been] placed in the scope," as it was found on the sixth floor.[6]

None of those problems would be publicized as they became known. But stories about the mail-order rifle soon filled the airwaves and newspapers, as if they were the final link in the chain of Oswald's guilt. On the other hand, news about evidence that raised the possibility of other assassins was summarily dismissed—and in some cases, even the physical evidence disappeared. One example is the skull fragment mentioned earlier, which was found on the median across from the grassy knoll, ten feet behind the position of JFK's limo—a location that could have indicated a fatal head shot from the front. The skull piece itself was from the back of JFK's head, which also tended to indicate that a shot from the front had blown the piece out of the back of his skull. The piece was found by a college student, then examined and photographed by three doctors, including the chief pathologist at the Methodist Hospital in Dallas. They forwarded it to Dr. Burkley in Washington, who gave it to the FBI, who also notified the Secret Service. The 2.75-by-2.2-inch piece from the back of JFK's skull then vanished, though its existence is confirmed by photographs and Congressional investigators. Apparently, the main autopsy physician was not told about the bone fragment.[7] On Saturday, November 23, he was still working on his first autopsy report when he first learned from a Parkland doctor that JFK's body had a throat bullet wound, under the tracheotomy incision.

The skull fragment is just one example of how the official story of Oswald as a "lone assassin," which dominated the Saturday newspapers and constant TV news coverage, was far different from what officials would say in private, or reveal much later. Newspapers that weekend cited Dallas Police Chief Curry as saying the case against Oswald was solid, but just a few years later Curry would admit: "We don't have any proof that Oswald fired the rifle, and never did. Nobody's yet been able to put him in that building with a gun in his hand."[8] According to *Vanity Fair,* Curry himself "believed two gunmen were involved" in the assassination, though not a hint of that belief appeared in the press that weekend or in the months to come.[9]

Even J. Edgar Hoover admitted to Lyndon Johnson, in a recorded phone call at 10:01 AM on November 23, that "the case, as it stands now, isn't strong enough to be able to get a conviction."[10] Yet the Saturday morning newspapers were conveying just the opposite impression by establishing the basic "lone assassin" scenario that some people still believe today. In hindsight, it seems absurd to think that all the relevant information about the shooting, and an unusual former defector like Oswald, could be uncovered less than twenty-four hours after the shooting—and that clearly wasn't the case. However, investigations that touched on covert matters would have to be conducted in secret, so as not to alarm the public or back LBJ into a corner regarding possible retaliation against Cuba or the Soviet Union.

In using their positions and media contacts to control the official release of information, key officials—including LBJ, Hoover, Bobby, the Secret Service, the Dallas Police, and the US military—were acting both in the national interest and in their own self-interest. The more attention focused on Oswald as a "lone nut" who hadn't acted on anyone else's behalf or with any confederates, the less chance the press or local law enforcement had of exposing leads or information that could cause problems with Cuba or Russia. For Dallas officials, limiting matters to the seemingly Marxist Oswald made the conservative city look better, and prevented any chance of exposing locals who might have used Oswald for their own purposes. The police had their man, and it was simply best not to look into evidence to the contrary because of the potentially troubling questions it could raise.

In some cases, as in squelching the story of the Tampa assassination attempt, top officials and agencies probably had to rely on press contacts to keep certain stories from being pursued. Fourteen years after Dallas, in generally more liberal times after Watergate and Vietnam, reporter Carl Bernstein would write in *Rolling Stone* that hundreds of journalists were involved in the "long-standing cooperation between the CIA and many media organizations, involving resource sharing, secrecy agreements, and covert operations. Among the media involved, he said, were the three major television networks; *Time* and *Newsweek* magazines; the *New York Times*; and the Associated Press and United Press International."[11] The vast majority of the CIA's press contacts have never been exposed, though a few memos have been declassified, listing various journalists as "unwitting collaborators" if they were fed information that they didn't realize originated with the CIA, and as "witting collaborators" if they did. Some Miami journalists covering anti-Castro operations even received their own CIA code names (AMCARBON-1, AMCARBON-2, etc.).[12]

Journalists withholding information from the public didn't have to be made aware of the JFK-Almeida coup plan, or the Cuba Contingency Plans to protect it. They could simply be told that certain information was too sensitive, could compromise US operations, or might force a confrontation with the Soviets—and just a year after the Cuban Missile Crisis, this last explanation might be all that was required, since Oswald's Soviet and Cuba connections had been so widely reported. We know that when information linking Oswald to David Ferrie started to surface during the weekend after JFK's murder, an NBC cameraman related that "an FBI agent said that I should never discuss what we discovered for the good of the country."[13] That same phrase, "for the good of the country," would be used to stop Dave Powers and Kenneth O'Donnell from revealing they had seen shots from the grassy knoll, and it was probably used to silence others as well. Longtime television journalist Peter Noyes was told by several "members of NBC News who covered the events in Dallas [that] they were convinced their superiors wanted certain evidence suppressed at the request of someone in Washington."[14]

Some US officials dealing with media assets might have been aware only that Oswald had been under US surveillance before the assassination, something that not only would have been embarrassing for the FBI, CIA, and Naval Intelligence if it were revealed, but also could expose the rather large domestic surveillance program those agencies ran, which was technically illegal. (Each time Congressional hearings threatened to fully expose those operations in the 1970s, the hearings were overshadowed by other events—first Watergate, and then the first revelations of the CIA-Mafia Castro assassination plots to the public.) Any official who actually had access to some of the surveillance might have believed Oswald acted alone, because the record showed it was unlikely he had any associates or contacts that US intelligence didn't know about. In fact, many of his associates were themselves of interest to US intelligence (which is why some of them helped with the surveillance). Some officials might have known that Oswald was some type of US intelligence asset, and simply thought he had turned "bad." All of these are reasons for officials to pressure certain journalists to withhold information, without requiring either the official or the journalist to be told about the JFK-Almeida coup plan.

The officially sanctioned story of "lone nut" Oswald that quickly emerged was limited to the evidence that had already become widely known. Anything else was quickly suppressed, like the newspaper article about the Tampa assassination attempt that appeared on Saturday, November 23. The article appeared only in the *Tampa Tribune;* it was based on information from Tampa Police Chief Mullins and also cited a White House Secret Service memo. The November 8 memo quoted in the article said a "subject made statement of a plan to assassinate the President . . . stated he will use a gun. . . . Subject is described as: white, male, 20, slender build." That description matches Lee Oswald's much better than the initial one issued in Dallas, which described the suspect as being much older and heavier. The sheriff of a county adjacent to Tampa confirmed in the article that officers had been "warned about 'a young man' who had threatened to kill the President during that trip."[15]

In the article, Chief Mullins mentioned another man at large, identified as a threat, and wondered "if the . . . two may have followed the Presidential caravan to Dallas." Mullins didn't know about the two men who had left Florida for Texas, with Rose Cheramie, shortly after the Tampa attempt. Also unknown to Mullins at that time, Gilberto Policarpo Lopez—the young Cuban exile linked to the Fair Play for Cuba Committee, who had so many recent parallels to Oswald—had indeed headed to Texas. Once Lopez was in Texas, Congressional investigators found that he "crossed the border into Mexico," then went to Mexico City and into Cuba, just as Oswald had tried to do in late September. Lopez used the same border crossing as Oswald, and apparently like Oswald on the return leg of his Mexico trip, "crossed [the border] in a privately owned automobile owned by another person."[16] Someone had to be helping each man, since neither owned a car or had a driver's license.

The description cited in the Tampa article is also close to Lopez's. Clearly, if JFK had been killed in Tampa, authorities would have already been primed to look for a suspect like Lopez or Oswald (whose

whereabouts the day before the Tampa attempt have never been determined; one unconfirmed report places him in Tampa, meeting with associates of Lopez). We noted previously an unconfirmed newspaper report
placing Lopez in Dallas on the day of the assassination. If films and
eyewitnesses had pointed so overwhelmingly to an additional shooter in
Dallas that they couldn't be ignored, Lopez probably would have been
fingered by one of the CIA assets working for Marcello, Trafficante, or
Rosselli. If the public found out that an accused shooter was a Cuban, or
that he had fled to Cuba, it's not hard to imagine the outcry that would
have resulted from Congress and the public for an invasion of Cuba.
We feel that's exactly what the mob bosses and their allies, like David
Morales and John Martino, had wanted to happen. They didn't care
if JFK's murder was blamed on one assassin or two—only that those
blamed were linked to Cuba.

Neither this *Tampa Tribune* article nor anything about the Tampa
attempt was ever brought to the attention of the Warren Commission or any of the later investigating committees, like the House Select
Committee on Assassinations. We discovered it only after reviewing
thousands of pages of newspaper microfilm in Tampa and Miami, pain-
stakingly reading through each edition (there were often several editions
in one day, especially during events like the Cuban Missile Crisis or
JFK's assassination).

When we contacted Mullins in 1996, he confirmed everything in the
article and provided additional information, as well as referring us to
more law enforcement sources who had been involved in dealing with
the Tampa attempt. (One high Florida law enforcement official provided
additional information about Trafficante's involvement in the attempt
and told us that Gilberto Lopez appeared to be an informant for some
government agency.) Chief Mullins, by then long retired, said he was
surprised he had never been contacted by reporters or government
researchers in the thirty-three years since the article appeared, and that
news about the Tampa threat had never been mentioned in any of the
reports about the JFK assassination. He felt frustrated by the fact that
many of his department's files about Trafficante had been destroyed
several years after he left office.[17]

We should point out that we don't think Gilberto Lopez was knowingly involved in JFK's death or the Tampa attempt. Moreover, based
on the descriptions, he was not one of the two men traveling with Rose
Cheramie. Given the many parallels between Lopez and Oswald that
we listed previously, both men were probably being influenced or

manipulated by the same type of individual, someone they trusted as an intelligence or law enforcement figure, who was actually working for one of the three Mafia chiefs. The same would be true for ex-Marine Vallee in Chicago. In the same way the Mafia bosses' plan to kill JFK in Chicago included not just one backup city, but two (Tampa and Dallas), they were prepared in case an accident or illness prevented one of their fall guys from being in the right place at the right time.

The *Tampa Tribune* article was small and on an inside page; it wasn't front-page news; just filler about an odd aspect of JFK's recent Tampa trip. But since all word of the Tampa threat had been kept out of the press, it quickly got the attention of the *Miami Herald* and the Associated Press. It's not hard to imagine the reactions of Bobby, Hoover, LBJ, the Secret Service, and McCone when they heard the Tampa threat had started to leak. Tampa had a large Cuban exile population, and a sizable minority of them supported Fidel; the Tampa chapter of the Fair Play for Cuba Committee was an actual organization, not a phony one-man front like Oswald had in New Orleans. While Lopez had apparently not yet surfaced as a suspect, he soon would, and the national-security implications were enormous. If the public found out that JFK had been targeted during his Tampa motorcade just four days earlier, the press and the public might not be so willing to swallow the official account of a lone, unaided assassin in Dallas. If word of the Tampa plans emerged, then the Chicago threat, which had contributed to JFK's decision to cancel his motorcade there, might also come out. It would look as if JFK had been constantly stalked by Cubans or by the "international communist conspiracy," the very thing LBJ had his aide order Texas officials to avoid mentioning.

Chief Mullins explained that he was never told why he had been ordered to cut off all mention of the Tampa threat to the press, which is one reason he was willing to talk to us about it in 1996. But in those days, as today, the Tampa police cooperated with the local FBI and Secret Service offices, and with other federal agencies like the CIA. Mullins therefore did what he was told. When the Associated Press and the *Miami Herald* attempted to follow up on the revelations in the *Tampa Tribune* article, they were confronted by a wall of secrecy. The *Herald* reported the next day that "the FBI, Secret Service, and local officers declined to discuss the matter." The Secret Service offered "no comment." As for the Secret Service memo quoted in the original *Tampa Tribune* article, it appears to have vanished from the official record. While it might be buried among the four million–plus pages of JFK files at the National

Archives, it could also have been one of the files covering the period of the Tampa attempt that the Secret Service would admit to destroying in January 1995. That was approximately six weeks after the authors had first informed the JFK Assassination Records Review Board about the newspaper article describing the Tampa attempt.

It took thirty-three years for any researcher or investigator to locate the first small article about the Tampa attempt, so other such articles might still be out there, perhaps appearing in only one edition of a newspaper. It took several days for all newspapers to completely adopt the official story, and in the meantime, other stories briefly emerged, only to quickly be shut down. On Monday, November 25, the *New York Post* reported that when Oswald went to Mexico, his "movements were watched at the request of a 'Federal agency in Washington' [according to] William M. Kline, assistant United States Customs Agent-in-Charge of the Bureau's Investigative Service." The following day, the *New York Times* reported from Mexico that Oswald's "movements were followed in Mexico by an unidentified United States Agency." The same day, the *New York Herald-Tribune* added a report from US Customs official Oran Pugh that the way Oswald was monitored at the border was "not the usual procedure."[18] These stories, which hinted at the tight surveillance of Oswald, were quickly squelched. The following year, the Warren Commission would obtain carefully worded denials from the Customs officials mentioned in the stories, though the subject would not be mentioned in the Commission's Final Report.

Another example of a story's slipping through the cracks in the early days was an Associated Press article saying "someone telegraphed small amounts of money to Lee Oswald for several months before the assassination."[19] Though private pressure usually worked to control stories in the media, just to make sure the message was abundantly clear, Hoover later issued a statement, carried by the *New York Times*, saying that Oswald had not been under surveillance by the FBI and was "neither a spy nor a saboteur."[20]

It's ironic that on Saturday, November 23, some newspapers were reporting information that was, in some ways, more accurate than many of Hoover's public statements. As we mentioned earlier, many editorials written the previous day—before much about Oswald was known—blamed JFK's murder on right-wing extremists. They were more correct than they realized, given the racist views of Marcello, his white-supremacist associates like Guy Banister and Milteer, and the far-right ties of others involved, such as Martino, Ferrie, and Masferrer, and those on the plot's periphery, like Artime and Rivero. Ironically, the statements of communist dictatorships in Cuba and Russia were in some ways closer to the truth than Hoover was. Far beyond the reach of Hoover's FBI, the official Soviet news agency, TASS, blamed "racists, the Ku Klux Klan, and Birchers." While not Klan members, both Banister and Milteer had close associates who were, and Martino was one of the most prominent speakers offered by the John Birch Society. Of course, the Russians had their own self-interest at stake in pointing the finger away from a seemingly lone communist assassin, as did Castro.

Fidel Castro was meeting with JFK's personal emissary, French journalist Jean Daniel, at Varadero Beach when they received word of JFK's death. In both his private and public statements, Castro indicated JFK's death was a very bad thing. Castro didn't mention the secret negotiations when he issued a public statement on Saturday, but he did blame JFK's murder on "'a macabre plan' prepared by United States right-wing extremists."[21]

In Washington, Richard Helms was trying to orchestrate critical cover-ups on two fronts, even as he tried to figure out what had really happened in Dallas. First, Helms had to be sure that no one—especially the CIA Director, President Lyndon Johnson, or Bobby Kennedy—learned of his unauthorized Castro assassination operations. Second, he also had to protect the CIA's authorized anti-Castro plots, ranging from the JFK-Almeida coup plan and AMWORLD to the far less developed AMTRUNK. Because there was some overlap between some of the operations (AMWORLD's Artime was part of both the JFK-Almeida plan and the unauthorized CIA-Mafia plots to kill Castro), he could use actions to protect the authorized plans to simultaneously hide—and even continue—his own unauthorized plotting.

First, Helms had to get control of all the CIA's material on Oswald. Historian Michael Kurtz has written that Hunter Leake, whom memos confirm was Deputy Chief of the New Orleans CIA office in 1963, told him "that on the day after the assassination, he was ordered to collect all of the CIA's files on Oswald from the New Orleans office and transport them to the Agency's headquarters in Langley, Virginia." Kurtz writes that:

> . . . [along with] other employees of the New Orleans office, Leake gathered all of the Oswald files. They proved so voluminous that Leake had to rent a trailer to transport them to Langley. Stopping only to eat, use the restroom, and fill up with gas, Leake drove the

truck pulling the rental trailer filled with the New Orleans office's files on Oswald to CIA headquarters. Leake later learned that many of these files were . . . 'deep sixed.' Leake explained that . . . the CIA dreaded the release of any information that would connect Oswald with it. Leake speculated that his friend Richard Helms, the Agency's Deputy Director for Plans, was probably the person who ordered the destruction of the files because Helms had a paranoid obsession with protecting the 'company.'[22]

Leake's remark about the "voluminous" files on Oswald makes sense, given the information from our independent source about the "tight surveillance" of Oswald, which was not known to Kurtz at the time of his interview with Leake. Buttressing Leake's credibility is the fact that no routine reports from the CIA's New Orleans office have ever surfaced about former defector Oswald's well-publicized pro-Castro activities in New Orleans during August 1963, despite the CIA's interest in both former defectors and the Fair Play for Cuba Committee. Also, Leake's statement to Kurtz that "Oswald indeed performed chores for the CIA during his five months in New Orleans during the spring and summer of 1963" fits with other information about Oswald's work for Banister: the remarkable amount of media coverage Oswald was able to generate in such a short time, followed by Oswald's meeting with CIA media expert David Atlee Phillips, who was also working on AMWORLD.[23] The last part is important, because it suggests that Oswald had some role in an authorized CIA operation like AMWORLD; otherwise, Helms couldn't have hoped to keep the efforts of Leake and "other employees of the New Orleans office" secret from McCone.

It's important to keep in mind that while Helms engaged in his cover-ups, several of the authorized and unauthorized operations were still active and viable. That meant that Helms had to find a way to conceal information while still preserving those operations and his options. He had to decide what to hide, and from whom, and what to reveal. Some of the decisions Helms made that day would become CIA dogma for decades, even as evidence emerged that the line Helms took couldn't possibly be true. As Dr. John Newman documented, this included the CIA's "decision soon after the assassination to deny that anyone within the CIA—including the Mexico station—knew of Oswald's visits to the Cuban consulate until after JFK's murder." CIA files declassified later show this claim was clearly false.[24]

Deceiving his own CIA Director, Helms apparently authorized Desmond FitzGerald, his head of Cuban operations, to tell McCone's executive assistant only that a CIA case officer had been meeting with Cubela in Paris when JFK was shot, and that FitzGerald himself had met with Cubela the previous month. FitzGerald didn't tell him anything about the assassination aspects of the Cubela operation, since McCone hadn't been told about that part of the plan. That meant McCone's assistant wasn't told about the poison pen the case officer tried to give Cubela, or about his promise to deliver high-powered rifles with scopes for Cubela to use in assassinating Castro, so McCone and his assistant probably saw little to be concerned about.[25]

However, McCone's assistant was struck by how emotional Fitz-Gerald was when he told him about Cubela. He told *Newsweek* editor Evan Thomas that "Des was normally imperturbable, but he was very disturbed . . . shaking his head and wringing his hands." He couldn't understand why FitzGerald appeared to be "distraught and overreacting," but he didn't realize how much crucial information FitzGerald was withholding from him and McCone. It's also revealing that Helms had FitzGerald tell McCone's assistant about the Cubela meeting, instead of Helms's telling McCone directly.

McCone was at least generally aware of Cubela, as were a few others outside of the CIA—but to them, Cubela was only someone who could look for others to help stage a coup, and who could provide intelligence on them. Other officials outside the CIA knew about Cubela in the same way, as one of "three persons who are in the [Cuban] military or who have highly placed contacts in such circles," as FitzGerald said in a meeting chaired by JFK just ten days before Dallas.[26] However, some of them, like Secretary of State Rusk and another source we spoke with, didn't yet know about the JFK-Almeida coup plan. Cubela wasn't part of Almeida's coup plan and hadn't been told about it, as is clear from newly declassified files and from our sources who worked on the plan. But Helms wanted to preserve Cubela as his own, unauthorized adjunct to the JFK-Almeida coup plan, so two days later he ordered FitzGerald to have Cubela's case officer remove a reference to the poison pen from a memo about the meeting.

As written, the Cubela memo seen by McCone obscures the subject of the scoped rifles by saying only that Cubela needed to be sent a seventy-five-pound cache of explosives that also included "weapons and ammo." It sounds like material for one of the small sabotage operations the CIA was still occasionally running, and there is no mention of assassination. This longer, more narrative memo—clearly designed to be read by someone like McCone—doesn't specifically mention the rifles with scopes, as does the much shorter, bare-bones operational memo.[27]

One reason Helms and FitzGerald probably felt they needed to hide the unauthorized portion of their actions involving Cubela and others was that the CIA's overall operations against Cuba were still very substantial. While not as extensive as it had been a year earlier, the effort was still a massive undertaking, run mostly from the huge Miami CIA station, but with especially sensitive portions run from Washington (by FitzGerald) and Mexico City (by Phillips). The whole program involved hundreds of agents and assets, some of whom were often infiltrated into Cuba or exfiltrated from it.

Declassified files from November 1963 are filled with the "AM" code names (which signify Cuban operations) of operatives and operations, many of which have never themselves been declassified. In addition to names we've explored—like AMWORLD, AMLASH (Cubela), and AMTRUNK—there were less important ones, like AMCOBRA, AMCLEOPATRA, AMHALF, AMFOX, AMCROW, AMCRUX, AMJUDGE, AMGLOSSY, and many dozens—perhaps hundreds—more, all active at the time of JFK's death. Secret drops of supplies, communications equipment, and arms were constantly being arranged and delivered. And all this was in addition to the support for the exile leaders that Bobby and Harry had selected for the JFK-Almeida coup plan (Artime, Ray, Menoyo, and Varona), who based their sometimes considerable operations outside the United States. Plus, there was CIA coordination with the Army's exile programs (like the Cuban exiles based at Fort Benning) and those of the DIA (which included Naval Intelligence). In that broad context, it's easier to see why Helms and FitzGerald felt they could hide a few small unauthorized operations.

Another important reason Helms felt he didn't have to reveal everything to Director McCone was that Helms was able to control the CIA's own internal investigations of JFK's assassination. Former *Washington Post* editor Jefferson Morley wrote that on November 23, "Helms called a meeting in his office, ordered his senior staff not to discuss the assassination, and announced that [John] Whitten would review all internal files on Oswald." Morley also said that "the following morning . . . Helms [delivered] Whitten's preliminary finding—that Oswald had acted alone—to President Lyndon Johnson." According to Morley, "Whitten's investigation continued—for the next couple of weeks, he and a staff of [thirty] worked almost around the clock, doggedly plowing through CIA cables from all over the world, scouring for new information. He forwarded the most interesting material to the White House, under Helms's name. He drafted a report on what the CIA knew about Oswald and began circulating drafts to the various offices in the operations directorate that had tracked Oswald at one point or another."[28]

However, beginning on November 23, Helms had started to withhold crucial information from Whitten, his own CIA investigator. Significantly, Helms was withholding more than just the information about his unauthorized assassination operations, like Cubela and the CIA-Mafia plots; Helms also didn't give Whitten the CIA's files about Oswald's written contact with the Fair Play for Cuba Committee (FPCC), something the FBI knew well (thanks to its illegal mail-opening and black-bag burglary operations), or about Oswald's well-publicized seemingly pro-Castro activities in New Orleans. While it's understandable that Helms would not tell his investigator about the unauthorized operations, it's less clear why he wouldn't tell him about Oswald's FPCC and New Orleans activities, which had been covered extensively in the national press in the wake of JFK's murder. One possibility is that the CIA files about those Oswald activities also involved Helms's unauthorized operations, the closely guarded JFK-Almeida coup plan, or the tight surveillance of Oswald. There are no indications Whitten was allowed to see all the Oswald files from the New Orleans office that Hunter Leake took to Washington, or the files about the CIA-backed Cuban exile group, the DRE, that Oswald interacted with in New Orleans.[29]

When Whitten finally complained to Helms and to Counter-Intelligence Chief Angleton, Whitten was sacked from the investigation and returned to his regular duties. (Morley notes that after this change of assignment, "Whitten's career stalled," and just over a year later, "he was kicked sideways into an unimportant job reviewing operations. He would not get a senior position" in the CIA, and would retire in 1970 to become a singer in Europe.)[30] Whitten's replacement was James Angleton, hardly a good choice from an objectivity standpoint, since one of his department's responsibilities had been to keep track of defectors like Oswald.[31] Instead of looking at Oswald's links to Cuban operations, Angleton focused on trying to tie Oswald to Russia, which kept Helms's secrets safe.

Whitten did get a chance to set the record straight almost fifteen years later, when he testified to Congressional investigators after the CIA-Mafia plots had been partially exposed. Though his testimony was kept classified until recent years, it sheds light on several CIA figures at the time of JFK's assassination. Whitten told investigators that if he had been told about Helms's CIA-Mafia plots, he would have focused on the Miami CIA station, run by Ted Shackley (who, by the time of Whitten's testimony, had become a very high-level CIA official). As for Helms's also withholding his unauthorized plots from the Warren Commission, Whitten said it was "highly reprehensible," and that Helms must have "realized it would have cost him his job and precipitated a crisis for the Agency" if it ever became known. Whitten also had extremely negative things to say about William Harvey, who was in charge of the CIA-Mafia plots for Helms until at least mid-1963. Whitten said that "Helms entrusting Harvey to hire a criminal to have the capacity to kill somebody violates every operation precept, every bit of operation experience, every ethical consideration." Whitten called Harvey a "ruthless guy . . . very dangerous." When Congressional investigators asked him if Harvey could have been part of a plot to kill JFK, CIA veteran Whitten didn't answer directly, but stated that Harvey "was too young to have assassinated McKinley and Lincoln."[32]

In addition to the Congressional investigators, many researchers have speculated that Harvey might have had a role in JFK's murder, though no evidence or confession has ever surfaced in that regard. Harvey had become a hero in the CIA for his work on the Berlin Tunnel in the 1950s, only to see his career come crashing down after Bobby Kennedy found out that Harvey had sent unauthorized commandos into Cuba at the height of the Cuban Missile Crisis (some accounts say that Harvey's team was an assassination squad, and that they did make an attempt to kill Fidel). Harvey had been running both the CIA-Mafia plots with Rosselli (with whom Harvey was very close) and European assassin recruiter QJWIN, as well as the CIA's ZRRIFLE "executive action" assassination program. But Bobby Kennedy thought Harvey was a "disaster," and so Helms had Harvey reassigned and replaced by Desmond FitzGerald in early 1963.[33] Harvey was eventually reassigned to Italy, though his activities in the United States during the rest of 1963 remain vague. He met with his drinking buddy Rosselli near Washington in June 1963, and the CIA admits they met (on a personal level) in 1964 and beyond.

Could Harvey have been involved in JFK's death, as Whitten seemed to imply? CIA veteran and former *Newsweek* Bureau Chief Bayard Stockton published a full-length biography of Harvey in 2006. Stockton had worked with Harvey in Europe and concluded that Harvey was probably not involved, though he seriously considered the possibility. Apparently, Stockton still had some doubts and information he couldn't resolve, because after he had turned in his book for publication, he contacted us by email about perhaps working together to investigate what he had found out about "Harvey's close association with Johnny Rosselli . . .

to see where it may lead us."[34] Before we could pursue it further with Stockton, he passed away of natural causes.

Harvey's actions in November 1963, and around the time of JFK's assassination, are not well documented, at least in CIA files that were shown to Congressional investigators. In some ways, Harvey would have had much less to lose than many by helping Rosselli with JFK's assassination, because Harvey had no official role in AMWORLD or the JFK-Almeida coup plan. At the same time, he would have been much less able to influence events and help with the assassination and cover-up than a confessed conspirator like David Morales. Also, because of Harvey's well-known feud with Bobby Kennedy, Harvey would have been a focus of Bobby's suspicion if strong evidence surfaced that pointed toward the CIA. Harvey had a much worse drinking problem than Morales—another factor that could have affected how much Rosselli and Trafficante would have utilized him in their plot. Rosselli could have simply taken advantage of Harvey—milking him for information during drinking bouts and manipulated him—without having Harvey knowingly involved in the plot. In the absence of evidence or a confession by Harvey, it's hard to be more definitive, though his actions detailed in later chapters indicate that he probably became aware at some point that Rosselli was involved in JFK's murder.

In looking at the CIA's actions during the weekend following JFK's murder, we should also consider the possibility that one or more of Harvey's CIA associates thought (then or later) that Harvey was involved, or worried that Harvey had been involved, with mobsters tied to JFK's assassination. In November 1963, the CIA's Miami Station Chief was Ted Shackley, who wrote in his autobiography how much he admired William Harvey, his "old boss," whom he "always regarded . . . as a mentor and friend." Harvey had actually convinced Helms to put Shackley in charge of the Miami station, launching Shackley into a higher-level CIA career that would last until 1979.[35] Shackley had even accompanied Harvey on one trip to take a trailerload of arms to Johnny Rosselli, in the spring of 1962.

Just after JFK's assassination, Shackley assigned an unusual agent to coordinate the Miami station's inquiries into JFK's murder. A recently declassified CIA memo says that "Anthony Sforza, AMOT case officer . . . received specific instructions from Shackley about how the AMOT service was to go about aiding in the investigation" of JFK's assassination.[36] Sforza had started working with David Morales in Cuba in the late 1950s. David Corn of the *Nation* says Sforza "operated in Havana under the cover of a professional gambler and cultivated contacts with the Mafia."[37] By 1963, Sforza was working at the Miami station under David Morales, whom he regarded as a brother.[38] Apparently, Sforza was one of the few Miami CIA agents who could actually travel safely into Cuba, and on the day of JFK's murder, he was going from Cuba to Mexico City as part of an operation with David Atlee Phillips to exfiltrate a very high-profile Cuban. Apparently, Fidel's sister Juanita was originally supposed to be brought out before the December 1 coup, but JFK's death caused a delay, and she didn't defect until the following summer.[39]

Sforza was also "fiercely loyal" to Shackley, which may be why Shackley chose Sforza to coordinate Miami's JFK assassination inquiry, using Morales's network of AMOT assets. However, choosing someone like Sforza, with ties to the Mafia and Morales, would also protect Shackley himself, and keep secret both his own contact with Rosselli and his involvement in the unauthorized portion of the Cubela operation. It would also safeguard Shackley's mentor, William Harvey. Not surprisingly, instead of looking at possible Cuban exile involvement in JFK's murder, Sforza's inquiry concentrated almost exclusively on trying to tie Fidel to JFK's murder. In the coming years, Shackley, Morales, and Sforza would continue to work together for the CIA in a variety of hot spots, from Laos to Vietnam to Chile, each country winding up much worse because of these men's lethal involvement. Harvey wasn't part of the clique in those years; his exclusion suggests that even lifelong admirers like Shackley saw reasons to keep their distance from him.

Another associate of William Harvey in the Castro plots, the CIA's spectral Counter-Intelligence Chief James Angleton, may also have had his own reasons to cover up, which would have also protected Harvey. In his Congressional testimony, Whitten said that Angleton had psychological problems. Worse, as author David Talbot noted, Whitten told the investigators that Angleton had ties to the Mafia and "had covered for them in federal investigations . . . and he had used them in Cuba operations."[40] Angleton's Mafia ties have been described by other authors, but his role with the Mafia in Cuban operations is missing from CIA accounts. Then again, recently released CIA files have shown those accounts, originally supervised by Helms or his associates, to have been woefully incomplete (leaving out, for example, Artime's work with the Mafia while he was working on AMWORLD).

British spymaster Peter Wright indicated one avenue that Angleton and Harvey may have pursued, which could help explain unusual

French activity in Dallas around the time of JFK's murder. As recounted in Wright's autobiography, in a discussion between Wright, Angleton, and Harvey that took place before Harvey was reassigned to Italy, Harvey brought up the subject of assassinating Castro, telling Wright, "We're developing a new capability in the [CIA] to handle these kinds of problems, and we're in the market for the requisite expertise." Wright says Harvey was looking for "deniable personnel," preferably foreign, who couldn't be traced to the United States. Wright suggested "the French. . . . It's more their type of thing, you know, Algiers and so on," and Harvey carefully wrote down Wright's recommendation, as Angleton looked on.[41] It was a good idea in some ways, since the French still had diplomatic relations with Cuba that would allow for easy travel, and at least one French heroin partner of Michel Victor Mertz still had a business in Havana.

Harvey's European assassin recruiter QJWIN was still on the payroll in November 1963, ostensibly working for FitzGerald with Helms's approval, even though the released CIA files make it appear as if QJWIN was being paid handsomely each month for producing no results. As we'll soon document, French assassin Michel Victor Mertz, who had worked undercover for French intelligence in Algiers, was deported from Dallas by the INS on the weekend of JFK's murder. Mertz had many parallels with QJWIN, which suggests that Mertz could have used QJWIN's identity or assistance in his operation.

If Angleton were involved with Harvey in an operation involving Cuba and the Mafia (perhaps through French gangster Mertz), then Angleton could have had much to hide after he took over the CIA's internal investigation of JFK's murder from Whitten. Based on most indications, Angleton thought the Soviets might have been behind Oswald, perhaps with Cuban assistance, and that Gilberto Lopez and the phony Cuban agent (Miguel Casas Saez) who had appeared to shadow JFK in Chicago, Florida, and Texas were involved. However, it's also possible that Angleton was just trying to divert attention and blame away from an operation for which he was at least partially responsible. Even historians agree that Angleton had psychological difficulties and became increasingly paranoid as the years went on (he eventually thought that even Henry Kissinger was a Russian agent). But Angleton also may simply have been trying not to look at areas that could have ended his own career.

In exploring the reactions and roles of CIA officials like Angleton, Shackley, Harvey, Sforza, Helms, and others, we aren't saying they were involved in the plot that killed JFK. Morales confessed his role before his death, but no evidence exists regarding the others. However, they still would have had ample reason to avoid or obstruct a genuine investigation into JFK's murder, for fear it could have exposed their own unauthorized actions. As with the Chicago and Tampa cover-ups, once they withheld certain information from superiors or subordinates, and from other agencies, they would always have to continue doing so.

Moreover, what were they, or others in the CIA, to do if they suspected one of their CIA associates—like David Morales—had been involved in JFK's murder? Because of their own ties to the CIA-Mafia plots, all the individuals listed above would have basically wrecked their careers if they had tried to expose a plot involving Rosselli and his associates. The same is probably true of others as well. In addition, there is a fine line between protecting a trusted CIA colleague from embarrassing, potentially career-ending revelations (like associating with Rosselli, or running a legitimate operation involving Oswald) and protecting them because you suspect they might have been used, knowingly or unknowingly, in JFK's assassination.

As for the Mafia bosses, they could always bring pressure if one or more CIA officials tried to point suspicion in their direction. Leaking the whole story of the CIA-Mafia plots to the press (even the foreign press) in the wake of JFK's murder would have essentially destroyed the public's faith in the CIA. But a more personal approach is the mob's style. Even without resorting to the numerous murders the Mafia would commit in the 1970s, other pressure could have been brought to bear by the mob.

David Talbot wrote that one of Bobby's aides, Adam Walinsky, talked in his oral history at the JFK Presidential Library about "some disturbing information . . . about high-ranking CIA officials" that the aide had relayed to Bobby. "The aide had been informed by a close friend—a psychiatrist at the National Institutes of Mental Health who treated 'the top CIA wives'—that the upper ranks of the intelligence agency were filled with sexually deviant personalities." Walinsky said the psychiatrist told him "the people who are running the CIA are really very very very sick and disturbed . . . real fetishes and crazy sado-masochistic behavior' . . . he was talking about the very top level people."[42] In the early 1960s, the revelation of such behavior, even at home, could end an official's career. If any of the officials pursued those activities with people besides their wives, they could also be subject to blackmail. The rarely publicized Mafia boss of Washington, D.C., Joe Nesline, was a close associate of

Carlos Marcello, who often stayed with Nesline when he visited Washington. Nesline was also involved in high-end call girl operations that generated blackmail potential, as well as income.

In fact, some in the CIA worried that exile leader Manuel Artime would be blackmailed in just such a fashion. The CIA not only illegally bugged Artime's safe house near Washington, but also discovered that he had a mistress.[43] According to David Corn, Shackley conducted an investigation that found Artime's mistress was "bisexual, had been a mistress to [former dictator] Batista in Cuba and a Venezuelan dictator, and had posed for pornography." CIA officials worried what might happen if someone decided to "leak the information to harm Artime's reputation," but in the end there was little they could do.[44] FitzGerald only asked AMWORLD official Henry Heckscher to talk privately with Artime, telling the exile leader that the affair packed "a considerable amount of political dynamite which his political opponents might be strongly tempted to set off."[45]

When Artime learned that JFK had been assassinated, he called a CIA officer. However, after briefly mentioning JFK's death, the rest of the CIA memo of Artime's call makes it seem like business as usual. Artime discusses various aspects of his operation with the CIA officer, almost as if Artime didn't think JFK's death would have any impact on his plans.[46]

Artime's reaction stands in stark contrast to Harry's reaction, for whom JFK's death essentially brought everything to a halt. Harry spoke to Bobby on Saturday, November 23, and arranged to meet with Bobby at his home, later that day or the next. Bobby was spending much time at the White House, and had pressing personal, family, and official duties, but Almeida was in place and waiting, so they had to decide what to do next.

As for the other Cuban exile leaders that Bobby and Harry had wanted for the coup plan, Tony Varona's actions around the time of JFK's death are unclear. Information soon surfaced that linked one of Varona's associates to a visit from Oswald on November 17, 1963, the day before the Tampa attempt. However, Varona, like the other exile leaders in the coup plan, wouldn't be investigated or interviewed by the FBI.

The day before JFK's death, one of Manolo Ray's boats had missed meeting a CIA boat to pick up military equipment to go into Cuba. As recorded in the documents released so far, Ray's explanation didn't satisfy the CIA.[47] It's possible the incident involved Ray's preparations for getting into Cuba for the coup, in which case important details might be missing from the released files, the same way the CIA withheld much about Ray from Congressional investigators. Ray's exile group, JURE, soon became embroiled in the matter of Oswald's visit to Silvia Odio, an operation that seemed designed to taint Ray and his organization.

According to a CIA report, Eloy Menoyo—the other very liberal exile leader for the coup—was getting ready to go into Cuba "sometime before 30 November 1963." This was said to be for "Plan Omega," an informal name some exiles on the periphery used for the JFK-Almeida coup plan. The CIA memo also says that Menoyo's associates had been talking to Carlos Prio about getting more financial backing. Prio, the corrupt former President of Cuba, was an associate of Trafficante and had been barred from the coup plan by Bobby and JFK.[48] The CIA's Miami station received two reports about Menoyo's group and JFK's death that tended to cast suspicion on Menoyo's operation. One of Morales and Sforza's AMOT informants "reported hearing" that "Menoyo commented 21 [November] 63 that 'something very big would happen soon that would advance [the] Cuban cause.'" While it sounds suspicious, as if Menoyo might have been referring to JFK's murder, a CIA official notes that "this remark, when taken out of context, is impossible to evaluate." The most likely explanation is that Menoyo was referring to the upcoming coup plan, something known to only a very few at the Miami CIA station (like David Morales). In the same CIA memo, vague suspicion is also directed at a member of Menoyo's group in Dallas.[49] While some exiles seemed to want to disparage Menoyo, the Miami CIA station seemed disinclined to take the comments seriously.

The bottom line is that Helms and others in the CIA were acting the same way officials (and businessmen) often do in a crisis: protecting themselves, their associates, and their organization first, then dealing with the crisis. Helms set the tone with his actions that weekend, and subordinates like FitzGerald and Shackley clearly got the message. However, their cover-ups would start to have serious ramifications, as new reports surfaced that threatened to trigger a conflict with Cuba and the Soviets.

Chapter Sixteen

On November 23, 1963, President Johnson, CIA Director McCone, and other top officials started getting ominous information from Mexico City indicating that Fidel Castro and the Soviet KGB were behind JFK's assassination. CIA officers in Mexico City, in particular David Atlee Phillips, had started sending the first of what would soon be a steady stream of reports that tried to incriminate Oswald by essentially saying he was working for Cuba or Russia. Since the United States hadn't immediately attacked Cuba after JFK's murder and Oswald's arrest, it was almost as if some people had decided more was needed to prod LBJ along. However, all of these reports would later be discredited, and most originated with or were promoted by associates of Morales, Artime, Trafficante, and Rosselli.

Even though the allegations were false, they sounded alarms not only during the weekend of November 23 and in the weeks that followed, but also through much of 1964, again in 1965, once more in the 1970s, and even later. The same long-discredited allegations would be raised again as recently as 2005, in a German television documentary. The first allegation has special resonance today because it led to US-sanctioned torture during interrogations in a foreign country.

When reading about these rumors, it's important to keep in mind the basic story that Richard Helms concocted on November 23, which remains the official CIA version of Oswald in Mexico City even today, long after declassified files, testimony, and interviews have shown it to be false: The Helms/CIA version claims the CIA didn't realize until after JFK's assassination that Oswald had visited the Cuban embassy when he was in Mexico City. Even though the CIA admits it photographed the people visiting the Cuban and Soviet embassies, it claims that no photos of Oswald were taken (the photos the CIA produced were of a much older, heavy-set man who has never been identified). And even though the CIA eventually confessed that it had tapped all the phone calls to and from each embassy with the help of the Mexican DFS (federal police), it claims the tapes of Oswald's calls were erased shortly after his visits, and before JFK's assassination.

Each of these assertions has been proven false by experts like former Army Intelligence Major and historian Dr. John Newman. As he carefully documented from CIA files and interviews, continuing work begun by the House Select Committee on Assassinations in the late 1970s, the official records reveal discrepancies about the number of visits Oswald made to each embassy, and raise questions about whether some of the visits were by someone impersonating Oswald. There are also differing accounts regarding the number of phone calls, but CIA records confirm that at least some, and probably all, of the phone calls were made by an imposter. This claim is easy to verify because Oswald spoke good Russian and no Spanish, while one of the callers pretending to be Oswald spoke Spanish and another spoke poor, broken Russian.[1]

Newman and other researchers have also established that, based on the files that have been released, much information is missing—either still withheld or destroyed. In the spring of 1964, two Warren Commission lawyers listened to the taped phone calls of "Oswald" that Helms and Mexico City CIA officer David Atlee Phillips claimed had been routinely erased before JFK's murder. Their existence at that time was also confirmed to *Vanity Fair* by the "senior CIA officer who had played [the lawyers] the tapes." We've noted that photos of the real Oswald in Mexico City did exist, as verified by the CIA's station chief there, Win Scott, and our own Naval Intelligence source, who saw the photos.[2] Congressional investigators received additional confirmation of Oswald photos in Mexico City from Win Scott's deputy and another CIA officer who used the name Joseph Piccolo.[3]

Some of Helms's cover-ups were based on legitimate national-security reasons, while others weren't. Helms and the CIA were initially reluctant to let even other agencies know that they had tapped both embassies' phones, though they eventually admitted it to the Warren Commission and Congress. We now know that the CIA also bugged rooms in the embassies themselves, something the CIA still doesn't officially confirm. (Cuban officials later discovered a bug in the arm of a chair in the Cuban ambassador's office.)[4] There is a good chance that rooms in the current Cuban and Soviet embassies are still being bugged under the same type of program today, so the fact that the CIA wants to conceal that tactic is somewhat understandable. On the other hand, it's important to keep in mind that information was available to at least some CIA officials when they were trying to evaluate the false allegations we'll soon detail.

However, even more information was withheld from other agencies (and from most parts of the CIA) starting on November 23 and for decades thereafter. The House Select Committee would complain in 1979 that "there is a possibility [that] a US government agency requested the Mexican government to refrain from aiding the Committee with this aspect of its work."[5] (Helms, Phillips, and Morales were no longer with the CIA at that time, though Shackley was still a high-level CIA official.) Even today, many files relating to Oswald's Mexico City visits are probably among the one million–plus CIA files related to JFK's assassination that are still being withheld, unless they were destroyed before Helms left the CIA.

It's significant that crucial information about Oswald and Mexico City was kept secret from most people in the CIA. As Dr. Newman and Jefferson Morley documented, some cables sent from CIA headquarters to the CIA's Mexico City office in the fall of 1963 contained accurate information, while some CIA cables clearly contained false information (for example, an inaccurate description of Oswald, or a statement that the CIA had compiled no information at all about Oswald since May 1962, even before his return from Russia). Newman and Morley located one former CIA official who signed off on both types of CIA cables. Years later, when shown the cables, she admitted, "I'm signing off on something I know isn't true." But the CIA official explained that Desmond FitzGerald's "SAS group would have held all the information on Oswald under their tight control." This meant that "if you did a routine check" on Oswald, some information "wouldn't show up." The CIA official stated that it was "indicative of a keen interest in Oswald, held very closely on a need-to-know basis." The official added, "I wasn't in on any particular goings-on or hanky-panky as far as the Cuban situation [went]."[6] That may be true from an operations standpoint, but newly declassified CIA memos show that during 1962 and 1963, this official was also a liaison between the CIA and the FBI regarding reports of criminal activity by CIA-backed Cuban exiles.[7] However, the criminal reports about exiles working for FitzGerald, like Manuel Artime's work with the Mafia, are missing and were probably under the same "tight control" FitzGerald exercised over the Oswald information.

As we've indicated, and documented in detail in *Ultimate Sacrifice*, Oswald's trip to Mexico City in September 1963 was probably his attempt to enter Cuba, as one of the assets the CIA was tasked with getting into Cuba for the upcoming JFK-Almeida coup plan.[8] That's what all of his pro-Castro publicity had been for in August 1963, and it was probably the subject of his meeting with David Atlee Phillips in Dallas a few weeks before his trip to Mexico. Oswald even took with him to Mexico an amazingly well-organized and detailed resume, which (aside from some misspellings) should have made him look like an attractive "catch" to the Cubans.[9] As we mentioned earlier, two other young men also linked to Artime associates went to the Cuban embassy in Mexico City around the same time, possibly as part of the same operation as Oswald. This type of operation would have been run by Phillips for Desmond FitzGerald, who reported to Helms. In addition to his regular duties for the CIA in Mexico City for Station Chief Win Scott, Phillips had additional assignments related to Cuba (like AMWORLD), for which he reported directly to FitzGerald. CIA Director John McCone would have been generally aware of this type of operation, since getting assets into Cuba prior to the coup had been the CIA's job since early summer 1963.

However, Oswald was impersonated in most, if not all, of his phone calls (and possibly his visit to one of the consulates) as part of an effort to both keep him from getting into Cuba and incriminate him after JFK's assassination. Mafia bosses like Rosselli and Trafficante were in a perfect position to carry out this plan. Their associate Richard Cain, a surveillance expert, had bugged a communist embassy in Mexico City the previous year for the CIA.[10] The Mexican federal police, the DFS, monitored the phone taps of the Cuban and Russian embassies for the CIA. The DFS was involved in drug trafficking with associates of Trafficante and Michel Victor Mertz, whose partners operated a heroin ring through Mexico City. Also, the DFS was involved in some of the interrogations that began on November 23, which included torture and allegations that were later shown to be false.

The first of these concerned Silvia Duran, whom Dr. Newman describes as "the secretary working in the Cuban consulate at the time of Oswald's visit to Mexico City."[11] On November 23, David Atlee Phillips (using one of his cover identities, Lawrence F. Barker) sent a memo saying that "in January 1962, Silvia Duran [was] seen in two cars with Texas plates. . . . Another Ford car [with] Texas plates . . . [was] seen in front of [the] residence [of her] brothers."[12] This memo would be followed by ever more incredible accusations that would eventually include Duran's entertaining Oswald at a "twist" party, having a torrid affair with Oswald, and working with Oswald on a plot to kill JFK.

In conjunction with other wild allegations that would start flowing on November 23 and continue in the following days, the stories not only were meant to emphasize Oswald's guilt, but also to pressure President Johnson to order an invasion of Cuba.

The CIA's Mexico City station asked the Mexicans to arrest Silvia Duran, who was a Mexican citizen; it's not clear whether this was Win Scott's idea, or if he was acting on behalf of David Atlee Phillips. The exact origin of all the accusations against Duran is still murky. The CIA memo said, "It is suggested that she be arrested as soon as possible by the Mexican authorities and held incommunicado until she can be questioned on the matter."[13] The CIA went on to "request [that] you ensure that her arrest is kept absolutely secret, that no information from her is published or leaked, that all such info is cabled to us."[14]

Richard Helms was caught off guard by Duran's arrest, and he wasn't part of whatever game was going on involving the wild accusations against her. According to a CIA report by Whitten, Helms's deputy immediately "ordered us to phone Mexi[co] and tell them not to [arrest Duran]." Helms's deputy ordered a cable to be sent to Win Scott in Mexico City, saying that the "arrest of Sylvia Duran is [an] extremely serious matter which could prejudice US freedom of action on [the] entire question of Cuban responsibility" for JFK's assassination. Helms did not want anything else coming out that could pressure the US to invade Cuba, and he probably knew enough about Oswald's closely watched trip to Mexico to know that there was nothing to the Duran allegations. However, the cable wasn't sent, because Win Scott told CIA headquarters it was already "too late to call off the arrest."[15]

The memo Phillips had sent about Duran's being seen in cars with Texas plates was "for possible use in connection [with the] interrogation [of] Duran," and her interrogation by the Mexican authorities turned out to be a nightmare.[16] Several years later, Duran told a trusted CIA informant that on November 23, 1963, during her interrogation, she was "beaten until she admitted that she had an affair with Oswald."[17] In a phone call bugged by the CIA a few days later, the Cuban ambassador to Mexico told Cuban president Dorticos that Duran "has black and blue marks on her arms, which she said she got during the interrogation process." A later CIA report of that conversation tried to soften the Cuban ambassador's remarks, translating them as saying that "Mexican police bruised Silvia Duran's arms a little [by] shaking her to impress her with the importance of his questions."[18]

Duran told Congressional investigators more of what her Mexican interrogators had asked and told her: "They tell me that I was a Communist . . . and they insisted that I was a very important person for . . . the Cuban Government and that I was the link for the International Communists—the Cuban Communists, the Mexican Communists, and the American Communists, and that we were going to kill Kennedy."[19]

It's important to remember that the DFS was simply asking questions (and making statements) that revealed what someone at the Mexico City CIA station had told them—probably Phillips or one of his associates and/or sources. The question is, was Phillips acting on his own, or was he being fed disinformation by one of his associates (like Morales) or his sources?

Duran was released that weekend, after she identified Oswald as the person she had dealt with at the Cuban embassy. Years later, she and the Cuban consul would both indicate that the man had actually not been Oswald, because he was much shorter, had blond hair, and was older than the real Oswald.[20] Where did the allegation about Oswald and Duran's affair originate? CIA files at the time said that Duran had had an earlier affair—with Cuban UN envoy Carlos Lechuga—that she later admitted to Congressional investigators. In the fall of 1963, Lechuga was a key player in the secret peace negotiations between JFK and Castro, through JFK's special UN envoy William Attwood.[21] It's as if someone in the CIA figured that tying Duran to Oswald would not only make Oswald and the Cubans look guilty, but also help to torpedo any secret peace negotiations that might continue after JFK's death. Despite the fact that Duran confirmed the story about her affair with Oswald only after being beaten, Win Scott later reported it to Washington as fact.[22]

However, just four days after Duran's release, and three days after Oswald's death, the CIA asked that Duran be arrested yet again—and even requested that Duran once more be interrogated "vigorously and exhaustively"—a polite way of saying "beaten." To keep it deniable, the next day the CIA sent a message saying, "We want the Mexican authorities to take the responsibility for the whole affair."[23] This time, Helms was on board, as was the FBI. An FBI memo sent to Clyde Tolson, the FBI's Deputy Director and Hoover's longtime live-in companion, said, "Mexican authorities [are] interrogating Duran vigorously and exhaustively. We agreed to this interrogation."[24]

What had changed between Duran's release and the new CIA demand that she be rearrested and tortured? The answer was additional incriminating (though eventually discredited) stories about Oswald that emerged from Mexico City, this time tying Oswald to the Soviets.

The CIA informed the FBI on November 23 about information that "indicated [Oswald] had been in contact with Valery Kostikov, Soviet Embassy, Mexico City, and that Kostikov had been tentatively identified as being with the department in KGB which handles sabotage and assassinations."

Within twenty-four hours after JFK's assassination, someone linked to the CIA's Mexico City station wanted it to appear as if Oswald were a pawn in a vast conspiracy, one that involved not just the Cubans, but also KGB assassination experts. However, in the coming days, this facade, too, would start to fall apart. By November 27, the CIA was able to confirm to the FBI only that Kostikov "is an official for the KGB," but had dropped the allegation about his being part of the KGB's assassination department.[25] It turned out that Kostikov just happened to be one of three officials at the embassy when Oswald visited it; he had actually helped to calm down the agitated Oswald. In the 1990s, after the fall of the Soviet empire, Kostikov and the other two officials would be interviewed extensively about Oswald's visit by journalists.

However, starting on November 23, 1963, and continuing for years, the allegations about Kostikov and Duran would be taken very seriously by LBJ, Hoover, McCone, and, for a time, even Bobby Kennedy. Congressional investigators later found that on November 23, James Angleton's CIA counter-intelligence staff prepared "a memo suggesting sinister implications of Oswald's Mexico City contacts."[26] Even Helms was so concerned on November 23 that he took the unheard-of step of telling the Mexico City CIA station to "feel free to abandon cables and talk plain English so that there can be no mistakes."[27] Helms knew the stakes were incredibly high, whether he was starting to believe some of the allegations or just wanted to ensure that things didn't get out of hand.

David Atlee Phillips seems to have been a central figure in these and other bogus allegations that kept springing up in the following days. The evidence suggests three possibilities: First, given Morales's confession to JFK's assassination, as well as his closeness to Phillips and frequent travel to Mexico City, it's possible that Morales was simply having information fed to Phillips that he knew would wind up with FitzGerald and Helms in Washington. Anything that made Oswald look guilty and could prompt the invasion of Cuba—which Morales knew had already been planned—would be good for Morales and his pal Rosselli. In this scenario, Phillips would basically have been a conduit for disinformation.

Second, it's possible that Phillips and some others in the CIA who weren't involved in JFK's assassination, but who did know that Oswald was a US intelligence asset, may have felt that Oswald was a turncoat who was responsible for JFK's murder. In that case, the CIA men might simply have wanted to release information that would help to prompt a US invasion of Cuba. (Arguing against this theory is the information pointing to the Soviets, which could have forced the United States into a serious conflict.)

The third possibility is that Phillips was a knowing participant in JFK's assassination, and this was part of the plot to make Oswald look even more guilty and to prompt the invasion of Cuba. One point that argues against this idea is that so much of the information links to Phillips that he would have come under great suspicion if the plot had started to unravel. In other words, if you know you're passing along bogus information, it seems preferable to put someone else's name on it so it can't be traced to you. To some degree, Phillips did just that, using his official Choaden and Barker cover identities, but higher-ups in the CIA knew or could have easily found out that those aliases were Phillips's. The same would be true for a new CIA director named after the 1964 elections or any time in the future.

In considering the above possibilities, one other potential link exists between Phillips and the release of incriminating information about Oswald and Mexico City: the incident we cited previously, when a member of the DRE, the exile group Phillips ran for the CIA, called Clare Booth Luce on Friday night, November 22, to mention Oswald's trip to Mexico. That trip wouldn't become known by the press until forty-eight hours after JFK's murder, so the DRE member had to have inside information. On the other hand, Phillips might have had nothing to do with the call or with passing to the DRE information about Oswald's visit to Mexico, since a CIA memo about Richard Cain said that "the DRE is a MOB-controlled organization, which, at times, seems to act independently of its monitor."[28] The capitalization of "MOB" for emphasis was in the original CIA memo, and the "monitor" it referred to could have been Phillips or his subordinate George Joannides, who handled day-to-day contact with the DRE.

Other information unrelated to Mexico, but incriminating to Cuba, began to surface on November 23. One of David Atlee Phillips's journalist associates, who had worked with Phillips in Havana, made sure the CIA was aware of remarks Fidel had made to AP reporter Daniel Harker in September 1963.[29] The tip to the FBI by Phillips's associate claimed Castro had said, "If the United States causes him difficulty, he has the facilities to 'knock off' United States leaders." [30] In his talk with Harker in Havana, Castro had condemned the exile raids against Cuba, which, despite denials to the press, were really backed by JFK. Harker wrote that Castro then said, "We are prepared to fight them and answer in kind. United States leaders should think that if they are aiding terrorist plans to eliminate Cuban leaders, they themselves would not be safe." [31] After Kennedy's death, Phillips's associate and others took Castro's remark as a threat to assassinate JFK, although the comment was not noted as such when the article first appeared.

Years later, Anthony Summers wrote that Castro told Congressional investigators "he never intended his words to be taken as a physical threat against [any] individuals in the United States." Instead, Fidel said "he probably meant to warn Washington that he knew of the plots against his own life and that it was 'a very bad precedent' which might 'boomerang' against its authors." [32] Fidel's former head of State Security, Fabian Escalante, says that what Castro really said was: "American leaders should be careful because the [anti-Castro operations] were something nobody could control." [33] Given that some men involved in the Castro assassination plots, like Morales and Rosselli, confessed to killing JFK, the Cuban dictator's explanation makes sense, especially since those admissions weren't revealed until years after Castro talked to the Congressional delegation. As several historians have pointed out, it would have made little sense for Fidel to do something that would risk having his country invaded in retaliation, just to make Lyndon Johnson president. While Summers notes that Fidel said that "any successor to President Kennedy was likely to be even tougher toward Cuba," he also points out an even more obvious argument that Castro did not make: "If Castro had really intended harm to President Kennedy, he would hardly have announced it to the [American] press two months in advance." [34]

Given the September 1963 timing of Fidel's remarks, it's important to reiterate that a confidential source who worked on the Cuba Contingency Plans, and with officials like FitzGerald and Rusk, told us that he and the others didn't see Fidel's remarks as threats against JFK. He said Fidel's comment had nothing to do with sparking the Cuba Contingency planning, and that he felt Castro had no role in JFK's death. [35] However, other high officials who were dedicated Cold Warriors were not so sure, and some in the CIA kept focusing on Fidel's comment to Harker into the next decade.

Years after JFK's death, another newspaper article from the weeks prior started to get attention; it might also help to explain Bobby's comments to McCone and to Haynes Johnson on November 22, which directed suspicion toward the CIA and CIA-backed exiles. Arthur Krock was a columnist for the *New York Times* who was quite close to JFK and Bobby. In his October 3, 1963, column, he had written about remarks another journalist had obtained from a "very high American official . . . who has spent much of his life in the service of democracy." Krock wrote that, according to this official, "the CIA's growth was 'likened to a malignancy' which the 'very high official was not sure even the White House could control . . . any longer.'" The official went on to say, "If the United States ever experiences [an attempt at a coup to overthrow the government] it will come from the CIA and not the Pentagon [since the CIA] represents a tremendous power and total unaccountability to anyone."[36]

The part about "total unaccountability to anyone" certainly applied to Richard Helms in 1963 and for the next decade. As for the "attempt at a coup," no credible evidence or confession has yet surfaced that definitely implicates any official in the CIA who ranked higher than Morales as a witting participant in JFK's murder. As pointed out by Dr. John Newman for PBS, the CIA's lies about Oswald and Mexico City "appear to have been invented to buttress the lone-assassin story—itself ostensibly created for the purpose of preventing war and saving millions of lives. Whether or not this also permitted conspirators to avoid the scrutiny of investigation—a possibility I take seriously—is something we will continue to debate."[37]

Chapter Seventeen

Based on the information that has been declassified so far, we cannot tell exactly when on November 23, 1963, top officials like McCone, LBJ, Hoover, and Bobby started learning about the incriminating information from Mexico City. CIA records claim that while McCone met with LBJ for fifteen minutes at 9:15 AM that day, the two did not discuss Cuba. Yet when LBJ talked with J. Edgar Hoover, just thirty minutes after McCone left, LBJ's comments and questions to Hoover made it clear that LBJ already knew about Oswald's visit to Mexico City. Keeping in mind that since McCone still had to bring LBJ up to speed on the top-secret JFK-Almeida coup plan, as well as other highly sensitive CIA anti-Castro activities, McCone's initial briefing to LBJ about Cuba would not have been well documented in the official records.

Also, given the length of time Bobby and McCone had spent talking the previous day, and the seriousness with which McCone viewed the Mexico City situation, it seems almost certain that McCone would have talked with Bobby about the situation sometime Saturday morning. How much McCone should tell LBJ about Bobby's control of the JFK-Almeida coup plan, and about the CIA-Mafia plots that both McCone and Bobby thought had ended a year and a half earlier, would also have been something they needed to discuss. Bobby certainly wouldn't want McCone to tell his adversary LBJ things that could be used as political ammunition against Bobby in the future. (Historian Michael Kurtz writes that just hours after JFK's death, Bobby called JFK's national security advisor at the White House and ordered him to "change the combinations on the slain President's files, to ensure that Johnson's people could not gain access to them.")[1] There was still the chance that Bobby could be elected president himself in less than a year, a possibility many oddsmakers would have given more credence to on November 23, 1963, than the actual landslide election of LBJ. McCone would have to manage a fine balancing act between informing and accommodating Bobby, while also telling LBJ what he needed to know. Since Bobby already had suspicions that some aspect of the anti-Castro operation had backfired against JFK, McCone likewise wouldn't be anxious to reveal information to LBJ that might cause LBJ to doubt McCone's abilities to keep running the CIA.

One thing that gave McCone some flexibility was the sheer volume of intelligence information about Cuba that LBJ had to be brought up to speed on—not just the JFK-Almeida coup plan and its many aspects (like AMWORLD), but also AMTRUNK, the CIA-DIA Task Force on Cuba, and the still-huge overall CIA effort against Cuba. Additionally, McCone had to update LBJ on the many other Cold War hot spots around the world, from Vietnam to Russia, China, and many more. In that context, McCone could tell LBJ as much as he thought he needed to know in the coming days and weeks, depending on how the Cuban and JFK assassination situations developed. At the same time, McCone would have to be sure to tell LBJ things that the new president could learn from other officials. When we interviewed Harry Williams, we were left with the distinct impression that after JFK's death, LBJ was not told everything about the coup plan with Almeida; that would only happen if LBJ decided to go forward with the operation.

McCone's November 23 memo for the record and his interview with historian William Manchester both say that in McCone's first official meeting with LBJ, the new president asked McCone to brief him each morning for the next few days, and McCone wrote that he did just that for quite some time.[2] This probably also helped McCone to see educating LBJ about the Cuba situation as a gradual process, not something that had to be done all at once. Still, the welter of detail about all the Cuba plans McCone knew about must have been a massive amount of data for the new president to absorb. Even seasoned historians have had trouble distinguishing AMWORLD from AMTRUNK from AMLASH, and figuring out where programs like the CIA-Mafia plots fit in. Imagine trying to learn all that as a new president, while also dealing with JFK's funeral, a parade of foreign dignitaries, and assuming all the regular presidential duties and responsibilities—from dealing with the press to handling Congress to developing (and promoting) a legislative agenda. It's clear that as the days and weeks passed, LBJ dealt with the Cuban issue by lumping much of it together in his mind as a product of Bobby Kennedy, and he would cautiously continue only some of the CIA's Cuban operations. Clearly, in those early days, starting on November 23, LBJ felt he had more pressing issues to deal with concerning Cuba: Oswald and Mexico City.

————

LBJ's 10:01 AM recorded phone conversation with J. Edgar Hoover on November 23 raises almost as many questions as it answers. While it's clear that LBJ had been briefed earlier about Oswald's trip to Mexico City, it also appears that LBJ had already discussed it with Hoover, and that this was a follow-up call. If so, the first LBJ-Hoover call about Oswald and Mexico City was never documented. Also, while we have transcripts of the 10:01 AM LBJ-Hoover call, the actual tape of their discussion has been erased. The tape isn't missing; officials at the National Archives confirm that the tape exists, and that it contains other LBJ calls. However, only the fourteen-minute 10:01 AM LBJ-Hoover call about Oswald, Mexico City, and JFK's assassination has been erased, making it impossible to know if more was said that isn't reflected in the written transcript.[3]

Odder still, during this conversation Hoover tells LBJ about a tape of the alleged Oswald Mexico City calls recorded by the CIA, and that "the tape [does] not correspond to this man's [Oswald's] voice." This is one of the Mexico City tapes that Helms and the CIA have officially maintained were erased many weeks prior to November 23, yet someone had listened to it before talking to Hoover. Yet the Mexico tape's existence couldn't account for why fourteen minutes of the LBJ-Hoover tape was erased, since mention of it remains in the transcript. So, why would this LBJ-Hoover call, and apparently only this call, be erased even after a transcript was prepared?

One possibility: If LBJ had already been briefed, even generally, about the JFK-Almeida coup plan (perhaps when he was also first told about the Oswald–Mexico City situation), and it was mentioned even in passing in the 10:01 AM conversation, that might have been grounds for LBJ or the CIA to have had that portion of the tape erased at a later date. Even into the 1970s, 1980s, and later, the Almeida portion of the coup plan was still considered extremely sensitive, since he was still in power, his work for JFK had never been exposed, and his family was still under CIA surveillance. On national-security grounds, in the interest of protecting an ongoing operation, it's much easier to doctor words in a transcript than it is to doctor a tape. Another LBJ-Hoover conversation, on November 29, included a very brief mention of "the Cuban operation," and a query about whether Oswald was connected to it "with money." Some historians believe "the Cuban operation" refers to an anti-Castro operation—and if that's true, an earlier and more extensive discussion between LBJ and Hoover about "the Cuban operation" on November 23 could explain why that call was erased. It's also possible that this particular portion of the tape was erased because it contained a reference (missing from the current transcript) to another top-secret aspect of JFK's assassination, such as the Tampa and Chicago assassination attempts, or the fact that Oswald was indeed a US intelligence asset. (Hoover mentioned Chicago three times in the first few minutes of the conversation, but only as the source of Oswald's rifle.)

Based on the transcript of the erased LBJ-Hoover call, LBJ seemed most interested in whether Hoover had "established any more about [Oswald's] visit to the Soviet Embassy in Mexico in September." That's when Hoover explained that the situation was "very confusing" because "the tape and the photograph of the man who was at the Soviet Embassy, using Oswald's name . . . do not correspond to this man's voice, nor to his appearance," indicating "there is a second person who was at the Soviet Embassy down there." In other words, Hoover was describing an imposter—or a co-conspirator.

In the course of their conversation, Hoover mentioned that the United States had a "secret operation" in which "no mail is delivered to the [Soviet] Embassy without being examined and opened by us," but doesn't yet mention the CIA-DFS bugging operations. Hoover twice told LBJ in the call that the case against Oswald wasn't very strong, and that Oswald had denied everything. LBJ asked for a written "synopsis" by the end of the day, which Hoover agreed to provide.

Based on this conversation and John McCone's notes, it's unclear whether LBJ and Hoover knew yet about the Kostikov/KGB assassination allegation and the Duran allegations and arrest, but if they didn't, LBJ soon would. Just over two hours after LBJ finished his call with Hoover, the President got together with McCone again for a longer meeting. McCone's official memo for the record says that at 12:30 PM (Eastern) he "went to the President's office . . . to tell him of the information from Mexico City." Based on later notes by McCone, this information included what was known at that time about the allegations involving Kostikov and Duran.[4]

If LBJ, or Hoover or McCone, had any qualms about the information they had withheld from the press the previous day, or about the pressure applied to Texas officials to avoid implicating Russia or Cuba, those qualms vanished when the Mexico City information surfaced. This meant that allegations or press reports from a foreign country could, if not handled properly, generate a clamor for retaliation against Cuba or Russia—a frightening prospect just a year after the Cuban Missile Crisis and barely twenty-four hours after the new president had assumed office.

These concerns help to explain some of Hoover's actions on November 23 and in the coming days and weeks. Congressional investigators found that on that day, Hoover had FBI headquarters cable all field offices to rescind the FBI's order of the previous day "to use all informants" to obtain information about JFK's murder.[5] Any real investigation of JFK's assassination essentially ended then. Apparently, for Hoover, the chance that informants or leads might turn up something implicating Cuba or Russia was simply too great. The decision had been made to simply put all the blame on Oswald. Agents in the field soon got the message. Therefore, when a witness like Arnold Rowland tried to tell the FBI that he and his wife had seen two men on the sixth floor of the Book Depository, one with a rifle, fifteen minutes before JFK was shot, the FBI "didn't seem interested at all." Summers writes that Roland said, "They told me it didn't have any bearing . . . on the case right then. In fact, they just the same as told me to forget it."[6] Numerous other witnesses reported having similar experiences, or worse—some were pressured or threatened with prosecution if they persisted in relating accounts that didn't support the "lone nut" theory.

Hoover was also learning officially about the JFK-Almeida coup plan for the first time that weekend. LBJ was no doubt sharing with his friend Hoover whatever he was being told about it by McCone. While the FBI had files on exiles like Harry (who sometimes talked to Miami FBI agents) that have never been released, and Artime (about whom very little has been released), Hoover was probably learning the full scope of the coup plan for the first time. For Hoover and LBJ, the coup plan gave Cuba and Russia the motivation to have taken action against JFK, a motivation that could never be revealed.

Concerns about Oswald and Mexico City, the Soviet Union, Cuba, and the JFK-Almeida coup plan also explain why Hoover barred the FBI's Latin American experts from participating in the JFK investigation. They should have had a leading role, since the average FBI agent didn't speak Spanish or have the experience and knowledge to quickly and effectively deal with the hundreds of Cuban exiles and exile groups who should have been interviewed. The exiles and their groups involved constantly shifting loyalties, alliances, offshoots, and command structures—confusing even to experienced historians and journalists— that could be unraveled only with the expertise of the FBI's Latin American experts. Those FBI experts would have known where and how to focus the Bureau's energy and resources, but were essentially barred from participating.

In excluding them, Hoover wanted to avoid having his Latin American experts uncover potentially explosive or embarrassing information. Without them, the released FBI files sometimes show confusion about Hispanic names and exile groups, which created a filing and cross-referencing nightmare that hindered the investigation. Also, at the time, racism was not uncommon in the FBI, which had few (if any) Hispanic agents, and no actual black agents. However, even if Hoover had wanted to conduct an all-out investigation into Cuban exiles associated with Oswald or JFK's murder, the poor level of cooperation between the CIA and the FBI at the time would have made that impossible. For example, when the FBI heard rumors of CIA-backed activity involving exile leaders like Artime and Ray, the CIA blatantly denied any support for those groups.[7]

Hoover eventually came to realize the CIA was lying to him about Oswald's Mexico City trip, as verified by a memo he wrote less than two months after JFK's assassination. Hoover raged in a handwritten note that "I can't forget CIA withholding the French espionage activities in USA nor the false story re: Oswald's trip in Mexico City, only to mention two of their instances of double dealing." Dr. Newman found that only "eighteen days after the assassination, [Hoover] censured, demoted, or transferred everyone in the FBI that had been touched by the Mexico City story."[8]

However, because of national security, Hoover had to maintain a grudging cooperation with the CIA and protect its secrets (just as the CIA had to protect Hoover's secrets). Hoover's relations with the Secret Service were better than his relations with the CIA, but not by much, since Hoover had long wanted to take over presidential protection from the Secret Service. Hoover was no doubt glad when LBJ had the FBI take control of all aspects of the JFK investigation, which also made it much easier to make sure leads embarrassing to the Bureau weren't publicized or pursued.

A good example of leads not pursued is the Chicago case mentioned earlier, when a Cuban exile who had been getting money from Felipe Rivero's Mafia-backed group said that the exiles would be able to buy arms "as soon as we take care of Kennedy." The exile also had ties to Phillips's DRE group, which a CIA memo said was also mob backed. Vincent Palamara found that when Chicago Secret Service agents like Joseph Noonan investigated, they became "uneasy that the Cubans might have some ties to the CIA." But just days after JFK's death, the FBI took over and the Secret Service had to drop its investigation. Former Senate investigator Bud Fensterwald wrote that Secret Service agents were ordered not "to discuss . . . the assassination and investigation with anyone from any other federal agency now or any time in the future."[9] The FBI essentially stopped investigating the exile group, thereby ensuring that no ties could be found that might lead to Cuban double agents, the Chicago JFK threat, or covert CIA operations.

On November 23, Hoover was also starting to utilize his extensive domestic surveillance network in the JFK investigation. It is now known that illegal FBI phone-tap operations were usually described in reports as information received from an unnamed informant. In Dallas, Hoover had apparently ordered wiretaps on the phone of the woman Marina Oswald had been living with, Ruth Paine. A November 23 phone call was intercepted between Ruth Paine and her estranged husband, Michael, in which he said "that he felt sure Lee Harvey Oswald had killed the President, but did not feel Oswald was responsible, and further stated, 'We both know who is responsible.'"[10] Both have denied having the conversation, and the FBI has never released the actual transcripts of that bugging operation. The conversation is known only because of one FBI memo that attributed the information to an unnamed informant. In later chapters, we will detail additional illegal domestic FBI surveillance as part of its JFK investigation, including an FBI break-in to bug Marina Oswald's bedroom.

Hoover had other cover-ups to maintain, unrelated to his official duties, even before Jack Ruby's actions on November 24 would escalate Hoover's concerns to a new level. By November 23, Hoover was no doubt becoming aware of the accusations coming out of New Orleans about his former Chicago FBI chief Guy Banister, and Banister's associate David Ferrie. Any connection between them and Oswald would be very embarrassing for the FBI, and Hoover's concern probably resulted in the gentle treatment of Banister following Ferrie's return to Dallas the following night.

Before JFK's murder, Hoover might have been aware of the decision not to tell Georgia FBI agent Don Adams—who was investigating Joseph Milteer's threats against JFK—any information about Milteer's threats being tape-recorded by a Miami police informant, or about the Tampa attempt that followed Milteer's threat.[11] That information would seem to have been crucial for Agent Adams's preassassination investigation of Milteer, but it was also withheld after JFK's death, even as the FBI's investigation of Milteer continued. After JFK's murder, the Milteer threat and any other serious threats against JFK in the FBI's files were almost certainly sought out by Hoover, who wanted to be sure the FBI hadn't missed anything that could embarrass Hoover and the Bureau. As for Milteer, he was still talking to the Miami police's informant, though Hoover and the FBI wouldn't find out what he was saying for several days.

The day after JFK's murder, Milteer was in South Carolina, talking to William Somersett (the Miami police informant). Milteer "was very happy over JFK's death" and said, "It happened like I told you, didn't it? It happened from a window with a high-powered rifle." Milteer also mentioned traveling recently to "Dallas, Texas, as well as New Orleans," which is not surprising, since Milteer knew Guy Banister, whose major client Carlos Marcello controlled the mob in both cities.[12] Milteer would make more provocative comments to the police informant the following day, just before Oswald was shot.

At least for a while, another well-traveled person linked to Marcello—French Connection heroin kingpin and assassin Michel Victor Mertz—was in Dallas on November 23, 1963. Mertz had recently been in Texas and Louisiana, using the name of an old adversary, Jean Souetre, while the real Souetre was in Spain. Mertz's alias was sure to trigger cover-ups by the CIA and FBI, since the real Souetre was wanted by French authorities because he'd participated in the 1962 attempt to assassinate Charles de Gaulle, which had left the French president's car riddled with bullets. While the real Jean Souetre was a fugitive in Europe in May 1963, a CIA official had filed a report about his meeting with Souetre, though Richard Helms decided in July 1963 to reject Souetre's overtures.[13] In the days leading up to JFK's trip to Dallas, former Senate investigator Bud Fensterwald discovered that "the FBI had traced [the man they thought was] Souetre to Dallas a day before the assassination and then lost him."[14] As Souetre told us, via French journalist Stephane Risset, the man in Dallas was actually Michel Victor Mertz, using Souetre's name.

Only one page of Mertz's CIA file has been released, and the following memo is just part of a much longer document that is still withheld. The memo was in response to FBI and French requests for information, and states that "Michel Mertz . . . had been expelled from the US at Fort Worth or Dallas 48 hours after the assassination of President Kennedy." The memo adds that the Frenchman "was in Fort Worth on the morning of November 22 [as was JFK] and in Dallas in the afternoon." It also provides the Jean Souetre alias, as well as that of a twenty-three-year-old aspiring French chef who was visiting Dallas at the time. However, official records confirm the chef was not deported and left Dallas legitimately.

This CIA memo was copied to Bobby Kennedy's FBI liaison, Courtney Evans. However, the memo wasn't sent until more than three months after JFK's assassination, meaning that Bobby probably wasn't aware of Mertz's presence in Dallas until that time. That tragic timing is compounded by the fact that a Bureau of Narcotics report says it received an anonymous letter, just a day after Mertz's deportation, that described heroin smuggling in Mexico City by one of Mertz's close associates, who also operated in Cuba.[15] But Bobby would never have all the pieces he would need to put together the story of Mertz. William Attwood's prize-winning *Newsday* series that exposed Mertz's heroin trafficking with Trafficante wouldn't appear until five years after Bobby's death; the CIA memo about Mertz's deportation from Dallas wouldn't be released until several years after the *Newsday* articles; and Souetre wouldn't reveal that Mertz had impersonated him until the early 1980s. It would also take our review of Fensterwald's files, and the release of the Bureau of Narcotics' internal history of the French Connection ("Project Pilot," first detailed by author Douglas Valentine in 2004), to finally complete the puzzle.

A Houston dentist who had known Souetre years earlier in France said he was interviewed by FBI agents who "told me that Souetre was in Dallas that day [of JFK's murder] and was flown out . . . as far as they were concerned, in a government plane. But there was no record whatsoever of the plane being there."[16] The FBI wouldn't find any record of Souetre's being "flown out" on a government plane, because the person in question was actually Mertz who'd been posing as Souetre. Also, when Mertz was picked up, he had switched to yet another alias, one guaranteed to get him deported back to familiar territory.

Virgil Bailey, an INS investigator in Dallas in 1963, told researcher Gary Shaw years later about "picking up a Frenchman in Dallas shortly after the assassination of President Kennedy." The man's description was very close to Mertz's, and he looked just a few years older than a cover identity Mertz often used. Based on age and description, the man Investigator Bailey remembered could not have been either the real Souetre or the young French chef. Bailey also recalled that "the Frenchman . . . had been tried in absentia in France and was under a death sentence for collaboration with the Nazis during World War II." Mertz could have picked up that alias from either of two of his heroin associates, Joseph Orsini and Antoine D'Agostino, who had both earned "a death sentence in absentia" for Nazi collaboration. (Orsini's nephew would later be arrested as part of the Fort Benning heroin bust that would eventually send Mertz, briefly, to prison.) Mertz's cover story apparently also tried to take advantage of the presence of the young French chef visiting Dallas, since Bailey thinks the man they arrested was "a chef or maitre d' in an unknown Dallas restaurant."[17]

Bailey's supervisor at INS at the time, Hal Norwood, recalled other aspects of the story. Norwood described the arrest of an "individual who might have been French which occurred shortly after the killing of the President. The Dallas police called INS and requested that they come to city jail to investigate a foreigner that they had in custody." Norwood thought Bailey "was one of the men he sent" to pick up the foreigner. "The man in question was a wanted criminal and shortly after INS took him into custody, the head of Washington INS investigations called requesting a pickup on the man. They were surprised that he was already a prisoner. . . . The Washington INS office was VERY interested in the man and called twice regarding him," according to the INS supervisor.[18]

Mertz's intelligence connections were enough to have the official paperwork suppressed later, especially if he or his associates were involved with QJWIN or another of Helms's unauthorized Castro assassination plots. The fact that the CIA discovered later that someone had been using the names of both Souetre and Mertz would also allow an official like Helms (or Angleton or Harvey) to ask INS officials to remove the information about the deportation from their files, on national-security grounds. In any event, it must have been deliciously ironic for Carlos Marcello to see the same INS that had once deported him, on the orders of Bobby Kennedy, now fly his heroin partner out of Dallas shortly after JFK's assassination.

Back in Washington, on the evening of Saturday, November 23, CIA Director McCone "called Secretary [of State] Rusk and reviewed with him the information received from Mexico City, most particularly the holding of a Mexican employee of the Cuban Embassy by Mexican officials for interrogation concerning Lee Oswald." McCone wrote in a memorandum for the record that he "explained to Rusk the information that we had transmitted to the FBI and to the authorities in Dallas. Rusk had not known of these developments prior to my communication with him."[19]

This call from McCone might have been when Rusk first learned about the JFK-Almeida coup plan, an operation so sensitive that McCone would not have included it in a routine office memorandum. When we interviewed Rusk, he indicated that he had first learned shortly after JFK's death that all of the planning he and other officials had been doing for months—for a Cuban coup and invasion—was for an "active" operation.[20] Before that, Rusk had thought the planning was so the United States would be ready just in case a powerful Cuban official was found to overthrow Fidel. Like other top officials present at JFK's big November 12, 1963, meeting about Cuba, Rusk had heard Desmond FitzGerald say, the "CIA is in touch with three persons who are in the military" in Cuba, and that the CIA was trying to get them "to talk and plot Castro's downfall."[21] We know from interviewing someone who worked with Rusk on one of Bobby's Cuban subcommittees that Rusk probably already knew about Rolando Cubela, but thought he was only a midlevel official with little power, whom the CIA was using to try to find a far more powerful Cuban official. Rusk and his associate never considered Cubela as someone who could actually stage a coup; they (along with McCone) had also not been told that Helms and FitzGerald were trying to convince Cubela to assassinate Fidel.

Our impression from talking to Rusk was that he was told briefly and generally about the JFK-Almeida coup plan within a day or so after JFK's death, and then learned more at a later time. Rusk was adamant in our interview that the "coup" and "second invasion" he had learned about after JFK's death were completely different from the Cubela operation, which would have required Rusk to have gained more than a passing knowledge of the JFK-Almeida coup plan.

Rusk also indicated in our interview that he was told about the coup plan not by Bobby Kennedy or one of his close associates, but in the course of his duties as Secretary of State. Rusk wasn't as close to Bobby Kennedy as some Cabinet officials who agreed to stay on under LBJ, such as Defense Secretary McNamara. Perhaps that's one reason Rusk was told about the coup plan after JFK's death, while some other officials, like McNamara, apparently weren't told at all. But even McCone couldn't tell Rusk everything, since Helms was withholding so much from his boss. (Helms would eventually withhold information directly from Rusk, when Rusk asked Helms in 1966 if the CIA had tried to use Cubela in an assassination operation. Helms told Rusk it hadn't, and Rusk wouldn't learn that Helms was lying until 1975. In stark contrast with his normally placid demeanor, Rusk's anger about being lied to by Helms was quite evident in our 1990 interview.)

A somber Bobby Kennedy took time out from his family and official duties for a private meeting with Harry Williams, who told us the meeting occurred within two days of JFK's death, placing it on either Saturday or Sunday. Almeida was still in Cuba, and his family was still outside of Cuba under US surveillance, but any plans for a coup were completely on hold. Harry says that Bobby "didn't say much," but told Harry that "things are going to change," now that Bobby no longer essentially ran Cuban operations and policy for the United States. Harry says he already knew that Bobby and "Johnson . . . hate[d] each other's guts," so Bobby's role and the plans would no doubt be very different.

Bobby didn't voice any suspicions to Harry about Artime or any other Cuban exiles, probably because by that time, Oswald's seemingly pro-Castro stance had been publicized extensively. In addition, Bobby knew about some of the information coming from Mexico City, which would have made him suspect, only briefly, that Castro might have had a hand in JFK's death.[22]

At the time, Harry didn't suspect any Cuban exiles; that would only come later, after he saw the ties between two of E. Howard Hunt's exile associates and Santo Trafficante. For the time being, Harry's suspicions were also directed at Fidel, especially once a Cuban exile linked to Artime and the CIA showed him a photo of Oswald going into the Cuban embassy in Mexico City. In 1992, when Harry told us about seeing the photo, he didn't know about our Naval Intelligence source who had described a similar photo. The accounts of Win Scott and other CIA personnel who saw the Oswald photo had also not been publicized or declassified at that time.

It's important to point out a significant difference between Bobby Kennedy and Richard Helms in the aftermath of JFK's murder. Helms would continue at least some of his unauthorized operations, hiding them from LBJ the same way he had hidden them from JFK and Bobby. In contrast, while Bobby withheld some information about the coup plan from LBJ, he didn't try to proceed with the plot behind LBJ's back, even after it became clear that Castro had nothing to do with JFK's death and that Almeida was still in place, unexposed, and willing to stage a coup. Harry still had a direct line of communication to Almeida that didn't require CIA assistance, and enough exile contacts (and goodwill from spearheading the release of the Bay of Pigs prisoners) that Harry could have gotten into Cuba even without the help of US authorities at Guantanamo. Once inside Cuba, Harry could have met with Almeida and proceeded with the coup. Bobby knew that all the planning and preparations for the invasion and post-invasion occupation had been completed, so LBJ would have had little choice but to commit the already trained and ready US forces if Almeida sent word of Castro's death. However, it appears that Bobby never even considered the option of going behind LBJ's back. Once it became apparent, by late December, that Almeida was still willing to go forward with the coup, Bobby would deal with LBJ directly on the matter.

In Dallas, the press was still feeding the public a steady diet of news stories, even as Chief Curry told tired journalists that Oswald's transfer to the county jail was being put off until Sunday morning. He assured them that if they were back by 10:00 AM, "they won't miss anything."[23] Earlier that day, CBS radio reporter Dan Rather had delivered the biggest scoop of his young career, when he told his listeners about being one of the very first journalists to see what would become known as the Zapruder film. Illustrating the power of suggestion, and most journalists' desire at the time to please authorities and network bosses, Rather described the movie this way: "I have just returned from seeing a movie which clearly shows the President's assassination . . . his head went forward with considerable violence."[24]

Of course, the film shows no such thing; instead, JFK's head jerks back and to his left. But it would be more than a decade before any of the American public could glimpse the actual film and many more years before the public could easily view and study clear copies of the footage. We should point out that Rather was allowed to see the film just once, and only at normal speed, and the grainy 8-millimeter home movie was nothing like the digitally enhanced version available today. But it does demonstrate that the "official" version of the shooting—three shots, all from the rear—was so prevalent among officials by Saturday that Rather believed that more than his own eyes.

Also in Dallas, Jack Ruby was getting ready to lay the groundwork for the following day, when his excuse for being near police headquarters at the time of Oswald's transfer would be that he had to wire $25 to one of his dancers, Karen Carlin. To begin preparing this cover story, Ruby had Carlin and several others go to Nichols Garage. All those involved in this meeting later gave authorities different accounts of what happened there. Carlin was willing to agree to whatever Ruby said, because the previous day, a Ruby associate had ordered her to meet him and threatened, "If you're not down here, you won't be around too long."

Karen Carlin arrived at Nichols Garage before Ruby did; then Ruby called the parking attendant and told him to loan Carlin $5—and be sure to time-stamp the receipt—for which Ruby would reimburse him. (The following day, Ruby's time-stamped Western Union receipt would be designed to "prove" that Ruby just happened to be near the police station when Oswald was being moved.) When Ruby arrived at the garage, his cover story was that he was supposed to loan Carlin another $25. But Ruby claimed he didn't have it and couldn't get it, ignoring the fact that his club and its safe were next door. The plan was for Ruby to wire Carlin the money the next day, from a Western Union office only one block from the police station where Oswald would be moved. It's clear this was only a cover story, since there were two Western Union offices much closer to Ruby's Oak Cliff apartment.[25] There was no need for Ruby to go all the way downtown to use the Western Union office near the police station—except for the fact that Ruby had to silence Oswald.

Chapter Eighteen

On November 24, 1963, at 10:00 AM (Eastern time), CIA Director McCone met with LBJ to tell him about "the Cuban situation," including "our operational plans against Cuba," according to McCone's notes.[1] However, the briefing was only twenty minutes long, and there was much to go over besides the JFK-Almeida coup plan and AMWORLD, so Johnson's understanding of Cuban operations was still in its early stages. LBJ and McCone no doubt also discussed the latest information from Mexico City about poor Silvia Duran and KGB agent Kostikov. Such information would keep LBJ worried about possible Cuban or Russian involvement in JFK's murder; in another meeting that weekend, LBJ asked former JFK aide Ted Sorenson, "What do you think of the possibility of a foreign government being involved [in JFK's assassination]?"

These concerns would drive LBJ's need for secrecy and his desire to limit any real investigation that might expose foreign links to JFK's murder that could generate a crisis with Russia or Cuba. Hence, the *Miami Herald* was unable to publish anything further about the Tampa assassination plot mentioned in the previous day's *Tampa Tribune*. In addition, no newspaper or TV station followed up on the *Miami Herald*'s intriguing November 24 newspaper story—which included many "no comment" responses from officials who didn't deny anything in the original *Tampa Tribune* story (some of which the *Herald* repeated). In hindsight, that type of story should have attracted attention from at least some other journalists, and perhaps it did. But nothing was ever published or broadcast, at least not for decades.

In South Carolina, white supremacist and Marcello associate Joseph Milteer was having breakfast with his friend William Somersett, unaware that Somersett was an informant for the Miami police. The subject of JFK's murder came up again, and "Milteer advised that they did not have to worry about Lee Harvey Oswald getting caught because he 'doesn't know anything.'" However, as if he needed to make sure, Milteer excused himself so that he could telephone someone.[2]

In Dallas, Jack Ruby was spruced up, dressed in his finest, for the spotlight he was sure to occupy after he completed his assignment. Ruby was probably nervous, but not about the length of time he might have to spend in jail after shooting Oswald. Under Texas law, for murders involving a "sudden passion," the sentence could be as brief as two years, with time off for good behavior, or even just probation.[3] Instead, Ruby was probably only worried that after he pulled out his gun and started shooting at Oswald, he might hit a policeman or a policeman might start shooting at him. Getting into the police station basement where the transfer would take place would be no problem for Ruby, since the FBI later acknowledged that "as a result of his friendship with a number of police officers, Ruby had easy accessibility to the Dallas Police Department."[4]

The executive director of the House Select Committee on Assassinations, former Mafia prosecutor G. Robert Blakey, said that "the murder of Oswald by Jack Ruby had all the earmarks of an organized crime hit."[5] Also, the Committee found that Ruby's shooting Oswald wasn't "spontaneous," and that Ruby probably had help entering the basement of the police station for the transfer.[6] The staffs of both the Committee and the Warren Commission focused particular attention on one of Ruby's policeman associates: Blakey "was convinced that Sgt. Patrick Dean had been the one that let Jack Ruby in the basement on the morning of the 24th."[7] Dean refused to testify to Blakey's Committee, and even told author Peter Dale Scott "of his longtime relationship with [Joe] Civello," the mobster who ran Dallas for Carlos Marcello. Scott also notes that Dean "was in charge of security in the Dallas basement when Oswald was murdered," and that Dean "later failed a lie detector test about Ruby's access to [the basement]." Dean also worked in narcotics, which Ruby was also involved in with Civello and Marcello.[8]

If JFK's assassination had occurred in Tampa, Ruby could have been assisted by Trafficante associate Police Sgt. Jack de la Llana. If JFK had been killed in Ruby's hometown of Chicago, Ruby could have turned to Trafficante and Rosselli associate Richard Cain, the chief investigator for the Cook County sheriff.

Even as evidence tying Oswald to Cuba and Russia was causing concern among officials in Washington, and would soon break in the press, Marcello continued with the plans to kill Oswald. If the main goal of JFK's death had been to provoke the invasion of Cuba, keeping the seemingly pro-Castro Oswald alive a while longer would have seemed a more logical choice, so that he could be the focus of an outcry to retaliate against Fidel. But since the main goal of killing JFK was to end the pressure on Marcello, Trafficante, and their associates, hence Oswald had to die—and soon. With the authorities still seeking David Ferrie, the whole plot could unravel and point to people working for Marcello, unless Oswald was killed. Marcello could make only limited efforts to contain Oswald's public statements and cooperation with police, which is why two attorneys linked to Marcello had been asked to represent the still lawyerless Oswald. But only killing Oswald could guarantee his silence.[9]

As had been planned the night before, at 10:19 AM (Central), dancer Karen Carlin in Fort Worth called Ruby's home, supposedly to ask him to send her money. It's doubtful that Ruby was there, since an earlier call to Ruby's home by his regular housekeeper was answered by someone who didn't seem to recognize her voice. At 10:45 AM, Ruby was talking to a TV crew in front of the police station, before heading to the Western Union office. At 11:00 AM, Sgt. Dean apparently removed police who had been guarding an interior door to the basement. Upstairs, in Detective Fritz's office, a small group of officials was questioning Oswald, but at 11:15 AM they were told their time was up. However, the transfer car wasn't in position, so the group with Oswald had to slow its passage toward the basement. The basement was packed with at least seventy policemen and forty newsmen. At Western Union, Ruby wired Carlin the money at 11:17 AM and then headed back to the police station, which was only a block away. The timing was tight for Ruby to have any hope of claiming a "sudden passion" defense, but he had plenty of associates who could signal when he should arrive. For example, one minute after Ruby left the Western Union office, his attorney entered the police station and saw Oswald coming out of the jail elevator. Ruby's attorney turned to leave, telling a police detective, "That's all I wanted to see."

Even with the crowds of press and police, no one ever claimed to have seen Ruby actually entering the police basement, which is one more indication that he must have had help in doing so. Ruby most likely entered the basement from the alley that runs between the Western Union office and the police station. One officer claimed to have seen "an unidentified white male" walk down the ramp into the basement, past Officer Roy Vaughn, who was guarding the ramp. But that officer failed a polygraph test, while Officer Vaughn, who consistently said he had not let Ruby down the ramp, passed his polygraph test.[10] Seven witnesses agreed with Vaughn.

Around 11:20 AM, Oswald walked through the door, flanked by two Dallas police detectives. As soon as he was visible, a car horn blew, and is audible on the news broadcast of the transfer. At 11:21, Ruby shot Oswald and the basement erupted in pandemonium. As Oswald was rushed to Parkland Hospital, the apprehended Ruby appeared to police officer Don Ray Archer as "being extremely agitated and nervous, continually inquiring whether Oswald was dead or alive." Oswald died at 1:07 PM, and it was only after Ruby was told that his victim had died that "Ruby calmed down," according to Marcello's biographer, John H. Davis. Davis notes that even after an officer told Ruby, "'It looks like it's going to be the electric chair for you' . . . Ruby immediately relaxed and even managed a wan smile." Officer Archer said "it seemed at that time that Ruby felt his own life depended on the success of his mission, that if Oswald had not died, he, Jack Ruby, would have been killed."[11]

Later that day, a Secret Service agent interviewed a "highly agitated" Karen Carlin. Carlin blurted out to the agent that "Oswald, Jack Ruby, and other individuals unknown to her were involved in a plot to assassinate Kennedy, and that she would be killed if she gave any information to authorities."[12] As Officer Archer had suspected, the same was true for Jack Ruby and members of his family. Ruby would soon be visited in jail by Dallas restaurateur Joe Campisi, an underboss for Marcello; Ruby had last seen Campisi at his restaurant on the night before JFK's murder. Campisi was also close to Sheriff Bill Decker, in whose custody Ruby would spend most of the rest of his life, reportedly in a cell overlooking Dealey Plaza. When Ruby was later asked in a polygraph examination if "members of your own family are now in danger because of what you did," Ruby said "yes." Ruby's sister later testified that Ruby worried about their "brother Earl being dismembered [and] Earl's children [being] dismembered [and their] arms and legs . . . cut off." At the time, a Chicago mobster associate of Richard Cain was well known in the underworld for that type of Mafia retribution; years later, Johnny Rosselli's legs were cut off after he was murdered.[13]

In South Carolina, Joseph Milteer had completed his phone call and rejoined his friend William Somersett. After the radio broadcast the news about Oswald's death, Milteer told his friend, "That makes it work perfect . . . now we have no worry."[14]

As Jack Ruby's name surfaced and started to reverberate through the back channels of law enforcement and intelligence, agencies ranging from the FBI to the CIA had new information to withhold from the public and from one another. Oswald's death also had an immediate and dramatic impact on the situation in Washington, since there would now be no public trial. This spawned more investigations, some of them secret, since the evidence gathered—and their final conclusions—would not have to be presented in open court.

One of the by-products of Oswald's death was the creation of what would become known as the Warren Commission. Sometimes misperceived as something solely created by LBJ so he could control the investigation, the Warren Commission was actually created because of the efforts of several of Bobby Kennedy's associates. Neither President Johnson nor J. Edgar Hoover wanted the Warren Commission, whereas Bobby's associates apparently saw some type of commission as preferable to having the whole investigation in the hands of LBJ and Hoover.

Within hours of Oswald's death, Hoover was talking to Nicholas Katzenbach, Bobby's trusted deputy Attorney General. While Bobby was consumed with funeral preparations and family matters, Katzenbach was essentially running the Justice Department. However, Katzenbach focused on areas like civil rights, and wasn't a specialist in the areas of organized crime or Hoffa, areas that were now especially relevant in light of Ruby's recent actions. Also, there is no evidence that Katzenbach was ever told about the JFK-Almeida coup plan, which had been withheld from all of Bobby's associates who weren't actively involved in the Cuba operation. Finally, it's not clear if Katzenbach was acting at Bobby's direction in pursuing the creation of what became the Warren Commission, or if he and other associates of Bobby were simply doing what they assumed the Attorney General would want them to do.

Hoover's memo of his conversation with Katzenbach on the afternoon of November 24 says, "The thing I am concerned about, and so is Mr. Katzenbach, is having something issued so we can convince the public that Oswald is the real assassin."[15] In later years, much attention was focused on the fact that Katzenbach seemed to be more interested in convincing the public that Oswald acted alone than in finding out if he was involved with others. Katzenbach stated his feelings even more strongly in a memo the following day to LBJ aide Bill Moyers, declaring, "The public must be satisfied that Oswald was the assassin [and] that he did not have confederates who are still at large." He even wrote, "Speculation about Oswald's motivation ought to be cut off, and we should have some basis for rebutting thought that this was a

Communist conspiracy or . . . a right-wing conspiracy to blame it on the Communists." In his private memo to Moyers, even Katzenbach notes that "the facts on Oswald seem [almost] too pat—too obvious (Marxist, Cuba, Russian wife, etc.)." Yet Katzenbach's main goal was "to head off public speculation or Congressional hearings. . . ."[16]

However, as reflected in Hoover's notes of his November 24 talk with Katzenbach, they disagreed about the best way to achieve that goal. Katzenbach "thinks that the President might appoint a Presidential Commission of three outstanding citizens to make a determination." Hoover "countered with a suggestion that we make an investigative report to the Attorney General . . . then the Attorney General can make the report to the President, and the President can decide whether to make it public." Hoover points out that to do otherwise could "complicate our foreign relations [because], for instance, Oswald made a phone call to the Cuban Embassy in Mexico City which we intercepted."[17]

We feel the evidence shows the latter concern is at the heart of Katzenbach's desire to convince the public Oswald acted alone, and to cut off speculation about anyone else who might have been involved. In that, Katzenbach shared the concerns of Hoover, LBJ, McCone, and other top officials as well, from Bobby to Rusk to General Maxwell Taylor. The only differences are that Katzenbach expressed his feelings in writing and was the least informed of the top officials just listed, all of whom had additional reasons to avoid any intensive investigation of Oswald's (and now Ruby's) associates.

As the struggle between Katzenbach's "pro-Commission" forces and Hoover and LBJ's "anti-Commission" forces played out in the coming days, Hoover was busy keeping a lid on connections to Ruby and Oswald that could embarrass the FBI. Ruby had been an official FBI informant in 1959, as part of an unusual sequence of events that coincided with Ruby's well-documented trips to Havana while Trafficante was under house arrest there. As we mentioned earlier, and documented at length in *Ultimate Sacrifice,* Ruby was running guns and other armaments to Cuba at the time with associates of Trafficante and Hoffa, and Ruby was probably one of the people using the alias "Jack La Rue," the mysterious man whom Bobby Kennedy's investigators were unable to find. At the time, Ruby was also acting as an intermediary for Marcello, in efforts to get Santo Trafficante released from house arrest in Cuba.

Just two days after Oswald's death, the FBI and the CIA learned that "a British journalist . . . John Wilson . . . gave information to the American

embassy in London that [in 1959] an American gangster named Santos...
was visited frequently by an American gangster type named Ruby."[18]
Wilson was a reliable witness who had testified before the US Senate
in 1959 about a young Salvador Allende (later president of Chile), and
Congressional investigators would eventually turn up information corroborating his account. However, in late 1963 and 1964, the FBI and CIA
did not want this information to be made public, so their main emphasis
was in trying to discredit Wilson.

In Dallas, just a few hours after Oswald's death, FBI Agent Hosty
was ordered to destroy the note Oswald had left for him a couple of
weeks earlier. He flushed it down a toilet, and its existence wouldn't
become known until 1975.[19] Hosty's name was also excluded from the
typed copy of Oswald's notebook that was sent to Washington. FBI
agents were also very harsh in dealing with the many leads that came
in regarding Ruby's Cuban gunrunning; some witnesses were threatened with arrest or prosecution if they persisted in their stories, even
though later investigations have shown their stories were accurate. On
the other hand, in a bizarre twist, the FBI used claims from several of
Ruby's Mafia associates as proof that Ruby had no ties to the Mafia. The
result was that the general public wouldn't link Ruby with the Mafia
for almost a decade and a half, and Ruby's ties to Cuban gunrunning,
which had continued into 1963, remain unknown to most of the public
even today.

Journalist Henry Hurt found that an analysis of FBI documents
provided to the Warren Commission "showed that at least 60 witnesses claimed that the FBI in some way altered what the witnesses
had reported." Journalists like Anthony Summers and Earl Golz found
other witnesses interviewed by the FBI who said the same thing. In at
least two instances, the FBI simply rewrote memos to completely change
their meaning—something an FBI agent would do only on orders from
the highest authority. We know this only because the National Archives
eventually released the original, unaltered memos.

In one case, a November 27, 1963, memo about Ruby originally cited
his link to Dallas mob boss Joe Civello. But in the version the Warren
Commission published, the final three paragraphs of the memo, which
cover Civello (and his ties to narcotics), are completely missing.[20] In
another instance of FBI document tampering, the FBI was trying to make
the case that Oswald used brown paper from the Book Depository to
wrap the rifle he allegedly carried to work on the day JFK was shot. The
published version of a November 30, 1963, FBI memo says that the Book

Depository paper was "found to have the same observable characteristics as the brown paper bag" found on the sixth floor after the shooting. However, the National Archives eventually released the original
version of the same FBI memo, which said the Book Depository paper
was "found not to be identical with the paper gun case" found on the
sixth floor.[21] The bottom line is that Hoover was using national-security
concerns to build a case against Oswald, avoid Ruby's Mafia ties, and
hide anything that might embarrass him or the FBI.

Once Ruby surfaced in the assassination saga on November 24, Hoover
had new worries. Hoover probably had reports on Ruby's links to
associates like Trafficante and Hoffa that he withheld from the Warren
Commission. The FBI definitely had reports of Ruby's fall 1963 visits
to Johnny Rosselli, who was under FBI surveillance at the time, which
were likewise withheld. If Hoover had FBI files searched for information about threats to JFK, he would have found that FBI informant Jose
Aleman had reported Trafficante's fall 1962 threat that JFK would be
"hit" before the next election. Recently released files make it clear that
Aleman continued to be an FBI informant in late 1963 and into 1964, as
part of the FBI's "Top Echelon Criminal Informant Program." Aleman
had met with his FBI handlers in the weeks prior to JFK's murder, as
confirmed by an October 23, 1963, memo to Hoover in which Aleman
"admitted [his] association with and business dealings with . . . Santo
Trafficante. . . . Aleman was cooperative throughout this interview and
has agreed to furnish information on a confidential basis relating to the
activities of [Santo] Trafficante."[22] In 1964, Aleman would continue to
provide information to the FBI about not only Trafficante, but also Trafficante's bodyguard, Herminio Diaz.[23] Faced with either revealing Aleman's report of Trafficante's threat to hit JFK (a threat not conveyed to
the Secret Service) or continuing to use Aleman as an informant, Hoover
chose the latter.

  Hoover had at least one other important JFK threat in his files, the one
involving Carlos Marcello that Ed Becker reported to the FBI in the fall of
1962. As Hoover received information on November 23 and 24 about the
allegations concerning David Ferrie and Guy Banister, the connection
to Marcello would have been inescapable. Yet this threat would also not
be revealed to the Warren Commission, apparently for the same reason
Hoover's New Orleans FBI kept its distance from Marcello.

  Hoover maintained his own set of "official and confidential files" of
the most sensitive and scandalous information, and one has to wonder

if all the sensitive files about Oswald, Ruby, Trafficante, Rosselli, and Marcello wound up there. Reportedly, all of the "official and confidential files" were destroyed by Hoover's longtime companion and right-hand man, Clyde Tolson, shortly after Hoover's death.[24]

Richard Helms at the CIA had even more reason than Hoover to be concerned about Jack Ruby, and to start covering up. Ruby's 1959 gun-running and trips to Cuba had placed him on the fringe of the original 1959 CIA-Mafia plot to kill Fidel Castro. Even the Colt Cobra pistol that Ruby used to shoot Oswald came from his activities during that era. The CIA-Mafia plot that began in 1959 had been brokered by Jimmy Hoffa, while then–Vice President Richard Nixon was running Cuba policy for Eisenhower. The 1959 plots preceded the more extensive and direct CIA-Mafia plots with Trafficante and Rosselli that began in the summer of 1960, in an attempt to assassinate Castro before the November 1960 presidential election. Helms had not been involved in the creation of either of those plots, which high-ranking CIA officials had authorized. But because Helms had continued the CIA-Mafia plots with Rosselli on an unauthorized basis, after telling Bobby Kennedy they had ended, Helms had to keep all of them secret, especially any of their ties to Jack Ruby.

The CIA, or the FBI, was probably behind the disappearance of files about Ruby from other government agencies. Author David Scheim said that "in 1958, Ruby wrote a letter to the State Department's Office of Munitions Controls 'requesting permission to negotiate the purchase of firearms and ammunition from an Italian firm' and the name 'Jack Rubenstein' was listed in a 1959 Army Intelligence report on US arms dealers. Although located by clerks of these two federal agencies in 1963, both documents are today inexplicably missing."[25]

While Helms was busy covering up CIA ties to Ruby and Oswald, he was simultaneously overseeing several CIA investigations. In addition to the Mexico City activities we cited earlier, the huge Miami CIA station (JMWAVE) reported that "following [the] assassination [of] President Kennedy, JMWAVE ran traces on all suspects or participants with negative results."[26] One can't help but notice the use of the plural "suspects" and "participants" for an assassination officially attributed to just one man. Then again, given the fact that confessed JFK assassination participant David Morales was the Chief of Operations for the Miami CIA station, it's not surprising that their search turned up only "negative results."

We mentioned earlier the internal CIA investigation that Helms originally assigned to John Whitten, until he complained that files had been withheld from him. Whitten was then replaced by CIA Counter-Intelligence Chief James Angleton, but there was apparently at least one more CIA investigation, which was conducted for LBJ. According to Congressional investigators, about a month after JFK's murder "the CIA report of [its] investigation [was] submitted to President Johnson," but they noted that there was "no indication that the Warren Commission received this document." (It's unclear whether this was the same report that Whitten started and Angleton finished.)[27]

Helms might have ordered at least one additional investigation or informal inquiry, but someone very close to him would have had to complete it. No thorough investigation of JFK's assassination, or of the role of CIA assets in it, could be conducted without the investigators' being told about at least some of Helms's unauthorized Castro assassination operations. While most of the Cuban exile leaders Bobby and Harry chose for the JFK-Almeida coup plan continued to receive CIA support during 1964, Tony Varona was unceremoniously dumped, for reasons not clear in his declassified CIA file. Varona, who had taken $200,000 from Rosselli's Chicago Mafia and then dealt with Trafficante associate Rolando Masferrer, was cut off by the CIA. Congressional investigators found that Varona left Miami in early 1964 and moved to New York, giving up his full-time work for the exile cause. Just months after that, a CIA memo cited a *New York Times* article about Varona that said he was earning money by selling cars in New Jersey at night.[28]

Legally, if Helms felt that Varona and any other CIA asset were involved in JFK's assassination, he didn't have to tell anyone. Author Peter Dale Scott found that an "agreement was in force from the mid-1950s to the mid-1970s, exempting the CIA from a statutory requirement to report [to the Justice Department] any criminal activity by any of its employees or assets." Declassified files indicate at least two other cases—one of which was QJWIN's termination—in which Helms may have sacked an agent because of links to JFK's assassination.

It's important to keep in mind that just as Hoover had to investigate JFK's assassination and conceal certain information while still running the FBI's usual operations, the same was true for Helms. The CIA's Cuban operations, both authorized and unauthorized, continued, even as Helms oversaw the CIA's own investigations and withheld important information from the FBI and the soon-to-be-created Warren Commission.

After Oswald's death, Naval Intelligence's goals changed radically. On the afternoon of November 24, the organization transitioned from shredding files about its "tight surveillance" of Oswald to conducting its own, secret internal investigation of JFK's assassination. Also involved were personnel from Marine Intelligence, and the operation was probably known to the head of the Defense Intelligence Agency, General Joseph Carroll. Our Naval Intelligence source participated in this secret investigation, aspects of which were later independently confirmed by the House Select Committee on Assassinations and by a former Navy man who was the son of a prominent admiral.

Our source "became part of a 6-week Naval Intelligence investigation into JFK's assassination." He said "their mission was 'Did [Oswald] do it?' not 'Who did it?'" As part of their investigation, Naval Intelligence personnel went to Dallas, but "they were forbidden to have anything to do with the autopsy." He said, "The result of the Naval Intelligence investigation was that [it] concluded Oswald was not the shooter, due to his skills, the gun, etc., [and that] Oswald was incapable of masterminding the assassination or of doing the actual shooting." The report's summary was "6–7 pages, with hundreds of supporting documents." Our source had "some knowledge that the CIA also conducted [its] own investigation," a fact that wasn't widely known when we talked to the source in 1991.

It's significant that Naval Intelligence had the same men involved with Oswald's "tight surveillance" conduct this secret investigation. On one hand, it kept Navy brass from having to let more Naval personnel know about the extensive surveillance Oswald had been under. On the other hand, the men were essentially investigating their own organization and their own work, and were hardly in a position to be objective if leads pointed to problems with some of those who had been providing information about Oswald (such as Guy Banister).

Our source "signed a disclosure agreement" after the investigation, and even after almost thirty years he would convey information to us only through a trusted intermediary.[29] The House Select Committee on Assassinations uncovered evidence of what appears to be a related Marine Intelligence investigation that reached similar conclusions. However, the US military stonewalled the Committee about critical information until the Committee's mandate expired. When we interviewed the US Navy Admiral's son, he independently claimed to have seen a copy of the Naval Intelligence report while he was stationed at a large US Navy base in the Pacific in the early 1970s. His account of the report's conclusions matched very closely those of our Naval Intelligence source.[30]

The Naval Intelligence investigation and its conclusions make sense in light of both the tight surveillance Oswald was under before JFK's death and the problems many experts have documented about the shooting skills required to assassinate JFK, and the poor quality of the Mannlicher-Carcano found in the Book Depository. As an internal Navy and Defense Intelligence Agency matter, it was probably important for officials involved with the surveillance of Oswald, and with whatever operations he participated in after he returned from Russia, to cover themselves with such an investigation. At the same time, the officials and those conducting the investigation were probably unaware that some of the people assisting with the surveillance and operations, like Guy Banister, were actually working for Carlos Marcello.

Early results from the Naval Intelligence investigation, or the fact that Naval Intelligence was keeping such close tabs on Oswald, might account for an unusual "top secret, eyes only" memo about Oswald. Less than two weeks after Oswald's death, even as LBJ and McCone were still worried that Oswald might have been acting for Cuba or the Soviets, "Gordon Chase of the National Security Council staff" implied that the "President's Special Assistant for national security Affairs," McGeorge Bundy (who had held the same position under JFK), was able to provide some type of "assurances re: Oswald" that he was not an agent for Castro. Only an official in an agency with access to the surveillance on Oswald, like Naval Intelligence or the CIA, could have given Bundy the information necessary to make such a claim.[31]

Following his brother's death, Bobby Kennedy had the most difficult task of all the people pursuing secret investigations of JFK's murder. Despite his sturdy and efficient manner immediately following JFK's murder, Bobby soon drained his reserves of strength and became a shattered, tortured man, according to those who saw him away from the public eye. Historian John H. Davis, Marcello's biographer, was a cousin of Jackie Kennedy who observed Bobby at the White House following JFK's funeral. In contrast to the stoic, solid demeanors of other family members—like Jackie, Ted, and Rose—Davis described Bobby as "a destroyed man . . . crushed by the death of his brother." Other Kennedy associates made similar observations. Yet at times Bobby would summon the resolve to have one of his trusted associates look into JFK's assassination. We've already noted his request to Chicago union expert Julius Draznin to look into Mafia ties to JFK's murder, even before Ruby surfaced in the case. That was just the first of several attempts Bobby made; others included investigations by his top Hoffa prosecutor, Walter Sheridan; his press secretary, Frank Mankiewicz; Daniel Patrick Moynihan, a former Los Angeles police chief; and at least one top Kennedy aide. However, in each case except one, the investigators weren't told about the JFK-Almeida coup plan or about the initial suspicions Bobby had voiced to McCone and Haynes Johnson.

We spoke to the one investigator for Bobby who did know about those activities. He told us of his belief in a conspiracy involving Marcello, Trafficante, and Rosselli, though he indicated his conclusion was based on information that started coming out only in the mid-1970s, facts that were unavailable to him or to Bobby in 1963 or 1964.[32] So, Bobby was left without definitive evidence, and at times seemed ambivalent about knowing what his investigators had uncovered. After all, there was little he could do with their conclusions without exposing Commander Almeida, revealing the Tampa and Chicago plots he had covered up, or giving Marcello or Hoffa ammunition to claim the US government's prosecutions of them were due to Bobby's suspicions of their involvement in JFK's murder. Bobby knew what type of evidence he would need to prosecute even a lower-level member of such a conspiracy, let alone a godfather like Marcello. Based on his later remarks to close associates, he knew that only the power of the presidency would allow him to conduct a truly thorough, secret investigation of his brother's murder. It may be no coincidence that even as he decided to run for president in 1968, Bobby was helping a journalist prepare a major exposé of Carlos Marcello.

While Bobby's focus would eventually settle on Marcello as being responsible for his brother's death, other suspects loomed in the days following Oswald's murder. We mentioned earlier Bobby's comment about the many associates Jack Ruby shared with Jimmy Hoffa. On November 26, Bobby Kennedy talked with Secret Service Agent Clint Hill, possibly to hear Hill's reaction to Powers's and O'Donnell's accounts of seeing shots from the grassy knoll.[33] With all the evidence coming out of Mexico City, Bobby considered Castro a possibility until at least December 9, 1963, along with "gangsters" and Hoffa.[34]

Bobby was aware of reports coming out of Chicago—some hinting at the Chicago plot, and another saying that "Ruby had recently been in Chicago [to] pick up a 'bundle of money' from Allen Dorfman, a close associate of Jimmy Hoffa." This account surfaced the day Ruby shot Oswald, and we are sure Bobby knew about it because it originated with his most trusted Hoffa prosecutor, Walter Sheridan.[35] As we discussed previously, we spoke with two eyewitnesses who saw Ruby receive approximately $7,000 from a Hoffa associate in Chicago, shortly before JFK's canceled November 2, 1963, motorcade there. Sheridan's report was apparently from someone familiar with that incident, at least on a secondhand basis. The Hoffa associate who gave Ruby the money wasn't Allen Dorfman. However, Dorfman did handle complicated financial transactions for Hoffa and the Mafia (he would later provide $500,000 to Richard Nixon to secure Hoffa's release from prison), and he may well have provided the untraceable cash to Hoffa's associate in 1963, to give to Ruby. Also, Allen Dorfman's father, Paul Dorfman, had known Jack Ruby for years. In fact, Robert Kennedy had written in his anti-Mafia book, *The Enemy Within*, about Paul Dorfman's takeover of a union that first cemented Hoffa's relationship with the Mafia. As Bobby described in his book, the union's takeover was accomplished after the union's "founder and secretary-treasurer was murdered." Not mentioned in Bobby's book, but confirmed by police files, is that a witness who kept his mouth shut about the murder at the time was a young Jack Ruby.

However, the reaction of another one of Bobby's Hoffa prosecutors to Sheridan's Ruby-Chicago story would set the tone for any allegations that surfaced that could expose secrets like the Chicago plot against JFK, or jeopardize ongoing prosecutions against the individuals Bobby felt might have been responsible for JFK's assassination. One of Bobby's top Justice Department prosecutors gave the order for "no further inquiry into this matter [because] the story would give Hoffa an opportunity to criticize the Justice Department for trying to tie Hoffa in with President Kennedy's murder."[36]

Bobby apparently struggled with himself over this issue at times, but in the end he seemed to decide that prosecuting targets like Hoffa and Marcello for specific, easier-to-prove charges was better than risking tainting any prosecution of them by linking them publicly to JFK's assassination without adequate evidence. Also, Bobby appears not to have told most of his Hoffa and Mafia prosecutors about things like the Chicago plot, which was yet another reason Chicago-linked allegations were not widely pursued or fully shared with the FBI. Hoover's comment on the whole Ruby-Chicago payoff matter was: "I do wish [the] Justice Department would mind its own business."[37]

———

Once the FBI took primary jurisdiction over JFK assassination matters, the Secret Service was, in many ways, the odd man out in the investigation. Yet it continued to monitor suspects like Chicago ex-Marine Thomas Vallee, though the released files about him are clearly incomplete. For example, Vallee, arrested in Chicago with a carload of weapons and ammo on the day of JFK's canceled motorcade, apparently wasn't even interviewed by the Secret Service or FBI after another ex-Marine, Lee Oswald, was arrested for JFK's assassination. This omission occurred despite the fact that Congressional investigators found a Secret Service "notation on November 27, 1963, of the similarity between his background and that of Lee Harvey Oswald." In spite of this apparent lack of interest, Congress found that the Secret Service maintained "a record of extensive, continued investigation of Vallee's activities until 1968."[38] It's likely that additional surveillance and investigative files about Vallee were kept with the other files about the Chicago and Tampa plots, none of which have been declassified or revealed to Congress.

This secrecy no doubt complicated the FBI's job when rumors of the Chicago plot surfaced among newsmen, some of whom had been aware of the threat and Vallee's arrest at the time, but had kept that information away from the public.[39] The Secret Service was less than forthcoming in dealing with its rival, the FBI, about such matters.[40] The FBI's main objective after JFK's assassination appears to have been to discredit such reports and ensure they didn't make it into print, a goal the Secret Service shared. Ironically, the source of some newspaper reports about Oswald visiting Chicago was Rosselli's associate Richard Cain, who was still feeding information to the CIA at the time. (CIA reports about Cain's activities for them in the weeks after JFK's death have never been released.)

The Secret Service also obtained records from other agencies. The Federal Bureau of Narcotics (FBN) headquarters file on Jack Ruby didn't contain much—"just that he was a source on numerous occasions, on unimportant suspects," and had been an FBN source "since the 1940s." As with the Dallas police, Ruby had been gaming the system, giving up small fish or problem dealers to gain information and protect his bosses. However, FBN agents say that Secret Service Chief James Rowley asked for Ruby's FBN file on November 25 and, after getting it, never returned it.[41]

After Ruby shot Oswald, things started looking up for Carlos Marcello, who no doubt felt even more relieved about Oswald's death than did

Joseph Milteer. Ruby had shown that he could keep his mouth shut about a murder investigation, and he knew that to cross Marcello would mean death not just for him, but also for his family. Despite Ruby's belief that he would get a light sentence, Marcello, Trafficante, and Rosselli made sure that Ruby would spend the rest of his life in prison, and possibly get the electric chair.

Former Mafia prosecutor G. Robert Blakey writes that shortly after Ruby shot Oswald, an associate of flamboyant attorney Melvin Belli got a "call from a Las Vegas attorney, saying that, 'One of our guys just bumped off the son of a bitch that gunned down the President. We can't move in to handle it, but there's a million bucks net for Mel if he'll take it.'"[42] The call didn't come from Johnny Rosselli, but it did come from his Las Vegas headquarters hotel, the Desert Inn. Belli soon took the case, and kept any mention of Ruby's Mafia contacts out of the trial. Instead of using Texas's "sudden passion" defense—the angle Ruby believed would secure him a short sentence even if he were convicted—Belli used a strange "psycho-motor defense" that had never been tried before. He lost, and Ruby was sentenced to death. Belli then went to Mexico City, where he met with a Mexican official whom the CIA says "directed drug smuggling."[43] Another CIA file says that Belli himself "was reportedly involved in illicit drug traffic."[44] Apparently, both Belli and Marcello got what they wanted. As Marcello's partner Jimmy Hoffa said in a TV interview after Ruby shot Oswald, Bobby Kennedy had become "just another lawyer."[45]

Marcello still had the Ferrie and Banister situation to worry about, but now that Oswald was dead and could never testify about working with them (or about meeting Marcello), that situation could be contained. Marcello's pattern of only using people in the JFK hit who had been— or were still—assets, informants, or agents for US intelligence or law enforcement agencies would again prove helpful. Banister—the former FBI chief for Chicago and once the number-two man in the New Orleans Police Department, and who had ties to Naval Intelligence through his friend Guy Johnson—could work behind the scenes to quiet the problem. After all, Banister had once worked with one of Bobby's top Justice Department associates, clearing suspected "reds" for employment. It wouldn't be hard for Banister to clear Ferrie, and himself, by saying their contact with Oswald was part of a legitimate US intelligence operation, and they had simply gotten burned by someone who turned out to be a turncoat. Banister wouldn't have said that to the three police officers who were eventually sent to interview him, but would have conveyed the national-security implications to their superiors and to Banister's higher-level government contacts.

For the federal agencies to investigate further would not only harm ongoing US covert Cuba operations, but also jeopardize each agency's extensive participation in the national domestic surveillance network. Later Congressional investigations would find that this network involved the FBI, CIA, military intelligence, and large police departments, which routinely tracked hundreds of suspects and thousands of individuals suspected of communist or leftist ties (along with a small but increasing number of white supremacists).

David Ferrie returned to New Orleans only after Oswald was dead. Ferrie and his associates were arrested the next day. Since Ferrie couldn't be sure what others might have said in his absence, he stuck to his improbable cover story about his recent Texas trip and denied knowing Oswald. However, Ferrie was careful in his interrogation to acknowledge potentially incriminating things others might have heard him say. For example, Ferrie admitted to the FBI that he had been very critical of JFK, and had even possibly said, "He ought to be shot." He also acknowledged being "critical of any President riding in an open car [since] anyone could hide in the bushes and shoot a President." Ferrie was also able to produce his library card when asked.[46]

There was no real investigation of Guy Banister. When three police officers went to his office, their report says that "Mr. Banister stated that he would not comment about this matter upon" advice of his attorney.[47] (The attorney isn't named, but it was probably Marcello's attorney, G. Wray Gill.) The three officers allowed their former boss to get by with that, especially since Banister's associate who had made the original allegation, Jack Martin, was an unstable individual who had started to back off from his initial claims. Martin probably realized that making accusations against two men who worked for Marcello wasn't going to get him anywhere in New Orleans.

We mentioned earlier that privately, the FBI told an NBC newsman that the story about Ferrie should not be broadcast, "for the good of the country." Publicly, the FBI issued an unusual statement to the press, which seemed to lay the arrest of Ferrie's associates solely at the feet of New Orleans District Attorney Jim Garrison. Garrison told a reporter for the *New Orleans States-Item* that the two young men "were picked up at the request of the Federal Bureau of Investigation and the Secret Service," and were being held for them. But the local FBI spokesman told the newspaper, "The FBI does not ask anyone to hold anyone for the FBI unless there is a warrant outstanding. There is no warrant outstanding, period."[48] The whole incident soon blew over, follow-up stories were kept out of the media, and Ferrie's name does not appear in the Warren Commission Report. However, Garrison maintained an interest in the case that would resurface three years later, with Ferrie as his first target.

Garrison later claimed that he once called Bobby Kennedy, some months after JFK's murder. Garrison told author C. David Heymann, "I told him some of my theories. He listened carefully, then said, 'Maybe so, maybe you're right. But what good will it do to know the truth? Will it bring back my brother?' I said, 'I find it hard to believe that as the top law man in the country you don't want to pursue the truth more ardently.' With this he hung up on me."[49] Bobby and his Mafia prosecutors didn't fully trust the District Attorney in Marcello's territory, and their relationship with Garrison would only get worse in the years to come.

Chapter Nineteen

The aborted investigations of Ferrie and Banister set the tone for how the FBI and other agencies treated any leads that threatened to tie Carlos Marcello to JFK's assassination. The CIA had its own links to Marcello and his associates to conceal, but Marcello's soft treatment by the Secret Service and Federal Bureau of Narcotics might have been influenced by the FBI's deferential approach to the mob boss. Marcello's biographer John H. Davis wrote that in the wake of JFK's murder, "no fewer than twelve persons associated with Carlos Marcello, or with some of his closest operatives, had been either arrested or questioned in connection with the assassination."[1] That list included both familiar names (Ruby, Oswald, Ferrie, Banister) and less-known Marcello lieutenants and family members. In the two decades since Davis wrote that passage, the total has increased as more suspects whom the FBI interviewed have been linked to Marcello (Martino and Milteer, for example). Yet Marcello himself was not questioned at the time, and it would be more than twenty years until an FBI supervisor secretly targeted the godfather because of JFK's assassination.

Marcello was not even interviewed about the two FBI reports detailed earlier: the one from November 26, about Oswald receiving money at Marcello's Town and Country restaurant; and the November 28 report linking Marcello's brother to talk of killing JFK.[2] While individual FBI agents and local supervisors might not have been able to fit together the various leads pointing to Marcello, it's hard to believe that the obsessive Hoover didn't notice the pattern.

Banister and Ferrie apparently covered their contact with Oswald by using legitimate US intelligence activities, so Hoover could have rationalized his inaction as protecting national security and the reputation of FBI veteran Banister, rather than as protecting Carlos Marcello or JFK's assassins. Hoover was enough of a Cold Warrior to believe that Oswald was a real Marxist, and may have viewed Oswald as a US intelligence asset who'd simply gone bad. That rationalization would have conveniently allowed Hoover to avoid confronting whatever damaging personal information Marcello had on the FBI director, as detailed by Anthony Summers in his landmark Hoover exposé, *Official and Confidential.*

J. Edgar Hoover's lax treatment of white supremacist Joseph Milteer after JFK's assassination has perplexed historians and researchers for years. Georgia FBI agent Don Adams, who investigated Milteer in the days before JFK's assassination and interviewed him afterward, was not told about the Miami Police's tapes of Milteer's threats against JFK, or the Tampa attempt to assassinate JFK. New information about links between Milteer and Marcello's associates might help to explain Hoover's easy handling of the white supremacist. Not until 2006 did Louisiana historian Dr. Michael Kurtz disclose information from three New Orleans witnesses, including the former New Orleans police superintendent, that tied Milteer to Guy Banister and another associate of Marcello.[3]

If FBI agents like Don Adams had been fully informed and allowed to pursue leads to their logical conclusion, the JFK plot might have unraveled, at least to the level of Milteer and Banister and Ferrie, which would have led to Marcello. However, Hoover clearly wanted to avoid investigating FBI veteran Banister and his associates, so any national-security concerns gave him the perfect excuse to avoid doing so.

The most logical course of action for the FBI after JFK's murder would have been to use phone taps or surveillance against Milteer, to learn more about his activities and associates. That would have also given the FBI more insight into the white supremacist movement, which the FBI had slowly started to target at Bobby Kennedy's urging. Possibly because Milteer's associates included Banister, that wasn't done. Instead, FBI officials sent Agent Adams to interview Milteer on November 27, 1963. Naturally, the report says Milteer "emphatically denies ever making threats to assassinate President Kennedy or participating in any such assassination. He stated he has never heard anyone make such threats." High FBI officials knew Milteer was lying to Agent Adams, and they had the Miami police tapes to prove it—yet Milteer was not arrested, and the active investigation of him was apparently dropped.[4]

Hoover would have known that sending an FBI agent to interview Milteer about his JFK comments would tip off Milteer that one of his associates was an informant. Perhaps that was the point, so Hoover wouldn't have to worry that Milteer might say something about Banister to Miami police informant William Somersett that could embarrass the

FBI. In fact, after Milteer was interviewed, he called Somersett. A worried and frantic Somersett then called his contact in the Miami Police Department, Detective Everett Kay, saying, "These people [the FBI] are going to get me killed by such actions."[5]

Ultimately, Hoover's handling of Milteer would result in another tragedy, in 1968, when Milteer would be a driving force in the assassination of Dr. Martin Luther King.

The FBI was far from the only agency with investigative shortcomings in the wake of JFK's murder, but it's interesting how many of the problems various agencies experienced involved Carlos Marcello's associates. After Michel Victor Mertz was deported from Dallas, he or his partners might have been behind a little-known incident that further diverted energy and resources away from the JFK investigation at a crucial time.

On Monday, November 25, leaders from around the world descended on Washington for JFK's elaborate state funeral. They included the French president, General Charles de Gaulle, target of more than a dozen assassination attempts in the previous four years, including the 1962 attempt linked to Jean Souetre and a 1961 attempt stopped by Michel Victor Mertz. According to John McCone, the CIA received "a high-priority report that there would be an attempt on General DeGaulle's life" during JFK's funeral. McCone told historian William Manchester that the "[ominous] reports came out of New York."[6] Former CIA agent Tom Tripodi says the reports involved four assassins "en route from Montreal."[7] The assassins were supposedly linked to the dissident group that included Jean Souetre, and were angry over de Gaulle's granting independence to Algeria.

It's not hard to imagine the reactions of Hoover and the FBI when they learned of the threat, since they had thought they had lost Souetre's trail in Texas shortly before JFK's murder (the FBI still didn't realize it was actually Mertz using Souetre's identity). Richard Helms might have had similar worries, due to Souetre's contact with the CIA several months earlier and his own memo about the matter. Also, Helms knew that prior to McCone's taking office, some US CIA officials had actually met with and supported Souetre's superiors in their attempt to overthrow de Gaulle.[8]

US officials, worried about yet another head of state being assassinated, would have turned to French Intelligence for assistance. French Intelligence had a trusted undercover operative with a proven track record of saving de Gaulle's life, an operative who spoke perfect, unaccented English and frequently traveled to America, where he maintained a residence in New York City: Michel Victor Mertz.

Agent Tripodi was never able to discover the source of the reports about assassins from Montreal. That city was a major base for Mertz, and the threat may have simply been a ruse by Mertz or his associates to divert investigative resources, or a chance for Mertz to appear to help US authorities. Jean Souetre confirmed to our French associate, journalist Stephane Risset, that there was no real attempt against de Gaulle by his group at that particular time, and that he was never in America during the 1960s.[9]

Carlos Marcello and his heroin associate Mertz stayed one step ahead of the law for years, by making careful plans and then ruthlessly executing them—but unforeseen problems did arise. Their roles in JFK's murder, and their heroin network, came very close to being exposed on the day of JFK's funeral, only twenty-four hours after Ruby murdered Oswald.

One of the lowliest members of their heroin network, Rose Cheramie, was well enough to talk to Detective Francis Fruge by Monday, November 25. While hospitalized at East Louisiana State Hospital, Cheramie had told Dr. Bowers—prior to JFK's death—that JFK would be killed. Dr. Bowers repeated Cheramie's remarks to Dr. Weiss, who was told by Cheramie herself that she worked for Jack Ruby.[10] Cheramie told Detective Fruge the same thing, also giving him detailed information about the heroin transaction her companions were to complete after taking care of things in Dallas. Cheramie named the ship and seaman bringing the drugs to Galveston, saying the deal would be consummated at the Rice Hotel in Houston. Fruge's superior gave her information to US Customs officials, who were initially very interested. In contrast, when Dallas Homicide Chief Fritz was informed of Cheramie's remarks about JFK and Ruby, he told Customs he was "not interested."[11]

Fruge and Cheramie flew to Houston to help Customs, and everything she said about the heroin operation checked out: Customs found her reservation at the Rice Hotel, and agents confirmed that the Dallas man holding Cheramie's child was a suspected drug dealer. Customs also verified the name of the ship Cheramie had provided, and the identity of the seaman smuggler. Author Larry Hancock found that Customs corroborated Cheramie's information about the Houston and Dallas Mafia families involved, which both "had records or reputations for narcotics [and] white slavery [prostitution]."[12]

Everything seemed set for a major heroin bust that could have tied members of Marcello's heroin network, like Ruby and Mertz, to JFK's assassination. It would have been the third bust in Marcello's South Texas territory in just over a year, following the October 1963 Laredo seizure and the 1962 Houston seizure bust, and would have dealt a serious blow to Marcello's heroin pipeline. Bobby's Justice Department was still prosecuting the first two seizures, but before it was told about Cheramie's information, the Houston investigation suddenly ground to a halt, for reasons that were never explained.

Customs lost track of the seaman they were tailing, and the agents didn't bother to interview the implicated local Mafia families or place them under surveillance. The Houston police entered the case and wanted to drop the investigation. The Secret Service became involved, and though its report about Cheramie is referenced in a Customs memo, no Secret Service files about Cheramie have ever been released.[13] Those weren't the only files about Cheramie that disappeared: Years later, Congressional investigators wrote that when they looked into the matter, "US Customs was unable to locate documents and reports related to its involvement in the Cheramie investigation, although such involvement was not denied. Nor could Customs officials locate those agents named by Fruge as having participated in the original investigation."[14]

On November 30, 1963, Customs dropped the case, despite having confirmed all of Cheramie's leads. Frustrated, Detective Fruge returned to Louisiana, and Cheramie was left on the streets of Houston. After reviewing all of the available material, we think it likely that someone in the Houston Police Department or Customs called off the investigation in order to protect Marcello's drug network. However, because the investigation closed so quickly, with no arrests, Cheramie was eventually able to resume some of her former contacts. She would lay low for a year, then try once more to get back at the heroin network of Marcello and Mertz—only to meet a gruesome fate.

In the days following Oswald's murder, Marcello, Trafficante, and Rosselli continued having associates plant disinformation implicating Castro in JFK's assassination; it would trickle out to the press and officials over the coming year, and beyond. The stories in small-market newspapers and radio, blaming Castro and hinting at the JFK-Almeida coup plan, were just enough to get the attention of US officials, but not enough to become major news stories. The mob bosses' actions forced top officials into a continuing cover-up about JFK's assassination, to prevent a public outcry to invade Cuba, and to avoid exposing Almeida.[15]

The most public spokesman for these efforts was John Martino. On

November 26, 1963, Martino began implicating Castro in JFK's murder and hinting at the JFK-Almeida coup plan in radio, newspaper, and magazine appearances. Martino was touring the country as a prominent member of the John Birch Society Speakers Bureau, ostensibly to promote his book *I Was Castro's Prisoner*. As noted earlier, Martino had worked with Trafficante, Rosselli, and Rolando Masferrer, and had met Carlos Marcello. It's unlikely that David Atlee Phillips or others in the CIA were behind Martino's publicity efforts, because Martino's book actually mentioned the name of Phillips's associate, David Morales, a fact that the CIA wanted to keep secret. In addition, Phillips was capable of generating much more publicity if he wanted to, and it seems unlikely that the CIA would have risked exposing the coup plan, since Helms would pursue a variation of it—with some of the same people, like Artime—for another year and a half.

Martino's phony stories started out mildly, claiming that Oswald had gone to Cuba in the fall of 1963, and had passed out pro-Castro literature in Miami and New Orleans. Those tales brought Martino a visit from the FBI on November 29, but he refused to identify his sources.[16] As press reports about the JFK investigation continued, Martino ramped up his rhetoric.

An article under Martino's name appeared in the December 21, 1963, issue of the right-wing journal *Human Events*, in which Martino took credit for revealing that "the Kennedy Administration planned to eliminate Fidel Castro. . . through a putsch, [and] the plan involved a more or less token invasion from Central America to be synchronized with the coup. A left-wing coalition government was to be set up, [and] the plan involved [the] US [military] occupation of Cuba." That was more than most high US officials in the Johnson Administration knew at the time.[17]

Martino knew about the involvement of Manolo Ray's JURE exile group, writing in the article that "Oswald made . . . approaches to JURE, another organization of Cuban freedom fighters, but was rejected." Three months earlier, Martino and Masferrer had been linked to the attempt to smear Ray's group by tying it to Oswald via the incident with Dallas JURE member Silvia Odio. When Martino's article was published, only the FBI and a handful of Odio's closest family and friends knew about Oswald's visit; nothing about it had appeared in the press.[18]

In Martino's first major article, he only hinted that Oswald was working for Fidel when he killed JFK. The following month, Martino revealed new details about the coup plan and implicated Fidel more directly, in a

January 30, 1964, *Memphis Press-Scimitar* article headlined: "Oswald Was Paid Gunman for Castro, Visitor Says." It quotes John Martino as saying, "Lee Harvey Oswald was paid by Castro to assassinate President Kennedy," and that the murder was in retaliation for JFK's "plan to get rid of Castro." Martino described JFK's coup plan with remarkable precision, including information from documents that wouldn't be declassified for more than thirty-five years: "There was to be another invasion and uprising in Cuba . . . and the Organization of American states . . . was to go into Cuba . . . and control the country until an election could be set up." Martino even knew that "since the death of Kennedy, the work on an invasion has virtually stopped."

We can only imagine the consternation Martino's increasingly provocative articles caused among some officials in Washington. They seem to have gotten the attention of J. Edgar Hoover, since FBI agents interviewed Martino yet again on February 15, 1964. In an era when presidents and Congress treated Hoover and his FBI with deference, Martino basically thumbed his nose at the agents. He declared that "President Kennedy was engaged in a plot to overthrow the Castro regime by preparing another invasion attempt against Cuba." But the frustrated FBI agents wrote that "Martino refused to divulge the sources of his information or how they might know what plans President Kennedy might have had."[19]

Other Trafficante associates also leaked information to the press and officials implicating Castro in JFK's murder, but none of these other leaks hinted at the JFK-Almeida coup plan. Martino was unique in that regard, probably because (by his own admission) he had actually been part of the assassination plot. Among the others planting stories implicating Castro was Trafficante's man Frank Fiorini, whose story appeared in a Florida newspaper on November 26, 1963, though Fiorini later admitted he'd gotten his information from John Martino.[20]

It's important to note that no credible evidence or testimony has yet turned up that identifies Fiorini as having played a role in JFK's assassination. Speculation that Fiorini was one of the "three tramps" arrested in Dealey Plaza has been disproven, as was an allegation that Fiorini, Oswald, and others drove from Miami to Dallas in the days before JFK's murder. (Numerous witnesses saw Oswald at work during that time.) A recent alleged confession by E. Howard Hunt places Fiorini in a position of trust within the CIA that he never had. Also, Fiorini was such a publicity seeker (resulting in his friendship with top columnist Jack Anderson) that no one as careful as Trafficante would have used him in any significant way in the JFK hit. However, Fiorini was a trusted mob asset, spreading disinformation about Oswald and Castro to divert attention from the real killers. Fiorini provided a steady stream of other information in 1963 and 1964 to another Trafficante man, CIA agent Bernard Barker (code-named AMCLATTER-1), but Fiorini didn't use Barker to spread his phony "Castro did it" stories to the CIA.

Others who spread stories tying Castro to JFK's assassination included Rolando Masferrer and drug-linked associates of Manuel Artime. With so many of Trafficante's and Rosselli's associates planting phony stories implicating Castro, it raises the question of whether they were also feeding phony stories to David Atlee Phillips. Because of their work together on AMWORLD (and earlier), David Morales knew what type of material Phillips would be receptive to, and that Phillips had a direct pipeline to Desmond FitzGerald, who could immediately bring information to Richard Helms's attention. Using Phillips as a pipeline for disinformation would allow it to reach very high levels, with more credibility, very quickly.

Other efforts to link Oswald and Ruby to Fidel were less sophisticated. These range from the fake "Pedro Charles" letter mailed to Oswald from Havana on November 28, 1963, to stories linking Ruby to Cuban plots. It's amazing how many dozens, sometimes hundreds, of pages of follow-up FBI and CIA memos were generated because of one or two obviously false letters or stories. It's likely that even more phony information implicating Fidel, with hundreds of pages of official follow-up memos, remains unreleased.

A well-timed leak that clinched the case against Oswald for much of the American press and public appears to have been part of the same disinformation plan as John Martino, since it also involved people who had worked for Carlos Marcello. By late November 1963, the mainstream news media focused on Oswald as JFK's lone assassin, and on Jack Ruby as a patriotic nightclub owner with no Mafia ties. However, we noted earlier the private concerns of officials like Dallas Police Chief Curry about the weak case against Oswald.[21] As if to provide officials with an ironclad case that Oswald was a cold-blooded killer, a new murderous accusation against him suddenly surfaced. Spread quickly by the US news media, it is still repeated today as evidence of Oswald's guilt as a "lone assassin."

The December 7, 1963, *New York Times* reported that on April 10, 1963, Lee Oswald—acting alone and using the same rifle found after JFK's murder—tried to assassinate recently retired General Edwin Walker, a far-right spokesman. The FBI claimed to have made the discovery in its December 3, 1963, interrogation of Oswald's widow, Marina. This news sealed the question of Oswald's guilt for most people.[22]

However, Walker's background, the evidence, and the actions of Marcello associates like Oswald and Ruby suggest a different interpretation of the shooting. General Walker became controversial in 1961, when JFK removed him from command of the 24th Infantry Division in Germany for indoctrinating his soldiers with inflammatory material from the John Birch Society. The group and its leader made ridiculous claims, saying that former president Dwight Eisenhower was "abiding by Communist orders, and consciously serving the Communist conspiracy, for all his adult life."[23]

General Walker resigned, and in September 1962, when James Meredith tried to become the first black student to enroll at the University of Mississippi, Walker's opposition march erupted into a riot that left two dead and seventy injured. The Kennedys had Walker arrested and placed under psychological observation, but after his release, he returned to his home in Dallas and ran for governor of Texas. Following his defeat, Walker continued making outrageous claims in speeches as he railed against the Kennedys, civil rights, and Castro. Walker flew the Confederate flag in front of his home and later made a well-publicized visit of support to Byron de la Beckwith, Medgar Evers' assassin.[24]

Walker was in the same far-right, racist circles as Marcello's associates John Martino, Guy Banister (whose close friend wrote a book about Walker), and Joseph Milteer.[25] Walker knew another Marcello subordinate, Jack Ruby. Walker's handyman told the FBI he saw "Jack Ruby visiting General Walker on several occasions. . . . Ruby called at the Walker residence on a monthly basis from December 1962 through March 1963. . . . Ruby stayed approximately one hour at Walker's home and talked with Walker behind closed doors." The Walker shooting occurred soon after Ruby's last visit to Walker's house.[26]

Also during the first three months of 1963, while Lee Oswald was in Dallas with Marina and working for the U-2 map firm Jaggars-Chiles-Stovall, Oswald began a series of unusual actions that led to his being blamed for JFK's murder. At least ten days prior to the Walker shooting incident, Oswald visited New Orleans on an unusual mission related to Cuba. An INS inspector told Senate investigators that prior to April 1, he interviewed Oswald in a New Orleans jail, where Oswald claimed to be a Cuban who couldn't speak Spanish.[27]

Earlier, Oswald had ordered his rifle and pistol through the mail (using an alias) and begun corresponding with the Fair Play for Cuba Committee (FPCC). Both the FPCC and mail-order guns were the subject of well-publicized Congressional hearings at the time; some speculate that Oswald was told his actions were assisting those efforts—something that was true for Martino and Fiorini. After the rifle arrived, Oswald had Marina take the infamous photograph of him holding the gun in one hand and newspapers from two rival communist groups in the other.[28] Oswald gave one of the photographs to his friend George DeMohrenschildt, the aristocratic White Russian who later admitted to being a CIA informant. Oswald also photographed the back of Walker's house, though the car tag of a 1957 Chevrolet was cut out before the Warren Commission published the picture.[29]

On April 6, 1963, a Walker aide told police he saw two prowlers near the house. Around the same time, another Walker aide saw a suspicious "Cuban or dark-complected man in 1957 Chevrolet," casing the property.[30] The FBI notes that one of the men who always accompanied Ruby on his visits to Walker had a "dark complexion."[31]

On the night of April 10, someone fired a rifle shot into a large window of Walker's house. A witness saw two men, in two cars, flee the scene. The next day's newspaper reported that Walker's window was shattered by a 30.06 bullet, a different caliber than that of Oswald's rifle. The burst of local and national publicity after the shooting earned Walker a few more months of national fame before he faded from view.[32] In 1976, the *Washington Post* reported the intolerant Walker's arrest for "making a homosexual advance to a plainclothes policeman in a men's room."[33]

After Oswald's death, Marina told the FBI that Oswald had gone out that evening and returned saying he'd shot at Walker, then buried his rifle. Oswald had no car or driver's license, so he would have had to take a bus or a cab, or walked each leg of the seven-mile journey to Walker's house—yet no one ever reported having seen anyone suspicious, carrying a rifle or a large package, in the vicinity.[34] The bullet recovered from Walker's home cannot be matched to Oswald's rifle, and even Walker said the Warren Commission's bullet was not the one he recovered.[35]

DeMohrenschildt told a writer for the *Wall Street Journal* that he informed the CIA about the matter shortly after the shooting, and one of DeMohrenschildt's friends says she told the FBI about it. Nine days after the shooting, DeMohrenschildt moved away from Dallas, and shortly after that, Oswald moved to New Orleans to live with his uncle "Dutz" Murret, a Marcello bookie.[36]

Despite the FBI's claim, Marina was not the first to link Oswald to the Walker shooting incident after JFK's murder—an article about it appeared on November 29, 1963, in the right-wing, West German newspaper *Deutsche National-Zeitung und Soldaten-Zeitung*. The newspaper had called General Walker six days earlier, the day after JFK's murder, and reached him in Louisiana, where Walker was giving a talk to the local White Citizens' Council (Milteer was a member of the Atlanta chapter).[37]

Walker liked to tell the dramatic story of how he avoided death by lowering his head only a moment before the bullet came whizzing by—but we have only Walker's word that he was even in the room at the time. Given the outrageous claims in Walker's speeches, his credibility seems doubtful. Walker told Dick Russell that his two young aides were involved in the shooting incident "one way or another." Ultimately, there is no proof the original shooting was anything more than a publicity stunt.[38]

Before Oswald's tie to the Walker shooting was reported in the US press, the *New York Times* quoted Walker "as having said that President Kennedy's assassination was a Communist plot organized by Cuban Premier Fidel Castro," the same line John Martino was propagating.[39] European writer Joachim Joesten points out that when most Americans first heard of JFK's death, they immediately suspected those in "the John Birch Society, the Ku Klux Klan, the White Citizens' Councils, General Walker's henchmen." But the timely leak of the Walker story steered suspicions away from those types—including Martino, Banister, and Milteer.[40]

The Walker story also diverted attention from Marcello and his many associates who had recently been questioned or arrested. Oswald was involved in the Walker incident somehow, but given the timing, Banister could have told Oswald it was something he had to do to be considered for his next assignment. The bottom line is that when the Walker story became public after JFK's murder, it was the final nail in the coffin proving Oswald's guilt to the American press and public.

Carlos Marcello, Santo Trafficante, and Johnny Rosselli needed to compensate those who had participated in JFK's murder, but they had to do so carefully to avoid attracting attention. Marcello was so cautious after his acquittal that he initially refused to pay the juror he had bribed, eventually giving him only $1,000 instead of the $25,000 he had promised. Because of David Ferrie's brief arrest, Marcello had to be even more careful in rewarding him. John Davis says that Ferrie began working for a Marcello-owned air-taxi service and, later, for a "Marcello-financed New Orleans air cargo service." Then Ferrie "suddenly turned up as the owner of a lucrative service station franchise in an ideal location . . . the FBI found that the franchise had been financed by Carlos Marcello."[41]

Some who later admitted their involvement in JFK's murder, like John Martino and David Morales, may have been rewarded though later business deals in Central America. Others, like Guy Banister, didn't receive a significant financial reward and had participated because they hated JFK and his support of civil rights. The same may have been true for Joseph Milteer, who in 1963 still had the inheritance from his father. Unlike Banister and Milteer, Michel Victor Mertz had no ideological stake in JFK's death and participated solely for money. Mertz was apparently well paid for his role in JFK's murder, and would soon begin an ascent to staggering wealth in France.[42]

Exile leader Tony Varona had already received $200,000 (well over $1 million in today's dollars) from Trafficante and Rosselli's associates three months before JFK's murder. The entire $200,000 was likely not all for Varona, and portions of it went to one or more of the other participants. However, laundering the money through the Kennedy-backed Varona, in a transaction that Trafficante/Rosselli associate Richard Cain reported to the CIA, helped to ensure that Helms and the CIA would later have to cover up much about the matter.

Varona's $200,000 may have been related to a problem with an identical amount that Santo Trafficante dealt with in early December 1963. Known about only in recent years, it raises the possibility that Frank Ragano, Trafficante's and Hoffa's attorney, was more actively involved in JFK's murder than he ever admitted. That idea would be consistent with the trust Ragano shared with Trafficante and Hoffa, and with the shield of attorney-client privilege, which could have been useful in plotting and paying for JFK's murder.

FBI files contain a report about a December 1963 dispute over the JFK assassination between Santo Trafficante, Frank Ragano, and a Tampa mob figure close to one of Trafficante's brothers. The FBI's source, a criminal who was a teenager at the time, later told the assistant US Attorney in Dallas what he saw at a Tampa club:

> Two men came in carrying briefcases; one I recognized as Santo Trafficante and the other I didn't recognize [until] a few years later, attorney Frank Ragano. [The owner] told me immediately I had to leave; [he was] screaming at me, so I walked out of the front door,

and, being nosy, I sneaked in the side door of the building. Anyway, both briefcases were opened with stacks of money in each one, and [the owner] was arguing with Santo, saying that was not their agreement, the money was $200,000 short, and he had already paid off the two men who killed President Kennedy.[43]

Much about the story checks out: The FBI's source named the club, the site of a book-making operation that the owner ran with one of Trafficante's brothers. The Tampa FBI said it was "well known [the club's owner was] associated . . . with organized crime."[44] The $200,000 figure cited in the FBI report matches the amount listed in CIA files as what Trafficante's associates gave Varona, but those CIA files had not been released when the FBI's source made his allegation.

In December 1963, the FBI's source tried to tell a policeman about seeing Trafficante and the money, but the officer "told me to keep my mouth closed because . . . it could get my family killed."[45] Years later, the FBI questioned the policeman, who admitted knowing the source but denied having heard the story about Trafficante. However, the FBI noted that it "had already received a similar story to the one" the source had told. The FBI files about the "similar story" have apparently never been released.[46]

The problem between the club owner, Trafficante, and Ragano was resolved, because the owner stayed partners with Trafficante's brother, while Ragano and Trafficante remained close for years. Before Ragano's death, he admitted to only limited involvement in JFK's murder: carrying messages between Hoffa, Marcello, and Trafficante.

In Ragano's autobiography, he described meeting with Carlos Marcello and Santo Trafficante in New Orleans approximately two weeks after JFK's assassination. Ragano said Marcello and Trafficante told him they hoped that Jimmy Hoffa would show his gratitude for JFK's murder. Marcello said, "When you see Jimmy . . . you tell him he owes me and he owes me big." An FBI memo quotes Ragano as saying, "While driving through New Orleans in Carlos Marcello's car . . . I heard Santo remark to Marcello, 'Carlos, the next thing you know, they will be blaming the President's assassination on us.'"[47]

Trafficante and Marcello knew that using CIA operatives and operations as part of their plot to kill JFK could keep them from being blamed for JFK's murder, and in the first week of December 1963, they took another step in that direction. In a possible continuation of the unauthorized CIA-Mafia plots to kill Castro, Trafficante bodyguard Herminio Diaz

reportedly returned to Cuba to assassinate Fidel.[48] Several years earlier, in Havana, Diaz had worked for Rosselli at a Trafficante-owned
casino, around the time that both mob bosses first became involved in
the 1960 CIA-Mafia plots. Diaz had left Cuba in July 1963, first going to
Mexico City, where David Atlee Phillips ran Cuban operations. After
arriving in the US, Diaz told the CIA in September 1963 that he wanted
to assassinate Fidel—and that he knew about Commander Almeida's
and Rolando Cubela's dissatisfaction. By October 1963, a CIA memo
confirms that Diaz had captured the interest of Desmond FitzGerald and
Ted Shackley, Chief of the CIA's Miami station, where Rosselli regularly
visited David Morales. In the 1990s, a former Cuban official claimed that
Herminio Diaz had been in Dallas for JFK's assassination; if true, Diaz's
work on the Castro assassination plots might have simply been a cover
for his role in JFK's murder.[49]

The December 6, 1963, attempt to assassinate Fidel Castro involving
Herminio Diaz was first documented in 2006 by author Larry Hancock.[50]
More CIA files have since been discovered, reporting the "wide rumor
of [an] assassination attempt against Fidel Castro after his TV appearance Dec. 6, resulting in [the] killing of [a] man next to him. Castro [was]
uninjured. Would-be killer at large."[51] Hancock quotes a CIA cable to
LBJ's national security advisor, McGeorge Bundy, that described "an
assassination attempt on Fidel Castro after his TV appearance on 12/6,"
reported by the wife of a Havana diplomat. CIA headquarters, likely
FitzGerald or one of his men, added a comment linking that attempt to
"continuing rumors of a plot to assassinate Castro which is connected
with Herminio Diaz."[52]

The CIA comment about Diaz is important, since FBI files show that
Diaz was trafficking narcotics for Trafficante around that time. CIA
records released so far about Diaz are clearly incomplete, raising the
possibility that Diaz was involved in activities involving the CIA that
Helms decided to keep hidden.[53]

Reports of an attempt to assassinate Fidel so soon after JFK's murder, especially one involving Trafficante's bodyguard, raise several
possibilities. By December 6, it was clear that the US was not going to
be rushed into a quick invasion of Cuba because of Oswald's seeming
ties to Cuba and Russia. Some Cuban exiles, and CIA personnel like
Morales, may have decided to remove Fidel themselves. Diaz still had
ties to Cuba, and Morales's Mafia-linked operative Tony Sforza could
travel freely in and out of Cuba. If Diaz was involved in the December
6 attempt, his participation could be seen as part of the unauthorized
CIA-Mafia plots to kill Castro.

Likewise, if Herminio Diaz was involved in JFK's assassination, linking him to the December 6, 1963, attempt to kill Fidel could inoculate him and his associates against scrutiny regarding JFK's murder. FitzGerald and Helms would worry that it might appear that an assassin trained by the CIA to kill Fidel had instead killed JFK. Even if the two CIA officials had not engaged Diaz directly, they would still worry that one of their operatives might have, and that anyone digging too deeply might uncover their unauthorized operations. From Trafficante's perspective, any of those possibilities were good. Even if Diaz's involvement, or the attempt itself, were just rumors, having them circulating at CIA headquarters and the White House was still a plus for Trafficante.[54]

Chapter Twenty

In late November and early December 1963, Richard Helms's career depended on how he and a few trusted subordinates handled several crucial matters. These ranged from continuing the CIA's operations against Castro to dealing with streams of suspicious information flowing through the CIA pipeline from Mexico City, stories that tried to link Fidel to JFK's assassination. Those tales were eventually discredited and Helms viewed them skeptically from the start, unlike high officials such as President Johnson and McCone. In the tense times following JFK's death, Helms may well have helped the US avoid a potentially deadly confrontation with Cuba and the Soviets. On the other hand, one has to wonder if he ever questioned the central role his Cuban operations chief in Mexico City, David Atlee Phillips, played in many of the suspicious stories.

Disinformation involving a young Nicaraguan named Gilberto Alvarado began flowing through David Atlee Phillips on November 26, 1963. On that day, at the American embassy in Mexico City, Alvarado claimed that two months earlier, he had seen Oswald receive $6,500 at the Cuban embassy "for the purpose of killing someone." Anthony Summers noticed that a phrase Alvarado attributes to Oswald matches the wording used in the Silvia Odio incident. Alvarado's accusations created a huge stir among high officials in Washington for more than a week, and US ambassador to Mexico Thomas Mann was convinced the account proved that Fidel was behind JFK's murder.[1]

Alvarado soon admitted he was lying—only to then claim that he wasn't lying. After failing a lie-detector test, Alvarado finally admitted that he was really a Nicaraguan intelligence agent. Summers writes that Alvarado "explains his presence at the Cuban Embassy" around the same time as Oswald by saying "he had been sent to Mexico to try to get to Cuba on an infiltration mission." The Alvarado investigation was dropped, and even though the CIA concluded that "Alvarado's allegation was indeed fabricated," some who want to blame JFK's death on Castro keep dredging it up.[2]

In addition to Alvarado and Oswald, a third unusual man visited the Cuban embassy around the same time; Summers says he "behaved as though he was on some sort of undercover mission in Mexico, and [his] movements ran parallel to Oswald's." Like Oswald and Alvarado, this individual "tried to get a Cuban entry visa." The young man then left Mexico, traveled to Dallas and New Orleans, and had met earlier with anti-Castro activists. Just as Alvarado worked for Nicaraguan Intelligence, this individual worked for Costa Rican Intelligence, which knew he "planned to infiltrate Cuba."[3]

One thread all three young men had in common was Manuel Artime, who had camps in Costa Rica and Nicaragua, and ties to their intelligence services.[4] Oswald, Alvarado, and the other man were apparently all on the same type of mission in Mexico City at the same time, trying to get into Cuba. But who controlled their movements—and gave Alvarado his phony story? Artime or David Morales (along with their mob associates) seem to be likely suspects, as does David Atlee Phillips.

Richard Helms received suspicious information about two more young men who went to Mexico City, trying to get into Cuba—only this time, the stories tied them more directly to events in Dallas. They were Tampa suspect Gilberto Policarpo Lopez and Miguel Cases Saez, the shadowy Cuban who had seemingly followed JFK to Chicago and Dallas. Helms did not take these allegations as seriously as Counter-Intelligence Chief James Angleton, who saw Lopez and Saez as part of a Castro conspiracy involving Oswald.[5]

Gilberto Lopez crossed the border from Texas into Mexico on November 23, 1963, but he didn't check into his Mexico City hotel until November 25.[6] His whereabouts between those dates are unknown; it was as if someone kept him secreted away until Oswald was dead and it was clear no evidence had emerged that required a co-conspirator. (Lopez "entered Mexico by auto," even though, like Oswald, he neither owned nor could drive a car.) An FBI report includes claims that "on November 27 last, Lopez departed Mexico City by special airplane for Havana, Cuba," and that Lopez had "a probable role" in JFK's murder.[7] However, the most incriminating information came from a "Covert American Source" in a Mexican ministry involved with the corrupt Mexican federal police (the drug-connected DFS). The story about Lopez's being "the only passenger [in a] special plane" to Havana fell apart under close examination three times: in late 1963, when it surfaced again in the spring of 1964, and in the late 1970s when it was debunked by the House Select Committee on Assassinations. Historian Richard D. Mahoney observed that Lopez's story seemed designed to trigger "what David Phillips, David

Morales, and Bill Harvey and the thousands of anti-Castro fighters in their training had demanded: a second invasion of Cuba."[8]

Some high US officials knew Lopez had left Tampa just three days after the attempt to kill JFK there, and that he had contact with the Fair Play for Cuba Committee, so it's not hard to see why they took the reports seriously at first. The FBI even tapped the telephones of people who had only brief contact with Lopez, which we describe in Chapter 22.

As the Lopez story rose through official channels, it was supplemented by stories about Miguel Casas Saez, who had appeared to shadow JFK while staying one step ahead of US authorities. Reports from Mexico said Saez was in Dallas when JFK was shot, then fled to Mexico City, where a Cubana Airlines plane was held for him for five hours. Saez then supposedly rode in the cockpit so the passengers wouldn't see him. Thirdhand accounts by David Morales's AMOT Cuban exile informants said the formerly poor Saez suddenly had money and American clothes once he returned to Cuba. Like Oswald and Lopez, Saez also had a Russian connection: He had taken a Russian-language course and "speaks Russian quite well," according to a CIA memo. (If true, it meant that like Oswald and Lopez, Saez would have also made a good patsy for a CIA assassination of Castro.)

Though the Saez allegations concerned US officials in the crucial early period after JFK's death, they eventually fell apart. When the initial report of the Cubana plane's being held was finally declassified, it didn't mention Saez at all. The most incriminating information in CIA reports was thirdhand, from sources of questionable reliability whose names are still withheld today. One CIA memo says that "in view of the vagueness of the original report [and its] unknown sources . . . I'd let this die its natural death, as the Bureau [FBI] is doing."[9]

Whether Saez was a real person or simply a creation of Morales's informants has never been established. If he was real, he might have been a Cuban on a low-level smuggling mission to the US who was simply manipulated so that his travels later looked suspicious. Trafficante and even Jimmy Hoffa engaged in these types of smuggling activities—one of Hoffa's lieutenants later wrote about "times when Jimmy asked that Castro send people over here to do little jobs for him."[10] After reviewing all of the available information, we conclude about Saez what we did about Gilberto Lopez: Neither man was knowingly involved in JFK's assassination, but their movements were probably being manipulated by someone who wanted it to appear as if they were.

None of the stories about Saez or Lopez were reported in the news media at the time. However, one of the long-secret CIA memos about Saez used wording similar to that from the Odio incident and the Alvarado allegation, saying that Saez "was capable of doing anything" after claiming "he had firing practice." As journalist Anthony Summers suggests, it was almost as if the conspirators in each instance were reading from the same script. The question is whether the authors were men like confessed conspirators Martino, Morales, and Rosselli, or whether they also included far more experienced writers like propaganda expert David Atlee Phillips and spy novelist E. Howard Hunt.

While dealing with the disturbing information about Saez, Lopez, and the others, Helms had to continue the CIA's efforts against Castro, including his own unauthorized attempts to assassinate Fidel. If one of his unauthorized attempts was successful, or those plots could be merged with plans authorized by the new president, it would give Helms additional cover. At the same time, Helms had to withhold crucial information from other agencies and investigators that could damage Helms, his associates, or the CIA.

Just one example among many, the following CIA memo from November 25, 1963, disproves one of Helms's cover stories to the FBI, LBJ, and eventually the Warren Commission: that no one in the CIA had ever expressed an operational interest in Oswald, even after he returned to the US with a Russian wife. The CIA agent who sent this still partially censored memo says that due to "the number of Soviet women marrying foreigners, being permitted to leave the USSR. . . . we eventually turned up something like two dozen similar cases [so] we showed operational intelligence interest in the [Lee] Harvey [Oswald] story."[11]

Even as Richard Helms withheld information like that from LBJ and Hoover, he was moving forward with some of his unauthorized Castro assassination operations. His European assassin recruiter, QJWIN, was still on the CIA payroll in December 1963 and would remain so for several months. CIA memos confirm that their plans were proceeding with Rolando Cubela as a result of his November 22 meeting in Paris, meaning that Helms was sure Cubela was not a double agent working for Castro.

We noted earlier the December 7, 1963, CIA memo about the weapons cache of shotguns, pistols, grenades, "C-4 [explosive]" and "rifles with scopes" that Helms approved for Cubela. The material was especially appropriate for an assassination attempt, and was slated to be delivered in January 1964 under David Morales's supervision. The memo was sent the day after the earlier-noted failed attempt to assassinate Fidel Castro by Santo Trafficante's bodyguard, Herminio Diaz, who had known of Cubela's desire to act against Castro since at least September 1963.[12]

President Johnson had to face a constant barrage of worrisome information in late November and December about Alvarado, Silvia Duran, KGB agent Kostikov, and other stories claiming that Castro or the Soviets were behind JFK's murder. Meanwhile, LBJ was still learning about the entire scope of JFK's covert operations against Cuba, from the CIA's AMWORLD and AMTRUNK to the US military's Cuban plans, to operations involving multiple agencies such as the CIA-DIA Task Force and the "Plan for a Coup in Cuba."

LBJ's reaction to this complex torrent of information about Cuba set him on a path that would ultimately have a tremendous impact on the US and future presidents: President Johnson decided to make Vietnam his main foreign-policy focus, instead of what he saw as the Kennedys' secret war against Cuba. Confronted with the problematic Mexico City information, and realizing the massive scope of Cuban operations he hadn't been told about while he was vice president, LBJ thought that making his stand against communism in Southeast Asia was simply a safer choice than Cuba. LBJ's decision would drive him from office in just over four years, and would ultimately cost fifty-seven thousand American lives.[13]

However, in contrast to common misperceptions, LBJ didn't immediately shut down all covert Cuban operations, nor did he start sending regular US combat troops into Vietnam in the coming days, weeks, or even months. It took a year and a half for each of those things to happen, and in the interim, LBJ kept his options open about Cuba.

CIA Director John McCone noted the turning point in a meeting LBJ had with his advisors on November 25, 1963, the day after JFK's funeral. In contrast to the overly optimistic assessment presented by the US ambassador to Vietnam, Henry Cabot Lodge, LBJ was much more cautious in the meeting. However, LBJ clearly liked what he heard about Vietnam better than the news about Cuba. The following day, LBJ authorized "covert action" against the North Vietnamese. However, those secret operations would prove no more effective than in Cuba and would help to trigger the Gulf of Tonkin incident in August 1964, which in turn led to the first US combat troops being sent to Vietnam in March 1965.[14]

LBJ stated his new focus in a December 2, 1963, memo to General Maxwell Taylor, saying, "It is clear to me that South Vietnam is our most critical military area right now."[15] LBJ also reversed JFK's decision to bring one thousand American "advisors" home from Vietnam, although former officials and historians still debate whether JFK had planned a real reduction, as the start of an eventual pullout, or whether it was merely a reduction on paper. (Most evidence supports the former.) However, LBJ couldn't ignore Cuba, especially while he continued to receive troubling information about it.

William Attwood, JFK's special envoy for peace efforts with Fidel Castro, got official confirmation on November 25 that Fidel was ready to begin talks. However, LBJ told him to "put the plans on ice for the time being." Though Attwood remained ready to pursue the plans, and Lisa Howard of ABC News would later prod LBJ to restart them, the peace effort had essentially died with JFK.[16]

One reason for LBJ's reluctance to pursue peace with Castro were the troubling reports about Oswald and Mexico City, as the Silvia Duran and Alvarado stories continued to unfold. After discussing them in a November 29 meeting with CIA Director McCone, LBJ said that while "he did not wish any repetition of [the Bay of Pigs] fiasco of 1961 . . . he felt that the Cuban situation was one that we could not live with and we had to evolve more aggressive policies." The next part of the declassified memo is still censored, so it's not known whether LBJ or McCone brought up the possibility of trying to use someone like Almeida, though McCone's later actions indicate it was something the CIA Director considered. That same day, LBJ asked J. Edgar Hoover "whether [Oswald] was connected to the Cuban operation with money," which historian Richard D. Mahoney believes was a reference to the Kennedys' anti-Castro "Cuban operation."[17]

On December 2, 1963, Cuba was at the top of McCone's agenda when he met with LBJ. McCone's notes say he brought up the idea of toppling Castro, "even to [the] possible invasion [of Cuba]"; in doing so McCone was laying the groundwork to soon prod LBJ to revive JFK's plan to stage a coup against Fidel.[18] In the early weeks after JFK's death, LBJ was at least open to listening to serious ideas about toppling Castro, possibly because he believed that Castro had something to do with JFK's murder. LBJ told his advisor Joseph Califano that "President Kennedy tried to get Castro, but Castro got Kennedy first."[19] However, we interviewed a US official who actively participated in high-level meetings about Cuba in 1963 and 1964, and had much more experience with Cuban operations than did LBJ. The official told us he was certain that Fidel was *not* involved in JFK's assassination, since "that possibility was looked at [and disregarded in the] days and weeks" after JFK's death.[20]

Even as John McCone and Richard Helms tried to convince President Johnson to continue AMWORLD and the CIA's other anti-Castro operations, LBJ was also consumed with trying to prevent Robert Kennedy's allies from stampeding him into appointing a blue-ribbon commission to investigate JFK's death. According to McCone's notes from a November 26, 1963, meeting with LBJ:

> The President noted with some considerable contempt the fact that certain people in the Department of Justice had suggested to him . . . that an independent investigation of the President's assassination should be conducted by a high-level group of attorneys and jurists. . . . President Johnson rejected this idea, and then heard that the identical plan was to be advanced in a lead editorial in the *Washington Post*. The President felt this was a deliberate plant and he was exceedingly critical. He personally intervened, but failed with [editor] Al Friendly and finally "killed" the editorial with Mrs. Graham [owner of the *Washington Post*].[21]

LBJ and other high-ranking officials used such heavy-handed interference with the press to suppress other unwanted stories about JFK's assassination. But the tide of political and public opinion soon became too great for LBJ to resist, especially when other investigations—from Congress to Texas—seemed imminent. LBJ finally resigned himself to the idea and decided that the panel should be headed by Earl Warren, Chief Justice of the US Supreme Court.

From a legal standpoint, LBJ's choice of the Chief Justice could have been a disaster: What if an accessory to Oswald was discovered, arrested, and put on trial? Given the suspicious reports from Mexico City, that was still a possibility. The verdict in Jack Ruby's trial could be appealed to the Supreme Court in the not-too-distant future. If Warren and his Commission had investigated or interviewed Ruby, Warren would have to recuse himself from such an appeal, leaving the court potentially deadlocked regarding Ruby's fate.

For LBJ, that prospect was outweighed by the more immediate fear of a nuclear holocaust. LBJ knew that if competing Texas and Congressional investigations exposed what appeared to be ties between Oswald and Castro or the Soviets, the call to retaliate would be overwhelming. Likewise, if those investigations revealed US plans to overthrow Fidel and invade Cuba, then Soviet or Cuban leaders would be under pressure to attack—and there were still rumors of Soviet nuclear missiles hidden in caves in Cuba.

Chief Justice Warren was mindful of the legal pitfalls of LBJ's request, and "refused at first to take the job even after both Robert Kennedy and Archibald Cox had asked him," according to historian John Newman. LBJ's recorded Oval Office conversations reveal that LBJ met with the Chief Justice, and initially Warren turned LBJ down—twice. LBJ said he then "pulled out what Hoover told me about a little incident in Mexico City." Newman writes that LBJ "told Warren this would make it look like Khrushchev and Castro killed Kennedy. LBJ said that Warren started crying and agreed to take the assignment." As Newman noted nine years later, in a documentary, Warren confirmed LBJ's account, "except for the tears. . . . Johnson felt the argument that Khrushchev and Castro had killed Kennedy might mean nuclear war."[22]

Like Warren, Georgia senator Richard Russell didn't want to join the new Commission. Russell had been LBJ's mentor in the Senate and was one of the few Congressional leaders who shepherded the CIA's budget through Congress. The CIA, military intelligence, and the FBI could depend on Russell to give them whatever they wanted, without asking questions. However, the senior senator from Georgia was very conservative, at a time when many conservatives considered Warren a traitor who should be impeached for his court decisions supporting school integration and banning official prayers in public schools. Newman writes that "when Russell said he didn't like Warren and refused . . . Johnson told him that he had no choice . . . that Oswald's apparent connection to Castro and Khrushchev had to be prevented 'from kicking us into a war that can kill forty million Americans in an hour.'" Russell finally told LBJ he would serve with Warren "for the good of the country."[23]

Others LBJ appointed to the Commission included Kentucky senator John Cooper; Congressmen Hale Boggs, of Louisiana, and Gerald Ford, of Michigan; disarmament official John J. McCloy; and former CIA Director Allen Dulles. According to historian Michael Kurtz, "Richard Helms personally persuaded Lyndon Johnson to appoint former CIA Director Allen Dulles to the Warren Commission."

Both Helms and Dulles knew about the original CIA-Mafia plots to kill Castro and still-ongoing operatives like QJWIN, first recruited under Dulles. Congressional investigators discovered that the CIA's James Angleton met with Dulles just before he joined the Warren Commission, and Richard Helms made Angleton his pointman to the Commission. That scenario would allow Helms, Angleton, and Dulles to withhold important information from the Warren Commission. Consequently, the Warren Report would contain no mention of the CIA-Mafia plots to kill Castro. None of the Cuban exile leaders involved in those plots, or in the JFK-Almeida coup plan, were ever interviewed by the Warren Commission.[24]

However, a couple of key Warren Commissioners were told, unofficially and in a general way, about at least the older CIA-Mafia plots to assassinate Castro. This news was probably intended to ensure that the investigation did not delve into any areas that might expose the plots. *Vanity Fair* found that "according to Earl Warren's son and grandson . . . the Chief Justice did know about the plots." The other Commissioner who indicated, years later, that he had been told something about the efforts to eliminate Castro was Gerald Ford.[25]

In contrast to Warren and Russell, Michigan Republican Congressman Gerald Ford quickly and eagerly agreed to serve on the Commission.[26] His history as a canny and ambitious politician is at odds with the clumsy, amiable image portrayed by comedians and the media. Most of the Warren Commissioners had demanding jobs that limited the time they could spend on the investigation, but Ford made it a point to be the most active Commissioner. He saw his appointment as a break for his career, one of the few ways in which a young, conservative Republican could gain notice in a Congress under firm Democratic control.

Ford wasted no time in using his new position to curry favor with the person who had replaced Bobby Kennedy as America's second most powerful man, J. Edgar Hoover. Just a week after the Warren Commission's first meeting, Ford went to one of Hoover's top aides, who wrote that Ford told him "he would keep me thoroughly advised as to the activities of the Commission. He stated this would have to be on a confidential basis." Five days later, Ford started delivering on his promise, and was soon telling his FBI contact that "two members of the Commission . . . still were not convinced that the President had been shot from the sixth floor window of the Texas Book Depository."[27] Hoover's Assistant Director, William Sullivan, later said that Gerald Ford "was our man on the Commission . . . it was to him that we looked to protect our interest and keep us fully advised of any development that we did not like . . . and this he did." While Ford's general role as an FBI informant has been known for years, almost all of his reports were kept classified until August 2008, when several were released.[28]

All of the members of the Warren Commission were respected establishment figures who could be counted on to maintain a good public face, despite any private doubts they might have. Except for Dulles, they had full-time positions aside from the Commission, leaving them little free time to seriously investigate areas the FBI had not already explored.

While the Commission hired a staff of lawyers, it essentially had to rely on the FBI for most of its investigations.

J. Edgar Hoover hated the idea of the Commission even more than LBJ did, and Hoover managed to essentially determine its conclusion before the Commissioners really had a chance to get started. On December 8, 1963, Hoover leaked the FBI's own assassination report, and used his extensive media connections to make sure it was front-page news. *Time* magazine said the FBI report

> . . . was expected to be forwarded to the Warren Commission some-time this week. It will indicate that 1. Oswald, acting in his own luna-tic loneliness, was indeed the President's assassin; 2. Ruby likewise was a loner in his role as Oswald's executioner; 3. Oswald and Ruby did not know each other; and 4. There is no proof of a conspiracy, either foreign or domestic, to do away with Kennedy.[29]

The Warren Commissioners were stunned. Representative Hale Boggs said privately that the FBI had "tried the case and reached a verdict" barely two weeks after JFK's murder.[30] Hoover put the Commissioners in a straitjacket: If they reached any other conclusions, they would be going up against the much admired FBI and its powerful Director.

Hoover's report on the assassination would undermine both the FBI's and the Warren Commission's actions in the coming year, even though the FBI report had severe problems. The FBI accounted for only the three shots it claimed Oswald fired—one that hit JFK in the back, one that hit him in the head, and one that hit Connally—but failed to acknowledge the shot that missed the limo entirely, hitting a curb far from the motorcade. The story might have ended there, except for the bullet fragment or chip from the curb that hit a bystander, who then talked to police and newsmen. This created the problem of a "fourth shot" that wouldn't go away. In addition, the FBI had only recently learned about, and had not accounted for, Oswald's visit to Manolo Ray supporter Silvia Odio in Dallas. In terms of Oswald's motivation, the FBI tried to steer clear of any political motivation that could raise the specter of Cuban or Russian involvement. It focused instead on Oswald's mother, evoking the "domineering, disturbed mother produces murderous son" scenario depicted in the popular film *Psycho*.[31]

Despite the authoritative nature of Hoover's report, even high-ranking FBI officials doubted its conclusions. *Vanity Fair* quoted William Sullivan, the FBI Assistant Director who also served as its Domestic Intelligence Chief, as saying, "There were huge gaps in the case, gaps we never did close." Those on the Warren Commission were dissatisfied as well: Senator Richard Russell said, "We have not been told the truth about Oswald." Congressman Hale Boggs was eventually even more blunt in his assessment, saying Hoover "lied his eyes out to the Commission—on Oswald, on Ruby, on their friends, the bullets, the gun, you name it."[32]

Russell and Boggs may not have realized it, but Richard Helms was withholding even more information from the Warren Commission. Even as the Commission had its first meetings, some of the top-secret anti-Castro operations Helms withheld from it were still unfolding.

For Commander Almeida in Cuba, the days after JFK's assassination must have been fraught with tension, especially when Harry told him Bobby had put the coup plan on hold. Some Cuban officials worried about an American attack because of Oswald's very public pro-Cuba stance, but Almeida had more reason to worry than most, because he knew the US was already prepared to invade. Even worse, within days of JFK's death, at least one rumor of a coup surfaced in Cuban government circles. The fact that two of Artime's Miami exile associates had recently reported rumors of a coup to their CIA contacts meant that Fidel's Miami agents might also have heard such rumblings. It's also possible that Castro's agents had detected the coup preparations of one of Almeida's allies in the Cuban government.

Almeida decided to leave Cuba, but in a way that would not arouse suspicion. On Thursday, November 28, 1963, a CIA memo was sent from the Miami station to McCone, reporting the "departure [of] 2 Britannias [airliners], probably for Algeria, with 170 Cubans aboard headed by Juan Almeida."[33] A large group of Cubans had gone to Algeria earlier that fall to show support for its leftist government.

Almeida's instincts, or inside information, were correct because just two days later, on Saturday, November 30, a CIA memo revealed that "a Western diplomat . . . had learned [from someone in the Cuban government] that Che Guevara was alleged to be under house arrest for plotting to overthrow Castro." This wasn't just some rumor off the street; the CIA said the "source" of the information about Che's involvement "in an anti-Castro plot" was a "trained observer of proven reliability who is a member of the Western diplomatic community in Cuba."[34] The timing of Che's arrest, just one day before the originally scheduled date for Almeida's coup, raises the possibility that Fidel had learned something about the coup and arrested one of those he thought responsible.

While it's possible Che was going to be an ally of Almeida for the coup, Fidel might have focused suspicion on Che for another reason. Three decades later, historian Jorge Castaneda first documented that Che had been making secret plans to leave Cuba in late December 1963, to return to his home country, Argentina, for an extended period of time. Che told only three of his most trusted subordinates about his plan, but not even they were not told why Che was leaving Cuba.[35] Had Castro found out about Che's plans to leave Cuba, put them together with reports of a possible coup, and decided to arrest Che?

As detailed in *Ultimate Sacrifice*, Che's problems with Fidel, the Russians, and Cuba's Communist Party were well known by the fall of 1963. Even William Attwood, JFK's special envoy for the secret peace talks, said in a November 1963 memo that "there was [a] rift between Castro and the [Che] Guevara . . . Almeida group on the question of Cuba's future course." Attwood wrote that Fidel's intermediary in Cuba told him that "[Che] Guevara . . . regarded Castro as dangerously unreliable; and would get rid of Castro if [Che] could carry on without [Castro] and retain his popular support."[36] With Castro's intermediary revealing such concerns about Che to Attwood, it's not surprising that Fidel would have arrested Che if word of a coup and assassination plot surfaced.

Che's house arrest probably lasted for only a short time, perhaps just a day or two. December 2 is one of Cuba's biggest holidays, the anniversary of the founding of the Cuban Army, whose first battle saw Almeida save his friend Che's life at the start of the Revolution. As Commander of Cuba's Army, Almeida was also considered its founder, so the Cuban public would definitely notice if he didn't appear for the celebration. Apparently, things had calmed down enough for Almeida to return from Algeria to be part of the celebration, something he would not have done if Almeida was worried that he was returning home to the same fate as Che. Almeida's only other choice would have been to make a public break with Fidel and defect, as he had wanted to back in March 1961.

The day after the big December 2, 1963, celebration, a CIA report says Almeida "expressed [his] despair" to a subordinate. The thirdhand report indicated Almeida's concern over possible American retaliation against Cuba. Almeida appeared to be laying the groundwork with the subordinate to explain why he might not take action against the US if they did invade.[37] Whatever his private worries, Almeida put on a good public face, and on December 6, 1963, the Cuban radio-news service noted Almeida's presence at a ceremony to install a new communications minister.[38]

In the second week of December 1963, John McCone and Richard Helms were still trying to get LBJ to continue JFK's efforts to overthrow Fidel. Since sensitive information took time to reach CIA headquarters from Cuba, McCone and Helms didn't learn about Che's house arrest until December 10, 1963, or about Almeida's despair until December 18. In the interim they pressed forward, and a December 9, 1963, CIA memo encouraged McCone to get LBJ to support "a coup in Cuba." The memo even mentioned JFK's November 18 speech in Miami, which had contained words intended for Almeida, and suggested that LBJ make similar remarks.[39]

The report of Che's arrest must have given McCone and Helms pause. However, by the time they learned about it, the information was ten days old. Almeida had already returned to Cuba from Algeria and had been seen in public. As long as Almeida was free, the coup could go forward. Apparently, the Joint Chiefs of Staff were still receptive, because they sent a memo asking if "dissatisfied Cuban military leaders represent a coup potential."[40]

LBJ planned to hold his first big meeting about Cuba on December 19, 1963, but the day before that, Richard Helms and Desmond FitzGerald got disappointing news: A CIA report said that Raul Castro had kicked Rolando Cubela (AMLASH) out of the Army. Cubela, never powerful to begin with, now was reported to "be doing nothing . . . and had no plans for the future."[41] Helms and FitzGerald could only hope that Cubela would be allowed to keep his travel budget and house at Varadero Beach next to Castro's, which turned out to be the case.

LBJ's December 19, 1963, meeting marked a major turning point in US policy and operations against Cuba. With at least sixteen people present, the gathering was far larger than Bobby's typical Cuba meetings, or even the big Cuba meeting JFK chaired ten days before his death. Notable by his absence was Bobby, which was probably no accident on LBJ's part. The meeting was President Johnson's clear signal that he was now calling the shots when it came to Cuba.[42]

President Johnson had learned at least the broad strokes of the JFK-Almeida coup plan, and in the meeting expressed "particular interest in the exploitation of discontent within the Cuban military." However, many at the meeting had never been told about Almeida (of the five representatives from the State Department, only Rusk had been told about Almeida), and since there had been no decision to go forward with the coup, the rest would not learn about it at this meeting. Thus, comments from the CIA were still subject to the same careful wording that had characterized JFK's last major Cuba meeting.[43] Still, the detailed presentation from FitzGerald probably contained some new information for LBJ, to supplement what LBJ had been learning in his almost daily meetings with McCone—which were often brief, had to cover the whole-world situation, and often concentrated on the disturbing information from Mexico City.[44]

Desmond FitzGerald initially discussed the CIA's support for the "autonomous anti-Castro groups" of "Manuel Artime [and] Manolo Ray." FitzGerald said these groups' purpose was to "conduct externally mounted raids on Cuba . . . to conduct internal sabotage, and to establish contact with dissidents." FitzGerald inaccurately told the meeting that "Artime will start operating out of Costa Rica and Nicaragua in February," ignoring the fact that Artime's camps had been operating and launching raids into Cuba since the early fall.

After being asked by LBJ, FitzGerald said the CIA had budgeted "five million" for the exile groups, with another "2 million" for other Cuban operations. Only under direct questioning from LBJ did FitzGerald cautiously address the matter of a coup. FitzGerald talked about the CIA's efforts to "establish contact with potentially dissident non-Communist elements in the power centers of the regime, with a view to stimulating an internal coup." FitzGerald noted the CIA had "been able to make an important penetration in the Cuban army," as well as others. He also said, "Any successful operation to overthrow Castro emanating from within Cuba will have to be supported by" these officials "if it is to have any real likelihood of success."

FitzGerald said the various "dissident elements, while willing to act, are not yet willing to act together." To an extent, this statement was true, since Almeida and AMWORLD were separate from the AMTRUNK operation, and they were all separate from the unauthorized Cubela assassination operation. FitzGerald, with Helms's approval, seemed to be laying the groundwork for combining those three operations—which was what both men would soon attempt to do.

The decisions LBJ announced in the meeting signaled a major shift. He didn't approve a previously planned attack on a Cuban power station, in part "because of the Soviet dimension"—his worry that such an attack would upset the Soviets. This decision represented a major difference in attitude between LBJ and JFK, who was usually willing to approve such raids as long as they were just a small part of the buildup to a coup against Fidel. Even worse for McCone, Helms, and FitzGerald, even after hearing about the exile groups and hopes for "an internal coup," LBJ made it clear that he was "most interested in economic denial actions [toward Cuba]." In other words, he wanted to focus on safe ways to impact Cuba's economy, instead of potentially risky coup plans or small hit-and-run attacks.[45]

The three CIA men could take solace only in the fact that LBJ allowed the funding for the exile groups to go forward, and didn't order them to stop their efforts with dissident Cuban officials. LBJ wanted to preserve his options with Cuba while minimizing the risk of antagonizing the Soviets or having a crisis with Cuba in the early weeks of his administration. If there was going to be a real effort to topple Castro, it was going to take someone besides McCone, Helms, or FitzGerald to convince LBJ to go through with it.

In the aftermath of his brother's murder, Bobby Kennedy struggled to cope with his overwhelming grief, while trying to maintain some of his official duties.[46] *Newsweek* editor Evan Thomas wrote that Bobby "seemed devoured by grief" that was "overwhelming [and] all-consuming."[47] The formerly intense dynamo was a shadow of his former self. One of his Mafia prosecutors, G. Robert Blakey, said that even months after JFK's death, Bobby "seemed absolutely devastated." Blakey came to feel that Bobby had some "terrible sense—is there something I did, or failed to prevent, that backfired against [JFK]?"[48] Joseph Califano also began "to believe that the paroxysms of grief that tormented [Bobby] after his brother's death arose, at least in part, from a sense that his efforts to eliminate Castro led to his brother's assassination."[49]

One of the National Security Council's Cuban subcommittees met on December 6, but Bobby no longer directed or approved their actions. In fact, he no longer had any role regarding Cuba. The following day, Bobby met with John McCone at 9:00 AM; McCone subsequently met with Secretary of State Rusk at noon, and with LBJ thirty minutes later. Given the sequence and people involved, the topic of all three meetings was probably Cuba, with McCone keeping Bobby informed about the subcommittees and operations the Attorney General had once controlled. McCone may have told Bobby and the others about the latest developments from Mexico City involving Oswald, Kostikov, Duran, and Alvarado (whose story had finally been exposed as fraudulent).

For at least three more days after that meeting, Bobby continued to think that Oswald could have been assisted by "Castro or . . . gangsters," as he told Arthur Schlesinger Jr. on December 9, 1963.[50] Due to the observations of Powers, O'Donnell, and Burkley, Bobby felt that there had to have been more than one shooter. As he reportedly told Democratic Party leader Lawrence O'Brien, "I'm sure that little pinko prick [Oswald] had something to do with it, but he certainly didn't mastermind anything. He should've shot me, not Jack. I'm the one who's out to get them." As false stories like Alvarado's fell by the wayside, Bobby soon abandoned any belief that Castro was behind his brother's murder.

Instead, Bobby focused on "gangsters," their associates like Jimmy Hoffa, and some Cuban exiles. According to a former Senate lawyer interviewed by author C. David Heymann, Bobby said it was "impossible that Oswald and Ruby hadn't known one another." Bobby also expressed anger at Cuban exiles who were "working for the mob. They blame us for the Bay of Pigs, and they're trying to make this look like a Castro Communist hit. I don't buy it. And I don't trust those guys at the CIA. They're worse than the Mafia."[51] Based on those comments, it's possible that Bobby played a role in Richard Helms's sacking Tony Varona from anti-Castro operations. As for the CIA, Bobby's close friend, publisher John Seigenthaler, said it became "clear that McCone was out of the loop—Dick Helms was running the agency . . . anything McCone found out was by accident."[52] Still, as Bobby told William Attwood, there were "'reasons of national security' for keeping a lid on the case."[53]

Bobby's ability to investigate his brother's murder was impaired not only by his personal grief and his need for secrecy, but also by his loss of power, as typified by the way J. Edgar Hoover treated him. According to historian Richard D. Mahoney, after JFK's death, Hoover "ordered his secretary to get rid of the phone on his desk that linked him to the Attorney General," and "the organized crime operation came to a halt." Mahoney writes that "as Bill Hundley, head of the Organized Crime Section, put it, 'The minute that bullet hit Jack Kennedy's head, it was all over. Right then. The organized crime program just stopped, and Hoover took control back.' Marcello had been right: Cut the dog's head off and the rest of it would die."[54]

Amidst his grief in December 1963, Bobby Kennedy made a major decision that would further strain his already rocky relationship with LBJ. Bobby decided he would try to persuade LBJ to continue the coup plan with Almeida. Harry Williams had received a communication from Almeida indicating that he was still willing to lead the coup. Harry was ready as well, and Bobby felt that a free and democratic Cuba would be the best memorial to his slain brother.[55]

Their first approach to President Johnson hinted at the problems to come. Harry tried to use his contacts in Cyrus Vance's office to arrange a meeting with LBJ. According to Harry, Vance's aide Joseph Califano told him that LBJ had first evoked the Kennedys' responsibility for the Bay of Pigs disaster, and had then declared, "I don't want to see any goddamn Cuban, especially that son of a bitch Williams." Apparently, LBJ had heard enough about the coup plan from McCone to wonder if JFK's death was some type of retaliation from Castro. Then, too, LBJ knew that Harry was a personal friend of Bobby, whom he still didn't trust.[56]

While Bobby had not attended LBJ's big December 19 meeting on Cuba, he was on good terms with several people who had, and he was no doubt disappointed by the results. Still, Almeida remained willing to proceed, and on December 26, 1963, Che Guevara made a television appearance in Cuba, showing that whatever issue had resulted in his house arrest had been resolved. In France, Cuban journalist Carlos Franqui had been waiting for something to happen regarding the coup. The longer he stayed in France, the greater the chance that Fidel might view Franqui's long absence with suspicion. By late December, it became obvious to Franqui that in the wake of JFK's death there wasn't going to be a coup, so he returned to Cuba. Fidel and Raul Castro didn't realize that Harry Williams and Bobby Kennedy were the ones who had arranged Franqui's sojourn to France, as part of the plan for the coup.

In early January, Harry and Bobby talked about trying one last time to get LBJ to continue with Almeida's coup plan. Since LBJ wouldn't see Harry, there was only one thing left to try: Bobby would have to swallow his pride, put his own feelings aside, and plead his case personally to LBJ. Their relationship had been terrible since 1960, when Bobby had managed JFK's campaign for the presidential nomination against LBJ and the other challengers. Their feelings toward each other had not improved during Johnson's tenure as vice president, and had been even worse since JFK's death, because Bobby felt that Johnson had moved into the White House and asserted control too quickly.

However, LBJ had tried to reach out to Bobby at times and perhaps that was why Bobby felt that talking to LBJ directly was worth a try. Also, we got the distinct impression from Harry that Bobby—and apparently McCone and Helms—had not told President Johnson everything about Almeida and the coup plan. There were apparently things that Bobby intended to tell LBJ only if he agreed to continue the plan. LBJ could become Bobby's political rival in the future, so it made little sense for Bobby to describe every aspect of his most sensitive plan to LBJ until after President Johnson had agreed to the coup.

Bobby's meeting with LBJ about the coup plan did not go well. Only the two of them were present, and Bobby later told Harry that LBJ listened sympathetically but made it clear that he would not continue with the plan. LBJ's decision also included ending the Cuban exile troop program at Fort Benning and Fort Jackson, since the exiles' real purpose had been to be among the first US troops into Cuba after the coup. However, LBJ did agree to keep funding Bobby's favored Cuban exile groups, in case they proved useful in the future. This was LBJ's way of preserving his options and asserting control: Formerly, Cuban operations had essentially been run by Bobby, through Army Secretary Cyrus Vance and Richard Helms. Now, Cuban operations would be primarily the CIA's responsibility, with McCone reporting to LBJ. Probably at Bobby's urging, LBJ agreed to meet with the leader of the Fort Benning Cuban American troops the following day, to break the news to him personally.

The leader of the Cuban American troops at Fort Benning was Second Lieutenant Erneido Oliva, later a Major General in the National Guard. Oliva had been second in command at the Bay of Pigs and was one of the men who presented JFK with the flag of the Brigade at the Orange Bowl ceremony. An Afro-Cuban, Oliva had been praised in a speech by JFK, who had planned to give Oliva a major role in the new Cuban provisional government after Almeida's coup. Oliva later wrote this account of his mid-January 1964 meeting with LBJ and Bobby:

> President Johnson . . . said that he really wanted to help Cubans recover their homeland from communism, but . . . the moment was not appropriate for any anti-Castro activity. He added that he was sorry to terminate the Special Presidential Program established by President Kennedy the previous year, but each Cuban officer would be given the opportunity to "stay in the service or find a new job."[57]

LBJ tried to refer Oliva to the Secretary of Defense, but Oliva tried one last time to get LBJ to change his mind. With Bobby sitting beside him, Oliva told LBJ:

> . . . as strongly as possible that the plans for Cuba established by the previous Administration were essential for the overthrow of Fidel Castro. But Johnson stayed firm in his decision. . . . At the Pentagon, Oliva and Kennedy were welcomed by Secretary of Defense Robert McNamara, Secretary of the Army Cyrus Vance, Army General

Counsel Joseph Califano, and Lieutenant Colonel Alexander M. Haig Jr. . . . Thus, with a short sixteen-minute meeting at the White House and twenty at the Pentagon . . . President Kennedy's plans for removing Castro from power were ended. . . . [58]

When Bobby met with Harry Williams to tell him about LBJ's final word, Harry took the news better than the Attorney General did. For Bobby, LBJ's refusal widened the already deep rift between them. Also, Bobby wasn't quite ready to give up the fight—though in light of LBJ's decision, he really had no options left. As Bobby struggled with his disappointment, he indicated to Harry that perhaps private funding could be found to keep Harry's effort alive, in case LBJ changed his mind or the situation in Cuba changed.

Harry had spent the last four years of his life in the fight against Fidel, often putting his family and business aside while risking his life. Even after suffering for a year in Castro's brutal prisons, Harry had been willing to put his life on the line yet again while he had the full support of President Kennedy and his brother, whom he'd come to consider a trusted friend. Now, that time had passed. Harry realized that LBJ would never give the same degree of support to Castro's overthrow as the Kennedys had. He and Bobby had done their best, and given it their all. Harry had sacrificed a lot, and Bobby even more, when JFK made the ultimate sacrifice.

In light of all that, Harry told Bobby that it was time to move on, to leave the task of bringing democracy to Cuba to others. Harry must have felt as if a tremendous weight had been lifted from his shoulders. Bobby had burdens enough without Cuba, and soon he came to see it Harry's way. From that time on, Bobby abandoned plans to stage coups, topple governments, and eliminate foreign leaders. He was beginning a new journey, one that would see him start to view the world, and his place in it, with a new perspective. It would also lead to his tragic murder just over four years later.

PART THREE

PART THREE

Chapter Twenty-one

Bobby Kennedy devoted the rest of his life to the pursuit of two goals, one very public and the other so private that it has become known only in recent years. Bobby's evolution into a champion of civil rights and the poor, which eventually included his stance opposing the war in Vietnam, has been widely chronicled. But another part of Bobby's life was conducted in secret and has not been fully documented until now. This quest, known only to a few of his closest associates, was his vigilant effort to discover who was behind JFK's assassination and bring them to some type of justice—without exposing Commander Almeida. Revealing the JFK-Almeida coup plan would not only cost the lives of the Commander and his allies in Cuba, but would also ruin the image of the slain president and his brother, Bobby—ending Bobby's chances of ever attaining the presidency, the only position that could allow him to conduct a truly thorough but secret investigation of JFK's murder.

Bobby Kennedy's deepening involvement in the civil rights movement is inexorably intertwined with his sometimes tumultuous relationship with Dr. Martin Luther King. Their relationship, which ended with Dr. King's death in 1968, lasted only eight years. It began during the 1960 presidential campaign, when Bobby and JFK may have saved Dr. King's life, while King helped propel JFK into office. *Newsweek* editor Evan Thomas wrote that "just two phone calls—one by JFK and one by RFK—decided the outcome of the election and determined the course of racial politics for decades to come."[1]

Two weeks before the 1960 presidential election, Dr. King had been convicted for staging a lunch-counter sit-in in Atlanta, and given a harsh prison sentence of four months at hard labor. According to Thomas, Dr. King was "hustled off in chains to a state prison deep in the Georgia backwoods." King's wife, Coretta, called a Kennedy aide and pleaded, "They are going to kill him . . . I know they are going to kill him."[2]

Mrs. King's concerns were real, since she knew that violence against blacks and their leaders was all too common. In January 1956, a bomb had been thrown at their home after King began leading a bus boycott in Alabama. Eleven months later, following the boycott's successful conclusion, a shotgun blast was fired into their home. A year after that, another bomb was thrown at their house.[3] The legal system offered little help, since Jim Crow laws limited the recourse of blacks; in addition, much of the South was still segregated, and some in law enforcement shared the racism of King's attackers.

Mrs. King's desperate plea reached JFK, who personally called to reassure her that he would try to help. JFK's call to Mrs. King during the tight 1960 presidential campaign was politically perilous: While the South was solidly Democratic, most Southern leaders were conservative and opposed civil rights. Yet as an issue of fairness and justice, JFK and Bobby felt something had to be done to help Dr. King. Just a few months earlier, Bobby had pushed for a pro–civil rights platform at the Democratic National Convention, and now he had the chance to turn those words into action.

Hurried, behind-the-scenes calls were made to Georgia's governor by JFK, and to King's judge by Bobby. However, the next day's newspapers reported only that King had been released after Bobby's call to the judge. Sparked by the Kennedys' actions, the shift of black voters away from the Republican Party of Lincoln, which had begun under Franklin Roosevelt, took a giant leap forward. Thomas writes that Dr. King's father, "an extremely influential Baptist preacher, openly shifted his endorsement from Nixon to Kennedy," and that on election day Kennedy carried "a half-dozen states in the East and Midwest . . . by very narrow margins [and] black turnout made the difference."[4]

After this promising beginning, the ensuing relationship between Bobby and Dr. King was often rocky. Dr. King pushed for rapid change, while the Attorney General and JFK moved cautiously, trying to lay the groundwork for JFK's reelection. Even slow progress was sometimes met with violence. On the night of JFK's June 12, 1963, televised speech to the nation as he prepared to introduce his civil rights bill, Mississippi civil rights leader Medgar Evers was shot and killed.

The Kennedys had to prod J. Edgar Hoover into action on that case and others. The FBI Director's racism has been well documented: As late as 1961, instructors at the FBI Academy used the "N-word" to refer to blacks and called the NAACP a communist-front organization. It was only pressure from Bobby that finally resulted in Hoover allowing the first blacks to enter the FBI Academy, in 1962.[5] FBI agents in the

South often stood by and watched when peaceful demonstrators were attacked, sometimes by the police themselves. Hoover's attitude set the tone for the FBI, and a former Atlanta agent later testified to Congress about the degree of racism he observed in the FBI's Atlanta office, particularly toward Dr. King.[6] A far different former FBI agent, Arthur Hanes (Sr.), was mayor of Birmingham in May 1963, when city authorities unleashed police dogs and fire hoses on peaceful demonstrators— and Mayor Hanes blamed King for the violence.[7]

Hoover hated Dr. King and constantly tried to portray him and his cause as communist. One of Dr. King's advisors had previously dealt with the American Communist Party, but even though Hoover knew that affiliation had ended by 1962, the FBI Director still pushed Bobby to approve phone taps on Dr. King. After Bobby tried unsuccessfully to persuade Dr. King to end his relationship with the advisor, the Attorney General finally gave in to Hoover's demands and approved limited phone surveillance on Dr. King in October 1963.

On November 22, 1963, Dr. King was at his modest Atlanta home when he saw the first televised reports that JFK had been shot. Joined by his wife Coretta, both watched in horror as the news filtered in. Dr. King said, "This is just terrible . . . I hope he will live." As JFK's death was announced, Dr. King could say only, "This is what's going to happen to me."[8]

After JFK's death, Hoover started bugging some of Dr. King's hotel rooms, setting in motion a campaign to discredit King that would last until the civil rights leader's death. President Lyndon Johnson reached out to King, meeting with him twice during LBJ's first months in office. However, while LBJ didn't explicitly authorize the hotel bugging, he also apparently didn't shut it down when he became aware of it. As for the Attorney General, whose authorization should have been required for the extra surveillance, Hoover hadn't bothered to ask Bobby.

In the early months of 1964, Bobby continued to be overwhelmed by his brother's tragic murder. Evan Thomas writes that Bobby's lingering grief left him appearing "wasted and gaunt." He cites JFK aide John Seigenthaler as saying that Bobby seemed "to be in physical pain, like a man . . . on the rack . . . he walked for hours, brooding and alone."[9] Bobby was consumed by keeping secrets he couldn't fully share with anyone, but decades later—after the Congressional disclosures of the 1970s—a few of Bobby's friends began to realize some of what he had gone through. Harris Wofford, a Kennedy aide before becoming a senator, said that for Bobby, "keeping from the public facts about the CIA, the FBI, and the Mafia crucial to the investigations of his brother's [murder] must have caused him special suffering."[10]

Bobby undoubtedly heard about Chief Justice Earl Warren's answer to a question about whether all of the material from his Commission would be made public. As the *New York Times* reported on February 5, 1964, Warren said, "Yes, there will come a time. But it might not be in your lifetime. I am not referring to anything especially, but there may be some things that would involve [national] security. This would be preserved but not made public."[11]

Perhaps such a public statement was Warren's attempt to encourage officials to share sensitive information with the Commission, with the assurance that it wouldn't be released in the foreseeable future. If so, that approach didn't work with Bobby, who revealed nothing to the Commission about Almeida, the coup plan, or his suspicions about CIA-backed exiles who might have sold out the plan to the Mafia. Bobby would make one indirect effort to focus suspicion on Jimmy Hoffa, but he would be stopped because of matters related to Cuba and Almeida.

Stymied in his pursuit of Marcello, Bobby had his prosecutors continue their trial of Hoffa in Chattanooga, with another Hoffa trial soon slated for Chicago. For Bobby, the associates Hoffa shared with Jack Ruby were too obvious to ignore. It's not clear whether Bobby ever realized that Ruby was probably the "Jack La Rue" he had searched in vain for only four years earlier. However, it must have been obvious to Bobby that Ruby had been involved in a murder that Bobby had mentioned in his book *The Enemy Within*. Union gangster Paul Dorfman had been implicated in that murder, and Paul's stepson, Allen Dorfman, was on trial with Hoffa in Chattanooga. Allen Dorfman's name had also been part of the Ruby-Chicago payoff rumor reported to Walter Sheridan just hours after Ruby shot Oswald.

Hoffa was shocked and furious when Sheridan had Teamster official Ed Partin take the stand against him in Chattanooga, because Hoffa knew the secrets he had confided to Partin, including talk of assassinating Bobby Kennedy in the summer of 1962. However, Walter Sheridan had warned Partin not to mention that during his testimony. Sheridan's fear was that in the wake of JFK's assassination, any mention of an attempt to kill Bobby (especially in a car) would be so prejudicial that Hoffa might be able to get a mistrial. Hoffa's lawyers realized the same thing, and though they pressed, they were unable to get more than a few words about it on the record, and nothing about the target's being Bobby

Kennedy. Still, in an obvious attempt to intimidate Partin, someone fired shots into his close associate's Louisiana home.[12]

Hoffa also had secrets he could expose, especially since one of his attorneys in Chattanooga was Trafficante's confidant, Frank Ragano. At one point when Partin was on the stand, he was asked about running guns to Cuba and dealing with high-ranking Cuban military officials. Bobby's men quickly shut down that line of questioning. Hoffa, Partin, and Ruby had all run guns to Cuba during the Revolution, but Bobby wanted to avoid the entire subject, since one of the Cuban military officials receiving such arms was Commander Almeida, who was still vulnerable in Cuba.

Though Allen Dorfman was acquitted, Hoffa was convicted and the Teamster president was sentenced on March 12, 1964. That same day, Puerto Rican Teamster official (and Hoffa enforcer) Frank Chavez sent Bobby a taunting letter, saying Chavez was taking up a collection from local Teamsters to "maintain, clean, beautify, and supply with flowers the grave of Lee Harvey Oswald."[13] Chavez had met with Jack Ruby in 1962, and in a few months Chavez would make his first attempt to kill Bobby Kennedy.

Chavez's letter may have been the final straw for Bobby, who decided to respond against Hoffa. Two days after Hoffa was sentenced, Jack Ruby received his death sentence in Dallas on March 14, 1964. Ruby immediately fired his lawyer, Melvin Belli, and hired high-profile Houston defense attorney Percy Foreman. But Foreman quit after just four days and wasn't replaced by anyone of national stature, so Ruby's appeals were not likely to be extensively covered by the media. Any information Bobby leaked to the press now could no longer affect Hoffa's or Ruby's conviction. So, a short time after Bobby learned about Chavez's letter, Bobby's associates began leaking stories to high-profile news outlets about Hoffa's summer 1962 plans to assassinate the Attorney General.[14]

The first story about Hoffa's plot to kill Bobby appeared on the front page of the *New York Times*, which proclaimed that Hoffa had been "plotting the assassination of Attorney General Robert F. Kennedy." Follow-up cover stories appeared several weeks later in America's leading news picture magazines, *Life* and *Look*. Bobby's well-coordinated PR offensive seemed designed to catch the attention of the American public—and surely of the Warren Commission and its staff.[15]

However, an article sympathetic to Hoffa was also in the works, and though it was in a much smaller magazine (the *Nation*), it included

Hoffa's lawyers' questions to Partin about running guns to high Cuban military officials. The article mentioned "a letter from one of Castro's generals to Partin, thanking him for help in training Castro's militia," and stressed how vehemently Bobby's prosecutors "shouted [their] objections."[16] Was Hoffa trying to send a subtle message to Bobby, threatening to expose Almeida or his associates? In this proxy war, via the press, Bobby knew that Almeida's life was at stake, so the Attorney General needed a truce.

In March 1964, an unusual and very informal summit meeting—which has never been explained—took place between Bobby and Hoffa at Dulles Airport in Washington, D.C. The last time the two men had met, Frank Ragano said, Hoffa had tried to strangle Bobby. This time, the two men talked as Hoffa's bodyguards looked on, while two Secret Service agents waited nearby for Bobby. The Attorney General did have one bargaining chip: keeping Hoffa's own gunrunning to Castro out of his next trial. At the time, the American public was so anti-Castro that such a revelation would have ruined Hoffa's "everyman" image. What kind of deal Bobby and Hoffa struck is not clear, but each side soon backed off from using the press to tie the other side to Castro or assassinations after the flurry of initial articles appeared.[17]

As for Cuba, Bobby kept in touch with Harry, though both men had given up any thoughts of a coup. Desmond FitzGerald noticed this change in Bobby when FitzGerald visited him on February 28, 1964. It was a courtesy call, suggested by John McCone, to make the Attorney General aware of current plans for Cuba. According to files reviewed by David Talbot, Bobby asked FitzGerald "whether or not the US could live with Castro." Bobby was persistent, but FitzGerald told Bobby that "it was not a good idea to explore the peace option with Havana."[18] Working through FitzGerald and Helms, Bobby made sure the CIA provided for Almeida's family members, who were still on their extended stay away from Cuba, their pretext still holding.[19] Bobby was probably unaware that E. Howard Hunt (and Barker) had helped to provide their initial support, a role Hunt was likely continuing.

Following Bobby's meeting with LBJ and Lieutenant Erneido Oliva about Cuba, Cyrus Vance had his men begin the process of shutting down the special training for the Cuban exile troops. Assisting Joseph Califano and Alexander Haig was a young Alexander Butterfield. Eight years later, those three men would be among a dozen veterans of the JFK-Almeida coup plan involved in various aspects of Watergate: Butterfield as the Nixon aide who revealed the taping system, Haig as Nixon's final Chief of Staff, and Haig's mentor Califano as attorney for the *Washington Post* and partner in the law firm representing the Democratic Party, whose Watergate offices were burglarized.

Lt. Oliva worked with Califano and Haig to phase out the special status of the Cuban American soldiers at Fort Benning and Fort Jackson. Oliva wrote that he "had to relate the devastating news to all Cuban exile personnel wearing an American military uniform." He said that "every Cuban officer and soldier was given the option, as individuals, to resign after the completion of his training or remain in active duty. Those who elected to stay were reassigned to regular units within the Army, Air Force, and Navy." Oliva resigned his commission (though he would eventually return to the military) and joined an exile group known by its initials as the RECE, which apparently was not funded by the CIA. While the RECE attracted some exemplary exiles, like Oliva, it was also joined by the dangerous Felipe Rivero.[20]

By January of 1964, Richard Helms was moving to consolidate the remnants of the JFK-Almeida coup plan into an operation, under his control, that included Manuel Artime's AMWORLD program, Manolo Ray's JURE exile group, and Eloy Menoyo's SNFE group. After Bobby and Harry's difficulty in getting those exile leaders to work together, it's ironic that FBI and CIA reports highlighted the cooperation of Artime, Ray, and Menoyo in the early part of 1964, as they briefly put aside their differences and coalesced under Helms's Cuban coordinator, Desmond FitzGerald. Personnel from AMTRUNK joined the operation, and Helms would soon add Rolando Cubela (AMLASH) to the mix.

Having such complete control allowed Helms to hide his unauthorized plots, like the assassination side of Cubela/AMLASH, by merging them with the authorized groups. For the time being, QJWIN remained on the payroll, though Johnny Rosselli's activities at the Miami CIA station appear to have ceased by 1964. Following the previously mentioned December 6, 1963, Herminio Diaz assassination attempt against Castro and the January 1964 termination of Tony Varona's support, Helms seems to have ended the CIA-Mafia plots. CIA files show that by early 1964, two veterans of the CIA-Mafia plots were still working together: David Morales was training Manuel Artime, who was lavish in his praise of Morales.[21]

Helms had more suspicions about the possible involvement of CIA personnel in JFK's death than he ever acknowledged officially to the

LEGACY OF SECRECY

Warren Commission or any of the Congressional investigations. In a rarely noted television interview in 1992, Helms admitted that "we checked [to] be sure that nobody [with the CIA] had been in Dallas on that particular day [of JFK's assassination]." Helms said they not only checked "at the time" but later, "when the Warren Commission was sitting."[22] Those investigations have never been released, so there's no way to know if Helms suspected Barker or other agents.

While Helms's initial suspicions may have centered on Varona and his associates, other CIA personnel would be quietly terminated or sent far overseas in the coming months. Such actions by Helms were technically legal at the time—even if he suspected CIA assets or agents were involved in murder, he was under no obligation to turn them over for prosecution. As former CIA agent Tom Tripodi observed about an unrelated 1963 murder case, CIA officials' attitude was "Look the other way. Don't get involved. Security rules supreme. It just didn't matter if murderers went free."[23]

As Helms tried to figure out whom he could still trust, his current Cuban operations were missing the three most important components that had been active under JFK: Bobby, Almeida, and Harry. Harry was no longer telling CIA officials like E. Howard Hunt what to do; instead, an almost poignant January 21, 1964, CIA memo describes Harry's final meeting with the same CIA case officer who had been working with Manolo Ray.

As for Ray, his JURE group was joined by Luis Posada Carrilles, who had just left the special Cuban American troop program at Fort Benning. Posada was far to the right of the more liberal Ray, and caused problems in JURE that would contribute to its eventual dissolution. Posada's later career for the CIA raises the possibility that he was an informant or provocateur in Ray's group, which the CIA had supported only because of the Kennedys. During 1964 and the years that followed, Posada remained close to a fellow ex-soldier from Fort Benning named Jorge Mas Canosa. Mas Canosa eventually became the top Cuban exile leader in the US, while Posada went on to a career of terrorist bombings that would include blowing up a Cubana airliner in 1976, a crime for which he was still being sought in 2008.[24]

At least officially, the CIA appeared to leave other Cuban exile groups out in the cold. LBJ had allowed support for Artime's and Ray's groups to continue, but on April 7, 1964, he ordered "all sabotage operations against Cuba [discontinued]." LBJ wanted the CIA to fund only a few groups, to give him options in dealing with Cuba, but he didn't want them taking actions that could force his hand. Other exile groups were not so lucky. A few weeks after JFK's death, someone at the Miami CIA station suggested to CIA headquarters that the small DRE exile group be added to AMWORLD, but this recommendation wasn't approved. Since Miami Chief Ted Shackley thought so little of the DRE, the suggestion probably came from David Atlee Phillips, who ran the DRE, or his associate David Morales. On the other hand, Congressional investigator Gaeton Fonzi says that Phillips continued his support for Alpha 66's Antonio Veciana, albeit under very deep cover.[25] At the time, Veciana was still working closely with Eloy Menoyo, who appears to have continued receiving some CIA support.

As Helms and FitzGerald worked to coordinate the Cuban operations they now controlled exclusively, attempts to assassinate Fidel Castro continued. In fact, Castro would later tell journalist Tad Szulc that there were more attempts to assassinate him under LBJ than there had been under JFK.[26] It's possible some of those unauthorized attempts were backed by the CIA under very deep cover, the same way Phillips supported Veciana, to give Helms and FitzGerald deniability with LBJ if problems arose.

Only in recent years have historians and researchers discovered that so many anti-Castro operations were going on while Helms was withholding crucial information from the Warren Commission. Helms had to be careful, since the earlier CIA-Mafia plots had been leaked to at least two members of the Commission, Warren and Ford. Perhaps significant is that Warren and Ford were the only Commission members to go to Dallas to interview Jack Ruby, whose pleas to go to Washington to testify were refused. Years later, Ford's inadvertent revelation of the CIA-Mafia plots, shortly after he assumed the presidency, would set off a chain of events that would expose some of the plots to the public for the first time.

It's possible that at least Earl Warren was also generally informed about ongoing CIA anti-Castro operations that LBJ had approved. A whisper about those activities to Warren, by Dulles or Angleton, could explain why the Commission never interviewed any of the important Cuban exile leaders, like Artime, Ray, and Menoyo, even though their names cropped up in important information the FBI provided to the Commission. This omission was especially glaring in the case of Ray and JURE, since Warren Commission staff would struggle for months with their investigation of Oswald's visit to JURE member Silvia Odio. The same is also true for John Martino, who was never interviewed by

Warren Commission staff about his remarks concerning a JFK-approved coup and invasion plan for Cuba, even though memos show that the staff knew about some of Martino's provocative remarks. It also appears that the Commission and staff never realized that Martino and his associates were linked to the Odio incident.

Warren had probably been told only about the CIA-Mafia plots that ran from 1960 to 1962, since the FBI was also aware of those, but it's doubtful that Warren was told that the plots had continued into 1963. Helms had no incentive to tell Warren something that remained hidden even from his own CIA Director, especially since problems with the plots kept coming up in early 1964. In April 1964, FitzGerald and Helms "terminated" (as in fired) QJWIN after news reports surfaced briefly in Europe, linking Jean Souetre and Michael Mertz to JFK's assassination. These news reports led to the inquiry that generated the only memo the CIA has ever released about Mertz, the one page (from a much longer, still withheld document) concerning his deportation that was quoted in an earlier chapter.

The European articles also caused the FBI to look for anyone with the name of, or a name similar to, Mertz who flew out of Dallas after JFK's assassination. However, no news about this was reported in America at the time, and it's not clear what, if anything, the Warren Commission was told about Mertz or Souetre. While the Commission received a few documents about the FBI's search in early 1964 for November 22, 1963, Dallas airline passengers named Mertz, those were just a handful of more than a hundred thousand pages of FBI files showered on the Warren Commission. Lacking more information from the FBI or CIA, Commission staffers probably didn't realize the significance of the documents.[27]

On March 2, 1964, Helms received reports of yet another Mafia plot to assassinate Castro, though he didn't tell McCone and Bobby about it until three months later. According to Congressional investigators, Helms wrote that CIA "officials have learned of several plots by exiles to assassinate Castro. Some of them are connected to the Mafia." However, Helms "does not mention [to McCone] the [earlier] CIA sponsored plots" with the Mafia. Helms said the March 1964 plots "involved 'people apparently associated with the Mafia' who had been offered $150,000 by Cuban exiles to accomplish the deed. Helms's memorandum stated that the sources of the reports were parties to the plots who had presumably given this information to CIA officials with the expectation that they would receive legal immunity if the plots succeeded."[28]

Three months later, in June 1964, Helms told McCone that, naturally, "the CIA representatives had told the Cuban informants that such action would never be condoned." Helms's delay in relaying this information begs the question of whether he was giving the plots three months to work, before finally informing his Director. Helms still had at least one possible pathway of information from the Mafia: Though Johnny Rosselli no longer went to the Miami CIA station, David Morales visited the Mafia don in Las Vegas in early 1964.[29]

Helms continued to withhold much important information from the Warren Commission, including the CIA's ongoing contacts with Rolando Cubela. More than a decade later, the Senate Church Committee would write that "it is difficult to understand why those aware of the operation did not think it relevant, and did not inform those investigating President Kennedy's assassination of possible connections between that operation and the assassination."[30] In hindsight, the motive for Helms's omission is clear: At the very least, revealing those connections would have cost Helms his job and probably would have made CIA officials like David Morales, and possibly even Helms himself, suspects.

Some Warren Commission staff members were already becoming frustrated with—and perhaps even suspicious of—the CIA. Congressional investigators later found that on March 12, 1964, there had been a "very important meeting between 6 Warren Commission staffers and 3 CIA men." During the meeting, Helms told the staffers that "two case officers would know for sure whether Oswald was an agent." The investigators, writing fifteen years later, found Helms's comment "very interesting," and wondered why Helms limited it to "just two officers. . . . Who were they, were they the only ones who had contact with Oswald?" In the meeting, Helms stated that "Oswald was not an agent," but said that the Warren Commission "would just have to take his word for it."[31]

Ever since a false report about Oswald's being an FBI informant had surfaced in January 1964, the Commission had been worried that Oswald had been an undercover operative for some US agency. They were not reassured when Hale Boggs asked fellow Commissioner and former CIA Director Allen Dulles if the CIA had "agents about whom you had no record whatsoever." Dulles answered that "the record might not be on paper," and that even if it was, it might be "hieroglyphics that only two people knew what they meant, and nobody outside the Agency would know."[32]

On April 30, 1964, the Warren Commission decided to have top officials from the CIA and FBI testify about the matter.[33] On May 14, Helms, McCone, and J. Edgar Hoover all testified to the Commission that Oswald wasn't an agent or informant for their agencies. In an extremely technical way, they were correct: As Helms would testify under oath in 1978, Oswald was the responsibility of the defense establishment, not the CIA. General Joseph Carroll, of the Defense Intelligence Agency, should have been subject to the same scrutiny, though it's unclear how much even he knew about Oswald's 1963 activities. Indications exist that the heads of Naval and Marine Intelligence knew more than General Carroll, but they never testified either. Essentially, each of the agencies was passing the buck to the other, leaving the Commission, and the public, in the dark.

Congressional investigators later noted that Helms blatantly lied to the Commission on several points.[34] The same day as Helms's testimony, one of Helms's CIA officials was also lying to the FBI about a report the bureau had received concerning Artime's AMWORLD camps in Guatemala. The FBI had learned that the "military forces in [Guatemala] were under the direct control of the US, that there are three military camps training mercenary forces which were originally organized for an invasion of Cuba." But on May 14, 1964, the FBI was told "it was the very strong opinion of CIA that the information [about the camps] is false. CIA officials speculated . . . the information may have been [planted] for deception or provocation."[35]

CIA files released in 1992 show that in 1964, affidavits had been prepared for Helms and three other CIA officials, in case the Warren Commission pressed them for more disclaimers about Oswald. The affidavits stated that Oswald "was not an agent, employee, or informant"; that the CIA "never contacted him, interviewed him, talked with him, or received or solicited any reports or information from him, or communicated with him, directly or indirectly, in any other way"; and that "Oswald was never associated or connected, directly or indirectly, in any way whatsoever with the Agency." There are blanks for the CIA officials to sign and for each affidavit to be sworn and notarized. However, only McCone signed an affidavit for the Warren Commission. Helms didn't sign his, and a note in the CIA file reads: "never sent to Commission."[36]

Although Helms lied and obfuscated about Oswald, the coup plan, and his unauthorized operations, he did tell the Warren Commission about troubling information that kept them concerned about a potentially devastating confrontation with the Soviets. A KGB officer named Yuri Nosenko, who had recently defected to America, claimed that he had read the KGB file on Oswald, and that it showed the Russians had no interest in Oswald. One of the CIA officers who helped Nosenko get from Europe to America was James McCord, the future Watergate burglar who also allegedly assisted Harry Williams with the JFK-Almeida coup plan.[37] Once Nosenko was in the US, a CIA memo confirms that Harry Williams's other CIA contact, "Howard Hunt, [was] told about the doubts regarding AEFOXTROT [Nosenko's] bona fides" on April 9, 1964.[38]

Richard Helms made sure Earl Warren knew that Helms and others in the CIA weren't certain that Nosenko was telling the truth about the KGB's lack of interest in Oswald. Helms pointed out that Nosenko might have been sent to the US as a false defector, a double agent. While the Warren Commission decided that Nosenko's testimony was too sensitive to mention in its report, Helms ordered the defector's interrogation to be stepped up.[39]

The way the CIA handled Nosenko in 1964, and for the next several years, evokes twenty-first-century concerns about the treatment of US prisoners at Guantanamo and in Iraq. Even Helms admits that Nosenko was held "in strict solitary confinement [and] subjected to various psychological pressures." This scenario went on for years, well after Helms became CIA Director. Yet in his autobiography, Helms tries to put the responsibility onto unnamed others for these actions, though he specifically exonerates James Angleton. In contrast, CIA Miami Chief Ted Shackley said in his autobiography that it was the paranoid Angleton who pressed for Nosenko's "abusive confinement"; Shackley also maintains that Nosenko was legitimate.[40]

From our perspective, Helms had much to gain from keeping Nosenko in solitary, with his status undetermined, for more than four years. As long as the Warren Commission and high officials like President Johnson thought the Soviets might be behind JFK's assassination, their fear of possible Soviet reprisals would keep them from pursuing investigations that could expose Helms's unauthorized operations, like the 1963 CIA-Mafia plots.[41]

Chapter Twenty-two

The lies and omissions of Helms, Hoover, and several agencies rendered any real investigation by the Warren Commission staff almost impossible. Because the Commission was still receiving reports implicating Fidel in JFK's murder, national-security concerns remained high. However, the Commission didn't realize that most of the reports were linked to associates of Manuel Artime and Santo Trafficante.[1] Because the Commission staff didn't know about Artime's work on AMWORLD and the CIA-Mafia plots with Trafficante, they didn't realize the "Castro did it" reports were disinformation designed to distract and divert them. That same lack of information caused Commission staff to dismiss reports about John Martino's accurate statements about JFK's planned coup and invasion, which may have been seen as the ravings of a far-right fanatic who was bitter about his time in Castro's prisons.

In *Vanity Fair*, Anthony Summers wrote that in an attempt to resolve the "Castro did it" stories, Earl Warren "dispatched staff counsel William Coleman on a secret mission. Coleman, who has spoken of the trip privately, [said], 'It was top-secret.' Asked to confirm or deny that he had met Castro, he said only, 'No comment.' What Coleman will say is that his mission helped convince him that Castro had nothing to do with the president's death."[2] No files about Coleman's "secret mission" have ever been released; they are just some of the sensitive Warren Commission files still being withheld, while others have been released only in recent years.

Quoted here are newly declassified files about the Warren Commission's largely unknown electronic surveillance of Marina Oswald. This surveillance included a break-in to bug her bedroom, delve into her sexual habits, and tap her phone. These files offer a rare glimpse of an all-too-common FBI practice at the time (and in later years), of invasive surveillance in the name of national security. It also shows how many files about JFK's death have been, and are still being, withheld from Congress and the public. Only a few memos have been declassified about this bugging operation, as well as one in Tampa, though more subjects were the targets of such surveillance.[3]

The phone taps on Marina resulted from a conversation between J. Edgar Hoover and Warren Commission General Counsel J. Lee Rankin, the investigation's executive director.[4] Rankin called Hoover on February 24, saying he would "hate to have [Marina] just run out on us," and that he wanted "a stake-out on her which would watch her and see who is visiting her." Hoover added helpfully that the FBI should "also consider getting a telephone tap in there." As he had done with Martin Luther King, the FBI Director went beyond Rankin's official request and apparently decided on his own to also install bugs (listening devices) in Marina's new residence. Hoover got approval for the phone taps from Attorney General Kennedy the same day.[5]

An FBI memo to Hoover states that "trespass was made to install" the bugs "on [the] night of 2/28/64, prior to subject moving to this house." After the FBI agents broke in, three bugs were "installed in the attic of subject's resident, in spaces above [the] ceiling light fixtures in [the] dining-living room area, in [the] kitchen, and in subject's bedroom." According to the FBI, "physical surveillance covering Marina" began four days prior to the break-in, utilizing "eight Agents . . . in cars." The phone taps began on February 29, while the secret bugs started picking up information on March 2, 1964, after Marina and her children had moved in. The electronic surveillance required an additional eight agents daily.[6]

Hoover wrote that he decided to end the Marina operation because the "coverage has embraced Marina Oswald's dealings with her attorney, [and] from a legal standpoint this is undesirable." However, Hoover told Rankin that "Marina Oswald's attorney . . . had indicated that he would keep the Dallas Office of the FBI fully informed of all information that would be of interest." Hoover also assured Rankin that he would "advise the President's Commission of any unusual activities on the part of Mrs. Oswald," meaning an FBI agent would continue to keep a close eye on Marina. The eight-man physical surveillance ended on March 9, 1964, while the phone tap and bugs were removed on March 12, probably after another FBI break-in.[7]

Agents prepared a full report containing all of the "take" from the phone tap and bugs, including "personal information concerning Marina Oswald's sexual desires and her sexual attraction" to one of her associates. (An FBI agent involved testified that the Bureau nicknamed Marina "hot pants.") However, Hoover didn't share the full report with the Warren Commission—he gave them only "pertinent information" by letter. The full report probably wound up in Hoover's "official and confidential" files, where he kept his most sensitive and scandalous information.[8]

In at least two other cases (probably more), the FBI tapped the phones of those involved in the JFK assassination investigation. One case involved a couple who were casual associates of Gilberto Policarpo Lopez, the Tampa suspect who went to Texas, Mexico City, then Cuba in late November 1963. If even casual associates of Lopez had their phones tapped, much closer associates of Lopez and Oswald were also likely being tapped.

In Marina's case, the FBI released memos about arranging the phone taps, but no transcripts; in contrast, transcripts of the Tampa couple were declassified, but not the memos about arranging the taps (or any authorization from Attorney General Kennedy). The Tampa transcripts were carbon copies that the Tampa FBI office transferred to the National Archives after the 1992 JFK Act, with the original transcripts going to FBI headquarters.[9]

In the interest of privacy, we won't name the couple involved. In general, the transcripts show the conversations of an intelligent left-wing couple and their friends about primarily mundane personal matters, but also about politics and the aftermath of JFK's death. They discuss how US officials had "pinned [JFK's death] on the Fair Play [for Cuba Committee] and communists, when they had no right to do so, and why didn't [US officials] say [Oswald] was a CIA man in the first place?" The FBI transcriber writes that "conversation continued re: Oswald being employed by the CIA."[10]

The FBI phone-tap transcripts start on December 5, 1963, and end on December 20, 1963. There is no indication that the FBI told the Warren Commission about them, since the Tampa threat had been withheld completely from the Commission. A stamp on the transcripts confirms CIA approval of their release and indicates that the CIA originally received copies, though the Agency never released or acknowledged any of those files.[11]

As for the CIA, it withheld from the Warren Commission, and probably from the FBI, its own bugging of the American safe houses near Washington, D.C., occupied by Cuban exiles such as Manuel Artime. Keeping in mind Artime's calls to and from Bobby Kennedy, it's likely that the CIA had phone taps on conversations involving the Attorney

General—surveillance that was not only illegal, but also certain to end Helms's career if Bobby or other US officials ever found out about it.[12]

The Warren Commission's investigative problems and failings have been amply documented over the years, most recently in Gerald D. McKnight's *Breach of Trust*, so we will focus on only a few important examples, involving organized crime, Bobby Kennedy, and the "magic bullet" theory.

Most writers have long assumed that Warren Commission counsel (now senator) Arlen Specter came up with the magic bullet theory, which holds that JFK's back wound, neck wound, and all of Governor Connally's injuries were caused by a single bullet that emerged in almost pristine condition, with very little visible damage, after shattering Connally's wrist bones and rib. However, Congressional investigators found that it was the main autopsy physician, Dr. Humes, who first "suggested both men could have been shot by one bullet."[13] Specter quickly embraced this theory because he needed it to account for all the wounds and avoid a conclusion of conspiracy. Since the Warren Commission claimed that Oswald fired only three shots, and one hit JFK in the head and one missed the limo entirely, either one "magic bullet" created all of the other wounds in JFK and Connally, or there had to have been more than one shooter.

Dr. Humes made his suggestion to Specter in early March 1964, and witnesses who clearly saw and heard shots from the grassy knoll were soon being pressured to change their testimony. We heard about that firsthand from JFK aide David Powers, who saw the shots from the knoll with fellow aide Kenneth O'Donnell, from their vantage point in the limo immediately behind JFK's. Both men told former Speaker of the House Tip O'Neill the same thing, as O'Neill recounted in his autobiography. O'Donnell, who was with Powers at the time, stated to O'Neill that he "told the FBI what I had heard, but they said it couldn't have happened that way and that I must have been imagining things. So I testified they way they wanted me to."[14]

When we interviewed Powers, he was head of the JFK Presidential Library, and said, "The Warren Commission was handed this theory on a [silver] platter, and anything that didn't conform with it, they just didn't take." Powers talked about how frustrated he was, trying to tell the truth while someone with the Warren Commission constantly interrupted him. Powers and O'Donnell were both interviewed on the same day, May 18, 1964, but while O'Donnell's testimony is printed in the usual transcript format, Powers' is represented only by a brief, tortuously worded affidavit. However, before they conformed to the official story, both Powers and O'Donnell did manage to get in brief indications of a shot from the knoll in front of them.[15]

As printed in the Warren Commission volumes, Powers's affidavit is unsigned by any witness and does not even bear the name of the official who oversaw its preparation. But the National Archives was able to locate the original copy for us, which shows that Arlen Specter prepared Powers's affidavit. Powers and O'Donnell's story leaked briefly in June 1975, when the *Chicago Tribune* reported that the two men were told they had to change their story "for the good of the country and global tranquillity."[16]

As for the magic bullet theory, many experts consider it physically impossible. A bullet from the Depository would have been coming down at a very steep angle, striking JFK's back almost six inches below the top of his collar. However, it exited from the hollow of JFK's throat, just below his Adam's apple, a higher position. For a bullet hitting JFK in the back to exit that high, JFK would had to have been leaning very far forward, at a thirty-degree angle, but films and photos clearly show that he hadn't leaned forward more than eleven degrees.

In addition, Connally's jump seat was actually lower than JFK's, so even if the bullet somehow managed to hit JFK's spine or some other bone (a scenario for which there is no evidence) and was deflected upward and out JFK's throat, it had to have magically changed course in midair and then dove down to hit Connally. That clearly didn't happen, since Connally can be seen in the Zapruder film holding his Stetson hat well after JFK has already been hit in the throat; Connally's wrist would have been shattered at that point if both men were hit by the same bullet.

The only way the "magic bullet" theory could be made palatable was if the back wound were changed into a back-of-the-neck wound. According to Josiah Thompson, the Warren Commission "staff let the autopsy doctor instruct a medical illustrator to raise the back wound from the back to the neck. Commission member US Rep. Gerald Ford then corrected a final draft of the panel's report to read 'neck wound' rather than 'back wound.'"[17]

Several Warren Commission staff members tried to do a thorough investigation, including delving into Jack Ruby's Mafia ties and Cuban gunrunning, but were stymied. As we mentioned earlier, the FBI intimidated several witnesses who tried to talk about Ruby's gunrunning, while FBI agents relied on Ruby's mob associates to say that Ruby had no mob associates. After the two Commission staffers investigating Ruby wrote a long memo to Rankin, outlining numerous problems and stonewalling by the FBI and by Richard Helms, they were barred from interviewing Ruby in Dallas.[18] The resulting interview by Earl Warren and Gerald Ford was marked by Ruby's saying, "Unless you get me to Washington, you can't get a fair shake out of me." Anthony Summers writes that "repeatedly, eight times in all, [Ruby] begged the Chief Justice of the US to arrange his transfer to Washington for further questioning and lie-detector tests." Warren and Ford refused, even when Ruby pleaded with them, saying, "Gentlemen, my life is in danger." Given Sheriff Decker's mob ties and Marcello's control of Dallas, Ruby's concerns were all too real.

The Warren Commission staff lost another important source of information when mob associates of Rosselli and Trafficante framed Chicago Secret Service agent Abraham Bolden. Based on information provided by two criminals he'd put in jail, Bolden was arrested on the day he went to Washington to tell Commission staff about the Secret Service's laxity, as well as the Chicago and Tampa attempts. One of Bolden's accusers worked for Sam DeStefano, a notorious associate of Richard Cain, the number-two man in the Cook County / Chicago sheriff's office. Richard Cain's brother, Michael, who detailed the declassified files on Richard in his book *Tangled Web*, says that Richard Cain had the "motive, means, and opportunity" to frame Bolden. Richard Cain was part of the Chicago Mafia, had worked with Rosselli and Trafficante on the CIA-Mafia plots, was an active CIA informant, and files show that he had infiltrated AMWORLD.

Abraham Bolden was sentenced to six years in prison, even though his main accuser later admitted to committing perjury in his testimony against Bolden. In addition, Bolden's judge was clearly biased against him, having told the jury that Bolden was guilty before their deliberations began. Even after that misconduct resulted in a mistrial, the same judge was allowed to conduct Bolden's second trial, which resulted in a conviction. Bolden has been fighting to clear his name ever since.

A Kennedy aide familiar with the JFK-Almeida coup plan told us that Bobby was aware of Bolden's plight, but couldn't do anything about it. The implication was that any interference by Bobby would have resulted in the exposure of the Chicago and Tampa attempts that he had kept secret. The resulting national uproar would have disclosed the reason for the secrecy—the JFK-Almeida coup plan—and put Commander Almeida at risk, potentially triggering a crisis with Cuba or Russia. Being unable to help Bolden no doubt only added to Bobby's pain and frustration.[19]

Bobby Kennedy, like so many others, also withheld important information from the Warren Commission. He avoided testifying by agreeing to provide a statement, which he agonized over for almost two months. It finally said that he "knew of no credible evidence to support the allegations that the assassination of President Kennedy was caused by a domestic or foreign conspiracy."[20] From a strictly legal standpoint, Bobby's statement was true, since he lacked hard evidence of the conspiracy involving the Mafia, Hoffa, and Cuban exiles, even though he strongly suspected them.

The Warren Commission investigation was essentially over by early June 1964. The original deadline for the staff to finish their reports was June 30, but after they complained, an angry Warren finally agreed to extend it to July 15. In the meantime, Bobby finally learned about CIA reports of the March 1964 Mafia plot to assassinate Fidel, and wanted an investigation, but his request went nowhere.[21]

Bobby was also focused on his political future. After deft political moves by LBJ ensured that the Democratic convention would not draft Bobby for vice president, Bobby decided to run for the Senate from his adopted home of New York. Two unusual things involving assassinations happened during Bobby's successful Senate run in the fall of 1964: ABC-TV journalist Lisa Howard, originally the spark for the peace attempts with Fidel Castro, turned against Bobby after learning he had been part of efforts to assassinate Fidel. In addition, Puerto Rican Teamster thug Frank Chavez made plans to kill Bobby, but Jimmy Hoffa apparently talked him out of it—for the time being. Three years later, Chavez would again try to assassinate Bobby.

Carlos Marcello, Johnny Rosselli, and Santo Trafficante saw their power and wealth continued to grow in 1964. Marcello was no doubt glad when Guy Banister died (of natural causes) in June 1964, even as the Warren Commission was trying to wrap up its work. Marcello hated blacks and civil rights, but when three young activists in Mississippi—James Chaney, Michael Schwerner, and Andrew Goodman—were killed by Klansmen in June 1964, J. Edgar Hoover reportedly had to turn to Mafioso Gregory Scarpa Sr. of the Columbo crime family to pressure one of the locals to reveal the location of the bodies.[22] Scarpa would have to get Marcello's permission to operate even briefly in Mississippi, but such assistance could only help Marcello maintain his good relationship with the local FBI.

Johnny Rosselli continued to be very successful in Las Vegas, especially since the massive crackdown Bobby had announced back in November 1963 had fizzled. Rosselli's status in Hollywood continued to increase, and he became a member of the prestigious Friars Club, an honor that would lead to major problems for him three years later.

Santo Trafficante likewise prospered, as did his part of the French Connection heroin pipeline. His henchman Herminio Diaz concentrated on his criminal and drug activity with Trafficante and wouldn't become involved in more plots against Castro until the following year. Trafficante's ties to exiles continued to pay off in intelligence, and in the summer of 1964 an exile FBI informant linked to members of Trafficante's organization once more got wind of the CIA's contacts with Rolando Cubela (AMLASH). Because the FBI didn't share this information with the CIA or the White House, the CIA remained unaware of how insecure its ongoing operation was.[23]

As Richard Helms continued to have Desmond FitzGerald meld parts of AMWORLD, AMLASH, and AMTRUNK together, both men were unaware of an even more serious breach of security that would help to doom their efforts. In September 1964, one of Fidel Castro's agents managed to infiltrate the security arm of Artime's organization. Unfortunately, Helms and FitzGerald were just beginning a major new push to topple Castro, but from that time forward, Fidel knew much of what Artime and the CIA were up to.[24]

Unaware of Castro's spy in Artime's group, Helms had FitzGerald forge ahead with their 1964 plots to topple Fidel. The very conservative Manuel Artime, and the liberal exile leaders Manolo Ray and Eloy Menoyo, found working together increasingly difficult. CIA files are full of their backbiting, insults, and complaints about one another. However, Ray and Menoyo were apparently willing to continue working with Artime because he got the lion's share of the CIA's funding and support. Artime worked with Ray because Ray had the connection to Rolando Cubela, an important fact left out of files that the CIA later provided to Congress. Without Almeida, Cubela appeared to be the only Cuban official willing to actively plot Fidel's elimination. The goal of Helms and FitzGerald (or of their subordinates E. Howard Hunt and David Atlee Phillips) seems to have been to get Artime and Cubela to meet face-to-face.

In late August 1964, two Cuban officials much higher than Cubela made it known to Artime's associates that they were willing to help with a coup in a limited capacity. In stark contrast to the risks Almeida had been willing to take the previous year, these two officials said they would "not conspire inside" Cuba because they were "afraid." Artime's case officer noted disdainfully that the two officials were willing only to "give information," and would "not try to assassinate [Fidel] themselves, because they are yellow."[25]

Even worse, the two officials had contacted an Artime associate who also worked with Santo Trafficante. Artime's case officer pointed out the Artime/Trafficante associate was "a walking security violation . . . he has already talked to too many people about his situation." However, to have any chance of succeeding, Cubela would need the help of other Cuban officials, so their names were kept in the mix. Also active in pursing this new avenue was Artime's second in command, Rafael "Chi Chi" Quintero, who was also in touch with Cubela.[26]

The CIA received sporadic reports of attempts or plots to kill Fidel in the fall of 1964. A plan involving Cubela, a Trafficante associate, and a Belgian rifle "equipped with a silencer" was called off. The Cuban who had been pushing for two years to have the CIA assassinate Fidel in the kitchen of his favorite restaurant (by hiding an assassin in the pantry) was finally arrested. One report described another attempt to assassinate Fidel, in which "one of his bodyguards was killed."[27] Even so, the CIA and exile plotting was still too unfocused to be effective.[28]

While Helms struggled to do something about Cuba, he was still fending off requests from the Warren Commission, which was trying to wrap up its work. The Commissioners had long missed their original deadline, but now LBJ was pressuring them to issue their final report well before election day. President Johnson faced the conservative Barry Goldwater, and while LBJ seemed to have a comfortable lead in the polls, he wanted to be sure that any doubts about JFK's assassination couldn't be used against him.

On September 15, Helms asked his deputy to write to Commission Counsel J. Lee Rankin, responding to a March 12 request for any information the CIA had about Jack Ruby. Helms himself had replied on June 8, saying the CIA had no information on Ruby. Given all of the reports about Ruby's trips to Cuba and his gunrunning, Rankin and his staff were appropriately skeptical and asked again, but Helms's deputy claimed the CIA had absolutely nothing on Ruby.[29]

Three days later, Helms himself admitted to Rankin that the CIA had received State Department documents about Oswald going back to November 1959, even though Helms had claimed earlier that the CIA had not opened its file on Oswald until 1960. But it was too late for Rankin to press Helms about the discrepancy, so Rankin let the matter drop.[30]

Helms still had not resolved the Nosenko situation, which left some of the Warren Commission members suspicious about possible Soviet involvement in JFK's murder. On September 7, 1964, Richard Russell, Sherman Cooper, and Hale Boggs went to Dallas to interview Marina Oswald again. Congressional investigators wrote that she "changed her story and altered testimony," which probably only added to the three Commission members' concern.[31]

Meanwhile, Warren Commission staffers and the FBI were under pressure to resolve the matter of Silvia Odio's visit from Oswald and two exiles a couple of months prior to JFK's murder. On September 16, the FBI apparently got a break. An anti-Castro soldier of fortune allegedly told "the FBI that he" and two friends "were the people who visited Sylvia Odio." The soldier of fortune knew Santo Trafficante and had been under house arrest with the mob boss in Cuba in 1959, before being asked to join the CIA-Mafia plots to kill Castro in the spring of 1963. The man's admission came just in time for the Warren Commission's last meeting, two days later.[32]

At that final meeting, three of the Commission members, led by Georgia senator Richard Russell, tried to include a dissenting opinion about the magic bullet theory. However, his effort failed, and the report was issued with no dissent. Over the next two days, the soldier of fortune changed his story and denied having visited Odio, as did his two friends, but it was too late to change the Commission's Final Report. [33] The Report was submitted to President Johnson on September 24, given to Hoover the following day, and released to the public on September 28, 1964. The press widely proclaimed the Warren Report, as it came to be known, to be the definitive account of Oswald's guilt as a lone assassin.[34]

In later years, four of the Commissioners (Russell, Boggs, Cooper, and McCloy) privately expressed doubts about the Report's conclusion. According to *Vanity Fair*, Richard Russell said he was "not completely satisfied in my own mind that he (Oswald) did plan and commit this act altogether on his own." Even though Louisiana congressman Boggs had his "political campaigns . . . heavily financed by Carlos Marcello," according to the head of the New Orleans Crime Commission, Boggs was one of the Commission's most skeptical members.[35]

Gerald Ford had expressed doubts privately to his fellow Commissioners, and he insisted on precise wording in the Report, saying the Commission had "found no evidence" of a conspiracy. But in public, Ford became the most vocal Commissioner proclaiming its accuracy. Ford wrote an article for *Life* magazine touting the report before its release, and declared "the monumental record of the President's Commission will stand like a Gibraltar of factual literature through the ages to come." He also wrote a book about the Commission, *Portrait of an Assassin*, that presented Oswald as a lone nut. Ford's public stance would impact his political career after he became president in 1974 (and ran for the office in 1976), since the release of any information that would undermine the Report's "lone assassin" conclusion would reflect badly on his judgment. In addition, Ford would later be less than truthful when testifying to Congress that he hadn't used classified files in writing his book about the Commission.[36]

Publicly, President Johnson embraced the Report's "lone assassin" conclusion, but "Johnson never believed that one person could have accomplished JFK's assassination," according to Joseph Califano, who left his position with Cyrus Vance to became one of LBJ's trusted aides. However, within three years, LBJ would broaden his suspicion, telling another aide that there was a "plot in connection with the assassination [and] the President felt that [the] CIA had something to do with this plot."[37]

Bobby Kennedy supported the Warren Report in his few, brief public comments on the subject, when students asked him about it during his 1964 Senate campaign. However, his friend Arthur Schlesinger Jr. said that in private, "Robert Kennedy had very serious reservations about the Warren Commission Report."[38] These reservations would only deepen in the months that followed, leading Bobby to initiate his own investigations into his brother's death.

Chapter Twenty-three

The American press's overwhelming support for the Warren Report in the fall of 1964 has been well documented. But far less known are the roles played by Richard Helms and E. Howard Hunt in shaping the media's coverage of the Warren Report, both in 1964 and in years to come. Even as Helms and Hunt continued their anti-Castro operations, their roles in dealing with the press and publishers have received surprisingly little attention over the years.

The mainstream press had several reasons to uncritically accept the Warren Report's conclusions, ranging from the distinguished nature of the Commission itself to the lack of counter-information easily available to the press in America. In those pre-Watergate days, the press often accepted government pronouncements at face value. Former FBI agent William Turner explained why even liberal and progressive media, more often skeptical of official explanations, generally defended the Report at the time and for years (sometimes even decades) afterward. When the Warren Report was released, the ultra-conservative John Birch Society and other far-right elements were pushing for Earl Warren's impeachment, due to his support for civil rights. For liberal publications to say anything bad about Warren's Commission would be like giving support to the Birchers.

Despite those factors, one might have expected to see some skeptical stories in the US mainstream press, but there were almost none. One often overlooked factor in the Report's almost universal acceptance by the American media was the CIA—Richard Helms and E. Howard Hunt in particular. Both Helms and Hunt played behind-the-scenes roles with the press and publishers during 1964 and afterward, and that likely applied to the reporting of matters relating to the CIA, Cuban exiles, and JFK's assassination. Helms used Hunt in two related roles—Cuban operations, and dealing with publishers and the press—during 1964 and for several years afterward. Hunt's background made him well qualified to take action if any word started to leak about covert CIA operations,

from the Cubela plot to the CIA-Mafia plots to any hint of US involvement with Almeida or his family.[1]

It's important to put in context the work Hunt, Helms, and their CIA
associates did with the media, since it not only impacted the press's and
the public's initial reaction to the Warren Report, but also influenced
coverage of JFK's assassination and related events for years to come—
especially when a wave of critical articles and books finally started
to appear in late 1966. By that time, the CIA's effort to manage press
coverage about JFK's assassination and the Warren Report would be
so extensive that Helms would have a fifty-three-page memo issued
detailing how CIA officials should bolster the "lone nut" theory in the
press.[2] No CIA press files from 1964 about the Warren Report have been
declassified, but a brief review of the facts—including a documented
CIA attempt to suppress a 1964 book about its covert operations—
provides insights into what Helms, Hunt, and other CIA officials were
likely doing.

Richard Helms didn't begin the CIA's manipulation of the press
in America, which started long before he became its Director. But he
did perfect and apply those techniques not only while he headed the
Agency, but even decades after he left it, as he rebuilt his own legacy
and prevented journalists from digging too deeply into his unauthorized 1963 Cuban operations. Helms's exceptional abilities in this regard
were partly a product of his own background as a reporter for UPI in the
1930s, when his one notable achievement was scoring a meeting with
German dictator Adolf Hitler.

Helms had seen how the power of the press could be used to help
the CIA achieve its goals, as it did in Guatemala in 1954, when Hunt,
Morales, and former newspaper publisher David Atlee Phillips were
essentially able to stage a coup via the press, with what some claim
were only a few hundred casualties. However, Helms had also seen the
press go on the attack, as in the aftermath of the Bay of Pigs disaster.
Though Helms had kept his distance from both of those operations, he
seemed determined to have the press on his side, and he was largely
successful.

Much of what we know today about the press and the CIA in the
1960s comes from the Senate Church Committee hearings of the mid-
1970s and a lengthy follow-up article by Carl Bernstein, which detailed
extensive information that then–CIA Director George H. W. Bush withheld from the Committee. For example, the Church Committee was able
to uncover that "the CIA maintained covert relationships with about 50

American journalists or employees of US media organizations" from the 1960s to the mid-1970s. However, Bernstein was able to document that there were actually "400 journalists who maintained covert relationships with the Agency." Bernstein writes that even that figure "refers only to those who were 'tasked' in their undercover assignments or had a mutual understanding that they would help the Agency or were subject to some form of CIA contractual control. It does not include even larger numbers of journalists who occasionally traded favors with CIA officers in the normal give-and-take that exists between reporters and their sources." In E. Howard Hunt's final autobiography, published after his death, Hunt confirmed Bernstein's much higher figures and the other information in his article.[3]

Bernstein found that "the CIA in the 1950s, '60s, and even early '70s had concentrated its relationships with journalists in the most prominent sectors of the American press corps, including four or five of the largest newspapers in the country, the broadcast networks, and the two major newsweekly magazines." One CIA official told Bernstein that the CIA's "files contained descriptions of about half a dozen reporters and correspondents who would be considered 'famous'—that is, their names would be recognized by most Americans."[4]

The Church Committee was able to uncover approximately twenty-five journalists employed by American firms who had "paid relationships" with the CIA. The Agency's practice of paying journalists (or, as Bernstein points out, placing active CIA employees in private media firms) persisted until well after Hunt and Helms had left the CIA. It would not be banned until 1976, and even then, CIA Director George H. W. Bush left key loopholes in place. However, then, as now, most journalists cooperated with the CIA not for money, but to obtain information, advance their careers, or out of patriotism.[5]

The Church Committee found that American journalists were just part of a "network of several hundred foreign individuals around the world who provide intelligence for the CIA and . . . attempt to influence foreign opinion through the use of covert propaganda." However, information that was spread to other countries sometimes found its way back to the US, apparently intentionally. As one CIA official told the Church Committee, "If you plant an article in some paper overseas," it could easily "be picked up and published by the Associated Press in this country." As Desmond FitzGerald stated in a CIA memo, that situation was "inevitable and consequently permissible." That meant CIA-backed stories attacking Warren Commission critics could be planted overseas, then picked up by US publications, and we will shortly detail one such example.[6]

Helms and the CIA sometimes didn't bother with such a circuitous route, since they could go directly to the highest reaches of the American media to get what they wanted. The Church Committee found that "not only journalists but even some of America's top editors, publishers, and network presidents regularly cooperated with the CIA in promoting or suppressing certain information." Bernstein named many of them, including the publishers of most of America's top news magazines and newspapers. In addition to confirming Bernstein's list, E. Howard Hunt later wrote that he "worked with some of these organizations" while he was a CIA official, a fact that was often overlooked in the wake of Watergate.[7]

Bernstein was able to cite an interesting source, who detailed how some CIA media assets were recruited. He writes that:

David Atlee Phillips . . . a former journalist himself, estimated in an interview that at least 200 journalists signed secrecy agreements or employment contracts with the Agency in the past twenty-five years. Phillips, who owned a small English-language newspaper in Santiago, Chile, when he was recruited by the CIA in 1950, described the approach: "Somebody from the Agency says, 'I want you to help me. I know you are a true-blue American, but I want you to sign a piece of paper before I tell you what it's about.' I didn't hesitate to sign, and a lot of newsmen didn't hesitate over the next twenty years."[8]

The CIA refused to tell the senators on the Church Committee "the names of its media agents or the names of the media organizations with which they are connected," and would instead provide only nameless "summaries of their . . . work with the CIA."[9] According to Bernstein, CIA Director Bush (acting for President Gerald Ford) ordered "the names of journalists and of the news organizations with which they were affiliated . . . omitted from the summaries."[10]

In the intervening thirty-three years, the names of a few journalists who were CIA assets have slipped out in declassified files. Ironically, one such journalist was Tad Szulc, who assisted the CIA with the AMTRUNK anti-Castro operation but seemed to specialize in exposing information the CIA didn't want to see printed. That may be why the CIA eventually allowed Szulc's name to be released, while still protecting others. By the fall of 1964, Szulc was no longer working on covert Cuban operations, as he had been when JFK was President. However, as Szulc would later report, E. Howard Hunt was still involved in the plots to assassinate Fidel Castro in 1964 and into 1965.

E. Howard Hunt's deep-cover role in working with Manuel Artime and the aftermath of the Almeida operation was linked to Hunt's little-known, more overt CIA role of working with publishers and the press. Hunt was one of the few CIA officials who testified with much specificity to the Church Committee about his actions in the 1960s with the press and publishers. Because of Hunt's Watergate conviction, the Church Committee had leverage over him that it lacked over other current and former CIA officials. Hunt later wrote that the Committee "identified me as an important figure in the [CIA's press] operation, pointing out [that] one of my ongoing responsibilities [was] to get certain books reviewed by particular writers who would be either sympathetic or hostile to works we hoped to popularize or suppress."

Though Hunt claimed, "Much of what I worked on [in the 1960s] was exposed in revelations [by the] Senate investigation in 1975," the CIA and Hunt actually withheld much information about his activities from the Committee. This included Hunt's work on the JFK-Almeida coup plan and with Artime on the Cubela plot to assassinate Castro. However, by combining Hunt's testimony with information from declassified files and the few revelations he included in his most recent autobiography, we can gain new insights into his and the CIA's activities during the mid- and late 1960s. These activities set the pattern for Hunt's role in Watergate, which stemmed from his work on AMWORLD and Helms's unauthorized plots to kill Castro.[11]

Once the Watergate investigations began, Helms ordered a CIA official to claim that Hunt had no role in Cuban matters after he withdrew from the Bay of Pigs operation, because he refused to work with exile leader Manolo Ray. As Harry Williams and other Kennedy associates, including Tad Szulc, confirmed, Hunt did continue to work on sensitive Cuban operations. However, because of Hunt's role in planning the Bay of Pigs fiasco, and his well-known antipathy toward the Kennedy-favored Ray, Hunt's role in Cuban operations was on a highly covert, "need to know" basis, even within the Agency.

Hunt's official position in 1963, and his cover for his Cuba work, was as the "Chief of Covert Action [for the CIA's] Domestic Operations Division." Hunt was an experienced writer and had helped former CIA Director Allen Dulles write his book *The Craft of Intelligence*. Hunt admits, "Most of my work involved publishing and publications, in which we supported an entire division of [one publisher] and subsidized books that we felt the American public should read." Hunt acknowledges that the CIA "also ran a couple of national newswire services and even published a popular series of travel books."[12]

Hunt's dealings with the press and publishers were useful for Richard Helms, because they allowed Hunt to monitor and potentially control leaks in the press about the JFK-Almeida coup plan, as well as about Helms's unauthorized Castro assassination operations. According to Carl Bernstein, CIA Director John McCone said that he was out of the loop regarding the CIA's extensive use of the press in operations and disseminating propaganda. McCone said he knew "nothing about any arrangements for cover the CIA might have made with media organizations [since] 'Helms would have handled anything like that.'" Bernstein points out that during "the Church Committee hearings, McCone testified that his subordinates failed to tell him about domestic surveillance activities or that they were working on plans to assassinate Fidel Castro."[13]

The vast majority of Hunt's CIA files from 1963 onward have never been released, and most were withheld from Congress. However, his position shows that he would have been involved in one high-profile attempt by Helms and the CIA to quash what they considered damaging information. The impending publication, in 1964, of *The Invisible Government*, by journalists David Wise and Thomas B. Ross, would have alarmed the CIA in general, but Helms and Hunt in particular. The book was the first objective look at the CIA that delved into topics like the CIA's 1954 coup against the president of Guatemala. It covered the Bay of Pigs operation extensively, including the roles of Manuel Artime, Tony Varona, Manolo Ray, and especially the Hunt-created Cuban Revolutionary Council. The book noted the training of some Cuban exiles in Louisiana, and even detailed the efforts of JFK's personal emissary to free three CIA agents from a Cuban prison in April 1963.

The Invisible Government covered too many sensitive subjects at a time when the Warren Commission had not yet issued its report. Helms had successfully kept the Warren Commission from questioning or investigating Artime, Ray, or Varona, or delving into the New Orleans branch of the Cuban Revolutionary Council that involved David Ferrie, so he would not have wanted a book drawing attention to those matters.

According to noted historian Thomas Powers, the CIA persuaded *Time* magazine's "bureau chief in Washington to" kill a cover story on *The Invisible Government*. According to one report, the CIA actually considered purchasing all copies of the book, until it realized that would simply cause the publisher to release a second printing. The book was published, but the CIA was able to suppress some of its publicity. The CIA's effort in 1964 set a pattern for what would happen in 1966, after the mainstream press finally started to question the Warren Report.[14]

In the fall of 1964, Bantam Books rushed more than a million copies of its paperback version of the Warren Report into print just after its release, while two books criticizing the "lone nut" theory of JFK's assassination were available only in small quantities from tiny publishers.[15] Both were of concern to the CIA, one in particular. The first critical book about the JFK assassination, Thomas Buchanan's *Who Killed Kennedy?*, was published in the US in 1964 after its British release, but it contained mainly speculation based on newspaper reports. The next critical book, *Oswald: Assassin or Fall Guy*, by Joachim Joesten, a left-wing European journalist and concentration-camp survivor, was of more concern to the CIA because Joesten had included an entire chapter entitled "Oswald and the CIA." It said Oswald may have been involved with US intelligence because the fact "that in the McCarthy era a young private in the Marines could study Marxism, learn Russian, and read Soviet newspapers without any adverse repercussions is a little too much for even the most naive person to accept." Joesten's book was quickly updated with an additional critique of the Warren Report that set the pattern for many books to come, by using information in the Report and its twenty-six supporting volumes to attack the Report's own "lone nut" conclusion.[16]

Both Joesten's and Buchanan's books first appeared in Europe, so the CIA and Helms could justify their actions because the books might negatively influence foreign opinion. The CIA even dug up Nazi files to use against Joesten, foreshadowing the more extensive efforts Helms and the CIA would launch against Warren Report critics just two years later.

In addition to his work with publishers and the press, E. Howard Hunt continued to work on Cuban operations in 1964. Hunt's long-standing experience with coups, starting with overthrowing the Guatemalan president in 1954, made him valuable to Helms. After that successful coup, Hunt tried to help foment a 1959 CIA coup in Uruguay, where Hunt was Chief of Station. However, Hunt angered the US ambassador and had to be reassigned. Hunt was made an early leader of the CIA's anti-Castro operations and became one of the first to press for Fidel's assassination.

Hunt worked extensively with Tony Varona, Manuel Artime, and other exile leaders on what became the Bay of Pigs operation. Hunt likely knew about, and may have played a part in, the CIA-Mafia plots, prior to the invasion. Shortly after Hunt's abrupt withdrawal over Manolo Ray, a never explained, last-minute miscommunication between the CIA and Tony Varona caused the CIA-Mafia assassination plot to fail just before the invasion, ensuring its defeat. The CIA has never acknowledged that Hunt had any role in the CIA-Mafia plots, but the same was also true for his best friend, Manuel Artime—until a CIA memo slipped through showing Artime was involved. Only weeks after the Bay of Pigs, Dominican dictator Trujillo's security chief alleged that Hunt had visited that country with Johnny Rosselli, just before CIA-backed plotters assassinated Trujillo. In addition, two of Hunt's associates—Barker and Varona—were working for Trafficante during the CIA-Mafia plots.[17]

Hunt's experience with Cuban operations and coups led Helms and FitzGerald to assign Hunt to work with Harry Williams on the JFK-Almeida coup plan. The CIA claims that Hunt didn't officially have a role with Artime, though the Agency admits that the two close friends remained in contact. However, Hunt's work with Almeida and several Artime associates make it almost certain that Hunt did have a covert role with Artime, possibly involving Artime's work in the CIA-Mafia plots.

After President Johnson scaled back Cuban operations in 1964, Hunt seems to have continued those roles. Hunt likely maintained a role in providing CIA support for Almeida's family, but with Almeida himself no longer actively involved in the coup plan, the focus shifted to Cubela. As noted earlier, the CIA's goal was to persuade Cubela and Artime to work together, and Spain was one of the key countries where those meetings could take place. According to Tad Szulc, after JFK's death, Helms had tried to appoint Hunt as the CIA's Deputy Chief of Station in Madrid. However, the US ambassador at that time was the same one Hunt had clashed with in Uruguay in 1959, and, in a rare move, he vetoed Hunt's appointment.[18] That meant that Hunt's role with Artime in Spain would have to be under very deep cover, which would set a pattern that Hunt would repeat during Watergate.

After almost a year of pain, the fall of 1964 brought good news for Bobby Kennedy. A month before Bobby's September 2, 1964, resignation as Attorney General to run for the Senate, Bobby heard that a key juror in the November 1963 Marcello trial had been bribed. Marcello initially refused to pay the juror he had arranged to bribe, since it would be suspicious if a leading juror suddenly had lots of money just after acquitting the godfather. After Marcello eventually paid the juror only $1,000 instead of a promised $25,000, the man went to the authorities. Shortly after that, the US Attorney in New Orleans learned that Marcello "had threatened to kill" the government's main witness during the same trial.

Bobby had left the Justice Department in the hands of his trusted deputy, Nicholas Katzenbach, who announced on October 6, 1964, that Carlos Marcello had been indicted for a conspiracy and obstruction of justice, including "seeking the murder of a government witness."[19] Four weeks later, Bobby won his race to become a New York senator. The first anniversary of JFK's death was no doubt full of anguish for Bobby, but it looked as if he might be able to find at least some measure of justice in the future.

Just over a year after JFK's murder, on November 30, 1964, the heroin network Carlos Marcello shared with Santo Trafficante and Michel Victor Mertz experienced a rare and very unusual setback. One of Mertz's trusted couriers had parked a Citroen car, loaded with heroin in hidden compartments, on the street near Mertz's townhouse on Boulevard Suchet in Paris. Mertz had lived well since JFK's murder, and this was one of the finer districts of Paris, home to the Duke and Duchess of Windsor. Since the car was filled with a million dollars' worth of heroin (street value), the courier was careful to disconnect the spark-plug leads and take the car's distributor cap with him, to make sure nothing happened to it overnight. The following day, the automobile would begin its journey to America, crossing the Atlantic on an ocean liner, as depicted in the classic book and film *The French Connection*. Mertz's other routes involved transport ships, or riskier border crossings into the US from Canada or Mexico.[20]

Mertz's Paris courier was stunned the next morning to find that Mertz's heroin-laden car had vanished. The street had been lined with cars, some more expensive than the Citroen, and thus more attractive to an ordinary thief. In addition, someone had gone to extra trouble to steal a car whose engine wouldn't start because of its missing distributor cap. Mertz's car had clearly been targeted, but by whom? The missing heroin never turned up, since French heroin distributors—like American law enforcement—were able to distinguish the output of the different French heroin labs. Mertz's deadly reputation in the French underworld was such that anyone familiar with his heroin network would know that stealing Mertz's heroin was tantamount to a death sentence. There were no warring factions in the French heroin trade at that time—Mertz and his allies reigned supreme. Mertz was also known for his ties to French Intelligence, which were yet another reason criminals in France didn't challenge him.[21]

Only weeks before the unusual theft of Mertz's heroin, CIA Director John McCone had shown a sudden interest in European assassin recruiter QJWIN, the former agent with so many parallels to Mertz. QJWIN had been paid through the Paris CIA station, and McCone requested they provide a "roundup of QJWIN Project and activities . . . and any knowledge you have of him" since his termination in April 1964 (after the CIA learned that Mertz had been deported from Dallas after JFK's assassination). McCone's October 1964 inquiry about QJWIN was sent within days of Mertz's obtaining a new US visa in Brussels, Belgium, where QJWIN had been living. However, for some reason, McCone quickly changed his mind and cabled Europe to "please destroy" his original request.[22] It might be relevant that one of Harry Williams's CIA contacts—a man who Harry felt was honest and tried to do the right thing—had been stationed in Europe just prior to his work on the JFK-Almeida coup plan, and was back in Europe at that time. Had McCone, Helms, or that CIA official learned that Mertz had been part of JFK's assassination, possibly through the QJWIN operation or the CIA's efforts to assassinate Castro?

Whether coincidental or not, Mertz's loss of a million dollars' worth of heroin just after the anniversary of his deportation from Dallas and JFK's murder was certainly poetic justice. It also put a brief dent in Trafficante and Marcello's heroin network, though it was only a foretaste of the disruption the two godfathers and Mertz would face the following year.

Chapter Twenty-four

By December 1964, Richard Helms, Desmond FitzGerald, David Atlee Phillips, and E. Howard Hunt were close to having their own coup plan, this time under the complete control of the CIA and not the Kennedys. By combining some of the remnants of JFK's original coup plan (Manolo Ray, Eloy Menoyo) with Artime's AMWORLD, AMTRUNK, and especially AMLASH (Rolando Cubela), they hoped to have a viable operation without the participation of Almeida, Harry Williams, or Bobby. The CIA officials also lacked the full support of President Johnson and even their own Director, John McCone, neither of whom was fully informed about the new scheme. But the ensuing actions of Artime, Menoyo, Cubela, and Che Guevara would soon result in three of the four losing their freedom, and would bring an end to massive US support for covert anti-Castro paramilitary operations.

While on a highly publicized trip to the UN in New York, Che Guevara had a private meeting on December 13, 1964, with *New York Times* journalist Tad Szulc, who had helped to originate the AMTRUNK operation. That was followed by Che's private meeting with former ABC newscaster Lisa Howard, who had lost her network job because of her outspoken opposition to Bobby Kennedy's Senate run. Lisa Howard had been frustrated in her efforts to get LBJ to continue JFK's attempts at secret peace negotiations, so she had arranged for Senator Eugene McCarthy to meet with Che at her apartment. However, a long-secret report about the meeting shows that McCarthy was clueless about what he was supposed to do with Che. After that meeting, Che left New York for an extended three-month trip overseas—and when Che returned to Cuba in March, he would be put under house arrest.[1]

On December 23, 1964, five days after Che left New York, CIA files say exile leader Eloy Menoyo was preparing to slip into Cuba, as part of a "[Castro] assassination plot." At the time, Menoyo was still working closely with Antonio Veciana, who Congressional investigators believe was carrying out the orders of David Atlee Phillips. Less than two weeks later, in early January, Fidel's forces captured Menoyo inside Cuba and charged him with conspiring "to kill Castro."[2]

In late December 1964, while Menoyo was getting ready for his mission into Cuba, Manuel Artime finally met in Spain with Rolando Cubela, officially merging the AMLASH operation with what was left of AMWORLD. They had two meetings, the last on December 30, 1964. Officially, Artime was being supervised by Henry Heckscher and another case officer, but Tad Szulc later wrote that Artime's good friends Barker and Hunt were also involved with the Cubela plot at that time. CIA files confirm that Artime's deputy, "Chi Chi" Quintero, was fully knowledgeable about the new joint operation. At Artime's second meeting with Cubela they discussed an array of Cuban officials who Cubela thought might help stage a coup, or support one after they had eliminated Fidel. It's clear from the notes of their talk that Almeida was not actively plotting with Cubela, and Cubela didn't realize that Almeida had been ready to lead a coup the previous year.

Artime later told a CIA associate that Cubela was incapable of leading a coup himself, so Helms and FitzGerald may have hoped that Almeida would join their plan at some point. The CIA had some leverage over Almeida, since his family was still outside Cuba and under covert CIA support and surveillance, likely with the assistance of Hunt, who had helped to arrange their original exit from Cuba. If the CIA needed to convince Almeida to support or participate in a coup, they could have threatened to reveal Almeida's work for JFK unless he cooperated. But the situation never reached that point, and Almeida never joined the new plots, a fact that allowed him to escape the fates of Che, Menoyo, and others. Besides, Almeida's own position and power had eroded over the past year, as had those of every high-ranking Cuban official except for Fidel and his brother Raul. Even if Almeida had wanted to stage a coup, it would have been far more difficult and risky by 1965 than it would have been under JFK.[3]

In early 1965, the CIA's support for Artime's camps in Central America was still a multimillion-dollar effort that CIA Miami Chief Ted Shackley described as "a fantastically large operation involving lots of people [and] substantial amounts of money." It was also incredibly insecure, since Castro's agent in Artime's security force and several of Trafficante's men like Barker knew much that was going on. Artime was friends with Trafficante operative Frank Fiorini, who gave the exile leader a powerful Magnum rifle with Artime's CIA code name engraved on it. The inscription called Artime "leader of [the] revolution" and was followed by Fiorini's name.[4]

In February 1965, Bernard Barker reported to the CIA that the "high-powered .300 Magnum rifle with telescopic lens that" Fiorini had given to Artime had been stolen from Artime's Miami home, along with "jewelry [and] documents." This security breach was coupled with CIA and FBI reports of two other Trafficante associates who knew about Artime's meetings with Cubela. One Trafficante associate tried to link Almeida's name to the Artime/Cubela plot, but it's clear from other files this wasn't true. The bottom line was that Trafficante was still in position to use Artime's covert work to achieve his own ends.[5]

Artime's initial plans with Cubela were not unrealistic. While Cubela had no real power in Cuba, he still owned his Varadero beach house near Fidel's seaside retreat, so a CIA memo discussed killing Castro "when he goes to Varadero." Cubela gave Artime "the details and exact locations where Fidel spends every Saturday and Sunday . . . at Varadero."[6] However, Artime and his deputy Quintero soon expanded the plans to grandiose proportions, envisioning a huge operation that involved not just assassinating Fidel at Varadero, but also having exile commandos storm ashore at the same moment to take the entire Cuban cabinet hostage. It was all slated for Cuba's annual July 26 holiday, and Artime made no provisions for dealing with the heavy Cuban security that always accompanied official celebrations. The plans were so over the top that they give credence to allegations that Artime was now simply milking the CIA for all he could get. From Central America came other reports of Artime's lavish lifestyle, huge sums spent on drinking and other recreational pursuits, profiteering, and outright theft.[7]

By this time, Artime was also reportedly getting involved in the drug trade.[8] Artime's activity paralleled what happened two decades later with some of Artime's associates like Quintero during Iran-Contra, when Congressional investigators and eventually the CIA's own Inspector General found that some CIA-backed Cuban exiles were involved with drug smugglers. The temptations were the same in 1965 as in 1985: When you have US intelligence assets and material covertly going back and forth between the US and Central America, the potential for transporting drugs is obvious. What investigators didn't realize in the 1980s and '90s was that some of Artime's men were not succumbing to a new temptation, but were continuing a pattern that had begun by 1965. According to some evidence, it had never really stopped, and continued into the 1970s and beyond, aided by associates of Artime and Santo Trafficante.[9]

In 1965, people working for Trafficante (or Fidel Castro) weren't the only ones able to develop contacts inside Artime's supposedly covert operation. Richard Helms was no doubt livid when he saw a January 25, 1965, article in the *Nation* that gave an all-too-accurate description of Artime's operation. Written by the *Miami Herald*'s Al Burt, the story even evoked aspects of the JFK-Almeida coup plan when it said that Artime's operation in Central America hoped "a coup could be engendered inside Cuba [and] that Castro might be assassinated." Burt even pointed out that JFK's November 18, 1963, Miami speech was "obviously intended for Cubans inside Cuba" who were part of Artime's operation. Official US support for Artime was documented when Burt detailed secret monetary transactions, including one for "$167,784 in a plain white envelope . . . issued on November 19, 1963" for Artime to buy "two World War II torpedo boats." These could have been used to get Artime into Cuba after the coup.

That publicity, the reported problems with Artime, and the insecurity of Cubela's involvement proved too much for Helms, and he began the gradual process of shutting down Artime's operation. Helms probably hoped that as long as Almeida was still in place and unexposed, the Cuban Commander might be willing to help the US at some point in the future.

On March 15, 1965, Che returned to Cuba from his three-month sojourn abroad, his first time back on the island since his secret meetings in New York with Szulc, Howard, and McCarthy. Che was reportedly placed under house arrest; some accounts even said that Che had been executed. It's not hard to see why Fidel would have been suspicious of Che, given Menoyo's capture on his assassination mission just after Guevara's unusual meetings in New York, plus the information from Fidel's undercover agent about Artime's meetings with Cubela to plan a coup.[10]

Unlike in late November 1963, this time Che Guevara would not return quickly to the limelight—instead, he would never be seen in public in Cuba again. Che wrote what was essentially his last will and testament, giving away all of his possessions and renouncing his government posts and power. Fidel Castro promised Che that the document would be read only after his death. Che was then exiled to Africa, as part of a doomed effort to aid rebels in the Congo who faced overwhelming odds. When Che was at his lowest point in Africa, Fidel staged a huge ceremony in Havana, and with Che's wife dressed in black sharing the stage, Fidel read Che's final statement. Rumors of Che's death were again rampant, and Che's compatriots say he was crushed when he heard of Fidel's betrayal. Che eventually returned to Cuba, but was kept away from the public until he left for his final exile to Bolivia, where he would meet his death in the fall of 1967 amidst Artime's AMWORLD associates.[11]

In 1965, as Harry Williams was readjusting to a normal life as a family man and mining engineer, he had an unexpected encounter with E. Howard Hunt, Manuel Artime, and Bernard Barker. Harry still occasionally saw or spoke with Bobby Kennedy, but he stayed away from anti-Castro activities, even though he was still revered by many exiles. Harry still avoided joining any of the exile groups, which helped him evade the infighting that plagued the exile community and would soon become explosive. But when Harry dropped by an exile's house in 1965 on an impromptu social visit, he found himself in the middle of a potentially deadly situation.

Harry's host welcomed him, believing Harry was there for a small meeting that was just starting. In the living room, Harry saw several AMWORLD veterans, including Hunt, Artime, and two exiles. Also present was Barker, whom Harry had learned was working for Trafficante. The men were getting ready to sell off the arms and equipment from Artime's huge program, which was being shut down. Harry told us in a later interview that he hadn't known anything about their plan, and that he advised them not to sell the armaments. He argued that the arms should be kept secure, in case the situation in Cuba changed and the weaponry was needed again.

Hunt, Artime, and the others wouldn't listen, because they wanted to keep all the money for themselves. They offered to cut Harry in for a share, but he declined. After that, the attitude of the men, except for Harry's friend, turned menacing. The situation was very tense as Harry excused himself, to leave. Harry told us that he felt glad to make it out the door alive. The arms and equipment were sold off, possibly through Bernard Barker's connections to Trafficante. Harry had also learned that both men were involved in JFK's assassination.[12]

CIA files say the total amount spent on AMWORLD was just over $7 million (over $35 million in today's dollars), though one former CIA official told *Newsweek* editor Evan Thomas that the total was $50 million.[13] Even if much of the material was sold or fenced for pennies on the dollar, that still would have been a substantial sum for Hunt, Artime, and the others. As detailed in Chapter 27, journalists have observed that by the following year, Hunt and his family appeared to be living well beyond the means of an ordinary CIA officer. Hunt ascribed his lavish lifestyle to money from his hack spy novels, but they never sold that well.

Helms or FitzGerald may have ordered Hunt to help liquidate the AMWORLD supplies, though it's unclear whether Helms knew that his protégé Hunt was pocketing some of the money. Helms might have felt that it was better for Hunt to dispose of the material quietly, rather than doing it openly, in a way that might reveal the CIA's massive support for Artime. If the Mafia were involved in selling the material, that might not have concerned Helms, since memos show that the CIA had considered using the Mafia as a cover for providing supplies to Artime the previous year. Plus, Artime had been part of the CIA-Mafia plots, so he already had a connection to the mob. Even if Helms knew that Artime and some of his associates were pocketing the money, Helms might have seen it as an appropriate reward, both for Artime's years of service to the CIA (including a year and a half in Cuban prisons after the Bay of Pigs) and to keep Artime from publicly protesting the US shutdown of his operation. It might also have been a type of hush money, to ensure that Artime didn't expose Helms's unauthorized operations to the press, or Congress.

Richard Helms would have wanted to keep the shutdown of Artime's operation as quiet as possible so that it wouldn't interfere with his own rising career. Helms was promoted to Deputy Director of the CIA on April 28, 1965. LBJ had grown tired of John McCone, who differed with him over Vietnam, so LBJ appointed Vice Admiral William Raborn Jr. as the CIA's new Director. Since US law mandates that either the number-one or number-two CIA official has to be a civilian, Helms was a logical choice to take the number-two slot. Helms's promotion was popular at the CIA, unlike the selection of Raborn, whose military style was resented by some in the Agency.

When McCone left the Agency, Bobby lost one of his better pipelines into the CIA; while not friends, he and McCone were cordial, and McCone kept Bobby up to date at times. Without McCone, Bobby had to depend on Desmond FitzGerald to keep him informed. Though they knew each other socially and played tennis, Bobby didn't realize that FitzGerald had been withholding important information from him since early 1963, including Rosselli's continuing work for the CIA and FitzGerald's Paris trip to meet Cubela while posing as Bobby's personal representative. As for Helms, he was civil to Bobby, but he felt an under-current of resentment that stemmed from the pressure Bobby had put on him regarding Cuba.

After Richard Helms was promoted, Desmond FitzGerald took Helms's old position as Deputy Director for Plans. These changes allowed them to continue concealing their unauthorized 1963 opera-tions, even as they started to scale back their anti-Castro programs. They had a relatively free hand because—in a reversal of JFK's policy—the CIA had primary control of all Cuban operations, while the US military and the DIA had only scattered exile assets.

Even though several high-profile Congressional committees inves-tigated E. Howard Hunt, numerous gaps and inconsistencies exist in Hunt's CIA records and in his testimony covering his service from 1963 until his supposed retirement in 1970. Both the CIA and Hunt admit that he and his family moved to Spain in 1965, though in testimony he was unusually vague about the year when such a major move had occurred (perhaps because he had traveled frequently to Spain before the move). According to Tad Szulc, E. Howard Hunt remained active in Cuban operations in 1965 with Cubela and Artime, even as most operations wound down. Buttressing Szulc's claim is the fact that Hunt later admit-ted that when the House Select Committee on Assassinations "asked for information about my work in Spain, the CIA told the Assassination Committee that there was none available, classified or not."[14] Likewise, the official reason given for Hunt's move to Spain is clearly a cover story, since—as noted earlier—he couldn't be officially assigned there.

CIA files confirm that Helms had Hunt technically resign from the CIA, while Hunt actually remained on the CIA's payroll, leaving Hunt free to pursue his assignment in Spain under deep cover. Some authors have pointed out that Hunt would do essentially the same thing several years later, when he would apparently resign from the CIA two years before Watergate. Hunt testified that his work in Spain was supervised directly by Helms's deputy. Near the end of his life, all Hunt would say about his activities in Spain was that he was working to develop "confidential relationships with influential Spaniards who would some day succeed Generalissimo Francisco Franco," the dictator who, with Adolf Hitler's backing, had taken control of Spain in the 1930s. If that was part of Hunt's assignment in Spain, it echoes not only what Hunt was doing at the time with Artime and Cubela regarding Castro, but also what Hunt had been doing previously with Harry Williams and Commander Almeida. Hunt's work in Spain may also have involved the CIA's ongoing support for Almeida's wife and children—though all of those files are still withheld, one of Almeida's sons later became a successful businessman in Madrid.[15]

Manolo Ray's group, JURE, fell apart over the course of 1965. Ray had been in touch with Cubela, since they had known each other previously in Cuba and were much closer politically than either man was with the extremely conservative Artime. However, Ray's men, including Luis Posada, grew increasingly frustrated over Ray's lack of progress, and Ray was apparently too cautious to tell them about Cubela. After JURE disintegrated, Ray returned to private life and Posada appears to have joined the RECE exile group.[16]

Some investigators, like Gaeton Fonzi, feel that Helms had a few CIA officers maintain a deep-cover relationship with certain exiles for covert operations, even after many exile assets started being phased out in 1965. That way, the CIA had deniable assets to use against Cuba, but the CIA's role was so well hidden that the Agency wouldn't be blamed if the exiles were captured or suffered a spectacular failure. Among those who continued to be supported even as Artime's operations wound down were Luis Posada and Antonio Veciana.

Alpha 66's Veciana apparently continued to deal with David Atlee Phillips (using the Maurice Bishop cover identity), but on a less frequent basis. This setup fit with Helms's new, more deniable approach, and since Cuban operations were winding down, Phillips was given a new position and a promotion. Helms and FitzGerald must have been satisfied with Phillips's work in the past year, because in late April 1965 they gave him his first Chief of Station post, in the Dominican Republic. This allowed Phillips to remain close enough to retain some involvement in Cuban operations, and the Dominican Republic had long been seen as a good base for CIA-backed operations against Castro. But Phillips's main focus was on the situation in the Dominican Republic itself, a hot spot that needed attention. The country's problems had been on the rise since the CIA-assisted assassination of dictator Trujillo in 1961. Though largely forgotten today, US Marines had landed in its capital, Santo Domingo, earlier in April 1965, just a month after the first official US combat troops arrived in Vietnam.[17]

By late 1965, Vietnam and other parts of the world increasingly occupied Richard Helms's attention. Cuba was becoming a much lower priority than it had been just a year earlier, but in only a few months, one of Helms's unauthorized Castro assassination operations would threaten to become front-page news.

Chapter Twenty-five

Compared to the dynamo he had been for much of his life, Bobby Kennedy spent much of 1965 and the early part of 1966 operating at half speed, still trying to deal with the loss of his brother. In terms of legislation, Bobby was not a notable freshman senator, but he tried to expand his horizons and seek new experiences. Bobby had always been a staunch anticommunist, but during a trip to South America he saw firsthand the terrible conditions miners had to endure. Bobby emerged from a tour of the pits proclaiming that if he had to work like that, he'd be a communist, too. Several writers have noted that Bobby rarely mentioned Cuba, except to express his admiration for Che Guevara.[1]

Bobby also rarely mentioned his brother's assassination, though he still had to contend with it. Troubling information from Mexico City implicating Fidel continued to trickle in, though there is no indication that Bobby took it seriously. However, he knew that Almeida was still in place in the Cuban government, and his family was still outside Cuba, so he didn't want to do anything to jeopardize them—or to expose what he and JFK had been planning with Almeida. That meant Bobby had to make sure he controlled important evidence. "On April 26, 1965, the Secret Service transferred the autopsy photographs and x-rays, and certain vital documents and biological materials, to the custody of the Kennedy family at the request of Robert F. Kennedy," according to Douglas Horne, former Chief Analyst for the JFK Assassination Records Review Board.[2] Bobby also obtained crucial physical evidence, such as JFK's brain and tissue samples.

Bobby believed it was up to him to decide what to do with government evidence about JFK's assassination. He summed up his feelings nine months later, when talking about the expensive bronze casket that had officially held JFK's body on the trip from Dallas to Washington. JFK had been buried in a mahogany casket, supposedly because this bronze casket had been damaged in some way. When Bobby told a General Services Administration official he wanted the bronze casket dumped at sea, the official said that would be destroying government property. Bobby declared, "I think it belongs to the family and we can get rid of it any way we want to." Based on files declassified in 1999, CNN reported that "the coffin, loaded with sandbags and riddled with holes, was taken from the basement of the National Archives . . . and dumped from an Air Force C-130 into the Atlantic Ocean at 10 AM on February 18, 1966."[3]

Even as Bobby took control of key evidence, he must have felt some measure of justice when he saw those he felt were involved in his brother's murder facing prison. Carlos Marcello was under indictment and facing an August 1965 trial for bribing a juror and threatening a witness at his November 1963 trial. Jimmy Hoffa had been convicted in his second trial, in Chicago, and only a flurry of appeals delayed the start of his long prison sentences for that conviction and the earlier one in Memphis. Sam Giancana went to jail in June 1965 for refusing to testify about the Mafia to a grand jury after being granted immunity, essentially ending Giancana's reign as Chicago's most powerful mob leader.[4]

Bobby also followed the struggle for civil rights and was evolving into one of its biggest public champions. However, 1965 was marked by increasing violence related to the cause. The previous year, LBJ had succeeding in passing the landmark civil rights legislation that Bobby and JFK had wanted, but blacks were still often prevented from voting, especially in the South. (One county in Alabama was 80 percent black, but no African-American resident of that county had been allowed to register to vote.)[5] LBJ, Bobby, and Martin Luther King all supported the new Voting Rights Act, but because it focused on the South, it would be difficult to get through Congress, where longtime Southern members wielded much power.

Dr. King's Nobel Peace Prize in late 1964 had further increased his stature, but it only generated even more resentment from FBI Director J. Edgar Hoover. Apparently due to pressure from LBJ, Hoover and Dr. King met at Hoover's office on December 1, 1964. Hoover touted to King the arrests of white supremacists who had murdered two civil rights workers in Mississippi, and King expressed gratitude when Hoover said the FBI would soon arrest the killers of three more civil rights activists (Chaney, Schwerner, and Goodman). King emerged from the meeting telling reporters that "the discussion was quite amicable."[6]

While Hoover tempered his public tirades against King, his private efforts against the civil rights leader continued. Hoover circulated a long report accusing King of being "a wholehearted Marxist," echoing the claims that the John Birch Society and white supremacists like Joseph Milteer had been making for years. Hoover's report went not only to LBJ, but also to the Secretaries of State and Defense, the Directors of the CIA and DIA, and Naval and Air Force Intelligence.[7]

Without telling LBJ, Hoover launched another covert attack against Dr. King, apparently designed to encourage him to commit suicide. Hoover had compiled portions of tapes his agents had recorded secretly in King's hotel rooms. He had William Sullivan, an assistant FBI director for the King operation, write an anonymous letter as if it were from a black man, telling King to "look into your heart . . . you are a colossal fraud and an evil, a vicious one at that. . . . King, there is only one thing left for you to do. You know what it is. . . . " The tape compilation and letter were then sent to King's office at the Southern Christian Leadership Council (SCLC) in Atlanta.[8]

The package sat unopened for a month before being forwarded to King's home, where Mrs. King was the first to read the letter and hear the tapes. However, most of the "highlights" were of poor quality, and it was hard to determine what was being said or who was saying it. With the support of Mrs. King and his advisors, Dr. King weathered the storm. The FBI tried to leak the story to the *New York Times*, but the paper wouldn't run it without comments from King or his staff, who refused to respond unless the *Times* revealed the FBI officials who were leaking the information. The *Times* refused to give up its FBI sources, so no story was written.[9]

Dr. King and other civil rights leaders had other enemies more deadly than Hoover. On January 18, 1965, King was attacked and punched by a member of the National States Rights Party, an often violent group linked to Joseph Milteer. Malcolm X was assassinated in Harlem on February 21, 1965, though most historians ascribe his murder to members of a rival faction within his own movement. That same month, police shot and killed a black demonstrator near Selma when he tried to defend his mother and eighty-two-year-old grandfather after both had been beaten by police. On March 6, 1965, state troopers on horseback attacked peaceful demonstrators in Selma, Alabama, on the Edmund Pettus Bridge. Soon afterward, a white Unitarian minister demonstrating in Alabama was beaten with a club and died from his injuries.[10]

Even Dr. King's triumphant march from Selma to the Alabama capital of Montgomery, which ended on March 25, 1965, was punctuated with violence when Viola Liuzzo, a white homemaker from Detroit who had been helping King's marchers, was shot twice in the face. Former

Birmingham mayor Arthur Hanes Sr. defended her killer. The articulate, Princeton-educated Hanes won an acquittal for him, which was one reason James Earl Ray would later enlist Hanes Sr. as his first defense attorney after Dr. King's assassination.[11]

According to Delmar Dennis, a Ku Klux Klansman turned FBI informant, Martin Luther King himself was targeted for assassination. The Klan group known as the White Knights, led by Sam Bowers, planned to kill King when he crossed a bridge in East Mississippi. They planned to use snipers and also dynamite the bridge. However, the Klan informant tipped off the FBI, and King avoided the area. The following year, the same group targeted King during a march through Mississippi and, according to the *Jackson Clarion-Ledger*, "killed a black man to lure King to the Natchez area." But that attempt also failed.[12] That same year, Joseph Milteer was speaking to Klan organizations in the South, and the Secret Service and FBI were still monitoring his movements whenever the president or vice president planned to visit the South.

The FBI was in the odd position of occasionally trying to protect Dr. King (due to pressure from LBJ) while at the same time carrying out Hoover's desire to destroy King's reputation. The previous year, when Bobby Kennedy was still Attorney General, the Justice Department had warned King of "credible reports of plans to assassinate him" on his trip to a Mississippi town known as a Klan base. Dr. King refused to cancel the trip, so Bobby called LBJ to get protection for the civil rights leader, since the Mississippi Highway Patrol refused to help. LBJ suggested the FBI, and Bobby had to sheepishly ask LBJ to make the call to Hoover, since Bobby "had no dealings with the FBI anymore." LBJ called Hoover, who agreed to have FBI cars travel behind and in front of King's.[13]

Hoover hated Dr. King, and many FBI agents and supervisors—especially in the South, but even in Washington—shared his racist views about King and civil rights. Some agents avoided that stain and tried to enforce the law. Still, Dr. King and his entourage so distrusted the FBI that by 1963, the FBI had stopped forwarding reports of threats against King to his office. In Atlanta, such reports were provided to Police Chief Herbert Jenkins, who was friendly with Dr. King's father. In other Southern cities, this lack of trust and cooperation presented a problem that would worsen in the coming years.[14]

The spate of violence against civil rights activists helped to propel passage of the Voting Rights Act on August 6, 1965, but many blacks outside the South saw it as too little too late. Simmering tensions over racism and poverty exploded just a week later, resulting in huge race riots in the Watts section of Los Angeles (leaving thirty-four dead) and in Chicago, where eighty people were injured. LBJ was crushed by the violent outbreaks, but Dr. King was more determined than ever to press for change, as was Bobby Kennedy.

The race riots had a large financial impact on Carlos Marcello's Mafia associates in Chicago and Los Angeles, because it disrupted their gambling and vice operations that preyed on minorities. As for Marcello himself, in the sweltering summer of 1965 in New Orleans, he focused his attention on the final days of his trial for bribing a juror and threatening to kill a witness. Those charges stemmed from his acquittal on the day JFK was assassinated, and this time the verdict was the same. Marcello was found "not guilty" on August 17, 1965, and was finally free of the charges and immense pressure that had dogged him since JFK and Bobby had taken office. Now that Bobby was no longer Attorney General and many of his Justice Department prosecutors had left, John H. Davis wrote that "Carlos Marcello was well on his way to becoming the wealthiest and most influential Mafia leader in the US." The Marcello organization's "estimated annual income of two billion dollars [made] it by far the largest industry in Louisiana."[15] In addition, Marcello's portion of the heroin network he shared with Trafficante had prospered for almost two years without suffering a major bust—but that was about to change.

The same month Marcello was acquitted, one of the lowest members of his heroin network attempted one last time to convince authorities to take action against Marcello's empire. Her efforts presaged a bust that would send one of the JFK assassination conspirators to prison, and begin a major shift in Marcello and Trafficante's heroin network that would eventually see Cuban exiles take an increasing role. In August 1965, sometime prostitute and occasional heroin courier Rose Cheramie told FBI agents that "individuals associated with the syndicate were running prostitution rings in several southern cities such as Houston and Galveston, Texas . . . furthermore, she claimed she had information about a heroin deal operating from a New Orleans ship."

Congressional investigators found that her story checked out, just as her November 1963 information had. An FBI "call to the Coast Guard verified an ongoing narcotics investigation of the ship" Cheramie had named. The prostitution ring Cheramie described sounds very much like an operation run by Marcello lieutenant Nofio Pecora (whom Jack Ruby, Cheramie's old boss, called just three weeks before JFK's murder).

However, as in 1963, local agents dropped the case—this time it was the New Orleans FBI, still notoriously lax in their treatment of Marcello. The Federal Bureau of Narcotics (FBN) in New Orleans also didn't pry into Marcello's heroin network.[16] If the FBI and FBN had seriously investigated Cheramie's allegations, they would have uncovered a heroin trail through New Orleans that reached all the way to France. This drug pipeline was about to be used again for a major delivery, which would eventually result in Michel Victor Mertz's finally going to prison.

However, Rose Cheramie didn't live to see Mertz, Marcello, or any of the men whose vice operations enslaved her go to prison. One month after Rose contacted the FBI in August 1965, she was killed. Congressional investigators noted that "ironically, the circumstances of Rose Cheramie's death are strikingly similar to the circumstances surrounding her original involvement in the assassination investigation," when she was left for dead by the side of the road shortly before JFK's murder. They found that "Cheramie died of injuries received from an automobile accident on a strip of highway near Big Sandy, Tex., in the early morning of September 4, 1965. The driver stated Cheramie had been lying in the roadway and although he attempted to avoid hitting her, he ran over the top of her skull, causing fatal injuries."[17] Though her official autopsy records had disappeared by the time investigators tried to find them, one extant medical file says that Rose had a "deep punctuate stellate [star-shaped] wound above her right forehead." Such a wound would not have been caused by a car or a tire, but could been caused by a pistol fired next to her skull.[18]

While Rose lay dying in a Texas hospital, Michel Victor Mertz hosted a party at his father-in-law's estate in France. In attendance was a US Army major, described by *Newsday* as "a close friend of Mertz," who suggested using a new contact to get a load of heroin into Fort Benning, Georgia, one of their regular smuggling points. A Warrant Officer moving to Fort Benning was offered $10,000 to have a special freezer shipped to the US as his own property. Told only that it contained diamonds, he agreed. In actuality, hidden in the freezer were two hundred small bags, each containing five hundred grams of almost pure heroin.[19]

The heroin-laden freezer would travel first by ship to Marcello's New Orleans, then by truck to Fort Benning. From there, Mertz's associates would take it to Miami, where the heroin would be distributed by one of Trafficante's men named Frank Dioguardi (Frankie Dio), who was also a Teamster associate of Jimmy Hoffa. One of Mertz's French smugglers who would meet with Dioguardi was given a Hispanic cover identity to use on his trip to Fort Benning, even though he spoke only French and English. The alias was "Almeida."[20]

After Mertz's heroin had left France, but before it arrived in the US, a French Inspector in Marseilles was tipped off about the shipment. The US Bureaus of Narcotics in New York and Washington were notified, and began shadowing both the heroin and Mertz's operatives. Five of them were arrested, including Dioguardi and the man using the "Almeida" alias. Mertz was identified as the source of the heroin, but it would take French authorities more than three years after the Fort Benning bust to finally arrest Mertz.[21]

On February 28, 1966, Rolando Cubela (AMLASH) was arrested in Cuba, due in part to information from Fidel's agent in Artime's camp. The CIA hadn't used Cubela for months, but Richard Helms would have been disappointed that Cubela's arrest also compromised the "entire AMTRUNK . . . network" in Cuba, according to a CIA memo. Gus Russo writes that Cubela was "arrested simultaneously [with] an important early recruit in the AMTRUNK project [who] was a co-defendant at Cubela's trial."[22] Eloy Menoyo, who had confessed after beatings a year earlier and was serving essentially a life sentence, was not part of Cubela's trial, possibly indicating that Fidel didn't realize Menoyo and Artime had been working together just prior to Menoyo's capture.

Castro made sure Cubela's trial was a highly publicized spectacle, but Che Guevara was conspicuously absent, even though he was apparently back in Cuba.[23] Almeida was present for Cubela's trial, and the CIA worried that its highest asset in Cuba might be exposed. Five days after Cubela's arrest was announced, a cable sent from the CIA Director's office said that CIA headquarters was "most interested [in] ascertaining Almeida's current status [in] view [of] AMLASH and other arrests." It asked for a friend of Almeida "to write . . . to Almeida in hopes of eliciting [an] interesting response."[24]

Almeida's name didn't come out in the trial, much to CIA officials' relief, as expressed in an April 14, 1966, memo saying there had been "no indication whatsoever that Rolando Cubela revealed anything more than his 'weakness, playboy attitude,' in plotting with a man like Manuel Artime to assassinate Fidel Castro. Under private interrogation to date there is no known possibility that Rolando Cubela has revealed the names of the real military leaders with whom he really was in contact. . . . None of these major individuals, whose names are known to us, have been arrested or detained."[25] Because of Cubela's public contrition, he was spared execution and sentenced to thirty years.

Richard Helms knew that as long as Almeida remained in place and unexposed, he had a possible asset to use in the future—if he could keep his job by hiding his unauthorized assassination schemes with Cubela from other US officials. The *New York Times* reported on March 6, 1966, that Cubela planned "to shoot Premier Castro with a high-powered tele-scopic rifle and later share [power] with Mr. Artime." Former FBI agent William Turner noted that when LBJ's Secretary of State Dean Rusk read about Cubela's arrest "in the *New York Times*, [he] demanded to know what the CIA's role might have been." The CIA's "Helms sent him a soothing memo stating that contact with Cubela had been confined to 'the express purpose' of intelligence gathering. 'The Agency was not involved with Cubela in a plot to assassinate Fidel Castro,' Helms wrote [to Rusk], 'nor did it ever encourage him to attempt such an act.'"[26]

Helms's statement was clearly false, as Rusk himself finally learned almost ten years later, when Senate hearings finally exposed Helms's Cubela assassination operation. When we spoke to Dean Rusk about this incident, his anger about Helms's deception was still quite evident. It was the only time in the interview when the consummate diplomat showed a flash of real emotion. Rusk felt the CIA had gone far beyond the scope of what the Johnson administration wanted, and then lied to him about it. His anger at Richard Helms also extended to information Helms gave him during the Warren Commission investigation, which, Rusk learned later, was also false.[27]

Three months after Cubela's arrest, a small group of exiles, including Trafficante's bodyguard, Herminio Diaz, and exile Tony Cuesta, appar-ently tried to get into Cuba to assassinate Fidel. In March 1966, during Cubela's trial, the CIA had heard that Herminio Diaz was planning to assassinate Fidel.[28] In the May 1966 landing, three of the men, including Diaz, were apparently killed, and two more were captured. One of those was Tony Cuesta, who was blinded and lost one hand in the attack. The Cubans identified one of Cuesta's three dead compatriots as Herminio Diaz—though it's unclear how they established his identity—and the matter seemed to end there.

Or maybe not. A CIA report written almost ten years later by Des-mond FitzGerald's former deputy says that while Herminio Diaz "was identified by Radio Havana as a member of a commando group killed while trying to land [in Cuba] for the purpose of assassinating Castro . . . in August 1973, an individual with the same name and year of birth was reportedly involved in narcotics trafficking in Costa Rica. A Cuban exile source stated that he believed subject [Herminio Diaz] to be identical with the narcotics trafficker in Costa Rica."[29]

Herminio Diaz had been involved in drug smuggling with Santo Trafficante, and Trafficante maintained a residence in Costa Rica that he used when investigations flared up in America. Could Herminio and Trafficante have arranged for Diaz's seeming death in 1966, by planting a fake ID on an exile who fit Diaz's general description and then tipping off Cuban authorities? According to British researcher John Simkin, during Tony Cuesta's long imprisonment in Cuba, "Cuesta realized he had been set up [by] people who organized the assassination of JFK." When Tony Cuesta was finally released in 1978 through the efforts of President Jimmy Carter, Cuesta told Cuban General Fabian Escalante that Herminio "had been involved in the assassination of President John F. Kennedy." Cuesta asked Escalante to keep the information secret until after Cuesta's death, and Escalante waited until 1995 to reveal it to a conference of US historians and officials.[30]

Whether or not Trafficante was tying up loose ends by having Diaz killed, or making it look like he was dead, Richard Helms was definitely cleaning house in 1966. LBJ had been dissatisfied with Admiral Raborn as CIA Director and had groomed Helms for the top spot. Richard Helms officially became CIA Director on June 30, 1966, putting him in the perfect position to ensure that his unauthorized activities under JFK and LBJ weren't exposed.

Helms "fired" Bernard Barker the following month, because he "was involved in certain gambling and criminal elements." (See the Special Addendum.) The heyday of Cuban operations was over, and the new focus was Vietnam and Southeast Asia, giving Helms an opportunity to send several of his operatives as far away as possible.

Six veterans of AMWORLD and the anti-Castro operations were shipped off to Laos in 1966, where the US had been waging a secret war for years. These included Artime's deputy "Chi Chi" Quintero, former Miami CIA Chief Ted Shackley, and (after an assignment in South America) David Morales.[31] Some writers have portrayed their transfer to Laos as a reward, giving them a choice assignment in an intelligence hotspot where their covert war expertise could flourish. However, living for long stretches in Laos's relatively primitive conditions was a long way from the poolside talks Morales and Shackley had formerly enjoyed in Miami. Also, Helms knew that their anti-Castro operations had been a failure at best, and at worst, somehow involved in JFK's assassination.

(Some historians have deemed the group's work in Laos, and then in Vietnam, equally disastrous.) As for Manuel Artime, though he was trained as a physician, he became a prosperous businessman, no doubt helped by the money and contacts he had gained from selling off the AMWORLD supplies. Artime traveled frequently to Central America, pursuing business ventures with the notoriously corrupt Somoza family, who ruled Nicaragua. (Marcello shared a Washington lobbyist with the Somozas.) Artime also apparently maintained his involvement in the narcotics trade, even as he continued to receive a regular salary from the CIA into 1966.[32]

Helms and the CIA would have been aware of several books about the JFK assassination slated for US publication later in 1966 that were highly critical of the Warren Commission's "lone assassin" conclusion. Coupled with a new development concerning Johnny Rosselli and his work for the CIA, those books might have made it seem wise for Helms to keep Morales and the other AMWORLD veterans as far away as possible from journalists and Congressional hearings. The impending US books critical of the Warren Report also meant that Helms's press and publishing expert, E. Howard Hunt, would be more useful back in the US.

Chapter Twenty-six

In the spring of 1966, Johnny Rosselli and Jimmy Hoffa began taking increasingly desperate measures to avoid prison, ultimately setting off a deadly chain reaction that would eventually lead to Rosselli's gruesome dismemberment murder, Hoffa's disappearance, and the slaying of Rosselli's patron Sam Giancana, all in the mid-1970s. Much sooner would come the brutal ax murder of Eladio del Valle, killed on the same day David Ferrie died, both in early 1967. All of those deaths would be linked to Santo Trafficante, Carlos Marcello, and the events surrounding JFK's assassination.

May 12, 1966, began as a typical morning in Beverly Hills for Johnny Rosselli, who had led a relaxed and affluent life since JFK's murder. A few months after the assassination, Rosselli had moved to a Beverly Glen Boulevard building that his biographers describe as having "some of the most beautiful and luxurious apartments in the nation." Rosselli's "suite of rooms on the eighth floor overlooked . . . the exclusive Los Angeles Country Club" and was near the Beverly Hills business district.[1] While Rosselli was taking a stroll near Rodeo Drive that morning, his serene world changed dramatically when two FBI agents confronted him. One of them uttered a name that sent a chill through Rosselli: Filippo Sacco.

The events that led to Rosselli's fateful encounter with the FBI had begun just weeks after JFK's death, when the FBI busted a midlevel Boston mob courier, who started giving the Bureau information to stay out of jail. The courier was careful not to tell agents his biggest secrets, but FBI surveillance finally revealed that the courier had worked for Rosselli for the past twenty-five years, taking money to the Mafia don's mother for her support. Rosselli couldn't visit his mother himself, because even though he was known as Johnny Rosselli in the power centers of Las Vegas and Hollywood, to his Boston family he was Filippo Sacco. An illegal immigrant who'd come to the US from Italy in 1911, Rosselli had changed his name to avoid a narcotics charge in the 1920s. Like Marcello, Rosselli was subject to deportation, something the FBI hadn't known about even when Rosselli was serving prison time in the 1940s for his Hollywood studio shakedown.[2]

Aware of how much trouble the US had in trying to deport Marcello, FBI agents built their case carefully for two years before finally confronting Rosselli in May 1966 on a Beverly Hills sidewalk. The Bureau offered Rosselli a deal if he became an informant for them, but he refused. Rosselli then called one of his first CIA contacts, Sheffield Edwards. Edwards had been one of two CIA officials responsible for bringing Rosselli into the CIA-Mafia plots to assassinate Fidel Castro in the summer of 1960.

A brief recap of CIA-Mafia plots is important, since several of the participants played increasingly crucial roles in the events of 1966 and beyond, culminating in the Watergate scandal. The plots had originally begun in 1959, with Jimmy Hoffa as the CIA's connection to (and cover for) the Mafia, but they had not succeeded. Much evidence shows that as the 1960 election approached, candidate—and vice president—Richard Nixon had pressed the CIA to step up its efforts to kill Fidel. E. Howard Hunt was also pushing the CIA to assassinate Castro around that time, and working closely with Nixon's top military aide for Cuba. CIA Security Chief Sheffield Edwards had looked first at using former Chicago FBI supervisor Guy Banister for a sensitive assignment as a "cover mechanism" in August 1960, before deciding to use former Chicago FBI agent Robert Maheu as the CIA's new conduit to the Mafia. Maheu and Banister had both worked with another former FBI agent, Carmine Bellino, after all three left the FBI in the early 1950s.[3]

By August 1960, Robert Maheu was doing increasing amounts of work for billionaire Howard Hughes, but since the CIA had helped to set him up in business in the mid-1950s, Maheu agreed to help the Agency. Maheu brought Johnny Rosselli into the plots; Rosselli then pulled in Giancana, who in turn brought in Trafficante (and, according to some evidence, Frank Fiorini). The hoped-for 1960 October surprise failed to materialize, but the plots with Rosselli and Trafficante continued. Just before the April 1961 Bay of Pigs invasion, the CIA-Mafia plots failed to kill Castro, due to CIA miscommunication regarding Tony Varona. The plots survived, and Sheffield Edwards eventually passed them off to William Harvey after Richard Helms decided to continue using Rosselli. However, it fell to Edwards to brief Bobby Kennedy on the plots in May 1962, after a wiretap scandal brought them to J. Edgar Hoover's attention. Edwards told Bobby that the plots had ended, though in reality

Helms was determined to continue them. Carlos Marcello told an FBI informant he had joined the CIA-Mafia plots as well.[4]

By the time Rosselli contacted Sheffield Edwards in May 1966, Edwards had retired from the CIA but still had high-level contacts at the Agency, from the days when he'd commanded seven hundred people as its Security Chief. Edwards immediately told a high-ranking CIA official about his talk with Rosselli. The smooth, dapper Rosselli had couched his concern to Edwards in nice language that made it sound as if he didn't want the CIA dragged into a messy situation, but Rosselli's real goal was clear: He wanted the CIA to get the FBI off his back and keep him out of jail.[5]

To make sure the CIA got the message, Rosselli also contacted his old pal William Harvey. Though the CIA admits that Rosselli and Harvey had remained in contact since 1964, Harvey no longer had much influence at the Agency. Rosselli's other contact with the CIA, David Morales, wasn't available, since he was on assignment in South America. Johnny Rosselli turned to a trusted friend, longtime Hoffa attorney Edward Morgan, for advice.[6] Rosselli and Morgan had a problem in common: the impending imprisonment of Jimmy Hoffa, whose final appeal was winding its way to the Supreme Court. Hoffa's Teamster Pension Fund was a major source of capital for the Mafia in Las Vegas, and losing it would have a huge impact on Rosselli and the Chicago Mafia he represented.

In addition to Rosselli's immigration trouble with the FBI, he had another, even more immediate problem. Rosselli's power flowed largely from Sam Giancana, but that too was at risk. Giancana had been in prison for almost a year for refusing to testify before a grand jury under grant of immunity. The grand jury's term was almost up, but the government could empanel a new one and keep Giancana in prison for another year. Control of the Chicago Mafia had already slipped from Giancana's grasp, though he was still a figure to be reckoned with—but another year could end even that, and greatly weaken Rosselli's clout.

For years, the decision to release Sam Giancana in May 1966 has been attributed to Bobby's successors at the Justice Department, but Congressional investigators found that the CIA actually played a part in Giancana's release. Richard Helms wanted to keep Giancana's role in the CIA-Mafia plots secret, but someone must have suggested that might not happen if Giancana faced another year in prison. Based on the timing, that someone was very likely Rosselli.[7]

Rosselli finally got some good news when Sam Giancana was quietly released on May 30, 1966. However, the event created a political firestorm in the press. Giancana, worried that the government might change its mind, fled to Mexico, where he was joined by longtime associate Richard Cain.[8] That left Rosselli to face his immigration problem without help from his formerly powerful patron. According to an FBI report, by June 1966, Rosselli "looked sick and worried and recently has not had his usual dapper appearance," despite the fact that the FBI observed a "very attractive blonde woman . . . staying at Rosselli's apartment" and "cooking his meals." Rosselli knew he needed a big score, a strong new patron, and a way to deal with his immigration problems—and soon.[9]

The roots of Rosselli's solution came from one of Hoffa's attempts to overturn his convictions. Hoffa felt that Bobby Kennedy had used illegal wiretaps against him. At that time, laws didn't allow wiretap evidence to be used in court—only phone records (demonstrating that a call was made to a certain number on a particular date) were admissible. Hoover's FBI utilized illegal and legal phone taps extensively, but the transcripts of even the legal taps, and the evidence gleaned from them, couldn't be used in court. If Hoffa could prove that his conviction was based on such evidence, he would go free.[10]

Hoffa had encouraged Missouri Senator Edward Long, one of his biggest supporters in Congress, to hold hearings on Justice Department phone taps, particularly those authorized by Bobby Kennedy. LBJ aide Bill Moyers told Richard Goodwin, Bobby's friend and now LBJ's top speech writer, that Long was "out to get Bobby" on behalf of Hoffa, and that LBJ was "egging him on" to get back at his political rival. Though Bobby still spoke approvingly of LBJ in public, several months earlier, Bobby had started to talk about the need for peace negotiations with Vietnam, and LBJ believed that his hated adversary was betraying him yet again.[11]

One of the witnesses that Senator Long's committee called was Robert Maheu, who had been involved in the bugging incident that first tipped off the FBI about the CIA-Mafia plots. At that point, Senator Long and the rest of Congress knew only about the bugging incident, not about the plots. Because of Maheu's increasing amounts of work for the reclusive Howard Hughes, he wanted to avoid doing anything that could damage that relationship. According to Rosselli's biographers, Maheu "contacted the CIA general counsel" about the matter. Richard Helms didn't want Congress finding out about the CIA-Mafia plots or the CIA's own illegal domestic surveillance, so the CIA's general counsel "persuaded Long to drop his demand that Maheu testify."

While it satisfied Maheu and Helms in the short term, this incident would have several important ramifications in the long run. Rosselli would see yet again how the threat of exposing the CIA-Mafia plots could be used to blackmail the CIA. Also, because Maheu retained his powerful position with Howard Hughes, Rosselli could use his relationship with Maheu to get to Hughes.

It's ironic that Senator Long's counsel for his Hoffa-inspired hearings was attorney Bernard Fensterwald. Apparently intrigued by what he heard from the CIA and observed while working for Long, Fensterwald would soon begin a quest to learn more. He would become one of the most important JFK assassination researchers, an attorney for figures like James McCord and James Earl Ray, and a leading Freedom of Information Act attorney who tried to pry crucial JFK files from reluctant agencies.

When Senator Long's hearings failed to produce the dramatic revelations that Jimmy Hoffa needed, the Teamster president turned to Carlos Marcello and Santo Trafficante for help. Though Trafficante was closer in some ways to Hoffa because they shared attorney Frank Ragano, Marcello had more power nationally. Later investigations showed that Marcello spent many of his days in his office at the Town and Country Motel, receiving requests from mob bosses, businessmen, and politicians who wanted his help. While most of those seeking his favor were from Louisiana and the surrounding states, some were from other regions of the country. As long as the deal was profitable and Marcello got his cut, he was happy to use his clout, muscle, and financial power to help himself by helping them.

Marcello and Trafficante would have also been very concerned about Rosselli's legal troubles and the loss of their old ally Giancana. Rosselli's influence in Las Vegas was still useful to the mob bosses, since their Mafia associates controlled most of the city's major casinos. Besides, after the Joe Valachi fiasco, they knew it was far better for Rosselli to remain free than to wind up in prison, where an aging Mafia don might say anything not to die. In addition, Rosselli's possible deportation would have had special resonance for Marcello, who potentially faced the same fate. The problems of Hoffa and Rosselli demanded that Marcello and Trafficante come up with an effective course of action.

FBI reports say that in June 1966, Carlos Marcello "visited Santo Trafficante at his Tampa, Florida home . . . [and] during this period Carlos Marcello and Trafficante had several lengthy private conversations." These talks had to be away from family and their usual associates, so the FBI notes that "Marcello and Trafficante sat alone in the backyard [of] Trafficante's home" for hours.[12]

Marcello and Trafficante had plotted and planned JFK's assassination for more than a year, but they didn't have that much time now. Just weeks after the two men strategized in Tampa, the FBI says, "over the July 4 weekend, Santo Trafficante . . . visited Carlos Marcello at his Churchill Farms Estate." At the same place where Marcello and Ferrie had plotted JFK's murder, "several lengthy private conversations occurred [while] Marcello and Trafficante walked out into the middle of the fields behind the main house and sat for many hours." The Mafia chiefs wanted to be sure there was absolutely no chance that their conversations were bugged. The plans they developed to aid Rosselli and Hoffa would unfold over the next several months and into early 1967.[13]

Richard Helms and Bobby Kennedy shared some of the same concerns about Long's hearings and Giancana's release, though each man was grappling with his own worries as well. Richard Helms had been forced to deal with the issue of the CIA-Mafia plots twice in only a month, and on June 24, 1966, a "summary of the operation [was] prepared by the [CIA's] Office of Security." The more people who knew even vaguely about the plots, either inside the CIA or out, the greater the chance the plans would leak, unraveling the cover-up Helms had managed so carefully on his climb to the CIA's highest post. Helms knew he would have to deal with the Rosselli matter at some point, but it wasn't as pressing as the Giancana and Maheu situations had been. In Rosselli's case, Helms would prove reluctant to play the same card a third time.[14]

Bobby Kennedy must have had mixed feelings about Sam Giancana's release. On one hand, a year in jail was a small price to pay for whatever role he'd played in JFK's murder. On the other hand, few high-level mobsters were ever imprisoned for any length of time, and almost never for a hit. Bobby also knew from his contacts in the Justice Department that Mafia prosecutions had fallen to less than half the number he had overseen in 1963. Finally, like Helms, Bobby didn't want the CIA-Mafia plots coming out. He was already struggling to not be tainted by Senator Long's surveillance investigation, and another scandal could end his political career. As Bobby would soon confide to trusted associates, becoming president was the only way he would really be able to find his brother's killers and bring them to justice.

Bobby faced other issues that, for him, were supplanting mob prosecutions. Though he had been an undistinguished freshman senator so far, his trip to South Africa in June 1966 seemed to reinvigorate him, and perhaps made him even more sensitive to the plight of minorities and the poor in the US.[15] He also saw with alarm what was happening in America in the summer of 1966: James Meredith, the first black student at the University of Mississippi, was shot in the back during a demonstration. Race riots broke out in Chicago and Atlanta. Martin Luther King denounced the "Black Power" advocates who had egged on the Atlanta rioters, only to be attacked by whites during a peaceful demonstration just outside of Chicago.[16] President Johnson's attention was increasingly consumed by Vietnam, so if LBJ's dream of a "Great Society" was to be fulfilled, some other leader would have to work with Dr. King and others to make it a reality.

Bobby now paid little attention to Cuba; LBJ also wanted to avoid bringing it back into the headlines before the 1966 Congressional elections. A 1966 FBI memo again raised the possibility that Soviet missiles were still in Cuba, something no president could prove wasn't true. In the wake of Cubela's imprisonment, any serious coup plans seemed out of the question. One of the Cuban officials who had approached the CIA in the summer of 1964 had been stripped of his rank and position, but at least he wasn't imprisoned like Cubela or Menoyo. By 1966, the CIA had no way of telling whether any of the disgruntled Cuban officials were safe to deal with.[17]

As a result, Richard Helms would have to keep the pot boiling with actions that stood little chance of blowing up in his face—and little chance of really changing things in Cuba. Operations to kill Castro and make small raids continued, but they were fewer and had to be more "deniable," looking as if they were staged only by exiles, not backed by the US. Unlike the CIA's usual covert efforts to acquire intelligence about Cuba, these operations had to be conducted under much deeper cover. As noted earlier, David Atlee Phillips apparently continued using his "Maurice Bishop" cover identity to deal occasionally with Alpha 66's Antonio Veciana, probably on trips to the US from his post as CIA Station Chief in the Dominican Republic. Congressional investigators found that Veciana was of interest to the DIA's Army Intelligence in 1966, so military intelligence may have been used as a cutout to hide Phillips's and the CIA's real role with Veciana.[18]

Various incidents made the news in Cuba, but received little coverage in the US: a supposed "CIA agent" captured in Cuba on June 1, 1966; a September bombing, by plane, of an electric plant being constructed in Cuba; and an American pilot reported as being "shot down and captured after dropping weapons and espionage equipment" into Cuba. It was hard to tell which were CIA operations and which were done solely by exiles—and that was the point, the way Helms knew it had to be from then onward.[19]

Most of the more established Cuban exile leaders were gradually being phased out in favor of a new, more violent generation. Even though Artime was involved in scandals, the CIA still paid him $5,000 per month until June 1966, when his payments dropped to $3,000 each month. There was talk in Miami's Little Havana that Harry Williams might come back to replace Artime, but it was only a rumor—Harry was devoting himself to his family and business. As for Artime, he agreed to officially terminate his relationship with the CIA at the end of 1966. Artime would pursue business interests, traveling widely in Central America and the Caribbean, while he continued to sell off some of the arms he had stolen from the AMWORLD supplies.[20]

Still in favor with the CIA was bomb expert Luis Posada, even though CIA files indicated his "involvement in [a] 1965 attempt to overthrow [the] Guatemalan government." That summer, the CIA had asked Posada to pass "silencers, C-4 explosive, [and] detonators to" a Miami organized-crime figure and to Norman Rothman, an associate of Santo Trafficante and Jack Ruby. Shortly after that, Posada was building "bombs for RECE and working directly with Mas Canosa," who would later reign as the top exile leader in the US for almost two decades. After Posada passed a lie-detector test, the CIA pronounced its bomb maker to be "of good character, very reliable, [and] security conscious." The CIA made him a Technical Supervisor, paying him $400 a month, and by September 1966, the Agency sent Posada to the Bahamas to look for a "suitable site for caching weapons."[21]

By the summer of 1966, the CIA was at least tolerating one Cuban exile whom the Kennedys had banned from US operations: Rolando Masferrer. The former Cuban death-squad leader wanted to invade Haiti, which could then be used as a base from which to attack Castro. Masferrer claimed the CIA had approved his effort—a statement that would be hard to believe if not for the fact that CBS was putting up $200,000 (more than $1 million in today's dollars) to buy the rights to film Masferrer's invasion of Haiti. As noted earlier, Carl Bernstein highlighted CBS's cooperation with the CIA at the highest levels in that era, so it's difficult to believe the network would have supported Masferrer if the CIA had not approved.

Even if the CIA didn't give its explicit approval to CBS, the Agency certainly could have stopped the venture by telling CBS that it was strongly opposed. It's possible that under the CIA's new, more covert backing of anti-Castro operations, Helms or FitzGerald wanted to see CBS take the risk. If Masferrer's plan worked, the CIA could use Haiti as a new base for anti-Castro operations. If Masferrer's plan failed, then CBS, not the CIA, would have a black eye.[22]

Masferrer's operation was a bizarre foreshadowing of the reality-TV trend of forty years later. Ostensibly, he planned to use Cuban exiles and Haitians to overthrow the cruel Haitian dictator Francois Duvalier (known as "Papa Doc"). Because Masferrer would then use Haiti as a staging ground for an invasion of Cuba, Cuban exiles had an incentive to risk their lives for the Haiti invasion.[23]

The venture with Masferrer turned into a fiasco for CBS: A young exile was hurt while CBS filmed his training, and he sued the network for a million dollars (though he ultimately settled for a fraction of that). In November 1966, a fake news report of an invasion surfaced, causing a Haitian hotel to threaten to sue for lost business. Rumors also sprang up that "Papa Doc" was going to pay Masferrer $200,000—and give him a base—in exchange for *not* staging the invasion. CBS executives finally pulled their support, though Masferrer continued his plan to invade Haiti. However, the sorry episode ended for years any serious investigation by the TV networks—not just of Masferrer, but also of any Cuban exile activity—which hindered the exposure of the exiles who had helped Trafficante and Marcello kill JFK.[24]

Chapter Twenty-seven

The summer of 1966 saw the first wave of American books critical of the Warren Report, and the reactions of Bobby Kennedy, Richard Helms, and J. Edgar Hoover would have far-reaching implications. Prior to that summer, only a smattering of books about the assassination—most of which initially appeared overseas—had criticized the Warren Report. The first significant critical book to originate in America was a paperback original, *The Unanswered Questions About President Kennedy's Assassination*. Written by veteran reporter Sylvan Fox, who would soon join the *New York Times*, the book generated little media attention. However, it was a solid work and advanced European author Joachim Joesten's pattern of using the Warren Commission's own Report and twenty-six volumes of evidence to pick apart their "lone nut, magic bullet" conclusion. By the summer and fall of 1966, Fox's book was followed by a host of well-documented, pro-conspiracy books, which also made use of the government's own evidence and testimony to make their case. These included attorney Mark Lane's *Rush to Judgment*, Sylvia Meagher's *Accessories After the Fact*, Josiah Thompson's *Six Seconds in Dallas*, and Edward Jay Epstein's *Inquest*.

Bobby Kennedy's friend, former JFK aide Richard Goodwin, was very impressed with *Inquest*, which focused on problems with the medical evidence and the "magic bullet." Goodwin not only wrote a glowing review of *Inquest* for the *Washington Post* that appeared on July 23, 1966, but Goodwin also declared that an "independent group should look at [Epstein's] charges and determine whether the Commission investigation was so flawed that another inquiry is necessary."

Goodwin's comments were the subject of an article in the next day's *New York Times*, which pointed out that he was "the first member of the President's inner circle to suggest publicly that an official re-examination be made of the Warren Report." The following day, Goodwin was at Bobby's New York apartment, trying to talk to him about *Inquest* and the need for a new investigation. However, Bobby could reply only, "I'm sorry, Dick, I just can't focus on it." Goodwin persisted, telling Bobby, "We should find our own investigator—someone with absolute loyalty and discretion."[1]

Bobby suggested, "You might try Carmine Bellino. He's the best in the country." Bobby had worked with the investigative accountant at the Justice Department, after originally using him as a Senate investigator to unravel Hoffa's and Marcello's complex criminal financial dealings. Bellino would have been ideal, given not only his experience with Bobby, but also his former work with Guy Banister and Robert Maheu. Years later, Bellino would help to lead the Senate Watergate investigators as they exposed the criminal activity of several AMWORLD veterans.[2]

The conversation between Bobby and Goodwin soon turned to other matters, but later that night, Bobby returned to the subject of the assassination. He said, "About that other thing. I never thought it was the Cubans. If anyone was involved it was organized crime. But there's nothing I can do about it. Not now." Four years after Richard Goodwin first wrote that account in 1988, he told Bobby's biographer, Jack Newfield, that Bobby had specifically pointed to "that mob guy in New Orleans."[3] It was as if Bobby couldn't bear to say the name of the man who had murdered his brother.

Perhaps it's just as well that Goodwin didn't pursue an investigation at that time using Bellino. As Goodwin told us in an interview when he confirmed the above account, he didn't know about the JFK-Almeida coup plan. Bobby couldn't tell him all about it because Goodwin still worked for his hated rival, Lyndon Johnson. In addition, Bobby didn't tell Goodwin that he had already attempted private investigations of JFK's murder, to no avail. However, Goodwin's pleas may have provided a spark that would ignite a new round of private investigations for Bobby in the coming months.[4]

In the meantime, the renewed public interest in JFK's murder spawned by the new books weighed increasingly on Bobby. On October 30, 1966, Bobby told Arthur Schlesinger that he "wondered how long he could continue to avoid comment on the [Warren] Report." Schlesinger wrote that while Bobby "believes that it was a poor job and will not endorse it . . . he is unwilling to criticize it and thereby reopen the whole tragic business."[5]

However, the rising tide of publicity due to the books didn't look like it would crest soon, and one book—Lane's *Rush to Judgement*—was soon high on the *New York Times* bestseller list. Bobby had to make sure the medical evidence was secure, so the day after his remarks to Schlesinger,

Bobby ordered the lawyer for the Kennedy estate to transfer much of the autopsy evidence to the official custody of the National Archives. However, Bobby didn't include the steel container that apparently held JFK's brain and tissue samples taken from around the wounds. Also missing from the transfer were some of the autopsy photos, including those of JFK's open chest and others official photographers had taken at the Bethesda autopsy; even today, these photos are not at the National Archives.[6]

FBI and Congressional files show that J. Edgar Hoover was very worried about the new books attacking the Warren Report's conclusions. Hoover and the FBI had plenty of intelligence failures to cover up, from Joseph Milteer to the Mafia threats against JFK to Jack Ruby's Mafia ties. The counteroffensive Hoover developed would include prominent journalists, a Supreme Court justice, and even electronic surveillance of members of Congress and critical journalists.

Hoover's use of the US media was probably even more sophisticated than that of Helms and the CIA. After all, Hoover had been ruling the FBI and using the media long before the CIA was created, having made himself a celebrity and turned "G-men" into movie heroes back in the 1930s. By 1967, a constant stream of books, articles, and even a weekly TV show praised the FBI and its Director. Helms's envy of the television program *The FBI* would eventually prod Helms to pressure Hollywood executive Jack Valenti to turn E. Howard Hunt's spy novels into a TV show, just weeks before Watergate. Only after J. Edgar Hoover's death would investigators find that the books Hoover had supposedly authored were actually written by FBI personnel at government expense, although Hoover had kept the proceeds.[7]

On November 13, 1966, Hoover had an internal FBI memo issued regarding how to deal with critics of the Warren Report. Intended only for use within the FBI, it makes a surprising admission, confirming that the FBI's "basic investigation was substantially completed by November 26, 1963," the day after Oswald's murder—inadvertently acknowledging the rush to judgment that critics claimed. The memo suggests that FBI media assets should stress the FBI conducted "approximately 25,000 interviews" This leaves out the fact (included in a CIA memo) that a number of those were actually "reinterviews" of the same witnesses, sometimes conducted because the interviewee was at odds with the FBI's hastily reached conclusion.[8]

More than a month before the FBI's November 13, 1966, anti-critics memo was issued, Hoover received what he considered a green light from LBJ in the matter, conveyed through Supreme Court Justice Abe Fortas. Declassified files show that Hoover had already long been waging a campaign against critics of the FBI and the Warren Report, so LBJ's message simply gave Hoover the presidential stamp of approval to do what he had already been doing.

On October 7, 1966, Clyde Tolson had written a memo to Hoover about his meeting that day with "Justice Abe Fortas in his chambers at the Supreme Court." Fortas had requested the meeting so that he could give Tolson some information for Hoover. Earlier that day, Fortas had met with LBJ, who was "extremely concerned regarding the rash of books" about JFK's assassination. LBJ was also concerned about William Manchester's forthcoming book authorized by the Kennedy family, *Death of a President*, fearing that it would make him look bad. LBJ's concerns were not surprising, given the impending 1968 election and the possibility that Bobby Kennedy might challenge LBJ from within his own party. Justice Fortas told Tolson that "Chief Justice Warren shared the concern of the President" about the books. Like LBJ, "Warren felt that [Hoover] should attempt to set the record straight by making information available to the public," since Warren believed that as Chief Justice, he shouldn't speak out publicly on the assassination. Warren was even willing "to make certain that various documents were declassified," and offered to personally deal with officials or agencies that might object to their release.[9]

Fortas said he was relaying LBJ's request for assistance to Tolson "on an extremely confidential basis" so that Tolson could take it to Hoover. Fortas was anxious to help and suggested that Hoover rebut the critics via "a book, a series of articles, or through the medium of one lengthy article. Justice Fortas also stated that he personally would be glad to line up a publication or publishing house through which a book or article could be handled." The mind boggles at the conflicts of interest the Fortas-FBI meeting represented. LBJ's use of a Supreme Court justice for such errands and back-channel dealings was a sign of the problems that would soon force Fortas from the Court.[10]

Dealing with a Supreme Court Justice about attacking critics was far from the most egregious action Hoover and his men took in that regard. According to Bud Fensterwald and Michael Ewing, "Senate investigators [later] established that FBI Director Hoover not only had prepared secret 'derogatory dossiers' on the critics of the Warren Commission over the years, but had even ordered the preparation of similar 'damaging' reports about staff members of the Warren Commission." One member of the Commission, Louisiana congressman Hale Boggs, would later charge on the floor of Congress that "certain FBI agents had tapped his own telephone, as well as the phones of certain other members of the House and Senate." After Boggs's death, his son would tell the *Washington Post* that "the FBI leaked to his father damaging material on the personal lives of critics of its investigation into John F. Kennedy's assassination."[11]

Hoover's investigation into the private lives of the critics had begun while the Warren Commission was still conducting its investigation. Fensterwald and Ewing, both veteran Congressional investigators, wrote that "Mark Lane . . . uncovered a February 24, 1964, Warren Commission memorandum [that] revealed that FBI agents had Lane's movements and lectures under surveillance, and were forwarding their reports to the Warren Commission." At that time, Lane was trying to represent the interests of Oswald and Oswald's mother to the Commission. Even in early 1967, "the official list of secret Commission documents then being held in a National Archives vault included at least seven FBI files on Lane, which were classified on supposed grounds of 'national security.' Among these secret Bureau reports were 'Mark Lane, Buffalo appearances.'"[12]

However, Hoover had the FBI do far more than just monitor Lane's travels. Fensterwald and Ewing point out that in 1975, Senator Richard Schweiker, of the Intelligence Committee, would reveal "new information from a November 8, 1966, memorandum by J. Edgar Hoover, relating to . . . the critics [in which] 'Seven individuals [were] listed, some of their files . . . not only included derogatory information, but sex pictures.'" Senator Schweiker found other FBI files from two months later showing "an ongoing campaign to personally derogate [critics of] the Warren Commission."[13]

Hoover's firm support of the "lone nut, magic bullet" conclusion of the Warren Report would far outlive him. Even decades later, when FBI agents question people about new evidence in the JFK assassination, they often refer to the Warren Report as the only officially accepted version of events, ignoring the 1979 conspiracy conclusion of the House Select Committee on Assassinations. However, the FBI wasn't alone in its quest to prevent broader investigations of conspiracy in JFK's assassination, since other federal agencies also had investigative and intelligence failures to hide.[14]

CIA Director Richard Helms would have been alarmed by the growing surge of JFK assassination books and articles questioning the Warren Commission's conclusions. Helms had to protect not only Almeida and the CIA's ongoing operations against Cuba, but also his own unauthorized Castro assassination plots that had backfired against JFK. But in the fall of 1966, his Deputy Director for Plans, Desmond FitzGerald, was in declining health, and David Atlee Phillips was still serving as CIA Station Chief in the Dominican Republic. So Helms turned to someone else who had every incentive to prevent the intelligence failures from 1963 from coming to light: E. Howard Hunt.

In the summer of 1966, Richard Helms ordered Hunt to return to the US from Spain and resume Hunt's important role in the CIA's dealings with publishers and the press. Hunt's and Helms's efforts would impact not only the CIA's response to the mounting media attacks on the Warren Commission, but also the unfolding coverage of Jim Garrison's JFK investigation, articles tying Johnny Rosselli and Joseph Milteer to JFK's murder, and coverage of the assassinations of Martin Luther King and Bobby Kennedy. The actions of Helms and Hunt in dealing with the press and leaks would lead to both men's involvement in Watergate, eventually landing Hunt in prison and costing Helms his position as CIA Director.

The emerging skepticism of the press and public regarding the Warren Report was a double-edged sword for E. Howard Hunt. It increased his value to Richard Helms, but raised the possibility that a journalist might come across Harry Williams or someone else who could implicate Hunt's associates in the events surrounding JFK's assassination. For the next six years, Helms made sure that Hunt was in a good position to keep that from happening.

Once the fallout from Cubela's trial had subsided in 1966, Hunt returned to the US, marking what he called "the beginning of the period that would make [him] a household name." During Cubela's public trial in Havana, Cubela had named Artime and the CIA's Madrid Station Chief as part of the plot, but neither Cubela nor any other witness had mentioned Hunt's real name or his code name, "Eduardo." Escaping notice, Hunt remained valuable to Helms and returned to the US apparently expecting great things and a very bright future.[15]

Hunt bought an estate twenty minutes from CIA headquarters that he described as a "sprawling horse ranch." Tad Szulc notes that its cost was "reported to have been $200,000," more than a million dollars in today's money. Szulc points out that "even with income from books and his CIA salary . . . Hunt could not have afforded that much." Szulc didn't realize that Hunt had profited from selling Artime's multimillion-dollar trove of CIA-supplied arms and supplies. Hunt's lavish lifestyle apparently didn't arouse the interest of the usually extremely observant CIA Counter-Intelligence Chief James Angleton, possibly because Hunt enjoyed CIA Director Helms's patronage and support.[16]

Hunt's primary objective for Helms, which he would maintain for the next six years, was to ensure that Helms's unauthorized 1963 Castro assassination attempts (primarily the CIA-Mafia plots, but also the CIA's backing for Cubela's plot and QJWIN) didn't become known to the press, public, or Congress—that would have destroyed both of their careers. Hunt's likely role in the CIA's continuing support for Commander Almeida's family outside Cuba provided a national-security basis for his actions. However, Hunt's role with Almeida was known only to a relative handful of CIA officials and wasn't a full-time job, so Hunt needed a more traditional position once he returned to the US to "officially" rejoin the CIA. (Hunt's phony resignation before going to Spain had been just a matter of paperwork, to provide cover.)

Helms's position as CIA Director allowed him to give Hunt a prestigious title and assignments, and Hunt's official position would soon be "chief of covert action for Western Europe," a key battleground in the Cold War. As he had in 1963, Hunt had an additional role as well: Congressional investigators found that Helms put Hunt "in charge of contacts with US publishers in the late 1960s." While much information was withheld from those investigators, they were able to discover a few examples of Hunt's handiwork, such as when Hunt arranged "a book review for an Agency book which appeared in the *New York Times* [that] was written by a CIA writer under contract."[17]

Not only are CIA operations targeting citizens inside the US forbidden by its charter, but also, since 1948, American laws have forbidden federal agencies from spreading propaganda inside the US. However, as one of Desmond FitzGerald's men later told *Newsweek* editor Evan Thomas, when it came to targeting the US news media, "we were not the least inhibited by the fact that the CIA had no internal security role in the U.S."[18]

After Watergate later triggered a series of Congressional investigations, Helms and the CIA would do a masterful spin job of downplaying Hunt's roles at the CIA, successfully depicting him as a bumbling loser whom Helms barely knew. Helms (and later, CIA officials) also downplayed the serious nature of much of Hunt's work by withholding from

Congress Hunt's important work on the JFK-Almeida coup plan, apparently on the grounds that it was an ongoing CIA operation because of Almeida's family. While we don't want to overstate Hunt's importance within the CIA, it's clear from the now available historical records that he retained Helms's trust and continued to perform important tasks for the Agency until Watergate. After Hunt's arrest in that matter, the American publishers and press Hunt had dealt with previously had no incentive to tout their own ties to Hunt, especially if they wanted to maintain their own reputations with the public or their relationships with the CIA.[19]

Hunt justified his CIA work with the media by saying the CIA "had a very real public relations problem within the U.S." Aside from a few exceptions, like *The Invisible Government*, the CIA seemed to get most of what it wanted from the American news media until late 1966. Then, the flood of books and articles questioning the Warren Commission coincided with the start of a gradual shift in the mainstream media away from unwavering support for the war in Vietnam. At the same time, the illegal activities of the CIA, FBI, and other federal agencies were starting to be exposed in progressive publications like *Ramparts* magazine.[20]

For Richard Helms, having Hunt working again with the press and publishers in 1966 offered him many of the same benefits it had in 1963. It gave Helms a trusted subordinate who could monitor books and the press for any leaks about Almeida's secret work for JFK, as well as any stories hinting at Helms's unauthorized Castro assassination plots involving Rosselli, Trafficante, and others. Hunt was the logical choice for Helms and Desmond FitzGerald, since Hunt had participated in those operations and it was in Hunt's personal and professional interest to make sure those matters weren't made public. By using Hunt, Richard Helms didn't have to make other CIA officials aware of the potentially career-ending information about his unauthorized Castro assassination operations.

Almeida remained in place and unexposed, and of potential benefit to the CIA if anything happened to Fidel Castro. Given Counter-Intelligence Chief James Angleton's concern about a "Monster Plot" involving possible Soviet moles in the CIA's upper echelons, it made little sense to tell additional CIA officials about Almeida or about Helms's unauthorized Castro assassination plots. That is why Helms continued to use the same small group of knowledgeable people (Hunt, Phillips, Morales, etc.) for certain sensitive operations, and continued drawing from that same small pool even though their results were often mixed (and disastrous or fatal for their targets).

The CIA continued a broad program of intelligence gathering and some covert action against Fidel Castro, and Hunt had the background and contacts to know whether any press or publishing plans might impact those operations. Hunt could also try to present a more positive view of the CIA in print, just as the Agency's image was starting to come under attack. According to Senate investigators, approximately 250 books written in English "were produced, subsidized, or sponsored by the CIA before the end of 1967." The investigators found that some of the books "were written by witting Agency assets" with access to "actual case materials," and at times, "the publisher was unaware" of the CIA's involvement.[21]

E. Howard Hunt actually wrote a few of those books, and two of his writing projects in particular are important in that regard. The first was Hunt's nonfiction take on the Bay of Pigs, called *Give Us This Day*, which Hunt began writing in 1966. Hunt claims he wrote the detailed, emotional account simply for his own pleasure, with no plans to have it published. However, Hunt's manuscript reads like a CIA response to the 1964 Kennedy-sympathetic book *The Bay of Pigs*, written by Haynes Johnson with Harry Williams and Manuel Artime, with the support of Bobby Kennedy. At a time when so much information about the CIA's role in the Bay of Pigs was still secret, it's hard to believe that Hunt would have devoted the time and energy needed to write such a book unless he had at least informal approval from his patron, Helms. Though Hunt's book about the fiasco would not be published until 1973, Hunt's CIA file says that he had submitted it to a publisher by mid-1968.[22] That raises the possibility that Hunt had completed the book so that it, or an advance excerpt, could have been used against Bobby Kennedy, if he ran for president in 1968 and tried to blame the CIA for the Bay of Pigs fiasco.

Hunt's other writing project in 1966 was a series of fiction books designed to cast the CIA in a good light. Neither the tawdry glitz of James Bond nor the bleaker depictions of the CIA in books and movies like *The Spy Who Came In from the Cold* were especially favorable to the CIA, so Richard Helms championed Hunt's idea for a series of CIA-approved spy novels. Helms kept copies of the paperbacks in his drawer to give to visitors, and nine novels appeared from 1965 to 1972, under the pseudonym David St. John, the name of Hunt's infant son.[23]

Chapter Twenty-eight

Carlos Marcello and Santo Trafficante dealt with the rising interest in JFK's assassination and the new conspiracy books by adapting the strategy they were developing to keep Jimmy Hoffa and Johnny Rosselli out of prison. Marcello and Trafficante's frequent meetings in the fall of 1966 and early 1967 allowed them to quickly respond to, and take advantage of, new developments. Beginning on September 21, 1966, a series of three meetings over three days in New York City showed Marcello, Trafficante, and the Mafia at the height of their post-JFK arrogance and power, though it ultimately sent the mob bosses (very briefly) to jail. The first conclave, revealed by Marcello to an FBI informant, has not been previously reported. Marcello said "the really serious meeting" occurred on the evening of September 21, and "that the New York Police would have 'seen some real power' if they had [known about it]."[1]

While Marcello identified that as the most important meeting, the one the following day at New York City's La Stella restaurant was very impressive. At the main table with Marcello and Trafficante were New York mob bosses Carlo Gambino, Joey Gallo, and Joseph Colombo, as well as eight more mob heavyweights from New York and Louisiana. Such an assemblage didn't pass unnoticed in Manhattan police circles, and the mob bosses were all arrested for consorting with mobsters (one another). After a humiliating strip search and several hours in jail, each was released on $100,000 bail and the charges were later dropped.[2]

On September 23, as if to show they were not intimidated, Marcello, Trafficante, Frank Ragano, Jack Wasserman (Marcello's lawyer), and three others returned to the same restaurant for lunch. Police showed up again, without arrest warrants but with a *New York Daily News* photographer. Just as Trafficante and Ragano had done on the night JFK was assassinated, the two raised their glasses in a toast—only this time, a photographer caught the moment on film.[3]

Marcello's arrogance was punctured on October 1, 1966, when he returned to New Orleans. The local FBI office was slowly overcoming its lax attitude about Marcello that had prevailed for years, and at the airport, an FBI agent confronted the godfather. Accounts vary as to the reasons for what happened next, but the physical act was well documented, by witnesses and a photographer: Marcello took a swing at the FBI agent and hit him. The resulting arrest and charges would dog Marcello for years, eventually sending him to a short stay federal prison.[4]

Journalists and historians have long debated the reason for Marcello's trip to New York for the highly unusual Mafia meetings. Those reasons range from the son of Marcello's predecessor demanding a bigger cut to squabbling between the New York Mafia families. Those or other concerns could have been factors, but because of what happened next, it's also likely that Jimmy Hoffa was on the agenda.

Soon after the meetings, a group of Mafia leaders reportedly authorized Marcello to spend up to $2 million to prevent Jimmy Hoffa from going to prison. Various leaders had contributed, and they decided that if anyone could keep Hoffa out of jail, it was Marcello.[5] This effort would guide much of what happened in New Orleans in the coming months, as a plan was put into place to keep Hoffa out of prison or to get him released once he was there.

Marcello's "spring Hoffa" plan, which he probably worked out with Trafficante at their long private meetings, was also part of their strategy to keep Johnny Rosselli from being deported. That would help to preserve the secret all four men shared: their roles in JFK's murder. The spate of books and articles criticizing the Warren Commission had not yet focused on the Mafia at all, or mentioned them by name, but that could happen at any time—unless the godfathers took some type of action to prevent it. They made sure their strategy to help Hoffa and Rosselli would also divert attention away from their role in JFK's murder and ensure that high US officials would have to keep covering up important information.

Trafficante kept up with national affairs and would have noticed the newspaper and TV polls that pitted Bobby Kennedy against LBJ in a hypothetical battle for the 1968 nomination, even though Bobby had made no public remarks suggesting he might run. Throughout the summer and fall, Bobby consistently beat LBJ in the polls. The worst nightmare for Trafficante and Marcello would be Bobby Kennedy as president, with the resources to conduct a thorough, secret investigation of his brother's murder. As president, Bobby Kennedy could declare martial law or (martial rule, as in Phenix City) and send the National Guard into their compounds and domains. If the Mafia dons' strategy to help Hoffa and Rosselli also damaged Bobby's presidential chances, all the better.

On October 5, 1966, the Texas Court of Appeals ordered a new trial for Jack Ruby, further complicating the situation for Marcello and Trafficante. The court was also considering a change in venue, meaning that Ruby would no longer be in a cell that reportedly overlooked Dealey Plaza (a reminder of what happened to those who crossed Marcello) and under the control of Sheriff Decker, an associate of Marcello's Dallas crime boss. On October 12, Trafficante went to Las Vegas, probably to meet with Johnny Rosselli about the events due to unfold. Soon after that, their plan began to be put into action. It's best to think of it as an evolving strategy, which changed to address new developments that would rapidly unfold in the coming weeks and months.[6]

Marcello, Trafficante, and Rosselli apparently came up with a three-pronged strategy that attempted to keep Rosselli and Hoffa out of jail, while neutralizing any current or future threat from Bobby Kennedy. Their plan's main goal was to avoid exposure of their roles in JFK's murder, whatever the cost: In the coming months and years, it became clear that they were willing to kill even high-profile targets, like government witnesses, in order to achieve their goals. Ultimately, like a pack of desperate jackals, they would even turn on one another.

It's important to keep in mind that Rosselli's Mafia position was lower than Marcello's or Trafficante's. While they were essentially godfathers of their respective territories, Rosselli was only a Mafia don whose main patron (Giancana) had left the country. So, while all three wanted to avoid suspicion, protecting Marcello and Trafficante would always take precedence.

The mob bosses' plan would box in Bobby Kennedy even further, limiting his ability to call publicly for any type of new investigation—and hopefully hurting his chances to run for the presidency in 1968. We mentioned earlier Senator Edward Long's hearings on electronic surveillance, designed to help Hoffa while hurting Bobby's reputation. Rosselli was laying the groundwork to strike even harder at an area sensitive to Bobby, one that would keep Bobby from leaking damaging information about the Mafia to reporters, since it would only support the distorted story Rosselli was about to spread.

To avoid immigration charges, Rosselli was pressuring the CIA to intervene on his behalf, depicting himself as a patriotic citizen who had helped the CIA and now needed its help. That ploy wasn't working with Helms, so the three mob bosses developed a story to float to a few high

US officials and to America's most powerful journalist. It was designed to alarm them, as well as the CIA and Bobby Kennedy, and would be especially effective for those who knew about the CIA-Mafia plots and/or the JFK-Almeida coup plan.

The basic story Rosselli would leak in late 1966, and on a much larger scale early the following year, was that Bobby Kennedy had been responsible for a 1963 attempt to kill Fidel Castro that had somehow boomeranged, killing his own brother. It was a more detailed version of the "Castro killed JFK" story that Rosselli and Trafficante associates like John Martino had been pushing mere days after JFK's murder. This story would hit Bobby Kennedy on several levels: It would associate his name with an assassination attempt in an era when that was unthinkable for most Americans; make Bobby responsible for his own brother's death; and threaten to expose Commander Almeida, still one of the highest-ranking officials in the Cuban government.

Helms and the CIA would be hit hard by the story, since Rosselli added some details from a real incident: the March 13, 1963, attempt to assassinate Fidel near the University of Havana, using mortars, bazookas, and machine guns. It had been one of two attempts to assassinate Fidel within a three-week period (the other was April 7, 1963), in which several of the participants had been captured. JFK's personal emissary, James Donovan, had been in Cuba around that time, trying to negotiate the release of twenty-one prisoners, including three CIA agents. These Castro assassination attempts had been totally unauthorized by, and unknown to, the Kennedys and CIA Director John McCone. Those plots wouldn't become public until several years later, after a Cuban government report detailing the attempts—and earlier ones under Vice President Richard Nixon—would help to trigger the Watergate break-ins.[7]

To tie the failed 1963 Castro assassination attempt to JFK's murder, Rosselli added a twist from a best-selling book and popular movie, *The Manchurian Candidate*, produced by Rosselli's friend Frank Sinatra. As Rosselli would tell the story, some of the captured Cuban exiles had been tortured and "turned" by their captors, then sent back to America to kill JFK.

In hindsight, it may sound like the wild tale it was. But the fact that it was couched in terms of a real operation that only a few high officials knew about gave it some credibility. Though skeptical at first, when the officials and journalists hearing the story found out that the CIA really had been conspiring with the Mafia, they thought the rest of the story might be true as well.

As with any good "con," the story the longtime gambling kingpins concocted played on the desires and fears of its targets. For LBJ, the tale offered dirt to use against Bobby Kennedy. For Bobby, it seemed to confirm his worst fear. For Cold Warriors like Hoover, it confirmed that communist Fidel had killed JFK.

The tale worked best when revealed cautiously, and only under carefully controlled circumstances, so the person hearing it couldn't ask Rosselli questions. Years later, when Rosselli testified under oath to Congressional investigators, he would downplay or deny the "turned-around assassins" story. Even so, the phony story would outlive Rosselli and both godfathers, continuing to resurface as fact in books and documentaries into the twenty-first century.

The false story's brilliance was not just its partial basis in reality, but also in the fact that if officials or the public ever saw evidence that linked Rosselli to those involved in JFK's murder, it would seem as if the Mafia don was just an innocent patriot, one whose associates had been "turned" and used by Fidel. Since Trafficante and Marcello had also worked on the CIA-Mafia plots, the same would be true if evidence tied them to those who had murdered JFK. The ultimate irony is that shortly before his own murder, Rosselli would admit to his attorney the true version of the story: that Trafficante's men involved in plots to kill Fidel had actually killed JFK, a confession that may have caused Rosselli's own murder.

The whole strategy to divert suspicion from the three Mafia bosses shared several characteristics with the JFK assassination plot: using intermediaries and cutouts; infiltrating operations; compartmentalizing information on a "need-to-know" basis; paying bribes; planning for contingencies and using backup plans to deal with evolving situations; and trusting that people would act in their own self-interest.

For example, Senator Russell Long of Louisiana (not to be confused with Senator Edward Long of Missouri, holding the wiretap hearings to help Hoffa) was used only on the Hoffa portion of the strategy, without being told about Rosselli's phony story. The Mafia and Hoffa had bought Russell Long the votes he needed to become Majority Whip in the Senate, so it's only natural that he would have wanted to keep Hoffa out of prison.

The mob bosses were quick to adapt their strategy to new developments, such as when they learned that the *New York Times* was investigating David Ferrie. Their resulting moves, detailed shortly, complemented what they were already doing with Rosselli's story and forced Richard Helms and other CIA officials into further cover-ups. Due to Helms's

1966 housecleaning, the mob bosses no longer had multiple information pipelines to and from the high levels of the CIA, as they did in 1963. Rosselli's friend Morales was out of the country, and William Harvey no longer enjoyed Helms's trust. However, there was at least one pipeline left, since Hunt remained close to Helms, and two Trafficante associates remained close to Hunt.[8]

Though their strategy had some risk, Marcello, Trafficante, and Rosselli had no choice but to try to find some leverage and get control of the situation. In addition to the rising tide of JFK conspiracy books, articles, and investigations, each of the three Mafia bosses had been arrested in recent months. They had to ensure that prosecutors wouldn't try to pressure them or their associates by digging into their possible roles in the JFK conspiracy. It was a matter of survival, and in their world only the most careful and ruthless survived. For any who doubt the Mafia bosses had the savvy to pull off their strategy, keep in mind that they were not characters from *The Sopranos*: Marcello ran a $2 billion operation ($12 billion in today's dollars), Trafficante was a major player in the multibillion-dollar French Connection heroin network, and Rosselli was about to best the world's richest businessman—Howard Hughes—in a series of casino deals.

Rosselli first floated his fake "Castro did it" story with some of the same people helping Hoffa, who were also involved in setting up Rosselli's first deal with Howard Hughes. As a trial balloon for bigger things to come, Rosselli used his old friend, Hoffa attorney Ed Morgan, to pass a brief version of the phony "turned-around assassin" story to another mutual friend, Hank Greenspun, the colorful owner of the *Las Vegas Sun* newspaper. Echoing the small-media-market strategy that John Martino had used in 1963 and 1964, the small *Sun* article attracted no national attention—except in Washington, which was Rosselli's real target. The FBI took notice, as did the CIA.[9]

Rosselli was also using Robert Maheu, who had originally brought Rosselli into the 1960 CIA-Mafia plots, to get close to Maheu's client Howard Hughes. The eccentric billionaire wanted to enter the Las Vegas casino business, and Rosselli needed a powerful ally with deep pockets if he was going to avoid prison or deportation. The way the story is usually told, based on court records, is that Rosselli helped to arrange for Hughes to move into the Desert Inn on November 27, 1966. The Desert Inn had been Rosselli's regular haunt for years, and Hughes was allowed to rent two entire floors of their best suites. This act was a sacrifice for the hotel/casino, since those suites were usually reserved for "whales," high-rolling gamblers whose losses yielded huge profits.

After two weeks, the mobster who supposedly controlled the hotel, Moe Dalitz, wanted Hughes out—but the billionaire didn't want to leave. Rosselli came up with a solution, based on the fact that Dalitz wanted to continue receiving loans from Hoffa's Teamsters Pension Fund. Rosselli asked Hoffa to call Dalitz and arrange for Hughes to stay, and suggested that Hughes buy the casino so he could stay as long as he liked. Howard Hughes then had Maheu arrange—with help from Rosselli, Morgan, and Greenspun—to buy the Desert Inn from Dalitz and his associates. But since Hughes had no experience running casinos, he left Dalitz and his crew in charge. Also on the fringe of the deal was Jack Anderson, the junior partner of America's leading news columnist, Drew Pearson.[10]

Everyone got what they wanted: Rosselli wound up with a $50,000 finder's fee, Hughes soon put Morgan on a $100,000 annual retainer, and Hughes owned the hotel/casino, while Dalitz and the Mafia stayed in charge where they were still able to skim profits. In addition, the powerful Hughes now owed a debt of gratitude to Rosselli and Hoffa. (Rosselli would not go to prison until after Hughes left Las Vegas and the country, following an acrimonious split with Maheu.) However, authors like George Michael Evica feel that Rosselli had set up Hughes and Maheu from the start, that Dalitz's complaints about extending the two-week stay were just an excuse, so that Rosselli and Hoffa could ingratiate themselves with Hughes while making it clear that Hughes needed to buy a hotel to have an assured base in Las Vegas.[11]

For the time being, Howard Hughes was satisfied with the deal, and soon Rosselli was brokering additional deals for him, helping Hughes buy the Sands (for which Rosselli received a $45,000 fee) and the Frontier (Rosselli got a gift-shop concession that netted him $60,000 annually). But because the Mafia men were left in place to run the casinos, they also skimmed and stole $50 million from Hughes over the next three years.[12]

However, none of the skim went to Rosselli, and he knew that if he were in prison or deported, even his finder's fees would be of little use. Rosselli would soon use Ed Morgan and Jack Anderson to ratchet up the pressure on the CIA, as well as on LBJ and Bobby, in an attempt to avoid that fate.

The recent flood of JFK assassination books had triggered new investigations by major newspapers and magazines in advance of the third anniversary of JFK's death. The last major reporter to look into the case had been Dorothy Kilgallen, a well-known TV personality and crime reporter for the *New York Journal-American*. In 1964, she scored an exclusive private interview with Jack Ruby in the chambers of Ruby's judge, after which she wrote a column calling Ruby "a gangster," a term journalists rarely applied to Ruby in those days. In early November 1965, she reportedly told a friend "she was going to New Orleans in five days and break the case wide open." But on November 8, 1965, she died at home of what was eventually determined to be a lethal combination of alcohol and barbiturates.[13]

A year later, other reporters had picked up the torch, and by November 1966 both the *New York Times* and the *New York Observer* had begun serious investigations into JFK's murder. Also looking into the case were two of America's leading magazines, *Life* and the *Saturday Evening Post*. This was a major reversal for some of these publications, whose coverage had previously been extremely supportive of the Warren Report and its "lone nut" scenario.[14]

The *New York Times* had begun its investigation by early November, and it quickly focused on David Ferrie and even Carlos Marcello. On November 21, Martin Waldron (no relation to the author), of the *Times* Houston Bureau, had developed enough information to write a stunningly detailed list of questions to the New Orleans Police Department. The thirty-two questions focused mostly on Ferrie, asking why he had been arrested in November 1963, what he'd been charged with, if he'd made a statement, and why the Warren Commission "did not call Mr. Ferrie as a witness." The *Times* especially wanted to know about any contact between Oswald and Ferrie, both in 1963 and going back to Oswald's days in Ferrie's Civil Air Patrol squadron.[15]

Some of the *Times*'s questions suggest the New Orleans police had been closer to charging Ferrie, and that their investigation continued far longer, than previously known. The *Times* letter said the "former Associated Press bureau chief in New Orleans . . . got the impression in late November 1963, that New Orleans police officials were convinced that Mr. Ferrie was involved in some manner in the Kennedy assassination, and that a biographical sketch was made available for use if and when Mr. Ferrie was so charged." Despite that fact that the official investigation of Ferrie was supposedly over by the end of November 1963, the reporter also asked about an incident in "February 1964 [when] police officers asked" a service station operator if he'd "seen Oswald being in the company of a man wearing a wig," like Ferrie.[16]

The *Times* also brought Marcello into the mix, inquiring about "reports that Mr. Ferrie has been acting as a pilot for Carlos Marcello, reputed to be involved in various shady enterprises in southern Louisiana." The answer to one of the reporter's questions involved Carlos Marcello, when he queried: "Where was Mr. Ferrie on the day President Kennedy was assassinated?"

As far as we can determine, the New Orleans police never answered the *New York Times*'s questions. Their responses would have gone a long way toward outlining the case that Congressional investigators and journalists would start to build against Carlos Marcello a decade later. However, the *Times* would soon fold its investigation, in part because of another inquiry its own questions helped to trigger: that of New Orleans District Attorney Jim Garrison.

The New Orleans police passed the *Times* questions to the District Attorney, putting the responsibility for answering them in Garrison's lap. As we noted earlier, on Monday, November 25, 1963, the New Orleans FBI had indicated to the press that its pursuit of Ferrie and his associates had been Garrison's responsibility. Even though the FBI—not Garrison—had interviewed Ferrie in 1963, when the *Times* or other reporters dug through old New Orleans newspaper files, Garrison appeared to be the one who had let Ferrie go.

Jim Garrison gave several different accounts of when and how he came to launch his investigation of JFK's murder in December 1966, an inquiry that would finally explode in the nation's press in late February 1967. However, Garrison never mentioned the *Times* questions from November 21, though they were clearly a major factor and our copy of the questions even came from Garrison's files. In early December 1963, Garrison told *Life* magazine's Richard Billings that Louisiana Senator "Russell Long [had] encouraged Garrison to take up [the] investigation [just a] couple of weeks earlier."

Senator Russell Long of Louisiana had long-standing ties with the Marcello organization.[17] The senator made remarks about his suspicions to others besides Garrison, as reported in the November 22, 1966, *New Orleans States-Item* in an article entitled "Second Person Aided Oswald, Long Asserts." It was quite unusual at the time for any member of Congress to make such claims, especially the second-ranking senator of the majority party. Within months, Senator Russell Long would be helping Marcello's associates in their attempt to get Hoffa released from jail.[18]

It might seem counterproductive for a Marcello-backed US senator to have pushed conspiracy to newspapers and to Garrison, but it makes sense in light of the strategy that Marcello, Trafficante, and Rosselli had apparently developed. The Mafia bosses wanted to divert attention away from themselves and toward a suspect that high officials, like LBJ and Hoover, had already shown a willingness to cover up in order to avoid: Fidel Castro.

While none of the recent JFK conspiracy books so far had mentioned Marcello or pointed suspicion even generally toward the Mafia, the *New York Times*'s investigation showed that it was only a matter of time before some journalist did so. From Marcello's associates in Houston and New Orleans, he was probably aware of the reporters' digging, even before it generated the November 21 letter about Ferrie and Marcello. Clearly, the mob bosses had to take action, not to simply stay ahead of the story, but to actually define the story.

First they concerned themselves with David Ferrie, since the *New York Times* wouldn't be alone in focusing on his arrest after JFK's murder. Instead of waiting until the press publicly linked Ferrie to Marcello, they decided to define Ferrie in terms of his intelligence ties to Cuban exiles. In today's terminology, they essentially "rebranded" Ferrie as a CIA anti-Castro operative, instead of as Marcello's pilot. That perception would not only force the CIA to withhold information about Ferrie and his associates, but would keep Bobby Kennedy silent as well. That's because Bobby had approved CIA funding for the New Orleans office of Tony Varona's Cuban Revolutionary Council (created by E. Howard Hunt), which had involved Ferrie.

Almost everyone the Mafia chiefs used in the original JFK conspiracy not only had ties to US intelligence, but also could have logically taken the fall for the assassination, if necessary. That would come in handy now, since Ferrie had been so publicly outspoken in his hatred of JFK after the Bay of Pigs debacle. If evidence convinced the public that a conspiracy must have happened, then the public and the press might logically accept a small plot that was limited to Kennedy haters Ferrie and Banister (now deceased), and to Ferrie's associate Oswald.

Chapter Twenty-nine

The JFK investigation of New Orleans District Attorney Jim Garrison, which began in late 1966, was controversial at the time and remains so today, even after being chronicled in numerous books and Oliver Stone's film *JFK*. Our focus is on aspects of Garrison's investigation that were not covered in that film or in most books—on facts that cast the Garrison affair in a new light. Having reviewed all of the relevant books, articles, and documents, we can say that Garrison emerges as neither devil nor saint. Though a larger-than-life character, Garrison was not a mythic, all-knowing hero—but neither was he the complete tool of Carlos Marcello.

Instances of Garrison's cozy treatment of Marcello and his associates are often cited, but most—though not all—have been explained by Garrison or his supporters. For each charge of complicity with the Mafia, Garrison's supporters can cite instances in which he acted against Mafia associates or turned down bribes the Marcello organization offered him, like a 1963 offer of $3,000 per week to allow slot machines in New Orleans. While Garrison certainly didn't wage a crusade against Marcello, or even publicly acknowledge his crime-lord status, the same would have been true of many big-city DAs in the 1960s, especially in cities as corrupt as New Orleans. Garrison did what officials in various cities did to survive politically: He essentially observed a truce with the local godfather, who, in Garrison's case, was one of the most powerful mob bosses in the country. To do otherwise would have certainly cost Garrison his position, if not more.

Jim Garrison had to begin his JFK investigation with David Ferrie because of the *New York Times*'s inquiry, but Garrison could have cleared and dropped Ferrie in a matter of days. Yet Garrison continued pressing Ferrie for more than two months, and some would say that targeting the man sitting with Marcello on the day of President Kennedy's murder was a courageous act, especially at that particular time and place. FBI files we detail later show that Garrison briefly even considered indicting

Marcello for JFK's murder. As with LBJ and Bobby, what Garrison said in public could be quite different from what he actually believed or said in private.[1]

Perhaps because Marcello wasn't sure he could completely control Garrison, associates of Trafficante and others tied to JFK's assassination infiltrated and compromised Garrison's investigation almost from the start. These infiltrators hugely impacted the direction of Garrison's investigation. Garrison seems to have begun his investigation with good intentions, apparently hoping that he could at least raise enough issues to spur the federal government to begin a new, real investigation—but he quickly became diverted and distracted.

Garrison also no doubt hoped the resulting publicity would boost his political profile. This hunger for the spotlight would be his downfall. Although Garrison initially tried to conduct his investigation in secret, he cut a deal with *Life* magazine in late November 1966, giving the publication inside coverage of his investigation in return for its assistance.[2]

The first major step in Garrison's investigation was having David Ferrie brought in for questioning on December 15, 1966. Interrogating Ferrie was John Volz, later the US attorney who would finally send Carlos Marcello to prison for a lengthy sentence. The attention on Ferrie no doubt worried Marcello, and within days, the first infiltrator volunteered to help Garrison. This was Cuban exile Alberto Fowler, who had made a suspicious call to Harry Williams in the hours following JFK's death, after stalking JFK with violent exile Felipe Rivero just before the attempt to kill JFK in Tampa.

The sophisticated and urbane Fowler was highly respected in New Orleans as its Director of International Relations, based at the Trade Mart. In that position, Fowler had worked with Clay Shaw, who had retired the previous year to pursue his avocation of restoring homes in the French Quarter. Fowler was still cordial with Shaw and had recently rented a house from him. As for Garrison, he needed all the help he could get, since he was still trying to conduct his investigation in relative secrecy and with limited resources. He especially needed someone who could speak Spanish and deal with Cuban exiles, so when Fowler volunteered his services, Garrison eagerly accepted.[3]

Fowler was only the first of several such volunteers who diverted Garrison's investigation away from Marcello, Trafficante, and their associates. Soon, Fowler brought in someone to help with Garrison's investigation who was allegedly linked to drugs, Trafficante, and JFK's murder. Later, even Rolando Masferrer and another Trafficante associate would provide information to Garrison. These were all people who should have been investigated themselves, but were instead influencing the course of Garrison's investigation.

Trafficante, Marcello, and Rosselli must have worried when the press announced on December 7, 1966, that a new trial had been ordered for Jack Ruby. Even worse for the Mafia bosses, the trial of their mutual associate Ruby would be held in Wichita Falls, Texas, away from Dallas and its mob-affiliated sheriff. Ruby had largely maintained his silence so far, just as he had done since 1939 about other mob hits and Mafia matters. However, due to Ruby's relative isolation while facing the death penalty, his mental state had declined and there was no way to know if Ruby might crack at some point, despite the apparent Mafia threats to harm his family.

On December 10, 1966, three days after the new trial was ordered, Jack Ruby was reported to be ill from lung cancer. The distraught Ruby, who had recently passed a physical exam with a clean bill of health, claimed that he had been injected with cancer cells.[4]

On December 10, 1966, Bobby Kennedy was distracted from any concerns about Ruby's upcoming trial—and what it might reveal—by two other matters. That day, J. Edgar Hoover leaked a report blaming Bobby for some of the FBI's electronic surveillance. Hoover's report was in response to Senator Edward Long's surveillance hearings that had been designed to "get Bobby" and aid Hoffa. One of the pretexts for Long's hearings had been lawsuits about an FBI surveillance effort in Las Vegas that had been leaked to the Mafia. (The source of the leak was never determined, but some authors think it might have been Hoover himself.)[5]

Bobby scrambled to respond to Hoover's disclosures, with only limited success. The general public and most journalists didn't distinguish between phone taps (which Bobby had sometimes authorized) and illegal break-ins to plant bugs (which Bobby apparently had not explicitly authorized). However, Bobby had listened to some tapes from bugging operations, though he claimed to aides that he thought they had been recorded by local law enforcement beyond his control. At that time, the press wasn't aware of Hoover's now well-documented practice of taking an Attorney General's authorization for limited phone taps and using that as carte blanche for break-ins and bugging, as Hoover had done with Dr. Martin Luther King. Bobby barely managed to cover himself in the press, but claims of his complicity in the surveillance damaged his reputation, especially with liberals. LBJ saw pushing the allegations against Bobby as one more way to constrain his rival's possible presidential aspirations.

In December 1966, Bobby's popularity also took a hit from another dispute being played out in the press: the impending publication of William Manchester's *Death of a President*, which Bobby and the President's widow, Jackie, had authorized. Months earlier, Bobby had been successful in having Manchester tone down some passages that depicted LBJ in an unflattering light, knowing they would only exacerbate the already bad situation between them. However, Jackie wanted additional changes about other matters, and in December 1966 she filed suit to stop publication of the book and upcoming excerpts in *Look* magazine. Bobby supported Jackie in his statements to the press and public, despite his own reservations about many of her concerns. In hindsight, it's interesting that Bobby tried to interfere only with the publication of a book that firmly endorsed the Warren Commission's lone-nut conclusion, and he didn't interfere with books that pointed to a conspiracy in JFK's murder.

Evan Thomas writes that "the only good news about the Manchester controversy [for Bobby] was that it pushed the bugging controversy off the front pages. The suit was settled . . . but the damage to" Bobby had been done, since it looked like he had tried to interfere with the press, and he "began to sink in the polls." Thomas points out that while Bobby had been leading LBJ by five points in presidential preference polls in the fall of 1966, by March 1967 the negative publicity had reversed the situation, and Bobby trailed LBJ by twenty-two points.[6] That would put Bobby in a very weak position when publicity about JFK's assassination became front-page news in late February and March 1967.

Ruby's impending move and trial, coupled with rising interest in JFK's murder due to the proliferation of conspiracy books and articles, may have contributed to Johnny Rosselli's patron moving even farther away from the US. In December 1966, former Chicago mob boss Sam Giancana left Mexico for Argentina, putting him well out of reach if the press or the trial uncovered Ruby's Chicago payoff. Giancana's move put Rosselli in an even weaker position, which would result in a humiliation that never would have happened just a few years earlier, when Giancana was at the height of his power.[7]

Johnny Rosselli's satisfaction over his impending casino deal with

Howard Hughes was dampened by his unexpected, but brief, arrest in Las Vegas on December 29, 1966. The charge was minor—a misdemeanor for not registering as a convicted felon—and Rosselli was bailed out almost immediately by his friend Hank Greenspun. However, the arrest reminded Rosselli of his precarious position as an illegal alien. The earlier leak to Greenspun about the Castro plots hadn't helped Rosselli, so the Mafia don made plans to ramp up the pressure considerably, with the help of Ed Morgan and Jack Anderson.[8]

Though Rosselli hadn't seen any positive results from his leak to Greenspun, the resulting article and his talks with his former CIA contacts Sheffield Edwards and William Harvey were affecting Richard Helms. They were also complicating the already difficult relationship between Helms's CIA and Hoover's FBI. A declassified memo from December 21, 1966, to Helms from the CIA's Director of Security (Howard Osborne, who had replaced Edwards) summarized the problem, saying the FBI had wanted to "subpoena . . . Edwards to appear before a Grand Jury to testify as to his last contact with Johnny [Rosselli]." The CIA strongly objected, since his doing so "would link this Agency and Rosselli and . . . lead to further and more embarrassing inquires." The FBI also wanted Edwards to pressure Rosselli to cooperate with the FBI with "the implied threat of deportation" if Rosselli refused. The FBI was told that this tactic "would be strongly resisted" by the CIA because the whole matter with Rosselli was "extraordinarily sensitive."[9]

Richard Helms gave his signed endorsement to the CIA's refusal to help the FBI, while the CIA's General Counsel pointed out that the issue had also come up regarding Maheu in Senator Edward Long's hearings and in Giancana's prosecution. While it must have looked to Helms as if this Rosselli problem would keep recurring, he didn't realize how soon it would threaten to become public, or that his Security Office would still be dealing with the Rosselli problem for years to come.[10]

Helms probably knew that Hoover was angling to find out more about the CIA-Mafia plots, to use as possible leverage against the CIA in their ongoing bureaucratic struggle for funding and power. Hoover knew about only a few parts of the CIA-Mafia plots, and would have relished getting Rosselli or the CIA in a position where he could learn the full story, something Helms had to prevent if he wanted to preserve his own position and reputation.

Because of Commander Almeida, Helms still had a thin veil of national security to hide behind in dealing with Hoover and the growing media publicity about a JFK conspiracy. Just five months earlier, a CIA memo had made it clear that "military leaders like Juan Almeida [still had] the respect and admiration of the troops," even though they were "supporting the regime more out of loyalty than [out] of conviction . . . without becoming influenced by Communist ideology."[11] As long as Almeida remained unexposed and subject to use in the future, Helms could rationalize (and potentially justify) anything that would keep secret the full range of operations the CIA had used in its attempts to eliminate Castro.

During the CIA's back-and-forth with the FBI over its refusal to help the FBI with Rosselli, Hoover had begun taking an interest in a Cuban exile who had once been a top aide of Commander Almeida. The former aide had come to the US a year earlier, was living in Miami, and had been extremely close to Almeida's family. As with the CIA-Mafia plots, Hoover had learned the broad outlines of the JFK-Almeida coup plan by 1966, probably from his friend LBJ, but there was still much he didn't know about the operation.[12] However, Richard Helms was determined to keep his secrets, from Hoover and even from President Johnson.

The recent surge of books and articles suggesting conspiracy in JFK's murder caused LBJ's White House counsel to propose reopening the JFK assassination investigation, as noted in a December 10, 1966, memo between LBJ aides Joseph Califano and Bill Moyers. The suggestion was to "convene a small (2–3) confidential task force" to look at "alleged circumstantial evidence of the existence and continuance of a conspiracy [and] events since the assassination [suggesting] a conspiracy." Despite the growing media attention, LBJ declined to pursue the idea. As for Richard Helms, he was determined to stem the growing tide of media coverage that generated the pressure for a renewed investigation of JFK's death.[13]

Chapter Thirty

In late 1966 and early 1967, Richard Helms and the CIA began a major new effort to counter critics of the Warren Commission. Most memos about the CIA's efforts to manage the media have never been released, but of the few that have been declassified, the one from January 4, 1967, is remarkable for its candor and length. This fifty-three-page memo detailed the CIA's plan to attack critics of the Warren Report's "lone assassin" theory. While the memo has been available to researchers for years, key portions have always been censored. This book marks the first time the uncensored version has been disclosed, providing new insights that were unavailable to earlier investigators. It allows us to see for the first time who wrote and approved the memo, which CIA divisions were involved, and what they personally had an interest in covering up.

While E. Howard Hunt didn't write the memo, his position of being "in charge of contacts with US publishers" for the CIA means he would have been responsible for helping to implement many of its recommendations. In this light, later CIA memos revealing the Agency's obsessive monitoring of books and articles about the Jim Garrison investigation (including those with even the briefest mention of Hunt associates, like Artime, Varona, and Harry Williams) take on new significance.[1]

It's important to look at the context surrounding the CIA's lengthy January 4, 1967, memo aimed at countering critics of the Warren Report. Prior to the surge of media interest in the JFK assassination that began in the summer and fall of 1966, the CIA had apparently dealt with the relatively few critical authors on an informal and low-key basis, one case at a time. However, by December 1966, a raft of books and articles presented an increasing array of evidence that contradicted the Warren Report's conclusion by using the Commission's own documents in its twenty-six supporting volumes, and a few additional files at the National Archives. Helms didn't know what new investigations this information might trigger, or where those investigations could lead—hence the need for a broader, coordinated attack by the CIA against the Warren Report's critics, detailed in this memo to CIA Station Chiefs.

The CIA's landmark January 4, 1967, memo was written before Jim Garrison's investigation was revealed to the general public, though it was surely known to the CIA. It was also written before Johnny Rosselli ramped up his approach to journalists. However, because Helms had the memo's framework in place, the CIA was able to respond more quickly and effectively to those developments and others. As this CIA memo was being developed, Jack Ruby was preparing to have a new trial, and the CIA no doubt worried about what new disclosures that could generate.

Ramparts magazine ran two short JFK assassination articles in its November 1966 issue, and a major piece in January 1967. Though *Ramparts* was a relatively small, progressive magazine, it became a major target for the CIA when it began developing another article for February 1967, one that had a more immediate impact on the Agency, the Johnson administration, and the national press.

Two days before the CIA's January 4, 1967, memo on attacking critics of the Warren Commission, the Agency learned that *Ramparts* was going to reveal that the CIA had for years secretly funded the National Student Association on America's college campuses. This would be the first revelation of the tip of a very large iceberg that eventually exposed the CIA's massive funding of a variety of domestic foundations, religious groups, unions, and other organizations.[2]

The CIA's reaction to that *Ramparts* story provides insights into how Richard Helms would implement his plan for dealing with Warren Commission critics. Desmond FitzGerald ordered a subordinate "to discredit the *Ramparts* editors any way he could. 'I had all sorts of dirty tricks to hurt their circulation and financing, [including] blackmail. We had awful things in mind, some of which we carried off,'" the former CIA official told Evan Thomas. According to Thomas, "possible examination by the Agency of *Ramparts* income tax returns was discussed." Thomas documented that "two hundred clandestine service case officers worked round the clock for two weeks on damage control."[3]

A rash of newspaper and television news stories appeared in the wake of *Ramparts'* revelation of the surreptitious CIA funding, causing an uproar among the public and Congress. President Johnson eventually appointed a special commission to look into the matter and quell the outrage, but because Richard Helms was a member, he was able to limit the committee's scope and recommendations.[4]

It was against that backdrop that the CIA memo detailing plans to deal with Warren Commission critics was issued and implemented. The only people aware of Helms's main goal for that effort were Helms himself, Desmond FitzGerald, E. Howard Hunt, and a few other CIA officials: to convince CIA personnel, from Station Chiefs to CIA officers, that attacks on the Warren Commission were an attack on the CIA itself. The overt result would be rallying key CIA personnel to defend the Warren Commission and to attack critics of its "lone nut" conclusion, no matter how well documented their books, articles, or arguments were. The covert result, known only to Helms and a few others, would be to make Helms's private worries the concerns of the CIA as an organization. That would prevent the exposure of Helms's unauthorized Castro plots and their ties to JFK's murder, without Helms's having to reveal those plots to additional CIA personnel.

While less than a dozen CIA officials knew about Almeida or about Helms's unauthorized Castro plots, hundreds (if not thousands) in the CIA were aware of other CIA operations that could be exposed if journalists seriously pursued the JFK assassination investigation. These activities ranged from the CIA's extensive domestic surveillance network (which might have been used to track a seeming former defector, like Oswald) to the CIA's operations against left-wing organizations like the Fair Play for Cuba Committee to the Agency's multimillion-dollar support for Cuban exile operations. It wasn't hard for most CIA personnel to see that promoting the Warren Commission's conclusion was a good way to protect the Agency from unwanted scrutiny.

Some CIA officials had other connections that a new JFK investigation could expose. The uncensored version of the CIA's January 4, 1967, memo shows for the first time that the memo was written and "pulled together by Ned Bennett of the CA [Covert Action] Staff in close conjunction with CI [Angleton's Counter-Intelligence]/R&A [Research and Analysis]." Bennett was an interesting choice because he had written an important article for the *London Spectator*, entitled "The Theories of Mr. Epstein," that trashed the book *Inquest* by Edward Epstein, the same book that Richard Goodwin had found so compelling. Bennett boasts in the memo that his *Spectator* article "has attracted widespread attention"—and he even attached the article to the memo as an example of the type of piece that could be written to attack critics, and as a resource whose arguments could recycled in other attacks.[5]

Ned Bennett was also interesting because CIA files show that in July 1962, Bennett had interviewed a former US serviceman who had just returned to America from a two-and-a-half-year defection to the Soviet Union, bringing with him a Russian wife and young child. This "redefector" (the CIA's term) was Robert Webster, one of seven Americans to defect to Russia within months of one another in late 1959 and 1960. Six of those, including Webster and Lee Harvey Oswald, became redefectors who returned to the US. Journalist Dick Russell noted the close parallels between Webster's and Oswald's defections: Webster defected to Russia two weeks before Oswald, and Webster returned to the US two weeks before Oswald. It was almost as if both ex-servicemen were on the same prearranged schedule, and Webster was a former Navy man, while Oswald was a former Marine with ties to Naval Intelligence. The fact that each returned with a Russian wife and new child makes the parallels even more suspicious. Russell points out that when Oswald was in Russia, he inquired about Webster at the US embassy, and the address for "Webster's Leningrad apartment building [was found] in [Marina Oswald's] address book" after JFK's death. Several authors and government investigators have speculated that Oswald and Webster (and the other redefectors) were all part of the same US intelligence operation.[6]

The CIA memo of Bennett's July 1962 interview with Webster raises a crucial question: If Webster was interviewed by the CIA after his return to the US, why wasn't Oswald interviewed, since his circumstances were almost identical? As we mentioned earlier, a CIA official suggested the "laying on of interviews" with Oswald after his return, and Richard Helms lied to the Warren Commission when he told them no one in the CIA had suggested interviewing Oswald. In 1964, James Angleton and his chief deputy were working with Helms on dealing with the Warren Commission, and the same people and departments helped to compile the January 4, 1967, CIA memo, furnishing "most of the themes" attacking critics. Also involved in preparing the memo was the Covert Action staff, and given the turf wars at the CIA, only Richard Helms could have ordered such a coordinated effort.

The official who signed off on the January 1967 anti-critics memo was Cord Meyer, the Chief of Covert Action, who reported to Helms and FitzGerald.[7] Aside from protecting CIA operations, Cord Meyer had an additional, personal reason to stifle further journalistic prying into JFK's life and death. In 1967, the American public was still eight years away from the first news reports of any extramarital affair by JFK, but Meyer's ex-wife had been one of JFK's more regular mistresses.

Cord Meyer and his wife, Mary, had divorced soon after the 1959 death of their son. Unlike her straitlaced husband, Mary was free-spirited and artistic. She was also the sister-in-law of JFK's good friend, *Washington Post* editor Ben Bradlee. According to historian Richard Reeves, JFK's affair with her lasted from February of 1962 until his death. Among Washington's social set, their liaison had not been that unusual.

In 1964, Mary Meyer was shot and killed during an apparent robbery.[8] By 1967, Cord Meyer had no desire to see the press dredge up his wife's death or affair with JFK, so he would have been glad to help Helms clamp down on Warren Commission critics.[9] While Cord Meyer's actions in 1967 have not been declassified, a later example shows what he probably did if information embarrassing to the CIA threatened to become public. In 1972, Meyer tried to suppress the publication of *The Politics of Heroin in Southeast Asia* by Alfred McCoy, which noted the drug trafficking of Santo Trafficante and associates of Manuel Artime.[10]

The CIA's January 4, 1967, memo encouraged the CIA "Chiefs, [of] Certain Stations and Bases," to have their personnel attack critics of the Warren Report, as well as to disseminate helpful information and propaganda supporting the Report's conclusion that Oswald acted alone. The memo opens with a four-page overview, supplemented by forty-nine pages of articles and additional information.

The CIA memo often does the same thing it accuses the Warren Report critics of doing: distorting the truth. Some of its claims are misleading or simply false, as is clear from reading all of the relevant books and articles the CIA memo refers to. The memo also ignores the fact that Helms and other top officials had withheld massive amounts of crucial information from the Warren Commission.

At times, the CIA memo resorts to McCarthy-esque Red baiting, smearing critics as being under the sway of communists. Those claims, along with others the memo details, would continue to be used against Warren Report critics (including members of Congress and government investigators) for decades to come, and even today. That's not because current authors who support the Warren Report are working for the CIA, but because the CIA's arguments and claims (some gathered from the press) were codified and recycled back to the press and then to the public, where they continue to keep resurfacing.

The title of the January 4, 1967, CIA memo is "Countering Criticism of the Warren Report." The CIA department that sent it was named "WOVIEW," a code name that has not previously appeared in any book.[11] The memo's aim "is to provide material for countering and discrediting

the claims" of Warren Report critics, whom the memo calls "conspiracy theorists." Many mainstream journalists still use that term today to
describe anyone who disagrees with the Warren Report. To provide legal
cover for a document that was distributed relatively widely within the
CIA, the agency claims the memo's purpose was "to inhibit the circulation of such claims in other countries," even though the CIA's earlier
action in regard to *Ramparts* and *The Invisible Government* illustrates that
the US was a primary concern. CIA Station Chiefs were told to

> discuss the publicity problem with liaison and friendly elite contacts
> (especially politicians and editors), pointing out that the Warren
> Commission made as thorough an investigation as humanly pos-
> sible, that the charges of the critics are without serious foundation,
> and that further speculative discussion only plays into the hands of
> the opposition. Point out that parts of the conspiracy talk appear to
> be deliberately generated by Communist propagandists.[12]

The CIA station chiefs were ordered "to employ propaganda assets
to answer and refute the attacks of the critics. Book reviews and feature articles are particularly appropriate for this purpose." Among the
attacks to be used against critics were claims they were "wedded to
theories adopted before the evidence was in," and were "hasty and inaccurate in their research." The opposite was true in many cases, since the
Warren Commission had to complete its inquiry in a matter of months,
and the FBI admits essentially completing its own investigation in four
days, while the critics had years to pore over material before arriving at
conclusions of conspiracy. The memo says critics should also be derided
as being "financially interested."[13] The CIA seems to resent that "Mark
Lane's *Rush to Judgment*, published on 13 August 1966, had sold 85,000
copies by early November," and suggests using his lucrative sales to
claim that all conspiracy writers were motivated by money—despite
that fact that several of the books cited by the CIA had sold only a few
thousand copies.

CIA personnel are told that "in private or media discussion," they
should claim that "no significant new evidence [underlining in original]
has emerged which the Commission did not consider." The CIA memo
does not acknowledge any possibility that journalists or investigators
might turn up information that was overlooked by, or unavailable to,
the Warren Commission or the FBI. It does not state that such evidence
should be evaluated or considered; it notes only that anyone disagreeing
with the "lone nut" conclusion should be countered and discredited.[14]

The CIA memo accurately observes that in the recent flurry of articles and books, "no new culprits have been convincingly identified." Helms and the FBI had withheld so much information from the Warren Commission that the Mafia was almost never mentioned, and the critics could mount only vague theories about the possible involvement of Cuban exiles or CIA personnel. The CIA memo is less accurate when it claims that "critics . . . place more emphasis on the recollections of individual eyewitnesses . . . and less on ballistic, autopsy, and photographic evidence." The Warren Commission's own twenty-six supporting volumes show that the Commission (and FBI) often cherry-picked witnesses and parts of their statements to support the Commission's case, and several of the critics' books did, in fact, make extensive use of "ballistic, autopsy, and photographic evidence."[15]

CIA personnel are told to point out to media assets "that Robert Kennedy, Attorney General at the time and John F. Kennedy's brother, would be the last man to overlook or conceal any conspiracy." It's sadly ironic that at the very time when the CIA memo was being issued, Bobby was getting ready to reactivate his own private investigations into his brother's murder. Plus, as Bobby had stated in Congressional testimony before JFK's assassination, the top men in the Mafia always insulate themselves in the case of mob hits, and prosecuting such a criminal conspiracy is almost impossible.[16]

The CIA memo makes a valid point regarding the overly large "mysterious death" lists some writers were using at that time, prior to the flurry of murders in the mid-1970s, the victims of which would include Giancana, Hoffa, Rosselli, and Nicoletti. It also tells CIA Station Chiefs that when they release propaganda supporting the Warren Report, they should emphasize the fact that "the Commission staff questioned 418 witnesses [and] the FBI interviewed far more people, conducting 25,000 interviews and reinterviews." (The fact that none of those interviews involved Cuban exile leaders working for the CIA or the Mafia is ignored.) CIA personnel are told that "reviewers of other books might be encouraged to add to their account the idea that, checking back with the Report itself, they found it far superior to the work of its critics." How many reviewers obeyed the CIA's directive, and how many of those reviews were placed by E. Howard Hunt, we can only wonder.[17]

It should be noted that the CIA's anti-critic memo was only a supplement to whatever efforts Helms, FitzGerald, and Hunt were pursuing as part of their usual contacts with publishers and the press. While pro–Warren Commission books would start appearing within months of the CIA memo's release, what role, if any, the CIA played in their production or promotion is impossible to discern. Those questions can be answered only when the files of Hunt, WOVIEW, and others are declassified.

The CIA memo's lowest point is when it helpfully details how Nazi files can be used to discredit author and Holocaust survivor Joachim Joesten, author of *Oswald: Assassin or Fall Guy* and other works criticizing the Warren Report. Bernard Fensterwald and Michael Ewing point out that "Helms' aides had used data on Joesten which had been gathered by Hitler's Chief of S.S. on November 8, 1937." The CIA's January 4, 1967, memo lists three places, including the National Archives, where CIA personnel or friendly journalists can obtain the Nazi information to use against Joesten.[18] The effort to discredit Joesten was part of a CIA approach to demonstrate that "some writers appear to have been pre-disposed to criticism [of the Warren Report] by anti-American, far-left, or Communist sympathies." Included in the list to smear are notables like England's Bertrand Russell.[19]

Helms succeeded in getting the CIA, as an organization, behind the cover-up he needed to conceal his own misjudgments and unauthorized activities, but the effects of Helms's effort would persist for decades: When Watergate triggered a series of Congressional inquires that started to expose the CIA's extensive use of the press, some of Helms's former subordinates and successors (including George H. W. Bush) used the press as part of a strategy to subvert and shut down those investigations. That allowed CIA manipulation of some press assets to continue during the Iran-Contra scandal, the first Iraq War, and the run-up to the second Iraq War. Helms's and Hunt's actions in the late 1960s mirror today's problems with news coverage of issues ranging from Iran to North Korea, where CIA "black propaganda," ostensibly targeted overseas, is widely reported in the American press.

As if the January 4, 1967, memo is still in force today, the CIA even now officially acknowledges only the Warren Report's findings, and ignores the conspiracy conclusions of Congress. Unofficially, a few former CIA officers tell journalists about the discredited "Castro did it" theory. Peter Dale Scott observes that only journalists who support the Warren Commission or "Castro did it" theories are treated by the CIA as "privileged authors, those who (unlike the rest of us) are able to interview CIA officers and quote from unreleased classified documents."[20]

The CIA and FBI were not alone in their effort to support the Warren Report and attack its critics. Both the Secret Service and the Defense Intelligence Agency may have made similar efforts to protect their reputation and operations, but their files in that regard have never been released. The bottom line is that many US agencies and officials had a variety of reasons to avoid reopening the JFK investigation in 1967, as well as in the aftermath of the 1968 assassinations of Martin Luther King and Bobby Kennedy, and in the years that followed.

Chapter Thirty-one

On January 3, 1967, Jack Ruby died at Parkland Hospital, three weeks after being diagnosed with cancer. His death, which occurred the day before the CIA issued its internal memo attacking Warren critics, was no doubt a relief to Richard Helms, since it eliminated the chance of any CIA secrets coming out at Ruby's new trial. Ironically, Ruby's death shared the front pages with bigger headlines about Rolando Masferrer's failed invasion of Haiti, which Masferrer had continued after CBS backed out. No journalist at the time noted that Ruby and Masferrer knew each other, or that both men had worked with Santo Trafficante.[1]

Marcello, Trafficante, and Rosselli must also have breathed a sigh of relief at Ruby's death, since it removed any possibility that the increasingly disturbed Ruby might blurt out something incriminating on the stand or to a journalist. His death allowed the three Mafia bosses to focus on diverting suspicion from themselves, keeping Rosselli and Hoffa out of prison, and trying to restrain Bobby Kennedy from taking action against them. As part of their efforts, they would soon have Rolando Masferrer feeding disinformation to New Orleans DA Jim Garrison.

In early 1967, Masferrer's drug-smuggling partner, Eladio del Valle, was being tracked down by the Garrison investigator recommended by Albert Fowler. Del Valle, Masferrer, and allegedly even Garrison's Florida investigator all had ties to Santo Trafficante. In 1963, del Valle had worked closely with David Ferrie. In the early 1990s, Cuban authorities would accuse del Valle of having been involved in JFK's assassination, along with Trafficante bodyguard Herminio Diaz.[2]

Trafficante's empire was thriving in many ways, from his profitable operations smuggling heroin and cocaine to the illegal *bolita* lottery, popular among Cuban exiles. Trafficante had long since given up any hope of reopening his casinos in Cuba, and was preparing to open a large casino in the Bahamas.[3] However, Trafficante's plans would all come crashing down if he were linked to JFK's assassination, so he couldn't afford for del Valle to become a person of interest, like Ferrie was. It was a dangerous situation for del Valle, since his partner, Masferrer, was under arrest and couldn't intercede with Trafficante on his behalf. The ruthless Trafficante would have been determined to squelch or spin any JFK conspiracy information coming out of his territory.

Possibly as a result of Trafficante's concerns, in early 1967 racist Joseph Milteer was briefly the focus of several newspaper articles about JFK's assassination. Most historians have overlooked these stories because they didn't mention Milteer by name, and because more dramatic events in New Orleans and Washington soon overshadowed the Miami articles. Thus the stories were only a brief blip on the national radar and Milteer was never identified in the media at that time. That left the white supremacist free to pursue his violent, racist agenda into the following year, when it would result in the assassination of Dr. Martin Luther King.

Although Milteer lived in the small South Georgia town of Quitman, he traveled frequently to Atlanta, and less often to Miami, New Orleans, and other towns in the South. For years, Milteer had subsisted primarily on a slowly dwindling inheritance, but by 1967 he and three associates in Atlanta had found a new way to fund their racist efforts while also lining their pockets: Each Friday, on payday, they waited just outside the gates of one of Atlanta's largest factories, a General Motors plant that employed more than seven thousand people. There, Milteer and his three partners collected money from some of the well-paid, unionized work force for a fund they claimed was to battle civil rights. Only their most regular contributors, once they trusted them, were told in confidence the money was really for a fund to kill Martin Luther King. An Atlanta race riot several months earlier had only increased their contributions. In actuality, Milteer and his partners were using most of the money to buy undeveloped mountain land in North Carolina, just over the Georgia border. (The full story of Milteer's involvement in King's murder begins in Chapter 38.)

Milteer had originally been drawn into the JFK conspiracy in 1963, probably by his racist associate Guy Banister, when reports surfaced about JFK's plans to give a speech in Atlanta more than two months before the President's visit to Dallas. That was around the time of Oswald's visit to an Atlanta Klan associate of Milteer, and calls by David Ferrie to Atlanta. Though JFK's Atlanta speech was canceled due to local officials' security concerns because of JFK's stance on civil rights, Milteer had remained a small part of the JFK plot. Milteer's involvement led to the November 1963 tapes and reports by Miami police informant William Somersett that were detailed in earlier chapters.[4]

Somersett had not been in contact with Milteer since December 1963, when an irate Milteer had called Somersett after being interviewed by FBI agents. Somersett had continued to be an informant for various agencies, since he was opposed to violence even though he was still extremely conservative politically. Somersett published a small, independent labor-union newspaper in Miami, which may have given Trafficante a way to influence him, directly or indirectly. Trafficante had ties to the Teamsters Union in Miami: He shared an office there with one of Hoffa's corrupt locals, and Trafficante was partners with at least two Miami Teamster–Mafia criminals.[5]

On January 26, 1967, J. Edgar Hoover told the director of the Secret Service that the Miami FBI office had just learned of an unusual request from the Miami Police Intelligence Unit: The police had asked Somersett if they could "release to the press information regarding the plot to assassinate [JFK] made by J. A. Milteer to [Somersett] on November 9, 1963." Somersett gave his okay to the Miami Police Intelligence Unit, "provided the informant's identity was concealed." After that, Somersett "was contacted by . . . a reporter for the *Miami News*," and Somersett "confirmed his conversation regarding the threat to President Kennedy."[6]

In a bizarre twist, to the reporter and consistently thereafter, Somersett spun the story of Milteer's talk of killing JFK not against the white supremacist, but to slam Bobby Kennedy. Somersett claimed that since he had told the government about Milteer's threat, Bobby should have taken action before Dallas—therefore, JFK's death was Bobby's fault. The FBI noted that Somersett's comments "indicated that . . . his story will be very critical of . . . Senator Robert F. Kennedy." We spoke to the *Miami News* reporter who broke Somersett's story, Bill Barry, who said that when Somersett had first approached him with the story in early 1967, it already had its anti–Bobby Kennedy angle.

Barry refused to include Somersett's anti-Bobby spin, and broke the story in the *Miami News* on February 2, 1967, headlined "2 weeks before JFK was Killed: Assassination Idea Taped." The *Miami News* article included Milteer's comments that JFK would be shot "from an office building with a high-powered rifle," and that "they will pick up somebody within hours afterwards . . . just to throw the public off." The article didn't identify Somersett or Milteer, though Milteer certainly would have recognized his comments.[7] Bill Barry's article also quoted

Milteer talking about a Klan associate who had "participated in the bombing of the Birmingham church" in 1963 that killed four young girls. The article also said Milteer's associate had "tried to get Martin Luther King [and] followed him for miles and miles, and couldn't get close enough to him."[8]

The Miami Police played the surveillance tapes for the news media the day the story broke. The next day, Barry and the *Miami News* published a second story on the matter, and the *Miami Herald* ran its first. However, despite the country's rising interest in a JFK conspiracy, the Miami story did not become major national news. The *Baltimore Sun* and a few major newspapers carried an AP version of the story, but it didn't generate any follow-up coverage in the national press, and soon the allegations vanished from even the Miami newspapers.

The most unusual aspects of the incident are how the story came out in the first place, and why it disappeared so quickly, before Milteer was named. Regarding the latter, it's possible that Hoover and the Secret Service contributed to the story's not becoming national news, since the Milteer affair didn't reflect well on either agency. Reporter Bill Barry told us he wanted to name Milteer in the articles and go to Georgia to interview Milteer, but officials at his newspaper denied both requests. Instead, Barry was taken off the Milteer investigation to work with one of Garrison's men pursuing dead-end leads. Soon, Barry was taken off the JFK assignment entirely. Left on his own to pursue Milteer, Barry might well have uncovered Milteer's ties to Guy Banister, or other important information. Since Milteer's name never surfaced in the press at that time, it left him free to pursue the King assassination plot with Carlos Marcello later in the year.[9]

The only official reaction to the Miami stories appears to have come from the Birmingham police, who came to Miami to listen to the portion of the tapes about the Birmingham bombing, and from the US Secret Service, which began a new investigation of Milteer—which would be closed several months later, after the Secret Service took no action. Also, even though the articles discussed JFK's Miami trip on November 18, none of them mentioned JFK's Tampa motorcade that same day. Just as federal officials had stonewalled the *Miami Herald*'s attempt to do an article about the Tampa threat two days after JFK's murder—and had squelched any follow-up about Tampa by the *Herald* or the *Tampa Tribune*—they may have put a lid on this Miami story for the same reason. None of the then recent JFK conspiracy books or articles had revealed the Tampa attempt, and Hoover and the Secret Service wanted to keep it that way. It's also interesting that the large FBI folder at the National Archives with the February 2, 1967, Milteer article also contains memos about Johnny Rosselli's 1966 and 1967 activities, as well as many files about Commander Almeida. It's as if whoever compiled this FBI folder knew, or suspected, that all those files were related.[10]

As for how the Miami Somersett-Milteer story was leaked in the first place, the FBI memo indicates that the Miami Police Intelligence Unit first approached Somersett about revealing the story. Given the violent reputation of white supremacists at the time, Milteer's associates in particular, it seems odd that Somersett would have willingly exposed himself to retaliation—unless he had something to gain. Even after the Miami newspapers dropped the story, Somersett kept pushing it, even talking about it on local television the following month. He even continued his anti-Bobby spin in a story in his own small labor newspaper, headlined "I charge Robert F. Kennedy with Murder."

If the Miami story were the only one blaming Bobby Kennedy for his brother's death, it might be more difficult to explain, but it was actually one of two being peddled at the same time; Johnny Rosselli was trying to leak the other. In fact, the Milteer story was printed at a time when Rosselli's effort to get his version into print in a major way seemed to have stalled, almost as if the leak about Milteer were a backup plan. In 1967, Rosselli's associate Santo Trafficante wielded tremendous influence in Miami, and still had a man in the Tampa Police Department, Sgt. Jack de la Llana, who headed the statewide Police Intelligence network. It would not have been difficult for Sgt. de la Llana to have learned about the Milteer tapes and Somersett's identity from the Miami Police Intelligence Unit, or for de la Llana to have influenced the Miami Unit's actions.

Trafficante would have been concerned about Jim Garrison's interest in David Ferrie, since Ferrie had spent significant time with Eladio del Valle in Miami during 1963, while dealing with his Eastern Airlines dismissal hearing. Perhaps Trafficante and Marcello were laying the groundwork to frame Ferrie as Banister's flunky who aided Milteer's racist plot to kill JFK. Blaming JFK's murder on right-wing extremists would have sounded logical to the public while also diverting suspicion away from the mob bosses. It's also possible that Garrison's investigator in Miami, or others, had learned of the existence of the Milteer tapes and the articles were an attempt to get the story out with an anti–Bobby Kennedy spin. Trafficante had been in New Orleans on January 30 and

31, plotting strategy with Marcello, just before the Miami Milteer story broke.

Santo Trafficante was arrested when he returned to Miami on February 3, 1967, the day the second Milteer article appeared. According to Frank Ragano, the godfather was arrested for vagrancy when he stepped off the plane at the Miami airport, even though he was "wearing an $800 silk Brioni suit and . . . had $1,000 in cash in his pockets and was on his way to his home in Miami."[11] Ragano paid Trafficante's bail within hours, and chalked up the arrest to harassment by the Dade County sheriff's office. However, the timing of Trafficante's arrest is interesting, and apparently, some officials were starting to suspect that Trafficante had had a role in JFK's death. The following month, Frank Ragano would write a letter to J. Edgar Hoover, saying that "some of the allegations involving Trafficante have been ridiculous." Author Dick Russell describes the rest of the letter as trying "to deflect any suspicion of Trafficante's involvement in the [JFK] assassination." Whose "suspicion" that was is not clear, since the press would not link Trafficante to JFK's assassination until well into the next decade.[12]

Three weeks before Trafficante visited Marcello, Trafficante had been in touch with Johnny Rosselli. Rosselli and Trafficante almost certainly discussed what Rosselli did next: revealing the CIA-Mafia plots, and the "turned-around assassins" cover story, to America's best-known investigative journalist, Drew Pearson.[13]

Drew Pearson wasn't just America's most famous muckraking reporter, whose "Washington Merry-Go-Round" column was read by fifty million people in six hundred newspapers.[14] Pearson was also known to be close to President Johnson and other powerful Washington figures, including Chief Justice Earl Warren. By revealing the Castro assassination plots and the "turned-around assassins" story to Pearson, Rosselli would show those in power that he wasn't bluffing, and that he wanted CIA help with his immigration problem. In addition, if Pearson printed the story, it would present the Mafia not as potential suspects in JFK's murder, but as patriots who had tried to help the US government— only to be caught up in a Bobby Kennedy plot that Castro turned to his own advantage. With this one crucial leak, Rosselli could help himself, deflect suspicion in JFK's assassination, and damage Bobby's political reputation.

To help spread the story, Rosselli used Edward Morgan, well known as an attorney for Jimmy Hoffa, even though Morgan wasn't handling

Hoffa's current appeal. Ed Morgan, a former FBI agent, was highly respected in Washington and could use attorney-client privilege to shield his contact with Rosselli. Pearson's junior partner, journalist Jack Anderson, was involved with Ed Morgan in yet another business venture with Howard Hughes, so Rosselli was essentially working with the same trusted people he'd used in the Hughes–Desert Inn deal.[15]

On January 13, 1967, Jack Anderson arranged for Drew Pearson to meet attorney Morgan and hear from "a client of his who was on the fringe of the underworld [how] Bobby Kennedy had organized a group who went to Cuba to kill Castro; that all were killed or imprisoned . . . that subsequently Castro decided to utilize the same procedure to kill President Kennedy." Pearson was amazed at the story, but Morgan was a distinguished attorney, who had helped direct the Congressional investigation of Pearl Harbor. Pearson wanted to take the story directly to President Johnson, and Morgan agreed.[16]

At the White House on January 16, 1967, Pearson told LBJ the story in a one-hour meeting. Pearson wrote in his diary: "I told the president about Ed Morgan's law client . . . Lyndon listened carefully and made no comment. There wasn't much he could say." LBJ didn't take the account very seriously at first, since he knew little or nothing about the CIA-Mafia plots and had only a partial understanding of Bobby Kennedy's and the CIA's extensive 1963 efforts to eliminate Fidel. Pearson told LBJ he didn't plan to write the story until November, when the statute of limitations on conspiracy ran out. LBJ suggested that Pearson take the story to Chief Justice Earl Warren; Pearson outlined the tale to a "decidedly skeptical" Warren on January 19, 1967.[17] However, Warren may not have wanted to let Pearson know that he had heard something about the CIA-Mafia plots when he headed the Warren Commission. Pearson asked Warren to meet with Morgan to hear more for himself, but Warren declined, saying he would refer the matter to the Secret Service.

Though Warren appeared skeptical to Morgan, the Chief Justice took the matter seriously enough to meet with the head of the US Secret Service, James Rowley. In Warren's private chambers at the US Supreme Court on January 31, 1967, he told Rowley the story of Morgan's underworld client. After the meeting, Rowley attempted to have his agents interview Morgan, who didn't keep the appointment. The attorney knew that spreading a story privately to LBJ or Earl Warren was one thing, but making statements to federal agents was quite another.[18]

Meanwhile, in Louisiana, a "Police Beat" column in New Orleans' main newspaper mentioned very briefly that Jim Garrison was looking into JFK's assassination. But an assistant DA cited in the column downplayed the inquiry's importance by making it sound routine, so the item received little attention in New Orleans and none nationally.[19]

Whether Rowley learned about that article is not clear, but he did receive word of the Miami Milteer article three days after his meeting with Warren. That triggered a new Secret Service investigation of Milteer, but little appears to have been done, and Rowley continued to sit on the story Warren had given him.

Bobby Kennedy didn't know that a story saying he was behind Castro assassination attempts was floating around Washington at the highest levels. The New York Senator was becoming more involved in Congressional issues, including his growing conviction that the war in Vietnam was wrong and the US needed to stop its escalation. On February 6, 1967, Bobby had a contentious meeting with President Johnson about the matter, in which LBJ accused Bobby of leaking news about a secret peace feeler from Hanoi. Bobby protested that he'd done no such thing, then argued that LBJ should stop the bombing of North Vietnam. The meeting ended badly, with Johnson saying he would end Bobby's political career and destroy Bobby's "dove friends."[20]

As the Rosselli-Anderson saga unfolds, it's important to keep in mind that for years, noted historians who had looked at the issue assumed that President Johnson eventually ordered Anderson and Pearson to publish Rosselli's story, as a way to get back at Bobby Kennedy over LBJ's differences with him regarding Vietnam. The fact that the story wasn't published right after LBJ's contentious February 6 meeting with Bobby helps to show that wasn't the case. As we'll detail shortly, President Johnson's now available White House tapes, the timing of Bobby's next confrontation with LBJ over Vietnam, and the Rosselli story's subsequent appearances all demonstrate that LBJ wasn't responsible for the story's ultimate release.[21]

On February 13, Secret Service Chief Rowley tried to toss the political hot potato of Morgan's JFK-Castro assassination story to his rival, J. Edgar Hoover. But the FBI Director told Rowley the FBI "is not conducting any investigation regarding this matter." The Bureau would, however, be willing to listen to Pearson, Morgan, or "Mr. Morgan's source" if they decided to "volunteer any information."[22]

For Johnny Rosselli, the wait must have been frustrating. His story had yet to find its way to his main target, the CIA, either through private channels or via Pearson's column. Headlines about JFK's assassination would soon explode across the front pages of America's newspapers, in a way unseen since the Warren Report's release—but they wouldn't be about Rosselli's story.

FBI reports confirm that around February 12, Carlos Marcello and Santo Trafficante met for three days in New Orleans. The FBI had finally developed several informants who, while not part of Marcello's inner circle, could provide basic information about the godfather's comings and goings, as well as Marcello's extensive use of pay phones to make and receive especially sensitive calls. One of the FBI's informants said, "Today Carlos Marcello feels he 'owns' [DA Jim] Garrison [though the] informant was not aware of any activities made between Marcello and Garrison." Just days after Marcello and Trafficante wrapped up their meetings, Garrison would become national news.[23]

The front page of the February 17, 1967, *New Orleans States-Item* blared, "DA Here Launches Full JFK Death 'Plot' Probe," signaling the start of the publicity barrage that dominated media coverage of the JFK assassination for the next two years. Coming on the heels of the recent books and articles indicating that a conspiracy murdered JFK, the article launched a firestorm of coverage across the country, and reporters were soon streaming into the Crescent City to cover the story. Garrison later claimed he had wanted to continue his investigation in secret and was not yet ready to have it publicized—but he didn't ask the newspaper to hold the story, when he was shown an advance copy before it went to press.[24]

On February 18, the New Orleans newspaper revealed that David Ferrie was a prime target of District Attorney Jim Garrison's investigation. Ferrie claimed he had sought out the reporter to tell his side of the story, so that he couldn't be "railroaded" by Garrison. More likely, Ferrie wanted to make sure his former employer Carlos Marcello knew he wasn't cooperating with the DA. None of the stories filed at the time, or in the coming weeks, mentioned Ferrie's work for Marcello in 1963, though Garrison's investigators and some journalists were aware of it.[25]

Garrison made a statement to the press that only attracted more national attention when he declared, "There were other people besides Lee Harvey Oswald involved [in JFK's murder, and] New Orleans was a factor in the planning. . . . We already had the names of the people in the initial planning . . . arrests will be made. Charges will be filed and convictions will be obtained." As would often be the case, Garrison's declarations went far beyond any evidence or witnesses he had in hand. Garrison's detractors call it political grandstanding and a play for publicity. His supporters say he was trying to smoke out conspirators by making them think he had more than he did, or that he was trying to prod federal authorities and Bobby Kennedy to investigate a New Orleans connection to JFK's murder—one that Garrison himself couldn't expose if he hoped to remain in office. Our assessment is that while his supporters' view had some validity at the start, the detractors' version came to be more and more true as the investigation dragged on.

The Garrison story developed a local angle in Miami, where on February 18 and 19, 1967, newspapers revealed that Garrison's investigators had been there for some time, looking for a Cuban involved with Oswald. Though none of those Miami articles mentioned the stories, printed just two weeks earlier, about the taped informant (Milteer) talking about JFK's assassination, they did point out that Garrison was using a Miami-based detective to search for Oswald's Cuban associate. While the New Orleans newspaper said the Miami detective was "a close friend of one of Oswald's Cuban friends," the detective denied that to the *Miami Herald*. Years later, Congressional investigator Gaeton Fonzi would write that a source told him it was the detective himself who "was in contact with Oswald," and that same detective "was . . . in Dealey Plaza on November 22nd [1963]."[26]

The Miami detective, brought into the case by Albert Fowler, was later alleged to have ties to organized crime and drug trafficking. The detective also served in an exile organization with Manuel Artime and would later be questioned about a terrorist bombing in the 1970s that involved Fowler's good friend Felipe Rivero. Garrison's original interest in Miami had been to find Ferrie's friend Eladio del Valle, but some authors believe the Miami detective played a role in diverting Garrison toward looking for other Cuban exiles with little or no connection to the case.[27]

Former Senate investigator Al Tarabocchia described Eladio del Valle as a "gun for hire" who was involved with "anything that had to do with smuggling, gunrunning." He said del Valle acted as "both a bagman and a hitman." Now the hitman himself must have been nervous once del Valle learned that the New Orleans DA was looking for him. His colleague Rolando Masferrer couldn't help, since he was still in legal hot water over his failed Haiti invasion. Their mutual partner in smuggling and the drug trade, Santo Trafficante, would not tolerate del Valle's becoming the focus of the same type of publicity now plaguing del Valle's old friend David Ferrie. If the Cuban reports are true about del Valle being involved in JFK's assassination with Herminio Diaz, then Trafficante couldn't let del Valle be found, let alone interviewed.[28]

Chapter Thirty-two

President Johnson, Richard Helms, and Bobby Kennedy had very different reactions to the news coming out of New Orleans about Garrison and
Ferrie. On February 18, the day after the news broke, LBJ called Acting
Attorney General Ramsey Clark to discuss Garrison and the story he'd
heard earlier from Drew Pearson. Clark had talked to one of Hoover's
top aides about the Garrison story the previous day, but LBJ seemed
much more interested in talking about Drew Pearson's story from Ed
Morgan, whom LBJ described as "Hoffa's lawyer." LBJ said the story
was about "a man brought into the CIA with a number of others and
instructed by the CIA and the Attorney General [Bobby Kennedy] to
assassinate Castro." The news from New Orleans now made LBJ take
the story more seriously.[1]

At CIA headquarters in Langley, Virginia, the public identification of
Ferrie hit Richard Helms hard. A former executive assistant to the CIA's
Deputy Director told Anthony Summers "he observed consternation on
the part of then CIA Director Richard Helms and other senior officials
when Ferrie's name was first publicly linked with the assassination in
1967 . . . and was told 'Ferrie had been a contract agent to the Agency
in the early sixties and had been involved in some of the Cuban activities.'"[2] In an earlier interview, the former executive assistant allegedly
said, "Helms stated that David Ferrie was a CIA agent and that he was
still an agent at the time of the assassination."[3] Helms no doubt started
taking steps to contain the situation and spin the news coming out of
New Orleans, using the CIA's extensive media assets as well as his personal high-level media connections.

Helms's career was finished if the Garrison investigation, or the media
coverage of it, exposed his unauthorized attempts to eliminate Fidel, or
any ties between CIA operations and JFK's murder. There were only a
few staff members in the CIA who knew those secrets, and to whom
Helms could turn for help and advice. In late February 1967, Desmond
FitzGerald was still the Deputy Director for Plans, though his health
and energy continued to decline. David Morales was on temporary

assignment in South America, before joining Ted Shackley in Laos. The increasingly alcoholic William Harvey had recently been recalled from Rome, due to his erratic behavior, and given a make-work project at CIA headquarters.[4] David Atlee Phillips was good with the press, but was still the Station Chief in the Dominican Republic. One of the few CIA insiders Helms could turn to for advice and spin control with the press and publishers was E. Howard Hunt. Because of Hunt's activities such as forming the Cuban Revolutionary Council, whose New Orleans branch had been involved with Ferrie, Hunt had just as much to lose as Helms if Garrison's investigation exposed Agency secrets.

While Bobby Kennedy shared some of Helms's desire to make sure the authorized 1963 plots to topple Fidel weren't exposed, Bobby also wanted to learn the full story behind his brother's murder. In late February and early March 1967, Bobby helped to launch two private investigations by his close associates, and monitored at least two more. One investigation covered the assassination in general, while three focused on Garrison, including one that would help to torpedo Garrison's investigation in the eyes of the public.

Ed Guthman, Bobby's former press aide at the Justice Department, who had since become a top editor at the *Los Angeles Times*, conducted one investigation. Guthman told author David Talbot he decided on his own to cover the Garrison affair, and assigned five reporters to cover the story. Guthman even traveled to New Orleans himself, but they all "concluded there was nothing to it." Guthman says Bobby "wanted to know what we had found out and I told him . . . my feeling was that it was possible [there was a conspiracy], but with Garrison, the evidence wasn't there."[5]

In 1967, former JFK special envoy William Attwood was editor-in-chief of *Look* magazine, *Life*'s chief rival. According to Talbot, after a meeting with Garrison in New York, Attwood "intended to throw the weight of *Look* . . . behind Garrison's investigation. He strongly encouraged [Bobby] Kennedy to commit himself to reopening the case. In response, Bobby told Attwood that he agreed his brother had been the victim of a conspiracy. 'But I can't do anything until we get control of the White House,' Kennedy told him." However, Attwood had a heart attack soon after talking to Bobby, and Garrison's investigation had already fallen into disarray when he returned to *Look* three months later. It would be five years before Attwood began an investigation that would finally expose Michel Victor Mertz in the American press, though as a heroin kingpin, not as part of JFK's assassination.[6]

In addition to monitoring Guthman's and Attwood's efforts, Bobby launched two investigations of his own, apparently in hopes of using the information once he became president. Bobby knew that coming out publicly in favor of a conspiracy prematurely, before clear evidence to substantiate it, could damage his reputation and possibly give Hoffa the ammunition he needed to avoid prison. It could also ruin Bobby's chances of ever occupying the White House, which he considered crucial for bringing any of JFK's assassins to justice. That meant that any investigation Bobby conducted before he was president would have to be done secretly, in a deniable fashion.

One of the trusted people Bobby turned to was Frank Mankiewicz, a journalist and attorney who in 1967 was Bobby's press aide. Shortly after the Garrison case became national news, Bobby told Mankiewicz, "I want you to look into this, read everything you can, so if it gets to a point where I can do something about this, you can tell me what I need to know."[7]

After reading all the books and articles he could get his hands on, and meeting with JFK researchers, Mankiewicz came close to uncovering the truth. He told David Talbot he "came to the conclusion that there was some sort of conspiracy, probably involving the mob, anti-Castro Cuban exiles, and maybe rogue CIA agents." However, when he tried to tell Bobby, "it was like he just couldn't focus on it. He'd get this look of pain, or more like numbness, on his face. It just tore him apart." What Mankiewicz probably didn't realize was that Bobby himself had come to a similar conclusion within days, even hours, of JFK's murder. Bobby withheld crucial information from Mankiewicz about his early suspicions and how they were linked to the JFK-Almeida coup plan. Also, as we'll see shortly, by the time Mankiewicz tried to give Bobby his conclusion, Bobby had new reasons to fear that too much about JFK's murder would come out too soon.[8]

Soon after Garrison's claims became public, while Mankiewicz was just beginning his investigation, another of Bobby's most trusted and experienced aides went to New Orleans to dig into the matter. It was Walter Sheridan, former head of the Get Hoffa Squad that had sent the Teamster leader to prison. What Sheridan did for Bobby in 1967 wasn't new. Sheridan's widow told David Talbot that her husband had helped Bobby look into JFK's murder before, and that they "continued working on the case even after Bobby left the Justice Department. The two of them would sometimes go back to the Justice Department to look over evidence together." However, Sheridan left the Justice Department in 1965 to work for NBC News as a producer and investigator. His widow said "the only thing Walter wouldn't do for NBC was to investigate the assassination," because that was something he and Bobby would only do together. Once the news about Garrison and Ferrie broke, they finally had the chance. Sheridan could go to New Orleans on behalf of NBC News, without appearing to work directly for Bobby Kennedy.[9] Talbot writes that Sheridan "began feeding [Bobby] information about [NBC's] investigation," one of several developments that would soon have a huge impact on Garrison's efforts.[10]

Perhaps the biggest turning point in Garrison's investigation came on February 21, 1967, when David Ferrie was released from protective custody. Ferrie had been at the Fontainebleau Hotel (where Trafficante often stayed), while Garrison weighed whether or not to charge him. Many have speculated about the reason for Ferrie's release, with some authors saying it was designed to scare Ferrie and prod him into turning on other conspirators. Even before the public learned of Garrison's investigation, the DA had told staff members that "Ferrie [was] talking about not having long to live." Ferrie was quoted as telling one of Garrison's investigators, "I'm a dead man," and his emotional condition declined rapidly under the stress.[11] It's also possible that Garrison saw releasing Ferrie from protection as the only way to get him to turn on Marcello.

Garrison's detractors point to problems with that scenario, since Ferrie was not placed under round-the-clock surveillance after his release, as he reportedly had been earlier. There were also reports that Garrison no longer saw Ferrie as important, and that his investigation had hit a dead end.

On the day of Ferrie's release, the *New York Times* ran an article picked up by other newspapers, in which Garrison said that because his investigation had been prematurely publicized, "arrests . . . are [now] most certainly months away." A Garrison staff member hinted at one New Orleans suspect in particular to the *Times*, but wouldn't name him. According to the *Times*, "one of the lawyers who served on the staff of the Warren Commission . . . said that the FBI had accumulated a 'great stack' of data on the alleged New Orleans suspect, and that the information indicated that the man had not seen Oswald in the months just before the assassination and had not been a part of any conspiracy." The *Times* also noted Garrison's connection to *Life* magazine, and observed that CBS News' Mike Wallace had been talking to Garrison for about "two weeks" regarding a CBS special on JFK's assassination. That meant

Garrison had been holding discussions with CBS even before his investigation was made public.[12]

In some newspapers, the *Times* article was headlined "JFK Death Link to Anti-Castro Plot Weighed," since the story told of a theory held by Garrison: "[that] President Kennedy's assassination grew out of a plot by anti-Communist forces to kill Premier Fidel Castro of Cuba. . . . The conspirators planned to send Lee Harvey Oswald to Cuba to kill Castro, and later decided to go after President Kennedy." This theory actually contained a few kernels of truth. Equally surprising, the Warren Commission staff attorney whom the *Times* consulted indicated that "the anti-Castro theory [was not] new," though the Warren Report mentions no theory describing Oswald as part of a plot to assassinate Castro. Garrison's theory, coupled with his focus on David Ferrie and Eladio del Valle, would have allowed Garrison to make real progress if he had been willing to investigate their bosses at the time of the assassination, Carlos Marcello and Santo Trafficante.

But everything changed on the morning of February 22, 1967, when David Ferrie's dead body was found at his home at 11:40 AM. The unusual circumstances surrounding Ferrie's death created a new firestorm of publicity, which Garrison played to the hilt. Garrison wrote that near Ferrie's body were "two typed suicide notes," and Ferrie's "signature on each note was also typed." One said, "To leave this life is, for me, a sweet prospect." The New Orleans coroner first determined that Ferrie's death must have occurred the previous evening. However, he had to change his finding after *Washington Post* reporter George Lardner revealed that he had interviewed Ferrie from midnight to 4:00 AM. The coroner determined the cause of death to be a brain aneurysm that caused a fatal cerebral hemorrhage. Essentially, David Ferrie had died of natural causes from a burst blood vessel, and he did have a history of high blood pressure. However, Garrison hinted at suicide and even murder. Yet another possibility given his medical condition is that the tremendous strain Ferrie was under, from knowing he had introduced Oswald to Carlos Marcello, and realizing the fate awaiting anyone who implicated the powerful godfather, might literally have caused Ferrie to worry himself to death.[13]

There was no debate about the cause of death for Ferrie's friend in Miami, Eladio del Valle. The *St. Petersburg Times* reported that "within hours of Ferrie's" body being discovered, "police said del Valle's body was found crumpled, beaten, and shot on the floor of his red Cadillac convertible . . . at the time, the death was portrayed as being mob-related." Richard Mahoney adds that del Valle "had been tortured, his head split open with an ax, and shot through the heart."[14] If Santo Trafficante was behind del Valle's "mob-related" death, killing him so quickly after Ferrie's death was ruthlessly efficient. Del Valle's murder was overshadowed by the news coverage of Ferrie's demise, and soon forgotten by the national press.

Bobby Kennedy was aware of Ferrie's connection to Marcello, since Bobby's Mafia prosecutors had encountered Ferrie in 1963 and earlier. After reading news reports about the odd circumstances of Ferrie's demise, Bobby called the New Orleans coroner at his home, to hear the details for himself.[15] On the day Ferrie's body was found, President Johnson was briefed on the situation in a phone call from Acting Attorney General Ramsey Clark. Clark revealed that Ferrie had called the New Orleans FBI four days before his death, saying "he was quite a sick man," and that he "wanted to know what the Bureau could do to help him with [Garrison]." Clark called the whole situation "a pretty sordid mess [that] sure took a bad turn today."[16]

Important developments in the Garrison case, and in Bobby Kennedy's life, would occur just a week after Ferrie's death—but before that, Bobby's old friend Haynes Johnson wrote an interesting summary of Garrison's case for the *Washington Star*. In an article researcher Paul Hoch provided, Haynes wrote on February 26, 1967, that a central "thread that winds through the story involves . . . John F. Kennedy's . . . problem of Cuba." Haynes expanded on the anti-Castro theory mentioned briefly by the *Times*, saying that Garrison's theory was:

> . . . that Oswald was working with an anti-Castro right-wing organization and actually intended to kill Fidel; that Oswald's publicly pro-Communist activities in New Orleans and his attempt to enter Mexico and secure a Cuban visa were a ruse to enable him to carry out that Castro assassination objective; that when Oswald was denied entrance to Cuba, the plot shifted and Kennedy, accused of letting down the anti-Castro Cubans at the Bay of Pigs, became the target. This theory has been examined at length in the past and has been discarded.[17]

Paul Hoch posed the question of who "examined at length" such a theory, since no investigation like that appears in the Warren Report. Haynes's article also details some of the anti-Castro activities of Guy Banister, David Ferrie, and the Cuban exile "organization created by the CIA" that shared their office building and activities. (We can only imagine what E. Howard Hunt, the creator of that organization, must have felt when he read that portion of Haynes's article.) The article never mentions Ferrie's and Banister's work for Carlos Marcello, which seems like an odd lapse for the usually thorough Haynes Johnson, who had won a Pulitzer Prize just a couple of years after working with Bobby, Artime, and Harry Williams on their *Bay of Pigs* book.[18]

Though no article on Garrison had mentioned Carlos Marcello yet, the Louisiana godfather would have known that some journalist was bound to report on his connection to Ferrie and Banister eventually, unless something was done. Oddly, after Ferrie's death Jim Garrison seems to have abandoned the theory Haynes and the *Times* had written about, in order to go in another direction. Garrison began focusing intently on what he had previously considered only a minor lead: After JFK's murder, a colorful attorney named Dean Andrews had claimed that while he was hospitalized, someone named Clay Bertrand had called him about representing Lee Harvey Oswald. Andrews later seemed to back away from his allegation in talks with the Warren Commission, though he did make other interesting comments about Oswald and never-identified Hispanic associates to the Warren Commission staff.

Often overlooked in 1967 was the fact that the jive-talking Andrews had been a minor attorney for Carlos Marcello. However, after Ferrie's death, Garrison apparently felt that he needed a live suspect. There were indications (later disputed) that Alberto Fowler's former coworker and landlord Clay Shaw had used the alias "Clay Bertrand," reportedly when he tried to help out New Orleans gays who had been arrested. Though Garrison didn't know it at the time, Clay Shaw had been a CIA informant until 1956, which was not unusual for the head of a bustling Trade Mart in a city like New Orleans, whose ports did a huge amount of business with Latin America and other foreign countries. According to CIA files, Shaw had occasional and brief, casual social contact with local CIA official Hunter Leake until 1965, when Shaw retired from the Trade Mart.[19]

Also unknown to Garrison in late February 1967 were reports that someone resembling Clay Shaw had been seen with Ferrie and Oswald in the small town of Clinton, Louisiana. Congressional investigators uncovered enough witnesses to find this incident credible, though others have pointed to racial politics that might have been responsible for the reports. (Oswald was supposedly trying to get a job at a local mental hospital at the time of a civil-rights voting drive.) Ferrie and Shaw may well have known each other through New Orleans' gay underground, and the same could have been true for Shaw and Oswald. Since Oswald didn't own a car or drive, if he did get to Clinton, someone would have to have driven him. But as with David Atlee Phillips's Dallas meeting with Oswald two months before JFK's murder, it makes little sense for Shaw to have allowed himself to be seen with Oswald in public (and with Ferrie) a couple of months before JFK's assassination, if Shaw had any knowing involvement in the murder.[20]

However, focusing attention on Shaw in 1967 was a good way to keep Garrison's investigation away from Carlos Marcello, and from Traffi-cante's ties to del Valle. It would also divert attention from Alberto Fowler's Cuban exile associates who should have been investigated, men like Felipe Rivero, Manuel Artime, and Tony Varona. Shaw's role as a low-level CIA informant would also force the CIA to cover up and withhold information if Garrison targeted him. So, on March 1, 1967, just as the Ferrie publicity had started to die down, Jim Garrison announced that Clay Shaw had been arrested for the murder of JFK, setting off a new wave of press coverage.

On March 1, 1967, the news about Clay Shaw's arrest was not foremost in Bobby Kennedy's mind since Bobby had just been informed that he was the target of an assassination plot. Jimmy Hoffa's brutal hench-man, Frank Chavez, had just left Puerto Rico with two thugs, headed for Washington and determined to kill Bobby. The Supreme Court had just declined to hear Hoffa's appeal—meaning the Teamster President would enter federal prison in only a week—and Chavez was determined to get his revenge on Bobby.[21]

We spoke to Justice Department prosecutor Tom Kennelly, who helped to uncover the threat, and he told us that because Chavez and his two men were armed, they took the threat very seriously. Washing-ton police located Chavez and his henchmen at a Washington hotel and put them under surveillance, while authorities ordered round-the-clock protection for Bobby Kennedy's Hickory Hill home in Virginia. Walter Sheridan's home received similar protection, since his family was still there while Sheridan was in New Orleans, investigating Garrison.[22]

Frank Mankiewicz was just beginning his secret investigation for Bobby into JFK's murder when the FBI showed him photos of Chavez and his two thugs, in case they came near Bobby's Senate office or press events. Mankiewicz told a journalist that while "we were sure looking for them" and everyone else was very concerned, Bobby "didn't want to talk about it."[23] The Chavez assassination threat undoubtedly impacted

Mankiewicz's nascent investigation. In light of Jack Ruby's many calls to mob associates and Teamster officials before JFK's death, it was enough information to point Mankiewicz in the right direction, even as he and others in Bobby's office watched for any sign of Chavez and his men. Mankiewicz was already familiar with the articles about Hoffa's talk of assassinating Bobby in a car in the South during the summer of 1962, and Mankiewicz may have also learned about the FBI report linking Chavez to Jack Ruby.[24]

Back in 1962, Hoffa had probably been thinking of Chavez when he talked about killing Bobby. In addition to possibly having Bobby shot, Hoffa had also mentioned using a "firebomb" to kill Bobby, after which the assassin could go to Puerto Rico to "hide out." Chavez, who was living in Puerto Rico in 1962, had previously been charged in one firebombing incident and was the top suspect in another. However, by the eve of his imprisonment in March 1967, Jimmy Hoffa felt the time wasn't right for an attempt on Bobby. The Teamster president had other important business to attend to, including Trafficante and Marcello's plans to keep him out of prison.

Frank Ragano, the lawyer Hoffa shared with Trafficante, had represented Frank Chavez successfully five years earlier. The day before Chavez and his cronies left for Washington in 1967, Ragano had arranged for Trafficante to talk to Hoffa from the payphone of a Miami Holiday Inn. Trafficante was still beyond the reach of almost all FBI phone taps, but he took no chances and used only random payphones for business. Ragano heard Trafficante's side of the conversation as the Tampa mob boss commiserated with Hoffa about Bobby Kennedy, saying, "That dirty son-of-a-bitch. Maybe he should have been the one to go instead of his brother. Yeah, I've talked to my friend in New Orleans and I will talk to him again. I'm sure he understands." Trafficante concluded his phone call with Hoffa by saying, "You'll be out before you know it."[25]

Trafficante and Marcello were getting ready to play two of their remaining trump cards to prevent Hoffa from serving a long prison sentence. As part of their strategy, Johnny Rosselli had leaked part of the same story he'd given Jack Anderson and Drew Pearson to someone in Jim Garrison's office and to a reporter with WINS, New York City's first all-news radio station. Since Anderson and Pearson hadn't run Rosselli's story, the mobsters hoped these new leaks would force the issue. In addition, Marcello would soon use some of the Mafia's $2 million Spring Hoffa fund, and Frank Ragano, in an attempt to bribe a key witness against Hoffa.

However, all that would be for naught if Chavez attacked Bobby at this critical time. Just six days away from reporting to federal prison, Hoffa couldn't afford to get mixed up in an assassination plot, so the task of reining in Chavez fell to Frank Ragano. The morning after the Hoffa-Trafficante call, Hoffa called Ragano and demanded that he come to Washington immediately to talk Chavez out of his ill-timed assassination plan. Ragano flew to Washington the same day.[26]

At Chavez's hotel, Ragano found Chavez and his two thugs "packing huge handguns in shoulder holsters." Ragano explained that if Chavez killed Bobby now, officials would easily figure out who had done it and why. An attempt on Bobby would ensure that Hoffa's prison life would be hell, and that the Teamster president would have to serve his entire thirteen-year sentence. Chavez admired Ragano's legal prowess and reluctantly agreed to call off the attempt. Still, Chavez concluded the meeting by saying of Bobby, "Sooner or later he's got to go."[27] Jimmy Hoffa shared that sentiment, and it was only Chavez's timing that he didn't like. In less than three months, Hoffa himself would be talking in prison about having Bobby killed—but it would be Chavez who was shot.

After Chavez returned to Puerto Rico with his men, Hoffa told Frank Ragano "to get in touch with Carlos [Marcello] and have him set up that meeting with Ed Partin," the government's prime witness against Hoffa. Hoffa hoped Partin could be bribed to declare that his testimony was false, or that the government had illegally wiretapped Hoffa during the trial. In return, Marcello would get a huge loan from the Teamster Pension Fund to build a new French Quarter hotel. Hoffa told Ragano that "Al Dorfman will take care of that while I'm gone. I told Al to give Carlos whatever he wants."[28]

With mere days remaining before Hoffa went to prison, Marcello and his men were already arranging an attempt to bribe Partin. An aide to Louisiana's governor set up a meeting between Partin and a close associate of Marcello. Marcello's man told Partin that if he changed sides and helped Hoffa, "the sky's the limit. It's worth at least a million bucks." During their talk, Marcello's associate called Allen Dorfman, explaining that while Dorfman was running the bribe attempt, Marcello was actually "holding the money." Marcello's man then boasted to Partin of Marcello's and Dorfman's political power, saying that they "had helped Senator Russell Long (of Louisiana) get elected whip" in the US Senate by paying for the votes of seven US senators.[29]

Marcello's man used a carrot-and-stick approach with Partin. While dangling the million-dollar carrot, he also told Partin that one or more Mafia hit contracts had been let on Partin's life. However, if Partin took the bribe and helped Hoffa, the Mafia would make sure he was protected. A few days later, when Partin proved reluctant to lie to help Hoffa, Marcello's envoy told him "that Jim Garrison was going to subpoena Partin in connection with his assassination probe." However, if Partin helped Hoffa, that subpoena could be avoided. Still, Partin refused.[30]

At the same time Allen Dorfman—the Teamsters' money supplier to the Mafia—was trying to bribe another key Hoffa witness to change his testimony. Dorfman's attitude and connections can be summed up by an encounter that took place the following year at a lavish dinner party at columnist Drew Pearson's Washington home. In addition to the political figures attending were Allen Dorfman and Frank Sinatra, who announced his opposition to Bobby Kennedy at the party. The *Washington Post*'s society reporter, Maxine Cheshire, covered the posh event and recognizing Dorfman, she told him, "I've heard you are here to try to get Jimmy Hoffa out of jail." Dorfman replied, "That's right, baby. I'm here to buy anyone who can be bought. Are you for sale?"[31]

On March 2, 1967, New York Senator Bobby Kennedy was wrestling with even more issues than Chavez's assassination threat, Marcello's attempt to bribe Partin, and Ferrie's recent death. Though Bobby's public-approval ratings and his relationship with LBJ were already at a low point, he took a step that risked making both much worse. That day, Bobby gave a major speech in the Senate in which he publicly broke with LBJ over Vietnam. Bobby announced his support for a suspension of the bombing of North Vietnam as part of an effort to bring that country into peace talks.

Bobby surprised many by apologizing in his speech for his past support of the war, saying that during JFK's administration he had participated in some of the decisions that had led to the current problem: "If fault is to be found, or responsibility assessed, there is enough to go around for all—including myself." Bobby's new position was a tremendous political risk, since the same day the other chamber of Congress defeated, by a resounding 372 to 18 votes, a nonbinding resolution to stop the bombing. LBJ was livid at Bobby's Vietnam speech, and the president gave two hastily scheduled talks that day in order to distract press attention from Bobby.[32]

Bobby had arrived at his stance on Vietnam after much soul searching, and it represented a major step in his political growth as a Senator. After his relatively low level of accomplishment during his first two years in the Senate, the speech marked a turning point that would see him come into his own in 1967 as a national political force to be reckoned with. Yet within hours of his courageous speech, he faced yet another public crisis, this one stemming from his brother's murder and his own secret work on the JFK-Almeida coup plan.

Chapter Thirty-three

Three related news reports about JFK's assassination that appeared on March 2 and 3, 1967, would have a tremendous impact not just on Bobby Kennedy, but also on Richard Helms, President Lyndon Johnson, and even later presidents Richard Nixon and Gerald Ford. For decades, most historians have focused only on Jack Anderson's explosive March 3, 1967, newspaper column about Bobby, Castro, and JFK's murder—but recently declassified files and presidential tapes now show the story emerged the day before, March 2, on radio and television in New York and Washington, D.C.

The story that broke on March 2 was Rosselli's tale that Castro had killed JFK in retaliation for Bobby Kennedy's secret efforts to assassinate Fidel, and its release was part of a coordinated effort by associates of Carlos Marcello and Santo Trafficante. The leaks to Jack Anderson, New York City's WINS radio, and Jim Garrison were designed to divert suspicion for JFK's assassination away from the Mafia dons, while also trying to keep Rosselli and Hoffa out of jail. They also wanted to damage Bobby politically, to lessen the chance he could run for president or lead a public outcry for a new government investigation into his brother's death. Aiding Rosselli in this effort was CIA official William Harvey, in the last, sad days of his once notable CIA career.

By the end of February 1967, Rosselli's initial leak to Anderson and Pearson—about Bobby's ordering CIA assassins to kill Fidel—had produced no tangible results. Though it had traveled to President Johnson, Chief Justice Earl Warren, Secret Service Chief James Rowley, and J. Edgar Hoover, Rosselli had nothing to show for it. So Rosselli's associates leaked parts of the same story to Jim Garrison and to a reporter with New York's WINS radio.

The version given to WINS radio was similar to Rosselli's Anderson leak and to a discredited tale briefly promoted in 1964 by associates of Trafficante, Masferrer, and Artime. These similarities have become clear only recently, since WINS didn't broadcast all the information it had. The station gave the unbroadcast portion to Texas governor John Connally, who relayed it to President Lyndon Johnson in a phone call recorded on LBJ's White House taping system.[1]

On March 2, 1967, at 9:55 PM, John Connally called his old friend LBJ from New York. Connally told LBJ there had been a "long story on [WINS] tonight . . . from a man who saw the files in Garrison's office . . . that there were four assassins in the U.S. sent here by Castro or Castro's people."[2] Since the two Texans had been in JFK's Dallas motorcade, they shared a personal interest in the WINS story.

Connally told LBJ confidential information from a WINS executive, who not only had "a team of reporters in New Orleans with Garrison," but also claimed to have two reporters in Cuba, though only for one day. The executive had explained to Connally the radio reporters "were working from different angles [but] came together with exactly the same story" implicating Castro. It's hard to believe that in just one day, or even several days, American reporters could turn up information inside Castro's Cuba that implicated Fidel's men in JFK's murder—and even LBJ would soon voice similar skepticism. More likely, someone had fed Rosselli's information to the reporters, since FBI files show that Rolando Masferrer and an associate of John Martino had fed a similar story to a New York City radio station three years earlier.[3]

The reporters' confidential information, which Connally said was "not going on the air," was that "six months after the Missile Crisis was over, the CIA was instructed to assassinate Castro." That time frame matches the one Rosselli gave to Pearson and Anderson, and it coincides with the start of the JFK-Almeida coup plan. Highlighting the anti-Bobby spin of Rosselli's tale, Connally said that JFK's "brother ordered the CIA to send a team into Cuba to assassinate Castro."[4]

Continuing to mirror Rosselli's story, Connally said, "Some of [the CIA team] were captured and tortured, and Castro and his people—and I assume Che Guevara—heard the whole story [and] one of Castro's lieutenants, as a reprisal measure, sent four teams into the US to assassinate President Kennedy." Laying the responsibility on one of Castro's lieutenants is a slight evolution of the original Rosselli story, probably to make it more politically palatable. If all the responsibility were placed on Fidel, LBJ and other high-ranking US officials would be trapped in the same box they were in just after JFK's murder, worrying about a public or Congressional outcry to invade Cuba and eliminate Fidel. However, putting the onus on a Castro lieutenant, who might have been acting on his own, relieved that pressure. Dropping Che Guevara's name into the story was a good touch, since by that time he had long since disappeared from public view.[5]

After Connally concluded his urgent story, LBJ told Connally a similar tale. After warning Connally, "This is confidential, too," LBJ explained he'd gotten "that story [from] one of Hoffa's lawyers [Ed Morgan, who] went to one of our mutual friends and asked him to come and relay that to us . . . just about like you have related it. A week or two passed, and then [Drew] Pearson came to me [and] told me [that Hoffa's lawyer] had told him the same thing."[6]

LBJ said he was skeptical of the story, and that Attorney General Ramsey Clark said there was nothing to it. However, LBJ said he had been "reconstructing the requests that were made of me . . . right after I became president," when LBJ was asked to continue the plans for a coup in Cuba. LBJ told Connally he was going to discuss this new information further with Attorney General Clark so that he and J. Edgar Hoover could "watch [the story] very carefully."[7]

LBJ told Connally that "some of these same sources" trying to prevent "this jail thing" for Hoffa "have [also] been feeding stuff to Garrison as they did here." Historian Michael Beschloss says that LBJ was worried that the story was being spread by "Hoffa's allies to keep the Teamster leader out of prison," by hoping "Johnson might be willing to intervene at the last minute at the price of tamping down public revelations about the CIA-Mafia conspiracy against Castro."[8]

One of America's most canny and astute politicians, LBJ worried that he and the others were being manipulated to keep Hoffa out of jail. LBJ didn't seem to realize that another goal was to divert suspicion for JFK's murder away from Rosselli and the other mob bosses, or that the story's anti-Bobby spin was designed not only to damage Bobby's reputation, but also to appeal to LBJ's hatred of Bobby. LBJ told Connally he didn't "know whether there's any [real] basis for [the story] or not. . . . I don't know how much of it is being fed out through their network . . . and how much of it anybody would know. It's pretty hard to see how . . . we would know directly . . . what Castro [actually] did."[9]

LBJ confided to Connally that he had talked to Supreme Court Justice Abe Fortas about the story. Fortas asked, "Who is it that's seen Castro and heard from Castro and knows Castro, that could be confirming all this?" Fortas found it suspicious that "we just hear that this is what he did, but nobody points to how we hear it." Fortas was appropriately skeptical about the story, but would soon become the focus of scandal himself and would have to resign from the Supreme Court because of his close relationship with LBJ.[10]

There is one important difference between the story Rosselli leaked to Anderson and Pearson, and the ones leaked to WINS and Garrison: the Mafia. Apparently, word about the Mafia's role with the CIA had been given only to Anderson and Pearson, back in mid-January. At that time, the Mafia angle had been needed to give Rosselli's story credibility and as a way to grab the attention of top officials, especially those who knew something about the CIA-Mafia plots. The Mafia part of Rosselli's tale worked most effectively when shared privately among officials like LBJ and Helms, as something they wanted to keep hidden. Things were different by late February and early March, when the Garrison investigation and Ferrie's death were in the headlines. The Mafia had so far escaped any mention in those matters, so it was better not to include the Mafia in the fresh leaks to Garrison and WINS. However, Jack Anderson already had the Mafia angle, and he wasn't about to be scooped on the story he'd had first.

As LBJ and Connally ended their call on the evening of March 2, 1967, Jack Anderson was getting ready to go on television to reveal Rosselli's story. He had already submitted an explosive column about the story, to run the following day in more than six hundred newspapers. Several factors figured into Anderson's decision to finally run the story he'd been sitting on for a month and a half. Anderson may have heard about the WINS story and wanted to salvage what was left of his exclusive. He later wrote that "we never conceded the field if there was a sliver of a chance that we could scoop the competition."[11] However, given the lead time necessary for a column syndicated to so many newspapers, including morning papers going to press by midnight, Anderson had probably written, edited, and submitted his column well before the WINS story aired. It's also possible that Anderson had come under additional pressure from Morgan to run the story, since Hoffa was only days away from having to report to prison.

Anderson ran Rosselli's story when his boss, Drew Pearson, was not just out of town, but out of the country. Pearson was on a tour of five South American countries with his friend Chief Justice Earl Warren. We now know from Drew Pearson's diaries that Pearson would not have run the story.[12] Anderson's decision to run it may also have been influenced by his business and personal ties to Rosselli's associates Ed Morgan, Robert Maheu, and Hank Greenspun.

Jack Anderson had other associates who could have been used to influence Anderson to run the story. Anderson was very close to Carlos Marcello's Washington lobbyist, who was also reportedly involved in the efforts to keep Hoffa out of prison. In addition, Anderson was a longtime friend of Frank Fiorini, Trafficante's operative who had spread a somewhat similar story he'd gotten from John Martino shortly after JFK's assassination. (In 1972, Anderson would pay Fiorini's bail after he was arrested as one of the Watergate burglars, under the name Frank Sturgis.)[13]

Decades later, Anderson would finally admit that by spreading Rosselli's story, he "may have been a card [Rosselli] was playing." As a Congressional report later concluded, "Rosselli manipulated the facts of the plots into the retaliation theory in efforts to force the CIA to intervene favorably into his legal affairs."[14] However, in March 1967, Anderson believed what he was hearing from the Mafia don, especially when William Harvey confirmed Rosselli's account. Harvey was still a CIA official at the time, though Anderson didn't realize that Harvey might have been acting more for himself and his friend Rosselli than for the CIA.[15]

Anderson was convinced he had a real scoop, since by March 2, 1967, he claimed to have "two memos from the CIA's most sensitive files, which summarize the whole operation."[16] An internal CIA Inspector General's report appears to confirm that Anderson and Pearson had at least one sensitive government memo about assassinating Castro.[17]

While much has been written about Jack Anderson's March 3, 1967, column, almost nothing has appeared about his first revelation of the story, on Washington's WDCA-TV at 10:55 PM on March 2. Anderson's revelation on their TV show *Expose* was discovered only recently because it was the subject of a newly declassified CIA memo. Such programs were regularly monitored by the CIA, a practice that continued at least into the 1980s, when the CIA had episodes of NPR's *Diane Rehm* radio show transcribed when they featured serious JFK assassination experts.

Anderson's Washington TV revelation on March 2 is important because the *Washington Post* decided not to carry his March 3 column with Rosselli's story, perhaps because the column reflected badly on Bobby Kennedy, who had good relations with the *Post*. Editor Ben Bradlee was close to JFK, and Bobby himself had written *Post* owner Katherine Graham the previous day about his Vietnam speech. However, the *Post* did carry a later Anderson column about the subject that criticized Bobby, so it's also possible that Anderson's televised preview of his column caught the attention of Richard Helms or one of his men, who then asked the *Post* not to run it.[18]

While Drew Pearson was a well-known media figure by the 1960s, having portrayed himself in Hollywood films like *The Day the Earth Stood Still*, his junior partner, Jack Anderson, was relatively unknown. But Anderson knew the Rosselli story had enough bombshells to make a name for himself, and it did. As recorded in the CIA memo of the broadcast, Anderson said that JFK

> ... was angered at the failure of the Bay of Pigs invasion and blamed [the] CIA. He quoted Kennedy as desiring to break up the Agency. [JFK] assigned his brother, the Attorney General, to watch over [the] CIA. Anderson implies Robert Kennedy controlled the Agency. The Attorney General, seeking revenge on Castro for the Bay of Pigs, planned through [the] CIA the assassination of Castro or considered it. Castro learned of the CIA plot to kill him, or obtained information which led him to believe such a plot existed. Castro arranged the assassination of the President in retaliation.[19]

In addition to Anderson's television appearance on March 2, 1967, he took one more step to ensure that he got credit for the scoop: He submitted the next day's column with a special by-line: "Today's column is by Jack Anderson." A few newspapers, like the *New York Post*, joined the *Washington Post* in not carrying the column, but most of the column's six-hundred-plus newspapers weren't so cautious. Johnny Rosselli's leaked information was soon being read by millions of people from coast to coast.[20]

Bobby Kennedy may have watched or heard about Anderson's TV broadcast, but he certainly found out about the following day's explosive newspaper column. Though the *Washington Post* didn't carry the March 3, 1967, column, out-of-town newspapers were plentiful in Washington, D.C., so Bobby would have been reading the bombshell column by the afternoon at the latest. The column's headline varied from newspaper to newspaper (in New Orleans, it was "Was JFK killed in CIA backfire?"), but Anderson wasted no time in making sure that readers knew they were looking at a shocking story about Bobby Kennedy. The column opened by saying:

> President Johnson is sitting on a political H-Bomb—an unconfirmed report that Sen. Robert Kennedy may have approved an assassination plot which then possibly backfired against his late brother.[21]

It's not hard to imagine Bobby's reaction, when he saw his own worst fears from the day of his brother's murder reduced to cold print in

America's most popular newspaper column. Bobby probably felt an initial burst of anger, followed by dread at the prospect that his secret plans and cover-ups might now be exposed—the coup plan with Almeida; the cover-up of the November 1963 Tampa and Chicago attempts—and that somehow, those events had boomeranged against JFK, resulting in his death.[22]

Anderson's column quickly made it clear that this wasn't idle rumor or wild speculation: "Top officials, queried by this column, agreed that a plot to assassinate Cuban dictator Fidel Castro was 'considered' at the highest levels of the Central Intelligence Agency at the time Bobby was riding herd on the agency. The officials disagreed, however, over whether the plan was approved and implemented." Bobby knew that was essentially true, but he also knew there had been not just "a plot," but rather, several efforts to eliminate Castro: the JFK-Almeida coup plan, the CIA's other authorized efforts like AMTRUNK, and the CIA's plots with the Mafia that Bobby had been told were stopped in May 1962.

Anderson made it clear that he also knew about the CIA-Mafia plots, writing, "One version claims that underworld figures actually were recruited to carry out the plot. Another rumor has it that three hired assassins were caught in Havana. . . . " The last sentence may have been confusing for Bobby, since it hinted at the spring 1963 attempts that he and JFK had not authorized or known about.

The next major point in Anderson's column was one Bobby had seen before. Though he no longer believed it, this leak by Johnny Rosselli would have a huge impact on relations between the US and Cuba for decades, one that persists to this day:

> The rumor persists, whispered by people in a position to know, that Castro did become aware of an American plot upon his life and decided to retaliate against President Kennedy.

While acknowledging that "whether the assassination plot was ever actually put into effect is disputed," Anderson points out that "some insiders are convinced that Castro learned enough at least to believe the CIA was seeking to kill him. With characteristic fury, he is reported to have cooked up a counterplot against President Kennedy."

This Anderson/Rosselli implication that Castro had orchestrated JFK's murder would continue to reverberate among official circles in Washington into the 1970s, '80s, and even today. Blaming Castro for JFK's death would be "whispered by people in a position to know" about some of the US's covert efforts against Fidel in 1963—among them

Alexander Haig, an aide to Cyrus Vance in 1963 who went on to become President Richard Nixon's Chief of Staff and Ronald Reagan's Secretary of State. Haig was one of the few officials eventually willing to state publicly his belief that Fidel had JFK killed. However, other high US officials believed—and probably still believe today—the same thing, not realizing that the story (and reports that seemed to back it up) originated with Johnny Rosselli's associates. Yet this belief among some officials is a major reason why, in 2008, Cuba is treated far more harshly than former US enemies like China and Vietnam.

While Bobby didn't fall for Anderson's "Castro killed JFK" claim, the column was filled with other worrisome information that Bobby knew was accurate:

> After the Bay of Pigs fiasco . . . the President's real watchdog was his brother, Bobby, who ended up calling the shots at the CIA. . . . During this period, the CIA hatched a plot to knock off Castro. It would have been impossible for this to reach the high levels it did, say insiders, without being taken up with the younger Kennedy. Indeed, one source insists that Bobby, eager to avenge the Bay of Pigs fiasco, played a key role in the planning.[23]

Of course, Anderson's source left out the fact that Bobby's role with the CIA applied only to Cuba and the operations he had authorized. The column also omits the US military's leading role in some 1963 anti-Castro operations. But Anderson's—or, rather, Rosselli's—true target was clearly Bobby. They went for the jugular by saying:

> Some sources consider Robert Kennedy's behavior after the assassination to be significant. He seemed to be tormented, they say, by more than the natural grief over the murder of his brother. . . . Four weeks after the tragedy, this column was told, Bobby was morose and refused to see people. Could he have been plagued by the terrible thought that he had helped put into motion forces that indirectly may have brought about his brother's martyrdom? Some insiders think so.[24]

Reading that statement must have been torture for Bobby, salt rubbed into the slowly healing wound of his grief over his brother's murder. It was all too accurate, but not in the way that Anderson (or his source, Rosselli) implied. Any guilt that Bobby felt would have been over the Mafia's infiltration of the JFK-Almeida coup plan, and the mob's use of certain elements of it to kill JFK.

Jack Anderson's repeated citing of unnamed "insiders" left Bobby boxed in. He didn't know who was talking to Anderson or what they knew. Was it a disgruntled US official who was simply confusing a jumble of Castro elimination plots? Or was someone deliberately deceiving Jack Anderson and Drew Pearson, trying to tie Bobby to the CIA-Mafia plots? Could it be LBJ, getting back at Bobby? At that time, Bobby had few people he could turn to for advice or counsel, since most of his associates hadn't been told about the coup plan with Almeida or the CIA-Mafia plots. Arthur Schlesinger, who didn't know about Almeida, observed Bobby shortly after the column and wrote that "an indefinable sense of depression hung over him, as if he felt cornered by circumstance and did not know how to break out."[25]

The rest of Jack Anderson's March 3, 1967, column was designed not for Bobby, but for other officials in both Washington and New Orleans. It noted Jim Garrison's JFK investigation, saying, "Insiders believe he is following the wrong trails." The column also addressed the fact that in 1967, it was still inconceivable to the average American that the US would try to murder foreign officials. (It would be another eight years before the American press widely reported such plots.)

Anderson dropped a couple of notable names to indirectly buttress his case, saying, "Those who may be shocked that the CIA would consider stooping to a political assassination should be reminded of the ugly nature of what Secretary of State Dean Rusk has called 'the back-alley struggle.'" Anderson also quoted "Clark Clifford, head of the President's Foreign Intelligence Committee," regarding CIA operatives who were captured and then "subjected to the most skillful, most fiendish tortures [and] reduced to animals." Clifford's comments unintentionally supported Rosselli's "turned-around assassins" story.[26]

Anderson foreshadowed today's debates about the use of waterboarding and other forms of torture against CIA prisoners when he wrote that "we also play rough" and cited a *New York Times* report that quoted "'one of the best-informed men in Washington on this subject' as saying: 'When we catch one of them (a Soviet or other agent), it becomes necessary to get everything out of them, and we do it with no holds barred.'" Besides laying more groundwork for Rosselli's story, those lines may have especially worried Richard Helms, who knew the CIA was still holding Soviet defector Yuri Nosenko in appalling conditions.

It's ironic that Richard Helms, who had withheld so much from Bobby and JFK, was one of the few people Bobby could turn to for help and information in the aftermath of Anderson's column. Bobby could at least talk freely to Helms about things like Almeida and the CIA-Mafia plots, which Bobby had withheld from his current advisors. At that time, Bobby knew far less about the article than LBJ, who knew at least that Anderson's information originated with "Hoffa's attorney," Ed Morgan. Helms could help Bobby find out who was talking to Anderson, so Bobby arranged to meet Helms for lunch the following day.

Before Bobby saw Helms, he had to deal with his own staff. According to journalist Sy Hersh, after reading Anderson's column, Bobby told his young assistants, Adam Walinsky and Peter Edelman, a bit about the CIA-Mafia Castro assassination plots, saying, "I didn't start it. I stopped it . . . I found out that some people were going to try an attempt on Castro's life and I turned it off." Frank Mankiewicz said Bobby "told me that there was some crazy CIA plan at one time for sending some Cubans in to get Castro which he called off."[27]

On March 4, 1967, when Bobby met Helms for lunch, he was probably glad that the major newspapers and TV networks had not yet followed up on Anderson's sensational column—whether due to pressure on the media from Helms and the CIA, or because Anderson's story was drowned out by news from New Orleans about Garrison. At their meeting, Bobby and Helms probably discussed what Helms had told—or was going to tell—LBJ about the CIA-Mafia plots, the 1963 coup plan with Almeida, and the current status of Almeida and his family.[28]

As for what Helms would tell LBJ about the CIA-Mafia plots, it appears that LBJ had learned very little about them at that point. However, Anderson's column would soon change that. If LBJ asked, Helms would at least have to give the president the same information LBJ could learn from J. Edgar Hoover. That would explain why, on the day of Bobby's lunch meeting with Helms, Bobby had his secretary call Hoover's office and ask for a copy of the FBI's May 7, 1962, memo about the CIA-Mafia plots.

Though this lunch is the only clearly documented meeting between Bobby and Helms after Anderson's first column, Bobby likely had further contact with Helms or one of his men, especially after Anderson's next column about the matter and LBJ's request that Helms give him a full report about the 1963 CIA-Mafia plots. Because the press was still speculating that Bobby might run for president the following year, Helms was in a delicate position: He couldn't offend Bobby, or else Helms might not be kept on as Director if Bobby became president—yet as LBJ's CIA Director, Helms couldn't appear to be too close to Bobby. Their subsequent contact on the matter was probably handled through

Desmond FitzGerald, the CIA's Deputy Director for Plans whom Bobby still saw socially. FitzGerald knew the secrets as well as Helms did, including those Helms still withheld from Bobby.

Once Richard Helms returned to CIA headquarters after his meeting with Bobby, he no doubt discussed the situation with FitzGerald. They both had much to lose if their unauthorized continuation of the CIA-Mafia plots in 1963 became known to LBJ or was exposed in the press. Their careers were on the line, to say nothing of the possibility of being dragged into Garrison's investigation.

Helms's actions regarding the matter for the next two weeks are not documented, but can be inferred from declassified files. In 2007, the CIA admitted that in the 1960s, it tapped the phones of Washington columnists Robert Allen and Paul Scott, suspected of "publishing news articles based on, and frequently quoting, classified [CIA] materials." A CIA memo says those phone taps were "particularly productive in identifying contacts of the newsmen . . . and many of their sources of information." Also disclosed in 2007 was that a few months before Watergate, Richard Helms himself had the CIA conduct covert surveillance of Jack Anderson and his assistants, including a young Brit Hume (now with Fox News), in order to find out who was leaking to them. The CIA admits the surveillance Helms ordered was "to determine Anderson's sources [of] highly classified Agency information appearing in his syndicated columns."[29]

Helms would have wanted to know who was leaking the CIA-Mafia plot information to Jack Anderson, and what other relevant information Anderson possessed that had not yet been published. As we'll detail shortly, the CIA was able to discover that Anderson and Pearson had additional sensitive information about the CIA-Mafia plots they had not yet printed. Given what the CIA did in similar circumstances, Helms may have ordered the CIA to use phone taps or physical surveillance on Anderson, which could have included FBI-style "black bag," surreptitious break-ins, which CIA veterans later used during Watergate. Helms could have rationalized such actions as necessary for national security, because the situation involved covert US operations against Cuba.

It's important to keep in mind that Helms's concerns about Anderson's column were occurring while the Garrison investigation in New Orleans was still unfolding. Garrison's inquiry was a major focus for Helms, and many CIA documents show that the Agency followed every twist and turn in Garrison's case, running checks on each person whose name surfaced not only in Garrison's investigation, but also in news reports or books about the case. This continued not just in 1967 and 1968, but for years afterward, until at least 1974. In addition, Helms was having the CIA make efforts to undermine or block Garrison, indirectly assist the defense of Clay Shaw, and influence how the news media covered the case. Amidst all that, Helms had to find the source of Anderson's leak, while trying to keep him and other journalists from publishing more damaging information about the CIA.

The ultimate effect of Anderson's column (and Garrison's investigation) was a high level of cover-ups and concealment almost unmatched since the immediate aftermath of JFK's assassination. Three years after JFK's murder, many of the same officials were once more trying to quietly investigate matters while simultaneously withholding information from the public and one another. Bobby, Helms, LBJ, and Hoover were again players in the drama, trying to discover things that Rosselli, Marcello, and Trafficante already knew.

Chapter Thirty-four

Johnny Rosselli had not gotten what he wanted from Anderson's first column: for the CIA to make the FBI back off on his immigration case. In addition, Marcello and Trafficante had not gotten the leverage they needed to keep their ally Jimmy Hoffa from going to prison, nor had there been any public backlash against Bobby Kennedy over Anderson's revelations. As a result, Rosselli got Anderson to publish another column, this time with one important element missing.

The next column by Anderson on Rosselli's story would eliminate any reference to the "underworld," meaning the Mafia. Unlike when Rosselli had first leaked his story to Anderson back in January 1967, the Garrison investigation was now grabbing headlines across the country, and New Orleans was filled with reporters from around the world. While the Mafia angle had been needed in January to grab the attention of high officials, now it could harm Marcello if Rosselli focused the reporters' attention on the Mafia, which had so far escaped blame in JFK's assassination.

While Drew Pearson was still traveling in South America with Earl Warren, Jack Anderson submitted his follow-up column on March 6, to run on March 7, the same day Jimmy Hoffa was scheduled to report to prison. Unknown to Anderson, on March 6 his first column was finally starting to have the impact Rosselli sought. On that date, LBJ's Attorney General, Ramsey Clark, received a detailed FBI report provocatively titled "Central Intelligence Agency's Intentions to Send Hoodlums to Cuba to Assassinate Castro."[1]

That memo was soon brought to LBJ's attention, and in it the FBI detailed much of what its top officials knew about the CIA-Mafia plots involving Johnny Rosselli, Sam Giancana, and Robert Maheu. The FBI said that Bobby Kennedy had been made aware of the use of the mobsters "to obtain intelligence . . . in Cuba" in May 1961, and that Bobby had learned of the operation's assassination aspects in May 1962, at which time he had "issued orders that [the] CIA should never again take such steps without first checking with [him]." The FBI also noted that William Harvey had met with Rosselli in June 1963, when Harvey claimed he finally shut down the operation.[2] (The FBI memo didn't mention the Bureau's surveillance of Rosselli in Miami in the fall of 1963, when he was working on the CIA-Mafia plots while meeting with David Morales and Jack Ruby—indicating those sensitive files were already being held separately from the main Rosselli FBI files.)

The FBI said that Rosselli had "used his prior connections with [the] CIA to his best advantage." According to the FBI, the CIA's Director of Security "admitted to us that Rosselli has [the] CIA in an unusually vulnerable position and that [Rosselli] would have no qualms about embarrassing [the] CIA if it served his own interests." Essentially, the CIA had taken the rare step of admitting to the FBI that Rosselli had the Agency over a barrel.[3]

LBJ had been skeptical of the Anderson/Pearson story, but Hoover's report confirmed that the CIA had indeed plotted extensively with Rosselli and the Mafia to kill Castro. This knowledge caused LBJ to take the whole matter much more seriously, and he would soon demand a full report from Richard Helms and tell the FBI to interview William Morgan. The resulting reports, coupled with the next day's Anderson column, would have a major impact on what LBJ believed about JFK's assassination—not just at the time, but for years to come, until his own death.[4]

The *Washington Post* ran Anderson's new revelations on March 7, 1967, even though they were tacked on to the end of a much longer story about Congressional corruption, where they would have been easy to cut. The column's main headline was about the unrelated Congressional story, but near the end was a subhead, "Castro Counterplot," that signaled the start of four short paragraphs updating the March 3, 1967, story. Anderson wrote that the publicity surrounding Garrison's investigation "has focused attention in Washington on a reported CIA plan in 1963 to assassinate Cuba's Fidel Castro, which, according to some sources, may have resulted in a counterplot by Castro to assassinate President Kennedy." He then added that "Sen. Russell Long (D-La.) has told us that Lee Harvey Oswald . . . trained with Castro revolutionaries in Minsk during his Soviet stay," and that "Long swore [the] information . . . is reliable."

It was highly unusual for a senator like Russell Long to be talking about such matters to Anderson, especially on the record, but it was no coincidence. Long was actively involved in Carlos Marcello's Spring Hoffa plan, and one of Marcello's associates likely leaked to Long the false claim that could tie Oswald to the "Castro counterplot" against JFK.[5]

Anderson's column in the *Post* concluded by saying his "sources agree that a plot against Castro definitely was taken up inside the CIA at the time. Sen. Robert Kennedy, D-N.Y., was riding herd on the agency for his brother. The report is that Castro got wind of the plot and threatened to find someone to assassinate President Kennedy."[6]

For Bobby Kennedy, Anderson's latest column must have seemed like another punch to the gut, amplifying his fear that Anderson's or Garrison's investigations might reveal his darkest secrets from 1963. Though he was a senator, Bobby's influence was at a low point in the current administration, so he would have to take steps on his own to keep crucial evidence beyond the reach of Anderson, Garrison, or LBJ. Anderson's new column must have tempered any satisfaction Bobby felt in knowing that Jimmy Hoffa was reporting to Lewisburg Federal Prison that day, to start his thirteen-year sentence.

For President Johnson, seeing Anderson's new story after receiving the FBI report about the CIA-Mafia plots was a sign that the matter wasn't going to go away on its own. LBJ would have to get all the information he could, since the 1963 date in the new column meant Anderson might be describing operations that had been going on when LBJ became president.

Neither LBJ, Bobby, nor Richard Helms would have wanted to see the story pursued. The same was true for J. Edgar Hoover, who could have easily leaked his report on the CIA-Mafia plots to the press—but didn't, probably so he could have something to hold over the CIA's and Bobby's heads. No other mainstream journalist printed any type of follow-up to Anderson's story, or even noted what Anderson had reported. Jack Anderson, on the other hand, knew he was onto something and would soon go to New Orleans to consult with Garrison and continue his digging.

For Richard Helms, the second Anderson story was apparently the last straw. Helms knew the small number of people involved in the CIA-Mafia plots, and it wouldn't have taken him long to pinpoint William Harvey, Rosselli's friend, as the likely source of at least some of the information in Anderson's story. According to later CIA Director William Colby, Harvey had been recalled from Rome "in February of 1967 [and] reassigned to CIA headquarters."[7] That was apparently when Harvey began talking to Jack Anderson, supporting Rosselli's story.

An account that "one of the CIA's most senior officers" gave to intelligence journalist David Martin said that not long after William Harvey returned to CIA headquarters, Harvey was asked to resign, after CIA personnel "began finding gin bottles in his desk drawer."[8] However, the CIA had previously used a noted mental-health facility near Towson, Maryland, for its officials who needed help. If Helms had really wanted to retain Harvey (still a legend in the CIA because of his work on the Berlin Tunnel project), he could have sent Harvey to that facility for a few weeks or months; one CIA official had stayed there for two years. The fact that the CIA didn't even attempt to get Harvey such treatment indicates that the request for Harvey's resignation was probably punitive.

For pension purposes, Harvey's official retirement date was set at the end of the year, but CIA files show that he was effectively out of the Agency long before that. These CIA files also show that Helms was right to be concerned about Harvey, since the former agent considered joining Ed Morgan's law firm (one account even says he did become affiliated with the firm).[9] The files also show that by 1967, Harvey's loyalty lay more with Johnny Rosselli than with the CIA. Harvey would later tell the CIA's Director of Security that "'Johnny' [Rosselli] was his friend," and "that he would not turn his back on his friends." Harvey explained that "he had told 'Johnny' at the outset of their association that if anything happened to 'blow the operation' that . . . 'Johnny' could not look to anyone other than Harvey for assistance."[10] Just weeks after Jack Anderson's second article, Harvey would suggest to the CIA's Security Director that "it would be a simple matter for the Director [Helms] to see Mr. [J. Edgar] Hoover personally and determine . . . what actual case the Justice Department had against Johnny [Rosselli]." That the disgraced Harvey would even suggest that Helms do such a thing shows the "unusually vulnerable position" Helms and the CIA were in because of Rosselli.[11]

Bobby Kennedy was also in a vulnerable position, and on March 14, 1967, he literally buried crucial medical evidence. JFK had originally been laid to rest next to the bodies of his infant son and daughter, in a relatively plain grave distinguished only by an eternal flame. In the summer of 1966 (during the first wave of JFK conspiracy books), work had begun on a more elaborate site twenty feet away, though some have wondered why it couldn't have been constructed around the original grave.

Bobby still possessed important medical evidence—including JFK's brain, tissue samples, and possibly X-rays and photographs from JFK's autopsy—that are not at the National Archives. In addition to whatever they might have revealed, Bobby had wanted to ensure that JFK's autopsy material never became a public spectacle. After Garrison's investigation became public and a grand jury was impaneled in New Orleans to investigate, Bobby's concerns must have increased. They would have grown even more when Clay Shaw was arrested on March 1, 1967, because that meant a trial could be held in the near future. Declassified US military memos show that activity for JFK's reinterment accelerated greatly that very day.[12]

By March 2, 1967, the relocation of JFK's grave was scheduled for that month, even though the new burial site wouldn't be completed until July. Within days, very detailed plans were drawn up for what was essentially a major military operation. As one author noted, once a New Orleans grand jury started considering the possibility of "exhuming [JFK's] body for a proper autopsy," plans were finalized in Washington to move JFK's body on the night of March 14, 1967. That evening, Gus Russo wrote that "300 military personnel arrived and closed Arlington National Cemetery to the public, clearing it of all unauthorized persons. An Army road block shut down Arlington Memorial Bridge [and] troops ringed the area."[13]

While a small, private memorial service was planned for the following morning, Bobby Kennedy, Frank Mankiewicz, Cardinal Cushing, and a few others were there to observe the excavation. Russo said, "The re-interment became the prime opportunity for a simultaneous re-burial of JFK's brain. Interestingly, in several newly surfaced photos of the late-night operation, a small box appears by the Kennedy graveside, at the feet of Cardinal Cushing."[14]

At the time of JFK's original autopsy, his personal physician, Admiral Burkley, had told two of the autopsy doctors that JFK's "brain, as well as tissue samples" would be given to "Bobby Kennedy for subsequent burial." Frank Mankiewicz told a Congressional investigator that JFK's "brain is in the grave. . . . Bobby . . . buried it when the body was transferred." JFK's secretary, Evelyn Lincoln, reportedly said to a friend that JFK's brain was "where it belongs."[15]

On the morning of March 15, 1967, LBJ joined Bobby, Jackie, and a few other family members and associates at the site for a private memorial service. The *New York Times* carried a UPI report saying that "the bodies of President Kennedy and his two dead children were quietly moved about 20 feet . . . under cover of darkness, and without word to the public [they were] reburied . . . in the center of the still unfinished memorial to the slain President."[16]

Three days after seeing LBJ at the ceremony, Bobby surprised his close associates by proclaiming that he was supporting LBJ in the next year's presidential election. Newspapers quoted Bobby as saying that LBJ "has been an outstanding president and I look forward to campaigning for him in 1968."[17] While Bobby's announcement disappointed his supporters, it makes sense in light of Bobby's weakened public support at that point: He had reversed his stance on Vietnam, faced controversies over bugging and Manchester's book, and worried about the still unfolding drama of Jack Anderson's revelations. Bobby knew that President Johnson had the upper hand in dealing with any fallout from Anderson's columns and Garrison's investigation.

News reports of Bobby's support for LBJ told Carlos Marcello and Santo Trafficante they had achieved the first big victory in their unfolding strategy. Their effort to compromise and divert Jim Garrison's investigation continued to go well, especially when Garrison took a trip to Las Vegas in early March. One of Marcello's associates paid for Garrison's room, though a long-rumored $5,000 gambling credit for Garrison turned out to be false.[18]

According to a CIA Inspector General's Report, "Jim Garrison, Edward Morgan, and Rosselli were all in Las Vegas at the same time. . . . Garrison was in touch with Rosselli; so was Morgan."[19] However, Garrison was not as bought and paid for as it might seem. It was not uncommon at the time for public officials to have their Las Vegas rooms comped by mob-owned casinos or covered by supporters. Regarding the CIA's assertion that "Garrison was in touch with Rosselli," Richard Helms was unable to say, during later questioning from Congressional investigators, where the claim had originated, and Garrison denied under oath ever meeting with Rosselli. The same was true for Rosselli when asked about meeting Garrison.

Johnny Rosselli was not a well-known Mafia figure to the public at that time, so if Rosselli were using an alias, Garrison could have met him without realizing the mobster's true identity. Likewise, Rosselli may have wanted the CIA to think he was meeting with Garrison, and Rosselli could have used William Harvey (who was interviewed for the CIA

Inspector General's Report) to plant the story. The CIA report includes an odd passage: "The Rosselli-Garrison contact in Las Vegas in March is particularly disturbing. It lends substance to reports that Castro had something to do with the Kennedy assassination in retaliation for US attempts on Castro's life." It's hard to see any basis for that reasoning in the Report but it does confirm that the CIA was very worried about Rosselli's sharing information with Garrison and Anderson—and the agency's fear worked to Rosselli's benefit.[20]

As for Garrison, the detailed notes of *Life* magazine reporter Richard Billings (who had almost daily contact with Garrison during much of the winter and spring of 1967) show that the District Attorney really did seem to be trying to solve the JFK assassination. However, the case defied simple explanation with the information that was available, so Garrison was constantly grasping at leads, changing directions, and shifting to new suspects. Garrison came close to what we now know to be the truth on several occasions, and within weeks of his Las Vegas trip would tell an FBI informant that he planned "to indict Carlos Marcello in the Kennedy assassination conspiracy because Garrison believes Marcello is tied up in some way with Jack Ruby." It's even possible that Garrison realized that someone in Las Vegas, or one of his volunteers in New Orleans, was trying to steer him away from organized crime, thus making him more suspicious of the mob. Certainly, Garrison didn't seem to buy the Castro retaliation story that Rosselli had told Jack Anderson.[21]

But whenever Garrison got close to the truth, something always happened. He was intentionally diverted, he let his ego get the best of him, or he seemed reluctant to really go after Marcello. Garrison later told filmmaker Oliver Stone that "he'd only met [Marcello] two brief times on social occasions," but Marcello's reputation was such that Garrison seemed privately torn over taking on the Mafia boss. The same week that Garrison talked about indicting Marcello, Garrison did arraign former low-level Marcello attorney Dean Andrews on perjury charges. However, on the same day, Garrison was successful in having the grand jury indict Clay Shaw for conspiring to murder JFK, taking his investigation permanently off course.[22]

While Garrison focused futilely on Clay Shaw, Shaw's former co-worker Alberto Fowler had a hand in torpedoing crucial parts of Garrison's investigation. Richard Billings's notes say that in early March 1967, Fowler claimed he was unable to convince Silvia Odio, or her sister Annie Odio, to cooperate with Garrison. Many years later, one of Fowler's associates would be identified as one of the two men who had visited Odio with Lee Oswald. Similarly, only after one of Fowler's men had located and interviewed Eladio del Valle, and after del Valle was brutally murdered, did Garrison learn that del Valle was "tied up with Santo Trafficante." Garrison quit using Fowler's associate at that point, but by that time Garrison had lost his only link between Trafficante and JFK's murder—and Trafficante's name would not be associated publicly with JFK's assassination until eight years later.[23]

Johnny Rosselli asked Ed Morgan to talk to Drew Pearson in mid-March, after Pearson had returned from South America. Morgan told Pearson he had seen Rosselli in Las Vegas, and that Rosselli had been "most indignant" about the stories Jack Anderson had written. Pearson wrote in his diary that Morgan told him Rosselli "will not cooperate in advancing the story any further." By that time, Rosselli had relayed two stories that Anderson had published and was content to let the situation play out quietly in Washington's corridors of power. Hoffa had already gone to prison, and while Rosselli had no official deal to avoid prosecution, the FBI was no longer actively pressuring him about the immigration matter. Rosselli's feigned outrage—that a journalist had actually run a story he'd been given—seems designed to make Pearson feel he wasn't being used, when he really was. (Rosselli would later leak more information to Anderson, further proof that Rosselli liked what Anderson had done.)[24]

Pearson also wrote in his diary that he originally thought Anderson's columns were "a poor story . . . and violated a confidence. . . . Finally, it reflected on Bobby Kennedy without actually pinning the goods on him." Author Max Holland points out that Pearson thought "the *Washington Post* and *New York Post* were right not to run the [first] column."[25] But Rosselli's fake indignation, coupled with others' reactions to the story, apparently made Pearson believe it was worth pursuing.

On March 13, 1967, Drew Pearson and Earl Warren met with LBJ at the White House. Before meeting with Pearson, LBJ met privately for forty minutes with only Earl Warren and LBJ's liaison to the FBI. A few days later, Pearson agreed to fund an almost two-week investigative trip to New Orleans, for Jack Anderson to meet with Jim Garrison. Clearly, Pearson wasn't upset with Anderson for running the Rosselli story and wanted to pursue it further. Now that Rosselli was no longer talking, Garrison seemed like the next best source.[26]

Four days after meeting with Pearson and Warren, LBJ had one of his aides tell FBI official Clyde Tolson that the FBI should "try to interview" Rosselli's attorney, Ed Morgan. Tolson protested, but LBJ insisted, so the FBI complied.[27]

The FBI's interview with Ed Morgan on March 21, 1967, provides an almost unfiltered version of Rosselli's tale, and is as close as we can get to hearing it from Rosselli himself. Some of its points were not in Jack Anderson's articles, but were heard by officials like President Johnson and had an impact on their later beliefs and actions. Rosselli's tale is the masterful spin job one would expect from a longtime force in Las Vegas and Hollywood, combining facts with fantasy designed to appeal to the intended audience (in this case, J. Edgar Hoover, LBJ, and worried CIA officials like Helms). Morgan made a convincing mouthpiece for the tale because he and Anderson probably believed Rosselli. Mounting confirmation that the CIA really had plotted with the Mafia would also suggest to officials that Rosselli might be right about Castro's having killed JFK.

It's clear from reading Morgan's story, as taken down by the FBI agents, that one of Rosselli's goals was to conflate the CIA-Mafia plots with the JFK-Almeida coup plan. That conflation can be seen in Anderson's columns, especially the second one, which cited 1963 as the date of the plot to kill Castro, and ascribed control of it to Bobby Kennedy. One sign that Rosselli succeeded in achieving this goal is the fact that Morgan's FBI interview, and memos about LBJ's reaction to Rosselli's story, are in a massive, 318-page FBI file at the National Archives that contains much of the FBI's information about Commander Almeida.[28]

Soon after Morgan's FBI interview began, he said his goal in talking to the agents was to get "complete immunity" for his clients from "some competent authority." Morgan claimed that such immunity was needed to keep some DA like "Garrison of New Orleans" from prosecuting his clients for trying to kill Fidel, a very unlikely scenario. Morgan's real goal was to try to prevent the FBI from using the immigration charges against Rosselli.[29]

To help hide the fact that the whole story was a ruse to acquire immunity for Rosselli, Morgan stressed to the FBI that he "was employed by more than one of those involved." That statement was technically true, since Morgan had earlier represented Robert Maheu and Jimmy Hoffa, in addition to Rosselli. However, in pushing the story to the FBI, Morgan was acting primarily on Rosselli's behalf.[30]

Morgan tried to convince the FBI that his clients' actions were noble by claiming that they were "substantial citizens, people who loved their country and had a high regard for the then President [Kennedy]." He stressed their "high ethical standard," and the fact that they had been "patriotically motivated" in helping the US against Castro, and were coming forward now only because their "conscience bothered" them. This was the same phony image Rosselli would later present when testifying to Congress.

In a revealing passage, Morgan got close to the truth when he said, "One client, when hearing the statement that Lee Harvey Oswald was the sole assassin of President Kennedy, 'laughs with tears in his eyes and shakes his head in apparent disagreement.'" Johnny Rosselli may well have laughed at JFK's murder, but not for the reasons Morgan thought.[31]

To conflate the CIA-Mafia plots with the real coup plan from 1963, and to explain how his clients could have found out that Castro had retaliated against JFK, Morgan told the FBI his clients had been

> ... called upon by a Governmental agency to assist in a project which was said to have the highest Governmental approval. The project had as its purpose the assassination of Fidel Castro. . . . Elaborate plans involving many people were made. These plans included the infiltration of the Cuban government and the placing of informants in key posts within Cuba.[32]

Rosselli knew that having Morgan mention the "infiltration of the Cuban government" would set off alarm bells with the high US officials who knew about Almeida. In addition, the "informants ... within Cuba" could explain how Morgan's clients learned about Fidel's retaliatory hit teams. The rest of Morgan's story was a clearer version of the account related in Anderson's columns.

The well-connected Morgan was aware of Hoover's insatiable thirst for inside information, so he suggested the possibility that the FBI could learn much more if it would give his clients "complete immunity." Morgan also slammed the CIA, saying that "it was inconceivable to him that an agency of the Government . . . has not [made] this most important data available to the Warren Commission."[33]

Morgan conveyed the information Rosselli wanted him to, while refusing to give up the mobster's name to the FBI. The FBI wasted no time in getting a summary of Morgan's interview to President Johnson and Attorney General Clark, setting off a chain of events that would echo into the next decade and beyond—and trigger yet another round of cover-ups by Richard Helms.

Chapter Thirty-five

President Lyndon Johnson received the results of the FBI's interview with Rosselli's attorney, Ed Morgan, on March 22, 1967. That evening, LBJ demanded a full explanation from CIA Director Richard Helms, but he didn't get one; instead, Helms gave an incomplete, often misleading account to the president who had appointed him.

Helms did with LBJ what he had done with other high-ranking officials, only more carefully and on a larger scale. Declassified files and Congressional testimony show that Helms had withheld information from, and lied to, a succession of officials about his unauthorized Castro assassination plots: President Kennedy, Attorney General Bobby Kennedy, then–CIA Director John McCone, the Warren Commission, and Secretary of State Dean Rusk. LBJ would fare no better, though Helms went to greater lengths to cover himself this time, withholding information from CIA investigators and even having internal CIA memos and testimony destroyed.

The limited, incomplete story Helms would allow the CIA's Inspector General to generate about the CIA-Mafia plots to kill Castro would become the object of presidential fascination and Congressional investigations, and large parts of it would remain beyond the public's reach for decades. Only in the 1990s would the almost uncensored report finally become available, and only later would files be declassified that showed just how much crucial information Helms had withheld from LBJ.[1]

That President Johnson asked Helms for the report is ironic, because LBJ was suspicious of the CIA—and not just for withholding information about the plots to kill Castro. According to a memo from a high-ranking FBI official, based on talks with top LBJ aide Marvin Watson, President Johnson "was now convinced that there was a plot in connection with the assassination [of JFK]. Watson stated the President felt that [the] CIA had had something to do with this plot." Perhaps Helms sensed LBJ's suspicion, or was told about it, resulting in Helms's decision to withhold crucial information.[2]

LBJ's worry that the "CIA had something to do with" JFK's assassination did not last long, and would apparently be dispelled by the incomplete report Helms made sure was generated. But President Johnson still harbored those doubts on the evening of March 22, when he met with Richard Helms at the White House. It was not the type of folksy chat LBJ sometimes utilized to get what he wanted. According to Helms's biographer, Thomas Powers, President Johnson did not ask for the report "idly or in passing." Instead, LBJ "asked directly, formally, and explicitly, in a tone and manner which did not [foresee] evasion," making it clear that he expected "an honest answer."[3] For good measure, LBJ also wanted Helms to address any CIA involvement in the assassinations of Vietnam leader Diem, in 1963, and Dominican dictator Trujillo, in 1961.

LBJ's formal request was one of two overriding factors that dictated the form of Helms's resulting report. First, LBJ's request would have to be referred to the CIA's Inspector General, Jack Earman, who had given Helms such a hard time in the summer of 1963 about the CIA's MKULTRA mind-control program. Second, how much LBJ told Helms about the information he had received from the FBI about the CIA-Mafia plots is not clear. While the CIA appears to have received copies of the FBI memos that went to LBJ and the attorney general, Helms didn't know what additional information J. Edgar Hoover might have shared privately with his friend LBJ. Helms was aware of earlier memos the CIA had provided to the FBI about the plots, after the FBI discovered parts of the plots in 1961 and 1962.

Richard Helms's report would have to account for everything he knew the FBI had, plus any additional information it might have uncovered without telling the CIA. At the same time, Helms would have to avoid detailing the most sensitive parts of his unauthorized Castro assassination plots. He would also have to make sure the report didn't reveal how Rosselli and other Mafia bosses had infiltrated and compromised the JFK-Almeida coup plan.

Helms chose to protect himself and some of his associates by withholding important information from the CIA Inspector General's investigation, and thus from LBJ and any later president who might ask to see the Report. From Helms's perspective, he had no other choice if he wanted to keep his job—and he had several ways to control, restrict, and direct the Inspector General's investigation. First, it was up to Helms to verbally convey LBJ's request to the Inspector General. By choosing his words carefully, Helms could shade his request so that it generated a lengthy report that addressed some of LBJ's concerns, while avoiding sensitive subjects that could cost Helms his career.

Like a savvy politician talking to a journalist, Helms relied on the strategy of not answering the question that was asked, but instead answering the question he wished had been asked. Peter Dale Scott has pointed out that the final Inspector General's report (henceforth called the IG Report) devoted scant attention to what LBJ had wanted investigated, which was primarily the story in Jack Anderson's columns on March 3 and March 7. Scott points out that the IG Report itself admits that Anderson's March 7 column "refers to a reported CIA plan in 1963 to assassinate . . . Castro," but Scott notes that less than 10 percent of the IG Report refers "to a 1963 plot at all, and that one is not the one Anderson was writing about."[4]

According to Scott, "less than a dozen lines" in the 133-page report "are devoted to" the main point of Anderson's columns, the "political H-bomb" about the alleged "counterplot by Castro to assassinate President Kennedy." He notes that the IG Report "wholly fails to investigate . . . the central theses [of the Anderson articles:] that Robert Kennedy authorized a CIA plot which then 'possibly backfired' against Kennedy."[5]

Instead of focusing on the main point of the Anderson articles as LBJ had wanted, Helms apparently directed the IG to focus on finding out who had leaked the information to journalists Anderson and Pearson, and what could be done about it.[6] Helms also worded the request—or controlled access to information—so that the investigation focused only on the summer 1960–1962 plots, which were made to look as if they had essentially ended by early 1963—well before JFK's assassination. That approach was safer for Helms than focusing on operations Bobby Kennedy had authorized, or the unauthorized CIA-Mafia plots Helms was running into the late fall of 1963.

LBJ no doubt hoped Helms would turn up information he could use against Bobby Kennedy to stop him from entering the race for president, but the IG Report is devoid of information that reflects badly on Bobby. In fact, there isn't much about Bobby in the IG Report at all, since Helms knew that the young Senator could become president at some point in the future. Evan Thomas talked to one of the two CIA staffers assigned to actually write the IG Report, a man who was definitely not a Kennedy partisan. The CIA man said he "simply never heard [Bobby] Kennedy cited as a mastermind [of operations to eliminate Castro] by any of the CIA officials he interviewed." Then again, Helms himself, who had much contact with Bobby about Cuban matters in 1963, was never interviewed for the IG Report.[7]

In protecting Bobby, Richard Helms was also protecting himself. Helms couldn't allow the IG Report to include information about the Mafia's penetration of the Almeida coup plan if he wanted to keep his job. Thus, the entire coup plan with Almeida is missing from the IG Report, as are the 1963 portions of AMWORLD (the code name appears nowhere in the Report) and the CIA's extensive support for Manuel Artime and Manolo Ray in the last six months of JFK's presidency. Omitting all of that information made it easy for Helms to hide the fact that Artime had been working on the CIA-Mafia plots at the same time that he was working on AMWORLD and the Almeida coup plan.

Richard Nixon had made a remarkable political comeback by 1967, and Helms knew he had an excellent chance of running for president in 1968. Hence, the IG Report does not mention Nixon's push, in 1959, for the CIA to find ways to eliminate Fidel. Also missing is any indication of Nixon's leading role regarding Cuba policy under President Eisenhower, or why the CIA-Mafia plots were ramped up so extensively three months before the 1960 election, when Rosselli, Trafficante, and Giancana were brought in. Ironically, throughout Nixon's presidency, he would press Helms and the CIA for information they had about those and related events, not realizing he had nothing to worry about from Helms's whitewashed IG Report.

Even after Helms assigned the report to the CIA's Inspector General on March 23, 1967, Helms had many ways to control and limit its content. In consultation with Desmond FitzGerald, Helms could withhold certain information and witnesses while making others more easily available. This tactic would ensure that the two IG investigators covered easily documentable high points, especially those the FBI already knew about, while steering the IG investigators away from information that could expose the extent of Helms's unauthorized plans or the Mafia's infiltration of Almeida's coup plan.

For example, even though CIA officer E. Howard Hunt was very active in the coup plan with Almeida, one of the two IG investigators would later testify to Congress that "at the time of our investigation in 1967, Howard Hunt's name did not come up."[8] Also, many CIA personnel who should have been interviewed were conveniently out of the country during the IG investigation, including David Morales, Ted Shackley, AMWORLD case officers like Henry Heckscher, and CIA employees who had worked closely with Artime like Rafael "Chi Chi" Quintero. Even though the IG Report mentions Artime's contacts with Rolando Cubela in late 1964 and 1965, Artime was not interviewed for the IG Report, even though he was still living in Miami. As a result, the investigators didn't learn about Artime's massive, $7 million AMWORLD effort or his Mafia ties. Manolo Ray wasn't interviewed, and his contacts with Cubela—first documented in *Ultimate Sacrifice*—are missing from the IG Report, even though recently declassified CIA files and Ray himself have now confirmed such contact. Especially glaring is that fact that investigators didn't talk to Tony Varona, though he and his contact with the Mafia were mentioned many times in the report. The Report contains no mention of the $200,000 Varona received from the Mafia in the summer of 1963.[9]

Helms may have felt entitled to withhold the material relating to the Almeida coup plan (such as AMWORLD, Hunt, and Harry Williams) because part of it was still technically an ongoing, highly sensitive operation. Almeida was still unexposed and in power (and soon to get a major promotion), and his family was still outside Cuba, receiving secret CIA support. Excluding current operations from the investigation on the basis that they could be disrupted enabled Helms to steer investigators toward older CIA operations that had originated before he became responsible for them.

Helms also worked to manipulate the IG investigation to his own advantage. He would be able to find out which sensitive files the investigators could find on their own, how those files meshed with what the FBI had, and how people who weren't involved in the original operations might interpret them. Helms would also use the IG Report's preparation as an excuse to destroy some of the sensitive material the investigators uncovered.

Essentially, Helms attempted what would later be termed a "limited hangout," allowing some negative material about the CIA to be disclosed to LBJ, but nothing that could get Helms fired. It's important to keep in mind that the Rosselli matter and Jack Anderson's investigation were still ongoing at the time of Helms's IG investigation. It was a fluid situation that limited what Helms could safely allow the Inspector General to see or investigate.

The first two weeks of April 1967 saw new developments involving Bobby Kennedy, Jack Anderson, and former CIA Director John McCone that further affected Helms and the IG investigation. On April 4, Jack Anderson told the FBI about his trip to New Orleans and his talk with District Attorney Jim Garrison. According to an FBI memo, Anderson had gone to New Orleans skeptical of Garrison, but Anderson "now believes there is some authenticity to Garrison's claims." Anderson said he had also spoken with LBJ's press secretary, who "was also convinced that there must be some truth to Garrison's allegations."[10]

The scenario Garrison outlined to Anderson involved Oswald's going to Mexico City in an attempt to get into Cuba for a CIA-approved plot to assassinate Fidel Castro. Oswald supposedly became "disillusioned and refused to go through with the plot to assassinate Castro," and was then set up to take the fall for JFK's murder. Garrison correctly linked David Ferrie to Oswald, but tried to make Clay Shaw the mastermind of the operation. Although Anderson was in New Orleans for two weeks, he didn't find—or at least didn't write about—the extensive links between Ferrie and Carlos Marcello in 1963.[11]

Jack Anderson told the FBI that Garrison was "willing to give the FBI everything . . . and let them finish the investigation." However, the FBI official who spoke to Anderson told the reporter that "the FBI would not under any circumstances take over the case." In contrast to Helms and the CIA, who were very concerned about Anderson, the FBI official wrote in his memo that there was "no need to make further contact with Anderson." Though the FBI appeared to have little interest in Anderson, Hoover was following the Garrison inquiry closely and giving LBJ regular updates.[12]

Drew Pearson, Anderson's boss, spoke to President Johnson the following day. LBJ had seen the results of Morgan's FBI interview and had talked with Helms, so he admitted to Pearson that "we think there's something to . . . Morgan's information. There were some attempts to assassinate Castro through the Cosa Nostra [the Mafia], and they point to your friends in the Justice Department." Pearson replied, "You mean one friend"—a reference to former Attorney General Bobby Kennedy.[13]

It must have been agony for Bobby Kennedy, waiting to see what Jack Anderson was going to write next and wondering when other news outlets would start investigating Anderson's revelations. Unlike LBJ, Bobby had no special pipeline to Pearson or Anderson to find out what was going on. Bobby must have been concerned when former CIA director John McCone told Bobby that Jack Anderson had just called him. According to Senate investigators, Anderson told McCone he was "preparing [yet another] column on Castro assassination attempts, implicating President Kennedy and Robert Kennedy."[14]

John McCone and Bobby apparently came up with a response that would protect both of them, as well as the CIA. McCone then talked "with Anderson at Robert Kennedy's request," after which "McCone dictated [an] April 14, 1967, memorandum" to Helms that likely mirrored what McCone had told Anderson. In it, McCone admitted only that in early August 1962, he recalled having heard in Project Mongoose meetings "a suggestion being made to liquidate top people in the Castro regime, including Castro." McCone said he "took immediate exception to this suggestion."[15]

In a small way, McCone and Bobby paralleled Helms's strategy with LBJ and the Inspector General, by shifting the focus away from 1963 and admitting a little in order to hide a great deal. It's ironic that at that very moment, Helms was allowing the IG Report to include admissions about some of the information he had withheld from Bobby and McCone, since he apparently hoped that neither man would ever see the report.

For reasons that are still unclear, Jack Anderson suddenly dropped his plans for another article. By then Anderson certainly knew he had a good story, based on LBJ's confirmation to Pearson and McCone's admission that the subject of assassinating Castro had surfaced during an official meeting in 1962. The CIA was somehow able to learn that Anderson and Pearson had additional "information, as yet unpublished, to the effect that there was a meeting at the State Department at which assassination of Castro was discussed and that a team actually landed in Cuba with pills to be used in an assassination attempt." The CIA's IG Report would confirm that "there is basis in fact for each of those . . . reports," but didn't indicate how the CIA knew what information the journalists possessed, or why they hadn't published it.[16]

It's possible that LBJ, after telling Pearson that Anderson's story had a factual basis, had asked or pressured Pearson not to pursue the story. In keeping with Richard Helms's strategy of trying to minimize stories unfavorable to the CIA or which questioned the Warren Report, Helms or other CIA officials may also have intervened with Pearson. Perhaps Morgan or Rosselli, or the associates they shared with Anderson, had conveyed the message that no more stories were needed at that point. Jack Anderson would not resume writing about the leaks from Johnny Rosselli for almost four years, when his articles were again connected with the legal problems of Rosselli and Hoffa, and would help lead to the Watergate scandal.[17]

Bobby Kennedy must have been relieved when it became apparent that Anderson's revelations had stopped and no other media outlets were pursuing the story. In April 1967, Bobby's political stock was at its lowest point, and any future office beyond the Senate seemed unlikely.

At the same time, Bobby was beginning another step in his sometimes painful transformation that would see him become a symbol of hope and inspiration for millions the following year.

While dealing with the McCone/Anderson matter, Bobby was still struggling with the profound effects of his recent trip to Mississippi. After listening to shocking testimony about hunger and poverty at his hearings in Jackson, Bobby had insisted on seeing the conditions for himself. The following afternoon, cameras were rolling as Bobby made an impromptu visit to dilapidated Delta shacks that housed poverty-stricken families. The cameras recorded Bobby's barely contained surprise and concern when the New York Senator asked a young boy what he'd eaten for lunch—and the boy said he hadn't had anything to eat.[18]

The cameras couldn't film clearly what happened inside one of the shacks, but it was a pivotal moment that gave Bobby the cause that would consume him until his death. Reporter Nick Kotz described the dwelling as "a dark windowless shack [smelling of] mildew, sickness, and urine. . . . There was no ceiling hardly [and] the floor had holes in it." Bobby noticed a little boy with "his tummy sticking out." Bobby picked up the boy and said, "My God, I didn't know this kind of thing existed. How can a country like this allow it?" When Bobby was unable to get a response from the starving child, an associate says that Bobby soon had "tears . . . running down [his] his cheek and he just sat there and held the little child . . . then he said, 'I'm going back to Washington to do something about this.'"[19]

At his Hickory Hill mansion that night, Bobby appeared "ashen faced," according to his daughter Kathleen. Bobby told nine of his ten children that "in Mississippi a whole family lives in a shack the size of this room. The children are covered with sores and their tummies stick out because they have no food. Do you know how lucky you are? [You should] do something for your country." Bobby was really talking to himself as much as he was to his children. What he had seen continued to torment him, and the following night, Bobby could no longer contain himself. He exploded in self-recrimination, telling the wife of an aide, "You don't know what I saw! I have done nothing in my life! Everything I have done was a waste! Everything I have done was worthless!"[20]

Bobby Kennedy channeled the shock of what he saw in Mississippi, and the lingering pain of losing his brother, into a new cause that re-energized him. Poverty, and all the ills that flowed from it, became his cause, his crusade. He pressured Congress and LBJ to increase funding for food programs, a demand that LBJ saw as just another of Bobby's attacks. Bobby made a high-profile appearance on NBC's *Meet the Press*, proclaiming, "If we can spend $24 billion for the freedom and liberty of the people in Vietnam, certainly we can spend a small percentage of that for the liberty and the freedom and the future of our own people in the United States." Bobby reached out to Martin Luther King, saying in a letter to him that when it came to the issues of poverty and hunger, "I cannot agree with you more that something must be done. If you have any suggestions, I would appreciate hearing from you."[21]

As Bobby moved closer to Martin Luther King's position on poverty and civil rights, Dr. King was moving toward Bobby's openly antiwar stance. On April 4, 1967, just a month after Bobby's first major antiwar speech, Dr. King delivered his own ringing denunciation of the war in his famous sermon at Riverside Church. Most historians and journalists say the trigger for Dr. King's change was his seeing a copy of *Ramparts* magazine on January 14, 1967. As described by Nick Kotz, the magazine's "story and pictures showing Vietnamese children who had been horribly maimed or killed by . . . napalm, dropped by US planes, [stunned] King, [who] resolved to speak out against the war."[22]

However, Dr. King was moving steadily in an antiwar direction even before he saw the magazine. The previous year, King had met and befriended Vietnamese Buddhist religious leader and peace advocate Thich Nhat Hahn, when he was in the US on a speaking tour arranged by the Fellowship of Reconciliation, a peace group that been helping King for years. Hated by both the US-backed Vietnamese dictator and the communist insurgents, King nominated Hahn for the Nobel Peace Prize on January 25, 1967. However, King proceeded cautiously in making public pronouncements against the war until the spiraling cost in lives—disproportionately minorities, due to college deferments more readily available to Caucasians—and money (needed to fight poverty) became too great.

Dr. King's April 1967 antiwar speech was eloquent and well grounded in fact, and it would have far-reaching implications. King condemned sending young black men "eight thousand miles away to guarantee liberties in Southeast Asia which they had not found in southeast Georgia and East Harlem." Ironically, South Georgia racist Joseph Milteer would use King's new antiwar stance to drive his collection of even more contributions to kill the civil rights leader.

After Dr. King's speech, he was criticized by some black leaders who were trying to keep the struggle for equal rights separate from the antiwar movement. The US news media were generally hostile to King's new position, as was President Johnson. After all the work President Johnson had done for civil rights, LBJ saw King's remarks as a betrayal, further fraying a relationship that had already become strained. LBJ would increasingly shift his focus away from his war on poverty, as he struggled to manage both the Vietnam war and the growing discontent in America's inner cities. J. Edgar Hoover seized upon King's new anti-war stance as a reason to increase his already extensive surveillance of the civil rights leader and his associates. Now that Dr. King was part of the antiwar movement, he became subject to even more illegal domestic surveillance from other federal agencies, due to the burgeoning efforts of US military intelligence and the CIA to monitor peace groups and demonstrators.

CIA Director Richard Helms was consumed increasingly by Vietnam in 1967—both the war there and covert efforts in neighboring countries like Laos—as well as by monitoring the growing antiwar movement. Helms and the CIA also had a dozen other hot spots and fronts in the Cold War, including ongoing covert actions against Cuba. However, in the short run, Helms's most pressing issue remained the IG Report about the Rosselli/Anderson situation, since its revelations could end his career.

By April 24, 1967, the Inspector General was starting to deliver its report to Helms in installments, while Helms continued to track the related matters of Cuban operations and the Jim Garrison investigation. A short time later, District Attorney Garrison subpoenaed Helms to appear before the grand jury in New Orleans. Helms felt obliged only to tell Georgia senator (and former Warren Commissioner) Richard Russell about Garrison's subpoena—which Helms then ignored. Though Russell's relationship with his former protégé, LBJ, had been strained over civil rights, they were still friends—and Helms knew that as long as the powerful Senator Russell approved of Helms's actions, Garrison could do nothing to compel Helms's testimony.

News reports monitored by the CIA and FBI indicated that Commander Almeida remained prominent in Cuba, helping to fill the vacuum created by Che Guevara's mysterious absence. UPI reported that on May 1, 1967, "Havana radio announced that Cuba's acting Armed Forces Minister, Major Juan Almeida, will preside over May Day ceremonies today, instead of Premier Fidel Castro. . . . Almeida recently was designated acting Armed Forces Minister in place of Major Raul Castro, the Premier's brother. The reason for that move never was explained."[23]

At the huge ceremony, Almeida revealed only that Che Guevara had been "serving the revolution somewhere in Latin America." He didn't say that Che was in one of the most rugged parts of Bolivia, trying to spark a small insurgency that even Bolivia's Communist Party didn't support. It was another doomed mission, even more poorly supplied and supported than Che's first exile to Africa.[24]

Richard Helms would have been pleased that Almeida was trusted with heading Cuba's big May Day celebration in Fidel's absence, since it indicated Almeida still had enough power in Cuba to be valuable to the US in the future. This knowledge undoubtedly allowed Helms to rationalize withholding from the Inspector General information about Almeida's secret work for JFK, and the CIA's ongoing covert support for Almeida's wife and children outside Cuba. That in turn gave Helms an excuse to also withhold the Mafia's infiltration of the Almeida coup plan from both the IG Report and President Johnson.[25]

The list of additional material Helms withheld from the Inspector General, or that Helms convinced the IG and his staff to not include, is immense: CIA assassination attempts against Castro in 1963; CIA contact with Rosselli in the summer and fall of 1963; the CIA's extensive 1963 support for and work with Artime, Varona, Ray, Menoyo, and Harry Williams; Artime's and Carlos Marcello's work on the CIA-Mafia plots; the Mafia's $200,000 payoff to Varona, and Varona's bringing Masferrer into the plot; CIA contact with Antonio Veciana; the 1963 activities of E. Howard Hunt, David Atlee Phillips, and David Morales; Oswald's contacts with CIA-backed exile groups; and much more detailed in the earlier chapters of this book and in *Ultimate Sacrifice*.

In a few cases (such as those of the 1959 CIA-Mafia plots and AMWORLD), a few vague words alluded to the missing operations; in other cases, information was simply ignored—or history rewritten—to accommodate the facts deemed safe to include. For example, the IG Report makes it sound as if the CIA needed to start using Johnny Rosselli and Santo Trafficante, in the summer of 1960, to find Cubans and exiles to assassinate Fidel. However, the two the CIA wound up with—Tony Varona and Juan Orta—had already been working for the CIA.

The story that emerged from the IG Report succeeded in separating the CIA-Mafia plots from JFK's assassination by claiming the plots had ended by early 1963. Only brief passages in the Report mentioned Helms's unauthorized operations, but nothing tied them to JFK's assassination.

The overall thrust of the IG Report was damage control, with a goal of discovering who was leaking information and how to stop the leaks. Ironically, the same concern would result from the next round of Rosselli revelations to Jack Anderson, and would set in motion the actions of E. Howard Hunt and the Watergate "plumbers," so named because their purpose was to find and stop leaks. Hunt's men would even consider killing Jack Anderson, and while the 1967 IG Report does have a section entitled "Should we try to silence those who are talking or might later talk?," the options considered in the IG Report weren't lethal.[26]

Some material was added after the Inspector General had completed the report, such as the March 7, 1966, memo in which Helms lied to Secretary of State Dean Rusk about the Cubela/AMLASH assassination plot. That plot was discussed extensively in the IG Report, and since Helms apparently realized Rusk might have told LBJ about the memo, he made sure it was included. Helms was probably confident that he could rationalize his lie to Rusk if need be, since Helms had withheld the most damaging information about the Cubela/AMLASH plots from the IG Report. The suppressed information ranged from Manolo Ray's contacts with Cubela to Manuel Artime's work with the Mafia when Artime was meeting with Cubela.

Helms had dealt with several presidents by that time, and he understood how they operated: LBJ was not going to read the 134-plus-page memo himself, and likely not even a several-page summary. The matter was so explosive that LBJ would probably not even have a trusted staff member read it for him. Helms therefore prepared a few pages of notes so that he could give LBJ a verbal summary. Congressional investigators later found that Helms hadn't bothered to prepare any notes about the CIA-Mafia plots or the Cubela plots that continued past mid-1963. Helms was at a loss to explain why when he testified to Congress, but he clearly never intended to detail for LBJ the CIA activities that were most relevant to Anderson's columns and JFK's assassination.

Helms went to the White House to brief LBJ orally about the IG Report on May 10, 1967, taking only his notes and not even a copy of the Report. While LBJ could have demanded to see it, Helms apparently hoped that by verbally emphasizing the sensitive nature of the CIA-Mafia plots he had inherited, LBJ would be content to trust Helms to keep the whole situation under wraps—and that was exactly what happened.[27]

Helms did not tell LBJ about details in the report like the poison pen the CIA tried to give to Rolando Cubela on the day JFK was killed. When Senator Frank Church asked Helms about that years later, Helms testified, "I just can't recall having done so." Helms tried to claim to

Church and the other senators that the Cubela operation hadn't been an assassination plot, but the senators had seen the IG Report by then and knew Helms was lying. At the time of this testimony, Helms and the CIA (including then-director George H. W. Bush) were withholding even more damaging information from the senators, including the Almeida coup plan and its infiltration by Mafiosi linked to JFK's assassination.

When Helms briefed President Johnson on May 10, 1967, the only other person at the meeting was LBJ's press secretary, probably in case the material ever surfaced in the news.[28] By the end of the briefing, LBJ was apparently content to let the matter rest with Helms, as long as it stayed out of the press. By feeding LBJ's suspicions of Castro, Helms's presentation also appears to have succeeded in removing the CIA from LBJ's list of suspects in JFK's assassination. In later years, LBJ would admit privately to a journalist that "we were running a damn Murder Incorporated in the Caribbean" and "Kennedy was trying to get Castro, but Castro got to him first."[29] Leaving LBJ with that impression would also help Helms justify his ongoing anti-Castro operations, which were proving more and more problematic.

After his meeting with LBJ, Helms held on to the IG Report for twelve days before returning it to the CIA's inspector general. Helms probably kept the report for as long as he did because his Cuban exile operations were in a sensitive phase, and because he wanted to make sure nothing new about the CIA-Mafia plots surfaced from Jack Anderson's or Garrison's investigation. On the following day, May 23, 1967, Senate investigators later found that "all notes and other derived source material of the IG Report are destroyed." Thomas Power writes that the destruction included "every scrap" of the inspector general's investigation: "every transcript of an interview, every memo, every note made by the investigators. The draft which Helms had read went into a safe, his briefing notes neatly attached to the front, and it stayed there, untouched and unread, until . . . 1973," after Richard Nixon had sacked Helms in the wake of Watergate. President Nixon had wanted access to material contained in the IG Report, but Helms had refused to give it to him.[30]

By mid-May 1967, Helms had succeeded in fending off LBJ's interest in the 1963 CIA plots involving the Mafia, plots that Helms must have suspected could have backfired against JFK. In addition, someone had persuaded Jack Anderson to stop writing articles about the matter, even though he still had important unused material. But what about the original catalyst for the affair, Johnny Rosselli?

Rosselli had finally gotten what he—along with Marcello and Trafficante—had wanted for almost a year. Page 132 of the IG Report relates a May 3, 1967, discussion between the CIA and the FBI's liaison to the CIA. The FBI liaison said that Rosselli had the "CIA 'over a barrel' because of 'that operation.' [The FBI liaison] said that he doubted that the FBI would be able to do anything about either Rosselli or Giancana because of 'their previous activities with [the CIA].'"[31]

In other words, because Rosselli had leaked his role in the CIA-Mafia plots to Jack Anderson, the FBI would have to hold off on pursuing the immigration charges that had surfaced one year earlier. Rosselli, Marcello, and Trafficante had achieved a major goal of the strategy they had begun developing the previous year.

Chapter Thirty-six

Richard Helms had extricated himself from the mess caused by mingling the CIA with the Mafia, which had contributed to JFK's assassination. Now, the same pattern was about to repeat itself in the coming months. Helms's increasingly unsettled Cuban operations would help to trigger a series of events leading to yet another high-profile assassination involving Carlos Marcello.

As JFK's murder had, this one would involve Cuban-exile gunrunning and drug trafficking. However, there would be major differences between the two assassinations, from the nature of Marcello's participation to the CIA's shifting role with Cuban exiles. By 1967, the CIA's anti-Castro effort had dwindled from what it had been just a few years earlier. With the massive escalation of intelligence operations in Southeast Asia and the high level of covert activity in other Cold War hot spots, Cuba was no longer the major focus it had been earlier in President Johnson's term. Even inside the US, Helms's increasing focus on domestic surveillance of antiwar critics was supplanting anti-Castro operations as the CIA's primary domestic operation.

However, Castro was still entrenched just ninety miles from the US, and looking for opportunities to export his revolution and influence. According to the FBI, almost a thousand Cuban exiles arrived each week in Miami, and there were "136,244 Cuban refugees . . . in South Florida."[1] The CIA still had to gather intelligence about Cuba and take what action it could against Fidel. Something could always happen to Fidel and Raul, creating an opening for Almeida. Given the usual shelf life of Latin American dictators, Fidel had already achieved a relatively long run—and in 1967, it would have been inconceivable to Helms that Fidel would remain in power for another four decades. Helms needed the CIA to maintain a network of exile operatives, in case an opportunity arose, while the Agency kept at least a small amount of pressure on Castro's regime.

As *Ramparts* had shown, cracks were starting to appear in the CIA's ability to manage the US news media, so it was more important than ever to hide the CIA's role in Cuban exile operations. Gone were the days when the Miami CIA station employed six hundred people who managed three thousand exile CIA assets and fifty corporate fronts.[2] While the CIA's covert Cuban operations were much better concealed by 1967, its assets—and former assets—were much harder to control.

While the 1967 Cuban operations of CIA Director Helms and Deputy Director for Plans Desmond FitzGerald were more deniable, the agency's looser control led to problems that sometimes made the news. Like Helms, FitzGerald had much more on his plate than just Cuba. In May and June 1967, FitzGerald and the CIA were able to accurately predict both the Six-Day War in the Middle East and Israel's quick victory, but those efforts took time and attention away from supervising officials overseeing Cuban operations.

Desmond FitzGerald's health was deteriorating, but he tried to put up a good front and continue his work. A CIA associate described Fitz-Gerald to Evan Thomas as looking "physically ill; his face was 'flushed and puffy' [because] FitzGerald was . . . suffering from a circulatory problem." FitzGerald had only a short time to live, and his health likely affected the lack of direction and supervision that plagued Cuban operations.[3] These management problems would lead to terrorist acts by Cuban exiles in the US and other countries, and some writers viewed those exiles as being out of control, as going beyond what their CIA case officers wanted. On the other hand, that may have been the impression Helms and FitzGerald wanted to create: that the exiles were acting on their own and were not under Agency control.

Even Cuban exiles the CIA admits were under its direct control at the time, like Luis Posada, were sometimes involved with the Mafia—with the CIA's knowledge, if not approval. For example, CIA files document that in the summer of 1967, Posada was dealing explosives with one Mafia figure who was later linked to a Marcello casino deal, and with another mobster who had worked for Trafficante and run guns with Jack Ruby.[4]

The CIA's less hands-on approach relegated many Cuban exiles to a gray area. Some CIA-backed exiles worked with non-CIA exiles, while former CIA assets seeking to continue the struggle against Castro began receiving support from sources whose backing (or US approval) was unclear. Still other exiles who had once been CIA assets had to simply find a new way to earn a living.

Given the Miami nexus of exile operations and Trafficante's continued presence there, it shouldn't be surprising that in 1967, drugs became an increasing problem among formerly—and perhaps some currently—CIA-supported exiles. According to noted intelligence journalist Joseph Trento, the problem became so widespread that by the following year, the Federal Bureau of Narcotics (FBN) would find "itself arresting scores of former CIA employees. These Cuban 'freedom fighters' were using their CIA training for a life of crime [and justifying] their actions by claiming that they were using the ill-gotten funds to continue the effort against Castro, an effort that the CIA had abandoned. Many of these men were working directly for Santo Trafficante."[5]

Tom Tripodi was a Federal Bureau of Narcotics agent assigned to the Miami CIA station's security office. He wrote that the CIA originally looked the other way when some exiles began smuggling car parts and other black-market goods to Cuba: "The CIA was happy, because the smuggling gave a sense of purpose and a means of funding to a group it had trained for a counter-revolution that every day seemed less likely to occur." However, now that the CIA had "instructed them in the fine art of smuggling, some of them applied their newly learned expertise to drug trafficking." Tripodi found that some exile drug "suspects employed many of the intelligence and security techniques they had learned from the CIA, making" the job of US drug agents more difficult. Yet for some exiles, the downsizing of anti-Castro CIA operations left "the drug trade as their only viable means of support."[6]

Former FBI agent Bill Turner has pointed out that the CIA's Miami operations had created a tradition of lawlessness. In addition to the fact that the CIA's charter forbade it from conducting operations on America soil, "every time a [CIA] boat left for Cuba or a plane dumped firebombs, the Neutrality Act was broken. . . . The transportation of explosives on the highways transgressed Florida law. The possession of illegal explosives and war *matériel* contravened the Munitions Act, and the procurement of automatic weapons defied the Firearms Act." The CIA even set up false corporations and filed false tax returns, all while quietly arranging "for nonenforcement. An elaborate recognition system was devised, and police, sheriffs, Customs, Immigration, Treasury, and the FBI all looked the other way."[7] Some exile assets knew the CIA had given massive support to Manuel Artime while he was smuggling drugs and working with the Mafia. In some ways, the Cuban exiles getting into drug trafficking and arms smuggling in 1967 were simply continuing an already established tradition.

Trafficante and his organization were no doubt happy to add such seasoned men to their drug network. Within a few years, this new exile influx would accelerate a major shift in the Mafia's heroin and cocaine networks, leading to new CIA exile drug scandals in the 1970s and '80s. But in 1967, the usual French Connection heroin routes through Mexico City and port cities like Montreal and New Orleans were still going strong. Because of Michel Mertz's political and intelligence ties, he had not yet been arrested for the earlier Fort Benning bust, so his allies in Montreal and Mexico were free to prosper.

The Montreal World's Fair that began in the spring of 1967, popularly known as Expo 67, was the unlikely catalyst for both Cuban-exile terrorism and a rise in Canadian heroin trafficking. It also helped to bring together drug running and gunrunning operations involving the Mafia, Cuban exiles, and far-right racists—including an escaped convict (detailed shortly) named James Earl Ray, who would soon travel from the US to England and Canada.

Felipe Rivero's Cuban Nationalist Movement (CNM) had only about a dozen members, but according to the FBI, it "claimed credit for acts of violence committed in England, Canada, and the United States." Rivero was the aristocratic-exile friend of Alberto Fowler, the sophisticated Cuban assisting Jim Garrison in 1967. Fowler's work for Garrison might be characterized more accurately as diverting suspicion from himself, Rivero, and other exiles who hated JFK. Garrison didn't know about Fowler's close friendship with Rivero, who had helped Fowler shadow JFK the day before the Tampa assassination attempt, nor was Garrison aware that just hours after Lee Oswald's arrest, Fowler had tried to spread disinformation about Oswald to Harry Williams. Instead, Garrison told *Life* magazine writer Richard Billings that "Alberto Fowler [was one of the] legit Cubans who have contempt for wildcat, outlaw Cubans."[8]

Both Fowler and Rivero had worked for the CIA during the Bay of Pigs operation, but by 1967 Rivero and his small but violent CNM exile group were similar to the more deadly racist groups in the South. Miami authorities described Rivero as a neo-Nazi; he was a Holocaust denier at a time when the Ku Klux Klan was stepping up its anti-Semitic violence. Anti-Semitism was just one trait that the Miami-based Rivero shared with white supremacists like Joseph Milteer, who made regular visits to Miami. Both men belonged to organizations that also trafficked in arms and explosives, and some of these deals were brokered by the Mafia. Both men also had associates involved in drug trafficking.[9]

It's important to stress that the vast majority of Cuban exiles didn't share Felipe Rivero's extremist politics. However, the violence of Rivero and his associates would drive many more moderate exiles out of the movement, leading to a wave of terrorist exile bombings and killings in the 1970s, including Rivero's terrorist bombing of Chilean diplomat Orlando Letelier in Washington, D.C.[10]

Exiles like Rivero had learned, or been told, to attack Cuban interests only outside the US, a policy that evokes CIA guidelines dating back to 1963. While there is no evidence that the CIA supported Rivero directly in 1967, some in the Agency would have liked his results: increasing psychological pressure on Cuban officials over their presence at Expo 67, with minimal damage and no loss of life—and no obvious connection to the CIA. Some writers feel that at various times the CIA was assisting, or at least tacitly approving, Rivero's associates. The idea is not inconceivable, since CIA files confirm that the Agency did employ bombers, like Luis Posada, at the time. The bottom line is that the hazy lines of CIA command and support allowed men like Rivero and Posada to operate, often with tragic results.

Seven months before the April 27, 1967, opening of Expo 67, one of Rivero's members allegedly used a bazooka to attack the Cuban embassy in Ottawa, Canada's capital. Just three weeks before the Expo's opening, the FBI had questioned the same Rivero operative and his brother about the Montreal bombings of a restaurant and a Canadian company that did business with Cuba.[11] The focus of exile violence shifted briefly to Mexico on May 3, 1967, when four people were wounded after someone threw a bomb into the car of Cuba's ambassador.[12]

According to the *Miami News*, US authorities arrested Felipe Rivero on May 12, 1967, and "charged [him] with threatening to blow up the Cuban pavilion at Expo 67."[13] The FBI said that Rivero's supporters tried to rally exiles in Florida for a general strike on his behalf, but when a more moderate exile group (RECE) "opposed the general strike and" urged "Cuban exiles to not participate . . . the office of RECE was bombed [and] almost completely destroyed." Two of Rivero's men were arrested for that bombing, but charges were later dropped against one of them.[14]

Rivero and his men had more plans for Expo 67 and Montreal: While Rivero remained in a Dade County jail, the FBI said that two of Rivero's men "went to Montreal, Canada, by automobile [and] at Expo 67 . . . placed a bomb under a bridge adjacent to the Cuban Pavilion. The bomb subsequently exploded." However, the bridge shielded the Cuban Pavilion from the blast. To ensure the incident garnered attention, Rivero's group issued a statement in Miami, proudly taking responsibility for the attack.[15] The FBI reported that four days later, on June 3, 1967, two of Rivero's men met with another exile leader and "Tony Varona [to discuss] a two-pronged plan to assassinate the Cuban Ambassador to Canada and to attack a Cuban ship in Montreal."[16]

Because of Rivero's bombing campaign, and information that the FBI picked up about additional exile attacks planned for Montreal and Expo 67, Canadian authorities had to increase the city's security—especially at Expo 67, where attendance would suffer if visitors did not feel secure. Yet a heavily armed presence would hardly yield the type of fun atmosphere that Expo organizers knew attendees wanted. Only one type of Canadian security wouldn't clash with, and would actually enhance, the Fair's festive atmosphere: red-jacketed officers of the Royal Canadian Mounted Police (RCMP).

Unfortunately, many of the RCMP members diverted to security duty at Expo 67 came from their expert narcotics squad, which was then dealing with a surge of heroin into Montreal and Toronto. While much of the world thinks of the RCMP as horse-riding Mounties, most of its members do the same type of investigative work as the FBI. The RCMP was close to tracking down the source of the new heroin surge, which involved members of the same Mertz/Trafficante/Marcello heroin network busted at Fort Benning the previous year. According to Canadian crime reporter Jean-Pierre Charbonneau, when Canadian authorities increased security, "experienced [narcotics squad] officers suddenly found themselves in scarlet RCMP tunics patrolling [Expo 67]. For six months the Narcotics Squad ceased functioning [thus creating] an unhoped-for opportunity for traffickers" in the summer and fall of 1967.[17] Felipe Rivero's bombing campaign hadn't produced major damage or deaths, but it did have the unintended effect of creating a rush to smuggle more heroin through Montreal. Seasoned criminals would soon be recruited to help with the increased narcotics traffic, among them James Earl Ray.

As 1967 progressed, two major personnel losses—Win Scott and Desmond FitzGerald—would further complicate Richard Helms's and the CIA's increasingly problematic anti-Castro operations. Win Scott was the CIA Station Chief in Mexico City, as he had been in 1963. Mexico City remained an important station for anti-Castro operations, since it both housed a Cuban embassy (subject to extensive electronic surveillance by the CIA) and offered regular flights to Havana, sometimes utilized by CIA agents like Tony Sforza, an operative for David Morales.[18]

Win Scott's biographer, Jefferson Morley, writes that in the wake of the IG Report and the CIA memo directing CIA Station Chiefs to support the Warren Report's "lone nut/magic bullet" theory, "Scott responded by ordering a comprehensive review of his Oswald files. Then he retired and wrote his memoir disputing the Warren Report." Morley thinks "Scott wrote his JFK conspiracy theory mainly to protect himself [because] he knew that top officials—including himself, Angleton, and . . . David Atlee Phillips—had far more knowledge about Oswald's travels and intentions than the American people could imagine."[19]

Scott's departure no doubt had a negative impact on anti-Castro operations, especially since Deputy Director for Plans Desmond FitzGerald's health was in sharp decline, though he still forced himself to show up for work each day. Even while Felipe Rivero remained in jail for attempting to blow up the Cuban Pavilion at Expo 67, CIA files confirm that the Agency continued to employ bombing expert Luis Posada. Posada was working with an alleged Mafia figure who would later manage a Las Vegas casino following a deal brokered by Carlos Marcello. According to a CIA report to the FBI on June 27, 1967, this man was "tied in with organized crime figures in [the] Miami area and also involved with 7 recent bombings in Miami." The man got "in touch with Posada" by going through Norman Rothman, who had worked for Trafficante in Havana and also run guns with Jack Ruby and Carlos Prio. The man "understands Posada [was] attached with [the] CIA and claims Posada supplied him with caps, primers, and C-4 explosives." The CIA admits its Miami headquarters had previously okayed Posada's work for the man, giving him "hand grenades and silencers."[20]

Perhaps someone in the CIA realized it might look odd for the US to prosecute bombers like Felipe Rivero while a bomber like Posada was a full-time CIA employee. A CIA memo claims "Posada [was] terminated 7/11/67 because he resigned from position as military coordinator for RECE. JMWAVE does not have current need." However, other CIA files place Posada's termination as a full-time employee in 1968, and, in any event, an Agency memo admits that the CIA rehired Posada almost immediately "as an independent contractor from 1968–75." Another CIA memo says the Agency retained "Posada [until] 2-13-76," even though three years earlier the CIA was "sure that Posada [was] involved with narcotics drug trafficking"—confirming previous reports that "Posada may be involved in smuggling cocaine . . . to Miami."[21]

All of this information had a three-part implication for CIA Cuban operations in 1967. First, the CIA was trying to downgrade its violent operatives to a less official status, while still using them. Second, CIA records, as in the case of Posada's service dates, were sometimes fudged or altered when the operative was linked to terrorism or political scandals—in Posada's case, that included his involvement in the bombing of a Cubana airliner, work for the CIA in Iran-Contra, and later attempts to assassinate Fidel Castro. Finally, drugs were an increasing aspect of anti-Castro operations in the late 1960s and early '70s, and the CIA did not regard drug trafficking (and contact with the Mafia) as a reason to terminate certain operatives. As the CIA had written about Manuel Artime and AMWORLD in 1964, perhaps the impression that covertly backed CIA exiles got their weapons and explosives from Mafiosi benefited the CIA more than the impression that the agency had provided them.[22]

The bottom line is that the CIA's method of operation made it increasingly difficult to determine which exiles were actually working for the CIA—and where their allegiance ultimately lay. That situation had been a problem while JFK was still alive, and it continued even as CIA supervision of exile operatives decreased. The soft treatment of some arrested exiles might indicate which Cuban exiles were supported or sanctioned by the CIA. Felipe Rivero's two men who had been arrested for firing a bazooka at the UN in 1964 were also questioned in the 1967 Montreal bombings and "arrested [in the Montreal case] by Jersey City PD for possession of explosives," according to a June 29, 1967, FBI report. However, both were released on only a small bond by July 10, 1967.[23]

In the summer of 1967, Felipe Rivero's men formed an alliance with another group, headed by Cuban exile Juan Bosch. A July 14, 1967, FBI report says that one of Bosch's men negotiated with a "Cuban exile arms dealer in Miami . . . to order .30 and .50 caliber machine guns, a 20 millimeter cannon, a 57 millimeter recoilless rifle, and a large amount of ammunition for these weapons." That arrangement might have been related to an incident two days later, in which author Jane Franklin writes that Cuban authorities captured several exiles in a speedboat who were "armed with high-powered rifles, cyanide bullets, and a plot to assassinate [Fidel]." On July 19, 1967, an FBI memo said that Juan Bosch and five of his men "were indicted in Miami . . . and charged with conspiracy to export arms." However, they were freed on $1,000 "recognizance bonds." Five days later, the FBI says, Bosch and some of his men were "indicted at Macon, [Georgia] . . . for attempting to export arms," yet they were freed once more on only "recognizance bonds."[24]

The soft treatment of Bosch, his men, and Rivero's associates by US authorities raise suspicion that their activities were approved at least tacitly by someone in the CIA. The same idea applies to Felipe Rivero, whom the FBI described on July 11, 1967, as "excludable and deportable"—yet he was never deported. Likely not approved by the CIA, however, were the six Cuban exiles who, according to the FBI, "hijacked a 380-foot ship in Miami" to use in an attack on Cuba; "their plan failed, and they escaped. They were indicted in Miami on 7/26/67."[25] That was the type of bad publicity the CIA didn't need.

By the summer of 1967, the CIA's anti-Castro operations were clearly approaching, or actually in, a state of disarray. FBI files are full of reports of bickering and backbiting between Cuban exile groups and leaders, some of which turned violent.

Things got worse on July 23, 1967, when Desmond FitzGerald, the CIA's Deputy Director for Plans, died of a heart attack, further disrupting the CIA's already problematic Cuban operations. Bobby Kennedy attended the funeral of the man he sometimes played tennis with, probably never realizing the secrets FitzGerald (and Helms) had withheld from him. Helms appointed his trusted former deputy Thomas Karamessines to take FitzGerald's position.[26] As for Cuban operations, Helms needed someone experienced, someone he could trust, to assume command and get them back on track. Just as Helms had turned to E. Howard Hunt almost a year earlier, when Helms needed someone seasoned to deal with the influx of new JFK conspiracy books, Helms called on another familiar associate he trusted, David Atlee Phillips.

Like Hunt, Phillips had the advantage of not only being experienced, but already knowing about (and having worked on) the CIA's most sensitive Cuban operation: AMWORLD and the coup plan with Almeida, the remnants of which still involved the ongoing covert monitoring and support of Almeida's family members outside Cuba. Phillips's experience with Cuban operations from the Bay of Pigs to AMWORLD, coupled with his background in journalism, would also make him useful in dealing with disclosures emerging from Jim Garrison's investigation. In fact, by October 1967, because of a new book mentioning Manuel Artime, Harry Williams, Tony Varona, and Alberto Fowler, Phillips would write a long memo about the cover-up of the CIA's secret Bay of Pigs base just outside of New Orleans.[27]

In addition, the deniable way in which Phillips controlled Cuban exile Antonio Veciana—by using the deep-cover identity of "Maurice Bishop"—typified the more hands-off model the CIA was beginning to use with more of its operatives. Finally, since Phillips had been involved with activities such as meeting Oswald, Helms would have known that Phillips had just as much reason to avoid publicity and squelch criticism of the Warren Report as Helms did.

For all of those reasons, from Helms's perspective, Phillips was a logical choice to take over the fight against Castro. Hunt could not assume that position, because he was busy managing the CIA's relationship with publishers and running covert operations for western Europe—and because of his problematic official history with Cuban operations. Phillips wrote in his published autobiography that within weeks of FitzGerald's death, he had left his post as Station Chief of the Dominican Republic and was back in the US, meeting President Lyndon Johnson and becoming the CIA's Chief of Cuban operations.[28] Soon, Phillips would have several AMWORLD veterans, including David Morales, pursuing a top Cuban target in Bolivia: Che Guevara.

It's important to point out that relatively few CIA files have been disclosed about the scope and extent of the CIA's Cuban operations from 1967 onward, in stark contrast to the information available about the period from 1959 to 1966. That might be because Phillips and other Cuban operatives were later involved in various aspects of Watergate and were investigated regarding JFK's assassination, while exiles like Posada and Rivero were linked to terrorist bombings in the 1970s that caused international incidents. It is this lack of CIA files that makes it difficult to determine which exiles were acting on their own, and which the CIA supported or sanctioned.

From the perspective of Phillips, Helms, and the CIA, their task in recruiting exiles had become more difficult. Fewer exiles, especially inspirational leaders, were willing to risk their lives in the fight against Fidel. Finding such men had not been easy in 1963, just months after the Bay of Pigs prisoner release and the Cuban Missile Crisis, but by 1967 it was even more difficult. Moderate leaders, like Harry Williams, had settled into family life and were building businesses, while others, like Manolo Ray, had moved away from Miami. The exiles who were willing to risk their lives, like Rivero and Bosch, were also harder to control and prone to violent attacks. That left Phillips with exiles like Posada and Antonio Veciana. Because the press, especially the emerging left-wing media, was starting to look at domestic CIA operations, Phillips would soon have both men based outside of the US—and eventually working together on an attempt to assassinate Fidel.[29]

Phillips's new assignment coincided with Hunt's becoming Chief of

European Covert Operations, meaning that both AMWORLD veterans had done quite well for themselves and had avoided the exile faced by some of their fellow former AMWORLD officials. Richard Helms was probably relieved once Phillips took over Cuban operations and could help to monitor developments in Jim Garrison's investigation, since Helms still had his hands full with Vietnam and increased domestic surveillance.

In May 1967, Carlos Marcello had an urgent matter to attend to: the first journalist to link him directly to JFK's assassination. The journalist's account being readied for publication had nothing to do with Marcello's ties to David Ferrie or Jack Ruby, or any of the disclosures from the Garrison investigation. Instead, it revealed Marcello's fall 1962 outburst about JFK, made to a few associates in what the godfather thought were the secure confines of his immense Churchill Farms property.

The writer was Ed Reid, a longtime crime reporter who had coauthored *The Green Felt Jungle* in 1963, the book that first exposed Johnny Rosselli's Las Vegas influence and lavish lifestyle. Assisting with the research on that book had been private detective Ed Becker, who in 1962 had gone with Marcello to Churchill Farms to discuss a business proposition. With Becker were two of Marcello's most trusted associates, Carlo Roppolo and Jack Liberto, Marcello's bodyguard and personal barber. Becker heard Marcello rage against Bobby Kennedy over what the godfather saw as Bobby's persecution of him. Marcello said that if he killed Bobby, JFK would simply send the US military after him—but if JFK were killed, then Bobby's power would be over. (Congressional investigators later confirmed Becker's account and found him credible.)[30]

By 1967, Ed Reid was working on his next book about the Mafia, *The Grim Reapers*, and Becker allowed Reid to recount a brief version of Marcello's threat against JFK, as long as the detective's name wasn't used. Since Becker said he had told two FBI agents about Marcello's 1962 threat, on May 6, 1967, Reid asked Los Angeles FBI officials about the incident, and showed them his manuscript.

Word traveled fast to Marcello's associates, and the next day, an intermediary for top Chicago Mafia attorney Sidney Korshak contacted the Los Angeles FBI office. Korshak, whom the Justice Department called one of "the most powerful members of the underworld," had been helping Johnny Rosselli and the Chicago Mafia bury damaging information since 1941. An expert at forcing Chicago's two largest newspapers to soft-pedal his mob connections, and a man with ties to Hollywood power brokers, Korshak was the ideal person to suppress Becker's Marcello revelation in Ed Reid's forthcoming book.[31]

Sidney Korshak tried to damage Becker's credibility and reputation to the FBI. Even though J. Edgar Hoover had told the Warren Commission that JFK's murder would remain an open case, and that "any information coming to us from any source will be thoroughly investigated," exactly the opposite happened in May 1967. Despite FBI files describing Korshak's Mafia ties, the Bureau failed to investigate Becker's story and accepted Korshak's allegations at face value. The FBI still had pending charges against Marcello for punching a New Orleans FBI agent, but it didn't bother to tell that agent or the New Orleans office about Becker's accusation against Marcello.[32]

Korshak's intermediary tried to intervene directly with Ed Reid, after which an FBI agent visited Reid and both tried to convince Reid to drop Becker's Marcello account. Neither succeeded, and Becker's account remained in the book. Reid's manuscript also contained the first detailed overview of Marcello's criminal empire, as well as sections about Santo Trafficante and Johnny Rosselli (though it didn't link those two to JFK's murder).

However, *The Grim Reapers* wasn't published until two years later, in 1969, long after the media had lost interest in Garrison's investigation, so the mainstream press gave the passage little attention. It's unclear if the efforts of Korshak, or others, had any effect on the book's delay. If Reid's information had been published earlier, at the height of the media's interest in Garrison, it could have turned the spotlight of suspicion toward Marcello.

Marcello, Trafficante, and Rosselli were achieving much of what they had been striving for by May 1967: The FBI had backed off Rosselli because of the leaks to Anderson, their names hadn't surfaced in the press as suspects in JFK's murder, and Bobby was publicly professing his support for LBJ. In addition, Marcello and Trafficante could take advantage of new heroin opportunities because of the Expo 67 situation in Montreal. While Rosselli didn't have a role in the heroin network, he could relax once more among the stars at Hollywood's Friars Club without worrying about his immigration status.

But a major piece of unfinished business for Rosselli, Trafficante, and especially Marcello was Jimmy Hoffa. Marcello had so far been unsuccessful in using the Mafia's $2 million fund to get Hoffa out of prison, but would soon increase his efforts. Hoffa, in Lewisburg Federal Prison since early March, was getting impatient—and focusing his anger on Bobby Kennedy. Hoffa still hoped that Marcello and his associates might come through; he knew how much they wanted to keep receiving loans from the Teamster Pension Fund. But Hoffa knew that if Bobby ever became president, his chances of getting out—or staying out—were nil. Hoffa probably feared that even if he were able to win release, as president, Bobby could simply have him prosecuted again ... and again, and again. Hoffa wanted to make sure that couldn't happen.

According to FBI files, on May 30, 1967, an inmate overheard Hoffa say "that he had a contract out on Senator Robert F. Kennedy." The inmate's account contained credible details, and "stated that on or about Memorial Day, 1967, he was in the dining hall at the Lewisburg Federal Penitentiary and at the table next to him was James Hoffa, who was talking to the two ... individuals [both Americans] of Italian descent." One of the individuals wasn't named, but his physical description and age ("55–58 years old") fit that of fifty-seven-year-old Mafia underboss Carmine Galante, Hoffa's closest mob confidant in prison. According to Ed Reid, Galante had been prosecuted when Bobby was Attorney General, and "sentenced to 20 years for conspiracy to violate the narcotics laws." Galante had "many associates in Montreal," and Hoffa expert Dan Moldea writes that Galante controlled a French Connection heroin route that extended "from Montreal to Toronto, Ontario, then to Windsor, and across the river to Detroit." That Montreal heroin route involved associates of Michel Victor Mertz, and Galante was aligned with both Carlos Marcello and Santo Trafficante.[33]

The Lewisburg inmate told the FBI that he'd overheard Hoffa telling the two Italian-Americans, "I have a contract out on Kennedy and if he ever gets in the primaries or ever gets elected, the contract will be fulfilled within six months." The inmate named two other criminals who'd also heard Hoffa's remarks that day. One was a bank robber, "originally from St. Louis, Missouri," who was slated to be paroled soon. Two weeks after hearing Hoffa talk about his contract on Bobby, the Lewisburg inmate was talking privately with the Teamster boss. Curious about Hoffa's earlier remarks, he casually "asked Hoffa what he thought about [Bobby] Kennedy. He stated Hoffa immediately began an emotional tirade over Kennedy's use of wiretapping and Hoffa's conviction and incarceration at Lewisburg. He ended the conversation by stating, 'Right now Kennedy's in no danger; but if he gets into a primary or gets elected, I won't say how or when, but he'll get knocked off.'"[34]

When the inmate talked to the FBI, he wasn't seeking a deal, special treatment, or publicity. Instead, he told the FBI that "in view of Hoffa's power and influence in this country, he feared for his life and under no circumstances would he testify to the above information." Another FBI report might tie into the inmate's story: John Davis writes that a year later, just weeks before Bobby's murder, "an inmate informant in . . . Lewisburg told the FBI that he had overheard Jimmy Hoffa and New York Mafia boss Carmine Galante, an ally of Carlos Marcello's, discussing a 'mob contract to kill Bob Kennedy.'" Names and other information in FBI memos about this matter are still censored, so how, or if, this information relates to the May 1967 Lewisburg report can't be determined. As we'll detail in Chapter 60, the FBI apparently didn't ask Hoffa about his May 1967 threat against Bobby for more than a year—until six weeks after Bobby's assassination.[35]

If Hoffa was making plans in May 1967 to have Bobby killed in case he ran for president, there was one assassin Hoffa couldn't use, a loose end he would have to take care of before his plans could proceed: Frank Chavez, Hoffa's enforcer, whom authorities knew had planned to kill Bobby Kennedy on two different occasions, most recently in March 1967. If any assassination attempt were made against Bobby in the coming year, Chavez would be an obvious and immediate suspect, one tied directly to Hoffa.

Shortly after Hoffa's May 1967 threat to have Bobby killed, Frank Chavez was mysteriously shot by his own Teamster bodyguard. Bobby's former prosecutor for the Chavez case, Tom Kennelly, later told a journalist that Chavez's "bodyguard just pulled out a gun and nailed him one day. . . . No one seemed to know what it was about." Kennelly told us that after the bodyguard "shot Chavez dead at his desk . . . he got some time, a couple of years," in prison. However, there is no record of Hoffa's taking any action against the bodyguard for suddenly murdering Chavez.[36] Frank Chavez could have been the victim of a random argument, but he may also have been the victim of bad timing—wanting to kill Bobby Kennedy just a few months too soon, in a way that would have clearly pointed to Hoffa.

Chapter Thirty-seven

By late May of 1967 in New Orleans, Jim Garrison was getting ready to reveal Marcello's role in JFK's murder, as well as the fact that JFK had approved a plot to assassinate Fidel Castro in 1963. Both of those Garrison findings are little known today, even among JFK scholars, despite having been reported (briefly) in local and national media. Their obscurity can be credited to Marcello's continuing efforts to divert Garrison, and to the role of Bobby Kennedy's close friend Walter Sheridan in an upcoming tide of negative publicity designed to discredit Garrison. Just as in 1963, in 1968 it was difficult to expose Marcello's role in JFK's murder without also revealing parts of the JFK-Almeida coup plan.

Garrison was telling a few journalists about the Mafia's role in JFK's murder by mid-May 1967. An FBI memo describes a Lafayette, Louisiana, television broadcast, called *Garrison and the Mafia*, that aired on May 22 and May 23, 1967, which said that Garrison "believed that organized crime . . . is responsible, along with other anti-Castroites, for the assassination." The TV report went on to say that "organized crime wanted the assassination to appear as though it had been done at the instigation of Castro, and this would . . . arouse the United States to a point where Castro would be removed from power in Cuba, thereby allowing reopening of the gambling casinos." The "report also mentioned that David Ferrie may have 'flown some missions for a very important member of the syndicate who has been a long-time resident of Louisiana.'" While the TV report didn't name Carlos Marcello, the FBI memo did.[1]

The Lafayette TV report showed that Garrison or one of his staff was close to uncovering the truth. However, before the Mafia angle received national publicity, Garrison dropped it, having apparently been diverted by Marcello. Within weeks of the TV report, Marcello's associates and Louisiana Senator Russell Long would provide Garrison with a new suspect, designed to deflect suspicion from Marcello, free Hoffa, and embarrass Bobby Kennedy: Edward Grady Partin, the main witness Bobby and Walter Sheridan had used to send Hoffa to prison.

It's tragically ironic that just a few months earlier, Bobby and Sheridan might have welcomed Garrison's focus on Marcello. But at the same time that the Lafayette television station was highlighting Garrison's Mafia suspicions, the national media was publicizing an area of Garrison's interest that Bobby wanted to remain hidden—especially in the wake of Jack Anderson's revelations. The New Orleans District Attorney was still going after Clay Shaw, but in mid-May 1967, the *New York Times*, UPI, and the *Washington Post* had begun reporting new angles in Garrison's investigation. Their news stories were summarized in a May 17, 1967, letter from J. Edgar Hoover to Attorney General Ramsey Clark. It said Garrison's thesis was "that Oswald was a CIA agent, was violently anti-Communist, and was recruited by CIA for an operation, approved by President Kennedy, the purpose of which was to assassinate Fidel Castro."[2]

Hoover was worried because other news stories reported that "Garrison claims that Oswald was probably a CIA agent who worked undercover with anti-Castro Cubans with the knowledge of Federal agents."[3] Articles in the *Washington Post* and *Washington Evening Star* were even more specific. As summarized in a June 2, 1967, memo to the assistant US attorney general:

> Garrison claims that Lee Harvey Oswald did not kill President Kennedy but that the President was assassinated by five anti-Castro Cubans who were angered over his handling of the Bay of Pigs invasion.... The assassins were former CIA employees.... Garrison has said that he does not believe the CIA planned the Kennedy murder, or knew of it beforehand, but that the CIA is making every effort to prevent his office from trailing or learning the whereabouts of the assassins.[4]

Those reports would also have alarmed CIA Director Richard Helms. The CIA's copies of the above memos about Garrison are grouped in a CIA file at the National Archives with earlier FBI memos from 1965 about reports from a Trafficante-linked exile about a "plot to assassinate Fidel Castro [involving] Major Juan Almeida."[5] Helms and the CIA had already been trying to stymie Garrison's investigation, but these new revelations would ensure that Helms would continue those efforts.

Garrison was getting close to the truth, especially when the above disclosures are coupled with his suspicion of Carlos Marcello, which had not yet appeared in the national press. Cuban exiles like Martino had been involved in JFK's murder, as well as CIA employees like David

Morales. JFK had in fact approved a plan that would have eliminated Castro, and Oswald apparently had some contact with that plan.

Unfortunately, Bobby Kennedy didn't trust Garrison. The FBI had planted his seeds of distrust in 1963, when the Bureau warned Bobby's Marcello prosecutors not to cooperate with Garrison. Decades later, Bobby's lead Marcello prosecutor, John Diuguid, told us that "in retrospect, Garrison had some interesting stuff [about Marcello] and perhaps we should have taken him more seriously."[6]

By May 1967 it was too late, even though Garrison's suspicions mirrored the findings of Bobby's secret investigators. As we noted earlier, Frank Mankiewicz concluded that JFK was murdered by "the mob, anti-Castro Cuban exiles, and maybe rogue CIA agents." According to John Davis, Walter Sheridan had "conducted an informal investigation and concluded guardedly that Marcello might well have been involved." According to Walter Sheridan's son, this search left Sheridan "'convinced' that President Kennedy had been killed by a conspiracy." Sheridan had been assisted in New Orleans by a former fellow Hoffa prosecutor, Frank Grimsley, who shared Sheridan's feeling that Marcello was behind JFK's murder.[7]

However, when Sheridan tried to tell Bobby what he'd found, Bobby stopped him and said he "didn't want to know." Frank Mankiewicz faced the same reaction whenever he tried to share his conclusions with Bobby. Neither Mankiewicz nor Sheridan was among the handful of Bobby's associates who knew about the JFK-Almeida coup plan, and keeping that crucial information from them probably also weighed heavily on Bobby.[8]

If Bobby didn't want to hear his own investigators' conclusions, he certainly didn't want Garrison airing JFK's plot to eliminate Fidel as part of a public spectacle, especially after Anderson's articles. Sadly, Garrison's focus on the Mafia and hints of Marcello's involvement weren't receiving national attention, so it's doubtful that Bobby was aware of them—and even if he was, his distrust of Garrison meant the prospect of joining forces with the publicity-seeking District Attorney just wasn't an option. Instead, Bobby became one of those determined to stop the Garrison inquiry by discrediting it.

By early June 1967, Bobby Kennedy had joined a long list of officials and influential people who wanted to see Garrison's investigation shut down before it revealed embarrassing or classified operations. In addition to NBC's Walter Sheridan, the list included LBJ, Helms, Hoover,

Attorney General Ramsey Clark, and undoubtedly other members of the intelligence community in the high levels of the DIA and Naval Intelligence. Two major television specials about Garrison were in the works, and some of those men may have exerted influence to ensure that the productions slammed the District Attorney while avoiding Garrison's suspicion of the Mafia and his attempt to tie CIA-backed Cuban exile assassins to a 1963 JFK-approved plan to eliminate Fidel.

Almost as if to counter the pro-conspiracy news coming out of New Orleans and the recent surge of JFK conspiracy books, CBS began preparing a special called *The Warren Report* in the spring of 1967. Former FBI agent William Turner was assisting Garrison at the time, and he was originally told by a CBS field producer that "We're going to let the chips fall where they may. I've been assured of that [by CBS officials]." It was to be "an objective look at the criticism [of the Warren Report] and [a] search for fresh evidence." Turner writes that a "CBS correspondent . . . reported that seven out of the eight teams sent into the field came back with a conclusion of conspiracy." However, before the special was finished, the field producer said, "The whole tone was changed so as to completely reinforce the Warren Report." Turner writes that the change came "after a phone call from Washington to [the] CBS President. . . . The caller was a high government official."[9]

The NBC *White Paper* special that Walter Sheridan produced apparently targeted Garrison almost from the start. Sheridan's wife says her husband had "decided that Jim Garrison was 'a fraud—a dishonest man, morally and intellectually' within twenty-four hours of his arrival in New Orleans." According to David Talbot, Sheridan felt Garrison "was trying to deflect the spotlight from . . . Marcello and . . . Hoffa." Given that Garrison had originally set his sights on Marcello's pilot, David Ferrie, Sheridan's assessment seems too harsh—at least in regard to the Garrison inquiry's early stages. Also, Sheridan had no direct ties to Garrison himself and was apparently unaware of the District Attorney's suspicions of Marcello.[10]

However, a Garrison staffer's defection sealed Sheridan's and NBC's low opinion of the DA. Eleven days before the special was to air, the former Garrison staff member personally told Bobby that "Garrison will never shed any light on your brother's murder." However, the ex-staffer was unable to explain Garrison's motivation for his investigation; in turn, Garrison claimed the man was not a major part of his investigation, but was "merely a chauffeur and photographer."[11]

Garrison supporters have documented how Sheridan and NBC's June

19, 1967, *White Paper* went to unusual lengths to skewer Garrison, some of which are detailed in William Turner's autobiography *Rearview Mirror*. While the show quite rightly noted Garrison's weaker witnesses and speculations, Garrison himself was not allowed to appear. Turner notes the "special . . . attacked [Garrison] with such unremitting hostility that the Federal Communications Commission ordered that he be allowed a half hour of network time in rebuttal under the Fairness Doctrine."[12]

CBS's four-hour *Warren Report* special, hosted primarily by Walter Cronkite, at least allowed Garrison a brief appearance, "where he held his own under a when-did-you-stop-beating-your-wife interrogation by Mike Wallace," according to Turner. However, the special was primarily a defense of the increasingly-under-attack Warren Report. One of the Warren Commissioners, John McCloy, was even allowed to comment on the show's "rough script."[13]

Numerous writers have noted many problems the show experienced in dealing with issues like the number of shots that hit JFK, and how quickly and accurately they were fired. For example, the show used outstanding shooters to attempt to duplicate the three shots attributed to Oswald, a relatively poor rifleman at the time he left the Marines. The show and the Warren Report said that Oswald had hit JFK with two of his three shots, but, as Michael T. Griffith noted, "not one of the eleven participating expert marksmen scored at least two hits out of three shots on his first attempt. Seven of them failed to do so on ANY of their attempts. Oswald would have had only one attempt."[14]

Even though the CBS show used a rifle that fired faster and was in better condition than Oswald's, more than a third of the attempts had to be disqualified "because of trouble with the rifle." To account for Oswald's amazing speed and accuracy, which the experts had trouble duplicating even under better conditions, the script could only have Walter Cronkite intone, "It seems equally reasonable to say that Oswald, under normal circumstances, would take longer [than the experts to fire]. But these were not normal circumstances."[15]

It's hard to determine how much of what Cronkite said was his own opinion, and how much was simply part of an approved script he had to use. Cronkite had only a few skeptical lines, such as noting that the Warren Commission "permitted the FBI and CIA to investigate themselves" about whether Oswald was a government agent. After the special aired, the field producer who had originally promised Bill Turner "an objective look" resigned from CBS.

Dan Rather gave a mixed performance in the special. He admitted he was not "totally convinced about the single-bullet theory" but said it

wasn't "necessary to the final conclusion of the Warren Commission"—
even though most experts agree that it is central to their "lone nut" conclusion. While he was overwhelmingly supportive of the Warren Report,
even Rather said he was "not content with the findings on Oswald's possible connections with government agencies, particularly the CIA."[16]

Neither the NBC nor the CBS show mentioned David Ferrie's work
for Carlos Marcello, and they didn't mention Marcello (or Trafficante
or Rosselli) at all. Also avoided was any talk of a JFK-approved plot to
kill Castro in 1963, even though Garrison's remarks about that had been
reported in high-profile newspapers the previous month. As a result of
the two specials, Garrison was largely discredited to the rest of the mainstream press. More than two-thirds of the commercial television stations
in America were affiliated with CBS or NBC, and after they broadcast
their high-profile support for the Warren Report, major reporters for TV,
newspapers, or radio were not going to risk their careers by supporting a conspiracy. Essentially, those two specials ended any attempts by
mainstream journalists to seriously investigate the JFK assassination
until 1975, in the wake of Watergate. The fallout from the 1967 NBC
and CBS specials would have a similar chilling effect on the media's
investigations of the assassinations of Bobby Kennedy and Dr. Martin
Luther King, the following year.

Even some of Garrison's former associates admit that he could be his
own worst enemy, due in part to his love of publicity. Garrison also had
a tendency to overreach the limited evidence available to him, while not
realizing that infiltrators like Alberto Fowler were affecting the direction of his inquiry. While Garrison does not appear to have taken direct
orders from Marcello, the godfather was able to use intermediaries to
influence Garrison by using infiltrators, informants, and political associates, like Senator Russell Long.

Bobby Kennedy, Walter Sheridan, and Garrison had all focused on
Marcello by May 1967, but the NBC special and other attacks by Sheridan ended any possibility of the three working together against Marcello. Coupled with the lack of support (and outright hostility) from the
government, this situation probably helped to drive Garrison closer to
those he should have been most wary of, figures seeking to use him for
their own ends. This pattern became apparent by late June 1967, when
Garrison leaked to the press that he was investigating Edward Grady
Partin, the federal government's key witness against Jimmy Hoffa,
thereby confirming Bobby's and Sheridan's worst fears.

From that point forward, Garrison's investigation seems to have been

hopelessly compromised. On July 7, 1967, Garrison even issued a warrant for Sheridan's arrest, for allegedly trying to bribe a witness against
Shaw. When Sheridan surrendered, Bobby Kennedy issued a statement
saying that Sheridan wanted "as much as, or more than, any other man
to ascertain the truth about the events of November, 1963," and that
Sheridan wouldn't "do anything which would in the slightest degree
compromise the truth." Sheridan eventually beat the charges.[17]

Though Clay Shaw's investigation and eventual trial would drag on
for another two years, Garrison's efforts increasingly became the grotesque sideshow some journalists claimed it was. However, several private citizens assisting Garrison (Turner, Fensterwald, and others) would
go on to play important roles in helping to expose the JFK-Almeida coup
plan and the Mafia's use of it to assassinate JFK. Garrison's investigative files, most of which were unrelated to Clay Shaw and never used at
trial, would also become an important reference for later Congressional
investigations and journalists.

Garrison suddenly focused on Hoffa informant Edward Grady Partin
in late June 1967 because Carlos Marcello was still trying to take advantage of the Mafia's $2 million Spring Hoffa fund (more than $12 million
today). If Partin could be induced or bribed to recant his testimony—or
claim the government had used illegal wiretaps to convict Hoffa—the
Teamster president would win a new trial, and likely his freedom.

Carlos Marcello summoned Frank Ragano to New Orleans so the
mob lawyer could meet with Partin personally. As a sign of the seriousness of the effort, Marcello himself drove Ragano to Baton Rouge to
see Partin. On the drive, Marcello was pulled over by a Louisiana State
Patrol officer who pointed out the expired tag on Marcello's Cadillac.
When the officer realized he had pulled over Carlos Marcello, the patrolman became apologetic. Ragano says Marcello asked the officer if he
"would buy the plate for me and bring it to my office." The patrolman
replied, "Yes, sir, I'd be glad to." Marcello gave the officer $20 for the
tag, plus another $100 in thanks, before continuing on his way with
Ragano.[18]

Ragano's meeting with Partin didn't produce the desired results, so
Marcello had his associates offer a bribe of $1 million, which Partin
declined. That was the most Marcello was willing to offer, even though
the Spring Hoffa fund contained twice that amount; the rest would have
been profit for Marcello. The effort to free Hoffa would soon involve
Senator Russell Long, Louisiana's governor, World War II hero and

B-movie star Audie Murphy, and Dallas media owner Gordon McClendon, a friend of both Jack Ruby and the CIA's David Atlee Phillips.[19]

Even though Marcello's 1967 efforts to free Hoffa were unsuccessful, Marcello still felt he deserved a huge loan from the Teamster Pension Fund, so that he could build a Las Vegas casino for himself and Trafficante, fronted by a seemingly legitimate business associate. Hoffa had left Allan Dorfman in charge of distributing such loans, but with Hoffa in prison, Dorfman became greedy, demanding a $500,000 fee and 25 percent interest in the casino. Marcello and Trafficante were outraged. A few weeks later, on July 26, 1967, in an upscale Chicago suburb, two masked gunmen blasted Dorfman's car with shotgun fire. Dorfman was driving but was uninjured. As Trafficante explained to Ragano, "If they had wanted to kill him they would have. This was just a warning."[20]

Marcello preferred dealing with Hoffa, but it became apparent that getting him out of prison would be a longer-term undertaking. The 1968 election would represent an opportunity, since it looked like Richard Nixon was going to run. Marcello and Hoffa had donated $500,000 to Nixon's 1960 presidential run, and Nixon would soon be seeking Teamster backing for his bid. Also, given both Hoffa's and Carmine Galante's ties to Marcello, it's likely that at some point Marcello was told of Hoffa's plan to kill Bobby Kennedy if he tried to run for president.

In the early summer of 1967, the future looked promising for Johnny Rosselli. A year earlier, he'd faced the possibility of deportation and the loss of his patron, Sam Giancana. Now he had a new financial source (Howard Hughes) and had recently gotten his cut from their first casino deal, with more in the works. Leaking the CIA-Mafia plots to Jack Anderson had worked as he'd hoped, and Rosselli's friend William Harvey was still able to feed him inside information from the CIA.

Even though he was in the clear, the sixty-three-year-old Rosselli wasn't ready to relax or back off from his illegal activities. A criminal for all of his adult life, Rosselli couldn't resist continuing a card-cheating scam at the prestigious Los Angeles Friars Club, where Frank Sinatra had sponsored Rosselli for membership in 1963. Since then, Rosselli's men had bilked some of the wealthy members—including comedian Phil Silvers and singer Tony Martin—for $400,000.

On July 20, 1967, the FBI raided the Friars Club in Los Angeles and found the electronic equipment Rosselli and his men used in their card-cheating scam. The government then used a grand jury to pressure Rosselli. Because of the still pending immigration matter, the Mafia don couldn't even answer when asked, "Are you . . . John Rosselli?" and instead had to plead the Fifth.[21]

Because of the high-profile nature of the case and the notables involved, a new criminal division chief at the US attorney's office in Los Angeles also used it to press the immigration case against Rosselli. Eight members of Rosselli's family were subpoenaed, followed by several of his Los Angeles friends. According to Rosselli's biographers, "on October 21, 1967, Rosselli was indicted on six counts for failure to register as an alien." Though "released on $5,000 bond," Rosselli and five codefendants would be indicted in December 1967 for the Friars Club charges. True to form, Rosselli's first reaction was to hire notorious hit man Jimmy "The Weasel" Fratianno to kill the main witness in the Friars Club case. However, that approach failed when the man went into the Federal Witness Protection Program, leaving Rosselli with few options.[22]

One option was his friend William Harvey, and CIA files reveal that Rosselli resumed meeting with William Harvey in the fall of 1967. In addition, one of Johnny Rosselli's codefendants hired prominent Los Angeles attorney Grant Cooper as his attorney of record. Cooper would soon mysteriously come into possession of illegal copies of the grand jury's testimony against Rosselli and the others. These transcripts would give Rosselli and his associates leverage over Cooper the following year—when Cooper volunteered to represent Sirhan Sirhan for shooting Bobby Kennedy.[23]

With his new spate of legal problems, Johnny Rosselli needed Carlos Marcello's help more than ever. The charges Rosselli faced could result in his deportation, and Marcello had a long track record of success in that area. Though in the summer of 1967 Bobby Kennedy wasn't actively talking about seeking the presidency, the press still speculated he might run in 1968. The prospect of a Bobby Kennedy presidency would be daunting to Rosselli, since the information he'd asked Ed Morgan to convey to Earl Warren and Jack Anderson could be contained in memos Bobby might see if he made it to the White House. It wouldn't be difficult for a Mafia expert like Bobby to learn that Rosselli was Morgan's source, and Rosselli could ill afford to have Bobby in a position where he could use trusted federal agents to secretly explore Rosselli's connections to the CIA and JFK's murder.

For Carlos Marcello, keeping Rosselli out of prison would help to ensure that Marcello's role in JFK's murder would never become public. Rosselli could still be of use to Marcello, potentially in Las Vegas (for casino deals) and in Los Angeles, where Bobby Kennedy was a frequent visitor. After Marcello heard about Hoffa's contract on Bobby, the godfather would have known that Rosselli's ties to Los Angeles could help to insulate him or Hoffa from any action they might need to take against Bobby, if he decided to run for president.

In late August 1967, Carlos Marcello would have worried about a two-part series slated for *Life* magazine that tied him to Jimmy Hoffa and District Attorney Jim Garrison. *Life*, America's leading photo-news weekly, was preparing a major exposé about Marcello's Spring Hoffa effort, and for most Americans it would be their first exposure to the New Orleans godfather.

J. Edgar Hoover learned of the forthcoming article because on August 7, 1967, he called the New Orleans FBI office, which replied the following day with an Urgent teletype. It confirmed that the FBI had interviewed one of Marcello's brothers and three Marcello associates about stories that had surfaced soon after JFK's murder. As detailed in Chapter 3, one story described Oswald's receiving money at Marcello's Town and Country Motel restaurant and another story was about a horse trainer who'd heard one of Marcello's brothers say, "The word is out to get the Kennedy family." Hoover apparently wanted to be prepared in case word broke about Carlos Marcello's ties to JFK's murder.[24]

Life magazine editor Richard Billings had been dealing with Jim Garrison since late 1966, but assigned another writer to do the two-part series on the Mafia. FBI veteran William Turner quotes FBI files as saying that writer was "'a great admirer of the Director [Hoover] and a very strong backer of the Bureau' who had been 'utilized' on 'many different occasions.'"[25] While Hoover no doubt tried to influence the articles, much of their content appears to have originated with Walter Sheridan, Bobby Kennedy's confidant.

Part I of the *Life* series appeared in the September 1, 1967, issue and behind a cover highlighting the psychedelic posters of Peter Max and Rick Griffin, readers got their first detailed look at Carlos Marcello and his "empire of Organized Crime." In addition to a dramatic, full-page, close-up photograph of Marcello looking powerful, the article detailed Marcello's Spring Hoffa bribe attempts with details only Walter Sheridan could have provided.[26]

From Sheridan and Bobby's perspective, the series appears to have had at least three goals. The first was to stall Marcello's Spring Hoffa attempts by exposing his efforts. The second was to outline Marcello's massive power and influence, as part of the greatest national exposure the publicity-shy Marcello had ever received. The article covered Marcello allies like Sam Giancana, who, *Life* notes, was still influencing the Chicago Mafia "from a hideout in Mexico," aided by "Richard Cain, a well-known former Chicago policeman." Though the article doesn't mention it, Giancana was helping to run the Mexican side of the heroin network that supplied Marcello. The article does not mention the CIA-Mafia plots that involved Giancana and Cain.[27]

It's interesting that an article featuring information from Sheridan, and that was certainly approved by Bobby, highlighted Marcello, Hoffa, and Giancana—three people whom Bobby suspected in his brother's murder. However, Part I of the *Life* series didn't mention JFK's assassination at all. The first public effort to tie Marcello to JFK's murder was still two years away, in Ed Reid's 1969 *The Grim Reapers*, though the *Life* article did mention mob lawyer Sidney Korshak.

Bobby and Sheridan's third goal became clear the following week, when *Life* ran Part II. In addition to providing more information about Marcello's criminal empire, this part of the story attempted to characterize Jim Garrison as being close to Marcello. Thus, the *Life* series can be seen as part of Sheridan's quest on Bobby's behalf to discredit Garrison. However, Part II contains nothing linking Marcello to JFK's assassination, and (like Part I) nothing tying David Ferrie to Marcello.[28]

Because the *Life* series appeared after the NBC and CBS attacks on Garrison, the stories generated no follow-up from other news media about Marcello, Ferrie, and JFK's assassination. By November 1967, *Life* would return to largely supporting the Warren Report in its JFK assassination anniversary issue. The next national magazine to feature Marcello would not appear until the following year, when Bobby Kennedy would take an even more direct role in guiding a Marcello story, shortly before his own murder.

Marcello weathered the *Life* series with no lasting damage or follow-up in the national media, and would soon reactivate his Spring Hoffa efforts. Marcello's charge of hitting an FBI agent was mired in the legal system and many months away from trial, so he quickly resumed his normal routine, which John Davis described as being "the chief executive of an invisible state." Based on FBI files, Marcello would often sit in his office at the Town and Country Motel, taking calls and seeing visitors ranging from prominent businessmen to the representatives of governors to other Mafia bosses. The requests ranged from "fixing a federal judge" to "helping a gang of drug smugglers" to complex casino and real estate deals.[29]

Other times, Marcello would authorize, or order his men to arrange, a hit. For example, in 1967, one of his "prominent syndicate gamblers, Harry Bennett, was shot dead by unknown killers not long after . . . Marcello's aides discovered he had met with a federal prosecutor and offered to help him in the government's investigation of the Marcello organization." Like Marcello's other hits, this case was never prosecuted. Two years later, after Bennett's assistant crossed Marcello, police discovered his "bullet-riddled body" in the same spot where Bennett's body had been found.[30]

In these hits and in Marcello's business dealings, his careful use of intermediaries, along with his power and fearsome reputation, insulated him from blame and stymied investigators. As Davis wrote, Marcello and his associates "seemed to feel he could get away with almost anything," including murder—and to a large degree, they were right.[31]

PART FOUR

PART FOUR

Chapter Thirty-eight

On July 17, 1967, an American career criminal named James Earl Ray arrived in Montreal after escaping from a Missouri prison almost three months earlier. Ray was forty years old, and a repeated loser whose only forte seemed to be an ability to escape from custody. He came from an extremely dysfunctional family of ten children, headed by an alcoholic mother. Born in the small town of Alton, Illinois, about twenty miles from St. Louis, Ray was first arrested in 1949, shortly after an early discharge from the Army. His theft of a typewriter netted him only a ninety-day sentence, but his $11 robbery of a cab driver in 1952 resulted in his being "shot by police and sentenced to two years in jail," according to author Philip Melanson. Forging money orders in 1955 earned Ray a stay in Leavenworth until early 1958. His 1959 robbery of $120 from a Kroger grocery store in St. Louis got him a twenty-year sentence in the Missouri state penitentiary, in Jefferson City. After three failed escape attempts, he finally succeeded on April 23, 1967, supposedly by hiding in a bread truck making a delivery to the prison.[1]

While in prison, Ray was described as having "superior" intelligence; though his achievement level was only that of a high school sophomore, he read a variety of books and magazines ranging from James Bond stories to *Time*. According to one of Ray's brothers, and confirmed by six of Ray's fellow inmates, Ray dealt drugs—apparently amphetamines ("speed")—in prison. When *Playboy* asked him in 1977 about prison drug dealing, Ray only replied "I've never been any type of big operator in drugs in Missouri." (Note his use of the qualifier "big," and the fact that Ray limited his answer to the state of Missouri.)[2]

Accounts vary greatly about whether Ray made only pocket money or a substantial amount in prison, but he was said to have a supplier outside of prison. According to Congressional investigators, one of Ray's

1. From this point forward, any use of the term "Ray" refers to James Earl Ray, and not to Cuban exile leader Manolo Ray, who is not connected or related to James Earl Ray in any way.

associates in prison at the time of his escape was John Paul Spica, who had been convicted for a 1963 contract murder. After having been in the same cell block and same tier as Ray, Spica testified that "he was acquainted with Ray." However, their relationship was more than a simple acquaintance, since "prison officials and other inmates . . . indicated a much closer friendship between Spica and Ray than Spica admitted." Ray himself wrote that he "got to know . . . a St. Louis guy named John Paul Spica, who was doing life for conspiracy to commit murder. He was said to have heavy mob connections."[3] A major player in the St. Louis mob in 1967 was Morris Shenker, Jimmy Hoffa's chief attorney at the time, and a key part of Carlos Marcello's Spring Hoffa attempt.[4]

According to the Justice Department, between James Earl Ray's April 23, 1967, escape from prison and his July 17 arrival in Montreal, he lived in Chicago, where he worked for "eight weeks as a dishwasher and cook's helper" at a restaurant in nearby Winnetka. Ray apparently wanted more money than his meager salary provided, so, the week of June 19, he quit his job and left town with a small amount of savings and a 1959 Chrysler he'd bought for $200. On July 14, 1967, Ray bought a similarly priced 1962 Plymouth in East St. Louis, transferred the tags from his old car, and headed for Canada the following day.

From that point until his capture in June 1968, Ray's extensive cross-country and globe-spanning travels and activities far surpass anything he (or his family) had ever done before, or anything one might expect of a criminal with his background. According to the 1977 Justice Department Task Force, which analyzed the FBI's original investigation, "a good deal of mystery still surrounds James [Earl] Ray . . . particularly the means by which he financed his life style and travels. . . . The Bureau should have pursued this line of the investigation more thoroughly." The Justice Department concluded that "the sources for Ray's funds still remain a mystery."[5]

The House Select Committee on Assassinations (HSCA) attempted to track Ray's funds, and strongly suspected that Ray participated in a July 13, 1967, bank robbery of $27,230 in Alton, Illinois, along with one of his brothers, who was convicted years later for a similar robbery. However, the Justice Department found that the FBI had "investigated the possibility that Ray participated" in the robbery, "but it was established that he was not a participant." Ray's attorney pointed out FBI files that fingered two criminals unrelated to Ray for the bank robbery, as well as the fact that Ray's fingerprints didn't match those connected with the robbery.

Ray's brother, who was implicated in the 1967 robbery by the 1978 HSCA hearings, took the unusual step of going to the Alton bank in 1978 to meet with the bank's managers, then to the Alton Police Department, where he offered to stand trial, waive any statute of limitations, and take a lie-detector test. The Alton police chief told Ray's brother, and reporters, that "he is not, and was not then, a suspect in the holdup."[6] James Earl Ray would soon be spending and traveling far beyond anything he could hope to earn legitimately, so if he hadn't gotten his funds from the robbery, where did they come from?

According to HSCA files, one of Ray's brothers revealed to a journalist the real source of Ray's funds between the time of his escape from prison, and his capture after King's murder—and why Ray went to Montreal in July 1967. He said that Ray "made money in dope. Told me he had [a] contact, made it in prison, in Montreal. Some guy who had been in [the same prison as Ray]. Guy would supply [Ray] with dope—[Ray] had contact [in] Detroit—ran it back and forth. Detroit–Montreal." According to this brother, Ray would make approximately $7,000 from running drugs over the next seven months.[7]

Ray was no longer dealing with amphetamines, known as speed or bennies. His brother said there was "no money in speed, bennies . . . it was heroin—that's where [the] money is." Ray would later claim he'd gone to Canada to escape to a country overseas, perhaps by getting a job on a merchant ship at Montreal's busy docks. However, HSCA files quote Ray's brother as saying that Ray "did not try to get [a] seaman's job," and that "when [Ray] went [to] Canada it wasn't to leave [the] country then—[he] went to work [in the] dope racket. 'I'm positive of that.'"[8]

James Earl Ray himself later admitted to Dan Rather that when he went to Montreal, "I met with some people. I thought they were possibly narcotics smugglers."[9] Ray's actions in Canada—and his similar, admitted smuggling later in Laredo, Texas, and in Mexico—mirror closely the drug-smuggling activities of the Canadian heroin courier busted in Laredo in the fall of 1963, detailed in earlier chapters. That courier had worked for Carlos Marcello's portion of the French Connection heroin network.

The heroin from the 1963 Laredo bust was chemically matched by US authorities to the drugs seized from a Houston ship in 1962. It was all part of the same heroin network involving Marcello that Rose Cheramie had told authorities about in 1963 and 1965, and that was busted at Fort Benning in late 1965. Michel Victor Mertz's associates supervised the operations in Canada, while American oversight of the Montreal–Toronto portion of the network was under the control of Carmine Galante, Marcello's ally and Hoffa's confidant in his Lewisburg prison.[10]

James Earl Ray's activities are almost a textbook case of a typical heroin courier for the heroin network allied with Marcello, but that eluded Congressional investigators, because the only definitive book on the Canadian heroin trade—*The Canadian Connection*, by Jean-Pierre Charbonneau—was never published in the US. Just like Ray, the 1963 Laredo heroin courier had originally been recruited in Canada, prior to his Texas–Mexico smuggling. Also like Ray, the 1963 Laredo courier had never smuggled heroin before, but was recruited because he knew a criminal associate of one of the traffickers. Before beginning the Mexican part of the smuggling, the 1963 Laredo courier had been told he would "have to change my car because the one I had was too old and I'd need a newer one." In the same way, Ray would be told after leaving Canada, but before heading to Mexico, that he would need to "get rid of the car I had (it was old)"—parentheses in original—in order to smuggle drugs between the US and Mexico.[11]

Ray's arrival in Montreal coincided with the need for new heroin smugglers. The traffickers were taking advantage of the decreased scrutiny caused by the reassignment of RCMP narcotics squad officers to provide security for Expo 67, caused in part by the Cuban-exile bombings and threats. Even before the summer 1967 heroin surge, the network of couriers, traffickers, distributors, and importers had been large: According to Charbonneau, it had imported "ten tons of heroin with a street value of $9 billion" in just the "previous five years."[12] But by July 1967, the RCMP's narcotics squad had been "reduced from 30 men to eight men, [creating] an unhoped-for opportunity for traffickers. . . . Montreal during the months of [Expo 67] festivities was a major, if not the major, port of entry for heroin on the continent." Eventually, the few Mounties who remained on "the Narcotics Squad realized that international traffickers had been taking advantage of the situation and so had Montreal dealers, who had started up new trafficking rings."[13]

James Earl Ray's involvement in the Montreal arm of the French Connection heroin network helps to finally explain two lingering mysteries about him. No investigation has ever come up with a reasonable explanation for how James Earl Ray found the alias Eric Starvo Galt, the main cover identity he would use for months. The same is true for three other aliases he used: Galt and those other aliases were all from real Toronto citizens who lived within a two-mile radius of each other. Three of the men even fit Ray's general description, and all four were legitimate businessmen with no criminal history. The real Eric Galt's middle name was St. Vincent, which he abbreviated for a time as "St. V.," with large circles for the periods. Thus, the middle name in a handwritten "Eric St. V. Galt" might have been misinterpreted to have "Starvo" as a middle name. However, neither the HSCA nor the FBI nor Canadian authorities could figure out how Ray obtained Galt's name, since Ray passed only briefly through Toronto on his way to Montreal, where he first used the alias. Galt was not in any newspaper or TV stories around that time, and the same was true for the three other Toronto men whose identities Ray would steal and use in the coming months.[14]

However, aliases are important for effective smuggling, and the Montreal heroin ring also ran an immigration and illegal-identity racket for "supplying false papers"—what would be called identity theft today. In addition to smuggling, the ring was also used for new Mafia recruits, immigrants fresh from Italy and Sicily who needed cover identities to avoid the well-publicized troubles of illegal immigrant Mafiosi like Marcello. This illegal-identity part of the heroin ring was run by three Mafiosi, including two longtime associates of Michel Victor Mertz, Marcello's heroin partner.[1] James Earl Ray's aliases and cover identities, stolen from the Toronto men, probably came from this identity-theft ring, which also ran heroin through Toronto.[15]

Shortly before Ray arrived in Montreal, the third Mafioso working in the identity division of the heroin ring had plastic surgery to make himself less distinctive and harder to recognize. Perhaps Ray heard about that, because several months later—just four weeks before Martin Luther King's murder—Ray would undergo plastic surgery in Los Angeles to make his nose less distinctive. That was something Ray, his family, or other associates had never done before.[16]

Ray's access to false identities would help not only in the short run, with his drug smuggling, but also in his eventually getting a fake identity that would be good enough to allow the fugitive to settle safely in the US or assume residence in a foreign country. In the short term, Ray's first and main false identity, Eric Starvo Galt, would help him in his drug smuggling. Either just before or just after Ray arrived in Montreal, he obtained a fairly sizable amount of money to tide him over until his first cross-border smuggling run the following month.

Ray later offered various accounts of how he obtained his first funds

---

1. One of the Canadian identity theft kingpins used an "Amusements" company as a cover; Marcello and Trafficante used similar amusement companies as covers, and so did a Marcello operative tied to Dr. King's murder as well as another man who would first find Ray's rifle after Dr. King was shot.

in Montreal, saying he robbed a Montreal brothel or a grocery store, but Canadian authorities identified no grocery store robberies within that time frame. Many of Ray's claims over the years have proven false, so we treat all of Ray's statements with caution unless we find corroborating evidence or testimony. As a career criminal, Ray often changed his story to avoid subjects and crimes he didn't want to discuss, such as the Mafia, heroin trafficking, and federal agents involved in Cuban exile operations. Ray's stories also evolved over time to fit emerging evidence or the claims of others.[1]

Ray mentioned various amounts when describing the haul from his alleged Montreal robbery, ranging from $800 to $1,700 (in today's dollars, $4,800 to $10,200). Given Ray's shifting stories about it over the years, he likely obtained the money in another fashion, perhaps from an initial smuggling run in Montreal that he didn't want to confess to. Realizing the questions it would raise and the mobsters it would anger, Ray always tried to avoid clearly admitting that he smuggled heroin, usually limiting himself to describing even obvious examples as only something that might have been drugs.[17]

James Earl Ray arrived in Montreal on July 17, 1967, and, as his brother noted earlier, Ray sought out a contact he'd made in prison, who was then in Montreal. The brother says Ray "must have made [a] drug contact in Canada," and was adamant that Ray "was running dope" there.[18] Ray initially registered at a Montreal hotel and began hanging around the seedier part of the waterfront area, known as a major importation center for the French Connection drug ring. Ray frequented the Neptune Tavern, and later claimed he made it known that he was looking for false identity papers to help him leave the country and that he was soon approached by a man, known to him only as "Raoul," who would supposedly guide Ray's actions over the next nine months.

Ray's physical descriptions of this "Raoul" varied over the years, though his supposed actions that Ray described remained relatively consistent. We believe, after reading all of the available material, that while Ray might have had a drug- and arms-smuggling contact who

1. The same also applies to the statements of Ray's brothers. In general, we look for one or more of the following in evaluating and accepting the statements of veteran criminals: 1. Independent corroborating evidence or testimony; 2. If it is an admission against interest (i.e., harmful to the criminal's own case), especially when the statements form a coherent and consistent pattern, even when they are made at different times; examples of the latter are Ray's drug smuggling and his cont acts in New Orleans; 3. The conditions under which the statements were made (i.e., is there a reason the criminal might have let their guard down or been comfortable in actually telling the truth).

used the name Raoul, the individual he describes is more likely a composite of two or more criminal figures Ray dealt with. Ray's first two attorneys, Arthur Hanes Sr. and Percy Foreman, came to the same conclusion: Foreman told noted author William Bradford Huie, "'Raul' . . . is the name Ray uses for any and all of his contacts and accomplices in crime between July 1967 and April 1968."[19]

A career criminal like Ray would most likely tell authorities about a named figure like Raoul only if:

1. He had been told to do so by a crime boss, in case he was ever caught, or

2. He thought doing so would keep him alive in prison; in other words, by letting the criminals he was working for know that if he or a family member was killed, then the true identities of the criminals he collectively called "Raoul" would be revealed by his attorney or a surviving family member.

Ray's extensive travels and activities from July 1967 until his capture two months after Martin Luther King's murder, in London in June 1968, demonstrate clearly that Ray had criminal associates during that time. As political science professor Phillip Melanson wrote, "The best evidence suggests that Ray was an unexceptional criminal who had exceptionally clever help."[20] To avoid buying into Ray's extravagant claim of a single, all-powerful "Raoul," we will usually refer simply to Ray's criminal contact or contacts when the evidence suggests that doing so is appropriate, and on the occasions when he obviously had help.

According to Justice Department files, Ray met his Montreal contact as early as the day after he arrived in the city, and things moved quickly after that. Given the expenditures he would soon make, Ray had definitely received money at that point. Since Ray would be trusted within weeks to smuggle heroin across the Canadian border into the US, his first Montreal job may have been a less dangerous smuggling venture. Seamen often brought heroin and other contraband into Montreal on ships, as in the Rose Cheramie case in Houston involving the same heroin network.

William Bradford Huie, the author *The Execution of Private Slovik* and other investigative works, pointed out that "Montreal is the easiest big city in the world to bring contraband into," but someone still had to retrieve the heroin from the seaman and then deliver it to the trafficker, who would then test it, repackage (and sometimes reprocess) it, and secure it in false-bottomed luggage or in cars for its later cross-border trip. Ray's proximity to the Montreal docks and the amount of money he soon had would be consistent with his helping with the short delivery from seaman to trafficker, all under the covert and watchful eyes of the trafficker's associates. Ray probably got this opportunity, as his brother said, from a former fellow inmate who trusted Ray, perhaps aided by the Mafia ties of John Paul Spica, his prison friend.[21]

The day after first meeting his Montreal contact, Ray signed a six-month lease on an apartment in the city, apparently thinking that Montreal would be a long-term base of operations for him. Ray expected his future to be bright, and, according to his brother, Ray "spent $300 on new clothes," the likes of which he had never owned before, including ordering a custom-tailored suit. Ray would continue meeting with his Montreal contact eight or ten times between late July and mid-August, but his first cross-border smuggling trip wouldn't be for several more weeks. In the meantime, Ray did something else he had never done before: He went to a posh resort called the Gray Rocks Inn.[22]

Ray's cover story was always that he went to Montreal hoping to immediately leave the country, but it was clearly not true, since Ray would soon return to the US with (by his own reluctant admission) more than enough money to buy a good fake passport and false identity that would have safely allowed him to leave North America. Ray also claimed that he was misinformed that in Canada he needed a Canadian citizen to vouch for him in order to get a passport. (The denizens of the seedy Montreal waterfront bars Ray frequented would have known that wasn't true.) So, in Ray's version of events, he went to the exclusive Gray Rocks Inn to find a woman who would vouch for him so he could get a passport. However, according to one of Ray's brothers, Ray was really "trying to get [a] rich girl at Gray Rocks. Not ID. It was the money he wanted."[23]

Just a few weeks earlier, James Earl Ray had been washing dishes in the back room of a restaurant, but on July 30, 1967, he went to the luxurious Gray Rocks Inn wearing a fine new suit and apparently hoping to bilk some unfortunate "rich girl." Since she would know Ray only by an easy-to-change alias and cover story, it would not have been difficult for Ray (rather, his alias) to seemingly vanish after he found a way to extract money from her. It's also possible that Ray intended to dupe a woman into helping with his upcoming cross-border smuggling, since a couple on a brief vacation would attract less suspicion than a lone man. (The 1963 Laredo smuggler from Montreal had his wife accompany him on his cross-border smuggling trips.) Ray, whose sexual experience was limited largely to receiving oral sex from men in prison or buying the services of prostitutes outside of prison, had even ordered a sex manual to aid him in his seduction.[24]

Though Ray went to one of Canada's finest resorts to bilk a wealthy girl, he actually met a woman of modest means who had gone to the resort's lounge in hopes of meeting a wealthy man. (The woman, from Ottawa, was staying at a less expensive hotel nearby; she went to the Gray Rocks lounge with a girlfriend.) Given the usual women Ray had associated with, the first journalist to track the woman down was surprised to find that she was "a most attractive . . . tastefully dressed and coiffured mature woman [who] at almost any resort . . . could have had her pick of the unattached men." In the early stages of a divorce, the woman said the shy Ray appealed to her.[25]

In the expensive surroundings, each thought the other was wealthier than they really were, and the woman spent the night with Ray. She and her friend were going to Expo 67 the following day, and they spent the next night with Ray at his somewhat seedy apartment in Montreal. Ray made excuses for the less-than-glamorous surroundings, and he saw the woman again in Ottawa ten days later. Ray claimed it was only on that day, August 18, 1967, that he learned she worked for the Canadian Department of Transport, and he abandoned his plan to ask her to vouch for him as the "guarantor" of his passport by swearing falsely that she had known him for two years. More likely, Ray simply decided it was too risky to try to use a government employee to help with his smuggling, or that she didn't have enough easily available money to bother stealing.[26]

Ray admitted that since at least early August 1967, he had been talking with his contact in Montreal about getting money and "travel documents" in return for assisting the contact "in crossing the border." Specifically, Ray agreed to "smuggle some unspecified contraband across the border," from Windsor, Ontario, to Detroit. Ray said the contraband would be "some packages [smuggled] in the car I had." Ray's eventual payoff would be big, "ten to twelve thousand dollars" ($60,000–$72,000 in today's dollars), though Ray was told that amount wouldn't come until later. If the Detroit–Windsor smuggling was successful, Ray testified that the big payoff was supposed to come after he did "something similar to that in Mexico" and his Montreal contact "went to New Orleans." According to the statements of Ray and one of his brothers, New Orleans was the focal point of Ray's drug smuggling.[27]

Congressional investigators wrote that from Windsor, Ray "smuggled two sets of packages across the border" on August 21, 1967. Ray said his contact had an attaché case from which he "removed three packages . . . and put them behind the back" of one of Ray's car seats. Ray's contact crossed the border first, in a cab. Ray passed through the checkpoint with no problem, then met his contact on a side street, where the man "removed the packages" and put them in his attaché case. The contact went into a bus station and came out without the attaché case, and told Ray they were going to repeat the procedure.[28]

Congressional investigators asked Ray about his contact: "When he gave you the narcotics the first time," how did he know "you wouldn't just take off with them?" Based on later talks with investigators, Ray replied that perhaps the first group of packages contained only flour, as a "dry run," a type of test, to see if he was trustworthy. While that's possible, it's doubtful that Ray would have been involved in the first place, unless he were seen as seasoned criminal with contacts who could vouch for him. For example, the 1963 Laredo heroin courier had been told by his trafficker they "had confidence in me because I was a [veteran] thief" and because another criminal "knew me." Ray claimed he never told his Montreal contact his real name, or that Galt was an alias, but Ray's brother's statements show that's not true. Ray started using the never explained Galt alias only after he got to Canada, and it was no doubt given to him to use in the same way the same drug traffickers had given the Laredo courier several aliases to use.[29]

During the smuggling run, Ray would have been under covert surveillance by one of the trafficker's associates, someone Ray had never met. For example, the 1963 Laredo heroin courier discovered that he had been subject to secret "surveillance for certain transactions" by the traffickers. The courier's bosses even told him later that the person secretly watching him said he "had been driving too fast," and that he should drive more slowly.[30]

Then, too, an experienced criminal like Ray would have known the lethal penalty for crossing a heroin trafficker. Ray had spent ten of the last dozen years in prison, had been part of the prison speed racket, and had inmate friends like the Mafia-linked Spica and another tied to the Montreal heroin trade. Since Ray was an escaped convict, the traffickers could be sure he wouldn't do anything to call undue attention to himself. Of the thousands of miles in heroin's journey, the few hundred yards at a border crossing are the most dangerous part, and Ray fits the profile of the type of expendable courier who would have been used. Comparatively speaking, Ray's three-package lot was appropriately small, befitting an initial cross-border attempt by a new courier. In contrast, just two months later, Montreal authorities would find a piece of "luggage . . . concealing 16 small plastic sacks, each containing a pound of white powder"—heroin that had been brought in by an experienced courier.[31]

During Ray's second run from Windsor to Detroit, shortly after the first, he had only one minor glitch at the border, when he "was stopped for a customs inspection [and had] to declare his television set" that he had bought in Montreal. After that, Ray met his contact on a side street just over the US border. As Congressional investigators detailed, Ray said he was given $1,500 "and a New Orleans telephone number which [he] could use" to reach his contact. Ray later alleged he had been expecting his contact to also give him a passport, but that statement is also false, since Ray admitted in testimony that he had not given his contact any type of photo of himself to use for a passport.[32]

Further confirmation for James Earl Ray's involvement in heroin smuggling comes from Percy Foreman, who would represent Ray after Dr. King's murder. Foreman had briefly represented Jack Ruby and, as William Bradford Huie wrote, had also "defended . . . members of the Mafia, some of whom direct the running of heroin across the Canadian border." Foreman told Huie that what Ray did "is standard operating procedure for bringing heroin in from Canada."[33]

In Detroit, Ray and his contact discussed their next steps, for which Ray expected his really large payoff of $10,000–$12,000 dollars. Ray said he was told this reward would involve smuggling "weapons into Mexico or [helping] in some way." Ray was ordered to "get rid of the car I had," since "it was old," and to "go to Mobile, Alabama, where we would meet." Ray said he talked his contact into allowing him to go to Birmingham instead, due to Ray's allergies. His contact was agreeable and said "he would finance a car plus living expenses" for Ray, as HSCA records note. Once again, this scenario parallels the experience of the 1963 Laredo courier for the same heroin network, after he left Canada for Mexico: A Trafficante associate told him that because the courier's "car . . . was too old," he "could advance me the money" to buy a new one, and he'd take it out of "the money I'd make working as a courier."[34]

As for the reason Alabama was chosen, and why Ray preferred Birmingham over Mobile, Ray's brother said that Ray had "contacts down there—Underworld."[35] Since the days of Phenix City, the Mafia underworld in Alabama had been subject to the influence of Carlos Marcello and his close associate Santo Trafficante, whose heroin routes transversed the state of Alabama. Depending on supply and demand, heroin could flow from Trafficante's Florida to Marcello's Louisiana, or originate in Mexico, Houston, or New Orleans and head to points east and north.[36]

Ray arrived in Birmingham on August 26, 1967, staying one night in a motel before renting a room as "Eric S. Galt." On August 30, after answering a want ad, Ray paid $1,995 in cash for a 1966 Ford Mustang. Ray's use of the money for a car in Birmingham undermines his later claims that he wanted to leave the US for a country like Rhodesia (now Zimbabwe) as soon as possible. In testimony, Ray said that "as a con, he knew phony passports were generally available for about a thousand dollars." Instead, the fugitive Ray used the money to purchase the car and remain in the US, when he could have bought a fake passport and still had enough money to leave North America. Ray would remain in Birmingham, apparently "on ice," waiting for his next assignment for more than a month.

Chapter Thirty-nine

Alabama remained a bastion of segregation in 1967, but neighboring states like Georgia were undergoing a transformation that mirrored America's troubled, sometimes violent progress on issues of race. Advances in the struggle for civil rights were used by some politicians and other leaders to polarize large segments of the population along racial lines, laying the groundwork for more violence. The two national leaders who were the focus of the most extreme emotions on the issue of civil rights were Bobby Kennedy and Martin Luther King.

By the summer of 1967, Bobby Kennedy had recovered from the controversies that had dogged him earlier in the year, and was once again ahead of President Lyndon B. Johnson in polls for the 1968 presidential race. However, Bobby continued to publicly support LBJ while resisting pressure from his friends and advisors to enter the race. Despite his growing differences with LBJ on Vietnam and the need for faster progress on programs to help the poor, Bobby was unable to explain clearly to advisors why he was unwilling to run against LBJ. He couldn't tell them that while Jack Anderson's revelations about his 1963 Cuban operations had stopped, Bobby didn't know what other information about him LBJ might have turned up in their aftermath. Bobby was reluctant to find out by running against LBJ and potentially stirring up the matter again.[1]

However, Bobby's increasing focus on civil rights and poverty in the wake of his Mississippi trip was slowly increasing his popularity, not just among minorities but also with poor whites and even liberals, who had long viewed Bobby with suspicion. Bobby's determination to aid the poor only increased when the New York senator found appalling poverty among migrant laborers in his own state. Since 1966, Bobby had championed the cause of California migrant leader Cesar Chavez, developing with Chavez the type of personal rapport and friendship Bobby had with Harry Williams. While Bobby's meetings with Cesar Chavez in California garnered headlines and resentment from conservative farm owners, Bobby's little-publicized discovery of horrible conditions in New York showed him that the plight of the poor was a national problem that needed national solutions. To Bobby, migrant-worker issues, civil rights, poverty, and even Vietnam were all one cause—that of standing up for the less fortunate who were held down by laws or force.[2] Though Bobby was not yet willing to challenge LBJ openly for the presidency, he could use his considerable powers of publicity to draw attention to the issues he cared about.

However, Bobby's growing public status as a champion of the down-trodden only fueled the hatred directed at him by the far Right and extreme conservatives. These hardliners still had roles in mainstream politics and large corporations, not only in the South, but also in other regions of the country. Developments in the summer of 1967 gave them new ammunition to use in stoking the racial fear and anger that they frequently directed toward Bobby Kennedy and civil rights leaders like Martin Luther King. LBJ appointed Thurgood Marshall, a key player in the landmark 1954 Supreme Court decision against segregated schools, to be the first black member of the court. Activist groups like the Black Panthers became more prominent, and the images of gun-toting black militants rattled segments of the white population. Young black men in the inner cities felt increasingly impatient for change after promises of Lyndon Johnson's "Great Society" antipoverty programs, and they were often receptive to more radical leaders like H. Rap Brown, the new head of the Student Nonviolent Coordinating Committee. Brown turned his back on Dr. King's nonviolence, reportedly telling a Black Power confer-ence that blacks should "wage guerilla war on the honkie white man" and declaring, "I love violence."[3]

For a variety of reasons, violence exploded in many of the nation's inner cities in the summer of 1967, most prominently in Newark and in Detroit, site of the most deadly race riot in US history until that point, with a death toll of thirty-eight and damage estimated at half a billion dollars. According to one account, "racial strife . . . erupted in 70 cities, including Atlanta, Boston, Philadelphia, Birmingham, New York, [and] Cincinnati."[4] Often overlooked are the race riots that summer in Tampa, Florida (in June), and in Memphis (on July 20)—along with those in Atlanta, they would have unexpected consequences for Martin Luther King.

For Georgia white supremacist Joseph Milteer, the summer 1967 race riots would have been both a blessing and a curse. In the short term, they might have boosted contributions from his supporters. While the racial troubles in Atlanta in the summer of 1967 didn't rise to the level of full-scale race riots (as the city had experienced the previous summer), riots in neighboring states like Tennessee, North Carolina, and Florida would have worried the white, blue-collar workers Milteer targeted, a fear he would have been able to exploit.

On the other hand, the riots would have increased the pressure on Milteer from his most extremist longtime contributors, who wanted to see Martin Luther King killed. Though Dr. King received a steady stream of death threats, there had been no recent public attempts on his life—nothing that Milteer could claim credit for. Milteer was sixty-five years old, and the money he collected for his anti-King, anti–civil rights efforts supplemented his slowly dwindling inheritance. The money Milteer had accumulated, plus his interest in the land his associates had purchased just across the Georgia border in North Carolina, would give him a financial cushion in his old age. By all accounts, Milteer was a true believer who wasn't just pushing his brand of racial hatred for money, but his golden years would be a nightmare if his most faithful contributors came to feel he'd bilked them. Some of his supporters were members of violent groups like the Klan, and Milteer knew what could happen to the targets of their wrath.

Before examining the steps taken by Milteer and his associates that led to King's death, it's important to put their actions in context by taking a snapshot of the racial politics of the time. Race relations and civil rights underwent a rapid transformation in the 1960s, with some racial conditions affecting the nation as a whole, while others were specific to parts of the South, like New Orleans, Atlanta, and Memphis. What happened in those cities in 1967 and early 1968 would cause Dr. King's assassination to be planned at that particular time and place.

In 1967, the majority of the country—even well-educated people and authority figures—held views that are considered racist today. On June 12, 1967, the day before LBJ appointed Thurgood Marshall to the Supreme Court, the court finally struck down laws in sixteen states barring interracial marriage. Many people today might be surprised to learn that as recently as 1967, three-fourths of the American public was against interracial marriage. The language of the Virginia Supreme Court justices, whose decision upholding the ban was reversed by the US Supreme Court, sounds shocking in hindsight. The supposedly distinguished Virginia justices said the ban was needed to stop "the corruption of blood" that might create "a mongrel breed of citizens" resulting in "the obliteration of racial pride" for the white race.[5]

Attitudes like that among mainstream leaders make it easy to see why the civil rights stands of Bobby Kennedy, Martin Luther King, LBJ, and JFK were considered so groundbreaking—and, by some, dangerous. The anti–civil rights John Birch Society had begun a slow decline after Barry Goldwater sought its support prior to his landslide loss in the 1964 presidential election, but many prominent citizens in the South and elsewhere were still members of groups like the loosely organized White Citizens' Councils. By 1967, some chapters were calling themselves simply Citizens' Councils, but their anti–civil rights, anti–Martin Luther King stance remained. The White Citizens' Councils have been described as "the Klan in suits and ties," and David Halberstam said their "members are respectable citizens of the community." That was especially true in the Deep South, where the Klan took on an increasingly blue-collar bent as its membership declined in the 1960s. Membership in the White Citizens' Councils also declined after its peak in the 1950s, but to a lesser extent, and it remained acceptable in many cities for prominent professionals and officials to be members.[6]

Though Halberstam points out that while the Councils gave the appearance of a "civic luncheon club [with] speakers from the ministry and the universities," their essential message was often similar to Stoner's and the Klan's. An Atlanta Citizens' Council member stated that Jews were responsible for the Holocaust and a synagogue bombing because they worshipped "the Baal of Socialism and Communism," while a Memphis member said, "The NAACP is the worst organization to come along since the one that crucified Christ."[7]

Most White Citizens' Council chapters, Birchers, and the Klan were avid supporters of former Alabama governor George Wallace, who in 1967 was gearing up for a presidential run the following year. While Wallace didn't think he could win, he thought he might be able to gain enough electoral votes to throw the election to the House of Representatives, where his block of votes could allow him to be a kingmaker.[8]

However, Wallace and his supporters present a more complex picture than appears on the surface. Most people don't realize that the NAACP supported Wallace when he first ran for governor—and lost. He switched his position, sought the support of the Klan and other racist groups, and won. Thus, Wallace's racist policies may have been more pragmatic pandering than his sincere beliefs. This notion raises an important point in the story of King's murder: Many professional racists also had a strong profit motive.[9]

According to one survey of the time, a quarter of Wallace's supporters had an unexpected second choice for president: Bobby Kennedy. Those people were supporting Wallace not necessarily because he espoused racism, but because he was an alternative to a political and economic system they felt had failed them. Their attitude resulted from seeing political and business leaders use racism to distract working families and the rural populace from issues like better schools, unions, improved access to medical care, and decent housing. For decades, those people were taught to blame black people, instead of unresponsive leaders, for their problems, but now a quarter of them were finally receptive to a solution beyond racism—hence their admiration for Bobby Kennedy.[10]

While it was openly acceptable to be a Wallace supporter in most parts of the country, Joseph Milteer aligned himself with a gamut of groups, including some that advocated more extreme forms of racism and violence. Like the prominent lawyer and the dentist who were his partners in the auto workers' scam and the King plot, Milteer belonged to the Atlanta White Citizens' Council, considered almost respectable in the city (it *was* respectable in most other Southern towns). Yet Milteer also served as a recruiter for the racist and anti-Semitic National States Rights Party of J. B. Stoner, an organization shunned by polite society.[11]

Stoner, who would later be convicted for the 1958 bombing of a black church, had caused whites to riot against blacks in 1964 in St. Augustine, Florida, following an appearance by Martin Luther King. After Dr. King's murder, Stoner would be James Earl Ray's third attorney and would employ one of Ray's brothers for a time. The FBI and Congressional investigators looked at Stoner in King's assassination, but no evidence ever surfaced that connected him to the murder. However, Stoner was in the perfect position to be used by Joseph Milteer after King's murder, as a conduit of instructions and information.

Joseph Milteer also had associates in the higher levels of the various Klan groups, which were responsible for most of the racial violence in the South. Mississippi was still rife with racial violence in 1967: In Meridian alone that year, five black churches were torched and the house of a Head Start teacher was shot up; National States Rights Party members were suspected by the FBI in all the attacks. Klan bombings were becoming more common, with six in Mississippi in the fall of 1967.[12]

However, the Klan as an organization was in decline and splintering, and thus was of little use to Joseph Milteer as a resource for finding someone to assassinate Martin Luther King. The Klan's violent reputation and the FBI's slow but increasing progress in bringing its members to justice were eroding its membership. In the 1950s, Klan membership in the South numbered in the tens of thousands, but it had declined dramatically by 1967. That year, a Memphis newspaper noted that one of the largest Klan groups had lost almost half of its members in less than a year. Even the Klan stronghold of Mississippi had only about five hundred active members, and unlike the White Citizens' Councils, most of them were no longer prominent businessmen or officials.[13]

The Klan could still muster an occasional large crowd for the television cameras, such as its July 6, 1967, rally in support of the Vietnam War at Stone Mountain, just east of Atlanta. The event attracted over three thousand people, including two thousand in Klan robes. But due to disinterest, infighting, and a desire to avoid FBI surveillance and infiltrators, the Klan was no longer one massive organization, but an increasingly fragmented number of smaller ones. The two largest Klan groups in Georgia were run by attorney James Venable and Calvin Craig. Much smaller, but more violent, was Joseph Milteer's Dixie Klan of Georgia.[14]

In 1963, Milteer's Dixie Klan had been described in a Miami police intelligence report as "an underground organization [and] offshoot of [the] hardcore membership of the KKK, John Birch, White Citizens' Council, and other groups." The report noted an informant's statement that in terms of "assassinations through rifles, dynamite, and other types of devices, this is the worst outfit he has ever come across." The organizations Milteer was connected to were also fervently anticommunist and especially anti-Castro, a fact that in 1963 had brought those groups into contact with CIA-backed Cuban exiles like John Martino. Milteer had been in contact with Guy Banister in 1963, when both Martino and Banister were documented associates of Carlos Marcello.[15]

However, by 1967 Milteer's Dixie Klan and the other Southern Klan groups were on the wane, even as Milteer's hardcore supporters increased their pressure on him to fulfill his promises to take lethal action against Martin Luther King. The demands were all the greater because the contributors to Milteer's four-man clique were based in Atlanta. Nationally, Dr. King's power and influence were being diluted as other black leaders emerged—a natural result as the civil rights movement matured. These figures ranged from newly elected African American senator Edward Brooke, of Massachusetts, to Cleveland's Carl Stokes (running to become the first black mayor of a major American city) to the leaders of more radical groups like the Black Panthers. While those leaders were increasingly in the news and the targets of racist anger (and for some, of FBI surveillance and operations), in Atlanta Dr. King was still the major focus. King and his actions made news locally as well as nationally, and rarely did a week go by that Atlanta TV stations and newspapers didn't feature stories about King.

The plot to kill Martin Luther King was spawned in Atlanta in 1967 because of factors that were also at work in other parts of the country, but were especially polarizing in Atlanta at that particular time. As the South's first large city to be integrated, Atlanta became a lightning rod for racist demagogues. Atlanta was a center for African American higher education, business, and organizations such as the SCLC—but that also made it a hotbed for those looking to exploit racial tensions.[16]

Atlanta's moderate leadership brought the city attention, business, and professional sports franchises, like the Braves and the Falcons, that bastions of segregation (such as Birmingham) lacked. Suddenly, white Atlantans who had never socialized with black people were with them at the integrated stadium or at Atlanta's huge new Six Flags amusement park. In just a few years, Atlanta appeared to transition from apartheid-like conditions to a degree of integration unheard of in the South—but simmering racial tensions remained. The more progress the city made, the more racist leaders could exploit those advances. Georgia switched from voting for JFK in 1960 to backing Barry Goldwater in 1964, and would soon back the even more extreme George Wallace in the 1968 presidential race.

By 1967, several factors were causing the racial situation in Atlanta to reach a critical point. Though the city was not known for racial violence, it occasionally flared and a racial killing occurred in Atlanta in January 1967: As the *New York Times* reported, unknown assailants shot dead the wife of a preacher, following an attempt to burn down their church.[17]

From the perspective of black pride and civil rights, King's proclamation of the new slogan "Black is beautiful" at the August 1967 conference of the Southern Christian Leadership Conference in Atlanta was a landmark event. However, the BLACK IS BEAUTIFUL signs that began to appear in the city also created more opportunities for racist leaders to exploit the angst of some white Atlanta citizens.

Like many other cities, Atlanta was in the midst of a major transition in education and housing that racists from Milteer to Georgia governor Lester Maddox exploited to their advantage. Restaurants had been integrated only recently, and Maddox's stand against that change had propelled him to the governorship.[18] Metro Atlanta schools had only just been desegregated by 1967, so many white students in the area were attending schools with black students for the first time, something most of their parents had never done.

As in cities across America, many of Atlanta's major real estate firms and speculators engaged in blockbusting, using scare tactics to panic middle-class whites into selling their Atlanta homes and fleeing to the suburbs. They essentially carved up the city, designating certain areas for blockbusting, while even black professionals were informally kept out of the more affluent areas that were home to real estate–firm owners and prominent Atlanta businessmen.[19]

In just a few years, Atlanta went from being majority white to majority black, while Milteer and his three partners exploited the strains of transition. They particularly targeted the General Motors plant in the Lakewood area of southeast Atlanta. The neighborhoods around the plant, where many of its workers lived, were hit especially hard by blockbusting. Depending on the number of shifts, the plant employed between 7,500 and 9,000 union workers, all members of the United Auto Workers (UAW). Union locals of that size, and the high-paying jobs they generated, were relatively rare in the South. Since the Great Depression, conservative Southern governors and legislatures had generally been hostile to unions. Organizing in industries like textiles had largely ground to a halt after the National Guard and state police fired on striking workers and their families in the mid-1930s. However, the economic boom of World War II and its aftermath brought a new wave of industry to the South, and Atlanta's more moderate leadership welcomed three huge auto plants. In addition to Lakewood, another General Motors plant had gone up in northeast Atlanta, and a Ford plant had been built near the growing Atlanta airport on the south side; the UAW represented all of them.

The UAW plants were among the relatively few places where Atlanta workers with a high school education or less could earn very high wages and exceptional benefits. Some workers traveled from as far away as Alabama, driving an hour and a half each way for the type of lucrative union jobs that were largely unavailable in eastern Alabama. Most workers lived much closer, many in the almost all white middle-class neighborhoods near each of the three Atlanta auto plants.

Ironically, the workers who lived in, or had moved to Atlanta from, the more depressed rural areas of Alabama and Georgia were some of the people most likely to support Milteer and his Citizens' Council associates, even though the Citizens Council had a long history of being anti-union and anti-labor. Yet many of those more rural, less educated workers had grown up under the sway of racist politicians like 1930s and '40s Georgia governor Eugene Talmadge (father of Georgia Senator Herman Talmadge), who had for years reportedly received a kickback on every Klan uniform sold in Georgia.[20] Those raised in such a racist atmosphere resented having to work alongside blacks at the integrated plants, since the UAW was an integrated union. Yet most workers had no other alternative that could provide nearly as well for themselves and their families.

Most UAW members in Atlanta had never worked with, lived beside, or gone to school with blacks—something racist leaders began exploiting in the mid-1950s, in the wake of the Supreme Court's decision to integrate schools and the resulting tumult in cities like Little Rock, Arkansas. According to labor historian John Barnard, "white racist organizations actively recruited and agitated in some southern plants and [UAW] locals," and "80 percent of the white members, including half of the officers of Local 988 in Memphis, joined the White Citizens' Council. In Atlanta, perhaps as many as 5,000 members in three large locals joined the Ku Klux Klan, which underwent a revival throughout the South in the mid-1950s, and a member of Local 34 [at the Lakewood General Motors Plant] was the Georgia Klan's Imperial Wizard."[21]

However, it's important to remember that even those figures represented just a small percentage of the overall workforce at all three Atlanta auto plants. By 1967, those Klan membership figures would have been just a fraction of their 1950s totals, mirroring the group's membership decline in the rest of the South. However, the integration of housing and schools that started in the mid-1960s had brought a new wave of resentment to some of the workers. While it was no longer fashionable to join the Klan, Milteer and his two associates in the local White Citizens' Council had found a new way to tap into the fears of some of the workers. Taking advantage of the worries being stoked by conservative state politicians and real estate firms, they gave the workers a way to fight back—by donating money from their substantial weekly paychecks to fight civil rights.

Milteer used a longtime auto-assembly worker at the Lakewood General Motors plant, Hugh R. Spake, as his front man for talking up Milteer's plans and helping collect the money each Friday. Spake had been a decorated veteran during World War II, but his friends and family had noticed a marked change in him after the death of his first wife. He became bitter at the world and focused his energy on the extreme conservative and racist causes he shared with Joseph Milteer. The two were joined in their activities at the Lakewood auto plant by a prominent Atlanta attorney and a local dentist, both members of the White Citizens' Council, though they were acting for themselves in their dealings with Milteer and Spake, not for the Council.[22]

There were several reasons why the Atlanta auto plants in general, and Lakewood in particular, were ripe for Milteer's efforts by 1967. The day-shift workers at Lakewood, those Milteer targeted most, had the greatest seniority. Most were children of the Depression, many were veterans, and they didn't mind the grueling assembly-line work because it allowed them to provide a good life for their families. But by 1967, their world was in flux on every front. Minorities were moving into their neighborhoods and schools, and the Democratic Party, which dominated Georgia, was changing from segregationist to pro–civil rights. At home, divorce was becoming more common, and their children were experimenting with interracial dating, drugs, and antiwar protests that had been unthinkable only a few years earlier. Milteer and his partners were ready to channel all of their anger and confusion into hating minorities.

Most of the Lakewood workers had originally lived in more rural areas, and because of blockbusting in their neighborhoods, they now felt uprooted again. Unlike the other two auto plants—one on the Northside, which was largely immune from blockbusting; and the Ford plant, far south and next to an interstate highway—the Lakewood workers had to relocate far from their plant. Many had to exchange a pleasant commute of a few minutes through tree-lined neighborhood streets to a grueling daily drive from the far suburbs—a transition that created more anger and resentment for Milteer and his associates to channel toward their cause.

Milteer's activities at Lakewood by 1967 were building on a tradition established in the early 1950s, when a Lakewood employee revitalized the Klan, and continued in 1964, when Lester Maddox had chosen the Lakewood neighborhood for the first "all-star" racist rally that launched his political success. Maddox welcomed George Wallace, Mississippi Governor Ross Barnett, and Klan Imperial Wizard Calvin Craig to address a crowd of more than ten thousand. The speakers so incited the crowd that two black men were beaten by the assemblage, to chants of "Kill 'em!"[23] (Again, it's important to stress that most Lakewood workers didn't participate in or support such actions, but some did.)

At lunchtime each Friday, thousands of Lakewood auto workers made a mad dash to cash their large paychecks. Upon their return, and when they got off work, Spake would be ready to collect money from the various contributors. Usually, Milteer's other partners—the attorney or the dentist (or both)—were also on hand, and once or twice a month, Milteer himself would be present as well. Milteer used his contacts and credibility with a wide range of racist groups to his clique's advantage. If a worker wanted to support the Klan without being an actual member, Milteer presented contributing to his clique as a way to do exactly that. If a worker wanted to support the more mainstream Citizens' Council, the presence of the attorney and the dentist helped in that regard. As a decorated veteran, Spake could frame the worker's contributions in patriotic terms, evoking General Joseph Walker and George Wallace's soon-to-be running mate, General Curtis LeMay.

The money Milteer's clique collected was all cash, so the exact amount they collected each week can't be determined, but it was substantial and had been accumulating since at least 1965. Milteer and his partners may have had someone like Hugh R. Spake at one or both of the other Atlanta auto plants, generating a similar take. However, the only one we can cite with absolute certainly is the Lakewood plant.[24]

Various literature was also available from Milteer and his associates: relatively crude newsletters and flyers that Milteer produced himself, polished publications obtained from the John Birch Society, material from the Klan, and J. B. Stoner's locally published *Thunderbolt* newspaper. Essentially, the workers who contributed were in three groups. The first and largest group was interested in trying to learn about—and counter—what they perceived as forces turning their tranquil world upside down with the integration of schools, housing, and government. A smaller number were interested in the more aggressive action represented by the Klan and Stoner's group. Out of that group, only the most trusted regular and substantial contributors would be told—after many months, and then only in the strictest confidence—that all the money wasn't just going to generally fight civil rights and Martin Luther King. Instead, they were told, it was really funding a plan to kill Martin Luther King.

Milteer and his partners had found a way to raise substantial amounts of money while avoiding the FBI and other law enforcement organizations' surveillance of groups like the Klan. The money was probably never reported for income tax purposes, and much of it was spent buying up undeveloped mountain land in North Carolina. Milteer's contributors were not part of a traditionally organized group, so authorities had no membership lists, offices to bug, or office phones to tap. There were no regular meetings or rallies that law enforcement could infiltrate. The union jobs were highly prized, especially the high-seniority day shift—where the men had often worked together for ten or twenty years—so planting an undercover informant in the workforce would have been difficult for the FBI, even if it had tried. Finally, if Dr. King were ever murdered, Milteer's most faithful contributors could be trusted to never boast to outsiders about their own role in funding it.

We spoke to a source who knew Spake well for more than a decade and witnessed, on many occasions, Spake with Milteer and his two Citizens' Council partners. This confidential source had wide-ranging contacts around the Lakewood plant, and learned that Spake and Milteer confided to their most trusted contributors that the funds were being used to finance Dr. King's assassination. Our source assumed it was the same type of racist boast and demagoguery he had heard for years—until the day after Dr. King's murder. That's when he learned firsthand that James Earl Ray called Hugh Spake that morning—and within hours, Joseph Milteer was with Ray in Atlanta.[25]

Chapter Forty

Joseph Milteer and his Atlanta accomplices initially tried to search beyond their immediate area and colleagues to find someone to kill Martin Luther King. FBI files show that in the year prior to Dr. King's murder, contracts to kill King were offered on at least three occasions—and each time, the contract was tied to either Atlanta or associates of Milteer and his partners.

Because the Klan groups had been shrinking, even as the FBI increased their infiltration efforts, using Atlanta or Georgia Klansmen for the hit could have been too easily traced back to Milteer's group. Another factor was the money being offered. Some Klansmen had committed murder—but not for money, according to William Bradford Huie, whose most recent books as of 1967 were *Three Lives for Mississippi* and *The Klansman*, both about real-life racial killings. Huie, who had interviewed several admitted Klan murderers, wrote that "Klansmen don't kill for pay. Nor do they pay killers. Klansmen kill from religious conviction. The average Klan killer attends church and has no previous criminal record." Huie also pointed out that while "Klansmen hated Dr. King . . . they didn't hate him so intensely in 1968 as they did in 1963 or 1964 or 1965," before other black leaders emerged to share the spotlight with King.[1]

Even in 1965, a $100,000 bounty on King, which FBI files say was floated at a May 1965 Klan meeting in North Carolina, was unsuccessful. Authors Larry Hancock and Stuart Wexler write that "the Klan screened candidates and had possibly picked an individual who would make an attack on King during a visit to North Carolina," but nothing came of it. The offer had originated with a southeastern Klan group, but the actual source of the funds could not be determined. This could have been an early effort from Milteer's Atlanta clique, taking advantage of the area where they were buying North Carolina land. If Milteer's group wasn't behind the offer, his extensive Klan connections and visits to North Carolina made it likely that he was at least aware of the 1965 offer—and its lack of success.[2]

By 1967, as the pressure increased on Joseph Milteer's group to take action against Dr. King, Milteer had other reasons to find a killer outside of Atlanta. Through his travels and network of contacts, Milteer would have been aware of the February 1967 articles about him in Miami, even though they omitted his name. Milteer probably assumed—and correctly—that the FBI or Secret Service would start looking at him as a result of the articles. Because of that, Milteer would have known it would be far better for him and his partners to locate an assassin by using their contacts in other cities, even outside the South.

Milteer was one of the relatively few racist leaders of the time with good contacts on most socioeconomic levels of the anti–civil rights movement. He had connections to the lowest level, the Klan; a step higher, to J. B. Stoner's National States Rights Party (NSRP); and higher still, by being a member of the Atlanta White Citizens' Council. The Atlanta chapter was part of a loose network of similar groups across the South, whose membership included professionals, leading businessmen, and officials who would never attend a Klan rally.[3]

The wealthier and more prominent members of the White Citizens' Councils were sometimes part of the highest economic level of groups opposing civil rights: Business organizations whose members were powerful executives at several top Southern companies. They reaped most of the financial benefits from the activities of the lower-level racist groups.

By the 1940s and '50s, it was no longer acceptable for Southern governors, the National Guard, sheriffs, or company security forces to shoot striking workers and their families, as had been done in the 1930s. However, as the *Mississippi Historical Review* noted, by the 1940s the Klan was helping to defeat union drives in the South. It's often overlooked that in addition to opposing civil rights, the Klan, Stoner's NSRP, the White Citizens' Councils, national groups like the John Birch Society, and certain business associations also preached a strong anti-union message. While the higher-level groups didn't take physical action against unions, they deflected workers' frustrations away from employers, racist politicians, and blockbusting real estate firms by instead directing their anxiety and anger toward blacks and their leaders.[4]

Congressional investigators spotlighted one of these high-level Southern business groups, whose president said in a speech after Dr. King's murder "that Martin Luther King brought his crime upon himself." The members of this group included an "assistant Vice President [of]

Southern Bell . . . Atlanta," a "Vice President [of] Mississippi Power & Light," and one of the highest executives at "Carolina Power & Light." In contrast to the inflammatory rhetoric found in publications from the Klan and in Stoner's *Thunderbolt* newspaper, this Southern business group's literature featured smoothly written, PR-savvy denunciations of the media's coverage of racism in the South and "communist infiltration of the Negro movement." They also favored ending union rights and sanctions against white-run Rhodesia. Although that business group was not part of Dr. King's murder, its agenda shows the scope of interests aligned against civil rights in 1967—and the House Select Committee on Assassinations (HSCA) discovered that one of its members had offered a contract on Dr. King's life.[5]

John Sutherland was a member of that business group and Congressional investigators found that he was also a member and "early organizer" of the White Citizens' Council in St. Louis. A St. Louis patent attorney, Sutherland had also looked into joining Stoner's NSRP and could have come into contact with Joseph Milteer either through the Citizens' Councils or via the NSRP, for which Milteer was a well-traveled organizer. Sutherland's wife was from Atlanta, and one of his colleagues in the St. Louis White Citizens' Council attended meetings of the NSRP and may also have had Klan contacts. Like Milteer, Sutherland was a true believer: One of his friends testified to the HSCA that "Sutherland was a 'diehard Southerner' who would 'never let the Civil War die.'"[6]

The HSCA found that in "late 1966 or early 1967 [a] relatively sophisticated and experienced criminal" in St. Louis named Russell Byers was approached by a Sutherland associate named John Kauffmann. A criminal himself, Kauffmann "asked [Byers] if he would like to earn $50,000" ($300,000 in today's dollars). That night, the two met with Sutherland at his home, a memorable setting whose den "had a rug replica of a Confederate flag. . . . Sutherland [wore] a Confederate colonel's hat." Sutherland was in his early sixties at the time, as was Kauffmann, and in spite of the silly hat, Sutherland was deadly serious.[7]

Byers testified that "Sutherland offered [him] $50,000 to kill Martin Luther King." When Byers asked who was putting up the money, "Sutherland said he belonged to a secret southern organization, and they had a lot of money." The HSCA investigated both the St. Louis White Citizens' Council and the business group mentioned earlier, and determined that they were not behind the offer. Sutherland himself would leave an estate of $300,000 when he died three years later, but that included his home, savings, stocks, property, and all assets—not really enough for him to have easily paid $50,000 himself (plus a finder's fee for Kauffmann). On the other hand, Milteer and his Atlanta White Citizens' Council partners, who included an attorney, did have "a lot of money" and needed someone "to kill Martin Luther King," preferably a hit man who couldn't be traced to their Atlanta clique.[8]

As for why Sutherland's associate approached Byers, the HSCA said that if Byers didn't want to accept the contract himself, Sutherland and Kauffmann felt Byers "could have established contact with people willing to accept the offer." Byers had no connection with any racist organization, but Phillip Melanson described him as a "St. Louis underworld figure." In fact, Byers's brother-in-law was John Paul Spica, then serving time at Missouri State Prison in Jefferson City for a contract murder—the same inmate whom James Earl Ray admitted he "got to know" and who had "heavy mob connections."[9]

Sutherland's associate Kauffmann had his own ties to that particular prison. In addition to his business ventures, which included owning a motel, the HSCA found that "in 1967 and 1968 . . . Kauffmann sold over 1 million pills illegally to undercover Federal agents [and] some of the illegal pills were delivered to the Missouri State Penitentiary in Jefferson City . . . where James Earl Ray was incarcerated." As we documented earlier, Ray used and sold amphetamines in the prison. The HSCA received reports naming a prison doctor as being "involved with Mr. Kauffmann in the distribution of amphetamines in the prison." They also found that "while Ray was pushing a food cart in the prison hospital, John Paul Spica, in fact, worked [for the suspected doctor] in the same hospital."[10]

Sutherland's associate, Kauffmann, engaged in a wide range of criminal activity in the St. Louis area, according to the HSCA. In addition to "dealing in drugs," he accepted "stolen property in exchange for room rent [and was] running a prostitution ring out of [his] motel." After a "Federal narcotics agent was [discovered] talking to an informant about Kauffmann," the "agent was ambushed and shot." The scope of Kauffmann's criminal activity indicates that he would have had some contact with the local Mafia, but there is no indication that the St. Louis Mafia itself was involved in the offer to Byers. At the time, St. Louis Mafia attorney Morris Shenker was busy representing Jimmy Hoffa and trying to help with Carlos Marcello's Spring Hoffa effort.[11]

It seems as if Sutherland was trying to reach out to the underworld through Kauffmann.[12] Sutherland's wife testified that her husband and Kauffmann were not close, and given Kauffmann's criminal background, it appears that Sutherland was simply paying Kauffmann to find a hit man. The HSCA interviewed a sheriff's informant who lived at Kauffmann's motel in 1967, who said he heard about "a standing offer to murder Dr. King." The informant testified that "if they were hard up for money, somebody would say, 'Well, we can always make $20,000 or $30,000 for killing Martin Luther King . . . for John.'"[13]

Sutherland didn't find a hit man. According to the HSCA, Byers turned down the contract without seriously considering it, and Kauffmann was soon "arrested and convicted for the manufacture and sale of amphetamines." The HSCA interviewed two other attorneys, one a judge, who testified that Byers had told them about the offer after King's death. The HSCA "uncovered enough evidence to be convinced that the Byers allegation was essentially truthful."

Though the HSCA documented four ways that James Earl Ray could have heard about the $50,000 Sutherland contract on King, including associates of Sutherland who knew one of Ray's brothers, they were unable to confirm any of them. They also couldn't find who was really putting up the money for the hit or any evidence that Sutherland's contract was put into operation. If James Earl Ray did hear about the contract in prison, there is no evidence Ray ever contacted Sutherland or Kauffmann, something the HSCA tried very hard to find.[14]

Our new information, unavailable to the HSCA, suggests a new possibility: that Sutherland's "secret Southern organization [with] a lot of money" might have been Milteer's Atlanta clique, or affiliated with it. Word could have been passed to St. Louis Citizens' Council member Sutherland from an Atlanta Citizens' Council member, such as Milteer or his partners. Word could also have traveled to Sutherland via Milteer's work for Stoner's NSRP. It might, or might not, be relevant that St. Louis had two large General Motors plants at the time, similar to the one where Milteer, Spake, and their two Atlanta associates collected money each week.

Sutherland's use of the criminal Kauffmann to reach "underworld figure" Byers was an attempt to offer a contract on King to the mob. If there was a connection between Milteer's group and the St. Louis offer, which we think is likely, then using Sutherland as a cutout didn't work. A more direct approach was needed, and the next time the underworld was contacted for a hit man to shoot King, it would be at a much higher level.

The next well-documented 1967 murder contract on King was offered shortly after the St. Louis offer, and has a direct connection to Atlanta; many of the following FBI files are quoted here for the first time. Just before the April 1967 release of an inmate at the federal prison in Leaven-worth, Kansas, FBI files say the man was told about a $100,000 contract on the life of Martin Luther King. The inmate, whose name (as well as his associates') is still withheld by the FBI, had been in Leavenworth since July 1965. A fellow prisoner, a former "Mississippi bootlegger [who] worked [with the inmate] in the shoe factory at Leavenworth, [learned the inmate] was going to Atlanta," so he told the inmate about the con-tract on King.[15]

The former bootlegger told the inmate "that $100,000 had been offered by the White Knights of the Ku Klux Klan of Mississippi . . . to be paid to anyone who would kill Martin Luther King." Specifically, the bootleg-ger told the inmate "that if, after his arrival at Atlanta, he could find out Martin Luther King's travel route and itinerary, he could earn $100,000 for himself."[16]

The inmate later told the FBI that the former bootlegger "instructed him to contact" a female associate at a certain company in Jackson, Mis-sissippi, regarding the contract. The bootlegger told the inmate he cor-responded with her and would tell her that the inmate "was 'okay.'" The FBI later determined that the bootlegger "had written often to" the woman in Jackson, "had received seven visits from [her, and] planned to work with [her] in the real estate business upon his release from Leavenworth."[17]

The Leavenworth inmate was apparently released on schedule in April, but by June 2, 1967, he was "an inmate of the county jail, Sherman, Texas." While there, he told an FBI agent about the contract on King. The FBI conducted a cursory investigation of the allegation over the next two months, including interviewing the woman in Jackson, who admitted writing to the Mississippi bootlegger in prison but denied any connec-tion with the Klan. When the FBI interviewed her again a year later, after King's death, she had a new excuse to account for talk of the $100,000 contract, claiming she was just speculating, and that the bootlegger must have "taken her casual statement seriously."[18]

The heavily censored FBI files don't say why the former Leavenworth inmate was in a Texas country jail, or whether telling the FBI about the King contract had anything to do with his release. But by the late fall of 1967, the former inmate was on parole while "living and working in the Atlanta, Georgia, area" as he had originally planned. As he later described to the FBI, the former inmate said that "around the first or second of December, 1967," as "he was leaving the Federal Building in Atlanta after having made his regular contact with his [parole] officer, he was hailed on the steps of the Federal Building by an individual unknown to him." The individual was described as "a white male, age 30–35, 5'10", 165–170 pounds, blond hair, cut medium short, and slightly wavy. . . . He was extremely well dressed in obviously expensive clothes."[19]

After getting the parolee's attention, "this person asked [by name] if he was" the former inmate who had been at Leavenworth, "and when he replied in the affirmative, this individual stated he had a message for him from" the still imprisoned Mississippi bootlegger who had revealed the "$100,000 [contract to] kill Martin Luther King." According to the FBI, "the person accosting [the parolee] on the steps of the Atlanta Federal Building" in a threatening tone said that "apparently somebody had done some talking." The former inmate realized that was a "reference to" his revelations to the FBI about the King murder contract. Having spent time in Leavenworth, the parolee knew the penalty for being a snitch, especially about a murder contract. The irony was that he was literally only steps away from federal authorities—but in those less security-conscious days, they were all inside the building and would be of little help if the mysterious man wanted him to take a ride.[20]

Before the frightened parolee could respond to the man's accusation, a friend "who had [driven the parolee] to the Federal Building called to him, from across the street." At the friend's call, "the unknown individual immediately walked away." He was apparently worried that the former inmate's friend "might be an FBI agent or police officer," and he "did not desire that his identity be learned."[21] The parolee was no doubt relieved by his friend's sudden appearance, and the threatening man's quick departure.[22]

Though out of immediate danger, "the more [the parolee] thought about this incident, the more alarmed he became. . . . He considered revealing [the] above facts to his parole officer at Atlanta but . . . he did not trust his parole officer too much and was afraid his parole might be revoked automatically. He also considered contacting the FBI office in Atlanta but decided against this." The parolee said he was worried because "the Ku Klux Klan was reportedly strong in that area [and] it was his understanding that [a] Deputy United States Marshal . . . who went to work about the time he started reporting to his parole officer at Atlanta, was supposed to be a member of the Ku Klux Klan."[23]

Fearing "for his life [the parolee fled] Atlanta shortly thereafter" and moved to Tampa, Florida, with his wife. He remained there, working, for the next eight months. He finally turned himself in to the FBI in early

August 1968 (four months after King's murder) because he was worried about his wife, who had become pregnant.[24]

The matter of the $100,000 contract and the threatening confrontation on the federal courthouse steps in Atlanta raise troubling questions. Who was the well-dressed man, and how did he learn that the parolee had told the FBI about the King contract? How did the man know the parolee would be leaving the courthouse at that particular time? Had the former inmate been tailed, or did the man (or his associates) have a contact who was privy to information about the FBI and federal parolees?

It makes little sense for the man to have risked confronting the parolee at the federal courthouse in Atlanta about a matter that the FBI had investigated and dropped four months earlier—unless the King murder contract was still an active issue. Given that the threatening man was "well dressed in obviously expensive clothes" and the public nature of the confrontation, the encounter was likely meant only to scare the parolee, in which case it succeeded. As for the mystery man, his age doesn't match that of Milteer, Spake, or their attorney partner, who were all older; a description of the dentist member of their clique isn't available. The parolee's description of the mystery man might indicate that he was dressed a step above the usual attorneys and bureaucrats at the Federal Building. If the parolee was suggesting that the man looked wealthy, he could have been describing some of Milteer's associates in the Atlanta White Citizens' Council. If the description was meant to imply that the man was a flashy dresser in expensive clothes, he could have been pointing to Atlanta nightclub operators and gamblers tied to the Dixie Mafia, at least one of whom was linked to Carlos Marcello.[25]

James Earl Ray would be in New Orleans, allegedly meeting with three Marcello associates, just two weeks after this Atlanta incident, as we'll detail shortly. While Ray and the parolee had both served time at Leavenworth, their stays were years apart, and there was no known connection between the two. The same is true for the Mississippi bootlegger at Leavenworth who originally mentioned the contract.[26]

As for the source of the $100,000 for the King contract, the conduit was said to be the White Knights of the Ku Klux Klan, the small, violent Mississippi group led by Sam Bowers, who was also linked to the 1965 offer in North Carolina. However, Bowers was a small-time businessman who didn't have that kind of money. Wealthy members of the Citizens' Council would have been cautious about giving it to him, because on October 20, 1967, Bowers was one of seven people convicted for the murders of civil rights workers Andrew Goodman, James Chaney, and

Michael Schwerner. Pulitzer Prize–winning journalist Jack Nelson noted that it was "the first time a Mississippi jury had convicted members of the Klan—and a white law enforcement officer as well—for crimes committed against civil rights workers."[27]

Bowers was thus occupied during much of the fall of 1967, and likely not an active participant in the contract on Dr. King. Bowers hated Jewish people as much as blacks and, while free on bond, would continue his violent behavior in late 1967 and 1968—he was caught in a car with a submachine gun in December 1967. Jack Nelson documented that Bowers' attacks focused primarily on bombings of Jewish homes and buildings, in conjunction with a small handful of trusted associates.[28]

Another prison report of a contract on Dr. King's life may shed additional light on the offers circulating at Leavenworth and in St. Louis. This FBI report concerned the Texas State Prison at Huntsville, and authors Hancock and Wexler note that it mentioned "$100,000 and the White Knights." The offer said that "interested parties were to make contact via cutouts, they were expected to 'case' King in Atlanta, and payment would be made only 'after' King were killed. Remarks were also made that would indicate that the bounty itself or the rumor of it was coming out of North Carolina." Hancock adds that $50,000 was also payable to the person handling only surveillance for the hit, but anyone involved had to have a certain level of criminal experience, at least at the level of armed robbery—hence the logic of spreading word of the contract in prisons. The FBI report also indicated that someone in law enforcement would be a contact for the hit, which might explain how the mystery man was able to find the Leavenworth parolee in Atlanta.[29]

The threads running through all the FBI reports of a contract on King—the large amount of money, links to members of the Klan and White Citizens' Council and organized crime, as well as to North Carolina and Atlanta—indicate a likelihood they were tied to the efforts of Milteer and his three Atlanta partners. However, none were effective in locating an appropriate hit man. While the White Knights' Sam Bowers was the focus of more legal pressure in October 1967, that same month Milteer was being freed from what little scrutiny he had been under from law enforcement since the articles about him had appeared in the Miami press back in February 1967.

On October 9, 1967, the Intelligence Division of the US Secret Service in Washington told the head of its Atlanta office that it had "reviewed" the file on Joseph Milteer and saw "nothing to indicate that this subject presents a danger to any person under our protective jurisdiction [and] that quarterly investigations should be discontinued at this time." The Atlanta office received a report about Milteer from their Valdosta office in South Georgia on October 10, and two days later told the Intelligence Division, "[We] heartily agree with you in this action," and that they would "discontinue [their] quarterly investigations" of Milteer. The FBI had been kept abreast of the Secret Service activities related to Milteer, and would have been told of the investigation's termination.[30]

Though the decision was legally justified, it's tragic that the Secret Service abandoned their Milteer investigation because they felt he wasn't "a danger to any person under our protective jurisdiction," without making some type of referral to another agency. A serious investigation of Milteer would have shown that he was still a danger to civil rights leaders like Dr. King, even if he was no longer an active threat to President Johnson or Vice President Hubert Humphrey. While racial attitudes in the Secret Service had likely progressed somewhat since Abraham Bolden's complaints in 1963 and 1964, problems persisted: In 2008, sixty black Secret Service agents were supporting discrimination suits, and the Associated Press reported a black "employee found a noose in one of the Secret Service's training centers," resulting in the suspension of a white agent.[31]

Even if the Secret Service felt Milteer was no longer a presidential threat and was thus out of its jurisdiction, it could have recommended that the FBI or the Georgia Bureau of Investigation continue to monitor Milteer. However, the Atlanta FBI office's attitude toward Milteer had been unusually tolerant dating back to 1963, when FBI agent Don Adams wasn't given crucial information about Milteer, the Miami police tapes, or the Tampa threat.

This raises the possibility that Milteer was aware that the Secret Service had closed its case on him, either from a contact in law enforcement or because agents stopped questioning his associates and neighbors. In later Congressional hearings, retired Atlanta FBI agent Arthur Murtagh testified about the racist attitudes of many agents and supervisors in the Atlanta FBI office in 1967 and 1968. Murtagh was part of the "security squad" in the Atlanta office, which handled "investigations of Black extremist organizations" that for the FBI, included Dr. King and the Southern Christian Leadership Conference (SCLC). The security squad was also responsible for "investigations of the Ku Klux Klan" and Cuban matters, including Cuban exiles. That meant the same FBI agents looking for informants in the Klan were also operating against King and the SCLC, creating an opportunity for racists who wanted to manipulate the system.[32]

Murtagh said that many agents in the Atlanta office and on the security squad were racists themselves, who saw King as the enemy. Another former Atlanta security squad agent admitted in later testimony that in 1968, he saw Dr. King's death as the "removal of a threat to our national security." This Atlanta agent admitted those feelings were based on "his own personal prejudice" and not "on anything [he saw] as an FBI agent."[33]

Hoover encouraged such attitudes, and they were all too common not just in the FBI but in other branches of law enforcement as well. When coupled with the fact that the FBI assigned those responsible for investigating the Klan to also run surveillance on King, it was a recipe for disaster. There is no evidence that the Atlanta FBI (or Secret Service) office was involved in King's assassination, something Rep. Carl Stokes and the House Select Committee on Assassinations looked at very closely. But it is possible that Milteer or his partners on the White Citizens' Council were able to exploit the racist attitudes of some agents and supervisors.

In 1967, law enforcement usually didn't consider the White Citizens' Councils to be a hate group like the Klan. While they weren't regarded as highly in Atlanta as they were in more conservative areas (where the Citizens' Councils evolved and persist to this day), they still provided a forum in which types like Milteer could network with respectable businessmen, professionals, and officials. FBI agents were barred from Klan membership, but it's unclear if there was any such policy about the White Citizens' Councils, since their views largely mirrored Hoover's.

Another way Milteer could have learned that the Secret Service had closed his case was through the Florida Police Intelligence Unit, since his case had originated in Miami. Trafficante's man Sgt. de la Llana headed the statewide unit that shared information with other states and federal authorities, he could easily have learned that Milteer's case had been closed. Both de la Llana and Milteer had been involved in the Tampa attempt on JFK, so they could have been in communication about this matter as well.[34]

The FBI agents in Atlanta were subject to the same fears about blockbusting and school integration that stoked contributions to Milteer's group, and those concerns were reaching a crescendo by October 1967. The school year which began that fall was the first in which Atlanta's schools were fully integrated, triggering an increased wave of "white flight" documented in Princeton historian Kevin M. Kruse's 2005 book of the same name about Atlanta. However, the school integration was based primarily on geographic location, meaning it didn't affect

Atlanta's affluent Northside, still largely closed to blacks. Even the governor's mansion, occupied by segregationist Lester Maddox, was moved from midtown (increasingly home to rooming houses and, soon, to James Earl Ray) to the exclusive Northside Buckhead area. In contrast, the middle-class areas surrounding the Lakewood General Motors plant were hit especially hard by blockbusting, causing massive transition and turmoil.[35]

While that upheaval probably increased contributions to Milteer's group, it also increased the pressure on him to have King killed, as he'd been promising his most faithful supporters for several years. Some of his supporters at the Lakewood auto plant were Klan members, and Milteer would have been all too aware of the August 25, 1967, murder of George Lincoln Rockwell, head of the American Nazi Party, by one of his own disgruntled followers. Milteer certainly wanted to see King killed, but even an attempt on King by a nonprofessional—an effort that Milteer could take credit for with his contributors—would help to ensure that Milteer didn't meet the same fate as Rockwell.

Apparently, Milteer hadn't been able to find a contract killer who couldn't be traced back to him by going through the prison grapevine, or through Bowers' White Knights, or by using Sutherland's approach to the lower levels of the St. Louis Mafia. The media coverage of Bowers' trial in Mississippi made using Klan members even more risky, and Milteer would have wanted to avoid recruiting anyone connected to groups he belonged to, like the Citizens' Council or Stoner's NSRP. Milteer had apparently tried to recruit someone with no ties to Atlanta or Georgia, by looking to North Carolina, Kansas, Texas, and Missouri—but it hadn't worked. His lack of success may have led to an attempted recruitment in Atlanta that had some similarities to the one in St. Louis.

In the fall of 1967, two men in Atlanta were offered $50,000 to kill Martin Luther King, according to testimony that the House Select Committee on Assassinations "concluded . . . was credible." The two men, the Powell brothers, were house painters who the Committee said had "a reputation for violence." They hung out at an Atlanta bar, where a mutual friend "told them he could put them in touch with a person who would pay a large sum of money to anyone willing to kill Dr. King. Several days later, at the same bar [the brothers] were approached by a white male who introduced himself only as Ralph." After explaining that he was the man their friend had told them about, "Ralph displayed an open briefcase full of money . . . said it contained $25,000 and promised that if they took the job, they would receive $25,000 more when it had been completed. The Powells hesitated to accept the offer" of $50,000 to kill Martin Luther King.[36]

Seeing their reluctance to accept the contract, "Ralph closed his brief-case and left the bar," and one of the brothers said they "never saw or heard from this person again." The other brother initially cooperated with Congressional investigators and passed a lie-detector test about the incident. But when it came time to give testimony, he refused, even when subpoenaed, saying "he feared for his life." He was so afraid to testify he "subsequently pleaded guilty to contempt of Congress for his refusal," rather than risk talking about the offer.[37]

The FBI hadn't learned about the incident until 1976, and was "unable to ... discredit the story," even after what it called "a full investigation." Two years later, the HSCA "conducted an extensive field investigation," pursuing leads the FBI had missed. They even released to the news media a sketch of "Ralph," whom the *Washington Star* described as "a hard-faced young man with dark hair," though the sketch produced no results. Investigators also tried to find links to the Sutherland St. Louis offer "because of their similarity and proximity in time," but were unsuccessful.[38]

At that time, Milteer and his small group were trying to find someone to assassinate Dr. King, and we believe it's likely they were behind the offer. Since it came after unsuccessful offers floated in other states, Milteer's group might have decided to try finding willing hit men closer to home. Also, as with the offers in St. Louis and the prisons, they didn't try to recruit someone with ties to any of the known racist organizations, a precaution that would protect Milteer and his partners after Dr. King's death. In addition, because of the cash they collected each week at the Lakewood plant, Milteer's group could easily have had the ready cash available for the offer. Finally, though the two brothers weren't seasoned criminals, Milteer was probably willing by this point to settle for some-one with a violent reputation, since even a failed attempt would give him credibility with his anxious contributors. That may be why "Ralph" had been willing to pay $25,000 in advance just for the Powell brothers to make the attempt.

However, like the earlier attempts to find a hit man, this one didn't work. While Milteer's group may have made a few other such approaches in Atlanta, Milteer's group couldn't have done many without attracting attention or risking making the offer to someone who might immedi-ately go to the police. Then, too, recruiting someone who lived in Atlanta carried a danger of investigators' being able to trace the recruit back to Milteer, Spake, or their two partners. Yet Milteer's group had few options left. Using a local Klansman could increase the pressure on the allies and organizations of Milteer and his associates, even if the plotters escaped detection. Hiring a hit man who was not an experienced criminal increased the chance he might talk or get caught.

Milteer's group needed a way to hire a seasoned criminal who had used guns before and knew how to keep his mouth shut. He should be someone who wasn't a longtime resident of Atlanta, or even Georgia, and who wasn't a member of any of the usual racist organizations—yet would still be willing to accept a contract to murder Dr. King. The hit man would need to be an experienced traveler, so he could stalk King and shoot him away from Atlanta. Killing Dr. King near his home or office in Atlanta could bring too much heat to Milteer's local associates, especially since Atlanta Police Chief Herbert Jenkins was on good terms with Dr. King's father. It would also help Milteer's group if the hit man worked for a powerful person or organization that the hit man wouldn't dare cross, even if he wound up in prison. Basically, Milteer needed a professional at arranging such things, someone with a proven ability to find hit men that could get away with even high-profile killings.

Joseph Milteer knew about such a man, having worked on his biggest hit back in 1963. Using Carlos Marcello to broker the contract on Dr. King would be expensive, but nothing else had worked, so Milteer and his partners apparently had no other option.[39]

Chapter Forty-one

Shedding important new light on Martin Luther King's assassination is the following 1968 Justice Department memo, which was withheld from Congressional investigators and is quoted here for the first time. The memo—based on confidential information, including that of a "well placed protégé of Carlos Marcello in New Orleans"—says "the Cosa Nostra [Mafia] agreed to 'broker' or arrange the assassination [of Martin Luther King] for an amount somewhat in excess of three hundred thousand dollars ($300,000) after they were contacted . . . by representatives of 'Forever White,' an elite organization of wealthy segregationists [in the] Southeastern states. The Mafia's . . . interest was less the money than the investment-type opportunity presented, i.e., to get in a position to extract (or extort) governmental or other favors from some well placed Southern white persons, including the KKK and White Citizens' Councils. Quitman . . . was said . . . to be a possible base of 'Forever White's' operations."[1]

The Justice Department memo says the Mafia group involved was based in New Orleans, and that two participants in the plotting were "Frank [C.] Liberto . . . a Memphis racketeer and lieutenant of Carlos Marcello, the southern Mafia chieftain in New Orleans," plus "Joe Carameci (phonetic)" who was described as a "professional" killer. When the Justice Department referred the information to the FBI after Dr. King's murder, the Bureau said "Joe Carameci" was "unknown to this office." Though not acknowledged in any of the FBI's King files, the Bureau had opened a criminal intelligence file on a "Frank Joseph Caracci" on October 9, 1967, almost six months before Dr. King's assassination. The FBI described him "as an associate of Carlos Marcello, New Orleans La Cosa Nostra leader."[2]

History shows that Frank Joseph Caracci was the type of Marcello operative who could be involved in a major hit. On November 27, 1963, the FBI had interviewed Caracci about his contacts with Jack Ruby in the five months before JFK's assassination. According to witnesses and phone records, Ruby had met with Caracci at least twice during that time, in addition to visiting and making eight phone calls to Caracci's nightclubs.[3]

The Justice Department memo about Marcello and the contract on Dr. King was sent to the Assistant Attorney General of the Civil Rights Division five months after King's murder, and will be covered in additional detail in Chapter 60. The memo was based on sources found by journalist William Sartor, described in the memo as "a contract writer for *Time* [magazine who] covered Memphis, particularly racial matters." The Justice Department investigator said that Sartor "appears to be known and trusted by those Negro leaders in Memphis with whom I have talked." After citing Sartor's most recent article in *Time*, the investigator says that Sartor "is a 'low key' fellow who is not apparently irrational or fanciful." In addition to the "protégé of Carlos Marcello," Sartor's sources in the underworld included "four or five petty racketeers in Memphis, New Orleans, and elsewhere."[4]

According to one of James Earl Ray's attorneys, in 1971 William Sartor was in Texas, completing research on what would have been the first book (or article) to tie Carlos Marcello to Dr. King's murder. But "the night before he was to interview a significant witness"—a nightclub owner Congressional investigators had linked to Marcello—Sartor was murdered. It took twenty-one years until the Waco, Texas, district attorney "officially declared [Sartor's] death a homicide."[5]

The essence of what Sartor's sources told him about Marcello's brokering the contract on Dr. King appears to be based on Milteer and his Atlanta associates. Sartor was getting his information about the plot second- and thirdhand, so some details are wrong. For example, he (or his source) assumed that the town of Quitman being discussed was the one in Mississippi, the state where Sartor lived, instead of Quitman, Georgia, the home of Joseph Milteer. But other sources and documents corroborate many aspects of Sartor's basic story.[6]

There are several reasons why it took forty years for any book or article to reveal the Justice Department memo about Marcello's "brokering" the contract to kill Dr. King for a group of "segregationists." Sartor's death no doubt had a chilling effect on his mob-connected sources. While the House Select Committee on Assassinations (HSCA) had some of Sartor's unpublished notes and his partial manuscript, the Committee never cited the Justice Department memo quoted above. The FBI apparently didn't give the memo to the HSCA, but we can't determine that with certainty, since the HSCA's files on Dr. King's assassination are sealed until the year 2029. At any rate, the HSCA appears to have not been aware of Sartor's most important sources, and was not informed by the FBI that one of Sartor's sources personally told a Justice Department investigator his story in 1968. When FBI agents summarized the Justice Department memo for Hoover in 1968, they left out the most important information about Marcello and the Mafia—and even this sanitized version appears to have not been given to the HSCA. Though the HSCA had investigated Marcello and Milteer closely for any connections to JFK's assassination, its 1979 report contained only a few lines dismissing Marcello as a suspect in King's death (for lack of evidence), and nothing at all about Milteer and Dr. King's murder.

Not until 1989 would Marcello's biographer, John H. Davis, first raise the prospect of Marcello's having a role in King's death in a widely available book. But the hundreds of pages Davis wrote about Marcello and JFK's murder overshadowed his few pages about Marcello's possible role in Dr. King's murder. When Congress unanimously passed the 1992 JFK Assassinations Records Act, it covered only government files about President Kennedy's murder, not those about Dr. King's.

In the 1990s, more ties between Marcello and Dr. King's death were exposed by James Earl Ray's last attorney, William Pepper, an associate of King who had the support of King's family. However, like any good defense attorney, he attempted to use the Marcello information to exonerate Ray. Pepper tried to blame King's murder on a massive conspiracy involving Army Intelligence, the FBI, the CIA, and the Memphis police. Because of that, and the use of some questionable sources, the press largely overlooked the Marcello aspect of the story.

Pepper won a 1999 civil court verdict for the King family, which found that a conspiracy involving Marcello killed Dr. King. In 2000, at the request of Coretta Scott King and her family, President Clinton and Attorney General Janet Reno had the Justice Department review the case and Pepper's evidence. However, their report didn't mention, let alone address, their Department's own 1968 memo about Marcello's brokering the King contract. The Justice Department's 2000 report left out much more relevant information, such as Marcello's detailed 1985 FBI confession to JFK's assassination, and the FBI's hundreds of hours of still-unreleased prison audio tapes of Marcello, which could shed additional light on both assassinations.[7]

We uncovered those Marcello files at the National Archives in 2006, where they had finally been released because of the JFK Act. The Sartor files about Marcello are also at the National Archives, and since early 2008 have been available on the Mary Ferrell Foundation's website (www.maryferrell.org). The Mary Ferrell site's computerized ability to search the text of hundreds of thousands of pages of documents—a feature that was not available to the FBI for decades—enabled us to find the relevant pages in a short time. The Sartor/Marcello documents are part of the FBI's files about Dr. King's assassination (codenamed MUR-KIN) that were released due to the efforts of attorneys specializing in the Freedom of Information Act, like Bernard Fensterwald and his law partner, Jim Lesar.

Four years after successfully pulling off JFK's murder, it is not surprising that two of the men involved considered working together again on another, much easier, high-profile hit. By the fall of 1967, of the dozen or so Marcello and Milteer associates who had participated knowingly in JFK's murder, several had died (Ferrie, Banister, Ruby, Herminio Diaz), and none of the others had talked. The Secret Service and the FBI were no longer investigating Milteer, and Marcello had escaped unscathed from the Garrison investigation and any fallout from the September 1967 *Life* magazine articles.

Since the media hadn't followed up on *Life*'s revelations, Marcello would soon resume attempting the Spring Hoffa bribes that the *Life* articles had tried to expose. The second *Life* article had destroyed what little credibility Garrison had left with the mainstream press, and the District Attorney was now focusing almost completely on Clay Shaw, who had no connections to Marcello. (The only other person to receive serious attention from Garrison was a right-winger from California, fingered by a Trafficante associate to take the heat off an alleged mob courier with a similar name.) Ed Reid's *Grim Reapers*, with its information about Marcello, was still two years away from publication, and in the fall of 1967 there was no way to know if it would ever see print.

Carlos Marcello still faced a pending charge of slugging an FBI agent at the New Orleans airport in 1966, but his trial was at least half a year away, and could be stalled by still more legal delays. In late 1967, the FBI's attitude about Marcello was in a state of flux. At the top, J. Edgar Hoover still refused to make Marcello a priority or authorize the kind of phone taps or planted bugs he had used against Martin Luther King and Marina Oswald. Regis Kennedy, the FBI agent who pronounced Marcello nothing more than a tomato salesman, was still in the New Orleans office, though he was in the process of retiring. It's hard to say if Regis Kennedy's feelings were his own or merely reflected what had been Hoover's policy on Marcello since the 1950s.[8]

While some of the New Orleans agents apparently shared Regis Kennedy's lax attitude toward Marcello, others—like those involved in the airport slugging incident—were at least trying to gather information against such an obvious target. Realistically, Hoover couldn't tell too many people in the FBI about whatever blackmail material Marcello had on him. So, as younger agents joined the Bureau, they couldn't understand why headquarters didn't go after the Louisiana godfather. New Orleans FBI files from 1967–1968 reveal an increasing number of low-level informants providing second- and thirdhand information about Marcello's movements. Perhaps some agents wanted to be ready for the time when their elderly FBI director finally retired or passed away, and they could at last go after Marcello in a serious way. Marcello might have been aware of some of the FBI's informants through Regis Kennedy, but the basic level of information most of the informants provided—Marcello lived here, drove there, stopped at this store, met with this longtime associate—would have given Marcello little cause for concern.

As we mentioned earlier, Marcello's workdays in 1967 consisted largely of receiving visitors at his office behind the Town and Country Motel, from mobsters (including Mafia chiefs from other parts of the country) to prominent businessmen to politicians, all making proposals or asking for help. Especially sensitive meetings took place in the farmhouse on his huge Churchill Farms estate, and Marcello frequently traveled to other parts of his empire for a firsthand look at land and business deals.

At some point in the latter part of 1967, Joseph Milteer was likely one of Marcello's visitors, asking what it would take for the godfather to arrange a contract on Martin Luther King. It wouldn't be the first time a white supremacist had considered such a thing. Congressional investigators reported that just six years earlier, the imperial wizard of the New Orleans Ku Klux Klan had told a Klan meeting that "Southern racial problems could be eliminated only by the murder of Dr. King and that he had a New Orleans underworld associate 'who would kill anyone for a price.'"[9]

Carlos Marcello's personal involvement in brokering a murder contract would essentially amount to having a few meetings with only trusted associates—his enormous power had grown from being extremely cautious in such matters. We know from the BRILAB informant and CAMTEX informant Van Laningham how Marcello typically operated when someone brought him a proposal. If it intrigued him, he would say he needed to talk to some people first, and would then get back to the person making the request. Like any good businessman or gambler, Marcello always tried to lay off most or all of the risk and actual work onto others. After checking with his appropriate associates, Marcello would make his decision. If he thought the rewards justified the risk (most of which would be borne by others), Marcello would come back with a deal—take it or leave it, with no negotiation. That's why the $300,000 figure (more than $1.8 million today) in the Justice Department memo may be accurate, and is considerably higher than the $50,000–$100,000 Milteer and his partners may have offered originally.[10]

In addition to the money, the Justice Department memo said, Marcello hoped to gain leverage over the "segregationists" for future deals or blackmail, but Marcello would have been willing to consider helping Milteer for other reasons as well. John H. Davis wrote about FBI wiretaps documenting that Marcello was "an avid racist" who hated African Americans from the time he began his Mafia career selling drugs in the black areas of New Orleans. His use of the n-word was constant, even when referring to black politicians, since Marcello saw blacks as "subhuman, chattel to be exploited [and was] vigorously opposed to civil rights . . . and detested its leaders." Carlos Marcello's close ally Leander Perez, Louisiana's powerful political boss, had established White Citizens' Council chapters in more than half of the parishes in the state, totaling one hundred thousand members. Marcello was "an enthusiastic supporter of the Ku Klux Klan" and tolerated black voters only because he could deliver their votes to his politicians.[11]

Because of Martin Luther King, Carlos Marcello's ability to control black voters and exploit them in other ways was starting to change. The race riots in the summers of 1966 and 1967 would have worried Marcello, especially the 1967 riots in Tampa, Memphis, and Atlanta, since they could be the harbingers of even more problems in the South. In the days before legal state lotteries, the Mafia's illegal lotteries, the "numbers" or "policy" rackets, targeted America's ghettos and minority communities. As with today's legal lotteries, they preyed disproportionately on poor and desperate minorities, many of whom gambled regularly in an attempt to win a better life for their families. Along with the sale of drugs to minorities, the numbers racket generated a steady cash flow for Marcello, some of which he used for regular payoffs to local officials. Any disruption to that steady stream of money—even something short of a riot, such as a demonstration or boycott—was bad for Marcello.

Carlos Marcello would have been concerned about the riot in Tampa because of his long-standing business associate Santo Trafficante, but the Memphis race riot on July 20, 1967, had a more direct impact on Marcello's bottom line. Marcello didn't control Memphis, as he did New Orleans or Houston, but he did wield influence there through the Memphis Mafia, sometimes called "the Cartel." Arthur Baldwin, a nightclub owner and "government informant who worked closely with the Marcello organization in Memphis," described that relationship to Ray's last lawyer. The Justice Department later confirmed "that Baldwin assisted the government in federal investigations."[12]

Marcello shared control of the state of Mississippi with the Memphis Cartel, which managed the northern third of the state, while Marcello controlled organized crime in the rest, including the state's main cities: Jackson, Gulfport, and Biloxi. According to journalist James Dickerson, the Cartel had diversified into "construction, land development, and various legitimate storefront businesses . . . but beneath that veneer of respectability operated the same old network of graft, extortion, and political corruption" that was familiar to Marcello. Microphone experts in the Memphis recording industry helped the Memphis Cartel pioneer the mob's use of electronic surveillance, giving it a degree of protection from law enforcement since "they knew more about the science of recording than did the FBI." Starting in the 1950s, Marcello had allowed the Cartel to set up legitimate businesses in New Orleans; in return they allowed Marcello "to form a joint venture with [Trafficante] for the transpiration and sale of illegal drugs in Memphis."[13]

Marcello had further ties to the city through the Liberto family, notably Memphis produce dealer Frank C. Liberto, who was named in the Justice Department memo. Liberto confirmed his Mafia ties to a witness and reminisced "that as a youngster he used to push a vegetable cart with Carlos Marcello in New Orleans." According to Marcello's biographer, John H. Davis, "the FBI determined that Frank's New Orleans brother was . . . an associate of Carlos Marcello." Also part of the clan was Jack Liberto, Marcello's bodyguard and barber. Jack Liberto had been present for Marcello's fall 1962 threat to kill JFK, and FBI files confirm that he was still working closely with Marcello in 1967 and 1968. These family connections, along with the involvement of both Marcello and Liberto in the produce business, gave the two mobsters a cover for working together: Soon after King's assassination, Frank Liberto told the FBI that he had to make "frequent trips to New Orleans for produce, has relatives in New Orleans, and discusses large sums of money when making produce purchases over the telephone."[14]

In addition to protecting his Southern cities from the effects of Dr. King's movement, Marcello had other reasons to seriously consider Milteer's proposal. Through a variety of law enforcement and political contacts, including Sgt. de la Llana, Marcello could easily have learned that Milteer's small group was not on the radar screens of law enforcement or the FBI—a fact that made cooperating with Milteer more attractive. Marcello would have had no qualms about aligning himself with white supremacists like Milteer, since he had used Milteer and Guy Banister in the JFK assassination.

Marcello could insist that Milteer and his group take on much of the risk, especially after the crime had been committed. Hence, when Ray would flee to Atlanta after King's death, Ray wouldn't contact a Mafioso; he would call Milteer's partner, Hugh Spake, instead, and Milteer himself would have to aid Ray's flight from Atlanta.

How long Marcello considered Milteer's proposal is not known, but he probably would have consulted his closest ally among America's mob bosses, Santo Trafficante—especially since working on the King hit could potentially affect the successful cover-up of their roles in JFK's assassination. The recent Tampa riots, coupled with the disruption caused to the drug route they shared in riot-torn Memphis, probably made Trafficante amenable to Milteer's proposal.

In every way, a hit on Martin Luther King would be simpler and far less risky than JFK's assassination. There was far less security for Dr. King than there had been for President Kennedy; on the few occasions King even had a security detail, it was usually small and unarmed. Other than in Atlanta, King rarely trusted local or state police in the South, so even if those officials heard any warnings or leaks about the hit, they were unlikely to be quickly or effectively passed along to Dr. King's men. Many Southern police forces did not yet bar Klan membership, and some public officials were either former KKK members or sympathetic to the cause, a potentially useful factor as long as the hit happened in a Southern city. By killing King in the South, Marcello and his allies would know which members of local law enforcement were on the take or amenable to a bribe. Also, in the South, even if the hit man were captured alive, he was not likely to be convicted—and on the chance that he were, his sentence would be light.

Using people from Marcello's highly secure, ruthless drug network had been effective in the JFK hit, and that strategy could be used again if Marcello brokered the King contract. The CIA's covert Cuban operations had been extremely useful in forcing an official cover-up after

JFK's murder, and there might be a way to tap into that again, though on a far smaller scale.

Compromising the government's domestic surveillance programs had been a key part of the JFK hit, and those programs had only increased by 1967. In 1963, that effort had been directed primarily at the person blamed for JFK's murder, Oswald, whose surveillance had involved the CIA, military intelligence, and the FBI. For King, it would be the reverse, since King himself was the subject of massive, often illegal domestic surveillance. That meant the best time to hit King would be not when he was routinely leaving his home or office, but when he was subject to an especially large amount of government surveillance. A hit then would force authorities to go into cover-up mode, not to protect King's killers, but to protect their roles in a huge domestic spy program that the America public wouldn't begin to learn about fully for another eight years.

Marcello could have found out about that surveillance through numerous ways. Once more, Trafficante's Sgt. de la Llana, coordinator of Police Intelligence for the state of Florida, provides a good example, since he shared information with intelligence units in other states, as well as with the FBI, Army Intelligence, and the CIA. Mississippi's Sovereignty Commission, an official racist state organization, collected intelligence on civil rights activists, antiwar protesters, and leftists in general, all under the guise of fighting communism. That intelligence was shared not only with state and local law enforcement, but sometimes with federal agencies in the state, including military intelligence. Marcello's political boss, Leander Perez, had been successful in persuading Louisiana to authorize the creation of a Sovereignty Commission largely under his control. Several other Southern states, like Florida, had similar bodies, and all could be used in learning about the surveillance directed at Dr. King. Those connections could also allow Marcello and his men to feed disinformation into the system before and after King's death, as they had done for JFK's murder.[15]

The FBI and military intelligence were large parts of the growing domestic surveillance network; both had been forced into cover-ups after JFK's murder, and the same could be done again. (The FBI's COIN-TELPRO operation in 1967 and 1968 is detailed in Chapter 45.) Using information not declassified until seven years after King's murder, journalist James Dickerson wrote that "by 1967 the U.S. Army" effort to "gather information about the political activity of American citizens [had grown to] 1,500 plainclothes agents . . . assigned to over 350 secret record centers." They assembled "information on individuals attending protest rallies, business executives who contributed money to political causes, and politicians who voted for unpopular legislation." According to Hancock and Wexler, the rationale was that "army surveillance [was] designed to provide early warning of demonstrations, rallies, and other gatherings which could lead to civil disturbances requiring the deployment of Federal troops." Martin Luther King—and even his wife—became prime targets, and information on them was shared with the FBI. According to Dickerson, several Southern cities were "designated a target city by the Army" for surveillance and operations, including Memphis.[16]

In 1963, Guy Banister had helped Marcello compromise the FBI, but four years later there were other ways to do that for the hit on Dr. King. Through Banister and Regis Kennedy, Marcello would have known that many in the FBI remained racist. Based on his public statements alone, J. Edgar Hoover clearly hated Martin Luther King, and because FBI headquarters had fumbled its investigation of Milteer so badly in 1963 (and again in 1967), the FBI would be loath to reveal its failings by following leads to Milteer, even if his name should surface in King's murder. The FBI would eventually be so compromised in their investigation of King's murder that some people would come to believe that J. Edgar Hoover and the FBI were behind King's murder. However, William Bradford Huie has pointed out that many of the people who believe that, including associates of Dr. King, don't realize that theory was originally put forth by James Earl Ray's third attorney, J. B. Stoner. Then again, even Huie didn't realize that Stoner was an associate of Joseph Milteer.[17]

Carlos Marcello would have considered all that, and more, before making a decision about helping Joseph Milteer and his group. Meanwhile, events would continue to unfold with his drug network, James Earl Ray, and the CIA that might have influenced Marcello's final decision.

Chapter Forty-two

In the fall of 1967, CIA Director Richard Helms had his hands full with the aftermath of Israel's Six-Day War in the Middle East, Cold War fronts from South America to Europe, and especially Vietnam. He was constantly under pressure from the US military to cut in half CIA estimates of communist forces in South Vietnam, even as the number of US forces there approached half a million. AMWORLD veterans like Ted Shackley and "Chi Chi" Quintero were handling secret operations in Laos, where heroin trafficking was booming. Helms was also overseeing the CIA's own rapidly expanding illegal domestic surveillance operation, which would soon be named Operation CHAOS.[1]

As writer Verne Lyon pointed out, CHAOS grew out of the CIA's early Cuban operations with exiles in the US. It became so large that by 1964, President Johnson had authorized the CIA to create "a new super-secret branch called the Domestic Operations Division (DOD), the very title of which mocked the explicit intent of Congress to prohibit CIA operations inside the U.S." E. Howard Hunt was one of those assigned to this new branch, one of whose responsibilities "was burglarizing foreign diplomatic sites at the request of the National Security Agency (NSA)," something Hunt did until shortly before the final Watergate break-in. Lyon writes that "by August 1967, the illegal collection of domestic intelligence had become so large and widespread that [Helms] was forced to create a Special Operations Group [that] provided data on the U.S. peace movement . . . on a regular basis." By that time, Martin Luther King had become a major part of that movement.[2]

The Chief of Special Operations was Tom Tripodi, who said it was "responsible for extralegal domestic covert activities." He writes that "some of the guys who later would be bagged in the Watergate affair worked for me. I understand that when I left the Agency, most of the functions of [Special Operations] were transferred to a unit supervised by E. Howard Hunt."[3]

Oddly enough, the turf wars that had raged between the CIA, the FBI, and military intelligence were reduced somewhat by the cooperation necessary for their often illegal domestic spying. For example, the CIA and FBI were still overwhelmingly white, whereas Army Intelligence could easily field black operatives when needed. According to Verne Lyons, the CIA also expanded its cooperation "with local police and their intelligence units . . . and began in earnest to pull off burglaries, illegal entries, use of explosives, criminal frame-ups, shared interrogations, and disinformation." While federal agencies still protected their turf, they also had to share information and sometimes coordinate surveil-lance. Domestic surveillance information could flow from the FBI to police intelligence to the 111th Military Intelligence Corps to the CIA and back again, all below the radar of the American public and most of Congress and the press.[4]

By fall 1967, AMWORLD veterans Hunt, David Atlee Phillips, and David Morales had helped Richard Helms better control two areas involving domestic operations. The CIA continued to closely monitor the Garrison investigation and the prosecution of former CIA informant Clay Shaw, hindering the former and aiding the latter. Mainstream press coverage of Garrison was rarely positive, though how much of that was due to CIA efforts, and how much was because of Garrison's own fail-ings, can't be determined. Most important for Helms, Garrison's activi-ties no longer threatened to reveal his unauthorized operations, like the CIA-Mafia plots and their tie to JFK's murder. Also, the Jack Anderson articles had stopped, and the Rosselli matter appeared to have quieted down after the Mafia don's recent legal troubles with the Friars Club. The surge of pro-conspiracy JFK books had also ended, replaced by the publication of a few anti-conspiracy "lone nut" books and articles, some of which slammed critics of the Warren Report along the lines suggested in the CIA's January 1967 anti-critics memo.

As for Cuban operations, David Atlee Phillips was taking control just as the CIA scored one of its biggest Cold War propaganda victories: the capture and execution of Che Guevara, with the help of several veterans of AMWORLD and the Almeida coup plan. Che had returned to Cuba after his exile to Africa, though he made no public appearances and the Cuban populace had no idea what had happened to him. After Rolando Cubela's trial, Che had been sent on his second doomed mission, this time to Bolivia.

Richard Goodwin, JFK's first Latin American aide, wrote that "it is hard to think of a place where a guerrilla war would have been more certainly doomed than the Bolivia of the mid-1960s. Everyone in Bolivia was poor. The oligarchy had been driven from the country in the revolution of 1952 and the land redistributed . . . thus the revolutionaries had no oligarchs to terrorize, no wealthy businessmen to hate, and no large landowners from whom the soil could be wrested." Goodwin adds, "Nor were the stocky brown Indians of Bolivia likely to follow a romantic white Argentine suddenly materializing from a place as foreign to them as New York City or London. 'The inhabitants of the region,' Guevara wrote shortly before his death, 'are as impenetrable as rocks . . . you talk to them, and in the depths of their eyes it can be seen that they don't believe.'" Goodwin said "the outcome was inevitable. Outside the protective citadel of the Cuban island [Che] became an open target."[5]

In Bolivia, Che not only lacked support from the Indian peasants he was supposed to be fighting for, he didn't even have the backing of Bolivia's Communist Party. In addition, Castro kept Che's presence in Bolivia a secret, so Che couldn't attract international support or volunteers. In short, Che's mission to Bolivia was a death sentence.[6] Two years after Che's execution, historian Daniel James noted widespread belief, in some parts of the world, that Castro was responsible for Che's death: "There is a school of thought which believes that Fidel betrayed Che. Fidel, so its reasoning goes, deliberately sent Che to his doom."[7]

James notes that Castro failed to provide Che with the aid and publicity he requested and even refused to communicate with Che, leading James to ask, "Why would Fidel abandon Che?" James documents that Castro didn't tell Cuba—or the world—that Che was leading the fight in Bolivia, even when Che sent messages he wanted read to the public on major Cuban holidays. As a result, Castro was "depriving Che of . . . supporters inside Bolivia, where they were desperately needed. . . . Che Guevara gained no supporters anywhere for the principal reason that they did not know of his existence. To the world, Che Guevara was still 'dead' or otherwise disposed of." Castro's "silence had the effect of helping to bury Che," according to James.[8]

Castro was apparently determined not to rescue Che from Bolivia, as he had in the Congo, no matter how bad things got. Historian Jorge Castaneda pondered this issue in his recent biography of Che: "There was no lack of Cuban commandos who would gladly have given their lives to save Comandante Guevara" on a rescue mission to Bolivia. Castenada adds that "Fidel . . . might well have decided that a Che martyred in Bolivia would better serve the Revolution than a Che living." For example, Castaneda points out that a year after Che's death, "in 1968, the Cubans attempted a similar rescue mission in Venezuela; they were able to save twenty-four surrounded guerillas."[9] Yet Castro did nothing to save Che from certain death.

Che's fatal exile to Bolivia may have been the culmination of the suspicion Fidel had harbored against him since November 30, 1963, the eve of the original date for Almeida's coup, when Fidel reportedly had Che placed "under house arrest for plotting to overthrow Castro." Che's second house arrest in March 1965, shortly after exile Eloy Menoyo's capture—and when Fidel was receiving reports about Cubela's plotting with Artime—followed by Che's subsequent exile to Africa, suggest that Fidel suspected Che was plotting with Menoyo, Artime, and the CIA. If so, Fidel badly misjudged the situation, much to Commander Almeida's benefit and Che's regret.

Bolivian and CIA forces captured Che Guevara on October 8, 1967. Artime's former lieutenant in the later stages of AMWORLD—CIA veteran Felix Rodriquez—wrote a firsthand account of his involvement in Che's death. He was one of what some reports say were several CIA agents present for Che's execution. Felix Rodriquez gave the cover name for his "CIA colleague" there as Eduardo.[10] Castaneda writes that after Che was captured, he said, "Don't shoot, I am Che Guevara and I am worth more to you alive than dead." According to Castaneda, Felix Rodriquez "recalled how Che seemed to think he would be tried and sentenced, but not shot." Former JFK aide Richard Goodwin later wrote, "I had seen enough of [Che's] personal vitality, his love of life, to believe that he would have preferred survival—even as a prisoner—to martyrdom." However, Felix Rodriquez "remembered how the prisoner [Che] blanched when he heard the news that his fate was sealed" and he would be executed.[11]

Felix Rodriquez saw how low Che had sunk by the time he was finally captured—Castro's lack of support had taken a harsh toll. Rodriquez wrote that Che's "clothes were filthy, ripped in several places, and missing most of their buttons. He didn't even have proper shoes, only pieces of leather wrapped around his feet and tied with cord." Somewhat incongruously, the ragged Che had only one item of real value: his expensive "Rolex GMT Master" watch, which Felix Rodriquez wears proudly to this day.[12]

While Rodriquez has said the CIA wanted Che alive, E. Howard Hunt later stated, "We wanted deniability. We made it possible for him to be killed ... it was just important that it was done."[13] Hunt never explained why it was more "important" that Che be killed instead of captured. However, Almeida was still in place and unexposed at the time, and remained potentially useful. If Che were alive and kept in Bolivian custody or allowed to get information to the media, the CIA had no way of knowing what he might say about Almeida or the CIA's work with Cubela. Congressional investigator Gaeton Fonzi writes that David Morales claimed he was "involved in the capture of Che Guevara in Bolivia" and that Morales, formerly Phillips' superior back in pre-Castro Havana, had become "David Atlee Phillips's most valuable action man." Larry Hancock confirmed that "Morales' Army cover documents do show him as being assigned to Bolivia [in 1967]." David Morales later confided to his attorney and close friend that he "had the Bolivian police arrest [Che and] told them to shoot him."[14]

Back in Cuba, Castro got word of Che's death—but oddly, he was "frankly euphoric" about it, according to journalist Carlos Franqui. Shortly after that, Franqui finally left Cuba for good and never returned. Ironically, if Fidel really did want Che dead, either because of suspected coup plotting or just to eliminate a rival, then Hunt, Morales, Phillips, and Helms helped to give Fidel what he wanted.[15]

While Che's capture and execution in early October 1967 was a high point for Helms and Phillips, the rest of their operations against Cuba remained in transition. Longtime assets like Luis Posada and Antonio Veciana were being moved to foreign bases, while Felipe Rivero and his violent associates still faced legal problems. Aside from a few well-documented cases—like Posada, who remained on the CIA payroll—historians and Congressional investigators had trouble identifying which exiles were working for the CIA and which were acting on their own.

Drug smuggling among the (seemingly) former CIA Cuban exile operatives whom Tom Tripodi wrote about continued to worsen, and exiles—along with the Mafia and racist groups—remained major buyers for illegal guns and explosives. The situation was rife with opportunities for any of those groups to exploit. One person who apparently became involved in anti-Castro operations at that time, while running both arms and drugs, was James Earl Ray.

Chapter Forty-three

In early October 1967, James Earl Ray was still living at a rooming house in Birmingham, Alabama, as he prepared to enter a new phase of his criminal career. According to notes Congressional investigators obtained from an interview with one of Ray's brothers, Ray's "contact in Montreal [had] put him in touch with a guy in Birmingham." Ray's purpose in "going to Birmingham [was to] establish residence [and] live there while [doing] drug runs." Ray's Montreal contact "put him in touch eventually with The Fence in New Orleans," an older criminal connected to the Mafia whom Ray had known more than a decade earlier.[1]

HSCA investigators found that while he was in Birmingham, Ray had ordered photographic equipment from a Chicago firm, that Ray described as "a new type of camera or movie and had something to do with distant movie taking and infrared." Ray also purchased a .38 pistol and obtained an Alabama driver's license using the alias Eric Starvo Galt. Driving his 1966 white Mustang, by far the nicest car he had ever owned, Ray left Birmingham for Mexico on October 6, 1967.[2]

Ray later testified that he started "to make a detour to Dallas to consult an old acquaintance from Leavenworth," who had been "a narcotic smuggler in Mexico." Ray wanted the former drug smuggler to tell him "how to handle the current situation." However, Ray began to worry that his old friend "may be under surveillance," so he decided not to go. Ray said he stopped in Baton Rouge, Louisiana, and called a number he had been given in New Orleans. The person answering said Ray was to go "to Mexico [and] gave me an address and gave me a name of a motel in Nuevo Laredo."[3]

Ray originally indicated the "Mexican operation was going to involve narcotics." But he later mentioned that it was "what [he] thought was a gun deal." What type of a gun deal? The answer may lie in a statement to the press that one of Ray's brothers later released, saying it was based primarily on his conversations with Ray.

According to the press statement, James Earl Ray said he "was working with agents of the Federal government . . . they told me that I was helping them to supply arms and guns to Cuban refugees to overthrow Castro and the Communists in Cuba. The reason why I made trips to Mexico was in regard to helping the agents of the Federal government to supply arms to Cuban refugees there to overthrow Castro."[4]

When that statement about James Earl Ray and Cuba was first released to the press in 1969, more than a year after his capture for King's murder, Ray went ballistic. That reaction was unusual, because Ray was usually quick to go along with any story that would exonerate him, no matter how wild. The statement also indicated that Ray thought he was help-ing Cuban exiles "overthrow Castro" while he was in Memphis when Dr. King was shot, and "that the federal agents merely used me to be the fall guy when they killed King. I now realize they had no interest in overthrowing Castro."[5]

That would seem to be in line with other stories Ray told to depict himself as an innocent patsy, but Ray's response to the statement's release was angry and unprecedented for the usually cool Ray. He immediately issued a signed notice disavowing it, and for a time Ray even banned the brother who released it from visiting him in prison.[6]

When the statement about Ray and Cuban operations was released in 1969, the American press and public were largely unaware that the US government even had "federal agents" helping Cuban exiles after the Bay of Pigs fiasco. It would be the mid-1970s before that started to become widely known, because of the CIA operatives and Cuban exiles involved in Watergate and the resulting revelations about the CIA-Mafia plots.

When Ray's brother released the statement, he was working for J. B. Stoner, and Congressional investigators seemed to feel that Stoner was behind it, though Ray's brother denied it. (Ray refused to allow Stoner to testify to the investigators.) However, Stoner had no known involvement with covert Cuban operations. On the other hand, Stoner's associate Joseph Milteer had dealt with Guy Banister, who had numer-ous contacts in anti-Castro operations.[7]

A decade after the statement's release, Ray's brother clarified to the HSCA what was still a touchy subject, testifying that he wrote the state-ment based on conversations he'd had with Ray, who would "agree with the general thrust of his statement [even if] he might disagree with the emphasis" of certain parts. For example, he said that that James Earl Ray "thought he was working for" the "Federal agents" regarding Cuba, but "he didn't know [for sure, and] that was just suspicion on his part."[8]

Ray's sensitivity about the matter might be explained by the fact that Cuban exiles were involved in both drugs and explosive violence in

1967, at the time of Ray's trip to Mexico, and in 1969, when the statement was released. While Marcello's heroin network was ruthless, equally fearsome were the reputations of Cuban exiles like Felipe Rivero, who didn't hesitate to try to blow up their former comrades.

Ten years after the original statement was released, Ray himself talked about Cuba to Congressional investigators. His testimony not only indirectly confirms the statement Ray tried to disavow six years earlier, but also provides a reason why someone might have thought Ray would be drawn to Cuban operations, aside from the chance to make money. Ray testified that in late 1967, a contact in New Orleans "told him their next venture would be a gunrunning operation into Mexico" that would involve "some type of military equipment, rifles, or something." After "that Ray would end up in Cuba, from where he would be able to book passage anywhere in the world he wanted to go." That should have appealed to a fugitive like Ray, though Ray claims he told his contact he "wasn't too interested in [going to] Cuba."[9]

If Ray felt he was involved with "Federal agents [trying] to overthrow Castro," his suspicions evoke the experience of Antonio Veciana with "Maurice Bishop" (likely the alias of David Atlee Phillips), and Oswald's contacts with Phillips and Guy Banister. In Veciana's case, drugs were eventually also involved. Ironically, Richard Helms revealed in his autobiography the way someone like Ray might have been recruited for a CIA Cuban operation. He wrote that "in the real world," a person sought out for "an operation like this would have been recruited by a cutout" using an alias, "who would say he was fronting for some well-heeled [Cuban] émigrés. . . . It would have been a cash-and-carry event—all cash and no checks." If caught, the person recruited "would [not] have anything to reveal but a sterile telephone number and a physical description of" the man using the alias, "who would have vanished the moment" problems developed. In his autobiography, Helms was writing about Watergate, not Ray, but his account evokes not only the story of Veciana and "Bishop," but also James Earl Ray's tales about the mysterious "Raoul."[10]

Ray probably had not yet been offered the contract on Dr. King when he went to Mexico, since he was still proving himself as a member of Marcello's heroin network. That network also involved Cuban exiles, Cuban operations, and other forms of smuggling. Just nine months after Ray's trip to Mexico, a familiar name was arrested in a smuggling operation on the Texas–Mexico border that used ex-cons and anti-Castro operations: Trafficante's operative Frank Fiorini.

According to the Justice Department, Fiorini's scheme "was really a conspiracy to smuggle stolen automobiles out of the United States" into Mexico, which Fiorini claimed was all leading up to "a commando raid on Castro's Cuba." Using "ex-cons and [those with] military [experience]"—the same kind of background Ray had—Fiorini smuggled stolen cars, apparently along with firearms, from Texas into Mexico. One of Fiorini's men in the car-smuggling operation had also helped Fiorini spread John Martino's phony stories after JFK's assassination. The smuggled vehicles were late-model American cars, including Mustangs; Fiorini's men would drive them across the border into Mexico, return to Texas, and drive another car over the border.

Frank Fiorini's scheme went on for quite some time and involved more than a hundred cars, after which Fiorini and some of his men were captured in British Honduras while supposedly en route to Cuba. However, according to the *Miami Herald*, Fiorini called "somebody in Washington," and subsequently "a Fort Lauderdale lawyer says he got a call 'from a man at the State Department'" about representing the men. Fiorini and his crew were all released, with no charges at the time. The lawyer said, "I gather it had the tacit approval of somebody in the government, or they would have been in trouble." Fiorini was not prosecuted until five years later, after he was arrested for Watergate.[11]

Fiorini's scheme was just part of a large, ongoing operation involving Mafia associates of Marcello and Trafficante, the corrupt Mexican Federal Police (the DFS), and the heroin network they shared. As Peter Dale Scott noted, Sam Giancana and Richard Cain were living in Mexico, and their mob was "simultaneously involved in smuggling stolen cars . . . in an international ring which appeared to overlap with narcotics operations." The ring would last from the 1960s to the 1980s, when "thirteen DFS officials were indicted in California," though the "DFS Director . . . was initially protected from indictment by the CIA."[12]

In the fall of 1967, James Earl Ray was just a very small cog in the Mafia's smuggling operation in Laredo, Texas, site of the October 1963 heroin bust of the Marcello/Trafficante/Mertz portion of the French Connection heroin pipeline. On October 7, 1967, Ray said he crossed the border in his Mustang at Laredo, and in Mexico he checked into a Nuevo Laredo motel frequented by criminals, the type of place "where the owner is somewhat under suspicion."

Ray admitted he smuggled something in a spare tire from the US into Mexico and said he was paid "$2,000 [more than $12,000 today] in $20 bills." In addition, Ray said he was promised his employers would eventually provide him with travel documents under another name and "enough money for me to go into business in a new country. He mentioned 10 or 12 thousand dollars. He also said it would involve taking guns and accessories into Mexico." With the man Ray called Raoul was "a Mexican, with Indian-like features." Ray planned to go to Los Angeles after he left Mexico, but he would remain south of the border for another month.[13]

Ray drove across Mexico, to Acapulco for a few days, then to Puerto Vallarta for the rest of his time. He frequented a Mexican prostitute and may have trafficked in marijuana, but the real money was in harder drugs. According to one of Ray's brothers, when he left Mexico for California in mid-November, Ray "hauled dope to LA." His brother said that Ray "carried the drugs on his person . . . and delivered them to someone at the St. Francis in Los Angeles."[14]

Apparently, Ray was well paid and expecting even bigger money soon, because in Los Angeles he rented an apartment on November 19, 1967, and soon began an unusual spending spree. It would include six visits to a clinical psychologist to learn about self-hypnosis (the practitioner was only one of several Ray would consult), $364 for dance lessons, and even plastic surgery. Ray had shown the mob he could handle jobs effectively, so they gave him more assignments, including one that would require him to drive across the country to New Orleans to meet with associates of Carlos Marcello.

Johnny Rosselli faced a new legal challenge on October 27, 1967, when "Rosselli was indicted under the Alien Registration Act" for being an illegal alien, according to G. Robert Blakey. Rosselli had been in the clear by May 1967 as a result of the pressure his leaks to Jack Anderson had generated on Helms and the CIA, but his recent Friars Club charges had helped to revive the immigration case.[15]

As he had done before, Rosselli turned to his old friend William Harvey for help. Rosselli called Harvey on the day of his indictment, asking Harvey to represent him, but he declined. However, Harvey still wanted to help his friend, so he tried to pressure the CIA's FBI liaison, Sam Papich, over lunch on November 6, 1967. Harvey became "incensed" when Papich suggested that he end his relationship with Rosselli. Instead, Harvey warned that if he cut off Rosselli, "the Agency could get itself in serious trouble"—which sounds like Harvey was threatening that he or Rosselli might reveal more about Helms's unauthorized operations to someone like Jack Anderson.[16]

Rosselli met with Harvey on November 26, 27, and 28, 1967. Though Harvey was technically with the CIA for retirement purposes until the end of the year, he was no longer an active agent. Harvey was bitter at the Agency and seemed to side completely with Rosselli. Apparently, he still had some influence in the Agency because within a couple of months, the FBI would be complaining about pressure to end Rosselli's prosecution.[17]

For Bobby Kennedy, the fourth anniversary of his brother's slaying was very different from the previous year. In the fall of 1967, Bobby constantly had to tell aides and the press that he wasn't going to challenge LBJ for the presidential nomination. Yet he made clear in his private comments (though much less so in public) that he was very critical of LBJ for not pursuing peace talks to end the conflict in Vietnam, or finding a way to scale back the war. Whatever had transpired with LBJ back in the late spring of 1967, when the Jack Anderson articles had stopped, still seemed to have Bobby in a straitjacket.

Bobby's appearance on CBS's *Face the Nation* on November 26, 1967, poignantly brought home his uneasy and almost untenable dichotomy. Just four days after the anniversary of his brother's murder, one almost surreal exchange reflected his lingering despair over JFK: Three newsmen, including Roger Mudd and the *New York Times'* Tom Wicker, pressed Bobby to resolve the apparent discrepancy between his opposition to the war and his support for LBJ. If Bobby wanted to end the war, wasn't it inevitable that he would have to challenge LBJ for the presidency?[18]

An obviously uncomfortable Bobby could only respond, "I don't know what I can do to prevent that or what I should do that is any different other than try to get off the earth in some way."[19]

The newsmen sat stunned for a moment before one of them said, "Senator, nobody wants you to get off the earth, obviously." They backed off, claiming, "Nobody is trying to put you on the spot, really." Of course, that's exactly what they were doing, yet they, like Bobby's own staff and advisors, simply couldn't understand why he felt he couldn't run—and Bobby couldn't tell them.[20]

Bobby probably noticed that instead of a rising tide of JFK conspiracy articles in the mainstream press, most had reverted to generally supporting the Warren Report and reporting skeptically, often with hostility, about Garrison's investigation. No one else in the news media had picked up on his leaks to *Life* about Carlos Marcello, meaning that the national press still had not linked the godfather and the Mafia to JFK's murder. Two months would pass before Bobby would try again to focus press attention on Marcello.

One article that certainly caught Bobby's attention was the December 6, 1967, *New York Times* report on Abraham Bolden. Headlined "Plot on Kennedy in Chicago Told," the story marked the first time the press had revealed anything about the attempt to kill JFK in Chicago three weeks before Dallas. Bolden was still in prison at the time, and his attorneys, including Mark Lane, had generated the article in an attempt to garner publicity for his appeal. However, the article produced little follow-up, and the story soon died (or was suppressed).[21]

For Bobby, the article would have been a painful reminder of the secrets that kept him from challenging LBJ. Based on our talk with a close Kennedy associate, it is clear that Bobby wanted to help Bolden— but Bobby knew that any action on his part would bring up matters that could prevent him from ever being in a position to bring JFK's killers to justice.[22]

Unnoticed by the general public, some private citizens were taking action. Bernard Fensterwald, former Senate investigator for Senator Edward Long when the CIA-Mafia plots had surfaced briefly in their private discussions, was now trying to aid Jim Garrison. He had interviewed William Somersett about Milteer, and would soon interview four Chicago newsmen, some of whom confirmed hearing about the plot to kill JFK in Chicago on November 2, 1963. Still, Fensterwald was an attorney, not a journalist, and he knew he needed all the facts before he tried to go public. At the time, it would have been hard for Fensterwald to see how Milteer's story fit in with the Chicago threat and the CIA-Mafia plots to kill Castro, especially since Garrison kept chasing (or being diverted to) so many blind alleys that needlessly complicated things.[23]

Also taking notice of the *New York Times* article about Bolden and the Chicago threat was the CIA, which generated a memo about the matter. The CIA memo contained information linking Cuban exiles to the Chicago threat, something that hadn't been mentioned in the *Times* article. The CIA's Bolden memo also brought up their former asset from 1963 and the CIA-Mafia plots, Richard Cain. Richard Helms was no doubt glad when the media did not pursue the *Times*'s revelation about Bolden and Chicago—though whether the CIA had anything to do with that is unclear, since the CIA's file on Abraham Bolden, and many of its records on Cain, have never been released.[24]

Chapter Forty-four

Carlos Marcello apparently decided to become involved in the hit on Martin Luther King, soon after the fourth anniversary of JFK's assassination. But unlike in JFK's murder, Marcello was not the driving force behind Dr. King's assassination. He was only the high-level broker for the contract from Milteer's small Atlanta group, and was extremely well paid to make sure the right people were in place to do the job.

If the information in the Justice Department memo is correct, the fee of $300,000 (almost $2 million today) that Marcello demanded is more than twice what Milteer's group had originally been willing to pay—but nothing else had worked, and Milteer knew the power Marcello could bring to bear on the murder and its aftermath. Because much of the Milteer group's money was invested in North Carolina mountain real estate, it likely took them some time to raise the $300,000 in cash. Other wealthy racist supporters, on the level of Sutherland in St. Louis and some referred to (though not by name) in the Justice Department memo, may have contributed as well.

For holding a few meetings, Marcello would clear the equivalent of nearly $1 million in today's dollars. He would also have the potential of getting even more from the leverage Marcello would gain over the racists putting up the money, as mentioned in the Justice Department memo. In a typical mob contract, Marcello would take at least half off the top for himself. The remainder would be used by whatever Mafia lieutenant was delegated the main task of coordinating the hit. That person would work with other trusted mobsters to hire the hit man and others needed, and to arrange bribes if necessary. By the time the hit man got his share of the money, it could be as little as $10,000 or $20,000.

Despite the money, Carlos Marcello would not have become involved unless he wanted King dead as well, and was certain his participation would not expose his role in JFK's murder. As for the latter concern, the fact that his name—or any mention of the Mafia—had failed to surface in the JFK anniversary's press coverage showed him that his efforts to divert and compromise Garrison had worked, leaving him with nothing to fear.

As for Martin Luther King, he had publicly declared the Mafia his enemy two years earlier, writing in the *Saturday Review* that

> Organized crime . . . flourishes in the ghettos—designed, directed, and cultivated by the white national crime syndicates operating numbers, narcotics, and prostitution rackets freely in the protected sanctuaries of the ghettos. Because no one, including the police, cares particularly about ghetto crime, it pervades every area of life.[1]

Black journalist Louis Lomax wrote that shortly before Martin Luther King was killed, Dr. King "was on the verge of exposing . . . the influence of the underworld in ghetto economic life [so] I was surprised [when] Martin did not disappear into Lake Michigan, his feet encased in concrete."[2]

As detailed in Chapter 41, Carlos Marcello had many reasons, both racial and financial, to want to eliminate Martin Luther King. Given all of those factors, it's not hard to understand why Marcello decided to broker Milteer's contract. Before making that decision, Marcello and his lieutenants in New Orleans, such as Frank Joseph Caracci or Jack Liberto (related to Memphis's Frank C. Liberto), would have carefully considered the people in their organization to find someone who could be used in the hit and could take the fall.

Once Marcello had agreed to broker the contract to kill Dr. King, it's possible that James Earl Ray was not his first or only choice, in the same way that Marcello had originally planned to kill JFK in Chicago or Tampa before finally succeeding in Dallas. Ray's last attorney, William Pepper, found three witnesses who said a Tennessee man named "Red Nix [who] knew Marcello and undertook various jobs for him [had] been given a new car and a rifle and paid $5,000 a week to track and kill King," with a promise of $50,000 "if he succeeded." Supposedly, the contract "came directly from New Orleans and Carlos Marcello."[3]

However, using someone like James Earl Ray had several advantages for Marcello and Milteer. Ray had no long-term ties to Marcello's organization and none at all to Milteer's white supremacist groups. In fact, someone would have the previously nonpolitical Ray suddenly become very active in supporting George Wallace's American Party, almost as if Ray needed to buttress the fact that he was clearly a racist. Unless he was acting under orders, it makes little sense for a fugitive like Ray to have called attention to himself in such a manner. On the other hand, Ray's seeming political involvement would help to convince the press and public that he had murdered Dr. King on his own, for racial reasons. The House Select Committee on Assassinations (HSCA) found that "while unsympathetic to the civil rights movement, he [Ray] did not manifest the type of virulent racism that might have motivated the assassination in the absence of other factors." Instead, "the Committee . . . concluded that the expectation of financial gain was Ray's primary motivation [because] historically, Ray was a financially motivated criminal."[4]

While "the Committee concluded that there was a likelihood of conspiracy in the assassination of Dr. King," and that "James Earl Ray assassinated Dr. Martin Luther King Jr. as a result of a conspiracy," it didn't have access to the information we have today, which shows Marcello's and Milteer's involvement.[5] James Earl Ray's connections to organized crime dated back to the 1950s, according to an inmate who served time with him at Leavenworth and the Missouri State Penitentiary. As recorded in FBI files, prior to being sentenced to Leavenworth in 1955, "Ray had another close friend . . . of Italian descent, apparently a 'big man' in the syndicate. This Italian had apparently operated with Ray in the past, and both he and Ray had engaged in handling stolen Postal money orders and travelers checks." Ray said he had "operated" in Illinois in the 1950s, engaging "in burglary and payroll jobs." The inmate said that "Ray mentioned underworld and hoodlum connections . . . in Chicago, Detroit, Tampa, and the Tijuana, Mexico area."[6]

The inmate "stated that Ray had a friend in New Orleans, Louisiana [whose name is censored in the FBI report], who was apparently a 'fence.'" This fact appears to confirm Ray's brother's account that Ray knew an experienced "Fence" in New Orleans. The inmate said "this man was well connected with the hoodlum element," but by 1968 he would have been in his late sixties. Still, the inmate felt that "this individual would definitely harbor Ray," even as a fugitive. After Dr. King's death, the inmate said "he would not be surprised if James Earl Ray was the murderer of Martin Luther King, however, he does not believe Ray would have killed King without being paid for it." (When the inmate told that to the FBI just three weeks after King's assassination, he "said he would not testify . . . because if he did . . . he would fear for his life." He spoke to the press and Congressional investigators, but not about Ray's ties to the Mafia.)[7]

James Earl Ray had been drawn into Marcello's heroin network the same way as other experienced, low-level criminals who had the right contacts. Starting in Montreal and continuing in Mexico, Ray had proved he could handle the travel, the secrecy, the drugs, and large sums of money without drawing attention to himself. Ray's long-standing habit of being tight-fisted with money was an asset in that regard—which was another reason why his spending spree in Los Angeles was so unusual for him. While Ray had been successful on recent smuggling runs, he wasn't an essential part of Marcello's organization and was the type of disposable felon who wouldn't be missed after Dr. King's murder.

For the hit on Martin Luther King, an outstanding shooter wasn't needed. Unlike with JFK, Dr. King had no mass of trained and armed security usually surrounding him, and there was no need to shoot King in a motorcade. The assassin could wait until King was a stationary target, so what was needed was someone who could patiently stalk him.

Since Ray had first been used in the Detroit–Toronto–Montreal heroin network under the control of Carmine Galante—the man whom Hoffa had told about his contract on Bobby Kennedy—it's tempting to speculate that Ray might have been considered for that operation. However, that contract would have been activated only if Bobby decided to run, and Bobby was adamant in his public statements in the fall of 1967 that he would not do so.

Because that heroin network specialized in providing aliases and cover identities, Marcello's associates could offer Ray something more than just money for participating in the hit on Dr. King. "Galt," as well as the other Toronto aliases Ray would soon use, were helpful in the US and were probably provided by Galante's Toronto associates. But the Mafia could also promise Ray secure travel documents (passport, visa, etc.) as part of a cover identity that he could use to establish himself in another country. Apparently, Ray envisioned himself running a bar in such a place with his stake from killing King, so he would enroll in bartending school.[8]

Some writers have speculated that Ray knew about the contract on King from hearing about it in prison, so it's possible that Ray may have been the one to initially approach associates of Marcello about it at some point. An FBI report claims that Ray told a fellow inmate at Missouri State Penitentiary that someone in St. Louis was offering $50,000 to kill Dr. King. Ray told the inmate he could also get $50,000 just for helping, and even if they got caught, as long as they killed King in the South, they would have no problems with a jury.[9] Ray could have heard about Sutherland's offer to Russell Byers, the brother-in-law of Ray's prison buddy John Spica. Also, Ray's brother later indicated in an interview that James Earl Ray knew that the King contract was somehow related to Leander Perez, the Louisiana political boss close to Carlos Marcello—

but Ray didn't know how to approach someone like Perez or his associates. Once Ray became part of Marcello's heroin network, however, that wasn't a problem.[10]

Because of the usually sympathetic nature of juries in the South, Ray apparently told one of his brothers that "it had to be a southern State where he killed MLK," and the "main thing was Alabama—but if not there, Memphis." Notably absent were Marcello's Louisiana and Milteer's Georgia. Mississippi at the time was the focus of too much FBI and Justice Department undercover activity to be considered safe for a secure hit.[11] Ray said at one point that after King was murdered, "he figured [there] wouldn't be [an] all-out manhunt because Hoover hated King [and] didn't want him [to] come [to] Washington," for a Poor People's March in the spring of 1968. That sounds like something Ray might have heard from someone who was aware of the FBI's massive effort against Dr. King.[12]

On December 15, 1967, James Earl Ray abruptly left Los Angeles for a cross-country drive to New Orleans. The HSCA felt that "Ray's trip to New Orleans . . . was significant. The abrupt nature of his departure from Los Angeles, the risks he took on the road, his receipt of money during the visit, and the speedy termination of his mission all indicated Ray's involvement with others in an important meeting with a preplanned purpose."[13]

Within three months of interviewing Ray following his capture, author William Bradford Huie told Ray's second attorney, Percy Foreman, that he "believed that the decision to kill Dr. King was made in New Orleans by someone other than Ray," and that after spending time in New Orleans, Ray "was directed to do the killing." Huie also "believed the FBI would make an arrest in New Orleans. In addition, when [Ray's first attorney] showed Ray the witness list, Ray was interested only in certain witnesses from Louisiana. None of the other witnesses interested him, but he looked carefully at every name from Louisiana."[14]

Ray would be worried about people from New Orleans during his trial for killing Dr. King because, as he told his brother, "it is dangerous down there in New Orleans. They get pretty mean down there." Ray's December 1967 trip to New Orleans was also a drug run, and his brother said that Ray knew "for sure about [the] dope business . . . from New Orleans to LA." But as the HSCA noted, Ray's actions before, during, and after his New Orleans trip were also probably connected to his involvement in the conspiracy to kill Dr. King.[15]

According to information from the Justice Department memo cited earlier that was apparently withheld from the HSCA, "'Charlie Stein, a petty racketeer connected with organized crime, contacted James Earl Ray in Los Angeles and told him that there were people in New Orleans whom he ought to talk to.' Sartor states . . . that 'Ray was told that the people he ought to talk to would help him with money and his fugitive status.'"[16]

Charles Stein would accompany Ray on his long drive to New Orleans. The Fifth Circuit US Court of Appeals describes Stein as "a former resident of that city [who] in the mid-1950s [had] worked at several bars in the French Quarter . . . where he managed and ran dice tables. In the early 1960s, he ran a prostitution ring that included his wife. During the same period, he was also reputedly involved in selling narcotics—a favorite Mafia activity in New Orleans, along with gambling and prostitution. Later, in 1974, Stein was convicted of selling heroin in California."[17]

When the FBI interviewed Stein soon after King's murder, Stein claimed "the first time he ever saw [Ray] was on the night of December 14, 1967," just before the drive with Ray to New Orleans. However, FBI agents were suspicious about Ray's white Mustang being seen at Stein's place of employment. When the FBI told Stein it "had information which indicated that he was possibly engaged in the sale of some type of drugs, Stein admitted to having been arrested in the past for narcotics violations."[18]

After Dr. King's murder, Stein went to ridiculous lengths to deny that he was still involved in drugs in 1967, even when FBI agents told him they knew "there was an unusually heavy amount of traffic into" his home, including "young men seen lying in a stupor in his backyard." The FBI confronted Stein with the accusation that "the trip he made with [Ray] to New Orleans [was] made by the two of them to procure drugs." Stein denied that, but admitted Ray could have been using amphetamines. That explains why Stein and Ray claimed they were able to drive straight through to New Orleans and back again, without stopping at a motel.[19]

Ray's cover story for the trip was that he needed to bring back two children from New Orleans for a woman he'd met at a bar in Los Angeles. However, Ray told Stein that wasn't his real purpose for the trip and that "he was not doing anyone a favor, because he had business to conduct in New Orleans." Of course, having children in the car on the way back would have made Ray and Stein appear far less suspicious if they were stopped.[20]

When the FBI first interviewed Stein after Dr. King's death, Ray had not yet been captured, and the FBI clearly knew enough about Stein's drug dealing to make life very difficult for him. Stein told the FBI that Ray "mentioned the name and address of the person he was going to see" in New Orleans, which Stein claimed not to recall. However, Stein said "the name was an Italian-sounding name, was a well-known name in New Orleans."[21]

Stein appears to have been hinting that Ray's contact was in the Mafia, as a way to get the FBI to back off, either by offering the Bureau a lead if it went easy on him or because he'd heard about the FBI's reluctance to pursue Marcello's organization. In either case, his gambit appears to have been effective. There is no indication that the FBI seriously investigated either Ray's mob-connected New Orleans friend, "the Fence," or the area of New Orleans that Stein said Ray intended to visit, "the Chalmette–Industrial Canal area of New Orleans."[22]

One of Ray's brothers said that in addition to "the Fence," James Earl Ray "had [another] contact in New Orleans . . . Eddie was his dope contact in New Orleans." Apparently, Ray was afraid of Eddie and his boss. After Ray's guilty plea for King's murder, Ray would ask his brother to call Eddie in New Orleans to "tell him everything was okay from James . . . he wanted Eddie to know he hadn't talked, wasn't going to talk." As another of Ray's brothers later stated, "If [Ray] did kill King he did it for a lot of money—he never did anything if it wasn't for money—and those who paid him wouldn't want him sitting in a courtroom telling everything he knows."[23]

Ray said that he met with someone in New Orleans to talk about "gunrunning into Mexico, and . . . Cuba." The HSCA also investigated a rumor that Ray met with three of Carlos Marcello's associates in New Orleans. (William Sartor uncovered information about the meeting after the earlier cited Justice Department report had been completed.) The HSCA, apparently lacking that report and its references to Sartor's sources who were close to Marcello and the Mafia, said it had "no information about how he discovered that such a meeting occurred."[24]

According to the HSCA, Sartor's unpublished manuscript named three people who allegedly met with Ray: "Sam DiPianzza, Sol La Charta, and Lucas Dilles were also at the meeting. DiPianzza and La Charta were described by Sartor as involved in organized crime, as well as avid racists. Dilles, also a racist, was allegedly connected with the late Leander Perez, Louisiana political boss and virulent segregationist."[25]

Sartor had apparently only been told the names of the men who met with Ray, and knew them only phonetically, but "further investigation by the [HSCA] revealed that the correct spelling for names of the persons alluded to by Sartor was Salvadore 'Sam' DiPianzza [and] Salvadore La Charda," and a New Orleans physician. "Sartor believed both DiPianzza and La Charda had direct ties to Marcello"; the HSCA was able to confirm that for DiPianzza. The HSCA called DiPianzza a "gambler and bookmaker with reputed connections to Marcello and other underworld figures . . . 3 weeks before the alleged meeting, DiPianzza was sentenced to 10 years in prison on a gambling conviction [but] was free on bond at the time of the alleged meeting." Also, "DiPianzza [was] unable to account for [his] whereabouts" at the time of the alleged meeting with James Earl Ray. As for Salvadore La Charda, Congressional investigators discovered he had worked for the "St. Bernard Parish Sheriff's Office [and] had no criminal record," but had "committed suicide in June 1968," the same month James Earl Ray was arrested for assassinating Dr. King.[26]

Because of a mistaken middle initial, the HSCA misidentified the physician who was apparently involved in the meeting. When two later authors quoted and cited that part of the HSCA report, the physician sued them in a New Orleans court in 1989. A federal judge dismissed his lawsuits in 1990, but the US Circuit Court of Appeals reinstated them in 1991, and the physician won a $2 million judgment from a New Orleans jury in February 1995. According to an interview with the physician's attorney, the publishers of both books later settled the suits for an undisclosed amount.[27] The doctor at the meeting was a different physician, who had the same first and last name but a different middle initial. This other physician was related by marriage to Carlos Marcello's sister, Rose.[28]

Sartor had reported that Ray's meeting took place at either Marcello's Town and Country Motel or the Provincial Motel in New Orleans. From December 17 to 19, 1967, the HSCA found that Ray had stayed at the Provincial, described by John H. Davis as "a mob hangout" at the time. Records for the Town and Country "were no longer available" to Congressional investigators. Finally, Ray admitted "to author William Bradford Huie that he left New Orleans with $2,500 in cash and the promise of $12,000 more for doing one last big job in 2 to 3 months." Dr. King was killed three and a half months later.[29]

Ray stayed in New Orleans from December 15 to December 22, 1967, but the HSCA says Ray never "described his activities during [the last] two days" of his visit. Marcello, Stein, and DiPianzza all denied to the

HSCA that any meeting with Ray took place. But we believe that the weight of the evidence, including material not available to the HSCA, shows that Ray became involved in the contract to kill Martin Luther King at that time.[30] Ray could have approached Marcello's people about the King contract after hearing about it in prison, or Marcello's lieutenants could have approached Ray after Milteer and Marcello had struck a deal—or it could have been a combination of the two. The bottom line is that when Ray left New Orleans, he was part of the plot.

Chapter Forty-five

After his cross-country trip to New Orleans and back, James Earl Ray returned to Los Angeles. He would remain there for the next three months, except for taking a brief New Year's Day trip to Las Vegas. It seems odd Ray would want to miss the Vegas New Year's Eve celebrations, especially given his recent free-spending ways, but on January 1, 1968, Ray probably had other business in the Mafia-dominated city.

During his early 1968 stay in Los Angeles, Ray became even more obsessed with self-hypnosis, and, following several sessions with his first therapist, he visited a new "psychologist-hypnotist" on January 4, 1968. Ray told William Bradford Huie that while he was in Los Angeles, he visited "seven other psychiatrists, hypnotists, or scientologists." At the time, self-hypnosis was in vogue as a way for people to lose weight, stop smoking, or accomplish other tasks for which they lacked the necessary willpower. Though Ray was an armed robber, he had never killed or even shot anyone, so it's possible he wanted help in learning how to focus his mind on his lethal goal.[1]

Ray continued his unusual spending spree in other ways, attending frequent dancing lessons and enrolling in bartending school on January 19, 1968, apparently in anticipation of running a bar in some exotic locale with his windfall from killing Dr. King. As for the money he was spending in Los Angeles, a 1977 Justice Department Task Force states that "the sources for Ray's funds still remain a mystery today."[2]

Until the time was right to assassinate Dr. Martin Luther King Jr., Joseph Milteer and Carlos Marcello needed ways to keep an eye on James Earl Ray in Los Angeles. They had to use people they could trust; they apparently chose two Los Angeles men who were later linked to Dr. King's murder. One of the men, Reverend Wesley Swift, was a longtime associate of Milteer, while the other man was tied to Ray by physical evidence and had worked with Marcello for years: Johnny Rosselli.

According to the FBI, Milteer's associate "Wesley Swift [was] the single most significant figure in the early years of the Christian Identity movement," which later evolved into today's Aryan Nations. Swift was also a fanatical racist who considered black people subhuman. Veteran journalist Peter Noyes wrote that Swift was "one of the most notorious right-wing extremists in California," created paramilitary groups, and "was also identified by the California Attorney General as a Ku Klux Klan organizer [and] a former KKK rifle team instructor." Swift even had a rifle range in his backyard.[3]

Joseph Milteer's ties to Swift dated back to at least 1963: Four days after JFK was assassinated, informant William Somersett gave a taped interview to Miami police about his conversations with Milteer. Somersett told police that after Milteer indicated that the JFK "conspiracy originated in New Orleans," Milteer "mentioned Dr. Swift very often [and said] what a great man he was." An FBI report confirms that Milteer was working closely with Swift at the time, and that the Bureau had received information on December 31, 1963, that "Milteer advised that he had been to the West Coast, where he was in contact with Dr. Wesley Swift [in] Los Angeles. Milteer stated that the meeting with Swift was very profitable," and that they were making more plans for the future.[4]

In March 1968, a young man named Thomas Tarrants, arrested three months earlier with Klan leader Sam Bowers for having "a machine gun . . . in a stolen car," jumped bail in Mississippi. According to Pulitzer Prize–winning *Los Angeles Times* correspondent Jack Nelson, Tarrants then "set out on a trip for the West, visiting the anti-Semitic Dr. Wesley Swift. . . . Tarrants would later testify [that in March 1968] he bought a rifle from Swift with plans to use it to shoot Martin Luther King. [Tarrants stated,] 'That was my ambition, to shoot Dr. King.'"[5]

According to the *Jackson Clarion-Ledger*, "at the time Tarrants met Swift . . . James Earl Ray was living in Los Angeles—about an hour away." Tarrants would apparently leave California around the same time as Ray, as we'll detail in Chapter 47. On March 23, 1968, Tarrants would reportedly be in Alabama, less than sixty miles away from Dr. King, though Ray would be much closer. After Tarrants spotted FBI agents at his house several days before Dr. King's murder, Jack Nelson writes that Tarrants fled to "a safe house located in the mountains near Franklin, North Carolina, staying with friends who were followers of Swift." Franklin is nine miles from Otto, North Carolina, where Milteer and his three Atlanta partners had been buying up mountain land with the money they collected at the Atlanta auto plant.[6]

Though Nelson wrote that "upon hearing the news [of King's murder] Tarrants danced for joy," Tarrants told the Jackson *Clarion-Ledger* in 2007 that he "had nothing to do with King's assassination" and was in Franklin, North Carolina, at the time. Tarrants also told the news-paper that while he didn't know of any plot to kill King involving Bow-ers' Klan associates, "I'm not saying they didn't," just that "I wouldn't have been told about it." On June 29, 1968, police shot Tarrants after he attempted to bomb the home of a Jewish leader in Meridian, Mississippi. His accomplice, attractive schoolteacher and avowed white supremacist Kathy Ainsworth, was killed. Tarrants was sent to prison, where he con-verted to mainstream Christianity, and was released shortly before the House Select Committee on Assassinations interviewed him. By then, Tarrants had renounced violence; he later became a prominent religious author, speaker, and leader.[7] We believe Tarrants' assertions that he was not involved in King's murder in Memphis, and that he didn't meet Ray. However, the cross-country proximity of Tarrants and Ray to Dr. King yields the possibility that Tarrants was being unknowingly manipulated or monitored by Milteer associates like Swift, perhaps in case anything happened to Ray before he could kill Dr. King.

Because Wesley Swift was willing to sell a rifle to kill Dr. King in early 1968, it's quite conceivable Swift would have aided his friend Milteer in the King assassination plot. This assistance could have involved his keeping track of James Earl Ray in Los Angeles, where Swift's church was located, or giving Ray a secure place to practice shooting, since no one has been able to document Ray's taking target practice in the years prior to King's murder. Swift died in 1971, though white supremacists and the Aryan Nations continue to lionize him.[8]

The other person tied to Milteer who could have helped with surveil-lance on James Earl Ray in Los Angeles was Johnny Rosselli. Both Mil-teer and Rosselli had been involved in JFK's assassination with Carlos Marcello, and each had met with Guy Banister in New Orleans in the summer of 1963. James Earl Ray definitely had some connection to Ros-selli, based on a hand-marked, detailed street map of Los Angeles that the FBI found in Ray's Atlanta room shortly after Dr. King's murder. The map, with its few markings, has long been known to authorities and was available to the House Select Committee on Assassinations.[9]

Compared with Marcello and Trafficante, the HSCA devoted rela-tively little time to Rosselli in its investigation of JFK's assassination, even though Rosselli's own murder had helped to launch the HSCA's investigation. Johnny Rosselli's name didn't surface at all in the HSCA's King investigation, and one reason for their lack of focus on Rosselli was that the CIA and FBI withheld important information about him from both the HSCA and the Miami police. The withheld information included AMWORLD exile leader Manuel Artime's work on Rosselli's CIA-Mafia plots in 1963, and FBI Miami surveillance reports on Rosselli from the fall of 1963, when Rosselli allegedly met twice with Jack Ruby. Further complicating matters was that Rosselli's slaying, tied to Trafficante, was an open murder case during the HSCA hearings. The HSCA also had not heard about Rosselli's confession to JFK's assassination, made to his attorney shortly before he was killed. The result was that no Congressional investigator checked the few marks on James Earl Ray's Los Angeles map to see if they were connected to Rosselli.[10]

James Earl Ray's detailed street map of Los Angeles had only ten marks on it, most in and around Beverly Hills—and one marked the block taken up by Johnny Rosselli's apartment building. Rosselli's lavish apartment was in the Glen Towers Building at 1333 South Beverly Glen, with Warnall Avenue behind it. During James Earl Ray's time in Los Angeles, he lived in and frequented considerably less affluent surroundings than the neighborhoods surrounding Beverly Hills. Ray lived in a seedy part of Hollywood when he first moved to Los Angeles, and on January 21, 1968, he moved three blocks, to the St. Francis Hotel on Hollywood Boulevard. The FBI described the St. Francis, where Ray had delivered his first heroin shipment in Los Angeles, "as a 'den of iniquity' teeming with prostitution and drug trafficking." Ray frequented a dive bar in the St. Francis called the Sultan Room and another bar nearby called the Rabbit's Foot—quite a contrast with the places Rosselli preferred, like Rodeo Drive and (until recently) the posh Friars Club.[11]

Ray's mark on Rosselli's building is unconnected to any of Ray's known activities and was so far away from Ray's usual haunts that the Rosselli connection seems beyond coincidence. Ray took maps seriously in the weeks and months prior to Dr. King's murder. An Atlanta map (with one of Ray's fingerprints), found at the same time as the Los Angeles map, had only four marks: one near Dr. King's office and church, one near Dr. King's former home, and one at Atlanta's Capitol Homes housing project, where Ray would abandon his Mustang when connecting with Joseph Milteer.[12]

In late 1967 and early 1968, Rosselli was in a difficult legal and financial situation and could not have refused a request from Carlos Marcello to help monitor James Earl Ray in Los Angeles. However, we do not posit a major role for Johnny Rosselli in Dr. King's murder—most likely, it was simply a matter of Rosselli's having some trusted mob associate keep a discreet eye on Ray and his activities to ensure that he was doing what he was told, and nothing more. An experienced criminal like Ray might have become suspicious of some of the people he was dealing with, or even noticed the covert surveillance, and the mark noting Rosselli's apartment could have been the result of Ray's seeing one of those people enter Rosselli's building. The same might have been true of the other marks on the map in the Beverly Hills area, where Rosselli often spent time and may have met someone keeping an eye on Ray.

According to Ray's controversial statement, discussed earlier, in early 1968 he was still "working with agents of the Federal Government" as part of the effort "to overthrow Castro." Ray had apparently indicated to his brother, "At a later time, if necessary, I will give more extensive proof about the federal agents with whom I was involved."[13] No such proof ever surfaced, either from Ray or from CIA files, but since Rosselli had been active for three years in anti-Castro operations for the CIA, Rosselli or his mob associates may have used that as a cover story to Ray, as a way to keep tabs on him.

Just before James Earl Ray went to Los Angeles, and right after Ray left the city for good, Johnny Rosselli had several meetings with his good friend William Harvey, the former CIA officer who still had many contacts in the Agency. Later in the spring of 1968, Rosselli would be linked to a Los Angeles hit involving another old CIA friend, David Morales. Harvey had formerly been involved in Cuban operations, and Morales had been active in covert Cuban activities as recently as the fall of 1967. Morales would soon be working again with several AMWORLD veterans in the Far East, but would make at least one trip to the Los Angeles area. The possibility exists that Rosselli used his CIA associates to arrange surveillance of Ray as part of what Ray thought were operations directed against Castro. If that were the case, we can only imagine the consternation and cover-ups that would result after Dr. King's murder—the same result Rosselli and Marcello had manipulated to occur after JFK's assassination. Ray would claim that all of his activities, from the fall of 1967 through his time in Los Angeles and up until his trip to Memphis, were part of these anti-Castro gunrunning activities.

Declassified CIA files from late 1967 and 1968 about operations against Cuba are very sparse, after they came under the control of Morales's close associate, David Atlee Phillips. The files that have surfaced show that although operations were not as extensive as they had been in their heyday in the mid-1960s, some covert actions were still being undertaken. One of the few CIA agents with even partially declassified files for that year is Luis Posada; however, his CIA records sometimes don't match, indicating either sloppy record-keeping not typical of the CIA, or later tampering, perhaps after Posada became the prime suspect in the terrorist bombing of a Cubana airliner in 1976.[14]

The CIA admits that after Posada was fired in 1967 (or 1968), the Agency rehired him as a CIA contractor in 1968, and he remained one until at least 1975 (or 1976). The CIA retained Posada despite a February 1968 CIA report saying that he had a "tendency [toward] clandestine sabotage activities." Four months later, the CIA expressed concern about Posada's "unreported association with gangster elements."[15] Cuba expert Ann Louise Bardach writes that while Posada was employed by the CIA in 1968, he "worked closely with" a violent associate of Felipe Rivero, still facing charges for the Expo 67 bombing. CIA files say that by April 1968, "Posada [would be] working on [a] case involving possible smuggling from Miami to Venezuela, involved" with a "Negro who infiltrated . . . black power groups in Miami."[16]

We are not suggesting that Posada, or the CIA as an organization, had anything to do with Dr. King's death. However, the violent, lightly documented (and thus deniable) milieu of CIA Cuban operations under David Atlee Phillips in 1968 created a situation that "gangster elements" like Rosselli and Marcello could use to their advantage. To add to the murky picture, in early 1968, the Federal Bureau of Narcotics was being transformed into the Bureau of Narcotics and Dangerous Drugs, creating disruptions that didn't make it any easier for agents to spot Ray's drug trafficking.[17]

Some CIA officials and officers viewed Martin Luther King as the enemy, a perception that could have made them susceptible to manipulation. The following CIA Security Office memo from March 1968 shows how some in the Agency viewed Dr. King:

> The FBI noted that Dr. King has shown not only a willingness, but even an eagerness, to accept Communist aid, to support Communist causes, to confer with high-ranking Communist functionaries, and to rely heavily upon the advice and direction of dedicated Communists with concealed affiliation . . . one of these Communist advisors wrote King's vicious denunciation of US policy in Vietnam. . . . According to the FBI, Dr. King is regarded in Communist circles as "a genuine Marxist-Leninist who is following the Marxist Communist line."[18]

Whether the CIA memo is racist or simply Cold War paranoia is not clear, but it's erroneous on most counts. For example, King's only advisor with a hidden tie to American communists severed those ties in 1963, a fact that J. Edgar Hoover was well aware of and that an intelligence agency like the CIA should have known as well.

Before Dr. King openly joined the antiwar movement in the winter of 1967, most CIA surveillance of him was apparently obtained from agencies helping the FBI with its monitoring of King, such as the Miami Police Intelligence Unit. Only one of those files appears to have been declassified; it says the Miami police weren't even telling the FBI they were giving information to the CIA.[19] By early 1968, the CIA had its own domestic surveillance targeting the antiwar movement, including Dr. King. However, the CIA's actions against King were mild compared with those of the FBI.

The Senate Church Committee of the mid-1970s described the FBI's vendetta against Dr. King as a "war." Using the same techniques it applied against Soviet agents, "the FBI collected information about Dr. King's plans and activities through an extensive surveillance program, employing nearly every intelligence-gathering technique at the Bureau's disposal. . . . FBI informants in the civil rights movement and reports from field offices kept the Bureau's headquarters informed of developments in the civil rights field."[20]

The FBI's attempt "to destroy Dr. King as the leader of the civil rights movement entailed attempts to discredit him with churches, universities, and the press"—and that extended to smearing Dr. King to Congress and government officials. A major part of the FBI's operations against King, and the rest of the civil rights and peace movements, was through COINTELPRO, short for Counter-Intelligence Program. Started in 1956, LBJ's pressure on Hoover in 1964 caused the FBI's "COINTEL-PRO–White Hate" program to begin targeting with increasing effectiveness groups like the Klan. Ironically, because of the FBI's growing domestic surveillance of the peace movement, its efforts against King had started to diminish somewhat by early 1967—until King came out strongly against the war. With Hoover's Cold War mindset, the FBI Director felt renewed justification in going after King, and the summer 1967 race riots allowed Hoover to expand his operations against the entire civil rights movement.

The FBI created a new program called "Black Nationalist-Hate Groups," which targeted the SCLC, the Congress for Racial Equality, the Student Nonviolent Coordinating Committee, the Nation of Islam, and the Black Panthers. Dr. King was personally added to the list in February 1968, after Attorney General Ramsey Clark turned down Hoover's January 2, 1968, request for more wiretaps on King and the SCLC.

Hoover had no legal justification for going after Dr. King, who constantly preached against violence while condemning both riots and revolution. Taylor Branch quoted Dr. King as saying that "riots just don't pay off," and he urged "his staff to combat the 'romantic illusion' of guerrilla warfare in the style of Che Guevara." But that didn't stop Hoover from targeting Dr. King through the sometimes all-too-willing press. At one extreme, *Parade* magazine helpfully asked the Bureau if it could say the FBI "has a great deal of titillating information about [King's] sexual activities." The request was denied only because Hoover wanted to maintain the fictitious notion that the FBI wasn't "furnishing information to the public" about King. At the other extreme, and in a far rarer effort, Richard Harwood at the *Washington Post* was apparently disgusted by yet another FBI attempt to give "reporters tape-recorded evidence of [King's] 'moral turpitude.'" So, in late February 1968, Harwood mentioned the FBI's tactic in a column which also suggested that "Hoover had become a pampered tyrant with homosexual leanings."[21]

Around the same time, Martin Luther King became quite depressed during a short trip to Acapulco. Branch found that Dr. King "stared alone from a high balcony until nearly dawn" and wouldn't tell a worried aide what was wrong. It's not known whether King was despondent over the FBI's latest sexual blackmail, the constant stream of death threats, or other pressures in the SCLC and his home life.[22]

The FBI propaganda and dirty-tricks war on Dr. King were relentless. As Nick Kotz noted, the FBI created serious programs with silly names, like GIP (Ghetto Informant Program), the "'Rabble Rouser Index' [for] the level of threat posed by specific individuals," and POCAM, launched on January 4, 1968. The latter was a twenty-one-city COINTELPRO effort to sabotage Dr. King's Poor People's Campaign.[23]

On March 6, 1968, Hoover began a new COINTELPRO initiative to "prevent the rise of a 'messiah' who could unify and electrify the military black nationalist movement." Along with Dr. King, other leaders targeted were Elijah Muhammad, of the Nation of Islam, and Stokely Carmichael. A typical FBI trick involved telling Carmichael's mother the Black Panthers were going to shoot her son, causing Stokely to leave the country. FBI offices were given deadlines to submit ways "to pinpoint potential troublemakers and neutralize them before they exercise their potential for violence." Taylor Branch pointed out that many agents chafed at the request, while others wondered, "What did Hoover's nobly dramatic words really mean?" To "neutralize" someone?[24]

The number of FBI officials and agents involved in these efforts in some capacity surely ran into the hundreds, and Hoover's pressure created a situation in which Milteer or Marcello could have used a racist FBI agent or supervisor, either knowingly or unknowingly. For example, on February 15, 1968, Dr. King was followed in Mississippi by both the FBI, ostensibly to protect him, and by agents of the state's racist Sovereignty Commission. It's not clear whether the two agencies were in competition or if they were cooperating and sharing intelligence on Dr. King, but they could have been doing both, depending on the agents involved. Another way in which Milteer could have compromised an FBI agent or supervisor was if the man had friends or family in one of the White Citizens' Council chapters. While most FBI agents at the time simply tried to do a good job, the example their own director set created the potential for problems.[25]

The FBI also had excellent contacts with most city and state police forces, which furthered the Bureau's reach. Because Hoover's request for federal wiretaps had been refused, Hoover would need those local contacts, as well as Army Intelligence and the CIA, to help monitor Dr. King. The total number of local and federal officials involved in all aspects of the surveillance and operations against Dr. King and his movements would number in the thousands, given the extensive paperwork that was generated in those pre–desktop computer days.

For the murder of Dr. King in the South, Milteer and Marcello could have utilized one or more law enforcement officials in some way. Milteer's involvement in the plot to kill Dr. King yielded access to law enforcement officials and officers who would not have helped the Mafia, but who were so racist they would have willingly accepted a bribe to assist somehow with Dr. King's elimination.

Marcello and Milteer could also take advantage of others in law enforcement and domestic surveillance without making them knowing players in the plot to kill Dr. King. As in the JFK hit, they could glean and feed information and disinformation to the right people, who could be expected to react predictably based on their past behavior. These factors are important to keep in mind as the story of Dr. King's assassination unfolds.

Chapter Forty-six

Martin Luther King was encouraged to develop his last great initiative, the Poor People's Campaign, by several key people—including Bobby Kennedy. The idea of bringing people to Washington not just for one demonstration, but for a longer stay, was not new. One of Dr. King's advisors had in mind the "Bonus Army" from the Great Depression, the desperate World War I veterans who camped near the Capitol—until, on the orders of President Hoover, General Douglas MacArthur ordered his troops to forcibly disperse them. A few years later, under President Roosevelt, the veterans finally got what they wanted. Nick Kotz writes that "an encampment of the poor also had been suggested by [Bobby Kennedy], who passed the idea on to Dr. King via Marian Wright, an NAACP lawyer."[1] Kotz, who covered Bobby's transformative trip to Mississippi, writes that the Senator "was becoming more involved in poverty issues as he considered challenging Johnson for the presidency." While Bobby's concerns for the poor were genuine, he told Wright that in addition to being a way to "dramatize the issues of poverty [it would] give President Johnson trouble, a possibility Kennedy viewed with some relish."[1]

Bobby still wrestled privately with the contradiction of wanting to run for president while being constrained by whatever implicit understanding had been reached with LBJ the previous spring—when Bobby began publicly supporting LBJ after the Jack Anderson articles stopped. While the evidence shows that LBJ did not instigate the articles, he may well have prevailed upon Drew Pearson and Jack Anderson to stop them, to avoid embarrassment to his own administration. LBJ likely conveyed to Bobby, through any of several intermediaries on good terms with both men, that Bobby's public support of LBJ would ensure that the articles didn't resume. The two adversaries probably struck no formal deal, but Bobby's public remarks since the spring of 1967 demonstrated clearly that Bobby knew what he had to say, at least in public. Even when Bobby increased his rhetoric involving poverty and maintained his antiwar stance, his comments to the press stopped short of attacking LBJ, for whom he publicly expressed nothing but support.

Many people, from some of Bobby's advisors to the crowds who greeted the Senator, wanted him to run for president, and the news media constantly brought up the subject. Finally, on the morning of January 30, 1968, Bobby Kennedy told a group of journalists that he would not seek the Democratic nomination for president "under any conceivable circumstances." According to Evan Thomas, Bobby's press secretary, Frank Mankiewicz, almost immediately "softened the statement to read 'any foreseeable circumstances.' But the damage had been done. [Bobby] was brutally ridiculed on two prime-time comedy shows, *Rowan and Martin's Laugh-In* [America's most popular TV show] and the [overtly liberal] *Smothers Brothers Comedy Hour*, for, in effect, chickening out." An advisor told Bobby "the columnists and [political] cartoonists" were also hitting him hard. Bobby was being attacked because his public statements in late 1967 and early 1968 were so divergent from LBJ's position that the press and public expected him to join the race. They couldn't understand why he wouldn't—unless he was afraid.[2]

LBJ was still far ahead of the only other declared Democrat in the race, Senator Eugene McCarthy, running on a peace platform. But all that started to change on the afternoon of Bobby's January 30 statement, when the White House began receiving word that Saigon was under heavy mortar attack, even though it was the start of Tet, the three-day Buddhist holiday period. Within hours, it was clear that a major offensive by the Viet Cong had begun, as the US embassy and diplomatic compound in Saigon became a battleground. According to Taylor Branch, "Seventy thousand guerrillas [some estimates place the number of enemy forces far higher] launched similar attacks of coordinated surprise in" most of Vietnam's provinces. These would drag on for weeks, "killing nearly four thousand American and six thousand South Vietnamese soldiers, plus an estimated 58,000 Communist soldiers and 14,000 civilians."[3]

Richard Helms's earlier capitulation to US military demands to reduce by half the CIA's estimates of Viet Cong forces played a role in the debacle. Those lower estimates may have led LBJ, and the press and public, to underestimate the Viet Cong's ability to mount a countrywide, coordinated attack on such a large scale. Even after the US eventually triumphed in what has come to be known as the Tet Offensive, Helms's artificially low estimates would continue to affect US planning for the war, since it appeared that American forces had killed a much larger percentage of the enemy than they really had.

By 1968, the American public had been hearing from officials and the press for years that US forces had nearly prevailed and troops would start coming home soon. In the week before Tet, the White House and the US military had issued especially optimistic assessments of the war that were carried by outlets from the Associated Press to the *New York Times*. But the Tet Offensive shattered the rosy image LBJ and his generals tried to depict. One infamous incident and image from Tet galvanized the transition of American feeling about the war: a starkly disturbing photograph, taken near a Buddhist temple, in which the South Vietnamese national police chief fired a pistol point-blank into the head of a suspect. After that, Branch says, US polls "recorded the most decisive single drop in American support for the Vietnam War." Conversely, McCarthy's support increased to 40 percent in New Hampshire, site of the first primary race, giving him a real chance of beating the incumbent president.[4]

As Bobby Kennedy said, "Tet changed everything." He was finally ready to make his move, though carefully. Just nine days after saying he wouldn't challenge LBJ for the nomination, Bobby finally broke the mold of the preceding months—he gave an antiwar speech on February 8, 1968, that criticized, directly, LBJ's handling of the war. Bobby's advisors noted the change immediately, and talk about his challenging Johnson increased. However, the most recent historian to chronicle Bobby's last campaign, Thurston Clarke, pointed out that "Ted Kennedy, Ted Sorensen, and other former JFK White House aides . . . were strongly opposed to his running."[5]

But the tide of American opinion seemed designed to force Bobby's hand. In the wake of JFK's assassination, Walter Cronkite had become America's must admired newscaster and on February 27, 1968, he broadcast from Vietnam and pronounced it a "quagmire." On March 6, Cronkite took the then unprecedented step of announcing his opposition to the war during his broadcast, using terms like "futile" and "immoral." This was a courageous act at the time, as other news anchors remained neutral or, like ABC's Howard K. Smith, encouraged an expansion of the war.[6]

By March 10, 1968, Bobby Kennedy had begun to tell aides and associates, like Ed Guthman and Cesar Chavez, that he was going to run for the nomination. On the advice of Senator George McGovern, he decided to hold his announcement until after the March 12 New Hampshire primary, to avoid splitting the antiwar vote with Eugene McCarthy, which would have guaranteed a decisive victory for LBJ. Meanwhile, Bobby had worked hard in the Senate on a bill to protect civil rights workers; it had finally passed on March 11, 1968. Also supporting the bill was LBJ—so, at least at a distance, they had finally found some common ground. Martin Luther King also backed the bill, marking one of the last times all three men publicly shared the same objective.[7]

On March 12, 1968, the political landscape shifted dramatically when LBJ mustered less than half the vote in the New Hampshire primary. Though he still won, with 49 percent to Eugene McCarthy's 42 percent, LBJ, like much of America, was stunned. The next day, Bobby announced for the first time that he was "reassessing" whether to run. But Bobby still had several matters to consider before actually announcing his candidacy—including whether there was still time to stop Dr. King from endorsing McCarthy before Bobby was even in the race.

Martin Luther King's latest problem with President Johnson had been over the report of the Kerner Commission, appointed by LBJ following the previous summer's race riots. Headed by Illinois Governor Otto Kerner, the commission found that racism and poverty had caused the riots, and recommended a wide range of programs to address the issues. When news of the report broke on March 1, 1968, Dr. King had embraced its findings, even saying he might call off his Poor People's March on Washington—then scheduled for April 22—if its recommendations were implemented.[8]

In contrast, LBJ tried to ignore his own commission, viewing its report as a slap in the face to his own civil rights efforts. LBJ was having problems enough trying to fund the Vietnam War, and thought the country couldn't afford the antipoverty programs the Kerner Report called for. By 1968, LBJ had reduced much of his originally ambitious funding for his Great Society programs in order to fund the war and balance the budget. But Dr. King saw clearly what had happened: Vietnam was siphoning needed funds away from America's inner cities, and he was determined to support another candidate for the Democratic nomination.[9]

On March 14, one of Bobby Kennedy's aides began trying frantically to reach Dr. King, who was going to Los Angeles to address the California Democratic Council. Though the council was endorsing Eugene McCarthy, Bobby hoped that Dr. King could be persuaded to delay announcing his endorsement until after Bobby had officially entered the race. On March 15, Bobby's aide finally reached King, who agreed to Bobby's request.[10]

Bobby also had to deal with Lyndon Johnson. There was no point in entering the race only to be greeted by a new series of articles by Jack Anderson about Bobby's 1963 Cuban operations and JFK's assassination. To deal with that, Bobby apparently pursued two strategies. One, whose results wouldn't be widely available until April, will be discussed in Chapter 54. The other was a little-known plan that could have dramatically changed the course of US history and perhaps saved Bobby's life. Evan Thomas described it as "a last-ditch attempt to keep Kennedy out of the race." Bobby had his aide Ted Sorensen offer the White House "a deal: If the president would appoint a special commission to figure out how to extricate the United States from Vietnam, RFK would not run."[11]

Sorensen negotiated for three days with LBJ's latest defense secretary, Clark Clifford. (Robert McNamara had turned against the war and announced his resignation the previous November.) By the time Clifford officially assumed office on March 1, 1968, he was no war booster, and declassified files and tapes show that even LBJ was coming to realize the war was essentially unsustainable, with five hundred US soldiers dying in Vietnam each week. The US commander in Vietnam, General Westmoreland, would soon be asking for two hundred thousand more troops, raising the total US forces to seven hundred thousand—and that was just to maintain the status quo, not achieve any type of victory. Even worse, the general said an additional two hundred thousand troops might be needed the following year, bringing the US presence to nine hundred thousand. Yet LBJ couldn't bring himself to give up his tight control, especially to a commission suggested by Bobby, so the negotiations ended on March 14 with no deal reached. Still, the discussions served to put LBJ on notice that Bobby was planning to challenge him. The Jack Anderson articles about Bobby didn't resume at that time, perhaps because LBJ was coming to his own dramatic decision.[12]

Bobby must have wrestled with one other consideration about entering the race: the possibility of assassination. As his brother Edward Kennedy admitted in 1996, "We weren't that far away from '63 and that was still very much of a factor." Jackie Kennedy told Bobby that she thought if he ran, "the same thing that happened to Jack" would happen to him, because "there was so much hatred in this country, and more people hate Bobby than hated Jack." But Bobby seemed determined to run and was not going to let fear dictate his life—even though Hoffa's operative Frank Chavez had planned to assassinate him only a year earlier, and Bobby's secret investigations had indicated that Carlos Marcello was behind JFK's murder.[13]

As if in defiance of such concerns, on March 16, 1968, Bobby entered the race for president in the same Senate hearing room where he had first grilled both Jimmy Hoffa and Carlos Marcello, nine years earlier.[14] There, Bobby read a speech written primarily by Ted Sorensen, but Bobby must have debated privately what he would do if he were elected—and could finally finish the job against Marcello and the other mob bosses that he and Jack had begun in that very room. Since Bobby's own secret investigations had pointed to Marcello in JFK's murder, that quest would be more important than ever.[15]

Chapter Forty-seven

In Los Angeles, James Earl Ray continued to engage in activities that were at odds with his past behavior during January, February, and March of 1968. That the fugitive was spending months in the United States was unusual enough, since he could have stayed in Canada or Mexico, where he wasn't a wanted man. But instead of laying low in Los Angeles, someone had Ray pursuing a variety of activities that left a well-documented trail, mostly as "Eric Starvo Galt," but sometimes under his real name, which he gave to his first hypnotherapist.

The high school dropout suddenly seemed consumed with learning in Los Angeles, from continuing his bartending classes to attending more dance lessons. Ray also enrolled in a correspondence course in locksmithing, which could be useful in case he had to gain surreptitious entry to get a good shot at Dr. King. Ray continued his interest in self-hypnosis, and his third hypnotherapist, the "head of the International Society of Hypnosis," said later that Ray "was impressed with the degree of mind concentration which one can obtain." Anxious to be sure that he could do what was necessary when the time came, Ray even bought and studied the books the hypnotherapist recommended.[1] Ray also tried writing for a female pen pal through a "swingers'" magazine, sending a photo of himself and eventually writing five letters.[2] In all, Ray met dozens of people in Los Angeles, who would later provide authorities with an image of him that was far different from what he really was—a low-level drug runner with mob connections.

In early March 1968, Ray's spending spree continued as he underwent plastic surgery, paying $200 in cash (more than $1,200 today) "to change my facial features so it would be harder to identify me though pictures circulated by law officials." Ray had his pointed nose altered, and planned to have his large, prominent left ear fixed as well, but later said he "didn't have time for the ear" because he had been summoned back to New Orleans.[3]

According to Ray, "in late February [1968, my contact] wrote and asked me to meet him at the bar we had met in before, in New Orleans, [and] that we would go from New Orleans to Atlanta, Ga." Ray said he made a follow-up telephone call to New Orleans, and when he spoke to his contact, he received "more detail in the phone call than I usually got." According to Congressional investigators, Ray assumed "this trip was going to be the first leg of the gunrunning deal mentioned" on his previous New Orleans visit, the deal involving Cuba that could net him $12,000 and a new identity, complete with passport. The investigators received evidence that Ray told an associate about going to New Orleans, saying he "had a deal down there about some stuff to go into Cuba."[4]

In preparation for the trip, Ray wrapped up his dealings in Los Angeles. When he graduated from bartending school on March 2, 1968, Ray closed his eyes in his graduation photo, thinking it would make him harder to recognize. (An FBI artist would draw in the eyes for its first wanted poster, which used the photo.) After Ray's last visit to the plastic surgeon, on March 11, Ray said he pushed his bandaged nose to one side, so it wouldn't match any description the surgeon might later give of him or his work.[5]

The day before leaving Los Angeles, Ray probably heard about Klan convictions in the burning death of Mississippi civil rights worker Vernon Dahmer, since it was front-page news in the *Los Angeles Times* on March 16, 1968. While four men were convicted, justice in such cases was so lax that one of them didn't have to start serving his life sentence until thirty years later. Eleven more men indicted for the slaying were not tried at all, and it would take until 1998 for Klan leader Sam Bowers, who ordered the murder, to finally be convicted.[6]

That's why Ray apparently told one of his brothers "it had to be a southern state where he killed MLK." Ray thought he stood an excellent chance of being acquitted, even if he were caught and put on trial, as long as he killed Dr. King in the South. Ray had said "the main thing was Alabama—but if not there, Memphis," a preference that became very important on March 16, 1968, when Dr. King arrived in Los Angeles on a trip that would also take him to Alabama and Memphis over the next three days.[7]

On March 17, 1968, James Earl Ray would be within three miles of Martin Luther King, who was giving a speech in Los Angeles. At the same time, Ray was submitting a change of address (to "General Delivery, Main Post Office") for his move to Atlanta. Even though Dr. King's visit was widely reported in the press, Ray claimed he didn't know King was in Los Angeles on March 17, 1968. While it does not appear that Ray planned to kill Dr. King in Los Angeles, he may well have done some quick surveillance, to see what King's security was like. The following days would begin a cat-and-mouse chase across much of the US, as Ray began actively stalking Dr. King.[8]

While Dr. King was finishing his foray to Los Angeles, a late change to his schedule added a trip to Memphis, where he would address striking garbage workers. Because Dr. King's flights had to be rescheduled, after he left Los Angeles King would detour through New Orleans. Ray admits he left the city that same day for New Orleans. One of Ray's brothers reportedly said, "When Jimmy left Los Angeles he knew he was going to do it."[9]

Ray was unusually vague about his solo drive to New Orleans, meaning he could have remained in Los Angeles another day or left late in the evening, giving himself plenty of time to watch Dr. King. Ray offered to take some boxes of clothes to New Orleans, for the small daughter of a Los Angeles relative of Charles Stein, but the narcotics-linked Stein didn't go with Ray on this trip.[10]

According to Congressional investigators, unlike Ray's last drive to New Orleans, "this trip east was leisurely and took several days. Ray stopped at a couple of unidentified motels at night," using his Galt alias. The investigators note skeptically that even though Ray claims he "was a full day late getting to New Orleans," he didn't bother to call his contact from the road to tell "him he was behind schedule." Ray arrived in New Orleans after Dr. King's brief detour there en route to Memphis, which probably was nothing more than a coincidence—unlike the stalking Ray was about to begin. After arriving in the Crescent City, Ray called the "contact number," only to be told the person he was supposed to meet had already left, and would meet him at a lounge in Birmingham, Alabama, the next day.[11]

Ray was hazy about whom he spoke with on the phone in New Orleans, though it was apparently someone he trusted, since Ray says he followed the person's orders. As noted earlier, Ray's two regular New Orleans contacts were his drug supplier, named "Eddie," and his longtime, much older acquaintance known as "the Fence." But the person Ray spoke to would have been acting as a cutout, an intermediary, for one of Marcello's men involved in the King hit, like Frank Joseph Caracci. As with JFK's assassination, this setup illustrates the value of using those involved in Marcello's already cautious and secure heroin network for the King hit. Whoever Ray talked to wouldn't had to have been a knowing part of the King hit contract; the person could have just been an experienced member of the drug pipeline, used to pass along messages securely.[12]

In Memphis on March 18, 1968, Dr. King addressed a rally for the city's striking black garbage workers, who had been laboring under appalling conditions. The workers were barred from having union representation, even though Memphis bus drivers, teachers, and police were allowed to have unions. As a result, their starting pay was only a nickel above the minimum wage, there was no overtime pay, and workers were allowed no breaks. Matters had come to a head six weeks earlier, when two workers died after seeking shelter from a rainstorm in a garbage truck, where they had been crushed.[13]

Martin Luther King had been so alarmed by the workers' plight, and their so-far unsuccessful strike, that he had agreed to squeeze in a visit and supportive speech before his planned trips to Mississippi and Alabama. Dr. King's Memphis speech, before a crowd of seventeen thousand, was a resounding success, so King's aide Andrew Young passed him a note saying he might want to revisit Memphis soon. Another aide, Ralph David Abernathy, got the crowd to wait while Dr. King returned to the rostrum to tell the delighted crowd, "I am coming back to Memphis on Friday, to lead you in a march through the center of Memphis." The following day, Dr. King began his previously planned tour through Mississippi and Alabama.[14]

James Earl Ray couldn't have had much advance notice about Dr. King's first speech to the Memphis garbage workers, and the same is true for Milteer and the Marcello associates working on the King hit. However, Dr. King's visits to Mississippi and Selma, Alabama, were a different story, since they had been publicized ahead of time to generate crowds and volunteers for his Poor People's March to Washington. Ray's accounts of his actions during Dr. King's tour are very inconsistent, and made Congressional investigators highly suspicious that he was tracking Dr. King. Ray told William Bradford Huie he was in New Orleans on March 21, and Huie noted that King's plans to be near Selma the following day were "reported in the New Orleans news media of March 21st." Ray left New Orleans that evening, heading for Birmingham, but claims "it was dark" so he instead "stayed in a motel . . . between New Orleans and Biloxi, Miss." Both cities were in the domain of Carlos Marcello, who also had influence in Alabama.[15]

Ray told Congressional investigators that "the next morning [he] was back on the road headed for Birmingham, but somehow he got lost and wound up spending the night in Selma, Ala.," on the night of March 22. As in Los Angeles, Ray maintained he had no idea that Dr. King was going to be near Selma, in the town of Camden. The investigators wrote that Ray "strongly denies . . . that he was in Selma because Dr. King was in the area; he says that he accidentally got off the main highway onto a smaller road to Montgomery, and that he spent the night in Selma simply because that happened to be where he was when it got dark." But in an exchange with William Bradford Huie, Ray essentially confirmed Huie's statement that Ray "spent the night in Selma, not because you got lost but because you were stalking Dr. King."[16]

In Selma, Ray may have been armed only with his pistol, since he had not yet bought the powerful rifle that would be found after Martin Luther King's murder. If so, Ray was likely still attempting only surveillance of Dr. King, trying to see firsthand the type of entourage and security King had in the South. Also, the packed and hectic nature of Dr. King's schedule for that tour would have made planning an effective hit difficult. Dr. King sometimes traveled by car, and other times in a small Cessna plane, and weather problems caused him to cancel some appearances in Alabama. Dr. King's previously announced return to Memphis on March 22 was canceled early that morning, before King had a chance to leave for the city, because of a rare March snowstorm. Selma's newspaper reported that after his Alabama trips, Dr. King would return to Atlanta. On the morning of March 23, Ray says, he headed for Birmingham in his Mustang to meet his contact before heading to Atlanta.[17]

James Earl Ray apparently arrived in Atlanta, a city he had never visited, on the evening of March 23, 1968. According to Ray, his contact was with him and directed him to a particular section of Atlanta. The HSCA described the "neighborhood of Peachtree and 14th Street" as being "inhabited by motorcycle gangs and narcotics dealers and [it] seemed to Ray to be a bad choice." However, that description is incomplete, and the area, known as Midtown, was then a unique blend of fading affluence and Atlanta's burgeoning hippie scene. The area had been home to Atlanta's governor's mansion until the previous year, and while some of the stately city homes retained their original residents, others had been turned into rooming houses.[18]

Atlanta's Midtown was a magnet for those in, aspiring to join, or wanting to observe the emerging counterculture. Young people from other neighborhoods and Atlanta's exploding suburbs came to the area to buy an array of drugs. However, this was Atlanta in 1968, not Haight-Ashbury, and those who looked "straight," like Ray, were still a majority in the area. Also, while integrated to a small degree, the area was still overwhelmingly white. The number of people, apartments, rooming houses, and crash pads meant that Ray wasn't likely to make a memorable impression on many people.

James Earl Ray said that "his contact was 'familiar with the area,'" and they found an appropriate rooming house for Ray on their third try, at 113 14th Street. Ray said his contact wanted him in "that particular area," rather than in that particular rooming house. After Ray had found a place to stay, his contact left on foot, which tends to confirm the contact's familiarity with the area. Ray says his contact showed up again the next morning and told him he might need Ray to drive him to Miami at some point.[19]

Ray's contact could have been familiar with the area because he lived in or was a frequent visitor to the city, either as part of Marcello's drug network or Milteer's racist activities. In fact, since Milteer would soon help Ray escape from Atlanta after Dr. King's murder—which involved getting Ray back to his Midtown rooming house—it's possible that Milteer himself, or a close associate, may even have guided Ray to the neighborhood. As a frequent visitor to Atlanta, Milteer would know it well and could have had his own car parked nearby when he left Ray.

On March 25, 1968, Martin Luther King and Bobby Kennedy both had the assassination of John F. Kennedy on their minds. Dr. King was in Manhattan that night, after an exhausting day spent planning the Poor People's March with advisors in New York City, followed by giving a speech to a convention of rabbis in the Catskills. Back in the city at the end of a long day, Dr. King baffled one of his advisors by wanting to get out of their car and take a shortcut by walking along the Manhattan streets in the cool night air. Harry Williams had worried about Bobby Kennedy's doing the same thing when they were together in New York City, because he worried that the Mafia might shoot Bobby. Five years later, Martin Luther King's advisor was similarly concerned, and told Dr. King it would be less dangerous to stay in the car, but King wouldn't be deterred. Martin Luther King explained his preference for walking by saying, "If they couldn't protect Kennedy, how can anything protect me?"[20]

Dr. King accepted the risks involved in his work, and his attitude about them ranged from quiet resolve to stoic resignation. Taylor Branch pointed out that even "in the face of constant death threats," Dr. King "didn't have a personal will." One of the reasons his wife, Coretta, rarely traveled with him was "to guarantee a surviving parent" in case he were attacked. In the coming days, death and sudden violence would increasingly be subjects Dr. King would have to confront.[21]

The day after Dr. King's comment about JFK, King made it clear to an advisor that Bobby Kennedy would have his support in the race for the Democratic nomination against LBJ and Senator Eugene McCarthy. Dr. King said that even though he was going to hold off on endorsing Bobby for the time being, "we have to be realistic enough to see that if there's any possibility of stopping Lyndon, it's going to be Kennedy." He explained that the patrician McCarthy didn't have enough support from "white working-class voters." Dr. King said that another reason Bobby "would be the stronger candidate to defeat Johnson [was] because he would draw some black support away from Johnson, but McCarthy would not."[22]

Oddly enough, on the day following Dr. King's remarks about Bobby, private comments made by President Lyndon Johnson showed that he had a similar assessment of Bobby's chances. Unknown to the country, the press, and most of his advisors, LBJ was thinking of withdrawing from the race. One day earlier, on March 26, 1968, LBJ had received an extraordinarily blunt and bleak assessment on Vietnam from a senior team of advisors, informally called "The Wise Men." They included former JFK advisors, like McGeorge Bundy, Cyrus Vance, and Maxwell Taylor, as well as distinguished military leaders, such as World War II's General Omar Bradley and the Korean War's General Matthew Ridgeway. All the Wise Men, aside from Taylor and Abe Fortas, told LBJ that the US "must begin the steps to disengage" from Vietnam.[23]

Richard Helms's decision to cut estimates of enemy strength in half wasn't known to most people in the meeting, but indirectly, it was a big factor in Vance's and others' decision to push for withdrawal. Helms had agreed to estimates asserting that there were 230,000 communist forces before Tet, yet the US military also claimed that 80,000 enemy had been killed, and another 240,000 wounded. The figures simply didn't add up—in the words of Arthur Goldberg, LBJ's UN ambassador, "Who the hell is there left for us to be fighting?" Yet the US commander in Vietnam, General Westmoreland, was still asking for two hundred thousand more American troops.[24]

Realizing the bleak prospects for the war and his presidency, the day after the meeting, LBJ discussed with advisor Joseph Califano the possibility of withdrawing from the race. In their talk, LBJ was surprisingly positive about Bobby Kennedy, given their fractious past. After Califano said he thought Bobby would beat LBJ's vice president, Hubert Humphrey, President Johnson mused:

> What's wrong with Bobby? He's made some nasty speeches about me, but he's never had to sit here. . . . Bobby would keep fighting for the Great Society programs. And when he sat in this chair he might have a different view on the war.[25]

LBJ went on to say that while Bobby would have trouble getting his programs funded by Congress, at least "he'll try." Califano was surprised when LBJ ordered him to not say anything bad about Bobby. LBJ told Califano to say simply that "you know him and he's had a brilliant government career."[26]

It wasn't as if the rift between LBJ and Bobby had healed, but apparently the shared goal of the recent civil rights legislation, coupled with the negotiations about a way to keep Bobby out of the race, had all had a positive effect. Each man was starting to see the other in a different light, in terms of the future. Then, too, LBJ knew that if he withdrew, Bobby and Dr. King would be the most effective people to push for the Great Society legacy he wanted to be remembered for.

Like the rest of the country, Bobby Kennedy didn't know that LBJ was considering pulling out of the race, and he was running as hard as he could in late March, struggling to make up for getting into the race so late. The Associated Press reported that on March 25, 1968, as Bobby was speaking to students at San Fernando Valley College in California, he was met by "a barrage of questions today on whether if elected President he would open the United States archives to reveal details of the assassination of his brother, President John Kennedy."

Bobby's carefully worded response was "I would not reopen the Warren Commission report. I have seen everything that's in there. I stand by the Warren Commission." Each of those statements is more or less accurate, without really saying that Bobby believed all, or even most, of the Report. It also didn't address the students' actual question about opening the assassination material in the archives.

The students picked up on that, and kept asking the original question. The AP says that Bobby "tried to ignore questions from students. He became obviously more distressed as they persisted. Finally, he said:

'Your manners overwhelm me. Go ahead, go ahead, ask your questions.'
A student shouted: 'Will you open the archives?'"

Bobby's response again ignored the actual question. But it reflected his private struggle between protecting his brother's legacy and Commander Almeida while also quietly investigating his brother's murder. Bobby replied, "Nobody is more interested than I in knowing who is responsible for the death of President Kennedy." Those were his final words on the subject, and the AP reported that Bobby never did say "whether he would open the archives."[27]

Chapter Forty-eight

On March 28, 1968, James Earl Ray was in Atlanta while Martin Luther King was on his way to Memphis to lead the striking garbage workers' demonstration. Ray's presence in Atlanta on March 28 is confirmed by a signed money order he purchased for the Locksmithing Institute. Because of the New York meetings described earlier, Dr. King had not been in Atlanta since Ray's arrival. William Bradford Huie believes Ray had used the time to locate Dr. King's home, office, and church, which he marked on the Atlanta map found later in Ray's room.[1]

According to James Earl Ray, his contact had returned, saying he wanted Ray to buy a powerful hunting rifle in Atlanta, but Ray claims he suggested going to Birmingham to purchase it so that he could use his Alabama driver's license under the name "Eric S. Galt" as ID. According to Ray's later assertions, the hunting rifle purchase was part of the gunrunning scheme, and Ray was to also price cheap foreign or surplus rifles. Later, Ray and his contact would supposedly show the high-quality hunting rifle to prospective buyers and tell them about the cheap surplus rifles. If the buyers were agreeable, they would put in an order for ten of the cheap surplus rifles, which Ray would then supply.

Ray's story, which evolved over time and repeated telling, makes little sense. Why would prospective clients buy cheap surplus rifles when they hadn't been shown an example of the merchandise? Also, when Ray finally did buy a high-quality hunting rifle in Alabama, he didn't use his "Eric S. Galt" Alabama driver's license, but another alias he made up (or was given)—which defeated Ray's stated purpose in making the three-hour drive to Birmingham.

What is certain, based on testimony and documentation, is that in Birmingham on March 29, 1968, James Earl Ray bought "a Remington .243 caliber rifle, Model 700 with a 2x–7x Redfield telescopic sight" while "using the name of Harvey Lowmyer." Lowmyer was not one of the four Toronto aliases, but was similar to a name known to one of Ray's brothers. Ray made the purchase at Aeromarine Supply, located across from Birmingham's airport, and he told the clerks he needed the rifle for deer hunting with his brother-in-law. Later that day, Ray called the shop to say his brother-in-law wasn't happy with the gun, and Ray exchanged it the next day for a more powerful weapon, "a Model 760 30-06 caliber Remington." Ray had the scope transferred to the new rifle, but it wouldn't fit in a Remington box, so the shop provided Ray with a Browning box large enough to hold it. The total price, which Ray paid in cash, was $248.59 (more than $1,500 today), including the scope and twenty cartridges for the rifle.[2]

Ray said his contact had told him to return the first rifle and then specified the right one to buy based on some literature Ray had picked up at the store. In addition, Ray says his contact had given him approximately $700 to buy the rifle and for other expenses. On these points, Ray was likely much closer to the truth. Ray may have been given general instructions about what type of rifle to buy, bought the wrong one, and then told exactly which more powerful weapon to purchase. Ray could not have test-fired the first rifle and found it wasn't powerful enough, because the Justice Department noted that it "could not be loaded," since that part of the rifle was "caked with a hardened preservative (cosmoline)."[3]

For those reasons and others, Ray was probably buying the rifle on someone else's advice or orders. Though Ray contended that buying the rifle in another state was his idea, doing so helped to ensure that the FBI could assert jurisdiction when Martin Luther King was killed. While shooting King outside of Atlanta was preferable for Milteer and his Atlanta partners paying for the hit, there was always the chance that the assassination might have to be done in Georgia. If Dr. King were shot in Georgia, and if the rifle also had been bought in the state, it might have been more difficult for the FBI to take control of the investigation. Bringing in the FBI would actually benefit Milteer and Marcello, since Hoover and the Bureau had so much to hide: their illegal surveillance and COINTELPRO operations directed at King, the racism of much of the Bureau—especially of Hoover and the Atlanta office—and even the FBI's past lax treatment of Milteer and Marcello, if leads should ever point their way. By having Ray live in one state and buy the rifle in another (and, as it turned out, having Dr. King shot in yet another), the FBI would have no trouble taking charge of an interstate crime.

As a long-term criminal, Ray could have easily obtained a potentially untraceable rifle from the underworld. It makes little sense for Ray, on his own, to have not only bought the rifle at a public store, but to have also called extra attention to himself with the rifle exchange and scope remounting. It all seems designed to have left a paper trail, and to make

Ray stand out as a customer. (It's even possible that Ray was intentionally given instructions that caused him to buy the wrong rifle the first time.) Marcello wouldn't have wanted authorities trying to trace Ray's rifle to the underworld, and Milteer wouldn't want white supremacist groups investigated as the possible source, and Ray's buying the rifle from a legitimate store solved both of those problems.

Ray stated that the $700 his contact gave him for the rifle purchase was part of the anti-Castro gun-smuggling operation. However, when authorities later interviewed the men at the shop who helped Ray, they said that he never asked about buying quantities of cheap foreign or surplus rifles. We suspect that Ray knew he was buying the rifle that would be used to kill Dr. King, and that it wasn't part of the anti-Castro operation. However, that doesn't mean that, aside from the rifle purchase, no such anti-Castro operation existed.[4]

One often-overlooked piece of evidence provides some support for Ray's Cuban gunrunning claims. When Ray's Remington rifle was found after Dr. King's murder, Congressional investigators say that Memphis police discovered in the same large bag "military ammunition . . . with machinegun link marks," that was different from the ammo used in Ray's rifle. Ray later said the military ammunition was part of the anti-Castro gunrunning scheme, but Aeromarine didn't sell such military ammunition, and despite years of investigation by the FBI, Justice Department, and Congress, its source has never been determined. It would be interesting to know if the military machine-gun ammo in James Earl Ray's bag was similar to that used by any of the CIA-backed Cuban exile groups. If so, its inclusion would have been a simple way for Marcello or Milteer to further stymie any thorough investigation of Ray's associates.[5]

Ray said that on March 30, 1968, while he was still in Birmingham at the Travelodge motel, his contact was getting ready to go to New Orleans. His instructions to Ray were to proceed to Memphis and register at the New Rebel Inn motel. Ray claimed he headed straight to Memphis from Birmingham, staying there until Dr. King's murder. However, Ray said it took him an unusually long time to drive the 241 miles from Birmingham to Memphis: four days, for a pace of just sixty miles per day. Ray claims it took him so long because he drove only "3 or 4 hours a day," but even that's implausible. While small Alabama towns sometimes had speed limits of twenty-five or thirty-five miles per hour, they were separated by long stretches of highway with speed limits of at least sixty. In addition, no documentation (receipts, motel records, etc.) has ever emerged for Ray's visits to the motels he claims he stayed at along the way.[6]

Instead, evidence confirmed by the Congressional investigators and the Justice Department clearly shows that after his rifle purchase in Birmingham, Ray returned to his Atlanta rooming house. On March 31, Ray paid his rent in person and on the same day, the rooming house operator also had Ray write out his name for their official records. On April 1, 1968, Ray dropped off his clothes at the Piedmont Laundry on Peachtree Street.[7]

Despite the evidence, Ray was always adamant that he didn't return to Atlanta after buying the rifle in Birmingham, but there are two likely reasons why Ray felt he had to lie about it. One might have been to conceal a meeting with Joseph Milteer or one of his associates in Atlanta. Such a contact would occur on April 5, and Ray never mentioned it, so he might well be covering up a similar contact a few days earlier. At some point during Ray's brief stay in Atlanta, either before he went to Birmingham or after, never explained evidence shows that Ray had a nice restaurant meal with someone in the city.[8]

An undated receipt for a meal for two, at a notable Atlanta restaurant on Peachtree Street, was later found in Ray's belongings by the FBI. The restaurant was "Mammy's Shanty," one of the few Atlanta restaurants at the time with a racist theme. In the wake of the desegregation of the city's restaurants, the racist image kept black customers away, so it would have appealed not only to Ray, but also to hardcore racists like Joseph Milteer and his Atlanta partners, such as Hugh Spake. As with his return to Atlanta after his Birmingham trip, Ray was evasive regarding the meal and whom he was with. When his first lawyer asked him about it, Ray denied knowing anything. But then, as he often did when evidence surfaced that he hadn't accounted for, Ray later claimed to his second attorney to have suddenly remembered having dinner on Peachtree with the mysterious Raoul. However, the receipt was for London broil, and Ray told William Bradford Huie that not only had he never "ordered London broil in a restaurant, he didn't even know what it was."[9]

There was another, related reason Ray was adamant that he hadn't gone back to Atlanta before heading to Memphis: because the well-traveled Martin Luther King had finally returned to Atlanta for the first time since Ray had initially arrived in the city. Ray didn't want to admit that he was stalking or surveilling Dr. King, who had come home to Atlanta following his disastrous March 28 trip to Memphis.

On March 28, 1968, Martin Luther King had returned to downtown Memphis to lead a demonstration to support the striking garbage workers. His visit was plagued by problems from the start, and delays with Dr. King's flight from New York caused him to arrive two hours after the march was supposed to begin. He walked into an already tense situation, with rumors of police brutality earlier that day and a group of young protesters, who called themselves "the Invaders," advocating for violent action. But all of the protestors were initially peaceful as Dr. King led the march down Beale Street, toward City Hall. Photographs of the day show the demonstrators with signs mounted on wooden sticks, the most notable proclaiming simply: I AM A MAN.

However, the young protesters soon shed their signs and began using the sticks to smash windows. Dr. King, at the head of the march, was shocked by the sounds of shattering glass, which meant that for the first time, one of his protests was turning violent. As a riot began to erupt around them, Dr. King's aides feared for his safety and found a car to drive him from the scene. Since Memphis police had blocked key roads after the melee started, Dr. King couldn't be taken to the place where he usually lodged in Memphis, the black-owned Lorraine Motel. Instead, the car made its way to the Holiday Inn–Rivermont Hotel— until recently, a whites-only establishment.

The morning rumor of police brutality had turned out to be unfounded, but once the riot started, the police lived up to it. Congressional investigators wrote that "tear gas was fired," and soon the police resorted to "nightsticks, mace, and finally guns," shooting four blacks, one fatally, and injuring sixty. There were 300 arrests, 150 fires, and Tennessee's governor called on 3,500 members of the National Guard to patrol Memphis and enforce a curfew.[10]

At the Holiday Inn, Martin Luther King appeared extremely depressed. As journalist Nick Kotz described, Dr. King told aide Ralph David Abernathy, "Maybe we just have to admit that the day of violence is here, and maybe we just have to give up, and let violence take its course." The following day, Dr. King told an aide that people would interpret the march-turned-riot "as a sign 'that Martin Luther King is at the end of his rope.'" He worried that his critics in the civil rights movement would soon be saying, "Martin Luther King is dead! He's finished! His non-violence is nothing. No one is listening to it."[11]

Dr. King returned to Atlanta and rallied his aides from around the country to figure out how to return to Memphis, prove that nonviolence could work, and then continue planning the still problematic Poor

People's March for late April. It was an ambitious undertaking, and some of the aides were in favor of King's returning to Memphis but not of the Poor People's March in Washington, while others favored neither. Jesse Jackson, Andrew Young, and Hosea Williams argued against the Washington march. A frustrated Dr. King abruptly left the meeting. He later returned, and after an intense ten-hour conference, all the aides had agreed to support the Poor People's March and the return to Memphis—which is why so many of Dr. King's aides would be there with him on April 4. However, the riot's aftermath had taken a toll on Dr. King, and the day after the marathon meeting, his associate Walter Fauntroy observed that King looked like a "spent force." (Fauntroy would later chair the Martin Luther King investigation for the House Select Committee on Assassinations.)[12]

J. Edgar Hoover was quick to exploit the Memphis riot in his campaign against Dr. King and other civil rights leaders. Taylor Branch writes that "within hours [the FBI] disseminated to 'cooperative news sources' a blind memorandum stating that 'the result of King's famous espousal of nonviolence was vandalism, looting, and riot.'" The next day "Hoover approved a second effort 'to publicize hypocrisy on the part of [Dr. King].'"[13]

One of these was an infamous memo chiding Dr. King for "leading the lambs to slaughter," then fleeing to the safety of "the plush Holiday Inn" instead of the Lorraine Motel, "owned and patronized exclusively by Negroes." When the memo was first revealed in the mid-1970s, some saw it as part of an FBI effort to get Dr. King to the Lorraine Motel as part of a massive assassination plot. But the House Select Committee on Assassinations found that theory wasn't true, since King often stayed at the Lorraine on his trips to Memphis and would have stayed there on his next trip regardless.[14]

The FBI continued waging its propaganda war against Dr. King and the other civil rights leaders and groups, as well as conceiving various dirty tricks. Branch found that Hoover wanted to tie Dr. King to both the Nation of Islam and boxer Muhammad Ali, who had refused military service in Vietnam in 1966. The head of Chicago's FBI office pointed out that blacks knew that Dr. King and the Nation of Islam weren't allied, and Ali was so popular that the FBI's plans "might backfire," but the autocratic Hoover ordered them implemented anyway. Mississippi's FBI office sent Hoover a proposal "to distribute leaflets skewing King as a fancy dresser who deserted his people," an idea that Hoover had under consideration at the time of Dr. King's murder.[15]

Such efforts sound almost silly in hindsight, but some American newspapers picked up on Hoover's propaganda. Branch points to the *Memphis Commercial Appeal*'s story headlined "Chicken à la King" and a *St. Louis Globe-Democrat* story that denounced Dr. King as "one of the most menacing men in America today." While not parroting Hoover's spin, even newspapers like the *New York Times* and the *Washington Post* took a cautious tone regarding Dr. King and his efforts.[16]

One day before Dr. King would return to Memphis, Hoover tried to use the Memphis riot as an excuse to get approval for more wiretaps against King and the SCLC. But LBJ's attorney general, Ramsey Clark, turned down Hoover's request, just as he had back in January, leaving Hoover even more dependent on his allies in the country's secret domestic surveillance network, from police intelligence units to military intelligence to the CIA.[17]

Members of the 111th Military Intelligence Group were sent to Memphis starting "on March 28, 1968," as documented by authors Hancock and Wexler. They write that "this Civil Disorder Operation (Lantern Strike) involved coordination with Memphis Police, the FBI, and the Tennessee National Guard . . . to monitor and respond to any civil disorder involved with . . . the sanitation workers' strike. Members of this group [would] maintain surveillance on Dr. King and were observing his rooms at the Lorraine Motel" when he returned to Memphis on April 3, 1968.[18] Because of the riot, Dr. King would be under unusually heavy official surveillance upon his return, a situation that could yield helpful opportunities for those able to penetrate the surveillance network for the Mafia.

One Mafia-affiliated person with access to intelligence about King was Sgt. Jack de la Llana, Trafficante's man on the Tampa police force, who could access information nationwide using the Law Enforcement Intelligence Unit (LEIU) or his direct contacts. De la Llana would also be able to feed information or disinformation into the intelligence system. His boss, Trafficante, shared the drug network through Memphis with Marcello and would not want to see it disrupted again.

Marcello's ally Johnny Rosselli also had ways to learn about or penetrate the government's domestic surveillance network. In late March 1968, Rosselli met with his old CIA friend, William Harvey. Such a meeting could have been helpful in case Rosselli's connection to James Earl Ray ever surfaced after Dr. King's murder. While Harvey was no longer in the CIA, his many high-level contacts in the Agency included the CIA's liaison with the FBI.[19]

The Memphis riots would have affected the plans of Joseph Milteer and Carlos Marcello. For Milteer, the Atlanta press coverage of the riots no doubt generated additional pressure on him, Hugh Spake, and their other two Atlanta partners. For Marcello, the riots would have confirmed his worst fears about the civil rights leader's potential for disrupting his Memphis drug network's profits and his Mafia allies' vice operations in that city, and potentially other cities in his territory. The riot could have accelerated the timing of Dr. King's assassination, in hopes that King would be killed before his next march could trigger another riot. Reports of the massive damages from the riot would be all the more reason not to kill Dr. King in Atlanta, which meant the assassination would happen in Memphis.

We cited earlier the Justice Department memo, withheld from the HSCA, which said that one person helping Marcello implement the King contract from the racist group was "Frank [C.] Liberto . . . a Memphis racketeer and lieutenant of Carlos Marcello," who had both family and business ties to the New Orleans godfather. One of the regular customers at Frank C. Liberto's Memphis produce store was black civil rights worker John McFerren, who had heard rumors that Liberto might have ties to the Mafia. On one shopping trip, "he overheard [Liberto] say about Martin Luther King: 'Somebody ought to kill that son of a bitch.'" Later, the FBI would talk to "Frank C. Liberto [who admitted he] may have made derogatory remarks about King because of the loss of revenues caused by his activities." Liberto also "admitted making [those] remarks . . . in the presence of their customers," further buttressing McFerren's credibility.[20] According to the Justice Department memo, "[James Earl] Ray's contacts in New Orleans were with Mafia–Cosa Nostra representatives who referred him to Frank [C.] Liberto."[21]

On March 31, 1968, the nation was hit with a bombshell when President Johnson announced at the end of his prime-time televised speech about Vietnam that he was withdrawing from the race for another term. His statement dramatically changed the political landscape for America, and for Dr. King and Bobby in particular. Earlier that day, Dr. King had delivered a rousing sermon at Washington National Cathedral, making comments indirectly criticizing LBJ, saying the US was in "one of the most unjust wars in the history of the world." At a press conference later that day, Nick Kotz writes, "King declared that he could not support President Johnson for reelection." King closed his remarks by saying he was going to return to Memphis on April 2, to "prove that nonviolent" protest could still work.[22]

At home in Atlanta that night, Dr. King was buoyed by LBJ's announcement that he was withdrawing from the race. According to Kotz, "the next morning, King decided to postpone the Poor People's Campaign." However, most historians, including Taylor Branch, cite information showing that the oft-delayed campaign was still progressing despite its many problems, which included finding enough volunteers to make the trek to Washington. Meanwhile, Dr. King's return to Memphis was rescheduled until April 3.[23]

Bobby Kennedy was probably just as shocked as the rest of the country by President Johnson's unexpected announcement. Perhaps because their recent negotiations via Sorensen and Clifford had been at least cordial, Bobby asked to meet with LBJ. President Johnson agreed to see Bobby and Sorensen on April 3.[24]

The meeting between Bobby Kennedy and President Johnson was as friendly as it was unlikely. The two long-standing adversaries seemed to make a genuine effort to gloss over, if not patch up, their differences. It probably helped that Bobby was accompanied by Ted Sorensen, whom LBJ admired and had originally wanted for his own administration. As Taylor Branch recounted, Bobby told LBJ, "Your speech was magnificent." Bobby "said he appreciated the heavy burdens on Johnson and regretted letting their difference leave him out of touch." Taking a share of the blame, Bobby said, "A lot of . . . the feud 'was my fault.'"[25]

After the mutual compliments, and LBJ's revelation that North Vietnam had just agreed to start the process leading to peace talks, Bobby got down to the political business both men knew so well. LBJ told Bobby he wouldn't be giving advice to his vice president, Hubert Humphrey, who was now making his own run for the nomination. According to Branch, LBJ said that "while reserving his options . . . he would try to stay out of the race." After delving into more political details, the meeting ended on a hopeful note as LBJ said that "he regarded all he had done as a continuation of the Kennedy-Johnson program—in education, poverty, and civil rights." Bobby replied, "You are a brave and dedicated man"—and then repeated the words, to make sure Johnson heard the compliment that few would ever have imagined just days earlier.[26]

LBJ's withdrawal from the race, his meeting with Bobby, and the start of the peace process with North Vietnam all raise two issues about Martin Luther King. The cordial meeting between the two former foes suggests that LBJ and Dr. King might have eventually had a similar rapprochement. Their antagonism had not lasted nearly as long as that between LBJ and Bobby, and even in the wake of the Memphis riots, LBJ had avoided publicly criticizing Dr. King by name, making only general comments about the need for protesters to obey the law. Their biggest difference was over the Vietnam War, which was now going to be the subject of negotiations with North Vietnam. However, disputes still existed between the two—most prominently, the need for enacting the Kerner Commission's recommendations, which Dr. King embraced but LBJ wanted to ignore. Dr. King's murder, the day after LBJ's meeting with Bobby, ended any possibility of seeing what might have developed between the two men who had done so much for civil rights.

LBJ's decisions to not seek another term and to begin the peace process with North Vietnam are also significant factors in evaluating Dr. King's assassination. Many of those who think LBJ was part of a huge government conspiracy to murder Dr. King ignore the fact that LBJ had dropped out of the race and started the peace process prior to King's murder. It's difficult to see what LBJ had to gain by Dr. King's death, but he certainly had a lot to lose. The resulting nationwide riots ended any chance of LBJ's cementing civil rights and fighting poverty as his major legacy, leaving his dream of a Great Society literally in ashes. That the Vietnam peace process had begun before King's assassination has been largely overlooked for decades, because LBJ's efforts were sabotaged in late October 1968 by Republican candidate Richard Nixon, as is now well documented by declassified files. Finally, black leaders like Rep. Louis Stokes, on the House Select Committee for Assassinations, looked for any signs that LBJ and other federal agencies were part of a plot to kill Dr. King, and concluded that no evidence existed for such a massive plot.[27]

Chapter Forty-nine

On April 1, 1968, Atlanta newspapers reported that Martin Luther King would soon return to Memphis for a peaceful demonstration. On April 3, 1968, around 7:00 PM, James Earl Ray checked into the New Rebel Inn, a motel on the outskirts of Memphis. Memphis was 398 miles from Atlanta by the most convenient route, meaning that Ray could have left Atlanta early that morning or the previous day. One of Ray's brothers later claimed to have received a call from him on April 3, in which Ray "just acted excited, jubilant."[1]

Many of Ray's actions over the following days and weeks have been the subject of controversy for decades. While we won't dwell on Ray's claims that have repeatedly been debunked or altered by him, we will cite information, uncovered by his various defense attorneys, that has withstood the test of time. Because of the FBI's bias against Dr. King, we try to use government reports that were both critical and skeptical of the FBI. These include the 1977 Justice Department Task Force Review and the House Select Committee on Assassinations, headed by African-American civil rights figures like Rep. Louis Stokes (a former prosecutor) and King associate Walter Fauntroy. In addition, we sometimes quote FBI reports that are at odds with what became the Bureau's official "lone assassin" story, or that appear to have been withheld from the HSCA. Finally, we cite the findings of independent researchers where they can be documented. While the HSCA found that many of the key facts surrounding Dr. King's murder can't be determined with scientific precision, the essential story that emerges is consistent with James Earl Ray's being part of a contract hit that Carlos Marcello brokered for Joseph Milteer and his Atlanta partners.

Martin Luther King's trip to Memphis on April 3, 1968, got off to a bad start that foreshadowed the difficulties to come. As Bobby Kennedy and LBJ were meeting in Washington, Dr. King was waiting in a commercial airliner at Atlanta's large Municipal Airport. There had been a bomb threat, which said, "Your airline brought Martin Luther King to

Memphis, and when he comes again a bomb will go off, and he will be assassinated."[2]

As was the FBI's usual procedure, it had not passed word of the threat to Dr. King. He first heard about it when the pilot finally announced they were ready for takeoff and blamed the delay on the threat against King. Since Dr. King already knew he was going into a very tense situation in Memphis, the bomb threat only magnified the strain he was under.[3]

When Dr. King finally arrived in Memphis, he checked into the Lorraine Motel, where, Congressional investigators confirmed, he had stayed many times before. Dr. King wound up in his usual room, number 306, in the newest part of the motel on the second floor. Its outdoor balcony, overlooking the parking lot, was typical for the time. The motel faced Mulberry Street, and anyone driving past it would have a perfect view of someone on the balcony. Across Mulberry Street were the backs of several older two- and three-story buildings, which faced a run-down portion of South Main Street. Numerous rear windows in those buildings also had an unobstructed view of the Lorraine Motel balcony.

More unobstructed views of the balcony were available from the roof and rear windows of Fire Station 2, where undercover black Memphis police officers, including Ed Redditt of the intelligence unit, had set up surveillance on Dr. King. Because of police behavior on his last visit (and before that, against the strikers), as well as his stance against armed security, Dr. King's group had refused protection from the Memphis Police. In addition, some of Dr. King's aides believed it was sometimes hard to tell whether local police were providing protection or running surveillance.

Military Intelligence was also running surveillance on Dr. King, and the FBI had an informant in Dr. King's entourage, later identified as an SCLC financial official. When Dr. King met with the young black militant group known as the Invaders, on the afternoon of April 3, he didn't realize that one of them—Marrell McCullough—was also an undercover Memphis police officer.[4]

Dr. King was under intense surveillance for two reasons. First was to monitor his actions leading up to his next large demonstration, planned for April 8. City officials were trying to stop the march with an injunction, which federal marshals served to Dr. King at 2:30 PM on April 3. Second was to protect him, since an attack on Dr. King by racists or even black militants (not a realistic threat, except in the minds of some white city officials) could trigger more rioting in a downtown business district still recovering from its previous turmoil.[5]

After an exhausting day of meetings, punctuated by thunderstorms and reports of tornadoes, Dr. King learned that the crowd expected for that night's speech at the Mason Temple was far smaller than his last crowd, only about two thousand people. Worried that Dr. King's support would appear to be sagging, the group instead sent Ralph David Abernathy to speak, accompanied by Jesse Jackson and Andrew Young. But the crowd was obviously disappointed by King's absence, so, despite the worsening weather (tornadoes would kill five people and demolish forty mobile homes around Memphis that night), Dr. King went to speak.

The last speech Martin Luther King ever gave, on April 3, 1968, was one of his greatest, full of emotion. Nick Kotz writes that, after praising the bravery of the striking workers and their families, Dr. King "told about his brushes with death as a civil rights leader," including the day in 1958 when he was stabbed in the chest in Harlem. After telling the crowd that the attending physician said the blade was so close to his heart that a sneeze would have killed him, Dr. King launched into a litany of all the important moments he would have missed "if I had sneezed."[6]

Dr. King had delivered those lines many times before and was on a roll that night, but as he said, "And they were telling me . . . " he paused. Suddenly, his tone shifted, and he became far more serious. He continued, saying, "It doesn't matter now. It really doesn't matter." He explained that when he'd left Atlanta that morning, there had been a bomb scare. After arriving in Memphis, "some began to say the threats—or talk about the threats—that were out, what would happen to me from some of our sick white brothers."[7] Dr. King couldn't have known how tragically accurate he was about "sick white brothers," such as Ray, Milteer, Marcello, and Spake, but the recent strains made his own mortality all too clear. King continued, saying, "I don't know what will happen now," then appeared to be fighting back tears as he declared, "We've got some difficult days ahead. But it really doesn't matter with me now.[8]

"Because I've been to the mountain top," Martin Luther King's voice rang out, even as it started to break with emotion. He said that "Like anybody, I would like to live—a long life—longevity has its place. But I'm not concerned about that now. I just want to do God's will. And he's allowed me to go up the mountain . . . and I've looked over. And I have seen the Promised Land. And I may not get there with you, but I want you to know tonight that we as a people will get to the Promised Land!" His expression softened as he added, "So I'm happy tonight. I'm not worried about anything. I'm not worried about any man. Mine eyes have seen the glory of the coming of the Lord!" The already rapturous crowd erupted as an exhausted and emotionally drained Dr. King fell into the arms of Abernathy, who helped him to his seat.[9]

On April 4, 1968, the daylong battle being fought in a Memphis court-room may have influenced the timing for the hit on Martin Luther King. The fight was over the injunction to stop not just Dr. King's planned April 8 demonstration, but any other march through the Memphis business district as well. Trying to get the injunction lifted was the SCLC, buttressed by additional attorneys from the American Civil Liberties Union. Some aides, like Andrew Young, were at the hearing as witnesses, while Dr. King remained at the Lorraine Motel, resting from his taxing schedule before making calls and having more meetings.

If the city of Memphis prevailed in court and the injunction were upheld, Martin Luther King could have returned to Atlanta at any time, since appeals to higher courts might take weeks. Should that happen, Marcello's representatives working with Ray on the King contract would lose a prime opportunity. Two independent sources referenced in the 1968 Justice Department memo, including one of journalist William Sartor's mob informants from New Orleans, said that "the assassination was originally scheduled to take place after the march for which Dr. King had returned to Memphis." That might make sense, because the march itself and the hours leading up to it would have called for very tight security, perhaps including thousands of National Guard troops, so getting to Dr. King—and getting away afterward—would have been difficult. Yet the period after the march, when the crowds had gone and those around Dr. King had relaxed, could have been an opportune time.[10]

As for who was helping Ray in Memphis, one of Sartor's named sources spoke about that directly to a Justice Department investigator in 1968. The informant was "a petty gambler with sources of information close to Frank [C.] Liberto," the Memphis produce dealer who worked with Carlos Marcello. The Justice Department investigator wrote that "in my presence," the named informant said that "Ray met Joe Cacameci at a Lion Service Station [in Memphis] on the night before or the day of the shooting." As we noted earlier, that person's actual name was likely Frank Joseph Caracci, a Marcello lieutenant who owned an amusement company in New Orleans. Caracci had been questioned after JFK's assassination about his contacts with Jack Ruby, and the FBI had opened an unrelated criminal-intelligence investigation on Caracci in the fall of 1967.[11]

Apparently because of the mobsters involved, the informant "expressed concern for the safety of his wife and children." Apparently, the FBI withheld the Justice Department account of this incident—like much of Sartor's other information about Marcello's brokering the hit contract for an out-of-state group of racists—from the HSCA, even though the Bureau did provide less important information about the frightened informant. The Justice Department memo also names a "professional killer" (and two of his aliases) said to be involved in the Marcello contract with Caracci. None of those names or aliases surfaced in the HSCA investigation and, like all the leads linked to Marcello, appear to have not been investigated seriously by the FBI—at least, based on the files released so far.[12]

Because of the court hearing that could cause Dr. King to leave Memphis as early as the night of April 4, the plan to kill King had to move fast. The Memphis newspaper said Dr. King was at the Lorraine Motel, and a radio news report even gave his room number. A copy of that Memphis newspaper, with Ray's fingerprint on it, would later be found among his possessions. According to the 1977 Justice Department Task Force, "Ray left the Rebel Inn before the 1 PM checkout time." His next two hours are unaccounted for. Then, "between 3:00 and 3:30 PM . . . a man generally answering Ray's description rented" a room at a flophouse "at 422 1/2 South Main Street." The back of that building faced the Lorraine Motel. Ray turned down the first room he was offered, on the first floor, but took the next room offered, on the second floor, without bothering to look inside first to check the view. If he had, he would have seen that to have an unobstructed shot at the balcony in front of Dr. King's room, he would have to lean far out of the window. Before accepting the room, Ray also didn't check out the shared bathroom at the end of the hall, which did have an unobstructed view.[13]

The fact that Ray didn't inspect either view first could indicate that he had been directed to the rooming house by someone who had, or who at least was more familiar with Memphis than Ray. Like Atlanta, Memphis was a city Ray had never visited before. Typically, in order to avoid problems, an out-of-town hit man will be given information about where to go and what to do. Ray registered under the name "John Willard," and was later unable to explain how he came up with the alias. "John Willard," like "Eric S. Galt," was one of four Toronto names of real men that Ray used as aliases. They all lived within two miles of each other, and three of the men generally resembled Ray. All four were legitimate businessmen with no criminal past, whose identities had been stolen—most likely by the Montreal/Toronto arm of the Marcello-linked drug network Ray had worked for, which also specialized in providing fake identities.[14]

Ray then left the rooming house and drove his Mustang to the York Arms Company store at 162 South Main Street, where, he later admitted, he bought "a pair of Bushnell binoculars for . . . $41.55." According to the Justice Department, Ray returned to the rooming house "by 5 PM at the latest [and] parked his Mustang" approximately four spaces south of the entrance to his flophouse. Ray also "had taken his zipper bag and bedspread to Room 5-B." However, Ray may have done more than buy binoculars while he was out—he could have also called Frank C. Liberto.[15]

On the afternoon of April 4, 1968, at approximately 4:30 PM, civil rights worker John McFerren entered Frank Liberto's produce market to buy stock for his "small country grocery store [located] in the hills [more than fifty miles] east of Memphis," as he had been doing every Thursday for at least two years. McFerren had originally begun making the long drives to Memphis to buy his supplies almost eight years earlier, when white merchants in his small county had refused to sell to black store owners. As recounted in *Time* magazine in 1960 and 1961, the situation came about after McFerren had been one of the leaders of an effort to increase black voting in the county, after white officials had "turned away every one of the . . . Negroes who tried to vote," even though the county was majority black.[16]

The following is based on an FBI report that included a detailed account of William Sartor's first interview with McFerren, later the basis for a shorter 1968 article in *Time* magazine. McFerren said that on April 4, "as he walked through the doorway he heard a man's voice from an office just off the hall. 'The man was screaming and I could hear his voice before I got inside. . . . I just stopped inside the doorway and listened for a moment . . . .outside the office where this man was screaming.'"[17]

The man McFerren later identified as Frank C. Liberto "kept screaming over the phone: 'Kill him. Kill him. I don't care how you do it. Kill the son of a bitch on the balcony.'" Another man, walking up the hall, noticed McFerren "and told me to go on inside the food locker and help myself." McFerren says he made sure he "obediently shuffled off," playing the "acquiescent [role] he adopted years ago for self-protection" when dealing with white businessmen. But "as he was leaving the [food] locker four or five minutes later, the phone in [Liberto's] office rang again." A man with a scar answered it and passed it to Liberto, who "was in no mood for further talk."[18]

Frank Liberto "sat with both feet on the desk and growled: 'Don't call me no more. And don't come near my place. You know my brother in New Orleans—he'll give you the $5,000. Don't bring your ass near my place again.'" McFerren says that Frank C. Liberto "slammed the phone down without waiting for a reply." John McFerren "made out like I didn't hear what he said. . . . Every time I go in there I play like I'm hard of hearing. . . . I went up and paid my bill and left. . . . I didn't want to stay around there."[19]

In 1978, Frank C. Liberto briefly affirmed his role in King's murder to someone he trusted. Each morning for the past year, the aging, extremely overweight Liberto had stopped once, sometimes twice, a day at a Memphis restaurant run by LaVada Whitlock Addison. He came in every workday for breakfast, and sometimes had a "beer or two" in the afternoon. According to Addison's sworn testimony, as described by Ray's last attorney William Pepper, Liberto "developed a friendship of sorts with [her] and he would occasionally be candid with her and her son," who would listen to Frank C. Liberto's complaints about his wife and mistress. Sometimes Addison would even "sit down at the table" to chat with Liberto. "On one occasion she recalled that something about the King assassination came on the television and Liberto calmly commented, partly to Mrs. [Addison] and partly to no one in particular, 'I had Martin Luther King killed.' Startled, she responded instantly . . . saying, 'Don't tell me such things,' and 'I don't believe it anyway.'"[20]

However, Mrs. Addison was apparently concerned enough to tell her son about the conversation. According to her son's sworn testimony as recounted by Pepper, he confronted Frank C. Liberto one afternoon at the restaurant, and Liberto responded by saying, "I didn't kill the nigger but I had it done." The son left for Canada soon afterward. While Addison's and her son's accounts would not become public for more than a decade after 1978, the HSCA questioned Liberto about the McFerren report that same year. Frank C. Liberto denied having had anything to do with Dr. King's assassination; he died later that year, apparently of natural causes.[21] Pepper also noted an FBI report that described how in the weeks before James Earl Ray had left Los Angeles, a man calling himself "J. C. Hardin" had left messages about contacting Ray with the manager of the St. Francis Hotel—the Los Angeles hotel to which Ray had delivered drugs after his return from Mexico. The FBI was never able to identify "Hardin," meaning the name was probably an alias, and Pepper pointed out that "Hardin" was Liberto's mother's maiden name.[22]

The Justice Department memo about Frank C. Liberto, based on Sartor's sources including a "protégé of Marcello," also said:

> . . . the original plan was that Ray would be arrested immediately after the shooting, tried, and acquitted. There was a change, however, perhaps as late as an hour before the shooting, due to a mix-up involving the money. Either the Mafia wanted him at large until the balance of the price was paid or, more likely, says Sartor, the shares of those in Memphis (Liberto and others) had not been paid, and it was they who wanted Ray at large [for leverage].[23]

The Justice Department memo also indicates why a Memphis policeman might have been involved. Sartor said that "information possessed by former [Memphis] Mayor Ingram concerning corruption in the Police Department suggests that" one or more "officers may have known of or participated in the conspiracy—because they were bribed or feared exposure." As likely happened with Officer J. D. Tippit in Dallas, any Memphis officer involved wouldn't have been fully aware of the plot—only told or manipulated to be at a certain place at a certain time to take, or not take, certain action. However, we still agree with the HSCA conclusion that no evidence has yet surfaced proving any Memphis officer's involvement. In fact, so many officers were in Dr. King's vicinity that it would have been difficult for one, two, or more to have done anything unusual without calling attention to themselves.[24]

Frank C. Holloman was one of the Memphis police officials who was investigated closely and cleared by Rep. Stokes and the HSCA. Holloman was the Fire and Police Director for the city of Memphis, and on April 4, 1968, he was trying to get Martin Luther King to leave Memphis. Years later, Holloman had attracted suspicion from some writers because in the late 1950s he had been an assistant to J. Edgar Hoover in Washington, D.C., before heading the Atlanta FBI office at the start of its anti-King activities.[25]

On April 4, Holloman testified in court on behalf of the city of Memphis as they tried to maintain the injunction against Dr. King's demonstration. Holloman told the court that not only had "white citizens of Memphis" written and called him to say they were "greatly agitated," but also that "there was a theft from a sporting good store last evening of guns and ammunition." Often overlooked by many writers, but pointed out by Taylor Branch, is that in open court Holloman cited "numerous threats that King would not survive" his demonstration in Memphis.[26]

Holloman was extremely concerned that another riot might be triggered in the still-recovering downtown area, and from the stand he rattled off "fourteen reasons why the march would endanger the half-million citizens in his charge," since he was "convinced that Dr. Martin Luther King, his leaders, or others cannot control a massive march of this kind." Memphis was a powder keg at the time, and would logically face another riot if Dr. King were attacked there. Holloman's career would be enhanced by stopping a riot, not starting one—hence his testimony that fateful day. After much investigation, the HSCA found misjudgments on Holloman's part, but no deliberate involvement in Dr. King's murder.[27]

The HSCA looked into two other incidents involving the police earlier that day, and found that the situations weren't as suspicious as some of Ray's attorneys had claimed. One event was the removal that day of black undercover officer Ed Redditt from his Fire Station 2 surveillance post across from the Lorraine Motel, and the other was the reassignment of the only two black firemen at the station. After investigating, Stokes and the HSCA concluded that "Redditt was removed because his superior perceived real danger to his safety." That day, Redditt received "a threatening phone call" at the firehouse, in addition to "another threat Redditt had received at the airport," and yet another threat transmitted to Memphis authorities by a Senate investigator. Moreover, even Redditt's removal still left another black undercover policeman on duty at the fire station. Redditt's removal was not part of any big conspiracy involving the Memphis police, but we don't rule out the possibility that someone outside the force made one or more of those threats to get Redditt away from Dr. King.[28]

Likewise, the HSCA determined that the removal of the only two black firemen at the fire station was not part of a conspiracy. Ironically, the HSCA concluded that the firemen's transfers "were made . . . out of a concern for the security of the surveillance post [and] Redditt himself was the person who initiated the request." The Memphis police were worried that the firemen, one of whom was "very sympathetic with the strike," might blow Redditt's cover.[29]

As 6:00 PM approached, the police forces near Dr. King were considerable. The HSCA found "53 to 66 law enforcement officers [were] within a mile of the Lorraine Motel," including six tactical (or "tact") units, each with three or four vehicles, designed "to respond to any disorder or emergency." By 6:00 PM, one of those tact units, with twelve officers, "was on a rest break at Fire Station 2." The fire station was about fifty yards from the Lorraine Motel. One officer was even closer: "Marrell McCullough, an undercover officer who was in the Lorraine parking lot," as a member of the Invaders militant group that had been negotiating with Dr. King and his men.[30]

Chapter Fifty

In a first-floor room at the Lorraine Motel, Martin Luther King was buoyed when Andrew Young returned from court to report that the hearing seemed to have gone well. The tension and fear of the previous night were gone, as four of King's men playfully attacked Young with pillows for not having kept Dr. King better informed throughout the day. Around 5:30 PM, their attorney arrived to say the march had been approved with conditions that satisfied King. As described by Taylor Branch, these included "a prescribed route, no weapons, and narrow ranks [so] the marshals [could] keep the spectators away."[1]

That began a fresh round of discussion among Dr. King and his men, about planning sessions scheduled over the weekend to finalize Monday's march, which soon ended so they could begin preparing for dinner. Dr. King and Ralph David Abernathy headed up to King's room at 5:40 PM. Once there, King pressed Abernathy to find a way to be in Washington on April 29 for the start of the lobbying portion of the Poor People's Campaign. They were soon joined by local Reverend Billy Kyles, who was hosting Dr. King for a home-cooked dinner that night.[2]

Downstairs shortly before 6:00 PM, Andrew Young and Jesse Jackson stepped out of their room, where Jackson had been leading a musical group, the Breadbasket Band. Dr. King went outside and leaned over the railing, calling out for Jackson "to come to dinner with me," but Kyles said that Jackson had already been invited. Jesse Jackson looked up from the parking lot and pointed out to Dr. King his group's saxophonist, Ben Branch.[3]

Martin Luther King recognized Branch, saying, "He's my man. . . . Ben, I want you to play my favorite song, 'Precious Lord, Take My Hand.'"[4]

Seconds later, a loud *CRACK* that sounded like a firecracker shattered the hopes and dreams of millions. It was 6:01 PM.

The 30.06 slug tore through the right side of Dr. King's face, severing his spine and throwing him backward. As he lay on the ground, one foot stuck through the balcony railing, Abernathy tried to comfort the dying man, saying, "Martin—it's all right. This is Ralph. Martin, can you hear me?"[5]

In the Lorraine Motel parking lot, volunteer driver Solomon Jones had just begun talking to Dr. King when the shot rang out. Andrew Young and another aide immediately pushed Jones to the ground. According to one account, an FBI report said that "to Andrew Young . . . the sound was a firecracker and it came from the bushes above the retaining wall across the street from the motel." The HSCA found that "others in the courtyard, including Ben Branch and Jesse Jackson . . . believed that the shot had come from the direction of the rooming house." The thick bushes were just below the rooming house, and because of a retaining wall, both the bushes and the rooming house windows were higher than the Lorraine's second-floor balcony.[6]

Across Mulberry Street, tenants on the second floor of the rooming house heard the gunshot. The HSCA found that "Charles Anschutz heard a shot, opened his door, and saw a man fleeing down the hallway from the direction of the bathroom." But he didn't get a good look at him, and "was unable to give a good description" to police. In about the past hour, Anschutz had "made two attempts to use the bathroom and found it occupied on each occasion." He was told by another second-floor tenant, Charles Stephens, "that the bathroom was being used by the new tenant in 5-B," which Ray had rented earlier.[7]

Charles Stephens shared a small apartment with his common-law wife, Grace Walden. On the day of the shooting, Stephens "heard a loud explosion that he recognized as a shot. After looking out the window toward the Lorraine Motel, he heard footsteps running in the hallway. He went to the door, opened it, looked out, and observed a man with something under his arm turning the corner at the end of the hallway. Stephens was sure the individual had come from the bathroom adjoining his apartment because of the loudness of the shot." While the man Stephens saw "fit the general description of James Earl Ray," he didn't get a good look at his face.[8]

Stephens' wife, Grace Walden, was bedridden; when police interviewed her "shortly after the shooting," she told them that the new "tenant of 5-B had been running back and forth between 5-B and the bathroom, and about 2 minutes before the shot was fired, he had returned to the bathroom. After the shot, the person in the bathroom ran down the hall toward the front of the building. She said she was sick, did not get out of bed that day, and did not see the man."[9]

James Earl Ray fled down outside stairs into a four-foot-wide alley that separated his small wing of the rooming house from the main building. That structure housed two other businesses, including the Canipe Amusement Company, two doors south of the rooming house entrance. Canipe Amusements' recessed entrance was slightly more than one car length north of Ray's white Mustang, which was parked on the same side of the street. Based on a reenactment, the Justice Department Task Force estimated it would have taken Ray forty-five seconds to clear the rooming house.[10]

Some experts think Ray stopped by his room to get his zipper bag after he ran out of the bathroom—otherwise, he would have had to lug it with him each time he went into the bathroom. But Ray's room was only two doors down from the bathroom, so stopping there to grab the bag would have added only a few seconds to his escape time. His bag probably hadn't been unpacked, since Ray later wrote in a letter that he brought his own blanket "in case he had to spend the night" in the flophouse. Since Ray had already checked out of the New Rebel Inn, he must not have intended to sleep in the flophouse room he'd rented three hours earlier—if things went according to plan.

Once on the sidewalk, Ray would have walked quickly down South Main Street toward his Mustang. The Justice Department estimates it would have taken him only fifteen seconds to get to his Mustang, which was just over forty feet away, south of Canipe Amusements. But before he reached his car, Ray apparently did something that has caused controversy for forty years—and that ensured his eventual capture. As the Justice Department described the situation, based on early interviews with three witnesses:[11]

> Guy Warren Canipe, Jr., in his place of business, Canipe Amusement Co. . . . heard a thud near the front door of his store, looked up to see a white male walk rapidly past his store going south . . . and, with the two customers in his store, went to the front door, where they observed a small white car, a Mustang according to the two customers, pull away going north from a curbside parking place just south of Canipe's store.

The thud Canipe had heard was the sound of a bundle being dropped; the man who apparently dropped it was described as "dressed in a dark suit . . . white, approximately 30 years of age with a medium build," and with a height and weight consistent with that of James Earl Ray, who said he was wearing a suit that day. The bundle contained "valuable pieces of evidence," including the rifle Ray had bought in Birmingham and "a blue zipper bag [containing] various toilet articles along with a pair of men's underwear with laundry tags, a pair of binoculars, two cans of beer, [and] a York Arms Company case sales receipt dated April 4, 1968."[12] Within several minutes, policemen swarmed the area and found the bag.

The large bundle of rifle, blanket, and zipper bag was a treasure trove of incriminating evidence. Ray's fingerprints, in addition to appearing on the Memphis newspaper mentioned earlier, were on the rifle (which had one spent shell in its chamber), its scope, the binoculars, and a beer can. In those pre–high-speed computer days, it could take weeks to match prints by hand, if they were on file, but it could be done eventually. Authorities were fortunate to get so many prints from the bundle, since they found no prints of Ray's in the rooming house—Ray had once bragged that he knew how to avoid leaving fingerprints. Ray's bag also contained his prison radio, which had his prison ID number scratched on it, though that would be overlooked until Ray had been identified through his fingerprints.[13]

The entrance to Canipe's was only a few feet deep, and the bundle was easily visible to anyone on the sidewalk. Assistant District Attorney John Campbell, who investigated the case in the 1990s, told an author that if Ray "had not dropped the bundle there, he might well have gotten away with the crime. It was that close to being a perfect assassination."[14] But the bundle was dropped, and just over three hours after Dr. King was shot, it was delivered to the FBI, "who immediately had it flown by agent courier to Washington for [the] laboratory examination" that would eventually help identify the fingerprints as James Earl Ray's.[15]

Debates have raged for years about why Ray dropped the bundle; Ray himself repeatedly claimed that someone else had dropped it to incriminate him. Then again, Ray claimed he hadn't known that Dr. King was at the Lorraine, despite the newspaper, with his fingerprint, that had an article about it. Ray also said he didn't know Dr. King had been shot when he left Memphis just after 6:00 PM, and that he'd left Memphis only because of "his instinctive fear of police and his concern that something had gone wrong with Raoul's gunrunning scheme."[16]

The main reason usually cited for Ray's dropping the bundle, rather than taking it to his car, just over a dozen feet away, is that he spotted a police car. Some authors say that as soon as Ray came out of the alley between the two buildings and turned left toward his Mustang, he saw the front of a police car, much farther down Main Street. According to this scenario, Ray walked a couple of car lengths down to the Canipe's entrance, dropped the gun/bundle on the sidewalk there, and continued walking one more car length to his Mustang. However, it would have been more logical for Ray to have simply dropped the bundle in the deep, narrow alley as soon as he saw the police car, rather than walking with it down the sidewalk and leaving his rifle in a far more visible place.

Attorney William Pepper says the police car in question really wasn't that close, or clearly visible, to Ray. The car belonged to Officer Emmett "Gene" Douglass, who broadcast the first alert about the shooting on his police car radio. Douglass later told the attorney he had been parked beside the fire station, which Pepper says "was set back about sixty feet from the sidewalk." CNN came up with a fresh angle in 2008, when correspondent Soledad O'Brien broadcast new information from Douglass, who had been parked next to the fire station, which was approximately 170 feet south of Canipe's Amusements. According to CNN, after hearing the shot and radioing the alert, Douglass got out of his car and started running north on Main Street, toward Canipe's. He stopped twenty or thirty feet away from Canipe's when a fellow officer called him, then Douglass turned and started heading away from Canipe's. While Douglass didn't see Ray or the bundle, Soledad O'Brien indicated that Ray could have seen Douglass running toward him, causing Ray to drop the bundle.[17]

Douglass's new statement may explain why Ray dropped so much incriminating evidence. Scotland Yard detective Alec East testified to the HSCA that while he was guarding James Earl Ray in England, Ray told him "he had seen a policeman or police vehicle and thrown the gun away."[18] However, Ray denied saying that. In addition, there are other factors to consider—such as why Ray didn't simply pick up the bundle when he saw that Douglass had turned away, since Ray was only one car length away from his Mustang and a perfect getaway.

There is also an issue of timing, based on a summary of Douglass's initial statement back in 1968. According to the Justice Department Task Force, "Douglass . . . heard the shot when it was fired. He immediately got out of the car and ran toward the rear of the fire station with the other men." That would have meant he was running away from Canipe's, not toward it. "After Patrolman Douglass realized what had happened, he returned to the lead car along with [another patrolman] and radioed the dispatcher that Dr. King had been shot. Douglass and [another patrolman] then drove the lead car south on South Main," taking them away from Canipe's, and eventually to the "entrance of the Lorraine Motel." Douglass "later drove the car [from the Lorraine] to the front of the buildings" that included Canipe's. Based on original police statements, the Justice Department report doesn't have Douglass running on foot toward Canipe's, and the elapsed time in which Douglass could have arrived near Canipe's is far greater than the one minute Justice says it took for Ray to get from the flophouse bathroom to his Mustang.[19]

One other anomalous detail about the incriminating bundle found at Canipe Amusements was provided in a later account by owner Guy Canipe. Arthur Hanes Jr., one of Ray's first defense attorneys, who later became a judge, interviewed Canipe as a possible witness for Ray. Hanes Jr. later testified that Canipe told him "the package was dropped in his doorway . . . about ten minutes before the shot was fired." Hanes Jr. was going to have Canipe appear for the defense at Ray's first trial, until Ray switched lawyers and pled guilty.[20]

Canipe's story that the bundle was dropped ten minutes before the shot would show that Ray was framed. However, that version of the story is greatly at odds with Canipe's initial statements to police and the FBI, as well as those of his two customers—all made soon after the shooting and prior to Ray's capture. We believe that Hanes Jr. was accurately conveying what Canipe told him, so the question is why Canipe would have changed his story to help Ray, after he'd first helped to direct suspicion toward him.

Canipe owned an amusement company, as did Carlos Marcello, mobster Frank Joseph Caracci, Santo Trafficante, and a kingpin of the Montreal heroin route that used Ray. (Sam Bowers, a likely Milteer associate, also owned one.) The Mafia found these companies to be useful cover, since they often provided jukeboxes in bars and supplied them with records on a regular basis. Those regular visits, and cash transactions, could cover for gambling, protection, money laundering, and other criminal pursuits. Author Larry Hancock has pointed out that little is known about Canipe himself, or any Mafia ties he might have had.

It's important to remember that the bag was dropped, and that Ray fled in his Mustang, just over a minute after the fatal shot was fired. Though there were dozens of the police in the general area, their first inclination was to head for the Lorraine Motel, not to the rooming house area.

In Fire Station 2, when the bullet struck Dr. King, black undercover patrolman "Richmond, who was manning the surveillance post in the rear of the station, yelled throughout the station that Dr. King had been shot." The tactical-unit patrolmen "all ran out the north side of the fire station and then east toward the rear of the fire station and the Lorraine Motel." From the back of the fire station, they had to "climb down the concrete wall and [run] across Mulberry Street to the Lorraine." The patrolmen quickly covered the Lorraine itself, but didn't seal off a two-block area around the Lorraine until five minutes later—four minutes too late to stop James Earl Ray.[21]

On the balcony, Dr. King lay dying. Photographs show undercover officer Marrell McCullough kneeling next to his body, along with Andrew Young. An officer asked where the shot came from, and a famous photo shows Young and the other aides standing as they all point in the direction of the rooming house across Mulberry Street.

Below the rooming house windows was a thicket-covered area, fronted by bushes along the top of the retaining wall that ran along Mulberry Street. After patrolmen climbed up the wall and searched the area, the Justice Department says, "about 10 feet up the alley" that ran between the two buildings of the rooming house, "they found two fresh footprints in the mud . . . subsequently, a plaster cast was made of each footprint. However, the footprints were never positively identified by either the Memphis Police or the FBI." According to William Pepper, the shoe size was large, approximately "13 to 13 ½."[22]

Ralph Abernathy said that by the time an ambulance arrived at 6:06 PM, police officers "cluttered the courtyard." The mortally wounded Dr. King lay unconscious as he clung to life, and Abernathy rode with him to the hospital. They arrived at 6:15 PM.[23]

Martin Luther King was pronounced dead at 7:05 PM.

Chapter Fifty-one

For forty years, many have wondered if James Earl Ray fired the fatal shot from the rooming house. Rep. Stokes and the HSCA concluded he did, though they were careful to point out that the direction and source of the shot could not be determined with scientific precision. No witness actually saw the shot come from the bathroom window, and no one in the rooming house watched Ray fire the rifle, or definitively identified him fleeing with the weapon. The autopsy might have provided conclusive information about the bullet's angle, and thus its origin, but the doctor who performed the autopsy said he didn't track the path of the bullet, so as not to further disfigure Dr. King.[1]

The bullet recovered from Dr. King's body could not be matched to, or excluded from, the rifle Ray had purchased that was left on the sidewalk in front of Canipe's. That was true for tests done in 1968 and for the most recent testing done in the 1990s. Apparently as a result of the first round of tests, the bullet that was removed from Dr. King in one piece is now in three pieces, further reducing the chance that authorities will ever be able to prove it did, or did not, come from Ray's rifle.[2]

A shot from the rooming house would not have been difficult for an experienced shooter. The motel's balcony was about 205 feet away from the bathroom window, but with the seven-power Redfield scope, the distance would have seemed like less than thirty feet. That's still a good shot for someone like Ray, who had no documented practice. If Ray acted alone and not as part of a conspiracy, the idea of his risking target practice with the rifle in some random part of the Alabama woods seems unlikely, given his chances of getting caught. The gun was loud, the bullets powerful, and he would have had to practice in daylight, increasing his chances of being seen. A simple arrest for trespassing could have meant the fugitive Ray's return to prison. On the other hand, since we feel that Ray was acting for Milteer in the contract that Marcello brokered, Ray could have had a safe place to practice either through someone like Milteer's associate Dr. Swift in California, or via one of Marcello's Mafia associates.

If the shot was fired from the bathroom window, as the HSCA concluded, then King's murder was simply a variation of two earlier assassination efforts linked to Marcello and Milteer: the JFK attempt planned
for Tampa and his murder in Dallas, both of which involved a shooter
firing from an open window. In the rooming house bathroom that Ray
shared, the window screen was pushed out, further indicating that a
shot was fired from there. Though the window had jammed when someone tried to raise it, leaving only a five-inch gap, positioning the rifle
and scope, then firing, would not have been difficult.[3]

Could someone besides Ray have fired from the bathroom window?
Second-floor tenant Grace Walden would later claim to have seen a
man who did not fit Ray's description in various ways, though, as we
noted earlier, she first told authorities she "did not see the man" at all.[4]
Her later descriptions didn't match Ray, but varied considerably. Usually she said he was white, but on the *Today* show in 1978, she said, "I
think he was a nigger." Grace Walden suffered from mental illness and
was institutionalized later in 1968, and some authors alleged that she
was committed because she wouldn't accept a $100,000 bribe to say she
had seen Ray. However, Stokes and the HSCA investigated the matter
closely, even having their staff review her medical records and talk to
her doctors. They concluded that all of her treatment "was based on
medical considerations and was not related to her role as a possible
witness," and that "because of the differences in Walden's statements
about whether she saw anyone at all, and if so whether the man she
saw was white or black, the Committee found that her testimony was
virtually useless."[5]

The HSCA was also cautious about the statements of Walden's
common-law husband, Charles Stephens, whose identification of the
man he saw fleeing down the hall seemed to grow more like Ray as time
passed. All accounts say that Stephens had been drinking that day, and
most say he was intoxicated to some degree, with some stating he was
"drunk." Keeping in mind that the rooming house was essentially a
flophouse, the reliability of the witnesses there was far from ideal.

It seems odd that a sniper would choose as his lair the shared bathroom on a floor where tenants often drank beer for much of the day.
There was nothing to prevent an irate tenant like Stephens or Anschutz
from banging on the locked bathroom door while—or just after—the
shot was fired, then getting a good look at whoever came out of the
bathroom, and what he was carrying. Then again, Ray wasn't an experienced hit man, and if Sartor's sources in the Justice Department memo

were accurate, a schedule change scarcely an hour earlier had sped up the hit's timing, putting additional pressure on the shooter.

Some of Ray's defense attorneys have said the shot came from the bushes below the rooming house windows. Such a shot would have been closer to the Lorraine, and therefore easier. But debates have raged for years about how thick the foliage was, and whether a shooter there would have been spotted easily by tenants looking out of their windows (police noticed several women peeking through those windows not long after the shots). Also, aside from the two footprints mentioned earlier, no other prints were found, as would have been expected if someone had gone through the area, especially given the recent very wet weather.[6]

Aside from Andrew Young's brief statement at the time, three other witnesses indicated seeing something in the area of the bushes, but there are issues with each of their stories. Volunteer driver Solomon Jones later testified to the HSCA that after he got up off the ground, where Young had pushed him when the shot rang out, "he saw a movement of something white and 'as tall as a human being' in the brush beneath the rooming house," but "for only a brief time. He did not see a head or arms; he could not tell whether the object was black or white, male or female." Since Jones didn't look at the brushy area until after he got up off the ground, as the police were starting to enter the area, the HSCA concluded that he likely saw one of the officers in the brush.[7]

On the day of the shooting, Jones gave varying accounts of what he saw: He told a reporter within minutes that "the shot came from the bushes 'over there,' pointing across Mulberry Street to the thick brush behind the rooming house." According to William Pepper, Jones told the Memphis Police "he saw a man heading back toward the rooming house," but "in a statement given to the media [that] evening [Jones] said he saw a man come down over the wall and onto or near the Lorraine property, only to drift away." At that point, Jones said he was "desperate to follow [the man, so] he tried to find a way out of the Lorraine Motel parking area, becoming hysterical when he couldn't find a clear path to drive out."[8]

Earl Caldwell, covering King's Memphis trip for the *New York Times*, later said he was standing in the doorway of his first-floor room at the Lorraine when he heard what sounded like an explosion. As William Pepper recounted, Caldwell "was looking at the brush area at the rear of the rooming house on the other side of Mulberry Street and saw a figure in the bushes, a white male wearing what appeared to be coveralls. The man was crouched or semi-crouched in the midst of the high bushes and was staring at the balcony . . . he didn't see a gun in the hands of the man, and he was quickly distracted by Solomon Jones, who began driving the car back and forth frantically in the driveway of the motel. When Caldwell looked back to the brush area, the man had disappeared.". However, critics of his account point out that Caldwell didn't go public with his story for years, and that he didn't mention it when author Gerold Frank interviewed him a year after Dr. King's murder.[9]

A minister with Dr. King said he saw "a puff of white smoke" coming from the bushes—but critics point out that the gunpowder in use at the time didn't generate smoke, and no other witnesses reported seeing the "puff."[10] Those are the only reports of activity in the bushes that have emerged after forty years that are even close to being credible. A few other stories surfaced at various times, but have been discredited. Ray's many defense attorneys tried to do their job, which was to cast reasonable doubt on their client's possible guilt, by using any testimony available. (Ray said he fired one of his attorneys because the lawyer was more interested in finding out the truth than in defending him.)

None of our work is based in any way on the claims of Lloyd Jowers, the owner of Jim's Grill on the first floor of Ray's rooming house. In the early 1990s, Jowers began telling stories about his involvement with another shooter and rifle, though his accounts varied greatly over time. A Tennessee civil jury found Jowers liable for the death of Dr. King in 1999, a case in which he essentially offered no defense and paid damages of $1. Jowers' and his associates' claims changed so much over the years, and lacked corroborating evidence, that even his supporters acknowledge that their stories are problematic. One of Jowers' biggest supporters, Ray's last attorney, William Pepper, wrote that "Jowers's impetuousness, often combined with his drinking, resulted in behavior which is used to undermine his credibility." Of another key witness involved in Jowers' story, Pepper wrote that her "credibility has been hurt as much by some of those working for me as it has by the agents of the state who wish to discredit her." The only thing that can be said with certainty about Jowers is that he was a gambling associate of Frank C. Liberto, so he may have heard about part of the plan or had some role in it. Jowers seemed motivated by a desire for financial gain, and started to go public with his story only in the wake of the success of Oliver Stone's *JFK*, when Carlos Marcello was near death.[11]

One alternate theory holds that Ray was doing only surveillance for the hit, an option mentioned in one of the earlier cited prison-bounty stories. In that scenario, either the real shooter set Ray up to take the fall, or Ray himself suddenly decided to make additional money by shooting

Dr. King, as well as doing the surveillance. However, the fact that Ray had to buy binoculars just an hour before the shooting indicates that he was poorly prepared if his main job was merely surveillance.[12]

After weighing all the evidence from the past forty years, it does appear that the shot came from the second-floor bathroom. However, it can't be stated with absolute certainty. We don't rule out the possibility that someone else tied to the contract was in the immediate vicinity, either helping Ray or ensuring that he was tied to the crime—or both. The HSCA also looked closely at the Memphis Police Department's performance in the wake of Dr. King's murder. While the Committee documented the department's bad decisions and its lack of a contingency plan for problems at the Lorraine—and pointed out things that could have been done more effectively—it didn't find any member of the Memphis police who was involved in Martin Luther King's assassination. As the assistant district attorney noted earlier, if the bag hadn't been dropped at Canipe's, Ray would have gotten away with "a perfect assassination"—and without any assistance from the police being required.

Because Memphis lies at the intersection of three states, within minutes of the shooting, Ray could have been in any of them. After confirming Officer Douglass's initial report, the dispatcher issued a system-wide alert at 6:03 PM. The HSCA found that "at 6:08 PM [a general] description of the suspect was broadcast as a young, well-dressed white male"—but by then, "Ray could have been in Arkansas." At 6:10 PM, the description of the suspected getaway car as a late-model white Mustang was broadcast (at least three were eventually stopped), but at that time, "Ray could have been halfway to the Mississippi state line." Even though "roadblocks were not established on major arteries leaving Memphis," they probably couldn't have been set up in time to stop Ray. Worse, "an all points bulletin for a white Mustang was never broadcast to . . . Arkansas, Mississippi, and Alabama," apparently because of problems the Memphis police had experienced with previous alerts to Mississippi.[13] Congressional investigators were able to debunk the story of the so-called "fake broadcast," originally thought to be part of a conspiracy. In addition, the HSCA found that the reason why the many police tactical units (with 49 to 110 vehicles) didn't join the search for the Mustang "was that their primary concern was with the rioting, firebombing, and looting that occurred throughout the city following news of the assassination."[14]

———

As James Earl Ray drove through Mississippi and toward New Orleans, riots exploded in more than a hundred American cities. The raw figures are staggering, but can't convey the true extent of the pain, suffering, and destruction that raged in the aftermath of Martin Luther King's murder: almost seventy thousand troops deployed, forty-five people killed (all but five of them black), twenty thousand arrested, and almost $50 million in property destruction. Outbreaks were especially bad in Washington, D.C., Detroit, Chicago, Baltimore, and Pittsburgh. Some riots lasted for days—in Chicago, they continued through the following week, until Mayor Richard Daley issued "shoot to kill" orders.[15]

Two large cities that seemed relatively immune to the widespread destruction were Atlanta, Dr. King's home, and Indianapolis. Bobby Kennedy had gone to Indianapolis to address a rally in what Evan Thomas called "the heart of the ghetto." While still in the air on the way to Indianapolis, Bobby learned that Dr. King had been shot. The news shattered whatever positive feelings he still had after the previous day's cordial meeting with LBJ. According to an aide, Bobby's "eyes went blank" and he "sagged" visibly. After he landed, Bobby learned that Dr. King had died.[16]

In the days before 24-hour TV news and radio networks, information traveled far more slowly. Many of the thousand or so people who were gathered to hear Bobby didn't know that Dr. King had been shot, let alone killed. Police officials were worried about a riot, so Bobby was advised to cancel his appearance. He went anyway, despite the fact that his police escort left as soon as he reached the predominately black part of Indianapolis.

As Bobby faced the crowd in the chilly night air, he was wearing one of JFK's overcoats, something he had begun doing at times after his brother's murder. It must have been a daunting prospect for a white politician to face an African American crowd and tell them their greatest and most beloved leader had just been shot and killed. But Bobby delivered what was perhaps his greatest speech—and without the aid of teleprompters or spin doctors:

> Ladies and gentlemen . . . I'm only going to talk to you just for a minute or so this evening, because I have some—some very sad news for all of you . . . I think, sad news for all of our fellow citizens, and people who love peace all over the world, and that is that Martin Luther King was shot and was killed tonight in Memphis, Tennessee.

Gasps, screams, and cries arose from the audience. Bobby continued, saying that "King dedicated his life to love and to justice between fellow human beings. He died in the cause of that effort. . . . For those of you who are black—considering the evidence . . . that there were white people who were responsible—you can be filled with bitterness, and with hatred, and a desire for revenge. . . . Or we can make an effort, as Martin Luther King did, to understand, and to comprehend, and replace that violence, that stain of bloodshed that has spread across our land, with an effort to understand, compassion, and love."

Speaking from the heart and drawing on the experience he and they knew all too well, Bobby said earnestly that

> For those of you who are black and are tempted to fill with hatred and mistrust of the injustice of such an act, against all white people, I would only say that I can also feel in my own heart the same kind of feeling. I had a member of my family killed, but he was killed by a white man.

After making it clear that he knew the kind of pain they were feeling, Bobby didn't talk down to his audience. Instead, he quoted his favorite poem saying, "My favorite poet was Aeschylus," the ancient Greek writer in whose words Bobby found solace after JFK's murder. He recited the poem, talking of pain that first brings despair, but eventually engenders wisdom. He closed by asking the audience to "return home, to say a prayer for the family of Martin Luther King . . . but more importantly to say a prayer for our own country, which all of us love—a prayer for understanding and that compassion of which I spoke."

After the speech, Bobby called Coretta Scott King and arranged to have Dr. King's body flown back to Atlanta.[17]

Chapter Fifty-two

After Martin Luther King's murder, James Earl Ray claims he left Memphis, driving south to New Orleans, but while he was in Mississippi, he began heading east to Atlanta, Georgia. New information, presented here for the first time, finally explains why Ray went to Atlanta and who helped him once he arrived. Ray's original explanations for his change of direction and destination were suspicious. He claimed that he first heard that Dr. King had been shot and killed over his car radio, which made Ray think "he was somehow involved in the assassination and that the police were looking for his white Mustang." Ray testified that he then decided to go to Atlanta to get his pistol, which he maintained he hadn't taken with him to Memphis.[1]

Congressional investigators and journalists found holes in Ray's story: First, the radio in his Mustang was found to be inoperable. Second, the HSCA thought it unlikely Ray hadn't taken his pistol with him to Memphis—or that he would have made an almost four-hundred-mile trip just to get it.[2]

By the very early morning of April 5, 1968, Ray was on his way to Atlanta, and would be in Canada the following day. The HSCA found that "Ray's decision to flee . . . to Atlanta, rather than directly north to Canada, was also significant, since it . . . created an increased risk of arrest." The Committee looked at two possible explanations. "First, Ray returned to Atlanta to receive money for the assassination. Second, there was highly incriminating evidence in Atlanta that Ray needed to eliminate before leaving the country." However, the HSCA could find no evidence to substantiate either possibility.[3]

Ray may well have originally headed toward New Orleans, intending to collect the $5,000 that Frank C. Liberto had mentioned over the phone the previous afternoon. Ray said that once he was in New Orleans, he planned "to telephone [his contact's] associates in that city." From there, Ray could drive to Mexico; one of his brothers said that Ray "had everything set up in Mexico for a life after killing King." Ray had spent far more time in Mexico than in Canada, and by all accounts, including his own, was much more comfortable south of the border.[4]

Exclusive facts about whom James Earl Ray contacted in Atlanta, information not available to the HSCA, finally help to explain Ray's actions. While Ray may have intended to go to New Orleans, get his payoff, and then go to Mexico, at some point he was ordered to Atlanta instead. As he had done before, Ray probably stopped at a pay phone to call his New Orleans contact. Because of the riots sweeping the country, and the outpouring of sympathetic press coverage about Dr. King's murder, the assassination was clearly having a far larger national impact than racists like Joseph Milteer and Carlos Marcello might have anticipated.

Marcello had only brokered the contract to kill King, and now it was too risky to have Ray drive through Louisiana to New Orleans, then drive through Marcello's Texas territory to Mexico. While authorities had not yet issued any good descriptions or sketches of Ray, such information could be released to law enforcement or the public at any time. By daybreak, it would be too dangerous to allow Ray to remain on the road in his white Mustang, a car that authorities were already looking for.

Marcello transferred the risk to those paying for the contract, Joseph Milteer and his three Atlanta partners. After Milteer had helped Ray in Atlanta, it would be safer for Marcello—and closer for Ray at that point—to have Ray go to Canada, rather than Mexico. It's important to remember that on as little as an hour's notice, the hit on King may have been moved up by as much as four days, to ensure it wasn't stopped by the court injunction. However, while Ray wasn't a professional hit man, Marcello and his lieutenants had decades of proven success in that area, and knew how to whisk someone out of the country—while avoiding blame themselves.

In addition, Atlanta was a safe destination that was relatively unscathed by the riots plaguing other parts of the country. In stark contrast to Memphis, Atlanta's mayor, Ivan Allan, was a moderate on race who, four years earlier, had helped to host Dr. King's lavish Nobel Prize banquet. Atlanta's police chief, Herbert Jenkins, was friends with Dr. King's father, the respected Daddy King, who presided over Ebenezer Baptist Church on Auburn Avenue, Dr. King's home pulpit. Since Atlanta was home to the now widowed Coretta Scott King and her children, it was as if the angry and distraught African American residents of even Atlanta's poorest neighborhoods—some near Auburn Avenue—felt it would be disrespectful to erupt in violence. Then, too, King hadn't been killed in their city, and they had no reason to think that anyone in Atlanta was involved with the murder.

Sadly, Joseph Milteer's instincts had been proven correct: It was better for him and his three partners to have had Dr. King killed outside of Atlanta. Now though, they faced the problem of what to do about James Earl Ray. According to Ray's account, he drove nonstop to Atlanta and threw out his expensive photographic equipment along the way.[5]

Ray arrived in Atlanta around 6:00 AM on April 5, 1968, twelve hours after he left Memphis. Ray's next action, well-documented by Congressional investigators and Atlanta police, was witnessed about 9:00 AM, when Ray was seen abandoning his car in an Atlanta housing project that was three miles south of his rooming house. Investigators have never been able to determine what Ray did in Atlanta between 6:00 and 9:00 AM on the day after King's murder, why he left his car in that particular place, and how he traveled the three miles to his rooming house.[6]

For the first time, exclusive new information answers those questions and helps to explain why Ray returned to Atlanta. Based on a witness who heard a portion of the call, we can now report that on the morning of April 5, James Earl Ray phoned Hugh R. Spake, Joseph Milteer's Atlanta partner. Our source remains confidential because racist associates of Milteer and his ally J. B. Stoner (later Ray's attorney) are still alive, and active in the sometimes violent white supremacist movement. Our source was not involved in any racist activities and has a long-standing reputation for honesty and integrity, with no criminal record. We verified that our source had known Spake for a long time, witnessed some of Spake's activities with Milteer, and was in a position to have heard a portion of Ray's call to Spake that morning.[7]

James Earl Ray phoned Hugh R. Spake on the morning of April 5 for assistance with his escape. However, it was a Friday, a regular workday for Spake at the Atlanta General Motors factory in the Lakewood neighborhood. Because of the workers' high hourly wages, plant management closely monitored and documented attendance, so if Spake's name ever surfaced in the investigation, it would certainly look suspicious if he had not been at work the day after King's murder. Friday was also payday, when Spake—often joined by Joseph Milteer—networked with his contributors. Milteer would later admit that he was in Atlanta that morning. However, because he and Spake were behind Dr. King's murder, they deliberately refrained from publicly celebrating his death. A knowing look and a calm demeanor would have been all that was needed by their most trusted, and now satisfied, longtime contributors. Those people knew the type of Klan associates Spake and Milteer were involved with, the kind of men who for decades had gotten away with murder in the South. That knowledge helped to ensure that even Milteer and Spake's most ardent contributors wouldn't boast publicly that their money had helped to kill Dr. King—in addition to the fact that any such confession would have made them accessories to murder.[8]

Witnesses document that at the Atlanta Housing project known as Capitol Homes, Ray's "Mustang was parked shortly before 9 AM [on] April 5, 1968, by a lone man matching [Ray's] description." The housing project was just south of Georgia's gold-domed State Capitol—and halfway between Ray's rooming house and the General Motors factory where Spake worked. According to witnesses, the man leaving the Mustang simply walked away and wasn't seen again. The late-model car, driven by someone not seen in the neighborhood before, attracted some notice at the time. But it would be days before the residents realized it had been abandoned, and almost a week before anyone called the police about the car.[9]

The housing project was an unusual place for James Earl Ray to ditch his car. At the time, Atlanta's housing projects were in the process of being integrated, and photos show that many, if not most, of the residents at that time were white. But Capitol Homes was three miles away from Ray's rooming house, too far for him to safely walk in broad daylight, since he couldn't be sure when a police drawing or photo of him might be issued. Yet Ray left his car only nine short blocks from Martin Luther King's church and SCLC office on Auburn Avenue, both in the heart of Atlanta's black business district, which Ray would have to pass on his way north to his rooming house.

Even after his face became well known, Ray was not reported as having been seen on any of the Atlanta buses running that day. Atlanta is not the type of city where taxis simply cruise in most areas. Although cabs would have been available several blocks from the housing project, at the State Capitol building, its grounds were always well covered by law enforcement. The governor's office at the Capitol was then occupied by ardent segregationist Lester Maddox, and, given the reports of riots in other cities, security was likely even higher than usual around the State Capitol. Atlanta police and the FBI later carefully canvassed all Atlanta taxi drivers. The only two who thought Ray might have been a passenger remembered taking him on short trips (one only two blocks) in the Midtown area near Ray's rooming house, three miles away—and those trips were at night, not during the day. No cab driver ever reported taking Ray to his rooming house or anywhere near Capitol Homes. So how did Ray get to his rooming house?[10]

Joseph Milteer, Hugh Spake's partner in the assassination plot, was in the area at that time, according to one of his close friends. After Milteer's death by explosion several years after Dr. King's murder, Miami reporter Dan Christensen found much of Milteer's correspondence still in his deserted house. He thought it odd that in all of Milteer's letters, there were only two lines about Dr. King's assassination. Christensen wrote that "more might have been expected because Milteer hated King. But no gloating . . . nothing," except for two lines in a letter written to Milteer by a racist friend from West Virginia. The letter was written just two weeks after Ray abandoned his car at Capitol Homes in Atlanta. Responding to what Milteer had told him earlier, the friend wrote that it "looks as though you [Milteer] and the hunted suspect [Ray] were in the Capitol area about the same time. They found a car there—they say."[11]

Milteer's friend was appropriately suspicious, and he wrote the letter the day James Earl Ray's name was first announced as a suspect. Given Ray's earlier call to Milteer's partner Spake, and the lack of any other known way for Ray to have safely traveled the three miles north to his rooming house, Milteer probably either drove Ray himself or observed from a safe distance while an associate did it. The actions and whereabouts that day of Milteer's two other Atlanta partners—the dentist and the attorney—are not known.[12]

Spake had to be at work that day until 3:30 PM, and Ray had reportedly left the city before that, after picking up his laundry (shortly after leaving Capitol Homes) and then stopping by his rooming house. However, Spake could have telephoned Milteer after Ray's morning call to him, relaying Ray's request for help; alternately, Spake could have given Ray a number where Milteer could be reached. Because of urban renewal, which had cleared out local residents for two recently completed construction projects (the Atlanta Braves' baseball stadium and a major interstate interchange), next to Capital Homes were several isolated side streets where Milteer could have picked up Ray without being seen by witnesses.

Ray himself was vague about how he got to his rooming house; he later testified that he "walked in the general direction of where I thought was the rooming house. I'm not certain how I found the rooming house."

Perhaps realizing how far that would have been, he changed his story immediately and said that maybe he "got a cab. I think I got a cab, yeah, I believe I did get a cab." But as noted earlier, despite law enforcement's exhaustive investigation of Atlanta cab drivers and companies, none were found who had driven Ray anywhere near Capitol Homes.[13]

Apparently, leaving his car and rerouting his escape to Canada were not part of Ray's original instructions. According to the HSCA volumes, one of his brothers said, "It wasn't [Ray's] plan to abandon his car and everything. His actual plan after Memphis was to go to Atlanta, pick up his stuff, and go to Mexico." But Mexico was a 1,100-mile drive away, and going anywhere in the wanted white Mustang was out of the question.[14]

At the rooming house, Ray quickly packed important items, like his pistol, and threw away others, such as his typewriter. He left behind several things, including two maps of Atlanta (one with marks near Dr. King's office and Capitol Homes) and two maps of Los Angeles (one unmarked, and one with Rosselli's apartment building marked), since he apparently had no plans to return to either city. Other abandoned items ranged from his portable television to a John Birch Society brochure.[15]

James Earl Ray's account of his movements for the next twenty-four hours is vague and contradictory, and they can't be definitively documented. Ray said he thought he recalled taking a cab to the bus station, checking a bag, visiting a tavern, then going back to the bus station. In one account, he said he left Atlanta at around 1:00 PM, while in another, he says it was between 3:00 PM and 5:00 PM. No actual documentation of his bus trips exists, and the only cab drivers who might remember Ray said they drove him at night, and nowhere near the bus station in downtown Atlanta. The fact that the bus station was almost two miles from Ray's rooming house makes it unlikely that he walked there. More likely it was Milteer (or his associate) who drove Ray from Capitol Homes to his rooming house also took him to the bus station.

In less than two weeks, Ray's face would be on television and the front page of almost every newspaper in the country. Yet even after weeks of such exposure—and, later, televised footage of Ray—no bus passengers or drivers came forward to say that they remembered seeing him. That lack of witnesses was in marked contrast to some of Lee Harvey Oswald's bus trips, where even two months later, some passengers remembered the relatively average-looking young man.

Before leaving Atlanta, Ray was probably given a small amount of

money, with the promise of more later—if he went where he was told
and did what he was ordered. That was the best way to maintain control
over Ray. In Atlanta, Ray got nowhere near the $5,000 he was supposed
to receive in New Orleans. The large amount of money that Milteer and
his Atlanta partners had put up for King's murder would have gone
to the contract's broker, Carlos Marcello, and to Marcello's designated
Mafia lieutenant. Marcello's organization was responsible for paying
Ray, though Milteer and his partners would have been able to come up
with expense money of several hundred dollars, perhaps even $1,000
($6,000 today), on short notice and without arousing suspicion or obtain-
ing it in a traceable way. Ray later told his brother that "he would never
have been caught if he had enough money—he expected [to] make [a]
big score in [the] U.S. before he left but too much heat, he couldn't."[16]

Not giving someone like Ray all, or even most of, the money promised
is consistent with how Carlos Marcello treated the juror he bribed in
November 1963, after the JFK hit. Depriving Ray of most of the money
would prevent him from having so much cash that he attracted attention,
being tempted to not follow orders, or becoming the victim of a robbery.
Also, if Ray were caught with a large amount of money, it would indicate
that he had backers and co-conspirators. A smaller sum wouldn't arouse
suspicion and couldn't be traced if Ray were captured.

Milteer helped James Earl Ray get as far away from Atlanta as possible. The following description of Ray's travels, based on his statements,
could be accurate, but he also may have omitted important information.
Ray said that he went by bus, train, and cab from Atlanta all the way to
Toronto, Canada. He claims he first took the "bus from Atlanta to Cincinnati, Ohio, on the 5th of April . . . arrived in Cincinnati about 1:30 AM
on the 6th of April," and went to another tavern. Ray then took a bus to
Detroit, arriving at 8:00 AM, still on April 6. He took a cab to the Detroit
train station, then another cab across the border to Windsor, Ontario,
getting "there about 10 or 11 AM." There appears to be no official record
of Ray's crossing the border, and he apparently used his "Eric S. Galt"
identity. No public alert had yet been issued for that name, though Ray
couldn't have known what confidential alerts might have been sent to
border crossings. Ray says that once he was in Canada, he took a train
and arrived "in Toronto about 5 PM on the 6th of April." He says he
then rented a room without giving his name, from a woman who had
trouble speaking English. She later confirmed renting the Toronto room
to Ray for $10 a week.[17]

Ray was now in a city he had only passed through before, part of the Montreal–Toronto drug pipeline of the French Connection heroin network he had worked for the previous summer. That part of the network also specialized in providing fake identities, and Ray soon began using two new aliases, Paul Edward Bridgeman and Ramon George Sneyd. Like Eric Galt and John Willard, both were real names belonging to businessmen with no criminal past. Ray claimed to have gotten them from birth announcements in newspapers, but the HSCA noted Ray had "contradicted himself" regarding parts of his story. Ray's version also doesn't explain why he would just happen to pick, from decades-old birth announcements, two men who in 1968 lived within the same two-mile radius as his previous aliases, Galt and Willard. More likely is that Ray obtained all four names from the same source in the drug network that he'd worked for.[18]

James Earl Ray would soon undertake a trek that was even more unprecedented for him than the previous year's journey from Illinois to Canada to Alabama to Mexico to Los Angeles, to New Orleans, back to L.A., to New Orleans again, then to Memphis. A month after arriving in Toronto, Ray would leave for London, England. From there, he would go to Lisbon, Portugal, stay two days, then return to London, where he would prepare for a trip to Belgium—all while he was the subject of a worldwide manhunt. The much vaunted reputation of the FBI and its Most Wanted list, which J. Edgar Hoover had carefully crafted for decades, would be made to look ridiculous by a two-bit escaped con from Missouri.

Chapter Fifty-three

On April 9, 1968, the eyes of the world were on Martin Luther King's funeral procession in Atlanta. Gathered behind a simple wagon, pulled by two mules, walked the four leaders vying to become the next president: Bobby Kennedy, Vice President Hubert Humphrey, Eugene McCarthy, and Richard Nixon. Joining the King family, associates, and assorted dignitaries were fifty thousand people from all walks of life. Most were black, but some whites walked beside them as well. Just three years earlier, such a huge integrated gathering in a Deep South city like Atlanta would have been unprecedented and, to some, unthinkable. Now, thanks to the professional baseball and football teams the city's moderate image had attracted, racially mixed gatherings of such size were no longer rare. Sadly, such a large, peaceful integrated march wouldn't have been possible in many large American cities at that time, that were still smoldering from the riots following Dr. King's slaying.[1]

Unknown to the thousands of somber marchers beginning the four-mile trek, their route took them within a few blocks of James Earl Ray's abandoned Mustang. It would take two more days for police to be called about the white car that had been sitting in the parking lot of Capitol Homes since the morning of April 5. Registered to "Eric S. Galt" in Alabama, the car was one more crucial piece of evidence in the FBI's massive search for the man who had shot Dr. King.

As two Congressional committees documented a decade later, the FBI's manhunt was both incredibly thorough and severely compromised. Many of the field agents did an amazingly well-documented job of investigative work, methodically piecing together the clues to Ray's identity and travels. But key officials in Washington, including FBI Director J. Edgar Hoover, made glaring lapses in the investigation that left important questions unanswered.

By April 5, the day after Dr. King's murder, the FBI had only two aliases for Ray: "Willard" (used at the Memphis rooming house) and "Lowmyer" (used for the rifle purchase). But each had been used only once, so neither led anywhere. Not until April 11, when the car was found and one of Ray's t-shirts was traced by a laundry mark to a Los Angeles cleaners, did the FBI learn his main alias, "Eric Starvo Galt." That led agents to "Galt's" former residence in Los Angeles, then to his dancing lessons and the bartending school. Though authorities talked to narcotics trafficker Charles Stein, he told them only generally about his trip to New Orleans with the man he claimed to know only as "Eric Galt." The bartending school graduation photo allowed the Birmingham gun clerks to ID "Galt" as the man who'd bought the rifle, and a money order traced from the Locksmithing Institute led to "Galt's" Atlanta rooming house in Midtown.[2]

Agents watched the rooming house covertly for a time, but on April 16, they made a surreptitious entry, obtaining food, clothes, and maps, including the marked Atlanta map with a clear fingerprint. By cross-checking that print, and one from the rifle, with those of fugitives fitting the general description from Memphis, the FBI announced on April 19, 1968—fifteen days after King's murder—that "Eric Starvo Galt" was an alias, and that James Earl Ray was wanted for King's murder.

In a Toronto bar on April 21, Ray claimed to have watched the dramatic announcement at the end of that week's episode of the popular TV drama *The FBI*, when he was officially added to the FBI's "Ten Most Wanted" list. Ray, now pretending to be George Ramon Sneyd, left for Montreal the next day, having already applied for a Canadian passport using his new alias. Ray stayed in Montreal for a week, claiming later that he didn't "associate with anybody" while he was there. Ray returned to Toronto to find that he finally had a Canadian passport, but on it, his "Sneyd" alias was misspelled as "Senya." Not wanting to wait the extra time needed to fix the error, Ray paid for a ticket to London and flew to England on May 6, 1968.[3]

The FBI's identification of Ray was a result of the diligent work of hundreds of field agents in the days immediately following Dr. King's murder. J. Edgar Hoover made some efforts in the right direction, like eventually asking the attorney general to approve wiretaps and surveillance on Ray's family, including one of his brothers. The brothers weren't tied to the conspiracy with Milteer and Marcello, but one of them had associates who might have led investigators to Milteer. However, when Attorney General Ramsey Clark didn't act on Hoover's request for a month, the FBI Director withdrew it.[4,5]

Hoover was often far off the mark in his other investigative efforts, and a week after the assassination he theorized to President Johnson that black leaders H. Rap Brown or Stokely Carmichael might have been behind Dr. King's murder. Hoover even had the FBI float a false story to Jack Anderson that someone connected to an alleged mistress of Dr. King in Los Angeles might have been behind the assassination.[6]

However, the longer James Earl Ray remained at large, the more pressure Hoover faced from LBJ, the press, and the public to find the real culprit, especially once Ray's real name and photograph were released. The fact that Ray had been an escaped fugitive at the time of Dr. King's murder, and had been traveling across the country for almost a year, made the Bureau look less than stellar.

While Hoover told LBJ and the attorney general early on that the killer had most likely acted alone, both the Director and other FBI officials remained somewhat open to the possibility of a conspiracy. A May FBI memo from Hoover said, "The possibility exists that subject was a hired assassin." To detect signs of a payoff to the hit man, Hoover even asked for agents in Atlanta, New Orleans, Birmingham, Los Angeles, and Memphis to talk to all banks in those cities in order to learn the identities of anyone withdrawing more than $10,000 in cash during the month of April.[7]

Just two days after Dr. King's murder, an assistant FBI director had said that "Los Angeles should keep in mind that King may have been killed by a hired assassin. In this connection [two lines mostly censored] should be kept in mind." It's not known whether the censored name was some Mafioso in Los Angeles, the type of mobster who routinely hired hit men, a King-hating fanatic like Milteer's friend Dr. Wesley Smith—or another type of suspect entirely. Even though Hoover and his top aides considered a conspiracy at least possible for a time, Hoover apparently didn't want to pursue leads that might lead to Johnny Rosselli, Carlos Marcello, or Joseph Milteer. Perhaps that's because all three had been problems for the FBI back in 1963 and again in 1967.[8]

On April 16, 1968, before the FBI had confirmed that "Galt" was in fact James Earl Ray, agents had found the marked Los Angeles map in Ray's Atlanta room. Given the methodical way FBI agents across the country followed even the smallest leads, it's very unusual that the marks on Ray's Los Angeles map were not run down and checked out, especially since the FBI knew by then that "Galt" had lived in Los Angeles for a time. If the locations marked were visited or cross-checked, agents would have noticed that one address was familiar to the FBI.[9]

Numerous FBI files prove that the Los Angeles FBI office and FBI headquarters were well aware that Rosselli lived in the Beverly Towers apartments on Beverly Glen, located at one of Ray's map marks. Since Rosselli had been living there since 1964 (and would continue to reside there until he finally went to prison in 1971), the fact that either a Los Angeles agent or a higher-level official in Washington didn't notice the familiar location is almost inconceivable. Some experts point out that the FBI was pursuing so many leads that perhaps it was simply overlooked, and that despite all the good work many agents did, some leads were bound to fall between the cracks. Still, it's hard to imagine a Los Angeles FBI agent either overlooking or deciding on his own not to call attention to the coincidence of addresses, especially given Hoover's fearsome reputation. The FBI had been getting information regularly on Rosselli's movements from a variety of mostly noncriminal informants, like his building's switchboard operators, for almost four years at that point.[10]

It's possible the Rosselli-Ray lead wasn't pursued because it could have complicated the FBI's role in Johnny Rosselli's upcoming trial on immigration charges, set for April 23, 1968, and his Friars Club trial slated for later in the year.[11] The evidence was overwhelming in each case, and the odds were high that Rosselli would be convicted in both. Any hint or indication that Rosselli was being investigated for the assassination of Martin Luther King could play into the hands of Rosselli's defense attorney. In Jimmy Hoffa's spring 1964 trial, he had tried without success to elicit testimony from a government witness about his 1962 threat to assassinate Bobby Kennedy. While it may seem counterintuitive that Jimmy Hoffa would try to bring that out in court, Hoffa's attorneys wanted to demonstrate that the government and Bobby Kennedy had a vendetta against him by planting such a wild story. Rosselli could have tried the same approach: claiming that the FBI couldn't find Dr. King's real killer, so they were now trying to scapegoat him for that crime, along with the other violations he was charged with.

Rosselli had also been a problem for the FBI in 1967, when Richard Helms and the CIA intervened with the FBI on Rosselli's behalf after the Jack Anderson articles appeared. Rosselli had also presented difficulties in the fall of 1963 after JFK's assassination, since the FBI had apparently noted the two Miami meetings between Rosselli and Jack Ruby, while Rosselli was working on the CIA-Mafia plot to kill Castro. In early 1968, officials in Washington (certainly the CIA) were pressuring the FBI about Rosselli, and recently retired CIA officer William Harvey had met with Rosselli in March 1968, just weeks before Ray's Los Angeles map was found.[12]

If the FBI did make the Rosselli connection based on Ray's marked map, it could have been not pursued, or buried, at the request of someone in the CIA, ostensibly on national security grounds relating to Cuba. Rosselli's old friend David Morales was still quite active in the CIA and made at least one visit to Los Angeles in 1968. At the time, Morales was between overseas CIA assignments, and apparently working on a personal project involving Rosselli. It's also possible that Hoover simply had any memos about the fact that Rosselli's building had been marked on Ray's map sent to Hoover's secret "official and confidential" files, many of which were destroyed after Hoover's death. That way, the information would never have to be provided to Rosselli's defense attorneys, and it couldn't embarrass the FBI.

John McFerren's statements regarding Memphis produce dealer Frank C. Liberto could also have been problematic for J. Edgar Hoover because they should have led to Carlos Marcello. On April 8, 1968, McFerren was persuaded to talk to Frank Holloman, an interview that resulted in the FBI's questioning McFerren. It's interesting to contrast the FBI's initial interview of McFerren with those by journalist William Sartor, and to see how the McFerren's story evolved and was slanted to a degree by the FBI. When the FBI first interviewed McFerren, their only visual representation of Dr. King's shooter was an FBI sketch, which diverged somewhat from a better-known drawing, by a Mexico City police artist, that appeared in many American newspapers. McFerren said the sketch resembled someone who had worked briefly at Liberto's produce market in the fall of 1968. However, McFerren was always clear that this person had a "jaundiced complexion, a rash or pockmarks on his neck," which Ray lacked. After photos of Ray were available, McFerren said one in a photo line-up "resembled" the man who'd worked at Liberto's in the fall, but that he wasn't sure and simply had "a gut feeling the man was an itinerant hood, probably laying low for a while." Sartor's first article about McFerren made it clear that there was "no way of knowing if" the man who'd worked briefly at Liberto's was Ray, and initial FBI memos accurately conveyed the tentative nature of McFerren's first identification.[13]

However, later FBI memos turned McFerren's cautious comments into a definite identification that was incorrect, which the FBI then used to discount the story about Liberto's yelling over the phone that we related earlier. (Years later, McFerren even adopted the FBI's version of his identification.) Similarly, when the FBI summarized William

Sartor's interviews with McFerren's and Sartor's underworld sources, the latter's references to Carlos Marcello weren't included in the summary; they were provided only as an attachment—which the FBI apparently never gave to Congressional investigators.[14]

J. Edgar Hoover had many reasons to be sensitive about any King leads that led to Carlos Marcello or his associates. The previous year, Hoover had been worried about the revelation in Ed Reid's *The Grim Reapers,* describing Marcello's fall 1962 threat to assassinate JFK, and the Director had tried unsuccessfully to get Reid to remove it. (The book would not be published until April 1969.) Reid's investigator, Ed Becker, who witnessed Marcello's outburst, maintained he had reported it to the FBI at the time—and there is some evidence that Becker did, though no FBI files have been found to confirm it.

Present at the Marcello threat that Becker heard was Jack Liberto, Marcello's lieutenant, who doubled as his personal barber and sometimes driver. FBI files from April 1968 discuss Jack Liberto's activities with Marcello. However, though the FBI interviewed Frank C. Liberto's brother and other family members in New Orleans as part of its King investigation, there is no indication that agents ever talked to Jack Liberto about it, or that the FBI looked at Jack's relationship to Frank. Naturally, Frank C. Liberto and his New Orleans relatives with whom the FBI spoke denied any connection to, or knowledge of, King's assassination. Their denials allowed the FBI to decide by April 22, 1968, while Ray was still at large, that no "further inquires along these lines are warranted"—even though by that time, the FBI knew that Ray had gone to New Orleans with a known drug trafficker who had lived in the Crescent City.[15]

Sartor, on the other hand, kept investigating and didn't shy away from those connected to Marcello. As for McFerren, he stuck to his story about Liberto's phone call, and a brief mention of the incident appeared in the press. After the FBI's inquiries in New Orleans about it, and after Ray was announced as the prime suspect, the Justice Department memo about McFerren and Sartor noted that McFerren was frightened by an unexpected visitor from New Orleans. Sartor described the New Orleans man as someone "who has been in the penitentiary . . . [was] involved in bootlegging . . . is believed to have murdered at least one man [and] it seems clear that he is mixed up in the rackets." The man was white and "well-dressed," drove up in a Cadillac, and actually reached out to shake McFerren's hand, something his family said that white folks never did there. The man's visit to McFerren seemed to have no real purpose, but it left McFerren feeling threatened and thinking the man "wanted to know what I looked like so he could point me out to some trigger man."[16]

Aside from Marcello's 1962 threat to kill JFK that Becker reported, J. Edgar Hoover had other reasons to avoid leads pointing toward Carlos Marcello. Like Rosselli, Marcello was facing trial in May 1968, for punching an FBI agent. If the reports Anthony Summers obtained are true, Hoover had gone easy on Marcello for years because of sexual blackmail. Younger FBI agents in New Orleans clearly wanted to go after the notorious New Orleans godfather and probably couldn't understand Hoover's reluctance—and the Director couldn't explain it to them. That's probably why one or more FBI agents arranged the public confrontation at the New Orleans airport, which resulted in Marcello's arrest.

Marcello's trial, slated for May 1968, appeared to be a rare slam-dunk case against the mob boss, since he had swung at the FBI agent in front of numerous witnesses and a photographer even captured the moment. But tying Marcello into the King assassination, before or during the trial, could have let Marcello assert what his friend Hoffa had wanted to do back in 1964: that he was simply being persecuted by the government.

The other reason Hoover might have avoided Carlos Marcello in the King investigation had to do with the JFK assassination. The FBI had interviewed fourteen associates of Marcello and his lieutenants after JFK's murder, but had never bothered to talk to Marcello himself about the JFK assassination or Ruby's shooting of Oswald. In April 1968, Jim Garrison's prosecution of Clay Shaw was still dragging on, and Hoover knew that less than a year earlier, Garrison had toyed with the idea of going after Marcello. The more the FBI stuck to the simple assault case and avoided looking at Marcello for anything assassination-related, the better the chance that the press and public would continue to overlook the FBI's failure to investigate Marcello before or immediately after JFK's death.

Even more glaring than the FBI's reluctance to investigate King leads pointing to Rosselli and Marcello was the FBI's seeming lack of interest in Joseph Milteer after the King assassination. Many FBI staff members had thought Milteer's associate J. B. Stoner a logical suspect in Dr. King's murder—but he had an airtight alibi. Stoner was in Meridian, Mississippi, at the time, holding a meeting in a barbershop that happened to be across the street from Meridian's FBI office. Agents were looking through a window at Stoner when they heard on the radio about Dr. King's shooting. FBI agent Jack Rucker said, "Damn, J. B. Stoner's got an alibi. If he wasn't down there right now, he'd be tops on our list of suspects." Instead, they had to watch as Stoner and his men celebrated the news. According to Jack Nelson, Stoner proclaimed, "He's been a good nigger since he got shot." Stoner would later say in his racist newspaper, the *Thunderbolt,* that "the white man who shot King . . . should be given the Congressional Medal of Honor and a large annual pension for life, plus a Presidential pardon."[17]

The FBI did investigate other violent racists in their files, including those affiliated with some of the same groups as Milteer, like a former "director of the National States Rights Party," Stoner's group for which Milteer had been an organizer.[18] But there is no sign in the FBI's King files that the Bureau interviewed or investigated Joseph Milteer, even though the FBI had had an open case on Milteer the previous year. As the FBI was fully aware at the time, and had been reminded just a year earlier, Milteer had even spoken on a Miami police undercover tape in November 1963 about an associate who tried to kill Dr. King.

Some of the names of racists the FBI investigated are censored in the released files, but Milteer's small hometown of Quitman, Georgia, coupled with the Mary Ferrell Foundation's online search capabilities, make it clear that Milteer is not named in any of the released FBI files, since the city of residence is almost always given for FBI suspects. One of the many investigative failings the HSCA noted was that "FBI files indicate only limited efforts to investigate the possible involvement of extremist organizations, such as the White Knights of the Ku Klux Klan of Mississippi," and other groups who "had demonstrated both a propensity for violence and a clear antagonism toward Dr. King."[19] But because Milteer in particular had recently figured so prominently in FBI files, his absence seems unusual.

If Milteer's name had ever surfaced publicly in the King assassination, it would have been a potentially career-ending embarrassment for Hoover. Imagine how it would look if the public learned that the FBI and the Secret Service had closed their case on Milteer eight months after newspaper articles detailed his talking about an earlier plot to kill Dr. King—just six months before King was actually murdered. Hoover and high-ranking FBI officials had also mishandled the Milteer investigation immediately before and after the JFK assassination, withholding important information from the agent sent to interview Milteer before JFK's murder.[20]

It's a tragedy that Milteer wasn't investigated in the aftermath of Dr. King's murder, since the FBI did get at least one report of a King assassination plot that might have involved Milteer's scheme. The FBI memo sent from Miami to Director Hoover quotes an informant as saying that "after [the] assassination of King [name censored] proceeded to Atlanta, Ga., and then to the residence of [name censored] who resides near Topton, N.C." Topton was just twenty miles from Otto, North Carolina, where Milteer and his partners had been buying up mountain land.[21]

It is possible that Milteer was investigated for Dr. King's murder, but then, to avoid potential embarrassment, those files were routed only to Hoover's private "official and confidential" files. The FBI could have secretly investigated leads in King's slaying involving Milteer, Marcello, and Rosselli, the same way the Bureau had handled the Tampa attempt to kill JFK on November 18, 1963. However, by 1968 the stream of articles in *Ramparts* by former FBI agent William Turner was a constant reminder to Hoover that any current agent could one day decide to expose the FBI's wrongdoing and mistakes. In some ways, it was better for Hoover to simply avoid having agents pursue leads pointing to Milteer, Marcello, or Rosselli, rather than risk generating information and files that could later damage the FBI and his reputation.

Some of Ray's defense attorneys, starting with J. B. Stoner, suggested that Hoover and the FBI were behind Dr. King's assassination. Rep. Louis Stokes and the HSCA looked at that possibility very closely and could find no evidence of their involvement. It would have been illogical for Hoover to kill Dr. King using people the FBI was helping to prosecute in trials only weeks away, like Marcello and Rosselli. It also wouldn't have made sense for Hoover to use Joseph Milteer in a plot to kill Dr. King, since his activities were known not just to the Secret Service and the Miami police, but also to *Miami News* reporter Bill Barry and his editors. Likewise, allowing a small-time hood like Ray to stay on the run for eight weeks across two continents would have been senseless for Hoover, since it harmed the reputation of Hoover's FBI. Finally, for the FBI to have requested that J. B. Stoner claim publicly that the Bureau was behind King's murder is irrational—but it makes perfect sense for Joseph Milteer to have his associate Stoner blame King's death on the FBI, to divert suspicion from the real culprits.

However, the HSCA and the Senate Church Committee documented such pervasive racism in some parts of the FBI that we don't rule out at least the inadvertent sharing of information between FBI agents, or supervisors, and associates of Milteer or Marcello. An Atlanta FBI agent in April 1968, Arthur Murtagh, later testified about the racist comments he heard in the office from some of his fellow agents. On the night of King's assassination, he was so upset by one Atlanta FBI agent's anti-King remarks that they got into an altercation in the parking lot after leaving the office.[22] Still, the presence of good agents like Murtagh illustrates how difficult it would have been for the FBI as an agency to have killed Dr. King.

Chapter Fifty-four

After Dr. King's funeral, Bobby Kennedy resumed his quest for the Democratic nomination for president. Before he left Atlanta, Bobby met with a group of black celebrities, including Bill Cosby and Sammy Davis Jr., along with black Georgia politicians like state senator Julian Bond. But the meeting didn't go smoothly, and some of the celebrities took so much credit for the civil rights movement that Cosby left in a huff. Bobby then met with former aides of Dr. King, including Andrew Young and Ralph David Abernathy. Young said the gathering was serious and blunt, but Bobby "handled himself well."[1]

Bobby resumed his grueling campaign schedule in the remaining primary states, but the danger he faced must have been even more apparent to him in the wake of Dr. King's murder, particularly because the assassin was still eluding authorities. In spite of the risk and what had happened to his brother, Bobby insisted on always riding in an open car. Just as he wore JFK's clothes at times, perhaps Bobby reasoned that if JFK had been brave enough to ride in an open limousine through Tampa while a reported assassin was at large, he could do no less. A week after Dr. King's murder, Bobby was visiting Lansing, Michigan, when he learned that police had spotted a gunman on a roof. An aide wanted to close the blinds in Bobby's suite, but the Senator replied, "Don't close them. If they're going to shoot, they'll shoot." When he left the hotel, Bobby made a point to step out of his limo and into the crowd.[2]

Bobby Kennedy traveled with only one security man, trusted aide Bill Barry (no relation to the *Miami News* reporter of the same name), who was unarmed. Barry says that Bobby told him he didn't want armed protection, or any intrusive or obvious security men or police. Walter Sheridan worried constantly about Bobby's lack of security, saying, "There wasn't anything you could do about it because he was uncontrollable, and if you tried to protect him he'd get mad as hell."[3]

Even before the King assassination, the press had been worried about Bobby's safety. After Bobby's very first campaign stop, journalist John J.

Lindsay told Jimmy Breslin and a group of reporters that while Bobby "has the stuff to go all the way . . . he's not going to go all the way. The reason is that somebody is going to shoot him. I know it and you know it. Just as sure as we're sitting here, somebody is going to shoot him. He's out there now waiting for him." According to Thurston Clarke, "one by one, the other reporters agreed. But none asked the most heartbreaking question: Did Kennedy himself know it?"[4]

Bobby was all too aware of the risks. Though they saw each other infrequently, Bobby had maintained his friendship with Harry Williams. Harry saw reporter Haynes Johnson occasionally and was friends with a Kennedy aide, which enabled Harry to meet privately with Bobby amidst the Senator's hectic campaign schedule. When Bobby and Harry spoke, the subject of Almeida and his wife and children always came up, but the CIA was still supporting them. Bobby's view on Cuba had softened since he and Williams had worked together, while Harry had no desire to reenter the world of covert Cuban operations, now increasingly the province of violent bombers like Felipe Rivero and Luis Posada.

Harry had not sought out Bobby to encourage him in his run for president in the hope that Bobby would reinvigorate the action to topple Castro. Instead, Harry had a different message for his old friend. Having seen the coverage of Bobby's huge crowds, Harry said, "You got thousands of people around you [but] if some son of a bitch comes out . . . and just starts shooting . . . " Harry didn't have any specific information, but said that "with all these Mafia people [still around], they [are] going to try to kill you."[5] At a small Hollywood gathering with Warren Beatty and Shirley MacLaine, novelist Romain Gary essentially told Bobby the same thing. Bobby's simple reply to Gary was "That's the chance I have to take."[6]

Some people hoped for what Bobby's friends feared. William Sullivan, the number-three man in the FBI at the time, wrote that in late April 1968, Bobby's "name came up at a top-level FBI meeting. Hoover was not present, and Clyde Tolson was presiding in his absence. I was one of eight men who heard Tolson respond to the mention of Kennedy's name by saying, 'I hope someone shoots and kills the son of a bitch.'" Other conservatives echoed that sentiment: According to Thurston Clarke, "the right-wing columnist Westbrook Pegler . . . welcomed the possibility that, as he put it, 'some white patriot of the Southern tier will spatter [Kennedy's] spoonful of brains in public premises before the snow flies.'"[7]

Bobby had many enemies because of his stance on civil rights and migrant workers, as well as his fights against Hoffa and organized crime. Among the remaining primaries, California was the biggest prize, and Bobby planned to make several trips there in April and May, before its June 4, 1968, primary. Migrant labor leader César Chávez, head-quartered in the small California city of Delano, had recovered from the nearly monthlong hunger strike he'd staged there. César Chávez worked across California to build support for Kennedy's campaign among migrants, Hispanics, and college students. When some of the students asked Chávez where Bobby had been when they were in New Hampshire, working for McCarthy in the first primary, Chávez always replied that Bobby "was walking with me in Delano!"

California's rich agricultural areas, like Delano, depended on cheap migrant laborers who often lived in appalling conditions. Delano police officials would later say that "[Bobby] Kennedy has been to Delano three times in this past year. Prior to Kennedy's visits the area was quiet and untroubled; however, since his visits there have been riots, strikes, and picketing. The wealthy farmers in the area all hate Kennedy [but] when Kennedy came to visit Chávez on his hunger strike, he refused to allow any local police to furnish him [with] any protection."[8]

In late April or early May, two Delano police officials overheard a boast by a wealthy local farmer, Roy Donald Murray, who frequently gambled large sums in Las Vegas. In uncensored files, quoted here for the first time and detailed later, Murray said that "he had pledged $2,000 . . . to be utilized to pay off a contract to kill Senator Kennedy," and that the Mafia "was behind the letting of the contract."[9]

In April 1968, the results of Bobby's most recent attempt to expose Carlos Marcello were on America's newsstands. The press hadn't followed up on Bobby's previous leaked exposé about Marcello, in the September 1967 issues of *Life* magazine, so Bobby couldn't resist helping a young writer for *Ramparts* magazine, Michael Dorman, who was working on an article concerning Marcello. Bobby had begun talking with Dorman back in February 1968, around the time he had first decided to enter the presidential race.[10]

Dorman's article was about a longtime political-payoff man, Jack Halfen, who provided Mafia money to politicians in both parties. Bobby had first started investigating Halfen in 1961, and Carlos Marcello was one of several prominent mob bosses Halfen worked for. The politicians Halfen claimed he funneled money to included John Connally, Supreme Court Justice Tom Clark, Texas Congressman Albert Thomas—and Lyndon

Johnson, while he was a leading senator in the 1950s. Halfen claimed to have funneled a million dollars to LBJ while he was in the Senate, to block certain gambling legislation.[11]

According to Gus Russo, Bobby had one of his aides assist Dorman with his research, and the journalist "received RFK's personal attention, meeting with the Senator in his office [where] 'Senator Kennedy was enthusiastic about the article.'" By 1972, Dorman would greatly expand his article into a book called *Payoff* that contained much more material about Marcello. According to Russo, a memo "obtained from the LBJ Library in 1992 . . . asserts that the Kennedys helped Dorman write his book, *Payoff*." Other memos from the LBJ library show that Johnson had an advance copy of the article, and knew that Bobby had an interest in it. In light of the article, the fact that LBJ had been so cordial to Bobby during their last visit is all the more remarkable.[12]

Marcello's friends in the Teamsters were as ruthless as ever, but also pragmatic. The $2 million fund to "spring Hoffa" from prison hadn't secured his release, and for Hoffa as well as his allies, the prospect of Hoffa's continued imprisonment during a Bobby Kennedy presidency would have been their worst nightmare. Evan Thomas documented that in the spring of 1968, after Bobby announced his run for the presidency:

> . . . a Teamster leader came to Senator Edward Kennedy proposing that the Teamsters would give RFK $1 million and help him at the polls—if RFK would . . . shorten Jimmy Hoffa's prison sentence. . . . RFK told brother Ted, "Well, you tell so and so that if I get to be president, then Jimmy Hoffa will never get out of jail and there will be a lot more of them in jail."[13]

Bobby Kennedy faced his first primary challenge in Indiana on May 7, 1968. Though Indiana was considered a conservative state, Bobby won, with 42 percent of the vote to Eugene McCarthy's 27 percent (the remaining votes went to the governor as a favorite-son stand-in for Hubert Humphrey). However, Bobby and his advisors believed he needed to do even better, so that he could head into the Democratic convention in Chicago with the momentum needed to secure the nomination. Neither Bobby nor any other candidate could win enough votes in the primaries to secure the nomination, so for Bobby, momentum was everything.[14]

The following week, in Nebraska, Bobby scored a more decisive victory over McCarthy—51 percent to 31 percent—but it still wasn't enough to drive his rival from the race. For Bobby, everything would come down to the two West Coast primaries: Oregon, on May 28, and especially California, on June 4. Bobby would need to win at least the latter to have any realistic hope of securing the nomination.[15]

Bobby visited California as much as possible, but he had to deal with several distractions during May, two involving President Johnson. On May 10, 1968, the preliminary peace talks with North Vietnam began, with Bobby's old Cuban operations subordinate Cyrus Vance as one of two US negotiators. In this instance, Bobby's goals coincided with LBJ's because if steps toward peace were soon announced, that would take much of the wind out of McCarthy's campaign, since the war was his main issue. For LBJ, securing a peace deal was his only chance to leave office on a high note—otherwise, his legacy would be the war he'd hugely expanded but couldn't win. President Johnson also knew a peace agreement was probably the only way to keep a Democrat in the White House, though LBJ wanted that person to be his vice president, Hubert Humphrey.[16]

Though Bobby and Johnson shared peace in Vietnam as a goal, Bobby probably suspected that LBJ had a hand with Hoover in new articles slamming Bobby by Drew Pearson that began appearing in late May. This time, the stories weren't about Cuba or JFK's assassination. As described by Evan Thomas, on May 22, 1968, Pearson printed the "allegation that RFK had paid off a witness in one of the Hoffa cases. Then on May 24 . . . Pearson revealed that RFK, as attorney general, had authorized wiretaps on Martin Luther King." It's unclear if the decision to leak the story originated with LBJ or if Hoover had first leaked it to an LBJ aide who brought it to President Johnson's attention. But LBJ certainly supported the leak and talked with Pearson in the White House six days before the story ran.[17]

Luckily for Bobby, one of the stories contained an error, saying that Bobby had not only approved phone wiretaps on Dr. King, but also approved placing "bugs" in King's hotel rooms. Since Bobby had approved the wiretaps but not the bugs, he was able to issue carefully worded denials giving Bobby enough wiggle room to evade most of the blame in the press, to the public, and even among many of his own staff.[18]

During his hectic May campaigning, Bobby also followed the trials of Carlos Marcello and Johnny Rosselli. Thanks to a change of venue, Marcello finally stood trial in Laredo, Texas, on May 20, 1968, for slugging the FBI agent in New Orleans in 1966. John H. Davis writes that "amid widespread rumors of tampering, the trial ended in a hung jury." Bobby could perhaps take solace that the Justice Department's new Organized Crime Strike Force was determined to retry Marcello on the same charges.[19]

How much Bobby suspected Johnny Rosselli in JFK's murder is not known, though in 1992, a close Kennedy aide indicated to us Rosselli's responsibility (along with Marcello's and Trafficante's). With Bobby's own investigations pointing toward Marcello, his Mafia associates, and those involved in anti-Castro operations, Bobby would have realized at least that Rosselli was a likely suspect. Rosselli was convicted in Los Angeles of failure to register as an alien on May 23, 1968, and would eventually be sentenced to six months in federal prison. First, though, Rosselli would have to stand trial again in Los Angeles, for the Friars Club charges that also involved four codefendants. Rosselli's attorney was working closely on the defense team's strategy with distinguished Los Angeles lawyer Grant Cooper, whose client in the trial had owned a Las Vegas casino. Cooper's client had also worked with Rosselli on an aborted hit scheme, to silence the key witness in the Friars Club case.[20]

In late May, Bobby alternated between campaigning in Oregon and in California, with the latter getting the lion's share of his attention, due to its huge slate of delegates. Though the state had recently elected conservative governor Ronald Reagan, Bobby's campaign had gone well, generally drawing huge and enthusiastic crowds as he rode in open cars and stopped to give talks. Security was a problem, and was almost impossible to manage effectively, especially in Los Angeles. Mayor Sam Yorty and Police Chief Ed Davis were extremely conservative, with Yorty considering Bobby "subversive." Bobby had openly criticized Yorty in Senate hearings following the 1965 riots in Watts, because of the deplorable conditions that had helped trigger the outburst. Yorty sometimes didn't bother to hide his racism, as when he used a slur to introduce a black Assistant Secretary of Commerce, and then made a point of wiping off his hand after shaking hands with the black official. Yorty's police chief, Edward M. Davis, continued the problems that led to the riots by resisting hiring minorities to serve on the force. There was a growing chasm of mistrust in 1968 between the police and liberals, minorities, and those opposed to the war—the very groups Bobby was trying to woo.[21]

During much of the time that Bobby was darting around the Los Angeles area, police security was almost nonexistent. Bobby had previously had a trusted friend in the LAPD, Captain James Hamilton, who had founded the LAPD's intelligence unit, but Hamilton had left the force to take a security job with the National Football League (and had since died), leaving no one to mediate the friction between the LAPD and Bobby's campaign. It would have been clear to anyone who attended Bobby's events that the police were not providing close security for the candidate, though officers were often stationed in the area for crowd control.

In an ordinary house in Pasadena on May 18, 1968, a twenty-four-year-old former aspiring jockey named Sirhan Bishara Sirhan was writing in his notebook, apparently as part of his interest in self-hypnosis. Sirhan loved horses but was a compulsive gambler who had been losing hundreds of dollars in recent weeks. In his notebook, Sirhan wrote "May 18, 9:45 AM," then scribbled "RFK must die" and "Robert F. Kennedy must be assassinated before 5 June '68." On the same page, Sirhan wrote more statements about assassinating Bobby, followed by "Please pay to the order of of of of of."[22]

As Bobby continued to dash around Los Angeles in between trips to Oregon, the security situation began to reach a critical point. Security usually went well when Bobby visited towns just outside of Los Angeles—like Pomona, on May 20, where he drew four hundred supporters to Robbie's Restaurant. There, a Pomona police officer kept an eye on a young couple who appeared suspicious, until a manager dealt with the problem. But security issues arose when Bobby was back in Los Angeles, as he was for a rally downtown on May 24 and for a small motorcade five days later. When Bobby's motorcade stopped at 9th Street and Santee, Bobby left his car and walked into the crowd, where he was soon mobbed. According to a Los Angeles police sergeant, when a motorcycle officer attempted to rescue Bobby from the crowd, an LAPD report says that "Kennedy and his aides berated the sergeant and told him that they had not asked for the assistance of the police."[23]

The police seemed to take that as a signal to back off even more, though accounts differ greatly about whether Bobby's staff rejected further police protection in Los Angeles. Though Bobby had a rally scheduled at Los Angeles's Ambassador Hotel on June 2, and his hoped-for victory party on the night of the California primary, on June 4, the Los Angeles police wouldn't have official security roles at either event.[24]

While Richard Nixon would later make the most effective use of television in the 1968 campaign, Bobby was adapting to the medium. On May 20, 1968, his campaign aired a documentary about Bobby in California and Oregon. Jewish voters were an important constituency for Bobby, especially in California, and the TV special talked in general terms about Bobby's support for Israel. On May 26, Bobby gave a speech at a Portland synagogue, urging the Johnson administration to "sell Israel the fifty Phantom jets she has so long been promised." The Jewish vote in Oregon wasn't large, but Bobby's speech was covered in Los Angeles area papers, which were read by his true intended audience. Bobby lost the Oregon primary on May 28, 1967, by six points to Eugene McCarthy, which made his winning California even more critical.[25]

Eugene McCarthy had been demanding a debate with Bobby, and one was finally scheduled for June 1, 1968, in San Francisco. By most accounts, Bobby did well, even when asked about wiretapping Dr. King. However, the moderator pointed out that on most issues, the candidates had few substantial differences.[26]

On June 2, 1968, Bobby Kennedy went to the Ambassador Hotel in Los Angeles for a rally, which seemed to go smoothly. That was good for Bobby and his staff, because the following day would be the most intense of their campaign so far, a 1,200-mile trek that would drive Bobby to the brink of exhaustion.

On June 3, Bobby went "from Los Angeles to San Francisco, back to Watts and Long Beach, on to San Diego, and back to [Los Angeles, all] in thirteen hours," according to Evan Thomas. The first problem arose that morning, as Bobby's small "motorcade crept through San Francisco's Chinatown"—when suddenly, a series of what sounded like shots erupted. Bobby's wife "dove for the bottom of the car," while Bobby, "standing on the rear hood of a convertible, remained upright and continued to wave to the surging crowd." But a journalist "who was running alongside the motorcade saw Kennedy's knees buckle" at the sound, which turned out to be only firecrackers. Even so, "Ethel was [so] badly shaken" that Bobby asked a reporter to comfort her while he continued to smile and wave.[27]

That night, after side trips to Watts and Long Beach, Bobby was in San Diego for a rally at the El Cortez hotel. The strain and pressure were getting to Bobby, and soon after beginning his speech to the crowd of three thousand, Bobby suddenly fell silent. Thomas wrote that Bobby "nearly collapsed. He abruptly sat down on the stage and put his head in his hands." NFL football star and friend Roosevelt Grier got Bobby "into a bathroom, where he threw up. He lay on the floor while Grier knelt and mopped his head." Then Bobby got to his feet and walked back to the stage, where he completed his talk, finishing with his classic words: "Some men see things as they are, and ask—why? I dream of things that never were, and I ask—why not?"[28]

Chapter Fifty-five

On June 4, 1968, California's primary was underway when the first exit polls at 3:00 PM showed Bobby Kennedy winning by eight points over McCarthy. Even if Bobby won the same day's primary in South Dakota, Humphrey would still have a big lead in delegates, though not a majority. A win in California could very well propel Bobby to the nomination, setting up a race in the fall with Richard Nixon that would echo the 1960 fight between JFK and Nixon.[1]

At 6:30 PM, Bobby—accompanied by his family and advisors—headed to the Ambassador Hotel, where he planned to greet his supporters in the Embassy Ballroom later that night, then talk to reporters in a smaller room. For his personal security, Bobby had only his one unarmed bodyguard, Bill Barry, plus athletes Roosevelt Grier and Olympic decathlon champion Rafer Johnson, both unarmed. Dan Moldea found the hotel had hired "18 security guards for crowd control," including eleven unarmed guards who worked for the hotel. The rest were armed guards hired for the night from Ace Security—again, for crowd control, not personal protection. There were no Los Angeles police officers at the hotel that night, though some were stationed nearby.[2]

The Ambassador Hotel was full of parties on the night of June 4, 1968, including several for large companies and other political races, for both liberal and conservative candidates. Sirhan Sirhan went to a private party first, after seeing a name he recognized from high school on the marquee. His former classmate wasn't there, so Sirhan said he "drank four Tom Collins." For the diminutive Sirhan, that was a lot of alcohol. It was almost as if he were steeling himself for a difficult upcoming task, using liquid courage to buttress the self-hypnosis he'd been studying. Bobby would leave Los Angeles the next day, June 5, and Sirhan had no way of knowing when Bobby would be back. After downing the drinks, Sirhan felt woozy, but went to his car and got his pistol.

Bobby watched TV coverage of the results anxiously with family, friends, and advisors in his suite on the Ambassador's fifth floor. By 11 PM, it finally looked like Bobby would be victorious. Less than an hour later, Moldea wrote that Bobby "took a freight elevator down to the kitchen [and] walked through the pantry and anteroom," toward the doors to the Embassy Ballroom.[3]

Hotel ballrooms and kitchens are often connected by a maze of hallways and pantries, used to whisk food and celebrities to waiting crowds. Gaining access to such areas is usually not difficult, especially if someone looks as if they belong there, either as a worker or someone dressed for business. In Sirhan's case, the fact that his darker skin and black hair made him look Hispanic helped, since he resembled the Ambassador's busboys and kitchen workers. Various other people also managed to get into the pantry area behind the ballroom, though some people were turned away. Guarding the pantry area was Ace Security guard Thane Cesar, armed with his own .38 pistol. However, Cesar was there only for crowd control, not as a bodyguard, and had only recently started working part-time for Ace at night to earn extra money.[4]

The plan was for Bobby to enter the Embassy Ballroom and make some remarks. He would then exit out the back door, turn right, go through some swinging doors into the pantry, past an ice machine, heading to the smaller Colonial Room to meet the press. While some thought that route was a last-minute decision made at the end of Bobby's speech, work by Larry Hancock shows the route had been known since at least 10:00 PM, an hour prior to Bobby's arrival at the ballroom. Hancock documented that several hotel "security personnel . . . stated [to law enforcement] that Kennedy staff had told them, well before the Senator arrived to make his address, that RFK would be exiting though the pantry."[5] Kennedy had to address the press in the Colonial Room, and there was no other effective way for him to get there, since walking off the stage and trying to exit through the packed ballroom wasn't a realistic option.

Shortly before midnight, Bobby entered the Embassy Ballroom to the rousing cheers of almost two thousand rapturous supporters. Bobby clearly relished his victory, but he talked about the themes close to his heart, including

> . . . the direction we want to go in the United States . . . what we're going to do for those who still suffer in the United States from hunger; what we're going to do around the rest of the globe; and whether

we're going to continue the policies which have been so unsuccessful in Vietnam. . . . We should move in a different direction. . . . My thanks to all of you, and now it's on to Chicago and let's win there![6]

As the crowd went wild and began chanting his name, a beaming Bobby left the stage and headed toward the ballroom exit to the pantry that would lead him to the waiting reporters.

Sirhan Sirhan had been seen carrying a drink as late as 10 PM. He later said he was drunk when he went into the press room in the Colonial Ballroom, where he stared at a teletype, which the teletype operator later confirmed. Sirhan claims he wandered into the Embassy Ballroom before Bobby arrived, looking for coffee to help him sober up, and that someone directed him to the pantry area. He says he spoke briefly to a brunette near the coffee urn.[7]

By midnight, Sirhan had left the coffee area and gone through the swinging doors that led to the pantry proper. Beyond a half wall in the pantry was an ice machine on the right and steam tables on the left.

Just before 12:15 AM on June 5, 1968, Bobby Kennedy and various staff, friends, and press left the Embassy Ballroom for the pantry area. Well-wishers followed, and there would soon be about seventy people in the pantry area. Ambassador Hotel maitre d' Karl Uecker took Bobby's right hand and led him toward the Colonial Room. Just behind Bobby, occasionally touching his arm, walked security guard Thane Cesar, his pistol holstered. Paul Schrade, Kennedy's friend with the United Auto Workers, followed a few feet behind. The group passed through the swinging doors into the main part of the pantry and past the half wall. Bobby was jovial, greeting hotel workers as he walked through the narrow pantry.

As Bobby stopped and turned to shake hands with two busboys, Karl Uecker noticed a young man emerge from behind the large ice machine on the right. Uecker thought it was another kitchen worker who wanted to meet Bobby—but it was Sirhan. Wanting to get Bobby to the press room as quickly as possible, Uecker nudged Sirhan against the steam table so he couldn't get to Bobby, who was still a few feet short of the steam table. But Sirhan raised his arm, holding a revolver in his hand. Sirhan stuck his gun to the left of the taller Uecker's head, pointing the pistol at Bobby as he said, "Kennedy, you son of a bitch!"[8]

Sirhan fired two shots, then Uecker grabbed Sirhan's "arm holding the gun" and pushed it "down towards the steam [table]." Uecker threw his "right arm . . . around his neck as tight as [he] could . . . pressing him against the steam [table]," as the maitre d' later testified to the grand jury. Sirhan's pistol never got closer than a foot and a half to Bobby, and now Sirhan was pinned to the steam table, with the assistant maitre d' now pushing against Uecker to hold Sirhan down—but Sirhan kept firing wildly.[9]

Sirhan's first bullet likely hit Paul Schrade, standing several feet behind Bobby. Bobby was hit next: One bullet flew harmlessly through his coat, but three found their target—two in his back, just behind his right armpit, and the most serious shot entered just behind Bobby's right ear. All the shots hitting Bobby entered from the back and had a steep upward trajectory. The coroner and LAPD all agree that they were fired from a distance of one and a half inches or less—a distance that is difficult to reconcile with the idea of Sirhan as the fatal shooter.[10]

Aside from the four shots at Bobby and one bullet that struck Paul Schrade, others in the pantry fell from the bullets that Sirhan continued to fire. According to Uecker, the "shooting stopped for just a moment," but then "I felt him shooting [again]." The pistol was wrenched from Sirhan's hand and left on the steam table. Though he was pinned down by an increasing number of people, Sirhan grabbed it and began trying to fire more shots, as if he was determined to fire all eight bullets in his pistol whether he was shooting at Bobby or not.[11]

By the time Sirhan's gun was empty, bullets had also struck student Erwin Stroll in the leg, ABC News executive William Weisel in the abdomen, artist Elizabeth Evens superficially in the head, and radio reporter Ira Goldstein. One shot passed harmlessly through Goldstein's pants leg, but the other struck him in the buttocks. Schrade and Weisel were the most seriously injured, though all five would recover.[12]

As might be expected of a part-time security guard hired only for crowd control, Thane Cesar "ducked and tried to take cover" falling forward onto the ground, according to Moldea. Cesar says he lay on the ground for about five seconds, then got up and briefly drew his .38 pistol, before reholstering it after seeing the crowd holding down Sirhan.[13]

As confusion reigned amidst the screams and panic and attempts to restrain Sirhan, Bobby Kennedy lay on his back on the ground, arms and legs splayed, a pool of blood growing under his right ear. Cesar's clip-on tie had come off and lay just over a foot away from Bobby's hand. Busboy Juan Romero kneeled beside Bobby, saying, "Come on, Mr. Kennedy, you can make it."

Bobby, his face ashen, asked weakly, "Is everybody all right?"[14]

Rosary beads were handed to Romero, who pressed them into Bobby's left hand, which Bobby held over his heart. That famous image was frozen in time by photographer Harold Burba, its eerie calm belying the fierce struggle taking place several feet away, as a growing number of Kennedy aides, friends, and others piled on to restrain Sirhan. Burba had begun taking photos only after Bobby fell, but fifteen-year-old student Scott Enyart had started taking pictures when Bobby entered the pantry. Enyart told police he was standing on a table photographing Bobby when "the shots started to be fired, and I took pictures and kept taking pictures."[15]

Athletes Roosevelt Grier and Rafer Johnson finally made their way through the panicked crowd with Bobby's wife, Ethel. As she knelt beside her bleeding husband, Grier and Johnson joined the struggle with Sirhan, who was held down by a group that included author George Plimpton and Bobby's security man, Bill Barry. The first LAPD officers had not yet arrived.[16]

Both inside and outside the pantry, credible witnesses saw individuals whose actions would later be the source of intense controversy. Nearly a dozen witnesses saw someone who could have been a second gunman, either in the pantry or fleeing the pantry after the shooting. In some accounts, the shooter had a weapon. For example, Larry Hancock cites the statements of

> Dr. Marcus McBroom, [who] had been standing [just outside the pantry] when he heard the first couple of gunshots. A young woman immediately ran past him into the Embassy room; she was wearing a polka-dot dress and shouting something as she passed. McBroom thought it sounded like "We got him!" or "We shot him!" but at that instant he was not certain. It became clearer to him as he saw the girl quickly followed by a young man. The man had a newspaper over his arm, but McBroom could see a pistol underneath. McBroom and an ABC cameraman both drew away upon seeing the gun. McBroom described the young man as an "Arab looking person" wearing a blue suit and sweating noticeably.[17]

In addition to those witnesses, numerous others reported a suspicious woman in a "polka dot dress" and some confirmed the same wording that Dr. McBroom heard her use. Before the shooting, to escape the heat and crowds, Sandy Serrano had been sitting on a metal emergency exit stairway at the rear of the Ambassador. Earlier, she had seen a young woman in a polka-dot dress enter through the exit with two men. Serrano later gave the FBI a very detailed description of the dress, since one of her friends had one just like it. After the shooting, she told the FBI the same woman and one of the men "came running down the stairs toward her." The woman in the polka-dot dress shouted, "We shot him—we shot him!" When Serrano asked, "Who did you shoot?" the woman replied, "Senator Kennedy!"[18] A worried Serrano tried to find someone to tell her story to, and eventually found Los Angeles Deputy District Attorney John Ambrose, who had gone to the hotel after hearing about the shooting on the radio. Ambrose immediately questioned her, decided she was sincere, and took her to talk with the police who had started to arrive at the Ambassador.

Completely independent of Serrano and Ambrose, one of the first LAPD officers on the scene, Sergeant Paul Sharaga, had a similar encounter. Six minutes after Bobby had been shot, Sgt. Sharaga arrived at the rear parking lot of the Ambassador. As documented by Dan Moldea, Sharaga said that after he headed toward the hotel, "an older Jewish couple ran up to me, and they were hysterical." The woman said they were leaving the hotel near the Embassy Ballroom "when a young couple in their late teens or early twenties, well dressed, came running past them. They were in a state of glee. They were very happy, shouting, 'We shot him! We shot him!'" When the older woman asked whom they had shot, the young girl said, "Kennedy, we shot him! We killed him!" The older woman told Sgt. Sharaga the girl was "wearing a polka-dot dress." Sharaga wrote down the couple's names (the Bernsteins), and "radioed in the description of the [suspects] a number of times, requesting that it be broadcast every fifteen minutes." Sgt. Sharaga's first call was recorded at 12:23 AM.[19]

Around the same time, the first LAPD officers arrived in the pantry. A physician had been tending to Bobby, trying to keep the blood flowing from his head injury so it didn't build up in his brain cavity. Sirhan was still being held down by Uecker, Grier, and the Speaker of the California State Assembly, Jesse Unruh. Seeing the uniformed officers, Unruh yelled, "We don't want another Dallas here! This one's going to stand trial! He's going to pay! No one's going to kill him!" Roosevelt Grier didn't want to turn Sirhan or the gun over to police, and released Sirhan only when an officer said the police "basically threatened Grier." Rafer Johnson carried Sirhan's pistol personally to LAPD headquarters, where he turned it over to authorities.[20]

At 12:28 AM on June 5, 1968, only thirteen minutes after Sirhan started firing, Bobby was taken from the Ambassador Hotel to an ambulance. He was first driven to Central Receiving Hospital to be stabilized, then transported to the nearby Good Samaritan Hospital, which had a much larger trauma unit. There, six surgeons worked feverishly on Bobby's most serious injury, trying to remove the bullet from his brain.

Meanwhile, Sgt. Sharaga had set up a command post at the Ambassador, ordering officers to "get identifications and license numbers of everyone entering or leaving the hotel grounds [for] investigating officers when they arrive." He sent a note about the Jewish couple and the girl wearing the polka-dot dress to a detective who had set up another base in the pantry. However, the acting chief of detectives soon told Sgt. Sharaga that his alerts about other suspects would be stopped because the only shooter had already been arrested. Radio logs show that the assistant detective chief ordered LAPD radio control to stop sending out the descriptions of the young woman and her male associate, saying we "don't want them to get anything started on a big conspiracy."[21]

Sirhan was first taken to the LAPD Ramparts station, the one closest to the Ambassador. Sirhan refused to give his name. The first detective that talked to Sirhan said "the suspect had no ID. Normally, I started thinking in terms of, maybe, a hit. That's typical." The lack of any ID would allow time for the hit man's confederates to flee or secure incriminating evidence.[22]

In his pockets, Sirhan had $10.66, plus four $100 bills. He also had two unfired bullets, one shell from a different type of .22 bullet, and an announcement for Bobby's June 2, 1968, rally at the Ambassador. He also had an article from a May 26 newspaper highlighting Bobby's opposition to Vietnam and support for Israel. Though the article lacked any mention of the Phantom "jet bombers" Sirhan would later claim were his main motivation for the shooting, the contents of his pockets quickly painted Sirhan as a shooter who had stalked Bobby because of his support for Israel, and instantly provided police with Sirhan's motive, means, and opportunity.[23]

That was convenient, since Sirhan continued to resist giving officers his name. He showed no remorse, and yielded only to small talk that didn't touch on Bobby's murder. Sirhan had seemed dazed at first, though accounts vary as to whether he appeared intoxicated. No Breathalyzer test was administered, and the only blood sample taken was later destroyed without being tested for alcohol or drugs. For someone who had never been arrested before, Sirhan seemed remarkably calm, and a

Ramparts detective wrote in his report that Sirhan "appeared less upset to me than individuals arrested for a traffic violation." Sirhan was soon taken to the main LAPD jail, but since none of the officers were able to get a name from Sirhan, he was booked and arraigned as "John Doe." He was finally identified the next morning, when his pistol was traced and two of his brothers went to police after seeing Sirhan's picture in the media.[24]

Robert F. Kennedy clung to life though June 5, 1968, but his injuries were too severe. He was pronounced dead at 1:44 PM on June 6. Bobby's press secretary, Frank Mankiewicz, made the announcement to a waiting world.

Meanwhile, three thousand miles away, something had made President Lyndon Johnson think of the Mafia as soon as he heard that Bobby had been shot in Los Angeles. On his White House notepad, LBJ scribbled, "[La] Cosa Nostra," "Ed Morgan," and "Send in to get Castro planning." LBJ must have thought there was some connection between Bobby's shooting and Johnny Rosselli's CIA-Mafia plot stories that Jack Anderson had described a year earlier. It's ironic that when those stories had appeared the previous year, Frank Mankiewicz had been conducting his secret investigation of JFK's murder for Bobby, which would point to "the mob, anti-Castro Cuban exiles, and maybe rogue CIA agents."[25] Three people who would eventually confess or be linked to Bobby's murder would also fit into that same group.

Chapter Fifty-six

Several issues continue to make Bobby Kennedy's assassination a topic of controversy and debate four decades after that tragic night at the Ambassador Hotel. Two of those issues—the number of bullets fired in the pantry, and whether Sirhan ever got close enough to fire the shots that struck Bobby—are central to whether or not there was another gunman that night.

Los Angeles coroner Thomas Noguchi concluded that all the shots that hit Bobby were fired at extremely close range, from the end of a gun barrel in "contact" with Bobby or "near contact." Shots leave a distinctive "burn pattern," a gunpowder tattoo based on how close the end of the barrel is to the target. In Bobby's case, extensive testing showed Noguchi that the head shot would have been "between one inch and one and a half inches" away from Bobby's right ear. Regarding the other shots that hit Bobby, Noguchi testified that the barrel was either touching his coat or not more than an inch away.[1]

Dan Moldea pointed out that, according to Karl Uecker, who was standing beside Bobby in the pantry and was the first to grab Sirhan's pistol, "Sirhan's gun never got closer than one and a half to two feet from the senator. Not a single witness who testified before the grand jury . . . or at Sirhan's subsequent trial said or would say that Sirhan's gun ever got closer to Kennedy than this."[2]

Unlike Martin Luther King's assassination, the actual shooting of Bobby was witnessed at close range by a large number of reputable people who saw Sirhan firing his pistol—and they were almost unanimous that it would have been physically impossible for Sirhan to have fired the shots that struck Bobby. The list includes noted journalist Pete Hamill, who said that Sirhan's gun was at least two feet away from Bobby. Kennedy campaign worker Lisa Urso told police that Bobby was between "three and five feet" away from Sirhan's gun. Other witnesses with a good view of the shooting said Sirhan didn't get closer than "three to six feet" to Bobby. Moldea points out that "the only witness to claim

Sirhan's gun was within a foot of Kennedy's head" was *Los Angeles Times* photographer Boris Yaro. But Yaro told the FBI he was looking at the scene through the viewfinder of his camera, which rendered Bobby and Sirhan "little more than silhouettes."[3]

Aside from Yaro, the fourteen witnesses who gave an estimate of the distance stated figures that made it impossible for Sirhan to have fired the shots that hit Bobby—and the vast majority of those witnesses have been remarkably consistent over the years.[4] Karl Uecker points out that Bobby never made it to the steam table before he was shot, and that Sirhan never passed the steam table to which Uecker pinned him, meaning there was simply no way for Sirhan to have fired the gun at Bobby from only an inch or so away.

The only explanation that accounted for how Sirhan could have fired the fatal shot was offered by Dan Moldea, who wasn't a witness but developed his theory in the 1990s after years of research. Moldea speculated that the witnesses saw only the first shot and, in the panic that followed, didn't realize that Bobby had been pushed (by the crowd behind him) closer to Sirhan—who, in this scenario, fired as Bobby turned away from him. However, with all those witnesses in a corridor that was little more than six feet wide, no one there reported seeing that happen.[5]

Significant problems also exist with the bullets and bullet holes in the pantry. The bullets recovered from Bobby and the other victims could never be matched to Sirhan's pistol. A later official review panel showed that early testimony from Sirhan's trial was erroneous, and no definitive match could be made to Sirhan's eight-shot revolver.[6]

Those conclusions lead to another problem: the number of bullets fired that night, since everyone agrees that if more than eight bullets were fired, there had to be another shooter. FBI veteran Bill Turner notes that the LAPD said seven slugs were recovered from the victims, and one was lost in the space above the ceiling. Thus, "the official LAPD position was that no bullets were found at the assassination scene, and other than an entry and exit hole in the ceiling caused by the lost bullet, there were no bullet holes on any of the doors or walls of the pantry." Yet crime scene photographs taken in the pantry do show bullet holes—and any additional bullet holes mean that someone besides Sirhan was firing.[7]

Many official LAPD and FBI photographs show bullet holes in the pantry, some with officers pointing at the holes, and others showing bullet holes marked by police. While these extra bullet holes appear to be in several locations, including the ceiling, the most notable were later described by FBI agent William Bailey. He said there were "two bullet holes in the center divider between [the] two swinging doors ... that Senator Kennedy came through on his way through the pantry." Other FBI agents had accompanied Agent Bailey when he conducted his inspection, and Bailey later stated in a sworn affidavit that "there was no question in any of our minds as to the fact that they were bullet holes ... and they definitely [contained] bullets." Dan Moldea says that "if Bailey ... is correct, then there is no doubt that at least two guns were fired that night." While Moldea thinks Bailey was mistaken, not only did others see the bullet holes, but one police officer also marked them, circling each hole and writing his badge number, as official photographs clearly show.[8]

Noted reporter Robert Wiedrich wrote a story about the extra bullet holes, that ran on June 6, 1968, the day Bobby died. Wiedrich said the "strip of molding, torn by police from the center [divider] of the double doors ... thru which Sen. Kennedy had walked [now] bore the scars of a crime laboratory technician's probe as it had removed two .22 caliber bullets that had gone wild" and been embedded in the wooden center divider. As for the center divider, it was booked into evidence on June 28, 1968—and destroyed (along with the ceiling tiles) a year later by the LAPD on June 27, 1969, after Sirhan's trial.[9] Those two extra bullets meant a total of ten shots, two more than Sirhan's eight-shot revolver could have fired, so they couldn't be entered into evidence as having come from the wooden divider without destroying the case against Sirhan as the lone shooter.

What became of the two bullets removed from the center divider? As Bill Turner, Larry Hancock, and others have pointed out, the LAPD reported having conveniently found two spent bullets in Sirhan's car, along with a box of unfired ammo. Hancock writes that "seven different experts studied the two bullets, and all found that they had 'wood' embedded in the nose, sides, and base." How or why the wood is on the two bullets has never been explained, and Sirhan had no memory of—or explanation for—having the two spent bullets in his car. But Hancock points out that the presence of wood on those bullets is consistent with the slugs' having been removed from the center divider.[10]

At least ten witnesses reported seeing a man with a gun, or what could have been a weapon, in the pantry at the time of the shooting, or fleeing the pantry just after. The witnesses were not referring to Sirhan or guard Thane Cesar, so if any of their reports are true, there was a second gunman involved. In addition to Dr. McBroom (cited earlier), who saw a man fleeing the pantry with "a newspaper over his arm [and] a pistol underneath," there are the statements of Lisa Urso, who was in the pantry.[11]

Urso saw a man wearing a "gray suit" who "had a gun and . . . put it back into a holster." The only guard in the pantry was uniformed security guard Thane Cesar, and Bobby's personal bodyguard, Bill Barry, wasn't armed. Witness Don Schulman also saw the man in a suit with a gun in the pantry. Author Larry Hancock has pointed out that Schulman was one of the few people who noticed that guard Thane Cesar had actually drawn his pistol after Sirhan started shooting; Cesar himself estimated he'd had it out for only about thirty seconds. As Hancock notes, in addition to seeing Cesar, "Schulman was also certain that he had seen men in regular clothes with drawn guns inside the pantry," something he tried repeatedly to tell authorities.[12]

However, witnesses who said they saw what might have been a second gunman were either ignored (like Urso) or questioned repeatedly and sometimes aggressively (like Schulman) until some backed off their stories. However, years later, when some witnesses were finally shown their recantations, as written by the LAPD, they denied ever backing off what they had seen (McBroom is a good example).[13]

It would have been possible for another gunman to have been inside the pantry prior to Bobby's arrival, since Moldea points out that "neither Cesar nor anyone else can explain how Sirhan managed to get into the kitchen pantry." Cesar himself "insisted, 'I was the only guard in the pantry, and I just never noticed him.' He added that during his time in the kitchen, he watched television with Roosevelt Grier and Rafer Johnson and listened to Milton Berle's jokes." Distracted by celebrities, Cesar could have missed someone else just as easily as he missed Sirhan, especially if the person were wearing a business suit and looked like a campaign aide or journalist.[14]

If there were a second gunman, how could he have shot Bobby in such a crowded space? Few viable answers have been offered over the years. However, after spending several years reviewing thousands of pages of the most recently available files, Larry Hancock offers the following possible scenario, after Bobby entered the pantry:

> As [RFK and his group] passed beyond a half wall which butted up against one side of a large ice machine, they came into Sirhan's view, and in a couple of steps Sirhan lunged at RFK. . . . The [other] shooter was probably standing at the half wall and slipped in behind RFK

and Cesar to fire the fatal shots after Sirhan fired the first couple of times. . . . This was when RFK was falling back from Sirhan—he had not even been hit at that point. It's probable that as two witnesses describe, the shooter had a pistol in his hand concealed under a folded newspaper and delivered the shots virtually execution style, without having to wave his gun or make it very visible at all.[15]

Ace Security guard Eugene Thane Cesar has been the subject of much controversy and investigation for decades, especially after Dan Moldea tracked him down in the 1980s. Moldea noted that Cesar "gave contradictory statements to the police and to the FBI about exactly when he drew [his] weapon," and one witness "claimed to have seen [Cesar] fire the gun" he drew. Moldea points out that Cesar repeatedly gave "different versions of his movements immediately after the shooting"; that he "owned a .22 caliber revolver similar to Sirhan's but gave false statements to the police about when he sold it"; and that "Cesar was a supporter of . . . George Wallace."[16]

However, Moldea also points out that Cesar "had no criminal record," had been "called in to work at the last minute" that night, and "volunteered to be questioned [and] offered to surrender the gun in his holster, a .38 caliber revolver, for police inspection during his questioning." In Cesar's favor, Moldea says, the security guard "voluntarily told the police that he owned the additional .22 revolver and gave them the name and address of the man" he'd sold it to, and cooperated with the police and the FBI, even offering to take a polygraph test. Cesar also allowed Moldea to interview him, and he took a polygraph test that Moldea arranged. That test asked many key questions, like "Were you involved in a plan to shoot Robert Kennedy?" Cesar passed with flying colors, so Moldea no longer considers him a suspect.[17]

One person that many find suspicious is the infamous "girl in the polka-dot dress" who crops up in so many witness accounts of that night, as well as in sightings on previous days with Sirhan. At least fourteen witnesses provided accounts of the attractive young woman. Their recollections of her appearance were generally consistent, except that some said she had dark-blond hair, while others said it was brown. While TV footage shows many women in polka-dot dresses at the Ambassador on the night Bobby was shot, this particular one is suspicious because she was usually seen with Sirhan prior to the shooting and/or fleeing with a taller man after the shooting.[18]

Four witnesses said she yelled something like "We killed him!"

and seemed happy about it. Why would an accessory to murder have boasted about such an act while fleeing? Some have speculated that the young woman was a gleeful white supremacist in the same vein as Kathy Ainsworth, mentioned in Chapter 45 and described by Pulitzer Prize–winning reporter Jack Nelson as an attractive young "school teacher by day and ruthless Klan bomber by night." Otherwise, it's difficult to imagine a murderess happily touting her crime in public unless she were on drugs, intoxicated, or psychotic.[19] Innocent explanations have been offered, ranging from far-right Republicans, attending other parties at the Ambassador, gloating over Bobby's death to someone's meaning "we" as a symbol of collective guilt for America at the time.[20]

The LAPD tried to come up with innocent candidates in or near the pantry. But the main one they found, Valeria Schulte, had worn a dress nothing like the one witnesses described—and, Philip Melanson points out, "her leg was in a cast from hip to ankle, and she walked with a crutch" the night of Bobby's shooting. Melanson observed that not only did none of the witnesses note that prominent fact, but the cast would have prevented Schulte from running in the way the suspect was described.[21]

The LAPD seemed to wish the whole "girl in the polka-dot dress" angle would go away. But Sandra Serrano had given a television interview about the girl before she went to police headquarters, so the news was already out and had to be dealt with. The LAPD questioned Serrano extensively, possibly more than it did any other witness, interviewing her twice on June 5, then again on June 7, when she also reenacted what she'd seen for the Secret Service and the FBI. Serrano was then reinterviewed on June 8 by the FBI, and on June 10 by the LAPD. All the while, she remained consistent. At that time, apparently only a few in the LAPD knew there were so many other witnesses who had seen the mysterious polka-dot-dress girl, and those officers and detectives were in a tight-knit group created just to investigate Bobby's murder, Special Unit Senator (SUS).[22]

Sandy Serrano stuck to her story, so on June 20, the only SUS polygraph examiner, Lieutenant Hank Hernandez, took Serrano out for a friendly dinner. Then he gave her two polygraph tests. The first lasted an hour. As Larry Hancock points out, "current guidelines for polygraph testing . . . specify that the examiner is required not to display or express bias in any manner regarding the truthfulness of the examinee prior to the completion of the testing, as failure to do so may generate false positives."[23]

The following are samples of Hernandez's techniques with Serrano, as he tried to get her to change her story before polygraphing her:

HERNANDEZ: Be a woman about this . . . don't shame his death by keeping this thing up. . . . I want to know why you did what you did.
SERRANO: I seen those people!
HERNANDEZ: No, no, no, no, Sandy. Remember what I told you . . . you're shaming him!
SERRANO: Don't shout at me![24]

After browbeating Serrano like that for an hour and fifteen minutes, Lt. Hernandez gave her the first polygraph test and Moldea notes that Hernandez "determined that the badly shaken Serrano had lied about the entire matter." She was then reinterviewed and finally, grudgingly, recanted what she had seen, saying she'd heard about the polka-dot-dress girl at the police station. Hernandez and the SUS were satisfied with her statement, though it ignored the fact that Serrano had told her story to the assistant district attorney even before she went to the police station. In addition, Hernandez and at least some in SUS knew that other witnesses supported Serrano's story.

In some ways, Serrano's treatment typified that of witnesses who didn't support the official "lone nut" version of Bobby's murder. Among those subjected to similar intense pressure was one of Sirhan Sirhan's brothers, though he had a criminal background and Sandy Serrano was simply a witness. Other witnesses weren't treated as badly, as far as we can tell from the files and tapes that weren't destroyed, but those who reported anything indicating that Sirhan had confederates were often subject to repeated questioning or harsh tactics. They were also frequently polygraphed by Lt. Hernandez, a procedure that witnesses supporting the "lone nut" scenario rarely underwent.[25]

The "lone nut" version was becoming the LAPD's official story less than an hour after Bobby had been shot, as demonstrated by the cancellation of the radio broadcasts of Sgt. Sharaga's description of the two suspects. The idea that the shooter had no confederates was apparently being set in stone before police officials even knew Sirhan's name, let alone what associates he might have.

Even as the official focus narrowed to an unaided Sirhan Sirhan, witnesses to the contrary were giving their accounts to the LAPD. Apparently, instead of keeping an open mind and trying to determine whether those reports were accurate, at least some LAPD officials decided to not run down, or to discount, leads that pointed to a conspiracy. Though key LAPD files, interview tapes, and photographs were later destroyed, many were preserved and released years, sometimes even decades, later. Starting in early 2008, the text of thousands of pages of LAPD (and some FBI) files about Bobby's murder can be searched online at the Mary Ferrell Foundation's website in ways not available to investigators in 1968 or to journalists in the 1980s or 1990s. These documents make it crystal clear that all of the LAPD's slanting, badgering, and harassment were geared toward witnesses who didn't support the "lone nut" conclusion. The question is—why?

Part of the answer may be the frequent tendency of police to look for evidence against an obvious suspect, rather than trying to develop evidence and run down leads that defense attorneys could later use to cast doubt on the prime suspect's guilt. As we detail later, police might also informally cover up information to protect city or federal officials. In Sirhan's case, it seems beyond coincidence that in the weeks and months just before Bobby's murder, the former aspiring jockey had suddenly developed ties to two of Los Angeles mayor Sam Yorty's good friends. In addition, at least one lead in a military intelligence file on Sirhan wasn't pursued by the LAPD.

Something the released files now show that was rarely fully appreciated in earlier decades is just how large and extensive the entire LAPD investigation really was. As with JFK's murder—which spawned secret investigations by the CIA, Naval Intelligence, and even Bobby Kennedy—the LAPD did extensively investigate certain conspiracy allegations regarding Bobby's death, but only for its own internal use. The LAPD sometimes withheld the results of these investigations from the press and the public for decades. For example, unknown to the public until recently, the LAPD generated an internal report of more than nine hundred pages about possible ties between the JFK assassination and Bobby's murder. However, since members of the Mafia were not officially considered suspects in JFK's murder at the time, that LAPD report included only a few fringe Mafia associates.[26]

Yet reading those reports today (or, in the case of those still withheld or destroyed, their partial summaries or indexes) raises new questions about leads that weren't fully explored. Some important leads were pursued only because of pressure on the LAPD from journalists Peter Noyes and William Turner. While there were members of the LAPD that seriously investigated the journalists' leads, others seem to have just gone through the motions so they would be able to counter any stories the journalists might make public.[27]

Being able to search and review the thousands of pages of LAPD files about Bobby's assassination today also reveals key areas that weren't pursued, or investigations that were aborted prematurely. The Mafia was a huge area that wasn't explored, even when obvious leads pointed in that direction. Dan Moldea quoted a key LAPD supervisor for SUS as saying that he "never supervised any phase of [looking into] a conspiracy allegation involving the mob." Related areas that surfaced briefly in the LAPD investigation but weren't seriously pursued include drug trafficking, Sirhan's gambling with a bookie, and the criminal ties of some of Sirhan's brothers.[28]

Why the LAPD or the FBI didn't fully explore those particular areas will become clear as the story of their investigation unfolds. First, however, it's important to remember that both agencies were involved at the same time with another high-profile assassination—that of Martin Luther King—and it was about to take a dramatic turn.

Congressional investigators found that after James Earl Ray arrived in London, he exchanged the return portion of his ticket for one to Lisbon, Portugal. Ray claims he was trying to get to Africa, perhaps Angola, to find work; if he couldn't get a job there, then he planned to go to "one of the English-speaking countries" in Africa, like Rhodesia or South Africa. But Ray left Portugal and returned to London on May 18, 1968. He later said he was running low on money and had only about $400 left (almost $2,500 today).[29] One of Ray's brothers said that Ray "didn't figure [there would] be that much heat. He was going to [white-run] Rhodesia. He was desperate in London. Had more heat on him than he ever dreamed of."[30]

In the manhunt for James Earl Ray, the FBI had asked the Royal Canadian Mounted Police (RCMP) to conduct a passport search in an attempt to match Ray's photo with those on passport applications. After reviewing 175,000 applications, finally on June 1, 1968, the RCMP found Ray's photo on his April 24 application under the name of "Ramon George Sneyd." Ray's handwriting and a fingerprint also matched. The travel agency where Ray had filed his application gave Canadian authorities information about Ray's airline ticket to London. This allowed authorities to follow Ray's trail to Portugal and back to London, where Scotland Yard ordered a passport watch for Sneyd/Ray.[31]

There is evidence that Ray may have committed a bank robbery in

London on June 4, 1968.[32] The next day, Ray moved to a very small hotel in the Pimlico area of London. Later, when the hotel's owner was cleaning Ray's room while he was out, the owner saw newspapers on Ray's bed open to articles about Bobby's assassination. Also, the owner said she took two phone messages for Ray that have never been explained, including one from a woman. Though Ray told the owner he was heading to Germany, he was actually planning to go to Brussels, Belgium. While in London, Ray called a British newspaper reporter and asked about getting to Belgium. Ray later claimed that he hoped to travel from Belgium to a white-controlled country in Africa, his ultimate destination.[33]

Ray went to Heathrow Airport on the morning of June 8, 1968, with his Brussels plane ticket, the equivalent of $117 in British currency, and his pistol. But when Ray presented his "Sneyd" passport on the morning of June 8, 1968, officials took action. Ray was arrested at 11:15 AM.[34]

James Earl Ray had come close to getting away with murder. For someone who had managed to elude authorities in the US, Canada, England, and Portugal for sixty-five days during an intense international manhunt, it seems odd that Ray never bothered to change his appearance by growing a beard or mustache (or lightening his dark hair). Not only would those changes have seemed logical once Ray's "wanted" photo was publicized worldwide, but doing so would also have kept the RCMP from identifying "Sneyd" as Ray. Instead, the only thing Ray had done to alter his appearance for his Canadian passport photo was to comb his hair a bit differently and wear the glasses he usually wore only for reading and driving.

The other factor in Ray's capture was that he was running out of money. If someone had wanted Ray to elude the worldwide search, providing him with money and a new alias (and ordering him to disguise himself) would have prevented Ray from being captured. Also, either remaining in teeming London or shipping out, under a new alias, on any of the hundreds of freighters that docked there regularly, would have been far safer for Ray than attempting to fly to Brussels. It's almost as if someone wanted Ray captured once the May 1968 trials of Carlos Marcello and Johnny Rosselli were over. A continued, massive manhunt was not in the interests of either Marcello or Joseph Milteer and his clique. It would have only put more pressure on racist groups affiliated with Milteer, and someone in law enforcement might have started looking seriously into the Mafia leads that journalist William Sartor was uncovering. The FBI had already started just such an investigation even before

Ray's capture, since Sartor would soon tell the Justice Department that the FBI had already visited some of his sources.[35]

As we noted earlier, according to the Justice Department memo cited here for the first time, some of Sartor's mob-linked sources told him that "either the Mafia wanted [Ray] at large until the balance of the [contract] was paid" by the racist group, or the mobsters in Memphis "had not been paid, and it was they who wanted Ray at large as a lever on higher-ups in the rackets." In any event, the mobsters told Sartor that "after the money problem was resolved, Ray deliberately permitted himself to be arrested in London with the understanding that he will be acquitted in Memphis."[36]

On June 6, 1968, a grieving Senator Edward Kennedy summed up the feelings of many Americans about the murder of his brother. As the body of Robert F. Kennedy was being flown from Los Angeles to New York City, Edward Kennedy talked to NBC TV newsman Sander Vanocur during the grim flight. William Turner wrote that, to Vanocur, "Edward Kennedy had remonstrated bitterly about the 'faceless men' who had been charged with the slayings of his brothers and Martin Luther King. . . . Always faceless men with no apparent motive. 'There has to be more to it,' Ted Kennedy had told Vanocur," who broadcast the Senator's comment after they landed.[37]

Bobby's body lay in state at Manhattan's St. Patrick's Cathedral until the morning of June 8, with lines of mourners stretching more than two dozen blocks. At a special Mass that morning, Coretta Scott King comforted Ethel Kennedy. Bobby's widow was both stoic and gracious; later, Mrs. King said, "I don't see how she has been able to go through this awful experience with such dignity." César Chávez and his men joined the other Kennedy friends, family, and associates for the Mass. Edward Kennedy gave a heart-rending tribute to his brother, saying in a voice quivering with emotion that Bobby "saw wrong and tried to right it, saw suffering and tried to heal it, saw war and tried to stop it."[38]

After Mass, a special train of twenty cars took Bobby's body to Washington, moving slowly as crowds lining the tracks watched and wept. It was night on June 8 by the time the funeral procession left Washington's Union Station, passing many national landmarks—two of which were especially significant. One was the Justice Department building, where Bobby had waged his war against Carlos Marcello, Jimmy Hoffa, and the Mafia. The other was Resurrection City, the encampment from the Poor People's March, which Martin Luther King's advisors had continued after their leader's murder. Without Dr. King's leadership and publicity clout, the effort was largely considered a failure, but Bobby Kennedy had been one of the only major politicians to support the attempt.[39]

After the funeral procession headed toward the burial site at Arlington National Cemetery, network television coverage was interrupted for the first report of James Earl Ray's capture. Former assistant FBI director William Sullivan later wrote that J. Edgar Hoover postponed the announcement of Ray's capture by "a full day," just so "he could interrupt Bobby's funeral." That Hoover delayed the announcement is likely, but he couldn't have put it off for an entire day, because Ray had been arrested in London only that morning.[40]

Bobby Kennedy was laid to rest in a somber ceremony late at night, under a full moon. His grave was about ninety feet down from the knoll that held the more elaborate resting place he had ordered for his brother the previous year. Later, across from Bobby's grave, a marble monument was erected that included the ancient Greek poem Bobby had quoted on the night Martin Luther King was shot:

> In our sleep, pain which we cannot forget falls drop by drop upon the heart until, in our own despair . . . comes wisdom.[41]

President Lyndon Johnson proclaimed the following day, June 9, 1968, a national day of mourning.[42]

Chapter Fifty-seven

In the days after Bobby's murder, the LAPD began piecing together the life of Sirhan Bishara Sirhan, some of which would be leaked to the press or come out at his trial. However, today a new and more complete picture of the life and 1968 activities of Sirhan Sirhan has now emerged, thanks to declassified files that became available in easily searchable form for the first time in 2008. When paired with the earlier work of Turner, Melanson, Moldea, and, most recently, Hancock, it presents a view of Sirhan that is at odds with the image of an enigmatic young man the media presented in 1968 or the proto–Middle Eastern terrorist some authors have tried to depict.[1]

Though Sirhan's family emigrated from East Jerusalem when he was thirteen, he was a quintessential American in many ways. Sirhan was raised a Christian, and he regularly drove his mother to the Baptist church where they both belonged. He lived in Pasadena with his mother and two of his four brothers. He liked to shoot pool and eat at Bob's Big Boy, where he loved to talk about horse racing. He also enjoyed visiting topless bars, and especially gambling on horses. As Sirhan now says, "I had as many all-American values as the next guy." He dreamed of getting a Ford Mustang to replace his weathered pink-and-white 1956 DeSoto. Sirhan told one of his friends that his main goal in life was to make lots of money.[2]

Though he was insecure about being short (his height is variously given as 5' 2" and 5' 4") and having little money, by the mid-1960s, Sirhan was on his way to fulfilling his dream of becoming a jockey. He worked as a horse walker at racetracks and breeding farms, including one connected to Cuban-born entertainer Desi Arnez, and eventually became an apprentice jockey. However, after Sirhan sustained two injuries caused by falls from horses (the first on September 24, 1966), his personality seemed to change, according to his family and friends. He became resentful of authority and developed an interest in mysticism, especially self-hypnosis.[3]

In late 1967, Sirhan had largely dropped from sight. An LAPD officer confirmed a mysterious three-month gap in Sirhan's life to William Turner, and an FBI summary says that Sirhan's mother was "extremely worried [because] she did not know his whereabouts for quite some time"—which was unusual because he usually lived at her house and spent much of his free time there. Sirhan didn't vanish completely, but he apparently stopped visiting his usual haunts and was away from home for stretches of time. Sirhan's activities have never been fully accounted for during that time, but once he returned home and to his usual routines, Sirhan's interest in self-hypnosis increased. It was as if Sirhan needed to learn self-hypnosis to focus on an important task, something he was afraid he might not be able to complete.

In some ways, Sirhan seems similar to Lee Harvey Oswald, since, on the surface, both young men seem like quiet loners, lost souls adrift in society. But upon closer inspection, both had unusual associates, engaged in seemingly contradictory actions in the months leading up to the respective assassinations, and were the subject of covert surveillance.

Sirhan was definitely under some type of covert surveillance prior to Bobby's assassination. LAPD reports show that after Bobby's murder, the department received information from "Military Intelligence in San Francisco . . . that Sirhan was a student at . . . Pasadena [Community College]." The memo then lists accurately all of Sirhan's earlier schooling, then says that "Sirhan active in gaining support for Shah of Iran's visit." However, no other released files about Sirhan mirror this comment about his support for the Shah. Such support also runs counter to Sirhan's professed beliefs, which were supportive of the Arab cause and not Israel, which the US-backed Shah supported. No CIA files about Sirhan have been released, nor have the reports that served as the basis for this brief Army Intelligence report, which, Philip Melanson notes, "seems clearly to have been in federal intelligence files before the assassination." This timeline indicates the existence of significant unreleased files and pre-assassination information about Sirhan that was never fully explored in the original investigation.[4]

Still more covert surveillance of Sirhan occurred in late 1967, about six months before Bobby's murder. A year after the assassination, secretly filmed sixteen-millimeter film footage of Sirhan surfaced, taken during his odd partial disappearance for three months in late 1967. The footage, found in the vacated office of a private detective in a "canister labeled 'Sirhan B. Sirhan—1967,'" showed Sirhan, filmed at a distance, walking on a Pasadena street. Sixteen-millimeter cameras and processing were quite expensive and not easy to obtain, unlike the much smaller eight-millimeter home-movie cameras of the time (such as the one Abraham Zapruder used). Sixteen-millimeter cameras were usually used for documentary films, or sometimes for crowd surveillance by military intelligence or police, where the film's higher resolution could allow for the recognition of individual faces even at a distance.[5]

While Sirhan did have a small claim for his horse fall pending with Argonaut Insurance at the time, Turner points out that "Sirhan's injuries had been minor and he did not claim to be disabled." Sirhan would receive $1,705 a few months later, and Argonaut Insurance "denied knowing anything about the film." In addition, the cost of hiring a private detective to track and film Sirhan using expensive equipment that was large and difficult to conceal wouldn't have made sense financially. The footage has never been explained.[6]

Sirhan had no criminal record when he was arrested, and at the time the press and public didn't view him as being connected to organized crime in any way—despite his compulsive gambling, his work around racetracks, and the fact that the two men who would soon become his main attorneys had ties to the Mafia.[7] Building on the leads journalists Peter Noyes and William Turner tried to persuade police to pursue in 1968, a fuller picture emerged gradually over the years, with some connections published here for the first time.

One of Sirhan's unusual associates among the racetrack crowd was a former jockey whom Sirhan knew by his alias, Frank Donneroummas. His real name was Henry R. Ramistella, and he had "a record of narcotics violations in New York and Florida," according to G. Robert Blakey, the organized-crime expert who directed the HSCA. Under his real name, Ramistella's jockey license had been revoked for giving "false testimony," so he obtained a new license in California as Frank Donneroummas. He had hired Sirhan to exercise and groom horses, and Sirhan worked for Donneroummas until December 1966, though Sirhan says he would sometimes see his former boss at the races after that. Sirhan says the man "always seemed to be having financial problems, which probably stemmed from his [heavy] gambling."[8]

Author David E. Scheim documented that the first racetrack where Sirhan worked was "a Syndicate meeting place," and that another track "was frequented by some of the nation's most infamous racketeers." That milieu was ripe for organized crime, which ran the illegal bookie network that extended gamblers credit for large bets in a way that legal betting couldn't. Scheim also noted "Sirhan's compulsive racetrack gambling and his heavy losses, particularly in the months before the assassination."[9] Dan Moldea quoted the LAPD as discovering that in the months prior to Sirhan's three-month disappearance, Sirhan "bet most of his salary on the horses, [and] a school acquaintance . . . described Sirhan as a heavy bettor, betting as much as sixty to eighty dollars on one race." Moldea points out that Sirhan "was making only $75 a week," though "the FBI . . . claimed that he made bets with a Pasadena book-maker [and] that Sirhan and his mother often argued about his gambling habit and the debts he accumulated."[10]

In Sirhan's private handwritten notebook, which police found after Bobby's murder, Sirhan had scribbled lots of seemingly random words and phrases; some say he wrote them when he was practicing self-hypnosis. On one notebook page, Sirhan wrote, "happiness," then repeated Donneroummas's name three times, followed by "please . . . please pay to 5 please pay to the order of Sirhan Sirhan the amount of 5. . . ." Scheim writes that "several other notations containing the phrase 'please pay to the order of Sirhan' were found in Sirhan's notebooks [a dozen times]—and references to Robert Kennedy or to 'kill' always appeared on these same pages." Also after Bobby's murder, envelopes were found on which Sirhan had written, "RFK must be disposed of like his brother was," and another saying: "RFK must be be be disposed of . . . properly Robert Fitzgerald Kennedy must soon die, die die. . . ." There are repeated references in the notebook to money, especially to the amount of $100,000. All of that led Scheim to ask, "Did someone in fact hire Sirhan to kill Robert Kennedy?"[11]

On February 15, 1968, Sirhan bought a gun for the first time in his life, an Iver-Johnson .22-caliber revolver—the pistol he would fire at Bobby Kennedy. One of Sirhan's brothers was with him and accounts differ among the seller, Sirhan, and the brother about who actually paid for the pistol—but all agree that Sirhan handled the weapon during the trans-action and Sirhan stated "the gun was for me." Though bought from a private individual for $25 on a street corner, it had a well-documented trail from manufacturer to stores to the person who sold it to Sirhan. Later, Sirhan was careful to point out that it was not one of the "cheap . . . Saturday night specials. But . . . was of good quality."[12]

As with James Earl Ray's rifle, Sirhan's handgun was not stolen or undocumented, so there would be no later suspicion that it had any

criminal ties. At the time Sirhan obtained his pistol, the press was speculating increasingly that Bobby might run for president, and Bobby was
already working behind the scenes to help with the *Ramparts* article
about Carlos Marcello. Bobby's campaign officials announced his entry
into the race on March 16, 1968.

In early April 1968, Sirhan Sirhan and two other apparently Middle
Eastern men went to the "Lock, Stock, 'n Barrel Gun Shop," where Sirhan
would eventually buy the .22 caliber bullets he fired at Bobby Kennedy. But that would be over a month later. On this trip, as described by
the woman who co-owned the shop with her husband, "three males of
foreign extraction entered the store" and one of them asked, "'Do you
have any .357 Magnum tank piercing ammo,' or words to that effect.
[My husband] replied, 'We don't have any.' The three then left." After
Bobby's assassination, the FBI showed her "a group of six photos [and]
I selected a photograph of Sirhan Bishara Sirhan and I am positive this
is a photo of the man who inquired about .357 Mag. tank piercing ammo
on or about April 3, 1968." While she thought photos of Sirhan's brothers
resembled the other two men, she was certain about Sirhan.[13]

Her husband remembered the incident similarly, saying that in April
1968, "three men entered the store [who] were short, dark, and foreign looking." He said that "they were very interested in the handgun
display . . . they approached my wife and asked her a question and then
she turned to me for assistance. . . . One of them asked me if we had
any armor piercing ammunition in the store. I do carry such ammunition, which I sell to law enforcement officers. After observing that these
men were not law enforcement officers I said that we did not have such
ammunition in stock. The three men then left." Unlike his wife, the man
was not able to identify Sirhan from photos. However, he said that "on
June 1, 1968," when Sirhan returned to the store to buy the .22-caliber
bullets he would fire at Bobby, the man saw "three short, dark, foreign-
looking persons talking to [his clerk]. From their appearance I thought
they were the same three persons who had been in the store on the April
15th date inquiring about the armor piercing ammunition." His wife
thought the date of Sirhan's visit was a bit earlier, but their stories seem
to otherwise match and be quite credible—and there is no question that
their shop sold the .22-caliber ammunition used in Sirhan's pistol.[14]

Why would Sirhan have wanted "armor piercing ammunition," for a
type of pistol he apparently didn't own? On April 10, 1968, Sirhan was
talking to "a Pasadena trash man, who made regular pickups at the
Sirhan family's house," according to Dan Moldea, citing LAPD records.

The presidential race came up, and the man told Sirhan he was going to vote for "'Kennedy.' Sirhan replied, 'Well, I don't agree. I am planning on shooting the son of a bitch.'" The trash man told police he thought Sirhan was exaggerating, and that he "did not take him seriously."[15]

There aren't many, if any, ordinary uses for "armor piercing" bullets. By the time of Sirhan's threat, Bobby Kennedy was becoming known for campaigning while riding in open cars, often standing to deliver his talks, even if the car was moving. If Sirhan considered shooting Kennedy from the crowds that surrounded Bobby while he stood in his car, Sirhan could have used armor-piercing bullets. They would easily penetrate the thin metal used for cars at the time, allowing his shots to find their target even if Bobby fell, or was pulled, to the floorboard or seat.

In early April 1968, while Sirhan was visiting the gun store and asking about armor-piercing bullets, he had seemingly realized one of his dreams: "to make a lot of money." Sirhan finally received $1,705 (more than $10,000 today) as his insurance settlement for his old horse-riding injury. Before becoming involved in the events leading to Bobby's assassination, Sirhan had talked of returning to community college, though he felt ashamed of his old pink DeSoto and longed for a Mustang that would impress girls. Now he finally had enough to pay cash for a good used Mustang and still have money left over to return to college in style.

But for some reason, having that much money didn't seem to matter to Sirhan anymore. He gave his mother some of the money, and let her hold much of it. He was soon gambling more than ever, and later in May, the LAPD noted that he was going to the racetrack and betting "nearly every day—and losing." It was as if the insurance money Sirhan had gotten wasn't enough to settle some huge debt he owed and he was desperate for a big score to get him out from under his obligation.[16] David E. Scheim noted a much earlier case that might have foreshadowed what happened to Sirhan: It involved a young man who bet heavily on horses, got himself into debt, and was forced by mobsters to fire a pistol from a crowd at a noted official while a mob hit man made sure the target was killed.[17]

Sirhan was not known to use or sell drugs, but one of his scribbled notebook pages contains the word "drugs" written four times, along with "danger" twice, as well as his own name.[18] In addition to the drug conviction of his former boss, whom Sirhan still saw at the races, Larry Hancock documented, based on LAPD files, that in the spring of 1968, Sirhan was living with a brother who "was still on probation from a conviction relating to the possession and sale of narcotics." Sirhan's brother "had served 9 months in jail for the felony conviction," and INS "was still actively engaged in efforts to deport [him] over his narcotics charge and conviction."[19]

Through his brother Adel, police files show that Sirhan knew a bar owner whom a "Federal Narcotics agent . . . stated [had been] arrested August 15, 1967, for narcotics." The man "admitted he knew Sirhan" and "said that he and other friends would occasionally meet Sirhan at the racetrack."[20] A man who "worked as an undercover agent for the Pasadena Police Department" told the LAPD that one of Sirhan's brothers "was pushing heroin and pot."[21] Still another one of Sirhan's brothers, Saidallah, had been arrested for attempted murder in 1963.[22]

Aside from Sirhan, most of his other brothers had run-ins with the law and contact with criminals. One brother's coworker told the LAPD that in mid- to late April 1968, Sirhan's brother said "he was so lucky and was showing me a wallet which appeared to have several $100 bills; in fact, it was full of $100 bills. I would guess several thousand dollars." But then, just a couple of weeks later, around May 1, 1968, Sirhan's brother "said he could kill himself that he had $5,000 a year ago and then he didn't have any."[23]

When he had lots of money, Sirhan's brother boasted to his coworker that "he had good information about horses and [asked] if I wanted any tips. He said his brother [Sirhan] was a jockey, but didn't say it was his brother who gave him the tips." Sirhan also boasted about having good tips on horses, yet Sirhan usually lost at the track. We can't help but wonder if Sirhan became deeply in debt to a mob bookie before receiving his insurance money, and was then given only one way to settle an amount greater than he could possibly hope to earn legitimately.

Sirhan's notebooks containing his odd writing were later found to have "one hundred thousand dollars," written several times, as if Sirhan was focused on that sum as part of his self-hypnosis. These were the same notebooks in which Sirhan wrote, "Please pay to the order" and, "Robert F. Kennedy must be assassinated." Getting lots of money for killing Bobby Kennedy wouldn't have done Sirhan much good while he was in prison, but he appears to have gotten the impression, or been told prior to the shooting, that his sentence for participating in Bobby's assassination would be minimal. Sirhan would later tell prosecution psychiatrist Dr. Seymour Pollack that he thought "he would get only two years in prison."[24]

In addition to the possible promise of lots of money, Sirhan's relationship with his large family, and especially with his mother, could also have been used to pressure Sirhan, by using threats to kill or harm them. As we'll detail in Chapter 58 for the first time, less than a month after Bobby's death, someone made an unusual attempt to murder one of Sirhan's brothers. Sirhan's situation is also reminiscent of Jack Ruby's remark about the lives of his relatives being threatened, since—like Sirhan—Ruby also waded into a crowd to fire at his target with a pistol.

As for Sirhan's motivation for deciding in May 1968 to kill Bobby Kennedy, facts show that it wasn't the Arab/Israeli conflict, as Sirhan would proclaim at length in court. Sirhan would later testify that he became determined to kill Bobby because of Bobby's support for Israel, as depicted in a May TV documentary Sirhan had seen, and the follow-up "promise" Bobby made, during remarks at a Portland, Oregon, synagogue, to sell fifty jet fighters to Israel. However, Sirhan's attorney Grant Cooper provided that motivation to Sirhan to use at the trial.[25]

Dan Moldea also found that the timing doesn't work for the claim. The documentary Sirhan referred to was shown on May 20, and only implied Bobby's support for Israel, while Bobby gave the Portland speech in which he mentioned the jet fighters on May 26, 1968. But Sirhan's notebooks show that on May 18, 1968, Sirhan was already writing repeatedly in his notebooks about killing Bobby, and had even specified his June 5, 1968, deadline for doing so.[26]

In contrast, Phillips Melanson found that Sirhan's notebooks contained "not a single reference to jets or bombers, not a single reference to Zionism, Israel, Palestine, [or any of] the terms Sirhan would spout at this trial as propelling him to murder." Melanson also points out that although Bobby's most serious challenger, Vice President Hubert Humphrey, also supported Israel, Humphrey is never mentioned in the notebooks. While in 1968 Sirhan didn't like Israel or Jews and was concerned about the Palestinians, he didn't join any Arab groups or attend demonstrations, or do any of the other things many other young Arab-Americans did at the time; Sirhan preferred to bet on horses. However, Bobby Kennedy's support for Israel and well-publicized courtship of Jewish voters in New York might have made Sirhan amenable to taking action against him in return for a large sum of money—especially if it meant paying off a debt to the Mafia that put his life, and the lives of his family, at risk.[27]

As for Sirhan's deadline of June 5, 1968, that was the day after California's June 4, 1968, primary, meaning Bobby would have been expected to leave California on that date. Assuming he won the primary and got the nomination, Bobby wouldn't have spent any significant time campaigning in California again until much later in the summer and into the fall—apparently too late for Sirhan.

Chapter Fifty-eight

———

Sirhan Bishara Sirhan might have started stalking Bobby Kennedy on May 20, 1968, when Bobby attended a luncheon for four hundred supporters at Robbie's Restaurant in Pomona, California, near Los Angeles. A Pomona police officer helping with security noticed "a young woman standing by the kitchen door of the restaurant, apparently trying to get inside." As Larry Hancock detailed from police and FBI reports, the officer told the young woman "the door was locked, and she then asked him which way Senator Kennedy would enter." The officer told her he "would probably go up the stairs to the second floor," where the luncheon was to be held.[1]

The officer later saw "the same young woman, along with a young man . . . climb over the stair railing behind people checking tickets at the foot of the stairs." However, they were intercepted by the restaurant's night manager, who had been called in to help with tickets. The woman claimed, "We are with the Senator's party," and was so insistent that eventually the night manager allowed them to pass. Later, he noticed that "the [young] man had a coat over his arm even though it was a very warm day," and that the couple remained at the back of the room, away from the main gathering of Kennedy supporters. When the night manager asked her why, the woman replied, "What the hell is it to you?" and he left them alone. The restaurant's owner also noticed the incident, though from a distance.[2]

The night manager later said "he was fairly certain the young man was Sirhan," and he would later "successfully [pick] out Sirhan's photo from a sample set of 25 young dark-skinned males." He described the woman as "medium blonde" with "a nice shape" and, at five-foot-six, somewhat taller than the man. He would later back away from his identification of Sirhan under questioning from the LAPD, though the Pomona officer had also seen the oddly behaving couple.[3]

Witnesses also spotted Sirhan at a rally for Bobby Kennedy in downtown Los Angeles on May 24, 1968. A clinical psychologist pointed out Sirhan to his wife, because he thought Sirhan was "out of character with the crowd, very intense, and sinister." At the next sighting of Sirhan at a public gathering, Bobby Kennedy wasn't present.[4] On May 30, 1968, two Kennedy campaign workers in Azuza, California, each independently recalled seeing Sirhan come into their office, along with a young woman and another young man. The woman was described as having an "excellent figure" and "dishwater blond" hair. Azuza is about fifteen miles west of Pasadena, where Sirhan lived at the time. One of the Kennedy volunteers said the man, whom she later identified as Sirhan, claimed to be from the Kennedy campaign office in Pasadena and asked if Bobby would be going there. After being told he would not, the two men and the woman left. Given both sightings of Sirhan with an attractive woman, it should be noted that while Sirhan was interested in girls and had had a couple of unrequited crushes in the past, he had no documented dates or girlfriends in 1968.[5]

In the middle of the afternoon of June 1, 1968, Sirhan Sirhan returned to the same gun shop near Los Angeles—Lock, Stock, 'n Barrel—that he had visited in April, when he had asked about armor-piercing ammo for a .357 Magnum. On June 1, two witnesses saw Sirhan in the shop again: the clerk who waited on Sirhan that day, and the shop's owner, who both said that Sirhan was accompanied by two young men who also appeared to be of Middle Eastern extraction. The gun shop's owner thought they were the same three-man group from April. The clerk, who hadn't been present for their April visit, told the FBI he sold Sirhan "two boxes of high-velocity .22 caliber long rifle bullets," with fifty shells in each box.[6]

Also on June 1, 1968, Sirhan signed in for two hours of target practice at the Police Department gun range in Corona, the town where Sirhan had previously worked at a couple of horse farms. Though the log book verifies Sirhan's presence, no one actually remembered seeing him there.[7] But Sirhan was observed firing his gun that same day, in the same general area, by an insurance executive and his son, who were hiking in the Santa Ana Mountains. They encountered a man later identified as Sirhan, taking target practice at tin cans. Sirhan was with a young brunette woman and a tall man with "sandy colored hair and a ruddy complexion." The insurance executive remembered the encounter because all three were quite "unfriendly [and gave him the] sensation that it would be possible for them to put a bullet in your back." He and his son quickly left the area.[8]

Two witnesses also saw Sirhan Sirhan at the Ambassador Hotel on June 2, 1968, during Bobby Kennedy's rally there. According to LAPD records, one witness actually knew Sirhan because he had worked close to Sirhan's last job. He recognized Sirhan near one of the ballrooms, while the other witness saw Sirhan in the hotel's Coconut Grove restaurant, where Bobby's rally was being held.[9]

That same day, Sirhan had been sighted at another of Bobby's Los Angeles campaign offices, on Wilshire Boulevard. Around 2:00 PM, two volunteers—a man and a woman—saw the man they later identified as Sirhan walk in. When the male volunteer asked Sirhan what he could do to help him, Sirhan pointed at a distinguished-looking older man in the office, saying, "I'm with him." The man Sirhan pointed to was a new volunteer named Khaiber Khan, a wealthy and prominent Iranian dissident who opposed the US-backed Shah of Iran and his brutal secret police, the SAVAK. After Sirhan left, the female witness said she noticed that her copy of Bobby's campaign itinerary had "disappeared from her desk."[10]

Khaiber Khan himself would later tell police that two days later, on June 4, he had seen Sirhan at around 5:00 PM at the same Wilshire campaign office. Khan said Sirhan was with a young woman "in her early 20s . . . with light brown or dark blond shoulder-length hair . . . 'a good figure, and nice legs.'" The woman was wearing a "light . . . dress with black or blue polka dots the size of a dime."[11]

Due to the American government's strong support for the Shah, Khan and his Iranian dissident associates were probably under some type of US surveillance. Sirhan's contacts with Khan meant that the same domestic surveillance would also pick up on Sirhan—which would later cause US agencies to cover up or destroy information after Sirhan was arrested as Bobby's assassin. The Army Intelligence memo had said that "Sirhan [was] active in gaining support for Shah of Iran's visit," but since the rest of its Sirhan file has never been released or acknowledged, it's not clear whether it referred to the Shah's imminent visit, slated for June 11, 1968. If it did, that would have provided all the more reason to have Iranian dissidents like Khan under surveillance—and for someone to take advantage of that by placing Sirhan in close proximity to Khan.[12]

Also on June 4, 1968, the day of the California primary, Sirhan was seen taking target practice with his pistol at the San Gabriel Valley Gun Club. He stayed until closing time, 5:30 PM. Sometime before leaving his house that day, Sirhan had thrown away an envelope on which he'd written, "RFK must be disposed of like his brother." That evening, Sirhan took his pistol when he went to the Ambassador Hotel.[13]

Even before Sirhan began stalking Bobby Kennedy in late May 1968, he had been linked to several people and groups that could have been expected to cause the LAPD or other officials to cover up Sirhan's involvement after he was arrested for shooting Bobby—and that's exactly what happened. Two of these connections were to the staunchly conservative mayor of Los Angeles, Sam Yorty.

Mayor Yorty had a friend named Jerry Owen, a small-time television preacher in Los Angeles whose show was called *The Walking Bible*, because of Owen's claim to have memorized the Bible. Sam Yorty appeared on Owen's show, was photographed with Owen in the mayor's office several times, and Yorty authorized the city to loan Owen "horse trailers and other city property." William Turner found several credible witnesses who placed Sirhan with Owen in May 1968, prior to Bobby's murder. Several of those witnesses later testified under oath in a civil trial about Owen's pre-assassination contact with Sirhan.[14]

As Larry Hancock summarized, "Jerry Owen ran horses at a ranch out in Orange County. . . . A number of people [said] they had personally heard Jerry Owen mention Sirhan and even saw Jerry with Sirhan (or someone looking very much like him). These people understood that Sirhan was doing minor jobs for Jerry, handling and feeding his horses. Their stories . . . don't show up in the internal police reports dealing with Jerry Owen." However, Turner found indications that the LAPD conducted a more intensive investigation of Owen's possible contacts with Sirhan than the released files reflect. After the assassination, Jerry Owen apparently tried to provide cover for his contact with Sirhan by telling police that he had first met Sirhan on the day of Bobby's murder, when he gave Sirhan a ride.[15]

Owen wasn't the only good friend of Mayor Yorty whom Sirhan contacted prior to the assassination. Mayor Yorty was a longtime follower of the charismatic and eccentric Manly Palmer Hall, whom William Turner described as a hypnotherapist who had "gained considerable publicity" by hypnotizing Hollywood actors. For twenty years, Yorty "had been a student of Hall, whom he regarded as a guru." As part of Sirhan's seemingly increased interest in the occult and self-hypnosis, Sirhan told Turner that "he remembered paying several visits to [Palmer Hall's] headquarters, an alabaster temple near Griffith Park [and] 'I remember seeing Manly Hall there himself there.'" Turner also notes that police found a copy of one of Hall's books in Sirhan's car after Bobby's assassination, but "the book mysteriously disappeared from the grand jury exhibits."[16]

LAPD detectives would, naturally, have tried to protect Mayor Yorty and his friends from being drawn into the Sirhan case, which raises the possibility that someone had made sure that Sirhan had those connections—and more serious ones—prior to Bobby's murder. Ironically, it would be Mayor Yorty himself who would publicly proclaim Sirhan a communist soon after Bobby's murder, saying that Sirhan "was a member of numerous communist organizations . . . [and] that Sirhan was sort of a loner who favored communists of all types." As Melanson pointed out, Sirhan belonged to no communist organizations, and Sirhan hadn't seen his only communist acquaintance for three years—until May 2, 1968. The man, a friend from Sirhan's college days, was Walter Crowe, who told the FBI "he had tried to interest Sirhan in Marxism or communism, but couldn't."[17]

When Crowe met with Sirhan at Bob's Big Boy on May 2, just over a month before Bobby's murder, Crowe had been under surveillance by the LAPD's intelligence unit—and likely also the FBI, since the Bureau later had more details about Crowe's meeting with Sirhan than records show that Crowe himself told the FBI or the LAPD. Crowe was not a significant communist figure, but he and his associates were some of the hundreds, if not thousands, of leftists targeted for surveillance by the LAPD, the FBI, the CIA, and military intelligence. Turner has written at length about the ultra-conservative mentality—a McCarthey-esque belief in the Red Menace—that pervaded the five-thousand-member LAPD in 1968.[18]

However, Turner also points out that, based on his own FBI experience and the files on Crowe, other young people with whom Crowe met would usually have been subjected to similar surveillance—or otherwise checked out—both in 1965 (when Crowe last saw Sirhan, at college) and in 1968. But there is no record that happened to Sirhan. Unless the FBI made an exception in Sirhan's case, for some reason, then Sirhan had been checked out or was under surveillance—and, like other information about him, those files were suppressed or destroyed after he was arrested for Bobby's murder.[19]

It's almost as if someone wanted authorities to think Sirhan was a communist, since that might put him under surveillance, or at least give the public and authorities some seeming motive for shooting at Bobby. Melanson points out that "Sirhan's notebook contained heavy doses of pro-communist, revolutionary zeal, and anti-Americanism, as if Sirhan were a member of the Communist Party or . . . interested in communist ideology. But he wasn't." However, that was only the second most frequent subject Sirhan scribbled about in his notebook. His primary topic was money and getting money, often very large sums.[20]

Before Bobby's murder, Sirhan had been tied to people who could trigger cover-ups by the LAPD or intelligence agencies—but after Bobby's death, the Mafia appeared to be a guiding force in Sirhan's actions. No more than four days after Bobby died, perhaps even before Bobby passed away, Sirhan picked Los Angeles attorney Grant Cooper to be his attorney—at the same time that Cooper was busy as part of the defense team for Johnny Rosselli's Friars Club trial. Although Cooper actually represented one of Rosselli's codefendants, a former casino owner (tied to a recent hit attempt by Rosselli), author Lisa Pease noted that Cooper "was in direct and extensive contact with Rosselli's lawyer" throughout much of 1968.[21]

Because of the way the press reported Sirhan's selection of Grant Cooper, the ties of Cooper to the Johnny Rosselli trial were largely overlooked at the time. But Cooper's representation of Sirhan would have a huge impact on Sirhan's trial, resulting in his receiving a death sentence and ensuring that future appeals were fruitless. Sirhan himself would later tell Dan Moldea that

> Grant Cooper conned me to say that I killed Robert Kennedy [acting alone and not as part of any conspiracy]. I went along with him because he had my life in his hands. I was duped into believing he had my best interests in mind. It was a futile defense. Cooper sold me out . . . I remember Cooper once told me, "You're getting the best, and you're not paying anything. Just shut up. I'm the lawyer and you're the client."[22]

Grant Cooper was a respected attorney who had no criminal record before joining the Friars Club defense team—but that changed when Cooper became involved with Rosselli and his codefendant. Secret grand jury transcripts about the case were somehow obtained and given to Grant Cooper, but authorities were never able to learn who provided them. Out of the five Friars Club defendants, Rosselli seems the most likely source because of his long-standing connections to both Los Angeles and the Mafia. The fact that Grant Cooper was later willing to face charges (and an eventual conviction) for illegal possession of the transcripts, rather than reveal their source, indicates they came from someone from whom Cooper feared retribution—and Rosselli was the only Mafioso among the Friars Club defendants. By giving the transcripts to Cooper instead of to his own attorney, Rosselli not only deflected suspicion away from himself, but also gained an important hold over Cooper.[23]

According to the *New York Times*, Sirhan picked Grant Cooper's name "from a list given him by [the] chief local counsel for the American Civil Liberties Union."[24] However, Rosselli's involvement explains why a pricey attorney like Grant Cooper would readily agree to represent Sirhan for free. Because Cooper would be busy with the Friars Club trial for months, he brought in Mafia attorney Russell Parsons to help on Sirhan's case. Dan Moldea notes that "Parsons was well known for serving as counsel to southern California mobster Mickey Cohen and members of his gang."[25] As he had with Cooper, Sirhan had selected Parsons' name from the list of lawyers provided by the ACLU local counsel—raising the possibility that someone had told Sirhan prior to Bobby's murder to select the two mob-connected attorneys. Parsons immediately agreed to represent Sirhan without being paid (at least, not by Sirhan).

Not reported at the time was the name of another lawyer Cooper originally tried to enlist to represent Sirhan, while he finished the Friars Club case: Washington power attorney Edward Bennett Williams, who had established his reputation representing Jimmy Hoffa. Williams still had the Teamsters as a client, though he hadn't been Hoffa's attorney for several years. Edward Bennett Williams had also represented Sam Giancana in his last bout with federal officials, helping to broker the May 1966 deal that allowed Giancana to go free in return for leaving the country and not divulging the CIA-Mafia Castro assassination plots. However, by 1968 Williams was trying to develop a more legitimate image, smoothing over his differences with Bobby Kennedy before his death and becoming a part owner of the Washington Redskins, so Williams declined Cooper's offer.[26]

That left Sirhan with two attorneys linked to the Mafia, though at the time the press largely overlooked their mob ties, for several reasons. First, the *New York Times* reported that Sirhan signed "the retainer for the two lawyers . . . sometime between Sirhan's arrest June 5 and June 10." But that news wasn't reported until June 20, and even then, only Parsons's name was released, not Cooper's. In the *Times* article that day, Parsons simply said that he would "be joined by another lawyer, whom he described as 'a very able man, a good lawyer who is involved in something right now in which it would be detrimental if his name were announced in connection with the Sirhan case.'"[27]

Parsons' Mafia ties stemmed mainly from earlier times, since by that time his primary mob client, Mickey Cohen, had been in prison for several years. The *Times* article of June 20, 1968, didn't mention the Mafia or Cohen, saying only that Parsons was "best known . . . for his defense of" a bookmaker, whose case helped to prevent the use "of evidence secured by placing hidden microphones in private homes without a search warrant."[28] On the same page, a much smaller article reported that the United States government had asked the country of Jordan not to allow "four Jordanian lawyers . . . to fly to Los Angeles to help the defense of Sirhan." Jordan complied with the US's request, leaving Sirhan's defense in the hands of two attorneys tied to the mob.

The *Times* article, headlined "Lawyer, 73, Agrees to Defend Sirhan Without Fee," could have given readers the impression that Parsons was simply an elderly attorney taking a case that might give him one last turn in the limelight, and that he would be the main attorney at trial, but Grant Cooper was actually calling the shots. It was Cooper who decided to bring in Russell Parsons on the case, saying that he'd "worked with Russ before."[29]

As Mafia expert David Scheim pointed out, Russell Parsons had not only "represented many Mob clients [but] had once been investigated himself by . . . Robert Kennedy." Parsons had called Bobby "a dirty son of a bitch," while praising former Los Angeles mob boss Mickey Cohen. When Parsons worked for Cohen, Scheim notes that Cohen had ties to the Ambassador Hotel dating back to "the 1940s," when Cohen "ran a major gambling operation there." In its secret internal reports, the LAPD did briefly take note of Parsons' Mafia ties years earlier, though the department apparently never investigated Cooper's link to the Mafia.[30]

Parsons had an initial, two-hour private meeting with Sirhan on June 19, 1968, so we can assume that from then on, Parsons and Cooper exerted a major influence on what Sirhan said and did. In contrast to Sirhan's lack of openness with LAPD investigators, Sirhan "would confide in Russell Parsons," according to defense investigator and journalist Robert Blair Kaiser.[31] Moldea writes that "Kaiser, a respected journalist and a former correspondent for *Time*, came into the case as an investigator—so that he could write about Sirhan's defense 'from the inside.'" Yet William Turner reports that whenever "Kaiser had tried to open the minds of the defense lawyers to the indications of a conspiracy, [he] had run up against a stone wall, [and Kaiser said that] 'Parsons simply would not talk about [conspiracy,] let alone pursue it.'"[32]

The unusual actions, and lack of action, by Parsons and Cooper in the time leading up to Sirhan's trial have been documented by many writers, but not at the time, only since the mid-1970s. William Turner points out their odd defense strategy of "not contesting the state's contention that Sirhan had acted alone."[33] Thus, all the evidence that authors and journalists later found to be so controversial—or missing—would never be tested at Sirhan's trial. Philip Melanson said this evidence included the many "eyewitness accounts that challenged whether it was physically possible for Sirhan to have inflicted Kennedy's wounds," and several witnesses who saw a second gunman. After a pretrial hearing on October 18, 1968, Russell Parsons would announce to the press that "'We have seen no evidence of a conspiracy.' An *LA Herald* headline the following day declared, 'Both Sides Agree Sirhan Acted Alone.'"[34]

To give the press and public a logical reason for Sirhan to have shot Bobby, Lisa Pease points out that "it was Cooper who supplied Sirhan the motive he lacked, claiming that Sirhan was angry that RFK was willing to provide jets to Israel." Melanson found it troubling that even though "Chief defense attorney Grant Cooper and . . . Russell Parsons decided on a diminished capacity plea," supposedly "in order to avoid the death penalty," they didn't try very hard "to obtain crucial audio tapes of Sirhan's interrogation sessions with police during the early morning hours following his arrest" that were central to such a defense.[35]

Decades later, Sirhan would finally admit to journalist Dan Moldea that "Cooper sold me out"—but even if Sirhan saw signs, in the summer and fall of 1968, that their defense wasn't going to be effective, Sirhan had no real choice but to go along with the two mob-linked attorneys. Because of Sirhan's experiences in the world of racetrack gambling, plus the criminal background and associates of some of his brothers, Sirhan would have known what happened to those who crossed the mob. Only two weeks after Sirhan first met with Russell Parsons, someone apparently attempted to murder one of his brothers, possibly to make sure that Sirhan realized what could happen to his family if he didn't cooperate.

In a well-documented but rarely noted incident, on July 3, 1968, Saidallah Sirhan was the victim of an unusual shooting. According to Pasadena police reports, at approximately 4:30 AM, while driving the Sirhan family's 1955 DeSoto on the Pasadena freeway, Saidallah noticed two cars signal each other with car horns. Saidallah sensed "he was possibly being followed" by the two vehicles. Soon, one of them—a late-model Volkswagen Beetle—pulled up along the right side of his car, while a 1959 Chevrolet came up beside his car on the left. The police report says that Saidallah was worried "that the two vehicles were attempting to box him in, in an attempt to slow his car." Then Saidallah "saw a hand gun being pointed out the [Volkswagen's] driver's window."[36]

Seeing the pistol, Saidallah "immediately let go of the steering wheel of his car and leaned over to the right, lying down on the front seat of his car," to get out of the way. Two shots were fired into Saidallah's car, both "through the right wind wing." Saidallah stayed down in the seat for about ten seconds as his car slowed, since he had also taken "his foot off the gas." When Saidallah looked up, he saw the Chevrolet turn left, while the Volkswagen turned right. Saidallah went straight ahead, to the Pasadena Police Department, to report the shooting, where at 4:45 AM it was written up as an attempted murder. Police recovered two bullets, which appeared to be from a .38-caliber pistol, from Saidallah's car. Saidallah told the Pasadena police that he had seen two men in the Volkswagen's front seat and two in the back, as well as the driver in the Chevrolet's front seat plus two passengers in the back. All seven individuals were white males, and Saidallah didn't recognize any of the men, or either of the cars.[37]

Police would never solve the shooting case, but they advised Saidallah to move from his apartment into his mother's house, where they already maintained a twenty-four-hour police guard. Before Saidallah could move to his mother's, however, he received a threatening phone call from an unidentified man, about five hours after the freeway shooting.[38]

Authorities were appropriately skeptical of Saidallah's stated reason for being out at 4:30 AM: to ask a female journalist for the *LA Free Press*, whom he'd met just once, over a month earlier, if she would write a story about him. Police confirmed that Saidallah had met the woman, as he claimed, but he admitted he had no appointment and knew that a court order prohibited "any story written about his family or himself at this time." Saidallah claimed that he went out as late as he did because "during the day there are too many people on the street . . . and he felt safer at 4:00 AM."[39]

Though Saidallah denied owning any type of gun, a couple of his associates whom police interviewed thought he owned a .38, but police couldn't confirm those assertions or find any such weapon. Saidallah had asked a female friend about buying .38 bullets for him shortly before the shooting, so the Pasadena police looked into the possibility that Saidallah had staged the incident. However, Saidallah offered to take a polygraph test about the incident and allowed his apartment to be searched without a warrant. Also, in analyzing the bullet paths, the

Pasadena police confirmed that the shots could have been fired from one moving car into another, as Saidallah described. Police noted that if Saidallah hadn't ducked after seeing the gun, "the [second bullet] would probably have passed through his neck."[40]

The timing of the incident, just a month after Bobby's shooting and two weeks after Sirhan met with mob lawyer Russell Parsons, is suspicious. While Saidallah was clearly not in the area to meet the *Free Press* writer, it's unlikely, by the same token, that he was mixed up in something like a drug deal gone bad—otherwise, there would have been no reason for him to go to the police, especially so quickly after the shooting. It's possible that Saidallah was being stalked, or had been lured to the largely deserted freeway at that particular time, when there would be no witnesses.

While someone may have wanted to kill Saidallah, it's also possible that they wanted only to scare him, to send a message to him—or to his brother in jail. Because the shooter allowed Saidallah to see the gun before he fired it—giving Saidallah time to duck—and the shooter stopped firing after just two shots, their goal was probably to frighten Saidallah, not to kill him. If so, it would evoke the incident, one year earlier, when Carlos Marcello and Santo Trafficante had two gunmen blast Teamster official Allan Dorfman's car in a Chicago suburb. Trafficante told his attorney that incident "was just a warning," because "if they had wanted to kill him they would have."[41]

In a bizarre parallel, noted here for the first time, Sirhan's mob attorney Russell Parsons had himself been the subject of a similar shooting. It occurred in 1940, before he became a lawyer for the Mafia, when Parsons was working as a prosecutor for the Los Angeles district attorney's office. As the *Los Angeles Herald-Examiner* reported, "Parsons was the target of two gunmen who fired at him ... on a street. ... One bullet broke a wind wing on the car, and another hit the engine." At the time of the hit, Johnny Rosselli was a very prominent member of the Mafia in Los Angeles. It was after the shooting that Parsons left the district attorney's office and started representing members of Mickey Cohen's mob.[42]

Saidallah was probably the toughest of Sirhan's brothers, and later threatened one of Parsons' investigators, a former policeman. Parsons and his investigator went to the police, saying Saidallah's threat might relate to a message left at their answering service by a "Mr. C. Sirhan" that said, "Step out of the case. If my brother is hurt, you will be hurt. I will kill you." However, Parsons told police he would handle the matter himself.[43]

Ultimately, Parsons wound up frustrating the LAPD by protecting Saidallah and the other brothers from participating in police lineups. This act left the LAPD unable to resolve whether Saidallah, or other brothers, were with Sirhan when he bought his bullets and asked about the armor-piercing shells, or if they were involved in sightings of a man with the girl in the polka-dot dress. The other matter in which Parsons deliberately stymied police was their investigation of possible ties between Sirhan and Jerry Owen, the preacher friend of Los Angeles Mayor Sam Yorty.[44]

At the time of Sirhan's trial, it didn't appear to the press that Cooper and Parsons were obviously throwing the case, which would have raised suspicion and provided grounds for Sirhan's future appeals. But years later, one of Sirhan's attorneys would claim that Cooper did precisely that.[45] Cooper was subject to pressure because of his indictment for the stolen grand jury transcripts in the Friars Club case. Parsons had a much longer history with the Mafia, but the fact that Saidallah's shooting incident was similar to the one involving Parsons meant that it could have served as a reminder to keep the seventy-three-year-old attorney in line.

Was the attack on Saidallah a message meant for Sirhan, to cooperate with his mob lawyers or see his family (or himself) killed? If so, Sirhan got the message. Moldea recounts that Sirhan launched into an "outburst on the opening day of his defense—which forced the judge to send the jury out of the courtroom [as Sirhan pleaded,] 'I, at this time, sir, withdraw my original plea of not guilty and submit the plea of guilty as charged on all counts.'" Sirhan stunned the court by saying, "I will ask to be executed . . . I killed Robert Kennedy willfully, premeditatedly, with twenty years of malice aforethought." Sirhan also asked that his two mob lawyers, Cooper and Parsons, "disassociate themselves from this case completely." Sirhan soon calmed down, but his outburst suggests someone who had resigned himself to take the fall to protect his family from harm.[46]

Grant Cooper was following orders from someone, but it clearly wasn't Sirhan. In hindsight, the most obvious person in a position to influence Cooper was Johnny Rosselli. But that fact wasn't obvious at the time, because while Sirhan's case was major news nationally and in Los Angeles, the Friars Club case involving Rosselli and Cooper was primarily a small, local story. In 1968 and 1969, the two cases were almost never connected in the national media, and even locally, the few times they were mentioned in the same article, it was mainly to note scheduling issues. If Rosselli were influencing Grant Cooper's defense of Sirhan, his sway could explain why two of Johnny Rosselli's associates would later apparently confess to being involved in Bobby Kennedy's assassination.

Chapter Fifty-nine

A decade after Bobby's murder, Carlos Marcello's brother Joseph would be discussing the Kennedys with FBI BRILAB informant Joe Hauser, a highly trusted business partner of Carlos Marcello. When the subject of John and Bobby Kennedy came up, Joseph Marcello declared to Hauser, "We took care of 'em, didn't we?"—implying that Carlos Marcello had a hand in eliminating Bobby, as well as JFK. On October 25, 1979, Hauser would record for the BRILAB operation a talk between Marcello and two trusted associates, including the number-two man in the Los Angeles mob. When one raised the subject of Edward Kennedy's running for president, Carlos Marcello shouted that "he better fuckin' not. He better stay the fuck out of it. . . . "[1]

The Los Angeles mobster replied, "What a fuckin' shithead dat brother of his, Bobby, was . . . bastard thought he was gonna put us all outa business, the motherfucker."

Marcello's associate said, "Yeah, so we put HIM outa business!" as all the mobsters laughed.[2]

Unlike in JFK's assassination, there is not a clear, unequivocal confession by Carlos Marcello to his being involved in Bobby Kennedy's assassination. Then again, unlike the mostly released BRILAB audiotapes, the hundreds of hours of CAMTEX audiotapes of Marcello that were secretly recorded in prison in 1985 have never been released—and crucial evidence about Bobby's assassination has disappeared or been destroyed by Los Angeles police. Still, by using only the evidence that was available twenty years ago, John H. Davis and David E. Scheim were able to make compelling cases that Marcello and the Mafia were involved in Bobby's murder. Aside from his close relationship to Mickey Cohen, Marcello said that he considered other leaders of the Los Angeles Mafia to be "personal friends of mine . . . good people. They part of the family."

Carlos Marcello had maintained his close ties to Jimmy Hoffa and the Mafia's $2 million "Spring Hoffa" fund. Hoffa shared Marcello's hatred of Bobby Kennedy, and on July 23, 1968, the FBI finally interviewed Hoffa about his earlier reported threats to have Bobby assassinated. In addition to the May 1967 and May 1968 threats we've mentioned, Dan Moldea wrote about another incident in June 1968, "eight days after Robert Kennedy's murder, [when] the FBI received information from a confidential informant that James R. Hoffa . . . had said [before the assassination], 'If Hoffa isn't out, Kennedy will never get in.'"[3]

When the FBI talked to Hoffa at Lewisburg Federal Prison, Hoffa did not directly deny making the threats to have Bobby killed, probably because he knew that lying to a federal officer was a crime. Hoffa also refused to "sign the waiver" saying that he had been informed of his rights. According to FBI reports, Hoffa was asked if "he had made the statement that he had a contract out on Senator Robert F. Kennedy, and if he, Kennedy, ever got in the primaries or ever got elected, the contract would be fulfilled within six months." In response, "Hoffa stated he would not answer such a 'stupid' allegation. He stated, 'You know as well as I do how many nuts there are in this place who would say anything.' Hoffa said, 'You have my statement,' and refused to comment further regarding this allegation or the assassination of Senator Kennedy."[4]

Hoffa's threats to assassinate Bobby Kennedy were not reported in the press at the time, and didn't start to become public knowledge until after Hoffa's disappearance, seven years later, and some are quoted in this book for the first time. If Hoffa's contract on Bobby were put into action, as a federal prisoner, Hoffa couldn't have played any significant role in implementing it—he would have needed others to do that.

In Chapter 54, we noted briefly police and FBI reports of a Las Vegas Mafia contract on Bobby. Around May 1, 1968, a wealthy rancher and farmer in Delano, California, named Roy Donald Murray was overheard by the Chief of Police and another officer saying that "he had pledged $2,000 . . . to pay off a contract to kill Senator Kennedy," and that the Mafia "was behind the letting of the contract." Quoted for the first time here, the Delano police confirmed that Murray had "supposed connections in Las Vegas" and was "a known gambler [who] frequently loses several thousands of dollars at a time when he visits Las Vegas, but this does not appear to bother him," indicating that the "prosperous cotton rancher" had money to burn.[5]

The two Delano police sources had heard Roy Donald Murray while he was drinking heavily at the local Elks Club. Murray said that "he received a telephone call from his 'Mafia,' friends in Las Vegas, requesting a contribution to help pay a $500,000 to $750,000 contract to assassinate Robert Kennedy. Murray stated that the assassination was to take place if it appeared Kennedy was to earn the Democratic presidential nomination." Murray said that according to the Mafia, "California was considered as the conclusive proof point of that probable nomination."[6]

Like many wealthy farmers in the area, Murray was upset about Bobby's support for migrant labor leader César Chávez, based in Delano. Local law enforcement supported the farmers, so Murray felt comfortable telling the policemen about his "friends [who] were members of the 'Mafia.'"[7] The two police officials who heard Murray's comments "discounted them as bragging on the part of Murray." The FBI did a cursory investigation after Bobby's murder—talking only to Murray, who denied contributing to the Mafia contract on Bobby—but made no attempt to interview Murray's Las Vegas associates. With Rosselli's long ties to Vegas, and Marcello's contacts with the other mob bosses represented there, it's likely that one or both knew Murray's "Mafia friends [planning] to assassinate Robert Kennedy."

In fact, given the reports of a contract on Bobby linked to Marcello, Hoffa, and the Mafia in Las Vegas—plus Grant Cooper representation of Sirhan—Johnny Rosselli could well have been involved in bringing the hit to fruition. Marcello's past history of eliminating people who got in his way, as well as his perfect track record of getting away with murder, could have convinced him that there was only one way to ensure that his hated enemy Bobby never achieved the presidency. Marcello had demonstrated in November 1963 that he was perfectly capable of having a Kennedy contract executed while he was on trial—and using Johnny Rosselli to help do it.

As with the contract on Dr. King, Marcello's role could have been to simply broker Hoffa's RFK contract to Rosselli's associates. It could have been even less substantial than that, on the order of contributing money (either Marcello's own or from the "Spring Hoffa" fund) or simply ensuring that things went smoothly between Rosselli and the new head of the Los Angeles Mafia. Horse walker Sirhan could have become involved through any of several of his associates who were connected to drugs or racetrack gambling, such as Frank Donneroummas.[8] Such a scenario evokes the incident cited in Chapter 3 regarding FBI files about a horse trainer for Carlos Marcello's brother, who in the summer of 1963 overheard Marcello's brother say, "The word is out to get the Kennedy family."[9] Marcello would have known that Bobby's frequent visits to Los Angeles meant that Rosselli's connections there could be very useful before or after such a hit. Plus—as we note shortly—by 1968, Rosselli needed money.

A snapshot of Johnny Rosselli in 1968, prior to Bobby's murder, shows that the Mafia don was in a unique position to have been used in a contract on Bobby Kennedy. Rosselli's legal and financial problems, coupled with his dislike for RFK, would have made him receptive to helping with such a hit.

Rosselli's power in the Mafia was in decline in early 1968 because his patron, Sam Giancana, had left the country in 1966 and hadn't returned. In addition, Rosselli had problems with the main Mafia family in Los Angeles and was starting to be cut out of the Las Vegas casino deals.

By March 1968, Rosselli was very worried not only about the Friars Club charges, but also about his immigration trial, scheduled for May. Rosselli had so far been frustrated in his attempts to pressure the CIA to intervene on his behalf. In March 1968, Rosselli had met with William Harvey, and Harvey then told the CIA "he has a very strong feeling that if either of the two trials that now threaten Johnny result in deportation, he will blow the whistle on the Agency." Because of his weakened position, and the locally high-profile nature of the Friars Club case, Rosselli was no longer trying to get both cases against him dropped. Rosselli's new demand to the CIA was much more realistic: to simply protect him from being deported if he were convicted.[10]

We know that CIA Director Richard Helms was told about Rosselli's new demand, as well as his earlier ones, because the CIA's Security Chief who met with Harvey wrote that he "told [Harvey] on numerous occasions . . . that I have passed his views on this to the Director."[11] Richard Helms knew what would happen to his career if Rosselli decided to "blow the whistle on" Helms's unauthorized operations from 1963. Helms's reaction to Rosselli's new demand can be gauged by the results: Rosselli's biographers discovered that a high FBI official wrote that in 1968, "certain efforts are being made to hamper the government's investigation into Rosselli." The biographers found that the United States attorney in Los Angeles said "unnamed people in the circles in Washington [are] saying that John was a patriotic citizen who deserved some form of consideration." Though Johnny Rosselli would be convicted in both trials, including the one proving that he was an illegal alien, Rosselli would never be deported.[12]

Rosselli was likely facing at least some prison time, and being trapped in federal prison while Bobby reassembled his Justice Department anti-Mafia team—and was free to engage in all manner of secret investigations—would have been Rosselli's worst nightmare. Bobby's quick, extralegal deportation of Marcello in April 1961 showed what the potential president was capable of, and would have been a sword of Damocles hanging over Rosselli's (and Marcello's) head as long as Bobby was in the White House.

Rosselli was involved in three attempted contract killings in early 1968, but only the King hit involving Carlos Marcello had been successful. Rosselli's first 1968 target had been the FBI informant in his immigration case, whose name Rosselli learned from Ed Morgan. Following the usual mob procedure for a hit, Rosselli got approval from his boss, Sam Giancana, then based in Mexico, and Giancana called the head of the Los Angeles Mafia to give his permission. However, the new Los Angeles mob boss was a former rival of Rosselli's and took no action. Rosselli let the matter drop, since he had a more important contract killing to worry about; but this time, Rosselli bypassed the usual Mafia hierarchy and hired his own hit man.[13]

For Rosselli's second 1968 attempt, he asked Jimmy "the Weasel" Fratianno, a notorious mob hit man, to kill the key witness in the Friars Club cheating scandal. According to Fratianno, George Seach was the "ex-convict [and] electronics engineer who had installed the cheating devices" at the club, and had agreed to testify against Rosselli and his four codefendants, including the former casino owner represented by Grant Cooper.[14] In January 1968, Rosselli discussed the hit with Fratianno in the Los Angeles office of Rosselli's attorney, Jimmy Cantillon. Rosselli and Fratianno talked in Cantillon's law library, where they felt safe from government surveillance—the type of secure location Rosselli could have later used when he met with Grant Cooper.

Rosselli complained to Fratianno about his greatly reduced income, caused by being cut out of his Las Vegas casino deals. Rosselli's codefendant, Grant Cooper's client, advanced the apparently cash-short Rosselli $2,000 in expense money for the hit, which he gave to Fratianno. Rosselli and Fratianno decided to do the hit in Las Vegas, where Rosselli still had influence; Fratianno hired a trusted mutual associate, Frank Bompensiero, to help with the killing. However, Rosselli's biographers write that, through Bompensiero, "the government had caught word of the contract [and the target] entered the federal witness protection program."[15]

Rosselli's first two 1968 hit attempts failed, but his involvement in a third was tragically successful: the Marcello-brokered contract on Martin Luther King. Johnny Rosselli's role with James Earl Ray, likely some type of monitoring, would remain secret for decades. Since Rosselli was tied to both Ray and Sirhan's attorney Grant Cooper, it's worth noting several interesting parallels between Ray and Sirhan. At the same time Ray had arrived in Los Angeles in 1967 and begun his unusual pursuit of self-hypnosis, Sirhan was deepening his long-standing interest in self-hypnosis—even as he started to engage in uncharacteristic behavior, such as trying to obtain armor-piercing bullets. It was as if both Sirhan and James Earl Ray felt they needed to learn self-hypnosis to focus on doing something they'd never done before. Both men had ties to the underworld and to people who dealt in narcotics, and within the space of six weeks, Sirhan bought his first pistol and Ray bought his first rifle. Both men used their respective weapons in assassinations linked not just to Rosselli, but also to Carlos Marcello.[16]

David Morales, Johnny Rosselli's old friend from the CIA, made a clear confession to being involved in Bobby Kennedy's assassination, telling his attorney Robert Walton that "I was in Los Angeles when we got Bobby." In 1968, Morales was in the process of transitioning from duty in Latin America to Southeast Asia. With CIA officials like Richard Helms and David Atlee Phillips concerned with their own problems, a supervisory gray area probably emerged that Morales exploited to his advantage—and that of his friend Rosselli. After Bobby's murder, Morales would ultimately wind up in Vietnam, working once again with AMWORLD veterans like Ted Shackley and soon helping future CIA Director William Colby with the massive CIA Operation Phoenix assassination program.

Two of Morales's closest friends say he still visited Los Angeles on occasion, where he had some family. As far as is known, Morales had no official CIA duties in the city, so whatever lethal business he did there was likely for himself and/or a crony like Rosselli, with whom Morales had worked closely on the 1963 CIA-Mafia plots to kill Castro. When those plots ended after their murder of JFK, Morales had continued to meet with Rosselli, sometimes in Las Vegas. In addition to the hatred of Bobby that Morales shared with Rosselli, Morales would have feared the possibility of Bobby Kennedy's being president, knowing it could yield secret investigations or CIA housecleaning that might expose Morales's (self-confessed) role in JFK's murder.[17]

Revealed here for the first time, based on CIA files only fully declassified in 2003, David Morales had an earlier plan for killing Fidel Castro—involving a shooter with a handgun in a pantry—that could have been applied to Bobby Kennedy. As we mentioned briefly in earlier chapters, from 1962 to 1964 the CIA had an asset in Cuba who wanted to assassinate Fidel at one of his favorite restaurants, the Montecatini. On each of his monthly visits, the egalitarian Fidel always went into the kitchen and pantry area to greet the busboys, dishwashers, and cooks. Because of the crowded conditions, the CIA file says that Fidel would leave his security escort "outside [so when Fidel] visits kitchen alone [and] chats with employees [Fidel] is 'a sitting duck.'"[18]

The restaurant's pantry/kitchen area was one of the only places where an assassin could get close enough to kill Fidel without having to get through his security detail of "about 20 [men] in about five cars." Fidel's security team would precede "the arrival of Fidel by 10 to 15 minutes and [make] an inspection of the locale [before taking] up strategic positions both inside and outside the restaurant. Even the waiters are watched individually and are followed around." However, there was a "closet partially under the stairs . . . used [as a pantry] for storage [where] a man could be hidden . . . comfortably." While the restaurant staff was small—"3 waiters, 1 bus boy, 1 Chef [owner], 1 cook, 2 dishwashers"—the Chef-owner and his wife were reputedly anti-Castro. They could have either allowed an assassin to hide in the closet, or hired the assassin as kitchen help. When Castro came through the kitchen and pantry area, the assassin could pull out a pistol and start firing away at Fidel, at close range.[19]

The initial pantry/kitchen assassination plan was sent to William Harvey on August 28, 1962, but the unfolding Cuban Missile Crisis and Harvey's subsequent removal likely prevented it from being considered seriously. The plan was raised again on November 8, 1963, but by that time, the JFK-Almeida coup plan and AMWORLD were already in place.[20]

As the CIA's Operations Chief for their Miami Station at the time, David Morales would have been involved in evaluating the pantry/kitchen plan. It presented two main problems: The small closet pantry might be able to hold only one assassin—and even if he were successful in killing Fidel, he would certainly be killed or captured by Fidel's security forces. Finding someone willing to sacrifice his life like that, someone who couldn't be traced to the CIA, wouldn't be easy. However, by the summer of 1964, the CIA might have been taking steps to implement the pantry / kitchen plan—but any chance of using it disappeared in August 1964, when a CIA asset learned the "owner [of the] Montecatini Restaurant, Havana, [was] arrested and imprisoned . . . to be tried for plotting against [the] life of [Fidel Castro]."[21]

In 1968, David Morales was in a good position to adapt the pantry / kitchen plan to use against Bobby Kennedy. Unlike Rosselli and Marcello, Morales was unfettered by suspicion or prosecution, and thus free from law enforcement scrutiny. In fact, especially in Los Angeles, Morales could wield important influence over some of those very same authorities.

Just as it had been in 1963, in 1968 the CIA was involved in a variety of activities that David Morales could have used to generate a cover-up after Bobby was murdered. For years, the CIA had maintained a special relationship with the Los Angeles Police Department, from helping with covert activities to training certain LAPD officers. Some of those officers later left the LAPD to work in Latin America, where David Morales had recently been very active. The CIA's especially close relationship with the LAPD had developed because of problems, dating to the 1950s, between the FBI and the city's police chief at the time.

According to William Turner, the LAPD was instrumental in the creation of "the Law Enforcement Intelligence Unit [LEIU], a network of big-city police departments across the country aimed at taking on the national crime syndicate." This network linked police intelligence units from Los Angeles to New Orleans to Tampa, but by 1968, these units "switched targets from organized crime to political dissidence." The CIA helped by having its "Clandestine Services Division" train officers from Los Angeles, Chicago, and other cities "in intelligence techniques." In return, the police aided the CIA with domestic operations like "surveillance and break-ins." Richard Helms's executive assistant described seeing a dozen LAPD officers at CIA headquarters in 1967, as "part of a 'sensitive project' . . . given the green light by the Director himself."[22]

Hank Hernandez, who intimidated witness Sandy Serrano during his grueling interrogation before polygraphing her, was one of the LAPD officers who not only received CIA special training but also performed assignments for the CIA. William Turner pointed out that "as a polygraph operator, Hernandez questioned the witnesses whose accounts indicated a [conspiracy]"—witnesses who were much more likely to be polygraphed than those who supported the official lone-assassin scenario. Hernandez was one of the key members of the LAPD's Special

Unit Senator (SUS) which conducted crucial interrogations about Sirhan, his family, his money, and his more unusual associates.[23]

Turner wrote that "Sergeant Hank Hernandez [who was] promoted to lieutenant in recognition of his status in [SUS] had CIA connections [and boasted] in a resume . . . that in 1963 he played a key role in [doing] training for the CIA in Latin America . . . and even received a medal from the Venezuelan government" for helping to fight "Fidel Castro's 'exportation' of the Cuban revolution." For that CIA assignment, Hernandez utilized "the usual cover of . . . the Office of Public Safety of the Agency for International Development (AID)," which "has long served as a cover for the CIA's clandestine program of supplying advisers and instructors for national police and intelligence services in Southeast Asia and Latin America." In 1968, the Chief Deputy Attorney General of California confirmed that information to Turner. [24]

Turner notes that Hernandez was just one of a small number of SUS officers who had such ties; another of whom apparently worked with an associate of David Morales. "In retrospect it seems odd," Turner writes, "that . . . policemen who doubled as CIA agents occupied key positions in SUS, where they were able to seal off avenues that led in the direction of conspiracy." Turner wrote those words in 1978, before he or other journalists knew about David Morales's work for the CIA or about Morales's friendship with Johnny Rosselli.[25]

Hank Hernandez's work for the CIA extended beyond Latin America and apparently outlasted the investigation of Bobby Kennedy's assassination. Lisa Pease pointed out that "during his session with Sandy Serrano, [Hernandez] told her that he had once been called to Vietnam, South America, and Europe to perform polygraph tests." Pease was told by "one of Hernandez's neighbors . . . how Hernandez used to live in a modest home in the Monterey Park area, a solidly middle-class neighborhood. But within a short time after the assassination, Hernandez had moved to a place that has a higher income per capita than Beverly Hills: San Marino. He came into possession of a security firm and handled large accounts for the government."[26]

Hank Hernandez, and others in SUS, didn't have to play a knowing part in the conspiracy. They or those higher in the LAPD hierarchy could simply have been told by someone like Morales that certain leads or associates of Sirhan involved national security and shouldn't be pursued or exposed, since they had no bearing on the case. Even though the SUS investigation was far bigger and more thorough in many areas than most people realized, the right words to a few key people—evoking national security concerns—would ensure that topics that could lead to Morales or his associates were avoided. Such arrangements could also ensure that certain proconspiracy witnesses could be grilled and polygraphed either until they changed their stories or until an SUS report was written saying that they had.

The key areas of evidence destruction and missing files center on the questions of whether more than one shooter was involved, and whether the Mafia or drug trafficking played some role. David Morales's involvement in Bobby's murder could account for many of those problems, such as the fact that the LAPD's Johnny Rosselli file was missing when the House Select Committee on Assassinations asked for it in 1978. Rosselli had been a major Mafia figure in Los Angeles since the late 1930s and was being actively prosecuted in 1968, so it's inconceivable that the LAPD didn't have a large file on him. Yet also in 1968, Rosselli was still pressuring the Agency, through William Harvey, over the CIA-Mafia plots to avoid deportation, which would have allowed a CIA officer like Morales to have the LAPD suppress its Rosselli file for reasons of national security.[27]

In 2008, anyone can search the LAPD's and FBI's raw reports online, to see how they were summarized in the final, internal SUS Report. We have found repeated examples where references to drugs and the Mafia were eliminated or minimized.[28] Other obvious subjects took an extraordinarily long time to pursue. Regarding Sirhan's drug-linked former boss, John H. Davis points out that it took the LAPD and FBI "ten months to find out who Donneroummas was, that his real name was Henry Ramistella, and that he had a criminal record."[29] By that time, Sirhan's trial was already underway.

The LAPD's forty-person SUS was in an extremely secure area that was not accessible to the average patrolman or detective.[30] Even within that unit, certain people, like Hank Hernandez and a few more, were essentially choke points whose decisions could determine what leads SUS pursued or which witnesses were viewed as credible. How people like Hernandez gained their prized positions is also unclear, since released files show that certain of these individuals were playing key roles very early in the LAPD's investigation of Bobby's murder, even before SUS was formed.

In 1968, the LAPD was helping the CIA—and military intelligence, and at times the FBI—in the extensive surveillance of "subversives," which by 1968 included a huge array of groups ranging from communists to "pro-Arab" groups to Iranian dissidents to civil rights activists to peace protesters. Sirhan had ties—however brief—to people in the first three groups in the months (and especially weeks) before Bobby's murder, connections that could have brought him under such surveillance. The CIA and other agencies would have been just as anxious to hide any pre-assassination surveillance of Sirhan and his associates as they had been for Oswald.[31]

In 1968, Helms and Phillips were still concerned with the Garrison investigation, which by then focused on the upcoming trial of former low-level CIA informant Clay Shaw, whom Garrison tied to David Ferrie through New Orleans' gay subculture. (The strong ties between Ferrie and Marcello no longer concerned Garrison and had so far escaped press attention.) In April 1968, the CIA generated a file card for internal use, saying that as far as Lee Harvey Oswald was concerned, until recently in the CIA:

> ... there had been no secret as far as anyone was concerned in regard to the fact that [Guy] Banister [and] David William Ferrie and subj [Oswald] may have known or been acquainted with one another.[32]

Much evidence shows that Helms and Phillips knew that Oswald actually worked with Banister and Ferrie in the summer of 1963—and that Phillips had met with Oswald, while Helms reportedly ordered Oswald's New Orleans files to be taken to Washington after JFK's assassination. Helms and Phillips would have been focused on preventing that information from coming out in Garrison's investigation, as well as on making sure the CIA's authorized and Helms's unauthorized anti-Castro operations weren't exposed. Rosselli played a key role in keeping the unauthorized operations from being revealed, giving Morales even more leverage to use if the SUS investigation came too close to Rosselli or his associates. Amidst all that, Helms and Phillips were also dealing with other problem areas, from Cuban operations (for Phillips) to domestic surveillance, Vietnam, Iran, and the Middle East; and other Cold War hot spots (for Helms). Helms and his subordinates probably would have welcomed whatever Morales could do to keep a lid on national security concerns during the SUS investigation.

Morales's intelligence background, coupled with Johnny Rosselli's Los Angeles ties and Carlos Marcello's national Mafia clout, meant that relatively few people would need to have been knowingly involved in Bobby's murder. Because of Morales's confession—which became known to researchers only through a privately printed book published in 1997—claims were made on a BBC program on November 20, 2006, that Morales and two other CIA associates were visible in videotape and films taken in the Ambassador's ballroom the night Bobby was shot. (These allegations were disproven the following year.) We feel that the cautious Morales would never have allowed himself to be visible in the Ambassador's ballroom, especially in front of cameras. Also, Bobby had met with Morales in the past and could have recognized him.

Because most of the CIA files on Morales are still classified, it's impossible to determine what his self-confessed role actually was. The same is true for Johnny Rosselli and Carlos Marcello, especially while so many of their CIA and FBI files—and tapes, in Marcello's case—remain unreleased. But the bottom line is that because of Sirhan's actions in the months prior to Bobby's murder and what the LAPD did in the shooting's immediate aftermath—followed by mob lawyers Cooper and Parsons taking control of Sirhan's defense—the final outcome of Sirhan's trial was a foregone conclusion months before it actually occurred.

In the summer and fall of 1968, as the Friars Club trial dragged on, Russell Parsons primarily handled Sirhan's pretrial defense while Grant Cooper represented one of Rosselli's codefendants. Parsons and Cooper had Sirhan enter a "not guilty" plea on August 2, 1968. On December 2, 1968, Rosselli and his four codefendants—including Cooper's client—were all found guilty in the cheating scandal. Cooper officially assumed command of Sirhan's defense the very next day, with sentencing in the Friars Club case still eight weeks away.

Defense investigator and journalist Robert Blair Kaiser noted Sirhan's preoccupation with large sums of money, even though "Sirhan never could explain the references in his notebook to money." Sirhan once told Kaiser, "You get me $100,000 [and] I could be pretty well set up." Yet when Kaiser encouraged Sirhan to really open up to him in their hundreds of hours of talks—so that Sirhan could make lots of money— Sirhan refused, and confided only in his mob attorneys. Kaiser was frustrated that he couldn't convince Cooper or Parsons to investigate conspiracy angles and the possibility that someone had paid Sirhan to kill Bobby. Later, Kaiser said that he realized, "What kind of defense would it be, to claim that your client was some kind of paid killer?"[33]

Kaiser wrote that "Grant Cooper once asked Sirhan about the money angle, and Sirhan" didn't deny it, and instead "answered with another question. 'If I got the money, where is it?'"[34] The answer to Sirhan's question was literally staring him in the face, since, as we noted earlier,

Cooper had told Sirhan, "You're getting the best [defense lawyers] and you're not paying anything."[35] In addition, it would have made little sense for anyone to have paid an amateur like Sirhan a substantial sum before the hit. As we pointed out earlier, Sirhan initially said he expected only a short sentence if he were caught and convicted, leaving plenty of time for him to be paid later. As it turned out, free defense from high-profile attorneys, and protection for his family from more shootings (and, for Sirhan, from attacks in prison), were apparently the only rewards Sirhan received.

Sirhan's trial began amidst much national publicity on January 7, 1969, but Grant Cooper was caught up in conflicts of interest from the start. The previous week, Cooper had been called before a new grand jury to testify about the illegal transcripts of the Friars Club grand jury that he had obtained mysteriously the previous year. According to a January 10, 1969, newspaper report, "Cooper did admit to the [grand] jury that he had lied to the Friars trial judge ... to protect his client," Rosselli's codefendant.[36] However, Rosselli's name was not mentioned in press accounts of Cooper's Friars Club problems or in regard to Sirhan's trial, press coverage of which quickly drove Cooper's own legal troubles from the news.

The possibility of jail time for Cooper wasn't resolved until almost four months after Sirhan's trial was over, when Cooper pleaded guilty and was fined only $1,000, even though he never revealed the source of the transcripts.[37] Cooper's distinguished legal career was still in jeopardy, and professional sanctions against him by the California Supreme Court remained hanging over his head for two more years.[38] Because of those circumstances, Johnny Rosselli and the Mafia had ample leverage over Cooper for the three crucial years after Bobby's murder.

As for Sirhan's own trial, many authors have pointed out that Cooper essentially capitulated to all of the prosecution's major points. As Lisa Pease pointed out, the result was that Sirhan's trial was "solely for the purpose of determining his sentence, not whether or not he really was guilty of the crime." Cooper simply ignored important prosecution problems, such as the autopsy's conclusion that Bobby had been shot from about an inch away, when no witness placed Sirhan that close. The defense apparently wasn't even given a copy of Bobby's final autopsy report until after the trial began. When an LAPD ballistics expert testified that only Sirhan's pistol and "no other gun in the world fired the evidence bullets," the defense didn't notice that the LAPD's test bullets were labeled as having been fired from a different pistol.[39]

Later official investigations found the ballistics evidence problematic: A 1977 report by the Los Angeles District Attorney's office said that "the apparent lack of reports, both written and photographic, either made . . . and destroyed, or never in existence, raised serious doubts as to the substance and reliability of the ballistics evidence presented in the original Sirhan trial." A 1975 court-authorized panel of ballistics experts concluded that the bullets from Bobby and the other victims could not be matched to Sirhan's pistol, and did not preclude the possibility that two guns had been fired.[40] Yet Cooper noted none of those problems, nor others, during Sirhan's trial, even though Cooper admitted three years later that he'd been "warned prior to the trial" by an experienced criminologist that the LAPD's ballistics expert "could not be relied upon," due to irregularities in an earlier case.[41]

Meanwhile, Cooper was still working on the Friars Club case. Four weeks after Sirhan's trial began, Rosselli and his codefendants were finally sentenced, on February 4, 1969, for the cheating scandal. The former Las Vegas casino owner who was Cooper's client received the longest sentence—six years and a $100,000 fine—while Rosselli received a five-year sentence and was fined $50,000. Rosselli got an additional six months for his earlier immigration conviction, to be served concurrently.[42]

On February 10, six days after Rosselli and the others were sentenced, Cooper tried to make a deal with Sirhan's prosecutor to end the murder trial. The prosecutor agreed to accept a guilty plea in return for sparing Sirhan the death penalty, because Sirhan's shooting had been so out of character for the young man that the prosecution's own psychiatrist could conclude only that Sirhan was psychotic—an assessment that fit perfectly with Sirhan's "diminished capacity" defense. But in a private conference with the District Attorney and Cooper, Sirhan's judge raised "the Oswald matter," in which people wondered what was "going on, because the fellow wasn't tried." The judge worried that if the prosecutor accepted the deal, the public "would say that it was all fixed; it was greased. So we will just go through the trial."[43]

That meant that Sirhan was on trial for his life, but even after Cooper began presenting the defense case, on February 28, 1969, Sirhan was opposed to portraying himself as insane or psychotic. Mental-health facilities could still be relatively primitive in those days, and apparently Sirhan feared spending the rest of his life locked away in an institution for the criminally insane more than he feared the death penalty (which Sirhan actually asked for during his February 25 outburst, mentioned earlier).[44]

Sirhan's case went to the jury on April 14, 1969, and he was convicted on April 17. The jury voted to give Sirhan the death penalty on April 23, and pronounced the death sentence on May 21, 1969.[45]

Without waiting for action to be taken on Sirhan's appeal, the Los Angeles Police Department was soon destroying critical evidence in the case. On June 27, 1969, the LAPD destroyed the ceiling panels and the door frames that had been photographed showing extra bullet holes, too many to have been made by Sirhan's bullets alone. The excuse the LAPD gave later was that the door frames were "too large to fit into a card file."[46]

Some 2,400 photos from the case were burned on August 21, 1969. Supposedly all were duplicates, yet crucial photos from the case are still missing, even today. We mentioned earlier the photos taken in the pantry during the shooting by fifteen-year-old Scott Enyart, who was standing on a table to get a good view of Bobby Kennedy. Larry Hancock writes that "Enyart eventually got back 18 prints, no negatives, and none of the photos taken in the pantry. After years of legal struggle, he was awarded the photos [from the pantry by the court]—which were then 'stolen out of the back seat of a courier's car' when the courier stopped to inspect a problem with a tire on the way to deliver them."[47] Without those photos—in the LAPD's possession, though what the pictures depicted was not mentioned in the LAPD's reports—we cannot know for certain if Sirhan did somehow manage to get close enough to Bobby to have fired the fatal shot, as Dan Moldea suggested.

Among the other evidence that was destroyed or is still missing, Philip Melanson lists "X-rays and test results on ceiling tiles and door frames, spectrographic test results [for bullets], the left sleeve of Senator Kennedy's coat and shirt, the test gun used as a substitute for Sirhan's gun during ballistics tests, and results from the 1968 test firing of Sirhan's gun." He also points to numerous missing tapes containing interviews of important witnesses, including those of eyewitness Paul Schrade; "twelve witnesses with information relating directly to whether Sirhan was accompanied by a female accomplice"; "five witnesses at a pistol range where Sirhan was target practicing the day of the shooting"; and "three associates of Sirhan's whose background . . . required probing for possible conspiratorial involvement." In some cases, reports refer to tapes that no longer exist, and in other instances, tapes do not appear to exist for witnesses who supposedly recanted their stories of having seen Sirhan with possible accomplices.[48]

———

In destroying or suppressing so much evidence soon after Sirhan's verdict, some in the LAPD were simply continuing what had begun less than an hour after the shooting: the depiction of Sirhan as a lone assassin with no accomplices. While much evidence seems to support that conclusion, its hasty adoption precluded a serious investigation of any backing Sirhan might have had.

Once LAPD officials had made their conclusions clear internally and to the press—that Sirhan had acted alone with no confederates—the essential nature of large institutions caused others on the force to support the conclusion—not just before and after Sirhan's trial, but even years later. This situation is similar to what happened in the JFK case with Hoover and the FBI, when field agents quickly realized that pursuing conspiracy leads was at odds with what headquarters wanted, and for thirty years the FBI's public stance continued to support that view. LAPD officers who backed the department's Sirhan-as-a-lone-nut conclusion in 1968 couldn't afford to admit later that they might have been wrong, if they wanted to see their careers—or those of their LAPD mentors—flourish. Decades later, the LAPD as an institution, including its members with no connection to the original investigation, would still take action to support its "lone nut" conclusions, not as part of a massively orchestrated cover-up, but to avoid embarrassment and scandal for the department.

Chapter Sixty

During the summer and fall of 1968 and into 1969, the investigation and pre-trial proceedings of James Earl Ray for Martin Luther King's assassination were going on at the same time as those for Sirhan Sirhan in Bobby's murder. News about Ray and Sirhan usually overshadowed reports about Jim Garrison's ongoing investigation of JFK's assassination in New Orleans, which was now hopelessly compromised and off-course, focusing almost exclusively on Clay Shaw.

At no time during the news coverage of any of those matters did the names of Carlos Marcello, Johnny Rosselli, or Joseph Milteer ever surface. The press and most investigators similarly ignored Santo Trafficante and Jimmy Hoffa. No mainstream reporter pointed out any possible connections between the three assassinations. Aside from a few public figures like comedian Mort Sahl, most commentators and newspeople in the US avoided even general comments on the apparent similarities between certain aspects of the assassinations of JFK, Bobby, and Dr. King.

After his capture on June 8, 1968, James Earl Ray spent the rest of June and much of July in London, awaiting extradition to the US for the murder of Dr. King. But even before his return to the US, Ray's legal defense started to become compromised by financial considerations and conflicts of interest. Over the next nine months, Ray would go through three attorneys, each with problematic connections to associates of Carlos Marcello or Joseph Milteer, who would help to ensure the roles of Marcello and Milteer weren't exposed.

While still in a British jail, Ray told an officer that he expected to profit from being involved in King's assassination. According to the officer's later testimony to the House Select Committee on Assassinations, Ray expected to be charged only with "conspiracy." Since the trial would be held in Memphis (or at least, if there were a change of venue, somewhere in the South), Ray might not be convicted at all—and even if he were,

Ray told the British officer, he expected to receive a sentence of only "ten to twelve years." Parole could reduce that time significantly, theoretically allowing Ray to emerge from prison a wealthy man.[1]

The British court appointed a solicitor for Ray, who asked the solicitor to contact two US attorneys whom Ray wanted to represent him. One was Arthur Hanes Sr., the former mayor of Birmingham, Alabama, known for winning acquittals for the four Klansmen accused of killing civil rights worker Viola Liuzzo. The other attorney was flamboyant Melvin Belli, the drug-linked attorney who had represented Jack Ruby. Despite their high profiles and fees, Ray told his British solicitor, "I'm not worried about their fees . . . even if it takes a hundred thousand dollars, I can raise it. They'll be taken care of."[2]

Melvin Belli passed on the chance to represent Ray, but Arthur Hanes Sr. was willing, and he flew to England.[3] Though he was a segregationist, Hanes Sr. was respected and admired in Alabama's legal and political circles. According to author Jeff Cohen, Hanes "was formerly a CIA contract employee," which is probably why Hanes had previously represented the widows of several Alabama pilots killed during the Bay of Pigs invasion, while they were flying for the CIA. The resulting compensation for the widows handled by Hanes had come from the Cuban Revolutionary Council, the group organized and managed by E. Howard Hunt and David Atlee Phillips.[4]

Throughout the time he represented Ray, Hanes later testified, he felt that "there was a conspiracy" in Dr. King's assassination, and that Ray had been a paid hit man. According to Cohen, on one occasion, Hanes "told the *Washington Post* that that if black militants weren't behind the murder [of Dr. King,] the CIA was." However, most of Hanes's public suspicions didn't implicate the CIA, and instead pointed toward Castro, as when he said, "My client is a tool of revolutionary groups financed by Cuba."[5]

Hanes's comments to reporters didn't cast suspicion on racist groups, perhaps for good reason. A former Klan leader told the HSCA that the United Klans of America had given Hanes $10,000, ostensibly to represent a small group of Klansmen in North Carolina, but in actuality to pay for Ray's defense. Hanes firmly denied the charge, but the HSCA found two independent sources that corroborated the surreptitious Klan payments to Hanes for representing Ray.[6] The involvement of North Carolina Klansmen in the scheme certainly raises the possibility that Milteer and his partners were involved in the payments, and Milteer almost certainly had associates in common with Hanes.

However, Hanes's motivation appears to have been primarily

financial, and Hanes was not knowingly part of the plot with Milteer. Even before Ray was extradited from England, Hanes had been
approached by William Bradford Huie, a noted author who was also a
prominent checkbook journalist. In his most infamous case, more than a
decade earlier, Huie had paid $4,000 to two of the Klansmen who killed
black teenager Emmett Till. Since a Mississippi jury had found the men
not guilty, Huie was able to buy and publish their account of the killing
in a popular national magazine. Huie told Hanes that Ray's story would
be worth at least ten times as much, and offered to pay them a $40,000
advance (almost $250,000 today) for the exclusive rights, against a 60
percent share of the profits. Hanes agreed, as did Ray.[7]

Even before Ray returned to the US, the publishing deal began to
affect Ray's defense and legal status. After the British court ruled that
Ray could be extradited, Hanes could have appealed and dragged out
the process, but he didn't. Perhaps he was influenced by the fact that
he wouldn't receive the $40,000 advance until Ray was back in the US.
In addition, Hanes was soon making side deals with Ray about that
advance, which resulted in a bigger share for Hanes. (Over the next
year and through changes in attorneys, Ray's share would dwindle to 18
percent, then lower still, until he eventually received none of the profits
from Huie's book.)[8]

Some authors have pointed out that Hanes also failed to take advantage of an English legal technicality that could have benefited Ray
greatly. British author Mel Ayton noted the "extradition treaty between
Britain and the United States which stipulated, 'A fugitive criminal shall
not be surrendered if the crime . . .' is one of a political character." Ayton
pointed out that "had any right-wing group in the United States claimed
responsibility for hiring Ray, or if Ray had claimed he had been hired by
any group or organization with a political agenda, he may have won his
[extradition] case and remained in Britain." Ray still might have had to
face robbery and firearms charges there, but those were far less serious
than the charge of first-degree murder.[9]

Hanes could have used that strategy even after Ray returned to the
US, since Ayton found that the treaty "also stipulated that once a fugitive had been extradited he cannot be charged with offenses other than
the crime with which he had been charged. Ray, therefore, could never
have been tried for 'conspiracy' or 'conspiracy to murder,'" since he had
been charged only with murder (and unlawful flight) in the extradition
request. Author Gerald Posner, whose book about Dr. King's assassination was far more objective and better documented than his book
on JFK's murder, wrote that "if, upon his return, Ray had admitted

his involvement, but instead claimed it was a conspiracy of which he was only the provider of the weapon or the getaway driver, the prosecutors could not have tried him." Even Ray eventually realized the legal maneuver Hanes should have employed, as Ray explained to Dan Rather in a television interview in 1977. However, an experienced criminal like Ray knew in 1977, and in 1968, that he could never admit the conspiracy he was really involved in, if he hoped to stay alive.[10]

With no appeal, Ray was returned to the US on July 19, 1968, three and a half months after Martin Luther King's murder. William Pepper noted that "tipped off about Ray's return, Memphis produce man Frank [C.] Liberto flew" out of Memphis, heading for Detroit.[11] Ray was soon being held at the Shelby County Jail in Memphis. When the jail's doctor asked Ray if he had shot Dr. King, Ray replied, "Well, let's put it this way: I wasn't in it by myself."[12]

Joseph Milteer had the means to potentially influence Hanes through intermediaries, using either mutual associates in groups like the Citizens' Councils or money from North Carolina—but one of Milteer's partners in the racist movement, J. B. Stoner, quickly began trying to become Ray's attorney. Soon after Ray's capture, Stoner made it clear to the press that he'd welcome the chance to represent Ray. Arthur Hanes Sr. told Ray to avoid Stoner, but the white supremacist was persistent, and by September 1968, the FBI discovered that Stoner had been writing Ray and offering to represent him for free. The FBI also received reports saying that Stoner was paying Hanes, but other files disprove that allegation, and Stoner admitted that his NSRP didn't have the money to pay an expensive attorney like Hanes for defending Ray. Despite Hanes's dislike of Stoner, by early October 1968, Stoner was able to visit Ray in jail.[13]

Meanwhile, William Bradford Huie continued his unique role as both a privileged defense investigator and a journalist, using information he obtained from Ray to run down numerous leads in the US and Canada. Huie managed to interview many witnesses before they had talked to the FBI, and his investigation far outpaced that of the Bureau on many fronts.

The FBI's past track record against Martin Luther King, and its unusual treatment of Carlos Marcello and Joseph Milteer, meant that no agency was in a position to do an objective, thorough investigation of James Earl Ray and Dr. King's assassination. No Southern law enforcement agency could do the job, and LBJ wasn't about to anger his longtime friend

Hoover by giving the investigation to another federal agency. However, it is possible that the FBI conducted a more thorough investigation of areas related to Milteer and Marcello than the released files indicate.

The FBI looked at the activities of other noted racists for any ties to Dr. King's assassination, but no such files for Milteer have ever surfaced, even though he was a logical and obvious suspect to investigate. Like any inquiries into Carlos Marcello's ties to King's murder—or Johnny Rosselli's apartment building's being marked on James Earl Ray's map—those files may have been sent to FBI headquarters and J. Edgar Hoover's "personal and confidential" files. Appeals were continuing in the Marcello and Rosselli cases, so any overt investigation of the two mob bosses could complicate their convictions. As with Milteer, Hoover also had embarrassing intelligence failures to hide regarding Marcello and Rosselli in the months before JFK's murder, further reducing any incentive for him to allow FBI field offices to pursue those leads. As when FBI investigators tried to follow conspiracy leads after JFK's assassination, it wouldn't take field agents in the King assassination investigation long to get the message, even if no overt orders to stop investigating were issued.

William Sullivan, an FBI assistant director in 1968, later said that he "was convinced that James Earl Ray killed Martin Luther King, but I doubt if he acted alone. . . . Someone, I feel sure, taught Ray how to get a false Canadian passport, and how to slip out of the country. And how did Ray pay for the passport and the airline tickets?"[14] Yet in spite of such a high-ranking FBI official's suspicions, the Bureau could not take advantage of the new law that Congress passed on June 19, 1968, which finally allowed "the use of court authorized electronic surveillance by law enforcement officers in certain . . . crimes, including murder." The HSCA noted that when President Johnson signed the bill, he announced that wiretaps would be confined "to national security cases," meaning that "a law which was passed in part because of Dr. King's assassination would not be considered by the FBI during the investigation of that crime."[15]

Still, the FBI could have relied on more traditional methods against obvious suspects, such as the racist or criminal associates of some of Ray's brothers, but the Bureau's efforts in that regard seem to have been very limited. As we noted earlier, the FBI did interview some of Sartor's sources, but the Bureau seemed more interested in trying to discredit their allegations than in fully investigating them.

Based on the Justice Department's memos about its very productive dealings with Sartor, Sartor clearly believed that much of his information would emerge during Ray's trial. Sartor was dealing with the deputy section chief of the Justice Department's civil rights division, for the central portion of the country, and Sartor expected that the government would use his sources in some way. He told the Justice Department attorney that "his informants will probably be willing to talk to [the Department], but that they will ask for money, immunity, or protection or all three." Lacking the inside access of a wealthy checkbook journalist like Huie, Sartor hoped to trade information with the Justice Department, and asked only that it "contact his principal informants through him," until they had a deal. As a sign of good faith, we noted earlier that he arranged for the Justice Department attorney to personally interview one of his confidential sources, about a mobster tied to James Earl Ray.[16]

The Justice Department's dealings with Sartor occurred in June, August, and September 1968, at which time the US Assistant Attorney General, Civil Rights Division, sent their information to J. Edgar Hoover. The official asked Hoover to "please follow out all leads indicated in the attached memorandum if you have not already done so."[17] From that point on, the FBI appears to have made no progress in pursuing Sartor's leads and sources.[18]

Instead, the reverse was true. By November 1968, the FBI wrote a memo stating that one of Sartor's sources said he hadn't given Sartor the information the journalist had claimed he had. The FBI's own memos show they knew that very source had personally repeated his information to the Justice Department attorney in Sartor's presence, but the FBI omitted that fact from the memo written for the record and later provided to the HSCA. Because the original Justice Department memos, and the FBI's copies of them, were withheld from the HSCA, the HSCA's Final Report referred to the man only as a "purported Sartor source."[19]

That source's reticence with the FBI in 1968 was understandable, since William Pepper says the man was threatened the following year with a knife, on the instructions of an associate of Frank C. Liberto, because of information the man had given Sartor. The source managed to talk his way out of the situation, but was reluctant to speak about the case for years afterward. Sadly, that source was "one of the last persons to speak with William Sartor" on the day before the journalist's 1971 murder, when Sartor was in Texas to meet with a man whom John H. Davis described as the former "chauffeur and bodyguard to Carlos Marcello."[20]

What happened to the FBI interviews of other Sartor sources is often not clear, as is true for much of the FBI's investigation in New Orleans in the aftermath of King's assassination. The FBI's internal summaries of the Justice Department reports eliminated or minimized most of the important information, such as that relating to Marcello or "Forever White," the small racist clique for whom he brokered King's murder. Searches of the FBI's King files have so far revealed no investigation of "Forever White," or interviews with Marcello or his close associates about the brokering allegation. There is no sign that the FBI tried to find or interview Sartor's prime source, described by the Justice Department as a "well-placed protégé of Carlos Marcello." Then again, the FBI had developed several of its own Marcello informants by that time—most of whom have never been identified—and one (or more) of them could have been talking to Sartor. One justification—or rationalization—for not pursuing the Marcello leads about King's murder was that it could have compromised other FBI sources, investigations, and the Bureau's recent conviction of Marcello for hitting an FBI agent.

FBI files do exist for a few of Sartor's other sources, like civil rights worker John McFerren. However, the FBI seemed determined to discredit his claims against Frank C. Liberto. Comments McFerren made hesitantly or tentatively were sometimes firmed up in FBI summaries, and then used by the FBI to dismiss much of what he said. Other obvious ties that needed to be investigated—such as any between Frank C. Liberto, in Memphis, and Marcello's aide Jack Liberto, in New Orleans— were apparently not explored by the FBI at all, even though the Bureau had been maintaining files on Jack Liberto since before King's assassination. There are other leads in the Justice Department's Sartor memo that the FBI apparently never pursued, and while some of the information may have been inaccurate, there was no way to know unless it was checked out.[21]

The HSCA pointed out that the FBI found various fingerprints in Ray's Mustang that weren't Ray's, yet it didn't seem to make a serious effort to identify them. Given the evidence available to the FBI in 1968, it would have been logical to check them against known violent racists in the places where Ray had stayed recently. While Milteer was probably too cautious to have left prints in Ray's Mustang, even today, it would be worthwhile to check the Mustang prints against those of Milteer, Spake, and their partners, as well as those of known Marcello associates, such as Frank Joseph Caracci, Frank C. Liberto, Jack Liberto, and others.[22]

In general, by the summer and fall of 1968, the FBI avoided or minimized information that indicated a conspiracy, despite Ray's incredibly far-flung travels, his unknown source of funds, and an FBI report saying the scope on Ray's rifle would have caused a shooter to miss by "4 inches left and 3 inches below," enough to at least call into question whether that rifle really was the murder weapon.[23] While the FBI spent inordinate amounts of time running down things like the manufacturer of the beer can found in Ray's bag dropped in the doorway of Canipe's Amusement company, it devoted seemingly little effort to uncovering troubling leads like the "military ammunition . . . with machinegun link marks" found in the same bag. Apparently, the FBI didn't bother exploring whether that ammunition connected Ray to the usual suspects who used automatic weapons: white supremacists, the Mafia, or CIA-backed Cuban exiles.[24]

As we noted earlier, William Bradford Huie uncovered many important facts about Ray's activities before the FBI did, in the months prior to King's murder. Sometimes Huie attempted to trade that information to the FBI, but other times the FBI first learned about some of Huie's discoveries when his explosive, three-article series began to appear in *Look* magazine, on November 12, 1968. At that time, Huie was firmly convinced that Ray had been part of a conspiracy and planned to title his eventual book *They Slew the Dreamer*.[25]

As James Earl Ray's trial was getting ready to start, Ray was understandably nervous that someone with the special access he and Hanes had given Huie was essentially proclaiming him guilty in one of the nation's biggest magazines. That was one reason why, less than two days before the scheduled start of his November trial, Ray fired Arthur Hanes Sr., hoping that in doing so, he would be rid of Huie.[26]

Ray's second American attorney was the well-known Percy Foreman, whose main concern also seems to have been money. If Ray thought that by getting rid of Hanes he'd be rid of Huie, he was wrong: Foreman said his fee would be $165,000, plus expenses. The attorney was soon dealing in percentages with Huie and even having Ray sign over to Foreman his Mustang and rifle, with an eye toward their eventual sale.[27]

In hindsight, Foreman was a logical choice, given what we know now about Ray and Marcello's heroin network. Based in Marcello's territory of Houston, Foreman had briefly been Jack Ruby's attorney. Foreman boasted to Huie that he had represented "members of the Mafia, some of whom direct the running of heroin across the Canadian border." As we noted earlier, that's why Foreman was able to tell Huie that Ray's actions in Canada "were standard operating procedure for bringing heroin in from Canada," and how Ray was probably recruited.[28]

Soon after Foreman took over, the way both Foreman and Huie viewed Ray's case changed. Huie went from believing in and writing about a conspiracy involving Ray's mysterious "Raoul," to writing that Ray had acted alone, with no confederates. In his third *Look* article, published five months after the second, Huie took the unusual step of saying his first two articles had been erroneous in their comments about a conspiracy. Percy Foreman would later testify that "there was no Raoul. Ray told me he invented him to feed conspiracy theories."[29] In private, Foreman didn't rule out a conspiracy, but said it wasn't his legal concern.

Ray later complained, and the HSCA confirmed, that Foreman did little to actually help his client. The HSCA said that "Foreman did not conduct a thorough and independent investigation into the death of Martin Luther King on behalf of Ray," and frequently used young interns to do important legal work.[30] Perhaps Foreman didn't want to expend too much effort, because he knew there wouldn't be a trial. On February 13, 1969, Foreman first suggested that Ray plead guilty. Ray strongly rejected the idea and was apparently planning on taking his chances with a Southern jury. Even if Ray were found guilty of murder and received a life sentence, he would be eligible for parole in thirteen years. But if he pled guilty in return for a life sentence as part of a plea bargain, according to Tennessee law, he wouldn't be eligible for parole for forty-five years.[31]

Foreman began pressuring Ray's family to encourage him to plead guilty, but they were against the idea as well. However, Foreman lied to Ray, telling him that his family was in favor of a guilty plea, in order to spare Ray the possibility of a death sentence. However, Foreman apparently didn't tell Ray that no one had been executed in the state of Tennessee for seven years, and that Memphis's Shelby County was an especially hard place in which to earn a death sentence.[32]

Ray was in a bind: The fact that Foreman wasn't doing a good job on his case could become a self-fulfilling prophecy if Ray went to trial, possibly yielding a death penalty for Ray. Also, given Foreman's previous clients, Ray might have thought that Foreman's plea recommendation represented the wishes of the underworld figures both men had worked for. On March 9, 1969, Ray agreed to Foreman's demand that he plead guilty.

The plea bargain was agreed to by Coretta Scott King, US Attorney General Ramsey Clark, and Tennessee Governor Buford Ellington. The following day in court, when Ray was asked if he was guilty of murdering Dr. King, Ray replied, "Yes, legally, yes."[33]

Within the criminal-justice system, that guilty plea would seal James

Earl Ray's fate for the rest of his life, while leaving many important questions unresolved. As Foreman was leaving the courthouse, he was asked about a conspiracy and replied, "I don't give a goddamn if there was a conspiracy or not. No. I never asked him that." Even one of the prosecutors who worked out the plea bargain later said, "Whether someone had paid him $25,000 to do it, I didn't know." The presiding judge, W. Preston Battle, soon indicated that Ray might have been part of a conspiracy, but said the plea deal was still the best solution, since "the trial would have muddied our understanding of the substantial evidence which established Ray as the killer." Battle and other officials seemed to feel that as long as the likely shooter was punished, it was better to move on than to look too closely at who might have paid Ray or been involved with him in the killing.[34]

On the other hand, Ray felt he'd been hung out to dry, and he soon began the quest that he would pursue for the rest of his life: to withdraw his guilty plea. Ray wrote a letter to Judge Battle on March 13, 1969, firing Foreman and asking for "a post conviction hearing." Now that he'd fired Foreman, Ray knew he had to be careful in asking to withdraw his plea and go to trial, so as not to arouse suspicion among the criminals who'd hired him. According to the HSCA volumes, on March 15, Ray told one of his brothers about "Eddie . . . his dope contact in New Orleans." Ray wanted his brother to "call [Eddie] and tell him everything [was] okay from James. . . . He wanted Eddie to know he hadn't talked, wasn't going to talk."[35]

Ray officially requested that his sentence be reversed on March 26. On March 31, Judge Battle died of a heart attack. Within days, Ray engaged a new attorney to continue his legal fight to avoid spending his life in prison: J. B. Stoner.[36]

Having Stoner become Ray's attorney in the critical time following Ray's guilty plea was a perfect situation for Joseph Milteer and his partners in King's assassination. Milteer had worked with Stoner for years, and would now have a direct means of influencing Ray and his legal strategy. Stoner was soon promoting to the press the theory that the FBI had killed Dr. King. One of Ray's brothers went to work for Stoner, and four months after Stoner became Ray's lawyer, Ray's brother made the statement, noted earlier, that Ray had been involved in gunrunning and Cuban-exile activities designed to overthrow Fidel Castro.[37]

While Stoner floated a variety of stories designed to both appeal to his base and worry officials, he worked with more competent attorneys on Ray's legal challenges. Various appeals were tried, to no avail. Likewise,

a lawsuit filed on Ray's behalf against Huie and attorneys Foreman and
Hanes was dismissed.

While J. B. Stoner was of no help to James Earl Ray, one of Ray's
brothers developed a close relationship with Stoner and worked for
him for more than a decade in a variety of positions, including driver
and bodyguard. When Stoner ran for governor of Georgia in 1970, Ray's
brother was Stoner's campaign manager. The moderate Jimmy Carter
trounced Stoner, who garnered just over 2 percent of the vote.[38]

Even as the Ray and Sirhan stories played out in the press, yet another
assassination trial was going on in New Orleans. On January 21, 1969,
Jim Garrison finally began his trial with Clay Shaw. While it exposed
much important information about the Kennedy autopsy, the magic bullet, and Oswald's unusual activities, the evidence against Shaw himself
was extremely thin. Shaw was acquitted on March 1, 1969, after the jury
deliberated for just forty-five minutes.

By the spring of 1969, when Sirhan's was the last of the three assassination-related proceedings remaining, America—or at least the mainstream press—seemed tired of such coverage. When Ed Reid's book
The Grim Reapers finally appeared in April 1969, the few paragraphs
about Carlos Marcello's 1962 threat to assassinate JFK received almost
no attention in the press, and none at all from network news. Marcello
had finally been convicted for assaulting an FBI agent, at his retrial in
Houston in August 1968, and received a two-year sentence. But Marcello's high-powered legal team immediately appealed and seemed well
poised to keep him from serving time anytime soon.[39]

By the summer of 1969, Carlos Marcello was still free on appeal and
making more money than ever with associates like Santo Trafficante.
Along with Rosselli's, their names had never surfaced in the press in
any of the coverage of the assassinations of JFK, King, or Bobby. Johnny
Rosselli still faced prison, but he was also free on appeal—and still had
potential leverage over the CIA to at least protect himself from being
deported on his immigration charge. Jimmy Hoffa was still in prison,
and for some reason had seemed unusually interested in following the
progress of the prosecution of James Earl Ray. Given Ray's extensive
criminal background and knowledge of what happened to snitches in
prison, in addition to the assassination attempt on Sirhan's brother, Marcello and the others could be confident that neither convicted assassin
would reveal anything that pointed in their direction.[40]

With the resolution of the cases against Sirhan, Ray, and Shaw, no government agency seemed to be actively investigating any of the three assassinations that had rocked the country over the past five years. The same was true for the major news organizations. With the help of organized crime, illegal campaign contributions from US companies and foreign governments, and scuttling a pre-election Vietnam peace agreement, Richard Nixon had been elected president in November 1968, and the Mafia had little to fear from his administration. Nixon had retained Richard Helms as CIA Director, a decision which would further ensure that information which might expose the Mafia's role in the CIA-Mafia plots and JFK's assassination would stay hidden. Helms had E. Howard Hunt and David Atlee Phillips well positioned to help him in that regard, while potentially problematic AMWORLD veterans like David Morales were stationed far away, in Southeast Asia.

While prospects for further government or press investigations into the murders of JFK, Bobby, or King looked bleak, important questions lingered. In some ways, Jim Garrison's best legacy was not his disastrous prosecution of Clay Shaw, but the information his investigators developed pertaining to other matters (never used in court) and the careers they pursued later. Some of the private citizens who had assisted Garrison were continuing their own investigations. These included former FBI agent William Turner, who learned that a Cuban exile named Harry Williams, who had worked for Bobby Kennedy, might have some interesting information. Washington attorney Bernard Fensterwald was organizing a group of people interested in the assassinations, and within a few years would become James Earl Ray's attorney. Former Senate investigator Harold Weisberg had continued his work after leaving Garrison, and would soon be the first journalist to name Joseph Milteer in relation to JFK's assassination.

Other private citizens and authors—Mary Ferrell, Sylvia Meagher, Paul Hoch, Dr. Cyril Wecht, David Lifton, Richard Sprague, Gaeton Fonzi, Peter Noyes, and several more—were also continuing their efforts, looking primarily at JFK's assassination but also aware of some of the lingering issues surrounding Bobby's and King's murders. While the government's legacy of secrecy had prevented the American public from learning the truth by the end of the 1960s, those men and women were essentially continuing Bobby Kennedy's quest to uncover his brother's killers.

PART FIVE

Chapter Sixty-one

As 1970 began, no one seemed close to exposing the roles that Marcello, Trafficante, and Rosselli had played in the assassinations of the sixties. It likewise didn't appear that anyone would discover Richard Helms's unauthorized plots between the CIA and the Mafia to assassinate Fidel Castro in 1963. No active government investigations were ongoing, leaving only a few independent journalists and private researchers to pursue leads in the murders of JFK, Martin Luther King, and Bobby Kennedy. However, the illegal activities of President Richard Nixon would change all that: In just a few years, the three Mafia bosses would be grilled by Congressional committees about the JFK hit, Rosselli would be gruesomely murdered, Helms would be fired and face prosecution, while Hunt would be in prison.

For fifty-nine-year-old Carlos Marcello, the start of the seventies saw his criminal empire continued to expand, even as he diversified into more legitimate businesses. However, Marcello still ordered contract killings, even while appealing his conviction and two-year sentence for slugging an FBI agent.[1] The Bureau had offered Marcello a deal to avoid prison, by providing information in just one other case, but Marcello refused. Marcello had backed Nixon for years, and one of Marcello's "fixers"—who treaded the thin line between politics and crime—was close to Nixon's own fixer, former mob attorney Murray Chotiner. According to John H. Davis, Marcello "and his lawyers pulled every string at their command to get Carlos's two year sentence reduced . . . to six months and made arrangements for him to spend that time at the Medical Center for Federal Prisoners in Springfield, Missouri."[2]

Marcello entered the Springfield facility on October 14, 1970. Since it was one of the least secure and most comfortable federal prisons, allowing more phone calls and visitors than others, Marcello had no trouble running his empire from prison. When he was released on March 12, 1971—after serving just five months—Marcello emerged much healthier and more fit, ready for what would be his most prosperous decade.

Even before Marcello entered prison in 1970, reporters whispered among themselves what they wouldn't print: that the New Orleans godfather was tied to JFK's murder. While covering a Marcello court appearance in 1970, journalist Peter Noyes heard "a newspaper reporter [say] 'There's been a lot of talk about that guy being involved in the Kennedy assassination.'"[3] In fall 1971, Noyes learned from the Los Angeles chief deputy district attorney that the Senate Judiciary Committee was holding secret hearings on JFK's and Bobby's assassinations, following California Senator George Murphy's remarks that "the killers of John and Robert Kennedy may have acted under orders from someone else." A Murphy aide confirmed the secret hearings to Noyes, who began writing a book about the assassinations, *Legacy of Doubt*. Most of the media ignored Noyes's book when it was published in 1973, even though it featured new information tying Marcello to JFK's slaying and raised troubling questions about Bobby's murder.[4]

William Sartor was also preparing a book in 1971, writing about Marcello's ties to Martin Luther King's murder. Sartor went to Waco, Texas, to interview Sam Termine, a nightclub owner and Marcello lieutenant who had once been Marcello's bodyguard and driver while serving as a decorated member of the Louisiana State Police. Sartor was killed the night before his interview with Termine, leaving his manuscript unfinished—but it wasn't until 1992 that the local district attorney ruled Sartor's death a "homicide."[5]

Unlike Marcello, Santo Trafficante didn't have legal issues to worry about, which allowed his operations to grow throughout the 1970s and into the early 1980s. Even though Jimmy Hoffa was still in prison, new Teamster president Frank Fitzsimmons made sure that associates of Trafficante and Marcello received generous multimillion-dollar loans from the Teamster Pension fund. The fifty-five-year-old Trafficante also greatly expanded his heroin network not just in America but internationally. Intelligence journalist Joseph Trento documented that after the Mafia chief made a 1968 trip to South Vietnam, Hong Kong, and Singapore, Trafficante[6]

decided to have his Hong Kong-based deputy . . . take control of every big Saigon nightspot catering to US servicemen. By 1970, [Trafficante's] Saigon-produced heroin was being sold directly to American GI's at bargain prices at each of these nightspots.[7]

Though largely forgotten today, the "Service Club Scandal" was major news at the time, because Trento points out that "by 1970, Congress estimated that a full fifteen percent of the US troops in Vietnam were hooked on heroin." Still, none of the mainstream press coverage linked Trafficante's name to the growing heroin problem or the service club scandal, allowing him to once again prosper by staying in the shadows. Trento finds it significant that AMWORLD veterans David Morales, former Artime aide "Chi Chi" Quintero, and CIA Station Chief Ted Shackley were stationed in Saigon as the heroin problem exploded.[8]

Trafficante's heroin network was undergoing a major shift by 1970, with Cuban exiles playing an increasing role, as France finally began to arrest some of their most notorious traffickers. Nixon's official reaction was to order the Bureau of Narcotics and Dangerous Drugs (BNDD) to crack down on US heroin trafficking.[9] Unofficially, Nixon would soon build his own small antidrug squad, one that included Trafficante associates like Frank Fiorini and Manuel Artime.[10]

As documented by many journalists in the 1970s, and more recently by Anthony Summers, Richard Nixon had numerous criminal ties, some dating back to the 1940s. By the time Nixon became president, several of his criminal business partners and contributors had links to Santo Trafficante. That may explain why Trento found that "the BNDD could not get the Nixon administration to go after Trafficante directly."[11]

Trafficante had casino interests in the Bahamas, as did several Nixon associates. Nixon's best friend, Bebe Rebozo—born in Tampa of Cuban parents and heavily involved in Nixon's business affairs—also had links to organized crime, though they were rarely reported in the press. Nixon's personal and business—and soon White House—affairs became so compromised by criminal associates that the corruption made a mockery of Nixon's public "law and order" stance so often extolled by Vice President Spiro Agnew.[12]

When US pressure finally resulted in the arrest of Michel Victor Mertz on November 24, 1969, for the 1965 Fort Benning bust, Mertz was too wealthy and powerful to suffer consequences for very long.[13] Mertz's long-standing ties to French Intelligence (SDECE) gave him far more leverage over the SDECE than Johnny Rosselli had over the CIA. Mertz was released from his initial jailing after just seven months but was then tried, convicted, and sentenced to five years for heroin trafficking in July 1971. However, *Newsday* reported he had to serve only eight months, even though Mertz's operation had shipped two tons of heroin, with a street value of $400 million, into the US in the past eight years.[14]

Because of the heroin epidemic in the US, *Newsday* publisher William

Attwood had devoted the resources of his newspaper to an unprecedented, globe-trotting narcotics exposé. Attwood had worked for JFK
and Bobby on Cuban matters, and though the prizewinning *Newsday*
series didn't mention any links between JFK's murder and Mertz, it was
the first American press exposure of Mertz's heroin trafficking—and his
soft treatment by the French government.[15]

Mertz's brief prison stints had little impact on Trafficante, since his
Cuban exiles filled the void left by the French arrests to such an extent
that *Newsday* reported the BNDD had discovered that 8 percent of the
1,500 Bay of Pigs veterans had "been investigated or arrested for drug
dealing." That total likely didn't include prominent exiles like Manuel
Artime, who would never be arrested for his drug trafficking activities,
and whose reach soon extended into the White House.[16]

At sixty-five, Johnny Rosselli was not doing nearly as well as Trafficante and Marcello. Rosselli not only faced five years in prison for his
Friars Club scheme and immigration violations but INS was again trying to deport him. Even worse, Rosselli's former partner in the Friars
Club scam, the casino owner, had turned states evidence and was giving information to the government. Prosecutors in Los Angeles used a
grand jury in an attempt to pressure Rosselli, but the Mafia don gave
only vague answers that didn't incriminate himself or anyone else.[17]

Rosselli's new attorney, Tom Wadden, once again pressed the CIA
to intervene for their former asset, at least enough to prevent Rosselli's
deportation. Toward that end, Rosselli had meetings with William
Harvey, CIA official Jim O'Connell, and Robert Maheu, recently fired by
Howard Hughes when the reclusive billionaire left the country.[18] One
CIA memo says that "on November 18, 1970 . . . Mr. Helms flatly refused
to intercede with INS on Rosselli's behalf." However, the CIA admits
"meeting with INS regarding the status of the deportation proceedings
[in] March 1971," and the INS deportation efforts were halted at that
time, after Rosselli entered prison on February 25, 1971. What happened
between November 1970 and March 1971 that caused Helms to change
his mind and help Rosselli?[19]

In a move that would change the course of Nixon's presidency, Johnny
Rosselli had resumed contact with columnist Jack Anderson on January
11, 1971. On January 18, Anderson ran the first of two new articles about
the CIA-Mafia plots, asking again, "Could the plot against Castro have
backfired against President Kennedy?" The new articles discussed "six
[CIA] attempts against Cuba's Fidel Castro," including those involving

CIA-trained "Cuban assassination teams equipped with high-powered rifles." Anderson said the Castro assassination plot he was writing about "began as part of the Bay of Pigs operation . . . to eliminate the Cuban dictator before the motley invaders landed." Anderson's linking the Bay of Pigs and the CIA-Mafia plots to JFK's assassination would hit Nixon especially hard. In addition, Anderson wrote that the plots continued until March 1963 and for the first time named some of the participants: Rosselli, Harvey, O'Connell, and Maheu.[20]

Anderson's column didn't mention Trafficante, Giancana, or David Morales—meaning that someone as knowledgeable as Helms would realize Rosselli had more bombshells to drop, if he chose. Even worse for Helms, Anderson had spoken to former CIA Director John McCone, who "vigorously denied that the CIA had ever participated in any plot on Castro's life. Asked whether the attempts could have been made without his knowledge, [McCone] replied: 'It could not have happened.'" Helms knew how much he'd kept hidden from McCone, more than Anderson had written about—which might help to explain the inaction of INS while Rosselli was in prison. Even though the US Attorney in Los Angeles requested that Rosselli not be deported until after he'd served his sentence, that doesn't explain why the INS didn't continue their proceedings while Rosselli was incarcerated, so they could deport Rosselli immediately upon his release.[21] Helms could have had the CIA intervene with INS to stall Rosselli's deportation on national security grounds, without leaving a paper trail.

In another odd twist, Rosselli's attorneys' plea to the original judge in July 1971, to reduce Rosselli's sentence because of his service to the CIA, was rejected in open court by the judge. Yet three months later, for no apparent reason and with no additional hearing, the judge suddenly took one year off Rosselli's sentence. Rosselli would wind up serving barely half of his original sentence.[22]

Jack Anderson's early-1971 columns about Rosselli also alarmed the Nixon White House, triggering concerns that would eventually lead to the Watergate scandal. The day Anderson's second column ran, Nixon's attorney general, John Mitchell, called Robert Maheu, who was being pressured by a grand jury at the time. Maheu immediately flew to Washington and told Mitchell what he knew about the CIA-Mafia plots. Maheu later told Anthony Summers that Mitchell was "shaking" when he finished, which explains why Mitchell let Maheu avoid the grand jury, in return for keeping the plots secret. Mitchell then had his assistant attorney general look for any Justice Department files about the plots. They hoped to prove that JFK and Bobby "had tried to kill Castro," to harm Edward Kennedy's chances of running for president. However, Summers points out that "Maheu's information about the CIA-Mafia plots . . . posed a threat as much to . . . Nixon as to the Kennedys."[23]

The Anderson stories also "triggered a spate of memos inside the Nixon White House," according to Peter Dale Scott. A February 1, 1971, memo to John Dean about "Jack Anderson's column" and "Maheu's covert activities . . . with [the] CIA" warned President Nixon that "Maheu's controversial activities . . . might well shake loose Republican skeletons from the closet." Nixon's young aides, like Chief Counsel John Dean and Chief of Staff H. R. Haldeman, didn't know about the CIA-Mafia plots, but they were worried about Maheu's involvement with Howard Hughes. Their worries ranged from money Nixon had received from Hughes to Maheu's friendship with Lawrence O'Brien, chairman of the Democratic National Committee, which was headquartered at the Watergate office complex. But Nixon's concerns about the Jack Anderson columns were even more serious than those of his aides.[24]

It has been long documented that in 1959 and 1960, Vice President Nixon was President Dwight Eisenhower's point man for Cuban operations. Peter Dale Scott, Anthony Summers, and other authors have made an excellent case (detailed in *Ultimate Sacrifice*) that pressure from Nixon spawned both the original 1959 CIA-Mafia plots brokered by Jimmy Hoffa (with Jack Ruby on their fringe), and the more extensive plots that began in the summer of 1960, with Maheu, Rosselli, Trafficante, Giancana, and Fiorini.

Rosselli's work for the CIA had continued through the time of JFK's assassination, when former Cuban president Carlos Prio—an associate of both Nixon and Trafficante—infiltrated part of the JFK-Almeida coup plan. A fall 1963 CIA memo says two of Prio's partners "have become associated [with] Richard Nixon in accordance with [a] Republican Party plan [to] bring up the Cuban case before [1964] elections."[25]

Nixon could ill afford to have it come out that his associates had infiltrated a plot that backfired on JFK, or that the CIA was plotting assassinations with the Mafia while he was vice president. Nixon had enough direct and indirect ties to Trafficante and Hoffa that—as H. R. Haldeman later indicated—Nixon probably suspected the CIA-Mafia plots that spawned the Bay of Pigs invasion were somehow tied to JFK's murder.[26]

Nixon couldn't share his concerns about the CIA-Mafia plots with most of his closest aides; perhaps he told only his chief domestic advisor, John Ehrlichman. However, Nixon's other aides were worried about other inside information Maheu might have told his friend O'Brien, whom they felt wanted to help Senator Edward Kennedy run for president in 1972. This included information about campaign contributions from Hughes to Nixon that totaled at least $100,000 and possibly much more.[27] While most Nixon aides worried about the money secrets O'Brien might know, Nixon's biggest concern was the CIA-Mafia plots.

To deal with the overall problem, Nixon aides John Dean and H. R. Haldeman turned to the Mullen Company, a Washington public relations firm. The company often worked for the CIA, offering services that included providing cover for CIA employees, and also counted Howard Hughes as a client. Robert Bennett (in 2008, a longtime Republican US senator from Utah) had recently taken over the firm. In a January 26, 1971, memo, Nixon aide Chuck Colson described Bennett as "a trusted and good friend of the Administration." Though he was not mentioned in that White House memo, working for Bennett at the Mullen Company was a man who had supposedly retired from the CIA the previous year, a figure whose name would soon be forever linked with those of Nixon, Dean, Colson, Haldeman, and Ehrlichman: E. Howard Hunt.[28]

E. Howard Hunt, who would figure so prominently in the Watergate scandal, had apparently left the CIA in 1970 to work for the Mullen PR firm at least in part because President Nixon was pressing Richard Helms on two fronts. As detailed by Pulitzer Prize–winning journalist Thomas Powers in his 1979 biography of Helms, the CIA Director had faced increasing demands from Nixon in 1970 for more CIA involvement in domestic operations against his critics.[29] Nixon also didn't want other federal agencies, or US military intelligence, to find out about his ever-increasing illegal campaign contributions, not just from Hughes, but from foreign governments (South Vietnam, the US-backed junta running Greece), large corporations, and mob-linked sources. The President and his staff tried to take control of the US government's large, mostly illegal domestic surveillance operation, with a view toward using it against Nixon's enemies and keeping damaging intelligence about the crimes of Nixon and his allies under their control.[30]

One solution Helms developed was to have CIA personnel perform such operations, but only after they were apparently no longer employed by the CIA.[31] As for who would be chosen for such assignments, Helms had another consideration. Even before the early-1971

Jack Anderson articles, Nixon knew the potential political problems that could be caused by the exposure of his role in the covert operations that developed into the Bay of Pigs. As Nixon Chief of Staff H. R. Haldeman wrote in his autobiography, President Nixon had been trying since just after he took office in early 1969 to get "all the facts and documents the CIA had on the Bay of Pigs."[32]

Amazingly, Helms had turned down the President's order, which had been conveyed by John Ehrlichman. After six months of waiting, Nixon commanded that Helms come to the Oval Office, so he could personally "give him a direct order to turn over" the material. However, after Nixon and Helms had "a long secret conversation" in private, Nixon told his staff "to forget all about [it]" and stop "trying to obtain" the Bay of Pigs information, though Nixon would soon change his mind.[33]

Helms's refusal, and the fact that the Republican Nixon had retained Helms as his CIA Director from the previous Democratic administration, raises the possibility that Helms had subtly blackmailed Nixon to keep his post in the new administration. Helms might have told Nixon that as long as he was CIA Director, he would make sure that material in CIA files embarrassing to the President (which Helms could have described only vaguely) would be kept secret. As Senator Howard Baker would say years later, after the Watergate investigation, "Nixon and Helms have so much on each other, neither of them can breathe."[34]

In 1960, E. Howard Hunt had been a key player in the political planning that led up to the Bay of Pigs, when he worked with Vice President Nixon's national security advisor, General Robert Cushman. In 1969, Nixon had appointed General Cushman to be Deputy Director of the CIA, under Helms—and yet Nixon still couldn't get the Bay of Pigs material.[35] Even so, Nixon's pressure on Helms continued, for both the material and for more domestic covert operations.

From that perspective, it's logical that Helms would turn to his trusted protégé, E. Howard Hunt, to help him deal with the two Nixon issues. Just as Hunt had apparently "retired" from the CIA in 1965, for his covert assignment to Spain at the time of the Cubela-Artime plots, Hunt once more appeared to retire from the CIA on April 24, 1970. Only 51, Hunt immediately joined the Mullen Company, which had long assisted the CIA. According to a handwritten note on Hunt's CIA retirement memo, Helms's Deputy Director for Plans told Hunt to "'stay in touch'—that the firm does provide cover" for CIA operatives.[36]

Declassified CIA memos, some possibly withheld from Watergate investigators, make it clear that even after his retirement Hunt was still involved in CIA matters. Four weeks after Hunt's "retirement," two CIA officials said a Covert Security Approval "under project QKENCHANT was requested concerning Mr. Hunt." Five months later, the "Corporate Cover Branch" of the CIA granted the "Covert Security Approval" allowing Hunt to be used for CIA operations.[37]

Peter Dale Scott summed up Hunt's CIA status after his official retirement date by saying "we now have the CIA's first post-Watergate memo on Howard Hunt, showing that in 1970 he had not retired from the CIA, but instead had been released on covert assignment to the Mullen Agency."[38] An internal CIA investigation—after Watergate and the firing of Richard Helms—found that during Hunt's first so-called retirement in 1965, when he went to Spain, "the statement disseminated for consumption within the Agency was that Mr. Hunt was retiring," but a former CIA official told investigators that "this was not generally believed" within the Agency.[39]

The bottom line is that after his "retirement," Hunt was available to handle domestic operations in a more deniable way for Helms. Much of the time, the CIA assisted Hunt as if he were still an Agency employee, supplying fake identities, a disguise, technical equipment, and photo processing. When Hunt asked the CIA "for an individual having skills in the area of locks and surreptitious entry [for a break-in involving] the Howard Hughes organization in Las Vegas," the CIA referred a former Agency employee to Hunt.[40]

Hunt could be useful not only in handling domestic operations Helms didn't want the CIA officially involved in, but also in dealing with Cuban matters, especially now that he was outside the chain of command that included Nixon's man General Cushman. The Mullen Company had previously handled "the public relations effort of a covert Agency activity known as the Free Cuba Committee."[41]

James McCord retired from the CIA four months after Hunt, establishing his own security firm before becoming Security Director for Nixon's Committee to Re-elect the President (CREEP), in September 1971. McCord has indicated in testimony and his own writing that his resignation from the CIA was genuine and has declined to comment (to us and to *Vanity Fair*) on Harry Williams's statements to William Turner that he worked with McCord and Hunt on Cuban matters in 1963.[42] A CIA memo says that on July 19, 1971, two months before McCord joined CREEP, E. Howard Hunt "joined the White House staff as a Consultant to President Nixon." However, Charles Colson says that Hunt was hired for his White House position on July 1, 1971.[43]

Hunt had been pursuing the White House position for quite some time. An Agency memo confirms Hunt's statement that when he "retired" from the CIA, the original plan was for Hunt to eventually head the Mullen Company. From that position, Hunt would have been able to perform and direct work for both the CIA and the Nixon White House. However, when Robert Bennett purchased the firm, those plans changed. Charles Colson told H. R. Haldeman that "early in 1971, Hunt and Bennett began visiting me from time to time to offer their services on a volunteer basis to help the White House in outside efforts or in political matters." Those activities could be characterized as dirty tricks, such as faking cables to look as if JFK had ordered the assassination of South Vietnam leader Diem just weeks before his own murder, then trying to leak the phony cables to *Life* magazine.[44]

After Watergate, Colson would realize that "all the time Hunt was on the White House payroll . . . Hunt's secretary was on the CIA payroll," leading Colson to ask, "Was Hunt, supposedly a retired CIA agent, actually an active agent while in the White House?" Richard Nixon harbored similar suspicions after Watergate, asking Haldeman, "[Did you know] that Helms ordered Bennett to hire Howard Hunt? Did you know that Hunt was on the payroll of the Bennett firm at the same time that he was on the White House payroll?"[45] Then again, Nixon likely had his own reasons to have originally approved the hiring of Hunt in 1971, since Hunt had been involved in many of the same Cuban operations leading up to the Bay of Pigs as Nixon had. John Ehrlichman—the only aide Nixon apparently confided in about what came to known as "the Bay of Pigs thing"—was the only White House official who interviewed Hunt before he was hired.[46]

By the fall of 1971, Nixon was again concerned about those operations, and on September 18, he ordered Ehrlichman to tell Helms he wanted "the full file [on the Bay of Pigs] or else." This time, Helms gave Nixon "three thin files," but not the IG Report about the CIA-Mafia plots, or the CIA's internal Kirkpatrick Report on the Bay of Pigs. Gus Russo notes that "Nixon and everybody else knew there was much more, but Helms never delivered."[47] This left Nixon in the dark on exactly how much Helms knew about his role with the CIA-Mafia plots, with Prio's associates in November 1963, and any ties those had to JFK's murder.

Nonetheless, in 1970 Nixon continued some US efforts against Fidel Castro. Hunt's friend Manuel Artime had met with Nixon about reviving his Central American camps, but wound up just helping Hunt with sensitive jobs.[48] Exile attacks on Cuba in March, April, and May of 1970 so worried Cuba that Castro had the Soviet Ambassador ask the US to reaffirm JFK's pledge not to invade Cuba. Nixon agreed, not realizing that Fidel had never complied with JFK's condition that Cuba allow UN inspections for weapons of mass destruction.[49]

Nixon's bigger concern in 1970 and 1971 was Chile, which would lead to its own scandal and to a little-known precursor to Watergate. Chile was about to elect its first socialist president, Salvador Allende, and to help prevent that Helms promoted David Atlee Phillips from head of Cuban operations to head of Latin America operations, putting him in charge of the CIA's Chile Task Force.

US efforts against Allende would be like a twisted version of the JFK-Almeida coup plan, involving some of the same people. JFK had wanted to overthrow a dictator and establish a democracy, while Nixon wanted a coup to replace Chile's democracy with a dictator. Working with Helms and Phillips on the coup was Artime's former case officer, Henry Heckscher, the CIA Chief for Chile. Ex–CIA Director John McCone was on the board of ITT, a US company that offered Helms and the CIA $1 million to block Allende's election. General Alexander Haig was involved as the aide to Nixon's national security advisor, Henry Kissinger. Even David Morales was soon deployed in Chile, to deadly effect. The general effort was code-named "Project Camelot."[50]

Unlike Commander Almeida in 1963, Chile's most admired General, Rene Scheinder, refused to be part of the coup plan and was killed by CIA-supported officers. Allende was elected, and praised by Fidel Castro, who planned to visit him in Chile. This led to a new CIA assassination attempt on Castro in 1971, involving Antonio Veciana and Luis Posada, and apparently also David Atlee Phillips. One aspect of the plan involved "a scheme to blame the assassination [of Fidel] on certain Russian agents." However, the plot failed, leading to a rift between Phillips and Veciana. Two years later, Phillips would end their relationship by giving "Veciana a suitcase [with] $253,000 in cash" as a reward for his years of service to the CIA.[51]

Chapter Sixty-two

Much of the conventional history about Watergate is incomplete, wrong, or continues the spin begun at the time to minimize Richard Nixon's crimes. The latter includes claims that the Watergate scandal was only about "a third-rate burglary" and that "the cover-up was worse than the crime." Countering these is a growing barrage of evidence, including Nixon White House tapes released in recent years (hundreds of hours remain unreleased). Many newer Nixon tapes are available as transcripts and in books, and it is almost impossible to read more than a few pages of Nixon's remarks—from the taping's start in 1971 until it stopped on July 12, 1973—without hearing him either planning a crime or talking about one that was actually committed. Nixon frequently talked with his aides about bribery, obstruction of justice, and illegal retaliation against perceived enemies—tax audits were a favorite, but break-ins were also discussed and used. And those are just the remarks Nixon made while he knew he was being taped—he was careful not to record even more sensitive conversations and documented criminal acts.[1]

There were actually numerous burglaries besides Watergate, and more than one break-in at that facility. Dozens of high officials—from Nixon's attorney general to his chief of staff—were prosecuted, and many sent to prison, for crimes that had nothing to do with the Watergate burglaries. Though dozens of books have detailed Watergate in depth, none has been able to document exactly what the burglars were really looking for. While we have room to cover Watergate only briefly, we finally answer that question, by focusing on something not covered in other books: the participation of a dozen people in various aspects of Watergate who were also involved in the events surrounding the JFK-Almeida coup plan and AMWORLD. They include several members of organized crime, who were also linked to JFK's assassination.

For a time in the early 1970s, the mainstream press reported on Nixon's Mafia ties, until they were overshadowed by the tidal wave of Watergate coverage that culminated with Nixon's resignation. Thus, while the *Los Angeles Times* would run a lead editorial entitled "Nixon, the Teamsters, the Mafia" a year after the final Watergate break-in, within a few years—and continuing today—political commentators and historians rarely mentioned Nixon's mob associates.[2]

One of the best examples of Nixon's work with the Mafia was his release of Jimmy Hoffa from prison, shortly before Christmas 1971. Most Mafia bosses were happy with new Teamster president Frank Fitzsimmons and had little desire to see Hoffa released, since Hoffa had favored Marcello's and Trafficante's Mafia families in the South. However, Teamster expert Dan Moldea found that large Teamster loans made to associates of Marcello and Trafficante (including Frank Ragano) yielded a compromise. Hoffa would be released—but would be prohibited from holding any Teamster office until 1980, leaving Fitzsimmons in control.[3]

Hoffa was furious when he learned of the condition, but there was little he could do at that time. He would have to wait for any type of revenge until January 1974, when his tip to government investigators would drag the CIA-Mafia plots and the Kennedy assassination into the Watergate investigation.

Nixon was careful not to document his illicit dealings with the Teamsters and the mob, but years later the *New York Post* described the FBI's discovery of a diary belonging to a New Orleans associate of Carlos Marcello's. An entry for January 5, 1973, said: "Fitz OK Al Dorfman chi ok.—Tony Pro Jersey ok ($500—to C. C. = nix OK)." According to A. J. Weberman, this showed "a payment [possibly $500,000] was made to Nixon through Charles Colson and had been okayed by Teamsters Allen Dorfman, Tony Provenzano [also a New Jersey mob boss], and Frank Fitzsimmons."[4] Former Nixon aide Chuck Colson later told journalist Dick Russell a theory he'd heard, that the Mafia "owned Bebe Rebozo, they got their hooks into Nixon early, and of course, that ties into the overlap of the CIA and the mob."[5]

As the broad range of White House crimes leading to the final Watergate break-in unfolded, Richard Helms and E. Howard Hunt took advantage of some of those operations to protect themselves. In the wake of Jack Anderson's early-1971 articles about the CIA-Mafia plots, Helms and Hunt had to be sure their problematic 1963 Cuban operations remained hidden. At the same time, Santo Trafficante had some of his men infiltrate Hunt's operation, just as he'd done for the JFK-Almeida coup plan in 1963. Trafficante no doubt wanted to protect his narcotics network, since Hunt's operatives were also targeting certain drug traffickers. But by having Barker, Fiorini, and Artime in Hunt's drug unit, Trafficante could also use them to prevent the exposure of anything that could uncover his role in the CIA-Mafia plots—and JFK's murder.

The White House "Plumbers" unit was created in 1971, ostensibly to plug leaks, not just within the administration but also from people like Daniel Ellsberg, the former RAND analyst who was trying to leak the Pentagon Papers (a massive Defense Department account of how the America public had been misled about the war in Vietnam). Most Watergate accounts list the first major break-in for Hunt's Plumbers as the September 1971 entry into the office of Ellsberg's psychiatrist, conducted by Cuban exiles working for Hunt and his comanager, former FBI agent G. Gordon Liddy.

However, Nixon's Oval Office tapes show the President had been considering Hunt for another break-in well before that and seemed to know that Hunt was right for such a task. On June 17, 1971, Nixon had begun talking about wanting to "blow the safe" of the Brookings Institute, a moderate Washington think tank, to see what material they had. On June 30, the day before Hunt officially joined the White House staff, Nixon ordered Haldeman to talk to "Hunt. I want the break-in. Hell, they do that. You're to break into the place, rifle the files, and bring them in."[6]

Even before Hunt officially joined the White House, he had begun preparing to use Nixon's operations to help protect his and Helms's secrets, by resuming contact with some of his former exile associates during the April 1971 tenth anniversary of the Bay of Pigs. Prior to that, Hunt had continued to maintain his close friendships with exiles like Artime.

Overtly, Hunt was using Cuban exiles in his Plumbers unit because— as explained by a Cuban exile to a later government investigating committee—"When Bay of Pigs operatives like Hunt moved [on] to Watergate, they sent for their old Cubanos. They work a little like a Mafia [and] when they want to issue . . . what looks like an anti-Communist contract, they contact us. We're reliable, intelligent, professional. And we're learning to keep our mouths shut [because] we fear the [CIA] . . . the [CIA] can drop a word and change your life."[7]

However, the real reasons Hunt used primarily Cuban exiles, and former anti-Castro operatives like Frank Fiorini (then using the name "Frank Sturgis"), was to protect the secrets Hunt and Helms wanted to stay hidden. For example, when Hunt heard that a female Cuban exile had information about Castro's reaction to JFK's assassination, he made sure that he, Fiorini, Hunt's former assistant Bernard Barker, and Cuban exile Eugenio Martinez (the CIA's top "boatman" for getting into Cuba in 1963, and still on a monthly CIA retainer) conducted their own investigation of the matter. Hunt gave his JFK assassination report to the White House and the CIA, but it was apparently one of several files taken from a White House safe and destroyed after Hunt's arrest. The Watergate committee was never told about it, though later Congressional investigators confirmed in 1978 that Hunt's JFK assassination report had existed.[8]

The White House dirty tricks operation had grown quite large by early 1972, as Nixon and his men targeted moderate Democratic presidential hopefuls like Edmund Muskie and Scoop Jackson. But with the support of Nixon, Hunt and Helms also focused on troublesome journalists like Jack Anderson. According to a 1975 memo prepared by Dick Cheney when he was President Ford's chief of staff (under Nixon, Cheney was deputy to White House Counsel Donald Rumsfeld), the CIA admitted that "from February 15 to April 12, 1972, 'personal surveillances' were conducted by the CIA on Jack Anderson and members of his staff [including] Brit Hume . . . the physical surveillances were authorized by Helms."[9]

That surveillance apparently didn't produce the desired result, because in March 1972, G. Gordon Liddy said that he and E. Howard Hunt talked about assassinating Jack Anderson. Liddy said they spoke with a former CIA doctor about getting a drug for "neutralizing" Anderson. The same doctor had provided the poisons for the Cubela and CIA-Mafia plots, and the *Washington Post* said Hunt's order from a senior White House official "to assassinate [columnist] Jack Anderson . . . was cancelled at the last minute."[10]

Just weeks earlier, Attorney General John Mitchell had asked Liddy if Hunt and his Plumbers could break into the office of *Las Vegas Sun* publisher Hank Greenspun. Journalist J. Anthony Lukas pointed out that one day before Mitchell's request, the *New York Times* had published an article saying "that Greenspun had (Howard) Hughes memos in his safe." Greenspun was friends with Anderson, Maheu, and Rosselli, and had been the first to publish a brief article hinting at Rosselli's story of the CIA-Mafia plots.[11]

Other break-ins linked to the CIA-Mafia plots—and thus potentially to JFK's assassination—were carried out by Hunt, his Cuban exiles, and Fiorini in May and June 1972. By that time, Hunt's group included a total of ten Cuban exiles, though only those soon to be arrested at the final Watergate break-in (Barker, Martinez, and locksmith Virgilio Gonzalez) are remembered today.[12] Three of Hunt's Plumbers group were also working for mob boss Santo Trafficante: Bernard Barker, Frank Fiorini, and Manuel Artime. Carl Shoffler, one of the officers who arrested Fiorini at the Watergate, told us that Fiorini later talked "off the record" about "knowing and working with Trafficante." Shoffler also said that Trafficante was very close to the reputed godfather of Washington, D.C., Joe Nesline, enabling Trafficante to monitor and even influence developments there.[13]

The Cuban exiles were motivated to help Hunt and the White House by being told their actions would help to defeat Castro, with the implication being that if Nixon won reelection, he could take stronger action against Fidel. George McGovern looked like the likely Democratic nominee—and McGovern's professed desire to negotiate with Fidel made his possible victory anathema to the conservative exiles. Hunt lied to the exiles, telling them McGovern was getting money from Fidel and that they needed to break into the Watergate offices of the Democratic National Committee to get proof.

The real goal of Hunt, Helms, and Nixon for the Watergate break-ins was to learn what DNC chairman Lawrence O'Brien knew about the CIA-Mafia plots against Fidel, which is also why Cuban exiles—and Fiorini, who'd been involved in the plots—had to be used. Aside from the fact that O'Brien was friends with Robert Maheu and might have notes of what he'd been told, the reason for the break-ins was for the Watergate burglars to find a specific document about the plots to kill Castro. Soon after the break-ins, Frank Fiorini described the document to his friend, journalist Andrew St. George, saying what

they were looking for in the Democratic National Committee's files, and in some other Washington file cabinets, too, was a thick secret memorandum from the Castro government, addressed confidentially to the Democrats . . . we knew that this secret memorandum existed—knew it for a fact—because the CIA and the FBI had found excerpts and references to it in some confidential investigations . . . But we wanted the entire document [which was] a long, detailed listing [of the] various attempts made to assassinate the Castro brothers.[14]

Fiorini described the document to Russell, saying it was more than a hundred pages long and had "two main parts," including information about "espionage and sabotage [by] the CIA and the DIA." Fiorini's information—obtained from Hunt, who likely got it from the CIA—would later be confirmed as fairly accurate.

Though Fiorini had a reputation as a braggart, there is good reason to believe him on this point: He described the document in print, in an interview published in *True* magazine in August 1974, one year before anyone else had ever publicly talked about such a document, or shown it to the world. That exposure didn't occur until July 30, 1975, when George McGovern issued a press release about the thick document he'd just received from Fidel Castro, following his May 1975 visit to Cuba.[15]

The Castro-McGovern document is very much as Fiorini described almost a year earlier, and is filled with detailed accounts of US-backed assassination attempts against Fidel. Almost a hundred pages long, it has the dates, names and photos of those captured, and photos of the some-times quite sophisticated arms and explosives used in the attempts.[16]

The 1975 version of the document lists familiar names and shows why Nixon, Helms, Hunt, and Trafficante would have been worried in 1972 about the report becoming public: Those named include Johnny Rosselli, Tony Varona (three times, the first during the CIA-Mafia plots), Manuel Artime (and several of his associates), Rolando Cubela, his CIA contact Carlos Tepedino, and Trafficante henchman Herminio Diaz. The account begins with a mid-1960 attempt (involving "a gangster . . . equipped by the CIA"), at the time when Vice President Nixon and Hunt were involved in CIA Cuban operations. The report ends with the 1971 attempt to assassinate Fidel in Chile, listing twenty-eight attempts in all. It included two attempts that Rosselli had hinted at in his disclosures to Jack Anderson: Helms's unauthorized plots to kill Fidel on March 13, 1963 (at the University of Havana), and April 7, 1963 (at Latin American Stadium).[17]

A couple of pages appear to have been added in 1975, reflecting then-ongoing Congressional hearings, but otherwise the detailed report is likely similar to the one Hunt described to Fiorini in 1972, which Fiorini then revealed in Dick Russell's 1974 article. The fact that Hunt (and Helms and Nixon) were willing to risk several break-ins to photograph a copy of it in 1972 indicates that while Hunt knew generally about the report, he and his patrons couldn't be sure exactly what was in it. The fact that Lawrence O'Brien might have a copy, or other information from Maheu about Rosselli and the CIA-Mafia plots, made O'Brien's office at the Watergate an irresistible and critical target for Nixon, Helms, and Hunt.

Jack Anderson's handful of articles over the past five years had generated no follow-up in the mainstream press, but more detailed or widespread news coverage of the CIA-Mafia plots from 1960, 1963, or 1971 could have cost Richard Nixon the election. To the majority of Americans in 1972, it was inconceivable that the CIA would try to assassinate a foreign leader, let alone use the Mafia to do it. Richard Helms knew that exposure of the CIA-Mafia plots and the other assassination attempts would cost him his career and reputation. Hunt likely realized it could also focus suspicion on him for matters related to JFK's assassination.

The possibility that the JFK-Almeida coup plan was listed in the document gave Helms and Hunt a thin reed of National Security justification—or rationalization—for their actions. But in trying to obtain a copy of the document and learn if O'Brien had it, Nixon would cost himself the presidency, Helms his career, and Hunt his freedom. While Trafficante would suffer no personal consequences for having his three men help with the operation, it would lead the godfather to order the murder of Rosselli four years after the break-in.

Confirmation of Fiorini's story came from Washington attorney Leslie Scheer, who would represent Johnny Rosselli when he testified in a closed hearing to Watergate investigators. Scheer told Rosselli's biographers that based on questions asked by the Congressional investigators, "the reason the break-in occurred at the Democratic Party headquarters was because Nixon or somebody . . . suspected that the Democrats had information as to Nixon's involvement with the CIA's original contact with Rosselli [and] felt that a document existed showing Nixon was involved with or knew what was going on with the CIA and the assassination of Castro and Rosselli's involvement. [The Watergate burglars] wanted to try to get this information that Nixon suspected [the Democrats] were going to use against him."[18]

Hunt used Cuban exiles (and Fiorini) to look for the document during the May and June 1972 break-ins because when going through files they would immediately recognize relevant names like Varona, Cubela, and Artime. Their anti-Castro backgrounds would also ensure their silence if they learned details of CIA assassination operations directed at Fidel. In early April 1972, two months before the final Watergate break-in, the CIA's Inspector General looked into the "activities of Howard Hunt and Manuel Artime in Miami and Nicaragua, Barker, Mrs. Hunt, [Tony] Varona [and Carlos] Prio," as part of an "Internal Review."[19]

Frank Fiorini told Dick Russell that he and the others "were looking for" the document not just at the Watergate, where they were arrested, but also "in some other Washington file cabinets, too." J. Anthony Lukas wrote that later government "investigators suspect that some of the Cuban-Americans may have been involved in burglaries at the" offices of Ambassador Orlando Letelier and others at the "Chilean embassy in Washington and the Chilean Mission to the United Nations that spring [as well as] a May 16 [1972] burglary of a prominent Democratic law firm in the Watergate."[20]

A June 28, 1972, memo by Deputy CIA Director General Vernon Walters (who replaced General Cushman) says that John Dean "believed that Barker had been involved in a clandestine entry into the Chilean embassy." A writer friend of Fiorini's confirmed that Fiorini told him "he took part in the Chilean embassy break-in," and a researcher for Bob Woodward wrote that one of the former CIA men arrested at the Watergate "expressed a belief that the Chilean embassy was bugged by the Administration, a belief then shared by officials of the embassy, and strengthened by the intruders' apparent knowledge of the [targeted] diplomats' movements."[21] Given Fidel's support for Allende's Chilean government, Hunt might have worried that Ambassador Letelier had been given a copy of the Castro assassination document to pass along to others in Washington. Fiorini said that in one of their non-Watergate break-ins, "we found a piece of" the Castro assassination document, but not "the entire thing," so it's possible that portion was found at the Chilean Embassy, prompting the next break-in, at the Watergate.

The Plumbers' first, unsuccessful, attempted break-in at the Watergate offices of O'Brien occurred eight days after the Chilean Embassy burglary, on May 22, with another failed attempt on May 23. The group finally succeeded at the Watergate on May 28, 1972. Anthony Summers writes that "Hunt's Cubans photographed papers [and] planted bugging devices . . . on two telephones." Fiorini said that "we looked high and low for this document" but didn't find it. As with the final Watergate bugging three weeks later, Nixon was far from Washington during the May attempts.[22]

Several important developments took place before the group returned to the Watergate for another burglary in June 1972. J. Edgar Hoover had died on May 1, 1972, and his "personal and confidential" files were reportedly destroyed soon after. In Laurel, Maryland, on May 15, 1972, Arthur Bremer shot George Wallace, who was running for the Democratic presidential nomination.[23] Wallace's injury removed a serious threat to Nixon's reelection, and though White House tapes show that

Nixon and Colson discussed planting leftist literature in Bremer's apartment after the shooting, no earlier connection between Nixon's men and Bremer was found.[24]

Richard Helms had several meetings in May 1972, including some with top entertainment executives, about turning E. Howard Hunt's spy novels into a weekly pro-CIA television series. That Helms pressed the issue several times that month is important, because it confirms the ongoing close relationship between Helms and Hunt, which is completely at odds with the image Helms would always present after Hunt's arrest. It also indicates the Watergate arrests were not engineered by Helms and the CIA, as many authors and officials have claimed, since Helms wouldn't tie himself and the CIA so closely to Hunt in May, knowing that Hunt would become infamous in June.[25] Also in May, Helms appointed former Miami Station Chief Ted Shackley to head the CIA's Western Hemisphere division. After Watergate, Shackley would make several suspicious trips to Miami and Mexico City—where much of the Watergate money was laundered—without telling the local CIA Station Chief.[26]

In addition to Artime, Haig, Hunt, and the others mentioned so far in this chapter, two more veterans of the covert war against Castro were in positions in 1972 that would let them play key roles in the aftermath of the Watergate burglaries. Alexander Butterfield had first worked with Haig and Joseph Califano to resettle the Cuban-American troops from Fort Benning. Charles Colson said Joseph Califano recommended that Butterfield be hired as a Nixon aide. By June 1972, Butterfield was responsible for arranging Nixon's extensive taping system—which he would dramatically reveal during questioning by Fred Thompson, just over a year after McCord, Barker, and the others were arrested.[27]

General Alexander Haig, working in Nixon's White House as Kissinger's aide in June 1972, had remained friends with his old boss from 1963, Joseph Califano. By June 1972, Califano was a partner at Williams and Connally, the powerful Washington law firm of Edward Bennett Williams. Though Williams had originally introduced Johnny Rosselli to Robert Maheu, and had represented Hoffa and Giancana (and still represented the Teamsters), Williams had spent his recent years building a more reputable image. At the law firm, Califano's clients included both the Democratic National Committee (target of the Watergate burglaries) and the *Washington Post*.[28]

Chapter Sixty-three

In events well-chronicled for decades, early on the morning of June 17, 1972, James McCord, Bernard Barker, Frank Fiorini, Eugenio Martinez, and Virgilio Gonzalez broke into the Watergate offices of the Democratic National Committee, while E. Howard Hunt and G. Gordon Liddy watched from across the street. Ostensibly, their mission was to fix or move a bug on the phone of Lawrence O'Brien's secretary, but they brought no additional bugging equipment. Instead, they had more than a hundred rolls of film, and Frank Fiorini later said, "Our assignment was to photograph 2000 documents that night." In addition to looking for the crucial Castro assassination document, Hunt had also told them to watch for "anything that had to do with Howard Hughes," which would include items about Robert Maheu. They were also looking generally for anything that could damage Nixon or hurt the Democrats.[1] For reasons still debated, the five burglars wound up being arrested by Carl Shoffler and others, while Hunt and Liddy fled.

Joseph Califano's key role in focusing attention on the Watergate story has been overlooked by most historians and journalists. At 5:00 AM on the morning of the arrests, Califano was called with news of the break-in at the offices of his client, the Democratic National Committee. According to Evan Thomas, Califano was told that "the burglars had been caught copying files and bugging telephones. Califano hung up and called another of [his] firm's clients, the *Washington Post*. Califano suggested to . . . the managing editor that the Watergate burglary might be a good story," setting in motion the coverage that would make Woodward and Bernstein famous. Califano's instincts and timing continued to be amazing later that morning, because after "Califano was told that the police had found the phone number of the Committee to Re-Elect the President on one of the burglars," Califano asked Williams, "What if this goes all the way to the White House?"[2]

The following evening, "Califano decided to file a suit for the Democrats against [CREEP]." Though little-remembered today, the suit was important because the pre-trial discovery process kept the story barely alive at a time when most American journalists continued to ignore the incident. In Califano's recent autobiography, he detailed for the first time the many extralegal and illegal steps the Nixon White House attempted in order to stymie the Democrats' suit.[3] Those were just some of the illegal actions authorized by Nixon, to ensure that Watergate wouldn't impact the 1972 presidential election.

Jack Anderson bailed Fiorini out of jail, while Hunt and Liddy were eventually tied to the break-in and arrested. Even before that, the Nixon White House was in damage control mode. On June 20, 1972, Richard Nixon called H. R. Haldeman and said to "tell Ehrlichman this whole group of Cubans is tied to the Bay of Pigs." A confused Haldeman asked, "The Bay of Pigs? What does that have to do with this?" Nixon simply said, "Ehrlichman will know what I mean."[4]

Three days later, in the Oval Office, Nixon told Haldeman, "Well, we protected Helms from one hell of a lot of things . . . Hunt will uncover a lot of things. You open up that scab, there's a hell of a lot of things . . . tell [the CIA] we just feel that it would be very detrimental to have this thing go any further. This involves these Cubans, Hunt, and a lot of hanky-panky that we have nothing to do with ourselves."[5]

Thus began Nixon's effort to get Helms to persuade the FBI to back off their Watergate investigation on national security grounds. Nixon later told Haldeman that "when you get the CIA people in say, 'Look, the problem is that this will open up the whole Bay of Pigs things again.' So they should call the FBI in and for the good of the country don't go any further into this case."[6]

Just before Haldeman was to meet with Helms and General Walters to discuss Watergate, Nixon said to "tell them that if it gets out . . . it's likely to blow the whole Bay of Pigs which we think would be very unfortunate for the CIA."[7] Helms had been reluctant to obstruct the FBI, even though three of those involved (McCord, Hunt, Barker) had worked for the CIA and another (Martinez) was still on monthly retainer for the CIA at the time of the break-in. So, Haldeman tried Nixon's suggestion during a June 23, 1972, meeting with Helms, saying, "The President asked me to tell you this entire affair may be connected to the Bay of Pigs and if it opens up, the Bay of Pigs may be blown."

Helms erupted in rage. According to Haldeman, there was suddenly "turmoil in the room, Helms gripping the arms of his chair leaning forward and shouting, 'The Bay of Pigs had nothing to do with this! I have no concern about the Bay of Pigs!'" Haldeman was "absolutely shocked by Helms' violent reaction [and] wondered what was such dynamite in the Bay of Pigs story?" Whatever it was, it worked, at least for a while, since Helms soon issued a memo saying the CIA was requesting the FBI "desist from expanding the investigation into other areas which may well, eventually, run afoul of our operations."[8]

Later, Haldeman said in his autobiography he realized that "in all those Nixon references to the 'Bay of Pigs,' he was actually referring to the Kennedy assassination." In other words, "when Nixon said, 'It's likely to blow the whole Bay of Pigs thing,' he might have been reminding Helms, not so gently, of the cover-up of the CIA assassination attempts on the hero of the Bay of Pigs, Fidel Castro—a CIA operation that may have triggered the Kennedy tragedy, and which Helms desperately wanted to hide."[9]

In later years, Richard Helms would make a point of telling journalists that he had never succumbed to pressure to get the FBI to back off from their Watergate investigation, something repeated by Stephen Ambrose and other historians. But the record clearly shows Helms did call off the FBI, at least for a time—all while withholding crucial information about the backgrounds of Hunt, Fiorini, and other Watergate participants from government investigators.

While many books, documentaries, and films have chronicled the basic facts of Watergate, some points remained unresolved. While there is a famous eighteen-minute gap in one of the crucial Nixon tapes, other tapes are missing entirely or also contain erasures. An example is the tape from the day when Nixon said that Watergate could "blow the whole Bay of Pigs thing." Anthony Summers discovered that tape, kept at the National Archives, had "at least six unexplained erasures."[10]

By the fall of 1972, Helms and the CIA had stopped helping the White House block the FBI on several fronts, though Helms continued to withhold information from investigators that could negatively impact him or the CIA. Nixon easily won reelection in early November, since Watergate was not a factor in the race. After his victory, Nixon began cleaning house, asking on November 5, 1972, for most of his officials to submit their resignations. Helms thought he would be an exception, but Nixon fired him at Camp David on November 20, 1972. Apparently Helms still had some leverage left, because he was able to get Nixon to appoint him as ambassador to Iran, a post he wanted that was also far from the Watergate investigations.

Richard Helms's last day at the CIA was supposed to be February 14,

1973, but Nixon moved the date up to February 2 on just two weeks' notice, so that new CIA Director James Schlesinger could take office. Helms and his secretary spent the next ten days destroying four thousand pages of transcripts from Helms's own office taping system, plus the tapes themselves. According to Helms biographer Thomas Powers, the destruction also included all of Helms's "personal records from six and a half years as Director," including everything relating in any way to Watergate. Because so many of the figures involved in Watergate had also been involved in the JFK-Almeida coup plan, the Mafia's infiltration of the plan, or the CIA-Mafia plots, this effectively allowed Helms to complete the cover-up he'd been conducting since 1963. There was no way his successor would have the information needed to really expose Helms, even if the new Director were so inclined. Helms didn't destroy the only copy of the IG Report, because it had left out so much crucial information and all of its supporting files had already been destroyed.[11] When coupled with the destruction of Hoover's private files the previous year, Helms's housecleaning put many details about the assassination of JFK, and likely some aspects of Dr. King's and Bobby's, permanently beyond the reach of history.[12]

Three months later, when new CIA Director Schlesinger issued an order for senior CIA officials to tell him about past or ongoing CIA activities outside its charter, he received almost seven hundred pages of misdeeds. Eventually named "The Family Jewels," the full list—kept secret until June 2007—was woefully incomplete, for several reasons. Aside from the unlikelihood that CIA employees and officials would willingly volunteer their most serious crimes or charter violations, there were also the ongoing Watergate investigations and prosecutions, as well as Schlesinger's own unpopularity (he would leave in less than two months and be replaced by William Colby). Most important, key officials and operatives knew how well Helms had essentially buried, or destroyed, the biggest secrets.[13]

It was perhaps poetic justice for Richard Helms that on February 7, 1973—five days after he finished destroying files and stepped down as CIA Director—Helms found himself testifying to Congress when the subject of Chile came up. Helms lied when asked if the CIA had provided help to those who opposed Allende in Chile, a false statement that would eventually bring him a criminal conviction.[14]

By fall 1972, Hunt had been making constant demands for hush money for himself and the others, which the White House supplied, using

Manuel Artime as a conduit. Artime—who would never be charged for Watergate or drug trafficking—used his protégé Milian Rodriguez to help launder the Watergate hush money. On December 8, 1972, Hunt's wife Dorothy was killed in an airline crash while carrying $10,000 in cash in her purse. After that, Hunt and the other defendants agreed to plead guilty, just as the Senate Watergate Committee was beginning its investigation.[15]

The White House's cover-up looked like it was going to hold—until James McCord wrote his famous letter to Judge John Sirica on March 19, 1973, saying the defendants had lied and that high officials, like Attorney General John Mitchell, were involved. For a time, Bernard Fensterwald represented McCord, until McCord says Fensterwald "introduced me to Tad Szulc, and the two men . . . sought to solicit information from me concerning CIA and concerning E. Howard Hunt."[16]

Nixon's position had looked strong in the fall of 1972, but by the spring of 1973, his situation was more difficult. The Senate Watergate investigators were starting to dig in, and McCord's letter to Sirica caused new prosecutions to be considered. Now that Hunt faced a long prison sentence, he demanded even more money, for himself and the others. When Dean told Nixon they might need a million dollars, Nixon replied, "we could get that . . . you could get it in cash. I know where it could be gotten [with] no problem. The money can be provided."[17] Where could Nixon get a million in cash?

According to the *Washington Star*, one answer came the following year, when "Alexander Haig"—by then Nixon's final chief of staff—ordered "a secret investigation of any Nixon connections with huge cash contributions from countries in the Far East [or] organized crime." The "Army's Criminal Investigation Command [found] strong indications of a history of Nixon connections with money from organized crime" and reports of multimillion-dollar contributions from top South Vietnamese officials.[18] Based on those findings, it's possible that some of Nixon's hush money came from associates of Santo Trafficante—and was being paid to (and distributed by) some of Trafficante's other associates, like Barker, Fiorini and Artime.

In the spring and into the early summer of 1973, the Senate Watergate Committee pressed forward while criminal prosecutions and the Democrats' civil suit continued. The committee chairman, North Carolina Senator Sam Ervin, was a conservative Southern Democrat who would ordinarily have been expected to support Nixon. However, the previous year, Ervin had tried to look into domestic surveillance by the US military, only to be stonewalled by the White House.[19]

Ervin was determined not to be obstructed again, with Watergate. His chief investigator, Carmine Bellino, was the same man Bobby Kennedy had recommended to Richard Goodwin as the ideal person to investigate JFK's assassination. In delving into Watergate, some of Bellino's investigators would actually interview several of those involved in JFK's murder.

Bellino and Ervin got the break they'd been hoping for when John Dean agreed to testify in open hearings against Nixon (on June 25, 1973) and when Alexander Butterfield revealed Nixon's taping system to the world in his testimony on July 16, 1973. From that time forward, despite all the issues with Special Prosecutors and matters of impeachment, it was simply a matter of time before Nixon would have to face some type of justice.

The Nixon tapes now available show that he was thinking of resigning as early as spring 1973, but it would take more than a year after the explosive Butterfield and Dean revelations for Nixon to finally step down. Descriptions of the prosecutions, battles over the tapes, and the "Saturday Night Massacre" resignation of Attorney General Elliot Richardson, are available in countless books and articles. Our focus is on the important events overlooked in those accounts, many of which had effects well beyond Watergate, such as several murders of Congressional witnesses in the mid-1970s.

Of all the millions of words written about Watergate at the time, only one largely ignored article mentioned an important part of Hunt's background that Helms had withheld from investigators: Hunt's work on the plots to assassinate Castro in the mid-1960s. Tad Szulc's February 1973 *Esquire* magazine article briefly described those operations (primarily the Cubela plots), saying they involved Hunt, Barker, Artime, and one other Plumber. No mainstream journalist followed up on Szulc's 1973 revelations, so he expanded on them the following year in a short biography of Hunt, saying that in the mid-1960s Hunt was "helping to coordinate [an] assassination plot" against Castro, which would be followed by Artime's arrival in Cuba. But Szulc couldn't write too much about the subject without drawing attention to his own covert work for JFK on AMTRUNK.[20]

Two interviews conducted in 1973 could have dramatically changed the course of Watergate events and possibly even exposed the JFK-Almeida coup plan. But neither made it into print at the time, so they remained unknown to Watergate investigators and Almeida's secret remained safe.

Researcher Richard E. Sprague interviewed Haynes Johnson on January 12, 1973, and the following quotes come from Sprague's handwritten notes. Aside from a few lines that appeared in a small newsletter in 1975, this is their first publication. According to the notes, Haynes said, "CIA-backed plans for [a] second Cuban invasion were going on in 1963." Haynes "knew RFK very well. He and Harry Williams called RFK a lot in 1963, because RFK had the CIA reporting to him and JFK." Harry was "the prime contact with the Cubans and other Florida groups by 1963 [and] knew and met all of the CIA people in Wash[ington] & Miami."[21]

Haynes Johnson told Sprague that "A meeting was held on Nov. 22, 1963 in Wash[ington] D.C. to discuss plans for Cuban operation . . . it was the most important meeting they had . . . at meeting were [CIA Executive Director Lyman] Kirkpatrick, Helms, Hunt, and Williams. Word of [JFK's] assassination came in [during the] meeting." Haynes knew something big was about to happen with Cuba, but hadn't been told about Almeida or the coup plan—though he did know that "RFK conducted his own investigation" into JFK's murder.[22] If any of this information involving Hunt and Helms had become widely known during the Watergate investigation, it would have changed American political history. Instead, when it was finally published in a small newsletter in 1975, it passed without notice.[23]

Journalist and former FBI agent William Turner interviewed Harry Williams on November 28, 1973. Harry told us later that he was shocked when the Watergate scandal erupted and he recognized former associates from 1963 like Hunt and Barker. Commander Almeida was still unexposed, but Harry had come to realize that one of Trafficante's men had used part of the coup plan for JFK's murder, so Harry tried to tell Turner as much as he could without endangering Almeida.[24]

In his long interview with Turner, Harry confirmed much of what Haynes Johnson had told Sprague. Without mentioning Almeida or a specific coup plan, Harry provided a wealth of additional information about Bobby's control of Cuban operations, their work together, and Harry's activities with Cyrus Vance, Joseph Califano, Alexander Haig, E. Howard Hunt, James McCord, and Bernard Barker. The names of Hunt, McCord, and Barker were still hot news items in November 1973, as Watergate continued to unfold, and an article about them by Turner at that time would have been big news. However, the 1973 interview wasn't published until 1981, when parts appeared in Turner's book *The Fish Is Red*, about the covert US war against Castro.[25]

As Watergate played out, AMWORLD veterans helped Nixon and Kissinger finally bring down Allende in Chile. David Atlee Phillips had become Chief of the Western Hemisphere Division and Henry Heckscher was still the Station Chief in Chile when General Augusto Pinochet led a US-backed coup against Allende. Though the CIA says Allende committed suicide on September 11, 1973, Allende's family and supporters say he was murdered—a claim supported by David Morales, who boasted to a close friend that he helped to kill the Chilean president.[26]

Due to political intervention from an unknown Washington official, Johnny Rosselli had been moved to a much more comfortable prison before he was finally released on October 5, 1973. At sixty-eight, Rosselli faced a relatively bleak future. Giancana was still in Mexico—primarily concerned with the drug network and gambling—and the mob powers in Chicago had Rosselli officially turn over his Las Vegas role to Tony "The Ant" Spilotro. With no part left to play in Las Vegas or Los Angeles, Rosselli moved to Florida, where he had family—and Santo Trafficante.[27]

Two months after Rosselli walked out of prison, his old compatriot from the CIA-Mafia plots, Richard Cain, was gunned down in Chicago. Eight months earlier, Cain had probably been involved in the murder of Sam DeStefano, the gangster who helped frame Secret Service agent Abraham Bolden in 1964, before he could talk to the Warren Commission.[28]

By Christmas 1973, Jimmy Hoffa had been out of jail for almost a year, but he still chafed at not being able to hold any Teamster office. Instead, he had to sit at home in Michigan, frustrated, while his replacement, Frank Fitzsimmons, rode in Air Force One with President Nixon.[29] Hoffa felt that he'd been betrayed, and someone had to pay. To get back at Nixon and add fuel to the slow-burning Watergate fire, Hoffa told a contact with the Senate Watergate Committee about the CIA-Mafia plots that had begun under Nixon's tenure. He also gave them the name of the man who could tell the investigators more: Johnny Rosselli.[30] Despite Bellino's past partnerships with Rosselli associates Robert Maheu and Guy Banister, Bellino wanted his men to grill the Mafia don.

Deportation proceedings against Rosselli had mysteriously stopped while he was in prison, but now Helms was out of the CIA, and by January 4, 1974, the INS was again targeting Rosselli. The INS pressure seemed designed to ensure Rosselli's cooperation when he was subpoenaed by the Senate Watergate Committee in February 1974. Setting a pattern that would last until his death, as long as Rosselli answered subpoenas, he wouldn't be deported.[31]

Johnny Rosselli's appearance had little impact on Watergate, but it triggered a series of events that would lead to his own murder, as well as those of Hoffa and Giancana. In late February 1974, Rosselli went to Washington to testify in secret. Thwarting Hoffa's intent, Rosselli's attorney said the Mafia don "offered nothing that would confirm Nixon's involvement in the CIA plots [with the Mafia] or shed any light on the motivations of the Watergate burglars." When Rosselli returned to Miami on February 25, 1974, he no doubt told Santo Trafficante he hadn't given investigators Trafficante's name or anything of importance.[32]

Three days after Rosselli returned to Miami, seventy-two-year-old Joseph Milteer died in a fire at his home. According to reporter Dan Christensen, "a gas heater in his home exploded" and "several days later, a small cache of arms and ammunition was uncovered in his car." The man who had informed on Milteer, William Somersett, had died in 1970. While Joseph Milteer was alive, Milteer's name was never linked in the press to Martin Luther King's murder in Memphis, and the same is true for all the FBI files discovered so far. The first time Milteer had been mentioned by name regarding JFK's murder had been in a small-press 1971 book by Harold Weisberg, which discussed the tapes of Milteer from November 1963. Judge Seymour Gelber later said that between 1971 and 1976, the Dade County state attorney's files on the Milteer case disappeared from a North Miami warehouse, even though they "consisted of thousands of pages of transcripts and documents."[33]

Heroin trafficking remained a hot topic in the news in 1974, and Sam Giancana's involvement in a narcotics ring eventually became too much for Mexican authorities. Giancana was suddenly and unceremoniously deported from Mexico on July 18, 1974, and returned to Chicago, where a grand jury was waiting for him.[34]

In Washington, pressure for impeachment kept building during the spring and summer of 1974. Former Warren Commissioner Gerald Ford had become vice president after Spiro Agnew had to resign for payoffs unrelated to Watergate. General Alexander Haig was by that time Nixon's chief of staff, and both Haig and Ford played crucial roles in the events that resulted in Richard Nixon finally announcing his resignation to a nationwide television audience on August 8, 1974. Gerald Ford was sworn in as president the following day, picking moderate Republican Nelson Rockefeller as his vice president. On September 8, 1974, many Republican officials breathed a sigh of relief when Ford issued a full pardon to Nixon, which was "unconditional for all crimes Nixon may have committed in the White House." Ford tried to quietly issue the pardon on a Sunday morning, but it was still controversial, because numerous prosecutions were still ongoing. The pardon removed the leverage prosecutors needed to get Nixon to testify in those cases, or about other officials who could only be indicted and prosecuted with Nixon's testimony. Ford's act helped to ensure that many of Watergate's mysteries would remain just that until after Nixon's death.[35]

E. Howard Hunt and his codefendants were not so lucky, and were among those who went to prison for their roles in Nixon's operations, Hunt for thirty-three months. More than two dozen Nixon aides and officials had been prosecuted, from Haldeman and Ehrlichman to those far less well-known.

The prosecution of one little-remembered official from the Watergate era would eventually lead to charges being brought against Santo Trafficante and Carlos Marcello, netting Marcello a conviction that would finally fulfill Bobby Kennedy's goal of sending the godfather away for a long prison term. In 1972, Nixon had appointed Richard Kleindienst as attorney general, to replace John Mitchell. Kleindienst would later be convicted for lying to a Senate committee. After Kleindienst's resignation, he became involved in what Dan Moldea described as "a multi-million-dollar insurance swindle involving the Teamsters." Moldea says that Kleindienst was "convicted with" an "insurance swindler" named Joe Hauser. Also involved in the scheme was Santo Trafficante, who was indicted, though he wouldn't go to prison. More importantly, to avoid prison Joe Hauser agreed to help the FBI. Hauser eventually became the first wired informant to get close to Carlos Marcello, as part of an FBI sting called Operation BRILAB (for "bribery and labor").[36]

Chapter Sixty-four

By fall 1974, the intense press and Congressional interest in Watergate began to fade—but less than six months after Nixon's resignation, new revelations in an article by Sy Hersh triggered a fresh round of inquiries. The hearings increasingly centered on JFK's assassination, and one investigation would spawn another until the end of the decade. At times the hearings came so close to exposing the truth that Santo Trafficante, Carlos Marcello, and their associates felt they had no choice but to have Congressional witnesses killed, sometimes on the eve of their testimony.

With Sy Hersh's December 22, 1974, article in the *New York Times*, the mainstream media finally began to expose what its headlines called the "Huge CIA [Domestic Surveillance] Operation" directed against antiwar critics in the US. CIA Director William Colby fired Counter-Intelligence Chief James Angleton the next day, but the firestorm had begun. To quell the furor, President Ford appointed a blue ribbon commission headed by Vice President Nelson Rockefeller, to look into the CIA's domestic activities. However, since most of the Rockefeller Commission's members were conservative establishment figures like Ronald Reagan, and its Executive Director was former Warren Commission counsel David Belin, charges of "whitewash" were inevitable. Though primarily devoted to domestic intelligence abuses, the commission soon started looking into JFK's assassination, to debunk reports that E. Howard Hunt and Frank Fiorini were two of the "three tramps" photographed in Dealey Plaza.[1]

After Watergate, Congress and the press were far quicker to investigate official wrongdoing, and the Rockefeller Commission soon found itself competing for headlines, witnesses, and documents with Congressional committees. Congress was already preparing to investigate the scandal uncovered by Hersh when President Ford met with a group of editors from the *New York Times* on January 16, 1975. Ford told them the Rockefeller Commission had to be careful not to expose certain past

CIA operations, "like assassinations." Ford quickly tried to qualify his remark, saying it was off the record, but word raced through journalistic circles, reaching Congress and adding CIA assassinations to their agenda.[2]

The Senate Select Committee on Intelligence was created on January 27 and chaired by Idaho Senator Frank Church. The Church Committee soon authorized a subcommittee devoted to the JFK assassination, headed by moderate Pennsylvania Republican Senator Richard Schweiker and including Colorado Senator Gary Hart. On February 19, 1975, the House created the Nedzi Committee. Soon to be called the Pike Committee, it too would delve into CIA assassinations, at times touching on the JFK assassination without realizing it.

The general public finally heard about President Ford's "assassinations" comment on February 28, 1975, during Daniel Schorr's CBS news broadcast. Schorr had also obtained from CIA Director William Colby an indirect confirmation of CIA assassination attempts against foreign leaders.[3] Even more attention focused on JFK's assassination after March 6, 1975, when Geraldo Rivera showed American TV audiences the complete Zapruder film of JFK's assassination for the first time, on his late-night ABC show, *Goodnight America*. Though of much poorer quality than today's digitally enhanced version, the film stunned audiences with their first glimpse of JFK being thrown back and to the left after being shot—indicating a shot from the front. (For the next decade, showings of the Zapruder film on TV would remain relatively rare.)[4]

Jack Anderson weighed in with new articles about the CIA-Mafia plots on March 10 and 13, having already named Johnny Rosselli as one of those involved. Four days later, *Time* magazine advanced the story by adding Sam Giancana to the plots with Rosselli and the CIA. To help deal with the increasing barrage of headlines about CIA assassinations and other misdeeds, in March 1975 David Atlee Phillips made arrangements to retire from the CIA. Since the press revelations could also uncover his own unsavory activities, Phillips immediately founded the Association of Retired Intelligence Officers, designed to counter the negative publicity the Agency was receiving.[5]

Richard Helms was called back from his ambassadorial post in Iran—where the Shah's regime had become even more brutal and repressive—to begin a series of increasingly intense rounds of testimony to the investigating committees. The Church Committee interviewed Helms on April 23, followed by the Rockefeller Commission staff on April 27, and culminating with a four-hour private session with the Rockefeller

Commissioners on April 28, 1975. Upon leaving, Helms saw CBS newsman Daniel Schorr. Fearing that the secret cover-ups he had maintained
since 1962 were about to unravel, Helms exploded in fury at the man
he blamed for making them public—Daniel Schorr. As described by
Schorr:

> Helms['s] face, ashen from strain and fatigue, turned livid. "You son-
> of-a-bitch!" he raged. "You killer! You cocksucker! 'Killer Schorr'—
> that's what they ought to call you!" Continuing his string of curses,
> he strode toward the press room.[6]

Helms was furious that his long-hidden secrets were being exposed,
and his use of the term "killer" could indicate his worry that the revelations of Schorr and the committees might result in the death of a CIA
asset. Since most of the publicity focused on the decade-old plots to
assassinate Fidel Castro, and most of the non-Mafia CIA assets from
those operations were either out of harm's way or already in Cuban
prisons (like Cubela and Menoyo), Helms may have been worrying (or
rationalizing) that a valuable asset like Almeida could be exposed and
killed.

Declassified files now make it clear that Helms lied to both committees about his unauthorized Castro assassination plots (admitting
only a limited amount of information) and completely hiding the JFK-
Almeida coup plan and most of AMWORLD (including its code name
and immense size). However, he wasn't the only one—in contrast to William Colby's carefully cultivated public image as being almost too forthcoming with Congress, according to the Church staff, "when it came to
the assassination plots . . . Colby closed the door" and wouldn't cooperate. Beginning a pattern to obstruct Congress that would be repeated
by the CIA with a later committee, Colby appointed Seymour Bolten—
Desmond FitzGerald's former assistant during the JFK-Almeida coup
plan and the CIA-Mafia plots—to be the CIA's liaison to the Church
Committee.[7] Thus, the person ostensibly helping the Committee
was someone who should have been interrogated and investigated
himself.

Even as the Rockefeller Commission issued its final report on June
11, 1975, the Church Committee intensified its efforts. On June 13, the
Church Committee again grilled Helms, this time exclusively about CIA
assassination plots, including those with the Mafia. His testimony was
in closed session, so the public had no way to know what he said—or
didn't say.

Santo Trafficante and Carlos Marcello must have worried about what might come out concerning the CIA's assassination plots, since it could expose their roles in JFK's murder. In the short term, Trafficante had the most to lose, since he'd played a much bigger role in the CIA-Mafia plots. Trafficante would have been especially worried when Sam Giancana was subpoenaed and slated to testify on June 26.

On July 19, 1975, Sam Giancana became the first of several Congressional witnesses to be murdered. The former mob boss was cooking a late-night meal for a trusted friend who was visiting Giancana's home in the Chicago neighborhood of Oak Park. His friend shot Giancana seven times with a silenced .22-caliber pistol, an unusually small gun for a mob hit. Five of the shots were around Giancana's chin and mouth, a sign that Mafiosi shouldn't talk.[8]

The gun was eventually traced to Florida, and some pointed the finger at Trafficante. One government informant, Charles Crimaldi, said that Giancana was killed by someone who worked for the CIA, though the hit man was acting on his own and not at the request of officials. Since several CIA assets and officials also worked with the Mafia, it could have been someone with ties to both the mob and intelligence.[9]

Giancana's murder made headlines across the country, adding urgency to the committees' investigations. The day after Giancana's death, CIA Director William Colby testified about CIA assassination plots, followed four days later by Johnny Rosselli. The transcripts—kept secret until the 1990s—show that Johnny Rosselli had mastered the art of saying a lot while revealing little, sticking to an incomplete version of the CIA-Mafia plots that mirrored the whitewashed version Helms had promulgated in his own testimony and in the 1967 Inspector General's Report. Jack Anderson wrote once more about Rosselli on July 7, and *Time* magazine ran an article touching on the original 1959 CIA Mafia plots that Hoffa had brokered—a story Hoffa himself had just leaked to someone with the Church Committee.[10] On July 17 and 18, the Church Committee once more interrogated Helms about assassination plots, in closed sessions.

Jimmy Hoffa was now in the crosshairs of the Committee, because of *Time*'s article about Hoffa's role in the 1959 CIA-Mafia plots. Trafficante, Marcello, and others couldn't afford to let Hoffa testify under oath about those or any other plots. On July 30, 1975, Jimmy Hoffa was spotted leaving a restaurant near Detroit, headed for what he thought was a meeting with New Jersey mobster Tony Provenzano, an associate of Carlos Marcello's. Hoffa was never seen again, and no body was ever found.[11]

Government informant Crimaldi said that "he had heard information that the same man that killed [Giancana] took care of Hoffa for the same reason: he knew about the Castro plots [and] it had been Hoffa who was the original liaison between the CIA and the [Mafia]."[12]

Rolando Masferrer was killed in a spectacular car bombing on October 31, 1975. His death could have been related to the Church Committee hearings or to the general upsurge of violence in Miami's exile community, fueled by politics and the expanding drug trade. A current article about JFK's assassination was on Masferrer's desk when he died. John Martino, Masferrer's mutual associate with Trafficante, had died of natural causes a few months earlier. In declining health, Martino had finally confessed his role in JFK's murder to two friends, his business partner and reporter John Cummings. The Church Committee apparently never learned about Martino or his published statements about the Kennedys' 1963 coup and invasion plan.

Johnny Rosselli used Jack Anderson to ensure he didn't meet the same fate as Giancana and Hoffa. Anderson's September 1, 1975, column said that Rosselli wasn't being deported because of his war record, helping Rosselli show Trafficante and Marcello that he wasn't getting preferential INS treatment because he was testifying. Rosselli was back in front of the Church Committee on September 22, ten days after Helms had faced the Committee yet again.

The CIA withheld a massive amount of information from the Church Committee, a situation that wouldn't change when President Ford fired William Colby and replaced him with George H. W. Bush, who'd headed the Republican National Committee during the latter stages of the Watergate investigation. At times, information found its way to the Committee from non-CIA sources—like the leads about the 1959 CIA-Mafia plots—only to hit a stone wall because the CIA withheld crucial information related to those leads. The Church Committee was never told about the JFK-Almeida coup plan, and thus knew nothing about the Mafia's infiltration of it. It received a few leads that could have pointed it in the right direction, if not for the information withheld by the CIA and other agencies.

On October 1, 1975, the Church Committee told the Justice Department it wanted "telephone logs derived from electronic surveillance" on seven people—including Trafficante, Tony Varona, Manolo Ray, and Harry Williams. Whoever tipped off the Committee had either worked with Bobby Kennedy or knew someone who had, because the memo lists

Harry's name as "Enrico Ruiz Williams." "Enrico" was Bobby's nickname for Harry, since he had trouble pronouncing Harry's first name, "Enrique." The Justice Department acknowledged having electronic surveillance on Trafficante, but it's not known what—if anything—they provided about Harry.[13]

At one point, the Church Committee asked the deputy attorney general for all the materials they had on "Major Juan Almeida," as well as Maurice Bishop (spelled "Morris"). This generated a document group, called the "Senstudy," of CIA files that had been given to the FBI. A dozen documents about Almeida were part of the Senstudy, all FBI copies of CIA documents, but the CIA did not provide their own copies of those documents to the Church Committee. These Almeida documents don't address the coup plan, but do talk about Almeida's dissatisfaction with Castro and his desire to defect shortly before the Bay of Pigs. However, the request for the Almeida documents was sent five days after the Church Committee completed its Final Report, so there was little the Committee could have done with the material—especially since Bush and the CIA were still withholding all information about the Almeida coup plan, AMWORLD, and Artime's involvement in the CIA-Mafia plots.[14] Inside the CIA, the small fig leaf of justification was no doubt that Almeida was still of potential value since he remained unexposed, plus the CIA's secret support for his family, which made the whole matter an ongoing operation. Ted Shackley probably oversaw that support after Phillips's resignation, since by 1975 Shackley was the highest CIA official remaining who had supervised 1963 Cuban operations.

While CIA officials withheld the most important information, they were usually quick to acknowledge more esoteric, unused assassination schemes, diverting attention from the plots that used high-powered rifles and might remind the public of JFK's murder. The CIA knew that unusual items like shellfish toxin would interest journalists and television audiences, and the increasingly publicity-hungry Senator Frank Church—eying a run for president in 1976—took the bait, holding two days of hearings on the poison.

In the fall of 1975, the Church Committee started to fragment for several reasons, in part because there was too much to investigate and too little information being provided. By this time, the Church Committee was investigating not only the CIA—in areas ranging from Chile to assassinations to domestic surveillance—but also the FBI and military intelligence. In addition, Church was investigating the FBI's COINTEL-PRO efforts against Martin Luther King. Their revelations helped to generate a 1977 Justice Department Task Force Report that critically reviewed the FBI's investigation of Dr. King's murder.

Leaks were another problem for the Committee. Though they didn't jeopardize real CIA operations, they did generate headlines—the most notable being the November 1975 leak about Judith Campbell, the woman who'd had relationships with JFK, Johnny Rosselli, and Sam Giancana. However, in some cases it's unclear if leaks came from Committee staffers or from one of the federal agencies being investigated.

One significant development for the Church investigation was when Schweiker and Hart's JFK subcommittee hired journalist Gaeton Fonzi in November 1975. What Fonzi assumed would be a weeks-long investigation would turn into a three-year quest involving both houses of Congress.

Fonzi and Hart were constantly frustrated by CIA stonewalling. Hart took particular interest in CIA assassin recruiter QJWIN. The CIA refused to tell the senator QJWIN's true identity, but when pressed it arranged for Hart to meet QJWIN in Europe. But after Hart flew across the Atlantic for the meeting, the enigmatic QJWIN failed to show up. After the Schweiker-Hart JFK subcommittee folded, a freedom of information lawsuit by Bernard Fensterwald would turn up one page from a CIA file about Michel Victor Mertz, the French assassin with so many parallels to QJWIN. Even that lone CIA page about Mertz came about only because of an order by Watergate Judge John Sirica. When Fensterwald's client Gary Shaw tried to get photos of Mertz from William Attwood's *Newsday* team, the newspaper found their one grainy photo of Mertz was no longer in the file.[15]

The CIA had used its considerable media assets and savvy, as well as David Atlee Phillips and his group, to counterattack Church and Congress. They got the ammunition they needed to eventually end Church's investigation when, on December 23, 1975, Greek rebels murdered Richard Welch, the CIA's Station Chief in Athens. The Ford administration, backed by CIA boosters in the press and Congress, claimed that leaks in the media had caused Welch's death. The charge was false, since Welch had been publicly identified as a CIA agent since 1969 and made no attempt to hide his home address—even though many Greeks were angry over US support for the brutal dictatorship that had ruled their country in the late 1960s and early 1970s. Though nothing in the Church

Hearings had prompted Welch's murder, a masterful spin campaign gave the opposite impression and helped to end the Church Committee's investigations in a matter of months.[16]

Before the Committee ended, David Atlee Phillips himself became embroiled in the Church investigations. In July 1974, Antonio Veciana had been arrested in a drug bust, telling an associate that "the CIA framed him because he wanted to go ahead with another attempt to kill Castro." Veciana was convicted and sentenced to twenty-seven months at the federal prison in Atlanta.[17] After his release, on March 2, 1976, Veciana told Gaeton Fonzi about his control agent, who used the name Maurice Bishop. It was Senator Schweiker himself who said on April 11, 1976, that a police artist drawing of Bishop—based on Veciana's description—looked like a CIA agent who'd testified to his committee: David Atlee Phillips.[18]

That began a cat-and-mouse game between Phillips and Fonzi that would last for three years, first in the Senate investigation and then in a new House committee. Veciana was always reluctant to definitively identify Phillips as Bishop. Phillips would dissemble and even lie in his sworn testimony to Congress, but to the frustration of Fonzi and other staff members, no perjury charges resulted.[19]

William Harvey also tried to obscure vital information in 1976, when he was working as an editor for publisher Bobbs Merrill, a subsidiary of ITT. That year, Bobbs Merrill was readying for publication a book by former Army Ranger Bradley Ayers, detailing his work with the CIA in south Florida in 1963 and 1964. Not bound by the usual strict CIA secrecy oath, Ayers's book mentioned Harvey (renamed "Harold"), Shackley, David Morales ("Dave"), and Johnny Rosselli. Using Rosselli's real name, Ayers described the mobster's exile sniper team and friendship with Morales. Later, Ayers said that someone at the publisher altered his book and he hadn't known that Harvey worked there.[20] In June 1976, the overweight, hard-drinking William Harvey died of heart problems.

On April 23, 1976, Johnny Rosselli testified to Richard Schweiker's small JFK subcommittee. When pressed, Rosselli admitted he had no facts to substantiate his Castro retaliation theory of JFK's murder. Though the Final Report of the main Church Committee was published that day, Schweiker was determined to continue his investigation, using Fonzi and his own office staff. Meanwhile, the Senate Intelligence Committee learned of other important information, such as the Cuba Contingency Plans from the fall of 1963 to deal with possible retaliation by Fidel, like the assassination of American officials. The Senate staffers had stumbled across a reference to the material in a Justice Department

file, since the CIA had not given their copies of the plans to the investigators. Tad Szulc even wrote an article about the Cuba Contingency
Plans that appeared in the *Boston Globe* and the *New Republic*, revealing
that "Robert Kennedy, the CIA and the FBI decided to keep from the
Warren Commission the fact that a special group had been set up to
protect American leaders from possible Cuban assassination plots." But
no other journalist followed up Szulc's work (until we did in the 1990s),
and it was dangerous for Szulc to write more without exposing his own
work on AMTRUNK.[21]

When the summer of 1976 began, the press suddenly appeared tired
of investigations of the CIA. Or perhaps they had gotten the message
that the Ford administration and conservative members of Congress
wanted such things stopped—and if Ford won the election, the reporters
could be frozen out for four years.

Senator Schweiker was determined to forge ahead and issued his JFK
subcommittee's report on June 23, 1976. Though largely ignored by the
news media, it was filled with important information, despite all the
material withheld by the CIA, FBI, and military intelligence. Schweiker
also planned to recall Johnny Rosselli for more testimony.

Facing more interrogation, from increasingly informed Senate staffers,
Rosselli would have consulted with his attorney, Tom Wadden. Rosselli
had another problem: During intense questioning, he had reportedly
given Congressional investigators Santo Trafficante's name. Rosselli
had to explain to Wadden why that, or further testimony, was so dangerous. According to historian Richard Mahoney, Rosselli confessed to
Wadden his "role in plotting to kill the President"—something Wadden
revealed only much later, to Bobby's former Mafia prosecutor William
Hundley.[22]

On July 16, 1976, Rosselli had dinner with Trafficante and told the
godfather he'd had to mention his name during his most recent testimony. Twelve days later, on July 28, 1976, Rosselli was seen alive in
public for the last time. When it was clear Rosselli was missing, Senator
Schweiker asked the FBI to look into the matter.[23]

On August 7, 1976, Rosselli's body turned up in a fifty-five-gallon oil
drum, found in a canal near Miami. Rosselli had been shot and stabbed,
had his legs cut off, and been stuffed in the oil drum. It was shot with
holes, so it wouldn't float, then weighted with chains, but somehow it
was still discovered. The police were officially baffled, and E. Howard
Hunt suggested that Fidel had killed Rosselli. However, three of Rosselli's associates said that Trafficante had ordered the gruesome slaying.[24]

Rosselli's murder was the kind of headline news that even the most jaded or intimidated reporter couldn't ignore, especially after Jack Anderson revealed information he couldn't tell while Rosselli was alive. In his September 7, 1976, column, Anderson wrote that Rosselli had said those involved in the CIA-Mafia plots had killed JFK and even hinted that shots from the grassy knoll were part of that plan.[25]

While the Senate Church Committee hearings had overshadowed those in the House, on September 17, 1976, amid the furor created by Rosselli's murder, Congress seized the initiative and created the House Select Committee on Assassinations. The HSCA was designed to investigate the assassinations of both JFK and Martin Luther King, the latter because of the FBI problems relating to King uncovered by the Church Committee. Unfortunately, the investigation's first nine months would be hampered by problems settling on a chief counsel to direct the probe and determining which member of Congress would chair the Committee. It would take until the following summer for the House Select Committee (HSCA) to finally have its permanent general counsel, G. Robert Blakey, creator of the RICO racketeering law and a former Mafia prosecutor for Bobby Kennedy.

While the public read stories about Rosselli's murder and the resulting Congressional investigation, other important stories played out in private. CIA Director Bush and the Ford administration, including his Chief of Staff Dick Cheney and Secretary of Defense Donald Rumsfeld, withheld crucial information from all of the investigating committees. Ford's reelection in 1976—and the careers of Bush, Cheney, and Rumsfeld—depended on nothing coming out that would make it look like Ford had been duped while on the Warren Commission or that he had been part of a deliberate cover-up. The CIA had so far revealed to the Church Committee only limited parts of AMTRUNK and the Cubela and CIA-Mafia plots, and nothing about the JFK-Almeida coup plan and AMWORLD.[26]

When the Miami police asked the CIA for information to help in their investigation of Rosselli's murder, the Agency was less than helpful. An internal memo shows the Miami Police had two pages of questions, including a request for the identity and whereabouts of a Cuban exile, code-named "B-1" in the Church Report, who had been involved with Rolando Cubela.[27]

On August 25, 1976, the Deputy Inspector General wrote to the Deputy Director of the CIA about the Miami police request. The Deputy IG said that "Artime and his group were supported by the CIA." Only because it was an internal communication not meant to ever be seen by outside eyes, the memo admitted that Artime "was used by the Mafia in the Castro operation. This information should not be released." Since the public knew that Rosselli had been the main Mafia figure "in the Castro operation," the CIA was refusing to provide information directly related to the Miami Police investigation of Rosselli's murder. The Artime-Mafia CIA memo was withheld from all Congressional investigations, until we revealed it in 2005's *Ultimate Sacrifice* and told a Congressional committee about it the following year.[28]

By the time the information in the memo left the office of CIA Director Bush (as part of a memo for US Attorney General Edward Levi), the sensitive portion about Artime and the CIA-Mafia plots had been deleted. Bush also made it clear to the Attorney General that he was reluctant to help the police with Rosselli's murder, claiming it was because of the CIA's "constraints on assistance to local law-enforcement authorities . . . and the [CIA's] proscriptions on police functions." The police were asking for basic information that Bush refused to provide, such as the name of the head of the CIA's Miami station in 1963. That was Ted Shackley, then a high CIA official working for Bush, who thus refused to give Shackley's name to the police.[29]

Former and current CIA exile Cubans were linked to two terrorist bombings that also triggered further cover-ups. On July 21, 1976, former Chilean Ambassador Orlando Letelier and his American coworker, Ronni Moffit, were killed by a car bomb in Washington, D.C. Numerous accounts linked several CIA assets to the murders, but often overlooked is information from Dade County officials which said that "at the time of the investigation, authorities believed that [Felipe] Rivero had planned Letelier's assassination in conjunction with Augusto Pinochet's security agents. Rivero was never charged or prosecuted due to a lack of evidence."[30] On October 6, 1976, a Cubana airliner carrying 73 people was blown up by a group that included associates of Luis Posada, who was arrested eight days later for the bombing. Scholars still debate whether Posada was working—officially or unofficially—for the CIA at the time. However, by the mid-1980s, Posada would be free and working with several AMWORLD veterans like "Chi Chi" Quintero in Iran-Contra.[31]

Jimmy Carter was elected president in November 1976, and though Bush wanted to remain as CIA Director, Carter appointed Admiral Stansfield Turner to replace Bush. Turner began a dramatic shake-up in the Agency by firing eight hundred people—though no foreign agents—from covert operations.[32] The reorganization left some longtime CIA personnel worried, and former CIA assets like Santo Trafficante must have been afraid of what old secrets the new CIA might give to Congress. Trafficante had been interviewed once by the Church Committee, with no record being kept at Trafficante's request, but he couldn't count on such consideration in the future.

Hit man Charles Nicoletti, an associate of Johnny Rosselli, was slated to talk to Congressional investigators. But on March 29, 1977, Nicoletti was "the victim of a mob assassination" in Chicago, according to the *Miami Herald*. They said Nicoletti "was pulled from his burning car . . . after being shot three times in the back of the head at point-blank range." The article mentioned that Nicoletti had once "been responsible for drawing up CIA-ordered plans for the assassination of Castro . . . in October, 1963."[33]

Gaeton Fonzi had gone to work for the new HSCA, and the day Nicoletti died, Fonzi was in south Florida to interview George DeMohrenschildt, the sophisticated White Russian who had been Oswald's best friend for a time. DeMohrenschildt had known not only Jackie Kennedy but also George H. W. Bush. Even as Fonzi spoke to DeMohrenschildt's daughter about arranging the interview, DeMohrenschildt was meeting with a writer for the *Wall Street Journal*, Edward Epstein, telling Epstein he'd told Dallas CIA official J. Walton Moore about Oswald's activities. That evening, before Fonzi could meet him, DeMohrenschildt committed suicide by putting the barrel of a .20-gauge shotgun in his mouth and pulling the trigger.[34]

About a week later, Fonzi had also planned to set up an interview in Miami with Carlos Prio, the mutual associate of Trafficante and Nixon. On April 5, 1977, before Fonzi could interview him, Prio committed suicide by shooting himself in the heart with a .38 pistol.[35]

That fall, Fonzi tried to arrange an interview with Manuel Artime after being tipped that Artime had "guilty knowledge" of JFK's assassination. Fonzi's partner talked to Artime in early November about arranging an interview, but Artime entered the hospital the following week, was diagnosed with cancer, and died two weeks later, on November 18, 1977, at only forty-five. Artime had become a player in Miami's exploding drug market, and his young accounting protégé, Milian Rodriguez, would become a major cocaine dealer in the Iran-Contra operation, which also involved Artime's former AMWORLD lieutenant "Chi Chi" Quintero.[36]

The following spring, Fonzi tried to track down David Morales, though the CIA made it hard for the HSCA to even determine Morales's CIA position in 1963. Two weeks after David Atlee Phillips and Antonio Veciana testified to the HSCA in executive session—and after Morales was added to the list of CIA personnel the HSCA wanted to interview—Morales died, apparently of natural causes, on May 8, 1978.[37]

In less than three years, Congressional investigations had been thwarted by the deaths of nine actual or potential witnesses, from the sensational murders of Rosselli, Giancana, Hoffa, Masferrer, and Nicoletti to the unexpected deaths of Morales, Artime, DeMohrenschildt, and Prio. Yet even after the headlines Harry Williams had seen, and the sometimes violent deaths of some he had known, he still volunteered to talk to the HSCA. Richard E. Sprague conveyed Harry's offer, but he never heard back from the HSCA.

While work proceeded on the JFK side of the HSCA, Fonzi noted that the "Martin Luther King [group] had a parallel staff of deputies, counsels, investigators and researchers."[38] However, James Earl Ray's attempt to retract his guilty plea and appeal his life sentence complicated matters, making Ray unwilling to cooperate in certain ways, such as by refusing to waive his attorney-client privilege with his former lawyer, J. B. Stoner.

On June 10, 1977, two months after Carlos Marcello's name was first connected to JFK's murder in the HSCA investigation, James Earl Ray and six fellow inmates escaped from the Brushy Mountain State Prison. Two days later, Ray was captured in a wooded area after traveling approximately eight miles. The HSCA later learned that as recently as 1975, one of Ray's brothers had been given $1,000 by a criminal that Ray had known in New Orleans.[39]

The remaining problems for Fonzi, Blakey, and the rest of the HSCA centered on the CIA and the Mafia. Richard Helms faced charges about lying to Congress that needed to be resolved before he could testify. After a major White House meeting about the issue in July 1977, Helms agreed to plead guilty to making a false statement to Congress and was fined $2,000 on November 4, 1977. Later that day, he went to a CIA reception where his current and former CIA colleagues donated an even larger amount. Helms was represented by Edward Bennett Williams, whose former law partner, Joseph Califano, was then Jimmy Carter's Secretary for Health, Education, and Welfare. Califano's former boss in

1963, Cyrus Vance—a key strategist for the JFK-Almeida coup plan—was Carter's Secretary of State.[40]

Trafficante had primarily pleaded the Fifth in his first HSCA appearance on March 16, 1977, but Blakey arranged to grant him and Marcello limited immunity, in an effort to get them to talk. The situation was complicated because Trafficante was under indictment for charges relating to the FBI's BRILAB investigation, while Marcello didn't realize his new business partner Joe Hauser would soon be a wired FBI informant for that operation. Nonetheless, Trafficante testified on November 14, 1977, and September 28, 1978, and Marcello testified on January 1978. Both gave cautious statements and denied having anything to do with JFK's murder.

The same month that Trafficante testified for the last time, author Dan Moldea had a revealing exchange with Frank Ragano, Trafficante's former attorney who had gone through a very acrimonious split with the Tampa godfather. Possibly as part of a Teamster effort to suppress Moldea's book, Ragano had offered Moldea a large sum for the rights to it. As part of their back and forth in September 1978, Moldea had his attorney ask Ragano about his book's theory that Hoffa, Marcello, and Trafficante were behind JFK's murder. Moldea was pleased to learn "that Ragano had corroborated my conclusions."[41]

In his book about the HSCA, *The Last Investigation*, Fonzi wrote about the constant struggle with the CIA for documents and access to personnel. Blakey tried to strike a middle ground, though he learned only in the 1990s about a 1978 incident with the CIA that made him realize how the Agency had deceived the HSCA.

Fonzi and his fellow investigators were interested in the DRE, a CIA-backed exile group Oswald contacted in August of 1963. While E. Howard Hunt had testified that David Atlee Phillips ran the DRE for the CIA, another agent handled their day-to-day supervision. The HSCA wanted to talk to that agent, but the CIA claimed they couldn't locate him. Around the same time, to help smooth out problems between the CIA and HSCA, the CIA called out of retirement Agent George Joannides, assigning him to be the CIA's liaison to the HSCA staff.[42]

What the CIA didn't tell the HSCA—and no one learned until Jefferson Morley discovered it in the 1990s—was that George Joannides had been the CIA official in charge of the DRE in 1963. Joannides started working for the HSCA in June 1978, but he never told the HSCA about his work with the DRE—or that he was the man they'd wanted to interview.

In 1981 the CIA gave Joannides a medal, but according to David Talbot, "today Blakey says that if he had known Joannides' background, he would have immediately relieved him of his duties and made him 'a witness under oath.'"[43]

What possible justification could Joannides and his superiors have used, to get authorization for such deceit from anyone in the CIA's chain of command? There is no reason to think the approval went as high as Director Stansfield Turner, since many longtime CIA officials regarded him as an outsider. On the other hand, the ambitious Ted Shackley had both the capability and the personal incentive to stifle the HSCA investigation. Shackley was the CIA's Deputy Director of Operations in 1978—comparable to Helms's 1963 position of Deputy Director for Plans—and Joannides had worked with the DRE while based at Shackley's JMWAVE CIA station in Miami in 1963.

Shackley might have had the same thin reed of a national security justification (or rationalization) Helms had used at times for his cover-ups, because of an unusual meeting at the UN just weeks before Joannides was recalled from retirement. America's UN Ambassador at the time, Andrew Young, reported to Secretary of State Cyrus Vance. On April 22, 1978, Young met at the UN with Commander Juan Almeida. Given the international publicity of the HSCA investigation, which often included coverage of the CIA's attempts to eliminate Fidel Castro, it's likely that Almeida wanted some assurance from Vance that his name would not be exposed by the investigation.

If some US official had asked the CIA to try to protect Almeida, it's not hard to image Ted Shackley taking that opportunity to also protect himself and his associates by having Joannides assigned as the CIA's liaison to the HSCA. Around the time of the Almeida UN meeting, three veterans of the JFK-Almeida coup plan—Varona, Phillips, and Morales—had been interviewed or were slated for an interview, and the HSCA was making constant requests for the files of Artime and others associated with AMWORLD. Joannides would have been the ideal candidate to make sure the HSCA didn't get too close to Almeida, while also protecting the secrets Shackley shared with Helms.

Other battles with the CIA drained the HSCA staff's time and energy, from their Mexico City investigation to Helms's testimony. Many critics charged that Helms had gotten off too easily for lying to Congress, and if he were caught lying under oath again, the Carter administration would have to punish him more harshly. A close reading of Helms's August 9, 1978, HSCA testimony shows that he was fairly candid about some things, saying that in 1963 "the US Government had a policy for many months of trying to mount a coup against Fidel Castro [and] these operations were known to the Attorney General of the United States [and to] the President of the United States [and] all kinds of people high up in the government." Helms added that "if you go through the records of those years, you will find the whole US government was behind this one." Helms knew that while the CIA was withholding much from the Committee, Cyrus Vance and the US military were also not being forthcoming about the 1963 plans. However, Helms also comes across in his testimony as incredibly arrogant, not willing to admit well-documented facts such as the assassination aspects of his Cubela operation.[44]

In addition to the CIA and US military, other agencies like the Secret Service and the FBI were keeping crucial facts from the HSCA, including everything about the Tampa attempt against JFK and most information about the Chicago attempt. The CIA stonewalled HSCA attempts to learn more about Gilberto Lopez, and the Defense Department did likewise regarding the Marine Intelligence investigation of Oswald, until the Committee's time had run out.[45]

Regarding Martin Luther King, the HSCA "concluded that there was a likelihood of conspiracy in the assassination of Dr. King" and that "the expectation of financial gain was Ray's primary motivation." The HSCA reached that conclusion despite investigating Joseph Milteer only for JFK's murder, not Dr. King's, and paying little attention to Marcello for King's assassination. That's because the FBI had apparently withheld the information given to the Justice Department about Carlos Marcello and the Mafia's brokering of the contract to assassinate Dr. King for a small clique of white racists.

As the House Select Committee on Assassinations rushed to finish its work on the JFK assassination, acoustic tests indicated there had been at least one shot from the grassy knoll. But those findings have been the source of much debate ever since, and we have not factored them into any of our findings. When the HSCA submitted its Final Report on March 29, 1979, its ultimate conclusion about JFK's murder was that it was likely a conspiracy, involving at least one shot from the grassy knoll. In addition:

> The Committee found that Trafficante, like Marcello, had the motive, means, and opportunity to assassinate President Kennedy.[46]

For both Marcello and Trafficante, the committee "was unable to establish direct evidence of Marcello's complicity." It could just as well have added "because of all the material the CIA, FBI, and other agencies withheld." The HSCA also recommended that the Justice Department pursue the matter further.[47] Within six years, the FBI would obtain a clear confession by Marcello to JFK's assassination—only to suppress it, until its full publication for the first time in *Legacy of Secrecy*.

Chapter Sixty-five

By 1980, as if exhausted by the five investigating committees that began with Watergate and ended with the House Select Committee on Assassinations, the government and the press had lost interest in the assassinations of JFK, Bobby, and Dr. King. This dormant phase would last for most of the decade. The Justice Department wasn't acting on the HSCA's request to follow-up on its leads, but the FBI's undercover BRILAB operation targeting Carlos Marcello still simmered just below the surface.

Before BRILAB erupted in the press, several former government investigators tried to sustain interest in the assassinations, in effect continuing the quest Bobby Kennedy had begun soon after his brother's murder. Former HSCA chief counsel G. Robert Blakey wrote an account of his inquiry, *The Plot to Kill the President*, that implicated Marcello and Trafficante more strongly than the HSCA's carefully worded conclusions had. His former investigator Gaeton Fonzi had been frustrated by CIA stonewalling and the lack of attention that Phillips, Veciana, and Odio received in the HSCA's Final Report—so he wrote a detailed article about it for the *Washingtonian* magazine, which he would later expand into a book, *The Last Investigation*. FBI veteran William Turner had seen publicity for his 1978 book *The Assassination of Robert F. Kennedy* apparently stymied by its publisher, but in 1981 he finally used portions of his 1973 interview with Harry Williams in his next book, *The Fish Is Red*.

Turner's *The Fish Is Red* included new information about JFK's assassination but was devoted primarily to offering the first book-length account of the US's secret war with Fidel Castro—a battle that was entering a new phase. After Ronald Reagan was elected president in November 1980, the undercover war between the US and Cuba began heating up again, with a new focus on Central America as the surrogate battleground. As the *San Francisco Chronicle* reported, Reagan's new Secretary of State, Alexander Haig, "regarded [the Sandinistas in Nicaragua and the rebels in El Salvador] as mere tentacles. He sought to go after the body of the octopus—Castro's Cuba. Proposals for forcing confrontation with Castro were repeatedly advanced by Haig."[1] As a result, half a dozen veterans of 1963 operations like AMWORLD—including Rafael "Chi Chi" Quintero and Luis Posada—became involved in US covert operations in Central America that would result in the Iran-Contra scandal. Commander Juan Almeida remained unexposed and high-ranking in the Cuban government—and potentially useful to the US at some point, if Castro should die, become ill, or be deposed. Almeida's family outside Cuba continued to receive covert support from the CIA.

On June 4, 1981, four black prisoners attacked and knifed James Earl Ray almost two dozen times, but the incident was little-noted in the press and created no new interest in Dr. King's assassination. Ray recovered and continued serving his life sentence. Sirhan Sirhan was also doing life, his death sentence having been thrown out with all the others in California because of an earlier Supreme Court decision.

By 1981, Carlos Marcello was feeling the full force of the FBI's BRILAB sting, which had grown out of the Watergate-era prosecution of Nixon's former attorney general Richard Kleindienst. Facing the biggest legal battle of his life, Marcello was under indictment in Louisiana for trying to bribe state officials in a multimillion-dollar insurance scam. In Los Angeles, he'd been indicted for trying to bribe a federal judge. Even worse, much of the evidence was in the godfather's own words, recorded by a bug and phone taps the FBI had finally placed in Marcello's office at the Town and Country Motel. They were augmented by secret recordings made by convicted insurance swindler Joe Hauser, who wore a wire for the FBI in hopes of securing an early release. He was aided by two undercover FBI agents, who pretended to be crooked businessmen in an elaborate operation that included a posh office for a phony company.[2]

In Miami, Santo Trafficante was under indictment for a $1 million fraud scheme involving a labor union. Both Trafficante and Marcello were also hit with RICO racketeering charges, using the statute that G. Robert Blakey had helped create. Trafficante would avoid conviction, but Marcello's luck had finally run out.

Marcello's BRILAB battles played out prominently in the national press, but the articles rarely mentioned his name in conjunction with JFK's assassination. The 1,200 hours of BRILAB recordings, along with unrecorded information from Hauser, contained only tantalizing hints about Marcello and JFK. They weren't mentioned in the press and were barred from the trial, at Marcello's lawyers' request, so they wouldn't prejudice the jury. Still, the jury was able to hear hours of Marcello discussing the blatant corruption and crimes he had been committing for years. Marcello was convicted in Louisiana on August 4, 1981, and in Los Angeles on December 11, 1981. The following year, he was sentenced to seven years for the Louisiana counts and ten years for the Los Angeles counts. His powerful attorneys did everything they could, but on April 15, 1983, Marcello's BRILAB appeal was denied and he was ordered to begin serving his sentence immediately.[3]

At age seventy-three, Marcello faced seventeen years in prison. He was initially sent to familiar territory: the US Medical Center for Federal Prisoners, in Springfield, Missouri, where Marcello had spent six months a decade earlier. The prison and its parklike grounds were designated as level one, meaning it was one of the least secure and most comfortable federal prisons. But after a year, Marcello was transferred to the maximum-security federal prison in Texarkana, Texas, an imposing level-three facility where most prisoners had few comforts. However, Marcello was not like most other prisoners, and he soon found ways to receive extraordinary privileges.

During Marcello's stay at Texarkana, he became the target of yet another undercover FBI sting operation: CAMTEX (for "Carlos Marcello, Texas"). As revealed for the first time in this book, CAMTEX resulted in Carlos Marcello's clear confession to having ordered JFK's assassination. In Chapter 3, we quoted Marcello's confession, made in front of two witnesses, as reported by the FBI's CAMTEX informant, Jack Ronald Van Laningham, who shared Marcello's prison cell in Texarkana. The following provides dramatic new information—quoted from declassified FBI files at the National Archives—about Marcello's admission, Van Laningham, and how the FBI recorded hundreds of hours of secret tapes of Marcello discussing his crimes.

The fifty-six-year-old Jack Van Laningham arrived in Texarkana from Tampa to serve an eight-year sentence for robbing a bank. (Not a career criminal, a remorseful Van Laningham had turned himself in to the Tampa FBI.) In a memo to the FBI, he wrote about his "crowded dorm with a hundred other guys . . . a TV lounge, and at the end of the hall lots of little rooms. I thought to myself, *If you behave you get one of the little rooms.*" Then "I saw a little man that looked like he just stepped out of a band box." The little man's "clothes were new and pressed and his shoes were shined. This guy was really sharp . . . a guy standing near me said, 'That's Carlos Marcello. He runs this place; a good friend to have.' It did not take long to see the guy was right. Marcello went where he pleased and did what he wanted. He had one of the little rooms, so I guess he was big time."[4]

Van Laningham saw that some "of the inmates hung around [Marcello], trying to get his attention." Marcello "was on the phone all the time," and Van Laningham thought "he must have a lot of friends to call." Several days later, Van Laningham sat down beside Marcello "in the lounge. He was reading a paper and did not notice me. When he finished reading he said, 'Hello, I'm Carlos Marcello.' I shook his hand and told him my name . . . he asked me if I had heard any news about" a governor who was being prosecuted for corruption. Marcello "got up to leave and said, 'If you need anything look me up.'"

That fateful meeting took place in March 1985, and Van Laningham wrote that as time passed, he and Marcello "became friends, in a strange sort of way . . . since I was older than most of the inmates, I guess he was drawn to me." At seventy-five, Marcello was the oldest inmate and Van Laningham the second-oldest; the other Texarkana inmates were all much younger.

Even after Marcello's imprisonment, his criminal empire continued, albeit at a reduced size. Marcello's biographer John Davis says that Marcello's "most trusted brother, Joe, was supposed to have taken over as de facto boss of what was left of the Marcello organization." The main goal of FBI agent Thomas Kimmel, who created and supervised the CAMTEX operation, was to find out how Carlos Marcello controlled his criminal organization from prison.

Kimmel arranged for veteran FBI agent Tom Kirk, nearing retirement, to work undercover on this one last assignment. Kirk would go to the prison on visiting day and appear to be Van Laningham's best friend. Kirk's "cover identity" would be that of a shady businessman hunting for opportunities, even if they were illegal. A local Texas FBI man, whom Kimmel described as "a terrific agent," would complete the team, working with Kirk, Kimmel, and Van Laningham. FBI headquarters in Washington authorized the CAMTEX operation against Marcello, since it echoed the BRILAB sting that had sent him to prison in the first place.

Despite Van Laningham's worries, the first few weeks went smoothly, and one visiting day Van Laningham casually introduced Kirk to Carlos Marcello. Van Laningham said, "Kirk thought that it was great that he could meet Marcello, but it was easy, as Marcello always wanted to be in the limelight."[5] They gradually began to draw Marcello into a series of illegal business schemes, detailed at length in the FBI files. But none worked, for various reasons, not the least of which was Marcello's caution.

So, Van Laningham explained, "the FBI asked the (Prison's) Unit Manager to move me into Marcello's room with him. Some days later this was accomplished."[6] Marcello's former roommate was moved to another cell, and now the FBI had installed Van Laningham in Marcello's private cell. This was an unparalleled opportunity for the FBI and the Justice Department, so it's not surprising that Van Laningham would soon be told that reports of his work were reaching even US Attorney General Edwin Meese.

After spending time as Marcello's roommate, Van Laningham had heard enough from the godfather to know that "the only thing Marcello was really interested in was getting out of prison. He had a standing offer with any attorney of a million dollars if they could get him released from prison." That knowledge gave the FBI a new goal for its sting, and Van Laningham was soon telling Marcello that his "best friend" (Kirk) knew someone in the Bureau of Prisons who could arrange a transfer to a more comfortable prison—for the right price.

After Van Laningham gave the FBI important information from Marcello about the trial of a governor, Agent Kirk told Van Laningham "he was going to report to his boss and try for a wiretap of the prison."[7] Van Laningham said, "Two weeks later, Kirk came to see me. He said, 'Well, a judge is going to give us a wiretap on this evidence.'"

Kirk told Van Laningham that "the Unit phone in the hall would be bugged and that I would have a bug in the room that I shared with Marcello. I was told to buy a Panasonic radio in the (prison) store. I bought the radio and [the Unit Manager] came to the room and said that he would have to take the radio away to see if it was legal for me to have. I called Kirk and he told me that the bug was being installed in the radio and it would be returned when they were finished. On the 17th of September," the Unit Manager "brought the radio back and told me that I could have it."

Once Van Laningham was alone with the specially modified transistor radio, he "thought to myself here I am in this little room with the head of the Mafia from New Orleans, with a radio with a bug inside. I was really scared. If I was found out, I was dead."[8]

Internal FBI memos, Kimmel, and other FBI sources all confirm Van Laningham's account of the dangerous bugging operation. A "Priority" memo sent from the Dallas FBI office to the Director of the FBI confirms that Van Laningham "was roommate of New Orleans organized crime boss Carlos Marcello at Federal Correctional Institution, Texarkana, Texas," and "was instrumental in furnishing probable cause to initiate Title III coverage of Marcello and prison telephone." The memo also confirms that Van Laningham "successfully introduced FBI undercover agent to Marcello."[9]

Kimmel verified that the "Title III" coverage approved by the judge covered both the special transistor radio and the phone tap. Van Laningham says the bugging operation against Marcello yielded "hundreds of hours" of tapes, something Kimmel also confirms. However, Kimmel told us that the FBI listened to every tape, but would transcribe a particular tape only if Marcello mentioned something of interest.

Van Laningham doesn't mention the JFK-Almeida coup plan in his notes in the FBI files, but he does say that Marcello "was always talking about . . . things I knew nothing about." It would be interesting to see if there are any comments about Cuba, Martin Luther King's assassination, or Joseph Milteer on the hundreds of hours of secret tapes Van Laningham made of Marcello, but they have never been released.

As Marcello and Van Laningham gradually grew closer over the following months, Marcello shared more of his background and experiences. By December 1985, after a Marcello family member had paid a bribe to soon move the godfather to a much better prison, Marcello had come to view Van Laningham as a trusted friend.[10]

"The last month that we spent together—December—we talked a lot," Van Laningham told the FBI. "Marcello seemed to be very upset about the Kennedys. This is all he would talk about. I was so tired of hearing about his so-called kidnapping that it played on my nerves. That is all he talked about, no matter where we were."

We noted earlier that Marcello had told Van Laningham and another trusted inmate from New Orleans about "his meeting with Oswald," and that Marcello "had been introduced to Oswald by a man named Ferris [Ferrie], Marcello's pilot." Marcello had also told them "about Jack Ruby, [whom] Marcello had . . . set . . . up in the bar business" in Dallas, and that "Ruby would come to Churchill Farms to report to Marcello."[11]

On December 15, 1985, Van Laningham and Marcello "were sitting outside in the patio" of the prison yard. Referring to the same trusted individual who had worked for Marcello's brother and had heard Marcello talk about Oswald and Ruby, Van Laningham wrote, "My friend came over to join us." (The friend/witness is named in one of the FBI files.) Marcello

LEGACY OF SECRECY

then embarked upon a blazing tirade about the Kennedys. After Marcello blurted out his admission of having JFK killed, he "stopped, realizing what he had said, and turned and walked over to some other inmates. My friend looked at me, and said, 'I don't know about you, but I did not hear anything.' My friend left, and I could see that he was upset. I was in shock. I never believed that the little man would admit that he had conspired to kill the President. We went back to our room and nothing else was said" about the matter, that day or the next.[12]

Marcello's confession quoted earlier in the book came from a detailed account in FBI files, written three years later by Van Laningham for the head of the San Francisco FBI. Yet it is remarkably consistent with the following internal FBI memo, written shortly after Marcello blurted out his confession. This FBI memo names Van Laningham but cautions that his name shouldn't be "disclosed in a report or otherwise unless [he has] to be a witness in a trial or hearing." It confirms that Van Laningham "has provided reliable information in the past." It goes on to say, "On December 15, 1985, he was in the company of Carlos Marcello and another inmate at the Federal Correctional Institute, Texarkana, Texas, in the courtyard engaged in conversation. Carlos Marcello discussed his intense dislike of former President John Kennedy as he often did. Unlike other such tirades against Kennedy, however, on this occasion Carlos Marcello said, referring to President Kennedy, 'Yeah, I had the son of a bitch killed. I'm glad I did. I'm sorry I couldn't have done it myself.'"[13]

The consistency of the wording, date, witness, and circumstances across three years give Van Laningham's statement a high degree of credibility. After telling the FBI about Marcello's admission, Van Laningham was willing to take a lie-detector test about it. Van Laningham had nothing to gain by making up such an admission, since he would antagonize the very FBI agents he was risking his life to help if he failed the test, or the witness denied it. Also, Van Laningham didn't try to leverage Marcello's JFK admission for anything else. Finally, by reporting Marcello's JFK confession to the FBI, Van Laningham increased the chance that Marcello would take potentially lethal action against him, if the godfather ever found out.

Given the trust that had developed between Marcello and Van Laningham—to the extent that Marcello had his family bribe Van Laningham's "best friend" (Kirk) to move Marcello to a more comfortable prison—it's not unreasonable that while raging against the Kennedys, Marcello would have impulsively blurted out the confession as he did such remarks. By that time, Van Laningham had become Marcello's trusted prison confidante. However, two days later, when Marcello was in a calmer frame of mind, he realized he needed to do something about his JFK revelation. After all, Marcello had for years kept a sign in his office that read: THREE CAN KEEP A SECRET, IF TWO ARE DEAD.

Van Laningham says that "on the 17th of December I was packing, to leave the next day" for the level-two Seagoville Prison near Dallas, where Marcello would soon follow. "Marcello was out making his calls. He came back into the room, and told me to sit down, that he had something to talk to me about. He said we have become good friends and I want to tell you a story; he was dead serious and I was scared. He said a Priest came to visit him from Italy, years before. The Priest was old Mafia. 'My son,' he said, 'if your enemies get in your way, you bury them in the ground, the grass grows over them, and you go on about your business.' He was telling me that if I crossed him, the grass would grow over me, as I would be dead. My god, if he had murdered the President, he would have no trouble with me."

While Agent Kimmel's report of Marcello's confession made its way up through official channels, he and the others continued with their sting against Marcello. A Marcello family member was to pay another bribe to have Marcello moved from Seagoville to the federal facility at Fort Worth, which John H. Davis described as "the paradise of the federal prison system, [a] minimum-security level-one facility" that even boasted a swimming pool and tennis courts.[14]

After the godfather was moved to Fort Worth, a member of Marcello's family was to pay Kirk a final bribe, for Marcello's early release from prison. Van Laningham said that "Marcello wanted out so bad he believed all that I told him." Marcello was grateful for what Van Laningham was doing, and told him "that after we were out, he was going to take me into his organization. He said that he would set me up in off-track betting in Georgia."

Marcello continued complaining to Van Laningham about the "running of his organization," which had been left in the care of his brother Joseph Marcello. Joseph simply lacked the ability to run such a huge criminal empire, though he enjoyed the increased prestige and money, now that the godfather was in prison. Marcello told Van Laningham "he would move me up [in his organization] and that I would be running things, as he trusted me. Here this man was offering me the world, and I was working with the Feds."

Van Laningham was soon transferred to a federal prison in California, where he began helping the San Francisco FBI on the important Ochoa drug case. Marcello's family member paid the bribe, and Marcello was moved to the Fort Worth facility. Now, only one step in the CAMTEX sting remained: persuading Marcello's family to pay the final bribe to Kirk, which was supposed to get Marcello released from prison. As weeks passed, Van Laningham waited anxiously for word that the bribe had been paid—and that Van Laningham was finally going to get his reward of freedom. But there was a problem.

Van Laningham was crushed to learn that while Marcello's family "paid the bribe money for the move, [they] would not pay the money to Kirk to get Marcello released." The reason was that a key Marcello family member "did not want [Carlos] out of prison, as he would have gotten kicked out of his soft job . . . he would have become a nothing." Marcello had railed to Van Laningham months earlier about this family member, saying he "was a disappointment to him."

Still, two bribes for the prison moves had been paid, so Van Laningham thought the FBI would soon file charges about those crimes. When time passed and nothing happened, Van Laningham began to think "The FBI did not seem to care what [Marcello] had done or what he was doing. I was risking my life and they were playing games."[15] Between the bribes and the other criminal activity Marcello had admitted to him and on tape, Van Laningham says Marcello and one family member "could have been convicted a dozen times with all the evidence that we put together."[16]

While Marcello sat in prison, his old partner Santo Trafficante made a startling confession to his old attorney. As Anthony Summers later reported in *Vanity Fair*, on March 13, 1987, the seventy-two-year-old Trafficante called Frank Ragano, to arrange a meeting for the following day. Trafficante had brought Ragano back into the fold, after smoothing over their acrimonious split in the 1970s, and in 1986 Ragano had helped Trafficante beat a federal RICO prosecution. But the Tampa godfather had fallen seriously ill, was facing risky surgery, and wanted to talk to his old confidant one last time.

During an hourlong drive in Ragano's car, away from family and any possibility of government bugs, Trafficante mused about his criminal career and their long association. According to Ragano, when the subject of John and Robert Kennedy came up, Trafficante said (in Italian), "Goddam Bobby. I think Carlos fucked up in getting rid of John—maybe it should have been Bobby." Ragano was stunned, but Trafficante repeated this admission, saying, "We shouldn't have killed John. We should have killed Bobby."

Four days later, Trafficante passed away. Ragano held a news conference in front of the Trafficante family home in Tampa's posh Parkland Estates. In discussing Trafficante's illness, Ragano mentioned his meeting with Trafficante four days earlier, as documented in a *Tampa Tribune* article published the following day. But Ragano wouldn't reveal Trafficante's confession to the public for almost five years, until 1992, and it wouldn't be detailed fully until his autobiography was published in 1994.

Trafficante's family remained silent when Ragano's allegation first surfaced, but in 1994 they denied Ragano's account to Anthony Summers and other journalists. They claimed Trafficante had been receiving medical treatment in Miami on March 13, and therefore couldn't have been in Tampa, where Ragano says his meeting took place. However, while medical records prove that Trafficante was in Miami receiving dialysis on March 12 and March 14, no medical records place him there on March 13. In addition, the March 18, 1987, *Tampa Tribune* article mentioning the March 13 meeting between Trafficante and Ragano is a near contemporaneous indication that some type of meeting between the two men did indeed take place. Also, as we've noted in earlier chapters, Ragano may well have played a role in a payoff for JFK's murder that he never admitted.

Just over two months after Trafficante's death, CAMTEX came to an end. By May 21, 1987, it was clear that Marcello's family was never going to pay the final bribe for Marcello's release. That night, federal marshals removed Marcello from his comfortable room at the Fort Worth prison. John H. Davis writes that Marcello was then "driven under heavily armed escort (back) to the federal prison at Texarkana."[17] Carlos Marcello had come full circle and was now back serving hard time where CAMTEX had begun.

To Marcello, his family, and his attorneys, the sudden move from level-one Fort Worth to the remote level-three Texarkana must have seemed like a nightmare. They no doubt tried to contact Kirk for an explanation, but his undercover role for CAMTEX had ended, and Agent Kimmel had left Tyler, Texas, by 1987.

In the first week of April 1988, as described in FBI files, Van Laningham "called Mr. Marcello's office," apparently to see what was happening to Marcello. But the person he spoke with "indicated to him in a very angry tone of voice that Mr. Marcello knew what he had done and of his cooperation with the FBI [and] hung up the phone" before Van Laningham could respond.[18] Van Laningham was frantic and remembered Marcello's threat, two days after his outburst about having JFK killed. Though he was halfway across the country, he knew enough about Marcello's associates and connections to realize he was in danger, especially while he remained in prison.

Fearing for his life, Van Laningham wrote the Justice Department in Washington. He listed the important information he had obtained for the FBI, including Marcello's JFK confession. Van Laningham said that "Kirk told me during the investigation that the Attorney General knew what was going on. And that I would be released when the case was over. . . . I did a good job and I put my life on the line for you."

Van Laningham also told the Justice Department, "Marcello knows all about what we did to him. He will never rest until he pays me back. . . . I also have a family to think of." He pointed out that for almost two years, "I have worked with the San Francisco FBI . . . and bad people have been put in jail. We are still working on some things that are very important. Agent [Carl] Podsiadly [said] if I am released I shall be working for him to put some drug dealers away." He pleaded with the Justice Department, saying, "You are responsible for me, I asked to be released. Given a new name and enough money to make a new start in my life after I have finished helping Agent Podsiadly." He pointed out that "a lot of mistakes have been made in the investigation of Carlos Marcello, but they were not my mistakes. . . . It has been two years [since his work against Marcello] and nothing has happened . . . why they have not been arrested?"[19]

When almost two weeks passed with no reply, Van Laningham wrote to FBI headquarters in Washington, D.C., on April 18, 1988. He told them about Marcello's discovery of his work for the FBI. He managed to persuade Agent Podsiadly, an FBI agent in San Francisco, to call one of the Texas CAMTEX agents. But the Texas agent said "he did not think that Marcello could have found out what we did to him, as all documents are sealed." Van Laningham reminded the FBI of Marcello's many "connections at Texarkana [that allowed him to] find out anything that he wants."

The frustrated Van Laningham couldn't understand why Marcello or his family had not been prosecuted, since "the Justice Department has all of the evidence that we gathered in the investigation . . . the bribe money that was paid to an undercover FBI Agent . . . all the tapes with hundreds of hours of conversations."

He reminded them about Marcello's JFK confession "that he had John Kennedy murdered," adding, "I believe that your office should make Senator Kennedy aware of this evidence." Van Laningham reiterated his willingness to "go on the stand against [Marcello and his family] any time that I was asked to do so."[20]

After Van Laningham failed to win his release at his July 6, 1988, parole hearing, he wrote an increasingly urgent series of letters to federal authorities throughout the summer of 1988. San Francisco FBI Agent Carl Podsiadly, who was receiving valuable information from Van Laningham for his case against the Colombian drug kingpin, weighed in on his behalf. Van Laningham also volunteered to take a lie-detector test about Marcello's JFK confession, as had been suggested by the Dallas FBI office.[21] Finally, Van Laningham also threatened to tell the news media about his work for the FBI against Carlos Marcello, and about the Justice Department's reluctance to use the secret tapes to prosecute Marcello or members of his family.[22]

At that very time, the FBI was becoming aware of a growing number of journalists and historians who were interested in Marcello, in advance of the upcoming twenty-fifth anniversary of JFK's assassination, in November 1988. John H. Davis had been in contact with the FBI regarding his upcoming biography of Carlos Marcello, since it featured the FBI extensively (often in an unflattering light), and he was seeking the release of FBI files and the BRILAB surveillance tapes of Marcello. Davis's book was scheduled for an early January 1989 release, just weeks after the twenty-fifth anniversary of JFK's death. The FBI would also have been concerned about a JFK special being prepared by Jack Anderson, slated to run in November 1988. A wide variety of officials and witnesses were being interviewed for the program, including Ed Becker, talking about Marcello's threat to kill JFK that had so concerned the FBI back in 1967.

Someone in Washington may have decided it was better not to add Van Laningham's explosive Marcello confession to the mix. By September 1988, Van Laningham had been given a firm release date in January 1989, ending any talk of his going to the press—and putting him beyond the reach of twenty-fifth anniversary coverage and any chance his information could be added to Davis's book or to launch its publicity.

The Informant appears to have received federal protection while he was on parole, because he was still helping FBI agent Carl Podsiadly with the case against the head of one of the world's largest drug-trafficking families. The drug kingpin was convicted in Colombia in 1991, apparently based on some information from Van Laningham. The following year, Van Laningham was released from parole, though all of his work against Marcello, and the secret Marcello tapes, would remain hidden away in FBI files. The drug kingpin was suddenly freed from his Colombia prison in 1996 without explanation—which was one reason we decided not to reveal Van Laningham's name in the first edition of *Legacy of Secrecy*.[23] (According to journalist Robert Perry, the kingpin's organization had been involved in drug trafficking linked to Iran-Contra and the CIA—at the very same time the FBI was keeping Van Laningham's Marcello information under wraps.)

Press coverage of the November 1988 twenty-fifth anniversary of JFK's assassination included several television specials, news reports, and high-profile articles that mentioned Carlos Marcello as one of several possible suspects—but none of the journalists knew the FBI was sitting on a trove of secret reports and tapes that included Marcello's confession. Because of that, some authors continued to blame JFK's murder on Castro, anti-Castro Cubans, wealthy Texas oil men, LBJ, Hoover, or the military-industrial complex, creating a confusing mix for mainstream journalists to sort through at the time.

Half a dozen television specials—involving newsmen ranging from Walter Cronkite to Geraldo Rivera—were aired around the anniversary, and several featured information about the Mafia. But the most influential would prove to be Jack Anderson's November 2, 1988, special, *American Exposé: Who Murdered JFK?* It focused extensively on Marcello, Trafficante, and especially Rosselli, though it appeared to endorse Rosselli's false claim that Castro was involved in JFK's murder. However, at the end of the program, Anderson revealed that thousands of JFK files remained unreleased, which started to generate a movement calling for their release. Because Anderson's special aired three weeks before the twenty-fifth anniversary, the movement was gaining traction by November 22, and was further fueled by the January 1989 release of John H. Davis's Marcello biography and other books. The push to release the files accelerated rapidly when Oliver Stone announced plans to dramatize the case in his film *JFK*. Essentially, the attention generated by the twenty-fifth anniversary reignited public interest in JFK's murder, eventually leading to action by Congress.

For Carlos Marcello, the most serious of the growing tide of accounts linking him to JFK's murder was the January 1989 release of John H.

Davis's *Mafia Kingfish: Carlos Marcello and the Assassination of John F. Kennedy*. Unlike most previous TV specials and books, Davis's biography presented Marcello not as one of many suspects in JFK's murder, but as *the* suspect. Even with so much material still withheld, Davis came remarkably close to outlining how Marcello had murdered JFK and used Jack Ruby in his plans.

Perhaps not surprisingly, in January 1989, Carlos Marcello had his first of several small strokes. He was transferred to Rochester, Minnesota's, Medical Center for federal prisoners.[24] There, on February 27, 1989, while Marcello was "in a semi-coherent state," an attendant overheard him say, "That Kennedy, that smiling motherfucker, we'll fix him in Dallas." The FBI didn't ask Marcello about his statement until September 6, 1989, when he denied "any involvement in the assassination of President Kennedy." Apparently, the Bureau didn't question Marcello at that time about his earlier remarks to Van Laningham.[25]

By that time, the debilitating effects of Marcello's strokes, compounded by Alzheimer's, were clear. One of the CAMTEX FBI agents told us he had not noticed any signs of the latter four years earlier, while listening to the Bureau's undercover Marcello tapes. Agent Kimmel said he thought some of Marcello's remarks in 1985 showed such indications; however, they weren't enough to stop the dangerous CAMTEX undercover operation, which continued for another six months. Marcello's statements, noted by Van Laningham in the FBI files, are usually accurate and consistent with facts not well known at the time. Van Laningham said Marcello was mentally "sharp" with no signs of Alzheimer's, and the aging godfather demonstrated a firm grasp of complex criminal matters in the 1985 accounts, prior to his 1989 strokes.[26]

Marcello was released from prison on October 6, 1989, after his BRILAB conviction was reversed unexpectedly. The government decided not to retry him, so Marcello, increasingly incapacitated from the strokes and his Alzheimer's, returned to Louisiana. By the time of his strokes, Marcello's empire had begun to break apart, and be taken over by his former associates, like Frank Joseph Caracci, because Marcello's brothers weren't capable of managing the organization.

Carlos Marcello died on March 2, 1993, at age eighty-three, after spending his final years at home, his mind ravaged increasingly by disease and his strokes. Marcello reportedly died peacefully in his sleep at his home; his death was a far cry from the bloody executions he had ordered for so many victims. His obituaries, such as the one the Associated Press ran, noted that "Marcello's name was often mentioned in connection with the assassination of [JFK], but he was never charged." It would take until 2008—and the publication of this book—for the public to know just how much information the FBI and the Justice Department had about the secret Marcello tapes, Marcello's confession to JFK's murder, and his talk of meeting with Oswald and Ruby.[27]

Around the time of Marcello's death, his name was linked publicly to Martin Luther King's assassination for the first time by Lloyd Jowers, an associate of Frank C. Liberto. Jowers ran a shop in Memphis across from the Lorraine Motel and below Ray's rooming house, but his stories often shifted and evolved over time. James Earl Ray died in prison in 1998, maintaining his innocence, and his belief in Raoul, until the end. In 1999, a civil trial jury in Memphis found in favor of the King family and decided that Jowers had been part of a Marcello-backed conspiracy. However, the following year, a Justice Department report on the case debunked many of Jowers' and his associates' claims. But the Department's report failed to mention information in its own files linking Marcello to the brokering of a hit contract on King for a small group of white racists—something that had not surfaced in the 1999 trial or in earlier Congressional investigations, nor in official efforts to declassify JFK files in the 1990s. At that time, Joseph Milteer had not been linked to either Marcello or to King's murder in Memphis, so he was not mentioned in the Justice Department's report.

Carlos Marcello's self-professed role with Trafficante and Rosselli in the CIA-Mafia plots was only revealed by John H. Davis in 1989, and was never addressed by Richard Helms or any of the relevant CIA officials. Before Marcello's involvement was exposed, legendary CIA spymaster James Angleton passed away in 1987 and David Atlee Phillips died in 1988. Shortly before Phillips's death, he told an associate that in JFK's murder, "there was a conspiracy, likely including American intelligence officers." Phillips's remarks wouldn't be published until six years later.[28]

The deaths of Angleton and Phillips left a dwindling number of people in a position to know about the darkest secret of Richard Helms and the CIA: how Helms's unauthorized 1963 CIA-Mafia plots had compromised the JFK-Almeida coup plan, and resulted in JFK's assassination. Michel Victor Mertz died in France on January 15, 1995, but the FBI and the CIA withheld the news of his death from a fresh set of government investigators, allowing Mertz's files to remain unreleased even today.

When Richard Helms died on October 23, 2002, he seemed to have taken his most important secrets to the grave. The media savvy, and political clout, of Helms and the CIA had successfully maintained his decades-long cover-up in the public eye, and rebuilt his reputation in the process. Helms's autobiography, released six months after his death, was even less revealing than Thomas Powers's 1979 biography: Helms devoted only one line to a brief mention of a 1963 coup plot against Fidel, and another to his belief that Fidel had not killed JFK.[29]

As we noted in *Legacy of Secrecy*'s introduction, E. Howard Hunt was somewhat more revealing in his 2007 autobiography, published after Hunt's January 23, 2007, death. Hunt essentially admitted that David Atlee Phillips had acted as Maurice Bishop, and that Richard Helms "made a confidant out of me [and I was] the first person" Helms told about "important events in his life." However, Hunt also said that Helms always kept his eye on "his future," and that if Helms were involved in something negative, "he would lie about it later."[30]

Hunt limited his JFK assassination revelations in the book to speculation, some of which was inconsistent with remarks he made to his son in a later-publicized tape. Other of Hunt's claims are demonstrably false. Hunt had tried to make millions selling his story to actor Kevin Costner before his death, and some of Hunt's account appears to have been cribbed from existing JFK conspiracy books, as he speculates about—but claims no direct knowledge of—a large conspiracy that could have included LBJ, Cord Meyer, William Harvey, David Phillips, David Morales, Frank Fiorini, and French hit man Lucien Sarti. Most tellingly, Hunt never mentioned—in his autobiography or in his son's tape—the Mafia ties of his closest friends, like Manuel Artime, or Artime's work on the CIA-Mafia plots. Likewise, Hunt avoided any mention of his work on the JFK-Almeida coup plan, even though the first revelation of it and Hunt's role had been published in *Ultimate Sacrifice* well before Hunt completed his autobiography.

Now that Helms and Hunt are dead, perhaps only two people are still alive that have significant firsthand knowledge about the operations that allowed Marcello, Trafficante, and Rosselli to infiltrate the JFK-Almeida coup plan and murder JFK. One is a man with a reputation for integrity, while the other worked for Trafficante on JFK's assassination. While some secrets died with the participants who have already passed away, or in records that were destroyed, other information has yet to be exposed. The Washington think tank OMB Watch found that "well over one million CIA records" pertaining to JFK's assassination remain unreleased. But despite a 1992 law requiring their release, the

CIA intends to keep them secret until at least 2017—unless the public and Congress demand action. Otherwise, as the history revealed in this book has shown, the legacy of secrecy surrounding the events of 1963 will continue to extact its tragic toll on America.[31]

Epilogue

The JFK assassination files still withheld today, material that could also shed new light on the murders of Martin Luther King and Bobby Kennedy, are inexorably intertwined with events in Cuba. That was true in 1963 just as it is in 2008, when several key players in the JFK-Almeida coup plan could still play important roles in resolving the forty-seven-year-old impasse between the US and Cuba. Developments from the late 1980s until today, involving both Cuba and the withheld files, help to illuminate why so much was secret for so long, and how each issue affects the other.

After serving twenty-one years in a Cuban prison, former exile leader Eloy Menoyo was released in 1986, the same year the last prisoner from the Bay of Pigs was released due to Senator Edward Kennedy's efforts. Commander Juan Almeida, still a revered figure in the Cuban government, was untainted by a 1989 drug scandal in the higher ranks of the Cuban military. However, several top officers were executed and others imprisoned, including some of Almeida's former protégés. One of them may have bartered for his life by revealing Almeida's secret work for JFK in 1963—because soon after the trials, Almeida largely disappeared from view in Cuba. There was no official explanation, though Almeida's absence was noted by exiles and journalists. Some rumors said Almeida had been executed, while others claimed he was under house arrest, trotted out only for rare public appearances before returning to custody.[1]

In the US, the success of Oliver Stone's film *JFK* in late 1991 amplified the growing movement to open the remaining assassination files. In an attempt to preclude Congressional action, President George H. W. Bush ordered the CIA to quickly declassify thousands of CIA files in 1992. The first few AMWORLD documents slipped through in the rush and were discovered at the National Archives by Dr. John Newman, then a Major with Army Intelligence and a respected historian. However, nothing would be published about AMWORLD, or the JFK-Almeida coup plan, until 2005, in *Ultimate Sacrifice*, so both subjects remained unknown to the public, Congress, and almost all historians.

With news about the push to release more files, and the passing of former exile (and Trafficante associate) Tony Varona, in 1992 Harry Williams began to open up to the authors about the JFK-Almeida coup plan and Trafficante's attempts to compromise it. Later that year, Congress unanimously passed the JFK Act, which created the JFK Assassination Records Review Board to identify and release the remaining files.

In November 1994, the authors informed the Review Board very generally about JFK's 1963 plans for a coup in Cuba, without revealing Almeida, and about the attempt to kill JFK in Tampa four days before Dallas. Six weeks later, the Review Board learned that—in violation of the JFK Act—the Secret Service had just destroyed files covering JFK's Tampa trip, and other important files. That destruction would not become public knowledge until 1998, and even today, most members of Congress remain unaware of it.[2]

By 1995, Commander Almeida had begun to resurface in Cuba. In the wake of the fall of the Soviet empire, Cuba was in dire financial straits, and Fidel may have been attempting to make his regime appear stable, by bringing back an admired figure. No official explanation for Almeida's return, or his several-year fall from grace, was ever given.

Harry Williams passed away on March 10, 1996, after the authors had interviewed him as a confidential source more than half a dozen times. He had detailed most of the JFK-Almeida coup plan and several attempts by Trafficante to penetrate it, and had even identified a man who worked for Trafficante and the CIA who was involved in JFK's murder. Though Harry's extensive CIA and FBI files remain unreleased, he lived to see a few declassified AMWORLD memos about himself, which detailed and confirmed information he had first revealed to the authors four years earlier.

In 1997, the Review Board declassified hundreds of pages of military files about JFK's 1963 "Plans for a Coup in Cuba" from the files of the Joint Chiefs of Staff and Joseph Califano, but none named Almeida—they referred only generally to the high-ranking Cuban officials who would lead the coup. However, after being contacted by a JFK Review Board official in late 1997 and 1998, the authors confidentially provided the official with the first information naming Almeida and AMWORLD. The Board's mandate expired in September 1998, and though it had released more than four million files, NBC News reported that "millions" of pages remain unreleased. Because of an arrangement between the Board, the FBI, and the CIA, more files trickled out over the following year, including dozens of key AMWORLD documents. But tens (or hundreds) of thousands of pages from that Mafia-infiltrated program remain unreleased, until at least 2017—and the CIA has indicated in court filings that it reserves the right to withhold JFK files even beyond that Congressionally mandated release date.[3]

In 2001, Commander Almeida was chosen over Raul Castro to appear in a sympathetic documentary about Fidel Castro, in which Almeida talked about the various CIA attempts to kill Fidel—but not his own. Almeida's appearance removed any doubt the CIA had that Fidel might not have learned of Almeida's secret work for JFK, ending any possibility that the CIA could use Almeida. The following year, a Miami newspaper article noted that Almeida's sons were prominent businessmen in Spain and Mexico. However, as long as the Cuban populace didn't learn about Almeida's secret work for JFK, he was still valuable to Fidel, since he was (and is) the highest-ranking black official in Cuba, where the majority of the population is of African ancestry. Almeida was also important to Fidel as a symbol around the world, especially in developing nations, as the leader of the Afro-Cuban movement. But he was not allowed to travel much outside the country, and even at small official ceremonies within Cuba, Almeida was always accompanied on stage by another official.

Not wanting to force Fidel to take action against Almeida, and assuming his files would remain secret until 2017, the authors and their publisher ensured that the first hardcover edition of *Ultimate Sacrifice*, published in November 2005, was factually correct, but didn't compromise Almeida's name or position. The book still outlined most of the coup plan and revealed AMWORLD in print for the first time. However, the day before the hardback went on sale, an official with the National Archives informed the authors that a formerly confidential file naming Almeida and detailing his work for JFK would be made available to the public.

It was inevitable that Almeida's identity and secret work for JFK would soon become known. A former Defense Department source said the best way to protect Almeida from retribution by Fidel was to publicize Almeida's work on the coup as thoroughly and widely as possible. So, an updated trade paperback of *Ultimate Sacrifice* was planned for fall 2006, with hundreds of additions that would fully detail Almeida's secret work with JFK and Bobby.

On July 31, 2006,with no advance warning, Fidel suddenly announced that he would undergo an operation for intestinal problems, and that he had placed his brother Raul in charge during his recovery. It was the first change in Cuban leadership in more than forty years, and it triggered rampant speculation that Castro was dead, dying, or permanently disabled. As days passed with no sign of Fidel, rumors about his fate continued to grow throughout the summer.[4]

Prior to the appearance of the trade paperback naming Almeida, his public role consisted largely of receiving the credentials of new ambassadors and attending various official ceremonies, though he was rarely featured prominently with Fidel. While he was still revered in Cuba as a hero of the Revolution and founder of the Cuban Army, and had a Vice President of State title that ranked him among a handful of officials just below Raul, Almeida had no real power and was not especially prominent at truly major ceremonies.

On September 22, 2006, columnist Liz Smith broke the news of the updated *Ultimate Sacrifice* trade paperback's revelations about Commander Almeida and JFK, and the book was in stores soon afterward. Almeida's appearance at the October 6, 2006, commemoration of the 1976 terrorist bombing of a Cubana airline showed that at least he hadn't been killed or imprisoned.[5] Almeida sat at Raul's right hand during the ceremony, a position that would not have been unusual in past years, except now Raul—not Fidel—ruled Cuba.

Cuba made no official comment about the new disclosures concerning Almeida in *Ultimate Sacrifice*, but the book had caught their attention. Former Cuban State Security Chief Fabian Escalante sent the following brief statement to a Dutch journalist for posting on a British website—that way, the average Cuban citizen, who lacked unrestricted Internet access, wouldn't see it. Escalante didn't contest any of our facts, and instead simply decried the revelations as "an active measure of the CIA . . . a dirty trick [with] no degree of certainty."[6] (Both authors want to make clear that they have never worked for the CIA.)

Fidel's absence from public view, and the continuing rumors of his death, worked to Almeida's advantage, limiting any type of action the Castro brothers could take against him. Given all the uncertainty about Fidel, if Almeida disappeared from view as well it would hardly instill confidence in the Cuban populace. While Raul hoped he could simply assume Fidel's power and position, it was by no means certain in those early days that the Cuban people would transfer their loyalty so easily. The more the Cuban government presented a united, "business as usual" front, the better. Also, it looked as if the situation with Fidel might create new opportunities for talks between Cuba and the US—until the Bush administration reiterated that it considered Raul Castro just as bad as Fidel. If the US wasn't going to talk to Raul, was there anyone in the Cuban government whom US officials might be willing to deal with?

One possible solution may have presented itself as Cuba began readying a huge celebration for December 2, 2006, both for the Cuban Army's fiftieth anniversary and for Fidel's eightieth-birthday celebration, delayed since August. But Fidel's announcement that he was too ill to attend the massive festivities in Havana fueled speculation that Fidel would never be well enough to resume power, truly marking the end of an era.

On December 2, 2006, Almeida was beside Raul Castro at the Havana celebration, attended by hundreds of thousands of cheering Cubans. Almeida led the parade with Raul and two other officials, and he remained at Raul's side on the reviewing stand while a huge band played a popular Cuban song Almeida had composed. Then Almeida remained on the stage as Raul delivered his speech, which included a rare olive branch for the US.[7]

American officials didn't seem to be getting the message, so Almeida also had a high-profile role in the May Day celebrations on May 1, 2007, heading the festivities for eight hundred thousand people in Cuba's second-largest city, Santiago de Cuba. On February 19, 2008, the eighty-one-year-old Fidel resigned from his post as Cuba's president, just before the election of new officials at Cuba's National Assembly, which officially cleared the way for the start of a new era. On February 24, Almeida was again seated beside Raul as Fidel's brother became President and Almeida was reelected as one of five Cuban Vice Presidents of State. The duo of Raul and Almeida repeated their side-by-side appearances on May Day 2008, and later at the huge Havana celebration for their "26th of July" national holiday.

It's almost as if Raul is saying to the US, "If you won't talk with me, why not talk with JFK's ally from 1963?" Currently, Eloy Menoyo has returned to Havana, having renounced the violence of the past to work for peaceful change. Manolo Ray remains a private businessman in Puerto Rico. Several Cuban-exile military veterans of AMWORLD and JFK's Cuban American training at Fort Benning have formed CAMCO, to reach out to military leaders inside Cuba. It would be the ultimate irony if some of the same people who worked for JFK in 1963, in both the US and Cuba, were key to finally realizing the dream he gave his life trying to achieve—a free and democratic Cuba.

Standing in the way of any true normalization between the US and Cuba is the continued withholding of "well over one million CIA records" and, no doubt, a substantial number of related files from the FBI, the Secret Service, the DEA, and the US military. Former officials like Alexander Haig maintain that Fidel Castro was behind JFK's murder, and such thinking will continue to influence the attitudes of powerful US officials, business leaders, and far-right Cuban-exile activists until all the files are released. Now that Almeida's identity has been revealed, there is no longer any legitimate reason for so many files to be withheld.

As *Legacy of Secrecy* has shown for the first time, releasing those JFK files—and their information about Marcello, Milteer, and Rosselli—is also crucial to fully resolve Martin Luther King's assassination. After the death of Hugh Spake on January 5, 2006, there may be no one left to prosecute for Dr. King's murder, but authorities should at least explore the possibility. Fully releasing all the JFK files, as required by law— especially those of Johnny Rosselli and David Morales—might also answer lingering questions about Robert Kennedy's assassination.

Congress has never taken any action regarding the CIA's deliberate 1978 deception of the House Select Committee on Assassinations, nor has it done anything about all the relevant files that a variety of agencies withheld from that Committee. Most current members of the House and Senate are unaware that the 1992 JFK Act failed to dislodge over a million relevant files, or that the Secret Service admitted destroying important files after the Act was passed. It's difficult to envision how federal agencies will take future Congressional investigations seriously when they continue to flout the will of Congress by withholding so many files whose release is required by law.

The amount of material yet to be declassified is vast, and the following few examples are just the tiny tip of a huge iceberg of secrecy—more withheld files are described or indicated in almost every chapter of this book. The most obvious example is the hundreds of hours of Marcello tapes recorded in 1985. Other pressing files that need to be released include the relevant files of all those individuals who have confessed to JFK's assassination: Marcello, Trafficante, Rosselli (especially his fall

1963 FBI Florida surveillance reports), David Morales, and John Martino. The complete 1963 CIA files of E. Howard Hunt, David Atlee Phillips, Desmond FitzGerald, and George Joannides should also be declassified, since each withheld crucial information from various government committees and commissions.

Other crucial JFK assassination files still withheld range from the CIA's and FBI's files on Harry Williams to the operational files of the multimillion-dollar AMWORLD program, especially those about Manuel Artime's work on the CIA-Mafia plots. The files of other Mafia figures linked to JFK's murder, like those of Michel Victor Mertz and Charles Nicoletti, should also be released. Naval Intelligence should still have a vast quantity of files about its secret JFK investigation and FBI-assisted surveillance of Oswald. All of the files about the Tampa and Chicago plots against JFK should be declassified. Framed ex–Secret Service agent Abraham Bolden is still fighting for a pardon after almost forty-five years, even as his own CIA file remains secret—as does much of the CIA file of Richard Cain, the Chicago Mafioso and CIA asset who may well have framed Bolden.

While the JFK Act covers only the files related to President Kennedy's assassination, three participants in that murder—Joseph Milteer, Carlos Marcello, and Johnny Rosselli—were also involved to some degree in the murder of Martin Luther King. That means releasing their files (FBI, CIA, DEA, Secret Service, Justice Department, military intelligence, etc.), and those of their associates from 1963–1968, should also yield new information about Dr. King's slaying. The same principle applies to Rosselli, Marcello, and David Morales regarding the murder of Robert F. Kennedy. Because *Legacy of Secrecy* has documented that some of the individuals who killed JFK remained free to help assassinate Dr. King and Robert Kennedy, simply enforcing the 1992 JFK Act is the quickest way to make sure that the most crucial information becomes available to the public at last.

SPECIAL ADDENDUM

Part I: Bernard "Macho" Barker, the Mafia, and the Murder of JFK

"Macho Barker—follow that name! He had something to do with the assassination of the President; follow that name! He's involved, I'm sure!"

In our November 1992 interview, the normally implacable Harry Williams practically shouted his revelation about Bernard "Macho" Barker. Harry was known for his calm demeanor even under pressure and had been relaxed during our three earlier interviews, so his excitement was surprising. When Harry blurted out his concern about Barker's involvement in JFK's murder, without prompting, it was as if a long-simmering volcano had finally erupted.

As Harry later explained, Barker had been working for godfather Santo Trafficante at the time of JFK's murder—at the very same time Barker was working with Harry on the JFK-Almeida coup plan. After JFK's assassination, Harry discovered that Barker's longtime relationship with Trafficante had stretched from before the Bay of Pigs invasion to Barker's infamous arrest at the final Watergate break-in.

The death of Bernard Barker on June 5, 2009, allows us to tell his full story for the first time, in this new edition of *Legacy of Secrecy*. Harry's revelations allowed us to build on the work of two Congressional investigators and Carlos Marcello's biographer, John H. Davis, who had previously documented ties between Barker and Trafficante, as well as with the godfather's associates like Jack Ruby. We have spent the last seventeen years quietly gathering information about Barker and even hinted at his involvement with JFK's murder and Trafficante in the first edition of *Legacy* in 2008. In this new trade paperback, we replaced those hints with actual information about Barker. Also, this Special Addendum contains Barker's whole story with much additional information, complete with endnotes for documentation.

In Part I of this Special Addendum, we describe how Barker sold out the JFK-Almeida coup plan to Trafficante. These revelations finally answer lingering questions not only about JFK's murder but also about other events involving Barker, ranging from the Bay of Pigs to the Watergate scandal. Part II provides new insights into Barker's role in Watergate and how that impacted the CIA files withheld from the Congressional investigations in the 1970s, many of which are still withheld today. While the rest of *Legacy* has focused largely on those who conceived and directed JFK's assassination at the highest level—Trafficante, Marcello, and Johnny Rosselli—focusing on Barker provides a different perspective, since he was on the ground (possibly even in Dealey Plaza), helping with the dirty work.

For decades, researchers have fruitlessly looked for solid evidence of a massive top-down, high-level government conspiracy involving the CIA in JFK's assassination. E. Howard Hunt has been the most intensely investigated figure in that quest, targeted by both government committees and independent journalists since the early 1970s, but all of those investigations have so far failed to turn up any solid evidence tying Hunt to JFK's murder. While we can now document much information about Hunt that the CIA has withheld over the years, none of it directly implicates Hunt in JFK's death. Much of the CIA secrecy involved protecting the reputations of officials like CIA Director Richard Helms, under the cover of protecting Commander Juan Almeida. Hunt himself added to the confusion, since his autobiography—after Hunt's January 2007 death—was full of major omissions, ranging from the Mafia ties of his closest friends, Barker and Manuel Artime, to the JFK-Almeida coup plan. The so-called "confession tape" Hunt left to one of his sons not only repeated those omissions but also added critical errors and speculation that were at odds with Hunt's autobiography. Both the autobiography and the tape raise more questions than they answer. No one who worked with John or Robert Kennedy, including those who knew about Hunt's work on the JFK-Almeida coup plan, ever told us that Hunt was involved in JFK's murder. However, the same isn't true for Hunt's assistant, Bernard Barker.

A house can be demolished from the top down, but it can also be brought down because of something gnawing away at the foundation, deep in the dark basement. Away from the light, operating in the shadows that engulfed both his professional and personal life for years, Barker was in the perfect position to help Trafficante and Marcello murder JFK in a way that forced cover-ups from Helms personally, from the CIA as an agency, and even from Bobby Kennedy. Barker's affection for Hunt may have been genuine—or Barker may have resented Hunt all the time that Barker played his servile lackey. Either way, Barker must have realized that Hunt's well-known dislike of the Kennedys and their aides would give Barker protection if Hunt learned about or suspected his aide's perfidy. It meant that Hunt could never expose his loyal aide Barker without revealing himself as an incompetent CIA officer or—by the early 1970s—as a suspect himself in JFK's murder.

For years, historians and the public have debated whether the Mafia, the CIA, or Cuban exiles were behind JFK's death. Barker demonstrates how one key man in the plot hatched by Trafficante and Marcello was in fact in all three groups. Even though Barker was only an average CIA agent, he worked for a variety of powerful and well-connected figures—from Trafficante to Richard Nixon's best friend, Bebe Rebozo, to E. Howard Hunt, protégé of eventual CIA Director Richard Helms. That allowed Barker to have a remarkable impact on the two most important presidential tragedies of the last fifty years.

Bernard Leon Barker, nicknamed "Macho," was born on March 17, 1917, in Havana, Cuba, to parents who were US citizens. From the start, Barker felt the influence of both countries, a duality that impacted the rest of his life. He went to high school in Farmingdale, New York, before enrolling in the University of Havana in 1940. The day after the December 7, 1941, attack on Pearl Harbor, Barker joined the US Army, later claiming he'd been the first Cuban American to enlist. Barker attained the rank of captain in the Army Air Corps, becoming a bombardier. According to his formerly secret CIA biography, Barker "flew sorties over Germany until he was shot down and taken as a prisoner of war." Captain Barker served sixteen months in a German POW camp until he was liberated by Russian forces.[1]

Barker eventually returned to Cuba. Beginning in 1950, CIA and FBI files show very different views of the man. According to one of Barker's several CIA files, in 1950 Barker became a "Sergeant in the Cuban Police Department in Havana," and E. Howard Hunt claimed Barker did so "at the request of the CIA." The CIA documents claim that while in the Cuban police, Barker "cooperated with [the] FBI representative at the American Embassy" and "assisted Treasury Department officials in breaking a drug-smuggling ring." The CIA even notes that Barker "received a commendation for . . . escorting" President Truman's wife Bess "on a visit to Cuba."[2]

The FBI's assessment of Barker stands in stark contrast to the CIA's rosy depiction of Barker as a crime-fighter. FBI files state from their first mention of Barker that he was involved with organized crime. According to an internal report prepared for FBI Director L. Patrick Gray a week after the Watergate break-in, "during the late 1940's, [Barker] became associated in gangster activities in Cuba." However, Barker's "gangster activities" were supposedly unknown to the CIA until 1966, even though he worked as a CIA agent from 1959 to 1966. At least, that's the story the CIA presented in the files about Barker that it gave to Congress for their numerous investigations of him, from Watergate to the House Select Committee on Assassinations.[3]

The FBI report notes that Barker's time in the Cuban police was "during the [Carlos] Prio regime," which may explain how Barker developed his Mafia connections in the first place. The last democratically elected president of Cuba, Prio was deposed in March 1952 by General Fulgencio Batista, remembered now for his corrupt ties to mob leaders like Santo Trafficante and Meyer Lansky. However, it's often overlooked that Prio and his allies, like Cuban senator Tony Varona, were corrupt as well. Since the Treasury Department could never confirm Barker's supposed role in "breaking a drug-smuggling ring" as the CIA claimed, it seems likely that Barker fabricated the story to cover his own ties to drug trafficking. Likewise, FBI records show the Bureau had no substantial contact with Barker in Cuba, as the CIA file claims. Much as Jack Ruby briefly used his status as an FBI informant to cover his work in Cuba for Carlos Marcello and Trafficante in 1959, Barker may have provided occasional information to the FBI in Havana as a way to cover for his own "gangster activities."[4]

Deposed President Carlos Prio left Cuba after Batista took over. Barker stayed in Cuba but left the police force, where he had been a sergeant and one of the Police Chief's assistants.[5] Later, according to Barker's CIA file and his own media interviews, Barker said that out of "personal spite" a State Department official in Havana decided to enforce a rule that anyone swearing allegiance to a foreign government cannot retain US citizenship. Barker and the CIA files made it appear that Barker's US citizenship was revoked only because he'd been an upstanding member of the Cuban police.[6]

However, in his Senate Watergate testimony, Barker started to admit that the real reason he lost his citizenship was that "some problem came up with a group of Cubans, of which I was in charge in the Cuban police department . . . this was denounced to the Embassy and one day I found out that my American citizenship had been taken away from me."[7] This sounds as if Barker or his men had been caught in some illegal activity, the US Embassy was told, and Barker quite logically lost his citizenship as a result.

In his testimony, Barker claimed that he'd been acting for the FBI during the operation, something the FBI denied. If Barker had been working with the FBI, it would have been easy for the Bureau to fix the problem with State Department. Instead, Barker testified that he then made a trip to the United States and saw the firm of "[Edward] Bennett Williams" to try to restore his citizenship (something that would take until 1967).[8] Barker was vague in his testimony about the exact year of this important trip. Perhaps that's because in the mid-1950s, Edward Bennett Williams began to represent members of the Mafia and their allies, building a client list that would include Frank Costello, Jimmy Hoffa, and Sam Giancana.[9]

According to an FBI report, back in Cuba, Barker became "a member of the Bureau for the Repression of Communism," part of Batista's brutal secret police.[10] He was probably only an asset or part-time operative, since from 1955 to 1958, Barker officially worked as a government housing inspector in Marianao, near Havana.[11]

John and Robert Kennedy's top Cuban exile aide, Harry Williams, didn't know Barker in Cuba, but his extensive contacts in the Cuban exile community—almost unparalleled by the mid-1960s, when Harry was regarded as a hero by Miami's Cubans—allowed him to learn much about the man he had to work with in 1963. According to Harry, he discovered that in Cuba in the late 1950s, Barker was known as "a dishonest inspector" who took bribes and was "known for cutting deals."[12]

Barker's reputation for dishonesty apparently represented no problem for the CIA, which officially recruited Barker in the spring of 1959. Earlier that same year, on New Year's Day, revolutionaries including Fidel Castro had overthrown Batista. The CIA was soon being pressed by Vice President Richard Nixon to eliminate Fidel. Though Nixon and Barker were at vastly different social levels, the resulting CIA efforts to assassinate Fidel by using the Mafia eventually linked the two men along sometimes parallel—and sometimes competing—tracks from 1959 until the Watergate scandal finally erupted in 1972.

Since Barker has been investigated by at least five Congressional committees and two additional government commissions, it is surprising that the name of the CIA officer who "originally handled" his "recruitment" has never been revealed. We have only his recruiter's CIA pseudonym, "Woodrow C. Olien," and several basic facts about him. These range from the recruiter's involvement in the 1954 CIA coup that overthrew the democratically elected government of Guatemala to his State Department cover at the US Embassy in Havana in 1959. Later, Barker's recruiter also helped in the run-up to the Bay of Pigs, dealing with exile leaders like Tony Varona, Manuel Artime, and Manolo Ray. By at least 1964, the CIA officer was also dealing with Rolando Cubela, the mid-level Cuban official code-named AMLASH whom the CIA wanted to assassinate Fidel.[13]

Based on released files, the list of candidates for the identity of Barker's recruiter is not large. It includes familiar names like David Morales and Henry Hecksher—both of whom rose to high positions in the US intelligence community—as well as Gerard Droller (a major planner of the Bay of Pigs under the alias "Frank Bender") and one of Cubela's case officers, who later became an official during the Reagan administration. Personnel information about CIA officers is often incomplete or contradictory, and no one candidate perfectly fits the description. However, all four of the prime candidates have one thing in common: they were among the relatively few CIA officers involved with plots to assassinate Castro. For the critical year of 1963, we found virtually no released CIA files mentioning "Olien," meaning he either took a leave from Cuban operations that year or (more likely) was involved in an extremely sensitive operation like the JFK-Almeida coup plan and AMWORLD, which is still mostly classified.[14]

Another startling fact about Barker's CIA file is that his official list of case officers—his CIA supervisors—for his entire CIA tenure (1959–1966) was "blacked out" before being provided to the House Select Committee on Assassinations. Usually, investigators were allowed to see uncensored CIA files, which were censored only before being released to the public. If there were just one or two particularly sensitive names, the CIA could have blacked them out before giving the file to the Congressional investigator. But in this instance, the entire list was withheld from Congress, as noted in writing by the investigator who saw it. The list was probably withheld because it was at odds with Congressional testimony given by CIA officials in the 1970s about Barker, Hunt, and others.

In addition to withholding the JFK-Almeida coup plan from Congress in the 1970s, the CIA also officially maintained that E. Howard Hunt had no involvement in anti-Castro activity after the Bay of Pigs and that Hunt was never involved in CIA assassination plotting, or with the Mafia or Cubela. The latter has always strained credibility, because Hunt wrote one of the first CIA memos calling for Fidel's assassination shortly before the start of the CIA-Mafia plots with Trafficante. Also, Hunt was in Spain in 1965, when his best friend, Artime (who was tied to Trafficante), was plotting assassination there with Cubela (who also knew Trafficante).[15] Now, two CIA memos have been uncovered linking Hunt to the Cubela assassination plot for the first time. We'll detail them shortly, but it's perhaps not surprising that one involves Barker's original CIA recruiter, the mysterious "Olien."[16]

Barker's first important job for the CIA in Cuba was helping to get Trafficante associate Tony Varona and Manuel Artime (a rising star in the resistance against Fidel) out of the country in late 1959. However, that achievement is not noted in most operational CIA summaries of Barker's work, indicating that it eventually became part of a file for some sensitive project whose records were later suppressed or destroyed.[17]

That project could well involve the CIA-Mafia plots to assassinate Castro. Those plots weren't publicly exposed or investigated until 1975, long after Watergate had made Barker and Hunt toxic for the CIA. By that time, Helms had destroyed sensitive files related to the CIA-Mafia plots on at least two occasions, in 1967 and 1973, meaning crucial information was missing from the Congressional investigations. However, Barker's work for Trafficante, combined with other new disclosures, makes it possible to rewrite the history of the CIA-Mafia plots, showing how they planted the seeds for both JFK's assassination and the Watergate scandal.

As noted earlier in *Legacy* and in Anthony Summers's Nixon biography, considerable evidence shows that Vice President Nixon, facing a tough race for the presidency in 1960 against likely Democratic nominee John F. Kennedy, pressured the CIA to increase their efforts with the Mafia to assassinate Fidel. Hunt's involvement in anti-Castro activities in 1960 and 1961 and beyond suggests that he played a role in the CIA-Mafia plots. Hunt has admitted to writing a memo in the spring of 1960 recommending the CIA "assassinate Castro before or coincident with the invasion" of Cuba by exiles. Soon after, he pressed his recommendation for Fidel's assassination in a meeting with General Robert Cushman, Vice President Nixon's military aide. (Years later, in the early stages of Hunt's Watergate operation, Nixon made Cushman the CIA's Deputy Director).[18]

In the summer of 1960, the CIA apparently briefly considered using

New Orleans private detective Guy Banister as their "cut out" (a deniable intermediary) to reach the Mafia. But a CIA memo says that Agency official Jim O'Connell decided to use "an alternative private detective company" instead, that of Robert Maheu, a former associate of Banister's.[19] O'Connell wanted Maheu to contact gangster Johnny Rosselli, whom O'Connell had met previously at Maheu's home. Rosselli wasn't known as a godfather (whose approval would be needed for such a major hit) or for being active in Cuba (aside from helping to manage one of Trafficante's casinos for a short time), but he could help Maheu and the CIA reach those who were.

On September 14, 1960, Maheu and O'Connell discussed Fidel's assassination with Rosselli, and soon afterward Rosselli introduced Maheu to his boss, Sam Giancana, and to Santo Trafficante, who had extensive connections in Cuba. Barker had moved to the United States in early 1960, and on September 21, 1960, a CIA memo quoted here for the first time stated that "Barker's best use is as assistant to Hunt," and the two men began working together.[20] If the CIA was not as ignorant as released files make them seem about Barker's "gangster activities in Cuba"—the ones so easily documented by the FBI—Barker could have been chosen to work with Hunt precisely because of those "gangster" connections.

By the following month, Trafficante's man Frank Fiorini (later known as "Frank Sturgis") would be linked to this CIA-Mafia plot. It's interesting to note that even with all the Congressional and press investigations of Fiorini and Barker after Watergate, how they first met has never been clearly established. The CIA-Mafia plots with Rosselli would eventually include associates of Barker's like Tony Varona and Manuel Artime, plus Trafficante's partner in crime, Carlos Marcello, all of whom were involved in JFK's assassination. By the fall of 1960, the nucleus of the small, tight-knit group who would later kill JFK was being utilized by the CIA to try to kill Fidel Castro. Trafficante and Rosselli would later claim they really weren't interested in killing Fidel, but their involvement with the CIA on the plot would prove helpful to the Mafia bosses when they decided to kill JFK, two years later.

It's long been documented that E. Howard Hunt was the political action officer for the Bay of Pigs operation as it developed in 1960 and early 1961. Hunt's friend David Atlee Phillips handled propaganda, while Gerry Droller coordinated the military training of the exile force, the size of which expanded dramatically after JFK won the election but before he took office. CIA files reveal that Bernard Barker had worked with all three men but became Hunt's top assistant.

E. Howard Hunt's main task was to assemble a select group of Cuban exile leaders into a CIA-created coalition called the Cuban Revolutionary Council (CRC), which would form Cuba's new government after Fidel's elimination. The CRC would eventually include a variety of former Cuban officials and rising stars, including Tony Varona and Manuel Artime. Headquartered in Miami, it would also have offices in cities with large Cuban exile populations, like New Orleans. As for Bernard Barker's role, journalist Haynes Johnson said that "Barker was [a] bagman in Miami [who] dispersed money to Cubans from CIA funds."[21]

Former FBI agent William Turner elaborated on Barker's activities: Barker's "task as Hunt's right-hand man was to deliver CIA cash laundered through foreign banks to the exile groups." In the process, Barker was learning techniques of money laundering that he could use in his later work for the CIA and Nixon. That may have ranged from the CIA's 1963 clandestine payment for Juan Almeida all the way to Watergate, when Barker laundered for Nixon $114,000 in illegal campaign contributions, some used for the Watergate break-ins.[22]

Barker's money laundering for the CIA helps to explain why the Agency would have tolerated, or perhaps even taken advantage of, Barker's ties to Trafficante. After all, the godfather's operations excelled at laundering large sums of cash. Barker's need to restore his citizenship may have given the CIA what they felt was a strong enough hold over Barker to ensure his loyalty to them over the Mafia. In fact, the CIA seems to have dragged their feet on helping Barker restore his citizenship—something a high-level call from the CIA to the State Department could have easily resolved—almost as if the CIA wanted some ongoing leverage over Barker. His citizenship would not be restored until several months after Barker's CIA career had been terminated.

Barker became very close to Hunt in the run-up to the Bay of Pigs. Frank Fiorini, later to work with both men on the Watergate burglaries under the name "Frank Sturgis," said that during the Bay of Pigs, "when [Barker] is around Hunt . . . Barker is like a valet. Servile . . . 'Sit here, Mr. Hunt, the sun won't bother you.' It's disgusting. 'Yes sir, Mr. Hunt, let me refresh your drink, sir.'" But Fiorini said that Barker didn't act that way just toward Hunt, but also toward "anybody that's over him." One wonders if Fiorini was indicating that Barker also acted that way toward their mutual boss, Santo Trafficante.[23]

Most CIA and FBI files about Hunt and Barker from the Bay of Pigs era remain unreleased, despite, or maybe because of, the investigations by the Kennedy administration and the CIA that began soon after the invasion's failure, plus three Congressional investigations in the 1970s. For example, the CIA has admitted that Hunt used the alias "Terence S. Crabanac" during the Bay of Pigs, as well as "Edward J. Hamilton," "Mr. Edwards," and "Eduardo J. Hamilton." "Crabanac" was placed into service in December 1960, the same month an earlier Hunt alias, Walter C. Twicker, had been compromised. For reasons never explained, Hunt had been assigned the additional "Eduardo" and "Edward" aliases on September 20, 1960, right after the CIA had their first meeting with Johnny Rosselli about the plot to assassinate Castro, just before Trafficante was brought into the plot. Perhaps that's why the CIA's "Eduardo" or "Mr. Edwards" files about Hunt were never given to Congress, even when they were specifically requested.[24]

Likewise, much remains withheld about Barker from the Bay of Pigs operation. We know his CIA cryptonym was "AMCLATTER-1" and one of his aliases was "Spencer O. Terteling," but none of Barker's operational files about his work as Hunt's assistant have ever been released. Barker may have used other aliases that have never been declassified; one of his CIA files shows that he may have also used the alias "Frank W. Zwerkling" or else worked with someone using that name. CIA agents often had several aliases at the same time, used for different operations or different tasks within the same operation. For example, David Atlee Phillips used at least five different identities, including "Lawrence F. Barker." Phillips used his "Barker" alias in Cuban operations even after Bernard Barker became involved in them, which seems unusual and potentially confusing. Perhaps Phillips worked closely enough with Barker to ensure there were no problems, the same way Hunt shared the "Eduardo" alias with his fellow CIA officer working on the JFK-Almeida coup plan.[25]

One reason for the Agency's withholding information about Hunt and Barker dating from the Bay of Pigs era could have been their involvement with the CIA-Mafia plots involving Johnny Rosselli and Barker's boss, Trafficante. While the official CIA version of the Bay of Pigs divided the planning into the three areas mentioned earlier, it left out the CIA's collusion with the Mafia and so did not detail how those efforts were coordinated with the rest of the operation. By the winter and spring of 1961, those plots had Rosselli and Trafficante dealing with Tony Varona, whose associate in Cuba had sufficient access to Castro to attempt poisoning him. Hunt's and Barker's close work with Varona at the time made them the most obvious choice to coordinate the assassination of Fidel with the Bay of Pigs invasion. As Barker said in a later interview for NBC, "Mr. Hunt personally always had the theory that the physical elimination of Fidel Castro was the proper way for the liberation of Cuba."[26]

E. Howard Hunt's practice of trying to press for Fidel's assassination is long and well-established, starting with his memo calling for Castro's murder that probably spawned the CIA-Mafia plots with Trafficante in 1960. Hunt continued his efforts to kill Fidel during his work on the JFK-Almeida coup plan in 1963 and his involvement in the Cubela Castro assassination plot with Artime in 1964 and 1965. (Most of Hunt's CIA files about those matters have never been released.) Hunt's involvement in the CIA-Mafia plots prior to the Bay of Pigs would be consistent with his track record. And if Hunt was involved, Barker would probably have been also.

Barker's close friend, CIA agent Eugenio Martinez, later talked about those who tried to distinguish between the plots to assassinate Fidel and other CIA efforts against Castro. Martinez, still on CIA retainer when he was arrested with Barker at the Watergate, was one of the CIA's master "boat men," an expert at getting CIA agents and assets secretly into Cuba. He told historians Taylor Branch and George Crile that

> There was an attempt by this country to overthrow Castro . . . there were plots. I took a lot of weapons to Cuba. Some of them were very special weapons for special purposes. They were powerful rifles with sophisticated scopes . . . rifles only used by snipers. They were not sent to shoot pigeons or kill rabbits. Everyone in the underground was plotting to kill Castro, and the CIA was helping the underground. I was with the underground, as well as with the CIA, so you could say I was involved in the plots, too, but that is all so obvious.[27]

Martinez's friend Barker may well have seen things the same way, only with the added twist that—unlike Martinez—Barker was working for Trafficante, who was himself actively participating in the CIA-Mafia plots to kill Fidel.*

It's long been known that Hunt pulled out of the Bay of Pigs operation shortly before the invasion, to protest the inclusion of moderate

---

* It's important to note that in contrast to Barker, Martinez has no ties to Trafficante, the Mafia or to the JFK assassination.

leader Manuel Ray in the CRC, but what that meant for Barker's CIA role in Miami is unclear. The CIA-Mafia plots failed in their effort to kill Fidel just before the invasion, and some attribute that failure to miscommunication involving Tony Varona. Given Barker's ties to Varona and Trafficante, he could well have played a role.

The CIA admits continuing to plot with Rosselli after the failure of the Bay of Pigs, and as noted on page 40, Rosselli was linked to a successful assassination shortly after the CIA-Mafia plots failed to kill Fidel. Brutal Dominican Republic dictator Rafael Trujillo was killed in May 1961 by plotters who had been receiving CIA assistance. In a book published only in Spanish, Trujillo's Security Chief alleged that the plot had involved both Johnny Rosselli and E. Howard Hunt, who had traveled together to the island prior to the assassination. If Hunt was involved, we're confident that Barker would have been as well.

Also linked to the CIA's efforts to oust Trujillo was a man who would play an increasingly large role in the lives of Barker and Hunt in future years: Charles Gregory "Bebe" Rebozo, Richard Nixon's best friend and business associate. In his well-documented Nixon biography, Anthony Summers writes that "shortly before [Trujillo] was assassinated" Bebe "Rebozo accompanied former Ambassador William Pawley on a secret mission to see . . . Trujillo." Pawley, famous for cofounding with General Claire Chennault World War II's "Flying Tigers," sometimes did favors for the CIA. He told William Turner that "this visit was [the result of a] CIA request [to ask] that Trujillo abdicate before events overtook him." After Trujillo refused the request of Pawley and Rebozo, the CIA intensified its efforts to assassinate the dictator and soon succeeded.[28]

Bebe Rebozo, who later was in business with Barker, was not a Cuban exile, but was born of Cuban parents in Tampa. *Newsday* found indications that Rebozo had been "involved in covert operations prior to the Bay of Pigs invasion." Journalist Howard Kohn wrote that "according to CIA sources, Barker and Rebozo met during the Bay of Pigs operation, when both were funneling money to the CIA-financed invaders." Rebozo, a businessman in Miami, would later be involved in complex, illegal financial and real estate transactions with both Barker and Nixon, apparently using the skills and connections he developed with Barker around the time of the Bay of Pigs.[29]

Like Barker, Rebozo was linked to the Mafia in Miami. Historian Richard D. Mahoney wrote that "Rebozo was a well-known figure in various mob families."[30] Anthony Summers documented that "[Meyer]

Lansky's name crops up . . . repeatedly in connection with Bebe Rebozo."
But Rebozo's mob connections wouldn't start to really take off until
he founded his own bank in 1964, and when his friend Richard Nixon
became president four years after that. In the early 1960s, Rebozo was
still a small-time operator, albeit one with a former two-term vice president as his best friend. Summers found a Miami Police Intelligence
memo from around the time of the Bay of Pigs that "cited a mob informant as saying Rebozo was running a numbers racket out of one of his
coin laundry businesses," while "fronting for" a mobster.[31]

Rebozo's Mafia ties might explain how he came to play one more
largely overlooked role in covert Cuban operations in the early 1960s,
one again involving Rosselli. A pilot who had first met Johnny Rosselli
and Trafficante operative John Martino in the late 1950s later told the
FBI that

> In March, 1963, he flew into Tampa, Florida, where he met Rosselli
> [and then] flew Rosselli and John V. Martino from Tampa to Rivera
> Beach, Florida . . . he learned that one Ambassador Pawley . . . was
> trying to arrange a raid to remove missile technicians from Cuba.
> He was under the impression that Pawley was organizing the raid
> through Rosselli, Martino, and . . . after the raid he flew Rosselli to
> Bimini Island where he was to meet with Pawley, Martino, and others.
> He stated that he learned that three weeks before this meeting, Paw-
> ley met at Bimini with Bebe Rebozo and Richard Nixon.[32]

As noted by Richard D. Mahoney and explained in *Ultimate Sacrifice*,
the "missile technicians" scam (code-named "Operation Tilt" by the
CIA) was part of an early mob plan to assassinate JFK. It was designed
to draw the CIA and the Kennedys into supporting an operation that
would later force the Agency and Bobby Kennedy into a cover-up, when
Operation Tilt appeared to be linked to JFK's murder.[33] Pawley had nothing to do with the assassination aspect and had simply been taken in by
the Mafia's phony "missile technicians" cover story.

Likewise, Nixon's and Rebozo's meeting with Pawley had nothing
to do with the assassination plans and was simply Nixon's attempt to
get inside information that could help his comeback in politics. By the
spring of 1963, Nixon had recovered from his failed race for governor of
California in November 1962 and had set his sights on the 1964 Republican nomination for president. The question of whether all the Soviet
missiles had been removed from Cuba was already a hot topic in Republican circles and was expected to be a major issue in the presidential

campaign. Nixon's meeting with Pawley—probably through Rebozo—was an attempt to get an inside story on an issue that could help his quest for the nomination, since the continued presence of Soviet missiles in Cuba would greatly embarrass the Kennedys. As we documented on page 175, Nixon would do something similar in November of 1963, when CIA files show that he would be part of an effort with Carlos Prio to infiltrate AMWORLD. In that case, as with Operation Tilt, Richard Nixon just wanted to get inside information about the Kennedys and AMWORLD for political gain, but that attempt would come back to haunt Nixon years later and help lead to Watergate.[34]

Linking Nixon to Pawley and Operation Tilt, even in a minor way, could have helped the Mafia if their plot to kill JFK had worked and Nixon had been elected president in 1964. However, Operation Tilt quickly fell apart and was soon replaced by another Mafia-backed sham Cuban effort, this one involving Bernard Barker.*

By the spring of 1963, Marcello, Trafficante, and Rosselli needed a way to force a cover-up after JFK's murder, not just by the CIA, but by also by Bobby Kennedy and the heads of other federal agencies. The CIA-Mafia Castro assassination plots were continuing, with attempts in March and April 1963. However, tying these to JFK's murder, as Rosselli would eventually do in his leaks to Jack Anderson, would only compromise certain CIA officials. Those plots had not been authorized by—and were unknown to—JFK, Bobby, and even CIA Director John McCone. They were known only to the level of Richard Helms, who had become Deputy Director for Plans after being left untainted by the Bay of Pigs fiasco. The Mafia needed a group that could involve Cuban exiles backed by the Kennedys, exiles whose activities would be reported on by the FBI and other federal agencies, all of whom would have to cover up those connections if they seemed linked to JFK's murder.

Spring 1963 presented an opportunity for the Mafia: The various Cuban groups were in a state of flux, just as the Kennedys were making it clear they were still interested in doing something about Fidel—but only with the aid of a few key exiles like Harry Williams. The Cuban Revolutionary Council begun by Hunt and Barker was in turmoil, and it would be summer before Tony Varona would assume control of the

---

* William Pawley would become the first of five witnesses to unexpectedly die in 1977 before they could be fully questioned about the JFK assassination by Congressional investigator Gaeton Fonzi. Pawley's suicide on January 7, 1977, was followed by the deaths of Charles Nicoletti, George DeMorhenschidt, and Barker associates Carlos Prio and Manuel Artime.

shell that was left. In the meantime, the CIA received a report in March 1963 saying that a group "of Cuban exiles in Chicago . . . were told the 'Nevada' group would help [them] since the US government could do nothing." According to another CIA memo, this Chicago exile group's support came from "gamblers in the West," specifically "large gambling interest backing," meaning the real owners of Las Vegas casinos. G. Robert Blakey pinpointed the source of funds more precisely, saying they came from "members of the underworld, whose gambling interests in Cuba had indeed been expropriated by Castro." The money probably involved Johnny Rosselli, the Chicago mob's point man in Las Vegas and Hollywood.

The front man for the new exile organization bankrolled by the Mafia was Paulino Sierra Martinez, a Cuban exile lawyer in Chicago who had previously not been a significant figure in exile circles. As briefly noted on page 161, his group was usually called by its initials, the JGCE, or "the Junta." Among the officers of Sierra's group was Felipe Rivero, the neo-Nazi who later that year would stalk JFK just five days before the President's murder. Eladio del Valle, Trafficante's Miami henchman who was close to David Ferrie in 1963, would also be tied to Sierra's group. A primary source for the CIA about the group was Bernard Barker, who passed along information from Frank Fiorini and other sources. Richard Cain was another CIA informant on JGCE's activities. Cain was the Mafioso and high official in the Cook County / Chicago Sheriff's Office who had worked on the CIA-Mafia plots with Rosselli and Trafficante.[35]

The JGCE was so mobbed up that its organized crime connections were noted in the first newspaper article about the group, which appeared in May 1963. Headlined "Gamblers Pop Out of Exile Grab Bag," the *Miami News* article quoted a participant in a recent Miami meeting as saying that "Chicago gamblers" had "offered $30 million" to help the exiles, in return for their overthrowing Fidel and forming "a government that will give back our investment with a reasonable profit." On one hand, the article made it easier for Sierra to get the ear of exile leaders in need of money. But on the other, the mob's clear backing—probably not intended to be publicly disclosed by Sierra, who wanted to make it look as if Chicago businessmen were putting up the money—would make it very difficult to recruit any exile leaders actually backed by the mob-fighting Kennedys.[36]

Three months after the newspaper article, Sierra made a direct approach to one of Bobby Kennedy's aides and to Harry Williams. But Sierra was shuffled off the State Department, like other groups deemed not suitable for inclusion in the Kennedys' JFK-Almeida coup plan. Though later Barker reported that Sierra made progress with a few groups like Alpha 66 and Eloy Menoyo's SNFE, Sierra and his group were effectively finished after JFK's murder. A CIA memo would indicate that the Mafia had essentially spent $50,000 to little effect, but in fact something better for Rosselli and his pals came along not long after Sierra's group was formed. The same May 19, 1963, *Miami News* article that headlined the start of Sierra's group included a subhead: "Bobby's Friend Another Hope." The article went on to describe Bay of Pigs veteran Harry Williams as "doing missionary work, probably with the blessing of Washington . . . a close friend of Attorney General Robert Kennedy, Williams has made numerous trips to Washington, New York, and Puerto Rico, talking to exile leaders." Soon the Mafia no longer needed to create a phony operation or exile group to use in JFK's murder, and instead of merely being an informant, Bernard Barker became a key player.

Cuban Army Commander Juan Almeida's offer to overthrow Fidel for JFK changed everything for Bernard Barker, as well as for his boss Trafficante's plans with Marcello and Rosselli to murder JFK. After the Bay of Pigs, Barker's career as a principal CIA agent seemed to wax and wane with the CIA-Mafia plots. The plotting was in a lull in the summer and fall of 1961, when the CIA seemed to have little interest in Barker. Since Barker had been indiscreet while passing out money for the Bay of Pigs, Cuban exiles now knew he worked for the CIA, a fact that limited his usefulness to the Agency. E. Howard Hunt, who was not working on Cuban matters in the summer of 1961, had to go to bat for Barker, recommending that he could still be valuable to the Agency in some capacity. By the winter of 1962, after William Harvey had taken over contact with Rosselli and with the blessing of Richard Helms had re-energized the CIA-Mafia plots, Barker was on a steady contract with the CIA. Working independently from Hunt, with a new official case officer, Barker was soon feeding Miami CIA headquarters with a steady stream of reports on exiles, including an increasing number from Frank Fiorini.

After Almeida's offer to the Kennedys in May 1963, Barker's old case officer (Hunt) was assigned to be one of two CIA officials working with Harry Williams. That Helms would give Hunt this assignment isn't too surprising, since Hunt's friend Manuel Artime and his old contact Tony Varona were the first two exile leaders to join Harry's and Bobby's coup plan. Years later, after Watergate broke, Hunt and Helms created a phony narrative to make it seem as if Hunt was adrift after the failure of the Bay of Pigs and was never again given an important CIA assignment because he was forever tainted by the debacle. However, even the released records about Hunt show that's not true, since within a few years Hunt would be "chief of covert action for Western Europe." In addition, only the CIA's top officials were forced to resign or had their careers curtailed after the failed operation. David Atlee Phillips certainly prospered in the Agency after the Bay of Pigs, and he hadn't even left the operation before the disastrous invasion, as had Hunt.

Assigning Hunt to help Harry made sense on several levels. From a security standpoint, it was wise to use someone who was not based at the CIA's huge Miami station, with its many agents, officers, and staff employees. Hunt's ostensible job was handling press and publications for the Domestic Operations Division. While parts of that job probably appealed to the hack spy novelist, no doubt he longed for more of the James Bondian action he wrote about, especially if it involved his long-time hope of eliminating Fidel. The CIA's Counter-Intelligence Chief, James Angleton, was extremely concerned that a high-level Soviet mole had penetrated the CIA, so having someone like Hunt work on the CIA's most sensitive operation—while using his Domestic Division job essentially as a cover—was good tradecraft. The fact that Hunt wasn't working on the JFK-Almeida coup plan full-time is probably the reason another CIA officer was also assigned to help Harry and why Hunt was allowed to resume having Barker as his assistant. Barker was based in Miami, where Harry lived, which made clandestine meetings convenient.[37]

Some in the CIA knew how close Hunt was to Artime, and a January 1963 CIA memo indicates their association was the reason that Hunt wasn't assigned to be Artime's official case officer, even before the emergence of Almeida. After Artime's AMWORLD side of the coup plan developed in the early summer of 1963, Henry Hecksher officially became Artime's case officer. Though AMWORLD was one of the most secret CIA operations, far more Agency personnel knew about it than about Almeida's identity. That ultrasensitive secret was reserved for a relative few CIA officers, an honor that it would make sense for Helms to bestow on his protégé, Hunt. Barker had learned to be more discreet since the Bay of Pigs and no doubt had ingratiated himself to Hunt once again during this sensitive new assignment.

Harry Williams met frequently with Barker and Hunt during the rest of 1963. He told us that for the JFK-Almeida coup plan "Barker was Hunt's assistant, very close to Hunt," and that Hunt worked extensively on the plan.[38] Another key Kennedy aide also confirmed that Hunt and Barker assisted Harry with the coup plan.[39] Though the released files do not reflect Hunt's work on planning the coup attempt, almost no operational files about Hunt from 1963 have been released, except for an old expense reimbursement involving Barker. However, Hunt himself has indicated how a CIA agent could be assigned to a Castro assassination project for which no paperwork exists (or has ever been released). We've written in earlier chapters about the likelihood that David Atlee Phillips was the mysterious "Maurice Bishop" who handled Alpha 66 and Antonio Veciana for the CIA—something Phillips and the CIA have always officially denied. However, in Hunt's 2007 autobiography, which the CIA reviewed and approved before publication, Hunt finally admits that his friend Phillips had indeed "helped support Alpha 66 [and] the organization's founder Antonio Veciana."[40] In terms of CIA paperwork, or the lack of it, the work of Hunt and Barker on the JFK-Almeida coup plan was probably handled the same way.

Harry explained that "to me it looked like Hunt had a lot of confidence in Barker and presented him as very much a man of action." Specifically, "Barker did dirty work for Hunt." What might that have included? Harry indicated the CIA handled three parts of the JFK-Almeida coup plan—and by "CIA," Harry meant either Hunt and Barker or the other CIA officer assigned to help Harry.* One CIA task was the $50,000 initial payment to Almeida, made to a foreign bank account, something Barker's money-laundering background could have facilitated. Another task was getting Almeida's wife and kids out of Cuba on a pretext, well before the projected coup date of December 1, 1963. They were safely out of Cuba—and under the surreptitious eye of the CIA—prior to November 22, 1963. Finally, there was the matter of setting up someone to take the blame for Castro's assassination, which Harry indicated was in the works but was something he didn't deal with.[41]

CIA travel records for Barker and Hunt for 1963 would be very helpful in determining their exact roles, but those have never been released. The CIA claimed they could find no records that Hunt had done any official travel during November 1963, but that seems unlikely. Regarding the number of meetings Harry had with Hunt and the other CIA officer assigned to help him, Harry said there were "dozens, from May to November [1963]."[42] For security reasons, almost all were held away

---

* Reported by William Turner and Anthony Summers in *Vanity Fair* to be James McCord, the CIA officer who became a Watergate burglar. McCord declined requests from Summers and the authors to comment on the matter.

from Miami, and Barker would sometimes help to arrange Harry's meetings with Hunt.

However, Harry noticed problems from the start with Barker, and his concerns only intensified the more he got to know him. He said Barker "was dishonest. I think the CIA knew" about Barker's criminal behavior, but the "CIA had to use that type of guy, too. That is part of the game." Harry explained that it "is dangerous [work]" and unless a person does it for patriotic reasons like himself without compensation, "not very many clean cut guys are involved."[43]

Harry said the fact that Barker "is a crook . . . was one of my [biggest] problems" in working on the coup plan.[44] It may have been more of a problem than Harry realized. Speaking of Santo Trafficante, Harry made it clear that "Barker was connected to him." In hindsight, that may seem like a huge red flag. But keep in mind that in 1963, one of Hunt's CIA associates had taken Harry to a meeting with Trafficante, where the godfather had tried to bribe Harry—supposedly so he could reopen his casinos if Harry's efforts against Castro were successful. Also, the CIA was still using Trafficante's associate, Johnny Rosselli, in the CIA-Mafia plots. Harry didn't realize at the time the danger that Trafficante represented to JFK—or to himself.[45]

Barker may well have played a role in trying to intimidate or kill Harry. In the incident we noted on page 55, in which former death squad leader Rolando Masferrer confronted Harry at Bobby Kennedy's Manhattan apartment, only someone like Barker could have let Masferrer know where Harry was. Barker and Masferrer had a mutual associate in Tony Varona, and all three were tied to Trafficante.

Likewise, the attempt to assassinate Harry in the restaurant in Guatemala City (mentioned on page 56) would have involved someone who knew Harry's travel schedule, and Barker was one of the few with access to that information. Harry had gone to Guatemala to visit Barker's friend Artime, who shows up frequently in Barker's 1963 CIA reports. We detailed the restaurant shooting in *Ultimate Sacrifice*, and we pointed out a similar Guatemala restaurant shooting that occurred years later, one that was linked to Artime when he was working with Barker.[46]

As 1963 progressed and the JFK-Almeida coup plan developed, Barker's CIA reports show him submitting a stream of information linked either to the mob or the coup plan. For example, Barker filed reports about a meeting between Artime and Varona to discuss unity, described Menoyo's "Plan Omega," and discussed the plans of Manolo Ray. Barker even submitted one "rumor" of a coup involving Ray and Commander

Almeida, just two weeks before the real coup with Almeida—slated for December 1, 1963—that Barker was actually working on.

Trafficante's man Fiorini was a constant source for Barker in 1963, sometimes telling him about his dealings with Artime. As noted earlier, Barker reported on Sierra's mob-backed "Junta" and Felipe Rivero, who would stalk President Kennedy the day before the attempt to assassinate JFK in Tampa.

Barker even reported on a little-known aspect of the ongoing CIA-Mafia plots to kill Fidel, one that involved Carlos Marcello. Barker's September 1963 CIA report reveals the plans of American mercenary Ed Arthur for a possible raid on Cuba. Arthur himself later confirmed a meeting in Miami that month with Sam Benton, a private detective who worked for Marcello, to discuss a raid that would assassinate Fidel Castro. Arthur says he backed out because he learned someone with the Chicago Mafia—and an associate of Johnny Rosselli—was involved.[47]

With so many connections to those involved in plotting the assassination of President Kennedy, it's no wonder that Barker himself was drawn into the plot to kill JFK.

"Barker . . . had something to do with the assassination of the President . . . He's involved, I'm sure!" Harry Williams almost yelled these words during our fourth interview with him, on November 13, 1992. It wasn't easy for Harry to say bad things about other Cuban exiles, especially if they were involved in the Bay of Pigs. He had made a point to mention Barker in each of our previous interviews, each time revealing more information about Barker's dishonesty. But Harry had been struggling with what he'd learned about Barker and JFK's murder for almost thirty years, and he could hardly contain himself when it finally burst to the surface.[48]

It had taken three interviews to build enough trust for Harry to finally tell us Almeida's name. Since then, Harry had learned that we were capable of uncovering additional information about the people and subjects he told us about. At that time, no files about AMWORLD or the "Plan for a coup in Cuba" had been released, and the JFK Act, which would trigger their disclosure, was in the news but had not yet been signed into law. However, we had accumulated thousands of pages of files and journalists' notes from private archives, hundreds of books and magazine articles, plus the reports and supporting volumes of the Warren Commission and House Select Committee on Assassinations. Harry knew by the time of our fourth interview that we were serious and would try to find out anything we could. His startling disclosure began for us a seventeen-year quest to find more information about Bernard Barker's involvement in JFK's murder.

Harry later told us that he "wouldn't be surprised of Barker was in Dallas when JFK was shot." That was an important statement because Harry—and we—were unaware at the time of two important indications of just such a thing.

Speculation originated in the 1970s that E. Howard Hunt was in Dallas when JFK was assassinated, initially because of Hunt's resemblance to one of the "three tramps" arrested after JFK's murder. However, the HSCA proved conclusively the tramp in question was much shorter and older than Hunt. That was further confirmed when the identities of the real tramps were finally released by the Dallas Police Department in the early 1990s. Hunt's inconsistent statements to various investigators about what he was doing in Washington at the time of JFK's murder, along with a lack of CIA documentation of his whereabouts, had also caused some to place Hunt in Dallas. Despite the speculation, we now know that Hunt was in Washington, in a top-secret critical meeting about the JFK-Almeida coup plan, with Harry Williams and other CIA officials. Since the coup operation was so secret that the CIA withheld it even from Congressional investigators in the 1970s, Hunt couldn't say anything publicly about the meeting. Therefore some journalists continued to pursue the possibility Hunt was in Dallas. Speculation also centered on Frank Fiorini as the tall tramp, but the HSCA and Dallas police records also proved that wasn't true.

Before the HSCA investigation, journalist Michael Canfield went to Dallas in April 1975 to talk to former Dallas deputy Seymour Weitzman, an important figure in the JFK investigation. Weitzman had helped find the rifle on the sixth floor of the Texas School Book Depository. He also witnessed the fragment of JFK's skull found in the grass, across from the grassy knoll. As we described on page 116, it's well-documented that Weitzman was one of the first law enforcement officials to reach the area behind the grassy knoll's picket fence. There he and another officer encountered a man claiming to be a Secret Service agent—even though no real agents were on the ground anywhere in Dealey Plaza.

It has been reported that soon after the Watergate arrests, Weitzman "had a nervous breakdown." Author Michael Canfield interviewed Weitzman in Dallas at "a home for aged war veterans." Canfield asked that Weitzman's doctor be present during the interview, but Canfield said that "Weitzman's memory seemed clear and sharp." Weitzman reviewed the day of JFK's assassination and described the man who claimed to be a Secret Service agent. He said the "agent . . . produced credentials and told him everything was under control" describing the agent as "medium height, dark hair and wearing a light windbreaker."[49]

Canfield then "showed him a photo of Sturgis [Fiorini] and Barker." Weitzman "immediately stated, 'Yes, that's him,' pointing to Bernard Barker." Just to be sure, "Canfield asked, 'Was this the man who produced the Secret Service credentials?' Weitzman responded, 'Yes, that's the same man.'" Weitzman even said he'd be willing "to make a tape recorded statement for official investigators." He was reluctant to do more and became fearful, saying, "So many witnesses have been killed . . . and two Cubans forced their way into my house and were waiting for me when I came home. I had to chase them out with my service revolver." However, the next day "Canfield made a poor quality tape recording of a telephone conversation with Weitzman in which he reaffirms the Barker identification."[50]

Some critics say that Weitzman's age and emotional illness make his identification questionable. Three years later, Weitzman's doctor felt his patient was not able to testify to the HSCA. But what about Barker's own statements about his whereabouts on November 22, 1963?

Canfield was party to a lawsuit involving E. Howard Hunt in which he and his coauthor obtained a sworn deposition from Bernard Barker. When their attorney asked Barker where he was on November 22, 1963, Barker initially remarked, "This is a question that came up during the Watergate Hearing." A review of Barker's Watergate testimony reveals no such questioning, but he could have been asked privately, perhaps after Johnny Rosselli's secret testimony brought the JFK assassination into the Watergate investigation.[51]

In Barker's deposition, he said that "since I was a Cuban Revolutionary Council agent, they would have me on record. I was working for the Agency, they know exactly everywhere I was, I reported to them daily." Barker was soon forced to clarify that he "didn't report necessarily every day, but just about every day I would get a call or assignment." That's not supported by the released files on Barker, but then they don't reflect his work as Hunt's assistant, either. Much of Barker's reporting consisted of calling in, which he could easily do from another city. In addition, the CIA would only know about Barker's travel if he asked for reimbursement, which was unlikely to occur if he were doing a job for Trafficante.[52]

Barker claimed to be at home, watching television at the time of the assassination, but he said no one but his family and friends could vouch for him that day. The attorney questioning Barker then "asked what soap opera he was watching at the time," and Barker replied that "he could not remember." The attorney then asked if Barker "heard of the assassination via a news flash." But Barker responded, "No," saying "I think I saw the parade, how the whole thing happened."[53]

If Barker "saw . . . how the whole thing happened," he didn't see it on live TV, or even on the news later that night. The motorcade wasn't broadcast live, even in Dallas. And the Zapruder film so well known today wasn't shown on TV at all until almost twelve years after JFK's murder. At the time of Barker's deposition, the film had been shown on TV a handful of times. In addition, the televised film was not the bright, colorful, and sharp restored version we're now used to. On the rare occasions it was shown, it was a grainy, dark copy of the somewhat fuzzy eight-millimeter film that looked nothing like the typical videotape or sixteen-millimeter news footage shown on TV at the time.[54]

According to a formerly secret HSCA memorandum about Barker, quoted here for the first time, "Barker was closely examined under oath by the [HSCA about] allegations under investigation by the Committee that Barker associates . . . Hunt and . . . Sturgis were in Dallas on November 22, 1963." We can't tell if the HSCA investigated Barker's possible presence in Dallas that day, because according to the National Archives website, as of July 2009, Barker's entire HSCA testimony remains unreleased. That is highly unusual, since even the testimony of far more senior CIA figures like E. Howard Hunt, Richard Helms, and David Atlee Phillips has been released in full. Generally for CIA figures, testimony is released and any sensitive terms or identities are censored—but it's remarkable that all of Barker's HSCA testimony remains secret.[55]

Even though the HSCA clearly conducted an investigation of Barker, it's not even mentioned in the HSCA's Final Report or in any of their supporting volumes. A six-page HSCA memorandum about Barker, recently discovered among the million-plus pages of files on the Mary Ferrell Foundation website, is the only indication Barker was investigated by the HSCA. However, the memorandum's biography of Barker does not mention the FBI report of Barker's gangster activity in Cuba, which may not have been provided to the Committee. There is no indication in the memo that the HSCA investigated Barker's Mafia ties.

The CIA withheld a large amount of material from the HSCA about the roles of Barker (as well as those of Hunt and Helms) in the JFK-Almeida coup plan, but they may have withheld other material as well.

A CIA Office of Security memo says that "3 sealed envelopes" were deleted from the Barker file given to the HSCA. The memo says that Barker had earlier been "of interest to the Senate [Church Committee that preceded the HSCA, but] prior to the release of Office of Security files to the [Church Committee] certain papers which were not to be made available were placed in sealed envelopes." Was the CIA hiding only information from Congress about the coup plan—or also files that linked Barker to the Mafia?

When Harry said that Barker "had something to do with the assassination of the President . . . he's involved, I'm sure!" he didn't mean that was true only if "Barker was in Dallas when JFK was shot." Harry made it clear he was referring to the fact that Barker had sold out the JFK-Almeida coup plan to Trafficante, who then used Barker somehow in JFK's assassination. We find the indications of Barker's presence in Dallas by Canfield and Barker's deposition interesting, but certainly not conclusive. If Barker was in Dallas on November 22, it wouldn't have been as a shooter; the mob bosses had professionals for that. As we noted on page 298, even Richard Helms had, for some reason, checked twice to see if anyone with the CIA "had been in Dallas on that particular day." However, there are other indications of Barker's involvement in JFK's murder for Trafficante.

"Bernard Barker [was] closely associated with organized crime, and specifically with two associates of Carlos Marcello's, Meyer Lansky and Santo Trafficante, Jr.," wrote Marcello biographer John H. Davis. Barker's ties to Trafficante were confirmed by former Senate investigator Bud Fensterwald and future Congressional investigator Michael Ewing. Davis also said that "Barker had been very much involved with the Cuban Revolutionary Council [CRC] in Miami, a Cuban exiles group that was closely linked to . . . New Orleans. This Louisiana group was supported by Carlos Marcello, who funneled his financial contributions to its leader, Sergio Arcacha Smith, through . . . David Ferrie."[56]

The small New Orleans office building that hosted the local branch of the CRC, the organization Barker helped to start prior to the Bay of Pigs invasion, was a nexus of activity for Lee Oswald and Guy Banister, the detective for Marcello whom witnesses say employed Oswald to do jobs for him in the summer of 1963. Gus Russo, a writer with numerous CIA sources, notes that "Banister was a key player in preparing the local Cuban exile contingent for the Bay of Pigs invasion . . . Banister's office was in the same building as Arcacha's CRC office and it is known that he saw David Ferrie, Arcacha's assistant, with some regularity." The address of the building housing the anti-Castro CRC in New Orleans was 544 Camp Street. That was the same address Oswald stamped on some of the pro-Castro leaflets he passed out in New Orleans in the summer of 1963 while working for Banister. Calls were even made from the building to Bobby Kennedy, because, as Arcacha told Russo, "Whenever we needed anything in New Orleans, I'd call Bobby Kennedy and he'd help us right away . . . I stayed in touch with him until the end."[57]

Twenty years ago John H. Davis wrote that "investigators also found credible links between Barker and Jack Ruby," and we now know that Ruby worked for Carlos Marcello. Fensterwald and Ewing point to an FBI report that Ruby had been involved in gunrunning with Barker's good friend Carlos Prio, who was also tied to Trafficante. Barker's close ties to Prio in the fall of 1963, when Prio was infiltrating Artime's AMWORLD part of the coup plan, are reflected in some of his reports to the CIA.[58]

Barker shared a secret trait with Jack Ruby—as well as with David Ferrie and Eladio del Valle—all of whom were involved in JFK's assassination and worked for Trafficante and Marcello. Cautiously explored here for the first time, Barker—like the other three—was a hebephile, an older man who preys on teenage males. Barker, who was married at the time of JFK's murder and had a child, carefully concealed his bisexuality. Barker's secret sex life is only relevant because his hebephilia—relatively rare in the general population—was shared by four of the dozen people knowingly involved in the mob bosses' murder of JFK. Though it could have been coincidence, the Mafia chiefs may have selected the men because their secret sexual lives gave the mob an additional hold over the men, since the consequences of exposure were so great.

The tangle of overlapping connections between these four middle-aged men is striking: Ferrie lived with del Valle in Miami during the early summer of 1963, when Ferrie was fighting his dismissal from Eastern Airlines for preying on teenagers. Del Valle and Barker resided in Miami and were involved with Trafficante. Ferrie worked for the CRC, which Barker had helped to start. Both Ferrie and Ruby worked for Marcello. Ruby and del Valle were involved in the same drug trafficking network. Their secret sex life was just one more thing the men had in common.

Harry carefully explained that Barker "corrupted a lot of young boys, you know what I mean? You know with the young boys? He worked for the CIA [but] did a lot of harm, especially to the reputation of the exile community." Harry pointed out that by "young boys" he meant that Barker targeted teenagers around the age of consent—otherwise Harry would have gone to the police. We should also point out that Harry was open-minded, especially for his time, and the gay or bisexual aspect of Barker's activities did not bother him. Though heterosexual, Harry was proud of having an openly gay friend before and during the Bay of Pigs invasion. Harry objected only to the age of Barker's teenage prey.[59]

Barker was married four times, but his longtime associate Frank Fiorini apparently alluded to Barker's secret life when he said in a published interview that "Barker tells everybody to call him 'Macho' . . . a man who is macho is supposed to be some kind of virile hard-charger. Calling Barker 'Macho' is like calling Liberace 'Slugger.'"[60]

That Barker was able to keep his dual sexual life secret from all but those who worked very closely with him says a lot about why he was a successful CIA agent for a time, and why he was even better at hiding his work for Trafficante. It also helps to show how he could deal with his involvement in JFK's murder.

Pulitzer Prize–winning reporter J. Anthony Lukas didn't know about Barker's secretive sex life when he analyzed Barker's carefully compartmentalized life, but he provides new insight into how Barker could commit the crimes he did. Lukas writes that

> In Miami, Barker led the life of a prosperous real estate man. But he had another life which he kept quite separate. Later, he [Barker] wrote about his two lives: "If I am asked my name on a mission, I give my operating name. That is not a lie; it is a cover. I am not Barker then. I am another person. It is a different dimension. I, Barker, would never go into a building in the dark of night, but . . . this other guy with a false name . . . could very well do this."[61]

Harry said that "Barker was very much against Kennedy," in contrast to the other CIA officer assigned to assist Harry, who "didn't hate JFK." Haynes Johnson, who knew Harry and Bobby Kennedy, noted the contrast between Barker and another Cuban exile CIA agent, Eugenio Martinez. Writing in the *Washington Post* about their appearance in a Bill Moyers special about the "Secret War" between the US and Cuba, Haynes said

> Bernard Barker and Rolando Martinez could not be more different. Barker comes over sneering, posturing, with an air of ugly venality as he defends the various illegal acts in which he participated. When

[journalist] George Crile remarks that it sounds like declaring war on the democratic system itself, with an analogy to the Nazis, Barker reacts venomously and angrily: "In other words we can't organize anything to defend ourselves. Huh? Because we are afraid that some people may call us Nazis. Then let us do nothing. I mean, this is what the Communists want you to think." [In contrast] Martinez speaks with disturbing eloquence, expressing in a rush of emotion so many doubts and so many contradictions and so many dilemmas.[62]

Barker's remarks are reminiscent of the neo-Nazi sentiments of Barker's associate Felipe Rivero and bring to mind Harry's comment that Barker's longtime friend Manuel Artime was so far to the right that he was practically "a Nazi." Still, why would Barker go so far as to actually participate in the murder of President Kennedy?

Trafficante and Marcello made the decision to kill JFK, but there were several reasons why Barker was not only following orders, but could also have been a willing participant. Based on all of the available information about Barker that we have studied for the past seventeen years, there appear to be three main reasons. One was the Bay of Pigs, on both a personal and a patriotic level. Barker's CIA associate David Morales, who confessed his role in JFK's murder, was known to his friends for vehemently raging against John and Robert Kennedy for the failure of the Bay of Pigs, and Barker probably shared those sentiments. On a more personal level, the failure of the Bay of Pigs represented a failed opportunity for Barker. When Barker was the CIA's covert bagman in Miami for the operation, he was at the height of his power and prestige in the Cuban exile community. If the invasion had somehow succeeded (which likely would have only happened if Fidel's assassination had caused JFK to send in US military forces), Barker could have expected to land a bigger role with the CIA and the new Cuban government, in a Cuba he had helped to liberate. Barker could therefore have blamed the Kennedys not only for the invasion's failure but also for his failure to achieve the success he craved.[63]

A second motivation for Barker could have been his worry that JFK would call off the JFK-Almeida coup plan at the last minute, in favor of the secret peace negotiations. It's clear that Barker knew about the secret talks because of the comment his best friend made when he and Barker appeared on a TV show together in May 1976. Barker and his friend were asked "about Kennedy's secret negotiations to reopen relations" with Cuba. Barker's friend—who was in the CIA with Barker in 1963—said that "we knew that thing was not gong to work!" The real question is how did lower-level exile CIA agents find out about JFK's highly secret peace attempt to Castro? Barker could have learned of them through Hunt, whose boss Desmond FitzGerald was in meetings where JFK's peace outreach was discussed.[64]

Barker's third motivation for participating in JFK's murder was probably money, a factor that helped to motivate other participants in the plot, like Jack Ruby and Michel Victor Mertz. Frank Fiorini stressed that Barker was concerned about accumulating and saving money, saying "Barker is the biggest Scrooge you ever saw" and giving many examples. Just three years after JFK's murder, Barker's desire for money would lead him to broker the illegal multimillion-dollar arms deal that we first mentioned on page 329.[65]

After Harry Williams told us Barker worked for Trafficante and had been involved in JFK's murder, he told us what he'd learned about the assassination, both from his extensive contacts in the exile community and his contacts with Barker. Regarding JFK's assassination, Harry told us, "No question there's a Mafia connection there . . . [Trafficante] is a Mafia guy and he was involved . . . the way I see it, he put [up] the money for some things," Given Barker's money-laundering background, he was in the ideal position to help with and manipulate money, since one of the main goals of Trafficante and Marcello was to tie JFK's assassination to the top-secret coup plan and AMWORLD, so that JFK's murder couldn't be fully investigated without exposing the plan to have Almeida overthrow Fidel. A good example was the bullet found in Oswald's rifle, which had been tied to pre-assassination reports in FBI and Treasury Department files about the coup plan, reports that were kept secret for more than thirty years.[66]

CIA memos confirm that "the Mafia" was considered by the CIA as a way to "cover CIA support . . . to AMWORLD bases." Barker was close friends with AMWORLD leader Artime, had experience hiding CIA support to exiles, and worked for Trafficante, so he was well-placed to assist with—and manipulate—the CIA's Mafia cover. It would have been easy for Barker to ensure that some of the CIA's money intended for Artime, money authorized by the Kennedys, was used in the JFK assassination plot. It's also interesting to note that Haynes Johnson dates Artime's involvement in the drug trade from around the time of those CIA-Mafia-AMWORLD memos. Laundering money intended for Artime through the Mafia might explain how Artime first became involved in Mafia drug trafficking. Also, the later tip to Senate investigators that Artime had "guilty knowledge" of JFK's assassination—which stops short of saying he was actively involved, but indicates he knew someone who was—could easily have been a reference to Artime's longtime friend Barker.[67]

Even when Harry Williams arranged to provide funds to two of the five main exile leaders for the coup plan, the money didn't come out of Harry's pocket. It was provided through the CIA, again giving Barker an opportunity to compromise the situation. One of the exile leaders to whom Harry gave money had already been involved in an earlier arms deal with Trafficante.[68]

Large sums of money were involved in aspects of JFK's murder. There was the $200,000 (over one million in today's dollars) that Mafia associates of Trafficante gave Tony Varona, and the identical figure for JFK's murderers in the briefcase that Trafficante, Frank Ragano, and another Tampa mobster argued over in December 1963 (see page 266). Even laundering smaller sums could have provided a chance for Barker to assist Trafficante, such as with the roughly $7,000 each obtained by Ferrie, Ruby, and Joseph Milteer prior to the assassination. (Given the earlier noted connections between Barker, Ferrie, Ruby, and Eladio del Valle, it would not be surprising if the latter received a similar sum in Miami.) In short, there were plenty of opportunities for Barker to help with JFK's murder even if he wasn't in Dealey Plaza or anywhere else in Dallas on November 22, 1963.

The main reason Trafficante used Barker in JFK's murder was because of his rare position as a CIA agent working on the ultra-secret JFK-Almeida coup plan, but Barker also fit the profile of others used in the JFK plot. Barker had longtime ties to organized crime, and so could be trusted to do his job and not talk or implicate his superiors, even if he were caught. Concepts like "need to know" and compartmentalization applied not only to Barker's intelligence job but also to organized crime. Like the other conspirators used by the Mafia bosses, if Barker were caught or implicated, he had his own clear motivation for killing JFK that the press and public would easily believe, one that wouldn't require further investigation. In Barker's case, it would have been because he was a Cuban exile angry over JFK's handling of the Bay of Pigs. Finally, Barker's intelligence job allowed him access to sensitive information and gave him the ability to feed disinformation into intelligence and law enforcement agencies.

Part II: Bernard Barker
and a New View of Watergate

JFK's assassination was a tragedy for America and the world, but it marked the start of a period of rising prosperity for Barker. His ascent would be threatened only by the exposure of the CIA-Mafia plots to kill Fidel and their tie to JFK's murder. Trying to plug that leak would lead Barker to the Watergate scandal and prison.

Barker's work on covert anti-Castro operations—and for Trafficante—didn't end after JFK's murder. On page 268, we discussed the CIA reports of an attempt to shoot Fidel Castro at a Havana TV station, on December 6, 1963. That assassination attempt was linked to Trafficante henchman Herminio Diaz, who was also linked to JFK's murder. Not surprisingly, Barker submitted a report about the rumored Castro shooting the following day.[1]

At least initially, Barker evaded the suspicion that Richard Helms apparently felt toward Trafficante associate Tony Varona, who was banished from a significant role in exile operations within two months of JFK's murder. Barker was given a lie detector test six months after JFK's assassination, but it appears to have had nothing to do with JFK's death. Even though Lyndon B. Johnson declined Bobby's pleas to continue the JFK-Almeida coup plan in January 1964, the new president continued to give official US support to Artime, Manolo Ray, and Eloy Menoyo, all of whom were discussed in CIA reports filed by Barker. Richard Helms seems to have greatly scaled back or ended the CIA-Mafia plots after JFK's murder. Though Miami CIA Operations Chief David Morales remained friends with Johnny Rosselli, Morales began working more closely with an appreciative Artime.

E. Howard Hunt's CIA "Fitness Report" covering the period from March 1963 to March 1964 is glowing, and some of the glory would be reflected on Hunt's main covert assistant, Barker. The Report pointed out that Hunt supervised seven CIA employees and the "fairness and precision of [Hunt's] management had patently won their respect and inspired their performance." While most of the Report clearly refers to Hunt's "expertise in the field of propaganda and publication" for the Domestic Operations Division, other parts could apply to his work with Barker on the JFK-Almeida coup plan. The Report praises Hunt's "objectivity and integrity" and his "habit of seeking maximum benefit for every dollar spent in time, effort or cash." The latter statement would soon prove to be true for Hunt and Barker in ways the CIA likely hadn't anticipated.

One reason CIA officials like Helms were happy about Hunt was that Commander Almeida remained in place and unexposed. With Harry Williams and Bobby Kennedy no longer involved in anti-Castro planning, Almeida was no longer actively plotting a coup against Fidel. Still, as long as Almeida remained unexposed, and while the CIA continued to covertly assist his wife and children outside Cuba, there was always a chance he could be used in the future. If something happened to Fidel even without CIA assistance—a reasonable expectation, given the historically volatile nature of Latin American politics at the time—Almeida could wind up running Cuba someday. Since the number of CIA officers that knew about Almeida was very small, Hunt probably continued to be involved in monitoring and covertly assisting Almeida's family, and if he was, it's also likely that Barker was helping him to some degree.

Apparently without telling LBJ, Richard Helms continued having his agents work with Rolando Cubela in 1964 and 1965 on the possibility of assassinating Fidel, with an eye toward eventually bringing Cubela together with Artime. Hunt has always denied working with Artime in 1964 and 1965, or having any connection to the Cubela plots, but knowledgeable journalists like Tad Szulc have long held that Hunt and Barker were part of the Cubela plot during that period. Szulc wrote that "Artime and Barker were involved . . . Hunt, according to the version with which I am familiar, was coordinating or helping to coordinate the assassination plot [involving] Rolando Cubela." The focus of the Cubela-Artime plotting was Spain, and as noted on pages 331 and 332, that fits with Helms's odd machinations of having Hunt pretend to resign from the CIA so he could be assigned to a never-disclosed covert CIA operation in Spain. Also, even though Artime's official case officer in 1963 and 1964 was Henry Hecksher, he apparently wasn't the only one supervising Artime. Gus Russo noted that "Artime's CIA case officer, Howard Hunt, received reports of Artime's 'lunches at Hickory Hill' [RFK's home]" during 1963.[2]

Barker's released CIA files don't reflect any of his work with Hunt from 1963 to 1965, but that's probably because Barker's actions for Hunt were filed under another alias. Barker's February 28, 1964, CIA contract extension by Desmond FitzGerald indicates that in addition to AMCLATTER-1 and "Spencer O. Terteling," Barker may have been using the name "Frank W. Zwerkling," but none of the Zwerkling files have ever been released. Likewise, none of Hunt's operational files for his best-known alias, "Eduardo," have ever been released—not from the Bay of Pigs, the JFK-Almeida coup plan, or from his work on the Cubela plot.[3]

But we recently discovered two memos that briefly mention "Eduardo" in connection with Cubela (code-named AMLASH-1). The first memo, from September 16, 1964, was sent from Madrid to the CIA Director and involves "Woodrow C. Olien," the CIA alias for the man who first recruited Barker. After talking about Cubela, "Olien" and the other man discuss someone code-named AMLASH-2, saying he doesn't look as useful for Cubela's Castro assassination plot as first hoped. As a result, the memo says that it's "quite likely 'Eduardo' will never appear to contact subject."[4]

A different memo says that "in January 65 when AMLASH-1 [Cubela] was in Madrid" he had dinner with three other Cubans, including one code-named AMLASH-3. "Contact instructions" were given to AMLASH-3 for meeting "someone he recognizes in the name of 'Eduardo.'" In the memo's next sentence, AMLASH-3 says he received three reports from Manuel Artime.[5]

Barker's 1964 and 1965 CIA reports remain full of information about Artime, Fiorini, and the few active exile groups. Though the general CIA effort against Fidel was winding down, Barker remained well-placed because he had good contacts in the exile groups still getting CIA support, which had all been part of the JFK-Almeida coup plan. Barker also continued his cover as a prize-fight manager to explain his trips to countries like Venezuela. Barker's lack of US citizenship was still a problem for him, but internal memos show the CIA didn't seem to expend much energy to resolve it.

The CIA even gave Barker special training that would later help him in the run-up to the Watergate burglaries. He was sent to New York for a special CIA course and then, according to J. Anthony Lukas, Barker "broke into New York City's Radio City Music Hall one night as part of a CIA 'test' of his surreptitious entry" skills.[6]

However, when it became clear to both the FBI and the CIA that at least two associates of Santo Trafficante (aside from Barker and Artime) knew about the Cubela operation by the spring of 1965, the CIA began winding down Artime's huge AMWORLD operation. Reports of lavish spending and criminal activity in the operation also contributed to its shut-down. After Cubela was arrested the following year, Cubela actually named Artime and several other CIA agents he had met (including "Olien") during his public trial in April 1966.[7]

Barker played the leading role in the sell-off of Artime's AMWORLD arms and supplies described on pages 329 and 330. Harry, who stumbled into a meeting about the sell-off by accident when he stopped by to see a friend, said "They sold everything . . . it was big money . . . I wouldn't be surprised if it was $5 million bucks." Harry said that Barker, Hunt, Artime, and at least two others "divided the money." Since CIA estimates of the US funds poured into Artime's operation range from $7 million to $50 million, Harry's figure might not be far off. There would no doubt be expenses and fencing fees, and the ill-gotten profits would have to be laundered to avoid taxes, which would reduce the total even more. Still, the amounts that Barker, Hunt, and Artime cleared would have been substantial.[8]

Harry said that Barker brokered the sell-off of arms, and he indicated that Trafficante was connected to the deal somehow, perhaps providing a link to his fellow mob boss, Meyer Lansky. Barker was a money launderer with no history of arms trafficking, so he would clearly have needed major help with the sell-off, both to complete such a large transaction and to avoid unwanted attention. Trafficante's involvement in facilitating the lucrative deal could have been his form of payment to Barker for the CIA agent's role in JFK's murder. From other cases, we know that Trafficante and Marcello tried to pay their operatives in the least traceable, most protected way possible. Helping Barker make a substantial sum on the deal could have been Trafficante's way of taking care of his payoff to Barker for JFK's murder right under the nose of the CIA—while ensuring that the CIA could never expose the payment without compromising Almeida's safety and causing an international incident. (Trafficante had put Helms and the CIA in a similar bind with their $200,000 payment to Tony Varona three months before JFK's murder.)[9]

Harry thought that he was lucky to get out of the meeting with Barker and the others alive, after telling the group he wouldn't be part of their deal and trying to get them to call it off. Later, trying to entice him once more, Barker essentially attempted to bribe Harry by asking him "to be his assistant. To help him [with the sell-off]." Harry declined, saying, "with friends like you I don't need any enemies." He "told Macho Barker that 'every time you do anything you hurt the Cuban community.'"[10]

After that, Harry had little to do with Barker but did continue to keep tabs on him, learning what Barker was up to and what he'd been involved in before Harry met him. (At one point, Harry's inquiries to other exiles about Barker and his associates may have triggered an erroneous rumor reported by a government informant, that Harry was getting ready to resume operations again.) Harry hadn't known that Barker was part of JFK's assassination at the time it happened, though he was troubled by some of Barker's behavior around that time. But Harry's suspicions became certainty as he learned more about Barker and his criminal activities. Using information obtained from his extensive contacts in the exile community, Harry discovered there was nothing temporary or excusable about Barker's work for Trafficante. Since Harry also kept up with Commander Almeida and the situation with Almeida's family, he realized that Barker couldn't even be investigated without exposing Almeida and the whole AMWORLD operation. There was nothing Harry could do but wait.

Richard Helms didn't have to wait to do something about Barker. President Lyndon B. Johnson appointed Helms as his new CIA Director in June of 1966, and Bernard Barker was terminated from the CIA the following month. Almost seven years later, after Watergate, Helms would testify under oath before the Senate Foreign Relations Committee that the CIA "fired" Barker at that time because "we found out he was involved in certain gambling and criminal elements."[11] In hindsight, one might think Helms's testimony that Barker, then notorious as a Watergate defendant, was involved in "gambling and criminal elements" in Miami would prompt questions about the Mafia and Trafficante. But it didn't, because Trafficante was virtually unknown to the general public at the time and the Mafia aspects of Watergate were almost never reported.

Still, it looked as if Helms was finally admitting to Congress what the FBI had known about Barker since 1950, and what Harry Williams had learned after working with Barker for just under a year. However, Helms soon corrected himself to the Senate and the press, since the CIA's official story about Barker after Watergate hadn't included any criminal behavior while Barker was in the CIA and neither did the files the CIA had given Congress.[12]

As noted earlier, the files about Barker given to Congressional investigators are clearly incomplete and sometimes inconsistent. Most CIA summaries of Barker's work for the Agency don't mention the reason Helms gave for "firing" Barker, and they read as though Barker was gently and nicely eased out of the Agency because he simply wasn't needed anymore. But one CIA file summary notes that a year before Barker was fired, his case officer expressed "concern that Barker may be becoming too involved with underworld elements."[13]

If one wanted to be generous toward Richard Helms, perhaps Helms realized or at least suspected Barker's role in the arms sell-off, or even in the JFK assassination. The first big wave of books and articles critical of the Warren Report had started to appear the same summer that Barker was fired. It's also interesting that Barker was fired even as his friend and former case officer, E. Howard Hunt, was returning to a lavish life in the United States following his mysterious assignment in Spain. On the other hand, Helms and the CIA may have simply had no more need for Barker after the disposing of Artime's arms, Cubela's arrest, and the end of the CIA-Mafia plots.

According to this CIA file, in July of 1966 Barker received a small CIA termination payment of $1,500 (a tiny fraction of what he got for the arms sell-off) and moved to Chicago. Little is known about Barker's time in Chicago, or even if he actually moved there. If he did, Barker was soon back in Miami—only this time he owned a growing real estate firm and built increasing political connections that included business deals with Richard Nixon's best friend, Bebe Rebozo. Barker's share from selling the AMWORLD arms no doubt helped him grow his business and attract more prominent business associates. Barker was also still involved with Trafficante, whose own criminal empire continued to grow and flourish, even as Trafficante spent more time in Miami and less in Tampa.[14]

Less than a year after Barker's termination, Richard Helms destroyed many of the files about the CIA-Mafia plots during the CIA Inspector General's investigation that was prompted by Johnny Rosselli's first leaks to Jack Anderson. The resulting IG Report, described in Chapter 35, was woefully incomplete, and was missing any mention of Barker, Hunt, "Eduardo," Almeida, Manolo Ray's contact with Cubela, and Rosselli's continued involvement in the plots after June of 1963. However, the process of having the report done gave Helms an opportunity to corral, and in some cases destroy, files that could have ended his career.

Barker had no known involvement in Bobby Kennedy's assassination in 1968. However, we documented in earlier chapters the possible con-

nection to Barker's old associate David Morales and a more definite connection to Trafficante's associate, Johnny Rosselli. Moreover, six years
after Bobby's murder, Barker made an odd comment in an NBC News
segment. According to an article in CIA files, Barker hinted to NBC of
"CIA knowledge of some strange connection between Cuban politics
and Robert Kennedy's death."[15] Barker's hint may have been accurate
in a way, since Bobby might have been killed to prevent any investigation into the links between the Cuban coup plan with Almeida and the
Mafia's murder of JFK. When Barker talked to NBC, he was only recently
out of prison and was trying to avoid further prosecution. Was his hint a
veiled threat, or an indirect request for help from the CIA or Trafficante?
We may never know, but Barker never had to return to prison after he
made his strange remarks linking Cuban politics to Bobby's death.

The seeds for Watergate were planted back in 1960 when the CIA-Mafia
plots with Trafficante and Rosselli first began under Vice President
Nixon. They began to germinate in 1963, with the growth of the CIA's
AMWORLD portion of the JFK-Almeida coup plan. CIA cables say that
Carlos Prio sent men to infiltrate AMWORLD, and one November 1963
CIA memo (cited on page 175) reported that Prio's men had "become
associated [with] Richard Nixon in accordance with Republican Party
plan [to] bring up the Cuban case before elections."[16] Nixon was simply
looking for a political advantage over JFK. Unfortunately for Nixon,
parts of AMWORLD were used by Trafficante, Rosselli, and Marcello
to kill JFK. Richard Nixon had nothing to do with JFK's murder, but his
need to hide his connection to Prio and AMWORLD at the time of JFK's
assassination—together with his role in spawning the CIA-Mafia plots
with Trafficante and Rosselli—would eventually lead to the Watergate
scandal.
    But before that happened, little-known events in 1968 and 1969, most
of them involving Bernard Barker or his associates, would lay critical
groundwork for the people who would play key, but often overlooked,
roles in Watergate. When you know more about that interconnected
group—which included Nixon, Rebozo, Barker, Artime, and others—
and what they were doing in the years before Barker's arrest at the final
Watergate break-in, many of the lingering mysteries about Watergate
become clearer.

By 1968, Bernard Barker was a fast-rising real estate businessman who
would soon have more than a dozen employees working for him. Barker

had become extremely well-connected, especially given the likelihood that Richard Nixon would win the November 1968 election. Thanks to the money from the arms sell-off, and to his contact with Trafficante, Barker's prospects were vastly more impressive than those depicted in his released CIA files, which just two years earlier portrayed him as someone who could only hope to get a low-level technical job after the CIA let him go.

Just as most people didn't realize that E. Howard Hunt had several ties to Nixon that predated Watergate until the publication of Anthony Summers's biography of Nixon, most historians are unaware of the pre-Watergate connections between Bernard Barker and those close to Nixon. We've noted that Barker's ties to Nixon's best friend, Bebe Rebozo, began during the buildup to the Bay of Pigs invasion, but their relationship really grew when Nixon sought the presidency. It's not widely known that during the 1968 campaign, Barker and Rebozo's main business partner, Edgardo Buttari, Sr., ran a group in Miami called "Cubans for Nixon-Agnew."[17] Rebozo was fifty-five when Nixon was elected, and Barker was just five years younger, so they were part of the same generation. Though Rebozo was born in Tampa, his parents were Cuban, but Rebozo tried to keep an arm's-length distance between himself and the often fractious world of exile politics. That's where his business partner Buttari and Bernard Barker came in handy for Rebozo.* And what was helpful for Rebozo was also helpful for his best friend, new president Richard Nixon.

Barker, Rebozo, Nixon, Buttari, and some of Barker's close associates were tied together in a series of complex, interlocking real estate deals and companies. Carefully organized to avoid legal or press scrutiny and protect Nixon's reputation, some of the deals surfaced in heavily detailed newspaper and magazine articles that appeared around the time of Watergate. However, they've been rarely noted since, both because they were so complicated and because the more dramatic developments of Watergate quickly overshadowed them.

For example, Anthony Summers learned that Barker and his best friend/business partner "were officers of real estate firms that acted in property deals for Nixon and Rebozo." William Turner found that *Newsday* had uncovered several unusual land deals in the 1960s and early 1970s involving Nixon and Bebe Rebozo and Miami's Keyes

---

* All of our references to "Buttari" or "Edgardo Buttari" only refer to Edgardo Buttari, Sr., not to his son, who had no involvement in any of the questionable matters discussed.

Realty. Barker's best friend/business partner was a vice president of Keyes Realty, which Nixon used "to broker the deal establishing the Florida White House on Key Biscayne." Barker's own real estate firm was "located in the Keyes building" and shared an important executive with Keyes. Barker's firm would later be "the corporate cover for the burglars in the Watergate break-in." Since Barker had run through much of the money from the sale of Artime's arms starting up his business, "Barker was financed in many of his real estate ventures by Bebe Rebozo." Turner notes that "Rebozo [was also] the silent partner to Richard Nixon" in various shady deals.[18]

Barker's associate Rebozo even lived in Nixon's Florida White House compound, occupying a house next to Nixon's. All the while, Rebozo was involved in various questionable or illegal business transactions: land deals with men tied to imprisoned Teamster leader Jimmy Hoffa, handling $195,000 in securities stolen by the Mafia, and using a mob boss to build a shopping center where one of Rebozo's tenants was Manuel Artime.[19] Santo Trafficante wasn't known for using complex deals to hide the true ownership of valuable real estate, but he had a close associate who was: Carlos Marcello. Perhaps that's why Summers was able to document that one of Rebozo's real estate partners made calls to associates of both Marcello and Trafficante.

While Barker was busy using Miami exiles to help get Nixon elected, his friend Artime was laying the groundwork for another chance to make money by going after Fidel. An FBI memo quoted here for the first time states that just before Nixon's election, "Artime claimed he had arranged an interview with . . . Richard M. Nixon, in order to establish the basis for a new plan which Artime hoped to put into effect." The FBI says that Artime got the interview with Nixon "through the assistance of [Buttari] who is acquainted with Mr. Charles G. 'Bebe' Rebozo . . . personal friend of President Nixon."[20]

Artime wanted Nixon to fund a new version of AMWORLD, telling the FBI's confidential informant that "he hoped to set up a training camp for Cuban exiles in Nicaragua." Artime said he had also "gone to Haiti . . . for the purpose of establishing a staging area for his future operations." The FBI memo said that according to information from Artime, "Mr. Rebozo would be the 'head man' for the next plan concerning Cuba."[21]

The FBI said that accompanying Artime on his 1968 and 1969 trips and participating in his efforts was a close friend of his, a Bay of Pigs veteran The Nation later described as being "an important Miami contact for the 'French connection' heroin ring," which revolved around Santo Trafficante. According to the FBI, Artime's heroin-connected friend owned real estate with Barker's associate, Edgardo Buttari, Sr.[22]

Artime's efforts appeared to be paying off, according to the FBI memo, because "on January 22, 1969 Artime . . . received word from [Buttari] a close friend of Mr. Rebozo, that in February of 1969, Artime would get the 'okay' signal." Artime explained to the FBI informant that "Buttari . . . was helping Artime so much in his contacts with Mr. Rebozo." Artime was so confident of success that he offered the exile FBI informant the position of Chief of Intelligence for this new operation, and Artime asked him to provide "10 additional names" of "prospective recruits."[23]

Artime's Cuban plans caught the eye of the FBI, which asked the CIA if he was again working for them. The Miami CIA office initially replied that they did have an "operational interest" in Artime. However, CIA headquarters told a different story. On January 6, 1969, a high FBI official received a memo about Artime, saying that "Mrs. Jane Roman, Central Intelligence Agency (CIA) advised . . . that CIA does not have any operational interest in the subject [or] plan to utilize Artime. [But the] CIA is interested in his activities and would appreciate receiving any information coming to our attention concerning [Artime]."[24]

Bebe Rebozo's FBI file calls "Barker [a] long-time operator for the CIA." After Nixon took office, Barker would take advantage of other Cuban exiles to help his own standing with Rebozo and Nixon. Barker continued to work closely with Buttari, whom the FBI says "was later called to Washington by the Nixon Administration to act as a consultant . . . when Nixon announced the blockade of Haiphong Harbor Buttari and Barker planned to take some action to support the Nixon administration. Barker called different exile groups around the United States and raised some money under the pretext it was for an operation against Cuba. The money was actually designated for pro-Nixon demonstrations to be held in Miami and other places."[25]

Just as Bernard Barker did E. Howard Hunt's "dirty work," Bebe Rebozo and his associates performed similar services for Richard Nixon. President Nixon had White House aides who could raise money for him, sometimes illegally, from the large corporate donors who usually wanted something in return. These ranged from $2 million from US milk producers wanting an increase in price supports to $400,000 from ITT to influence the location of the 1972 Republican convention. But for even more illicit types of donations, Nixon used Rebozo.[26]

William Turner points out that it's long been known that billionaire Howard Hughes funneled "$100,000 in $100 bills to . . . Bebe Rebozo as a Hughes post-election 1968 'campaign contribution' to Nixon," for help with his casinos and an airline purchase.[27] However, it's often overlooked that the contribution first involved Rebozo and attorney Edward P. Morgan, who helped Johnny Rosselli leak his CIA-Mafia plot stories about the JFK assassination to Jack Anderson. J. Anthony Lukas wrote that Rebozo had a Nixon associate first raise "the matter with Edward P. Morgan, a Washington attorney" in the "summer of 1968," even before Nixon's election. Senate Watergate Committee records cited by author Peter Dale Scott show that money started flowing to Hughes's top aide, "Robert Maheu, for possible payment to Nixon, beginning July 30, 1968." (In some ways, Hughes-Maheu-Rosselli-Morgan-Anderson formed an interconnected group the same way Nixon-Rebozo-Buttari-Artime-Barker-Trafficante and a few of their associates did.) The Hughes loan, and the CIA-Mafia plot stories Rosselli had leaked to Anderson, would soon come back to haunt Nixon.[28]

While many of Nixon's illegal campaign contributions were eventually tracked by Congressional investigators and journalists, and he sometimes discussed them on his White House tapes, that's not true for the money Nixon received from mob bosses and their associates. Even when the contributions are known from testimony—or when their results are clear, as in the case of Nixon's release of Hoffa—Nixon was smart enough not to mention them on his taping system or to leave a paper trail. There are a few vague references, such as Nixon's comment to John Dean that he knew where to get a million dollars for hush money, or $300,000 for two of his fired aides, but Nixon never mentions the source of his illicit funds.

Here is one source, which supplements the *Washington Star* article discussed on page 725, which reported that after an investigation ordered by General Alexander Haig, the "Army's Criminal Investigation Command [found] strong indications of a history of Nixon connections with money from organized crime." Author Dan Moldea found that

> a former Nixon aide, not privy to the Haig investigation, says that one of his associates in the White House mentioned to him . . . Nixon's possible "organized crime involvement." That conversation involved "a massive payoff" from those in [the] "Army Service Club scandals in Vietnam," during 1969 or 1970. The aide says that the Service Club rip-offs "involved the Mafia and millions of dollars," and that the main focus of the interest by "someone high up" in the White House

was on whether "the top Mafia guy" who ran "all these things in Southeast Asia" had made payoffs to Nixon. The crime figure, he says was "the one who was apparently known as the so-called mastermind or architect of the Southeast Asian drug trade . . . who was very powerful and very well known as a mob leader."[29]

Moldea pointed out that "according to government narcotics experts, the central figure in the Indochina-Golden Triangle narcotics traffic was Santo Trafficante." He then cited what another official said about Nixon's organized crime connections:

> "The whole goddam thing is too frightening to think about," says a Justice Department official. "We're talking about the President of the United States . . . a man who pardoned organized crime figures after millions were spent by the government putting them away, a guy who's had these connections since he was a congressman in the 1940s."[30]

The ties of Nixon's friend Rebozo to Trafficante associates like Barker, Artime, and the "Miami contact for the 'French connection' heroin ring" mentioned earlier would have made it easy for Rebozo to arrange such payoffs to Nixon from Trafficante. When Nixon was at his Florida White House, Rebozo frequently visited, he lived next door, and the men often went out on a large boat, far from prying eyes or ears.

However, keeping a lid on Nixon's illegal activities took a major turn in January 1971, when Jack Anderson ran two new columns about the CIA-Mafia plots and JFK's assassination, which said the plots started before the Bay of Pigs. For the first time, Anderson named Johnny Rosselli, as well as Howard Hughes aide Robert Maheu and ex-CIA officer William Harvey. We discussed those columns, and the reactions of Nixon's men, on pages 704–707, showing how they led to E. Howard Hunt's work for Nixon in what started as the "Plumbers Unit" (to plug unauthorized leaks) and led to Watergate. Nixon had secrets related to the columns that he wanted to keep hidden, as did CIA Director Richard Helms. Hunt was the ideal person to help both men, with his primary loyalty probably going to his CIA patron Helms, even though Hunt had supposedly "retired" from the Agency (for the second time in five years). Of course, Hunt's ultimate loyalty would have been to himself, since the subjects in Anderson's columns impacted him as well.

It's important to look for the first time specifically at Barker's role in the events leading up to Watergate in the context of his work for Traf-

ficante and the links of both men to Rebozo and his associates. Clearly,
Rebozo had much to hide, most of it related to Nixon or the mob or both.
However, Rebozo was the one far more likely to face charges and go
to jail if their illegal business and campaign activities became known.
There was also the more serious matter of Rebozo's links to those in the
drug trade with Trafficante, like Artime and the Miami exile involved
in the "heroin ring."

For Trafficante and Barker, the Anderson-Rosselli columns represented an extra threat: any more information could eventually lead to
the exposure of their involvement in JFK's murder (and would eventually cause Trafficante to have Rosselli murdered to ensure his silence).
For the next year and a half, in the months leading to the Watergate
arrests, Trafficante would have Barker do essentially the same thing
Barker had done during the JFK-Almeida coup plan. Barker would work
on the most secret operations of a president and the CIA (specifically
those of Richard Helms), while also advancing Trafficante's interests
and protecting the godfather from exposure. As in 1963, while Barker
would have wanted to help Hunt or Nixon when possible, Barker's
main loyalty would have been to Trafficante. It was simply a matter of
self-preservation.

Even though Barker potentially had far more powerful allies than
the average Cuban exile businessman, he still had reason to fear Trafficante. Barker's boss Hunt worked in Nixon's White House, and was
the protégé of the CIA Director, while Barker was business partners with
Nixon's best friend. But Barker would have done whatever Trafficante
wanted, because he knew the godfather had been able to get away with
murdering the president of the United States—and then the prime suspect, while he was in police custody.

As with the JFK-Almeida coup plan, Barker didn't have a leading role
in the Plumbers operations leading to Watergate (though he was more
highly placed than he had been in 1963), but Barker was in the right place
at the right time to serve Trafficante's needs. Helms had been positioning Hunt to eventually work for the White House well before Hunt was
officially hired. Hunt has told at least a dozen times how he reconnected
with Barker for the tenth anniversary of the Bay of Pigs in April 1971,
telling him things were getting started again about Cuba and with a new
operational group to be backed by the Nixon White House.[31]

The problem with Hunt's story is that he was not offered a job by
the White House until two months *after* he claims he reconnected with
Barker about the job. Also, a CIA file first noted by Peter Dale Scott

shows clearly that Hunt was still being used by the CIA (with a "Covert Security Approval for use by Central Cover Staff") months after he had apparently retired from the Agency.[32] The weight of the evidence demonstrates that Hunt was still working for Helms (under deep cover, as he had in Spain in 1965) after his retirement and even after Hunt started working in the White House. Some of Hunt's operations would be beneficial to the CIA as a whole, by taking the pressure off Helms to have the CIA perform Nixon's illegal political operations. Even making sure the JFK-Almeida coup plan wasn't exposed could be construed as being good for the administration and for the CIA. But some of Hunt's actions—especially making sure the CIA-Mafia plots weren't fully exposed—would be of particular benefit to his mentor, Helms.

It's logical that Hunt would turn to Barker as his number two, regardless of what doubts Helms might have had about him. Barker had made Hunt wealthy for a time, and Hunt trusted him. Then too, Barker had the same incentive as Hunt to make sure sensitive information didn't become widely known, from the full extent of the CIA's plotting with the Mafia to the JFK-Almeida coup plan.

The original plan Hunt explained to Barker in April 1971 was much larger than what eventually developed, even though the full extent of Watergate and related operations has never really been established. Hunt originally told Barker that his new operation "would reactivate 120 CIA veterans." The total never came close to that, but most people don't realize that at least a dozen rarely noted Cuban exiles (including Artime and Prio) were involved, in addition to those eventually arrested at the Watergate.[33] There are some indications that the total was much higher. In any event, as Barker said in a later interview, "I recruited the men and started the training."[34]

Barker worked for Hunt for free (aside from expense reimbursement), even though Hunt and G. Gordon Liddy were reportedly paid more than a thousand dollars for each break-in. Barker claimed he did it out of patriotism and because he hoped the operation would eventually topple Castro, and while those likely were factors, the normally tight-fisted Barker's largesse is probably more attributable to the fact he was also doing it for Trafficante.

It's logical, then, that one of the first people Barker recruited would be another Trafficante man, Frank Fiorini, by then using the name "Frank Sturgis." FBI reports say that "Fiorini has the reputation among Cuban exile activists of being a most untrustworthy, discredited, unsavory gangster type" and "of being a mercenary with Mafia type connections."[35] Another early recruit was Manuel Artime, who was part of Trafficante's drug network.

Some of the other Cuban exiles Barker recruited weren't linked to the Mafia, though they often had ties to those who were. For example, an HSCA file notes that Virgilio Gonzalez, "the professional locksmith" used on the main Watergate break-in, was "an old friend of former Cuban President Carlos Prio," who was tied to Trafficante.[36] Prio himself worked with Barker and Hunt on some of their projects, and both men would visit Prio shortly before the first Watergate break-in. William Turner writes that Prio also "became head of Cuban-Americans for Nixon-Agnew [and directed] a goon squad that roughed up antiwar demonstrators."[37]

To recruit and motivate the other Cuban exiles, Barker told them their work was all building toward action to remove Fidel Castro. Barker said that Hunt "mentioned something about planning for the second phase of the Bay of Pigs around the beginning of Nixon's second term."[38] That sounds unlikely, but it is true that, as Anthony Summers writes, when Nixon became "President in 1969, he promptly ordered the CIA to step up covert action against Castro at a time it was being wound down . . . in 1971 the CIA supplied a consignment of African swine fever virus to . . . anti-Castro operatives, who then smuggled it into Cuba. An outbreak of the disease followed six weeks later, requiring the slaughter of half-a-million pigs to avert an epidemic."[39] We want to stress that "swine fever virus" is confined to pigs and is different from the "swine flu" that is currently a major health concern.

However, the CIA was engaged in deadlier pursuits under Nixon. Based on Hunt's recent disclosure, it appears likely that the CIA— specifically David Atlee Phillips—was behind the 1971 attempt to assassinate Fidel Castro in Chile by Alpha 66's Antonio Veciana.[40] Later, other veterans of the JFK-era secret war against Fidel, like David Morales and Henry Hecksher, would be involved in the 1973 overthrow of Chile's leftist elected government of Salvador Allende (resulting in Allende's death) after Chilean general René Schneider was assassinated when he refused to stage an Almeida-like coup against Allende.

In 1971 and 1972, Hunt and Barker's group planned other assassinations, some as part of Nixon's expanded "war on drugs," which had the odd effect of increasing drug consumption and the coffers of Santo Trafficante. Author Henrik Kruger wrote an entire book documenting how Nixon's drug policies, reshuffling of federal drug enforcement, and involving his Plumbers in "drug enforcement" weakened some of the more traditional French Connection distributors while building up the Miami-based arm of the network, run by Cuban exiles working for Santo Trafficante. Kruger's work builds on that in the Pulitzer Prize–winning exposé by *Newsday* that first revealed the heroin trafficking of Michel Victor Mertz.

Congressional investigator Gaeton Fonzi wrote that "It has been suggested that Nixon's anti-drug campaign was, in actuality, a bid to establish his own intelligence network." Much evidence supports that view, since Hunt's Plumbers Unit employed Lou Conein, the controversial former CIA man. Conein would soon run a Special Operations group for the Drug Enforcement Administration whose duties included, according to Fonzi, "assassinating the key drug suppliers in Mexico." While Conein worked with Hunt, the *Washington Post* said their operations "stretched . . . far over the boundaries of legality."[41]

One of those plots included planning the assassination of Panamanian dictator Omar Torrijos. Jack Anderson would later write that "Hunt told a Boston television interviewer that there was 'concern' over Panama's drug smuggling and therefore, that 'if Torrijos didn't shape up and cooperate, he was going to be wasted.'" Hunt said, "the people in the Plumbers unit . . . had that as part of their brief." Anderson found that a "Dade Country, FL, investigation" had interviewed "Manuel Artime," who tied Barker to the plot. Artime said "he was working with Barker in Panama." Anderson quoted Senate investigator Michael Ewing as saying they'd discovered "a front, with a fictional subsidiary in Panama, linked to . . . Barker."[42] During a later deposition, when Hunt was asked, "Did you indicate to the press that you had knowledge of a plot to kill Omar Torrijos?" Hunt answered, "Well, I probably did."[43]

Torrijos wasn't assassinated by Hunt and Barker's crew, and neither was Jack Anderson, who was himself the reported target of an assassination plot by Hunt and Barker in 1972. However, other killings may have been linked to members of the Plumbers, such as one reported in the *New York Times* in 1972. That involved an official who was shot in a Guatemala City restaurant by two men with pistols, as almost happened to Harry Williams nine years earlier when he went to visit Artime. The slain official had recently begun dealing with Manuel Artime.[44]

It would have been easy for Barker to motivate exile members of the Plumbers by telling them that hit teams trained to slay drug lords could eventually be turned against Fidel. And if the slain drug kingpins had been competition for Trafficante, so much the better for Barker's ultimate boss.

Fiorini confirmed aspects of the drug assassination component of the Plumbers Unit, and he was also involved in a small investigation of JFK's murder undertaken by Hunt and Barker. Concerning the interview of a servant in Castro's household at the time of JFK's assassination, Hunt later testified that "I provided a raw report and submitted it to the Chief of the Western Hemisphere Division." After confirming Barker's role in the woman's interview, Hunt said, "I had part of that typed up in the White House and eventually sent a summary of it or a transcript over to CIA, and I may have accompanied that with a cassette tape."[45] The existence at one time of Hunt's report was confirmed by Congressional investigators, but the CIA has never been able to produce a copy. This is just one example of the many files involving Hunt and Barker that either are still withheld or were destroyed by Richard Helms before he was essentially fired by Nixon after the Watergate scandal.

Bernard Barker's role in Watergate could fill its own book, and what follows is meant only to supplement the highlights we covered in Chapters 61–63. As 1972 progressed, pressures were building on Nixon, Rebozo, Helms, Hunt, and Barker. Jack Anderson had written about Howard Hughes's payment the previous August, saying, "the money was delivered . . . to Bebe Rebozo, a Nixon confidant."[46] An FBI memo shows the Bureau interviewed Rebozo on March 9, 1972, apparently about another matter, but Rebozo stalled them, saying they should talk to Buttari.[47]

But a bigger problem was the Cuban report about CIA attempts to assassinate Fidel that was reportedly circulating in Washington by the spring of 1972. Later that year, Frank Fiorini described the report in an interview he gave to Andrew St. George. Congressional investigators confirmed the report's existence when they secretly interviewed Johnny Rosselli in January 1974. The report wasn't released to the public until 1975—three years after Fiorini had described the report in detail to St. George, and one year after Fiorini's interview was published.

Fiorini stressed in his interview with journalist Andrew St. George that the Cuban report about the CIA's Castro assassination plots was their main target at the Watergate and other locales. However, Fiorini said the Watergate burglars were watching for other items as well: "We were looking for everything . . . our assignment was to photograph 2,000 documents that night." They wanted "any document with money on it . . . anything that had to do with Howard Hughes . . . damaging rumors about Republican leaders [and] everything that could be leaked to the press with a damaging effect to the McGovern people." Fiorini was probably more credible than usual in this interview with Andrew St. George. It was conducted with no attorney or spin doctor present, and Fiorini didn't even want it published. While sitting in jail, Fiorini told St. George, "If you attempt to publish what I've told you, I am a dead man." (Perhaps that's why St. George waited almost two years to have the interview published.) Fiorini was unusually candid with St. George, whom he'd known since the late 1950s. Fiorini was so comfortable that at one point in the interview, he even slipped up and admitted that he and Hunt had met during the Bay of Pigs planning, something that Fiorini and Hunt denied every other time they were interviewed by journalists or gave testimony. Hunt finally admitted it was true shortly before he died.[48]

It's clear that the Cuban report about the CIA's Castro assassination plots was the main goal of Barker and the other burglars. If they found the other items they were keeping an eye out for, that would be icing on the cake, but they weren't the kinds of things for which Nixon would have been willing to risk his presidency. While some writers theorize Watergate was only about the $100,000 Hughes gave Rebozo, that wouldn't explain why there were break-ins at places like the Chilean Embassy in Washington. A high-level CIA memo says that John Dean linked Bernard Barker to the break-in at Chile's Embassy, which occurred shortly before the first Watergate break-in in May 1972.

In addition to that burglary and the others listed on page 719, there were reports of even more. J. Anthony Lukas wrote that in May 1972, just prior to the initial unsuccessful Watergate break-in, Hunt and Barker's team cased and made plans to bug "the offices of McGovern's two top aides, Frank Mankiewicz and Gary Hart." Five years earlier, Mankiewicz had secretly investigated JFK's assassination for Bobby Kennedy, while Hart would soon be part of a Senate committee investigating the CIA-Mafia plots and JFK's murder. According to Lukas, Hunt ordered Barker to get ready for a break-in to bug Mankiewicz and Hart's offices on Memorial Day 1972 and told him photographing documents would be part of the mission. Lukas also pointed out that aside from their main target at the large Watergate office/hotel/apartment complex, Barker and the other Watergate burglars were "mentioned in connection with a May 16 burglary of a prominent Democratic law firm in the Watergate, whose members included . . . Sargent Shriver, John Kennedy's brother-in-law."[49]

Other reported break-ins have been linked to Barker and his group, and the fact that there were so many helps to explain why eventually one was almost bound to fail in a major way. (There had already been small failures, such as the first two unsuccessful attempts to break in to the Watergate.) Some writers have claimed the final Watergate break-in was intentionally sabotaged, but no one loyal to Nixon would have done so, and the same goes for anyone working for the CIA or who was personally loyal to Helms. No evidence has ever emerged to show that one of the burglars was a Democratic plant. It's very likely that since so many burglaries were being attempted in an increasingly short time frame, some catastrophic failure was almost inevitable. Andrew St. George broached the idea more than thirty years ago, writing that "the idea behind the Watergate break-in does not seem so absurd if we keep in mind that it was never meant to be a one-shot operation."[50]

The Cuban report about CIA Castro assassination plots that Barker and the others were looking for explains why certain people were chosen for the Watergate operations, as well as Nixon's references to the "Bay of Pigs thing" on White House tapes. The shared secret between Nixon, Hunt, Barker, Fiorini, and Artime was the CIA-Mafia plots with Trafficante and Rosselli. Those had begun as Vice President Nixon's 1960 "October Surprise" and then continued in the greatly expanded operation that became the Bay of Pigs invasion. By November 1963 most of the same people had some tie to Artime's AMWORLD, which CIA memos say Carlos Prio was infiltrating in an operation linked to Richard Nixon. By the spring of 1972, Nixon knew he would be in a simply untenable situation if his politically motivated skullduggery in 1960 or 1963 should be exposed by the Democrats—or by Jack Anderson or Chile's leftist government (in retaliation for Nixon's covert operations against it or the attempt to kill Fidel there in 1971). Nixon apparently felt he had to use more political skullduggery to make sure that didn't happen.

In some ways, Richard Nixon in 1972 was like Bobby Kennedy in 1963. Like Bobby, Nixon was busy with the regular duties of his office; his covert operations were not part of his official position. At best, they could receive only a small amount of his attention in a typical day, and often none at all for days at a time. As with Bobby, underlings were doing things that Nixon probably didn't realize or fully understand. Just as some might say that Bobby lost JFK because he was trying to do too much on too many different fronts, it could be said that Nixon would lose the presidency in much the same way. Just as the Kennedys seemed more concerned about Castro in the fall of 1963 than the general public (something the Republicans hoped to change in 1964), Nixon may have been more worried about the emergence of the CIA-Mafia plots than his base would have been. The fact that a dozen people who were working on—or had infiltrated—Bobby's November 1963 coup plan with Almeida were later involved in various aspects of Watergate completes the parallel. The fact that Almeida was still in place and unexposed also gave certain officials and agencies the national security excuse to keep so much about the Watergate participants from the press and public.

According to the FBI, two weeks before the Watergate arrests Hunt met with Artime in Miami and spent the night at his home.[51] After Watergate, Artime would launder and help to distribute some of the hush money to the burglars. Before the break-in, Barker laundered $114,000 worth of Nixon "campaign contributions" of questionable legality, including some from an associate of George H. W. Bush. Barker ran the money through the bank account of his Miami real estate firm, and some of the funds would be used for the burglaries. Barker apparently kept $2,500 of the money for his trouble.[52]

According to investigators and Frank Fiorini, Bernard Barker committed some of the key errors that led to the arrest of Barker, Fiorini, Eugenio Martinez, Virgilio Gonzalez, and James McCord at the Watergate early on June 17, 1972. (E. Howard Hunt and G. Gordon Liddy, monitoring the operation from nearby, would be arrested later.) Fiorini primarily blames his longtime associate for the break-in's disastrous failure. He told Andrew St. George that Barker's cheapness was one factor, since it was the inexpensive tape Barker provided that was first noticed by the Watergate security guard, even though

> there were a dozen ways of keeping that lock open—ways that would not have been spotted. Barker was just as stupid about his goddamn walkie-talkie . . . his only job was to keep his ear to that goddamn walkie-talkie, listening to our lookout across from the Watergate in case there was any outside problem . . . But Barker [is] too cheap to install a fresh battery in the thing before an operation; no, he keeps the old battery going week after week by never turning up the volume . . . the night we got arrested, the minute we get safely inside the [Democratic National Committee office at the Watergate] Macho turns the volume of his walkie-talkie all the way down . . . saving the battery. He also kept us from picking up the first warning calls from the lookout across the street [who] saw the unmarked police car arrive, saw the cops begin turning up the lights on one floor after another . . . we suspected nothing until finally Barker heard

the footsteps of the cops pounding outside our door and [finally] turned up his walkie-talkie. Hunt was stationed in another section of the Watergate complex and his voice came in, squeaky with tension, "Alert! Alert! Do you read me? Clear out immediately" . . . but by then it was too late: the cops were in the corridor. Barker saved his damn walkie-talkie battery and blew our team.[53]

Barker and the others committed additional errors that resulted in their arrests. British researcher John Simkin compiled a list of the mistakes committed by each of those involved with the burglaries. Barker's most famous mistake was having his address book on him when he was arrested; in it were the initials "WH HH" and Hunt's phone number at the White House. It's often overlooked that Eugenio Martinez also had an address book containing a similar entry.[54]

Simkin pointed out that part of the $114,000 Barker had laundered was found on him and eventually was traced through his bank account to Nixon's campaign committee (CREEP), creating a link between the burglary and the White House. Also, after the first successful Watergate break-in, Barker had the film they'd taken of Democratic documents developed at a commercial camera shop in Miami, whose owner was suspicious and contacted the FBI. Finally, Barker "had his hotel key in his pocket" when arrested, which "enabled the police to find traceable material in Barker's hotel room."[55]

Simkin lists Barker as committing six critical errors, compared to eight for Hunt and seven for McCord and Liddy. But Barker could have also influenced some of the errors Hunt committed (and vice versa), making Barker an often-overlooked figure in the operation's exposure, which led to numerous prosecutions of Nixon administration illegality not directly related to the break-ins.[56]

It's not hard to imagine Harry's shock when he saw news of the arrest of his old associate Barker—and later, when Harry recognized E. Howard Hunt's picture after Hunt was linked to the break-in. (Harry had only known Hunt under his CIA alias of "Eduardo" when they worked together in 1963.) Soon after, Harry heard in Miami's Cuban exile community about Artime's efforts to provide financial assistance to the burglars. The involvement of Barker, Hunt, and Artime—the people he'd worked with on the JFK-Almeida coup plan—seemed beyond coincidence.

But, with Almeida still in place, high in the Cuban government and unexposed, Harry thought there was little he could do. He did give an interview to William Turner in 1973, just after the tenth anniversary of JFK's murder, though he was careful not to mention Almeida or reveal too much about the coup. Harry mentioned Hunt and Barker, but information from the interview wasn't published until 1981, after the Watergate-mania of the early and mid-1970s had long faded.

Rather than viewing all the machinations of Watergate's aftermath as a grand scheme with one person pulling the strings, as some have suggested, it's now clear that most of the participants simply acted to protect their own interests. Sometimes those interests aligned, and sometimes they didn't. A good example is Nixon's June 23, 1972, "Smoking Gun" audiotape, the one whose eventual release over two years later finally triggered his resignation. The information we've revealed about Barker puts a new spin on Nixon's desperation to have the CIA put a stop to the FBI's investigation of the break-in. Barker isn't referred to by name—just lumped in with "the Cubans"—but Hunt is. Keep in mind Barker's role as Hunt's assistant in the Bay of Pigs (probably including the CIA-Mafia plots), the JFK-Almeida coup plan, and Watergate, as Nixon says,

> we protected Helms from one hell of a lot of things . . . Of course, this Hunt will uncover a lot of things. You open that scab, there's a hell of a lot of things and that we just feel that it would be very detrimental to have this thing go any further. This involves these Cubans, Hunt, and a lot of hanky-panky that we have nothing to do with ourselves. . . . Look, the problem is that this will open the whole, the whole Bay of Pigs thing . . . [just tell the CIA that] the President believes that it is going to open the whole Bay of Pigs thing up again. And, because these people are plugging for, for keeps and that they should call the FBI in and say that we wish for the good of the country, don't go any further into this case, period![57]

It's clear how Nixon planned to use Hunt's CIA past as leverage to get CIA Director Richard Helms to help him. It worked for a time, just not long enough to save Nixon.

One set of questions to which we may never find definitive answers is how much Richard Nixon knew about Bernard Barker. When—and how much—did Nixon know about Barker's ties to Rebozo? How much did Nixon know about Barker's CIA work for Hunt? What about Barker's ties to Trafficante? Some of that information would have come from Rebozo, so it's beyond the usual White House tapes and Watergate testimony. It's plausible that Nixon learned at least some of Barker's connections after the fact, because Rebozo would want help making sure they weren't exposed. Anthony Summers cited Nixon's White House tapes, which showed that

> Bebe Rebozo's name kept being mentioned on the tapes . . . in a
> way that suggests Nixon was nervous about his friend's vulner-
> ability. At one point, while discussing the fact that Howard Hunt's
> name had turned up in two of the burglars' contact books, [Nixon]
> suddenly asked an odd question: "Is Rebozo's name in anyone's
> address book?"[58]

As for E. Howard Hunt, after Watergate he appears to have been essentially protecting the interests of the CIA in general and Helms in particular, since the CIA Director was vulnerable on many of the same points
as Nixon. Hunt probably assumed Barker had Hunt's interests at heart,
together with those of Barker's former employer, the CIA. But Barker
was probably primarily protecting the interests of Trafficante, as was his
associate Fiorini. Barker also had to protect himself, since he had been
involved with Trafficante in JFK's assassination.

Barker's friend Artime made out fairly well after Watergate. By
spreading hush money after the arrests, Artime was able to help Barker
and Hunt and their families. In the process, he also made sure that his
drug trafficking with Trafficante wasn't exposed. The hush money also
helped to ingratiate Artime with Nixon. Fensterwald and Ewing documented that "the Senate Watergate Committee investigation disclosed
that President Nixon had personal knowledge of Manuel Artime's early
hush money payments to the Watergate burglars" and that's probably
why "Artime was invited by the Nixon Administration to attend the
second inauguration of President Nixon."[59] According to Haynes Johnson, Artime's assistant at the time, Milian Rodriguez, reported that the
amounts distributed to Barker and the others were much larger than
most investigators realized. Milian Rodriguez later used the skills he
first learned with Artime and the hush money to become a major drug
trafficker and Iran-Contra figure.[60]

G. Gordon Liddy is known for saying the least of any of the Watergate
defendants during their prosecution. But an often overlooked reason is
that Liddy was the least informed of all the Watergate burglars, since
he shared none of the others' CIA anti-Castro background. Years later,
Liddy had to testify in civil trials related to Watergate. In one, the Associated Press reported that Liddy "testified that he was kept in the dark
about the 1972 break-in he helped organize . . . he learned afterward that
the 1972 burglary was not an attempt to tap phones." Instead, "Liddy
testified that the break-in mysteriously turned from one of a skeleton
crew quickly bugging the office to one with a full crew of burglars and
a load of photographic equipment," which is consistent with Fiorini's
account.[61]

In another trial, Liddy revealed more about the Watergate burglars, and at least some of his description could apply to Barker. Liddy testified that "Mr. Hunt, to impress upon me the high caliber of these individuals, stated that they had accounted among them for a substantial number of deaths . . . he indicated that these . . . Cuban individuals were connected in some way with organized crime."

In hindsight, it's amazing that Watergate didn't mushroom into a big scandal before the 1972 election. Much of the credit goes to the effective spin control of the White House and Richard Helms's CIA. Deals were cut, by people like Bob Bennett, head of the CIA front company Hunt had worked for prior to going to the White House. Bennett, currently a US Senator from Utah, essentially fed information to Bob Woodward in return for the *Washington Post*'s going easy on the CIA. That cemented a good relationship between Helms and the *Post* for years.[62]

Richard Helms lost his job after the election, and as mentioned on page 724, Helms spent his last ten days as CIA Director in January 1973 destroying a vast quantity of information, including his own office tapes and transcripts. Much of the information about Hunt and Barker was probably lost forever at that point. However, the operations both men were involved in—the Bay of Pigs and AMWORLD—were so large that many related files probably still exist. In addition, the FBI surely had extensive files on each man, only some of which they would have shared with the CIA.

Helms and the CIA were sometimes just lucky. J. Anthony Lukas pointed out that "the *New York Times* assigned the Watergate story at first to its Latin American specialist, Tad Szulc, who spent valuable days tracking down the ties Bernie Barker and his men had to Cuban exile groups in Miami."[63] Szulc uncovered a lot, but most of it went into one long *Esquire* article and his Hunt biography, not onto the front pages of the *Times*. Other mainstream reporters failed to pursue his revelations about Hunt and Barker and the CIA's plans for a second invasion with Cubela. If it had been possible for someone to put Szulc's revelations about Barker and Hunt together with Turner's interview with Harry Williams and Richard Sprague's interview with Haynes Johnson, much of Barker's background might have come out decades sooner. At the time, though, no one person had all the pieces.

According to the *New York Times*, in January 1973, Bernard Barker pleaded guilty "to seven charges of conspiracy, burglary and wiretapping" and on November 19, 1973, "Judge John J. Sirica . . . sentenced

Barker to a prison term of 18 months to six years."[64] Two weeks after Barker's sentencing, NBC News reported that the Miami-Dade County prosecutor was seeking "more information on Bebe Rebozo's bank [from] Bernard Barker."[65]

However, an investigative report in *Rolling Stone* reported that "Bebe Rebozo escaped indictment in Watergate despite strong circumstantial evidence of tax evasion and bribe taking. One reason, according to CIA sources, is that CIA officials sanctioned his plea of 'national security' when the special prosecutor's office began investigating Rebozo's" business affairs.[66]

Rebozo was with Nixon at the White House when the President made his decision to resign. Nixon was pardoned a month later, on September 8, 1974, by President Gerald Ford. Nixon was home free, since Ford's unconditional pardon was for ANY crimes Nixon might have committed in the White House, even those that might come to light later. The same was essentially true for Bebe Rebozo. The pardon took the spotlight away from Nixon and from his personal friends, since prosecutors no longer had any incentive to go after them in hopes they'd "flip" and testify against Nixon. In the case of someone like Rebozo, even if he were prosecuted, Nixon could simply claim that he as president had ordered Rebozo to do the offending act, since Nixon himself was immune to prosecution.

Financially, Nixon had made out well as president. The *St. Petersburg Times* noted Nixon's net assets when he took office were $307,141, but had increased to almost a million dollars just over four years later. (Despite his presidential salary, Nixon only "paid $782 in federal taxes in 1970 and $878 in 1971.") It is possible that Nixon made even more, since Jack Anderson reported that both Nixon and Bebe Rebozo hid money in Swiss banks. Compared to Nixon, Rebozo made out even better, seeing his net worth increase at least six-fold during his friend's term in office, to a reported total of $4.5 million.[67]

Santo Trafficante probably made out best of all financially, and unlike his underlings Barker and Fiorini, Trafficante didn't have to spend a single day in prison, even though he was prosecuted because of an offshoot of the Watergate prosecutions.

Bernard Barker was released from prison in January 1974 so that he could pursue an appeal. The following month, after a tip from Jimmy Hoffa, Johnny Rosselli had to give secret testimony to the Watergate Committee behind closed doors, starting him on a road that would eventually lead Trafficante to order his execution. Barker's own testimony had been in a public session, on May 24, 1973, so it was clear to Trafficante that Barker had said nothing that could endanger the godfather or his associates.

A CIA memo shows that on March 10, 1974, Barker called the CIA, saying he was worried because a "newsman had just . . . indicated that Ambassador [Richard] Helms testified that Mr. Barker [was] formerly associated with criminal and gambling elements." In fact, Helms had so testified a year earlier, while being confirmed as ambassador to Iran, but his testimony had just been released. However, Helms worked with the CIA to quickly issue a retraction before the news media started investigating Barker's Mafia ties.[68] Barker got more good news on July 11, 1975, when Judge Sirica reduced the sentences of Barker and his Cuban exile codefendants to time served. Barker was a free man.

Also in the summer of 1975, Barker was working on a book with authors Taylor Branch (later a noted biographer of Martin Luther King) and George Crile (best known for the book that inspired the movie *Charlie Wilson's War*). Their book with Barker was going to be called *Cuban Terror and the CIA*. A description of the book says it would include "the firsthand experience of" Cuban exiles "from the Bay of Pigs to Watergate" including "buggings, assassinations, spy operations . . . the Cubans participated in CIA conspiracies that included the Mafia." The advertising copy says, "Cuban Americans told their stories to Branch and Crile out of loyalty to Bernard Barker and Eugenio Martinez, around whose lives this book is built." It was slated to run "240 pages [with] 16 pages of photographs"—but it would never be published.[69]

A Cuban exile CIA asset tipped the Agency off about the book after Barker claimed to the asset that the CIA had approved the project. Barker had lied, and the CIA sent Barker a stern letter on June 20, 1975, reminding him of the CIA secrecy oath included in his April 1960 CIA contract. Barker's book was apparently cancelled. When Branch and Crile wrote a lengthy article for *Harper's Magazine* in August 1975 about the CIA's anti-Castro operations, for some reason Barker wasn't mentioned even though Eugenio Martinez was extensively quoted. As a former CIA employee, Martinez would have been subject to the same secrecy rules as Barker—so why was he included, and Barker not?[70]

The week before the CIA's letter to Barker about his book discussing "assassinations [and] CIA conspiracies involving the Mafia," Richard Helms had to testify to the Senate Church Committee in private about the CIA-Mafia plots to assassinate Fidel. The following week, Sam Giancana was murdered before he could testify to the Committee, in a killing linked to Trafficante. Barker's real boss, Trafficante, was also linked to Jimmy Hoffa's murder, the following month.

Demand for Watergate books was still so high that any book by Barker, even one gutted by the Agency, would have sold. But Barker probably figured that no amount of sales was worth risking his life. On October 28, 1975, Walter Cronkite reported on CBS news that even though Barker owed "$86,000 in attorney's fees" and "the Florida Real Estate Commission wants to revoke his license," Barker had to settle for a job as a Miami Sanitation inspector for $10,000 a year. At least Barker would get to have a "badge and arrest those who violate the sanitation code"—not bad for someone who'd only recently been released from prison. Barker was luckier than another Trafficante associate linked to JFK's murder: Rolando Masferrer. Three days after Barker started his sanitation job, Masferrer was killed in a car bombing. Barker never published a book, and he limited his publicity to occasional TV shows.[71]

In August 1976, Johnny Rosselli was brutally murdered, apparently on the orders of Santo Trafficante. Starting in 1977, Barker saw a spate of deaths of those linked to JFK's murder or to Trafficante, including the suicide of his friend Carlos Prio and the sudden, fatal illness of Manuel Artime before he could testify to the House Select Committee on Assassinations. Trafficante finally had to testify to the HSCA in November 1977 and September 1978, but he gave up only a few things of tangential importance, even after being given immunity. David Morales had died in May 1978 before he could testify. But Barker himself had to testify on August 29, 1978. He likely said nothing crucial, but it's hard to tell, since Barker's entire testimony remains secret.

While some of Barker's old CIA associates got renewed life during the Iran-Contra operation in the 1980s, Barker missed out on the action, though he was able to get a better job in Miami, as a building inspector. Barker remained silent about anything that really mattered, even after his old boss Trafficante died in March 1987. There was no way for Barker to capitalize on any of the secrets he knew without potentially implicating himself in JFK's murder. Instead, Barker took an early retirement when he turned sixty-four, to avoid facing a hearing about accusations that he'd been "loafing on the job." Barker's old friend and case officer, E. Howard Hunt, kept Barker's secrets out of his own 2005 autobiography and his so-called confession tape. Both are suspect because, among other things, they also omit the Mafia ties of Hunt's close friends, Manuel Artime and Bernard Barker.[72]

———

What Harry Williams told us in 1992 pushed us to piece together Barker's story over the next seventeen years. Later in the 1990s, the JFK Assassination Records Review Board began to release important files about Barker. We confidentially told a high official with the Review Board about the importance of Barker in 1997, while telling him about AMWORLD. In early 1998 that official said the CIA had agreed to release Barker's entire CIA file—but if it has been declassified, it hasn't shown up yet in the National Archives. So far, only the clearly incomplete files the CIA gave to the House Select Committee are available.

Still, information about Barker is slowly emerging, such as his CIA cryptonym, AMCLATTER-1, which we were the first to publish in *Ultimate Sacrifice* (2005). The updated trade paperback of that book included a couple of hints about Barker's role for Trafficante in JFK's murder, and the hardback edition of *Legacy of Secrecy* provided many more. We had much additional material, but new files about Barker and his associates were becoming available online, in easily searchable form, at the Mary Ferrell Foundation website. We wanted to be able to review all of those files before finally releasing our work about Barker to the public. Bernard Barker's death prompted a flurry of activity and gave us many sleepless nights, working to prepare the Special Addendum about Barker you're now reading.

We are confident that much additional material about Barker and his associates is among the "over one million CIA records" that remain unreleased. That figure came from someone who worked with the Review Board, as part of a study by the distinguished Washington watchdog group, OMB Watch. The more than "one million CIA records" no doubt include many thousands of pages related to AMWORLD and the JFK-Almeida coup plan, as well as the Mafia's infiltration of it. Under the 1992 JFK Act, all of the Barker files should be released. Unfortunately, even with a change in administration and a new CIA Director, the CIA is still fighting full implementation of that law, specifically in a lawsuit about the files on CIA officer George Joannides, who oversaw a Cuban exile group that had a run-in with Oswald.[73]

The CIA's file of Barker's work on the JFK-Almeida coup plan, and all of his time as Hunt's assistant, should be declassified. Even if Richard Helms destroyed a good portion of Barker's files in 1967 and 1973, the operations involving Barker were so extensive that some important material would remain. Likewise, the complete pre-Watergate FBI file on Barker, especially from 1963, could shed much light on Barker's work for Trafficante. We know that Barker is in Bureau files from 1963 because Miami FBI agents told Harry Williams they were keeping an eye on him that year, and they would have noted Harry's meetings in Miami with Barker. In addition, Barker was so active in passing out laundered money prior to the Bay of Pigs that he must have shown up on the FBI's radar screen at that time. In the same way, information about Barker and his criminal associates should appear in the files of the DEA, Treasury Department, and Justice Department as well as the military intelligence services that were involved in anti-Castro operations in the early 1960s.

This Special Addendum has pointed to many other files about Barker—and his associates linked to JFK's murder—that should be released to the public. But unless enough people demand enforcement of the JFK Act from the Obama administration and/or Congress, those files might not be released until 2017 or even later. A 2008 CIA filing in the Joannides lawsuit said the Agency reserved the right to withhold files beyond 2017, even though the JFK Act mandates release of even the most sensitive JFK assassination files by that date.[74]

A final note about Barker's legacy: For too many people, hearing the expression "Cuban exiles" evokes thoughts of suspects in JFK's assassination. Bernard Barker's participation in that murder caused a certain stigma to be borne by all Cuban exiles. Because we can now focus attention only where it is warranted—on Barker and his criminal associates—we hope our efforts will help to remove that unwarranted stigma from all other Cuban Americans.

Part III: What You Can Do to Get All the Assassination Files Released

It's tragic that all the JFK assassination files weren't released before Bernard Barker's death, since he was one of the last living participants who was knowingly involved in JFK's assassination. He should have had to testify about those events before Congress or to knowledgeable federal investigators. Forcing testimony by granting immunity to potential witnesses could be much more effective today than when the House Select Committee on Assassinations granted immunity to Santo Trafficante and Carlos Marcello in 1978. (Trafficante did let some interesting information slip out, even while denying any involvement in JFK's murder.) In 1978, both godfathers were at the height of their power, with high-caliber attorneys to handle the HSCA and a string of recent murders to keep other conspirators quiet. Also in 1978, certain high officials at the CIA who had risen under Richard Helms had little incentive to cast their former boss or their Agency in a bad light. A few of those CIA officials, like Ted Shackley, had actually worked on operations being investigated by the HSCA, like CIA-Mafia plots, giving them even more incentive to be deceptive. Almeida was still unexposed in 1978, and protecting him apparently gave CIA officials like Shackley an excuse to keep important information from the HSCA.

All of that is different today. But if the JFK Act isn't fully enforced and the files aren't released soon, more potential witnesses like Barker will be lost forever. One big change since the first publication of *Legacy of Secrecy* has been the election of Barack Obama, who pledged to run a more open government. Steps to implement that policy with public input began in the late spring of 2009, though those pressing extremist political views quickly overwhelmed the website for public input. Still, the White House website at www.whitehouse.gov allows citizens to send their concerns to President Obama's staff, and it also posts updates on his efforts to reduce needless government secrecy. Even agencies like the FBI—which have shown a marked reluctance to release their most important files about Marcello, Trafficante, Rosselli, and their associates—might finally comply with the law if ordered to by President Obama.

Leon Panetta had a relatively progressive track record before becoming Obama's CIA Director, and he might be more open to releasing CIA files even if they show past intelligence failures or indicate the involvement of Agency personnel like Barker and David Morales in JFK's murder. Panetta had not worked for the CIA prior to becoming Director, making him similar in some ways to the CIA's Director during the HSCA investigation, Stansfield Turner. However, the drawback of bringing in an outsider to become CIA Director is their sometimes limited ability to control the actions of their far more experienced CIA subordinates. Stansfield Turner had his hands full trying to reform a reluctant Agency, and there is no evidence that he knew about or ordered the CIA's extensive deception of the HSCA. We can only hope that Panetta fares better with the Agency he now heads.

Congress should also be concerned about the federal agencies that have still not fully complied with the JFK Act, seventeen years after the Senate and the House passed it unanimously. As noted in the Epilogue, simply enforcing the JFK Act will also release many important files about the assassinations of Dr. Martin Luther King and Robert Kennedy. A number of committees could hold hearings if enough members of the public demand them. In both the Senate and House, the most likely committees would be those for Appropriations, Budget, Intelligence, and the Judiciary. The Senate's Homeland Security and Governmental Affairs Committee and the House's Oversight and Government Reform Committee could also have jurisdiction. Because of the Cuban aspect of the story, any committees involving trade with Cuba should also want to have all the files released; those include Foreign Affairs in the Senate and the House's Foreign Relations Committee, as well as the Ways and Means Subcommittee on Trade.

The "Tell Congress" link on the home page of www.legacyofsecrecy. com will take you to a page with a link at the bottom that will help you find your member of Congress and Senators, learn how to contact them, and see what committees they are on. Even if they aren't on one of the above committees, they can still help by contacting their colleagues who are, or their chamber's leadership. Short, polite emails, letters, or calls would be most effective.

Releasing all the JFK assassination files is an important way to ensure that history doesn't keep repeating itself. That includes not only the

US-Cuba relationship—largely frozen since JFK's murder—but also the recent assassination plots against President Obama. Unfortunately, a surge in extremist activity and violence accompanied his election. The Associated Press found that "one of the most popular white supremacist web sites [Stormfront], got more than 2,000 new members the day after [Obama's] election." The FBI saw a nearly 50 percent increase in requests for gun permits in the weeks after Obama's win, and by April 2007, the Department of Homeland Security said "rightwing extremists are harnessing [Obama's] election as a recruitment tool." They concluded "that lone wolves and small terrorist cells embracing violent rightwing extremist ideology are the most dangerous domestic terrorism threat in the United States."[1]

To realize the magnitude of that threat, one has only to recall Bernard Barker's words, as noted by journalist Haynes Johnson: "some people may call us Nazis." Add to that the near-Nazi political beliefs of Barker's friend Artime (said to have "guilty knowledge" of JFK's murder) and the neo-Nazi actions of Barker's associate Felipe Rivero, who stalked JFK. They weren't white supremacists in the mold of Georgia's Joseph Milteer, who played a small role in JFK's death and a much larger role in Martin Luther King's assassination. But they all shared a mindset that could be used by powerful men who feel they have compelling reasons to assassinate a president.[2]

Most Americans don't realize how many arrests have been made in connection with plots—mostly by white supremacists—to assassinate President Obama. There have been arrests in Tennessee, Arkansas, California, Florida, North Carolina, Colorado, Mississippi, New Hampshire, Illinois, and Maine. Some of the plots resemble the plots to kill JFK and Dr. King described in this book. The November 4, 2008, arrest of a man near Chicago with a carload of weapons—including not only "handguns and ammunition" but also "an assault rifle"—evokes the November 2, 1963, arrest in the Chicago plot to kill JFK, described on page 74. A Maine extremist who plotted a "dirty bomb" attack during Obama's inauguration was able to pursue his plan because he was wealthy through an inheritance, much like Joseph Milteer. The arrest and prosecution near Memphis, Tennessee, of what the AP called "two white supremacists charged with plotting to kill President-elect Barack Obama" is all too reminiscent of what Milteer arranged to be done to Martin Luther King in Memphis in 1968.[3]

Aside from the Tennessee case, almost none of the other Obama assassination plot arrests have received national press attention. The Secret Service generally likes to avoid publicizing such arrests in order to prevent copycat attempts. Yet most of today's members of the Secret Service, or other law enforcement agencies, have never had the chance to learn an important lesson of history: how the cover-ups of the plots to kill JFK in Tampa and Chicago enabled Marcello, Trafficante, and their men to kill JFK in Dallas. That's because so many files about JFK's murder remain secret even today.

We hope today's generation never has to know the shattering pain and shock of the assassinations that shook America and the world back in 1963 and 1968. One sudden tragedy like 9/11 is more than enough. Yet even that might have been avoided had the lessons of history been learned from JFK's murder. As we pointed out on the final page of *Legacy*'s Overview, the report on the intelligence failures before the 9/11 tragedy quoted FBI and CIA files that were hauntingly similar to those that preceded JFK's assassination. The best way to ensure that history does not go on repeating itself is for all agencies to comply with the law and finally release all of the files related to JFK's assassination.[45]

Late breaking news: As this updated edition was being readied for printing, the official Cuban press reported that Commander Juan Almeida had died at 11:30pm on September 11, 2009, at the age of 82. The Cuban government declared September 13 a National Day of Mourning and Raul Castro led the mourners at Almeida's wake.

With the death of Commander Almeida, there is now no remotely legitimate reason for the CIA to continue to withhold an estimated one million records related to JFK's assassination from Congress, the press, and the public.

Photographs and Documents

The following are just a few of the thousands of pages of government files used in writing Legacy of Secrecy, *and links to more can be found at legacyofsecrecy.com. CIA and FBI files are from the National Archives and have been declassified.*

Carlos Marcello, for decades the absolute godfather of Louisiana, whose influence stretched from Dallas to Memphis. By 1985, Marcello was a federal prisoner because of the FBI BRILAB sting, begun in the wake of Watergate (*AP, detail*).

FEDERAL BUREAU OF INVESTIGATION

Date of transcription ___3/7/86___

      On March 4, 1986, JACK RONALD VANLANINGHAM, Inmate, SEAGOVILLE FEDERAL CORRECTIONAL INSTITUTE, was interviewed and provided the following information:

      A confidential source who has provided reliable information in the past furnished the following:

      On December 15, 1985, he was in the company of CARLOS MARCELLO and another inmate at the FEDERAL CORRECTIONAL INSTITUTE (FCI), Texarkana, Texas, in the court yard engaged in conversation. CARLOS MARCELLO discussed his intense dislike of former President JOHN KENNEDY as he often did. Unlike other such tirades against KENNEDY, however, on this occasion CARLOS MARCELLO said, referring to President KENNEDY, "Yeah, I had the son of a bitch killed. I'm glad I did. I'm sorry I couldn't have done it myself."

Marcello made this confession to a trusted associate—Jack Ronald Van Laningham—who was an FBI informant, in front of another named witness who also had the godfather's trust. The FBI suppressed Marcello's confession for more than a decade, and this edition marks the first disclosure of the uncensored files, with the FBI informant's name.

Van Laningham was part of a previously unknown FBI undercover sting, codenamed CAMTEX, revealed here for the first time. As part of the sting, the FBI had Van Laningham become Marcello's cellmate, and he got the godfather to pay bribes to an undercover FBI agent, in return for being moved to more comfortable federal prisons.

Marcello didn't realize at the time that his cellmate was an FBI informant. Van Laningham was considered so reliable that a federal judge approved Title III taps on the prison phones and a bugged transistor radio for Marcello's cell. The resulting "hundreds of hours" of tapes of Marcello are still withheld by the FBI.

Van Laningham wrote the following account for the Bureau, of Marcello's admission of having "several meetings with Oswald" before JFK's murder and that Marcello had set Jack Ruby up in business in Dallas. Not long after making his confession, Marcello threatened Van Laningham's life if he ever revealed what Marcello told him. Though fearful, Van Laningham reported Marcello's remarks to FBI agents and even offered to take a lie detector test. Though more than a dozen associates of Carlos Marcello and his men were interviewed by authorities soon after JFK's murder, Marcello himself was not interviewed or investigated by police or the FBI at the time. Marcello's name does not appear in the Warren Report.

```
lot. Marcello seemed to be very upset about the Kennedys. This is all he would
talk about. I was so tired of hearing about his so caled kidnaping, that it
played on my nerves that is all he talked about no matter where we were. I had
another friend at Texarkana that had worked for Marcellos brother as a bar ten
der. The little man would let him come to our room and they would talk about
New Orleans for hours. One night Marcello was talking about the Kennedys. He
told me and my friend about a meeting with Oswald. He had been introduced to
Oswald by a man named Ferris, who was Marcellos pilot. He said that the had
taken place in his brothers resturant. He said that he thought that Oswald
```

```
crazy. They had several( tings wit         fore he   t town. He also told
about Jack Ruby. Marcello had met him in U... Texas. He  t him up in the bar
business there. He said that Ruby was a homo son of a bitch but good to have around
to report to him what was happening in town. Marcello told us that all the police
were on the take, and as long as he kept the money flowing they let him operate any
thing in dalas that he wanted to. Ruby would come to churchill farm to report to
marcello so the little man knew what was happening all the time. Marcello talked
```

The FBI files document that Van Laningham grew close enough to Marcello that the godfather told him about many of partners in crime, including Tampa godfather Santo Trafficante and Teamster leader Jimmy Hoffa. Marcello, Trafficante, and Hoffa had been close since the 1950s and sometimes shared the same attorney, Frank Ragano.

The following report from FBI files, written by Van Laningham, recounts Marcello's revelation to him of a previously unknown meeting between Marcello and Hoffa shortly before Hoffa's disappearance. The informant wrote that he believes Marcello was involved in Hoffa's murder. Hoffa vanished in July 1975, while the US Senate was investigating JFK's assassination and the CIA's plots with the Mafia to assassinate Fidel Castro. The CIA-Mafia plots to kill Fidel had involved Hoffa, Trafficante, Marcello, and Chicago mob boss Sam Giancana (murdered the month before Hoffa), and Las Vegas mobster Johnny Rosselli.

```
teamsters union Jimmy Hoffa was released from prison. Hoffa wanted the union back.
A lot of people tried to talk to him to change his mind. The Kansas City people
knew that he would not go along with the pension loan from the temsters union.
Marcello told me that he was asked to talk to Hoffa. The were great friends so
it was believed that if any one could get to Hoffa it was Marcello. Marcello in
vited Hoffa down to Churchill farm a place he had in New Orleans and still owns.
Marcello wanted the union boss from Louisiana to talk to Hoffa also. Hoffa came
to see Marcello and was put up at churchill farm. Marcello and Nick Cevella
```

Johnny Rosselli, the Chicago Mafia's point man in Las Vegas and Hollywood, had been involved with Marcello since the 1950s. Rosselli admitted his "role in plotting to kill the President" to his attorney Tom Wadden. Soon after, Rosselli—preparing to testify again about JFK's assassination to a Congressional committee—was the victim of a brutal dismemberment murder, linked to Santo Trafficante (*HSCA*).

Tampa godfather Santo Trafficante, Marcello's close associate, confessed his role in JFK's murder shortly before his own death to his trusted attorney, Frank Ragano. *Legacy of Secrecy* contains new information indicating that Ragano played a more active role than he ever admitted in JFK's assassination (*HSCA*).

Bernard Barker, best known as a Watergate burglar, also worked for Trafficante. Barker was a CIA agent from 1959 to 1966, while also working for the Mafia. According to an aide to Robert Kennedy, Barker helped to assassinate JFK.

> Barker reportedly has theory that Castro using the bolita racket to fund agents in the U.S. CO expresses concern that Barker may becoming too involved with underworld elements.

The CIA claims not to have known about Barker's mob ties, except for the one instance in the above 1965 CIA memo, even though a CIA Director testified to Congress that Barker was fired for his underworld involvement. But the FBI memo below shows the Bureau had known about Barker's "gangster" activity since the late 1940s.

> BeRand Leon Barker   B march 17-1917- Havana Cuba 7/a
> BERNARDO L. BARKER, age about 45 to 55, of Cuban origin, served in the U. S. Air Force during World War II, was shot down over Germany, and became a prisoner of war. After the war he returned to Cuba and served as a sergeant in the Bureau of Investigations during the PRIO regime. During the late 1940's, he became associated in gangster activities in Cuba. (U)
> 45

Marcello, Trafficante, and Rosselli got away with murdering JFK because a dozen of their men had infiltrated John and Robert Kennedy's top-secret plan to overthrow Fidel Castro on December 1, 1963. The following is just a small sample of the files and operatives discussed in Legacy of Secrecy.

> It also has been reported to me that Commander Juan Almeida, who is Chief of Fidel's army, actually is very much disgusted with the Communistic situation, and is about to defect. This Almeida told to Manuel Ray, who is head of an anti-Castro Movement inside Cuba.

The roots of JFK's coup plan began in 1961, before the disastrous Bay of Pigs invasion. More than a month before the debacle, this February 20, 1961, CIA memo shows that Cuban Army Commander Juan Almeida offered to defect and help the US. The CIA didn't take Almeida up on his offer, because they were using Rosselli and Trafficante in a plot to assassinate Fidel Castro.

In December 1962, JFK welcomed home the Bay of Pigs prisoners, thanks to the efforts of Robert Kennedy and Cuban exile Enrique "Harry" Ruiz-Williams. JFK is seen here greeting Manuel Artime (far left), the leader of the Cuban exile prisoners (*JFK Library*).

By May 1963, Almeida—still Commander of the Cuban Army—was secretly working with Harry Williams (far right), Robert Kennedy, and JFK to stage what would appear to be a "palace coup" against Castro. Artime (far left) joined the coup plan, with support from the CIA, his best friend, E. Howard Hunt—and Hunt's assistant, Bernard Barker (*AP, detail*).

Enrique "Harry" Williams (left) in 1992 with co-author Thom Hartmann, in a photo taken by Lamar Waldron after their second interview. Harry and other Kennedy aides told the authors the CIA had only a supporting role in the JFK-Almeida coup plan. That included arranging for a large payment to Almeida, helping to get his wife and children out of Cuba on a pretext, and making sure someone could "take the fall" for Fidel's death—preferably someone who appeared to be a Russian or Russian sympathizer.

Harry talked frequently with his good friend Robert F. Kennedy about the coup plan. There are dozens of calls between the two in the Attorney General's phone logs. The one on the left shows back-to-back calls by "the President" and "Enrique Williams" to RFK on 5-13-63, just after Almeida first contacted Harry about staging a coup for the Kennedys. The log on the right shows calls by CIA official Richard Helms and Harry to RFK, three days before the CIA issued their first detailed memo about Artime's part of the coup plan, codenamed AMWORLD.

Planning "for a coup in Cuba" skyrocketed after the Kennedys began working with Almeida, and nine drafts of the coup plan were completed in just three months. (Excerpt shown below.) The US military had a leading role, but only a handful of officials trusted by the Kennedys—including Joint Chiefs Chairman Gen. Maxwell Taylor and Army Secretary Cyrus Vance—knew about Almeida. Other top US leaders thought the expanded planning with State and CIA was "just in case" a high official could be found to stage a coup.

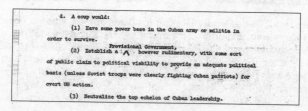

> d. A coup would:
>
> (1) Have some power base in the Cuban army or militia in order to survive.
>
> (2) Establish a **Provisional Government,** however rudimentary, with some sort of public claim to political visibility to provide an adequate political basis (unless Soviet troops were clearly fighting Cuban patriots) for overt US action.
>
> (3) Neutralize the top echelon of Cuban leadership.

RYBAT TYPIC YOBITE AMWORLD

1. NASIN ELIAS HAS ASKED NAVY IN GUANTANAMO BASE TO PASS
FOLL MSG TO █████

2. GENERAL UPRISING SCHEDULED FOR 1 DEC   PARTICIPATING
GROUPS FND. MRR AND MD.

The JFK-Almeida coup was eventually set for December 1, 1963, to be followed by an invited US invasion, to help keep order and prevent a Soviet takeover. The above detail is from a CIA memo sent by Director John McCone on the morning of November 22, 1963.

Richard Helms (left), CIA's Deputy Director for Plans in 1963, was the key official overseeing covert operations. In addition to supporting the JFK-Almeida coup plan, Helms continued to use Rosselli in the CIA-Mafia plots to assassinate Castro—but without telling his own CIA Director, JFK, or Robert Kennedy. CIA officer E. Howard Hunt (top right), Helms's protégé, was heavily involved in the JFK-Almeida coup plan. Bernard Barker was Hunt's assistant for the operation. Hunt's friend, CIA officer David Atlee Phillips (bottom right), assisted Artime in the coup plan (AP/HSCA-CIA/ Fonzi).

In case Fidel Castro found out about the coup plan and tried to retaliate, Robert Kennedy had a secret committee make plans in the fall of 1963 for what to do about the possible "assassination of American officials." Both Marcello and Trafficante told trusted associates that JFK had to be killed in order to end Attorney General Robert Kennedy's intense prosecution of them. The Kennedys had barred the Mafia from the coup plan, or from reopening their casinos in Cuba after the coup, but a dozen associates of Marcello, Trafficante, and Rosselli infiltrated the coup plan.

Seven associates of the mob bosses, including Bernard Barker and David Morales, worked on parts of the JFK-Almeida coup plan. Morales (right) was Operations Chief for the CIA's huge Miami Station. While helping with AMWORLD, Morales also worked with his good friend, Johnny Rosselli. Morales later admitted a role in the murders of JFK and RFK (*Fonzi*).

John Martino was a low level CIA asset in 1963, with no role in the JFK-Almeida coup plan. But Martino worked with Trafficante, Rosselli, and Marcello—and the above FBI file shows that Martino had learned about JFK's plan to invade Cuba. Years later, Martino confessed his role in JFK's murder to trusted associates shortly before his death.

In the fall of 1963, John and Robert Kennedy were using Manuel Artime in the coup plan; his part of the operation was codenamed AMWORLD, as shown in this detail from a later CIA memo (top). But the Kennedys didn't know Artime was tied to the Mafia and was part of the CIA-Mafia Castro assassination plots that Helms was hiding from them. All of the CIA files about Artime and the Mafia were withheld from Congressional investigators, and most are still classified, despite the 1992 law requiring their release.

On November 18, 1963, Trafficante, Rosselli, and Marcello planned to kill JFK during his long motorcade in Tampa. But Trafficante's inside man on the Tampa police tipped him that authorities had learned of the threat, so he cancelled the hit. Tampa's Police Chief told us the Floridan Hotel (left) was the likely site for the shooting. JFK and RFK kept the threat out of the press. On November 22, 1963, the same assassination plan was used in Marcello's territory of Dallas, with at least one shot fired from the Texas School Book Depository (right) (*Chris Barrows/Mary Ferrell Foundation*).

The infamous "grassy knoll," just moments after JFK was shot. Two JFK aides directly behind JFK's limo clearly saw and heard shots from the knoll, but one of them—Dave Powers—told us they were forced to alter their testimony for the Warren Commission. Both men confirmed the account to Speaker of the House Tip O'Neill (*JFK Library*).

Dallas gangster Jack Ruby, who worked for Marcello and knew Trafficante, silenced Oswald on November 24, 1963, in front of a live TV audience. An FBI report states that after his arrest, Ruby said "an invasion of Cuba was being sponsored by the United States government" (*HSCA*).

Robert Kennedy was usually at odds with Lyndon Johnson, but after JFK's murder, both men had to cover up important information to prevent "World War III" and to protect Commander Almeida in Cuba. However, LBJ refused Robert's request to continue the coup plan, further straining their already bad relationship (*LBJ Library*).

Dean Rusk, Secretary of State for JFK and LBJ, told us—and confirmed to *Vanity Fair*—that he only learned about the coup and invasion plan after JFK's murder. Prior to that, he and most other top officials thought their planning was merely a contingency exercise in case a high Cuban official offered to stage a coup (*LBJ Library*).

President Johnson receiving the report of the Warren Commission, the first of at least six government commissions and committees to investigate JFK's murder. J. Edgar Hoover, Richard Helms, Robert Kennedy, and military intelligence withheld massive amounts of information from the Commission about the JFK-Almeida coup plan, Ruby and organized crime, and the plot to kill JFK in Tampa. This allowed Marcello, Trafficante, Rosselli and their men to remain free to pursue their criminal activities (*LBJ Library*).

Dr. Martin Luther King and Robert Kennedy had a sometimes difficult relationship, but Robert grew into a tireless champion of civil rights and an advocate for the poor—all while deadly violence against blacks and civil rights workers in the South continued (*JFK Library*).

Joseph Milteer was a Georgia white supremacist tied to two associates of Marcello. Milteer was recorded on police undercover tape prior to JFK's murder, talking about JFK being shot by a high-powered rifle from a building. Hoover botched the investigation of Milteer, who was never arrested. Milteer then began working with Hugh R. Spake and two other partners to collect money in Atlanta each week to pay for the murder of Dr. King (*HSCA*).

New information about Joseph Milteer recently came to light: nine large boxes of his papers and photographs in a South Georgia courthouse, most untouched since they were reviewed by the House Select Committee on Assassinations in 1978. Georgia attorney James W. Hall, Jr. and his son, Andrew Hall, allowed the authors use of the material, shown here for the first time.

Joseph Milteer in 1971, three years after helping to pay for the assassination of Martin Luther King. Milteer was a key link between the violent radicalism of J. B. Stoner and the Klan, and the more respectable White Citizens Councils.

The new material puts Milteer in a new light. While he lived in South Georgia at the time of JFK and King's murders, Milteer was educated in business at a New York college, where he is shown here in 1922. A review of hundreds of Milteer's papers from four decades reveal him to be smart, articulate, shrewd, and ruthless.

Milteer's papers were left when he died in 1974, and they were unlikely to contain any smoking guns, since he had been linked by name to the assassinations of JFK and Dr. King in a 1971 book. However, one box did contain these shells, including a live .38 Special bullet. According to the FBI, Milteer carried a loaded .38 with him whenever he traveled.

Milteer supplemented his inheritance by becoming a traveling salesman, but he was also a professional white supremacist who sometimes dealt in arms. In the early 1960s, private buyers of large quantities of shady arms included Milteer's fellow racists, the Mafia and anti-Castro Cubans.

For a traveling salesman who drove thousands of miles a year, it was odd the boxes contained only one hotel receipt. It was for November 23, 1963, the day after JFK's murder. Given the unconfirmed reports that Milteer was in Dallas when JFK was shot, it was almost as if he kept the receipt as an alibi.

With Milteer at the Columbia, SC, hotel was an informant for the Miami Police Department, who said Milteer talked about using JFK's murder as another excuse for his anti-Semitism. This is a mild example of Milteer's self-printed white supremacist rants.

On this card, Milteer has written the address and phone number for another professional reactionary, General Edwin Walker. After JFK's murder, publicity about Oswald's possible role in a shooting incident involving Walker helped to incriminate Oswald to the press and public.

his sources, with three unimportant exceptions, beyond
saying that they include four or five petty racketeers
in Memphis, New Orleans, and elsewhere and one well
placed protege of Carlos Marcellos in New Orleans.

Ray's contacts in New Orleans were with Mafia-
Cosa Nostra representatives who referred him to Frank
Leberto (or Liberto), a Memphis racketeer and lieutenant
of Carlos Marcellos, the Southern Mafia chieftan in New
Orleans. Leberto owns or works at the Scott Street
Produce Market where John Wererren of Somerville allegedly overheard a man speaking on the telephone say, on or
about the day of the assassination: "Shoot him on the
balcony, shoot him anywhere; and go to New Orleans for
your money, don't come back here."

According to Sartor's informants, the Cosa Nostra
agreed to "broker" or to arrange the assassination, for
an amount somewhat in excess of three hundred thousand
dollars ($300,000), after they were contacted in the

These excerpts from a long Justice Department memo, which the FBI withheld from Congressional investigators, supports other information showing that Marcello brokered the assassination of Dr. King for a small group of white racists. Milteer turned to Marcello after previous attempts to recruit a hitman failed.

Much information shows that small-time career criminal and prison escapee James Earl Ray became a low-level drug runner for Carlos Marcello's drug network. From his prison escape in April 1967, until his capture in England in June 1968, Ray would travel thousands of miles across the US, Canada, and Mexico, in addition to flying to England and Portugal.

CURRENT RESIDENCE

ROSSELLI maintains a residence in Los Angeles,
California, at Apartment 803 Glen Towers Apartments, 1333
South Beverly Glen Boulevard, where he has non-published
telephone number GR 4-0198. The published telephone number
of the Glen Towers Apartments is 474-4526.

ROSSELLI makes numerous trips to Las Vegas,
Nevada, and in nearly every instance, he has resided at
the Desert Inn Hotel in Las Vegas.

From November 19, 1967, to March 17, 1968, Ray stayed in Los Angeles, except for a drug run to New Orleans and a brief trip to Las Vegas. Johnny Rosselli also lived in Los Angeles at that time, at the Glen Towers Apartments, where many FBI files (example above) show he was constantly monitored by the Bureau. After Dr. King's murder, the FBI found a map belonging to Ray that had Rosselli's apartment building marked on it, but no mention of that connection was made to the public or to Congressional investigators.

After Dr. King's murder in Memphis on April 4, 1968, James Earl Ray fled to Canada—but not before taking a 400-plus mile detour south to Atlanta. *Legacy of Secrecy* reveals for the first time that when Ray arrived in Atlanta on the morning of April 5, 1968, he called Joseph Milteer's partner, Hugh R. Spake, to get help and money from Milteer. Ray was soon in Canada, and from there he would fly to England, then Portugal, and back to England. His two-month sojourn as the world's most wanted fugitive embarrassed J. Edgar Hoover and the FBI.

Before Ray was captured, Robert Kennedy was shot in Los Angeles, early on the morning of June 5, 1968, after winning the California primary in his quest for the presidency. Questions remain about whether Sirhan Sirhan was the only shooter in the pantry/kitchen area of the Ambassador Hotel, and about Sirhan's criminal associates, in light of reports of a contract on Robert Kennedy tied to the Mafia.

Sirhan's revolver held only eight bullets; all were accounted for by the Los Angeles Police Department, which claims there were no bullet holes in any of the pantry door frames—otherwise, there had to be more than one shooter. However, photos of the crime scene show extra bullet holes that cannot be accounted for by Sirhan's bullets. Los Angeles Coroner Thomas Noguchi measures two bullet holes in a pantry doorframe (left). Close-up of the bullet holes, circled by and with the initials of an Los Angeles Sheriff's Deputy (right) (*Mary Ferrell Foundation*).

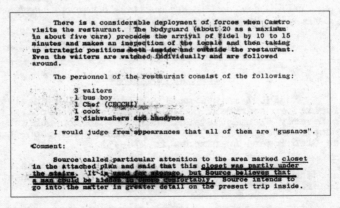

The above 1962 CIA document, about a plan to assassinate Fidel Castro at a restaurant, by hiding a pistol-wielding assassin in the pantry, is shown here for the first time. Miami CIA Operations Chief David Morales would have been involved in the plan, which was abandoned in 1964. David Morales apparently later confessed to having a role in Robert Kennedy's assassination. Morales's friend, Johnny Rosselli, was being prosecuted in Los Angeles at the time of RFK's assassination—and one of the members of the defense team became Sirhan Sirhan's main attorney.

While Sirhan's lead attorney, Grant Cooper, was busy with the case involving Johnny Rosselli and a Las Vegas casino owner, Russell Parsons, a longtime attorney for LA mobster Mickey Cohen, aided Sirhan. Years earlier, Parsons had originally worked for the LA District Attorney, until he changed sides after being shot at one night, through the "wind wings" (side vents) of his car.

Sirhan Sirhan's brother, Saidallah, was shot at through the wind wings of his car late one night, just weeks after RFK was assassinated. At the time, Saidallah had been creating problems for Sirhan's defense and wanting to talk to the press. After Sirhan was shot at on an LA freeway, he drove to the Pasadena Police Department, and part of their lengthy report is shown below.

WHEN THE FIRST SHOT WAS FIRED THROUGH THE RIGHT WIND WING, THE VICTIM LEANED TO HIS RIGHT IN AN ATTEMPT TO AVOID BEING HIT AND HE THEN HEARD THE SECOND SHOT WHICH FOLLOWED IMMEDIATELY AFTER THE FIRST SHOT AND ALSO CAME THROUGH THE RIGHT WIND WING. AFTER THE SECOND SHOT HAD BEEN FIRED, THE THREE VEHICLES WERE AT GLENARM ST. AND THE CHEVROLET TURNED LEFT ON GLENARM ST. AND THE V.W. TURNED RIGHT. THE VICTIM CONTINUED NORTH AND CAME TO THIS DEPARTMENT TO REPORT THE INCIDENT.

THE PROJECTILES FIRED BY THE SUSPECTS WERE RECOVERED BY THE UNDERSIGNED AND TAKEN AS EVIDENCE. SEE ATTACHED PHYSICAL EVIDENCE FORM.

A year before RFK's murder, FBI files say the imprisoned Jimmy Hoffa stated there was a hit contract on RFK if he ever ran for president. When the Bureau questioned Hoffa after RFK's assassination, Hoffa—apparently worried his threat might have been recorded—didn't explicitly deny it.

Information was previously reported that about Memorial Day, 1967, while confined in the U. S. Penitentiary, Lewisburg, Pennsylvania, JAMES RIDDLE HOFFA was alleged to have made a statement that he had a contract out on Senator ROBERT F. KENNEDY, and if he, KENNEDY, ever got in the primaries or ever got elected, the contract would be fulfilled within six months.

The LAPD and FBI also learned that a wealthy California rancher had told two law enforcement officers about a Mafia contract on RFK from Las Vegas. However, there is no evidence the FBI or LAPD ever interviewed the rancher's Las Vegas Mafia "friends."

On this occasion [redacted] advised the group that he had received a long distance telephone call from friends in the Las Vegas area requesting a contribution from him to help pay a one half to three quarter million dollar contract to assassinate ROBERT KENNEDY. [redacted] stated that the assassination was to take place if it appeared KENNEDY was to gain the Democratic Presidential nomination, and that California was considered as the conclusive proof point of that probable nomination.

[redacted] bragged that he had offered $200 towards this contract. He intimated that these friends were members of the "Mafia". He further stated that he told the people from Las Vegas that he could probably drum up at least $50,000 to

Watergate involved twelve veterans of the JFK-Almeida coup plan, including Bernard Barker, who had ties to Nixon that pre-dated Watergate. Shown above is a page from the document one of the burglars—Trafficante bagman Frank Fiorini, a.k.a. Frank Sturgis—said they were really after. The long Cuban memo described many CIA attempts to assassinate Fidel Castro, starting in 1960 when Richard Nixon was Vice President. That year Nixon, President Eisenhower's point man on Cuba, hoped to use the Mafia's assassination of Castro as the original October Surprise, to propel him past JFK in the November 1960 election.

The Watergate investigation eventually encompassed JFK's assassination, and Johnny Rosselli testified to the Watergate Committee in a private session. More commissions and committees followed, but five witnesses were murdered, among them (clockwise from top left) Trafficante drug associate Rolando Masferrer; Jimmy Hoffa; Rosselli's old Mafia boss Sam Giancana; Chicago hit man Charles Nicoletti; and Johnny Rosselli. There were four more sudden deaths of witnesses before they could testify, including those of Manuel Artime and David Morales (*Richards/Spartacus/HSCA/NARA*).

In the wake of Oliver Stone's JFK, Congress unanimously passed the 1992 JFK Act, creating the JFK Assassination Records Review Board to release the remaining files. According to the Review Board's final report, in January 1995—six weeks after the authors first informed the Board about the Tampa threat and JFK's coup plan—the Secret Service admitted they had just destroyed files covering the time of JFK's Tampa trip and other important files. Even today, a report by the government watchdog group OMB Watch says that "well over a million CIA records" are still unreleased.

Commander Almeida was more prominent in Cuba than ever after the revelation of his secret work for JFK in the authors' previous book, *Ultimate Sacrifice*. Almeida was often at the side of Raul Castro at Cuba's largest events, including the time when Raul issued a rare olive branch to the US. Almeida died on September 11, 2009.

However, several Cuban exile allies of JFK from 1963 are still alive and working to resolve the impasse between the US and Cuba. It's possible that John and Robert Kennedy's dream of a democratic Cuba—the cause of so much secrecy over the past forty-six years—could yet come to pass (*AP*).

Accused Agent Says JFK Guards Were Lax

CHICAGO, May 21 (UPI) — A Secret Service agent charged with trying to sell a government report said yesterday he is being framed because he intended to reveal details of heavy drinking and "general laxity" among agents assigned to President Kennedy.

Abraham Bolden, 29, who in 1961 became the first Negro assigned to the Secret Service detail guarding the President, outlined his charges in a news conference at his home here.

FILE SALE

He is charged with trying to sell a confidential file to a man indicted in the alleged counterfeiting of $50000,000 in bonds and checks.

Mr. Bolden said he told another agent two weeks ago:

ABRAHAM BOLDEN

The tragic case of Abraham Bolden is still affected by the withheld JFK assassination files. The first black presidential Secret Service agent, personally selected by JFK, Bolden was framed by the Mafia and arrested on the day he went to Washington to tell Warren Commission staff about the Chicago and Tampa attempts, and Secret Service laxity. Even though the main witness against Bolden later admitted committing perjury, Bolden still had to serve years in prison. Bolden has been fighting to clear his name for 45 years, but most of his CIA and FBI files remain secret, as do those agencies' files about the Tampa attempt and the Chicago mobsters who framed Bolden (*AARC/HSCA*).

Acknowledgments

Legacy of Secrecy wound up three times longer than originally planned, because so many people helped us find so much important new material. Unfortunately, the book's current length doesn't leave us enough room to detail the fantastic assistance of everyone who helped, but we'll try to at least mention everyone.

Counterpoint publisher Charlie Winton is the person most responsible for shaping this book, allowing us an extra year to write it with all the material we wanted to include. He is both a hands-on publisher and a knowledgeable editor, with a football coach's skill at bringing out the best in those he works with. His contribution can't be overstated, and his wife, Barbara, and their family often sacrificed nights, weekends, and vacations so that work could proceed. Charlie's outstanding staff at Counterpoint has been integral to making this book possible, especially Laura Mazer, Sharon Donovan, Abbye Simkowitz, and Julie Pinkerton. Kudos also to the excellent copyediting team of Annie Tucker, Elizabeth Mathews, Katie Vecchio, and Greta Baranowski. Cover designer Sarah Juckniess made it all look good, as did Web wizard John Spriggs.

The encouragement and support of my father, Clyde Waldron, was instrumental in bringing the project to fruition. His interest in history was shared by Thom's father, Carl Hartmann, who passed away in 2006. Thom uses that love of history in his many books and his daily *Air America* radio show, expertly produced by his wife, Louise Hartmann (www.thomhartmann.com).

Brad Strickland took time from his own career as a successful novelist and English professor to edit the entire manuscript, and I learned a great deal from him in the process. Paul Hoch provided valuable feedback on the factual underpinning for the book, keeping me focused on being as accurate as possible. But neither is responsible for any less than stellar wording or interpretation of fact—that responsibility rests with us.

Larry Hancock is one of the most conscientious and objective writers in the field today, and was generous in sharing his own research and observations. His upcoming project with Stuart Wexler will provide new insights into the assassinations of both Martin Luther King and Robert Kennedy. Hancock and Wexler work with Debra Conway and Sherry Fiester to put on the impressive JFK Lancer conference in Dallas, and their Web sites (www.larry-hancock.com and www.jfklancer.com) are full of valuable information and documents.

The most extensive online resource for research—and many of the documents contained in *Legacy of Secrecy*—is available at the website of the Mary Ferrell Foundation (www.maryferrell.org). Continuing the work of the late grand dame of JFK research, the foundation's Tyler Weaver and Rex Bradford make available the world's largest online archive of US government files about the assassinations of JFK, RFK, and Dr. King. The site spotlights many of the most important documents in *Legacy* and *Ultimate Sacrifice*, along with video clips of Lamar Waldron talking about both books.

The Foundation also works with Jim Lesar and the Assassination Archives and Research Center (www.aarclibrary.org), one of the earliest JFK research facilities, founded by Lesar with the late Bud Fensterwald. Lesar is one of the country's premiere Freedom of Information attorneys, still battling the CIA and FBI for important documents. Another valuable online resource is the JFK, RFK, King, and Watergate forums run by John Simkin at Spartacus Educational (www.spartacus.schoolnet.co.uk/JFKindex.htm), which feature photos from the collection of James Richards of many of those chronicled in *Legacy*.

The staff at National Archives II in College Park, Maryland, home to more than four million pages of JFK files, have always been incredibly helpful. We have also made use of the extensive online resources of the National Security Archives, located at George Washington University (www.gwu.edu/~nsarchiv). The website of The King Center (www.thekingcenter.org) has valuable information about life and tragic death of Martin Luther King.

Columnist Liz Smith was the first journalist to tell the public about *Legacy's* revelations, and she continues in the best tradition of Jack Anderson, being the first to break important stories. Literary icon Gore Vidal has been generous in his praise of our work, both in print and on film, for which we are very grateful. We are likewise appreciative of fine actor and comedian Richard Belzer's interest and encouragement.

Earl Katz, Richard Foos, and Stuart Sender are spearheading a documentary project based on the JFK revelations in *Legacy*, while writer and producer Stephen Kronish is working to bring *Ultimate Sacrifice's* story of Johnny Rosselli to the screen. German Public Television's *The Kennedy Murder* featured author Waldron looking at Marcello's JFK confession at the National Archives, and we'd like to thank its producers, Joerg Muellner, Jean-Christoph Caron, and Britta Reuther. Their documentary also included Senator Edward Kennedy, Gore Vidal, and former Mafia prosecutor Ronald Goldfarb.

Mr. Goldfarb's consideration and knowledge are always much appreciated. We are also grateful to his former fellow prosecutor, G. Robert Blakey, for taking the time to speak with us. The work of Congressional investigator and journalist Gaeton Fonzi continues to be a source of inspiration, as does that of ex-FBI agent William Turner. Turner's pioneering work on the assassinations of JFK and RFK, and the Kennedys' secret war against Cuba, were a major influence on *Legacy*. We are also grateful for the help of former Secret Service agent Abraham Bolden, and hope to see him one day receive the pardon he so richly deserves.

Authors whose work we relied on a great deal include Peter Dale Scott, Anthony Summers and Robbyn Swan, Dan Moldea, John H. Davis, John Newman, and Dick Russell, and we encourage our readers to seek out any and all of their work. Mike Cain was a source of valuable information about the Chicago Mafia and his half-brother, Richard Cain. Robert Dorff's pivotal work on the case of David Morales was crucial. From England, Paul Byrne was very helpful on the Tampa and Chicago aspects of the case, while French journalist Stephane Risset provided crucial information about Michel Victor Mertz. Australia's Kate Willard was generous with her time and excellent research.

Gordon Winslow continues to be a fountain of information about Cuban exiles in general, and Rolando Masferrer in particular. Vince Palamara contributed valuable work about the Secret Service and Bolden. Two important researchers passed away before publication of *Legacy*: George Michael Evica, an early influence on our work, and Jim Olivier, who made important discoveries about Rose Cheramie.

We've admired the work of Mark Crispin Miller for a long time, and his support is greatly appreciated. Mark Karlin's excellent news site, buzzflash. com, continues to be a source for important information often overlooked by mainstream news sources.

We are grateful to all those we interviewed during our research. While we can't list them all, the following people lived important parts of the history we write about: Thomas K. Kimmel, Dean Rusk, Pierre Salinger, J. P. Mullins, Senator Gary Hart, Tom Kennelly, Marvin Loewy, John Diuguid, Richard Goodwin, Antonio Veciana, and Don Adams. We'd like to thank all of our confidential sources, some of whom risked their careers, or more, to speak with us.

Susan Barrows and Chris Barrows were unfailingly helpful. Ashley Zeltzer's photography never fails to amaze. Jim Steranko's interest and encouragement have been part of this project since the beginning.

The work of the following people was useful in our research, even though at times we may differ with some in our conclusions: Edwin Black, Dan Christensen, Gary Shaw, Jefferson Morley, David Talbot, Michael L. Kurtz, Tim Gratz, CAMCO, Ian Griggs, Walt Brown, Jerry Rose, A. J. Weberman, Frank DeBenedictis, Jake Shepard, David Scheim, Jim Allison, Scott Malone, Michael T. Griffith, David Corn, Gus Russo, Allan Holzman, Doug Smith, David Lifton, Evan Thomas, Josiah Thompson, Ed Becker, Charles Rappleye, Warren Hinckle, Michael Benson, Bradley Ayers, Gary Mack, Jerry P. Shinley, Don Bohning, Michael Coffey, Wim Dankbaar, David Kaiser, Jeff Bowman, and William Pepper.

In addition to those listed previously, we'd also like to thank the following people, who either aided our research or helped to spread the word about *Legacy*.

South Georgia attorney James W. Hall, Jr., and his son Andrew were generous with their time and effort in allowing us access to their work and photographs of the nine boxes of material from white supremacist Joseph Milteer. While going through the boxes at the courthouse, it was interesting to find that Milteer was considered an extremist and outcast in the South Georgia town where he lived. It's both ironic and appropriate that today Milteer's home district is represented by an African-American Congressman, Sanford Bishop.

It was an honor to speak with Civil Rights figures like Dr. C. T. Vivian, Congressman Louis Stokes, and Valerie Jackson. Thanks also go to Rep. John Lewis and his Communications Director, Brenda Jones.

Our research has been aided by far too many to mention, but special thanks are due to Dr. Cyril Wecht (for his decades of investigation), Zapruder film expert Rollie Zavada, and Jack Ronald Van Laningham.

In addition to the wonderful and understanding folks at Charlie Winton's Counterpoint mentioned earlier, we'd like to thank Kristy Bohnet, Tiffany Lee, and Elizabeth Mathews for their help.

For developing and producing an excellent show featuring *Legacy* for the Discovery Channel, our thanks go to the people at NBC's Peacock Productions: Knute Walker, Caroline Christopher, Elizabeth Fischer, Lloyd Fales, Payal Bawa, Brad Davis, and Rick King.

We're also grateful to CNN (Jason Carroll and Bob Ruff) and Fox (Clayton Morris and Megan Macdonald). Kristin O'Connor produced an amazing summary of *Legacy* for New York's WPIX, while in Atlanta, thanks go to WAGA's "Good Day Atlanta" and WSB's Monica Kauffman.

For journalists, it's hard to beat the longevity and consistent quality of Liz Smith, who is now appearing online at wowowow.com. Thanks also go to *Vanity Fair*'s Wayne Lawson, Michael Hogan, and Rob Sheffield. Ron Rosenbaum's piece on *Legacy* was an unexpected surprise from a writer we've long enjoyed.

Publisher's Weekly and Michael Coffey are to be commended, as is Carl Hartman of the Associated Press, for getting the details right even on a tight deadline. Jon Waterhouse not only wrote a great article and review for the *Atlanta Journal-Constitution*, but also spread the word on his radio show. The former editor of that newspaper, Hank Klibanoff, was generous with his time, as was Jerry Mitchell.

Margie Burns is one of the better internet journalists, and she can be found at www.margieburns.com. We also appreciate the work of Jane Ann Morrison, Scott Acton, and Bill Simpich.

Radio publicists Leslie Rossman and Emily Miles Terry helped us obtain so much radio coverage that it's impossible to thank everyone. But special kudos go to Ian Punnett, George Noory, and Anne Silberman at *Coast to Coast*; Lionel and Lynn Shaw for Air America, Joey Reynolds (and Albert Wunsch and Tom Lynch); KPOJ's Paul, Carl, and Christine; and Shawn Taylor at the Thom Hartmann Show.

Special thanks also go to Bev Smith, Joe Madison, Reggie Bryant, Gary O'Brien, and Peter Werbe. In Canada, our favorite radio is done by Andrew

Krystal and Bill Dicks, and Brent Holland. We also appreciate Canadian publicist Jennifer Lynch.

For getting the word out over YouTube, Kelly Winton made the most-watched *Legacy* video, while Joe Friendly put up the most.

Everyone in Australia was just super, and that includes Henry, Emma, and Susan at Scribe; journalist James Campbell; too many fine radio hosts to list; and researchers like Mark Brigden and Kate Willard. So many people have been supportive in trying to spread the word, from George DiCaprio in LA to Sharon O'Connell in NYC.

Finally, we'd like to thank anyone we forgot, and all those who spend long hours digging through files and searching for the truth.

Lamar Waldron
Thom Hartmann
October 1, 2009

Notes

All government documents cited in these endnotes have been declassified and are available at the National Archives II in College Park, Md., near Washington, D.C. Information about many of them, and full copies of a few, are available at the National Archives and Records Administration Web site, and a link to their site is available at legacyofsecrecy.com. Most of these files can be viewed at maryferrell.org, using the document numbers or dates provided.

Regarding the interviews the authors conducted for this book: for brevity and consistency, the interviewers are generally referred to as "we," even if only one of the authors was present for that particular interview. Within quotes used in the book, for clarity we have often standardized names, commonly used terms, and date formats. Frequently used terms:

> HSCA = House Select Committee on Assassinations
> HSCA King = House Select Committee on Assassinations, Investigation of the
>   Assassination of Martin Luther King Jr.
> NARA = National Archives and Records Administration JCS = Joint Chiefs of Staff.

INTRODUCTION

1. We give hundreds of examples in this book and in *Ultimate Sacrifice*, (New York: Carol & Graf Publishers, 2005), for example: Army copy of Department of State document, 1963, Record Number 198-10004-0072, Califano Papers, declassified 7-24-97. CIA memo, AMWORLD 11-22-63, #84804, declassified 1993. 2. Army document, summary of plan dated 9-26-63, Califano Papers, Record Number 198-10004-10001, declassified 10-7-97; Army copy of Department of State document, 1963, Record Number 198-10004-10072, Califano Papers, declassified 7-24-97; interview with Harry Williams 7-24-93; interview with confidential C-Day Defense Dept. source 7-6-92. 3. From the John F. Kennedy Presidential Library, NLK 78-473, declassified 5-6-80. 4. LBJ call to Richard Russell 11-29-63, quoted in Michael R. Beschloss, *Taking Charge* New York: Simon & Schuster, 1997), p. 72. 5. Robert Kennedy testimony (and other public comments at the time) to hearings by the US Senate Permanent Subcommittee on Investigations on Organized Crime and Illicit Traffic in Narcotics, 9-25-63; Ed Reid, *The Grim Reapers* (New York: Bantam, 1970). 6. David Talbot, *Brothers: The Hidden History of the Kennedy Years* (New York: Free Press, 2007), p. 314. 7. In addition to concerns about Hunt by some of our confidential sources, the late E. Howard Hunt was extremely litigious, his lawsuits aided by files that his former employer, the CIA, withheld both from Congress and from opposing counsel. 8. Marcello: FBI contact investigation 3-7-86, FD-302 declassified 6-98 and on file at the National Archives; Rosselli: Richard D. Mahoney, *Sons & Brothers: The Days of Jack and Bobby Kennedy* (New York: Arcade, 1999), p. 229; Trafficante: Frank Ragano and Selwyn Raab, *Mob Lawyer* (New York: Scribners, 1994), pp. 344-62. For all three Mafia bosses, there is extensive corroborating evidence throughout *Legacy of Secrecy*. 9. "A Presumption of Disclosure: Lessons from the John F. Kennedy Assassination Records Review Board," report by OMB Watch, 2000, available at ombwatch.org.

CHAPTER ONE

1. "A Presumption of Disclosure: Lessons from the John F. Kennedy Assassination Records Review Board," report by OMB Watch, 2000, available at ombwatch.org. 2. Seymour M. Hersh, "Aides say Robert Kennedy told of CIA Castro plot," *The New York Times*, 3-10-75. 3. Investigation of Improper Activities in the Labor or Management Field, Senate Select Committee Hearings, 6-30-59; Ruby's 1959 activities are documented at length in Lamar Waldron and Thom Hartman, *Ultimate Sacrifice*, (New York: Carol & Graf Publishers, 2005), chapter 32. 4. Dan E. Moldea, *The Hoffa Wars: Teamsters, Rebels, Politicians, and the Mob* New York: SPI, 1993), p. 108. 5. Gus Russo, *Live by the Sword: The Secret War against Castro and the Death of JFK* (Baltimore: Bancroft Press, 1998), p. 163. 6. Joseph A. Califano, Jr., *Inside: A Public and Private Life* New York: Public Affairs, 2004), pp. 115-29; interviews with confidential Kennedy aide source 3-17-92 and confidential Kennedy Foreign Policy source 4-18-96. 7. Evan Thomas, *Robert Kennedy: His Life* (New York: Simon & Schuster, 2000), p. 159. 8. JCS 202-10001-10171. 9. Chase and Lerman, *Kennedy and the Press* New York: Crowell, 1965), pp. 333-39; John F. Kennedy address at Rice University 9-12-62, from Public Papers of the Presidents of the United States, v. 1, 1962, pp. 669-70; Laurence Chang and Peter Kornbluh, eds., *The Cuban Missile Crisis 1962* (New York: The New Press), 1992. 10. Interview with confidential

Kennedy C-Day official source 3-17-92; William Attwood memos 11-8-63 and 11-22-63. **11.** Clifton Daniel, *Chronicle of America* (Liberty, MO: JL International Publishing, 1993), p. 800. **12.** JCS 202-10001-10171. **13.** "Cuban Exiles in New Drive for Unity to Topple Castro," *The New York Times*, 5-11-63, citing 5-10-63 AP report. This was one of three similar articles that came out around the same time. **14.** RFK Oral History at the JFK Library; Edwin O. Guthman and Jeffrey Shulman, eds., *Robert Kennedy: In His Own Words: The Unpublished Recollections of the Kennedy Years* (Toronto, New York: Bantam, 1988), pp. 376, 377. **15.** Evan Thomas, *Robert Kennedy: His Life* (New York: Simon & Schuster, 2000), pp. 238-39. **16.** Robert Kennedy phone logs at the National Archives. **17.** Harry Williams interviews 4-92, 7-24-93. **18.** Declassified ZR/ RIFLE notes of William Harvey, also cited in Senate Church Committee Report, *Alleged Assassination Plots Involving Foreign Leaders* (New York: Norton, 1976). **19.** CIA 104-10315-10004, AMWORLD memo 6-28-63, declassified 1-27-99. **20.** *Foreign Relations of the United States*, vol. XI, Department of State, #370. **21.** Arthur Schlesinger, Jr., *Robert Kennedy and His Times* (New York: Ballantine, 1979), p. 598-600. **22.** Church Committee Report, vol. V, pp. 20, 21, 31, citing CIA Memorandum for the DCI, "Considerations for US Policy Toward Cuba and Latin America," 12-9-63; Foreign Relations of the United States, vol. XI, Department of State, #388, 12-19-63. **23.** Gus Russo, *Live by the Sword* (Baltimore: Bancroft Press, 1978), p. 276; note that the wording could not have been intended by JFK for Rolando Cubela/AMLASH, because Helms admitted that he never told JFK, or Bobby, about the Cubela assassination operation. **24.** CIA Document 12-6-63, from Director, released during the 1993 CIA Historical Review Program, courtesy Dr. John Newman. **25.** CIA cable to Director from Rio de Janeiro, 9-13-63. **26.** Army document, Summary of plan dated 9-26-63, Califano Papers, Record Number 198-10004-10001, declassified 10-7-97; interview with Dean Rusk 1-5-90; interview with confidential Naval Intelligence Investigator source 10-27-91; Tony Sciacca, *Kennedy and His Women* (Manor, 1976), pp. 83-90. **27.** Haynes Johnson, "One Day's Events Shattered America's Hopes and Certainties," *Washington Post*, 11-20-83. **28.** CIA 104-10308-10283; 104-10308-10274. **29.** CIA #104-10308-10098, declassified 9-18-98. **30.** CIA #104-10308-10098, declassified 9-18-98. **31.** Phillips' entire novel proposal has not been published, but portions have appeared in other sources, such as Anthony and Robbyn Summers, "The Ghosts of November," *Vanity Fair*, December 1994, p. 139. While Phillips proposal appears to be for a novel, it could also be for a movie or play. **32.** FBI memo, New York to Director, 6-2-65. **33.** CIA memos from 1963 through 1965 show that Almeida remained close to Raul Castro even as Almeida's command over Cuba's Army gradually eroded. **34.** HSCA vol. X, March 1979, p. 77; interview with Harry Williams 2-24-92; interview with confidential C-Day Defense Dept. source 7-6-92; interview with confidential Kennedy C-Day aide source 3-17-92. **35.** Army document, summary of plan dated 9-26-63, Califano Papers, Record Number 198-10004-10001, declassified 10-7-97; Joint Chiefs of Staff document, dated 12-4-63 with 11-30-63 report from Cyrus Vance, 80 total pages, Record Number 202-10002-101116, declassified 10-7-97. **36.** CIA 104-10308-10198; Fabian Escalante at Nassau Conference cited in *AARC Quarterly*, Fall 95/Winter 1996 issue. **37.** Confidential Kennedy Foreign Policy source 4-18-96. **38.** Part of the DR later evolved into an anti-Castro group based outside Cuba, called the DRE (Directorio Revolucionario Estudiantial). **39.** Confidential Kennedy Foreign Policy source 4-18-96. **40.** CIA 104-10309-10008. **41.** CIA cable from (censored) source to Director, 10-30-63. **42.** Interview with Dean Rusk, 1-5-90; Confidential Kennedy Foreign Policy source, 4-18-96. **43.** Foreign Relations of the United States, vol. XI, Department of State, #376, 11-12-63. **44.** CIA 104-10306-10024.

CHAPTER TWO

1. Joseph A. Califano, Jr., *Inside: A Public and Private Life* (New York: Public Affairs, 2004), p. 119. **2.** Ibid, p. 125. **3.** Califano Papers 198-10004-10001, declassified 10-7-97; 198-10004-10072, declassified 7-24-97; JCS 202-10002-101116, declassified 10-7-97. **4.** Ibid. **5.** Ibid. **6.** Ibid. **7.** Harry Williams 7-24-93; interview with confidential C-Day Defense Dept. source 7-6-92. **8.** Califano Papers, 198-10004-10001, declassified 10-7-97; 198-10004-10072 declassified 7-24-97; JCS 202-10002-101116, declassified 10-7-97. **9.** Richard Reeves, *President Kennedy: Profile of Power* (New York: Simon & Schuster, 1993), pp. 305, 306. **10.** CIA 104-10308-10113. **11.** While General Carroll probably wouldn't have appreciated knowing his conversations were being reported to the CIA, his own associates were engaged in similar high-level surveillance. In Joseph Califano's recent autobiography, he points to a time in June 1963 when he and his superior, Army Secretary Cyrus Vance, "secretly ran all" of "the White House and Justice Department...communication lines through the Army war room. Sitting there, Vance and I were able to listen to any conversations the President or Attorney General had...Because we assumed Robert Kennedy would have objected to our eavesdropping, we never let him know." Joseph A. Califano, Jr., *Inside: A Public and Private Life* (New York: Public Affairs, 2004), p. 109. **12.** Interview with confidential Naval Intelligence investigator source 10-27-91. **13.** Department of the Army documents dated 9-14-63 and 9-27-63, provided by the State Department, in SSCIA record number 157-10005-10372 dated 3-27-76, declassified 2-18-94. **14.** Ibid; 11-12-63 the John F. Kennedy Presidential Library, NLK 78-473, declassified 5-6-80. **15.** Army document, summary of plan dated 9-26-63, Califano Papers, Record Number 198-10004-10001, declassified 10-7-97. **16.** *The New York Times*, 12-3-63 (87:4); interview with Harry Williams, 2-24-92. **17.** Evan Thomas, *Robert Kennedy: His Life* (New York: Simon & Schuster, 2000), pp. 177, 178, 238, 239; Haynes Johnson, "One Day's Events Shattered America's Hopes and Certainties," *Washington Post*, 11-20-83; Haynes Johnson with Manuel Artime and others, *The Bay of Pigs: The Leaders' Story of Brigade 2506* (New York: Norton, 1964), many passages. **18.** CIA 104-10274-10447. **19.** CIA 104-10274-10391; CIA 104-10274-10412; CIA 104-10274-10408; CIA 104-10275; CIA 104-10274-10446. **20.** NARA 1994.03.17.10:45:20:220005, CIA 104-10235-10266; CIA Memorandum "Manolo Ray Rivero Meeting of 24-25 September 1963," declassified 2003; JMWAVE to CIA Director AMWORLD 11-23-63; Interviews with Harry Williams 2-24-92, 7-24-93. **21.** While the term "CIA-Mafia plots" is used by historians, it does not mean the plots were sanctioned by, or known to, the national Mafia commission. Only the named mob bosses were involved in the plots, which were largely secret from most of the nation's Mafia chiefs. **22.** William Scott Malone, "The Secret Life of Jack Ruby," *New Times*, 1-23-78; Gaeton Fonzi, *The Last Investigation* (New York: Thunder's Mouth, 1994), p. 373; Bradley Ayers, *The War that Never Was* (Canoga Park, Calif.: Major Books, 1979), pp. 58, 59. **23.** CIA Office of Security Varona File Summary, Record Number 180-10144-10405, declassified 8-23-95; CIA Confidential Information Report, 8-30-63; Document ID number1993.07.29.17:58:19:340059, declassified 7-29-93. **24.** CIA 104-10048-10173; Peter Dale Scott, *Crime and Cover-Up: The CIA, the Mafia, and the Dallas-Watergate Connection* (Santa Barbara, Calif.: Open Archive Press, 1993), pp. 16-18; Peter Dale Scott, *Deep Politics and the Death of JFK* (Berkeley: University of California Press, 1993), p. 120; Anthony Summers, *Conspiracy* (New York: Paragon House, 1989), pp. 293-304; Anthony Summers, *Not In Your Lifetime* (New York: Marlowe & Co., 1998) p. 236; interview with Lauren Batista and Alberto Fowler by Jim Alcock, Assistant District Attorney, 2-5-67. Note that reports vary about the number of camps, and their affiliation with the ammo dump. **25.** CIA #104-10098-10093, 10-31-63 AMWORLD Dispatch, declassified 6-20-96; CIA 104-10061-10115 pp. 89-91; CIA 104-10072-10234l; HSCA 180-10110-10016, pp. 10-12, 81, 82. **26.** E. Howard Hunt, *Give Us This Day* (New Rochelle: Arlington House, 1973), pp. 11, 12; Tad Szulc, *Compulsive Spy* (New York: Viking, 1974), p. 93. **27.** CIA 104-10275-10033. **28.** Ray and Mary La Fontaine, "The Fourth Tramp," *Washington Post*, 8-7-94; FBI airtel to "Director, FBI" from "SAC, San Antonio", 11-8-63, HSCA #1801007810062, declassified 11-29-93; FBI airtel to "Director, FBI" from "SAC, San Antonio," 11-1-63; HSCA #1801007810064, declassified 11-29-93; HSCA #1801007810066, FBI document to "Director, FBI" from "SAC, San Antonio;" Ray and Mary La Fontaine, *Oswald Talked: The New Evidence in the JFK Assassination* (Gretna: Pelican, 1996), pp. 207, 282, 286; CIA document, HSCA, Record Number 180-10143-10209, CIA Segregated Collection, Agency File Number 28-43-01, declassified 8-16-95; FBI airtel to Director, FBI from SAC, Dallas, 11-29-63, HSCA #1801007810057. Documents provided by Bill Adams. **29.** Staff and editors of *Newsday, The Heroin Trail* (New York: New American Library, 1974), pp. 114-19; Douglas Valentine, *The Strength of the Wolf: The Secret History of America's War on Drugs* (London, New York: Verso, 2004), pp. 364-71. **30.** Richard D. Mahoney, *Sons & Brothers* (New York: Arcade, 1999), p. 278. **31.** Larry Hancock, *Someone Would Have Talked* (Southlake, TX: JFK Lancer, 2006), pp. 314, 315. **32.** See http://mcadams.posc.mu.edu/morley1.htm. **33.** Memorandum by Bud Fensterwald, submitted to the US Justice Department, 7-13-82. **34.** Harry Williams interviews 4-92, 7-24-93; See Gus Russo, *Live by the Sword: The Secret War against Castro and the Death of JFK* (Baltimore: Bancroft Press, 1998), many passages. **35.** CIA 104-10434-10267 and CIA 104-10434-10283, both declassified 11-18-98. **36.** CIA 104-10295-10152, cable from JMWAVE to CIA Director McCone 12-3-63, declassified 5-19-99. **37.** Richard Helms with William Hood, *A Look Over My Shoulder: A Life in the Central Intelligence Agency* (New York: Random House, 2003), pp. 226, 227. **38.** CIA #104-10098-10093, 10-31-63 AMWORLD Dispatch, declassified 6-20-96; CIA 104-10061-10115, pp. 89-91; CIA 104-10072-10234l; HSCA 180-10110-10016, pp. 10-12, 81, 82; Gaeton Fonzi, *The Last Investigation* (New York: Thunder's Mouth, 1994), many passages. **39.** In 1961, CIA files showed that Phillips had been part of an operation with CIA officer James McCord that targeted the FPCC. In 1962, the CIA and FBI began jointly targeting the FPCC with a high-level informant, illegal break-ins, and mail surveillance, operations that continued into the fall of 1963. According to Dr. John Newman, the CIA "blocked an attempt by the [Senate] Church Committee in 1975 to find out . . . to whom such information had been circulated," so it's not clear how much Phillips was involved with the 1963 FPCC efforts. **40.** HSCA 180-10142-10307. **41.** John Simkin, David Morales biography at the British educational website www.spartacus.schoolnet.co.uk. **42.** Ibid; Joseph J. Trento, *Prelude to Terror: The Rogue CIA, and the Legacy of America's Private Intelligence Network* (New York: Carroll & Graf, 2005), p. 47. **43.** John Simkin, David Morales biography at the British educational website www.spartacus.schoolnet.co.uk; see also Larry Hancock, *Someone Would Have Talked* (Southlake, TX: JFK Lancer, 2006), many passages. **44.** Ibid Simkin and Hancock. **45.** Cuban Officials and JFK Historians Conference, 12-7-95. **46.** Larry Hancock, *Someone Would Have Talked* (Southlake, TX: JFK Lancer, 2006), pp. 128, 129. **47.** Harry Williams interviews 4-92, 7-24-93, and others. **48.** Anthony and Robbyn Summers, "The Ghosts of November," *Vanity Fair*,

12-94; Warren Hinckle and William Turner, *The Fish Is Red: The Story of the Secret War Against Castro* (New York: Harper & Row, 1981) pp. 153, 299, 303, 304. **49.** Tad Szulc, *Compulsive Spy: The Strange Career of E. Howard Hunt* (New York: Viking, 1974), pp. 77, 78. **50.** L. Gonzales-Mata, *Cygne* (Grasset, 1976). **51.** Thomas Powers, *The Man Who Kept the Secrets: Richard Helms & the CIA* (New York: Knopf, 1979), p. 62. **52.** Interview with Harry Williams, 2-24-92. **53.** CIA 104-10163-10258. **54.** WPLG-TV (Miami) Wright and Rinker interview Bernard Barker and Eugenio Martinez, 5-22-76.

CHAPTER THREE

1. US House of Representatives, *The Final Assassinations Report of the Select Committee on Assassinations* (New York: Bantam Books, 1979), pp. 208, 213. **2.** Interviews with confidential Kennedy aide source, 3-17-92. **3.** Charles Rappleye and Ed Becker, *All American Mafioso* (New York: Barricade, 1995), pp. 148-51; Stephen Schlesinger and Stephen Kinzer, *Bitter Fruit: The Story of the American Coup in Guatemala* (Garden City: Doubleday, 1982), pp. 234-36; Richard H. Immerman, *The CIA in Guatemala: The Foreign Policy of Intervention* (Austin: University of Texas Press, 1982), p. 200. **4.** Dan E. Moldea, *The Hoffa Wars: Teamsters, Rebels, Politicians, and the Mob* (New York, SPI, 1993), pp. 153, 154. This wasn't the first time that particular Ruby associate was linked to the assassination of a government official. Moldea writes on p. 153 that "In 1947 . . . the [Chicago] police captain who instigated [an] indictment" of this Ruby associate for another murder "was found dead in his garage, his jaw torn off by a .45 caliber bullet." The original murder indictment "was dropped" after "two witnesses against" the Ruby associate "were murdered" and "two others refused to testify." **5.** Ibid. **6.** Ibid, p. 108. **7.** House Select Committee on Assassinations Report, pp. 176, 177. **8.** Charles Rappleye and Ed Becker, *All American Mafioso* (New York: Barricade, 1995), pp. 237, 238; HSCA vol. IX p. 77-86. **9.** Dan Christensen "Court Secrecy Practices at Center of Drug Boss's 11th Circuit Appeal, *Daily Business Review*, 11-22-04. **10.** FBI contact investigation 3-7-86, report dictated 3-6-86, FD-302 declassified 6-98 and on file at the National Archives. **11.** Letter from informant to Carl Podsiadly, FBI, San Francisco office, 6-88. **12.** Ibid. **13.** Ibid. **14.** Ibid. **15.** John H. Davis, *Mafia Kingfish: Carlos Marcello and the Assassination of John F. Kennedy* (New York: McGraw-Hill, 1989), p. 522. **16.** Anthony and Robbyn Summers, "The Ghosts of November," *Vanity Fair*, 12-94. **17.** John H. Davis, *Mafia Kingfish: Carlos Marcello and the Assassination of John F. Kennedy* (New York: McGraw-Hill, 1989), pp. 120, 121. **18.** Letter from informant to Carl Podsiadly, FBI, San Francisco office, 6-88. **19.** Richard D. Mahoney, *Sons & Brothers* (New York: Arcade, 1999), p. 229. **20.** John H. Davis, *Mafia Kingfish: Carlos Marcello and the Assassination of John F. Kennedy* (New York: Signet, 1989), pp. 158-59; David E. Scheim, *Contract on America: The Mafia Murder of President John F. Kennedy* (New York: Zebra, 1989), p. 123. **21.** John H. Davis, *The Kennedy Contract* (New York: Harper Paperbacks, 1993), p. 253. **22.** Seth Kantor, *The Ruby Cover-Up* (New York: Zebra Books, 1992), p. 108. **23.** Warren Commission Exhibit #1697, Warren Commission Hearings vol. XXIII, p. 335, Warren Commission Documents vol. IV p. 529, all cited in David E. Scheim, *Contract on America: The Mafia Murder of President John F. Kennedy* (New York: Zebra, 1989), pp. 141-42. **24.** Warren Commission vol. XIV, p. 150, HSCA vol. IV, p. 198, 498 & vol. IX, p. 69, all cited by A. J. Weberman, ajweberman.com. **25.** HSCA vol. IX, p. 191. **26.** Charles Rappleye and Ed Becker, *All American Mafioso* (New York: Barricade, 1995), pp. 237, 238; HSCA vol. IX, pp. 77-86. **27.** Interviews with John Knight, Sr., 1-10-06 and 6-13-06. While a bystander told Knight the mobster from Los Angeles visiting Marcello was the well-known Mickey Cohen, it had to be Johnny Rosselli or another Los Angeles mob associate of Marcello, since Cohen was in prison at the time. **28.** John H. Davis, *Mafia Kingfish: Carlos Marcello and the Assassination of John F. Kennedy* (New York McGraw-Hill, 1989), many passages. **29.** CIA 104-10315-10004, 6-28-63 AMWORLD memo, declassified 1-27-99; Bradley Ayers, *The War that Never Was* (Canoga Park, Calif.: Major Books, 1979), pp. 58, 59. **30.** FBI 62-109060-251; FBI 62-109060-7077 2.26.73; FBI 62-109060-5815 10.13.67 cited by A. J. Weberman at ajweberman.com. **31.** Warren Commission Exhibit #2818. (In mid-December 1963, after JFK's death and LBJ put C-Day on hold, Ruby placed the date for the invasion in May 1964.) **32.** *Independent American*, 8-12-63. **33.** John H. Davis, *Mafia Kingfish* (New York: McGraw-Hill, 1989), many passages; Banister files at the Assassination Archives and Research Center, Washington, D.C.; Miriam Ottenberg, *The Federal Investigators* (Englewood Cliffs: Prentice-Hall, 1962), p. 93. **34.** Anthony Summers, *Not In Your Lifetime* (New York: Marlowe & Co., 1998), p. 233; *People and The Pursuit of Truth*, vol. 1, No. 1, 5-75. **35.** Ibid Summers, p. 236. **36.** CIA file card, "Oswald, Lee Harvey" R 6R05270089 from Oswald's CIA file 201-289248. **37.** Phone interview with confidential high Florida law-enforcement source 12-10-96.

CHAPTER FOUR

1. Carl Sifakis, *The Mafia Encyclopedia* (New York: Facts On File, 1987), pp. 325, 326; Douglas Valentine, *The Strength of the Wolf: The Secret History of America's War on Drugs* (London, New York: Verso, 2004), p. 471 U.S. Senate, McClellan Committee Hearings (officially Investigation of Improper Activities in the Labor or Management Field, Senate Select Committee Hearings), 6-30-59. **2.** Allen Friedman and Ted Schwarz

Power and Greed: Inside the Teamsters Empire of Corruption (New York: F. Watts, 1989), pp. 132, 154; Joseph Franco with Richard Hammer, *Hoffa's Man: The Rise and Fall of Jimmy Hoffa as Witnessed by His Strongest Arm* (New York: Prentice Hall, 1987), pp. 197, 198. **3.** Staff and editors of *Newsday, The Heroin Trail* (New York: New American Library, 1974), pp. 109-18; Project Pilot cited by Douglas Valentine, *The Strength of the Wolf: The Secret History of America's War on Drugs* (London, New York: Verso, 2004), pp. 315-18, 331, 332, 366, 367, 370, 371. **4.** Jack Newfield, "I want Kennedy killed," *Penthouse* 5-92. **5.** Harry Williams interview, 7-24-93. **6.** Senate Committee on Government Operations, Permanent Subcommittee on Investigations: Organized Crime and Illicit Traffic in Narcotics, Sept./Oct. 1963. **7.** Douglas Valentine, *The Strength of the Wolf: The Secret History of America's War on Drugs* (London, New York: Verso, 2004), p. 298. **8.** Senate Committee on Government Operations, Permanent Subcommittee on Investigations: Organized Crime and Illicit Traffic in Narcotics, 10-15-63. **9.** Phone interview with confidential high Florida law-enforcement source, 12-10-96. **10.** Senate Committee on Government Operations, Permanent Subcommittee on Investigations: Organized Crime and Illicit Traffic in Narcotics, 10-15-63. **11.** Phone interview with confidential high Florida law-enforcement source, 12-10-96. **12.** Fabian Escalante at Nassau Conference, also cited in *AARC Quarterly*, Fall 95/Winter 1996 issue. **13.** Dick Russell, *The Man Who Knew Too Much* (New York: Carroll & Graf, 2003), pp. 459, 460. **14.** CIA 104-10215-10321, cable to CIA Director, 9-17-63. **15.** Larry Hancock, *Someone Would Have Talked* (Southlake, TX: JFK Lancer, 2006), p. 337. **16.** CIA 104-10215-190316. **17.** Larry Hancock, *Someone Would Have Talked* (Southlake, TX: JFK Lancer, 2006), p. 337. **18.** CIA 104-10169-10006, memo to CIA Director, 8-6-73. **19.** Dick Russell, *The Man Who Knew Too Much* (New York: Carroll & Graf, 2003), pp. 459, 460. **20.** Harry Williams interview 7-24-93; other references withheld to protect source's family. **21.** Larry Hancock, *Someone Would Have Talked* (Southlake, TX: JFK Lancer, 2006), p. 49. **22.** Ibid, pp. 481-94. **23.** 1967 Inspector General's Report on the CIA-Mafia plots; William Scott Malone, "The Secret Life of Jack Ruby," *New Times* 1-23-78; Charles Rappleye and Ed Becker, *All American Mafioso* (New York: Barricade, 1995), many passages. **24.** Ibid Rappleye and Becker, pp. 120, 121. **25.** Ibid, pp. 248, 249. **26.** Bradley Ayers, *The War that Never Was* (Canoga Park, Calif.: Major Books, 1979), pp. 58, 59; Sylvia Meagher, *Accessories After the Fact: The Warren Commission, the Authorities, and the Report* (New York: Vintage, 1992), p. 107. **27.** Ibid, Ayers. **28.** Interview of Robert Plumlee 6-4-92, apparently by Robert G. Vernon. We tend to focus on those parts of Plumlee's story that have remained most consistent over the years and those parts for which there is some independent corroboration. **29.** Larry Hancock, *Someone Would Have Talked* (Southlake, TX: JFK Lancer, 2006), many passages. **30.** Michael L. Kurtz, *The JFK Assassination Debates* (Lawrence, KS: University Press of Kansas, 2006), pp. 209-15. **31.** Warren Commission Document #657 **32.** Richard D. Mahoney, *Sons & Brothers: The Days of Jack and Bobby Kennedy* (New York: Arcade, 1999), pp. 271-73. **33.** Larry Hancock, *Someone Would Have Talked* (Southlake, TX: JFK Lancer, 2006), many passages. **34.** Michael L. Kurtz, *The JFK Assassination Debates* (Lawrence, KS: University Press of Kansas, 2006), pp. 209, 210. **35.** CIA 1993.08.05.12:35:37:460006. **36.** Staff and editors of *Newsday, The Heroin Trail* (New York: New American library, 1974), pp. 109-18; Project Pilot cited by Douglas Valentine, *The Strength of the Wolf: The Secret History of America's War on Drugs* (London, New York: Verso, 2004), pp. 315-18, 331, 332, 366, 367, 370, 371. **37.** Hilaire du Berrier, Fensterwald files at the AARC. **38.** Fensterwald affidavit for the Justice Department, 7-7-82. **39.** Gary Shaw phone interviews with Robert Greene of *Newsday*, 5-11-79 and 5-17-79. **40.** Senate Committee on Government Operations, Permanent Subcommittee on Investigations: Organized Crime and Illicit Traffic in Narcotics, 9-63, 10-63. **41.** Fensterwald files, James P. Kelly interview 12-11-79; manuscript reference to K. Walsh. **42.** BBC News.com article 10-10-01. **43.** The parallels between Michel Victor Mertz and QJWIN are listed at legacyofsecrecy.com. **44.** CIA 1994.03.11.16:07:16:500005, CIA: 1994.03.11.16:05:55:410005. **45.** Background report on the travels of Mertz, with dates and places of entry and exit from the US, Bud Fensterwald Mertz files at the Assassination Archives and Research Center. **46.** Fensterwald affidavit for the Justice Department, 7-7-82. **47.** US Treasury Dept. letter to US Secret Service by Senior Customs Representative Aurelien Chasse, 11-29-63. **48.** CIA 104-10419-10342.

CHAPTER FIVE

1. *Chicago Daily News* interviews 5-28 and 5-29-68, from the files of Bud Fensterwald at the Assassination Archives and Research Center in Washington, D.C. **2.** CIA 104-10309-10008; Vincent Michael Palamara, *The Third Alternative* (Pennsylvania: 1993), chapter 10; Bernard Fensterwald interview of Abraham Bolden 3-29-68; HSCA Document #180-10070-10273, interview of Secret Service Agent Abraham Bolden by HSCA staffers Jim Kelly and Harold Rese; Bernard Fensterwald interview of Abraham Bolden 3-29-68. **3.** These are just a few of the references about the Chicago plot, which is detailed extensively in Lamar Waldron and Thom Hartman, *Ultimate Sacrifice*, (New York: Carol & Graf Publishers, 2005), chapters 50-52; phone interview with Pierre Salinger 4-10-98; phone interviews with Jim Allison 4-15-98 and 4-16-98; Edwin Black article, *Chicago Independent*, 11-75; CIA memo for Director of Security, subject: Cain, Richard Scully,

12-19-69, declassified 1992; HSCA 180-10105-10393, Secret Service memo 3-29-63, declassified 12-1-93; Bud Fensterwald, "The Case of Secret Service Agent Abraham W. Bolden," *Computers and Automation,* 6-71; HSCA Report, p. 231; UPI article 5-21-64; HSCA 180-10070-10273 interview with Abraham Bolden 1-19-78, declassified 1-5-96; Vincent Michael Palamara, *The Third Alternative* (PA, 1993) many passages; CIA F82-0272/1, 82-1625 (4); CIA 104-10308-10209, declassified 9-21-98; F82-0272/2: cable to CIA Director from (censored), 1-64. **4.** Michael J. Cain, *The Tangled Web: The Life and Death of Richard Cain* (New York: Skyhorse Publishing, 2007), many passages; HSCA 180-10105-10393, Secret Service memo 3-29-63, declassified 12-1-93; CIA memo for Director of Security, subject: Cain, Richard Scully, 12-19-69, declassified 1992; CIA memo for "Chief, LEOB/SRS" from Sarah K. Hall 12-11-67; CIA memo to Chief, SRS from M. D. Stevens, 10-9-67, declassified 1992; 12-12-67 CIA memo to Director of Security, #272141. **5.** Frank DeBenedictis, "Four Days before Dallas," *Tampa Bay History,* Fall/Winter 1994; *The New York Times,* 11-19-63; *Tampa Tribune,* 11-17-63; Mary Evertz, "John F. Kennedy: The Exhibition," *St. Petersburg Times,* 11-11-99. **6.** These are just a few of the many references for the Tampa attempt, which are detailed at length in Lamar Waldron and Thom Hartman, *Ultimate Sacrifice,* (New York: Carol & Graf Publishers, 2005): phone interview with J. P. Mullins 12-10-96; phone interview with high Florida law-enforcement source 12-10-96; HSCA 180-10074-10394, cited in JFK Assassination Records Review Board Update presentation by Joseph Backes at the 1996 JFK Lancer Conference. **7.** "Threats on Kennedy Made Here," *Tampa Tribune,* 11-23-63; "Man Held in Threats to JFK," *Miami Herald,* 11-24-63: It is bylined, "Tampa (UPI)," so it may well have appeared in other newspapers. **8.** Phone interview with Blanche Andrea Leon 3/2/96; Skip Johnson and Tony Durr, "Ex-Tampan in JFK Plot?" *Tampa Tribune,* 9-5-76; CIA 104-10075-10006. **9.** HSCA Report, pp. 118-21; 12-4-63 "secret" "classified message" from the office of CIA Director John McCone (though signed by Richard Helms) about the Tampa suspect and not wanting "to blow the [censored] operation," declassified 4-6-94, Document ID 1994.04.06.10:28:12:530005; numerous Lopez files from the CIA Russell Holmes work files collection and the Assassination Archives and Research Center. Much more about Lopez is detailed in Lamar Waldron and Thom Hartman, *Ultimate Sacrifice,* (New York: Carol & Graf Publishers, 2005). **10.** Miami Police Intelligence files; Michael L. Kurtz, *The JFK Assassination Debates* (Lawrence, KS: University Press of Kansas, 2006), pp. 218-19. **11.** Dan Christensen, "JFK, King: The Dade County links," *Miami* magazine, 12-76; HSCA Report, p. 232; Miami Police Department transcript of 11-9-63 Milteer conversation with William Somersett; phone interview with confidential high Florida law-enforcement source 12-10-96; Miami Police interview with William Somersett transcribed 11-26-63. **12.** Michael L. Kurtz, *The JFK Assassination Debates* (Lawrence, KS: University Press of Kansas, 2006), pp. 218, 219. **13.** Note that Commander Almeida had been in the Sierra Maestra mountains with Fidel Castro, unlike Rolando Cubela; *The New York Times* 11-19-63; *Marietta Daily Journal* 11-19-63; Gus Russo, *Live by the Sword: The Secret War against Castro and the Death of JFK* (Baltimore: Bancroft Press, 1998), p. 275. **14.** Ralph Martin, *A Hero For Our Time* (New York: Fawcett Crest, 1988), p. 503, cited in Vincent Michael Palamara, *Survivor's Guilt: The Secret Service & the Failure to Protect the President* (Pennsylvania: 2005), p. 21. **15.** "International relations chief Alberto Fowler dies at 58," *New Orleans Times-Picayune,* 12-30-87; *U.S. News & World Report, 1-7-63;* Statement of Alberto Fowler in the Office of the District Attorney 1-23-67; memos by Harold Weisberg on file at the Assassination Archives and Research Center; *New Orleans Times-Picayune,* 11-22-73; Harry Williams interview 2-24-92. **16.** Phone interview with confidential high Florida law-enforcement source 12-10-96. **17.** HSCA vol. X, pp. 199-205; Larry Hancock, *Someone Would Have Talked* (Southlake, TX: JFK Lancer, 2006), pp. 461-70; Statement of Mr. A. H. Magruder, taken by Det. Frank Meloche and Sgt. Fenner Sedgebeer, 2-23-67; John H. Davis, *Mafia Kingfish* (New York: Signet, 1989), pp. 606, 607; HSCA vol. X, pp. 198-205; Ronald Goldfarb, *Perfect Villains and Imperfect Heroes* (New York: Random House, 1995), pp. 139, 140; John H. Davis, *The Kennedy Contract* (New York: Harper Paperbacks, 1993), pp. 54, 55.

CHAPTER SIX

1. Michael Benson, *Who's Who in the JFK Assassination: An A-to-Z Encyclopedia* (New York: Citadel, 1993), pp. 329, 330; Robert Oswald testimony Warren Commission vol. I, pp. 264-469; John Edward Pic testimony Warren Commission vol. VIII, pp. 196-202; Greg Parker article 10-21-04; Robert L. Oswald, "He was my brother," *Look,* 10-17-67; Herbert Philbrick, *I Led Three Lives* (New York: Grosset & Dunlap, 1952); Roger M. Grace, "Channel 11 Loads Its Schedule with Syndicated Shows," *Metropolitan News-Enterprise,* 1-22-2003; Wesley Britton, "They were Communists for the FBI," August 2004, and Britton also cites Daniel J. Leab, *I Was a Communist for the F.B.I.: The Unhappy Life and Times of Matt Cvetic* (University Park: Pennsylvania State University Press, 2000). **2.** Anthony Summers, *Not In Your Lifetime* (New York: Marlowe & Co., 1998), pp. 234, 235; Anthony Summers, *Conspiracy* (Paragon House, 1989), p. 125; Dick Russell, *The Man Who Knew Too Much* (New York: Carroll & Graf, 2003), p. 126. **3.** Cindy Adams, *New York Post,* 2-12-92, cited by Michael Benson, *Who's Who in the JFK Assassination: An A-to-Z Encyclopedia* (New York: Citadel, 1993), p. 110. **4.** Michael L. Kurtz, *The JFK Assassination Debates* (Lawrence, KS: University Press of Kansas, 2006), pp. 149, 150. **5.** Gaeton Fonzi, *The Last Investigation* (New York: Thunder's Mouth, 1994), p. 191. **6.** Anthony Summers, *Not In Your Lifetime* (New York: Marlowe & Co., 1998), pp. 82, 83, 152-59. **7.** Ibid, pp. 82, 83, 152-72, and others; Warren Hinckle and William Turner, *Deadly Secrets* (New York: Thunder's Mouth, 1992), pp. 193, 194. **8.** Michael L. Kurtz, *The JFK Assassination Debates* (Lawrence, KS: University Press of Kansas, 2006), pp. 149, 150. **9.** CIA 104-10310-10208. **10.** Michael L. Kurtz, *The JFK Assassination Debates* (Lawrence, KS: University Press of Kansas, 2006), pp. 162, 240. **11.** Ibid, p. 163. **12.** Ibid, p. 184. **13.** Ibid, pp. 159, 186. **14.** Ibid, p. 184. **15.** Ibid, pp. 185, 186. **16.** Lisa Pease, article in *Probe*, vol. 3, No. 3, March/April 1996. **17.** E. Howard Hunt deposition, 11-3-78, document #180-10131-10342, declassified 2-9-96; Joseph B. Smith, *Portrait of a Cold Warrior* (New York: Ballantine, 1981), pp. 229, 230; John Newman, *Oswald and the CIA* (New York: Carroll & Graf, 1995), pp. 95, 236, 240-44. **18.** Michael L. Kurtz, *The JFK Assassination Debates* (Lawrence, KS: University Press of Kansas, 2006), p. 165. **19.** Interview with Antonio Veciana, 5-2-93. **20.** Michael L. Kurtz, *The JFK Assassination Debates* (Lawrence, KS: University Press of Kansas, 2006), p. 161. **21.** Interview with confidential Naval Intelligence investigator source 10-27-91; article about Win Scott in *Washington Post* 3-17-96. **22.** Peter Dale Scott, *Deep Politics III* (online excerpt available at maryferrell.org); Douglas Valentine, *The Strength of the Wolf: The Secret History of America's War on Drugs* London, New York: Verso, 2004), many passages. **23.** Anthony Summers, *Not In Your Lifetime* (New York: Marlowe & Co., 1998), p. 289. **24.** Warren Commission vol. XVI, Exhibit #102, pp. 441-42. **25.** Ibid. **26.** Skip Johnson and Tony Durr, "Ex-Tampan in JFK Plot?" *Tampa Tribune*, 9-5-76; Dr. Jerry D. Rose, "J. B. Stoner: An Introduction," *The Fourth Decade*, November 1995 FBI teletype 11-27-63, Springfield to Director and Dallas. According to the FBI report, the secretary said Oswald's visit happened in the summer of 1962 or 1961, but the New Orleans TV reference clearly places it in 1963. **27.** Sylvia Meagher, *Accessories After the Fact: The Warren Commission, the Authorities, and the Report* (New York: Vintage, 1992), pp. 45-63; Seth Kantor, *The Ruby Cover-Up* (New York: Zebra Books, 1992), pp. 386-89; Anthony Summers, *Conspiracy* McGraw-Hill, 1980), pp. 87, 88; Henry Hurt, *Reasonable Doubt* (New York: Henry Holt, 1987), pp. 96, 97. **28.** David Atlee Phillips, *The Night Watch* (New York: Atheneum, 1977), p. 12. **29.** CIA 104-10240-10337 shows that the torn-bill technique was also used for Manuel Artime as part of AMWORLD, so that he could identify his intelligence contact; interview with Antonio Veciana, 6-2-93; Ronald Goldfarb, *Perfect Villains and Imperfect Heroes* (New York: Random House, 1995), pp. 139, 140. **30.** Richard D. Mahoney, *Sons & Brothers: The Days of Jack and Bobby Kennedy* (New York: Arcade, 1999), p. 418. **31.** *San Jose Mercury News*, 9-28-88. **32.** Anthony Summers, *Conspiracy* (New York: McGraw-Hill, 1980), pp. 105-7; G. Robert Blakey and Richard N. Billings, *The Plot to Kill the President* (New York: Times Books, 1981), pp. 21, 363.

CHAPTER SEVEN

1. Ronald Goldfarb, *Perfect Villains, Imperfect Heroes: Robert F. Kennedy's War against Organized Crime* New York: Random House, 1995), pp. 139-42. **2.** Wallace Turner, "Las Vegas: Casinos Get Millions in Loans from Teamsters Fund," *The New York Times*, 11-22-63. **3.** Army document, from Director of Foreign Intelligence to Office, Secretary of the Army attn: Mr. Joseph Califano, General Counsel; Dec. 11, 1963, Califano Papers, Record Number 198-10004-10011, declassified 10-7-97. **4.** Haynes Johnson, "One Day's Events Shattered America's Hopes and Certainties," *Washington Post* 11-20-83. **5.** Interviews with Harry Williams 2-24-92, 4-92. **6.** Gus Russo, *Live by the Sword* (Baltimore: Bancroft Press, 1978), p. 272. **7.** CIA 104-10236-10350. **8.** Anthony and Robbyn Summers, "The Ghosts of November," *Vanity Fair*, 12-94; Anthony Summers, *Not In Your Lifetime* (New York: Marlowe & Co., 1998), pp. 310, 449; William Turner interview with Harry Williams 11-28-73; Warren Hinckle and William Turner, *The Fish Is Red: The Story of the Secret War Against Castro* (New York: Harper & Row, 1981), pp. 153, 218. **9.** Church Committee vol. V, p. 101. **10.** Church Committee vol. V, p. 19. **11.** CIA, Inspector General's Report on Plots to Assassinate Castro, 1967, p. 93a. **12.** Noel Twyman, *Bloody Treason* (Rancho Sante Fe, CA: Laurel Publishing, 1997), p. 451. **13.** Gaeton Fonzi, *The Last Investigation* (New York: Thunder's Mouth, 1994), pp. 389, 390. **14.** Ibid, pp. 384, 385; Noel Twyman, *Bloody Treason* (Rancho Sante Fe, CA: Laurel Publishing, 1997), pp. 402, 427. **15.** Nassau Conference Report, *AARC Quarterly*, Fall 1995-Winter 1996. **16.** Richard D. Mahoney, *Sons & Brothers: The Days of Jack and Bobby Kennedy* (New York: Arcade, 1999), p. 229; Larry Hancock, *Someone Would Have Talked* (Southlake, TX: JFK Lancer, 2006) many passages. **17.** Cuban Officials and JFK Historians Nassau Conference, 12-7-95; John Simkin, David Morales biography at the British educational website www. spartacus.schoolnet.co.uk. **18.** David Corn, *Blond Ghost* (New York: Simon & Schuster, 1994), p. 85. **19.** Wayne Smith comments on BBC "Newsnight" report 11-20-06; Eric Hamburg, *JFK, Nixon, Oliver Stone, and Me* (New York: Public Affairs, 2002).

CHAPTER EIGHT

1. Michael Dorman, *Pay-Off* (New York: Berkley Medallion, 1973) and John H. Davis, *Mafia Kingfish: Carlos Marcello and the Assassination of John F. Kennedy* (New York: Signet, 1989), several passages. **2.** David E. Scheim, *The Mafia Killed President Kennedy* (New York: SPI Books, 1992), pp. 140, 141. **3.** Ibid, p. 192. **4.** Phone interview with John Diuguid, 9-30-04. **5.** FBI report re Hugh Ainsworth, 11-25-63. **6.** Michael Benson, *Who's Who in the JFK Assassination: An A-to-Z Encyclopedia* (New York: Citadel, 1993), pp. 89, 215, 216; Mark Lane, *Rush to Judgment* (New York: Fawcett Crest, 1967), p. 223. **7.** Seth Kantor, *The Ruby Cover-Up* (New York: Zebra Books, 1992), pp. 55-63. **8.** Phone interviews with Jim Allison 4-15-98 and 4-16-98. **9.** HSCA vol. IX, p. 1100; Douglas Valentine, *The Strength of the Wolf: The Secret History of America's War on Drugs* (London, New York: Verso, 2004), pp. 310, 311; John H. Davis, *Mafia Kingfish* (New York: McGraw Hill, 1989), p. 74; David E. Scheim, *The Mafia Killed President Kennedy* (New York: SPI Books, 1992), pp. 125, 126. **10.** William Turner, "The Inquest," *Ramparts*, June 1967. **11.** Warren Commission Exhibit #1505; Warren Commission Exhibit #1697, cited in Scheim, *Contract on America: The Mafia Murder of President John F. Kennedy* (New York: Zebra, 1989) pp. 141-42; Warren Commission Hearings vol. XXIII, p. 335; Warren Commission Documents vol. IV, p. 529; Seth Kantor, *The Ruby Cover-Up* (New York: Zebra Books, 1992) p. 31. **12.** FBI 44-24016-275; C.Ray Hall Warren Commission Exhibit #3; FBI DL 44-1639; LL R: BC D-cove page, cited by A. J. Weberman. **13.** William Manchester, *The Death of a President, November 20-November 25 1963* (New York: Harper & Row, 1967). **14.** Anthony Summers, *Not In Your Lifetime* (New York: Marlowe & Co., 1998), pp. 459, 460; HSCA vol. XIII, pp. 37, others; Anthony Summers, *Conspiracy* (New York: McGraw-Hill, 1980), p. 602; Henry Hurt, *Reasonable Doubt* (New York: Henry Holt, 1987) several passages. **15.** William Scott Malone, "The Secret Life of Jack Ruby," *New Times*, 1-23-78. **16.** Richard D. Mahoney, *Sons & Brothers: The Days of Jack and Bobby Kennedy* (New York: Arcade, 1999), pp. 229, 408. **17.** Senate Committee on Government Operations, Permanent Subcommittee on Investigations: Organized Crime and Illicit Traffic in Narcotics, Sept./Oct. 1963; Carl Sifakis, *The Mafia Encyclopedia* (New York: Facts On File, 1987), pp. 154, 155. **18.** Charles Rappleye and Ed Becker, *All American Mafioso* (New York: Barricade, 1995), p. 248. **19.** Frank Ragano and Selwyn Raab, *Mob Lawyer* (New York: Scribners, 1994), p. 147. **20.** HSCA vol. V, pp. 303, 314, 315, 319, 320, 373, 374. **21.** Dick Russell, *The Man Who Knew Too Much* (New York: Carroll & Graf, 2003), pp. 459, 460. **22.** Larry Hancock, *Someone Would Have Talked* (Southlake, TX: JFK Lancer, 2006), p. 1. **23.** Anthony and Robbyn Summers, "The Ghosts of November," *Vanity Fair*, Dec 1994. 24. Ibid. 25. Larry Hancock, *Someone Would Have Talked* (Southlake, TX: JFK Lancer, 2006) p. 1. 26 CIA 1993.08.05.12:35:37:460006.

CHAPTER NINE

1. Sylvia Meagher, *Accessories After the Fact: The Warren Commission, the Authorities, and the Report* (New York: Vintage, 1992), pp. 106-10. **2.** Ibid. **3.** Anthony Summers, *Conspiracy* (New York: Paragon House, 1989), p. 77. **4.** Dallas Police Report re: Eddie Piper, 2-17-74. **5.** Anthony Summers, *Conspiracy* (New York: Paragon House, 1989), p. 77. **6.** Ibid, p. 42. **7.** Ibid, p. 43; Larry Hancock, *Someone Would Have Talked* (Southlake, TX: JFK Lancer, 2006), p. 72. **8.** Warren Commission Exhibit #2089 **9.** Anthony Summers, *Conspiracy* (New York: Paragon House, 1989), p. 80. **10.** Ibid, p. 44. **11.** Warren Commission vol. XXIV. **12.** Anthony Summers, *Conspiracy* (New York: McGraw-Hill, 1980), pp. 58, 59. **13.** Ibid, p. 29. **14.** Josiah Thompson, *Six Seconds in Dallas* (New York: Berkley Medallion, 1976), p. 155. **15.** G. Robert Blakey and Richard N. Billings, *The Plot to Kill the President* (New York: Times Books, 1981), p. 13. **16.** HSCA 180-10099-10491 **17.** Anthony Summers, *Conspiracy* (New York: McGraw-Hill, 1980), p. 37. **18.** HSCA 180-10074-10079 **19.** William Manchester, *The Death of a President* (New York: Harper & Row, 1967), chronology on inside front cover; Henry Hurt, *Reasonable Doubt* (New York: Henry Holt, 1987), p. 14; Josiah Thompson, *Six Seconds in Dallas* (New York: Bernard Geis, 1967), pp. 51-62. **20.** Interview with Dave Powers 6-5-91 at the John F. Kennedy Presidential Library; Ibid Hurt. **21.** Anthony Summers, *Conspiracy* (New York: Paragon House, 1989), p. 19. **22.** HSCA 180-100882-10452, cited in JFK Assassination Records Review Board Update presentation by Joseph Backes at the JFK Lancer Conference, 11-96. **23.** Michael L. Kurtz, *The JFK Assassination Debates* (Lawrence, KS: University Press of Kansas, 2006), pp. 30, 119; David S. Lifton, *Best Evidence: Disguise and Deception in the Assassination of John F. Kennedy* (New York: Carroll & Graf, 1988) several passages. **24.** Josiah Thompson, *Six Seconds in Dallas* (New York: Bernard Geis, 1967), pp. 72-73, 292-95. **25.** Anthony Summers, *Conspiracy* (New York: Paragon House, 1989), p. 24. **26.** Michael L. Kurtz, *The JFK Assassination Debates* (Lawrence, KS: University Press of Kansas, 2006), pp. 25, 47, 48; Michael Benson, *Who's Who in the JFK Assassination: An A-to-Z Encyclopedia* (New York: Citadel, 1993), pp. 172, 173. **27.** Anthony Summers, *Conspiracy* (New York: Paragon House, 1989), p. 29.

CHAPTER TEN

1. Statement of Forrest Sorrels, 11-28-63. **2.** Mark Lane, *Rush to Judgment* (New York: Fawcett Crest, 1967) p. 34. **3.** Michael Benson, *Who's Who in the JFK Assassination: An A-to-Z Encyclopedia* (New York: Citadel, 1993), p. 172. **4.** Warren Commission Decker Exhibit # 5323, p. 540. **5.** Mark Lane, *Rush to Judgment* (New York: Fawcett Crest, 1967), p. 33. **6.** Anthony Summers, *Conspiracy* (New York: McGraw-Hill, 1980), p. 82. **7.** Warren Commission Exhibit #2003 p.222; Michael Benson, *Who's Who in the JFK Assassination: A*

A-to-Z Encyclopedia (New York: Citadel, 1993), p. 367. **8.** Mark Lane, *Rush to Judgment* (New York: Fawcett Crest, 1967), p. 27. **9.** Josiah Thompson, *Six Seconds in Dallas* (New York: Bernard Geis, 1967), pp. 163, 164. **10.** Ibid, pp. 185, 186, citing 7H106-107. **11.** Anthony Summers, *Conspiracy* (New York: Paragon House, 1989), p. 50. **12.** Ibid, p. 51. **13.** Michael Benson, *Who's Who in the JFK Assassination: An A-to-Z Encyclopedia* (New York: Citadel, 1993), p. 172. **14.** Anthony Summers, *Conspiracy* (New York: McGraw-Hill, 1980) pp. 58, 59. **15.** Mark Lane, *Rush to Judgment* (New York: Fawcett Crest, 1967). **16.** Robert MacNeil, ed., *The Way We Were: 1963, the Year Kennedy Was Shot* (New York: Carroll & Graf, 1988), p. 195. **17.** Anthony Summers, *Conspiracy* (New York: Paragon House, 1989), pp. 24, 27. **18.** David S. Lifton, *Best Evidence: Disguise and Deception in the Assassination of John F. Kennedy* (New York: Carroll & Graf, 1988), p. 18. **19.** Ibid. **20.** Anthony Summers, *Conspiracy* (New York: Paragon House, 1989), p. 23. **21.** Ibid, p. 29. **22.** Mark Lane, *Rush to Judgment* (New York: Fawcett Crest, 1967), p. 31. **23.** For example, witness Ruby Henderson heard four shots (Warren Commission Exhibit #2089), while Secret Service agent Kellerman said "there have got to be more than three shots"; Anthony Summers, *Conspiracy* (New York: Paragon House, 1989), p.19. **24.** Josiah Thompson, *Six Seconds in Dallas* (New York: Berkley Medallion, 1976), p. 179. **25.** Anthony Summers, *Conspiracy* (New York: Paragon House, 1989), p. 78. **26.** Michael Benson, *Who's Who in the JFK Assassination: An A-to-Z Encyclopedia* (New York: Citadel, 1993), pp. 89, 215, 216; Mark Lane, *Rush to Judgment* (New York: Fawcett Crest, 1967), p. 223. **27.** Ibid Benson, pp. 23, 24. **28.** Warren Commission document #385; Josiah Thompson, *Six Seconds in Dallas* (New York: Bernard Geis, 1967), pp. 304-11, 314, 315. **29.** Robert MacNeil, *The Right Place at the Right Time* (New York: Penguin, 1990), pp. 207, 208. **30.** Don Thomas, "Rewriting History: Bugliosi Parses the Testimony," http://www.maryferrell.org. **31.** HSCA vol. IX, several passages; Anthony Summers, *Conspiracy* (New York: Paragon House, 1989), pp. 452-54. **32.** Anthony Summers, *Not In Your Lifetime* (New York: Marlowe & Co., 1998), p. 10. **33.** Dr. Carrico, Oral History, Sixth Floor Museum. **34.** Michael Benson, *Who's Who in the JFK Assassination: An A-to-Z Encyclopedia* (New York: Citadel, 1993), p. 360. **35.** Dr. Gary Aguilar and Josiah Thompson, "Magic Bullet," at historymatters.com. **36.** Anthony Summers, *Conspiracy* (New York: Paragon House, 1989), p. 8. **37.** William Turner presentation abstract, COPA Conference 10-94. **38.** Anthony Summers, *Conspiracy* (New York: McGraw-Hill, 1980), p. 115. **39.** Henry Hurt, *Reasonable Doubt* (New York: Henry Holt, 1987), pp. 163, 164. **40.** Michael T. Griffith, "Why Would Oswald have stopped Tippit," 1997 web article. **41.** Henry Hurt, *Reasonable Doubt* (New York: Henry Holt, 1987) p. 163; Ibid Griffith. **42.** Ibid Hurt, pp. 165-68. **43.** Anthony and Robbyn Summers, "The Ghosts of November," *Vanity Fair*, Dec. 1994. **44.** Jack Anderson and Daryl Gibson, *Peace, War, and Politics* (Forge, 2000), p. 117. **45.** Henry Hurt, *Reasonable Doubt* (New York: Henry Holt, 1987), p. 164. **46.** Michael T. Griffith, "Why Would Oswald have stopped Tippit," 1997 web article. **47.** Michael L. Kurtz, *The JFK Assassination Debates* (Lawrence, KS: University Press of Kansas, 2006), p. 49. **48.** Anthony Summers, *Conspiracy* (New York: Paragon House, 1989); Henry Hurt, *Reasonable Doubt* (New York: Henry Holt, 1987); Sylvia Meagher, *Accessories After the Fact: The Warren Commission, the Authorities, and the Report* (New York: Vintage, 1992); Mark Lane, *Rush to Judgment* (New York: Fawcett Crest, 1967). **49.** Anthony Summers, *Not In Your Lifetime* (New York: Marlowe & Co., 1998), p. 75. **50.** David E. Scheim, *Contract on America: The Mafia Murder of President John F. Kennedy* (New York: Zebra, 1989), p. 55; Michael Benson, *Who's Who in the JFK Assassination: An A-to-Z Encyclopedia* (New York: Citadel, 1993), p. 146. **51.** Mark Lane, *Rush to Judgment* (New York: Fawcett Crest, 1967), p. 161; Larry Harris, "The Other Murder," *Dateline Dallas*, 11-22-63. **52.** Dale K. Myers, *With Malice: Lee Harvey Oswald and the Murder of Officer J.D. Tippit* (Oak Cliff Press, 1998), chapter 6. **53.** CIA 104-10240-10337, 7-9-63 memo from Henry D. Hecksher. **54.** G. Robert Blakey and Richard N. Billings, *The Plot to Kill the President* (New York: Times Books, 1981), p. 19; Jim Garrison, *On the Trail of the Assassins* (New York: Sheridan Square Press, 1988), pp. 95-117; Henry Hurt, *Reasonable Doubt* (New York: Henry Holt, 1987), p. 18. **55.** Anthony and Robbyn Summers, "The Ghosts of November," *Vanity Fair*, Dec. 1994. **56.** Sylvia Meagher, *Accessories After the Fact: The Warren Commission, the Authorities, and the Report* (New York: Vintage, 1992), pp. 94-133. **57.** Henry Hurt, *Reasonable Doubt* (New York: Henry Holt, 1987), p. 90; Anthony Summers, *Conspiracy* (New York: Paragon House, 1989), p. 106. **58.** CIA 1993.08.04.16:20:46:530028. **59.** Earl Golz, "Confidential: The FBI's File on JFK-Part Two," *Gallery*, 12-82. **60.** Seth Kantor, *The Ruby Cover-Up* (New York: Zebra Books, 1992), p. 62.

CHAPTER ELEVEN

1. "A Presumption of Disclosure: Lessons from the John F. Kennedy Assassination Records Review Board," report by OMB Watch, 2000, available at ombwatch.org. **2.** William Manchester, *The Death of a President, November 20-November 25, 1963* (New York: Harper & Row, 1967), p. 196. **3.** Ibid. **4.** Richard Helms with William Hood, *A Look Over My Shoulder: A Life in the Central Intelligence Agency* (New York: Random House, 2003), pp. 226-244; we fault Helms for providing incomplete information to his co-author. **5.** CIA, Inspector General's Report on Plots to Assassinate Castro, 1967, p. 94. **6.** CIA 104-10306-10017; PFIAB 11-22-63 notes at National Archives and at maryferrell.org. **7.** Richard Helms with William Hood,

A Look Over My Shoulder: A Life in the Central Intelligence Agency (New York: Random House, 2003), p. 228
8. Thomas Powers, *The Man Who Kept the Secrets: Richard Helms & the CIA* (New York: Knopf, 1979), many
passages; see also Richard Helms testimony to the HSCA and Church Committee, as discussed in Chapter
64. **9.** Inspector General's Report on Plots to Assassinate Castro, 1967; CIA "Response to Item Comments
on Draft Report," 6-13-76, in the National Archives, from the files of Anna-Marie Kuhns-Walko; CIA 104-
10434-10267 and CIA 104-10434-10283, both declassified 11/18/98; Bradley Ayers, *The War that Never Was*
(Canoga Park, CA: Major Books, 1979), pp. 58, 59; William Scott Malone, "The Secret Life of Jack Ruby,"
New Times 1-23-78; Many QJWIN files at the National Archives, including his November 1963 payroll
records in 1994.04.06.10:47:29:710005 and his 1964 termination notice in 1993.08.13.08:39:48:560024. **10.** E.
Howard Hunt deposition, 11-3-78, document #180-10131-10342, declassified 2-9-96; 9-25-63 CIA memo
about 9-12-63 CIA call regarding Cain and the DRE. **11.** John Newman, *Oswald and the CIA* (New York:
Carroll & Graf, 1995) many passages; Jefferson Morley, "What Jane Roman Said," accessed 12-02 at http://
mcadams.posc.mu.edu/morley1.htm; Win Scott article in the *Washington Post*, 3-17-96. **12.** Interview with
confidential Kennedy aide source 3-17-92. **13.** CIA 104-10295-10152, cable from JMWAVE to CIA Director,
McCone 12-3-63, declassified 5-19-99. **14.** Bradley Ayers, *The War that Never Was* (Canoga Park, CA: Major
Books, 1979), pp. 58, 59. **15.** CIA 104-10172-10096, Ted Shackley to Desmond FitzGerald memo. **16.** CIA
104-10308-10283; 104-10308-10274; CIA 104-10308-10283; 104-10308-10274. **17.** Phillips' entire novel pro-
posal has not but published, but portions have appeared in other sources, such as Anthony and Robbyn
Summers, "The Ghosts of November," *Vanity Fair*, December 1994, p. 139. **18.** CIA 104-10004-10199. **19.**
Douglas Valentine, *The Strength of the Wolf: The Secret History of America's War on Drugs* (London, New
York: Verso, 2004), p. 300. **20.** G. Robert Blakey and Richard N. Billings, *The Plot to Kill the President* (New
York: Times Books, 1981), p. 61. **21.** CIA 104-10408-10029; CIA 104-10308-10080. **22.** Some might point to
the resentment Helms felt at the CIA only having a supporting role in the JFK-Almeida coup plan, or
his worry that JFK might call off the plan at the last minute, as reasons for Helms to assassinate JFK. But
having JFK killed in Dallas wasn't necessary to ensure the coup plan went forward. All Helms would
have had to do was to wait a couple of days until Harry Williams was slipping into Castro's Cuba (with
the aid of the CIA or Naval Intelligence) and have Harry killed. Killing one man on a covert mission
is much simpler and less complicated than killing the President of the United States in broad daylight.
Harry wasn't going to try to contact the US from inside Cuba (it was too risky); he would simply meet
with Almeida and await the coup. Once Harry was dead, Helms could have simply gone ahead with his
unauthorized Castro assassination operation. **23.** Thomas Powers, *The Man Who Kept the Secrets: Richard
Helms & the CIA* (New York: Knopf, 1979), p. 115. **24.** Ibid, p. 315 **25.** Gus Russo, *Live by the Sword: The
Secret War against Castro and the Death of JFK* (Baltimore: Bancroft Press, 1998), p. 303. **26.** David Corn,
Blond Ghost (New York: Simon & Schuster, 1994), p. 98; CIA 104-10110-10243. **27.** Douglas Valentine, *The
Strength of the Wolf: The Secret History of America's War on Drugs* (London, New York: Verso, 2004), pp. 371-
366. **28.** Ted Shackley, *Spymaster: My Life in the CIA* (Washington, DC: Potomac Books, 2006), p. 72. **29.**
David Corn, *Blond Ghost* (New York: Simon & Schuster), 1994, p. 105. **30.** Ibid, pp. 107, 108. **31.** CIA 104-
10306-10017, 4-10-64 interview with McCone, declassified 9-19-98. **32.** Ibid. **33.** Ibid; Arthur Schlesinger
Jr., *Robert Kennedy and His Times* (New York: Ballantine, 1979), pp. 655, 656.

CHAPTER TWELVE

1. CIA 104-10306-10017; Arthur Schlesinger, Jr., *Robert Kennedy and His Times* (New York: Ballantine,
1979), p. 665. **2.** Ibid, p. 664. **3.** McCone claimed later in testimony that he never mentioned Castro in his
afternoon meeting with Bobby, but we now know that McCone—and other CIA officials—were briefed
prior to their testimony, and only testified to match the documents they knew the Committee had been
provided. See Thomas Powers, *The Man Who Kept the Secrets: Richard Helms & the CIA* (New York: Knopf,
1979), p. 342. **4.** CIA 104-10306-10017, 4-10-64 interview with McCone, declassified 9-19-98. **5.** CIA 104-
10163-10258, CIA 104-10308-10113. **6.** NARA #179-40005-10028; David Talbot, *Brothers: The Hidden History
of the Kennedy Years* (New York: Free Press, 2007), pp. 8, 21, 414. **7.** Thomas Borstelmann, *The Cold War and
the Color Line: American Race Relations in the Global Arena* (Cambridge, MA: Harvard University Press,
2003). **8.** CIA 104-10306-10017; G. Robert Blakey and Richard N. Billings, *The Plot to Kill the President* (New
York: Times Books, 1981), p. 20. **9.** Haynes Johnson, "One Day's Events Shattered America's Hopes and
Certainties," *Washington Post* 11-20-83. **10.** Interview with Harry Williams. 2-24-92. **11.** Ibid, and 4-92; CIA
Document 12-6-63, from Director, released during the 1993 CIA Historical Review Program, courtesy Dr.
John Newman. **12.** CIA #104-10308-10098, declassified 9-18-98; Don Bohning, *The Castro Obsession: US
Cover Operations Against Cuba, 1959–1965*, (Washington: Potomac Books, 2005) p. 227. **13.** CIA 104-10408-
10029; CIA 104-10308-10080. **14.** Many have been declassifed, though some Barker files are still withheld,
including under his CIA code-name AMCLATTER-1: 180-10144-10221; CIA 104-10217-10287; 104-10237-
10005; CIA 104-10163-10258. **15.** Interviews with Harry Williams 2-24-92, 4-92, 2-21-95. **16.** CIA 104-10241-

10023, Henry Hecksher to Desmond FitzGerald 9-27-63. **17.** William Manchester, *The Death of a President, November 20-November 25, 1963* (New York: Harper & Row, 1967), chronology on inside covers; Anthony and Robbyn Summers, "The Ghosts of November," *Vanity Fair*, Dec. 1994. **18.** Haynes Johnson, "One Day's Events Shattered America's Hopes and Certainties," *Washington Post* 11-20-83. **19.** Haynes Johnson phone calls 6-16-92, 5-07. In Haynes Johnson, "Rendezvous with Ruin at The Bay of Pigs," *Washington Post* 4-17-81, when very briefly mentioning RFK's phone call, Haynes's wording indicated RFK made the "one of your guys" comment to Harry, but in his far more detailed account in the same newspaper on 11-20-83 and in his comments to us, he has made it clear that RFK made the comment to him. **20.** Haynes Johnson, *Sleepwalking Through History* (New York: W. W. Norton, 2003), p. 271. **21.** David Talbot, *Brothers: The Hidden History of the Kennedy Years* (New York: Free Press, 2007), p. 6. **22.** Ibid; Peter Dale Scott, *Crime and Cover-Up: The CIA, the Mafia, and the Dallas-Watergate Connection* (Santa Barbara, CA: Open Archive Press, 1993), pp. 8, 9, 53. **23.** Haynes Johnson, "One Day's Events Shattered America's Hopes and Certainties," *Washington Post* 11-20-83. **24.** Interviews with Harry Williams, 2-24-92, 4-92, 7-1-92; minute-by-minute transcript, NBC News, 11-22-63. **25.** Joan Mellen, *A Farewell to Justice* (Dulles, VA: Potomac Books, 2005), p. 67. **26.** *New Orleans Times-Picayune,*11-22-73. **27.** Statement of Alberto Flower in the Office of the District Attorney, 1-23-67; Harold Weisburg memos on file at the Assassination Archives and Research Center. **28.** Joan Mellen, *A Farewell to Justice* (Dulles, VA: Potomac Books, 2005), p. 67. **29.** Memo re: Paulino Sierra, 8-63. **30.** CIA 104-10235-10252. **31.** Joseph J. Trento, *Prelude to Terror: The Rogue CIA, and the Legacy of America's Private Intelligence Network* (New York: Carroll & Graf, 2005), pp. 79, 80. **32.** Files from Dade County Manager's office, discovered by Dade County Archivist Gordon Winslow. **33.** Ann Louise Bardach, *Cuba Confidential* (New York: Random House, 2002), p. 142. **34.** Anthony and Robbyn Summers, "The Ghosts of November," *Vanity Fair*, Dec. 1994. **35.** HSCA Secret Service interviews declassified by the Assassinations Records Review Board, cited by Vince Palamara in *Deep Politics* magazine 4-97. **36.** Michael L. Kurtz, *The JFK Assassination Debates* (Lawrence, KS: University Press of Kansas, 2006), p. 214. **37.** CIA 104-10429-10231. **38.** CIA memo, JMWAVE to Director, JFK 80T01357A, 11-22-63. **39.** CIA memo to FBI Director 1-18-77, declassified 9-23-88. **40.** Anthony and Robbyn Summers, "The Ghosts of November," *Vanity Fair*, Dec. 1994. **41.** Phone interviews with Naval Intelligence surveillance source, 10-27-91 and 12-9-91. **42.** 4-2-64 FBI memo by T. N. Goble, cited in *Echoes of a Conspiracy* 7-22-88. **43.** Phone interviews with Naval Intelligence surveillance source, 10-27-91 and 12-9-91. **44.** Phillips' entire novel proposal has not but published, but portions have appeared in other sources, such as Anthony and Robbyn Summers, "The Ghosts of November," *Vanity Fair*, 12-1994, p. 139. **45.** Bernard Fensterwald memo of 8-21 conversation with investigative journalist, on file at the Assassinations Archives and Records Center in Washington, DC. **46.** Anthony Summers, *Conspiracy* (New York: Paragon House, 1989), p. 61. **47.** CIA 104-10308-10113. **48.** Deane J. Allen, DIA Historian, "Overview of the Origins of DIA," 11-95. **49.** We spoke briefly to McNamara about it by phone, 5-07, and he declined to review any of the documents that have been declassified about Almeida or the coup plan. **50.** JCS 202-10002-10180; James P. Hosty, Jr., *Assignment: Oswald* (New York: Arcade Publishing, 1996), p. 219; *U.S. News & World Report*, 3-15-93.

CHAPTER THIRTEEN

1. John H. Davis, *Mafia Kingfish* (New York: Signet, 1989), pp. 198, 199; phone interview with John Diuguid 9-30-04. **2.** Anthony and Robbyn Summers, "The Ghosts of November," *Vanity Fair*, 12-94. **3.** Frank Ragano and Selwyn Raab, *Mob Lawyer* (New York: Scribners, 1994), p. 146. **4.** Phone interviews with Jim Allison 4-15-98 and 4-16-98. **5.** FBI Airtel to Director, 10-1-74. **6.** Larry Hancock, *Someone Would Have Talked* (Southlake, Tex.: JFK Lancer, 2003), p. 92; Hosty has denied making the remark. **7.** Ibid, p. 68 and others. **8.** *White Book of the John Birch Society for 1963*, many passages. **9.** Michael R. Beschloss, *Taking Charge* (New York: Simon & Schuster, 1997), p. 22; call between LBJ and Hoover, 11-23-63, 10:01AM. **10.** Church Committee Report, vol. V, p. 74. **11.** For example, CIA 104-10227-10257, FBI memo to Director, 6-11-63. **12.** FBI memo, DeLoach to Mohr, 6-4-64. **13.** *The Murder of JFK: A Revisionist History*, MPI DVD, 2006. **14.** Larry Hancock, *Someone Would Have Talked* (Southlake, TX: JFK Lancer, 2006), p. 71. **15.** Anthony and Robbyn Summers, "The Ghosts of November," *Vanity Fair*, Dec. 1994. **16.** No compelling reason has yet surfaced for Hoover (or LBJ or the CIA or the Secret Service or the Joint Chiefs) to have gone to the trouble of killing JFK in public, and risk causing World War III by blaming his death on Oswald, just to get JFK out of office a year early. **17.** *The Murder of JFK: A Revisionist History*, MPI DVD, 2006. **18.** http://www.presidency.ucsb.edu/. **19.** We only note for the sake of completeness that there is an unconfirmed report from a Dallas witness who claims that she saw E. Howard Hunt and a Nixon aide with Nixon at the airport on the morning of 11-22-63, shortly before the former Vice President left Dallas. Though it suggests the possibility that Hunt was trying to get Nixon out of Dallas prior to JFK's motorcade, the report is highly suspect. The report was made long after the fact, during the Watergate investigations, and the Nixon aide whom the witness claims she recognized was John Ehrlichman. **20.** CIA document,

JMWAVE to Director, 12-5-63, released in 1994 by the CIA Historical Review Program. **21.** John H. Davis, *Mafia Kingfish* (New York: Signet, 1989), p. 199. **22.** FBI report 11-25-63, 94-448-12; HSCA vol. X, pp. 113, 114; Anthony Summers, *Conspiracy* (New York: McGraw-Hill, 1980), pp. 497, 506. **23.** Peter Dale Scott, *Deep Politics and the Death of JFK* (Berkeley: University of California Press, 1993), p. 329. **24.** Ibid; David E. Scheim, *Contract on America: The Mafia Murder of President John F. Kennedy* (New York: Zebra, 1989), p. 62; G. Robert Blakey and Richard N. Billings, *The Plot to Kill the President* (New York: Times Books, 1981), pp. 46, 397; Anthony Summers, *Conspiracy* (New York: McGraw-Hill, 1980), p. 483; HSCA vol. X, p. 113. **25.** FBI report 11-25-63, 94-448-12; Anthony Summers, *Conspiracy* (New York: McGraw-Hill, 1980), pp. 497, 506. **26.** Michael Benson, *Who's Who in the JFK Assassination: An A-to-Z Encyclopedia* (New York: Citadel, 1993), pp. 284, 285. **27.** Phone interview with John Diuguid, 9-30-04. **28.** Miami Police Intelligence interview with William Somersett, transcribed 11-26-63. **29.** HSCA vol. X, pp. 198-205. **30.** Gaeton Fonzi, *The Last Investigation* (New York: Thunder's Mouth, 1994), p. 112. **31.** Ibid; Fonzi interview 1-16-76 with Silvia Odio from the National Archives, in Jim DiEugenio "Sylvia Odio vs. Liebeler & the La Fontaines," *Probe*, Sept.-Oct. 1996. **32.** Ibid Fonzi, p. 113; Warren Commission Document #1546, p. 213; NARA 124-10158-10186; Warren Commission Document #1546; Warren Commission vol. XI, pp. 367-389; Larry Hancock, *Someone Would Have Talked* (Southlake, TX: JFK Lancer, 2006) pp. 40-46, many others. **33.** Frank Ragano and Selwyn Raab, *Mob Lawyer* (New York: Scribners, 1994), pp. 147, 148. **34.** Ibid, p. 148. **35.** Phone interview with confidential high Florida law-enforcement source, 12-10-96.

CHAPTER FOURTEEN

1. Richard D. Mahoney, *Sons & Brothers: The Days of Jack and Bobby Kennedy* (New York: Arcade, 1999), p. 295. **2.** David S. Lifton, *Best Evidence: Disguise and Deception in the Assassination of John F. Kennedy* (New York: Carroll & Graf, 1988), pp. 157, 160, 161. **3.** Interview with Dave Powers 6-5-91 at the John F. Kennedy Presidential Library; William Novak, *Man of the House: The Life and Political Memoirs of Speaker Tip O'Neil* (New York: Random House, 1987), p. 178. **4.** Michael L. Kurtz, *The JFK Assassination Debates* (Lawrence, KS University Press of Kansas, 2006), p. 39; Henry Hurt, *Reasonable Doubt* (New York: Henry Holt, 1987), p. 49 **5.** HSCA interview with Francis O'Neill, 1-10-78. **6.** William Matson Law, *In the Eye of History* (Southlake, TX: JFK Lancer Productions, 2005), pp. 124, 125, 130. **7.** Ibid, pp. 35, 43, 51. **8.** Ibid, p. 84. **9.** Dr. George Burkley's Oral History at the JFK Presidential Library. **10.** Gus Russo, *Live by the Sword: The Secret War against Castro and the Death of JFK* (Baltimore: Bancroft Press, 1998), p. 325. **11.** *Washington Post*, 11-23-63 **12.** David S. Lifton, *Best Evidence: Disguise and Deception in the Assassination of John F. Kennedy* (New York Carroll & Graf, 1988), pp. 403-407. **13.** Ibid, photo section following p. 282. **14.** Michael Benson, *Who's Who in the JFK Assassination: An A-to-Z Encyclopedia* (New York: Citadel, 1993), p. 138; Michael L. Kurtz, *The JFK Assassination Debates* (Lawrence, KS: University Press of Kansas, 2006), p. 86. **15.** David S. Lifton, *Best Evidence: Disguise and Deception in the Assassination of John F. Kennedy* (New York: Carroll & Graf, 1988) pp. 590, 595, 646, 647; HSCA vol. VII, p. 15. **16.** William Matson Law, *In the Eye of History* (Southlake, TX JFK Lancer Productions, 2005), pp. 132, 133. **17.** Ibid, pp. 258, 1259; David S. Lifton, *Best Evidence: Disguise and Deception in the Assassination of John F. Kennedy* (New York: Carroll & Graf, 1988), p. 651. **18.** Douglas Horne, Press conference presentation, May 15, 2006; also Horne e-mail report, May 21, 2007. **19.** William Matson Law, *In the Eye of History* (Southlake, TX: JFK Lancer Productions, 2005), pp. 186, 220. **20.** *Cape Cod Today*, 3-20-07. **21.** William Matson Law, *In the Eye of History* (Southlake, TX: JFK Lancer Productions 2005), p. 47; David S. Lifton, *Best Evidence: Disguise and Deception in the Assassination of John F. Kennedy* (New York: Carroll & Graf, 1988), p. 607. **22.** Alexander M. Haig, Jr., with Charles McCarry, *Inner Circles How America Changed the World: A Memoir* (New York: Warner Books, 1992), pp. 113, 114. **23.** Joseph A. Califano, Jr., *The Triumph & Tragedy of Lyndon Johnson: The White House Years* (New York: Simon & Schuster 1991), pp. 13, 14. **24.** Department of the Army document dated 9-14-63 provided by the State Department in SSCIA record number 157-10005-10372 dated 3-27-76, declassified 2-18-94. **25.** Alexander M. Haig Jr., *Inner Circles: How America Changed the World: A Memoir* (New York: Warner Books, 1992), p. 116. **26** Anthony Summers, *Conspiracy* (New York: Paragon House, 1989), p. 409. **27.** Larry Hancock, *Someone Would Have Talked* (Southlake, TX: JFK Lancer, 2006), p. 289; John Simkin citing Henry Wade testimony to the Warren Commission June 8, 1964 at www.spartacus.schoolnet.co.uk. **28.** Larry Hancock, *Someone Would Have Talked* (Southlake, TX: JFK Lancer, 2006), p. 305. **29.** Dan Rather with Mickey Herskowitz, *The Camera Never Blinks* (New York: Ballantine Books, 1978), many passages; Bob Schieffer in "JFK: Breaking the News," PBS, 11-20-03. **30.** Jack Anderson column, *Washington Post* 9-7-76. **31.** Travis Kirk, cited by A J. Weberman, at ajweberman.com. **32.** Anthony Summers, *Not In Your Lifetime* (New York: Marlowe & Co., 1998), p. 253. **33.** Anthony Summers, *Conspiracy* (New York: Paragon House, 1989), p. 98; interview transcript with Jesse Curry from British television show Panorama, on file at the Assassination Archive and Research Center. **34.** Ibid Summers, p. 414. **35.** William Manchester, *The Death of a President, November 20-November 25, 1963* (New York: Harper & Row, 1967), p. 333. **36.** Anthony Summers, *Conspiracy* (New York: Paragon House, 1989), p. 58. **37.** *New Orleans Times-Picayune*, 3-23-56 and 3-31-56.

CHAPTER FIFTEEN

1. Richard D. Mahoney, *Sons & Brothers: The Days of Jack and Bobby Kennedy* (New York: Arcade, 1999), p. 417. **2.** Michael J. Cain, *The Tangled Web: The Life and Death of Richard Cain* (New York: Skyhorse Publishing, 2007) many passages; HSCA vol. X, p. 172, 193; *Chicago Tribune* 12-28-73, p. 16; Peter Dale Scott, *Deep Politics II* (Skokie, Ill.: Green Archive Publ., 1995), p. 132; CIA Office of Security Varona File Summary, Record Number 180-10144-10405, declassified 8-23-95; CIA memo, 3, 272, 992, released 1993; CIA "Process Sheet for OO/C Collections" from Cain's file, reports number 28925 and 28499, both released in 1993; CIA Memo for Chief, Western Hemisphere Division, Subject: Salvadore Giancana and Richard Cain, 1-10-74, released 1994. **3.** Bernard Fensterwald, "The Case of Secret Service Agent Abraham W. Bolden," *Computers and Automation*, 6-71. **4.** CIA memo for Director of Security, subject: Cain, Richard Scully, 12-19-69, declassified 1992. **5.** Sylvia Meagher provides a good summary in *Accessories After the Fact: The Warren Commission, the Authorities, and the Report* (New York: Vintage, 1992). **6.** Ibid, pp. 102, 106, 107. **7.** David S. Lifton, *Best Evidence: Disguise and Deception in the Assassination of John F. Kennedy* (New York: Carroll & Graf, 1988), pp. 503-04; Michael L. Kurtz, *The JFK Assassination Debates* (Lawrence, KS: University Press of Kansas, 2006), pp. 25, 47, 48. **8.** Tom Johnson, *Dallas Morning News*, 11-6-69. **9.** Anthony and Robbyn Summers, "The Ghosts of November," *Vanity Fair*, 12- 94. **10.** Michael R. Beschloss, *Taking Charge* (New York: Simon & Schuster, 1997), p. 23. **11.** Roger S. Peterson, *Declassified*, American History, 8-96, citing Carl Bernstein, *Rolling Stone*, 10-77. **12.** CIA 104-10048-10124. **13.** Peter Noyes, *Legacy of Doubt* (New York: Pinnacle Books, 1973), pp. 116-18. **14.** Ibid, pp. 117, 118. **15.** "Threats on Kennedy Made Here," *Tampa Tribune*, 11-23-63. **16.** Church vol. V, p. 62. **17.** Phone interview with J. P. Mullins 12-10-96; phone interview with high Florida law-enforcement source 12-10-96. **18.** "Oswald made visit in September to Mexico," *The New York Times* 11-25-63, p. 8; Sylvia Meagher, *Accessories After the Fact: The Warren Commission, the Authorities, and the Report* (New York: Vintage, 1992), pp. 311, 312. **19.** Larry Hancock, *Someone Would Have Talked* (Southlake, TX: JFK Lancer, 2006), p. 247. **20.** Ibid. **21.** Jean Daniel articles, *New Republic*, 12-14-63, 12-21-63; *Milwaukee Journal*, 12-24-63. **22.** Michael L. Kurtz, *The JFK Assassination Debates* (Lawrence, KS: University Press of Kansas, 2006), p. 162. **23.** Ibid. **24.** John Newman, "Oswald, the CIA, and Mexico City" at pbs.org. **25.** Evan Thomas, *The Very Best Men: Four Who Dared: The Early Years of the CIA* (New York: Simon & Schuster, 1995), p. 307. **26.** Evan Thomas, *Robert Kennedy: His Life* (New York: Simon & Schuster, 2000), p. 449. **27.** CIA 104-10295-10152. **28.** Jefferson Morley, *Washington Monthly*, 12-03. **29.** Ibid. **30.** Ibid. **31.** Ibid. **32.** David Talbot, *Brothers: The Hidden History of the Kennedy Years* (New York: Free Press, 2007), pp. 275, 276. **33.** RFK Oral History at the JFK Library; Edwin O. Guthman and Jeffrey Shulman, eds., *Robert Kennedy: In His Own Words: The Unpublished Recollections of the Kennedy Years* (Toronto, New York: Bantam, 1988), p. 379. **34.** Email to the authors from Bayard Stockton, 12-8-05. **35.** Ted Shackley, *Spymaster: My Life in the CIA* (Washington, DC: Potomac Books, 2006), pp. ix, xvi, 55, 68. **36.** CIA 104-10423-10226. **37.** David Corn, *Blond Ghost* (New York: Simon & Schuster, 1994), p.262. **38.** John Simkin, David Morales biography at the British educational website www.spartacus.schoolnet.co.uk. **39.** CIA 104-10423-10226. **40.** David Talbot, *Brothers: The Hidden History of the Kennedy Years* (New York: Free Press, 2007), p. 276. **41.** Peter Wright, *Spycatcher* (1987), cited at www.spartacus.schoolnet.co.uk. **42.** Adam Walinsky Oral History, JFK Presidential Library, cited by David Talbot, *Brothers: The Hidden History of the Kennedy Years* (New York: Free Press, 2007), p. 439. **43.** CIA 104--10110-10243. **44.** David Corn, *Blond Ghost* (New York: Simon & Schuster, 1994), p. 98. **45.** CIA 104-10241-10071. **46.** CIA 104-10241-10126. **47.** HSCA vol. X, p. 78. **48.** CIA 1993.08.04.16:20:46:530028. **49.** CIA 104-10429-10231.

CHAPTER SIXTEEN

1. John Newman, *Oswald and the CIA* (New York: Carroll & Graf, 1995), pp. 356, 35, many others. **2.** Interview with confidential Naval Intelligence investigator source 10-27-91; Anthony and Robbyn Summers, "The Ghosts of November," *Vanity Fair*, 12-94. **3.** Gaeton Fonzi, *The Last Investigation* (New York: Thunder's Mouth, 1994), p. 295; HSCA 180-10142-10353. **4.** Anthony Summers, *Not In Your Lifetime* (New York: Marlowe & Co., 1998), p. 264. **5.** John Newman, *Oswald and the CIA* (New York: Carroll & Graf, 1995), p. 377. **6.** Ibid, several passages; Anthony Summers, *Not In Your Lifetime* (New York: Marlowe & Co., 1998), p. 384. **7.** Confidential Kennedy Foreign Policy source, 4-18-96. **8.** See Lamar Waldron and Thom Hartman, *Ultimate Sacrifice*, (New York: Carol & Graf Publishers, 2005), chapters 45-46. **9.** Mentioned in the *Warren Report*, Oswald's resume is available online at ajweberman.com. **10.** *Chicago Tribune* 12-28-73, p. 16; Peter Dale Scott, *Deep Politics II* (Skokie, IL: Green Archive Publ., 1995), p. 132. **11.** John Newman, *Oswald and the CIA* (New York: Carroll & Graf, 1995), p. 356. **12.** CIA 104-10169-10458. **13.** Peter Dale Scott, *Deep Politics III* (online excerpt available at maryferrell.org), citing TX-1915 of 11-23-63; NARA #104-10015-10055 PS#64-43. Cf. MEXI 7029 232048Z; NARA #104-10015-10091 PS#78-94. **14.** Michael Benson, *Who's Who in the JFK Assassination: An A-to-Z Encyclopedia* (New York: Citadel, 1993), p. 119. **15.** John Newman, *Oswald and the CIA* (New York: Carroll & Graf, 1995), p. 412. **16.** CIA 104-10169-10458. **17.** Peter Dale Scott, *Deep Politics II* (online excerpt available at maryferrell.org), his note 48. **18.** Ibid, citing XAAZ-17958 10 Dec 63; Summary of Oswald case prepared for briefing purposes; NARA #104-10018-10040 PS#62-142. **19.** Peter Dale Scott, *Deep Politics III* (online excerpt available at maryferrell.org), citing HSCA vol. III, pp. 86, 91. **20.** John Newman, *Oswald and the CIA* (New York: Carroll & Graf, 1995), p. 413. **21.** Ibid, pp. 279-82. **22.** Peter Dale Scott, *Deep Politics III* (online excerpt available at maryferrell.org), his note 49 **23.** John Newman, *Oswald and the CIA* (New York: Carroll & Graf, 1995), several passages. **24.** Ibid, p. 409. **25.** FBI memo, Brennan to Sullivan, 11-27-63. **26.** HSCA 180-10142-10036. **27.** Larry Hancock, *Someone Would Have Talked* (Southlake, TX: JFK Lancer, 2006), p. 285. **28.** CIA memo 9-25-63 about 9-12-63 CIA call regarding Cain and the DRE **29.** Larry Hancock, *Someone Would Have Talked* (Southlake, TX: JFK Lancer, 2006), p. 236. **30.** Ibid, citing FBI memo. **31.** Anthony Summers, *Conspiracy* (New York: Paragon House, 1989), pp. 410, 411. **32.** Ibid pp. 410-412. **33.** Larry Hancock, *Someone Would Have Talked* (Southlake, TX: JFK Lancer, 2006), p. 236. **34.** Anthony Summers, *Conspiracy* (New York: Paragon House, 1989), pp. 410-12. **35.** Confidential Kennedy Foreign Policy source, 4-18-96. **36.** Arthur Krock, "The Intra-Administration War in Vietnam," *The New York Times*, 10-3-63. **37.** John Newman, "Oswald, the CIA, and Mexico City," at pbs.org.

CHAPTER SEVENTEEN

1. Michael L. Kurtz, *The JFK Assassination Debates* (Lawrence, KS: University Press of Kansas, 2006) pp. 13, 14. **2.** CIA 104-10306-10018; 104-10306-10017, p. 14. **3.** "The Fourteen Minute Gap," essay by Rex Bradford and documentary by Tyler Weaver, at maryferrell.org; Larry Hancock, *Someone Would Have Talked* (Southlake, TX: JFK Lancer, 2006), p. 284; **4.** CIA 104-10306-10018. **5.** HSCA 180-10142-10036. **6.** Anthony Summers, *Not In Your Lifetime* (New York: Marlowe & Co., 1998), p. 38. **7.** For example, see FBI 124-10285-10066. **8.** John Newman, "Oswald, the CIA, and Mexico City," at pbs.org. **9.** HSCA Secret Service interviews declassified by the Assassinations Records Review Board, cited by Vince Palamara in *Deep Politics* magazine 4-97; Bernard Fensterwald interview of Abraham Bolden 3-29-68. **10.** FBI 105-82555-1437. **11.** Phone interview with Don Adams, 6-14-06. **12.** Miami Police Intelligence interview with William Somersett, transcribed on 11-26-63 and additional Miami police files; Dan Christensen, "JFK King: The Dade County links," *Miami* magazine 12-76. **13.** CIA 104-10419-10342 and related papers in the CIA's Russell Holmes work files. **14.** Fensterwald affidavit for the Justice Department, 7-7-82. **15.** "Project Pilot," pp. 21, 67 cited in and quoted from Douglas Valentine, *The Strength of the Wolf: The Secret History of America's War on Drugs* (London, New York: Verso, 2004), p. 328. **16.** Dick Russell, *The Man Who Knew Too Much* (New York: Carroll & Graf/R. Gallen, 1992), p. 561. **17.** Virgil Bailey phone interviews with Gary Shaw 4-26-80, 4-28-80; additional information from the files of Bud Fensterwald; Jean-Pierre Charbonneau, *The Canadian Connection* (Ottawa: Optimum, 1976) pp. 47, 262; Senate Committee on Government Operations, Permanent Subcommittee on Investigations: Organized Crime and Illicit Traffic in Narcotics Sept./Oct. 1963. **18.** Gary Shaw interview with Hal Norwood, 4-28-80. **19.** John McCone Memorandum for the Record, 11-25-63. **20.** Interview with Dean Rusk, 1-5-90. **21.** Foreign Relations of the United States vol. XI, Department of State, #375 and #376, 11-12-63; Evan Thomas, *Robert Kennedy: His Life* (New York: Simon & Schuster, 2000), p 449. **22.** Arthur Schlesinger, Jr., *Robert Kennedy and His Times* (New York: Ballantine, 1979), p. 664. **23.** G. Robert Blakey and Richard N. Billings, *The Plot to Kill the President* (New York: Times Books, 1981), p. 320. **24.** *The Murder of JFK: A Revisionist History*, MPI DVD, 2006. **25.** Michael L. Kurtz, *The JFK Assassination Debates* (Lawrence, KS: University Press of Kansas, 2006), p. 18.

CHAPTER EIGHTEEN

1. CIA 104-10306-10018. **2.** Miami Police Intelligence interview with William Somersett, transcribed on 11/26/63 and additional Miami police files; Dan Christensen, "JFK, King: The Dade County links," *Miami* magazine 12-76. **3.** Gus Russo, *Live by the Sword: The Secret War against Castro and the Death of JFK* (Baltimore: Bancroft Press, 1998), p. 498. **4.** FBI memo, DeLoach to Mohr, 6-4-64. **5.** Peter Dale Scott, *Deep Politics and the Death of JFK* (Berkeley: University of California Press, 1993) p128. **6.** Michael T. Griffith cited HSCA in "Just the Facts," 2001. **7.** Article by Tim Smith in *Deep Politics* vol. 3 #4, 7-98. **8.** Peter Dale Scott, *Deep Politics and the Death of JFK* (Berkeley: University of California Press, 1993) citing personal telephone conversation, October 1979. **9.** Anthony Summers, *Conspiracy* (New York: Paragon House, 1989), p. 311 **10.** FBI 124-10273-10448. **11.** Blakey and Billings, op. cit., p. 324; Summers, *Conspiracy* (McGraw-Hill, 1980) p. 483; John H. Davis, *Mafia Kingfish* (New York: Signet, 1989), p. 603. **12.** Michael Benson, *Who's Who in the JFK Assassination: An A-to-Z Encyclopedia* (New York: Citadel, 1993), p. 72. **13.** Warren Commission vol. XIV, pp. 471, 596, 597; Carl Sifakis, *The Mafia Encyclopedia* (New York: Facts On File, 1987), pp. 103, 104. **14.** Miami Police Intelligence interview with William Somersett, transcribed on 11/26/63 and additional Miami police files; Dan Christensen, "JFK, King: The Dade County links," *Miami* magazine 12-76. **15.** J. Edgar Hoover FBI memo, 11-24-63. **16.** Gary Cornwell, *Real answers: The True Story* (Spicewood, TX: Paleface Press, 1998), pp. 143-53. **17.** J. Edgar Hoover FBI memo, 11-24-63. **18.** CIA memo 85657, 11-28-63. **19.** Anthony Summers, *Conspiracy* (New York: Paragon House, 1989), p. 396; G. Robert Blakey an

Richard N. Billings, *The Plot to Kill the President* (New York: Times Books, 1981), p. 63. **20.** David E. Scheim, *Contract on America: The Mafia Murder of President John F. Kennedy* (New York: Zebra, 1989) citing Warren Commission Document #84, p. 91 and Warren Commission Exhibit #1536. **21.** Henry Hurt, *Reasonable Doubt* (New York: Henry Holt, 1987), photo section showing 11-30-63 FBI memo. **22.** Airtel to Hoover from SAC Miami, 10-24-63. **23.** FBI Airtel to Hoover from SAC Miami, 7-30-64. **24.** Anthony Summers, *Official and Confidential: The Secret Life of J. Edgar Hoover* (New York: G. P. Putnam's Sons, 1993), many passages. **25.** David E. Scheim, *Contract on America: The Mafia Murder of President John F. Kennedy* (New York: Zebra, 1989), p. 221. **26.** CIA 1993.08.04.16:20:46:530028. **27.** HSCA 180-10142-10036 (HSCA timeline). **28.** HSCA vol. X, p. 59; CIA document from HSCA, Record Number 180-10141-10419. **29.** Phone interviews with Naval Intelligence source, 10-27-91 and 12-91. **30.** Ibid; HSCA vol. XI, pp. 542-551. **31.** *Foreign Relations of the United States*, vol. XI, Department of State, #384, 12-3-63. **32.** Interviews with confidential Kennedy aide source, 3-17-92. **33.** David Talbot, *Brothers: The Hidden History of the Kennedy Years* (New York: Free Press, 2007), p. 22. **34.** Arthur Schlesinger, Jr., *Robert Kennedy and His Times* (New York: Ballantine, 1979), p. 664. **35.** FBI memo from Handley to Rosen 11-24-64, released 6-18-94. **36.** A. J. Weberman, citing FBI 44-24016-112,1247; 62-109060-1528; FBI DC-44-1639 BL-E-cover pg; FBI CG 44-645-DWS: p. l6, cover page B. **37.** A. J. Weberman, citing FBI DC-44-1639 BL-E-cover pg; FBI CG 44-645-DWS: p. l6, cover page B. **38.** HSCA Report, p. 231; FBI Airtel to Director, 10-1-74. **39.** FBI teletype 12-8-63 C62-6115-55; FBI 12-9-63 B62-6115-69. **40.** Warren Commission document #149, 12-10-63 FBI memo. **41.** Douglas Valentine, *The Strength of the Wolf: The Secret History of America's War on Drugs* (London, New York: Verso, 2004), pp. 309, 310. **42.** G. Robert Blakey and Richard N. Billings, *The Plot to Kill the President* (New York: Times Books, 1981), p. 325 **43.** Seth Kantor, *The Ruby Cover-Up* (New York: Zebra Books, 1992), pp. 415, 416. **44.** CIA 104-10435-10001. **45.** Walter Sheridan, *The Fall and Rise of Jimmy Hoffa* (New York: Saturday Review Press, 1972), p. 300. **46.** Warren Commission Document #87 **47.** New Orleans Police Report #K-12634-63. **48.** *New Orleans States-Item*, "Two arrested for Federal Agents here," 11-25-63. **49.** David Heymann, *RFK: A Candid Biography of Robert F. Kennedy* (1998).

CHAPTER NINETEEN

1. John H. Davis, Mafia Kingfish: Carlos Marcello and the Assassination of John F. Kennedy (New York: McGraw-Hill, 1989), p. 298. **2.** FBI 124-1200-33; CD 301, pp. 286-93. **3.** Phone interview with Don Adams 6-14-06; Michael L. Kurtz, The JFK Assassination Debates (Lawrence, KS: University Press of Kansas, 2006), pp. 218, 219. **4.** Miami Police Intelligence memo 12-4-63; Peter Dale Scott, Paul L. Hoch, and Russell Stetler, eds., The Assassinations: Dallas and Beyond: A Guide to Cover-Ups and Investigations (New York: Vintage, 1976), pp. 133, 134; Phone interview with Don Adams 6-14-06; Dick Russell, The Man Who Knew Too Much (New York: Carroll & Graf/R. Gallen, 1992), p. 552. **5.** Ibid. **6.** CIA 104-10306-10017. **7.** Tom Tripodi, Crusade: Undercover Against the Mafia and KGB (Washington, DC, Brassey's, 1993), p. 87. **8.** The Strength of the Wolf: The Secret History of America's War on Drugs (London, New York: Verso, 2004), p. 270; Andrew Tully, CIA: The Inside Story (New York: William Morrow, 1962), pp. 45-53; Bernard Fensterwald affidavit for the Justice Department 7-13-82; "De Gaulle Plot Reported," UPI in Dallas Morning News 6-15-75; CIA 104-10419-10342. **9.** Letters from Souetre and other information provided by French journalist Stephane Risset to the authors in 1998; Bernard Fensterwald affidavit for the Justice Department 7-13-82. **10.** Michael T. Griffith, "Just the Facts," web article 2001. **11.** Larry Hancock, Someone Would Have Talked (Southlake, TX: JFK Lancer, 2006), pp. 462-66. **12.** Ibid. **13.** Ibid. **14.** HSCA vol. X, pp. 199-205. **15.** The way the stories were leaked indicates that the Mafia was their driving force. Had CIA officials floated the stories to stampede the U.S. into invading Cuba, it would have generated the stories in major markets all at once. In fact, David Atlee Phillips and E. Howard Hunt had participated in such an intense publicity strategy in 1954, in order to topple Guatemala's elected government. **16.** FBI 124-10033-10074. **17.** John Martino, article in Human Events, 12-21-63. (Note: Any ghostwriter involved in the article would have only been using the information given to him by Martino, and that writer would have had no knowledge of Martino's criminal activities). **18.** Harold Weisberg interview with Colonel Castorr, on file at the Assassinations Archives and Records Center; FBI memo to J. Edgar Hoover, 7-31-59; Warren Commission Document #1553D, pp. 1, 3. **19.** Warren Commission Document #657. **20.** Anthony Summers, Conspiracy (New York: Paragon House, 1989), p. 423. **21.** "A Sad and Solemn Duty," Time Magazine, 12-13-63. **22.** FBI memo, DeLoach to Mohr, 6-4-64. **23.** "Touched," Time magazine, 4-15-66. **24.** Dick Russell, The Man Who Knew Too Much (New York: Carroll & Graf, 2003), p. 195; Joachim Joesten, Oswald: Assassin or Fall Guy? (New York: Marzani & Munsell, 1964), pp. 150, 151. **25.** Ibid Russell, p. 199. **26.** Warren Commission, Document #1015. **27.** The Inspector was transferred out of New Orleans in 4-1, so Oswald's visit had to have been before that date, in March or even earlier; see Church Committee Report, vol. V, p. 91. **28.** The subjects of the photographs, the gun, and the communist groups are covered at length in many passages in: Henry Hurt, Reasonable Doubt (New York: Henry Holt, 1987);

George Michael Evica, And We Are All Mortal: New Evidence and Analysis in the John F. Kennedy Assassination (West Hartford, CT: Evica, 1978); Sylvia Meagher Accessories After the Fact: The Warren Commission, the Authorities, and the Report (New York: Vintage, 1992). **29.** Anthony Summers Conspiracy (New York: Paragon House, 1989), pp. 205-17. Ibid, p. 214. **31.** Warren Commission Document #1015 **32.** Bernard Fensterwald, Jr., and Michael Ewing, Coincidence or Conspiracy (New York: Zebra Books, 1977), p. 570. **33.** Ibid, p. 571. **34.** Even disassembled, Oswald's rifle was 35 inches long and weighed ten pounds; see Sylvia Meagher Accessories After the Fact: The Warren Commission the Authorities, and the Report (New York: Vintage, 1992). **35.** Joachim Joesten, Oswald: Assassin or Fall Guy? (New York: Marzani & Munsell, 1964), p. 162. **36.** Dick Russell, The Man Who Knew Too Much (New York: Carroll & Graf, 2003), pp. 196-207; Anthony Summers, Not In Your Lifetime (New York: Marlowe & Co., 1998), pp. 124, 161-71, 292, 421, 422. **37.** Ibid Russell, pp. 198-201; the German newspaper report was noted by the Warren Commission. **38.** Ibid Russell, pp. 198-207. **39.** The New York Times, 12-2-63 **40.** There is no evidence that Walker was involved in JFK's assassination, and he probably saw the April 1963 shooting as a one-time publicity stunt. **41.** John H. Davis, Mafia Kingfish: Carlos Marcello and the Assassination of John F. Kennedy (New York: McGraw-Hill, 1989), pp. 300-302. **42.** Staff and editors o Newsday, The Heroin Trail (New York: New American Library, 1974), pp.109-18; 2007 and 2008 phone interviews with Larry Hancock; Larry Hancock, Someone Would Have Talked (Southlake, TX: JFK Lancer 2006); HSCA vol. X, pp. 110-36. **43.** FBI 124-10273-10442. **44.** FBI 124-10273-10448; Tampa mafia article a www.weeklyplanet.com. **45.** FBI 124-10273-10442. **46.** FBI 124-10273-10442; FBI 124-10273-10448. **47.** FB 62-109060-5099 cited at ajweberman.com; the FBI memo dates the remarks to 4-67, not 12-63 as Ragano says in his book. While it's possible Trafficante made similar remarks four years apart, it's also possibl Ragano didn't want to disclose the full extent of what he, Trafficante, and Marcello really talked about **48.** 1993.07.31.08:55:58:710059; Larry Hancock, Someone Would Have Talked (Southlake, TX: JFK Lance 2006), p. 337. **49.** Larry Hancock, Someone Would Have Talked (Southlake, TX: JFK Lancer, 2006), p.141 CIA 104-10215-190316. **50.** Larry Hancock, Someone Would Have Talked (Southlake, TX: JFK Lancer, 2006 p. 337. **51.** CIA 104-10308-10164. **52.** CIA 157-10005-10186 to McGeorge Bundy, 12-20-63. **53.** In the summe and early fall of 1963, CIA reports about Diaz are rather detailed, but by 12-63, only scattered mention of Diaz become common, with references being made to other CIA information about Diaz which ha not been released. Also, FBI files show information about Diaz's criminal activities in 1964—sometime reported on by Jose Aleman—that is not reflected in the CIA files released so far. **54.** Possibly related t the Diaz attempt against Castro was an unusual meeting Trafficante had in Miami around the same time with Lewis McWillie, the man Jack Ruby called his "idol." (see 10-1-76 Trafficante testimony to Churc Committee.) Like Herminio Diaz, McWillie had worked at Trafficante's Havana casinos. McWillie ha been involved with Ruby and on the fringe of the CIA-Mafia plots in 1959, 1960, and in the spring of 196. McWillie was linked by the FBI to two 1959 gun-running associates of Jack Ruby and had been involve in Cuban deals with Ruby in 1959 and 1960, when Ruby went to Havana to see Trafficante during th initial CIA-Mafia plots. In May 1963, Ruby had shipped a pistol to McWillie while Rosselli was workin on the CIA-Mafia plots. By December 1963, McWillie was working at a Nevada casino, when he suddenl traveled across the country to meet with Trafficante in Miami. See also 1993.07.31.08:55:58:710059); Larr Hancock, Someone Would Have Talked (Southlake, TX: JFK Lancer, 2006), p. 337.

CHAPTER TWENTY

1. Anthony Summers, Conspiracy (New York: Paragon House, 1989), pp. 415-419, 518; John Newma Oswald and the CIA (New York: Carroll & Graf, 1995) many passages; Robert Sam Anson, "They' Killed the President!": The Search for the Murderers of John F. Kennedy (New York: Bantam, 1975), p. 25 Warren Commission Document #1084. **2.** HSCA 180-10142-10340. **3.** Anthony Summers, Not In You Lifetime (New York: Marlowe & Co., 1998), pp. 442, 443. **4.** Anthony Summers, Conspiracy (New Yor Paragon House, 1989), p. 600. **5.** Joseph J. Trento, The Secret History of the CIA (Roseville, CA: Prim 2001), pp. 226, 227. **6.** Warren Commission Document #205; Church Committee Report, vol. V, pp. 3 61-63; Skip Johnson and Tony Durr, "Ex-Tampan in JFK Plot?," Tampa Tribune, 9-5-76. **7.** FBI teletype fro SAC Dallas, declassified 2-17-93. **8.** Richard D. Mahoney, Sons & Brothers: The Days of Jack and Bobb Kennedy (New York: Arcade, 1999), p. 418. **9.** CIA F82-0272/1, 82-1625 (4); CIA F82-0272/2; 1-64 cable CIA Director from (censored); CIA memo declassified 8-16-93, still partially censored; CIA F82-0278 (th document number is hard to read, and might be F82-02781). **10.** Joseph Franco with Richard Hamme Hoffa's Man: The Rise and Fall of Jimmy Hoffa as Witnessed by His Strongest Arm (NewYork: Prenti Hall, 1987), p. 198. **11.** CIA 104-10018-10052. **12.** CIA 104-10215-190316. **13.** Almost half of those casualti would come after presidential candidate Richard Nixon sabotaged LBJ's peace talks with North Vietna in 10-68. **14.** John McCone "Memorandum for the Record," 11-25-63, CIA 104-10306-10018; David Scheim, Contract on America: The Mafia Murder of President John F. Kennedy (New York: Zebra, 198 pp. 305, 306. **15.** JCS 202-10002-10175. **16.** Anthony Summers, Conspiracy (New York: McGraw-Hi

1980), p. 453. **17.** CIA 104-10306-10018 (McCone-LBJ meetings); Richard D. Mahoney, Sons & Brothers: The Days of Jack and Bobby Kennedy (New York: Arcade, 1999), p. 303; Michael R. Beschloss, Taking Charge (New York: Simon & Schuster, 1997), pp. 55-57. **18.** CIA 104-10306-10018. **19.** Joseph A. Califano, Jr., The Triumph & Tragedy of Lyndon Johnson: The White House Years (New York: Simon & Schuster, 1991), p. 295. **20.** Confidential Kennedy Foreign Policy source, 3-6-95. **21.** CIA 104-10306-10018. **22.** John Newman, "Oswald, the CIA, and Mexico City" at pbs.org. **23.** Ibid; Michael R. Beschloss, Taking Charge (New York: Simon & Schuster, 1997), pp. 66-72. **24.** HSCA 180-10142-10036, Church Report, Book V, pp. 58-59; Michael L. Kurtz, The JFK Assassination Debates (Lawrence, KS: University Press of Kansas, 2006), p. 173; HSCA 180-10142-10036, Church Report, Book V, pp. 58-59. **25.** Anthony and Robbyn Summers, "The Ghosts of November," Vanity Fair, Dec. 1994; Gus Russo, Live by the Sword: The Secret War against Castro and the Death of JFK (Baltimore: Bancroft Press, 1998), pp. 373, 374, citing comments to the BBC. **26.** Michael R. Beschloss, Taking Charge (New York: Simon & Schuster, 1997), pp. 64, 65. **27.** FBI report, DeLoach to Mohr, 12-17-63. **28.** Interviews with confidential Kennedy aide source, 3-17-92; G. Robert Blakey and Richard N. Billings, The Plot to Kill the President (New York: Times Books, 1981), pp. 76-77. **29.** "A Sad and Solemn Duty," Time Magazine, 12-13-63. **30.** Michael L. Kurtz, The JFK Assassination Debates (Lawrence, KS: University Press of Kansas, 2006), p. 21. **31.** The Murder of JFK: A Revisionist History, MPI DVD, 2006. **32.** Anthony and Robbyn Summers, "The Ghosts of November," Vanity Fair, 12-94. **33.** CIA 104-10075-10256. **34.** CIA cable to Director, 12-10-63, CIA 104-10076-10252, declassified 8-95; David Corn, Blond Ghost: Ted Shackley and the CIA's Crusades (New York: Simon & Schuster, 1994), p. 110. **35.** Jorge G. Castaneda, Compañero: The Life and Death of Che Guevara (New York: Vintage, 1998), pp. 250-54. **36.** Memorandum to National Security Council Staff, 11-63; Memorandum from William Attwood to Gordon Chase, in Foreign Relations of the United States #379. **37.** CIA 104-10400-10200, declassified 10-31-98, p. 39 citing information from 12-3-63. **38.** CIA report of their monitoring of Cuban news media, report dated 12-9-63. **39.** David Corn, Blond Ghost (New York: Simon & Schuster, 1994), pp. 110, 433; CIA Record #104-10076-10252, dated 12-10-63. **40.** JCS 202-10001-10073, declassified 4-9-98. **41.** JFK 1994.04.26.11:46:50:000007. **42.** In addition to reviewing the declassified meeting notes of participants, we interviewed one of the officials who attended. **43.** Don Bohning, The Castro Obsession: US Cover Operations Against Cuba, 1959-1965 (Washington: Potomac Books, 2005), p. 242. **44.** CIA 104-10306-10018. **45.** Army document 12-19-63, Califano Papers, Record Number 198-10004-10013, declassified 10-7-97; Foreign Relations of the United States, vol. XI, Department of State, #388, 12-19-63. **46.** Evan Thomas, Robert Kennedy: His Life (New York: Simon & Schuster, 2000), pp. 282, 283. **47.** Ibid. **48.** David Talbot, Brothers: The Hidden History of the Kennedy Years (New York: Free Press, 2007), p. 266. **49.** Joseph A. Califano, Jr., Inside: A Public and Private Life (New York: Public Affairs, 2004), p. 126. **50.** Arthur Schlesinger, Jr., Robert Kennedy and His Times (New York: Ballantine, 1979), p. 664. **51.** www.spartacus.schoolnet.co.uk citing C. David Heymann, RFK: A Candid Biography of Robert F. Kennedy (1998). **52.** David Talbot, Brothers: The Hidden History of the Kennedy Years (New York: Free Press, 2007), p. 87. **53.** Anthony and Robbyn Summers, "The Ghosts of November," Vanity Fair, 12-94. **54.** Richard D. Mahoney, Sons & Brothers: The Days of Jack and Bobby Kennedy (New York: Arcade, 1999), p. 304. **55.** Interviews with Harry Williams 2-24-92, 4-92, 2-21-95. **56.** Ibid, 2-24-92. **57.** Erneido Oliva, "The End of Kennedy's Final Plan to Overthrow the Castro Regime," at camcocuba.org. **58.** Ibid, Oliva.

CHAPTER TWENTY-ONE

1. Evan Thomas, *Robert Kennedy: His Life* (New York: Simon & Schuster, 2000), p. 100. **2.** Ibid Thomas, pp. 100-103. **3.** Mark Lane and Dick Gregory, *Code Name "Zorro"* (New York: Pocket Books, 1978), p. 18. **4.** Evan Thomas, *Robert Kennedy: His Life* (New York: Simon & Schuster, 2000), pp. 100-104. **5.** Anthony Summers, *Official and Confidential: The Secret Life of J. Edgar Hoover* (New York: G. P. Putnam's Sons, 1993), p. 59. **6.** HSCA vol. VI, pp. 91-129. **7.** Gerald Posner, *Killing the Dream* (New York: Random House, 1998), p. 49. **8.** Nick Kotz, *Judgment Days* (New York: Houghton Mifflin, 2005), p. 3. **9.** Evan Thomas, *Robert Kennedy: His Life* (New York: Simon & Schuster, 2000), p. 282. **10.** Harris Wofford, *Making Sense of the Sixties* (Pittsburgh, PA: University of Pittsburgh Press, 1992), p. 6. **11.** *The New York Times*, 2-5-64. **12.** Walter Sheridan, *The Fall and Rise of Jimmy Hoffa* (New York: Saturday Review Press, 1972), p. 327. **13.** Ibid, p. 35. **14.** Seth Kantor, *The Ruby Cover-Up* (New York: Zebra Books, 1992), pp. 292, 293. **15.** *Life* magazine, 5-15-64; *Look* magazine 5-19-64; Dick Russell, *The Man Who Knew Too Much* (New York: Carroll & Graf, 2003), pp. 336, 337; *The New York Times*, 4-12-64. **16.** *The Nation*, 4-27-64. **17.** Ibid; David Talbot, *Brothers: The Hidden History of the Kennedy Years* (New York: Free Press, 2007), p. 263, 264; Gus Russo, *Live by the Sword: The Secret War against Castro and the Death of JFK* (Baltimore: Bancroft Press, 1998), p. 575. **18.** Ibid Talbot, p. 272. **19.** Interviews with Harry Williams, 2-24-92, 4-92. **20.** Erneido A. Oliva, *Why Did the Assault Brigade 2506 give its flag to President Kennedy for Safekeeping?* and *History of the Cuban Unit Organized During the Cuban Missile Crisis*, both at www.camcocuba.org. **21.** CIA 104-10241-10065, provided by Larry Hancock. **22.** Richard Schlesinger interview of Richard Helms, *48 Hours*, CBS, 1992. **23.** Tom Tripodi, *Crusade: Under-*

cover Against the Mafia and KGB (Washington, DC, Brassey's, 1993), p. 4. **24**. Ann Louise Bardach, *Cuba Confidential* (New York: Random House, 2002), many passages; "Venezuelans in Florida Bolster Expatriate Support for Luis Posada," *Sun-Sentinel*, 9-1-08. **25**. HSCA Chronology 180-10142-10036; Gaeton Fonzi, *The Last Investigation* (New York: Thunder's Mouth, 1994), pp. 136-39, many others; CIA JMWAVE to Director cables, 12-63. **26**. Tad Szulc, *Fidel: A Critical Portrait* (New York: Morrow, 1986), p. 600. **27**. Fensterwald affidavit for the Justice Department, 7-7-82. **28**. HSCA Chronology 180-10142-10036. **29**. HSCA Chronology 180-10142-10036. **30**. Church Committee vol. V, p. 72. **31**. HSCA Chronology 180-10142-10036. **32**. Warren Commission Executive Session transcript, 1-27-64, p. 144. **33**. See Warren Commission Executive Session transcripts and article at maryferrell.org. **34**. CIA 104-10018-10052; HSCA vol. XI, p. 64. **35**. CIA 104-10419-10021. **36**. CIA 1993.06.26.09:00:44:900550. **37**. The McCord family website says when McCord was a "Senior CIA Security Officer in Europe he headed a team which secretly whisked out of Europe and across national borders one of the most significant and controversial KGB officers ever to defect. This was [after] the assassination of President John F. Kennedy and the defector was highly wanted by the Warren Commission because of the vital information he possessed." See mccordfamilyassn.com; Warren Hinckle and William Turner, *The Fish Is Red: The Story of the Secret War Against Castro* (New York: Harper & Row, 1981), p. 153; McCord declined to speak about Harry Williams when called by one of the authors. McCord had no connection to the harsh treatment Nosenko received in America. **38**. CIA memo 8-9-73 by Director of Security Bruce L. Solie, cited by A. J. Weberman. **39**. Richard Helms with William Hood *A Look Over My Shoulder: A Life in the Central Intelligence Agency* (New York: Random House, 2003), pp 238-44; Ted Shackley, *Spymaster: My Life in the CIA* (Washington, DC: Potomac Books, 2006), pp. 92, 93 **40**. Ibid. **41**. Ibid.

CHAPTER TWENTY-TWO

1. Examples include the phony information from John Martino and Frank Fiorini; the DFS and Phil lips from Mexico City; and allegations in Warren Commission Exhibit #1444 that were traced back to Rolando Masferrer and associates of Manuel Artime. **2**. Anthony and Robbyn Summers, "The Ghosts of November," *Vanity Fair*, 12-94. **3**. See many examples in Anthony Summers, *Official and Confidential: The Secret Life of J. Edgar Hoover* (New York: G. P. Putnam's Sons, 1993) and William W. Turner, *Rearview Mirror* (Granite Bay, CA: Penmarin Books, 2001). **4**. David Wise, "Secret Evidence on the Kennedy Assassination," *Saturday Evening Post*, 4-6-68; HSCA Chronology 180-10142-10036. **5**. FBI 124-10369-10005, declassified 3-3-99; Gus Russo, *Live by the Sword: The Secret War against Castro and the Death of JFK* (Baltimore: Bancroft Press, 1998), pp. 349, 569. **6**. FBI 124-10369-10005, declassified 3-3-99. **7**. Ibid. **8**. Ibid; Gus Russo, *Live by the Sword: The Secret War against Castro and the Death of JFK* (Baltimore: Bancroft Press, 1998), pp. 569 **9**. I suggest: FBI memos dated 12-4, 12-5, and 12-16-63, declassified 5-17-94. **10**. Ibid. **11**. Ibid. **12**. CIA 104-10109-10188. **13**. HSCA Chronology 180-10142-10036. **14**. Interview with Dave Powers 6-5-91 at the John F. Kennedy Presidential Library; William Novak, *Man of the House: The Life and Political Memoirs of Speaker Tip O'Neil* (New York: Random House, 1987), p. 178. **15**. Warren Commission vol. VII, pp. 440-56, 472-74. **16**. Photocopy of original, signed affidavit of David Powers, signed and witnessed by Arlen Specter, provided by National Archives 2-5-99; "Probe of agency raises new questions in Slaying of JFK," *Chicago Tribune*. 6-75. **17**. Josiah Thompson, "Bugliosi picks only the evidence that backs his argument," *Pittsburgh Post-Gazette*, June 30, 2007. **18**. Seth Kantor, *The Ruby Cover-Up* (New York: Zebra Books, 1992) pp. 303-10. **19**. Interviews with confidential Kennedy aide source, 3-17-92. **20**. David Talbot, *Brothers: The Hidden History of the Kennedy Years* (New York: Free Press, 2007), pp. 276-78. **21**. HSCA Chronology 180-10142-10036. **22**. Tom Hays, "Mob girlfriend testifies at FBI trial," Associated Press, 10-29-07. **23**. Church Committee vol. V, p. 72; FBI Airtel to Hoover from SAC Miami, 7-30-64. **24**. Claudia Furiati, *ZR/Rifle: The Plot to Kill Kennedy and Castro* (Melbourne, Australia: Ocean Press, 1994), p. 150. **25**. CIA 104-10308-10084. **26**. Ibid. **27**. CIA 104-10308-10205; CIA 104-10308-10283. **28**. Don Bohning, *The Castro Obsession: U.S. Cover Operations Against Cuba, 1959–1965*, (Washington: Potomac Books, 2005), many passages **29**. HSCA 180-10142-10036; Seth Kantor, *The Ruby Cover-Up* (New York: Zebra Books, 1992), p. 309 **30**. HSCA 180-10142-10036. **31**. HSCA 180-10142-10036. **32**. Howard Kohn, "Execution for the Witnesses, *Rolling Stone*, 6-2-77; Ibid; Dick Russell, "Loran Hall and the Politics of Assassination," *Village Voice*, 10-3-77. **33**. HSCA Chronology 180-10142-10036; Mary Ferrell Foundation website at maryferrell.org. **34**. Ibid HSCA Chronology. **35**. Anthony Summers, *Not In Your Lifetime* (New York: Marlowe & Co., 1998), p. 31 the others were Sherman Cooper, Russell, and McCloy; John H. Davis, *Mafia Kingfish* (New York: Signet 1989), p. 344. **36**. Anthony and Robbyn Summers, "The Ghosts of November," *Vanity Fair*, 12-94; Bernard Fensterwald, Jr., and Michael Ewing, *Coincidence or Conspiracy* (New York: Zebra Books, 1977), p. 134. **37** Joseph A. Califano, Jr., *The Triumph & Tragedy of Lyndon Johnson: The White House Years* (New York: Simon & Schuster, 1991), p. 293; FBI memo, DeLoach to Tolson, 4-4-76. **38**. Anthony Summers, *Conspiracy* (New York: Paragon House, 1989), p. 493.

CHAPTER TWENTY-THREE

1. See many passages in Thomas Powers, *The Man Who Kept the Secrets: Richard Helms & the CIA* (New York: Knopf, 1979), and E. Howard Hunt with Greg Aunapu, *American Spy* (Hoboken, NJ: John Wiley & Sons, 2007). **2.** CIA 104-10404-10376. **3.** Church Committee vol. I, part 10, pp. 192-99; Carl Bernstein, "The CIA and the Media," *Rolling Stone*, 10-20-77; E. Howard Hunt with Greg Aunapu, *American Spy* (Hoboken, NJ: John Wiley & Sons, 2007), p. 150. **4.** Ibid Bernstein. **5.** Church Committee vol. I, part 10, pp. 192-99; Ibid; E. Howard Hunt with Greg Aunapu, *American Spy* (Hoboken, NJ: John Wiley & Sons, 2007), pp. 150-53. **6.** Ibid Church, p. 198; Ibid Hunt with Aunapu, p. 149. **7.** Ibid Church, pp. 192-99; Ibid Hunt with Aunapu, p. 150, citing "The CIA and the Media," *Rolling Stone*, 10-20-77. **8.** Carl Bernstein, "The CIA and the Media," *Rolling Stone*, 10-20-77. **9.** Church Committee vol. I, part 10, p. 195. **10.** Carl Bernstein, "The CIA and the Media," *Rolling Stone*, 10-20-77. **11.** E. Howard Hunt with Greg Aunapu, *American Spy* (Hoboken, NJ: John Wiley & Sons, 2007), pp. 148, 49. **12.** *The New York Times*, 2-24-67 cited by Lisa Pease; E. Howard Hunt with Greg Aunapu, *American Spy* (Hoboken, NJ: John Wiley & Sons, 2007), p. 148; **13.** Carl Bernstein, "The CIA and the Media," *Rolling Stone*, 10-20-77. **14.** Thomas Powers, *The Man Who Kept the Secrets: Richard Helms & the CIA* (New York: Knopf, 1979), p. 420. **15.** Robert Sam Anson, *"They've Killed the President!": The Search for the Murderers of John F. Kennedy* (New York: Bantam, 1975), p. 70. **16.** Joachim Joesten, *Oswald: Assassin or Fall Guy?* (New York: Marzani & Munsell, 1964), pp. 125, 128. **17.** E. Howard Hunt, *Give Us This Day* (New Rochelle: Arlington House, 1973); L. Gonzales-Mata, *Cygne* (Grasset, 1976); CIA 104-10408-10029, 8-25-76, CIA memo; Warren Hinckle and William Turner, *The Fish Is Red: The Story of the Secret War Against Castro* (New York: Harper & Row, 1981), pp. 75-77. **18.** Tad Szulc, *Compulsive Spy: The Strange Career of E. Howard Hunt* (New York: Viking, 1974), pp. 77, 78, 96, 97. **19.** John H. Davis, *Mafia Kingfish: Carlos Marcello and the Assassination of John F. Kennedy* (New York: McGraw-Hill, 1989), pp. 300, 301. **20.** Pierre Galante and Louis Sapin, *The Marseilles Mafia: The Truth Behind the World of Drug Trafficking* (London: W. H. Allen, 1979), pp. 41-55. **21.** Ibid. **22.** CIA 1994.03.11.16:07:16:500005; JFK 1993.08.13.08:39:48:560024.

CHAPTER TWENTY-FOUR

1. Tad Szulc, *Fidel: A Critical Portrait* (New York: Morrow, 1986), p. 599; Jorge G. Castañeda, *Compañero: The Life and Death of Che Guevara* (New York: Knopf, 1997), p. 275. **2.** Gaeton Fonzi, *The Last Investigation* (New York: Thunder's Mouth, 1994), many passages; CIA document, HSCA, Record Number 180-10143-10209, CIA Segregated Collection, Agency File Number 28-43-01, declassified 8-16-95; Enrique G. Encinosa, *Cuba: The Unfinished Revolution* (Austin: Eakin, 1988), p. 196. **3.** CIA #104-10308-10098; see other 1964 and 1965 Artime (AMBIDDY, AMWORLD) and Almeida declassified files online at maryferrell.org. **4.** HSCA #157-10014-10046; for the Artime/Fiorini rifle document, the file number is hard to read but appears to be CIA 180-10142-10307. **5.** Rifle: The file number is hard to read but appears to be CIA 180-10142-10307; HSCA vol. X, p. 184; FBI memo, New York office to Director, 6-2-65. **6.** CIA #104-10308-10098. **7.** Don Bohning, *The Castro Obsession: U.S. Cover Operations Against Cuba, 1959-1965* (Washington: Potomac Books, 2005) p. 227; Evan Thomas, *Robert Kennedy: His Life* (New York: Simon & Schuster, 2000), p. 238. **8.** Haynes Johnson, *Sleepwalking Through History* (New York: W. W. Norton, 2003), p. 271. **9.** *Hearings Before the Subcommittee on Terrorism, Narcotics, and International Communications of the Committee on Foreign Relations*, United States Senate, 1987, 1988; also see CIA drug reports by CIA Inspector General Frederick Hitz, 1-29-98 and 10-98, cited by Robert Parry, 10-29-04, consortiumnews.com. **10.** Tad Szulc, *Fidel: A Critical Portrait* (New York: Morrow, 1986), p. 603; Felix I. Rodriguez and John Weisman, *Shadow Warrior* (New York: Simon and Schuster, 1989), p. 133. **11.** Jorge G. Castaneda, *Compañero: The Life and Death of Che Guevara* (New York: Vintage, 1998), pp. 279, 296, 316-18; Daniel James, *Che Guevara: A Biography* (New York: Stein and Day, 1969), pp. 154, 155; *El Che: Investigating a Legend*, 1997, directed by Maurice Dugoson. **12.** Interviews with Harry Williams, 7-24-93, 2-21-95. **13.** HSCA #157-10014-10046; Evan Thomas, *Robert Kennedy: His Life* (New York: Simon & Schuster, 2000), p. 238. **14.** Tad Szulc, *Compulsive Spy: The Strange Career of E. Howard Hunt* (New York: Viking, 1974), pp. 96, 97; E. Howard Hunt with Greg Aunapu, *American Spy* (Hoboken, NJ: John Wiley & Sons, 2007), p. 156. **15.** Ibid. **16.** HSCA 180-10143-10078; 1994.04.06.10:30:14:250005. **17.** David Atlee Phillips, *The Night Watch* (New York: Atheneum, 1977), pp. 144, 155; Gaeton Fonzi, *The Last Investigation* (New York: Thunder's Mouth, 1994), several passages.

CHAPTER TWENTY-FIVE

1. Arthur Schlesinger, Jr., *Robert Kennedy and His Times* (New York: Ballantine, 1979), p. 861; Evan Thomas, *Robert Kennedy: His Life* (New York: Simon & Schuster, 2000), pp. 309, 310; Richard Goodwin, *Remembering America: A Voice from the Sixties* (Boston: Little, Brown, 1988), p. 530. **2.** Douglas P. Horne, Press Conference remarks, 5-15-06. **3.** "New documents reveal first JFK casket dumped at sea," CNN, 6-1-99; David Lifton, *Best Evidence: Disguise and Deception in the Assassination of John F. Kennedy* (New York: Carroll

& Graf, 1988), many passages. **4.** Charles Rappleye and Ed Becker, *All American Mafioso* (New York: Bar ricade, 1995), p. 259. **5.** Nick Kotz, *Judgment Days* (New York: Houghton Mifflin, 2005), p. 321. **6.** Ibid pp. 232, 233. **7.** Ibid, pp. 234-40. **8.** Ibid, pp. 246-47. **9.** Ibid, pp. 246-49. **10.** Juan Williams, *Eyes on the Prize* (New York: Penguin, 1987), p. 265; Mark Lane and Dick Gregory, *Code Name "Zorro"* (New York: Pocke Books, 1978), pp. 18, 19. **11.** Ibid Williams, p. 284; Nick Kotz, *Judgment Days* (New York: Houghton Mifflin 2005), p. 325; Gerald Posner, *Killing the Dream* (New York: Random House, 1998), p. 49. **12.** Jerry Mitchell "Book probes MLK killing," *Clarion-Ledger*, 12-30-07. **13.** Taylor Branch, *At Canaan's Edge: America in the King Years 1965-68* (New York: Simon & Schuster, 2006), pp. 177, 178. **14.** Ibid, p. 178. **15.** John H. Davis *Mafia Kingfish* (New York: Signet, 1989), p. 353. **16.** HSCA vol. X, pp. 199-205. **17.** Ibid. **18.** *Rambling Rose* by Chris Mills, available at maryferrell.org. **19.** Pierre Galante and Louis Sapin, *The Marseilles Mafia: The Truth Behind the World of Drug Trafficking* (London: W. H. Allen, 1979), pp. 65-83; Douglas Valentine, *The Strength of the Wolf: The Secret History of America's War on Drugs* (London, New York: Verso, 2004), pp. 364-67 Staff and editors of *Newsday*, *The Heroin Trail* (New York: New American Library, 1974), pp. 114-16. **20.** Ibid **21.** Ibid. **22.** CIA document: Warren Hinckle and William Turner, *Deadly Secrets* (New York: Thunder's Mouth, 1992), p. 289; CIA document: 4-25-77, Record Number 104-10400-10123, Russ Holmes Work File Subject: AMTRUNK Operation, declassified 12-26-98; Gus Russo, *Live by the Sword: The Secret War against Castro and the Death of JFK* (Baltimore: Bancroft Press, 1998), p. 247. **23.** *The New York Times* and several Cuban-sponsored publications printed accounts of the trial. **24.** JFK 1994.05.16.14:12:04:280005. **25.** CIA MFR 4-14-66 cited by A. J. Weberman. **26.** Warren Hinckle and William Turner, *Deadly Secrets* (New York Thunder's Mouth, 1992), p. 289; Peter Dale Scott, Paul L. Hoch, and Russell Stetler, eds., *The Assassinations Dallas and Beyond: A Guide to Cover-Ups and Investigations* (New York: Vintage, 1976), p. 363 citing *The New York Times*, 3-6-66. **27.** Interview with Dean Rusk 1-5-90; Anthony and Robbyn Summers, "The Ghost of November," *Vanity Fair*, 12-94, p. 105. **28.** CIA 104-10169-10090. **29.** CIA 104-10102-10087. **30.** Cuban Officials and JFK Historians Nassau Conference, 12-7-95; Nassau Conference Report, *AARC Quarterly* Fall 1995-Winter 1996. **31.** Larry Hancock, *Someone Would Have Talked* (Southlake, TX: JFK Lancer, 2006) many passages. **32.** Haynes Johnson, *Sleepwalking through History* (New York: W. W. Norton, 2003), p. 271 interview with Harry Williams 7-24-93.

CHAPTER TWENTY-SIX

1. Charles Rappleye and Ed Becker, *All American Mafioso* (New York: Barricade, 1995), p. 250. **2.** Ibid, pp. 259 64. **3.** Banister: see CIA #104-10109-10370 for 8-26-60 and 9-21-60 CIA memos about considering using Banister and his small detective firm as a "cover operation" for an unspecified project (A. J. Weberman notes that at that time CIA "Headquarters files #201-428810 and EE-28810 were opened, and file #222918F-SB/2 was opened on Guy Banister Associates."); for Banister-Bellino, see Joe Oster state ments in Banister files at the Assassination Archives and Research Center, Washington, DC. For Nixon' role in Cuban operations at the time, see Anthony Summers with Robbyn Swan, *The Arrogance of Power The Secret World of Richard Nixon* (New York: Viking, 2000), many passages; for Maheu's role, see Inspector General's Report on Plots to Assassinate Castro, 1967. **4.** Inspector General's Report on Plots to Assassinat Castro, 1967; John H. Davis, *Mafia Kingfish* (New York: McGraw-Hill, 1989), p. 87. **5.** Charles Rappleye and Ed Becker, *All American Mafioso* (New York: Barricade, 1995), pp. 261-63. **6.** Ibid; CIA #104-10133-10005 **7.** G. Robert Blakey and Richard N. Billings, *The Plot to Kill the President* (New York: Times Books, 1981 p. 152. **8.** Ed Reid, *The Grim Reapers* (New York: Bantam, 1970), p. 292; William Brashler, *The Don* (New York: Ballantine, 1977), p. 304. **9.** FBI 124-10221-10200. **10.** Ed Reid, *The Grim Reapers* (New York: Bantam 1970), p. 160. **11.** Evan Thomas, *Robert Kennedy: His Life* (New York: Simon & Schuster, 2000), p. 329. **12.** FB 124-10204-10205. **13.** FBI 124-10204-10205. **14.** CIA, Inspector General's Report on Plots to Assassinat Castro, 1967. **15.** Evan Thomas, *Robert Kennedy: His Life* (New York: Simon & Schuster, 2000), pp. 320-23 **16.** Clifton Daniel, *Chronicle of America* (Liberty, MO: JL International Publishing, 1993), pp. 810-12. **17.** FB 124-10280-10088. **18.** HSCA vol. X, pp. 37-56. **19.** Jane Franklin, *The Cuban Revolution and the United State A Chronological History* (Melbourne, Australia: Ocean, 1992), pp. 77, 78. **20.** CIA 180-10142-10307. **21.** HSC 180-101432-10215. **22.** Carl Bernstein, "The CIA and the Media," *Rolling Stone*, 10-20-77. **23.** Warren Hinckl and William Turner, *Deadly Secrets* (New York: Thunder's Mouth, 1992), p. 301-09. **24.** Ibid.

CHAPTER TWENTY-SEVEN

1. Richard Goodwin, *Remembering America: A Voice from the Sixties* (Boston: Little, Brown, 1988), pp. 462-65 **2.** Ibid. **3.** Jack Newfield, "I want Kennedy killed," *Penthouse*, 5-92. **4.** Authors' interview with Richar Goodwin, 4-15-98. **5.** Arthur Schlesinger, Jr., *Robert Kennedy and His Times* (New York: Ballantine, 1979 p. 664. **6.** Henry Hurt, *Reasonable Doubt* (New York: Henry Holt, 1987), p. 57 **7.** Anthony Summers, *Official and Confidential: The Secret Life of J. Edgar Hoover* (New York: G. P. Putnam's Sons, 1993), many passages **8.** Rosen to DeLoach FBI memorandum, 11-13-66. **9.** Tolson memo re: meeting with Justice Fortas, 2pm

10-7-66. **10.** Ibid. **11.** Bernard Fensterwald, Jr., and Michael Ewing, *Coincidence or Conspiracy* (New York: Zebra Books, 1977), pp. 99, 100; *Washington Post*, 1-21-75 **12.** Ibid Fensterwald, pp. 101, 102. **13.** Ibid, pp. 103. **14.** US House of Representatives, *The Final Assassinations Report of the Select Committee on Assassinations* (New York: Bantam Books, 1979), pp. 208, 213. **15.** E. Howard Hunt with Greg Aunapu, *American Spy* (Hoboken, NJ: John Wiley & Sons, 2007), p. 157. **16.** Tad Szulc, *Compulsive Spy: The Strange Career of E. Howard Hunt* (New York: Viking, 1974), pp. 100, 103; E. Howard Hunt with Greg Aunapu, *American Spy* (Hoboken, NJ: John Wiley & Sons, 2007), p. 157. **17.** Church Committee vol. I, part 10, p. 198; Ibid Hunt with Aunapu, pp. 149, 157. **18.** U.S. Information and Educational Exchange Act of 1948, commonly known as the Smith Mundt Act; Evan Thomas, *Robert Kennedy: His Life* (New York: Simon & Schuster, 2000), pp. 330, 408. **19.** Tad Szulc, *Compulsive Spy: The Strange Career of E. Howard Hunt* (New York: Viking, 1974), p. 104; Hunt CIA personnel files released to the National Archives in 1993 and 1994. **20.** E. Howard Hunt with Greg Aunapu, *American Spy* (Hoboken, NJ: John Wiley & Sons, 2007), p. 148. **21.** Church Committee vol. I, part 10, p. 193. **22.** E. Howard Hunt with Greg Aunapu, *American Spy* (Hoboken, NJ: John Wiley & Sons, 2007), p. 158; memo titled "Everette Howard Hunt, Jr." in CIA file at the National Archives declassified as part of the 1994 CIA Historical Review Program. **23.** E. Howard Hunt, *Undercover* (New York: Berkley Publishing, 1974), p. 133; Jim Lesar, "Valenti/Helms Plan for CIA Television Show" *AARC Quarterly*, Fall 1995/Winter 1996; CIA memo quoted by A. J. Weberman.

CHAPTER TWENTY-EIGHT

1. FBI 124-10204-10205. **2.** John H. Davis, *Mafia Kingfish* (New York: Signet, 1989), pp. 353-56. **3.** See "Lucchese Crime Family Epic, Part II" at www.crimelibrary.com. **4.** John H. Davis, *Mafia Kingfish* (New York: Signet, 1989), pp. 356-59. **5.** Sandy Smith, "The Fix," *Life* magazine, 9-1-67. **6.** G. Robert Blakey and Richard N. Billings, *The Plot to Kill the President* (New York: Times Books, 1981), p. 324; Charles Rappleye and Ed Becker, *All American Mafioso* (New York: Barricade, 1995), p. 276. **7.** *Miami Herald*, 7-31-75; Frank Sturgis interview by Andrew St. George, *True* magazine, 8-74. **8.** One of those Trafficante associates was Manuel Artime. **9.** John H. Davis, *Mafia Kingfish* (New York: Signet, 1989), p. 367; CIA, Inspector General's Report on Plots to Assassinate Castro, 1967; 124-10333-10036. **10.** Charles Rappleye and Ed Becker, *All American Mafioso* (New York: Barricade, 1995), pp. 279-82. **11.** Ibid, pp. 281-83; George Michael Evica, *And We Are All Mortal: New Evidence and Analysis in the John F. Kennedy Assassination* (West Hartford, CT: Evica, 1978), several passages. **12.** Ibid Rappleye and Becker, pp. 283-85. **13.** David E. Scheim, *The Mafia Killed President Kennedy* (New York: SPI Books, 1992), pp. 41, 42. **14.** Sid Blumenthal and Harvey Yazijian, *Government by Gunplay* (New York: Signet, 1976), pp. 216, 217; David Talbot, *Brothers: The Hidden History of the Kennedy Years* (New York: Free Press, 2007), p. 318. **15.** Martin Waldron letter to the New Orleans Police Department, *The New York Times*, 11-21-66. **16.** Ibid. **17.** Walter Sheridan, *The Fall and Rise of Jimmy Hoffa* (New York: Saturday Review Press, 1972), p. 408; Richard Billings' New Orleans Journal at www.jfk-online.com; John H. Davis, *Mafia Kingfish* (New York: Signet, 1989), many passages. **18.** Ibid Sheridan, p. 492. **19.**

CHAPTER TWENTY-NINE

1. New Orleans FBI memo, 6-10-67; Carl Oglesby, "The Conspiracy that won't go away" *Playboy*, 2-92. **2.** Richard Billings' New Orleans Journal at www.jfk-online.com. **3.** Joan Mellen, *A Farewell to Justice* (Dulles, VA: Potomac Books, 2005), several passages. **4.** Seth Kantor, *The Ruby Cover-Up* (New York: Zebra Books, 1992). **5.** Evan Thomas, *Robert Kennedy: His Life* (New York: Simon & Schuster, 2000), pp. 328, 329. **6.** Ibid, pp. 327, 330, 331. **7.** Ed Reid, *The Grim Reapers* (New York: Bantam, 1970), p. 292. **8.** Charles Rappleye and Ed Becker, *All American Mafioso* (New York: Barricade, 1995), p. 280. **9.** 1993.07.01.11:26:17:340800. **10.** 1993.07.01.11:26:17:340800. **11.** FBI copy of CIA memo 124-10285-10054. **12.** FBI 124-10285-10058; FBI 124-10280-1011. **13.** Joseph A. Califano, Jr., *The Triumph & Tragedy of Lyndon Johnson: The White House Years* (New York: Simon & Schuster, 1991), pp. 295, 377.

CHAPTER THIRTY

1. David Phillips memo to Chief, CI/R & A: CIA OGC 67-2061, CIA MFR 2.14.68 Sarah K. Hall, cited in A. J. Weberman web book chap. 7. Rosemary James and Jack Wardlaw, *Plot or Politics* (New Orleans: Pelican Publishing, 1967) was the book in question. See also CIA #104-10406-10022; CIA #104-10435-10007. **2.** Evan Thomas, *Robert Kennedy: His Life* (New York: Simon & Schuster, 2000), pp. 330, 408. **3.** Church Committee vol. I, part 10, p. 185; Ibid. **4.** Ibid Thomas. **5.** CIA 104-10404-10376; CIA 104-10209-10156; Lee Harvey Oswald CIA Soft File, p. 201. **6.** CIA 104-10182-10075; Dick Russell, *The Man Who Knew Too Much* (New York: Carroll & Graf, 2003), pp. xxviii, 126. **7.** CIA 104-10404-10376; CIA 104-10209-10156; Lee Harvey Oswald CIA Soft File, p. 201. **8.** Richard Reeves, *President Kennedy: Profile of Power* (New York: Simon & Schuster, 1993), pp. 291, 606, 626, 707. **9.** Ibid, pp. 291, 606, 626; later claims have her persuading JFK to try LSD. **10.** Alfred W. McCoy, *The Politics of Heroin* (Brooklyn: Lawrence Hill Books,

1991). **11.** CIA 104-10404-10376; CIA 104-10009-10024. **12.** CIA 104-10404-10376. **13.** CIA 104-10404-10376. **14.** CIA 104-10404-10376. **15.** CIA 104-10404-10376. **16.** CIA 104-10404-10376. **17.** CIA 104-10404-10376. **18.** Bernard Fensterwald, Jr., and Michael Ewing, *Coincidence or Conspiracy* (New York: Zebra Books, 1977), pp. 102, 103; CIA 104-10404-10376. **19.** CIA 104-10404-10376. **20.** Peter Dale Scott, *Deep Politics III*, excerpts available at maryferrell.org.

CHAPTER THIRTY-ONE

1. Warren Hinckle and William Turner, *The Fish Is Red: The Story of the Secret War Against Castro* (New York: Harper & Row, 1981), several passages. **2.** Cuban Officials and JFK Historians Nassau Conference, 12-7-95; Nassau Conference Report, *AARC Quarterly*, Fall 1995-Winter 1996; Dick Russell, *The Man Who Knew Too Much* (New York: Carroll & Graf/R. Gallen, 1992), pp. 292, 293, 507, 518, 537, 546, 641, 702, 703. **3.** Ed Reid, *The Grim Reapers* (New York: Bantam, 1970), pp. 99, 16. **4.** *Atlanta Journal-Constitution*, 11-25-66 and 11-26-66; Dr. Jerry D. Rose, "J. B. Stoner: An Introduction," *The Fourth Decade*, 11-95; FBI Atlanta Field Office file 105-3193, 12-1-63; David Ferrie long-distance phone record, p. 16, on file at the Assassination Archives and Research Center. **5.** Dan E. Moldea, *The Hoffa Wars: Teamsters, Rebels, Politicians, and the Mob* (New York: SPI, 1993), several passages. **6.** Hoover to Director, U.S. Secret Service, 2-3-67. **7.** Bill Barry, "2 weeks before JFK was Killed: Assassination Idea Taped," *Miami News*, 2-2-67. **8.** *Miami News*, 2-3-67, cited in FBI 124-10183-10239. **9.** Bill Barry interview, 2008. **10.** FBI #124-10183-10239. **11.** FBI 124-10209-10451; Frank Ragano and Selwyn Raab, *Mob Lawyer* (New York: Scribners, 1994), pp. 226-28. **12.** Dick Russell, *The Man Who Knew Too Much* (New York: Carroll & Graf, 2003), p 544. **13.** G. Robert Blakey and Richard N. Billings, *The Plot to Kill the President* (New York: Times Books, 1981), 384 **14.** Max Holland, *The Kennedy Assassination Tapes* (New York: Knopf, 2004), p. 392. **15.** George Michael Evica, *And We Are All Mortal: New Evidence and Analysis in the John F. Kennedy Assassination* (West Hartford, CT: Evica, 1978), p. 230. **16.** Treasury Department/Secret Service memo to J. Edgar Hoover, 2-13-67. **17.** Max Holland, *The Kennedy Assassination Tapes* (New York: Knopf, 2004), p. 396. **18.** Treasury Department/Secret Service memo to J. Edgar Hoover, 2-13-67; Ibid, pp. 389, 390, 416. **19.** Ibid Holland, pp. 389, 390. **20.** Richard D. Mahoney, *Sons & Brothers: The Days of Jack and Bobby Kennedy* (New York: Arcade, 1999), p. 332. **21.** For an example, see Evan Thomas, *Robert Kennedy: His Life* (New York: Simon & Schuster, 2000). **22.** Treasury Department/Secret Service memo to J. Edgar Hoover, 2-13-67; Hoover letter to Rowley, 2-25-67. **23.** FBI 124-10209-10451. **24.** James Kirkwood, *American Grotesque* (New York, NY: Harper Perennial, 1992), p. 141. **25.** Max Holland, *The Kennedy Assassination Tapes* (New York: Knopf, 2004), pp. 389, 398. **26.** Gaeton Fonzi, *The Last Investigation* (New York: Thunder's Mouth, 1994). **27.** Generally, see Larry Hancock, *Someone Would Have Talked* (Southlake, TX: JFK Lancer, 2006) and Gaeton Fonzi, *The Last Investigation* (New York: Thunder's Mouth, 1994). **28.** Dick Russell, *The Man Who Knew Too Much* (New York: Carroll & Graf, 2003), p. 182; Warren Hinckle and William Turner, *Deadly Secrets* (New York: Thunder's Mouth, 1992), pp. 233, 270, 321.

CHAPTER THIRTY-TWO

1. Michael R. Beschloss, *Taking Charge* (New York: Simon & Schuster, 1997), pp. 561-63. **2.** Anthony Summers, *Conspiracy* (New York: Paragon House, 1989). **3.** *People and the Pursuit of Truth*, vol. 1 No. 1, May 1975. **4.** Gaeton Fonzi, *The Last Investigation* (New York: Thunder's Mouth, 1994), p. 425; David C. Martin, *Wilderness of Mirrors* (New York: Harper & Row, 1980), pp. 186-89. **5.** David Talbot, *Brothers: The Hidden History of the Kennedy Years* (New York: Free Press, 2007), pp. 322, 323. **6.** Ibid, 314. **7.** Ibid, 312, 313. **8.** Ibid **9.** Ibid, 325-326. **10.** Ibid, 312, 313. **11.** Jim Garrison, *A Heritage of Stone* (New York: Berkley Medallion, 1975), pp. 110, 111; G. Robert Blakey and Richard N. Billings, *Fatal Hour* (New York: Berkley Books, 1992) p. xxii. **12.** "JFK Death Link to Anti-Castro Plot Weighed," *The New York Times*, 2-21-67, cited in *Miami News*, 2-21-67. **13.** Jim Garrison, *A Heritage of Stone* (New York: Berkley Medallion, 1975), p. 111; "Facts Don't Jibe in Ferrie Death," UPI, 2-23-67; James Kirkwood, *American Grotesque* (New York, NY: Harper Perennial, 1992), p. 142. **14.** *St. Petersburg Times*, 12-31-91; Richard D. Mahoney, *Sons & Brothers: The Days of Jack and Bobby Kennedy* (New York: Arcade, 1999), p. 338. **15.** Phone interview with John Diuguid 9-30-04; Ronald Goldfarb, *Perfect Villains, Imperfect Heroes: Robert F. Kennedy's War against Organized Crime* (New York: Random House, 1995), pp. 74, 147; Gus Russo, *Live by the Sword: The Secret War against Castro and the Death of JFK* (Baltimore: Bancroft Press, 1998), pp. 402, 403. **16.** Michael R. Beschloss, *Taking Charge* (New York: Simon & Schuster, 1997), p. 564. **17.** Haynes Johnson, "The New Orleans 'Plot'," *The Washington Sunday Star*, 2-26-67 and Paul Hoch letter 10-11-92. **18.** Ibid. **19.** 1994.05.09.10:43:33:160005. **20.** HSCA Report, pp. 142, 143. **21.** Walter Sheridan, *The Fall and Rise of Jimmy Hoffa* (New York: Saturday Review Press, 1972), pp. 406-08. **22.** Authors' interview with former Justice Department prosecutors Marvin Loewy and Thomas Kennelly, 11-4-93; Ibid, pp. 408-09. **23.** Ibid Sheridan; manuscript from the Billings Brown/Turner holdings on file at the Assassination Archives and Records Center. **24.** FBI report, 12-2

3, San Juan, Puerto Rico; Dan E. Moldea, *The Hoffa Wars: Teamsters, Rebels, Politicians, and the Mob* (New York, SPI, 1993), pp. 163, 164; David E. Scheim, *The Mafia Killed President Kennedy* (New York: SPI Books, 1992), p. 124. **25.** Frank Ragano and Selwyn Raab, *Mob Lawyer* (New York: Scribners, 1994), p. 191. **26.** Ibid, pp. 191-94. **27.** Ibid. **28.** Ibid, pp. 193, 194. **29.** Walter Sheridan, *The Fall and Rise of Jimmy Hoffa* (New York: Saturday Review Press, 1972), pp. 407-11. **30.** Ibid. **31.** Ibid, pp. 443, 444. **32.** Evan Thomas, *Robert Kennedy: His Life* (New York: Simon & Schuster, 2000), pp. 334, 335; Max Holland, *The Kennedy Assassination Tapes* (New York: Knopf, 2004), p. 409.

CHAPTER THIRTY-THREE

1. Harold Weisberg, *Oswald in New Orleans: Case of Conspiracy with the C.I.A.* (New York: Canyon Books, 1967), pp 256, 257. **2.** Michael R. Beschloss, *Taking Charge* (New York: Simon & Schuster, 1997), pp. 565-66; Max Holland, *The Kennedy Assassination Tapes* (New York: Knopf, 2004), pp. 404-09. **3.** Warren Commission Exhibit #1444. **4.** Michael R. Beschloss, *Taking Charge* (New York: Simon & Schuster, 1997), pp. 565-66; Max Holland, *The Kennedy Assassination Tapes* (New York: Knopf, 2004), pp. 404-09. **5.** Ibid. **6.** Ibid. **7.** Ibid. **8.** Ibid. **9.** Ibid. **10.** Ibid. **11.** Ibid Holland, p. 414. **12.** Ibid, p. 415. **13.** Ibid; see also several passages in Walter Sheridan, *The Fall and Rise of Jimmy Hoffa* (New York: Saturday Review Press, 1972) and Peter Dale Scott, *Deep Politics and the Death of JFK* (Berkeley: University of California Press, 1993). **14.** Inspector General's Report on Plots to Assassinate Castro, 1967. **15.** Jack Anderson column, 9-13-76; Charles Rappleye and Ed Becker, *All American Mafioso* (New York: Barricade, 1995), p. 271; **16.** Gus Russo, *Live by the Sword: The Secret War against Castro and the Death of JFK* (Baltimore: Bancroft Press, 1998), p. 446. **17.** CIA, Inspector General's Report on Plots to Assassinate Castro, 1967, p. 112. **18.** Evan Thomas, *Robert Kennedy: His Life* (New York: Simon & Schuster, 2000), p. 334, others. **19.** CIA 104-10438-10038. **20.** Max Holland, *The Kennedy Assassination Tapes* (New York: Knopf, 2004), pp. 414, 415; Anderson's byline was noted in some newspapers, like the *San Francisco Chronicle*, but not others, like the *New Orleans States-Item*. **21.** *New Orleans States-Item*, 3-3-67, p. 25. It's essential to note that the most important analysis of Jack Anderson's 3-3-67 and 3-7-67 columns was first done by Peter Dale Scott in the 1970s, in *Crime and Cover-up*, and in the 1990s, in *Deep Politics II*. As with all of his work, both are highly recommended. **22.** Richard D. Mahoney, *Sons & Brothers: The Days of Jack and Bobby Kennedy* (New York: Arcade, 1999), p. 333. **23.** *New Orleans States-Item*, 3-3-67, p. 25. **24.** Ibid. **25.** Richard D. Mahoney, *Sons & Brothers: The Days of Jack and Bobby Kennedy* (New York: Arcade, 1999), p. 333. **26.** *New Orleans States-Item*, 3-3-67, p. 25. **27.** Arthur Schlesinger, Jr., *Robert Kennedy and His Times* (New York: Ballantine, 1979), p. 532. **28.** Inspector General's Report on Plots to Assassinate Castro, 1967, p. 66. **29.** See the so-called CIA "Family Jewels," p. 21, 27, available in the National Security Archive's Electronic Briefing Book No. 222.

CHAPTER THIRTY-FOUR

1. Hoover to Attorney General memo, 3-3-67. **2.** Ibid. **3.** FBI 124—10183-10239; Hoover to Attorney General memo, 3-3-67. **4.** Max Holland, *The Kennedy Assassination Tapes* (New York: Knopf, 2004), p. 416. **5.** Walter Sheridan, *The Fall and Rise of Jimmy Hoffa* (New York: Saturday Review Press, 1972), several passages. **6.** The *Washington Post*, 3-7-67. **7.** SSCIA 157-10011-10025. **8.** David C. Martin, *Wilderness of Mirrors* (New York: Harper & Row, 1980), pp. 188, 189. **9.** Gus Russo, *Live by the Sword: The Secret War against Castro and the Death of JFK* (Baltimore: Bancroft Press, 1998), p. 446. **10.** CIA 104-10122-10306. **11.** CIA 104-10133-10005. **12.** William E. Kelly, "The Exhumation and Reinterment of JFK" *Dateline: Dallas*, Spring/Summer 1993. **13.** Ibid; Gus Russo, *Live by the Sword: The Secret War against Castro and the Death of JFK* (Baltimore: Bancroft Press, 1998), p. 405. **14.** Ibid Russo, p. 406. **15.** Ibid, pp. 328, 389, 390, 404-06. **16.** William E. Kelly, "The Exhumation and Reinterment of JFK," *Dateline: Dallas*, Spring/Summer 1993. **17.** *The New York Times*, 4-18-67 in Max Holland, *The Kennedy Assassination Tapes* (New York: Knopf, 2004), pp. 421, 422. **18.** *Life* magazine 9-8-67; William W. Turner, *Rearview Mirror* (Granite Bay, CA: Penmarin Books, 2001) p. 169; Joan Mellen, *A Farewell to Justice* (Dulles, VA: Potomac Books, 2005), p. 256. **19.** Inspector General's Report on Plots to Assassinate Castro, 1967, p. 120. **20.** Ibid, p. 127. **21.** Carl Oglesby, "The Conspiracy that won't go away," *Playboy*, 2-92. **22.** Oliver Stone and Zachary Sklar, *JFK: The Documented Screenplay* (New York: Applause Books, 1992), p. 217. **23.** Richard Billings' *New Orleans Journal* at www.jfk-online.com, 3-67. **24.** Max Holland, *The Kennedy Assassination Tapes* (New York: Knopf, 2004), p. 415. **25.** Ibid. **26.** Ibid, p. 416. **27.** FBI 124-10183-10239. **28.** FBI 124-10183-10239. **29.** FBI 124-10183-10239. **30.** FBI 124-10183-10239. **31.** FBI 124-10183-10239. **32.** FBI 124-10183-10239. **33.** FBI 124-10183-10239.

CHAPTER THIRTY-FIVE

1. CIA, Inspector General's Report on Plots to Assassinate Castro, 1967; for example, among the material Helms withheld from LBJ was the involvement of Manuel Artime in the CIA-Mafia plots, and the Mafia's payoff of $200,000 to Tony Varona in the summer of 1963. **2.** Dick Russell, *The Man Who Knew Too Much*

(New York: Carroll & Graf, 2003), p. 414. **3.** Thomas Powers, *The Man Who Kept the Secrets: Richard Helms & the CIA* (New York: Knopf, 1979), p. 136. **4.** Peter Dale Scott, *Deep Politics II* (Ipswich, MA: Mary Ferrel Foundation Press, 2003), pp. 66-67. **5.** Ibid. **6.** CIA, Inspector General's Report on Plots to Assassinate Castro, 1967, pp. 120-23. **7.** Evan Thomas, *Robert Kennedy: His Life* (New York: Simon & Schuster, 2000) p. 336. **8.** SSCIA 157-10011-10019. **9.** CIA files about Manolo Ray are available at maryferrell.org, including those under his CIA code-name of AMBANG (sometimes given as AMBANG-1); online interview with Manolo Ray, 2-9-06, arranged by John Simkin, www.spartacus.schoolnet.co.uk. **10.** Dick Russell *The Man Who Knew Too Much* (New York: Carroll & Graf, 2003), pp. 413, 414. **11.** Ibid. **12.** Ibid. **13.** Max Holland, *The Kennedy Assassination Tapes* (New York: Knopf, 2004), p. 416. **14.** U.S. Senate, Select Committee to Study Governmental Operations with Respect to Intelligence Activities, *Alleged Assassination Plots Involving Foreign Leaders* (New York: Norton, 1976), p. 164. **15.** Ibid; Richard Reeves, *President Kennedy Profile of Power* (New York: Simon & Schuster, 1993), p. 713. **16.** CIA, Inspector General's Report on Plots to Assassinate Castro, 1967, p. 6. **17.** Peter Dale Scott, *Deep Politics II* (Ipswich, MA: Mary Ferrell Foundation Press, 2003), p. 68. **18.** Arthur Schlesinger, Jr., *Robert Kennedy and His Times* (New York: Ballantine 1979), p. 855; Taylor Branch, *At Canaan's Edge: America in the King Years 1965-68* (New York: Simon & Schuster, 2006), p. 598. **19.** Ibid Schlesinger. **20.** Evan Thomas, *Robert Kennedy: His Life* (New York: Simon & Schuster, 2000), p. 339. **21.** Arthur Schlesinger, Jr., *Robert Kennedy and His Times* (New York: Ballantine 1979), pp. 856, 859; Taylor Branch, *At Canaan's Edge: America in the King Years 1965-68* (New York: Simon & Schuster, 2006), p. 599. **22.** Nick Kotz, *Judgment Days* (New York: Houghton Mifflin, 2005), p. 371. **23.** FB 124-10280-10110. **24.** FBI 124-10280-10110. **25.** Richard Helms with William Hood, *A Look Over My Shoulder A Life in the Central Intelligence Agency* (New York: Random House, 2003). **26.** CIA, Inspector General' Report on Plots to Assassinate Castro, 1967, p. 128. **27.** Max Holland, *The Kennedy Assassination Tape* (New York: Knopf, 2004), p. 418. **28.** Thomas Powers, *The Man Who Kept the Secrets: Richard Helms & th CIA* (New York: Knopf, 1979), p. 179; Ibid. **29.** Ibid Powers. **30.** Church Committee vol. X, p. 106; Ibid p. 180. **31.** CIA, Inspector General's Report on Plots to Assassinate Castro, 1967, p. 131.

CHAPTER THIRTY-SIX

1. Miami FBI memo, 8-7-67. **2.** William W. Turner, *Rearview Mirror* (Granite Bay, CA: Penmarin Books 2001), p. 206. **3.** Evan Thomas, *The Very Best Men: Four Who Dared: The Early Years of the CIA* (New York Simon & Schuster, 1995), p. 332. **4.** HSCA #180-10143-10215. **5.** Joseph J. Trento, *Prelude to Terror: Th Rogue CIA, and the Legacy of America's Private Intelligence Network* (New York: Carroll & Graf, 2005 pp. 44-45. **6.** Tom Tripodi, *Crusade: Undercover Against the Mafia and KGB* (Washington, DC, Brassey's 1993), pp. 4, 129-32, 169. **7.** William W. Turner, *Rearview Mirror* (Granite Bay, CA: Penmarin Books, 2001 p. 208. **8.** Interviews with Harry Williams 2-24-92, 4-92, 7-1-95; Richard Billings, *New Orleans Journal*, a www.jfk-online.com. **9.** Miami FBI memo 8-7-67; *Miami Herald* 4-17-05; Dade County Manager's Offic files on Felipe Rivero, found by former Miami-Dade County Archivist Gordon Winslow and availabl at his Cuban Information Archives website; Michael L. Kurtz, *The JFK Assassination Debates* (Lawrence KS: University Press of Kansas, 2006). **10.** Ibid Dade County files. **11.** Jean-Guy Allard, "The Miami Mafi in Canada," *Granma*, 4-16-04; after being questioned by the FBI, neither brother was charged. **12.** Jan Franklin, *The Cuban Revolution and the United States: A Chronological History* (Melbourne, Australia Ocean, 1992), pp. 79, 80. **13.** *Miami News*, 5-23-67. **14.** Miami FBI memo, 8-7-67. **15.** Ibid. **16.** Ibid. **17.** Jean Pierre Charbonneau, *The Canadian Connection* (Ottawa: Optimum, 1976), pp. 249-51. **18.** CIA 104-1007 10179. **19.** Ken Silverstein, "Six Questions for Jefferson Morley on *Our Man in Mexico*," *Harpers*, 4-17-0 **20.** HSCA 180-101432-10215. **21.** Ann Louise Bardach, *Cuba Confidential* (New York: Random Hous 2002), p. 183; CIA 104-10068-10010; HSCA 180-10143-10215. **22.** CIA 104-10408-10029, 8-25-76, CIA mem 23. Miami FBI memo, 8-7-67. **24.** Miami FBI memo, 8-7-67; Jane Franklin, *The Cuban Revolution and th United States: A Chronological History* (Melbourne, Australia: Ocean, 1992), p. 80. **25.** Miami FBI mem 8-7-67. **26.** Evan Thomas, *The Very Best Men: Four Who Dared: The Early Years of the CIA* (New York: Simo & Schuster, 1995), p. 333; Gaeton Fonzi, *The Last Investigation* (New York: Thunder's Mouth, 1994), p. 42 **27.** David Phillips memo to Chief, CI/R & A: CIA OGC 67-2061, CIA MFR 2.14.68 Sarah K. Hall, cited i A. J. Weberman web book chap. 7; Rosemary James and Jack Wardlaw, *Plot or Politics* (New Orleans: Pel can Publishing, 1967) was the book in question; see also CIA #104-10406-10022; CIA #104-10435-1000 **28.** David Atlee Phillips, *The Night Watch* (New York: Atheneum, 1977), pp. 185-87. **29.** HSCA vol. X, pp. 4 54. **30.** Charles Rappleye and Ed Becker, *All American Mafioso* (New York: Barricade, 1995), p. viii; Joh H. Davis, *The Kennedy Contract* (New York: Harper Paperbacks, 1993), pp. 34-35. **31.** David E. Schein *The Mafia Killed President Kennedy* (New York: SPI Books, 1992), pp. 258, 259. **32.** John H. Davis, *Maf Kingfish* (New York: Signet, 1989), p. 236; Ibid. **33.** FBI Los Angeles Field File 58-156, pp. 331-37; Dan Moldea, *The Hoffa Wars: Teamsters, Rebels, Politicians, and the Mob* (New York: SPI, 1993), pp. 64, 87, 110, 18 187; Ed Reid, *The Grim Reapers* (New York: Bantam, 1970), p. 291. **34.** FBI Los Angeles Field File 58-15

p. 331-37. **35.** Ibid; John H. Davis, *Mafia Kingfish* (New York: Signet, 1989), p. 384; FBI Memo, 7-23-68. **6.** Walter Sheridan, *The Fall and Rise of Jimmy Hoffa* (New York: Saturday Review Press, 1972), p. 408; Hoffa manuscript from Assassinations Archives and Records Center collection, p. 42; Tom Kennelly interview by the authors, 11-4-93.

CHAPTER THIRTY-SEVEN

. New Orleans FBI memo, 6-10-67. **2.** CIA 104-10419-10021, Russ Holmes Work File, declassified 8-26-98: Edgar Hoover memo to Attorney General Ramsey Clark, 5-17-67. **3.** CIA 104-10419-10021, Russ Holmes Work File, declassified 8-26-98: letter to Assistant Attorney General, 6-2-67, citing UPI 5-8 and 5-9-67; *The New York Times*, 5-10-67. **4.** *Washington Evening Star*, 5-22 and 5-26-67. **5.** FBI memo, New York to Director, -2-65. **6.** Phone interview with John Diuguid, 9-30-04. **7.** John H. Davis, *The Kennedy Contract* (New York: Harper Paperbacks, 1993), p. 154; Evan Thomas, *Robert Kennedy: His Life* (New York: Simon & Schuster), 338; interview with business associate of Frank Grimsley, 1-30-08. **8.** Ibid Davis; David Talbot, *Brothers: The Hidden History of the Kennedy Years* (New York: Free Press, 2007), p. 312. **9.** William W. Turner, *Rearview Mirror* (Granite Bay, CA: Penmarin Books, 2001), pp. 157, 158. **10.** David Talbot, *Brothers: The Hidden History f the Kennedy Years* (New York: Free Press, 2007), pp. 326, 327. **11.** Ibid. **12.** William W. Turner, *Rearview Mirror* (Granite Bay, CA: Penmarin Books, 2001), pp. 160, 161. **13.** Ibid, p. 161; Oliver Stone and Zachary klar, *JFK: The Documented Screenplay* (New York: Applause Books, 1992), p. 494. **14.** Michael T. Griffith, Just the Facts," 2001. **15.** Oliver Stone and Zachary Sklar, *JFK: The Documented Screenplay* (New York: Applause Books, 1992), p. 493. **16.** William W. Turner, *Rearview Mirror* (Granite Bay, CA: Penmarin Books, 001), p. 158. **17.** Walter Sheridan, *The Fall and Rise of Jimmy Hoffa* (New York: Saturday Review Press, 1972), . 420. **18.** Frank Ragano and Selwyn Raab, *Mob Lawyer* (New York: Scribners, 1994), p. 195. **19.** Walter Sheridan, *The Fall and Rise of Jimmy Hoffa* (New York: Saturday Review Press, 1972), pp. 414-55. **20.** Frank Ragano and Selwyn Raab, *Mob Lawyer* (New York: Scribners, 1994), p. 198. **21.** Charles Rappleye and Ed Becker, *All American Mafioso* (New York: Barricade, 1995), p. 287. **22.** Ibid, pp. 286-89. **23.** Ed Reid, *The Grim Reapers* (New York: Bantam, 1970), pp. 188-90; David E. Scheim, *The Mafia Killed President Kennedy* New York: SPI Books, 1992), pp. 359, 360. **24.** John H. Davis, *Mafia Kingfish* (New York: Signet, 1989), pp. 63, 364. **25.** William W. Turner, *Rearview Mirror* (Granite Bay, CA: Penmarin Books, 2001), p. 168. **26.** *Life* magazine 9-1-67; Walter Sheridan, *The Fall and Rise of Jimmy Hoffa* (New York: Saturday Review Press, 972), many passages. **27.** *Life* magazine, 9-1-67. **28.** Ibid; Martin Waldron letter to the New Orleans Police Department, *The New York Times*, 11-21-66. **29.** John H. Davis, *Mafia Kingfish* (New York: Signet, 1989), p. 352, 353. **30.** Ibid, pp. 351-53. **31.** Ibid.

CHAPTER THIRTY-EIGHT

. Philip H. Melanson, *The Murkin Conspiracy* (New York: Praeger, 1989), pp. 165, 166. **2.** Gerald Posner, *Killing the Dream* (New York: Random House, 1998), pp. 131-134. **3.** US House of Representatives, *The Final Assassinations Report of the Select Committee on Assassinations* (New York: Bantam Books, 1979), . 480; Gerald Posner, *Killing the Dream* (New York: Random House, 1998), p. 139. **4.** Dan E. Moldea, *The Hoffa Wars: Teamsters, Rebels, Politicians, and the Mob* (New York: SPI, 1993), p. 175; Walter Sheridan, *The Fall and Rise of Jimmy Hoffa* (New York: Saturday Review Press, 1972), pp. 415, 453; Shenker had been the conduit for paying Missouri Senator Edward Long $160,000 to hold his wiretap hearings the previous year, designed to help Hoffa and embarrass Bobby Kennedy. **5.** FBI Martin Luther King, Jr. Main File 00-106670, Section 103, p. 110. **6.** Ibid, p.108; HSCA King vol. III, p. 597; William F. Pepper, *Orders to Kill* (New York: Carroll & Graf, 1995) pp. 107-109. **7.** HSCA King vol. VII, pp. 347, 351-355, 360, 368, 369; should be noted that in some of his testimony to the HSCA, Ray's brother disavowed certain of the comments he had made earlier to the journalist. **8.** HSCA King vol. VII, pp. 347, 351-355, 360, 368, 369, 76. **9.** HSCA King vol. III, p. 16. **10.** Dan E. Moldea, *The Hoffa Wars: Teamsters, Rebels, Politicians, and the Mob* (New York: SPI, 1993), pp. 64, 87, 110, 186, 187; Ed Reid, *The Grim Reapers* (New York: Bantam, 1970), 291; HSCA vol. X, pp. 199-205; Goldfarb, *Perfect Villains and Imperfect Heroes* (New York: Random House, 1995), pp. 139-142; Douglas Valentine, *The Strength of the Wolf: The Secret History of America's War a Drugs* (London, New York: Verso, 2004), many passages. **11.** HSCA King vol. III, p183; Jean-Pierre Charbonneau, *The Canadian Connection* (Ottawa: Optimum, 1976), pp. 202, 203. **12.** Ibid, pp. 246-249. **13.** id, pp. 251-253. **14.** Philip H. Melanson, *The Murkin Conspiracy* (New York: Praeger, 1989), pp. 6-16, 52, many others. **15.** Jean-Pierre Charbonneau, *The Canadian Connection* (Ottawa: Optimum, 1976), pp. 04, 451. **16.** FBI Martin Luther King, Jr. Main File 100-106670, Section 103, p. 86. **17.** Ibid, Section 103. **18.** id; HSCA vol. VII, pp. 347-376. **19.** William Bradford Huie, *He Slew the Dreamer* (New York: Delacorte Press, 1970), pp. 37, 38. **20.** Philip H. Melanson, *The Murkin Conspiracy* (New York: Praeger, 1989), p. 125. . William Bradford Huie, *He Slew the Dreamer* (New York: Delacorte Press, 1970), p. 36; Jean-Pierre Charbonneau, *The Canadian Connection* (Ottawa: Optimum, 1976), pp. 199-247. **22.** HSCA vol. VII, pp.

347-376; Gerald Posner, *Killing the Dream* (New York: Random House, 1998), pp. 166, 167. **23.** HSCA vol III, pp. 174-183; HSCA vol. VII, pp. 347-376. **24.** FBI Martin Luther King, Jr. Main File 100-106670, Section 103; HSCA vol. VII, pp. 347-376. **25.** William Bradford Huie, *He Slew the Dreamer* (New York: Delacort Press, 1970) cited by Gerald Posner, *Killing the Dream* (New York: Random House, 1998), pp. 163, 164. **26** Gerald Posner, *Killing the Dream* (New York: Random House, 1998), pp. 161-166; HSCA King vol. III, p 180. **27.** Ibid HSCA, pp. 177-183. **28.** HSCA King vol. III, p182. **29.** Jean-Pierre Charbonneau, *The Canadia Connection* (Ottawa: Optimum, 1976), pp. 202, 203. **30.** Ibid, p. 252. **31.** Ibid. **32.** HSCA King vol. III, p 183. **33.** William Bradford Huie, *He Slew the Dreamer* (New York: Delacorte Press, 1970), p. 51. **34.** HSCA King vol. III, p. 183; Jean-Pierre Charbonneau, *The Canadian Connection* (Ottawa: Optimum, 1976), pp 202, 203. **35.** HSCA vol. VII, pp. 347-376. **36.** Many passages in the following: Staff and editors of *Newsday The Heroin Trail* (New York: New American Library, 1974); Douglas Valentine, *The Strength of the Wolf: Th Secret History of America's War on Drugs* (London, New York: Verso, 2004); John H. Davis, *Mafia Kingfis* (New York: Signet, 1989).

CHAPTER THIRTY-NINE

1. Evan Thomas, *Robert Kennedy: His Life* (New York: Simon & Schuster, 2000), pp. 348, 349. **2.** Arthu Schlesinger, Jr., *Robert Kennedy and His Times* (New York: Ballantine, 1979), pp. 852, 853. **3.** Clifton Danie *Chronicle of America* (Liberty, MO: JL International Publishing, 1993), p. 815. **4.** Ibid. **5.** Taylor Branch, *A Canaan's Edge: America in the King Years 1965-68* (New York: Simon & Schuster, 2006), p. 622. **6.** Meliss Ray Greene, *The Temple Bombing* (New York: Addison-Wesley, 1996), pp. 152-155. **7.** Ibid. **8.** J. Anthon Lukas, *Nightmare: The Underside of the Nixon Years* (New York: Bantam Books, 1977), pp. 2, 3, 199-20. **9.** This is not to say that many of those political figures weren't also racists, simply that they had strong financial and political incentive to stir racial hatred. *George Wallace: Settin' the Woods on Fire o The American Experience,* PBS, 2000. **10.** Evan Thomas, *Robert Kennedy: His Life* (New York: Simon & Schuster, 2000), pp. 375, 376. **11.** FBI memo by Don Adams, 12-1-63; Peter Dale Scott, Paul L. Hoch, an Russell Stetler, eds., *The Assassinations: Dallas and Beyond: A Guide to Cover-Ups and Investigations* (Nev York: Vintage, 1976), p.133. **12.** "The FBI, COINTELPRO-White Hate and the Decline of Ku Klux Kla Organizations in Mississippi, 1964-1971," *Mississippi Historical Review.* **13.** Ibid. **14.** Patsy Sims, *The Kla* (Lexington, KY: University Press of Kentucky, 1996); Miami Police Intelligence interview with Willia Somersett, transcribed 11-26-63 and additional Miami police files; Dan Christensen, "JFK, King: Th Dade County links," *Miami* magazine, 12-76. **15.** Dick Russell, *The Man Who Knew Too Much* (New Yor Carroll & Graf/R. Gallen, 1992), pp. 547, 548; Michael L. Kurtz, *The JFK Assassination Debates* (Lawrenc KS: University Press of Kansas, 2006), pp. 209-215, 218, 219, **16.** Kevin M. Kruse, *White Flight: Atlan and the Making of Modern Conservatism* (Princeton, NJ: Princeton University Press, 2005), p. 14; "The FB COINTELPRO-White Hate and the Decline of Ku Klux Klan Organizations in Mississippi, 1964-1971, *Mississippi Historical Review.* **17.** "Wife of Negro Minister Shot to death in Atlanta," *The New York Time* 1-30-67. **18.** That race was not as cut-and-dried as it seems. Though beaten in the general election by moderate Republican who didn't quite get the required majority of the votes, Maddox had been installe in office by the conservative Georgia legislature. **19.** Kevin M. Kruse, *White Flight: Atlanta and the Ma ing of Modern Conservatism* (Princeton, NJ: Princeton University Press, 2005), many passages. **20.** Whi confirmation of that claim remains elusive, Eugene Talmadge's use of the Klan to intimidate black vote and incite violence are well documented in Stetson Kennedy's, *The Klan Unmasked* (Gainesville, FL: Un versity Press of Florida, 1990). **21.** John Barnard, *American Vanguard: The United Auto Workers during th Reuther Years, 1935–1970* (Wayne State University Press, 2005). **22.** All information about Spake relatin to Milteer and King's assassination comes from confidential interviews conducted from early 1976 (whe author Lamar Waldron was briefly employed at the Lakewood General Motors Auto Plant) to 2007. F general background on Spake, see this account by former Atlanta newspaper editor Doug Monroe: "A old friend passes on without the balm of religion," *Creative Loafing,* 1-11-06. **23.** Kevin M. Kruse, *Whi Flight: Atlanta and the Making of Modern Conservatism* (Princeton, NJ: Princeton University Press, 2005 p. 221. **24.** Confidential interviews 1976-2007. **25.** Ibid; Dan Christensen, "JFK, King: The Dade Count links," *Miami* magazine, 12-76.

CHAPTER FORTY

1. William Bradford Huie, *He Slew the Dreamer* (New York: Delacorte Press, 1970), p. 14. **2.** *Martin Luth King / The FBI File;* Micheal Friedley and David Gallen, p. 22, cited by Larry Hancock and Stuart Wexl *Seeking Armageddon: Religious Terrorism in the 1960s and the effort to kill Martin Luther King,* (advance man script, 2008). **3.** HSCA King vol. VII, p. 297. **4.** "The FBI, COINTELPRO-White Hate and the Decline Ku Klux Klan Organizations in Mississippi, 1964-1971," *Mississippi Historical Review.* **5.** HSCA King vc VII, pp. 251, 270-292; the individual was acting on his own behalf, not that of the business organizatio

6. HSCA King vol. VII, pp. 250-251, 297, 302. **7.** Ibid, p249; US House of Representatives, *The Final Assas-inations Report of the Select Committee on Assassinations* (New York: Bantam Books, 1979), p. 474. **8.** HSCA King vol. VII, pp. 249-251. **9.** US House of Representatives, *The Final Assassinations Report of the Select Committee on Assassinations* (New York: Bantam Books, 1979), pp. 472, 480; Gerald Posner, *Killing the Dream* (New York: Random House, 1998), p. 139; Philip H. Melanson, *The Murkin Conspiracy* (New York: Praeger, 1989), p. 15; HSCA King vol. VII, p. 293. **10.** HSCA King vol. VII, pp. 250, 295. **11.** Ibid, p. 250-251; US House of Representatives, *The Final Assassinations Report of the Select Committee on Assassinations* (New York: Bantam Books, 1979), p. 475. **12.** Ibid. **13.** Ibid. **14.** HSCA King vol. VII, pp. 249, 250; US House of Representatives, *The Final Assassinations Report of the Select Committee on Assassinations* (New York: Bantam Books, 1979), pp. 472, 475. **15.** FBI St. Louis SAC memo to J. Edgar Hoover, 8-12-68; Memphis FBI memo, 8-27-68; FBI Director memo to SAC Memphis, 8-21-68. **16.** Ibid. **17.** Ibid. **18.** Ibid. **19.** Ibid. **20.** Ibid. **21.** Ibid. **22.** Ibid. **23.** Ibid. **24.** Ibid. **25.** Ibid; regarding Atlanta nightclub owner linked to Marcello, see Atlanta Field Office Files 11-63 and 12-63. **26.** Philip H. Melanson, *The Murkin Conspiracy* (New York: Praeger, 1989), p. 165; FBI St. Louis SAC memo to J. Edgar Hoover, 8-12-68; Memphis FBI memo, 8-27-68; FBI Director memo to SAC Memphis, 8-21-68. **27.** Jack Nelson, *Terror in the Night* (New York: Simon & Schuster, 1993), p. 64; Taylor Branch, *At Canaan's Edge: America in the King Years 1965-68* (New York: Simon & Schuster, 2006), p. 647. **28.** Ibid Nelson, many passages. **29.** Larry Hancock and Stuart Wexler, *Seeking Armageddon: Religious Terrorism in the 1960s and the effort to kill Martin Luther King,* (Advance manuscript, 2008) cites *Martin Luther King / The FBI File*; Micheal Friedley and David Gallen, pp.512-514; phone interview with Larry Hancock, 5-22-08. **30.** NARA U.S. Secret Service 180-10091-10217, cited by John McAdams. **31.** Eileen Sullivan, "New Material filed in on-going lawsuit alleging racism in the Secret Service," Associated Press, 5-9-08; Rebecca Carr, "Noose allegedly found at Secret Service Training Center," Cox Newspapers, 5-28-08. **32.** HSCA vol. VI, pp. 101-127. **33.** Ibid. **34.** Miami Police Intelligence interview with William Somersett, transcribed on 11-26-63 and additional Miami Police files; phone interview with confidential high Florida law-enforcement source 12-10-96. **35.** Kevin M. Kruse, *White Flight: Atlanta and the Making of Modern Conservatism* (Princeton, NJ: Princeton University Press, 2005), many passages. **36.** HSCA Report, pp. 394-395. **37.** Ibid. **38.** Ibid; *Washington Star,* 7-31-78. **39.** Michael L. Kurtz, *The JFK Assassination Debates* (Lawrence, KS: University Press of Kansas, 2006), pp. 218, 219.

CHAPTER FORTY-ONE

1. Justice Department memo 9-17-68, cited in 11-5-68 Memphis FBI memo. **2.** Ibid; FBI 124-10301-10270; the October 1967 FBI file refers to him only as "Frank Caracci," but by 1-24-69, the FBI is using his full name "Frank Joseph Caracci." **3.** David E. Scheim, *The Mafia Killed President Kennedy* (New York: SPI Books, 1992), pp. 123, 278, 284, 286. **4.** Justice Department memo 9-17-68, cited in 11-5-68 Memphis FBI memo. **5.** William F. Pepper, *Orders to Kill* (New York: Carroll & Graf, 1995), pp. 239, 249, 487. **6.** Justice Department memo 9-17-68, cited in 11-5-68 Memphis FBI memo. **7.** Justice Department Investigation of Recent Allegations Regarding the Assassination of Dr. Martin Luther King, Jr., 6-00. **8.** HSCA vol. IX, pp. 70, 71. **9.** HSCA Report, p. 383. **10.** John H. Davis, *Mafia Kingfish* (New York: Signet, 1989), many passages; letter from Informant to Carl Podsiadly, FBI, San Francisco office, 6-88. **11.** Ibid Davis, pp. 375-377; James Dickerson, *Dixie's Dirty Secret* (Armonk, NY: M. E. Sharp, 1998), p. 39. **12.** FBI 124-10200-10264; Justice Department Investigation of Recent Allegations Regarding the Assassination of Dr. Martin Luther King, Jr., 6-00; William F. Pepper, *Act of State* (New York: Verso, 2003), pp. 46, 48-50, 134, 231; John H. Davis, *Mafia Kingfish* (New York: Signet, 1989), pp. 378-380. **13.** James Dickerson, *Dixie's Dirty Secret* (Armonk, NY: M. E. Sharp, 1998), pp. 6, 7, 14, 25. **14.** FBI 124-10200-10264; Justice Department Investigation of Recent Allegations Regarding the Assassination of Dr. Martin Luther King, Jr., 6-00; William F. Pepper, *Act of State* (New York: Verso, 2003), pp. 46, 48-50, 134, 231; John H. Davis, *Mafia Kingfish* (New York: Signet, 1989), pp. 378-380; FBI memo Rosen to DeLoach, 4-22-68 (part of the large file, with no identification number or RIF, titled "Department of Justice, Civil Rights Referrals, Attachment D). **15.** James Dickerson, *Dixie's Dirty Secret* (Armonk, NY: M. E. Sharp, 1998), pp. 16-33, 39, 119-120. **16.** Ibid, pp. 134-137; FBI file #62-08052-12 (Coretta Scott King); Larry Hancock and Stuart Wexler, *Seeking Armageddon: Religious Terrorism in the 1960s and the effort to kill Martin Luther King,* (advance manuscript, 2008). **17.** William Bradford Huie, *He Slew the Dreamer* (New York: Delacorte Press, 1970), p. 203.

CHAPTER FORTY-TWO

1. Ray McGovern, "CIA Officer on the Agency's Days of Shame," *CounterPunch,* 2- 13-03; Alfred W. McCoy, *The Politics of Heroin* (Brooklyn: Lawrence Hill Books, 1991), many passages. **2.** Verne Lyon, "Domestic Surveillance: The History of Operation CHAOS," *Covert Action Information Bulletin,* Summer 1990; Gaeton Fonzi, *The Last Investigation* (New York: Thunder's Mouth, 1994), p. 426. **3.** Tom Tripodi, *Crusade: Undercover Against the Mafia and KGB* (Washington, DC: Brassey's, 1993), pp. 146-148. **4.** Tampa

FBI 6-30-65 memo re: JURE; David Raziq and Mark Greenblatt "Inside the FBI's Secret Files on Corett
Scott King," 8-30-07, KHOU-TV, Houston; FBI file #62-108052-12; Larry Hancock and Stuart Wexler, *Seek
ing Armageddon: Religious Terrorism in the 1960s and the effort to kill Martin Luther King* (advance manuscrip
2008). **5.** Richard Goodwin, *Remembering America: A Voice from the Sixties* (Boston: Little, Brown, 1988), pp
205, 206. **6.** For Che Guevara, see generally: Hugh Thomas, *Cuba: Or, Pursuit of Freedom* (London: Eyr
& Spottiswoode, 191); Daniel James, *Che Guevara: A Biography* (New York: Stein and Day, 1969); Jorg
G. Castaneda, *Companero: The Life and Death of Che Guevara* (New York: Vintage, 1998). **7.** Ibid James, pp
284, 285. **8.** Ibid, p. 301. **9.** Jorge G. Castaneda, *Companero: The Life and Death of Che Guevara*, (New York
Vintage, 1998), p. 386. **10.** Felix Rodriquez and John Weisman, *Shadow Warrior,* (New York: Simon & Schus
ter, 1989), p. 171; this "Eduardo" does not appear to have been E. Howard Hunt. **11.** Jorge G. Castaneda
Companero: The Life and Death of Che Guevara, (New York: Vintage, 1998), pp. 399, 404; Richard Goodwin
Remembering America: A Voice from the Sixties (Boston: Little, Brown, 1988), p. 207. **12.** Felix Rodriquez an
John Weisman, *Shadow Warrior,* (New York: Simon & Schuster, 1989), pp. 165-169. **13.** Ann Louise Bardach
"E. Howard Hunt talks about Guatemala, the Bay of Pigs, and what really happened to Che," Slate.com
10-6-04. **14.** Gaeton Fonzi, *The Last Investigation* (New York: Thunder's Mouth, 1994), pp. 309, 373, 376, 38;
389; Larry Hancock, *Someone Would Have Talked* (Southlake, TX: JFK Lancer, 2006), p. 418; Noel Twyman
Bloody Treason (Rancho Sante Fe, CA: Laurel Publishing, 1997), p. 466. **15.** Jorge G. Castaneda, *Companer
The Life and Death of Che Guevara,* (New York: New York: Vintage, 1998), pp. 387, 404.

CHAPTER FORTY-THREE

1. HSCA King vol. VII, pp. 355, 359. **2.** Ibid, vol. III, pp. 184-187. **3.** Ibid, pp. 189, 190. **4.** HSCA vol. VI
pp. 453-456. **5.** Ibid, p. 453. **6.** Ibid, pp. 347-376. **7.** Ibid, pp. 453-456. **8.** Ibid. **9.** HSCA King vol. III, pp
204, 205. **10.** Richard Helms with William Hood, *A Look Over My Shoulder: A Life in the Central Intelligen
Agency* (New York: Random House, 2003), p. 12. **11.** *Miami Herald*, 9-2-73; 1993.07.02.11:49:06:40080(
12. Peter Dale Scott, *Deep Politics II* (Ipswich, MA: Mary Ferrell Foundation Press, 2003), pp. 117, 118, 13:
13. HSCA vol. III, pp. 191-193. **14.** Ibid; HSCA vol. VII, pp. 347-376. **15.** G. Robert Blakey and Richar
N. Billings, *The Plot to Kill the President* (New York: Times Books, 1981), p. 385. **16.** CIA 104-10133-1007:
17. Ibid; CIA 104-10122-10293; CIA 104-10122-10306. **18.** Evan Thomas, *Robert Kennedy: His Life* (Nev
York: Simon & Schuster, 2000), p. 351; Taylor Branch, *At Canaan's Edge: America in the King Years 196!
68* (New York: Simon & Schuster, 2006), p. 657. **19.** Ibid. **20.** Ibid. **21.** *The New York Times*, 12-6-6'
22. Interviews with confidential Kennedy aide source, 3-17-92. **23.** Bernard Fensterwald interview wit
Somersett, 6-5-68, courtesy Don Adams; *Chicago Daily News* interviews 5-28 and 5-29-68, from the files (
Bud Fensterwald at the Assassination Archives and Research Center in Washington, D.C. **24.** CIA mem
to Director of Security, 12-12-67, #272141. **25.** Martin Luther King, "Beyond the Los Angeles Riots. Ne:
Stop: The North," *Saturday Review*, 11-13-65, cited in David E. Scheim, *The Mafia Killed President Kennea
(New York: SPI Books, 1992), p. 341. **26.** Ibid Scheim, pp. 341, 342, citing Louis Lomax, *To Kill a Black Ma
p. 165. **27.** William F. Pepper, *Act of State* (New York: Verso, 2003), p. 50. **28.** US House of Representative
The Final Assassinations Report of the Select Committee on Assassinations (New York: Bantam Books, 1979
p. 486. **29.** Ibid. **30.** FBI file #44-38861, 5-17-68. **31.** Ibid; see also Gerald Posner, *Killing the Dream* (Nev
York: Random House, 1998), pp. 132, 136. **32.** Jean-Pierre Charbonneau, *The Canadian Connection* (Ottaw
Optimum, 1976), p. 294. **33.** Gerald Posner, *Killing the Dream* (New York: Random House, 1998), p. 13'
34. HSCA vol. VII, p. 355; Martin Luther King traveled to Chicago on two dates (5-19-67 and 6-12-67) whe
James Earl Ray was in the city: HSCA King vol. III, p. 592. **35.** HSCA vol. VII, p. 347-376. **36.** Ibid. **37.** U
House of Representatives, *The Final Assassinations Report of the Select Committee on Assassinations* (Ne'
York: Bantam Books, 1979), p. 486. **38.** William Bradford Huie, *He Slew the Dreamer* (New York: Delacor
Press, 1970), p. 191, though Huie later changed his mind and decided that Ray had acted on his ow;
39. HSCA vol. VII, pp. 347-376. **40.** Justice Department memo 9-17-68, cited in 11-5-68 Memphis FI
memo. **41.** United States Court of Appeals, Fifth Circuit #941 F.2d 280, 8-23-91. **42.** FBI LA 44-1574. **43.** Ibi
44. Ibid. **45.** Ibid. **46.** Ibid. **47.** HSCA VII, pp. 347-369; United States Court of Appeals, Fifth Circuit #94
F.2d 280, 8-23-91. **48.** HSCA King vol. III, pp. 204, 205. **49.** HSCA Report, pp.387-388. **50.** Ibid. **51.** "Doct
Wins Libel Suit over Marcello Book," *New Orleans Times-Picayune*, 2-4-95; 2008 phone interview wit
Lanny R. Zatzkis. **52.** We'll release the references once all the affected parties have passed away. **5**
HSCA Report, p. 387. **54.** HSCA vol. III, p. 205; Ray likely had accepted the contract, but there is anoth
possibility. In noting the earlier contract mentioned in one of the prisons, where substantial funds we:
available for someone willing to track Dr. King without being the trigger man, author Larry Hanco(
speculated that Ray may have originally joined the plot just to provide surveillance on Dr. King. Ray
expensive camera equipment might support that possibility. But we believe, as does Hancock, that Ra
was a knowing part of Dr. King's assassination, and likely fired the fatal shot. **55.** William Bradfor
Huie, *He Slew the Dreamer* (New York: Delacorte Press, 1970), pp. 91-97. **56.** Martin Luther King Justi(

Department Task Force Report, 1977, p. 100. **57.** FBI Megiddo Report; Peter Noyes, *Legacy of Doubt* (New York: Pinnacle Books, 1973), p. 199. **58.** Transcript of Miami Police Intelligence Unit interview with William Somersett 11-26-63; Miami FBI report, "RE: Constitutional American Parties of the United States," 1-1-64. verify sp? **59.** Jack Nelson, *Terror in the Night* (New York: Simon & Schuster, 1993), pp. 139-141. **60.** Ibid Nelson; Jerry Mitchell, "Book probes MLK killing" *Jackson Clarion-Ledger*, 12-30-07. **61.** Ibid Nelson, pp.119, 139-141; Ibid Mitchell. **62.** www.israelect.com/reference/WesleyASwift/sermons/. **63.** FBI Laboratory to FBI Memphis, 4-23-68 report, FBI file #44-38861. **64.** Here are just a few of the many FBI files showing their interest in Rosselli and knowledge that he lived in the apartment building at 1333 South Beverly Glen from 1964 through 1970: August 1964 LA 92-113-C; FBI 124-10215-10222, 12-21-64; February 1966 LA 92-113; 11-27-1970 #92-367. **65.** Martin Luther King Justice Department Task Force Report, 1977; HSCA vol. III, p. 199; Gerald Posner, *Killing the Dream* (New York: Random House, 1998), pp. 297, 209, 210. **66.** FBI Laboratory to FBI Memphis, 4-23-68 report, FBI file #44-38861. **67.** HSCA King vol. VII, p. 453. **68.** Ann Louise Bardach, *Cuba Confidential* (New York: Random House, 2002), p. 183; CIA 104-10068-10010; HSCA 180-10143-10215. **69.** Ibid. **70.** HSCA CIA Posada Summary, p. 2, citing #92192, 4-16-68. **71.** Douglas Valentine, *The Strength of the Wolf: The Secret History of America's War on Drugs* (London, New York: Verso, 2004), pp. 456, 457. **72.** CIA Office of Security, Charles Kane, AD/OS 3-15-68, cited by A. J. Weberman. **73.** CIA 104-10125-10199, 7-15-66. **74.** Final Report of the Select Committee to Study Governmental Operations with respect to Intelligence activities, Book III. **75.** Taylor Branch, *At Canaan's Edge: America in the King Years 1965-68* (New York: Simon & Schuster, 2006), p. 708. **76.** Ibid. **77.** Nick Kotz, *Judgment Days* (New York: Houghton Mifflin, 2005), pp. 383, 386, 387, 388. **78.** Taylor Branch, *At Canaan's Edge: America in the King Years 1965-68* (New York: Simon & Schuster, 2006), pp. 708, 709. **79.** Ibid, pp. 694, 695. **80.** Nick Kotz, *Judgment Days* (New York: Houghton Mifflin, 2005), p. 383. **81.** Taylor Branch, *At Canaan's Edge: America in the King Years 1965-68* (New York: Simon & Schuster, 2006), p. 680; Evan Thomas, *Robert Kennedy: His Life* (New York: Simon & Schuster, 2000), p. 356. **82.** Ibid Branch, pp. 680-682. **83.** Ibid, pp. 676, 680-682. **84.** Evan Thomas, *Robert Kennedy: His Life* (New York: Simon & Schuster, 2000), p. 357; Thurston Clarke, *The Last Campaign: Robert F. Kennedy and 82 Days That Inspired America*, (New York: Henry Holt and Company, 2008). **85.** Clifton Daniel, *Chronicle of America* (Liberty, MO: JL International Publishing, 1993), p. 819; Taylor Branch, *At Canaan's Edge: America in the King Years 1965-68* (New York: Simon & Schuster, 2006), p. 710. **86.** Thurston Clarke, *The Last Campaign: Robert F. Kennedy and 82 Days That Inspired America*, New York: Henry Holt and Company, 2008); Nick Kotz, *Judgment Days* (New York: Houghton Mifflin, 2005), p. 391; Ibid Branch, p. 711. **87.** Ibid Branch, pp. 705, 706. **88.** Ibid, pp. 674, 675. **89.** Ibid, pp. 717, 718. **90.** Evan Thomas, *Robert Kennedy: His Life* (New York: Simon & Schuster, 2000), p. 359; Nick Kotz, *Judgment Days* (New York: Houghton Mifflin, 2005), p. 397. **91.** Ibid. **92.** Thurston Clarke, *The Last Campaign: Robert F. Kennedy and 82 Days That Inspired America*, (New York: Henry Holt and Company, 2008); Evan Thomas, *Robert Kennedy: His Life* (New York: Simon & Schuster, 2000), p. 361. **93.** Taylor Branch, *At Canaan's Edge: America in the King Years 1965-68* (New York: Simon & Schuster, 2006), pp. 713-715; Ibid Thomas, p. 360.

CHAPTER FORTY-FOUR

1. Martin Luther King, "Beyond the Los Angeles Riots. Next Stop: The North," *Saturday Review*, 11-13-65, cited in David E. Scheim, *The Mafia Killed President Kennedy* (New York: SPI Books, 1992), p. 341. **2.** Ibid Scheim, pp. 341, 342, citing Louis Lomax, *To Kill a Black Man*, p. 165. **3.** William F. Pepper, *Act of State* (New York: Verso, 2003), p. 50. **4.** US House of Representatives, *The Final Assassinations Report of the Select Committee on Assassinations* (New York: Bantam Books, 1979), p. 486. **5.** Ibid. **6.** FBI file #44-38861, 17-17-68. **7.** Ibid; see also Gerald Posner, *Killing the Dream* (New York: Random House, 1998), pp. 132, 136. **8.** Jean-Pierre Charbonneau, *The Canadian Connection* (Ottawa: Optimum, 1976), p. 294. **9.** Gerald Posner, *Killing the Dream* (New York: Random House, 1998), p. 139. **10.** HSCA vol. VII, p. 355; Martin Luther King traveled to Chicago on two dates (5-19-67 and 6-12-67) when James Earl Ray was in the city: HSCA King vol. III, p. 592. **11.** HSCA vol. VII, p. 347-376. **12.** Ibid. **13.** US House of Representatives, *The Final Assassinations Report of the Select Committee on Assassinations* (New York: Bantam Books, 1979), p. 486. **14.** William Bradford Huie, *He Slew the Dreamer* (New York: Delacorte Press, 1970), p. 191, though Huie later changed his mind and decided that Ray had acted on his own. **15.** HSCA vol. VII, pp. 347-376. **16.** Justice Department memo 9-17-68, cited in 11-5-68 Memphis FBI memo. **17.** United States Court of Appeals, Fifth Circuit, #941 F.2d 280, 8-23-91. **18.** FBI LA 44-1574. **19.** Ibid. **20.** Ibid. **21.** Ibid. **22.** Ibid. **23.** HSCA VII, pp. 347-369; United States Court of Appeals, Fifth Circuit, #941 F.2d 280, 8-23-91. **24.** HSCA King vol. III, pp. 204, 205. **25.** HSCA Report, pp.387-388. **26.** Ibid. **27.** "Doctor Wins Libel Suit over Marcello Book," *New Orleans Times-Picayune*, 2-4-95; 2008 phone interview with Lanny R. Zatzkis. **28.** We'll release the references once all the affected parties have passed away. **29.** HSCA Report, p. 387. **30.** HSCA vol. III, p. 205; Ray likely had accepted the contract, but there is another possibility. In noting the earlier contract mentioned in one of the prisons, where substantial funds were available for someone willing to track Dr. King without being the trigger man, author Larry Hancock speculated that Ray may have originally joined the plot just to provide surveillance on Dr. King. Ray's expensive camera equipment might support that possibility. But we believe, as does Hancock, that Ray was a knowing part of Dr. King's assassination, and likely fired the fatal shot.

CHAPTER FORTY-FIVE

1. William Bradford Huie, *He Slew the Dreamer* (New York: Delacorte Press, 1970), pp. 91-97. **2.** Martin Luther King Justice Department Task Force Report, 1977, p. 100. **3.** FBI Megiddo Report; Peter Noyes *Legacy of Doubt* (New York: Pinnacle Books, 1973), p. 199. **4.** Transcript of Miami Police Intelligence Unit interview with William Somersett 11-26-63; Miami FBI report, "RE: Constitutional American Parties of the United States," 1-1-64. verify sp? **5.** Jack Nelson, *Terror in the Night* (New York: Simon & Schuster 1993), pp. 139-141. **6.** Ibid Nelson; Jerry Mitchell, "Book probes MLK killing" *Jackson Clarion-Ledger* 12-30-07. **7.** Ibid Nelson, pp.119, 139-141; Ibid Mitchell. **8.** www.israelect.com/reference/WesleyASwift sermons/. **9.** FBI Laboratory to FBI Memphis, 4-23-68 report, FBI file #44-38861. **10.** Here are just a few of the many FBI files showing their interest in Rosselli and knowledge that he lived in the apartment building at 1333 South Beverly Glen from 1964 through 1970: August 1964 LA 92-113-C; FBI 124-10215-1022? 12-21-64; February 1966 LA 92-113; 11-27-1970 #92-367. **11.** Martin Luther King Justice Department Task Force Report, 1977; HSCA vol. III, p. 199; Gerald Posner, *Killing the Dream* (New York: Random House 1998), pp. 297, 209, 210. **12.** FBI Laboratory to FBI Memphis, 4-23-68 report, FBI file #44-38861. **13.** HSCA King vol. VII, p. 453. **14.** Ann Louise Bardach, *Cuba Confidential* (New York: Random House, 2002), p 183; CIA 104-10068-10010; HSCA 180-10143-10215. **15.** Ibid. **16.** HSCA CIA Posada Summary, p. 2, citing #92192, 4-16-68. **17.** Douglas Valentine, *The Strength of the Wolf: The Secret History of America's War on Drug* (London, New York: Verso, 2004), pp. 456, 457. **18.** CIA Office of Security, Charles Kane, AD/OS 3-15-68 cited by A. J. Weberman. **19.** CIA 104-10125-10199, 7-15-66. **20.** Final Report of the Select Committee to Study Governmental Operations with respect to Intelligence activities, Book III. **21.** Taylor Branch, *At Canaan's Edge: America in the King Years 1965-68* (New York: Simon & Schuster, 2006), p. 708. **22.** Ibid **23.** Nick Kotz, *Judgment Days* (New York: Houghton Mifflin, 2005), pp. 383, 386, 387, 388. **24.** Taylor Branch, *At Canaan's Edge: America in the King Years 1965-68* (New York: Simon & Schuster, 2006), pp. 708, 709. **25.** Ibid, pp. 694, 695.

CHAPTER FORTY-SIX

1. Nick Kotz, *Judgment Days* (New York: Houghton Mifflin, 2005), p. 383. **2.** Taylor Branch, *At Canaan's Edge: America in the King Years 1965-68* (New York: Simon & Schuster, 2006), p. 680; Evan Thomas, *Robert Kennedy: His Life* (New York: Simon & Schuster, 2000), p. 356. **3.** Ibid Branch, pp. 680-682. **4.** Ibid, pp. 680-682. **5.** Evan Thomas, *Robert Kennedy: His Life* (New York: Simon & Schuster, 2000), p. 357; Thurston Clarke, *The Last Campaign: Robert F. Kennedy and 82 Days That Inspired America*, (New York: Henry Holt and Company, 2008). **6.** Clifton Daniel, *Chronicle of America* (Liberty, MO: JL International Publishing, 1993) p. 819; Taylor Branch, *At Canaan's Edge: America in the King Years 1965-68* (New York: Simon & Schuster 2006), p. 710. **7.** Thurston Clarke, *The Last Campaign: Robert F. Kennedy and 82 Days That Inspired America* (New York: Henry Holt and Company, 2008); Nick Kotz, *Judgment Days* (New York: Houghton Mifflin 2005), p. 391; Ibid Branch, p. 711. **8.** Ibid Branch, pp. 705, 706. **9.** Ibid, pp. 674, 675. **10.** Ibid, pp. 717, 718 **11.** Evan Thomas, *Robert Kennedy: His Life* (New York: Simon & Schuster, 2000), p. 359; Nick Kotz, *Judgment Days* (New York: Houghton Mifflin, 2005), p. 397. **12.** Ibid. **13.** Thurston Clarke, *The Last Campaign: Robert F. Kennedy and 82 Days That Inspired America*, (New York: Henry Holt and Company, 2008); Evan Thomas *Robert Kennedy: His Life* (New York: Simon & Schuster, 2000), p. 361. **14.** Taylor Branch, *At Canaan's Edge: America in the King Years 1965-68* (New York: Simon & Schuster, 2006), pp. 713-715; Ibid Thomas, p. 360

CHAPTER FORTY-SEVEN

1. Gerald Posner, *Killing the Dream* (New York: Random House, 1998), p. 208. **2.** Martin Luther King Justice Department Task Force Report, 1977. **3.** Gerald Posner, *Killing the Dream* (New York: Random House 1998), pp. 212, 213. **4.** HSCA vol. III, pp. 204-208; HSCA Report, p. 354. **5.** William Bradford Huie, *He Slew the Dreamer* (New York: Delacorte Press, 1970), pp. 97, 98, 104. **6.** Taylor Branch, *At Canaan's Edge: America in the King Years 1965-68* (New York: Simon & Schuster, 2006), p. 712. **7.** HSCA vol. VII, pp. 354, 37 **8.** William Bradford Huie, *He Slew the Dreamer* (New York: Delacorte Press, 1970), p. 100. **9.** Taylor Branch *At Canaan's Edge: America in the King Years 1965-68* (New York: Simon & Schuster, 2006), pp. 717, 718; HSCA vol. VII, pp. 347-376. **10.** HSCA vol. VII, pp. 354, 594; HSCA vol. III, p.208; Gerald Posner, *Killing the Dream* (New York: Random House, 1998), p. 217. **11.** HSCA vol. III, pp. 207-209. **12.** Ibid. **13.** Taylor Branch, *At Canaan's Edge: America in the King Years 1965-68* (New York: Simon & Schuster, 2006), pp. 630, 681, 69 698; Woody Baird, "King slaying stained Memphis for years," Associated Press, 4-2-08. **14.** Ibid Branch pp. 718, 719. **15.** HSCA vol. III, pp. 208-209. **16.** Ibid, p. 209; William Bradford Huie, *He Slew the Dreamer* (New York: Delacorte Press, 1970), pp. 101-107. **17.** HSCA King vol. III, p594; Taylor Branch, *At Canaan's Edge: America in the King Years 1965-68* (New York: Simon & Schuster, 2006), pp. 720-722. **18.** HSCA vol. III, pp. 211, 212. **19.** Ibid. **20.** Taylor Branch, *At Canaan's Edge: America in the King Years 1965-68* (New York: Simon & Schuster, 2006), pp. 724, 725. **21.** Ibid, p. 677. **22.** Nick Kotz, *Judgment Days* (New York: Houghton Mifflin, 2005), p. 398; Ibid, p. 729. **23.** Ibid, pp. 727, 736. **24.** Ibid, pp. 727, 728. **25.** Joseph A. Califano, Jr., *The Triumph & Tragedy of Lyndon Johnson: The White House Years* (New York: Simon & Schuster, 1991), p. 268. **26.** Ibid. **27.** "Questions to Kennedy on assassin," Associated Press, 3-26-68.

CHAPTER FORTY-EIGHT

1. HSCA King III, 207-22; William Bradford Huie, *He Slew the Dreamer* (New York: Delacorte Press, 1970). **2.** Martin Luther King Justice Department Task Force Report, 1977, p. 79. **3.** HSCA vol. III, 216-222; Ibid. **4.** HSCA Report, pp. 307, 308. **5.** Ibid. **6.** HSCA vol. III, pp. 222-25; Gerald Posner, *Killing the Dream* (New York: Random House, 1998), p. 223. **7.** Martin Luther King Justice Department Task Force Report, 1977, pp. 79, 80. **8.** Confidential interviews 1976-2007; William Bradford Huie, *He Slew the Dreamer* (New York: Delacorte Press, 1970), p. 110. **9.** Ibid Huie. **10.** HSCA Report, p. 280; Nick Kotz, *Judgment Days* (New York: Houghton Mifflin, 2005), pp. 401-402; Taylor Branch, *At Canaan's Edge: America in the King Years 1965-68* (New York: Simon & Schuster, 2006), pp. 730-733. **11.** Ibid Kotz, pp. 402, 403. **12.** Ibid, pp. 406, 407. **13.** Taylor Branch, *At Canaan's Edge: America in the King Years 1965-68* (New York: Simon & Schuster, 2006), pp. 734, 735. **14.** Ibid; HSCA Report, pp. 409-411. **15.** Ibid. **16.** Ibid Branch, pp. 744, 745. **17.** Ibid, p. 735. **18.** Larry Hancock and Stuart Wexler, *Seeking Armageddon: Religious Terrorism in the 1960s and the effort to kill Martin Luther King,* (advance manuscript, 2008). **19.** CIA 104-10133-10071. **20.** Rosen to DeLoach, 4-22-68 (part of the large file, with no identification number or RIF, titled "Department of Justice, Civil Rights Referrals, Attachment D); William F. Pepper, *Orders to Kill* (New York: Carroll & Graf, 1995), pp. 132, 133. **21.** Memphis FBI memo, 11-5-68, citing 9-17-68 Justice Department memo. **22.** Nick Kotz, *Judgment Days* (New York: Houghton Mifflin, 2005), pp. 409, 411. **23.** Ibid, p. 411. **24.** Taylor Branch, *At Canaan's Edge: America in the King Years 1965-68* (New York: Simon & Schuster, 2006), pp. 750, 751. **25.** Ibid. **26.** Ibid. **27.** HSCA Report, pp. 407-459; Anthony Summers with Robbyn Swan, *The Arrogance of Power: The Secret World of Richard Nixon* (New York: Viking, 2000), pp. 297-308.

CHAPTER FORTY-NINE

1. Martin Luther King Justice Department Task Force Report, 1977, p. 80; HSCA Report, p. 298; HSCA vol. VII, pp. 347-376; Gerald Posner, *Killing the Dream* (New York: Random House, 1998), p. 225. **2.** Nick Kotz, *Judgment Days* (New York: Houghton Mifflin, 2005), p. 411; Taylor Branch, *At Canaan's Edge: America in the King Years 1965-68* (New York: Simon & Schuster, 2006), p. 752. **3.** Ibid. **4.** Ibid Branch, pp. 753-755. **5.** Ibid. **6.** Nick Kotz, *Judgment Days* (New York: Houghton Mifflin, 2005), pp. 412, 413; Taylor Branch, *At Canaan's Edge: America in the King Years 1965-68* (New York: Simon & Schuster, 2006), pp. 756-58. **7.** Ibid Branch. **8.** Ibid. **9.** Ibid. **10.** Memphis FBI memo 11-5-68, citing 9-17-68 Justice Department memo. **11.** Ibid; HSCA Report, p. 388. **12.** Ibid. **13.** HSCA Report, pp. 298, 299; Martin Luther King Justice Department Task Force Report, 1977, p. 80. **14.** Jean-Pierre Charbonneau, *The Canadian Connection* (Ottawa: Optimum, 1976), p. 294; Philip H. Melanson, *The Murkin Conspiracy* (New York: Praeger, 1989), pp. 13, 14; as Melanson points out, the only other connection between the real Galt and the real Willard, who like all four of the Toronto businessmen had no criminal past, was that each had visited Miami the previous year, traveling through Georgia and Tennessee. **15.** Martin Luther King Justice Department Task Force Report, 1977, p. 81; Gerald Posner, *Killing the Dream* (New York: Random House, 1998), diagram "A Graphic Analysis of the Assassination." **16.** "Freedom Village," *Time,* 8-8-60; "Wrongs beyond Rights," *Time,* 1-6-61. **17.** Attachment to 4-22-68 FBI memo DeLoach to Rosen, subject MURKIN. **18.** Ibid. **19.** Ibid. **20.** William F. Pepper, *Orders to Kill* (New York: Carroll & Graf, 1995), pp. 379, 380; William F. Pepper, *Act of State* (New York: Verso, 2003), p. 145. **21.** Ibid. **22.** William F. Pepper, *Act of State* (New York: Verso, 2003), pp. 247, 317; William F. Pepper, *Orders to Kill* (New York: Carroll & Graf, 1995), p. 247. **23.** Memphis FBI memo 11-5-68, citing 9-17-68 Justice Department memo. **24.** Ibid. **25.** Frank Holloman Collection, 1937-1992. Memphis/Shelby County Public Library and Information Center. **26.** Taylor Branch, *At Canaan's Edge: America in the King Years 1965-68* (New York: Simon & Schuster, 2006), p. 759. **27.** Ibid. **28.** HSCA Report, pp. 418-424. **29.** Ibid. **30.** Ibid, pp. 424, 425.

CHAPTER FIFTY

1. Taylor Branch, *At Canaan's Edge: America in the King Years 1965-68* (New York: Simon & Schuster, 2006), p. 764. **2.** Ibid, pp. 765, 766. **3.** Ibid, p. 766. **4.** Taylor Branch, *At Canaan's Edge: America in the King Years 1965-68* (New York: Simon & Schuster, 2006), p. 766; Nick Kotz, *Judgment Days* (New York: Houghton

Mifflin, 2005), p. 414. **5.** Ibid Kotz, p. 415. **6.** Gerald Posner, *Killing the Dream* (New York: Random House, 1998), p. 31, citing MURKIN ME, Sub. D., Section 1, p. 106; HSCA Report, p. 292. **7.** Ibid HSCA Report, pp. 291, 311. **8.** Ibid, pp. 291, 310. **9.** Ibid, p. 312. **10.** Martin Luther King Justice Department Task Force Report, 1977, pp. 81, 82. **11.** Ibid. **12.** Ibid, pp. 50, 51. **13.** William F. Pepper, *Orders to Kill* (New York: Carroll & Graf, 1995), pp. 128, 287. **14.** Gerald Posner, *Killing the Dream* (New York: Random House, 1998) p. 331. **15.** Martin Luther King Justice Department Task Force Report, 1977, p. 51. **16.** HSCA Report, p. 300. **17.** "Black in America: Eyewitness to Murder: The King Assassination," CNN 4-5-08; William F. Pepper, *Orders to Kill* (New York: Carroll & Graf, 1995), pp. 214, 215; Gerald Posner, *Killing the Dream* (New York: Random House, 1998), p. 331. **18.** "Black in America: Eyewitness to Murder: The King Assassination," CNN, 4-5-08. **19.** Martin Luther King Justice Department Task Force Report, 1977, pp. 40-42. **20.** James W. Douglass, "The King Conspiracy Exposed in Memphis," *The Assassinations: Probe magazine on JFK, MLK, RFK , and Malcolm X*, James DiEugenio and Lisa Pease, eds. (Feral House, 2003). **21.** Martin Luther King Justice Department Task Force Report, 1977, pp. 40-42; HSCA Report, p. 426; "Black in America: Eyewitness to Murder: The King Assassination," CNN, 4-5-08. **22.** Ibid Task Force Report, p. 43; William F. Pepper, *Act of State* (New York: Verso, 2003), p. 117. **23.** HSCA Report, p. 285; Mel Ayton, *A Racial Crime* (Las Vegas: ArcheBooks, 2005), p. 45.

CHAPTER FIFTY-ONE

1. HSCA Report, pp. 290, 291, 293. **2.** HSCA Report, pp. 295, 296. Gerald Posner, *Killing the Dream* (New York: Random House, 1998), pp. 271, 272. **3.** Ibid Posner, p. 330. **4.** HSCA Report, p. 312. **5.** HSCA Report, pp. 312-315. **6.** Martin Luther King Justice Department Task Force Report, 1977. **7.** HSCA Report, pp. 285, 292; William F. Pepper, *Orders to Kill* (New York: Carroll & Graf, 1995), pp. 185, 253. **8.** Ibid; William F. Pepper, *Act of State* (New York: Verso, 2003), p. 118. **9.** William F. Pepper, *Orders to Kill* (New York: Carroll & Graf, 1995), pp. 184, 185; Ibid Pepper, *Act of State*, p. 118; Gerald Posner, *Killing the Dream* (New York: Random House, 1998), p. 269. **10.** Ibid, Pepper, *Act of State*, p. 117; Ibid Posner, p. 272. **11.** William F. Pepper, *Orders to Kill* (New York: Carroll & Graf, 1995), pp. 229, 239; Ibid, Pepper, *Act of State*, pp. 315, 316. **12.** Larry Hancock helped to evaluate these alternate scenarios. **13.** HSCA Report, pp. 426, 427. **14.** Ibid. **15.** Clifton Daniel, *Chronicle of America* (Liberty, MO: JL International Publishing, 1993), p. 820. **16.** Evan Thomas, *Robert Kennedy: His Life* (New York: Simon & Schuster, 2000), p. 366. **17.** Ibid, p. 367.

CHAPTER FIFTY-TWO

1. HSCA Report, pp. 300, 301. **2.** Ibid; Gerald Posner, *Killing the Dream* (New York: Random House, 1998) p. 238. **3.** HSCA Report, p. 302. **4.** HSCA vol. VII, p. 300, 356. **5.** HSCA Report, p. 301. **6.** Martin Luther King Justice Department Task Force Report, 1977, pp. 1, 82, 83. **7.** Ibid Task Force Report; Confidential interviews, 1976-2007. **8.** Ibid interviews. **9.** Martin Luther King Justice Department Task Force Report, 1977. **10.** "Atlanta Cabbies Remember Galt," *The New York Times*, 4-17-68; "New Clue Here Hints at King Murder Plot," *Atlanta Journal Constitution*, 4-17-68; "The Face Was Thinner," AP, 4-17-68. **11.** Dan Christensen, "Assassinations: Miami Link, Part II," *Miami Magazine*, 10-76. **12.** Ibid. **13.** HSCA vol. III, p. 243. **14.** Ibid, pp. 347-376. **15.** FBI Laboratory to FBI Memphis, 4-23-68 report, FBI file #44-38861. **16.** HSCA vol. VII, pp. 347-376. **17.** Martin Luther King Justice Department Task Force Report, 1977, pp. 82, 83; HSCA vol. III, p. 245; Gerald Posner, *Killing the Dream* (New York: Random House, 1998), pp. 239, 240. **18.** HSCA vol. III, pp. 246, 247; Ibid Posner, pp. 240, 241.

CHAPTER FIFTY-THREE

1. Nick Kotz, *Judgment Days* (New York: Houghton Mifflin, 2005), p. 419. **2.** Mel Ayton, *A Racial Crime* (Las Vegas: ArcheBooks, 2005), p. 55; William F. Pepper, *Orders to Kill* (New York: Carroll & Graf, 1995) p. 36; Gerald Posner, *Killing the Dream* (New York: Random House, 1998), p. 244. **3.** Ibid; HSCA vol. II, pp. 96-98. **4.** HSCA Report, pp. 445-449. **5.** Taylor Branch, *At Canaan's Edge: America in the King Years 1965-68* (New York: Simon & Schuster, 2006), p. 769. **6.** FBI Murkin Director to SACs, 5-21-68. **7.** FBI Murkin 4-6-68 cited in Mel Ayton, *A Racial Crime* (Las Vegas: ArcheBooks, 2005), p. 185. **8.** FBI Laboratory to FBI Memphis, 4-23-68 report, FBI file #44-38861; William F. Pepper, *Orders to Kill* (New York: Carroll & Graf, 1995) p. 37. **9.** Here are just a few of the many FBI files showing their interest in Rosselli and knowledge that he lived in the apartment building at 1333 South Beverly Glen from 1964 through 1970: 8-64 LA 92-113-C; FBI 124-10215-10222, 12-21-64; 2-66 LA 92-113; 11-27-1970 #92-367. **10.** Charles Rappleye and Ed Becker, *All American Mafioso* (New York: Barricade, 1995), p. 290. **11.** CIA 104-10133-10071. **12.** FBI Murkin Rosen to DeLoach, 4-22-68; William F. Pepper, *Act of State* (New York: Verso, 2003), p. 13. **13.** HSCA Report, p. 660. **14.** FBI 124-10200-10264 4-26-68; FBI Murkin Rosen to DeLoach, 4-22-68 (part of the large file, with no idendification number or RIF, titled "Department of Justice, Civil Rights Referrals, Attachment D

5. Memphis FBI memo 11-5-68, citing 9-17-68 Justice Department memo. **16.** Jack Nelson, *Terror in the Night* (New York: Simon & Schuster, 1993), p. 119; US House of Representatives, *The Final Assassinations Report of the Select Committee on Assassinations* (New York: Bantam Books, 1979), p. 469. **17.** FBI Murkin SAC Atlanta to Director and Memphis, 5-21-68. **18.** HSCA Report, p. 451. **19.** NARA 180-10091-10217. **20.** FBI Miami memo to Director, 8-6-68. **21.** HSCA vol. VI, pp. 91-129.

CHAPTER FIFTY-FOUR

1. Arthur Schlesinger, Jr., *Robert Kennedy and His Times* (New York: Ballantine, 1979), pp. 943, 944. **2.** Evan Thomas, *Robert Kennedy: His Life* (New York: Simon & Schuster, 2000), pp. 356, 368. **3.** Arthur Schlesinger, Jr., *Robert Kennedy and His Times* (New York: Ballantine, 1979), p. 968. **4.** Thurston Clarke, *The Last Campaign: Robert F. Kennedy and 82 Days That Inspired America*, (New York: Henry Holt and Company, 2008). **5.** Interview with Harry Williams, 2-24-92. **6.** Evan Thomas, *Robert Kennedy: His Life* (New York: Simon & Schuster, 2000), p. 384. **7.** William Sullivan with Bill Brown, *The Bureau* (New York: Pinnacle Books, 1982); Thurston Clarke, *The Last Campaign: Robert F. Kennedy and 82 Days That Inspired America*, (New York: Henry Holt and Company, 2008). **8.** LAPD SUS Report, p. 859, FBI report regarding Delano police interview /6/68, FBI interview of Donald Roy Murray 6-7-68. **9.** Ibid. **10.** Thurston Clarke, *The Last Campaign: Robert F. Kennedy and 82 Days That Inspired America*, (New York: Henry Holt and Company, 2008).. **11.** An expanded account of Dorman's article can be found in Michael Dorman, *Pay-Off* (New York: Berkley Medallion, 1973); Gus Russo, *Live by the Sword: The Secret War against Castro and the Death of JFK* (Baltimore: Bancroft Press, 1998), pp. 283, 413-15, 579. **12.** Ibid. **13.** Evan Thomas, *Robert Kennedy: His Life* (New York: Simon & Schuster, 2000), pp. 374, 375. **14.** Ibid, p. 375. **15.** Ibid, pp. 377, 382. **16.** Clifton Daniel, *Chronicle of America* (Liberty, MO: JL International Publishing, 1993), pp. 821, 823. **17.** Evan Thomas, *Robert Kennedy: His Life* (New York: Simon & Schuster, 2000), p. 386. **18.** Ibid, pp. 378-80. **19.** John H. Davis, *Mafia Kingfish: Carlos Marcello and the Assassination of John F. Kennedy* (New York: McGraw-Hill, 1989), p. 322. **20.** Charles Rappleye and Ed Becker, *All American Mafioso* (New York: Barricade, 1995), p. 290; G. Robert Blakey and Richard N. Billings, *The Plot to Kill the President* (New York: Times Books, 1981), p. 385—some sources say the date of the verdict was 5-24. **21.** Evan Thomas, *Robert Kennedy: His Life* (New York: Simon & Schuster, 2000), p. 25; William Turner and Jonn Christian, *The Assassination of Robert F. Kennedy* (New York: Carroll & Graf, 2006), p. 161. **22.** Dan E. Moldea, *The Killing of Robert F. Kennedy* (New York: W. W. Norton & Company, 1995), p. 122; Larry Hancock, *Incomplete Justice*, article series on the Mary Ferrell Foundation website, maryferrell.org. Note that Hancock's article comes with a large number of actual documents from FBI and LAPD files, just some of the thousands of pages of RFK assassination files on the website. **23.** Ibid Hancock; Ibid Moldea, pp. 24, 25. **24.** Ibid. **25.** John H. Davis, *The Kennedys: Dynasty and Disaster* (New York: S.P.I. Books, 1992), pp. 653-55; Ibid Hancock ; Ibid Moldea, p. 122. **26.** Evan Thomas, *Robert Kennedy: His Life* (New York: Simon & Schuster, 2000), p. 386. **27.** Ibid, pp. 24, 25. **28.** Ibid, p. 26.

CHAPTER FIFTY-FIVE

1. Evan Thomas, *Robert Kennedy: His Life* (New York: Simon & Schuster, 2000), p. 387; Dan E. Moldea, *The Killing of Robert F. Kennedy* (New York: W. W. Norton & Company, 1995), p 26. **2.** Ibid Moldea, p. 25, 32. **3.** Ibid, p. 25. **4.** Ibid, pp. 30-33, many others. **5.** Larry Hancock, *Incomplete Justice*, article series Part One, on the Mary Ferrell Foundation website, maryferrell.org. **6.** Dan E. Moldea, *The Killing of Robert F. Kennedy* (New York: W. W. Norton & Company, 1995), pp. 25, 26. **7.** Ibid, pp. 29, 30. **8.** Philip H. Melanson, *The Robert F. Kennedy Assassination* (New York: Shapolsky, 1991), p. 19; Dan E. Moldea, *The Killing of Robert F. Kennedy* (New York: W. W. Norton & Company, 1995), p. 93. **9.** Ibid Moldea, pp. 93, 94. **10.** Philip H. Melanson, *The Robert F. Kennedy Assassination* (New York: Shapolsky, 1991), p. 19; Ibid, many passages. **11.** Ibid Moldea, pp. 46, 47. **12.** "The Other Gunshot Victims," Associated Press at msnbc.com; Lisa Pease, "Sirhan and the RFK Assassination," *Probe Magazine*, March-April and May-June, 1998; Ibid Moldea, p. 43. **13.** Ibid Moldea, pp. 207, 210, 211, 284. **14.** Philip H. Melanson, *The Robert F. Kennedy Assassination* (New York: Shapolsky, 1991), p. 20; Ibid, p. 311, writes that Bobby said, "Is Paul alright?" **15.** Ibid Melanson; Moldea, pp. 36-37. **16.** Ibid Moldea, pp. 46, 47. **17.** Larry Hancock, *Incomplete Justice*, article series on the Mary Ferrell Foundation website, maryferrell.org. **18.** William Turner and Jonn Christian, *The Assassination of Robert F. Kennedy* (New York: Carroll & Graf, 2006), pp. 70-73. **19.** Dan E. Moldea, *The Killing of Robert F. Kennedy* (New York: W. W. Norton & Company, 1995), p. 40; Larry Hancock, *Incomplete Justice*, article series on the Mary Ferrell Foundation website, maryferrell.org. **20.** Ibid Moldea, pp. 47, 48. **21.** Ibid Moldea, p. 59; Larry Hancock, *Incomplete Justice*, article series on the Mary Ferrell Foundation website, maryferrell.org. **22.** Ibid Moldea, p. 75. **23.** Ibid, p. 52; Philip H. Melanson, *The Robert F. Kennedy Assassination* (New York: Shapolsky, 1991), p. 196. **24.** Ibid Moldea. **25.** Evan Thomas, *Robert Kennedy: His Life* (New York: Simon & Schuster, 2000), p. 392; David Talbot, *Brothers: The Hidden History of the Kennedy Years* (New York: Free Press, 2007), p. 312.

CHAPTER FIFTY-SIX

1. Dan E. Moldea, *The Killing of Robert F. Kennedy* (New York: W. W. Norton & Company, 1995), pp. 8? 88. **2.** Ibid, p. 93. **3.** Ibid, pp. 97, 98; also Lisa Pease, "Sirhan and the RFK Assassination," *Probe Magazin* March-April and May-June, 1998. **4.** Fourteen witnesses who gave distance estimates that appear t eliminate Sirhan as the shooter: Aubrey, Burns, Cesar, DiPierro, Hamill, Lubic, Minasian, Patrusky, Pere: Romero, Schulte, Uecker, Urso, and Yaro. **5.** Dan E. Moldea, *The Killing of Robert F. Kennedy* (New Yor) W. W. Norton & Company, 1995), pp. 93, 312, 313. **6.** Lisa Pease, "Sirhan and the RFK Assassination, *Probe Magazine*, March-April and May-June, 1998. **7.** William Turner and Jonn Christian, *The Assassin tion of Robert F. Kennedy* (New York: Carroll & Graf, 2006), p. 178. **8.** Dan E. Moldea, *The Killing of Robe F. Kennedy* (New York: W. W. Norton & Company, 1995), pp. 268, 269, 318. **9.** Ibid, pp. 256, 268, 269, 31: **10.** Larry Hancock, *Incomplete Justice*, article series on the Mary Ferrell Foundation website, maryferrel org. **11.** Ibid. **12.** Philip H. Melanson, *The Robert F. Kennedy Assassination* (New York: Shapolsky, 1991 p. 65; Larry Hancock, *Incomplete Justice*, article series on the Mary Ferrell Foundation website, maryferrel org; Dan E. Moldea, *The Killing of Robert F. Kennedy* (New York: W. W. Norton & Company, 1995), sever. passages. **13.** Ibid Melanson, p. 61-86; Ibid Hancock. **14.** Dan E. Moldea, *The Killing of Robert F. Kennea* (New York: W. W. Norton & Company, 1995), p. 207. **15.** Larry Hancock summary provided to author 11-27-06. **16.** Dan E. Moldea, *The Killing of Robert F. Kennedy* (New York: W. W. Norton & Company, 1995 p. 198, 199. **17.** Ibid, many passages. **18.** Philip H. Melanson, *The Robert F. Kennedy Assassination* (Nev York: Shapolsky, 1991), many passages; Larry Hancock, *Incomplete Justice*, article series on the Mary Ferre Foundation website, maryferrell.org. **19.** Jack Nelson, *Terror in the Night* (New York: Simon & Schuste 1993), photo section, p. 2; Patsy Sims, *The Klan* (Lexington, KY: University Press of Kentucky, 1996 p. 236. **20.** Mel Ayton, "Review of Shane O'Sullivan's *Who Killed Bobby*" and the DVD: *RFK Must Die*, Hi tory News Network, 6-15-08; Mel Ayton, "RFK Assassination: New Revelations from the FBI's 'Kensal Files," History News Network, 5-26-08; Mel Ayton, "The Robert Kennedy Assassination: Unraveling th Conspiracy Theories," crimemagazine.com, 5-8-05 and 9-6-05. **21.** William Turner and Jonn Christia *The Assassination of Robert F. Kennedy* (New York: Carroll & Graf, 2006), p. 261; Ibid **22.** See many pa sages in Philip H. Melanson, *The Robert F. Kennedy Assassination* (New York: Shapolsky, 1991) and Wi liam Turner and Jonn Christian, *The Assassination of Robert F. Kennedy* (New York: Carroll & Graf, 2006 **23.** Larry Hancock, *Incomplete Justice*, article series on the Mary Ferrell Foundation website, maryferre. org. **24.** Dan E. Moldea, *The Killing of Robert F. Kennedy* (New York: W. W. Norton & Company, 1995), p. 11 **25.** William Turner and Jonn Christian, *The Assassination of Robert F. Kennedy* (New York: Carroll & Gra 2006), p. 265. **26.** LAPD SUS Report, available at maryferrell.org. **27.** Ibid. **28.** Dan E. Moldea, *The Killir of Robert F. Kennedy* (New York: W. W. Norton & Company, 1995), p. 116; regarding the drug contac of some of Sirhan's brothers, one of several examples is LAPD SUS Report, pp. 1019. **29.** HSCA vol. I pp. 98-100; Philip H. Melanson, *The Murkin Conspiracy* (New York: Praeger, 1989), p. 167; Gerald Posne *Killing the Dream* (New York: Random House, 1998), pp. 248, 249. **30.** HSCA vol. VII, p. 347-76. **31.** Mart Luther King Justice Department Task Force Report, 1977, pp. 60, 61. **32.** HSCA vol. III, pp. 98-100; Phil H. Melanson, *The Murkin Conspiracy* (New York: Praeger, 1989), p. 167; Gerald Posner, *Killing the Drea* (New York: Random House, 1998), pp. 248, 249. **33.** Ibid HSCA; Ibid Melanson; Martin Luther King Justi Department Task Force Report, 1977, pp. 60-62; Ibid Posner, pp. 248-50. **34.** Ibid Justice Department; Ib Posner, pp. 249, 250; Mel Ayton, *A Racial Crime* (Las Vegas: ArcheBooks, 2005), p. 5. **35.** Memphis FBI mem 11-5-68, citing 9-17-68 Justice Department memo. **36.** Ibid. **37.** William Turner and Jonn Christian, *T. Assassination of Robert F. Kennedy* (New York: Carroll & Graf, 2006), pp. xxxii, xxxiii. **38.** Arthur Schlesinge Jr., *Robert Kennedy and His Times* (New York: Ballantine, 1979), pp. 982-84; Evan Thomas, *Robert Kenned His Life* (New York: Simon & Schuster, 2000), pp. 392-94. **39.** Ibid; Nick Kotz, *Judgment Days* (New Yor Houghton Mifflin, 2005), p. 422. **40.** William Sullivan with Bill Brown, *The Bureau* (New York: Pinnac Books, 1982). **41.** Evan Thomas, *Robert Kennedy: His Life* (New York: Simon & Schuster, 2000), pp. 392-9 Nick Kotz, *Judgment Days* (New York: Houghton Mifflin, 2005), p. 422. **42.** Dan E. Moldea, *The Killing Robert F. Kennedy* (New York: W. W. Norton & Company, 1995), p. 99.

CHAPTER FIFTY-SEVEN

1. Thousands of searchable government files about Bobby's assassination, as well as those of JFK and [King, are available through the Mary Ferrell Foundation at maryferrell.org. **2.** Dan E. Moldea, *The Killi of Robert F. Kennedy* (New York: W. W. Norton & Company, 1995), pp. 26, 27; see also many passages Philip H. Melanson, *The Robert F. Kennedy Assassination* (New York: Shapolsky, 1991) and William Turn and Jonn Christian, *The Assassination of Robert F. Kennedy* (New York: Carroll & Graf, 2006). **3.** Ibid Molde pp. 103-106. **4.** Philip H. Melanson, *The Robert F. Kennedy Assassination* (New York: Shapolsky, 1991), p. 29 citing LAPD chronology. **5.** William Turner and Jonn Christian, *The Assassination of Robert F. Kennedy* (Ne York: Carroll & Graf, 2006), p. 223; also note that the newest type of home movie camera at the tim

Super-8, was far smaller (and thus easier to conceal) than the large and bulky 16-mm camera used to film Sirhan, with film and processing for Super-8 being a fraction of the cost of 16-mm. **6.** William Turner and Jonn Christian, *The Assassination of Robert F. Kennedy* (New York: Carroll & Graf, 2006), p 223. **7.** Ibid, p. 224; also, note that Sirhan apparently didn't disappear completely, but enough to make his mother worry. **8.** G. Robert Blakey and Richard N. Billings, *Fatal Hour* (New York: Berkley Books, 1992), p. 429; Dan E. Moldea, *The Killing of Robert F. Kennedy* (New York: W. W. Norton & Company, 1995), pp. 104, 105, 294, 297. **9.** David E. Scheim, *The Mafia Killed President Kennedy* (New York: SPI Books, 1992), p. 349. **10.** Dan E. Moldea, *The Killing of Robert F. Kennedy* (New York: W. W. Norton & Company, 1995), p. 105. **11.** David E. Scheim, *The Mafia Killed President Kennedy* (New York: SPI Books, 1992), pp. 349, 350; Philip H. Melanson, *The Robert F. Kennedy Assassination* (New York: Shapolsky, 1991), p. 160; Ibid, p. 108. **12.** Ibid Moldea, pp. 80. 293. 294. **13.** FBI interview with D. Herrick, 6-21-68. **14.** FBI interview with B. J. Herrick, 6-20-68. **15.** Dan E. Moldea, *The Killing of Robert F. Kennedy* (New York: W. W. Norton & Company, 1995), p. 107, citing LAPD files. **16.** Ibid Moldea, p. 105. **17.** The case involved Johnny Rosselli's Chicago Mafia associates, and David E. Scheim writes that a young man named Giuseppe Zangara had bet heavily on horse and dog racing, and had brief contact with a drug operation. At the same time, Chicago mayor Anton Cermak was trying to run Capone's mob out of Chicago. Zangara ran "into trouble with the Syndicate and [had] been given a choice: shoot Cermak or be killed or tortured himself." The Mafia plot was confirmed by the "president of the Chicago Crime Commission," a prominent Chicago judge who was friends with the mayor, and was even confirmed by the mayor himself, before he died after being shot. Chicago mobster Roger Touhy explained how the Cermak hit was done, to noted sociologist Saul D. Alinsky, a member of the prison board: In 1933, Mayor Cermak was in Miami, in a car with President-elect Franklin Roosevelt. "In the crowd near Zangara was another armed man—a Capone killer. In the flurry of shots six people were hit—but the bullet that struck Cermak" didn't come from Zangara's pistol, but "was fired by the unknown Capone man who took advantage of the confusion to accomplish his mission." **18.** Philip H. Melanson, *The Robert F. Kennedy Assassination* (New York: Shapolsky, 1991), photo-document pages. **19.** LAPD interview with subject 6-25-68, cited in Larry Hancock, *Incomplete Justice*, article series on the Mary Ferrell Foundation website, maryferrell.org.; "Brother of Sirhan fights deportation," *Los Angeles Herald-Examiner,* 6-20-68 (Night Final edition), p. A-3; we don't mean to imply that this brother had anything to do with a contract to kill Bobby. **20.** Interview by Sgt. Bowles, 6-8-68, File # I-93; LAPD SUS, p. 1019. **21.** LAPD interview 7-25-68, I-1831. **22.** LAPD SUS Report, p. 343. **23.** Ramparts Detective Division Raaegep interview, 6-6-68. **24.** Sirhan notebooks, California State Archives; Larry Hancock, *Incomplete Justice*, article series on the Mary Ferrell Foundation website, maryferrell.org, citing Robert Blair Kaiser, *RFK Must Die* (Nw York: Grove Press, 1970), p. 471. **25.** "The Other Gunshot Victims," Associated Press, at msnbc.com; Lisa Pease, "Sirhan and the RFK Assassination," *Probe Magazine*, March-April and May-June, 1998; Dan E. Moldea, *The Killing of Robert F. Kennedy* (New York: W. W. Norton & Company, 1995) **26.** Larry Hancock, *Incomplete Justice*, article series on the Mary Ferrell Foundation website, maryferrell.org; Ibid Moldea, p. 122. **27.** Sirhan notebooks, California State Archives; Philip H. Melanson, *The Robert F. Kennedy Assassination* (New York: Shapolsky, 1991), pp. 152, 156, 157: Melanson notes that the only thing even close is Sirhan's repeated writing of the name "Nassar," the Egyptian leader admired by many young Arabs.

CHAPTER FIFTY-EIGHT

1. Larry Hancock, *Incomplete Justice*, article series on the Mary Ferrell Foundation website, maryferrell. org. **2.** Ibid. **3.** Ibid: SUS indicates officer "said he did not feel the man he observed was Sirhan"; Philip H. Melanson, *The Robert F. Kennedy Assassination* (New York: Shapolsky, 1991), pp. 218-218. **4.** Dan E. Moldea, *The Killing of Robert F. Kennedy* (New York: W. W. Norton & Company, 1995), p. 107, 109. **5.** Larry Hancock, *Incomplete Justice*, article series on the Mary Ferrell Foundation website, maryferrell.org; William Turner and Jonn Christian, *The Assassination of Robert F. Kennedy* (New York: Carroll & Graf, 2006), p. 222. **6.** FBI Arnot interview 6-18-68. **7.** Dan E. Moldea, *The Killing of Robert F. Kennedy* (New York: W. W. Norton & Company, 1995), p. 109. **8.** William Turner and Jonn Christian, *The Assassination of Robert F. Kennedy* (New York: Carroll & Graf, 2006), p. 222. **9.** Dan E. Moldea, *The Killing of Robert F. Kennedy* (New York: W. W. Norton & Company, 1995), p. 109; Larry Hancock, *Incomplete Justice*, article series on the Mary Ferrell Foundation website, maryferrell.org. **10.** Philip H. Melanson, *The Robert F. Kennedy Assassination* (New York: Shapolsky, 1991), pp. 278, 279. **11.** Ibid, pp. 273-285: While some have tried to place Khan at he center of a large Iranian conspiracy to kill Bobby, no evidence has surfaced to support that. According o one account, Khan had met with Bobby's close aides Walter Sheridan and Pierre Salinger on June 3 at he Ambassador Hotel and, as an opponent of the repressive Shah, Khan had every reason to want to see omeone like Bobby—with his concern for Human Rights—elected president. Lisa Pease, "Sirhan and the RFK Assassination," *Probe Magazine*, March-April and May-June, 1998. **12.** Ibid Melanson, 273-85, 291. **13.** Dan E. Moldea, *The Killing of Robert F. Kennedy* (New York: W. W. Norton & Company, 1995), p. 26;

Ibid Melanson, p. 160. **14.** William Turner and Jonn Christian, *The Assassination of Robert F. Kennedy* (New York: Carroll & Graf, 2006), pp. 118, 119. **15.** Larry Hancock, *Incomplete Justice*, article series on the Mary Ferrell Foundation website, maryferrell.org; Ibid, many passages. **16.** Ibid Turner and Christian, pp 224, 225. **17.** Ibid, pp. 155, 156, 292-96. **18.** Ibid. **19.** Ibid. **20.** Ibid, p. 156. **21.** Lisa Pease, "Sirhan and the RFK Assassination," *Probe Magazine*, March-April and May-June, 1998; David E. Scheim, *The Mafia Killed President Kennedy* (New York: SPI Books, 1992), p. 359; Charles Rappleye and Ed Becker, *All American Mafioso* (New York: Barricade, 1995), p. 289; Ovid Demaris, *The Last Mafioso* (New York: Bantam, 1981) pp. 251-54. **22.** Dan E. Moldea, *The Killing of Robert F. Kennedy* (New York: W. W. Norton & Company 1995), p. 301. **23.** David E. Scheim, *The Mafia Killed President Kennedy* (New York: SPI Books, 1992), p. 359 Charles Rappleye and Ed Becker, *All American Mafioso* (New York: Barricade, 1995), p. 289; Ovid Demaris *The Last Mafioso* (New York: Bantam, 1981), pp. 251-54. **24.** Robert Windler, "Lawyer, 73, Agrees to Defend Sirhan Without Fee," *The New York Times*, 6-20-68. **25.** Dan E. Moldea, *The Killing of Robert F. Kennedy* (New York: W. W. Norton & Company, 1995), p. 116. **26.** Evan Thomas, *The Man To See* (New York: Simon & Schuster, 1991), pp. 197-99; Lisa Pease, "Sirhan and the RFK Assassination," *Probe Magazine*, March-April and May-June, 1998. **27.** Robert Windler, "Lawyer, 73, Agrees to Defend Sirhan Without Fee," *The New York Times*, 6-20-68. **28.** Ibid. **29.** Ibid; Lisa Pease, "Sirhan and the RFK Assassination," *Probe Magazine* March-April and May-June, 1998. **30.** David E. Scheim, *Contract on America: The Mafia Murder of Presiden John F. Kennedy* (New York: Zebra, 1989), p. 331. **31.** Dan E. Moldea, *The Killing of Robert F. Kennedy* (New York: W. W. Norton & Company, 1995), p. 134. **32.** Ibid, p. 119; William Turner and Jonn Christian, *The Assassination of Robert F. Kennedy* (New York: Carroll & Graf, 2006), p. 105. **33.** Ibid Turner and Christian p. 159. **34.** Philip H. Melanson, *The Robert F. Kennedy Assassination* (New York: Shapolsky, 1991), pp. 24 61-121, 62-86, many others; Ibid Turner and Christian, pp. 104, 105. **35.** Lisa Pease, "Sirhan and the RFK Assassination," *Probe Magazine*, March-April and May-June, 1998; Ibid Melanson, p. 26. **36.** RFK LAPD Microfilm, vol. 47, Pasadena Police Department Report on Saidallah Sirhan, 7-3-68. **37.** Ibid. **38.** Ibid **39.** Ibid. **40.** Ibid. **41.** Frank Ragano and Selwyn Raab, *Mob Lawyer* (New York: Scribners, 1994), p. 198 **42.** *Los Angeles Herald-Examiner*, 6-20-68, p. A-3. **43.** LAPD interview with Russell Parsons, 9-25-68 **44.** Ibid. **45.** Authors' interview with Lawrence Teeter, JFK Lancer Conference, 2006. **46.** Dan E. Moldea *The Killing of Robert F. Kennedy* (New York: W. W. Norton & Company, 1995), p. 121; Lisa Pease, "Sirhan and the RFK Assassination," *Probe Magazine*, March-April and May-June, 1998.

CHAPTER FIFTY-NINE

1. John H. Davis, *Mafia Kingfish* (New York: Signet, 1989), pp. 485, 504-505. **2.** Ibid. **3.** Dan E. Moldea *The Killing of Robert F. Kennedy* (New York: W. W. Norton & Company, 1995), p. 117. **4.** FBI Los Angeles Field File 58-156, pp. 331-337 (RFK Assassination: L.A.F.O. #56-156: Sub File X-5, vol. 18); FBI Airtel from New York to Director, 10-15-68 **5.** LAPD SUS Report, p. 859, 6-6-68 FBI report regarding Delano police interview, 6-7-68 FBI interview of Donald Roy Murray. In case Murray had a son or other relative with a similar name, we want to make it clear that all of our references are to the Roy Donald Murray, born on 2-18-21 and who died in 3-73. **6.** Ibid FBI interview. **7.** Ibid; According to *American Heritage*, in the mid-1950s, Johnny Rosselli had a lucrative sideline bilking big spenders at Las Vegas casinos—so it's not hard to imagine the cash-strapped Rosselli (or his associate) trying to make some extra money after hearing Murray denounce Bobby in Las Vegas. **8.** David E. Scheim, *The Mafia Killed President Kennedy* (New York: SPI Books, 1992), pp. 349, 350; Philip H. Melanson, *The Robert F. Kennedy Assassination* (New York: Shapolsky, 1991), p. 160; Dan E. Moldea, *The Killing of Robert F. Kennedy* (New York: W. W. Norton & Company, 1995), p. 108; we don't mean to imply that any of Sirhan's brothers were involved with in the contract to kill Bobby. **9.** John H. Davis, *Mafia Kingfish: Carlos Marcello and the Assassination of John F Kennedy* (New York: McGraw-Hill, 1989), pp. 131-133. **10.** CIA 104-10133-10071. **11.** CIA 104-10133-10071 **12.** Charles Rappleye and Ed Becker, *All American Mafioso* (New York: Barricade, 1995), p. 289. **13.** Ibid p. 288, 289. **14.** David E. Scheim, *The Mafia Killed President Kennedy* (New York: SPI Books, 1992), p. 359 Charles Rappleye and Ed Becker, *All American Mafioso* (New York: Barricade, 1995), p. 289; Ovid Demaris *The Last Mafioso* (New York: Bantam, 1981), pp. 251-54. **15.** Ibid Rappleye and Becker. **16.** For Sirhan, see William Turner and Jonn Christian, *The Assassination of Robert F. Kennedy* (New York: Carroll & Graf 2006), p. 224; see also many passages in Philip H. Melanson, *The Robert F. Kennedy Assassination* (New York: Shapolsky, 1991) and Dan E. Moldea, *The Killing of Robert F. Kennedy* (New York: W. W. Norton & Company, 1995); for James Earl Ray, see HSCA vol. III, pp. 196-206 and William Bradford Huie, *He Slew the Dreamer* (New York: Delacorte Press, 1970), many passages. **17.** Noel Twyman, *Bloody Treason* (Rancho Sante Fe, CA: Laurel Publishing, 1997), p. 471. **18.** CIA 104-10308-10274, 2003 CIA release; the spelling of "Montecantini" is also used. **19.** CIA 10308-10272, 2003 CIA release; CIA 104-10308-10283; 104-10308 10274. **20.** Ibid. **21.** Ibid. **22.** William Turner and Jonn Christian, *The Assassination of Robert F. Kennedy* (New York: Carroll & Graf, 2006), pp. xxvi, xxvii, 275, citing *Los Angeles Herald-Examiner* 1-12-76. **23.** Ibid, pp. 46

54. **24.** Ibid, pp. 65-67. **25.** Ibid, pp. 66-67. **26.** Lisa Pease, "Sirhan and the RFK Assassination," *Probe Magazine*, March-April and May-June, 1998. **27.** LAPD response to 5-31-78 letter from G. Robert Blakey, Chief Counsel HSCA, requesting files on Rosselli and other figures of interest. Rosselli is name number #155 on the list of LAPD responses, and beside his name is a large, handwritten "No" meaning they have no files; in contrast, the LAPD says on the same sheet "Yes" they do have three files on East Coast mob figure Tony Provenzano. **28.** SUS, p. 1019; also, the way the Mafia aspect of the Roy Donald Murray story was diminished in later LAPD summaries. **29.** John H. Davis, *The Kennedys: Dynasty and Disaster* (New York: S.P.I. Books, 1992), p. 671. **30.** Dan E. Moldea, *The Killing of Robert F. Kennedy* (New York: W. W. Norton & Company, 1995), p. 100, 101. **31.** Church Committee volumes on "Intelligence Activities and the Rights of Americans"; Sy Hersh, *The New York Times*, 1-7-79, cited in Henrik Krfger, *The Great Heroin Coup: Drugs, Intelligence & International Fascism* (Boston: South End Press, 1980), p. 74; William W. Turner, *The Police Establishment* (New York: Tower, 1968), pp. 60-90. **32.** CIA card 100-300-017, 4-9-68, for Oswald 201-289248. **33.** Robert Blair Kaiser, *RFK Must Die* (New York: Overlook Press, 2008) pp. 182, 380. **34.** Ibid, p. 380. **35.** Dan E. Moldea, *The Killing of Robert F. Kennedy* (New York: W. W. Norton & Company, 1995), p. 301. **36.** UPI story from 1-10-69 *Columbia Missourian*. **37.** *Los Angeles Times*, 8-7-69, 8-26-69, 9-24-69. **38.** *Los Angeles Times*, 7-2-71. **39.** Lisa Pease, "Sirhan and the RFK Assassination," *Probe Magazine*, March-April and May-June, 1998; also many passages in Dan E. Moldea, *The Killing of Robert F. Kennedy* (New York: W. W. Norton & Company, 1995) and William Turner and Jonn Christian, *The Assassination of Robert F. Kennedy* (New York: Carroll & Graf, 2006) and Philip H. Melanson, *The Robert F. Kennedy Assassination* (New York: Shapolsky, 1991). **40.** Ibid Moldea, p. 143, 176, 177. **41.** William Turner and Jonn Christian, *The Assassination of Robert F. Kennedy* (New York: Carroll & Graf, 2006), pp. 157, 158. **42.** Charles Rappleye and Ed Becker, *All American Mafioso* (New York: Barricade, 1995), pp. 291, 292. **43.** Dan E. Moldea, *The Killing of Robert F. Kennedy* (New York: W. W. Norton & Company, 1995), p. 120. **44.** Ibid, pp. 120, 121. **45.** Ibid, p. 123. **46.** William Turner and Jonn Christian, *The Assassination of Robert F. Kennedy* (New York: Carroll & Graf, 2006), p. 178; Philip H. Melanson, *The Robert F. Kennedy Assassination* (New York: Shapolsky, 1991), p. 45. **47.** Ibid Melanson, p. 20; Dan E. Moldea, *The Killing of Robert F. Kennedy* (New York: W. W. Norton & Company, 1995), pp. 36-37; Larry Hancock, *Incomplete Justice*, article series on the Mary Ferrell Foundation website, maryferrell.org. **48.** Ibid Melanson, pp. 103-105.

CHAPTER SIXTY

1. Mel Ayton, A Racial Crime (Las Vegas: ArcheBooks, 2005), pp. 207, 208. **2.** HSCA Report p. 451; Ibid, p. 210; Gerald Posner, Killing the Dream (New York: Random House, 1998), p. 49. **3.** As noted earlier, Arthur Hanes, Sr., was assisted in the case by his son, Arthur Hanes, Jr. However, in our discussion of Ray's defense, we refer only to the actions of Arthur Hanes, Sr., and nothing he did or that we write about should reflect in any way on Arthur Hanes, Jr. **4.** Jeff Cohen, "The Assassination of Martin Luther King" in Sid Blumenthal and Harvey Yazijian, Government by Gunplay (New York: Signet, 1976); Memphis Commercial Appeal, 7-28-68 and Martin Waldron article in The New York Times 1973, both cited by A. J. Weberman; Mel Ayton, A Racial Crime (Las Vegas: ArcheBooks, 2005), p. 210. **5.** Ibid Cohen; Gerald Posner, Killing the Dream (New York: Random House, 1998), p. 49. **6.** Ibid Posner, p. 50. **7.** Ibid, pp. 49-55. **8.** Ibid. **9.** Mel Ayton, A Racial Crime (Las Vegas: ArcheBooks, 2005), pp. 211, 212. **10.** Ibid; Gerald Posner, Killing the Dream (New York: Random House, 1998), pp. 50, 51. **11.** William F. Pepper, Orders to Kill (New York: Carroll & Graf, 1995), p. 486. **12.** Gerald Posner, Killing the Dream (New York: Random House, 1998), p. 61. **13.** Mel Ayton, A Racial Crime (Las Vegas: ArcheBooks, 2005), pp 211, 212; FBI Murkin memo, 9-23-68; Ibid, p. 62. **14.** John H. Davis, Mafia Kingfish: Carlos Marcello and the Assassination of John F. Kennedy (New York: McGraw-Hill, 1989), p. 381. **15.** HSCA Report. p. 453. **16.** Justice Department memo 9-17-68, cited in 11-5-68 Memphis FBI memo, pp. 64, 68. **17.** Justice Department to Hoover memo, 9-22-68. **18.** HSCA Report, p. 388. **19.** Ibid. **20.** William F. Pepper, Orders to Kill (New York: Carroll & Graf, 1995), pp. 206, 240; John H. Davis, Mafia Kingfish: Carlos Marcello and the Assassination of John F. Kennedy (New York: McGraw-Hill, 1989), p. 140. **21.** In addition to not investigating Marcello, Rosselli, and Milteer for the King assassination, one of the most obvious leads not perused by the FBI is the group, which supposedly used the Mafia to broker the King contract: the wealthy group of racists in the Southeast known as "Forever White." Based on the FBI files released so far, the Bureau appears to have not investigated any of these four leads, or tried to see if any of them were connected (for example, Milteer and "Forever White"). There could well be information in FBI files that could shed light on these matters, even forty years later. **22.** William F. Pepper, Orders to Kill (New York: Carroll & Graf, 1995), pp. 228, 287. **23.** William F. Pepper, Act of State (New York: Verso, 2003), p. 276. **24.** HSCA Report pp. 307, 308. **25.** Gerald Posner, Killing the Dream (New York: Random House, 1998), pp. 58-61, 253. **26.** Ibid, p. 62. **27.** HSCA Report, pp. 318, 319. **28.** William Bradford Huie, He Slew the Dreamer (New York: Delacorte Press, 1970), p. 51. **29.** Gerald Posner, Killing the Dream (New York: Random House, 1998), p. 253; New

York Daily News 6-14-77, cited by A. J. Weberman. **30.** HSCA Report, p. 319; Ibid Posner, p. 64. **31.** Ibid Posner, pp. 65, 66. **32.** Ibid. **33.** Ibid, pp. 69, 71. **34.** Ibid. **35.** HSCA King vol. VII, pp. 347-76; Ibid, pp. 71, 72. **36.** Ibid Posner. **37.** Martin Luther King Justice Department Task Force Report, 1977, p. 88. **38.** Gerald Posner, Killing the Dream (New York: Random House, 1998), p. 255. **39.** John H. Davis, Mafia King- fish: Carlos Marcello and the Assassination of John F. Kennedy (New York: McGraw-Hill, 1989), p. 322 **40.** FBI transcript of Dan Rather interview with James Earl Ray, p. 349.

CHAPTER SIXTY-ONE

1. The *Sun Herald* (Mississippi) and the Baton Rouge *Advocate* (12-3-89, 12-7-89) reported that in just the first two months of 1970, Marcello's hits included the murders of Jack Howard Joy and Donald Lester "Jimmy" James—and as usual for Marcello, "no one [was ever] convicted of [either] murder." **2.** Michael Dorman, *Pay-Off* (New York: Berkley Medallion, 1973), p. 114; John H. Davis, *Mafia Kingfish* (New York Signet, 1989), pp. 398, 399. **3.** Peter Noyes, *Legacy of Doubt* (New York: Pinnacle Books, 1973), pp. 141-43 **4.** Ibid, pp. 15-18. **5.** Congressional investigators later documented that Termine was long-time friends with Lee Harvey Oswald's mother and uncle, Marcello bookie "Dutz" Murret—HSCA vol. IX, pp. 115-17 John H. Davis, *Mafia Kingfish* (New York: Signet, 1989), pp. 140, 448; William F. Pepper, *Orders to Kill* (New York: Carroll & Graf, 1995), pp. 239, 249, 487. **6.** Ed Reid, *The Grim Reapers* (New York: Bantam, 1970) p. 300. **7.** Joseph J. Trento, *Prelude to Terror: The Rogue CIA, and the Legacy of America's Private Intelligence Network* (New York: Carroll & Graf, 2005), p. 45. **8.** Ibid, pp. 45-47. **9.** Henrik Krfger, *The Great Heroin Coup: Drugs, Intelligence & International Fascism* (Boston: South End Press, 1980), pp. 122, 123, many others **10.** Ibid, p. 161. **11.** Anthony Summers with Robbyn Swan, *The Arrogance of Power: The Secret World of Richard Nixon* (New York: Viking, 2000), many passages, especially the criminal ties of many of Nixon's associates, including his best friend, Bebe Rebozo; Joseph J. Trento, *Prelude to Terror: The Rogue CIA, and the Legacy of America's Private Intelligence Network* (New York: Carroll & Graf, 2005), p. 45. **12.** Ed Reid, *The Grim Reapers* (New York: Bantam, 1970), p. 115; Anthony Summers with Robbyn Swan, *The Arro- gance of Power: The Secret World of Richard Nixon* (New York: Viking, 2000), many passages. **13.** Staff and editors of *Newsday*, *The Heroin Trail* (New York: New American Library, 1974), p. 115: The Pulitzer Prize winning-series in *Newsday* noted that "at the time of his arrest" Mertz owned a "farm-hunting lodge of 1,445 acres equipped with...a private plane landing strip," a "luxury apartment on Boulevard Suchet in Paris," and various other property in France and Corsica, as well as his own private plane. **14.** Ibid, pp. vii viii, 111-15. **15.** Ibid. **16.** Ibid, p. 169. **17.** Charles Rappleye and Ed Becker, *All American Mafioso* (New York: Barricade, 1995), pp. 294, 295. **18.** CIA memo 8-9-76, subject: Johnny Rosselli. **19.** Ibid. **20.** Charles Rappleye and Ed Becker, *All American Mafioso* (New York: Barricade, 1995), pp. 294-96; Peter Dale Scott, *Crime and Cover-Up: The CIA, the Mafia, and the Dallas-Watergate Connection* (Santa Barbara, CA: Open Archive Press, 1993), pp. 26, 27; Peter Dale Scott, *Deep Politics II* (Ipswich, MA: Mary Ferrell Foundation Press, 2003), p. 68; Peter Dale Scott, Paul L. Hoch, and Russell Stetler, eds., *The Assassinations: Dallas and Beyond: A Guide to Cover-Ups and Investigations* (New York: Vintage, 1976), pp. 375-80. **21.** Ibid. **22.** Ibid Rappleye, pp. 300, 301. **23.** Anthony Summers with Robbyn Swan, *The Arrogance of Power: The Secret World of Richard Nixon* (New York: Viking, 2000), p. 197. **24.** Peter Dale Scott, *Crime and Cover-Up: The CIA, the Mafia, and the Dallas-Watergate Connection* (Santa Barbara, CA: Open Archive Press, 1993), p. 26. **25.** CIA document, JMWAVE to Director, 12-5-63, released in 1994 by the CIA Historical Review Program; from "Carlos Prio Socarras [soft file]" **26.** H. R. Haldeman with Joseph DiMona, *The Ends of Power* (New York: Dell, 1978), pp. 67-70. **27.** Anthony Summers with Robbyn Swan, *The Arrogance of Power: The Secret World of Richard Nixon* (New York: Viking, 2000), pp. 279-82. **28.** See Senate Watergate Hearings, Book 8 pp. 3369-71. **29.** Thomas Powers, *The Man Who Kept the Secrets: Richard Helms & the CIA* (New York: Knopf, 1979), many passages. **30.** Anthony Summers with Robbyn Swan, *The Arrogance of Power: The Secret World of Richard Nixon* (New York: Viking, 2000), many passages. **31.** Generally, see Anthony Summers with Robbyn Swan, *The Arrogance of Power: The Secret World of Richard Nixon* (New York: Viking, 2000); Peter Dale Scott, *Deep Politics and the Death of JFK* (Berkeley: University of California Press, 1993); and Peter Dale Scott, *Crime and Cover-Up: The CIA, the Mafia, and the Dallas-Watergate Connection* (Santa Barbara, CA: Open Archive Press, 1993). **32.** H. R. Haldeman with Joseph DiMona, *The Ends of Power* (New York: Dell, 1978), pp. 53, 54. **33.** Ibid. **34.** Ibid, 54. **35.** Anthony Summers with Robbyn Swan, *The Arrogance of Power: The Secret World of Richard Nixon* (New York: Viking, 2000), p. 480 and others. **36.** CIA 104-10119-10163. **37.** CIA 104-10119-10320; CIA 104-10119-10317. **38.** See Peter Dale Scott's new introduction to *Deep Politics and the Death of JFK* (Berkeley: University of California Press, 1996). **39.** CIA 104-10103-10042; in 1970 Hunt apparently observed a few more formalities, like interviewing with a couple of other firms before being hired by The Mullen Company. But the CIA investigators later found that in those interviews, Hunt appeared to be going through the motions and hadn't really tried to "sell himself." At the same time, they found that Richard Helms himself "was listed as a character reference on Mr. Hunt's resume and that M

Helms signed a letter of recommendation…on Mr. Hunt's behalf." In 1970, Hunt would have welcomed the potentially lucrative private sector assignment, because one of his daughters had developed a medical condition that had drained the family's finances. See Tad Szulc, *Compulsive Spy: The Strange Career of E. Howard Hunt* (New York: Viking, 1974), pp. 100, 103; E. Howard Hunt with Greg Aunapu, *American Spy* (Hoboken, NJ: John Wiley & Sons, 2007), p. 157. **40.** CIA 104-10103-10042; See also Senate Watergate Hearings, Book 8, pp. 3383-89. **41.** CIA 104-10103-10042. **42.** Anthony and Robbyn Summers, "The Ghosts of November," *Vanity Fair*, 12-94; James W. McCord, Jr., *A Piece of Tape* (Rockville, MD: Washington Media Services, 1974), many passages; authors' call to McCord, who declined to speak, 3-6-95. **43.** CIA 104-10119-0317. **44.** H. R. Haldeman with Joseph DiMona, *The Ends of Power* (New York: Dell, 1978), pp. 190-96. **45.** Ibid, 189-195. **46.** Ibid, 163. **47.** Peter Dale Scott, *Deep Politics II* (Ipswich, MA: Mary Ferrell Foundation Press, 2003), p. 58; Gus Russo, *Live by the Sword: The Secret War against Castro and the Death of JFK* (Baltimore: Bancroft Press, 1998), p. 423. **48.** FBI #124-10284-10085; FBI 124-10284-10086. **49.** Jane Franklin, *The Cuban Revolution and the United States: A Chronological History* (Melbourne, Australia: Ocean, 1992), pp. 86-88. **50.** David Corn, *Blond Ghost* (New York: Simon & Schuster, 1994), many passages. **51.** HSCA vol. X, pp. 40, 43, 44; Gaeton Fonzi, *The Last Investigation* (New York: Thunder's Mouth, 1994), p. 137.

CHAPTER SIXTY-TWO

1. Stanley I. Kutler, *Abuse of Power* (New York: The Free Press, 1997), many passages. **2.** Richard D. Mahoney, *Sons & Brothers: The Days of Jack and Bobby Kennedy* (New York: Arcade, 1999), p. 383. **3.** Dan E. Moldea, *The Hoffa Wars: Teamsters, Rebels, Politicians, and the Mob* (New York: SPI, 1993), pp. 261, 262, 292-94. **A.** J. Weberman at ajweberman.com citing the *New York Post* 11-16-79. **4.** Bernard Fensterwald, Jr., and Michael Ewing, *Coincidence or Conspiracy* (New York: Zebra Books, 1977) pp. 132, 133. **5.** Stanley Kutler, *Abuse of Power* (New York: The Free Press, 1997), pp. 3, 6. **6.** SSCIA 157-10011-10071. **7.** Michael wing and Peter Kross, HSCA 11210419, cited by Gary Buell. **8.** Dick Cheney memo #1781000410114, 4-3-75. **9.** Peter Dale Scott, *Deep Politics II* (Ipswich, MA: Mary Ferrell Foundation Press, 2003), p. 68, citing Liddy's *Will*, pp. 407-08; Gaeton Fonzi, *The Last Investigation* (New York: Thunder's Mouth, 1994) citing *Washington Post*, 9-21-75. **10.** J. Anthony Lukas, *Nightmare: The Underside of the Nixon Years* (New York: Bantam Books, 1977), p. 241. **11.** Ibid, p. 265. **12.** Phone interview with Carl Shoffler, 12-14-93; Peter Dale Scott, *Deep Politics and the Death of JFK* (Berkeley: University of California Press, 1993), pp. 56, 111, 145, 238-40, 367, 368; interviews with Harry Williams 7-24-93, 2-21-95. **13.** Frank Sturgis interview by Andrew St. George, *True* magazine, 8-74, p. 74. **14.** George McGovern Press Release 7-30-75. **15.** Cuban report, released 7-30-75 by the office of Senator George McGovern. **16.** Ibid, many passages. **17.** Charles Rappleye and Ed Becker, *All American Mafioso* (New York: Barricade, 1995), p. 307. **18.** CIA IG File #18 Tab #1, cited by A. J. Weberman. **19.** J. Anthony Lukas, *Nightmare: The Underside of the Nixon Years* (New York: Bantam Books, 1977), p. 266. **20.** Peter Dale Scott, Paul L. Hoch, and Russell Stetler, eds., *The Assassinations: Dallas and Beyond: A Guide to Cover-Ups and Investigations* (New York: Vintage, 1976), p. 99. **21.** Anthony Summers with Robbyn Swan, *The Arrogance of Power: The Secret World of Richard Nixon* (New York: Viking, 2000), pp. 408-10; Frank Sturgis interview by Andrew St. George, *True* magazine, 8-74, p. 74. **22.** Stanley I. Kutler, *Abuse of Power* (New York: The Free Press, 1997), p. 38. **23.** In an odd coincidence, later court testimony in an unrelated case showed that Arthur Bremer knew the sister of Jerry Owen, the television preacher tied to Sirhan Sirhan. See William Turner and Jonn Christian, *The Assassination of Robert F. Kennedy* (New York: Carroll & Graf, 2006), pp. 265-67. **24.** Jim Lesar, "Valenti / Helms Plan for CIA Television Show," *AARC Quarterly* Fall 1995-Winter 1996. **25.** David Corn, *Blond Ghost* (New York: Simon & Schuster, 1994), p. 261; Ted Shackley, *Spymaster: My Life in the CIA* (Washington, DC: Potomac Books, 2006), p. 265. **26.** Dick Russell, "Charles Colson," *Argosy*, 3-76. Len Colodny and Robert Gettlin, *Silent Coup* (New York: St. Martin's Paperbacks, 1992), pp. 329-33. **27.** See many passages in Evan Thomas, *The Man To See* (New York: Simon & Schuster, 1991) and Joseph A. Califano, Jr., *Inside: A Public and Private Life* (New York: Public Affairs, 2004).

CHAPTER SIXTY-THREE

1. Frank Sturgis interview by Andrew St. George, *True* magazine, 8-74, p. 74. **2.** Evan Thomas, *The Man To See* (New York: Simon & Schuster, 1991), p. 269. **3.** Ibid; Joseph A. Califano, Jr., *Inside: A Public and Private Life* (New York: Public Affairs, 2004), many passages. **4.** Gus Russo, *Live by the Sword: The Secret War against Castro and the Death of JFK* (Baltimore: Bancroft Press, 1998), p. 422. **5.** Ibid, p. 422, 423. **6.** H. R. Haldeman with Joseph DiMona, *The Ends of Power* (New York: Dell, 1978), p. 61. **7.** Ibid. **8.** Thomas Powers, *The Man Who Kept the Secrets: Richard Helms & the CIA* (New York: Knopf, 1979), p. 302; Ibid, pp. 64, 67-70. **9.** Ibid Haldeman and DiMona, pp. 67-70. **10.** Anthony Summers with Robbyn Swan, *The Arrogance of Power: The Secret World of Richard Nixon* (New York: Viking, 2000), p. 432. **11.** Thomas Powers, *The Man Who Kept the Secrets: Richard Helms & the CIA* (New York: Knopf, 1979), pp. 313-15. **12.** Anthony Summers, *Official and*

Confidential: The Secret Life of J. Edgar Hoover (New York: G. P. Putnam's Sons, 1993), pp. 423, 424. **13.** Se
the so-called CIA "Family Jewels," available online at the website of the National Security Archive, i
their Electronic Briefing Book No. 222. **14.** Thomas Powers, *The Man Who Kept the Secrets: Richard Helms*
the CIA (New York: Knopf, 1979), p. 351. **15.** Peter Dale Scott, *Deep Politics and the Death of JFK* (Berkeley
University of California Press, 1993), p. 306; NARA 1993.07.15.17:17:48:710610. **16.** Ibid. **17.** Anthon
Summers with Robbyn Swan, *The Arrogance of Power: The Secret World of Richard Nixon* (New York: Vikin;
2000), p. 445. **18.** Jeramiah O'Leary, "Haig Probe: Did Nixon get Cash from Asia," *Washington Star*, 12-!
76. **19.** Karl E. Campbell, *Senator Sam Ervin* (Chapel Hill, NC: University of North Carolina Press, 2007
many passages. **20.** Tad Szulc, "Cuba on our Mind," *Esquire*, 2-73; **21.** Haynes Johnson interview note
by Richard E. Sprague, 1-12-73, donated to the Assassination Archives and Records Center. **22.** Ibi
23. *People and the Pursuit of Truth* newsletter 5-75. **24.** Interviews with Harry Williams 7-24-93, 2-21-9!
William W. Turner, *Rearview Mirror* (Granite Bay, CA: Penmarin Books, 2001), pp. 210-15. **25.** As note
earlier, McCord has never acknowledged any 1963 work with Hunt or Williams, and he declined to spea
with the authors or *Vanity Fair*'s Anthony Summers about the matter. **26.** Noel Twyman, *Bloody Treas*
(Rancho Sante Fe, CA: Laurel Publishing, 1997), p. 467 and others. **27.** Charles Rappleye and Ed Becke
All American Mafioso (New York: Barricade, 1995), pp. 301-05. **28.** Michael J. Cain, *The Tangled Web: The Li*
and Death of Richard Cain (New York: Skyhorse Publishing, 2007), several passages. **29.** David E. Schein
The Mafia Killed President Kennedy (New York: SPI Books, 1992), pp. 366-67. **30.**   Dan Moldea artic]
in *Clandestine American*, vol. 3, #2, July-Aug/Sept.-Oct. 1979, p. 9. **31.** Charles Rappleye and Ed Becke
All American Mafioso (New York: Barricade, 1995), pp. 305-07. **32.** Ibid. **33.** Dan Christensen, "JFK, Kin;
The Dade County Links" *Miami Magazine*, 9-76; Dick Russell, *The Man Who Knew Too Much* (New Yor!
Carroll & Graf/R. Gallen, 1992), p. 552. **34.** William Brashler, *The Don* (New York: Ballantine, 1977), p]
331-33. **35.** Clifton Daniel, *Chronicle of America* (Liberty, MO: JL International Publishing, 1993), p. 84
36. Dan E. Moldea, *Dark Victory* (New York: Penguin, 1987), p. 338; David E. Scheim, *The Mafia Kille*
President Kennedy (New York: SPI Books, 1992), p. 367; John H. Davis, *Mafia Kingfish* (New York: Signe
1989), p. 465.

CHAPTER SIXTY-FOUR

1. Those reports were later shown to be untrue, though the real identities of the tramps were not di
covered in Dallas Police files until the early 1990s. **2.** Daniel Schorr, *Clearing the Air* (Boston: Hought
Mifflin, 1977), pp. 143, 144. **3.** Dick Russell, *The Man Who Knew Too Much* (New York: Carroll & Gra!
R. Gallen, 1992), p. 728; Loch K. Johnson, *A Season of Inquiry: Congress and Intelligence* (Chicago: Tł
Dorsey Press, 1988), p. 278. **4.** Michael Benson, *Who's Who in the JFK Assassination: An A-to-Z Encycloped*
(New York: Citadel, 1993), p. 381. **5.** Gaeton Fonzi, *The Last Investigation* (New York: Thunder's Mout
1994), pp. 157, 345, 346; one of the co-founders with Phillips was Jack Ruby's friend, Gordon McLendo
6. Daniel Schorr, *Clearing the Air* (Boston: Houghton Mifflin, 1977), p. 147. **7.** Loch K. Johnson, *A Season*
Inquiry: Congress and Intelligence (Chicago: The Dorsey Press, 1988), pp. 47, 55. **8.** John Kidner, *Crimale*
Contract Killer (Washington, DC: Acropolis Books, 1976), pp. 217-18; William Brashler, *The Don* (Ne
York: Ballantine, 1977), pp. 341-50. **9.** Charles Rappleye and Ed Becker, *All American Mafioso* (New Yor
Barricade, 1995), p. 311; John Kidner, *Crimaldi: Contract Killer* (Washington, DC: Acropolis Books, 197€
pp. 217-20. **10.** Dan Moldea, article in *Clandestine American*, vol. 3, #2, July-Aug/Sept.-Oct. 1979, p. 9.
11. Ibid; also Dan E. Moldea, *The Hoffa Wars: Teamsters, Rebels, Politicians, and the Mob* (New York: SPI, 199:
many passages. **12.** John Kidner, *Crimaldi: Contract Killer* (Washington, DC: Acropolis Books, 1976), p. 21
13. SSCIA 157-10006-10421. **14.** SSCIA 157-10005-10432. **15.** Phone interview with Gary Hart 5-4-98; Da
Bodine, "Was Expelled Frenchman Assassin?" *Cleburne Times-Review*, 11-21-77; memo of conversati
between Gary Shaw and *Newsday* journalist Robert Greene, 5-11-79, provided by Gary Shaw. **16.** Lo
K. Johnson, *A Season of Inquiry: Congress and Intelligence* (Chicago: The Dorsey Press, 1988), pp. 161, 16
179-85. **17.** HSCA vol. X, pp. 41-42. **18.** Gaeton Fonzi, *The Last Investigation* (New York: Thunder's Mout
1994), several passages. **19.** Ibid. **20.** David C. Martin, *Wilderness of Mirrors* (New York: Harper & Ro'
1980), p. 221. **21.** FBI 124-10271-10082; Tad Szulc, "An Eye for An Eye: The Death of JFK," *New Republ*
6-5-76. **22.** Richard D. Mahoney, *Sons & Brothers: The Days of Jack and Bobby Kennedy* (New York: Arcad
1999), p. 229. **23.** Charles Rappleye and Ed Becker, *All American Mafioso* (New York: Barricade, 199!
pp. 318-21; Jack Anderson, columns, 8-27-76 and 9-7-76. **24.** Ibid Rappleye and Becker, pp. 8, 9, 321, 325-2
25. Jack Anderson, columns, 8-27-76 and 9-7-76. **26.** U.S. Senate, Select Committee to Study Government
Operations with Respect to Intelligence Activities, "Alleged Assassination Plots Involving Foreign Lea
ers" (New York: Norton, 1976); Church Report vol. V, officially titled *The Investigation of the Assassination*
President John F. Kennedy: Performance of the Intelligence Agencies. **27.** CIA104-10408-10029. **28.** CIA104-1040
10029. **29.** CIA memo from Director George (H. W.) Bush to U.S. Attorney General, 10-14-76. **30.** Dac
County Manager's Office files on Felipe Rivero, found by former Miami-Dade County Archivist Gord

Winslow and available at his Cuban Information Archives website; *New Orleans Times-Picayune*, 11-22-73. **31.** HSCA vol. X, pp. 43, 44; Ann Louise Bardach, *Cuba Confidential* (New York: Random House, 2002), many passages; CIA 104-10068-10010; HSCA 180-10143-10215. **32.** Stansfield Turner appearance on CNN, 7-14-04   **33.** *Miami Herald*, 4-1-77; Michael Benson, *Who's Who in the JFK Assassination: An A-to-Z Encyclopedia* (New York: Citadel, 1993), p. 313. **34.** Gaeton Fonzi, *The Last Investigation* (New York: Thunder's Mouth, 1994), pp. 192, 193. **35.** Ibid, p. 77; HSCA 180-10108-10069. **36.** Ibid Fonzi, p. 40, 41; David Corn, *Blond Ghost* (New York: Simon & Schuster, 1994), p. 118. **37.** HSCA vol. X, pp. 37, 48; Gaeton Fonzi, *The Last Investigation* (New York: Thunder's Mouth, 1994), p. 433. **38.** Gaeton Fonzi, *The Last Investigation* (New York: Thunder's Mouth, 1994), p. 209. **39.** Philip H. Melanson, *The Murkin Conspiracy* (New York: Praeger, 1989), p. 167; HSCA vol. VII, p. 360. **40.** Thomas Powers, *The Man Who Kept the Secrets: Richard Helms & the CIA* (New York: Knopf, 1979), p. 349. **41.** Dan E. Moldea, *The Hoffa Wars: Teamsters, Rebels, Politicians, and the Mob* (New York: SPI, 1993), p. 432. **42.** Jefferson Morley, "What Jane Roman Said," 12-17-02. **43.** David Talbot, "The man who solved the Kennedy assassination," Salon.com, 11-22-03. **44.** HSCA vol. IV, pp. 158, 159, 173, 174. **45.** HSCA Report, pp. 118-21, plus additional files at the Assassination Archives and Research Center; HSCA vol. XI, pp. 539-51. **46.** U.S. House of Representatives, *The Final Assassinations Report of the Select Committee on Assassinations* (New York: Bantam Books, 1979), pp. 208, 213. **47.** Ibid, p. 208.

CHAPTER SIXTY-FIVE

1. Joseph Kraft article in *San Francisco Chronicle*, 4-20-83. **2.** John H. Davis, *The Kennedy Contract* (New York: Harper Paperbacks, 1993), 213-219; G. Robert Blakey and Richard N. Billings, *Fatal Hour* (New York: Berkley Books, 1992), pp. xxxvii, xxxviii, xxxix, xliv. **3.** Ibid. **4.** Letter from Informant to Carl Podsiadly, FBI, San Francisco office, 6-88, available at the National Archives. **5.** Letter from Informant to Justice Department, 4-6-88, available at the National Archives. **6.** Letter from Informant to Carl Podsiadly, FBI, San Francisco office, 6-88, available at the National Archives. **7.** Ibid. **8.** Ibid. **9.** Priority FBI memo from Dallas office to FBI Director, 11-88, available at the National Archives. **10.** Letter from Informant to Carl Podsiadly, FBI, San Francisco office, 6-88, available at the National Archives. **11.** Ibid. **12.** Ibid. **13.** FBI contact investigation 3-7-86, report dictated 3-6-86, FD-302 declassified 6-98 and on file at the National Archives. **14.** John H. Davis, *Mafia Kingfish: Carlos Marcello and the Assassination of John F. Kennedy* (New York: McGraw-Hill, 1989), p. 562. **15.** Letter from Informant to Carl Podsiadly, FBI, San Francisco office, 6-88, available at the National Archives. **16.** Letter from Informant to Justice Department, 4-6-88. **17.** John H. Davis, *Mafia Kingfish: Carlos Marcello and the Assassination of John F. Kennedy* (New York: McGraw-Hill, 1989), p. 565. **18.** Letter from Senior Case Manager, Federal Correctional Institution, Dublin, CA, to FBI agents, 6-21-88. **19.** Letter from Informant to Justice Department, 4-6-88. **20.** Letter from Informant to FBI headquarters in Washington, 4-18-88, available at the National Archives. **21.** Priority FBI memo from FBI San Francisco Office to FBI Director, Washington, 9-88, available at the National Archives. **22.** As for why the FBI never prosecuted Marcello or his family using the CAMTEX information, Agent Kimmel told us the bribes to move Marcello might have been considered entrapment by a jury. Another FBI agent who was involved added that convicting a family member for the bribe would have been difficult, since defense attorneys could have portrayed it sympathetically, as an attempt to make the elderly patriarch more comfortable in his final years. The agent added that if Marcello's brother had approved the funds to actually spring Marcello, they would have had a better case—but that never happened. It's also possible that political considerations in the Reagan administration, far above the level of those agents, kept the information from being used against Marcello, his family, or associates like the governor, since parts of Marcello's information and CAMTEX also crossed over into the ongoing Savings and Loan scandal and Iran-Contra. **23.** Dan Christensen "Court Secrecy Practices at Center of Drug Boss's 11th Circuit Appeal, *Daily Business Review*, 11-22-04. **24.** John H. Davis, *The Kennedy Contract* (New York: Harper Paperbacks, 1993), pp. 220, 221. **25.** Noel Twyman, *Bloody Treason* (Rancho Sante Fe, CA: Laurel Publishing, 1997), pp. 298, 299; FBI 124-10253-10112 and FBI Dallas 175-109 3-3-89, both cited by A. J. Weberman. **26.** Letter from Informant to Carl Podsiadly, FBI, San Francisco office, 6-88, available at the National Archives. The only point in the Informant's extremely lengthy account of his talks with Marcello that might indicate Marcello's advancing years is when the Informant writes one sentence as if David Ferrie is still alive. It can't be determined if that was simply an assumption on the Informant's part or if it was based on something Marcello said—that can only be clarified when the "hundreds of hours" of CAMTEX audio tapes are released. **27.** John H. Davis, *The Kennedy Contract* (New York: Harper Paperbacks, 1993), p. 221. **28.** Larry Hancock, *Someone Would Have Talked* (Southlake, TX: JFK Lancer, 2006), pp. 181, 182. **29.** Richard Helms with William Hood, *A Look Over My Shoulder: A Life in the Central Intelligence Agency* (New York: Random House, 2003), p. 229; Christopher Marquis, "Richard Helms, Ex-CIA Chief, Dies at 89, *The New York Times*, 10-23-02. **30.** E. Howard Hunt with Greg Aunapu, *American Spy* (Hoboken, NJ: John Wiley & Sons, 2007), pp. 135, 144. **31.** A Presumption of Disclosure: Lessons from the John F. Kennedy Assassination

Records Review Board," report by OMB Watch, 2000, at ombwatch.org; "'Denied in Full': Federal Judge Grill CIA Lawyers on JFK Secrets," *Huffington Post*, 10-22-07, which says, "Even though the JFK Act state that all assassination records must be made public by 2017, a top CIA official noted in a court filing tha the Agency has the right to keep as many as 1,100 still-secret JFK records out of public view beyond tha date."

EPILOGUE

1. "Cuba releases from jail last prisoner of ill-fated Bay of Pigs invation," *The San Diego Union*, 10-19-8(for the drug scandal, see many passages in Andres Oppenheimer, *Castro's Final Hour*, (New York: Simo & Schuster, 1992); Juan O. Tamayo, *Miami Herald*, 9-1-97; Cuba Transition Project report, Institute fc Cuban and Cuban-American Studies at the University of Miami; interviews with Harry Williams 2-2 92, 4-92, 7-24-93. 2-21-95. **2.** Lamar Waldron's written testimony sent on 11-9-94 for the Review Board 11-18-94 public hearing in Dallas, on file at the National Archives and noted in the Review Board's 199 Annual Report; Kennedy Assassination Records Review Board *Final Report*, 1998. **3.** *NBC Nightly New* with Tom Brokaw 9-29-98; "A Presumption of Disclosure: Lessons from the John F. Kennedy Assassinatio Records Review Board," report by OMB Watch, 2000, at ombwatch.org; "'Denied in Full': Federal Judge Grill CIA Lawyers on JFK Secrets," *Huffington Post*, 10-22-07. **4.** Jeff Franks, "Castro announces surgery Reuters, 11-29-96. **5.** "Chief of Cuba's Armed Forces Raul Castro attends event in honor of victims (Cuban downed airliner in Havana," Reuters story and photo, 10-7-06. **6.** Fabian Escalante message, 10-0(posted by Wim Dankbaar on the JFK Forum at www.spartacus.schoolnet.co.uk; Wim Dankbaar e-ma confirmation 11-06 to authors. **7.** Frances Robles, "Raul Castro asserts leadership at big brother Fidel birthday party," McClatchy Newspapers; Cuban media reports, all 12-2-06: *Periodico 26*; *Granma*; *Prens* Latina Latin American News Agency.

SPECIAL ADDENDUM
Part I: Bernard "Macho" Barker, the Mafia, and the Murder of JFK
1. CIA 180-10144-10219. **2.** CIA 180-10144-10219. **3.** FBI 124-10280-10440. **4.** FBI 124-10280-10440; CI 124-10289-10440. **5.** Marcelo Fernandez-Zayas, "A Man Called Macho," *Guaracabuya*, www.amigospai guaracabuya.org. **6.** CIA Office of Security file NARA 1993.08.02.09:58:48:810060. **7.** Senate Waterga Committee (officially the Senate Select Committee on Presidential Campaign Activities) testimony (Bernard Barker, May 24, 1973. **8.** Senate Watergate Committee testimony of Bernard Barker, May 24, 197 **9.** Evan Thomas, *The Man To See* (New York: Simon & Schuster, 1991), pp. 92-96, 104-120, 186-210. **10.** F| memo 6-22-72, from SAC Miami (139-328). **11.** CIA 180-10144-10219. **12.** Interview with Harry Willian 7-24-93. **13.** CIA 104-10183-10184; CIA 104-10247-10068. **14.** CIA 104-10061-10115; CIA officers often ha four or five official cover identities, each used for certain operations, so "Olien" was likely only one his pseudonyms. That means that other potential candidates, such as David Atlee Phillips, can't be rule out. In addition, sometimes more than one CIA officer used the same name for a particular operation- like "Eduardo" during the JFK-Almeida coup plan—so it's possible that more than one person used th "Olien" cover identity. **15.** Tad Szulc, *Compulsive Spy: The Strange Career of E. Howard Hunt* (New Yor Viking, 1974) and E. Howard Hunt with Greg Aunapu, *American Spy* (Hoboken, NJ: John Wiley & Son 2007), each several passages. **16.** CIA 104-10183-10184. **17.** CIA 180-10144-10219; E. Howard Hunt wi Greg Aunapu, *American Spy* (Hoboken, NJ: John Wiley & Sons, 2007), several passages; Marce Fernandez-Zayas, "A Man Called Macho," *Guaracabuya*, www.amigospais-guaracabuya.org. **18.** E. Hov ard Hunt, *Give Us This Day* (New Rochelle: Arlington House, 1973), pp. 38-40. **19.** CIA 104-10109-1037 CIA 104-101-9-10370. **20.** HSCA 180-10144-10219. **21.** Haynes Johnson interview notes by Richard Sprague, 1-12-73, donated to the Assassination Archives and Records Center. **22.** Haynes Johnson inte view notes by Richard E. Sprague, 1-12-73, donated to the Assassination Archives and Records Cente Warren Hinckle and William Turner, *Deadly Secrets* (New York: Thunder's Mouth, 1992), p. 56. **23.** Frai Sturgis interview by Andrew St. George, *True* magazine, 8-74. **24.** CIA 104-10120-10353; Fred D. Thom son, *At That Point In Time* (New York: Quadrangle, 1975), pp. 158, 159. **25.** Ibid; CIA 104-10194-10051; T| CIA sometimes makes a distinction between cover names that are aliases (usually used for outside wor and those that are pseudonyms (usually used in internal CIA records), but to simplify things we use tl general term "alias" for both. **26.** Bernard Fensterwald, Jr., and Michael Ewing, *Coincidence or Conspira* (New York: Zebra Books, 1977), p. 517. **27.** Taylor Branch and George Crile, "The Kennedy Vendetta *Harper's*, 8–75. **28.** Anthony Summers with Robbyn Swan, *The Arrogance of Power: The Secret World Richard Nixon* (New York: Viking, 2000), p. 496; Warren Hinckle and William Turner, *Deadly Secrets* (Ne York: Thunder's Mouth, 1992), p. 192. **29.** Howard Kohn, "Strange Bedfellows: The Hughes-Nixo Lansky Connection," *Rolling Stone*, 5-20-76; Anthony Summers with Robbyn Swan, *The Arrogance of Pow The Secret World of Richard Nixon* (New York: Viking, 2000), p. 496. **30.** Richard D. Mahoney, *Sons*

Brothers: The Days of Jack and Bobby Kennedy (New York: Arcade, 1999), pp. 383-385. **31.** Anthony Summers with Robbyn Swan, *The Arrogance of Power: The Secret World of Richard Nixon* (New York: Viking, 2000), p. 112, 127, 128. **32.** 8-31-76 FBI report from Phoenix, Arizona, in Bebe Rebozo files posted at fbi.gov. On the memo, the FBI hand-corrected the phonetic spelling of "Polly" to accurately read "Pawley." **33.** Richard D. Mahoney, *Sons & Brothers: The Days of Jack and Bobby Kennedy* (New York: Arcade, 1999), pp. 271-273. Marcello's territory was also linked to "Operation Tilt," since the FBI memo said that "Subsequent to the above raid, he was instructed to pick up $15,000.00 at Miami, which was to be used for the purchase of guns from the New Orleans, Louisiana area." **34.** CIA document, JMWAVE to Director, 2-5-63, released in 1994 by the CIA Historical Review Program. **35.** CIA 180-10145-10362; CIA 1994.03.04.09:39:50:340005; Peter Dale Scott, "Pinning Dallas on RFK: Milteer, the DRE and Richard Cain." **36.** FBI 124-90006-10038. **37.** Harry Williams interviews 4-92, 7-24-93; for background on Angelton, see Tom Mangold, *Cold Warrior* (New York: Simon & Schuster, 1991); for Hunt see: E. Howard Hunt with Greg Aunapu, *American Spy* (Hoboken, NJ: John Wiley & Sons, 2007). **38.** Harry Williams interview 7-24-93. **39.** Interviews with confidential Kennedy aide source 3-17-92. **40.** E. Howard Hunt with Greg Aunapu, *American Spy* (Hoboken, NJ: John Wiley & Sons, 2007), p. 135. **41.** Harry Williams interviews 4-92, 7-24-93, and others. **42.** William Turner interview with Harry Williams 11-28-73. **43.** Harry Williams interview 7-24-93. **44.** Interview with Harry Williams 2-24-92. **45.** Harry Williams interviews, 2-24-92, 7-24-93. **46.** For a detailed account of the attempt to shoot Harry, see the authors' *Ultimate Sacrifice* (Berkeley: Counterpoint, 2007), pp. 511, 512; for the later shooting linked to Artime see *New York Times* 6-18-72 p. 11, 6-27-72 p. 43, 7-13-72 p. 9, (as cited by A. J. Weberman), and Henrik Krfger, *The Great Heroin Coup* (Boston: South End Press, 1980), p. 161. **47.** John M. Lesar, "Ed Arthur—Soldier of Fortune," *Soldier of Fortune*, 5-78; Mike Wales, *Ed Arthur's Glory No More: Underground Operations from Cuba to Watergate* (Westerville, O.: Dakar, 1975), pp. 80-84. **48.** Harry Williams interview 11-13-92. **49.** Michael Canfield and Alan J. Weberman, *Coup d'état in America* (New York: Third Press, 1975), pp. 56, 57 and www.ajweberman.com/nodules2/nodulec22.htm. **50.** Ibid; in the account of the same interview at www.ajweberman.com/nodules2/nodulec22.htm, Weitzman is quoted as saying, "I can't remember for sure, but it looked like him. Couldn't swear it was him though . . . anyway so many witnesses are dead . . . two Cubans once forced their way into my house and waited for me when I got home. I had to chase them out with my service revolver . . . I feared for my life." **51.** www.ajweberman.com/nodules2/nodulec22.htm. **52.** Ibid. **53.** Ibid. **54.** Many years later, after frequent showings of the restored version on television and in the Oliver Stone *JFK* film, some people convinced themselves they'd seen the JFK assassination televised live. Shelly Winters, in her autobiography, is one documented example. But at the time of Barker's deposition, that scenario was highly unlikely, because the film was so infrequently shown and the film before restoration was of such poor quality compared to a typical TV newscast. **55.** HSCA Barker report: 180-0142-10061; Barker's HSCA interview has been assigned the Record Number 180-10103-10225 by the National Archives. But when the authors checked the National Archives web site in July 2009, the site said Barker's entire 87-page HSCA interview transcript is still "Postponed In Full" even though the file is "Unclassified." **56.** John H. Davis, *Mafia Kingfish* (New York: Signet, 1989), pp. 401, 410; Bernard Fensterwald, Jr., and Michael Ewing, *Coincidence or Conspiracy* (New York: Zebra Books, 1977), pp. 512, 513. **57.** Gus Russo, *Live by the Sword: The Secret War against Castro and the Death of JFK* (Baltimore: Bancroft Press, 1998), pp. 140-144. **58.** John H. Davis, *Mafia Kingfish* (New York: Signet, 1989), p. 410; CIA 180-10144-10219 and others. **59.** Harry Williams interviews, 2-24-92 and 11-13-92. Harry told us that his gay friend, who was short and weighed only 130 lbs., stood his ground during the fierce fighting of the landing at the Bay of Pigs. In contrast, Harry's 220 lb. radio operator ran away when the shooting started. Harry later told his gay friend that he deserved two medals—one for one for bravery under fire and one for having the courage to be openly gay at that time. **60.** Elinor J. Brecher, "Watergate 'plumber' was a hero to exiles," *Miami Herald*, 6-6-09; Frank Sturgis interview by Andrew St. George, *True* magazine, 8-74. **61.** J. Anthony Lukas, *Nightmare: The Underside of the Nixon Years* (New York: Bantam Books, 1977), p. 265. **62.** Haynes Johnson, *Washington Post*, 6-10-77. **63.** For general information about Barker during the Bay of Pigs, see E. Howard Hunt, *Give Us This Day* (New Rochelle: Arlington House, 1973); Tad Szulc, *Compulsive Spy* (New York: Viking, 1974); and E. Howard Hunt with Greg Aunapu, *American Spy* (Hoboken, NJ: John Wiley & Sons, 2007). **64.** 5-22-76 WPLG-TV program (Miami ABC affiliate). **65.** Frank Sturgis interview by Andrew St. George, *True* magazine, 8-74; Harry Williams interviews, 2-24-92 and 7-24-93. **66.** Harry Williams interview 7-24-93. **67.** Gaeton Fonzi, *The Last Investigation* (New York: Thunder's Mouth, 1994), pp. 40, 41; CIA 104-10408-10029 8-25-76 CIA memo; CIA 104-10308-10080, declassified 4-18-98.; Haynes Johnson, *Sleepwalking Through History* (New York: W. W. Norton, 2003), p. 271. **68.** NARA 1994.03.17.10:45:20:220005, CIA 104-10235-10266; CIA Memorandum "Manolo Ray Rivero Meeting of 24-25 September 1963," declassified 2003; JMWAVE to CIA Director AMWORLD 11-23-63; Interviews with Harry Williams 2-24-92, 7-24-93. Also CIA 1993.07.22.08:55:23:460530, cited by A. J. Weberman.

Part II: Bernard Barker and a New View of Watergate

1. CIA 104-10076-10181. **2.** Tad Szulc, *Compulsive Spy: The Strange Career of E. Howard Hunt* (New York Viking, 1974), p. 97; Gus Russo, *Live by the Sword: The Secret War against Castro and the Death of JFK* (Baltimore: Bancroft Press, 1998), p. 171. **3.** CIA 104-10194-10051. **4.** CIA 104-10183-10184. **5.** CIA 104-10216 10437. **6.** J. Anthony Lukas, *Nightmare: The Underside of the Nixon Years* (New York: Bantam Books, 1977) p. 264. **7.** NARA 1994.05.16.14:12:04:280005. It's not clear from CIA 104-10246-10068 if Cubela met "Olien under that alias or under "Olien's" real name. **8.** Harry Williams interviews, 2-24-92 and 7-24-93; HSC 157-10014-10046; Evan Thomas, *Robert Kennedy: His Life* (New York: Simon & Schuster, 2000), p. 238 **9.** Harry Williams interviews, 2-24-92 and 7-24-93. **10.** Harry Williams interview 7-24-93. **11.** Bernar Fensterwald, Jr., and Michael Ewing, *Coincidence or Conspiracy* (New York: Zebra Books, 1977), p. 512 **12.** CIA 1994.03.03.15:12:02:470005. **13.** HSCA CIA 180-10144-10219; the more detailed files about Barker' associates that supposedly generated that "concern" seem thin and don't really deal with "underworl elements." **14.** HSCA CIA 180-10144-10219. **15.** 1993.06.24.15:08:04:340800, which contains an article by Milton Viorst titled *The Mafia, the CIA, and the Kennedy Assassination.* **16.** CIA document, JMWAVE t Director, 12-5-63, released in 1994 by the CIA Historical Review Program. **17.** Cited by A. J. Weberma at www.ajweberman.com/nodules2/nodulec22.htm **18.** Warren Hinckle and William Turner, *Dead* *Secrets* (New York: Thunder's Mouth, 1992), pp. 338, 339, 352, 353; Anthony Summers with Robbyn Swar *The Arrogance of Power: The Secret World of Richard Nixon* (New York: Viking, 2000), p. 496. **19.** Warre Hinckle and William Turner, *Deadly Secrets* (New York: Thunder's Mouth, 1992), pp. 354, 355. **20.** FB 124-10284-10086. **21.** FBI 124-10284-10086. **22.** FBI 124-10284-10086; Penney Lernoux, "The Miami Conne tion: Golden Gateway for Drugs," *The Nation,* 2-18-84. **23.** FBI 124-10284-10086. **24.** FBI 124-10284-1008! **25.** 6-22-72 FBI memo, from Bebe Rebozo files (Part 6, p. 1) online at fbi.gov. **26.** Warren Hinckle and Wi liam Turner, *Deadly Secrets* (New York: Thunder's Mouth, 1992), p. 360. **27.** Warren Hinckle and Williar Turner, *Deadly Secrets* (New York: Thunder's Mouth, 1992), p. 338. **28.** J. Anthony Lukas, *Nightmare: Th Underside of the Nixon Years* (New York: Bantam Books, 1977), p. 154; Peter Dale Scott, *Crime and Cove Up: The CIA, the Mafia, and the Dallas-Watergate Connection* (Santa Barbara, Calif.: Open Archive Pres 1993), p. 64. **29.** Dan E. Moldea, *The Hoffa Wars: Teamsters, Rebels, Politicians, and the Mob* (New York: SP 1993), p. 351, 352. **30.** Ibid. **31.** Tad Szulc, *Compulsive Spy: The Strange Career of E. Howard Hunt* (New Yor Viking, 1974), pp. 128, 129; Senate Watergate Committee testimony of Bernard Barker, May 24, 197. **32.** 6-19-72 CIA report titled "Everette Howard Hunt, Jr." **33.** Warren Hinckle and William Turner, *Dead* *Secrets* (New York: Thunder's Mouth, 1992), p. 352. **34.** "A Man Called Macho by Marcelo Fernandez Zayas," *Guaracabuya,* www.amigospais-guaracabuya.org. Barker testified that he was not paid for th break-ins. On the other hand, Hunt "was being paid $3,000 per break-in, while Liddy received $2,500, according to Hunt's most recent autobiography—see E. Howard Hunt with Greg Aunapu, *American Sp* (Hoboken, NJ: John Wiley & Sons, 2007), p. 205. **35.** HSCA 124-10289-10440. **36.** Ibid. **37.** Warren Hinck and William Turner, *Deadly Secrets* (New York: Thunder's Mouth, 1992), p. 356. **38.** Anthony Summe with Robbyn Swan, *The Arrogance of Power: The Secret World of Richard Nixon* (New York: Viking, 2000 p. 509. **39.** Anthony Summers with Robbyn Swan, *The Arrogance of Power: The Secret World of Richard Nixc* (New York: Viking, 2000), pp. 508, 509. **40.** E. Howard Hunt with Greg Aunapu, *American Spy* (Hoboke NJ: John Wiley & Sons, 2007), p. 135; Gaeton Fonzi, *The Last Investigation* (New York: Thunder's Mout 1994), p. 137. **41.** Gaeton Fonzi, *The Last Investigation* (New York: Thunder's Mouth, 1992), pp. 70, 7 **42.** Jack Anderson column, *Atlanta Journal-Constitution,* 12-16-77. **43.** A. J. Weberman at www.ajwebermar com/nodules2/nodulec22.htm. **44.** *New York Times* 6-18-72 p. 11, 6-27-72 p. 43, 7-13-72 p. 9, (by A. J. Webe man); Henrik Krfger, *The Great Heroin Coup* (Boston: South End Press, 1980), p. 161. **45.** A. J. Weberma at www.ajweberman.com/nodules2/nodulec22.htm. **46.** FBI Rebozo file at fbi.gov, citing Jack Anderso column, *Las Vegas Review-Journal,* 8-6-71. **47.** FBI Rebozo file at fbi.gov, part 5. **48.** Frank Sturgis intervie by Andrew St. George, *True* magazine, 8-74. **49.** J. Anthony Lukas, *Nightmare: The Underside of the Nixo Years* (New York: Bantam Books, 1977), pp. 260, 261, 266, 267. **50.** Frank Sturgis interview by Andrew S George, *True* magazine, 8-74. **51.** HSCA 124-10289-10440. **52.** J. Anthony Lukas, *Nightmare: The Underside* *the Nixon Years* (New York: Bantam Books, 1977), pp. 193, 194. **53.** Frank Sturgis interview by Andrew S George, *True* magazine, 8-74. **54.** John Simkin, Watergate article at the British educational website ww spartacus.schoolnet.co.uk. **55.** Ibid. **56.** Ibid. **57.** We have condensed this Nixon transcript and smoothe some wording to make it easier to understand. A complete transcript is available at: www.bjornetjeneste dk/teksterdk/watergate.htm. **58.** Anthony Summers with Robbyn Swan, *The Arrogance of Power: T. Secret World of Richard Nixon* (New York: Penguin, paperback edition), p. 444. **59.** Bernard Fensterwal Jr., and Michael Ewing, *Coincidence or Conspiracy* (New York: Zebra Books, 1977), pp. 517-519. **60.** Hayn Johnson, *Sleepwalking Through History* (New York: W. W. Norton, 2003), pp. 270, 271. **61.** "Liddy Testifi in Defamation Case," Associated Press, 7-1-02. **62.** Howard Kohn, "Strange Bedfellows: The Hughe Nixon-Lansky Connection," *Rolling Stone,* 5-20-76. **63.** J. Anthony Lukas, *Nightmare: The Underside of th*

Nixon Years (New York: Bantam Books, 1977), p. 368. **64.** Bernard Barker obituary, *New York Times*, 6-6-09. **65.** http://tvnews.vanderbilt.edu. **66.** Howard Kohn, "Strange Bedfellows: The Hughes-Nixon-Lansky Connection," *Rolling Stone*, 5-20-76. **67.** *St. Petersburg Times*, 2-22-74; John Simkin, Watergate article at the British educational website www.spartacus.schoolnet.co.uk. **68.** CIA 104-10256-10287. **69.** CIA Office of Security File 1993.08.02.09:58:48:810060; also NARA 1994.03.03.15:12:02:470005. **70.** Ibid; Taylor Branch and George Crile, "The Kennedy Vendetta," *Harper's*, 8-75. **71.** http://tvnews.vanderbilt.edu. **72.** Hunt article in *Rolling Stone*, 4-2-07; Bernard Barker obituary, *New York Times*, 6-6-09. **73.** Jefferson Morley, "Dead Spy's JFK Files Pose a Test for Obama's FOIA Order," *Talking Points Memo*. **74.** The CIA initially made their assertion of being able to withhold JFK assassination records beyond 2017 in a 2007 filing—see "'Denied in Full': Federal Judges Grill CIA Lawyers on JFK Secrets," *Huffington Post*, 10-22-07.

Part III: What You Can Do to Get All the Assassination Files Released

1. Eileen Sullivan, "Obama has more threats than other presidents-elect," Associated Press, 11-14-08; NBC News reports 11-08; Eileen Sullivan, "Homeland Security chief defends agency risk report," Associated Press, 4-16-09. **2.** Haynes Johnson, *Washington Post*, 6-10-77. **3.** Woody Baird, "Tennessee: Men accused in Obama plot plead not guilty to new charges," Associated Press 11-26-08; Mark Price, "Local man sentenced for threatening Obama," *Charlotte Observer*, 6-8-09; Brad Jacobson, "Legal experts question US Attorney's decision not to prosecute Obama 'assassination plot,'" *Raw Story*, 10-31-08; Annie Sweeney and Frank Main and Chris Fusco, "Chicago-area man arrested with guns, ammo," *Chicago Sun-Times*, 11-4-08; "Police probe possible threat to Obama," UPI, 11-5-08; Jeremy Gantz, "Calif. Man charged for threatening Obama's life over Yahoo," *Raw Story*, 1-9-09; "Man is arrested in Obama threat," *New York Times*, 1-17-09; *Bangor News* reports cited by Stephen C. Webster in "Report: Slain US Nazi hated Obama, had parts for 'dirty bomb,'" *Raw Story*, 3-9-09. **4.** Eric Lichtblau, "FAA alerted on Qaeda in '98, 9/11 Panel said," *New York Times*, 9-14-05; Eric Lichtblau, "9/11 Report cites many warnings about hijackings," *New York Times*, 2-10-05. **5.** Eric Lichtblau, "FAA alerted on Qaeda in '98, 9/11 Panel said," *New York Times*, 9-14-05; Eric Lichtblau, "9/11 Report cites many warnings about hijackings," *New York Times*, 2-10-05.

Index